Children's House
Montessori School, Inc.
P.O. Box 1271
Eau Claire, WI 54702-1271

The World of the Child

Karen Owens
College of Lake County
Illinois

Merrill, an imprint of
Macmillan Publishing Company
New York

Maxwell Macmillan Canada
Toronto

Maxwell Macmillan International
New York   Oxford   Singapore   Sydney

Cover photo: J. Taposchaner, 1990
Editor: Linda A. Sullivan
Developmental Editor: Linda Kauffman Peterson
Production Editor: Linda Hillis Bayma
Art Coordinator: Peter A. Robison
Photo Editor: Anne Vega
Cover Designer: Russ Maselli
Production Buyer: Patricia A. Tonneman
Illustrations: Academy Artworks, Inc.

This book was set in Palatino by Carlisle
Communications, Ltd. and was printed and bound by
Arcata Graphics/Halliday. The cover was printed by
Lehigh Press, Inc.

Macmillan Publishing Company
866 Third Avenue
New York, NY 10022

Macmillan Publishing Company is part of the
Maxwell Communication Group of Companies.

Maxwell Macmillan Canada, Inc.
1200 Eglinton Avenue East, Suite 200
Don Mills, Ontario M3C 3N1

Library of Congress Cataloging-in-Publication Data
Owens, Karen.
     The world of the child / Karen Owens.
        p.   cm.
     Includes bibliographical references and
     indexes.
     ISBN 0-675-21336-3
     1. Child development. 2. Child psychology.
     I. Title.
HQ767.9.O84   1993
305.23'1–dc20   92-9837
                                            CIP

Printing: 1 2 3 4 5 6 7 8 9   Year: 3 4 5 6 7

Photo credits: Alaska Stock, p. 303; AP/Wide World
Photos, pp. 15, 541; The Bettman Archive, pp. 19, 21,
24; Andy Brunk, pp. 287, 559, 573, 581, 588, 610, 614;
Cleo Freelance Photography, pp. 78, 156, 594; Betty
Crowell/Faraway Places, p. 294; Culver Pictures, Inc.,
p. 9; Department of Psychology, George Washington
University, p. 179; Robert Finken, pp. 38, 42, 46, 51,
83, 170, 181, 193, 200, 229, 232, 240, 245, 252, 255, 266,
280, 326, 342, 346, 354, 357, 378, 426, 432, 438, 441,
449, 464, 470, 503, 510, 534, 556, 607; Lynn Gilmer,
p. 599; Audrey Gottlieb/Monkmeyer Press Photo
Service, p. 104; Harvard University News Office,
p. 516; Bruce Jennings, p. 602; Donna Jernigan/
Monkmeyer Press Photo Service, p. 490; Bruce
Johnson/Macmillan, p. 131; Valerie Beardwood Kunze,
p. 369; Jean-Claude LeJeune, pp. 263, 362; Mark
Madden/KS Studios, p. 283; Riverside Methodist
Hospitals, Columbus, pp. 74, 133, 339; Barbara C.
Schwartz, pp. 84, 109, 141, 153, 162, 169, 173, 207,
210, 248, 259, 262, 290, 310, 323, 329, 340, 374, 382,
385, 404, 422, 442, 475, 480, 484, 501, 527, 531, 536,
540, 566, 596, 605; Michael Siluk, pp. 60, 418, 578, 590;
Skjold Photographs, pp. 64, 389; Stanford University
Psychology Department, p. 23; Barbara Stimpert,
pp. 71, 87, 92, 152, 216, 218, 315, 505; UPI/Bettman
Newsphotos, pp. 10, 168; Ulrike Welsch, pp. 2, 102,
114, 206, 276, 334, 397, 409, 448, 453, 456, 549;
Zimbel/Monkmeyer Press Photo Service, p. 214; Gale
Zucker, pp. 111, 146, 284, 308, 522.

To my children
as they embark on new journeys in their lives:

Eric Owens—success in college
Gordon Owens—with your bride, Meade

Welcome to the new edition of *The World of the Child*. With renewed interest and enthusiasm, I have revised the text that will serve as your introduction to the growth and development of children and adolescents. Improvements and additions to the last edition have been combined with some of its unique features to present a text that introduces you to new information, gives you practical examples of how the content applies to growing and developing children, and challenges you to think about issues that affect the lives of children as they grow up in our society today. What I have presented is relevant to students in education, health care, human ecology, and psychology, as well as to those students who may one day, as parents, engage in one of the most important tasks of their lives: bringing up mentally healthy and happy children.

PRESENTATION AND ORGANIZATION

A BALANCED PRESENTATION OF THEORETICAL, EMPIRICAL, AND APPLIED ISSUES

Despite the great variance in teaching approaches and topics emphasized in a child development course, there are two elements that are important for you to be exposed to during the course of your study. One is a strong emphasis on empirical studies and theoretical foundations, and the other is exposure to practical applications of the theory and research. I have written the text with this in mind so that you will leave the course with a solid knowledge of the theory and research that supports the field, but also, as importantly, with a practical knowledge of how this research is interpreted in the everyday lives of children and adolescents.

UP-TO-DATE RESEARCH

Since the field of child growth and development is a rapidly changing scientific discipline, up-to-date studies must be presented to reflect the growing knowledge of children's development. Over 50% of the research studies that I've cited in this edition are new, 30% of which were conducted in the 1990s. Although recent research is included, classical studies in the field are presented as well.

Similarly, segments in each of the chapters reflect new research: expanded coverage in such areas as the effects of day care on infants under the age of 1 year, perinatal AIDS, adolescent AIDS, and fathers and child-rearing responsibilities, just to name a few. Because the area of information processing has grown substantially since the first edition, it now appears in a separate chapter. The information processing approach to gender-role development, social cognition, and social development is also reflected in these chapters.

Since it is also important for you to discover that research is not flawless and that just because something appears in print does not make it flawless, a complete section on developing the skills necessary to evaluate research from a critical standpoint has been added to Chapter 1. Moreover, when research is presented in the text, limitations of the research and cautions are noted.

CROSS-CULTURAL STUDIES

Since we now live in an increasingly global society, it is important for you to learn about children in other cultures. Each of the chapters offers research conducted in other countries to help you develop a broader, less ethnocentric perspective on children's development.

ORGANIZATION

To give you a fuller grasp of the concepts and theories presented in the book, I have organized the material in a topical fashion. I think you will better understand the continuity and coherence that reflects the true nature of a child's growth and development by viewing the content in this integrated way. In presenting the material topically, each important aspect of children's physical, cognitive, social, emotional, and moral development, like an important piece of a complex puzzle, is examined. This edition also contains expanded coverage of the significant developmental changes that occur in infancy, early childhood, middle childhood, and adolescence in each of these specific topic areas. Hopefully you will emerge from the course with an understanding of the total growth of the child, as the areas overlap and sometimes transcend the categories of age ranges and chronological designations.

SYSTEMS VIEW OF CHILD DEVELOPMENT

Since I have presented child growth and development to you in an integrated, topical way, it naturally makes sense to focus on the different systems that operate in the child's world. Since none of us grow or live in a vacuum, it is important to recognize the influences that affect our individual growth. In the text, I have looked at development as organized into the many situational settings or contexts that affect a child's life.

Children's development is influenced by biological, family, social, economic, and cultural contexts, and children's behavior is affected by events at all levels of this system. Chapter 2 and 3, new to this edition, specifically introduce you to the multidimensional, contextual world of children's development.

TEXT FEATURES

Each chapter is structured to maximize your exposure to the concepts and realities of a child's growth and development. I begin the first 15 chapters with an item called "Children's Thoughts" which gives you insight into the feelings and per-

ceptions of children in their everyday world. Other sections and features offer practical suggestions based on the main topics discussed in each of the chapters.

STUDYING CHILDREN

Each chapter offers "Studying Children" activities that you can perform with children, based on theory and research, so you can apply information firsthand and learn more about children's behavior.

FOCUS ON APPLICATIONS/FOCUS ON ISSUES

Each chapter also offers a "Focus on Applications" feature which discusses topics such as "Dealing with the Anorectic Child at Home," "Assessing Children's Self-Esteem," and "How to Help Today's Rushed Child." To help you develop your curiosity and analytical thinking skills, each chapter has "Focus on Issues," a section that helps you understand issues in the field. These features appear under such titles as "Separating for the Sake of the Children," "Are Men and Women Truly Liberated?" and "How Can We Infer Emotional States in Infants?"

PRACTICAL IMPLICATIONS

Each chapter concludes with a "Practical Implications" section that presents the practical side of dealing with children as they grow and develop.

The text, in addition, includes a glossary and list of key terms and a complete reference list for further study.

ENHANCING YOUR CRITICAL THINKING

New to this edition is "Enhancing Your Critical Thinking," which appears at the end of each chapter. The primary objective of these exercises is to have you read current journal articles or chapters from books and answer questions or engage in activities that will promote analytical thinking. Each activity falls into one of four categories and offers you the opportunity to further investigate topics about which you are curious. The four types of critical thinking activities are as follows:

Broadening Your Knowledge presents you with topical resources that you can consult to learn more about topics of special interest from the chapter.

Firsthand Experiences ask you to explore, through reflection or direct participation, special topics from the chapter and investigate your personal beliefs and attitudes about these topics.

Critical Thinking activities offer you alternatives and extensions of chapter content and encourage you to reflect, analyze, and evaluate the resources presented.

Personal Growth selections challenge you to apply the material to your own life and extend the concept and principles in a way that allows you to make personal decisions about your life and your development.

I hope your encounter with your text and course offers you new perspectives and allows you to apply the principles of child growth and development to any personal or professional endeavor that involves the ever-changing world of children and adolescents.

ACKNOWLEDGMENTS

I would like to express my appreciation to Linda Peterson, Senior Developmental Editor, and Linda Bayma, Senior Production Editor, for their diligent efforts in transforming my manuscript into this text.

I would also like to acknowledge the contribution made by the following reviewers who offered their scholarly advice during my revising of *The World of the Child*:

Gene V. Elliott, Glassboro State College (New Jersey)
Oney D. Fitzpatrick, Jr., Northern Arizona University
Lauren Heim, University of Michigan
Joan E. Herwig, Iowa State University
Lois E. Muir, University of Wisconsin—La Crosse
Rob Palkovitz, University of Delaware
Cheri Raff, Centralia College (Washington)
Nicholas Santilli, John Carroll University (Ohio)
E. Dean Schroeder, Laramie County Community College (Wyoming)
B. Lynn Tillman, University of Houston—University Park

Karen Owens

Brief Contents

Special Features

Contents

The World of the Child

PART I

Children and Adolescents in Contexts of Development

CHAPTER 1

Studying Children: Past, Present, and Future

CHILDREN'S THOUGHTS

On who Sigmund Freud was . . .

Sigmund Freud was a scholar who was of great intelligence. He, although having intelligence, was slightly on the crazy side. He dazzled readers with his psychological theories, and he was a great writer and poet. Through his insights, he gained knowledge that no one else had ever imagined or thought of before. A hermit by age 17 he lived in poverty for most of his life and his only connection with the real world from the small island that he lived on in the Pacific was his writings. Freud was a man troubled and brilliant. Somehow it always seems that brilliance comes from the troubled; maybe their depression or whatever makes them strive harder. Who knows I'm only 13, not quite yet a philosopher.

Kurt, age 13

Sigmund Freud was a psychologist, said to be one of the best. He has wrote many books on the subject of psychology to my understanding. However, I wouldn't know this if it wasn't for the former T.V. show entitled "M*A*S*H." Sigmund Freud makes periodic visits with the M*A*S*H unit.

Heidi, age 10

CHAPTER OUTLINE

KEY TERMS

Infanticide
Tabula rasa
Theory
Unconscious mind
Preconscious
Id
Ego
Superego
Pleasure principle
Reality principle
Perfection principle
Psychosexual stages
Fixation
Epigentic principle
Psychosocial stages
Behaviorism
Classical conditioning
Operant conditioning
Positive reinforcer
Negative reinforcer
Imitation
Scientific method
Hypothesis
Generalizability
Random sampling
Confounding variables
Case study
Survey
Naturalistic observation
Experimental method
Variable
Independent variable
Dependent variable
Experimental group
Control group
Multivariate analysis
Correlational method
Longitudinal study
Cross-sectional study
Cohort

Welcome to the fascinating world of children and adolescents! We are about to embark on a journey in which we explore, like individual pieces of a complex puzzle, each important aspect of children's physical, cognitive, social, emotional, gender, and moral development. The interrelatedness of each developmental facet is emphasized so that students of developmental psychology can see the child as an integrated whole.

Developmental psychology is a rapidly growing and changing scientific discipline. Not that long ago developmental researchers viewed children as small passive creatures whose behavior was primarily shaped and molded by the principal caregiver, in most cases, mom. The mother influenced the child, who was viewed as having a passive role in the developmental process.

Bell (1979) was one of the first developmental psychologists to point out the fallacy of this model. He suggested that researchers focus on the interactive relationship between the mother and child.

Today, it is recognized that the caregiver and infant engage in a constant two-way flow of influence and that the relationship between the caregiver and the child is an interactive one. Robert Cairns (1990) points out, however, that the idea of bidirectionality does not assume that mothers and children exercise equal influence over each other:

> The evidence from the past 20 years indicates that if influence is a two-way street, one direction is a four-lane expressway, and the other an alleyway. Moreover, the weight of influence depends not only on the context and the interaction that is being assessed but also on the age-developmental status of the participants and their momentary status. (p. 25)

Researchers have broadened the scope of their knowledge by studying reciprocal influences between not only mother and child, but also father and child. Fathers, prior to the 1970s, were virtually ignored in developmental research as they were not considered potent forces in influencing children's development. The father was seen simply as a secondary figure and, at the very most, played a supporting role for the mother. As you shall see, contemporary research does not support this image of the father as the helpless parent with little talent for or interest in child rearing. Moreover, researchers are studying reciprocal influences among all family members. As active members in an intimate, organized social system, mothers, fathers, and children influence the whole family system, and, of course, are influenced by all family members.

In addition, those studying children's development incorporated the concept of the actively thinking child. Rather than being faithful recorders of adult instructions, children are now seen as capable of eliciting, maintaining, and modifying their environment and the behavior of others.

Developmental theories in the 1990s have suggested that children create their own experiences from the opportunities afforded by their rearing environment. Scarr (1992) has proposed that children make their own environments in three ways: "First children's genes necessarily are correlated with their environments because parents provide both, so that their experiences are constructed from opportunities that are correlated positively with their personal characteristics" (p. 8). For example, parents who like to read and read well are likely to go to the library, subscribe to magazines and newspapers, and read to their children. These parents are more likely to expose their children to this world of literacy more so than parents who have reading problems. Thus, the reading abilities of parents, continues Scarr, are likely to be correlated with the reading abilities of their children and with the environments parents provide for their children. Second, children evoke from others responses that are correlated with their own characteristics. To illustrate, cheerful infants tend to evoke positive interactions from parents and other adults. Finally, children actively select environments that are correlated with their interests, talents, and personality characteristics. An outgoing toddler, for example, seeks the company of others.

Research in child development is no longer confined to studying children in one context, such as the family. Children's development, Bronfenbrenner (1979) points out, is best understood from an ecological or contextual point of view; that is, children's development is influenced by biological, family, social, and cultural contexts. These contexts, as seen in Figure 1.1, are best viewed as concentric networks of interrelated systems.

At the core of these concentric circles is the child's biological makeup. Children are not simply blank slates on which experience determines and writes their personalities. Children are born with genetic propensities that influence their development. Moreover, as we will see, children may actively seek certain environmental experiences that match their genetic propensities. Surrounding the biological context is the family, which comes in various forms: traditional (mom, dad, sister,

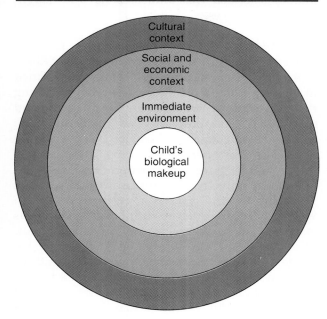

FIGURE 1.1   Children's Contexts of Development

Bronfenbrenner (1979) has suggested that children's development is influenced by biological, family, social, and cultural influences.

Source: From *The Ecology of Human Development* by U. Bronfenbrenner, 1979, Cambridge, MA: Harvard University Press.

brother), single-parent, stepparent/blended, and foster families. Although children's initial experiences occur in the immediate family context, as children get older, their experiential horizons broaden to include the social context: school, media, peers, and friends. Finally, to truly understand children's development, we need to study cultural influences. The particular cultural milieu in which children are reared has a profound influence on their development. Thus, a child's personality actively influences, and is influenced by, each of these interrelated contexts of development. This text reflects these new developmental approaches to studying children. Children are viewed as active problem solvers in mutually influential biological, family, social, and cultural systems.

In this chapter we'll begin our exploration into children's development by examining child-rearing practices, which have varied greatly over the centuries. Before scientific inquiry of childhood, child-rearing practices were largely influenced by philosophical and religious views and dogmas. A brief account of some of these views will help to put present-day attitudes and methods into perspective.

Next, some of the theories on childhood proposed after the science of child development was established are explored. When you consider the complexities of the child, it is not surprising that many theories were offered to account for different aspects of children's development. Faced with many influential factors, developmental psychologists narrow the focus of their investigation to a few aspects that they consider to be important. The psychoanalytic theories of Freud and Erikson, the learning theory of Watson and Skinner, and the cognitive-developmental approach of Piaget will be discussed. All these theories have had a prominent affect in influencing adults' treatment of children.

Although developmental psychologists may disagree on which aspects of children's behavior need to be studied, they do generally agree on the importance of studying children in a systematic and objective way. Therefore, the third section focuses on the scientific methods used by developmental researchers to explain children's development.

PERSPECTIVES ON CHILDHOOD BEFORE SCIENTIFIC INQUIRY

What was it like to be a child in times past? Throughout history, children have been regarded in various ways: as parents' property, as miniature adults, as innately evil, as blank slates, and as needed workers.

ANCIENT GREECE AND ROME

Information about attitudes toward children and childhood in ancient Greece comes from Plato's *Laws* and Aristotle's *Politics*. Borstelmann (1983) points out these philosophers "were concerned about corruption in politics and sought to devise ways of child rearing that would assure selection of better governing officials" (p. 6). Plato was convinced that parents were not capable of rearing their children properly. He believed that all children should be separated from their parents early in life and that the state should control child rearing and education. His ideal society was a *meritocracy,* in which an individual's position in life (regardless of a child's gender or economic position) would be decided by objectively determined merit. Aristotle, Plato's most outstanding student, agreed for the most part with Plato's philosophy about children, but he did not feel children should be taken away from their parents. The privacy of home life needed to be encouraged and protected; the family was essential to personal and social stability (French, 1977).

Life was grim for children in both ancient Greece and Rome. Most children did not survive infancy, and some were deliberately put to death by their parents. Although **infanticide** was both legally and culturally approved, it seems to have been restricted to children who had evident birth defects or were excess progeny, especially females. Once a child was accepted into the home, however, his or her position was secure (Greenleaf, 1978).

Discipline was harsh. "Antiquity is full of devices and practices unknown to later times, including shackles for the feet, handcuffs, gags, three months in the block and the bloody Spartan flagellation contests, which often involved whipping boys to death" (de Mause, 1974, p. 42). Children were considered to be their parents' property and were often sold into slavery (Aries, 1962).

A young girl in ancient Greece and Rome probably married before her 15th birthday and more than likely became pregnant soon after. Her husband had complete control over her and her status was little better than that of a child. The girl's husband was not completely independent either. A Spartan husband, for example, had to live in an army barracks until age 30, and only then could he establish his own home. Independence came late

for a Roman as well. A Roman family was a patriarchal family. The father was all-powerful; his influence extended well into his sons' and daughters' married lives.

THE MIDDLE AGES

Ancient times came to an end with the fall of Rome in the 5th century. Culture and commerce declined in Western Europe for the next 500 years. During the 11th century the economy began to expand once again, and progress was made on many fronts. The treatment of children, however, remained woefully behind.

The Middle Ages was a period of superstition, ignorance, brutality, and disease. Children were generally deemed of little importance, not even worthy of record once born. Infant mortality was extremely high. Borstelmann (1983) points out, "Estimates of death during the first year of life suggest that one, sometimes two, of every three children born died in their first postnatal year, a figure that did not change until after the middle of the 1700s" (p. 10). Even if a child did survive, her life was still precarious. Influenza, bubonic plague, and smallpox epidemics, to name a few, raged. Since childhood diseases were so rampant during the first 7 years of life, parents made little or no emotional or educational investment in their children until after their seventh birthday.

The life of medieval children was difficult even if they survived infancy. They often were beaten, neglected, and afforded no rights at all. "Legally, children were put in the same class as servants who had no civil rights and considered to be the parents' personal property. They were often disposed to monastery or marriage without even being consulted" (Greenleaf, 1978, p. 40).

With the exception of lovemaking and war, the daily activities of a child of the Middle Ages were the same as those of an adult. Children ate the same food, wore the same clothing, played the same games, used the same language, and performed the same labor as the adults. As late as 1780 England, 7-year-olds could be and were convicted for any of the more than 200 crimes for which punishment was hanging (Borstelmann, 1983).

Regular school attendance was impossible because of the medieval practice of children working in the fields with their parents. Some lower-class boys attended choir schools, where they learned to read Latin and the basics of writing. Schools were not for the rich, who were tutored at home. The poor went to school so that they could find a place in the world (Schorsch, 1979). Upper-class boys thought a formal education was a social handicap; they didn't need to learn a trade. Girls did not go to school because it was believed that they did not possess reason. Furthermore, they were regarded as deceptive and possessed of "tricky temperaments." The treatment of girls remained inferior to that given boys from cradle to grave.

THE RENAISSANCE

Thirteen hundred to the early 1600s were years of major economic and religious transitions. Scientific discoveries, inventions, voyages to unknown lands, and artistic endeavors moved Western Europe out of the Middle Ages into the Renaissance. Despite progress in the quality of life during this period, there weren't any significant improvements in the status of children. Generally, children were regarded as unimportant; they were considered to lack wit, strength, and intelligence and were likened to old men, foolish women, and drunks.

Some historians maintain that the nuclear family—a father, mother, and children—developed during the 17th century (Aries, 1962). In medieval times, every activity of family life—work, amusement, prayer, education—radiated under the direction of the lord from the manorial center. In this lord-serf system, strong loyalty to kinship networks existed; neither individuality nor privacy was valued. The family and family house did not exist. Aries (1962) contends that a conception of childhood as a world, distinct from the adult's, was not possible until nuclear family boundaries became distinct from kinship networks. During the 17th century, the nuclear family evolved, bringing with it the recognition of childhood as separate and different from adulthood.

This awareness led to the expansion of schooling under church auspices. Sons of the poor and middle class increasingly sought economic status through education. Even well-to-do families dropped their negative attitudes toward formal education. Aristocratic families now expected their sons to become educated in public schools.

COLONIAL AMERICA IN THE 17TH CENTURY

In colonial America there was a need to keep every child alive, because success depended on an increasing labor force. Throughout the colonial period, children were considered primarily as workers who were needed to clear the land, sow seed, and harvest the crops. As a result, children, for the most part, received little education.

The pervasive Calvinistic image of colonial children was that they were innately sinful and ignorant. Calvinists believed the newborn child to be full of the "pollutions of sin." Similarly, they viewed the first strivings of a 2-year-old toward independence, which we now recognize as essential to a child's growing mastery of himself and understanding of the world, as a clear manifestation of that original sin (Beekman, 1977).

Pious parents were faced with two tasks: instruction and discipline. They thought they should be strict, and they worked diligently to break the child's will, subdue the evil spirit, and provide scriptural foundations. Seventeenth-century America could be called the age of the whip. Children were taught to revere their parents and to fear not living up to their parents' expectations (Cable, 1972).

Although parents believed that children were evil and sinful, they did think that children were at least partly rational creatures who with proper training could learn to act piously and according to reason. That human effort could eradicate sin and ignorance is one of the rays of light that occasionally broke through the clouds of 17th-century Calvinism.

WESTERN EUROPE—17TH AND 18TH CENTURIES

There emerged among 17th- and 18th-century intellectuals of Western Europe a dramatically different view of human nature. This period came to be known as the Enlightenment because of great changes in religion, politics, science, and education. The child was now thought to be a distinctive and not unimportant being. Moreover, there was a surge in interest in education. Grammar schools were established within 12 miles of almost every family. Girls, however, were still not considered worthy of education. For both the poor and the privileged, girls' training consisted first of learning domestic skills and only secondarily reading and writing (Despert, 1965).

The 18th century was characterized by a willingness of parents to be close to their children, a change occasioned in part by greater confidence in infant survival and in part by the educational theories of John Locke and Jean Jacques Rousseau. Unlike the Calvinists and their negative image of children, these two men believed that children were not born evil. During the Age of Enlightenment, the writings of Locke and Rousseau were widely read and accepted. Their works were highly influential in helping to usher in the great and innocent "age of the child."

Locke (1693/1964) believed that heredity had no influence in predetermining the child's course or quality of development. The child's mind, according to Locke, is like a blank tablet, a **tabula rasa,** on which experience writes, thereby creating the child's personality. Locke urged parents to observe each child and try to adjust education to his or her unique personality. Locke rejected the "spare the rod and spoil the child" philosophy that had been used so unquestioningly in previous times. Instead, he recommended the use of praise and commendation for children's successes, and a "cold and negative countenance" for their failures.

Rousseau (1762/1911) believed that children were naturally good and, provided they were not corrupted by an evil environment, could develop into paragons of virtue. Stating that education had a corrupting influence on children, he virtually wrote off education as a manipulative device of an evil society. He observed that many defects found in children's bodies and minds came from society's desire to make adults of them before their time. He concluded that nature provided children with the necessary learning tools, and he urged schools to become more flexible and less rule-governed. However, Rousseau believed that higher education was useless for girls because they were incapable of logical reasoning. He viewed girls as bound by tradition to bring comfort and love to those around them.

In his book *Emile,* Rousseau talks of learning more about children and the psychological principles that created a radically new vision of children. Emile was Rousseau's sanctified child educated by his natural environment. Rousseau urged parents to be more respectful of childhood and to allow children to be more "natural." Although Rousseau offered virtuous advice for parents and schools, he had no special credentials to dispense educational advice. He failed miserably as a tutor and consigned his five illegitimate children to foundling hospitals.

THE INDUSTRIAL REVOLUTION

Although children had always worked, they had done so in the fields and shops near their homes. During the Industrial Revolution (1780–1900), children began to work in factories further away. The *Industrial Revolution* described widespread economic changes that occurred in parts of Europe and America. Economies that were once solely dependent on farming and crafts now became industrialized. Great numbers of children worked in airless, insect-infested factories, meat-packing plants, and coal mines for 14 to 16 hours a day. In 1880, the United States census revealed that one million children between the ages of 10 and 15 were holding jobs.

Things were worse in England, however. Children as young as 4 were often used as chimney sweeps or in the coal mines because their small bodies could fit into the narrow flues and coal seams. If they survived the hazardous work and grew too big, they were simply turned out into the streets.

Poor children in England from the ages of 7 to 21 were often indentured virtually without pay to textile mills. As inmates of poor houses, 50 or more children were crammed into bare barracks and fed so poorly that they often raided pigsties in order to get food (Greenleaf, 1978). Of work, duties, and responsibilities, there is ample evidence; of joys and amusements, there is none.

During the 1830s the factory system had abused children to such an extent that finally the first child protective laws were passed. The Factory Act, for example, set a 12-hour-per-day limitation in factories, made some provisions for schooling, and required some changes in factory hygiene.

PERSPECTIVES ON CHILDHOOD AFTER SCIENTIFIC INQUIRY

It is not only difficult to pinpoint the precise beginnings of scientific child development but also equally difficult to narrow the list of prominent names associated with its inception. Most child development specialists, however, would agree that Charles Darwin was a vital force in establishing child development as a science (Kessen, 1965; Charlesworth, 1992). In 1859, Darwin wrote *On the Origins of the Species*. In this book he drew a parallel between human evolution and the development of the child. Darwin believed that the development of the child repeats the development of the species and is a living reflection of the human species' evolution. Although this idea was later rejected, Darwin was the first to believe that studying children's development was important in order to study human behavior.

G. Stanley Hall is another prominent name associated with systematic study of children's behavior. Among other achievements, Hall was the first to devise and refine the questionnaire method in studying large groups of children. In addition, he was the founder of a child study institute at Clark University in Worchester, Massachusetts, in 1891. At about the same time in France, Alfred Binet and Theophile Simon were laying the foundations for child development at the Sorbonne by devising an objective, standardized intelligence test.

Other prominent scholars entered the field and began to systematically study children and to pro-

Darwin showed an extreme interest in studying children.

pose individual theories charting the course of children's development. A **theory** is a formulation to explain underlying principles of certain observed phenomena that have been verified to some degree.

Three major theories have had a significant impact on the field of child development, each emphasizing a different aspect of children's development. The psychoanalytic theories of Sigmund Freud and Erik Erikson emphasize personality development and stress the importance of unconscious conflicts and biological instincts in the determination of children's development. The learning theories of John B. Watson and B. F. Skinner focus on environmental determinants of behavior and stress the role of reinforcement in shaping a child's behavior. The cognitive theory of Jean Piaget is concerned with the development of thought processes or reasoning and stresses the child's active role in determining his developmental level. Let's begin our discussion of these theories with Freud's "pleasure-seeking" child.

SIGMUND FREUD'S PLEASURE-SEEKING CHILD

It has been suggested that theorists' lives and work experiences cannot be separated from their theories. It is interesting not only to describe a given theory but also to see how life may have led to the development of the ideas. Freud's long life has been surveyed by the foremost English psychoanalyst, Ernest Jones, and brilliantly related in a three-volume biography. Freud's theory pertaining to children's sexual and aggressive drives, to the importance of early experiences to later development, to the ways the unconscious mind influences children's behavior may have been derived from his personal as well as clinical experiences as a therapist (Rieff, 1961).

Sigmund Freud was born in Freiberg, Moravia, now a part of Czechoslovakia, in 1859, and was raised in Vienna, Austria. He graduated from medical school in 1881 and became a research associate to a professor of physiology. It was a job that paid very poorly, eventually forcing Freud to go into private practice, where he specialized in the treatment of neurotic disorders (Jones, 1953). Freud's patients, primarily women, suffered from symptoms that Freud then classified as hysteria. (Hysteria was a general category that referred to a host of symptoms, such as psychological blindness, deafness, paralysis of limbs, for which there were no organic reasons.)

Freud's theory on the Oedipus complex germinated as he listened to the sexual fantasies verbalized by these troubled women. Several patients reported that they had been seduced by their fathers. Freud concluded that such thoughts of sexual activities were only a dream wish on the part of the child, uncovered by the adult later in life.

In 1984, a psychoanalyst who briefly headed the Freud archives, Jeffrey Masson (1984), charged that Freud had lied and that his patients had truly been victims of actual sexual abuse in childhood. Masson claimed that Freud had covered up the

Despite the fact that Freud observed few children in a clinical setting and none in a traditional experimental design, his theory emerged as one of the most important influences on child development in the 20th century.

truth to advance his theory. These charges were widely denounced by Freudian scholars on the grounds that Masson had offered little convincing evidence (Gay, 1988).

Freud (1920/1957) discovered that he, too, had this same sexual dream wish toward his mother. Through self-analysis and analysis of his dreams as a youth, Freud traced his experiences as a young boy. It appears that Freud experienced a deep love for his mother and jealousy for his father. When Freud was born, his father was 40 years old; his mother (his father's third marriage) was only 20. His father was somewhat strict and authoritarian. Freud recalled as an adult the childhood hostility, hatred, and rage he felt toward his father. Freud's mother, however, was slender and attractive, protective and loving. Freud felt a passionate, sexual attachment to her. He often had dreams, phenomena that Freud characterized as the royal road to the unconscious mind. Freud interpreted the symbols of his boyhood dreams as manifestations of his love for his mother and jealousy toward his father—the typical Oedipus complex as embodied in Freud's theory (Jones, 1953). Thus, Freud's theory was formulated initially on an intuitive basis, drawn from his own experiences and memories. It was then constructed along more rational lines through his work with patients, examining their childhood experiences and memories through case studies and analysis of their dreams.

Freud's practice continued to grow, and more and more people began to pay respectful attention to his work. During the 1920s and 1930s, Freud reached the pinnacle of his success, but at the same time his health began to deteriorate. From 1923 until his death 16 years later, Freud underwent 33 operations for cancer of the mouth. In late September 1939, Freud confided to his physician, Max Schur, "Now it's nothing but torture and [life] makes no sense any more" (Schur, 1972, p. 529). Schur administered three injections of morphine over the next 24 hours, each dosage greater than necessary for sedation. Freud's years of pain were finally over.

The Conscious and Unconscious Mind Freud (1938/1973) proposed the view that the mind consists of conscious and two unconscious aspects. The conscious mind represents those aspects of our personality of which we are aware. By the **unconscious mind,** Freud meant a sort of mental receptacle for ideas too anxiety-producing for the conscious mind to acknowledge; they are, therefore, pushed voluntarily (suppressed) or involuntarily (repressed) into the unconscious mind. While the individual cannot recall these ideas at will, they continue to influence her thinking, feel-

ing, and behavior. Some mental material, although not directly conscious, is stored and can be brought rather easily to the conscious level. This third level Freud called the **preconscious.** Within these levels of consciousness are three processes known as the id, ego, and superego that interact and produce our personalities: patterned or characteristic ways of behaving (see Figure 1.2).

The **id** is the level of personality that contains all human motives and emotions such as love, aggression, fear, and so on. The id is our unconscious mind; it is primitive and illogical. The childlike id wants immediate gratification; it wants what it wants now! The id's inability to always produce the desired object leads to the development of the **ego,** the mind's avenue to the real world. The ego is the rational level of personality that slowly emerges and becomes noticeable after the child's first birthday. The ego guides the basic impulses for behavior that arise from the id. In a sense, it functions as the executive in dealing with real-life events and balances the irrational demands from the id and superego. Above all, the ego's decision making involves the delay of energy discharge. The **superego** represents ideals on morals and manners. The superego consists of the conscience, which reminds us of the "should-nots," our inter-

---

FIGURE 1.2 The Id, Ego, and Superego

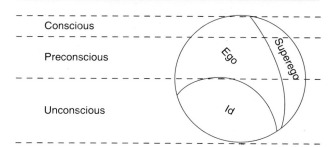

The id resides in the unconscious mind; the ego and superego are partly conscious, preconscious, and unconscious. For example, when we experience guilt or self-doubts without being aware of the causes, it is the unconscious workings of the superego.

Source: Adapted from *The Ego and the Id* by S. Freud, 1923/1974, London: Hogarth.

nal judicial system. The superego strives for perfection and is not satisfied with less. It is, like the id, unrealistic (Bettelheim, 1983).

The id operates on the **pleasure principle,** seeking gratification and avoiding pain. Freud believed that all behavior is dominated by sexual and aggressive drives. Human beings are born with untamed instinctual forces that push for discharge. Society's role is to tame those forces, and to transform them into energies that are usable for constructive purposes. Parents are missionaries bringing civilization to unsocialized natives. The ego, on the contrary, operates on the **reality principle,** rational analysis of the situation and realistic reduction of the id's need state. The superego operates on the **perfection principle,** guiding the person's behavior according to socially desirable values. The superego incorporates many of the values taught by parents. In conflict situations, such as the one represented in Figure 1.3, each of these drives strives to have its needs met (Freud, 1905/1953).

Instincts   An instinct is a basic element of Freud's theory. Instincts are the motivating, propelling force of personality that drives behavior and deter-

mines its direction. Instincts have two interrelated elements: a biological need state and an inborn psychological representation—a wish. To illustrate, the biological need state that relates to the experience of hunger is a drop in the glucose level in the bloodstream. Psychologically, hunger is represented as a wish for food. These elements combine to form an instinct to eat food when food is needed. Instincts, then, may be thought of as needs seeking appropriate satisfactions.

When the body is in a state of need, a person experiences the condition of tension. The aim of an instinct is to satisfy the need and thereby reduce the tension. According to Freud, people are continually motivated to restore and maintain equilibrium—to eliminate the tension and keep the body tension-free.

Instincts can be grouped into two bipolar categories: the life instincts (growth and satisfying needs for food, water, air, and sex) and the death instincts (destruction, unconscious wishes to die, and aggression).

Psychosexual Stages   One of Freud's most influential ideas is that the adult personality is shaped by early childhood experiences. He proposed that

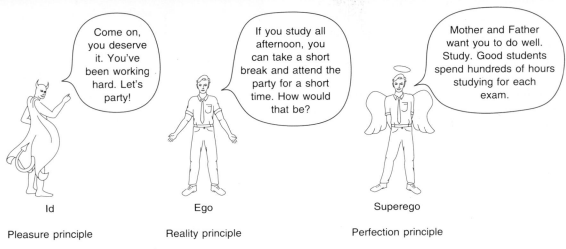

FIGURE 1.3   Conflict situation: You have been invited to a party, but unfortunately you have a mid-term exam tomorrow.

Come on, you deserve it. You've been working hard. Let's party!

If you study all afternoon, you can take a short break and attend the party for a short time. How would that be?

Mother and Father want you to do well. Study. Good students spend hundreds of hours studying for each exam.

Id

Ego

Superego

Pleasure principle

Reality principle

Perfection principle

children travel through several **psychosexual stages** in which sexual instincts associated with different erogenous zones are particularly important. Freud believed that the development of the personality (psyche) was crucially influenced by the manner in which the child learned to expend sexual energy (libido) from one psychosexual stage to the next. How a child comes through each stage, according to Freud, depends on how the mother handles her child's sexual impulses and behavior. If children, for example, receive too much gratification or too little in each of the stages, they fixate. **Fixation** implies stagnation within a particular stage, resulting in the inability to move on to a more mature way of interacting with the world. To pass through these stages successfully, with no psychological conflicts or tensions, requires an optimal amount of gratification at each stage. Freud placed considerable emphasis on the importance of the first three psychosexual stages. He felt that

the first five or six years were of great importance in determining the adult personality (Fine, 1979). These stages and the concept of fixation account for ways libidinal energy might become centered on the person's body. If fixation occurs, the person is predisposed to seek tension reduction later in life by resorting to forms of behavior that were of greatest significance during earlier stages of development. A child who is weaned too early, for example, may experience urges to eat and drink to excess as an adult. Table 1.1 provides a summary of the psychosexual stages and the developmental outcomes of fixation at each stage.

What then is the role of parents who wish to guide their children's growth in ways that promote positive adjustments? Based on Freud's theory, parents should

(a) recognize the nature of instinctual urges and accept the desirability of permitting expression of the urges; (b) recognize normal psychosexual

TABLE 1.1 Psycho-sexual Stages			
Stage	**Fixation**	**Developmental Outcome**
ORAL (BIRTH–2 YEARS) Child gums, mouths, and bites everything in sight. Breast is source of pleasure.	Child weaned from bottle or breast too early or too late.	As adult, will be dependent, gullible, ready "to swallow" anything. Excessive eating, drinking, kissing, and smoking behaviors.
ANAL (2–3 YEARS) Anus is source of pleasure.	Child is severely toilet trained or undertrained.	As adult, overly neat, always on time, stingy, stubborn, never disobeys orders. Excessive sloppiness.
PHALLIC (3–6 YEARS) Phallus, or penis, is most important body part.	Child fails to identify with the same-sex parent.	Homosexuality.
LATENCY (6–12 YEARS)	No sexual fixations occur during this stage.	
GENITAL (12–ADULT) Genital area is primary zone of pleasure.	No sexual fixations occur during this period.	

Source: From *The Ego and the Id* by S. Freud, 1923/1974, London: Hogarth.

stages of development and the sorts of conflicts the child faces at each stage; and (c) provide at each developmental stage enough opportunities for the child to satisfy instinctual drives within an atmosphere of understanding, but not furnish so much that the child becomes fixated at that point and is unwilling to move to the next stage. (Thomas, 1979, pp. 252–253)

Evaluation of Freud's Theory   Note, on the positive side, that Freud's theory brought up the fact that children have sexual pleasures and fantasies long before they reach adolescence (Fromm, 1980). Before Freud, children were thought to be innocent, "sexless" creatures. In addition, Freud's theory has helped us see that children's pleasure drives, propelled by the id, often conflict with parental or societal demands. Today, it is thought that while the unconscious mind motivates children's behavior, children's egos play a more influential role in directing their behavior than Freud believed.

One of the most significant ideas in Freud's theory was the realization of the need for maternal acceptance and affection (Fromm, 1980). Prior to Freud, parents accepted the notion that they should care for children's physical needs; after Freud, parents became aware of children's needs for love and affection as well.

On the negative side, Freud's theory seems to overemphasize biological drives and has an unnecessarily dim view of human potential. A model of a child as an energy system totally propelled by drives is questionable. Similarly, children of today are not seen as bundles of id, but as alert, active, and responsive.

Some of the problems in accepting Freud's theory as a valid reflector of children's development include the source of his data (a small sample of an atypical group of adults); his methodology (theory based on recollections of his patients' childhood memories); and the fact that he did not directly test children during their years of growth. Moreover, many aspects of Freud's theory are not verifiable. One reason for this is that psychoanalytical terms such as *ego, id,* and *superego* are ambiguous and removed from observable and measurable behavior. The theory cannot be substantiated or confirmed by direct observation or assessment.

It has been over 50 years since Freud's death, and during this time his theory has been continually scrutinized, embellished, revised, and criticized. Freud was a pioneer, giving to the fields of psychology and child development a wealth of ideas about human behavior. Freud is remembered by most as a genius whose ideas had an overwhelming impact on humanity. It is on his shoulders that the succeeding psychologists stand.

ERIK ERIKSON'S IDENTITY-SEEKING CHILD

Erik Erikson was a student and a follower of Freud. He, however, embellished and expanded Freud's theory to emphasize the role that culture plays in personality development. Although Erik Erikson was strongly influenced by Freud, their theories differ in important ways. Whereas Freud was concerned with personality development in the psychosexual stages of the first five years of life, Erikson was concerned with personality development in psychosocial stages during the total life cycle. Erikson's scheme centered on understanding different aspects of our social selves, unlike Freud's, which centered on sexuality. Unlike Freud, who was primarily concerned with the unconscious mind, Erikson was concerned with the social aspects of personality, and emphasized the role of the ego in children's development. Erikson changed the focus of psychodynamic theory from an emphasis on the gratification of pleasure (id) to an emphasis on successful adaptation (ego).

Erikson's own life history is one he feels has had a distinct bearing on the development of his theoretical outlook. He was born in 1902 to Danish parents. Shortly before his birth, his parents separated and his mother moved to Germany. Three years later she married the man who was her son's pediatrician. Erikson considered himself to be German; his stepfather was German, and he lived in Germany. His mother was Jewish, however, and this ethnic and religious combination caused Erikson difficulties in school. Despite the fact that Erikson became a German superpatriot, he was rejected by his anti-Semitic classmates. The tall, blond boy was not accepted at the synagogue either (Watson, 1971).

While Erik Erikson believed in many of Freud's ideas, he embellished and broadened Freud's theory.

The man who gave us the concept of identity crisis went through several such crises in his earlier years. During his early 20s, Erikson dropped out from society for awhile and wandered throughout Germany and Italy, reading, recording his thoughts in a notebook, and observing life around him. He studied art for a short period of time, but soon left art school to resume his wandering and to search for his identity. Erikson later wrote, "No doubt, my best friends will insist that I needed to name this crisis and to see it in everybody else in order to really come to terms with myself" (Erikson, 1975, pp. 25–26).

At the age of 25, Erikson began his training in psychoanalysis under the tutelage of Freud's daughter, Anna. Six years later, he and his new wife moved to Boston, Massachusetts, where he set up a private practice specializing in the treatment of children. Throughout his professional career Erikson continued to pursue his interest in identity formation by studying Native American tribes and World War II veterans. He became convinced that these men were suffering from confusion of identity as to who and what they were as a result of being "uprooted" from their culture. Thus, Erikson's theory, which centered on the ego as it develops through various psychosocial stages searching for a sense of identity and completeness, paralleled his own experiences as a youth and his later experiences as a psychoanalyst.

Epigenetic Principle Erikson created the **epigenetic principle,** which refers to the observation that "anything that grows has a ground plan, and . . . out of this ground plan the parts arise, each part having its time of special ascendancy, until all parts have arisen to form a functioning whole" (1959, p. 52). Thus, some sort of blueprint must exist at conception containing instructions for all the developmental changes that will occur and how they will be sequenced. In fetal development, for example, certain organs of the body appear at certain specified times and eventually "combine" to form a child. Personality, according to Erikson, develops in a similar way.

Psychosocial Stages Erikson proposed that human development consists of a series of periods in which some issue is particularly prominent and important. In his view, people experience a psychosocial crisis, or conflict, during each of the eight **psychosocial stages.** A crisis is a turning point, a period when the potential for growth is high but a person is also quite vulnerable. Erikson sees a crisis as a struggle between attaining some adaptive psychological quality versus failing to obtain it. Individuals negotiate each stage by developing a balance, or ratio, between the two qualities for which that stage is named. Successful negotiation of a stage, however, does imply the balance is weighted more toward the positive value than the negative value.

Successful resolution in each of these stages strengthens the ego and prepares one to face the next crises. Inadequate resolution invariably continues to haunt a person and affects his ability to function and to cope. Failure or difficulty in establishing what is required at one stage does not condemn anyone to complete failure in the next stage, although developmental progress can be slowed or made more difficult to achieve. Thus, a crisis is not resolved once and then forgotten. Rather, resolutions of previously encountered conflicts are reshaped at each new stage of psychosocial development. Although early psychosocial crises in Erikson's theory are similar to the psychosexual stages articulated by Freud, Erikson's interpretation adds a strong social element (Kacerguis & Adams, 1980).

The first stage, which Erikson labeled the *cornerstone of the vital personality,* is known as *basic trust versus mistrust* (birth to age 2). The infant's task is to reach out to the social environment for nurturance, with the expectation that her longing will be satisfied. The degree of trust that the infant develops depends on the quality of care she receives. Infants who are cuddled, played with, talked to, and whose needs are met when they arise, whose discomforts are quickly removed, develop a vital sense of trust that the world is safe and reliable. Infants who receive inconsistent and unreliable care develop a basic mistrust, which may lead, in adulthood, to a basic fear and withdrawal from interpersonal contact and a dread that one's social needs cannot or will not be met. An adult who experienced the conditions for trust during infancy greets the world with fundamental hope; one who did not greets the world with a sense of doom.

Just when children have learned to trust or mistrust their parents, they must learn to exert a degree of independence. This stage is known as *autonomy versus shame and doubt* (ages 2 to 4). Children discover that they have a mind and a will of their own. To develop autonomy and a firmly developed will in children, parents need to recognize children's needs to climb, open and close, push and pull, hold on and let go. Children increasingly demand to control their own behavior,

but they do not have a keen sense of judgment about their capabilities. They need to be protected from excesses while being granted autonomy in matters they can handle. A successful resolution of this stage gives the individual the capacity to be loving and cooperative, yet firm in dealing with others. Overprotection, lack of support, restricting children's freedom of movement, impatience, or continually doing things for children that they can do for themselves can lead to children developing a sense of shame and doubt, which later may be expressed either in too much conscience or in flagrant disregard of social convention.

Children 4 or 5 years old are ready to engage in constructive activities under their own initiative. The major achievements of increased social mobility, language development, and the expansion of imagination set the stage for *initiative versus guilt.* If explorations, projects, and activities are generally effective and rewarded by their parents, children develop a sense of competence. In later years, the child who manages this stage well is capable of imagining alternative futures. The potential problem at this period is guilt. If children's motor activity is considered bad, their questions viewed as bothersome, their play activities regarded as stupid, they develop a sense of guilt over self-initiated activities in general. As adults they may either continuously try to prove themselves to others, or they may be hypercritical of everything concerning themselves and others.

In the fourth stage, *industry versus inferiority* (ages 7 to puberty), children master activities that are essential for functioning in society. When children are encouraged to build things, to cook, and to experience, and they are praised for their results, industry is enhanced. Children who learn that they are skilled tend to take the sense of competence with them throughout their lives. When children are not praised for their accomplishments, when projects and activities are viewed as messy and children a nuisance, their sense of inferiority is reinforced.

The fifth stage, *identity versus role diffusion,* is, according to Erikson, the most dynamic, complex, and significant stage of all. Young adolescents develop a multitude of new ways of looking at and thinking about themselves and their world. They attempt to bring together all the things they have learned about themselves as students, sons, daughters, friends, and workers, and they begin to develop a sense of what they are and where they are going. The process of self-definition is not construed as one in which there should be a static end point, rather, it is an ongoing process reflecting change as needed throughout the life span. Those who successfully resolve the identity crisis have a strong sense of their values and directions, and are at peace with whom they have become. Those who fail this suffer from identity confusion, and are directionless, or merely adopt, without analysis, the roles imposed on them.

The next three stages go beyond the ages of interest in this book, but for a complete presentation of Erikson's theory, they are discussed in Table 1.2. Each stage of development contributes its own unique virtue to the human personality: Infancy contributes to faith, early childhood to power, preschool to purposefulness, school age to efficiency, adolescence to commitment, young adulthood to love, adulthood to responsibility, and old age to wisdom.

Erikson further suggested that basic strengths are developed with the successful resolution of crisis at each of the eight psychosocial stages. *Hope*, growing out of stage one, basic trust, is the persistent belief that desires can be satisfied. It is a sense of confidence that is maintained in spite of temporary setbacks. *Will*, an irrevocable determination to exercise both freedom of choice and self-restraint, develops out of autonomy. *Purpose* develops from initiative and involves a sense of courage to envision and to pursue important goals. *Competence* develops from industriousness and involves the exertion of skill and intelligence in the pursuit and completion of tasks. *Fidelity*, which grows out of identity cohesion, involves the maintenance of basic loyalties, a sense of duty and sincerity in relations with others. *Love* develops from intimacy and is considered by Erikson to be one of the greatest strengths. *Care* emerges from generativity and involves a broad concern or solicitude toward others.

The final strength, *wisdom*, arises out of ego integrity. Wisdom conveys to the next generation an integration of experience best captured by the word *heritage*.

Evaluation of Erikson's Theory   Erikson's theory is subject to some of the same criticisms as Freud's. Erikson relied on subjective data built out of his own experiences and recollections of patients in therapy. Research on his theory has not substantiated or refuted its ideas and explanations. One of Erikson's strongest ideas is his emphasis on social and cultural influences on development. Another, perhaps his main contribution, lies in his delineation of development and crises of the healthy personality, with an emphasis on normal rather than on abnormal development. His ideas about the nature of children are optimistic.

JOHN B. WATSON'S CONDITIONED CHILD

Early American psychologists dismissed such hidden, internal agents as Freud's id and ego as unfortunate leftovers from the magical thinking of the Middle Ages. The first American psychologists ushered in a new era of pragmatic adherence to fact rather than speculative imagination. John Broadus Watson was an American psychologist who sought to bolster the scientific character of psychology. Contrary to Freud and Erikson, Watson argued that any science of behavior must be based on observable events (Cohen, 1979). His approach to studying behavior is known as **behaviorism.**

Watson (1914) set out to demonstrate the relevance of purely behavioral procedures to the study of child behavior. He began his work with newborn infants and the analysis of the conditioning of emotional responses. The experiment on which Watson embarked was to become one of the enduring classics.

Classical Conditioning   Albert, an 11-month-old child, was shown a small, white rat. Just as Little Albert reached out to touch the rat, Watson banged on a steel bar with a hammer. As Watson describes the experiment, "The infant jumped violently, and fell forward, burying his face in the mattress." The

TABLE 1.2 Psychosocial Stages	Stage	Developmental Outcome
	BASIC TRUST VS. MISTRUST (BIRTH–2 YEARS)	Degree of trust child develops depends on the quality of care child receives. Infants who receive consistent and reliable care learn to develop sense of trust.
	AUTONOMY VS. SHAME AND DOUBT (2–4 YEARS)	Parents need to recognize the child's need to run, climb, and explore to develop sense of independence. Severely restricting child's freedom can lead to sense of doubt about his or her own abilities.
	INITIATIVE VS. GUILT (4–7 YEARS)	Parents need to recognize child's need to engage in constructive activities under own initiative. If explorations, activities, and projects are not rewarded, or if child feels he or she is overstepping the limits set by parents, the child may feel guilty.
	INDUSTRY VS. INFERIORITY (7 YEARS–PUBERTY)	Sense of duty and accomplishment; child develops academic and social competencies. Excessive competition, personal limitations, or other conditions that may lead to failure result in feelings of inferiority. Praising children for accomplishments leads to feelings of industry and self-competency.
	IDENTITY VS. ROLE CONFUSION (ADOLESCENCE)	Adolescents try to figure out "Who am I?" They establish sexual, ethnic, and career identities or are confused about what future roles to play.
	INTIMACY VS. ISOLATION (ADULTHOOD)	Young adults seek companionship and love with another person or become isolated from other people.
	GENERATIVITY VS. STAGNATION (ADULTHOOD)	Adults are productive, performing meaningful work and raising a family, or they become stagnant and inactive.
	INTEGRITY VS. DESPAIR (OLD AGE)	People try to make sense out of their lives, either seeing life as a meaningful whole or despairing at goals never reached and questions never answered.

Source: From *Identity: Youth in Adolescence and Crisis* by E. Erikson, 1968, New York: Norton.

infant reached for the rat again, and as he did so Watson banged again. "Again the infant jumped violently, fell forward and began to whimper." Watson showed Albert the rat three times at the same time the loud noise was made. The child "puckered his face and cried. Then I let him quiet down. Again the assistant brings in the rat. This time something new develops. No longer do I have to rap the steel bar. *He shows fear at the sight of the rat.* He makes the same reaction to it as he makes to the sound of the steel bar. He begins to cry and turn away the moment he sees it" (Watson, 1928, pp. 52–53). This process is known as **classical conditioning,** and according to Watson, this study demonstrates that feelings are a product of classical conditioning.

In classical conditioning, an unconditioned stimulus (unlearned, innate) produces a reflexive response. For example, during a physical examination, the doctor taps your knee with a small rubber hammer and your leg reflexively jerks. When the unconditioned stimulus is continually paired with a conditioned stimulus (learned, neutral at the start), people eventually respond to the conditioned stimulus in the same way they did to the unconditioned stimulus. In this example, if the doctor were to whistle the first five notes of Beethoven's Fifth Symphony (conditioned stimulus) and then tap a person's knee (unconditioned stimulus), and the doctor continued to do this for a number of trials, eventually the doctor could just whistle and the person's leg would jerk. The essential characteristic of classical conditioning is that a previously neutral stimulus becomes capable of eliciting a response similar to the unconditioned stimulus because of its repeated association with that stimulus.

Child-care Advice   Watson considered all emotions, not just fear, to be obstacles to adaptive behavior and a happy life. Moreover, he maintained that love and affection expressed toward children cause them to be dependent on attention from others, to remain stuck with infantile emotional responses, and unable to handle a job effectively. The baby who is cuddled too much will become an adult who always needs to be pampered and coddled. Watson (1928) believed that scientific evidence showed that children should get very little kissing and hugging. Children should never be kissed, never be hugged, and "never let them sit on your lap (p. 32)." If there has to be any kissing, let it be on the forehead. He felt it far better to shake hands.

In his influential, best-selling book *Psychological Care of Infant and Child*—Dedicated to the First Mother Who Brings Us a Happy Child—Watson (1928) pointed out other ways of raising children. In so doing, he became a symbol for a "modern," scientific approach to child rearing during the 1920s and 1930s. According to Watson, parents need to give children more freedom. They should

Parents today reject John B. Watson's cold and non-emotional approach to child rearing. Contemporary parents recognize that showing affection and warmth is important in producing emotionally healthy children.

not be constantly keeping an eye on the child. If they are unable to do this then they should use a periscope. If they use a periscope the children would not know they were being watched and might develop independent habits. Parents are too authoritarian and emotional when disciplining their children; they need to be less emotional and more objective.

Watson's modern child-care suggestions may not have been solely derived from his scientific endeavors. Perhaps his own experiences as a child led him to these conclusions. Watson was the fourth child born to Emma and Pickens Watson.

Emma, as a staunch member of the Baptist Reedy River Church, did not believe in smoking, drinking, or dancing. She did not believe in showing affection toward her children, the older three children anyway. She doted on John, however, who was very close to his father. Unfortunately, his father's main interests in life were swearing, drinking whiskey, and chasing women. When Watson was 13, his father left home. John was devastated and felt betrayed. Emma now doted on John even more. John felt very ambivalent about this, both basking in it and fretting over it. Perhaps the close relationship with his mother and a father who later betrayed him are the reasons for Watson's cold and austere child-care advice.

Evaluation of Watson's Theory   Perhaps the most salient weakness of Watson's theory is the assumption that development is a mechanistic process. The behavioristic approach to investigating and explaining development is based on the mechanistic model in which humans are conceived as functioning *as if* they are machines. Human beings are reacting to stimulation (internal or external forces) in a way predictable from the knowledge of the forces impinging on them and from knowledge about their genetic makeup.

Watson appears to have based a great deal of his theory on one subject and one experiment—Little Albert. "This was what Watson relied on to establish the validity of his proposal that the conditioned response was the key to understanding the development of human behavior. We are aghast today to see the uncritical acceptance this study received" (Stevenson, 1983, p. 216).

In retrospect, we do see that Watson opened a new era in psychology. His theory effected a complete change in psychology from Freud's nonempirical approach to an objective study of behavior.

B. F. SKINNER'S MECHANICAL CHILD

Operant Conditioning   Proceeding along Watsonian lines, B. F. Skinner (1974) does not concern himself with studying internal motives in order to explain behavior. Skinner (1972) maintained that all behavior is a result of classical and operant conditioning, with the larger part of behavior being learned via operant conditioning. In **operant conditioning,** subjects are active, that is, they *operate* on the environment. (In classical conditioning remember that subjects are *passive*; that is, things are done to subjects, who have very little control over their behavior.) Moreover, in operant conditioning, subjects' behavior is voluntary, as compared with classical conditioning, which involves involuntary behaviors (reflexes). In operant conditioning, subjects' behavior is determined by its consequences. If the consequences are rewarding, the chances are that children will repeat the behavior the next time they are in a similar position. Consequences that are not rewarding or painful cause individuals to be less likely to repeat the behavior.

Individuals, however, have very little control over their environment. Skinner rejects the idea that internal agents allow us to make independent and free choices. Just as people deserve no credit for inherited qualities, Skinner maintains they can take no credit for what they become after being born; factors simply exist and have effects. In neither case do people freely choose or decide what conditions will affect them or what they become. For Skinner, there is no ego that eventually will enable people to take over and give deliberate, conscious, rational directions to their lives. People are never really free; their "choices" are dependent on their basic genetic structure and, very importantly, on their exposure to a multitude of environmental conditions (Skinner, 1981).

Skinner emphasizes the importance of rewards in shaping behavior. *Reward,* however, is a term that Skinner would find imprecise. What most people think of as a reward is a **positive reinforcer,** which can be anything that makes it more likely that people will repeat a response. Words of praise, bear hugs, money, a piece of Fanny Farmer candy are all *potential* reinforcers. For example, a mother may increase the probability that her son will eat his spinach if she reinforces him with his favorite chocolate-covered bon bon when his spinach has been eaten. In this case, the bon bon is a positive reinforcer; it is a consequent event after a desired behavior.

B. F. Skinner was known as a radical behaviorist because of his extreme emphasis on the importance of the environment in shaping one's behavior.

Sometimes children behave in a certain way so that they can stop an unpleasant situation. A **negative reinforcer** removes a condition previously in effect to increase the probability of a response. If, for example, a first-grade teacher is screaming at her students to take their seats, they may all scramble for their respective desks in order to stop Miss Schultz's tirade. In this illustration, children sitting in their seats is negatively reinforced by the removal of the teacher's screaming.

A child's personality, as defined by Skinner, is considered to be the result of the individual's reinforcement history and genetic makeup (although Skinner was not concerned with studying genetics). Although Skinner never actually set forth a theory of child development, his thinking does stress the importance of the environment and positive reinforcement in a child's development. Parents should, according to Skinner, shape children's behavior systematically by reinforcing desired actions and ignoring undesirable ones.

Perhaps Skinner's views on the power of reinforcement, programming individuals to exhibit the right behaviors, and his advice on not using physical punishment stem in part from his early childhood experiences. In his words, "I do not believe that my life shows a type of personality à la Freud, or a schedule of development à la Erikson. There have been a few abiding themes but they can be traced to environmental sources" (Skinner, 1983, p. 25). Burrhus Frederic Skinner was born in a small railroad town in northeastern Pennsylvania known as Susquehanna in 1904. He describes his early home environment as quite warm, secure, and stable. He remembers his father as always seeking praise from others and his mother as being concerned with establishing right from wrong behaviors. She evidenced great alarm if her son demonstrated any tendency to stray from the path she had so clearly pointed out. Young Fred was never physically punished by his father, and he recalls being physically punished by his mother only once (she washed Fred's mouth out with soap for swearing).

As a youth, Skinner spent many hours designing and constructing machines: wagons, slingshots, a steam cannon, and model airplanes (prophetic, perhaps, of his later view that people function as if they were machines). His adult interest in the study of animal behavior may also have been derived from Skinner's catching and making pets of an assortment of animals: turtles, lizards, and chipmunks.

Skinner attended a small liberal arts school, Hamilton College, where he majored in English. After graduating, he spent 2 years in full-time literary endeavors. This period, however, was rather unproductive and Skinner gave up writing and turned to Harvard and psychology, receiving his Ph.D. in 1931. Skinner then spent 9 years at the University of Minnesota. During this time, he was remarkably productive and subsequently was recognized as one of the major experimental psychologists of his time. Skinner returned to Harvard to teach and remained there until his death in 1990.

Evaluation of Skinner's Theory   Many of the major criticisms of Skinner's theory of personality center on the following points: The theory fails to explain how innovative or creative acts occur. For example, how does a brilliant symphony or novel arise? Skinner's theory also neglects many important aspects of behavior. Behaviorists often ignore the importance of the unobservable aspects of human behavior such as emotions and unconscious processes. They tend to discredit feelings or ideas that do not fit neatly into the controlled experimental situation. To focus on laws of observable behavior is a narrow approach, making it very difficult to really grasp the human condition.

Skinner also extends the conclusions he derived from animal experiments—primarily with rats and pigeons—to humans without accounting properly for differences of intellectual quality among the species. Generalizations from a group of pigeons to human society are difficult to accept. Skinner has also been attacked for his implicitly mechanistic philosophy of humans whose performances are controlled and who are the products of their past conditioning experiences.

However, his learning principles (the power of immediate feedback and reinforcement) have had wide practical applicability in mental and penal institutions and schools. Skinner points out the importance of the effect of environment and helps us see that certain behaviors are the result of the immediate environment rather than of deeply rooted problems or inborn drives. He draws attention to the power of reinforcement. His theory has generated a remarkable variety of research efforts. Skinner, as do other behaviorists, emphasizes the need to define terms carefully and to run controlled experiments. Such a contribution has made psychology more of a science.

ALBERT BANDURA'S IMITATING CHILD

Many behaviorists no longer give the environment the primary position in controlling behavior.

Whereas Skinner holds that the environment influences behavior directly, social learning theorists maintain that individuals are the active agents who interact with their surroundings. The behavior of the organism and environmental events are interconnected determinants of each other. The environment may affect individual behavior, but individuals may also influence the environment; they are, therefore, freer to monitor and control their own actions. Thus, people are viewed less mechanistically than was done by earlier learning theorists.

Emulating Others   Albert Bandura received his Ph.D. in clinical psychology from the University of Iowa. After a year of postdoctoral clinical training, Bandura joined the psychology department at Stanford University. In 1974 he was elected to the presidency of the American Psychological Association. In the course of his research at Stanford University, Bandura's social learning theory has been refined and expanded to include imitation and identification, social reinforcement, behavior change through modeling, and vicarious reinforcement.

Bandura (1977; 1991) stresses that many kinds of behavior are learned simply by observation. Thus, the concept of **imitation** plays a key role. By observing others, the child forms a conception of how new behavior patterns are performed; later, this conception, or symbolic construction, of the new behavioral response guides the individual's actions. The appearance of social learning had a refreshing, immediate appeal, for the theory saw children as social creatures who do learn a great deal—whether language, eating habits, or mischief—from observing what others say and then emulating them.

Although Skinner maintains that children only reproduce behaviors that are directly reinforced, Bandura states that children also learn when reinforcement is only vicarious. For example, if Jean observes that Bill is rewarded by the teacher for saying please, she too will say please in a similar circumstance. This nonreinforced type of learning is given a central role in social learning theory. "Studying Children" provides you with an exper-

Albert Bandura is one of the major architects of social learning theory.

STUDYING CHILDREN

IMITATION

Do children only imitate behaviors that are directly reinforced or is Bandura correct when he suggests that imitation also takes place when reinforcement is only vicarious? Try this experiment with two children: Have one child observe while you and the other child are working on assembling a puzzle. Directly reinforce the child you are working with every time he or she puts a puzzle piece in the correct place. Say nothing to the other child. Later, have the children each construct another puzzle. Which child, if either, performs better in solving the puzzle?

---

iment that will enable you to evaluate whether children imitate more readily in reinforced as compared to nonreinforced learning conditions.

Bandura (1991) further asserts that adequate attention must be given to cognitive and motivational factors as determinants of behavior. Cognitive processes play a central role in regulating what children attend to, how they describe or think about what they see, and whether they repeat it to themselves or lodge it in memory.

Some developmental trends in imitation then are apparent. Young infants' modeling, or imitative behaviors, are mainly instantaneous, whereas older children, because of their more sophisticated cognitive functioning, can store and recall after extended periods of time. As language and coding schemes become more advanced, children's abilities to profit from models are enhanced. Children without an adequate coding system will fail to store what they have seen or heard. Older children are able to pay attention to pertinent cues.

Evaluation of Bandura's Theory   Unlike Skinner, Bandura is not subject to being criticized for devaluing the role of cognition. However, he has been criticized for slighting hereditary factors. One of the major contributions of Bandura's social learning theory has been his extensive effort to introduce into experimental settings conditions more analogous to real-life social environment and to acknowledge that human beings have cognitive, symbolic capacities that allow them to regulate their own behavior and to some degree control their environment rather than to be completely controlled by it. He has broadened the conception of personality development by pointing out that classical and operant conditioning account for only part of behavior and development. Observation, in the forms of modeling, imitation, and vicarious experience, is also an influential determinant of children's behavior.

JEAN PIAGET'S THINKING CHILD

The problem of how thinking develops in children attracted the attention of the brightest talents of the discipline, one of whom was Jean Piaget. Piaget was born on August 9, 1896, and died September 16, 1980. Although he remembered his mother as energetic and kind, he also remembered her as having a neurotic temperament that made family life troublesome. As a direct consequence of his mother's poor mental health, Piaget started foregoing play for more serious work. Perhaps he was trying to take refuge in a real but private world. For example, he wrote and published, at the age of 10, a one-page article on the albino sparrow. He was a precocious boy who by his teens had already developed an intense interest in biology. At age 21 he received his doctorate in biology from the University of Neuchatel in Switzerland; by then he had published over a dozen professional papers on his biological studies. This early specialization in biology had a lasting influence on Piaget's conceptions of the development of thinking.

Jean Piaget was interested in studying children's thinking patterns at various stages of development.

Stages of Cognitive Development   Piaget investigated and described how infants, children, and adolescents organize their thoughts. Piaget categorized this continuous process of cognitive development into four periods of cognitive growth: sensorimotor (birth to 2); preoperational (2 to 7); concrete operational (7 to 11); and formal operational (11 to 15). Each stage is associated with the appearance of certain kinds of behaviors and reasoning strategies. Although each new stage represents an advancement in the way children reason about their environment, limitations are also apparent until children reach the last stage of formal thinking.

How do children develop more sophisticated reasoning strategies that allow for cognitive growth and enable them to progress from one stage to the next?

The Mechanisms of Cognitive Development   *Logical structures* are aspects of thought that reflect developmental change in the child, and as such they are the building blocks of cognitive development. Logical structures refer to the way in which children organize *schemes,* or information they already know. In this sense, logical structures determine how children process information and what they are capable of understanding. Children process bits of information from their environment into their existing schemes. This process is known as *assimilation.*

Children are continually working toward establishing harmony, *equilibrium* in Piagetian terms, between themselves and their environment. If they encounter some task, experience, or situation that cannot be readily assimilated, one of two consequences can be expected. The first is that the event is not assimilated at all. It is ignored or passed by. The encounter with the environment simply does not register on the child. The second possible consequence is not outright rejection but dissatisfaction or disequilibrium and continued efforts to achieve a match. So it is that schemes, under pressures from perceived realities of the environment, are altered in form or are multiplied to accommodate for the lack of an adequate match. Piaget used the term *accommodation* to identify this process of altering or modifying existing schemes to permit the assimilation of events that would otherwise be incomprehensible.

As children progress, more sophisticated schemes are formed, providing them with more efficient reasoning skills and adaptability to their surroundings. If the structural components of the child's cognition did not change with differential exposure and learning, development would not occur.

Piaget's study of cognitive development breathed fresh life into how thought and logic develop in children. He depicted children as active problem solvers—striving to act on and to master the environment. His extremely comprehensive approach to the development of thought expanded understanding of children's thinking.

Table 1.3 provides a summary of the main points discussed in each of the theories presented. No one theory offers a complete, comprehensive picture of child development. Each theory has, however, something to contribute to the field as a whole: unique ideas, observations, and evidence. Taken together, they can give us considerable insight into understanding children's development.

DAVID ELKIND'S RUSHED CHILD

In the 1990s, it appears that children's status is elevated compared with the past. Children no longer work long hours. Some experts say that children are not treated as special individuals (Elkind, 1981a; Winn, 1983). David Elkind (1988), for example, suggests that childhood is no longer considered to be a sheltered, special, and formative time and that we are witnessing its disappearance.

It doesn't take a social scientist's keen eye and experimental expertise to observe that children are growing up faster and faster. The language, games, clothing, sexuality, and tastes of children and adults have become barely distinguishable. Precocious knowledge, independence, and assertiveness characterize many children today. Sometimes it's easy to get the impression that children are just more mature these days. This is not so, however, if maturity is characterized as the ability to share, to sacrifice, and to love unselfishly. On

the sharp statistical rise are teenage suicide, pregnancy, alcoholism, drug use, child prostitution and pornography, truancy, and criminality. Why is this happening?

Elkind's (1981b) work is pertinent here. While his perspectives on today's child do not really qualify as a theory in the Freudian or Skinnerian tradition, his observations enable us to complete our perspectives on childhood by looking at children in the 1990s. Elkind (1981b) maintains that the changes in society and adult life-styles are prominent reasons for the disappearance of childhood. The 1990s has witnessed a rise in two-career families and a mounting divorce rate that has led to single-parent families. Moreover, the media place children and adults in the same symbolic world. Media, including books, films, and television, portray young people as precocious and present them in explicitly sexual or manipulative situations.

Children are readied for each new milestone in their development by being given systematic practice. Preschoolers, for example, are given practice in the technical requirements of the reading process (known as *reading readiness*) because in order to be prepared a child must read as soon as possible. The push to early academic achievement is but one area of contemporary pressures on children. Another may be the push to do it all—be a superkid. Be a star basketball player, tennis hero, and so on. Sometimes children practice these other skills before and after school. Sometimes they go to specialized training summer camps. Remember when kids went to camp to have a good time boating, swimming, hiking, playing team sports just for fun? Many children still do attend camps like these, but increasingly children are told not to "fritter away" childhood by engaging in activities merely because they are fun.

The social changes that helped to bring about children's new integration into adult life—divorce, single-parenting, two-parent incomes, increasing dominance of the media in children's lives—cannot be reversed. However, these social phenomena may be modified to work better for the family (see "Focus on Applications").

TABLE 1.3 **Theories of Children's Development**				
	Freud	**Erikson**	**Skinner**	**Piaget**
MAJOR AREA OF CONCERN	Personality development.	Ego development.	Environmental effects on behavior.	Development of thought and reasoning in children.
SOURCES OF DATA	Subjective accounts of childhood from his patients and his own self-analysis.	Analytic interviews.	Lab settings.	Observation, clinical interviews, experiments.
BASIC PREMISES	Human beings motivated to reduce tensions produced by sexual and aggressive drives; unconscious mind directs and controls behavior: Children go through psychosexual stages.	Each stage of life produces psychosocial crisis that we must solve in order to function effectively at a later stage of development.	Environment crucial factor in determining behavior; consequences of our behavior (+, −, neutral) shape our personality.	Children active explorers seeking to establish harmony between what they know and what they experience.
NATURE OF HUMAN BEING	Basically evil and savagelike.	Positive.	Neutral—whether good or evil determined by environmental experiences.	Active problem solvers.
CONCEPTIONS OF DEVELOPMENT	Psychosexual stages; first 5 years important to later behavior.	Psychosocial stages that span a lifetime.	Continual action of environment on individual; no stages of development.	Qualitative stages; sensorimotor to formal.
SOURCES OF PROBLEMS	Fixation during psychosexual stages; repressed sexual and aggressive drives.	Too much attention or not enough in each stage can result in maladjustment.	Excessive punishment can lead to undesirable behaviors.	Nonstimulating environment; not recognizing child's developmental level.
CRITICISMS	Small, nonrepresentative sample; too much emphasis on the unconscious mind.	Theory difficult to prove.	Too much emphasis on environment and not enough on internal factors.	Small sample; ages appropriated for various stages may not be correct.
CONTRIBUTIONS	Early experiences may influence later behavior.	Relationships with parents and peers important.	Importance of environment and reinforcement.	Younger children's reasoning strategies differ from older children's.

WAYS OF STUDYING CHILDREN'S DEVELOPMENT

The theories previously discussed offer a valuable base for studying children's development. However, rather than just guessing about how and why children's thinking patterns or behavior changes, theorists use the **scientific method** as their chief source of investigation. If you wished to study a particular aspect of children's behavior, for example, gender differences in children's mathematical ability, you would begin with careful observations,

FOCUS ON APPLICATIONS

How to Help Today's Rushed Child

Parents need to realize that children are not their psychological equals, and that children really don't prosper when treated as such. Parents should be encouraged to take a more authoritative position in the family. I do not mean authoritarian like a ruling despot, or one who makes rigid rules in a detached, controlling way. Rather, I am referring to an authoritative disciplinarian who maintains the role of authority and operates from the advantage of his or her superior knowledge. Such a parent is willing, in an accepting way, to reason and explain to children.

Children should be protected from life's unpredictabilities. They need to feel the protectiveness of their parents and other adults. Under the adult's careful supervision, children can sense that they are separate, protected, and special. As Winn (1983) points out, the desirability of children's exposure to evil, violence, injustice, and misery is questionable. Today, parents "divorce and marry, struggle for economic survival, rail against political corruption, [and] agonize over depleting natural resources and ecological destruction" (p. 38). Many parents make no attempt to shield their children from these complex affairs. Rather than face the truth that they are incapable of hiding these subjects from children, parents believe that it is *harmful* to their children to do so. Those who believe that protecting children is impoverishing them are making a questionable assumption: that children have the same ability to assimilate and utilize knowledge and experience as adults do. Winn (1983) suggests:

Children need to feel secure in the certainty that children are children and adults are adults and that in spite of the "wretchedness" they might glimpse in their world, they can still remain in a different state, untouched by it. Children should be allowed the simple pleasures of play, imagination, curiosity, and pursuit of adventure — in the most adverse circumstances. (p. 46)

Perhaps the recognition that a highly complicated civilization such as ours cannot afford to shorten the period of nurture and protection of its immature members will restore a real childhood to the children of future generations.

followed by reading research, and talking to others. Eventually, after this careful preliminary research, you would formulate your **hypothesis:** "Boys tend to display higher spatial ability than girls." A hypothesis is a specific prediction of behavior that can be tested. Next, you would want to try to prove or disprove the hypothesis. You are now faced with trying to decide which method of research to use. There are several alternatives: case studies, surveys, questionnaires and interviews, naturalistic observations, correlational research, or the experimental method. Moreover, as a researcher, you are interested in events that have immediate or long-term consequences. There are

several ways in which you could study development over a period of time: using a longitudinal, cross-sectional, or a cross-sequential design. After you have conducted the research, you draw conclusions from your research. In order for you to fully understand the strengths and weaknesses of the various research methods, it first will be necessary to discuss certain criteria that are necessary for conducting valid and reliable research.

EVALUATING RESEARCH

There are certain basic requirements in conducting research. As a student it is important for you to be aware of these criteria so that you can evaluate critically the results of the studies you may read about in journals, magazines, and newspapers. It is important for you to be aware of the problems in research, not necessarily so that you simply disregard any study that does not meet some very high standard of research quality, but rather so that you are able to judge the strengths and limitations of each study, and in turn, its validity and reliability. The major criteria to look for when evaluating research are generalizability, sampling, subject and experimenter bias, and controlling for confounding variables.

Generalizability   **Generalizability,** also called *external validity,* refers to the extent to which research findings may be applied to broader populations or settings. In other words, how valid are these findings when applied to other people, cities, institutions, and so on. Since social science, like other sciences, strives for explanations that are useful and valid over a wide range of circumstances, generalizability of the findings is crucial.

A population refers to all "members of any well-defined class of people, events, or objects" who, for research purposes, are designated as being the focus of investigation (Kerlinger, 1986, p. 52). For example, if you are interested in studying the effects of day care on the social development of preschoolers, all preschoolers attending day care would be your population. Because it is doubtful that the entire population can be tested, a sample must be used that presumably provides results similar to those that would have been obtained if the entire population had been studied. Thus, a major sampling concern in research is whether the sample is *representative* of a larger population.

Sampling   A representative sample means that all nationalities, religious groups, socioeconomic status, occupations, and ages are representative in proportions similar to the entire population. Thus, a pivotal concern in research is to make sure that the sample is representative so that findings from this sample can be generalized to the larger population. Research on social issues such as child abuse is often used to draw inferences about broader groups than those included in the study,

so that findings can be translated into suggestions for social policy. Because of this, it is critical that sampling limitations be recognized. Unfortunately, some researchers have made the mistake of generalizing from small, unrepresentative samples to the entire population of children.

Random sampling is often used to make sure that the sample is representative of the entire population. Random sampling is a selection process whereby each individual in the population has an equal chance of being chosen as a subject for the research. Because each person has an equal chance of being selected, it is presumed that the population characteristics will be represented, essentially, to the degree that they exist in the population. Because chance is used to construct the sample, random sampling substantially reduces the possibility that a biased or nonrepresentative sample will be selected.

How many subjects are needed when conducting research? There is no set number of subjects required under all research conditions. Given different circumstances, larger or smaller samples may serve adequately. In general, however, it appears that the best answer to the sample size question is to use as large a sample as possible. A large sample is more likely to be representative of the population, and the data are more likely to be more accurate and precise. Size alone, however, does not guarantee accuracy.

Subject Bias   When respondents know they are being observed or studied, it is always possible that they react to this awareness in ways the researcher does not anticipate. To illustrate, in the 1930s a study was carried out at the Hawthorne Electrical Company (Roethlisberger & Dickson, 1939). The investigators asked if various improvements in working conditions would lead to an increase in productivity of workers making electrical equipment. A group of workers was placed in a separate room, and their productivity was measured after such changes as better lighting, longer rest periods, or greater financial incentive. Each change in working conditions was associated with an increase in productivity. When the workers returned to their original working conditions, productivity still increased. The investigators argued that these subjects were highly motivated to work harder because of the extra attention they had been given.

Another type of reactive effect occurs when the participant feels that certain responses are expected. In these situations, respondents or subjects, having little or no information about the hypotheses being tested, try to figure out the "real" purpose of the study, and act in ways that fulfill what they perceive to be the expectations of the investigator. For example, in one study (Orne, 1962), subjects were asked to read an instruction card after completing each page of addition problems. In every instance the card instructed the subjects to tear up the work just completed. The experimenter expected the subjects to stop when they realized that all the instruction cards were the same, but, in fact, they continued for hours. When interviewed later, the subjects indicated that they viewed the task as part of a legitimate experiment, perhaps having to do with some sort of endurance test. Unless the experimenter has taken special precautions to conceal the purpose of the experiment, bright, discerning subjects can often correctly (and incorrectly) figure it out.

Experimenter Bias   Substantial bias can be introduced by the investigator. Such bias may be the subtle result of hoping to find support for a favored hypothesis. As a corollary to the demand effect present in subjects, investigators may unintentionally convey their expectations. Second, experimenters differ in gender, skill, technique, personality, and other factors, all of which can influence the subjects in different ways.

A technique for minimizing experimenter bias (and subject bias as well) is the *double-blind procedure*. In using this technique neither the subjects in the research project nor those taking measures know the hypotheses of the research or the characteristics of those they are measuring. For example, if we are measuring the side effects of a certain drug, some subjects are given the drug; others are given a placebo. In using the double-blind procedure, neither the patients nor those examining them know whether they were given the real drug or the placebo.

Controlling for Confounding Variables   Control in social science research can be achieved either by (a) the elimination of **confounding variables** or (b) the measuring of these variables in order to ascertain their effects. Confounding variables are variables that could influence the behavior or performance of the subjects or the dependent variable. To illustrate, in an experimental design, the independent variable is manipulated under conditions in which all the other variables are controlled in order to see the effect of this independent variable on some dependent variable of interest. For example, a researcher concludes from his study that single-parenting causes academic problems in children. In order to be sure that this interpretation is correct, the researcher must make sure that he has controlled for variables that may influence children's academic achievement.

Some earlier studies on the effects of single-parenting on children's academic achievement, for example, did not control for socioeconomic class, a variable known to influence academic achievement. However, when children from single-parent and two-parent families from the same socioeconomic class were compared, no differences in academic achievement were found. When conducting research, then, it is important to make sure that it is the independent variable (in this case, single parenting) that is producing the changes or differences found in the dependent variable (academic achievement). Thus, the subjects in the experimental and control groups need to be as similar as possible on all variables known to have an influence on the dependent variable. The independent variable should be the only way in which the groups differ.

Second, it is important to measure the effects of relevant "third variables." For example, various investigators have suggested that interparental conflict, socioeconomic status, and the quality of the parent-child relationship explain a greater proportion of the variance in the correlation between divorce and child-behavior problems. By measuring the effects of these important variables, the researcher avoids the mistake of attributing adjustment outcomes to divorce per se rather than the series of conditions, or third variables, associated with it.

RESEARCH METHODS

Developmental psychologists have various research methods available to them: case studies, surveys, naturalistic observation, experimental method, and correlational method.

Case Studies   The distinguishing feature of a **case study** is there is a sample size of one. It could be one person, one organization, one society, or one church. While a sample of one means that the researcher can examine a particular case in great detail and depth, that same sample of one introduces definite limitations. It must be determined to what extent findings can be generalized. It could always be argued that the findings refer to the idiosyncrasies of this case, and thus provide little general explanation or prediction.

The second major limitation of the case study is that using one case alone prohibits comparison. If the researcher is interested in the differences between high-quality and low-quality day care, at least two cases are needed to make a comparison. The solution, of course, is to study a second case. Although the addition of cases can give research an added dimension, generalizability is still likely to be limited. Case studies are also limited in their ability to find causal relationships. They can, however, stimulate hypotheses and systematic research.

Surveys   Although the case study focuses its attention on only one case, the **survey** is designed to investigate many cases at once. The researcher using a survey method wishes to know how a particular phenomenon is distributed throughout the population. Basically, to survey means to describe the characteristics of any given phenomenon in a population. Surveys may address whether variables are related to each other, and in surveys covered over time, whether some variables occur prior

to others. Because no variables are manipulated and all confounding variables are not held constant, surveys do not show causality. The strength of the survey lies more in the generalizability of its findings than in its fulfillment of the criteria to ascertain cause.

The survey method is commonly thought to be synonymous with the use of *questionnaires* and *interviews* as methods of data collection. The interview and the questionnaire utilize the question-asking approach. These instruments can be used to obtain information concerning facts, beliefs, feelings, intentions, and so on. Although both the interview and questionnaire make use of the question approach, they differ in important ways.

In an interview, data are collected through face-to-face or telephone interaction between the interviewer and the respondent. The questionnaire obtains information through the respondent's written response to a list of questions. Each method has advantages and disadvantages. For example, the interview provides flexibility. The interviewer has the opportunity to observe the subject and the situation in which he or she is responding. Questions can be repeated or their meanings explained. The interview can also press for additional information if the subject's response is confusing or incomplete. A greater completion rate is another advantage of the interview. The low return rate of the questionnaire (typically around 40%) may not only reduce the sample size but also may bias the results. The important question for the researcher is how these nonresponses affect the generalizability of the findings. If you are surveying attitudes toward working mothers, for example, and had a large number of female nonrespondents who were too busy or not at home, you would suspect that those who failed to respond to the questionnaire differ significantly from those who cooperated. The main disadvantage of interviews is that they are more expensive and time-consuming than questionnaires.

Questionnaires and interviews use two types of questions: open-ended and closed. An open-ended format allows the subjects to respond freely; the closed-question format provides the subjects with alternative response options. A limitation of the closed question is that it does not provide much insight into whether respondents have any information or any clearly formulated opinions about an issue. Of course, a combination of the two types of questions may be used.

Another problem with interviews and questionnaires is the possibility that respondents are not telling the truth or are distorting their actual beliefs or facts about their lives. In such instances the respondent may be more concerned with answering "the right way" or socially desired way than in giving true attitudes or behaviors. Researchers need to be concerned about such matters, the representativeness of the population being surveyed, and reliability and validity in assessing the questionnaires and interviews used in surveys.

Naturalistic Observation   Any analysis of behavior requires observation. It is a basic tool and method used in gathering information. At times, observation is done in a laboratory setting, but, because many psychological variables cannot be observed there, it is sometimes better to turn to **naturalistic observation:** watching children in their natural environments (home or school, for example). In conducting this kind of research, no attempt is made to change or control the environment of the children being studied. You can, however, select both the subjects and situations you wish to observe.

To illustrate, let's say your hypothesis is that "Boys exhibit more aggressive behaviors, such as shoving, pushing, and hitting others, than do girls." We could then observe children's interactions in a free-play situation and record the number of shoving, pushing, and hitting behaviors observed in boys and in girls.

Observing children for scientific study may be more difficult than you expect, as you may find out in performing the "Studying Children" experiment.

Naturalistic observation may also be used when it is unethical to subject children to various experimental situations. For example, if you wanted to study the effects of maternal separation, you could use a sample of children who are enrolled in day-

---

STUDYING CHILDREN

OBSERVATION

With another student, go to a nursery school or to the park. Begin watching the children from a specific location for 10 minutes and write down everything you notice. Later, compare your notes with your colleague. You may find that each of you noticed different things and perhaps reported them differently. For example, what you thought was a friendly pat, your partner may have seen as a hostile shove.

Sometimes observations may be invalid because people tend to interpret a child's behavior rather than report it. Sometimes observations are invalid because people try to observe too much. Next time, you and your partner should agree on specific behaviors that you will observe (e.g., how many times these children talk to the teacher and how many times they talk to their peers). Pick out one or two target children and observe and record these behaviors only. Is there more agreement in your observations this time?

---

care centers and observe and compare their behavior to children who remain at home with their mothers.

Information about children in natural settings is crucial for a complete science of children's development. It does, however, suffer from some drawbacks. The main disadvantage of this method is that it does not indicate cause and effect. Because you cannot manipulate or control the environment, you cannot be sure which factor (or factors) is determining the outcome. A second disadvantage is observer bias. Some researchers may want to prove their hypothesis so badly that their observations are clouded by their subjectivity, their own thoughts, feelings, and ideas. That is, they actually "see" boys as being more aggressive when in reality they are not. Having more than one observer may help to alleviate observer bias. When two or more observers agree, the observations are said to be reliable.

Experimental Method   An experiment differs from other types of scientific investigation in that, rather than searching for naturally occurring situations, the experimenter *creates* conditions necessary for observation. By using the **experimental method** you can manipulate the environment to provide a precise test of your hypothesis. Thus, the link between cause and effect is clearer than in naturalistic observation. Generally, in the experimental method, you observe the effects of a particular variable under study. **Variables** are factors that are controlled and measured in an experiment. The researcher tries to establish a causal link between two variables; that is, the experimenter tries to show that one variable is *the* variable that is causing the observable effect in the subjects. In order to do this, the experimenter will manipulate and control one variable, known as the **independent variable,** and observe some change in the subject's resultant behavior—the **dependent variable.** It is called *dependent* because the experiment is designed so that any change in this factor *depends* on change in the independent variable.

An **experimental** and a **control group** are often used in this type of design. The experimental group receives the independent variable; the control group does not. This difference is used for comparison. Both groups are matched as closely as possible; that is, variables such as age, gender, and socioeconomic background are controlled for similarity. If the two groups are equal in every respect except for the independent variable that is added to or deleted from the control group, any differences appearing between the two groups can be attributed to the independent variable. By carefully matching groups on all variables except the one you are going to investigate, you can control for the effects of these *confounding variables.* Without control, it is impossible to evaluate unambiguously the effects of the independent variable. The main objective of the experimental method is to keep all other variables constant so as to understand the impact of the independent variable(s) on the dependent variable(s).

Fortunately, all differences between groups do not require rigorous control. Aspects in which situations differ that are irrelevant to the purpose of the study can be ignored. To illustrate, say an experiment is being conducted to study differential effects of two methods of teaching reading. It is impossible to have two absolutely identical groups. The experimenter, however, seeks to establish two groups that are as similar as possible with respect to those variables related to reading achievement, such as motivation or general intelligence. Other variables, such as athletic ability or height, are unrelated to reading achievement, so they are ignored.

The experimental method works something like this: Suppose you wanted to test the hypothesis "If nursery-school children are exposed to soft, relaxing music (Brahms, for example), then they will tend to participate in quiet activities (working with puzzles, looking at books) during free play." First, select your sample of children and place half in the experimental group and half in the control group. Each of your subjects in these groups is as alike as possible so that you can make sure that it is your independent variable (relaxing, soft music) that is producing the behavior. The experimental group hears Brahms music during free-play time and the control group does not (see Figure 1.4).

During your experiment record the types of activities in which the children from the experimental group and the control group participate. Note from your observations that children in the experimental group engage in significantly more quiet activities, such as looking at picture books and playing with puzzles, than do children in the control group. (*Significant* here means that the different behaviors observed in the two groups are unlikely to have occurred by chance.) Have you proved your hypothesis? In this experiment you have. Conclusions are not based on the results of one study, however. Further replication is necessary to establish the validity (truthfulness) of the hypothesis. Try the experiment in "Studying Children" for a better understanding of how the experimental method works.

The chief advantage of the experimental method is that it allows you to control for other intervening variables, thus providing you with clues to causal relationships. In the experimental design, the independent variable is manipulated under conditions in which all other variables are controlled in order to see the effect the independent variable

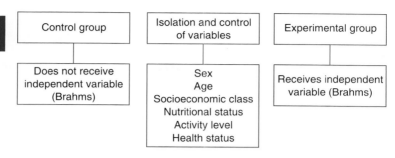

FIGURE 1.4   The Experimental Method

Control group
Does not receive independent variable (Brahms)

Isolation and control of variables
Sex
Age
Socioeconomic class
Nutritional status
Activity level
Health status

Experimental group
Receives independent variable (Brahms)

Dependent variable: Types of play activities

STUDYING CHILDREN

THE EXPERIMENTAL METHOD

Your hypothesis is "Children between the ages of 7 and 11 can learn the definitions of abstract concepts if they draw a picture that reflects the meaning of the word." Select a sample of two boys and two girls of the same age for the control group and two boys and two girls for the experimental group. Give both groups a list of five new vocabulary words and their definitions. Two of the vocabulary words should be abstract nouns such as liberty, justice, horizon, truth. The control group is to write the words and their definitions. The experimental group is to write the words and their definitions plus draw a picture that illustrates the abstract nouns. Two days later, give the children the vocabulary test. Which group has a higher percentage of correctly defining the abstract nouns? Based on your experiment, is this hypothesis true?

has. By establishing such cause-effect relationships, you operate within the bounds of a natural science and go on to establish relevant laws. Unless experimenters control for extraneous variables, you can never be confident of the relationship among the variables of the study.

The disadvantage is that experiments conducted in this situation can be rather artificial. As a result, the structured laboratory situation may elicit behaviors from children different from those evoked in the natural setting. In the previous example, children may react differently in their home sur-

roundings when Brahms is played. Although much information can be obtained about the relations between discrete aspects of children's behavior, the experimental situation, by design, does not begin to approximate the total environment in its intricate complexity.

Although many people tend to associate experiments with highly controlled laboratory settings, it is not necessarily so. A field experiment, for example, is one that takes place in a naturally occurring situation. A field setting might be a classroom in which a new teaching method is introduced. The dependent variable might be students' knowledge of a particular academic subject after exposure of the teaching method. The major advantage of this setting over that of a laboratory experiment is its increased reality.

Although the experimental method is designed to answer cause-and-effect questions—Can the presence of the independent variable x cause a change in the dependent variable y?—rarely can children's behavior be attributed to a single cause or variable. Rather, behavior is a result of interconnected effects. Research seeks to describe these effects with procedures that are sensitive to these complexities. The effects of two or more different variables are considered in these experimental designs rather than just one. The advantage is that **multivariate analysis** utilizes information about the relationship among variables. For example, you may wish to know the relationship of several background characteristics such as social class, urban-rural residence, parental relationship, gender, and age to drug addiction. In this case, there are many independent variables, and one dependent variable for which explanation is sought. Or, you may wish to know the relationship of gender and age to drug addiction and juvenile delinquency. This problem has two dependent variables. Obviously, these designs are quite complex but then so is children's behavior. Behavior is determined by multiple variables, and multivariate analysis research is designed to analyze the behavior in terms of multiple causes and effects.

Correlational Method   In some cases, the independent variable cannot be manipulated. For example, if your hypothesis is "Children with high IQs are more creative," IQs cannot be manipulated by research. In this case, all we can do is measure IQ and correlate it with creativity. The **correlational method** attempts to measure the relationship between two or more events, conditions, or situations; it is expressed in terms of a direction (positive or negative) and size of the relationship. For example, if you tested five children (in practice, you would use a larger sample), you might find their scores were as follows:

Child	IQ Test Score (95 to 105 is average)	Creativity Test Score (highest score = 15)
Jean	125	14
Bob	118	11
Dave	100	7
Dan	98	6
Mike	95	4

In analyzing the scores, you can say that it looks as if there is a positive correlational relationship between IQ and creativity. When a child receives a high score on the IQ test, he also receives a high score on the creativity test. In contrast, low IQ scores are correlated with low scores on creativity tests. High IQ and creativity appear (in your hypothetical study) to be correlated.

One serious drawback is that many people seem to think that because two variables are correlated one *caused* the other. The correlational method cannot generate the kinds of conclusions that controlled experimental research generates. In this case, a high IQ does not *cause* one to be highly creative. The correlational method simply points out that an association between two variables has been found. Table 1.4 summarizes research methods in developmental psychology.

RESEARCH DESIGNS

Most researchers are interested in developmental changes that occur over a period of time. In studying developmental changes, the investigator must decide whether to focus on behaviors that accompany age change with the same individuals over time—a **longitudinal study**—or, on behaviors that reflect age differences among individuals at given points in time—a **cross-sectional** study.

Longitudinal Studies   Studies that follow people over time are called longitudinal studies. You may ask the question, "Do children who are verbally proficient at a young age continue to display high language skills?" In order to test the hypothesis, you may make repeated observations and give language proficiency tests to the same group of children over an extended period of time. By doing so, you gain valuable information regarding the stability or instability of a behavior.

The main advantages of this method are that it allows direct analysis of age changes and, because individuals are compared with themselves at different periods of time, there are fewer problems with the sample itself. Subjects do not have to be carefully sorted out and matched each time. The major disadvantage is that it is costly in money and time. Another limiting factor is that over time original subjects may move, get sick, or drop out of the experiment. Changeovers in staff can also occur. In addition, the fact that children are taking tests over a period of 4 or 5 years could enable them to become quite proficient test takers. That is, the repeated testing itself could cause an increase in performance.

Cross-sectional Studies   A method that is quick and less expensive is the cross-sectional research design. In this design, groups of individuals of different ages are observed and/or measured on some particular behavior at one point in time (see Figure 1.5). It is assumed that when large numbers of

TABLE 1.4	Summary of Research Methods in Developmental Psychology		
Method	**General Approach**	**Advantages**	**Disadvantages**
CASE STUDY	Carefully describes all relevant aspects in a sample size of one	Examines a particular case in great depth and detail	Provides little general explanation or prediction
SURVEY	Designed to measure many cases at once; thought to be synonymous with the use of questionnaires and interviews	Examines how a particular phenomenon is distributed throughout the population	Respondents may refuse to participate In assessing validity and reliability need to be concerned about representativeness of sample
NATURALISTIC OBSERVATION	Analysis of behavior through observation without intrusion	Provides information from "real life"situations	Causal inferences are speculative
INTERVIEW	Subjects give verbal responses of their thoughts, attitudes, and behaviors	Systematic data can be gathered	Verbal responses of subjects may be inaccurate
EXPERIMENTAL	Manipulates the environment to provide precise test of hypotheses	Can control for confounding variables, thus providing clues to causal relationships	Responses from subjects may be different in a testing situation than those encountered in a natural setting
CORRELATIONAL	Determines relationships among variables	Can uncover relationships among variables	Cannot show causality

children are chosen at random, the differences found in the older age groups are a reflection of how the younger children will develop, given time. In this case, test children's language proficiency skills by using a sample of fourth-, fifth-, and sixth-graders. Each of these groups is referred to as a **cohort.** A cohort group represents a generation of individuals, and comparisons are made between generation groups.

One drawback to the cross-sectional design, known as the *cohort effect,* is that not all the differences observed between the cohorts are the result of age. The differences may reflect other cultural or historical factors that distinguish members of different cohorts. If, for example, we tested groups of people at ages 20, 30, 40, 50, and 60 about their attitudes toward sex, we may find that as people get older they tend to become more conservative. Can these differences be a result of age, or could they be a result of the experiences peculiar to each of the cohorts? A 60-year-old, for example, was raised in a Victorian-style cultural milieu. Thus, it

is often difficult to separate the effects of age from those of the historical period. Similarly, this method does not allow you to study continuity in behavioral changes in a particular individual, only behavioral differences among groups of individuals. Finally, if you do not control for important variables in making your subjects similar (health, education, socioeconomic class) your results may not be valid. Therefore, it is important to use similar groups of people at different age levels being investigated.

Cross-sequential Studies A design that incorporates cross-sectional and longitudinal studies may eliminate either's disadvantages. Suppose you wondered if children's conceptions of friends change over time. You can conduct a study to test this idea. In 1986, a group of 4-, 5-, and 6-year-olds are asked to describe their friends. You note that these children use highly personal and concrete constructs to describe their friends: "We play together." "She gives me things."

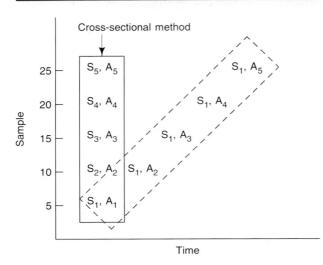

FIGURE 1.5 Cross-sectional versus Longitudinal Research Designs

A longitudinal design involves following the sample (S_1) through all ages (A_1–A_5). A cross-sectional method involves multiple samples (S_1–S_5) of different ages (A_1–A_5).

Source: From *Life-span Developmental Psychology* (p. 115) by P. B. Baltes, H. W. Reese, and J. R. Nesselroade, 1977, Belmont, CA: Wadsworth. Copyright © 1977 by Wadsworth Publishing Company, Inc. Reprinted by permission of Brooks/Cole Publishing Company, Pacific Grove, CA 93950.

A longitudinal component is added when these same children are tested 4 years later at ages 8, 9, and 10. You note that these children now use less personal and more abstract constructs such as "She is kind." "He is smart." Using cohorts at different age levels greatly reduces the amount of time needed to gather information about a particular behavior, and, at the same time, provides useful information regarding behavioral differences at different ages and within a given age.

ETHICS IN CHILD DEVELOPMENT RESEARCH

No matter what research method is used, strict adherence to ethical standards in planning and conducting the research is most important. Dennis (1935) attempted to show that many children's abilities emerge without practice, experience, or encouragement. Dennis and his wife raised two foster children in an extremely restrictive environment. Until the babies were 6 months old, the adults kept impassive faces when interacting with them, "neither smiling, nor frowning, and never played with them, patted them, tickled them . . . nor spoke (p. 18)." They provided them with no toys nor did they prop them up or turn them over.

It should be pointed out that Dennis tried to design his research in an ethical manner. He firmly believed that behavioral development came automatically with maturation, which is essentially determined by heredity. Thus, Dennis did not expect that the children would be harmed in any way by their deprivation of stimulation. Today, however, most of us would agree that his research was not ethical.

What of contemporary research, however? Is it acceptable to subject children to minor stress for research purposes? What about questioning adolescents about their sexual experiences? Is it ethical to use deception in research, for example, misinforming the child about the purpose of the experiment? In 1984, the placing of a baboon's heart into the chest of little "Baby Fae" made headlines and raised some questions on ethics. For a closer look at the ethics involved in this operation see "Focus on Issues."

To make sure that research is ethical, particularly when dealing with human beings, the American Psychological Association (1968) adopted a document outlining ethical procedures. Following are some of the points mentioned in that document:

No matter how young the child, he has rights that supercede those of the investigator.

The experimenter must outline the research with respect to participants and show concern for their dignity and welfare.

All participants must be informed about all features of the research that might influence their willingness to participate.

The experimenter must respect the participant's freedom to decline to participate or discontinue the experiment at any time.

FOCUS ON ISSUES

Baby Fae

The disturbing facts about this experiment with Baby Fae had nothing to do about animal rights or violating the separateness of man and animal species. The truly controversial issue concerned the means and the ends used.

According to Charles Krauthammer in an article written for *Time* magazine:

It turns out that . . . the doctors at Loma Linda had not sought a human heart for transplant. The fact betrays their primary aim: to advance a certain line of research. As much as her life became dear to them, Baby Fae was to be their means. . . .

To give Baby Fae a human heart would have advanced the cause of children in general very little. But it might have advanced the cause of *this* child more than a baboon's heart, which, given the imperfect state of our knowledge, was more likely to be rejected. . . . One does not have to impute venal motives—a desire for glory or a lust for publicity—to wonder about the ethics of the choice. The motive was science; the research imperative. . . .

Consent is the crucial event in the transition from therapy to experiment. It turns what would otherwise be technological barbarism into humane science. . . . To be used by others is to be degraded; to give oneself to others is to be elevated. . . .

Infants who can decide nothing, are the difficult case. (If Baby Fae had volunteered for her operation, the ethical questions would evaporate.) Since infants are incapable of giving consent, the parents do so on their behalf. In Baby Fae's case what kind of consent did they give? If her parents thought that the operation might save their child (*that is,* that it was therapeutic), they were misled. There was no scientific evidence to support that claim. The longest previous human survival with a heart xenograft was $3\frac{1}{2}$ days. (Baby Fae lived 17 more.). . . .

If, on the other hand, the parents had been told that the purpose was to test a procedure that might help other babies in the future (that is, that it was experimental), what right did they have to volunteer a child—even their child—to suffer on behalf of humanity? . . .

Baby Fae was a means, a conscripted means, to a noble end. This experiment was undertaken to reduce not her suffering, but, perhaps some day, that of others. But is that really wrong? Don't the suffering babies of the future have any claim on us? How do we reconcile the need to advance our knowledge through research, with the injunction against using innocents for our own ends?

Whether this case was an advance in medical science awaits the examination of the record by the scientific community. That it was an adventure in medical ethics is already clear.

Source: Charles Krauthammer, "The Using of Baby Fae," in *Time* Magazine, December 3, 1984, pp. 87–88. Copyright 1984 Time Warner Inc. Reprinted by permission.

The experimenter must make certain that there are no damaging effects or consequences of the experiment. (pp. 1–3)

In addition, many universities and other research facilities have an ethics advisory committee consisting of researchers representing several disciplines. These researchers review investigations that involve human subjects and attempt to ensure that the experiment is in accordance with the highest ethical standards.

PRACTICAL IMPLICATIONS: WILL THE CORRECT THEORIST PLEASE STAND UP?

A number of theories about the nature of children's development have been discussed. An important question that remains to be answered is, Why is it important to study these theories? One reason for understanding the various theories is that they provide a framework for studying children. Given the vast number of events and conditions that influence children's development, theories are needed to help give shape to an otherwise large and unmanageable collection of data. As such, theories can be likened to a special pair of glasses through which children and their development are observed.

Look at a hypothetical example to see how these special lenses work. Seventeen-year-old Sally has become belligerent toward her parents. She is continually having fights with them about her schoolwork. The main area of dissension is her poor grade in English. According to her parents, she needs to study more. If you don your "Erikson glasses," you may explain her behavior in one way: Sally is more than likely going through an identity crisis, trying to find herself and establish her sense of independence. If you exchange these glasses for your Skinnerian hornrims, you see Sally from a different perspective: Sally's argumentative behavior undoubtedly is being reinforced somehow; maybe the only time she gets attention at home is when she brings home a poor grade in English. Your Piagetian glasses enable you to focus on another perspective: Sally does not have an adequate background in English and consequently she is unable to assimilate the new material. Thus, she is doing poorly in English.

The situation—Sally doing poorly in English—remains the same, but the way you *perceive* that

Each of the major theorists would view Sally's behavior from a different perspective, and each would offer different reasons as to why Sally is not doing well in English.

situation changes with each switch of eyeglasses. When you view children's behavior through different lenses, you perceive different meanings of their behavior. Understanding theories will show how variations in perspective can lead to markedly varied interpretations of development. Theories then can be used by students of child development as tools to help them better understand children's development. Theories enable you to step outside a particular way of viewing behavior. You can examine behavior from other major perspectives simply by exchanging your glasses. In addition, theories provide a backdrop against which to examine and evaluate your ideas about children.

You must also be aware, however, that theorists propounding a certain philosophy on children's development may be somewhat "nearsighted" in studying children's development; that is, the

adoption of a specific theory may direct an investigator's focus on a particular subset of the entire domain of variables. As a result, relevant variables may be overlooked, and interpretations that run counter to theoretical assumptions may go unnoticed or de-emphasized (Walker & Emory, 1985). For example, behaviorists believe that in studying children's behavior, you need to be concerned with only observable events. Therefore, unobservable aspects of behavior such as motivations or emotions may be ignored. Likewise, Freudians view human action as largely determined by unconscious processes; powerful, irrational motives; and the child's early identification with the parents. Their research will be guided by this conception and the "facts" influenced by it. Theories are ways of seeing the world, and once you accept the design of a theoretical orientation, events may be interpreted in light of that orientation.

REVIEW OF KEY POINTS

Beginning in ancient Greece and Rome, children were subject to a low level of care. Infanticide was common, children were put out in the fields to work when they were very young, and parents had complete control over their children's lives. Children's education until the 18th century was spasmodic and primarily for lower-class males so they could improve their station in life. Children in the New World were considered first and foremost as workers. Adults took for granted that they were ignorant and sinful. The job of parents was to discipline and instruct. After several centuries, and affected dramatically by the works of Locke and Rousseau, childhood was finally considered to be a separate and special time.

Sigmund Freud viewed the infant as being born with a collection of unconscious sexual and aggressive drives that supply energy and direction for behavior. All development may be seen as the result of changes in the way psychic energy is channeled and organized as the child journeys through the first three psychosexual stages. Freud maintained that the bulk of people's personality is unknown to them; that is, it resides in the unconscious mind. Erikson, however, emphasized the role of the ego as it develops throughout the psychosocial stages. Watson stated that stimuli in the environment force organisms to behave or incite them into initial action. He proposed that classically conditioned responses were the key to understanding human behavior. Skinner agreed that behavior is controlled by the eliciting stimuli (classical conditioning) and by stimuli that reinforce responses (operant conditioning). Skinner spent much of his time studying specific environmental cues under which a given behavior is likely to occur. Bandura's social learning theory stressed the importance of observation and imitation in producing various behaviors. Piaget traced the development of the intellect, beginning with reflexive behavior in early infancy to the abstract thinking found in late adolescence. It was also pointed out that children today are growing up faster and faster. Recognizing the "child" in children and protecting them from life's unpredictabilities was recommended.

Scientific methods and procedures are used in studying children. In order to conduct valid and reliable research, certain criteria should be met: namely, using large numbers in samples, making sure the sample is representative of the target population; choosing samples randomly; controlling for experimenter and subject bias; and controlling or accounting for confounding variables. Scientific methods and procedures used in studying children are case studies, surveys, questionnaires, the experimental method, naturalistic observation, and the correlational method. Case studies use a sample of one and provide little general explanation. Thus, they are particularly vulnerable to questions of generalizability. Case studies can, however, give an in-depth, detailed coverage of the phenomena under study. Surveys are designed to reach large numbers of people and generally involve the use of questionnaires, interviews, and observations. The experimental method involves an experimental group and a control group. The experimenter manipulates the independent variable (received by the experimental group) and then observes and compares the behavior or performance in each of these groups. Because this method may be artificial (children may not always act the same way out of the laboratory setting), naturalistic observation may be used. The chief disadvantage of the naturalistic method is lack of control. An experimenter may at times use the correlational method, in which the relationship between two or more factors is observed.

In longitudinal experimental designs, behavior is observed at successive time periods. In cross-sectional designs, groups of children of different ages (cohorts) are observed at one point in time. Sometimes a combination of these two methods is used, which helps to cancel out the drawbacks of each. To make sure that the highest ethical standards are followed in conducting research on human beings, ethics advisory boards review prospective research to ascertain that the rights of the participants supercede those of the investigators.

Theories are logically related statements about the nature of children's development and as such provide a means of understanding it from various perspectives. If you consider the large amount of data on children's behavior, you see that theories help organize and systematize the volumes of information about children. However, you must also be aware that the adoption of a single theory may direct an investigator's focus to a particular subset of the entire domain of variables. Thus, relevant variables pertaining to children's behavior may be overlooked.

ENHANCING YOUR CRITICAL THINKING

Firsthand Experiences

Ways of Studying Children

Children are fascinating creatures to observe but, as noted in the text, there are some problems and limitations to observational methods. There are also some effective techniques you can use to make observations of children more reliable. Herbert F. Wright (1960) discusses observational techniques in "Observational Child Study" in P. H. Mussen (Ed.),

Handbook of Research Methods (pp. 92–104) (New York: Wiley). Observe children before reading the article and after, and see how his suggestions have helped you in your observational skills.

Critical Thinking

Analyzing Theory

Nye, R. D. (1979). *What is B. F. Skinner really saying?* Englewood Cliffs, NJ: Prentice-Hall.

Robert Nye presents a highly readable summary and critique of Skinner's theory. Not only does Nye provide, in his words, "a clear, concise picture of what Skinner said in various writings . . . so that individuals can decide for themselves whether or not the Skinnerian approach has value," but he also compares pertinent points of Skinner's theory with Sigmund Freud's psychoanalysis and Carl Rogers' humanism. Which theory has the most value to you and why?

Analyzing Research

The following periodicals are good sources for selecting and reading current research in the field of developmental psychology. Go to the library and select an article from one of these journals; critique it according to the points mentioned in the text for analyzing research. Write down the strengths and limitations of the study. Based on your evaluation of the article, how valid and reliable are the findings presented in the study?

Annual Review of Psychology (reviews significant studies that have appeared during a given year)

Child Development

Developmental Psychology

Adolescence

Journal of Experimental Child Psychology

CHAPTER 2

Biological and Family Contexts of Development

CHILDREN'S THOUGHTS

On genes . . .

They are little things in your blood, and they tell your mind to give you brown hair or blue eyes. Like mine did. They also can make you short or tall, or smart or dumb.

Kevin, age 10

On divorce . . .

My parents were divorced about two years ago. I live with my mom. It's better now than when they first got a divorce. I really felt alone. I tried to think of ways to get them back together. I wondered if I would be divorced when I was older like my Mom. I don't think about these things so much anymore. But, I wish I'd see my dad more, he doesn't visit as much as he use to.

Jean, age 12

These children's thoughts introduce you to the topics of concern in this chapter: biological and family contexts of development. Kevin's ideas about genes exemplify a genetic determinist's point of view—genes (and to a very little extent, environment) determine behavior. In contrast, an environmental determinist holds a rigid adherence to an environmental explanation of behavioral development. The latter view has been pervasive in the United States. Presently, the trend is to move away from a strict environmental approach by incorporating research that analyzes genetic influences on behavioral development. Care must be taken, however, that the swing from environmental determinism is not replaced by genetic determinism.

In discussing children in the family context, the changing U.S. family and how the situations of divorce, single-parenting, blended families, and maternal employment affect the function of the family and the individuals within it will also be examined.

THE BIOLOGICAL CONTEXT OF DEVELOPMENT

There has been much controversy over the relative influence of inborn or genetic factors and environ-mental or experiential factors on the development of an individual's behavior and propensities. In particular, the debate has centered on the question, "How do inborn factors compare with environmental factors in contributing to an individual's personality and intellectual development?" The nature-nurture controversy has continued to tease and beguile the most brilliant developmental minds.

Genetic determinists argue that genetic endowment is the major influential factor in determining children's development; the behaviorists argue from quite a different school of thought, placing the environment as the major force in guiding children's future social and cognitive interactions. Today, most developmental psychologists put these either-or positions in perspective. Everyone must have both a viable gene complement and an environment in which the genes can be expressed over development. Thus, the question is not which one determines an individual's behavior, but in what manner.

BEHAVIORAL GENETICS

Research in understanding how environmental and genetic factors influence behavior and development has its base in **behavioral genetics.** In particular, behavioral genetics focuses on the nature and organization of genetic material and the way in which genetic material controls the development of traits during a person's life. It seeks to answer such questions as, "How wide are the boundaries set by heredity for various aspects of development (cognitive abilities, personality traits, etc.)?" "How do environmental forces influence the way these aspects will manifest themselves in children's personalities?" A mountain of data has been accumulated, much of it during the 1980s and 1990s. Most of this research has focused on three domains: intelligence, personality, and mental illness.

Studies examining hereditary and environmental influences on intelligence and personality are often based on studies of fraternal and identical twins. Identical twins (monozygotic twins) develop from one fertilized egg. Early in development, the contexts of the single egg develop into two embryos, usually enclosed in a single fetal membrane. Identical twins have the same genetic structure. Fraternal twins (dizygotic twins) are a result of two ova being released and fertilized. Dizygotic twins share a variable number of genes in common (50% on the average). Behavioral geneticists view development as the process through which your **genotype** (the set of genes you inherit) is expressed in your **phenotype** (your observable or measurable characteristics).

STUDYING ENVIRONMENTAL AND HEREDITARY INFLUENCES

Two major methods for studying environmental and hereditary effects are (a) the *twin design*, in which identical twin resemblance is compared with fraternal twin resemblance, and (b) the *adoption design*, in which genetically related individuals reared apart and genetically unrelated individuals reared together are studied.

Psychologists study twins by comparing the similarity, or **concordance,** of identical twins with the similarity of fraternal twins. In examining the concordance of identical and fraternal twins on some variable such as intelligence, statistical techniques for determining relationships between cer-

tain variables known as correlational procedures are used. The correlation coefficient is an estimate of the direction and magnitude of the relationship. Two variables may be positively correlated, negatively correlated, or unrelated. A perfect correlation is expressed as 1.0; if it is a positive correlation, it means that if one twin scores high on an IQ test, the other twin also scores high on the IQ test. A perfect negative correlation occurs when one twin scores high, and the other twin scores low. Correlational coefficients in educational and psychological measures, because of the complexity of these phenomena, seldom reach these maximum points. A moderate correlation would be between .40 and .60. It needs to be pointed out that correlation does not imply causation. If you say that creativity is highly correlated with intelligence, for example, you are not saying that creativity causes intelligence, just that the two variables are related.

Researchers not only examine similarities, but also are interested in analyzing differences. In this case, researchers are trying to explain what percentage of the **variance** in a certain behavior is accounted for or explained by another factor or factors. To illustrate, the circle in Figure 2.1 represents the total variance in intelligence; that is, which factors explain the individual differences (variance) that are found in children's intelligence. The area marked G (genetic) shows that 50% of the total variance in intelligence is due to individual differences in children's heritability. This means that genetic differences among individuals account for about half of the differences in individuals' performance on IQ tests. About 30% of the variance is due to **shared family environment,** marked Es on the chart, which includes such factors as shared parental attitudes, education, socioeconomic factors, and so forth. Approximately 10% of the variance is due to **nonshared family environment,** marked Ens, which includes experiences unique to the individual. Ten percent is error of measurement.

INTELLIGENCE

More behavioral genetic data has been obtained for IQ than any other trait. To what extent are chil-

FIGURE 2.1

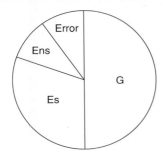

Proportions of IQ variance due to heredity (G), shared environment (Es), nonshared environment (Ens), and error of measurement

Source: From *Nature and Nurture: An Introduction to Behavioral Genetics*, by R. Plomin. Copyright © 1990 by Wadsworth, Inc. Reprinted by permission of Brooks/Cole Publishing Company, Pacific Grove, CA 93950.

dren's intellectual abilities (those measured by IQ tests) influenced by heredity? You could assume that if genetic factors play a role, then monozygotic twins' IQs would be more highly correlated than dizygotic twins' IQs.

IQ and Identical and Fraternal Twins   The higher concordance of monozygotic twins relative to dizygotic twins on standard tests of intelligence is a well-established finding (McGue & Bouchard, 1989; Wilson, 1983). Numerous studies have demonstrated a positive relationship between the average percentage of genes in common (by descent) and resemblance in mental ability.

Erlenmeyer-Kimling and Jarvik (1963) concluded that the closer the family relationship, the higher the concordance of IQ. The concordance between IQ scores was .49 for brothers and sisters, .53 for dizygotic twins, and .87 for identical twins. Nichols (1978) compiled 211 studies of intelligence that compared the resemblance of identical and fraternal twins. The mean correlation of general intelligence was .82 for monozygotic twins and .59 for dizygotic twins. Segal's (1990) study provides

further support for a genetic influence on general intelligence. The Wechsler Intelligence Scale for Children-Revised was administered to 103 sets of twins from Chicago and New York. Segal found a greater full-scale IQ concordance with monozygotic twins (.85) relative to dizygotic twins (.42).

The concordance between twins reared together and twins reared apart has been studied. Identical twins reared apart are rare; all the world's literature adds up to fewer than 100 pairs. (However, one ongoing study in the United States and two studies in Scandinavia are tripling that number; more will be discussed later.) Studies of twins have typically reported correlations between IQ scores of identical twins reared apart that are quite substantial and appreciably greater than those for fraternal twins reared in the same home. Bouchard and his colleagues (Bouchard, 1990; Bouchard & McGue, 1981; Bouchard, Scarr, & Weinberg, 1991) report an average correlation of .86 on IQ tests for identical twins reared together and .76 for identical twins reared in different families. The fact that these twins are nearly as similar intellectually as twins reared together is a rather startling finding, which is interpreted as testifying to the primacy of genetic influences in the determination of intelligence. Underlying this interpretation is the assumption that twins reared apart are experiencing widely different environments, so that substantial similarity between them must be attributable primarily to their common genetic endowment.

IQ and Adopted Children   The adoption of children with biological backgrounds that are different from their adopting parents and each other provide yet another opportunity to evaluate the impact of heredity and environment on children's intelligence. In one kind of adoption study, researchers compare the behavioral characteristics of adopted children with those of their biological and adoptive parents. Skodak and Skeels's (1949) report of a longitudinal adoption study of IQ is one of the most frequently cited studies in developmental psychology. The IQ scores of adopted children tested 4 times between infancy and adoles-

The science of behavioral genetics seeks to find the extent to which intelligence is influenced by heredity.

cence were compared to the characteristics of both their adoptive parents and their biological parents. The results of the study were impressive: The correlation between the IQ of 63 biological mothers and their adopted-away children indicated increasing hereditary influence during childhood, and reached .45 when children were adolescents. In early childhood, the adopted children's IQs were 20 to 30 points above the mean IQ of the biological mothers; however, at age 13 the child-adoptive parent IQ correlation had dropped to a mere .04.

Two ongoing longitudinal studies of cognitive development are the Texas Adoption Study and the Louisville Adoption Study. In the Texas Adoption Study (Horn, Loehlin, & Willerman, 1979), 1,230 members of 300 Texas families that had adopted one or more children from a church-related home for unwed mothers were studied. Persons tested included the adopted child, the adoptive parents, and other available biological or adopted children in the family. At the time of testing, the index children were between 3 and 14

years old. Approximately 10 years later, 259 adopted children in 181 of the families were located and retested as were 93 biological children of the adoptive parents. The findings of this study showed that adopted children resembled biological mothers more than lifelong providers. The data showed that the average correlation between adoptive parents' and adopted children's intelligence test scores was .19; a correlation of .48 between intelligence test scores of biological parents and their children who had been adopted was found. Second, children from higher-IQ unwed mothers surpassed those from lower-IQ unwed mothers, even though the intellectual potential in their environment was compatible.

In reanalyzing the data from the Texas Adoption Study, Loehlin, Horn, and Willerman (1989) reached the general conclusion that the popular view of genetic effects as being fixed at birth and environmental effects as changing was incorrect for the trait of intelligence in this population during these developmental years. These researchers maintain that shared family environment effects occur early in childhood and persist to a degree in the phenotype; however, the shared family environment has a decreasing influence on IQ as children get older. Changes in genetic expression, however, continue at least until late adolescence. A near-zero correlation based on adult adoptees in Denmark was obtained in one study (Teasdale & Owen, 1984), again suggesting very little influence of shared family environment on IQ measured after adolescence. Genetic factors not only contribute directly to children's development, but also mediate the effects of the environment (Braungart, Plomin, DeFries, & Fulker, 1992).

Thus, heritability increases substantially during childhood and may increase further during adolescence. Genetic effects account for about 15% of the variance in infant mental test scores, and by early school years, increase in importance to 40% of the variance. Increasing heritability means that the phenotypic variance of IQ scores is increasingly due to genetic differences, as can be seen in Figure 2.2.

The Continuing Influence of Genes   The Louisville Adoption Study also yields estimates of the contribution of shared family environment decreasing from 70% at age 3, to 30% to 40% in middle childhood, and 20% at age 15. The Louisville Twin Study was a longitudinal study initiated several years ago; at present there are 494 pairs of twins who have made regular visits to the study for testing. Wilson's (1983) elegant longitudinal work with twins from the Louisville Adoption Study demonstrates that not only mental ability level but also the timing of developmental events are under significant genetic influence. Mental development proceeds at different rates in different children. Just as children show spurts and plateaus in physical growth, they also show variations in the rate and timing of intellectual growth. Figure 2.3 shows the trends in mental development during early childhood for two monozygotic (MZ) and two dizygotic (DZ) pairs of twins. Even in patterns of intellectual ability and in rates and timing of intellectual growth, monozygotic twins are more similar than dizygotic twins.

FIGURE 2.2   Life-span Profile of Genetic and Shared Environmental Influences on IQ

Heritability increases substantially during childhood and may increase further during adolescence. Genetic effects account for about 15% of the variance in infant mental test scores and, by the early school years, increase in importance to about 40% of the variance.

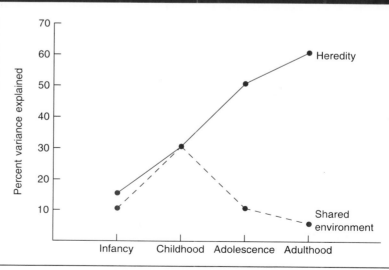

Source: From *Nature and Nurture: An Introduction to Behavioral Genetics*, by R. Plomin. Copyright © 1990 by Wadsworth, Inc. Reprinted by permission of Brooks/Cole Publishing Company, Pacific Grove, CA 93950.

FIGURE 2.3   Trends in Mental Development During Early Childhood for Two Monozygotic (MZ) Pairs and Two Dizygotic (DZ) Pairs

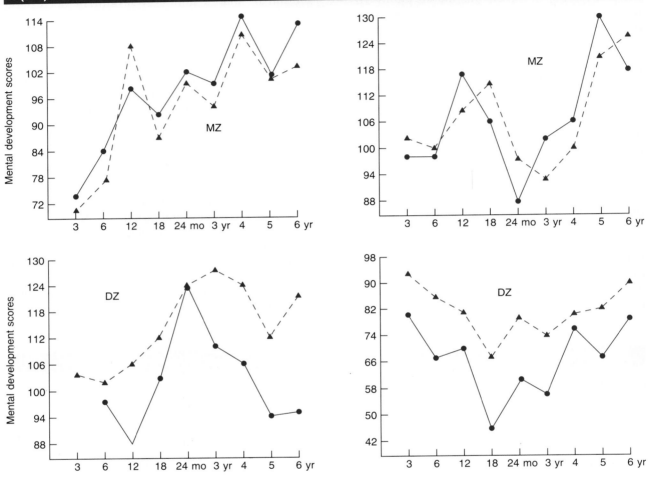

Source: From "The Louisville Twin Study: Developmental Synchronies in Behavior" by R. S. Wilson, 1983, *Child Development, 54,* p. 301. © The Society for Research in Child Development, Inc. Reprinted by permission.

The remarkable synchrony of the developmental patterns furnishes compelling evidence that genes "turn on and off" during development. This study shows that the influence of genes is manifest not only at conception, but also that developmental processes are subject to continuing genetic influences. Wilson (1983) concludes by saying:

The message from these results seems clear: There is a strong developmental thrust in the growth of intelligence that continues through adolescence and is guided by an intrinsic template or ground plan. The template is rooted in genetic processes that act throughout childhood and adolescence. . . . In this sense, developmental genetic processes are most sharply displayed in the long term—they produce continuing re-finements in the phenotype until the process is completed, and at that point the zygotes display concordance values closest to expectations from the genetic model. (p. 314)

The cumulative effect of being raised together in the same home appears not to offset the level of similarity commensurate with the extent of shared genotype—in the case of these unrelated adopted siblings, close to zero. Wilson's (1983) study appears to endorse the basic theme found in other studies: that intelligence as ultimately realized in adolescence is powerfully affected by developmental genetic processes that steadily move each individual toward a targeted end point.

Hereditary and Environmental Influence on Specific Abilities Although behavioral, genetic analyses of general intelligence have been reported, little is known about the genetic and environmental origins of individual differences in specific cognitive abilities. Plomin and his colleagues have recently reported data on specific abilities in early and middle childhood (Cyphers, Fulker, Plomin, & DeFries, 1989; Plomin, 1986, 1990). The analysis is based on data collected from 201 adopted and 209 nonadopted children tested at age 3; 192 adopted and 209 nonadopted children tested at age 4; 163 adopted and 142 nonadopted children tested at age 7; and the biological and adoptive parents of these children. The results suggest the existence of substantial genetic influence for verbal and spatial abilities and less so for perceptual speed and memory. These results are exciting because they suggest the existence of some genetic continuity from early childhood to middle childhood for specific cognitive abilities.

Similarly, report card grades show substantial genetic influence. For example, in one study school grades were obtained for 352 pairs of identical and 668 pairs of fraternal 13-year-old twins in Sweden (Husen, 1959). The identical and fraternal twin correlations were, respectively, .72 and .57 for reading, .76 and .50 for writing, .81 and .46 for arithmetic, and .80 and .51 for history. As you can

see, higher correlations were found for identical twins than for fraternal twins, which again gives support to the role of genetic influences on academic performance.

Twin studies of academic achievement test scores also show substantial genetic influence. For example, the largest twin study in the United States utilized data from the National Merit Scholarship Qualifying Test (Loehlin & Nichols, 1976). The twin correlations for English usage, mathematics, social studies, and natural sciences are listed in Table 2.1 and components of variance are illustrated in Figure 2.4. The results are quite similar to those for specific cognitive abilities.

As you have seen, other adoption studies show results comparable to Wilson's: Adoptive children ultimately match their natural parents more closely than their adoptive parents, although at the early ages they may show an initial association with the qualities of the adoptive home. Furthermore, when two unrelated infants are adopted into the same home, they may show similarities in mental development at early ages, but at adolescence their correlation lapses to zero. In the case of adopted children, Scarr and Weinberg (1977) have presented conflicting data. These researchers found that African-American children (N = 176) adopted by white families tended to have IQs

TABLE 2.1 Twin Correlations for Tests of Scholastic Achievement

| Test | TWIN CORRELATIONS | |
	Identical (1300 pairs)	Fraternal (864 pairs)
English Usage	0.72	0.52
Mathematics	0.71	0.51
Social Studies	0.69	0.52
Natural Sciences	0.64	0.45

Source: From "Personality Resemblance in Adoptive Families" by J. C. Loehlin and N. C. Nichols, 1976, *Behavioral Genetics, 11,* 309–330. Copyright 1976 by Plenum Publishing Corporation. Reprinted by permission.

FIGURE 2.4

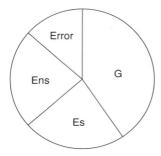

Components for variance for scholastic achievement due to heredity (G), shared environment (ES), nonshared environment (ENS), and error of measurement.

Source: From *Nature and Nurture: An Introduction to Behavioral Genetics*, by R. Plomin. Copyright © 1990 by Wadsworth, Inc. Reprinted by permission of Brooks/Cole Publishing Company, Pacific Grove, CA 93950.

higher than their genetic parents. Those adopted before the age of 1 scored 110 on IQ tests, about 20 points higher than comparable children from the African-American community.

The evidence supporting the existence of genetic influences on human cognitive abilities is overwhelming. Analyses of twin data indicate that the data cannot be explained without allowing for genetic effects and that the magnitude of these effects are such that approximately 50% of the variance in IQ is associated with genetic differences among individuals. The error surrounding this estimate may be as high as 20%, so it seems that the heritability of IQ scores is between 30% and 70%. Nonetheless, even if the heritability of IQ scores is at the bottom of this range, it is a remarkable finding. To explain 30% of the variance of anything as complex as IQ is an important achievement. If half of the variance of IQ scores is due to heredity, the other half is due to environment. Much of the environmental variance appears to be of the type shared by family members (Plomin, 1990).

Environmental Assessment   Does all the research suggest that the quality of the home environment

is inconsequential? Not at all. The contribution of the parents, whether natural or adoptive, is in helping their children reach the fullest extent of their abilities by creating an atmosphere of enthusiasm for learning, and in adapting their expectations to the child's capability. As Wilson (1983) notes,

> The wide diversity within families emphasizes the importance of giving each child full opportunity for development and indeed of making sure that the opportunity is taken. The ultimate goal is the maximum realization of each child's intelligence coupled with a sense of satisfaction and personal accomplishment in its use. There is no better way to foster such development than by a supportive and appropriately stimulating family environment. (p. 313)

PERSONALITY

It is more difficult to demonstrate significant genetic variance in personality than in cognitive variables. One reason for personality differences may be that personality characteristics are difficult to define and measure. Second, rarely are personality characteristics an all-or-nothing phenomena. That is, individuals express degrees of certain traits such as friendliness, outgoingness, or shyness. Moreover, the dynamic interaction between the individual and the environment that shapes personality is highly complex. There are, however, some convergent findings from a number of studies that confirm the existence of a genetic component in children's social characteristics.

Almost all knowledge regarding environmental and genetic causal influences on stable personality traits comes from studies of twins reared together. On the genetic side, regardless of the trait studied, the correlation for dizygotic twins has approached .25, and that for monozygotic twins has approached .50 (Goldsmith, 1983; Nichols, 1978), showing that genetic factors contribute to personality makeup. Fifty percent of the variance, however, is due to environmental influences, measurement error, and nonsystematic changes in the trait over time. Research has shown that genetic factors make a more significant contribution to traits such as extroversion, neuroticism, activity level, inhibition or fearfulness, altruism, and cooperation (Eaves, Eysenck, & Martin, 1989; Lytton, Watts, & Dunn, 1988).

Extroversion and Neuroticism Much research has considered two dimensions of personality that represent major clusters of behavior: extroversion and neuroticism. Longitudinal studies of children from birth to adolescence and studies of twins and adopted children suggest that the inclination to be friendly, outgoing, sociable and lively (extroverted) or moody, anxious, and irritable (neuroticism) is influenced by heredity (Goldsmith & Campos, 1990; Wilson & Matheny, 1986).

A review of the research involving over 25,000 pairs of twins for these two dimensions yields average heritability estimates exceeding .50 for both extroversion and neuroticism (Henderson, 1982). In a twin study involving a Swedish sample of 4,987 identical twin pairs and 7,790 fraternal twin pairs from 17 to 49 years of age (Floderus-Myhred, Pedersen & Rasmusson, 1980), the identical and fraternal twin correlations were .51 and .21 for extroversion, respectively, and .50 and .23 for neuroticism.

As noted, extroversion and neuroticism are global traits that encompass many dimensions of personality. The core of extroversion is sociability, or gregariousness, which is the extent to which individuals prefer to do things with others rather than alone. The key component of neuroticism is emotionality—the tendency to become aroused easily to fear and anger. From infancy to adulthood, these two traits, and one other—activity level—have been proposed as the most heritable components of personality (Plomin, 1990). Activity level is the preference for different kinds and amounts of stimulation. Some individuals seem to crave excitement and activity; others prefer a more tranquil kind of existence. It appears that monozy-

Studies of twins suggest our inclination to be sociable and outgoi... by heredity.

gotic twins are more similar than dizygotic twins in seeking (or not seeking) stimulation.

Kagan, Reznick, Clarke, Snidman, and Garcia-Coll (1984) maintain that heritability influences social inhibitedness and uninhibitedness. Children who were either socially inhibited or uninhibited when first tested at 21 months tended to remain relatively inhibited or uninhibited when retested at 4 and 5½ years of age. It was also discovered that inhibited children often displayed intense physiological arousal, for example, high heart rates, in response to novel stimuli, while the uninhibited children were barely phased.

There is some evidence that altruism is influenced by heritability. Rushton, Fulker, Neale, Nias, and Eysenck (1986) found that measures of altruism and aggression (traits expected to be heavily influenced by socialization processes) both had heritabilities of about .50 and no shared family environment influence. Segal (1990) compared monozygotic and dizygotic twins as interactive participants in a variety of social contexts. The cooperative and competitive behaviors of 47 IQ-concordant twin pairs between 6 and 11 years of age were observed during the completion of joint ojects or tasks. Monozygotic partners provided king evidence of greater cooperation, relative to otic partners. Monozygotic twins expended antly greater efforts for their partners on erent tasks than dizygotic twins, strongly g that a more altruistic spirit is operative ese pairs.

Research has also shown that gen-ect individuals to seek out environ-ost compatible with their biolog-s (Plomin, 1990; Wilson, 1983). en called *niche picking*. Children t, or create environs that they ren who are genetically pre-ted, for example, may ac-ny of others. As the child more freedom in select-notype may be more hildhood and adoles-he intelligence find-ings that adopted children are closer in intelligence scores to biological mothers than to their adopted mothers later in childhood. Starting from a common home environment, the offspring disperse in selecting their niches, and the directions reflect the range of intrinsic capabilities represented among the offspring (Wilson, 1983).

Nonshared Family Environment Contrary to what most of us would think is the finding that less than 1% of the environmental variance in personality is explained by shared family environment. That is, environmental variance works in a way very different from how the environment was thought to work. The environment primarily operates to make children growing up in the same family different from, rather than similar to, one another (Dunn & Plomin, 1990). Growing up together in the same family does not make siblings similar in personality. Even an event that affects every individual in the family will not be experienced in the same manner by each individual. Research indicates that siblings perceive that their parents treat them quite similarly; other research suggests that parents themselves perceive that they treat their children similarly (Daniels, Dunn, Furstenberg, & Plomin, 1985). Nonetheless, it is the nonshared family environment that influences personality. This conclusion was also reached by another group of researchers. Loehlin and Nichols (1976) found that greater similarity in twins' experiences could account for only a small fraction of the monozygotic twins' similarity in personality. Tellegen, Lykken, Bouchard, Wilcox, Segal, and Rich (1988) administered the Multidimension Personality Questionnaire measuring 11 primary personality dimensions to 217 monozygotic and 114 dizygotic reared-apart twin pairs. They conclude that personality differences are more influenced by genetic diversity than they are by environmental diversity.

Alcoholism Studies continue to shed light on heritability of other personality characteristics, for example, alcoholism, a rather complicated area of inquiry, since research shows that "situational" alcoholism caused by environmental factors such as war and unemployment skews the findings. Conventional wisdom holds that about 25% of the male relatives of alcoholics are problem drinkers themselves, as compared with less than 5% of the general population. Perhaps the best evidence for a genetic link comes from an adoption study in Sweden, which found that the adopted sons of alcoholic birth fathers were 4 times more likely to grow up to be alcoholic than were members of a control group (Bohman, Sigvardsson, & Cloninger, 1982).

Mental Illness   Recent adoption and twin studies also suggest that there's a genetic link to most, but not all, forms of schizophrenia. In one study (Gottesman & Shield, 1982), a significantly higher concordance for schizophrenia between members of identical twin pairs than for members of fraternal twin pairs was found. They found that of 28 pairs of identical twin pairs there was a 42% concordance for schizophrenia. The concordance for fraternal twin pairs was only 9% for a sample of 34 pairs. The likelihood that a child or sibling of someone with schizophrenia will develop the disorder is about 12% — 12 times higher than the risk for everyone else. If one identical twin has schizophrenia, the other has a 50% chance of developing the illness. Researchers suspect that a constellation of genes, working in combination with environmental forces, triggers the illness.

Both adoptive and twin studies confirm that clinical depression, particularly the bipolar manic-depressive variety, has a strong genetic component. If one identical twin suffers from bipolar manic depression, the other has a 79% likelihood of having the same disorder. Among fraternal twins, that correlation is only 19%.

CAUTIONS ABOUT TWIN AND ADOPTION STUDIES

There are some complicating factors in adoption studies that confound findings. Delayed separation from biological parents is one such factor. It invalidates an adoption design if early environmental influences are important to development of traits being studied. In the intellectual domain, the early adoption work of Skodak and Skeels (1949)

suggests a substantial role for early environment in raising the average IQ of a group of adopted children. Selective placement of children in homes resembling those they would have had with their biological parents is a problem because it elevates correlations used to estimate the influence of genetic and environmental factors in intellectual development.

Second, the unrepresentativeness of both adoptive parents and parents who give up their children for adoption represents another set of difficulties. Adoptive parents are usually favorably selected on a host of desirable characteristics including emotional stability, employment history, and socioeconomic class. This restriction in environmental variance could limit the generalizability of adoption results. Because adoptive agencies will continue to use these procedures, it will always be possible to say that, had some of the children been placed in particularly undesirable homes, the observed environmental effects would have been larger.

DIRECTNESS AND INDIRECTNESS OF T INFLUENCE OF HEREDITY

Several years ago, Anastasi (1958)
best way to view the nature-n
in terms of a directness an
more directly heredit
narrower will be t
For certain tra
tion, Down
deafness, t
be very na
great influ
syndrome
ment, it
exceed
helped
the sam
deafne
sight o
room
acteris
netic fac
to environ

(Waddington, 1968). Waddington used the term *chreod* to express the idea more succinctly: A chreod is a "fated" or predetermined, virtually fixed, developmental pathway.

In keeping with the systems view of this text, in which development is viewed as hierarchically organized into multiple contexts, Gottlieb (1991) suggests that canalization can take place not only at the genetic level, but also at all levels of the developing system. As can be seen in Figure 2.5, the most important feature of the systems view is the recognition that the genes are an integral part of the system and that their activity (i.e., genetic expression) is affected by events at other levels of the system, including the developing organism's environment.

Gottlieb's *experienced canalization* theory suggests that genes are part of the developmental system and are not inviolate or immune to influences from other levels of the system. For example, Gottlieb found that mallard duck embryos had to hear their own vocalizations prior to hatching if they were to show their usually highly specific behavioral response to the mallard maternal assembly call after hatching. If the mallard duck embryo was deprived of hearing its own or siblings' vocalization, it lost its species-specific perceptual specificity and became as responsive to the maternal assembly calls of other species as to the mallard hen's call. The fact that the ducklings have to hear their own (or siblings') vocalizations to show the species-specific responsiveness to their respective maternal calls raises the possibility that exposure to such vocalization also plays a canalizing role in development. Gottlieb's developmental systems theory, in contrast to Waddington's (1968) view of canalization, reflects the integration of experiential and genetic factors.

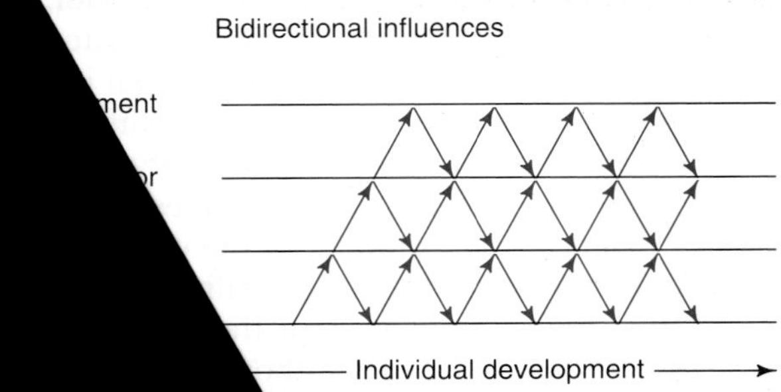

THE FAMILY CONTEXT OF DEVELOPMENT

As active members in an intimate, organized social system, children influence the family system and, of course, are influenced by the family and its members.

CHANGING FAMILY LIFE-STYLES: CHILDREN IN DIVORCED FAMILIES

The divorce rate continues to rise. What impact does divorce have on children? It appears that the initial period of divorce and parental separation is profoundly difficult for all children. Even when parents have been caught in severely unhappy marriages, their children usually do not want the divorce to occur and suffer as a result of the divorce. In recent years, researchers have moved away from viewing divorce as a static event that has pathogenic effects on children. Rather, current investigators are viewing divorce as a process of events. They are focusing on the diversity of children's responses prior to, during, and after the dissolution of marriage, and on the factors that facilitate or disrupt children's adjustment during the parents' marital transition. There are several factors that appear to relate to whether children make (or fail to make) a healthy adjustment to their parents' divorce: children's developmental status, the quality of the ex-spouse's relationship, custody

FIGURE 2.5

Bidirectional influences

...ment

...or

Individual development ⟶

...evelopmental systems view showing a ...teracting components in which there ...ottom-up" bidirectional influences.

...alization of Behavioral Develop-..., *Developmental Psychology*, ...erican Psychology Associa-

arrangements, the quality of the parent-child relationship, children's gender, and the support systems available to the family.

Children's Developmental Status Although divorce tends to be difficult for all children, Wallerstein and Kelly (1980) found that children of varying ages responded somewhat differently to the divorce of their parents. Approximately 131 children between the ages of 2½ and 18 years from 60 families in a high divorce area of northern California were studied over a 5-year period after the decisive marital separation. A 10-year follow-up study has been conducted.

Effects of Divorce on Infants and Toddlers The results of a handful of recent studies indicate that even infants and toddlers react negatively to parental stress and conflict. Three-month-olds have been found to respond negatively to simulated acts of maternal depression (Cohn & Tronick, 1983), while 1½ to 2½-year-olds have reacted to naturally occurring and simulated instances of interparent conflict with distress and attempt at active intervention (Cummings, Iannotti, & Zahn-Waxler, 1985). A frequently replicated finding is that infants younger than 2 years have been found to develop anxious-ambivalent or anxious-avoidant attachments to single mothers, particularly when these mothers are stressed and have limited access to social support.

Effects of Divorce on Preschool Children Preoperational thinkers center on particularly salient stimulus properties, are unable to coordinate information about states transformations, confuse their own and others' subjectivity, and have difficulty differentiating between inner motives and outer actions or appearances (Piaget, 1975). With this type of information-filtering system, preschoolers' reasoning about parental divorce has several distinctive features. These children are more likely to focus on one parent's physically moving away rather than on interparental incompatibility. Preschool children tend to become frightened and confused, rendering them especially vulnerable.

The most frightened children are those who had not received any explanation of the events in the family. Over three fourths of the children in the Wallerstein and Kelly (1980) study received insufficient explanations for the divorce, and it was these children who most frequently regressed and showed fear.

When children do not receive adequate explanations, they are at the mercy of their own conclusions. They are apt to believe that they are personally responsible for their parents' separation. This belief of being responsible for the parents' divorce may be the result of the child's special, magical kind of thinking. For example, young preschool children believe that they can cause things to happen just by thinking them. Similarly, they believe that events that happen together cause one another. A child will become attached to a blanket or teddy bear that brought comfort once, because the child now believes that it causes or necessarily brings about comfort. Similarly, children may feel that Daddy has left because they did not clean up their room, or brush their teeth often enough. Preschoolers need to be assured and reassured that they did not cause their parents to separate as well as being given adequate explanations about the divorce. This helps to reestablish the child's fractured world. Telling children about an impending divorce is discussed in "Focus on App..."

Preschool children, as a result of divorce, tend to exhibit an ... ical contact with adul... worry that their ... are afraid ... and find th... return fro... school, th... ness, an... who are... press th... fered du...

Acute... grown toy... whining, cr... served in you... ter a divorce. ...

FOCUS ON APPLICATIONS

How to Tell Children about Divorce

Both parents should talk to the children together. This reduces the tendency to blame the other parent. Children feel more secure.

Tell them one or two weeks before one parent moves out of the home. To tell the children too soon is to foster reconciliation fantasies. The longer the parent remains, the more the child believes the event will never happen. Telling the child a few days before does not allow enough time to adjust.

Begin with honesty, explaining the reasons for divorce appropriate to the age of the child. You might begin by saying, "Maybe you've seen that Mom and Dad haven't been too happy with each other for some time." You don't have to elaborate the minute details that children won't understand.

Parents need not fear openly expressing their emotions. Don't be afraid to cry. Tears are an expression of love. When adults cry in front of children they're giving their children permission to cry as well.

Let children express anger and resentment. This reaction is normal; children should not be punished for it.

Explain what life may be like in the future as best you can. If you know you're going to sell your home, share that information. By supplying details of common, everyday experiences, children can feel a sense of stability about their future.

Source: From *Children under Stress* (pp. 86–87) by D. C. Medeiros, B. J. Porter, and D. Welch, 1983, Englewood Cliffs, NJ: Prentice-Hall.

child needs to go back in development and mark time for a while in order to gain strength for the next step forward. Regression is not the favored ~~ial~~ response for the older preschool child (3¾ to ~~Many~~, however, become irritable, whiny, and

~~ce~~ seems to have a substantial effect on the ~~play and their ability to get along with~~ ~~study of 48 middle-class, white pre-~~ ~~ren from divorced families and a~~ ~~of 48 from nondivorced families,~~ ~~ox, and Cox (1978) found that, in~~ ~~wing divorce, disruptions were~~ ~~and social relations for boys~~ ~~se effects had largely disap-~~ ~~ars after the divorce; how-~~ ~~ore intense and enduring~~ ~~ns of children from di-~~

vorced families were less socially and cognitively mature; they showed less imaginative play; they also did less playing and more watching than children from intact families. In the year following divorce, both boys and girls showed high rates of dependent, help-seeking behavior and acting-out behaviors (temper tantrums, physical aggression toward other children). This, again, was more enduring in boys than in girls. An experiment similar to Hetherington et al.'s is described in "Studying Children." Try it to see if you also observe important differences in the way children from recently divorced families play as compared with children from intact families.

Although the children in Hetherington et al. (1978) and Wallerstein & Kelly (1980) studies had been distressed and frightened, and had represented the age group most severely troubled by

STUDYING CHILDREN

EFFECTS OF DIVORCE IN PLAY SITUATIONS

Have a nursery school teacher point out two children for you to observe. One child should be from an intact family; the other child from a home in which the parents have recently separated. (The status of these children should not be known to you until after you have completed your observations.) For approximately 20 minutes, observe these children in a free-time play situation. Note the children's social interactions with their peers. After the observation, examine your notes. Does the child from the divorced family situation tend to play by himself? Does the child display less mature play? Is he less imaginative in his play as compared with the child from an intact home situation? Does the child from the divorced home show more acting-out behaviors?

family crisis at the time of the study, the results of a follow-up study paint a different picture (Wallerstein, Corbin, & Lewis, 1988). Most of the original sample of preschool children in the Wallerstein and Kelly study, who were now 12 to 18 years of age, had no memories of their intact, predivorced families. The researchers note that the cognitive immaturity that created profound anxiety for children who are young at the time of their parents' divorce appears to prove beneficial over time. Ten years after the divorce, these children have fewer memories of either parental conflict or their own fears and suffering, and they typically have developed a close relationship with the custodial parent. What emerges is the very interesting possibility that children who are very young at the marital breakup are considerably less burdened in the years to come. They carry fewer memories of unhappiness and conflict between the parents and almost no memories of the intact family or their fights and suffering at the time of divorce. In addition, they appear to be very optimistic about the future.

Wallerstein et al.'s (1988) findings are noteworthy for a number of reasons. First, they contradict Freud's critical period hypothesis, which states that events happening before the age of 5 are more potent than later events in determining subsequent development. Second, they point out how important longitudinal research is, and how caution must be taken in predicting future development from data taken at one point in time.

Effects of Divorce on Children in Middle Childhood
Like their younger counterparts, older children experience considerable initial pain and anger when their parents divorce. Children who are between the ages of 6 and 10 no longer feel that they are personally responsible for their parents' divorce, but they still feel abandoned and rejected. They appear, however, to be better able to receive, sift through, and absorb the shocking news that their parents are going to separate. In fact, Wallerstein and Kelly (1980) noted that these children interviewed with "presence, poise and courage," and seemed to exhibit an ease and comfortableness in talking about their parents' divorce. One of their major concerns was that they would not be able to continue in activities that they valued and would have to give them up because of the financial stresses of divorce.

Children in middle childhood tend to define divorce in psychological terms, and frequently cite parent incompatibility or changes "on the inside" as a reason for the divorce (Kurdek, 1981; Neal, 1983). Unlike young children, school-aged children usually tell friends about the divorce.

Effects of Divorce on Adolescents Some parents feel that it may be best to wait to get a divorce until their children are older—in their teens. Wallerst... and Kelly (1980) found, however, that this time has a profoundly dist... olescents. The event st... front in every w... loss of face the d... peers. They becon... culties when their ... and feel powerless... they often strike back... is causing the divor... emptiness, fearfulness,... chronic fatigue, and tro...

Because the marital rupture occurs at an age when the adolescent is preoccupied with sex and the search for a partner, these issues become centers of anxiety. A number of adolescents become overtly anxious about their parents' sexuality— suddenly now visible—where before the divorce it could be denied. The relative invisibility of sex in the intact family reinforces the adolescents' capacity to deny that their parents have sexual needs (it's comforting to think of parents as old and sexless). Parental dating causes adolescents to see that their parents are sexual beings and this produces a great deal of discomfort and anxiety for many of them.

Both sons and daughters in divorced families tend to be given more responsibility, independence, and power in decision making than those in nondivorced families. Divorced mothers tend to monitor their children less closely than do mothers in nondivorced families. In the words of Weiss (1979), these children tend to "grow up faster."

One thing that is clear from Wallerstein and Kelly's (1980) study is that divorce can affect children in adverse ways. But, if the marriage is characterized by strife and strain, isn't it better for the children if parents do divorce? See "Focus on Issues."

The generalizability of these findings may be limited because of methodological errors. Most studies, for example, have involved small samples that vary widely in terms of the length of time passed since the parents' separation. That the majority of studies have included only white children and their parents is especially distressing considering that the percentage of divorced and single-parent situations is higher for nonwhites than for whites. The bias toward middle-class families is so problematic, because the negative consequences of divorce for children and parents have been linked to a decrease in financial resources available to the single parent (Zill, 1978). Most of the studies used the unstructured method in which children respond to regarding various aspects of the divorce. interviews often provide clinically rich information, they often show low reliability and do not control for subject and experimenter bias.

Quality of Ex-spouse's Relationship   The existence of a negative relation between ongoing parental conflict and childhood adjustment has been well documented. High levels of interparental conflict have been shown to be related to increases in the behavior problems of toddlers (Jouriles, Pfiffner, & O'Leary, 1988), school-aged children (Shaw & Emery, 1987), and young adolescents (Long, Forehand, Fauber, & Brody, 1987).

Therefore, another salient factor influencing children's adjustment is whether the parents engage in cooperative behavior or in combative interchanges (quarrels, sarcasm, demeaning the other parent, physical abuse). Continued parental discord has had an extremely negative influence on children, and seems to lead to consequences that markedly affect the establishment of a secure representational world, a healthy adaptive behavior, and developmental progression (Cummings, Pellegrini, Notarius, & Cummings, 1989).

Long and Slater (1988) examined the relation between continued high interparental conflict following divorce and reduced interparental conflict following divorce with 55 children between the ages of 11 and 15 years. The results indicated that children in the high-parental-conflict group reported significantly higher levels of adjustment difficulties. The nature of these difficulties included academic problems, internalizing problems (high anxiety, withdrawal), and externalizing problems (conduct disorders).

Data suggest that the ability of parents to handle differences in their relationships through appropriate conflict management and communication skills contributes to their child's well-being (Allison & Furstenberg, 1989). McCombs and Forehand (1989) studied 71 adolescents, 11 to 16 years of age, in order to find which factors appear to have a particularly strong effect on academic achievement. Two family factors, taken together, accounted for 33% of the variance between those

FOCUS ON ISSUES

Separating for the Sake of the Children

Do children in one-parent households function better than those in nondivorced families characterized by marital discord? This is a critical question, and the answer is particularly relevant because it bears on issues such as whether parents should stay together or separate for the sake of the children.

Hetherington (1989) found that in the first year following divorce, children in divorced families functioned less well than those in the high-discord nondivorced families. In this period, children from divorced families were more oppositional, aggressive, lacking in self-control, distractible, and demanding of help and attention both at home and in school than were children in nondivorced families with high rates of marital discord. At the end of 2 years, however, more acting out, aggressive behavior and less prosocial behavior such as helping, sharing, and cooperation was found in boys from conflictual nuclear families than in boys from divorced families.

The impact of divorce seems more pervasive and long lasting for boys than for girls. Differences between the social and emotional development of girls from divorced and nondivorced families with low conflict had largely disappeared by 2 years after divorce. Although the behavior of boys from divorced families had greatly improved over the 2-year period following divorce, and was less disruptive than that of boys from stressful nuclear homes, Hetherington (1989) points out that the boys still functioned less well than children from low-stress nondivorced families. There was still considerable conflict in the mother-son dyad, and at school the boys were more socially isolated, verbally aggressive, immature, and less constructive in play.

Thus, it appears that divorce, in the long run, may be more advantageous when the marriage is characterized by a high degree of conflict. This remains true only if the divorce results in a termination of conflict between the parents, which cannot be assumed to happen. Wallerstein et al. (1988), for example, found that conflict between the parents often survives the legal divorce by many years. In fact, a rather high proportion (approximately one third of her sample of 36 boys and 36 girls) continued to experience open parental discord even 10 years after the dissolution of the parents' marriage.

Current evidence suggests that interparental conflict, whether in intact families or in divorced families, is the most salient factor in creating childhood behavior problems (Zill, 1988). Hetherington (1989) points out that children from broken or intact homes characterized by interparental conflict are at a greater risk than are children from broken or intact homes that are relatively harmonious. When parents continue to engage in bitter battles, children feel unable to master the resulting stress and psychic pain.

who were high and low academic achievers: the absence of conflict observed by the adolescents between their divorced parents, and a positive relationship with their mothers.

Exposure to parental discord repeatedly has been associated with the development of problems of control (aggression, cor⸱ (Block, Block, & Gjerde, 1⸱ mings, 1989; Whitehead, ⸱ through which adults' angr⸱ ence aggressiveness is throu⸱ or stress, particularly in bo⸱

(1985) found that adults' angry behavior was emotionally arousing for 2-year-olds and was linked with increasing aggressiveness in play between children following exposure. Children from high-parental-discord homes tend to play at a lower level with peers, display more negative peer interactions, and have worse health (Gottman & Katz, 1989).

Various theoretical frameworks suggest that parental conflict influences a child's adjustment indirectly by altering some aspect of the parent-child relationship. Fauber, Forehand, Thomas, and Wierson (1990) found in their study of 97 adolescents and their mothers that parental conflict increased the risk of antisocial or coercive behavior. They also found that parental conflict produced laxed parenting, particularly maternal monitoring of the child's behavior. The authors suggested that as parental conflict escalates, parents become increasingly absorbed in the marital problems and begin to pay less attention to the child. The child may "learn" that acting out is an effective attention-getting strategy that thus becomes more likely to be emitted in response to perceived parental withdrawal.

Custody Arrangements   There is some evidence, scant though it may be, that school-aged children adapt better in the custody of a parent of the same sex (Camara & Resnick, 1988; Zill, 1988). Boys in the custody of their fathers are more mature, social, and independent, are less demanding, and have higher self-esteem than do girls in their fathers' custody. Boys do tend to be less communicative and less affectionate. However, whether boys are in the custody of either mothers or fathers, they show more acting-out behaviors than do girls.

Some studies have shown that children benefit from contact with both parents after the divorce, provided there is a low conflict level between the parents. For example, it was found in one study (Ash & Guyer, 1986) that the child's adjustment to the divorce was related not to the type of custody

...en experience a great deal
...ty when mothers and fa-
...tinually display angry

(joint, father, or mother) but to the quality of the current interparental relationship. Joint custody in and of itself may not benefit children's adjustment. When parents continue to engage in acrimonious battles, joint custody may just prolong the children's involvement in hostility and conflict, thus making their adjustment to divorce much more difficult. There is no evidence that encouraging or mandating joint custody and frequent visitation through the legal system either diminishes hostility between those parents who are severely disputing such arrangements, or increases their cooperation in parenting their children (Kline, Tschann, Johnston, & Wallerstein, 1989).

Some studies have found evidence that children who have more frequent access to both parents during custody and visitation disputes were more emotionally troubled and behaviorally disturbed (Kline et al., 1989). More verbal and physical aggression appears to be generated between parents when children have more frequent access arrangements. The higher incidence of parental conflict to which children are exposed is associated with their increased vulnerability to being caught and used in the parental disputes; this, in turn, partially explains the higher incidence of emotional and behavioral problems. The level of parental conflict and its sequelae are not the only factors implicated in children's postdivorce disturbances. Kline et al. (1989) also found that

> the more often children have contact with their parents in distressed families, the more problematic is their adjustment, regardless of the level of interparental aggression. Children of severe divorce disputes appear to be more symptomatic in response to living in and making transitions between parental homes, even when their parents are not fighting. (p. 437)

The investigators continue by saying,

> It appears that some jurisdictions are ideologically more committed to encouraging joint custody and frequent visitation. In light of the research findings, it is important to review these attitudes and policies continually, not only in light of new evidence, but from the perspective of the accumulating body of related research findings. (p. 437)

Parent-Child Relationship   Another possible mediating factor in children's adjustment to divorce is the relationship between the parent and child. Hess and Camara (1979) studied the possible mediating effects of the parent-child relationship on the adjustment of children, ages 9 to 11, following divorce. The data suggest that the quality of the parent-child relationship is a significant factor in predicting a child's postdivorce functioning. They found that a good relationship with both parents (versus a good relationship with one or with neither parent) is the most powerful mediating situation for children experiencing divorce.

More recently, Wierson, Forehand, Fauber, and McCombs (1989) provided further support for the Hess and Camara (1979) finding regarding the buffering effects of a good parent-child relationship on a sample of 41 adolescent males (ages 10 to 15). Adolescents in the divorced/good relationship group did not differ significantly from the intact/good relationship group on measures of cognitive, social, and behavioral functioning. It remains uncertain as to what mechanisms this buffering effect is activating. Perhaps a good relationship, suggest Wierson et al. (1989), allows for support and creates security such that the adolescent does not feel as personally threatened by the divorce. Howes and Markman (1989) found that the quality of the relationship with the mother was a stronger indication of children's adjustment than that with the father. Because mothers are likely to spend more time with the child, it makes intuitive sense that disturbances in that relationship may be more destructive to the child.

Children's Gender   One of the most consistent findings is that boys are more negatively affected by divorce than girls. Girls tend to recover faster from the divorce of their parents. Boys, on the other hand, take longer to recover from effects, and they show greater emotional, and academic areas show more sustained, nonco behaviors even 2 to 3 years aft turbances in social and emotional have largely disappeared 2 years

Some researchers have suggested that the problems manifested by boys may, in fact, have occurred long before the marriage breakup (Block et al., 1986). In an ongoing longitudinal study, these researchers took advantage of the fact that some children in their sample would experience divorce. In fact, 40% of the families did divorce or separate. They had, then, a record of behavior of boys and girls (ages 3 to 7) in a variety of areas before separation occurred. Boys from families that eventually divorced were, prior to the divorce, exposed to significant amounts of conflict between the parents, and this parental discord was related to their being more aggressive, impulsive, and full of misguided energy before the separation. The behavior of girls was found to be notably less affected.

A finding about gender differences contradictory to the Block findings was reported by Doherty and Needle (1991), who studied the well-being of an older sample: adolescents before and after a parental divorce. The sample consisted of adolescents who were administered self-report measures of psychological adjustment. Forty-eight adolescents experienced the disruption of their parents' marriage during this time. Data were collected at an average of 12 months before the separation and 5 months after the divorce. The control group consisted of the 578 adolescents in the original sample whose parents remained continuously married.

Girls tended to show their negative consequences prior to the separation and did not appear to decline further after the divorce. The marital disruption itself did not appear to create more negative consequences for girls than they had already experienced. For boys, however, the main consequences appeared to occur after the divorce. The authors suggest that adolescent boys may be able to buffer themselves emotionally during the stressful preseparation period, but can no longer sustain this stance after the divorce, when their life-style has changed significantly and they experience a decrease in the quantity and sometimes the quality of parental supervision.

Thus, the matter of gender differences among [ ]n in response to divorce is not clear-cut but [ ]ay depend importantly on the timing of [ ]ring the divorce process (Zaslow, 1988).

Moreover, gender differences may depend on the adjustment variables being examined. The negative effects of divorce on boys may be due to the preponderant use of measures of externalizing behavior, which generally will show greater difficulties for boys (Zaslow, 1989).

The aggressive, acting-out, noncompliant behavior seen in boys may be due, in part, to the fact that they are exposed to more parental conflict than are girls. Morgan, Lye, and Condron (in press) indicate that parents tend to argue more in front of males than they do in front of females. The investigators also reported that families with sons are 9% less likely to divorce than families with daughters. This may be due to fathers being more involved with sons, or because mothers may be more reluctant to raise males on their own.

Another explanation is that boys tend to receive less support and nurturance and are viewed in a more negative way by mothers and teachers in the period immediately following the divorce than are girls. Divorced mothers of boys report feeling more stress and depression than do mothers of girls, and so may reflect this in their treatment of sons.

Some researchers have suggested that boys from divorced families may not be doing as well as boys from nondivorced families because of "diminished parenting" (Hetherington, 1989). Divorce may reduce the parental attention and supervision available to children, thus disrupting the intellectual environment of the home, supervision of homework, and communication with school. It is not uncommon for custodial mothers to become less supportive and more punitive in dealing with their children, particularly boys (Kline et al., 1989). This may have an immediate effect on academic work, particularly when combined with ongoing interparental conflict that may have already reduced attention.

Social Support Systems   Support systems can serve as sources of practical and emotional support for both parents and children experiencing divorce (Hetherington, in press). Schools and day-care centers, for example, can offer stability to children by providing warm, structured, predictable environments. School personnel can validate feelings of self-control and competence. Wolchik, Ruehlman, Braver, and Sandler (1989) showed that at high levels of stress, children with high support from nonfamily and family adults tend to report fewer adjustment problems than children with low support. It is interesting to note, however, that at the lowest level of stress, children with high support from nonfamily adults were significantly more poorly adjusted than were children with low support. The authors suggest that high support from nonfamily adults may be associated with more adjustment problems in these children because they may view this aid as a message that they have problems, which may influence children's assessments of their functioning.

CHANGING FAMILY LIFE-STYLES: CHILDREN IN SINGLE-PARENT FAMILIES

The number of single-parent households has more than doubled since 1970, and the majority of children in single-parent households (90%) live with their mothers (Bureau of the Census, 1988). About three quarters of the single-parent households result from divorce or separation of married couples, although a growing minority are composed of never-married mothers and their children. It is estimated that approximately 50% of the children born in the 1980s will experience their parents' divorce and will spend an average of 5 years in a single-parent home before their custodial parent's remarriage (Hetherington, Stanley-Hagan, & Anderson, 1989).

Currently about 60.1% of all African-American children live in female-headed households (Anthony, Wiedemann, & Chin, 1990). Of these children, 70% are poor compared with 24% of African-American children who live in two-parent families. Furthermore, African-American children spend more time than white children in a single-parent family before making the transition to a two-parent family and are much more likely to remain in a single-parent family for the duration of childhood (Duncan & Rodgers, 1987).

Because only one parent is present in the home, single-parent families have been thought to be in trouble. The common belief was that children from "broken" homes tended to have more academic, emotional, and behavioral problems. The single-parent household was assumed to be the cause of the child's low self-esteem, achievement problems, inappropriate gender-role behavior, and immaturity. A one-to-one causal relationship was assumed between single-parent life-styles and all kinds of psychological problems found in children.

The major problem with these early studies was that they failed to control for important variables, such as socioeconomic status, the custodial parent's access to social supports, the involvement of the noncustodial parent, or the relationship between the parents before and after the breakup. Research today is studying single-parent families while controlling for important variables.

Despite the common misconception that in any group of disturbed children a large number of them will be from single-parent homes, research indicates that intervening variables play a more significant role in determining single parents' and their children's adjustment than the absence of one parent. Economic deprivation appears to be an important variable (Daly & Wilson, 1985; Wolfe, 1987). Moreover, Gelles (1989) found that child abuse is more likely to occur in single-parent, poverty-stricken homes. He also found that the rate of severe and very severe violence toward children was higher among single fathers than among single mothers, and the highest risk for abuse occurred in fathers earning less that $10,000 a year.

Moreover, economic variables appear to play an important role in determining children's social and academic achievement. When children from one-parent and two-parent homes at similar economic circumstances are compared, little difference is found in children's school performance and their social adjustment (Dornbusch et al., 1985). Thus, living with one parent may not necessarily be th~ most important factor that affects a ~~ opment, but rather the econ countered by single parents. A tors, not just the absence of a p. psychological problems in child

It may also take time to ac parenting situation. Dreman, (1990) discuss three stages that sir to experience following the actual divorce: aftermath, realignment, and stabilization. In the aftermath period, which lasts for about 2 years, single parents tend to feel highly defensive, and their sense of competence and control over life events is low. In the realignment stage, single parents tend to feel less defensive, and undergo an "emotional divorce" in which they become more accepting of their situation. The last stage, stabilization, which occurs 3 to 4 years after divorce, is characterized by more positive attitudes about themselves, feelings of control, and an ability to develop more favorable attitudes about remarriage (Herz Brown, 1988).

CHANGING FAMILY LIFE-STYLES: CHILDREN IN BLENDED FAMILIES

Each year in the United States about one-half million children are involved in a remarriage, adding to the 7 million stepchildren under 18 (Reid & Crisafulli, 1990). Stepfamilies cannot operate as traditional families do—it takes more flexibility and dedication. Approximately 75% of divorced mothers and 80% of divorced fathers remarry, and the divorce rate in remarriages is about 50% higher for second marriages than for first marriages. Thus, many children are exposed to a series of marital transitions and household organizations following their parents' initial separation and divorce.

The first problem in remarriage situations appears to be difficulties with the children (Crosbie-Burnett, 1983). Sometimes it is hard for children to adapt to the new situation, which may make life difficult for the parents. For example, children may have a special bond with the solo parent following the marital dissolution and feel betrayed when he or she remarries. If the parent marries too soon, the child may not have had enough time to adjust to the divorce before having to adjust to the remarriage. Some children continue to harbor wishes that their "real" parents will get together—a new marriage obviously undermines this possibility.

Following remarriage, many children evidence a [emer]gence of problem behavior (Bray, 1988; Hetherington & Clingempeel, 1988). The younger child [is] able to eventually form an attachment

A blended family is one in which one or both spouses have been married in the past and have brought children from the first marriage to live in the newly arranged stepparent family.

with a competent stepparent and to accept the stepparent in a parenting role. Most younger children in supportive homes with "normal" conflict levels eventually accept a warm and involved stepparent. Developmental tasks facing adolescents, however, may make them especially vulnerable and unable to adapt to the transition of remarriage (Brand, Clingempeel, & Bowen-Woodward, 1988). In addition, because older children have more confidence and resources for fighting back, they may confront or question some aspects of family roles and functioning that younger children would not (Brown & Hobart, in press).

Do stepchildren differ from their counterparts in intact families? Santrock (1982) studied 36 families, half of whom had a girl and half of whom had a boy between the ages of 6 and 11. One third of the group consisted of divorced mothers who had remarried (the stepfather group), one third consisted of mothers who had not remarried (the mother-custody group), and one third were intact families. Parents were observed interacting with their children in a lab setting. It appears that the entrance of a stepfather into a previously father-absent home has a positive effect on boys' cognitive and personality development. This effect on boys was also noted by Wallerstein and Kelly (1980), who noted that for boys the entry of a stepfather triggered excitement, growth, and a rapid attachment. (A similar process may occur for girls when a stepmother arrives in a previously mother-absent home.) Girls in stepfather families, however, showed more anxiety than girls in intact families.

Whereas boys experience more pervasive problems in postdivorce adjustment, some studies report that girls have more problems adjusting to remarriage. For example, Hetherington (1989) found that preadolescent boys in families with stepfathers are more likely than girls to show improvement on measures of adjustment. In contrast, girls who often have close relationships with their custodial mothers and considerable independence may find stepfathers disruptive and constraining, and view them as intruders or competitors for their mothers' attention. Zaslow (1988, 1989) found that "boys tend to show more pervasive effects of divorce [than girls] except in postdivorce family forms in which a stepparent is present" (1989, p. 137).

Although mothers and stepfathers view sons as extremely difficult, the son's behavior improves over time. Boys whose mothers had been remarried for over 2 years showed no more aggressive, noncompliant behavior in home and school than boys in nondivorced families. Daughters tend to exhibit more demandingness, hostility, coercion, and less warmth toward both remarried mothers and stepfathers. While their behavior tended to improve, 2 years after the remarriage these girls

STUDYING CHILDREN

SUCCESSFUL BLENDED FAMILIES

Interview three or four children of varying ages from blended family situations. Ask them to describe some of the reasons why blended families are successful. What advice would they give to children in newly formed blended families to help them to adjust to the new situation? Any commonalities found in the children's responses?

were still more antagonistic and disruptive with their parents than were girls in two-parent families.

Discipline is a thorny issue. Some children resent having a stepfather or stepmother telling them what to do. Both remarried mothers and fathers report poor family communication, less effective problem resolution, less consistency in setting rules, less effective discipline, and less family cohesion in the early months of remarriage (Bray, 1988). Stepfathers who initially spent time establishing relations with stepsons by being warm and involved, but not asserting parental authority, may eventually be accepted by their stepsons. Acceptance of the stepfather by the stepdaughter, however, is uncorrelated with his behavior toward her and more difficult to obtain (Hetherington, 1987). The best strategy, according to Hetherington (1987), is for the stepparent not to make an active attempt to initiate, shape, and control children's behavior, but rather to be supportive of their mother. Later, the stepfather may become more authoritative, which leads to constructive long-term outcomes, at least for boys. Open communication between the children and the marital pair concerning many issues—including discipline—seems to be essential. Other factors that lead to a successful blended family are discussed in Table 2.2. What are children's feelings abo~~
ate a successful blended family
Children" experiment to find c

CONTEMPORARY TRADITIO

Taubin and Mudd (1983) make
servations about the future of tra

TABLE 2.2   Successful Blended Families

Jeannette Lofas, head of the Stepfamily Foundation, lists ten steps for new stepparents to bear in mind during the often difficult first year of living in a stepfamily.

1. Recognize that the stepfamily will not and cannot function as does a natural family. It has its own special dynamics and behaviors.
2. Recognize the hard fact that the children are not yours and they never will be. We are stepparents, a step removed; still, in this position, we can play a significant role in the development of the child.
3. Super-stepparenting doesn't work. Go slow. Don't come on too strong.
4. Discipline styles must be sorted out by the couple. They need to work out what the children's duties and responsibilities are. What is acceptable behavior, and what are the consequences when children misbehave? The couple works out jobs and family etiquette together.
5. Establish clear job descriptions for the parent and stepparent and their respective children. What specifically is the job of each one in this household?
6. It is vital to the survival of the parent to understand expectations for each member, especially the primary issues that produce upset—for example, money, discipline, the prior spouse, visitation, authority, emotional support, and territory and custody.
7. There are no ex-parents—only ex-spouses. Learn how best to handle the prior spouse.
8. Be prepared for the conflicting pulls of sexual and biological energies within the step-relationship. In the intact family, the couple comes together to have a child. The child is part of both parents, and generally pulls the parents' energy together for the well-being of the child. In stepfamilies, blood and sexual ties can polarize the family in opposite energies and directions.
9. The conflict of loyalties must be recognized as normal right from the beginning and be dealt with. Often a child who is just beginning to have warm feelings toward the new stepparent will pull away and negatively act out. He feels something like this: "If I love you, that means that I do not love my real parent."
10. Guard your sense of humor and use it. The step situation is filled with the unexpected. Sometimes we won't know whether to laugh or cry. Try humor.

Source: From *Our Endangered Children: Growing Up in a Changing World* by Vance Packard. Copyright © 1983 by Vance Packard. By permission of Little, Brown, and Company.

Alternative family life-styles will continue to exist, but so will traditional families. Unlike Bronfenbrenner's (1986) belief that traditional families may be a thing of the past, many social scientists believe that family commitments will persist in our society; the family is not an "archaic remnant of a disappearing traditionalism (p. 727)." "Over 95% of the adult population still marry at some point in their life and more than 60% will remain married" (Taubin & Mudd, 1983, p. 259). In addition, 3 out of 4 individuals say they are happy in their present marital situation. Similarly, when individuals were asked "How would you evaluate your own marital happiness?" only a small percentage reported that they were "not too happy."

Although there is less stability in contemporary relationships, fewer external pressures to remain married, and more available family life-style alternatives, few persons maintain nontraditional family life-styles for more than a short period of time. Marriage and remarriage occur as individuals seek the desired permanence, happiness, connectedness, and continuity.

Taubin and Mudd (1983) do point out that the contemporary traditional family will emphasize equality and a sharing of responsibilities. The days of the dominant husband and submissive wife are over. Contemporary traditional families are ones that will provide for individual growth and expression. Current trends indicate that contemporary families will be a two-paycheck family with fewer children. Stability and quality are still strong motives underlying family formation and a permanent marriage is still, for most, the ideal way of achieving these goals.

CHILDREN IN DUAL-WAGE-EARNER FAMILIES

The rate of working mothers has steadily increased among women of almost all ages. The current rate of maternal employment for two-parent families with school-aged children is 71% (Hoffman, 1989). This rate increases modestly each year. The most impressive recent change in maternal employment rates, however, has been among mothers of preschool children and infants. As of 1988, 56% of mothers with children under the age of 6 were in the labor force. Employed mothers of infants under 1 year of age represent the fastest growing subgroup, escalating from 31% of all women with infants under 1 year in 1976 to 52% in 1990 (U.S. Bureau of Labor Statistics, 1989). Assuming that the present labor force trends continue, it is predicted that by 1995, two thirds of all preschool children and three fourths or more of all school-aged children will have mothers in the work force (Hofferth & Phillips, 1989). That is, 15 million preschoolers and 34 million school-age children may have mothers who work outside the home.

Effects of Maternal Employment on Infants and Toddlers What distinguishes recent research from previous research is the focus on the effects of mothers working on their infants and toddlers. In particular, considerable attention has been given to the relationship between the mother's employment status during the first year of the child's life and the type of emotional bond, or *attachment* relationship, that emerges between infant and mother. It is widely held that an infant's attachment relationship to the mother emerges at ap-

proximately 7 months of age, with its quality being a product of the preceding months of interaction. A wealth of empirical data now documents the power of 12- to 18-month evaluations of the security of the mother-infant attachment relationship and the child's concurrent as well as later functioning in a variety of areas.

Studies of the relation between maternal employment and the quality of infants' attachments have led to inconsistent findings. Some studies have found no association between the mother's work status and the quality of the infant's attachment to her (Easterbrooks & Goldberg, 1985; Hock, 1980). In contrast, some investigators have found higher rates of insecurely attached infants among those mothers who were employed (Barglow, Vaughn, & Molitor, 1987; Chase-Lansdale & Owen, 1988). However, in reviews that have combined subjects across studies (Belsky, 1988), it has been found that full-time employed mothers are more likely than part-time employed and nonemployed mothers to have insecurely attached infants.

The results of studies addressing the issue of short- and long-term effects of mothers working full time, and subsequent full-time day care for the infant, have been unclear enough to allow varied interpretations. Belsky (1988), interpreting the available data, claims that full-time maternal employment involving daily separations between mothers and infants put infants at risk for developing insecure attachment bonds. Clarke-Stewart (1989), evaluating the same studies, concludes that there is insufficient evidence to support this claim.

The overwhelming impression of attachment studies is that maternal employment is not so robust a variable that it can be related to child outcomes. It operates through its effects on the family environment and the child-care arrangements, and these are moderated by parental attitudes, family structure, and other variables. It is these variables that may explain the higher percentage of insecurely attached infants among full-time employed mothers. For example, one explanation is that full-time maternal employment during the early months may be a stress that, when combined with other stresses, can interfere with the mother-infant relationship.

Another possibility is that the type of measures used to assess the quality of attachment may not be applicable to infants of employed mothers. The Strange Situation Test is the standard test used. The measure assumes that the situation of entering an unfamiliar room, meeting a new person, and experiencing two brief separations from the mother is anxiety producing for infants and activates attachment behavior. While its validity has been established for children reared in home care, its validity has not been established for employed-mother families. The idea is that mild stress is the key to assessing how secure the base of attachment is. The experiences encountered in the Strange Situation Test may not produce anxiety or mild stress in the child, and thus the child's behavior may not be a basis on which to judge the attachment relationship. Field (1991) observed 80 infants, toddlers, and preschoolers before, during, and after separations from their mothers. Data indicate that children in her study seemed to adapt to repeated separations; that is, they no longer exhibited stressful reactions to mother leaving, which lends support to the suggestion that the Strange Situation Test may not produce anxiety in children used to repeated separations from their mothers.

Belsky and Braungart (1991), on the other hand, also tested the hypothesis that children with early and extensive day-care experience are less stressed by the Strange Situation Test on a sample of 20 infants from middle- and working-class two-parent families. Eleven of these infants had histories of extensive nonparental care in their first year of life (more than 20 hours per week), and nine averaged less than 20 hours per week of routine nonparental care in their first year. Contrary to propositions advanced by Field (1991) and Clarke-Stewart (1989), Belsky (1988) found that infants with extensive nonparental care experience whimpered, fussed, and cried more and engaged in object play less in each reunion episode than their counterparts with less nonparent care experience. Belsky and Braungart (1991) conclude,

Clearly it remains untenable to argue that elevated levels of avoidance and insecure-avoidant attachment classifications in the case of infants with early and extensive daycare histories are a function of the fact that these children are less stressed by the separations designed into the Strange Situation Test and that they engage in more independent exploratory behavior than other children with the same insecure attachment classifications but different child care histories. (p. 571)

A third explanation is that mothers who obtain employment early in the infant's life are less sensitive to the child's attachment needs. Finally, mothers' attitudes about employment or staying home could affect their behavior toward their children and subsequently the type of attachment relationship. In one study (Hock & DeMeis, 1990), for example, it was found that mothers who preferred employment but remained at home showed higher scores on depression and stress inventories than mothers whose employment status was consonant with their preferences.

The issue of whether early day care is hazardous to children's development is really not the issue. Maternal employment is a reality. Discussing whether infants should be in full-time day care or not is superfluous. It is important to know how to make their experiences at day care and at home supportive of their development and of their parents' peace of mind, a topic that will be discussed in "Practical Implications."

Consistencies may be seen as emerging across studies that have included fathers as well as mothers in observations of employed- and homemaker-mother families. Most studies have reported a tendency for parents in employed-mother families to interact somewhat less with their children than parents in families with homemaker mothers (Zaslow, Pedersen, Suwalsky, & Rabinovich, 1989). Other researchers (Stuckey, McGhee, & Bell, 1982) have reported that when observed at home, parents from dual-income families engaged in less frequent verbal behavior and quiet play with their children than parents in single-income families. Sons of homemaker mothers, but daughters of employed mothers, receive more parental attention in terms of caregiving, punishing, and active play (Zaslow, Pedersen, Suwalsky, Cain, & Fivel, 1985).

Effects of Maternal Employment on School-aged Children and Adolescents Research presents a fairly consistent finding that daughters of working mothers are higher achievers than daughters of nonworking mothers, and that they show more positive adjustment on several indexes (Armistead, Wierson, & Forehand, 1990). Sons of working mothers, as with daughters, are less stereotyped in their view of what each sex is like; they see women as more competent than do sons of nonworking mothers, and they see men as warmer. Furthermore, in several studies the sons of working mothers have had better social and personality adjustment scores on various standards (Paulson, Koman, & Hill, 1990). The picture for boys' academic achievement, however, is not uniformly reassuring, and findings differ by social class. Recent findings suggest that the mother working outside the home is associated with lower academic achievement for sons from middle-class homes, but not in low-income families (Gold & Andres, 1978; Hoffman, 1989).

The studies of maternal employment among poor families have consistently found that a working mother contributes positively to the achievement of children. For example, Woods (1972) found in a ghetto school that fifth-grade children of employed women had higher IQs and better teacher ratings than a matched sample of children of nonemployed mothers.

Why should lower achievement be observed in middle-class boys? A reasonable hypothesis is that in lower-income families the income generated by the mother's work may result in a standard of living that offsets any negative consequences for boys that might ordinarily result from her working. In higher-income families, however, the mother's income may not make the crucial difference for the family's quality of life and thus may not add enough to compensate for disincentives to academic achievement arising from the mother's involvement in work outside the home (Crouter, MacDermid, McHale, & Perry-Jenkins, 1990; Lamb, 1984).

Maternal employment seems more beneficial for girls than for boys; some studies help to explain why this is so. Bronfenbrenner, Alvarez, and Henderson (1984) found in their study of 3-year-olds that in families where mother worked, daughters got more attention than sons and were described very positively by their mothers. Their sons were described in less positive terms. The most positive pictures are given for daughters of mothers employed full time. The opposite pattern was found for nonemployed mothers. This is a rather different picture from the traditional situation of favoring sons found in homes when mother does not work. Perhaps sons are more difficult to deal with at the end of mother's day than are girls.

Very few studies of maternal employment during adolescence have found negative effects, and most have found positive ones. Daughters of working mothers tend to be more outgoing, independent, active, highly motivated, and appear better adjusted on social and personality measures (Stevens & Boyd, 1980). Both sons and daughters of working mothers show more competent social behavior, have a strong sense of personal worth, better family relations, and better interpersonal relations at school.

Possible negative effects of maternal employment include the possibility that working mothers have less time to monitor their adolescent's behavior, which increases the risk of negative peer influences (Patterson & Forgatch, 1987). In a recent study (Dusek & Litovsky, 1988), 11th and 12th graders perceived greater control from parents in families with nonemployed mothers than in families with employed mothers. Also, children and adolescents of employed mothers may feel rejected and/or overburdened by household chores, which could place a strain on the mother-child relationship (Montemayor & Clayton, 1983). To illustrate, the self-reports of 174 11- to 14-year-olds revealed that they carry out moderate to high levels of family responsibility (taking care of younger children, preparing meals, working in the yard, doing laundry) and moderate to high levels of personal management tasks (doing homework without being reminded, earning own money, getting to school on time) than a group of young adolescents from homes in which mothers were not employed (Keith, Nelson, Schlabach, & Thompson, 1990).

Positive and Negative Consequences of Maternal Employment Just a generation ago experts would more than likely have recommended that a woman contemplating work outside the home should consider the answers to these questions: Will my working result in a happy child, a satisfied husband, a companionable home life, a better community? Or, will my working cause my youngster to feel deprived of a normal happy childhood, or my husband to feel he is an inadequate provider? Because of my decision to work, will the community eventually have to deal with a broken home or a potentially delinquent child? Three decades ago, the working mother (especially one with younger children) was considered selfishly derelict in her maternal responsibilities, and her husband was considered an inadequate provider and weak, because he "permitted" her to go to work.

Current attitudes toward maternal employment are more accepting. For example, it has been found that although society has long recognized the importance of work as a validating activity for men, evidence suggests that it is now becoming increasing salient for women as well. Studies of employed mothers have shown that they express higher levels of self-esteem, competence, and a general satisfaction with life than mothers not engaged in paid employment (Hoffman, 1986).

Full-time mothering may not always have a positive effect. One longitudinal study (Moore, 1975), begun in the 1950s, indicated that full-time mothering had its vulnerabilities even then. It was found that boys who experienced full-time mothering during preschool years were more competent intellectually but also more conforming, fearful, and inhibited as adolescents. In addition, the educated, nonworking mother may overinvest her energies in her children, bringing an excess of worry and discouraging independence in them (Birnbaum, 1975).

Going back to work is much more complicated than signing a W-2 form. Yogev (1983) points out that there are several problems faced by a dual-career family. There is a scarcity of time—for relaxing, socializing, intimacy with spouse, quality interaction with children. There is the financial stress of having to pay for and find supplemental child care.

Some mothers may experience feelings of guilt for leaving their children. Sometimes there is a great deal to contend with—more, perhaps, for the families with preschool children. Hock and De-Meis (1990) label mothers' feelings of sadness, loss, anger, and guilt related to their employment *maternal separation anxiety*. In their study of 209 mothers (average age 26 years), they found that women who were employed, but preferred to be home, showed significantly more maternal separation anxiety evidenced by symptoms of depression and higher levels of stress than mothers who wanted to be employed and were.

One final note on the positive side for working mothers is that a working mother and a father who helps with child-rearing chores may provide more effective role models and socialize their children in ways that emulate their parents' nonstereotypic behaviors. Not long ago, the socialization experiences of boys and girls reflected the expectation that girls would spend most of their adult lives as mothers and boys would be breadwinners. The fact that children of employed mothers tend to be more egalitarian and less stereotyped in their gender-role concepts would have been interpreted as an adverse effect of maternal employment. Not so today.

While the effects of maternal employment must take into account factors such as the age of the child, race, family structure, socioeconomic class, circumstances leading to work, and the mother's attitude toward work and toward the family, the most frequently supported conclusion documented by research since 1960 is that, taken by itself, the fact that a mother works outside the home has no universally predictable effects on the child. The majority of studies indicate that *satisfaction* with one's role, be it employed mother or full-time homemaker, is associated with more effective child-rearing experiences and outcomes (Bronfenbrenner et al., 1984). Moreover, Alvarez (1985) found that when mothers viewed their employment outside the home as an important means of maintaining a sense of self, they tended to describe their children in positive ways. The way in which mothers view their children possibly plays an important part in how these children are treated.

Maternal Employment and Fathers The changes in women's roles, particularly their increased participation in work outside the home, have been accompanied by ideological changes concerning fathers' roles in child care and child rearing. Research has increasingly recognized fathers and have addressed various aspects of their role. The father of the 1990s is (or should be) very involved in the daily care and rearing of his children. However, there is not a great deal of empirical evidence that supports this image. Consider these figures concerning the degree of fathers' involvement in two-parent families, in which mothers are not employed outside the home. According to Lamb and Oppenheim (1989), "fathers tend to spend about 20% to 25% as much time as mothers do in *engagement* (direct, one-to-one interaction) with their children. In terms of being accessible to their children (available whether or not interaction is actually

taking place), fathers spend about one third as much time as mothers do. Perhaps the biggest discrepancy between paternal and maternal involvement is with responsibility, defined as providing appropriate care at all times. Fathers tend to help out when 'it is convenient' " (p. 12).

The picture does not significantly change when we view fathers' engagement and accessibility when mothers are employed outside the home. "The figures for direct interaction and accessibility average 33% and 65%, respectively" (Lamb and Oppenheim, 1989, p. 12). (The proportion cited here goes up, not because fathers are doing more, but because mothers are doing less.) As for responsibility, the fact that mothers work outside the home doesn't affect fathers' level of involvement with their children. Even when mothers worked over 30 hours a week in paid employment, the amount of responsibility assumed by fathers appears negligible. The frequency with which fathers actually engage in child-care activities seems largely unaffected by the changes in ideology and women's work patterns.

In comparing fathers' involvement with home and child care, it can be seen in Figure 2.6 that

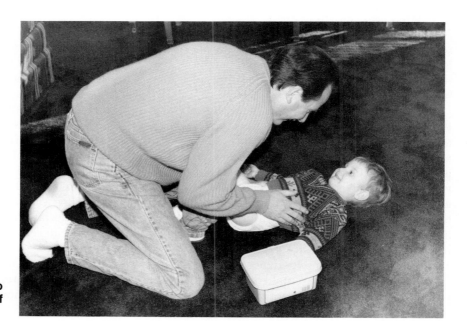

For some families, child care is no longer just the responsibility of the mother.

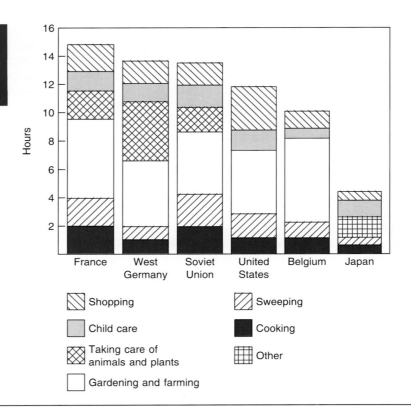

FIGURE 2.6   Husband's Participation in Child Care and Housework in Hours per Week in Six Countries

Legend:
- Shopping
- Child care
- Taking care of animals and plants
- Gardening and farming
- Sweeping
- Cooking
- Other

Source: From *Child Development and Education* in Japan, ed. Harold Stevenson, Hiroshi Azuma, Kenji Hakuta. Copyright 1986 by W. H. Freeman and Company. Reprinted with permission.

fathers in six different countries tend to spend the least amount of time in cooking and child care. Fathers from France spend the most time in home-related chores; Japan, the least.

What determines fathers' involvement with their offspring? Lamb and Oppenheim (1989) point out some important determinants of fathers' involvement. One of the most consistent predictors is their motivation, or the extent to which fathers want to be involved. Jordan (1990) interviewed 56 expectant and recent first-time fathers and found that the men in this investigation wanted to be involved parents, but they did not believe they had the knowledge, skills, or support to do so. They felt alone in their experience and without resources to enact the parental role as they ideally would have chosen. Their motivation, Jordan comments, was impressive. Baruch and Barnett (1983)

found that the fathers' attitude toward the quality of fathering they had received was important. This often involved negative modeling; fathers wanted to be close to their children because their own fathers were distant.

Second, fathers' perceived skills and self-confidence in carrying out child-care chores or relating to their children are also factors. In particular, fathers need to perceive that they are able to read their children's signals, know what they want, know how to respond appropriately, and what expectations are realistic. Contrary to the notion of maternal instinct, parenting skills are usually acquired "on the job" by both mothers and fathers. Because mothers are on the job more than fathers usually are, they become more sensitive to their children, more in tune with them, and more aware of each child's characteristics.

The third factor that influences paternal involvement is maternal support, that is, mothers encouraging fathers to become involved. When fathers are encouraged to help, their involvement is more frequent and of higher quality. When fathers are forced to be highly involved without wishing to be so, the quality of fathering may not be as high. It is interesting to note that in one study (Grossman, Pollack, & Golding, 1988) it was found that 60% to 80% of the mothers did not want their husbands to be more involved. Supposedly greater involvement would change the power balance and other attributes of the marital relationship. A factor not mentioned by Lamb and Oppenheim (1989) that may be influential in determining fathers' child-care involvement is that fathers may believe that their way of being involved is through their paid employment, which provides security and the material things their families need.

Finally, fathers' involvement with their children may relate to mothers' employment status. Crouter and Crowley (1990) studied 73 families in which mothers primarily worked inside the home as homemakers and 74 families in which mothers worked outside the home at least 15 hours a week. The target children in each of these families was a fourth or fifth grade boy or girl. Three components of fathers' involvement were (a) interaction, that is, the father's direct contact with the child through shared activities, (b) availability, meaning the father's accessibility for possible direct interaction, and (c) responsibility, that is, the father taking charge of making child-care arrangements and meeting other needs of the child. The central findings of this research were that overall amounts of time were low, with 17% (N = 26) of fathers engaging in no dyadic activities with their children. In single-earner families, the pattern of involvement was gender-typed, with fathers spending almost 3 times as much time with sons as with daughters. The pattern for dual-earner fathers was more egalitarian. In single-earner families, fathers worked longer hours, which resulted in reduced availability for interacting with their children. Moreover, fathers most often engaged in passive (e.g., television viewing) and didactic (e.g., homework) activities with their school-age children.

These findings suggest that fathers' involvement, in terms of time spent with their offspring, is not strongly related to mothers' employment status. The findings also suggest that fatherhood has not changed considerably from the traditional role represented in the 1950s.

PRACTICAL IMPLICATIONS: SHOULD MOTHERS WITH INFANTS WORK FULL TIME?

In the section on maternal employment, it was pointed out that significantly more infants of mothers working full time in outside employment were classified as insecurely attached. Researchers continue to debate whether full-time maternal employment, and subsequent full-time day care for the infant, leads to insecure attachment classifications. The pertinent issues are not being addressed in these debates. Maternal employment is a reality. The U.S. Bureau of Labor Statistics (1989) estimates that by 1995 the labor force participation rate of women in their 20s and 30s, the childbearing years, will reach 80%.

One of the pertinent questions then is how can employed parents balance these dual demands of work and child care. Sweden stands at the forefront of advanced, industrialized societies in its recognition of the dilemmas of employed parents as a public rather than private issue and its adoption of a number of structural reforms. The United States has no major federally mandated parental leave nor other legislative benefits facilitating childbearing and child rearing.

Moen (1989) considers some of Sweden's policies. Parental insurance permits father or mother to take a 6 months paid leave of absence on the birth of a child, and to receive, typically, 90% of their normal wage. The parental leave benefit is paid for by the Riksforsakringsverket (Social Insurance Board) rather than by employers directly. Parents of children under 8 years old have the right to reduce their working time to 6 hours a day with proportional reduction in wages. Two thirds of mothers with preschoolers are working part time; however, they receive all the fringe

It is important that the mother feel happy in her role, whether she works inside or outside the home.

benefits of full-time employees. There is a high degree of flexibility and discretion available over work schedules.

Another basic support for working parents is the provision of government-supported child-care assistance. Five different arrangements are available: day nurseries (caring for children from 6 months to 7 years), part-time groups (3 hours of activities for 6-year-olds), recreation centers (providing before- and after-school care), small, home–day nurseries (offering family day care for up to four children), and open preschools (which enable nonemployed parents and children to meet together under trained leadership). The responsibility for these child-care programs is assigned to the local government, and they are located in residential neighborhoods.

The United States tends to take a negative view of government-supported programs; Sweden, however, views the absence of adequate parental support and child care as harmful. Studies have shown that problems with child care can reduce productivity, increase absenteeism, and contribute to low morale and high levels of stress among workers. Providing more public and private resources for quality child

care is regarded by many people as one of the most important issues for the 1990s.

Some mothers have to work out of necessity, some are working by choice, and some may be working because they may feel that "just being a mother" is not a respected and highly valued role. Mothers have been encouraged to become laundry

STUDYING CHILDREN

HAPPY IN HER ROLE

Interview three or four mothers with children between the ages of 5 and 10 who either work outside the home or are full-time homemakers. Ask them to cite positive and negative points about their working outside or inside the home. Are they happy in their role? Then interview one child of each of these mothers. How does he or she feel about Mom working or staying home full time? What positive or negative factors do the children cite about their moms working or staying home? Is there a correlation between mothers being happy (or unhappy) in their roles and children's positive (or negative) reactions to their moms' role?

dropouts and seek *real* fulfillment in the real world. A generation ago, women were told that the only way to be a self-fulfilled person was through motherhood. Today, the message appears to be that freedom comes from a career outside the home. Women need not be pressured by cultural dicta. More importantly, women need to feel good about what they are doing, happy in their role (a positive or a negative perception about one's role is a predominant factor in providing effective child-rearing experiences and outcomes), whether it be as a mother, a career person, or a combination of the two (try the experiment in "Studying Children.")

REVIEW OF KEY POINTS

Behavioral genetics is the study of the role played by genetics in influencing intelligence and personality. Research has shown that approximately 50% of the variance in intelligence is accounted for by genetic factors. In support of this statement, studies have shown that identical twins' IQs are more highly correlated than fraternal twins' IQs. Other studies have demonstrated that adopted twins resemble their biological mothers' IQ more than that of lifelong providers. The shared family environment has a decreasing influence on IQ as children get older.

Convergent findings suggest that genetic factors make a contribution to personality characteristics such as extroversion, neuroticism, activity level, inhibition or fearfulness, altruism, and cooperation. A consistent finding is that the common shared family environment accounts for only 1% of the variance in personality. Personality differences are more influenced by the nonshared family environment—unique experiences that children share with none of the family members.

Examination of various life-styles—divorce and single-parenting—revealed that several factors affect whether children make a healthy adjustment: children's developmental status, the quality of the ex-spouse's relationship, custody arrangement, the quality of the parent-child relationship, children's gender, and social support systems available to the family. One of the most consistent findings is that boys are more negatively affected by divorce than are girls, as exemplified in their aggressive, acting-out, noncompliant behavior, and girls are more negatively affected by remarriage, demonstrated by their antagonistic behavior toward mother and stepfather.

The rate of working mothers has steadily increased, particularly for mothers with infants and toddlers. A significantly higher percentage of infants of full-time employed mothers, as compared with full-time mothers, are labeled insecurely attached. The general consensus from these studies is that full-time maternal employment (and subsequent full-time day care for infants) is not so robust a variable that it can be related to child outcomes.

ENHANCING YOUR CRITICAL THINKING

Broadening Your Knowledge

Genetics

Plomin, R. (1990). *Nature and nurture: An introduction to behavioral genetics.* Pacific Grove, CA: Brooks/Cole.

A highly readable introduction to the wonderful world of genes and chromosomes. If you tend to be an environmentalist, that is, you are inclined to place a great deal of emphasis on environmental forces in shaping behavior, read this book. After reading it, your views on behavior are likely to reflect a more balanced, interactional point of view.

Fathers

Lamb, M. E., & Oppenheim, D. (1989). Fatherhood and father-child relationships: Five years of research. In S. H. Cath, A. Gurwitt, & L. Gunsberg (Eds.), *Fathers and their families* (pp. 11–26). Hillsdale, NJ: The Analytic Press.

Perhaps you believe (as many students do) that fathers have become more involved in child-rearing responsibilities. Lamb and Oppenheim review some highlights of research done on fathers' involvement. Reading this chapter will help students learn more about the extent and nature of paternal involvement.

Firsthand Experiences

Divorce

Wallerstein, J. S., Corbin, S. G., Lewis, J. M. (1988). Children of divorce: A ten-year study. In E. M. Hetherington & J. Arasteh (Eds.), *Impact of divorce, single-parenting, and stepparenting on children* (pp. 198–214). Hillsdale, NJ: Erlbaum.

A good book to read on divorce and its effects on children. Each chapter is written by an authority in the field. What are some conceptions that you have about the effects of divorce on children? Interview some of your friends about their opinions. Write these comments down before reading this chapter. Does research back up what you and your friends have written?

Social and Cultural
Contexts of Development

CHILDREN'S THOUGHTS

On . . . "Are you motivated to do well in school? If so, why? If not, why?"

I am not motivated to do well in school. School is boring.
Sam, age 15

Doing well in school is critical. We are jeopardizing our own future, if we mess up in school. So I really study hard. If we are going to get ahead in life, we have to have a good education.
Rogelio, age 12

KEY TERMS

Peer group
Achievement motivation
Internal locus of control
External locus of control
Learned helplessness
Collectiveness
Individualism
Amae

The social contexts of development involve extrafamilial settings such as supplemental day care, the world of peers, socialization forces such as television, and the school setting. This chapter begins by looking at the effects of day care on children's social and cognitive development. Next, how peers influence children's development is examined, and then such issues as how television influences children's prosocial and aggressive ways of behaving, their beliefs about social groups, and how commercials influence children's (and subsequently their parents') buying habits are discussed. School is another important context of development. Why is it that some children are motivated to do well in school, and others, such as Sam, appear to find school a boring and unmotivating setting?

The cultural context of development is discussed. Developmental psychologists realize that child development cannot be understood unless it is known how children grow up in different cultures. Studies of cultural differences have helped to explain how children are affected by the culture in which they live. Japan's child-rearing and educational practices are compared and contrasted to those in the United States.

SOCIAL CONTEXTS OF DEVELOPMENT

SUPPLEMENTAL CARE

Not surprisingly, with the increased number of women working outside the home, a substantial number of children need supplemental care. As Figure 3.1 illustrates, the number of preschool children declined until about 1980; however, since then it has steadily increased. Labor force participation by mothers of preschool children has also steadily increased over the same period.

Since the early 1970s, the proportion of children younger than 6 with mothers in the labor force has increased by nearly 80%, from 29% in 1970 to 51% in 1988 (Hofferth & Phillips, 1987; U.S. Bureau of Labor Statistics, 1988). In the United States, there are approximately 20 million children under the age of 6; the mothers of about 10.5 million of those children are in the labor force (National Issues Forum, 1989). The largest increase in the past decade was in the proportion of children under the age of 1 year with mothers in the work force, which rose 65% between 1976 and 1987 (Wingert & Kantrowitz, 1991). Hofferth (1989) has predicted that by 1995 there will be just under 15 million preschool children with mothers in the labor force.

FIGURE 3.1   Preschool Children with Mothers in the Labor Force, 1970–1995

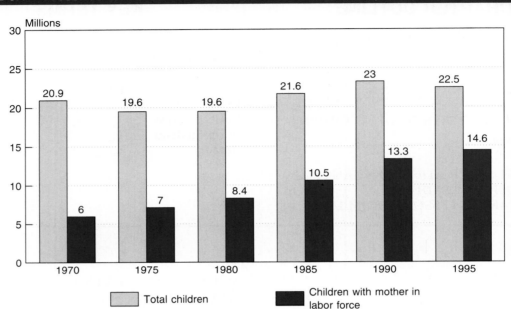

Source: From "What Is the Demand for and Supply of Childcare in the United States?" by Sandra Hofferth, 1989, *Young Children*, July, p. 29. Copyright 1989 by the National Association for the Education of Young Children. Reprinted by permission.

Types of Child Care   Of the 10.5 million children of working mothers in 1985, 37% were cared for in someone else's home by relatives or nonrelatives and 31% were cared for in their own homes by relatives or nonrelatives. Approximately 23% were placed in day-care centers or preschools, and 8% were cared for by their mothers while they worked (Hofferth, 1989). Among young, dual-earner married couples, 30% of the full-time workers and nearly 40% of the part-time workers used some type of shift schedule that enabled the spouses to share the care of their children.

Fathers provide the care for about one third of the preschool children who are cared for by their relatives. "Fathercare" has remained essentially stable over the past 2 decades. Use of organized child-care facilities (nursery schools, day-care centers) by employed mothers, however, increased substantially and sharply from 16% in 1982 to 23% in 1988. According to the U.S. Bureau of the Census (1990), only 24% of all preschool children can be accommodated in approved facilities. Socioeconomic status and child-care arrangements are closely related. Poor parents cannot afford high-quality programs and tend to use either low-quality care or informal arrangements with non-trained persons. The dominant mode of child care in the United States for various age levels is displayed in Figure 3.2.

School-age children may need care while the parents are working, but programs for school-age children are not widely available, nor are they used by a majority of parents. By the time children reach 8 years of age, reported use of "self-care" rises sharply. A study of children in the Minneapolis metropolitan area conducted by Hedin (1987) concluded that about half of the children in grades K to 3, about two thirds of those in grades 4 to 6, and about 80% of those in grades 7 and 8 were home alone or with siblings after school. The need for before- and after-school care is apparent.

FIGURE 3.2 What Arrangements Have Been Made for the Preschoolers?

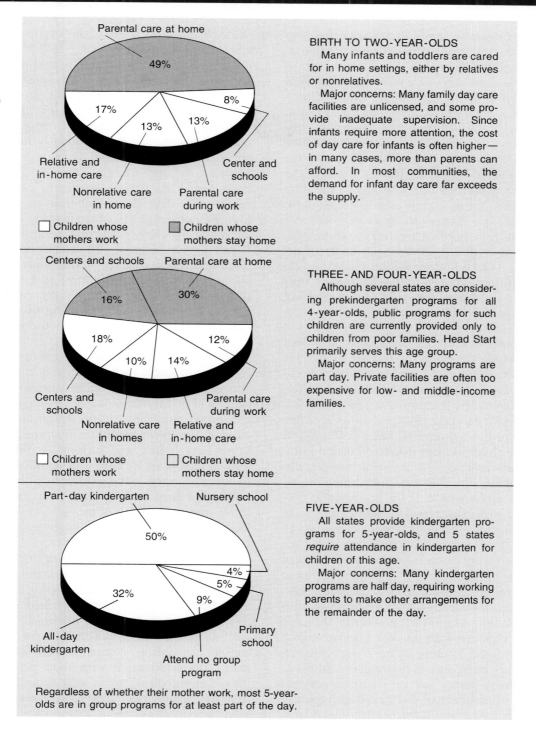

BIRTH TO TWO-YEAR-OLDS

Many infants and toddlers are cared for in home settings, either by relatives or nonrelatives.

Major concerns: Many family day care facilities are unlicensed, and some provide inadequate supervision. Since infants require more attention, the cost of day care for infants is often higher—in many cases, more than parents can afford. In most communities, the demand for infant day care far exceeds the supply.

Parental care at home — 49%
8% — Center and schools
Parental care during work — 13%
Nonrelative care in home — 13%
Relative and in-home care — 17%

☐ Children whose mothers work
▨ Children whose mothers stay home

THREE- AND FOUR-YEAR-OLDS

Although several states are considering prekindergarten programs for all 4-year-olds, public programs for such children are currently provided only to children from poor families. Head Start primarily serves this age group.

Major concerns: Many programs are part day. Private facilities are often too expensive for low- and middle-income families.

Centers and schools — 16%
Parental care at home — 30%
12% — Parental care during work
14% — Relative and in-home care
Nonrelative care in homes — 10%
Centers and schools — 18%

☐ Children whose mothers work
☐ Children whose mothers stay home

FIVE-YEAR-OLDS

All states provide kindergarten programs for 5-year-olds, and 5 states *require* attendance in kindergarten for children of this age.

Major concerns: Many kindergarten programs are half day, requiring working parents to make other arrangements for the remainder of the day.

Part-day kindergarten — 50%
Nursery school — 4%
5%
Primary school
Attend no group program — 9%
All-day kindergarten — 32%

Regardless of whether their mother work, most 5-year-olds are in group programs for at least part of the day.

Source: From *The Child Care Dilemma* (p. 6) by National Issues Forum, 1989, Dubuque, IA: Kendall/Hunt. Reprinted by permission of the Charles F. Kettering Foundation.

Effects on Cognitive and Social Development
With the increased number of children in alternative care settings, there has been an increased interest in the short- and long-term effects of child care. Before you review the studies on day care, a note of caution is necessary. Much of the evidence comes from high-quality, university-based day care, which is not the most common alternative care arrangement used by parents. Because few parents have access to these settings, much of the research cannot be safely generalized to the day-care situations most infants really experience. Available data are flawed in other respects; for example, day care is often treated as a homogeneous context, when it includes an array of arrangements. Time of entrance into day care is often not reported. Finally, only a few researchers have followed children for extensive periods of time, and thus little is known about the long-term effects.

With regard to children's cognitive development, the available evidence indicates that for middle-class children day care has neither beneficial nor adverse effects on intellectual development (as measured by standardized tests). For economically disadvantaged children, however, day care may have positive effects. Lally (1974) found that day-care children from poorly educated families performed better on the Stanford-Binet Intelligence Tests than did their matched home-reared counterparts. Golden et al. (1978) studied 400 children from low socioeconomic classes who were given the Bayley Developmental Index at 18 months and the Stanford-Binet at 36 months. Half of the children were reared at home and half were enrolled in one of the 31 infant day-care programs. Children enrolled in the day-care programs performed significantly better than youngsters who remained at home. Moreover, intellectual levels of 131 of these children were assessed semiannually until they entered kindergarten. These children continued to outscore home-reared children. Thus, university-based day care helped prevent the decline in intellectual performance typically observed in socioeconomically disadvantaged families. Burchinal, Lee, and Ramey (1989) also con-cluded from their study of socioeconomically disadvantaged children that "good" day care positively affects the overall preschool cognitive level of socioeconomically disadvantaged children.

Another study, directed by Clarke-Stewart (1989), involved 150 2- to 4-year-old children from a mixture of home backgrounds and a variety of care arrangements, including at home with parents or baby-sitters, and in day-care centers, nursery schools, and day-care homes. The children were tested on various measures of intellectual competence such as remembering numbers, identifying photographs of objects, using play materials, solving problems, copying designs, and so on. On all these measures of intellectual competence, a clear difference was found between children in home care (with parent, sitter, or day-care home provider) and children in center care (nursery school, day-care center), favoring those in center care. This occurred for both boys and girls, after as little as 6 months in day care.

Field (1991) studied the relationship between attendance in stable high-quality day-care programs and grade school behavior and performance on a sample of 56 11-year-olds from mixed ethnic backgrounds (Caucasian, African American, Hispanic). All children in the sample had started full time (8 hours/day) before age 2. Results indicated that time in quality infant care was significantly related to being assigned to the gifted program and receiving higher final math grades. The importance of these studies is that they provide evidence of possible intellectual benefits in high-quality day care for high-risk populations.

Day care continues to have both positive and negative effects on social development. Belsky and his colleagues (Belsky, 1988; Belsky & Steinberg, 1982) found that children who had experienced day care were more peer-oriented than home-reared children. Vlietstra (1982) found that full-day preschool children, compared with half-day children, interacted more with their peers and displayed more prosocial as well as aggressive and assertive behaviors. Increased interaction may have provided greater opportunities for conflict, leading to more aggressive behaviors.

Children in full-time day care tend to be more prosocial and more aggressive toward their peers.

Some studies have shown that children with extensive day-care experience tend to be less cooperative with adults, more active, and somewhat more aggressive toward their peers and teachers (Rutter, 1981; Siegal & Storey, 1985). Vandell and Corasaniti (1990) found that children with intensive child-care experiences since infancy were as toddlers rated by teachers and parents as having poorer peer relationships, work habits, and emotional health, and as being more difficult to discipline. Other studies have shown that children enrolled in day care tend to be more sociable with their peers as preschoolers (Howes, 1988) or generally more socially competent (Andersson, 1989). On the positive side, some studies show that day-care children are prosocial and peer-oriented; on the negative side, these children tend to be uncooperative with adults and more aggressive.

Contrary to the mixed results on social development in the United States, Andersson (1989) found that 8-year-old Swedish children (N = 119) who entered day care as infants (prior to their second birthday) were more socially competent (more cooperative, more persistent, more independent) than late-entry (after age 2) and home-reared children. In a follow-up study of these children at age 13 (Andersson, 1992), social competence was rated highest for those children who entered day care before the age of 1; at age 13 social competence was rated lowest among those without out-of-home care. Andersson concludes that the high quality of Swedish day care may account for the differences found in social development cross-culturally.

Andersson's studies (1989; 1992) also focused on the cognitive effects of day care. Children who entered day care before age 2 were, at ages 8 and 13, more cognitively competent (performed better on verbal tests and in school subjects) than children with late-entry day care and home-reared children. Andersson, again, stresses that the negative effects of day care may only be applicable to poor quality day care.

In support of Andersson's research, Howes (1990) studied early entry (before first birthday) and late entry (enrolled between 12 and 48 months), high-quality and low-quality day care, and children's subsequent social and cognitive development during kindergarten. She found in her study of 89 middle-class U.S. children that those who entered low-quality child-care centers as infants had the most difficulties with peers as kindergartners and were rated by their teachers as more distractible and less task-oriented. Those who entered high-quality child-care centers as infants (early entry) did not appear different from children who entered day care later or home-reared children. Figure 3.3 compares the magnitude of the differences among groups at different ages' entry into day care for social adjustment and cognitive competence. These data suggest that early-day-care children are not disadvantaged if they experience high-quality care.

Similarly, in a study done by Field, Masi, Goldstein, Perry, and Parl (1988), preschoolers who had started day care within the first 6 months of life were compared with preschoolers who had started later than 6 months (but still in the infancy period). The two groups attended the same high-quality infant-care center. The children were compared on their reunion behaviors with their parents, their peer interactions, and their teachers' and parents' ratings of their behavior. The results of this study suggest that early- and late-entry infants showed no differences in attachment (reunion) behavior. However, the children with more months of day-care experience were more socially interactive with their peers. Teachers and parents gave those children who had received more quality infant day care higher ratings on emotional well-being, attractiveness, and assertiveness.

Other studies on social adjustment have shown that infants and toddlers tend to exhibit more sociable behavior when they were enrolled in child-care arrangements with stable, as opposed to unstable, caregivers (Howes & Stewart, 1987), with caregivers trained in child development as opposed to untrained caregivers (Howes, 1983), and with more adult caregivers per child (Howes & Unger, 1989). Other factors associated with high-quality day care are listed in Table 3.1.

Thus, there appears to be a growing consensus that the quality of day-care programs is a salient factor in influencing children's adjustment. Analysis of the current research on day care suggests that the amount of day care and age of entry may not be as important to children's social and cognitive competence as the quality of day care (Wingert & Kantrowitz, 1991).

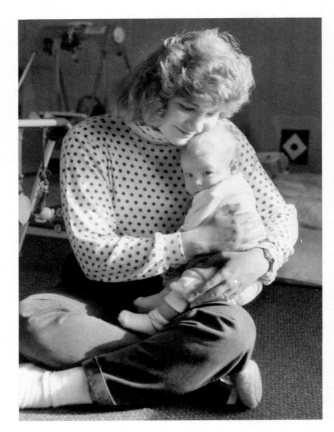

The quality of day care appears to be an important factor in determining children's later cognitive and social adjustment.

FIGURE 3.3   Social Adjustment of Children with Varying Child-care Histories

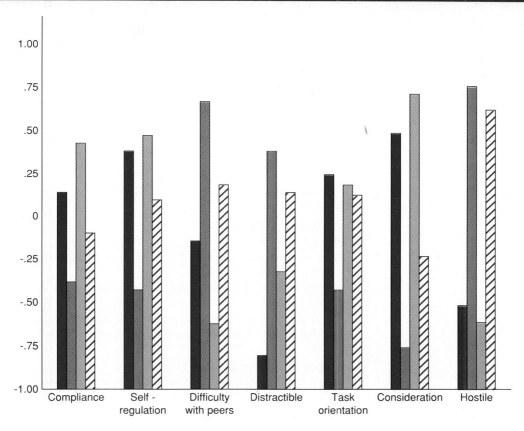

1. entered high quality child care when less than 12 months old
2. entered low quality child care when less than 12 months old
3. entered high quality child care as an older child
4. entered low quality child care as an older child

Source: From "Can the Age of Entry into Child Care and the Quality of Child Care Predict Adjustment in Kindergarten?" by Carollee Howes, 1990, *Developmental Psychology, 26* (2), p. 299. Copyright 1989 by the American Psychological Association. Reprinted by permission.

PEER GROUPS

The **peer group** is rivaled only by the family as the child's major developmental context. The peer group generally consists of three to perhaps a dozen children whose individual members have a feeling of belonging. The term *peer group* charac-terizes children who have regular contact with one another and more or less share the same attitudes and values (Hartup, 1983). As socializing agents, peer groups contribute uniquely to the growth of the individual—group interactions help children learn how to relate to others, develop social con-

TABLE 3.1   Checklist for Day-care Centers

HEALTH AND SAFETY

Adults—no smoking in the same room with children

Floors carpeted or have nonskid covering

At least one adult present at all times to supervise children

Detergents, medicines, drugs kept out of reach of children

Records kept on each child (emergency phone numbers, medical information)

PHYSICAL SPACE

Individual space (locker, drawer, cubicle) for each child to store personal belongings

Dark and quiet space to allow children to nap (shades or curtains can be closed, cots can be set up in separate area)

Toileting area easy for children to get to

Physical space not overcrowded (not too many children, or too much large equipment)

MATERIALS, EQUIPMENT, AND ACTIVITIES

Attractive and well-written story and picture books

Materials and equipment for quiet play (books, puzzles) and for active play (riding toys, climbing structures)

Some of the following materials: paints, crayons, pencils, paste, clay or dough, sand, water, scissors, paper

In outdoor play area, two or more of the following: blocks, cartons, or boards for building, sandbox and sand toys, slides, riding toys, seesaw, balance beam, tires

TEACHERS, ADULT STAFF, AND CAREGIVERS

Enough adults to provide individual attention (probably at least one for every six children, more for children under 3 years)

Use of encouragement, suggestion, and praise by adults, rather than orders, commands, prohibitions, criticism, or reprimands

Adults teaching children sometimes, but not all the time

Adults with some training in child care and child development

Source: Reprinted by permission of the publishers from *Daycare* by Kathleen A. Clarke-Stewart, Cambridge, Mass.: Harvard University Press, Copyright © 1982 by Kathleen A. Clarke-Stewart.

trols, acquire social values, and develop social skills commensurate with others in the group. Peers are the transmitters of child culture.

Peers provide the context through which children move from childhood parental dependencies to a sense of autonomy and connectedness with the greater social network (Erikson, 1968). Peers are trusted critics; they provide stability in times of stress or transition and sometimes function as therapeutic confidants. In these groups, children see themselves as free and equal agents. Both Sullivan (1953) and Piaget (1962) proposed that peer relations, in particular children's relationships with friends, are a major and positive force in social development.

Perhaps the most important thing children learn from their peer interactions is how to control and regulate their behavior. Peers may strengthen ex-

Peers are a source of companion-ship and recreation.

isting behaviors and attitudes, establish new ones, or weaken those that are in conflict with peer-group values. As a result of the group's sometimes tactless, brutal, and blunt comments (children are not particularly noted for their subtlety and tact!), children learn that some of their behaviors need to change if they are going to survive as members of the peer group. Children must recognize that *some* conformity is desirable and that sometimes the needs of others must take precedence over their own desires. They learn the ability to control and regulate their behavior and that they must consider the reactions of other group members, which come to have a great moderating effect on what children do and say. Because of children's emotional ties and the security they derive from the group, most children begin to bring their own behavior in line with group standards. The net effect is that they become less egocentric. With increasing age, various patterns of peer-group interactions emerge.

Infancy   Today a sizable number of babies have regular contacts with other babies and young children. Anecdotal accounts show that from 20% to 60% of 6- to 12-month-old U.S. babies see other

babies more than once a week (Vandell & Mueller, 1980). Social responsiveness among these young infants is often unpredictable. One early investigator (Buhler, 1927) characterized infants during the first few months of life as being "socially blind." We know differently now.

The older infant shows more social responsiveness to other infants. The developmental sequence appears to be that looking appears first, followed by touching and reaching (emerging at around 3 to 4 months), smiling and vocalizing (occurring around 6 months), followed by coordinated social acts (imitating the other infant and playing simple games). When crawling emerges, babies may follow one another. Vandell (1980) suggests that a growing interest in peers begins to develop after the onset of sitting and crawling. Throughout these early months, smiling and reaching increases, convincing many investigators that these activities are true social behaviors.

In the second year of life, social interaction becomes more common, coordinated, and complex. Sustained social exchanges occur during this time. There is no evidence, however, that children are sought out as social objects or that they serve necessary or unique functions in socialization (Hartup, 1983). Children now engage in activities such as exchanging toys, chasing and being chased, and leading and following. One can observe toddlers engaging in object-related social acts; that is, toddlers coordinate toys with age-mates in unified messages. For example, they will look expectantly at another toddler while simultaneously banging on a drum. Through the coordination of banging and intently gazing, the youngster seems to be asking, "What will you do if I do this?"

Early Childhood   As toddlers become preschoolers and improve their verbal facilities, their peer group interactions increasingly involve trading words rather than objects. Observations suggest that child-child interactions begin to resemble adult social behaviors. That is, preschoolers maintain eye contact with the child and vocalizations are positively correlated in social interaction (Savitsky and Watson, 1975).

Greater and greater investment in peer relations continues throughout the preschool years. Preschoolers' bids for attention are more commonly directed toward peers than toward teachers or adults. Immature social actions are replaced by more efficient, smooth interactions, as more and more time is spent in peer interaction. Peer social interaction diversifies and true mutual give-and-take behavior begins to develop. First friendships are made, cooperative play increases, and first groups are formed. These increases in sociability are a major achievement in the preschool period.

Middle Childhood   Peer relations have become central to the child's social world, as revealed by children's self-consciousness about the impressions that others have of them and the importance they give to their peers. Children in middle childhood begin to exist in two worlds: the adult world and the peer world.

By age 8 or 9, many children become members of a group of peers, often called the gang. During the early years of middle childhood (6 to 9), children usually participate in informal groups. The gang is a relatively stable or enduring group of individuals who interact, share common goals and values, and whose behavior is governed by mutually agreed-on rules (Hartup, 1983). Membership is usually homogeneous, consisting of children from the same socioeconomic status and age. Stable same-sex peer groups begin to emerge in preadolescence (Coleman, 1981; Hallinan, 1980). The importance of being in a group increases during this time, tapering off during the late teen years (Brown, Eicher, & Petrie, 1986). Members of the group eagerly adopt the gang's values, manners, attitudes, and even their speech patterns.

While children in early childhood tend to engage in egocentric thinking (they have a difficult time perceiving things from another person's point of view), school-age children recognize that others have viewpoints different from their own. The decrease in egocentric thinking is a result of the interaction of increased cognitive ability and the growing desire of the individual to cooperate with others. This decline in egocentrism undoubtedly helps children interact more effectively with peers. Conversations between peers become better coordinated as egocentrism declines. There are, however, certain limitations in children's ability to infer motivation and intent in the action of other children.

From middle childhood on, children engage in a wide range of activities. Zarbatany, Hartmann, and Rankin (1990) found that the most important activities were noncontact sports, watching television or listening to tapes, talking on the telephone, physical games, going to parties, and hanging out. Table 3.2 lists the activity preferences of preadolescents. Zarbatany et al. (1990) conclude that these peer activities serve three major functions for preadolescents: (a) they provide a context for sociability, enhancement of relationships, and a sense of belonging; (b) they promote concern for achievements and integrity of the self; and (c) they provide opportunities for instruction and learning.

Adolescence   Adolescent groups tend to differ from middle childhood groups in several ways. Children's groups are often neighborhood friends or classmates; adolescent groups tend to include a broader array of members and tend to be more formalized than children's groups. Children's groups are same-sexed. In fact, as you know, children show a marked disdain for those of the op-

TABLE 3.2   Mean Importance and Amount of Time Spent in Activities Overall and by Gender

Activity	IMPORTANCE			TIME SPENT		
	All Children	Boys	Girls	All Children	Boys	Girls
Noncontact sports	.85	1.00	.69	5.17	5.67	4.64
TV/records	.83	.82	.83	5.39	5.38	5.39
Conversing	.73	.67	.81	6.76	6.69	6.83
Telephone	.67	.54	.81	5.63	4.85	6.47
Physical games	.65	.69	.61	5.26	5.43	5.08
Parties	.63	.69	.56	2.41	2.54	2.28
Hanging out	.53	.54	.53	6.57	6.87	6.25
Acting silly	.48	.46	.50	5.12	4.95	5.31
Shopping	.41	.23	.61	2.23	1.43	3.08
Cards/board games	.39	.49	.28	3.81	4.13	3.47
Contact sports	.37	.62	.11	3.15	4.21	2.00
Baby-sitting	.36	.21	.53	2.20	1.59	2.86
Secrets	.33	.26	.42	3.69	3.18	4.25
Clubs (e.g., Scouts)	.32	.31	.33	2.11	2.03	2.19
Play with pets	.31	.36	.25	3.80	3.85	3.75
Academic	.27	.26	.28	5.15	4.85	5.47
Arts and crafts	.25	.21	.31	2.63	2.36	2.92
Travel to/from school	.24	.31	.17	5.57	5.26	5.92
Walking at school	.23	.23	.22	5.65	5.36	5.97
Eating	.21	.28	.14	3.53	3.31	3.78
Fashion talk	.20	.03	.39	1.92	.49	3.47
Class clean-up	.16	.18	.14	3.69	3.54	3.86
Waiting for a ride	.11	.15	.06	4.23	3.85	4.64
Homework	.09	.08	.11	1.37	.97	1.81
Fighting	.09	.13	.06	1.87	1.92	1.81
Church	.08	.00	.17	1.07	.59	1.58
Stopping fights	.07	.10	.03	1.40	1.46	1.33
Trading things	.05	.08	.03	1.20	1.33	1.06
Housework	.04	.03	.06	1.08	.59	1.61

Note.—Importance scores indicate the proportion of subjects endorsing an item (range is 0 to 1), whereas amount of time spent in activities ranges from 0 (never) to more than once a day (7). For all children, importance scores differing by .28 or more and time-spent scores differing by 1.32 or more are significant at the .01 level (Tukey's HSD test). Gender means that are underscored are statistically different at $p < .003$ using a variant of the Bonferroni inequality. *Number* = 75.

Source: From "The Psychological Functions of Preadolescent Peer Activities" by L. Zarbatany, D. P. Hartmann, and D. B. Rankin, 1990, *Child Development, 61*, p. 1072. © The Society for Research in Child Development, Inc. Reprinted by permission.

posite sex. Eight-year-old Ryan may loudly refuse to attend Chuck's birthday party because some girls were invited. Later, in adolescence, Ryan may react quite differently: "A party? Great! Any girls coming?" In adolescence we see a shift from single-sex groups to mixed or cross-sex groups.

Adolescent peer groups are also characterized by exclusivity, impermeability, and hostility toward nonmembers (Gavin & Furman, 1989). In general, these qualities appear to serve as mecha-

nisms to differentiate between members and nonmembers and to create status differences. Girls report greater intimacy and emotional investment in their friendships than boys (Hallinan, 1980). In contrast, boys show more aggression in their relationships than girls (Maccoby & Jacklin, 1978). Boys also engage in more status and dominance struggles (Savin-Williams, 1976).

Adolescent groups range in size from the two-person friendships popular among early adolescent girls to increasingly larger groups more pop-ular in middle or late adolescence. One variety is the small and exclusive *clique* made up of individ-uals with similar interests. It usually consists of three to four persons of the same sex and provides companionship and security. The importance of being in a popular clique increases in early adoles-cence. The sense of belonging gained by member-ship in a popular group may allow teens to feel secure in the social arena, bolstering their sense of identity as they seek to separate from the family unit. It is estimated that 70% to 80% of adolescents belong to cliques (Dunphy, 1963). A larger, more impersonal peer group is the *crowd,* which gener-ally consists of 10 to 20 members who share com-mon interests in social activities. Crowds are hetero-sexual, unlike cliques, which tend to be one-sexed. Groups of cliques generally comprise the crowd.

A well-known study by Dunphy (1963) supports the notion that opposite-sex participation in

groups increases during adolescence. Dunphy's work, as well as more current research (Berndt, 1982), shows that in late childhood, boys and girls participate in small, same-sex cliques. As they move into the early adolescent years, the same-sex cliques begin to interact with each other. Gradu-ally, the leaders and high-status members form further cliques based on heterosexual relation-ships. Eventually, the newly created heterosexual cliques interact with each other in large crowd ac-tivities too—at dances and athletic events, for ex-ample. In late adolescence, the crowd begins to dissolve as couples develop more serious relation-ships and make long-range plans that may include engagement and marriage. A summary of Dun-phy's ideas is presented in Figure 3.4.

TELEVISION

Television is a familiar companion to children. Nearly every U.S. household has a television set

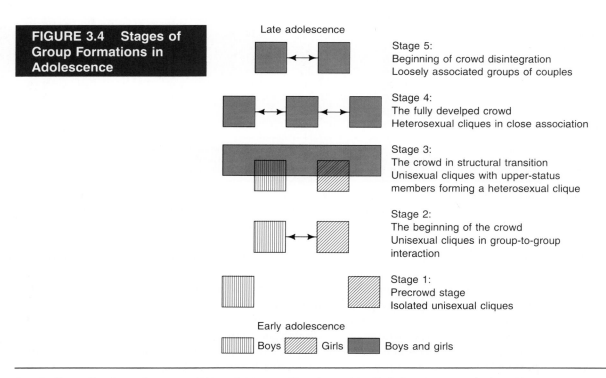

FIGURE 3.4 Stages of Group Formations in Adolescence

Late adolescence

Stage 5:
Beginning of crowd disintegration
Loosely associated groups of couples

Stage 4:
The fully develped crowd
Heterosexual cliques in close association

Stage 3:
The crowd in structural transition
Unisexual cliques with upper-status members forming a heterosexual clique

Stage 2:
The beginning of the crowd
Unisexual cliques in group-to-group interaction

Stage 1:
Precrowd stage
Isolated unisexual cliques

Early adolescence

Boys   Girls   Boys and girls

Source: From "The Social Structure of Urban Adolescent Peer Groups" by D. C. Dunphy, 1963, *Sociometry, 26,* p. 236.

(98%), and several households (52%) have more than one (A.C. Nielsen Co., 1988). Children spend a great deal of time watching television. Between the ages of 2 and 18, children watch an average of over 3 hours of television per day. They spend more time watching television than in any other single waking activity, including going to school, and being with family and friends (Parke & Slaby, 1983).

Viewing Time   Preschool children spend an average of 27.9 hours per week watching television (more than one third of their waking time). Averages tell only part of the story; variations among individuals are extremely high. For example, the range of total hours viewed in 1 week was from zero to 75 hours. Moreover, individual differences in viewing were quite stable over time (Huston, Watkins, & Kunkel, 1989). Older children, 6- to 11-year-olds, spend 24.5 hours per week.

It appears that the total time children spend watching television is stable and that this pattern is established in early childhood. The amount of television that children watch at ages 3 to 5 was generally the same amount of television they watched at 5 to 7 years of age. For example, 3-year-olds who watched 2 to 3 hours of television a day also watched the same number of hours of television a day when they were 5 years old (Huston, Wright, Rice, Kerkman, & St. Peters, 1990). These consistencies may reflect the influence of family environments in which adults and older siblings have stable habits of television use to which children are exposed early in life. Whatever the reason, the finding is important because the acquisition of television-viewing patterns established in early childhood appears to have long-term implications.

Similarly, the types of shows that children watch also show a pattern of stability. For example, children who tend to watch humorous cartoons watch comedy shows at a later age. Many children prefer adventure types of cartoons and continue to prefer these types of shows when they are older. Try the "Studying Children" experiment.

Because watching television is usually defined as presence in the room with the television on, it

STUDYING CHILDREN

TELEVISION VIEWING PATTERNS

Interview three or four 10- to 12-year-olds. Begin by asking them what kind of television shows they watch now. Then ask them to recall what shows they watched when they were younger (as 5- or 6-year-olds). Is there a correlation between earlier viewing preferences and what they watch today? For example, if they watch action-oriented shows now, did they tend to watch similar types of programs when they were younger?

could signify active, concentrated attention, or passive, shallow exposure. However, videotapes of home viewing (Anderson, Lorch, Field, Collins, & Nathan, 1986) showed that children between the ages of 3 and 7 attended visually to the television set 50% to 70% of the time that they were in the room. Attention tends to peak at around 80% in late childhood (ages 10 to 12).

Effect on the Family   The primary importance for television, according to Bronfenbrenner (1967), lies "not so much in the behavior it produces as the behavior it prevents, and the behavior that can be prevented is family interaction—the talks, the games, the family festivities, and arguments through which much of the child's learning takes place and his character is formed" (p. 170). There is only one study that examines the effect of television on patterns of family interaction, and that study was done by Maccoby (1951). She summarized her results as follows: "The nature of the family social life during a program could be described as 'parallel' rather than interactive, and the television set does seem quite clearly to dominate family life when it is on" (p. 428). Given the massive expansion of television since then, it is perhaps time to follow up on Maccoby's study.

How much time do children spend watching television with their family? Lawrence and Wozniak (1989) studied 151 children ranging in age from 6 to 17, who were living in two-parent, two-child families. It was found that children spend

It appears that television prevents family interactions.

60% of their total viewing time (or 75 minutes a day) watching television with other members of the family. The entire family averages 18 minutes per day watching television together (14% of total viewing time). Other coviewing patterns and percentages of children's total viewing time were as follows: child with sibling, 40 minutes per day (30%); child with mother, 11 minutes (8%), and child with father, 17 minutes (18%). The study confirmed that children spend the majority of their time viewing television without the moderating influence of a parent as a coviewer.

Use as an Educator   If you look at the foods children eat (sugar cereals, candy, snacks), the clothes they wear (designer jeans, particular kinds of sneakers), the toys they play with (He-Man figures, Barbie Dolls, Transformers), the expressions they use ("It's awesome," "Hey, Dude"), you can see the vast potential of television in terms of shaping language, values, and morals. Similarly, because of its appeal and widespread availability, television has enormous potential for teaching academic, cognitive, and social skills. Planned pro-

grams designed to teach began to be widely noticed in the late 1960s with pioneers such as "Sesame Street" and "Mister Rogers' Neighborhood." Careful evaluations have demonstrated that such programs are often (though not always) effective. Field experiments demonstrate that viewing "Mister Rogers'" leads to increased prosocial behavior, task persistence, and imaginative play (Stein & Friedrich, 1975).

In two large-scale evaluations of "Sesame Street," the target audience of preschool children learned many of the skills and concepts taught on the program (Ball & Bogatz, 1970). Even a skeptical interpretation of the data concluded that children learned letter and number skills from unaided viewing (Cook, Appleton, Conner, Shaffer, Tamkin, & Weber, 1975). Viewing at ages 3 and 4 is associated with improved vocabulary, and prereading skills at age 5 (Rice, Huston, Truglio, & Wright, 1987). After broadcasts of "Reading Rainbow," a program designed to encourage reading, sales and library use of the featured book rose dramatically. "Freestyle," a series designed for 9- to 12-year-olds, succeeded in expanding this age group's concept about gender roles and careers (Johnston & Ettema, 1982).

Whether intended or not, television can and does teach about social behavior and social groups. Programs designed for children and adults often convey a highly stereotyped and distorted social world in which being male, youthful, beautiful, and white are valued, and being female, old, handicapped, dark-skinned, or foreign are not valued (Greenberg, 1986; Liebert & Sprafkin, 1988). When positive, counterstereotyped models are available, nonstereotypical role learning occurs (Wroblewski & Huston, 1988).

African Americans tend to be given minor roles, often cast in an unfavorable light as swindlers, villains, drug addicts, or very poor people who work at service occupations. They are shown as prone to violence or involved in illegal activities (Liebert & Sprafkin, 1990). Do these negative portrayals affect children's attitudes toward African Americans? Graves (1976) showed both African American and white children a series of cartoons in which African American people were portrayed positively (as competent, trustworthy, and hardworking) or negatively (as inept, lazy, and powerless). On a later test of racial attitudes, both African American and white children became more favorable toward African Americans if they had seen the positive portrayals. But when the depictions of African Americans were negative, an interesting racial difference occurred. African American children once again became more favorable in their racial attitudes, while white viewers became less favorable. The way African Americans are portrayed on television may have a striking effect on the racial attitudes of white viewers, whereas the mere presence of African American television characters may be sufficient to produce more favorable attitudes toward African Americans among a young African American audience.

Television and Aggression The effects of television violence have been investigated more thoroughly than any other television issue. During their television viewing time, children between the ages of 5 and 15 will have witnessed some 18,000 violent acts. (These violent acts average 1 per minute in standard television cartoons.) How does viewing aggression or violence on television affect these children? Experts have repeatedly concluded that there is a small but reliable causal effect of television violence on aggressive behavior. The American Psychological Association (APA) (1985) and many other professional organizations have endorsed this conclusion.

Eron (1982) obtained data from more than 400 youngsters at 9 years of age and again at 19 years. The measures included peer ratings of aggressions, self-reports of aspects of television viewing, and information on family background and parental practices. The results of this longitudinal study showed that, for boys, a preference for viewing violence on television at age 9 was significantly linked to aggressive behavior 10 years later. In fact, of the great variety of other socialization and family background factors measured, viewing television violence was the best single predictor of aggressive behavior in late adolescence. Research suggests that for boys, the watching of violence is likely to have both an immediate and a long-term, cumulative effect on building aggressive habits (Eron, Walder, & Lefkowitz, 1971). Singer and Singer (1980) have shown that longitudinal relationships between watching violence on television and exhibiting aggressive behavior last 1 year or more in preschoolers. Eron (1982) has found that a long-term relationship clearly exists between the viewing of televised violence and the viewer's subsequent aggression.

Recent research, however, supports the theory that television violence may have an effect on aggression but it is likely to exert such an effect only on children who are genetically predisposed to develop aggressive personalities (Lynn, Hampson, & Aga, 1989). The genotype-environment correlation and interaction theory posits that there are two processes by which genetic propensities determine personality and behavior. Genotype-environment correlation is the means by which parents transmit their characteristics to their children by both genetic and environmental mechanisms. The genotype-environment interaction is a second process by which genetic predisposition determines personality and behavior. This is the means by which genetically different children react differently to the same environment in accordance with their genetic propensities. The thesis of this theory is that some parents provide a deleterious family environment in which a high level of aggression and the viewing of television violence are constituents. The high aggression would be transmitted to children both genetically and environmentally. Thus, violence on television only affects certain individuals who are genetically predisposed to adopt aggressive television characters as models.

Exposure to televised violence tends to decrease the viewer's behavioral and physiological responsiveness to aggression produced by others. For example, grade-school children, while watching "real-life" aggression on a television monitor (two boys fistfighting) were found to show fewer physiological changes (increased heartbeat, sweaty palms) than those watching an equally arousing but nonviolent championship volleyball game (Thomas, Horton, Lippincott, & Drabman, 1977). This finding suggests that children become hardened to violence after seeing a great deal of it. As Parke and Slaby (1983) point out, however, "Although diminished physiological responsiveness parallels the evidence of diminished behavioral responsiveness, the potential link between the two has not been investigated" (p. 604).

Television and Prosocial Behavior If viewing aggression plays an important role in producing aggressive behavior in children, is the opposite also true? That is, if children view prosocial behaviors on television, will their helping and sharing behavior, for example, increase in frequency? Data on the helpful aspects of television are nowhere near as extensive as the evidence on the harmful aspects. It appears, however, that children generally have little trouble recognizing the prosocial themes in entertainment programs. Interviews with hundreds of elementary school children who had viewed episodes of various programs with prosocial themes revealed that approximately 90% of the young viewers could remember at least one prosocial message ("Be nice to other people." "Sharing

is good to do.") up to 5 hours after seeing the show (Columbia Broadcasting System, 1979).

Prosocial programs also influence behavior. One study found that second- and third-grade children were more cooperative on verbal problem-solving measures and on helping behaviors after viewing an episode of "The Waltons" (Baran, Lawrence, & Courtright, 1979). Another study found that 4th- through 10th-grade children who viewed a program in which the hero coped constructively with a personal problem were subsequently more likely to help a peer than were children who viewed an aggressive or neutral program (Collins & Getz, 1976).

Friedrich and Stein (1975) studied the effects of prosocial programming on 73 kindergarten children. The first purpose of the study was to assess the effects of viewing prosocial behavior on television; the second purpose was to test whether training procedures such as verbal labeling and role playing increase the children's ability to include prosocial conduct in their behavioral repertoire. Four groups of children were shown a series of four television programs from "Mister Rogers' Neighborhood." One of these groups engaged in activities that were irrelevant to the program; one received verbal-labeling training in which the themes from the program were labeled in storybooks; one group received role-playing training in which the themes were rehearsed using hand puppets; one group received both verbal-labeling and role-playing training. The fifth was a control group that saw neutral television programs (nature films) and engaged in irrelevant activities.

The results of the study provide clear evidence that children learned the prosocial content of the television programs and generalized that learning to a number of real-life situations. The verbal labeling had the greatest impact on verbal measures of learning and generalizing program content for girls. Role-playing training increased helping behaviors for boys. The greater impact of verbal labeling on girls may be due partly to girls' finding listening to a story and responding verbally a more appealing activity. Likewise, boys, who tend to be more physically active, may learn more when engaging in active role playing.

Commercials   Children are a targeted market for advertising toys, cereals, candy, and other foods. A convincing body of research accumulated during the 1990s demonstrated that preschool children typically fail to distinguish program material from advertising. Children below the age of 8 do not understand the persuasive intent of advertising and are, therefore, particularly vulnerable to its appeals. Children older than 8 are more aware of the purposes of advertising, but they are still apt to be persuaded by appeals that are subtly deceptive or misleading (Kunkel, 1988). Both data and the continuing investment in advertising to children by food and toy companies provide ample evidence that advertising is effective in its ultimate goal: selling products. Some marketing strategies designed to meet motivational needs are presented in Table 3.3.

Advertising direct to children promotes toys and foods; the majority of the foods advertised contain large quantities of sugar and/or fat. On Saturday morning network programming, commercials and program promotions occupy 15% of each hour (Condry, Bence, & Scheibe, 1987). Weekday children's programs on independent channels have typically included about 12 minutes per hour (20%) of nonprogram content, including commercials.

It is interesting to note that in earlier years, toys were often developed from program characters and themes as an afterthought. Now, programs are created as an integral part of the design and merchandising of a toy. The latest extension of this trend is interactive programming, for which a toy can be purchased to interact with a signal from the program. Although interactive technology could be used for prosocial or education purposes, its first commercial incarnation was high-tech weaponry that allowed the viewer to shoot or be shot at by the figures on the television set (Huston et al., 1990).

SCHOOL

School is a social institution, reflecting the culture of which it is a part and transmitting to the young an ethos and a world view as well as specific skills and knowledge. Children spend years in school as members of a small society in which there are tasks to be done, people to relate to, and rules that define the possibilities of behavior. Such experiences affect several aspects of children's behavior: their sense of self, beliefs of competency, morality, and their conceptions of a social system beyond the family.

Achievement Motivation   Children's learning potential is influenced by a number of variables. Motivational factors exert a profound influence on children's academic performance. **Achievement motivation** is defined as the "energizing force" that stimulates children to act and determines the vigor and persistence of that action. Young children appear to have an abundance of this energizing force, evidenced by toddlers who derive great pleasure from mastering their environments.

Children's Conceptions of Their Abilities   Self-perceptions of ability figure prominently in virtually every cognitive theory of achievement motivation (Heckhausen, 1982). Ability perceptions are assumed to affect behavior and learning and thus to have practical educational importance (Stipek & MacIver, 1989). Ratings of competence are close to the maximum in the early grades, and decline thereafter (Beneson & Dweck, 1986). There is some evidence for a particularly steep decline in early adolescence (Harter, Whitesell, & Kowalski, 1987).

When children enter kindergarten and first grade they have a positive conception of themselves as competent beings (see "Studying Children"). They tend to underestimate the difficulty of a task, tend to hold and maintain high expectancies, are less apt to focus on negative outcomes, and view their ability as extremely high (Parsons, 1978). In fact, most kindergartners and first-graders rank themselves at or near the top of their class (Nichols, 1979). Their ratings of their classmates mirror the teacher's ratings (Stipek, 1981).

How might we explain young children's typically high ratings of their competence as compared with older children's more negative ratings? This may occur because three major factors come into play: (a) younger children do not differentiate ability from effort; that is, they do not have a concept

TABLE 3.3   Marketing Strategies for Each Level in Maslow's Hierarchy of Needs

Needs	Products	Specific Themes
Self-actualization	Education, hobbies, sports, some vacations, gourmet foods, museums	*U.S. Army:* "Be all you can be." *U.S. Home:* "Make the rest of your life . . . the best of your life." *Outward Bound School:* "Challenges, adventure, growth."
Esteem	Clothing, furniture, liquors, hobbies, stores, cars, and many others	*Schaeffer:* "Your hand should look as contemporary as the rest of you." *St. Pauli Girl:* "People who know the difference in fine things know the difference between imported beer and St. Pauli Girl. . . ." *Cricketeer:* "Cricketeer: Because the quality of your clothes should equal the quality of your life." *Cadillac:* ". . . those long hours have paid off. In recognition, financial success, and in the way you reward yourself. Isn't it time you owned a Cadillac?"
Social (Belongingness)	Personal grooming, foods, entertainment, clothing, and many others	*Atari:* "Atari brings the computer age home" (with a picture of a family using an Atari home computer). *Oil of Olay:* "When was the last time you and your husband met for lunch?" *J. C. Penney:* "Wherever teens gather, you'll hear it. It's the language of terrific fit and fashion. . . ." *AT&T:* "Reach out and touch someone."
Safety	Smoke detectors, preventive medicines, insurance, social security, retirement investments, seat belts, burglar alarms, tires, safes	*Sleep Safe:* "We've designed a travel alarm that just might wake you in the middle of the night—because a fire is sending smoke into your room. You see, ours is a smoke alarm as well as an alarm clock." *General Electric:* "Taking a trip usually means leaving your troubles behind. But there are times when you just might need help or information on the road. And that's when you need HELP, the portable CB from GE." *Alka-Seltzer:* "Will it be there when you need it?"
Physiological	Limited in the United States, generic foods, medicines, special drinks and foods for athletes	*Campbell Soup:* "Soup is good food" (with copy that stresses the nutritional benefits of soup). *Raisins:* "Thank goodness I found a snack food kids will sit for. And mothers will stand for." *Kellogg's All-Bran:* "At last. Some news about cancer you can live with" (with copy that stresses the role of fiber in the diet).

Source: Adapted excerpt from *Consumer Behavior*, Fifth Edition, by James F. Engel, Roger D. Blackwell, and Paul W. Miniard, copyright © 1986 by The Dryden Press, reprinted by permission of the publisher.

of ability as a stable trait that limits the effectiveness of effort; (b) older children tend to judge themselves in comparison with their classmates; and (c) children become more dependent on adults' evaluations of their skills.

Effort and Ability   Young children's poorly differentiated concept of ability was demonstrated in a study done by Stipek and Tannatt (1984). The authors reported that 40% and 15% of kindergartners and first-graders, respectively, referred to social behavior when they were asked to explain the "smartness" ratings they gave their classmates. Thus, according to some children, smart classmates shared their toys, and classmates who were not smart bit other children.

STUDYING CHILDREN

WHO'S WHO IN THE CLASSROOM?

Ask three or four kindergarten children and first-graders who they feel is the smartest, the nicest, the cutest or most handsome, the best at games in the classroom. Do many of these children cite themselves for most of these categories?

Even after children have begun to differentiate social and cognitive competence, they do not have a concept of intellectual competence that is as narrow as that of most older children. In Stipek's interview studies, many of the second- and third-graders discussed work habits (e.g., neatness, effort) to explain their assessments of their own and their peers' ability in school (Stipek, 1981; Stipek & Tannatt, 1984).

In addition, children do not differentiate between effort and ability. (Typically, these studies have used *ability* as a general term entailing capacity to reason as well as knowledge about the task at hand. Effort is seen by these researchers as a factor that must be taken into account in judging ability.) Young children tend to believe that ability is similar to a skill, and it is increased through one's own instrumental behavior, like practice or effort. Young children, for example, insist that even when the child who achieved a higher performance outcome also exerted less effort, the one who tried harder, nevertheless, must be smarter (Nichols, 1979). Subsequently, older children tend to conceive of ability as a stable trait, unaffected by effort. Thus, these children infer from identical performance outcomes that the child who exerts less effort must be the smarter.

Older children no longer conceive of intelligence as a repertoire of skills that can be endlessly expanded through their efforts. Rather, they learn to see intelligence as a global, stable entity whose adequacy is judged by their performance. Intelligence is thought of as fixed and unalterable—it is something you inherit (Heckhausen, 1982). The concepts of effort and ability have been widely used in analyzing achievement motivation in U.S. children.

The development of the concept of ability as a stable trait is especially important to understand because it has implications for children's behavior in academic contexts. Two studies have demonstrated that young children's persistence on academic tasks does not decline as a consequence of failure until the fifth or sixth grade (Miller, 1985; Rhodes, Blackwell, Jordan, & Walters, 1980). The Miller (1985) study provides direct evidence indicating that the debilitating effect of failure is associated with the development of a concept of ability as a stable trait.

Recent studies have suggested that children's perceptions of the cause of their failure mediates their expectations for future success in learning situations and the types of goals they set (Connell, 1985). Stipek and Hoffman (1980) studied high-, average-, and low-achievement children in three first-grade and three third-grade classes. Twenty subjects in each of these grades were given an anagram task consisting of letters from a Scrabble game. The children were told that they would be asked to make a word from 10 different sets of letters.

Before the first trial, the experimenter showed children a card with rows of pluses and minuses, representing scores from 0 to 10. The children were then asked to indicate how many of the 10 "puzzles" they expected to do. The letters were placed in the stand and the children were asked to make a word. None of the letter combinations formed a word, so failure was assured. At the end of 45 seconds, the experimenter said, "That puzzle wasn't solved." The children were reminded of failures by looking at the rows of minuses. They were then asked, "Were the puzzles not solved because (a) you weren't careful (effort) or (b) you are not good at this (ability)?" Finally, children were asked how well they would do if they had 10 more anagrams to do.

Results suggest that children's perceptions of the cause of past performances mediated their expectations for future success. Children who attributed their lack of success on this task to lack of ability reported that they would not do well on the next series of anagrams. The experimenters point out that by the end of third grade, poor perfor-

FOCUS ON APPLICATIONS

More Homework Time—Better Grades

Children's innate ability, quality of educational programs offered, socioeconomic class, and parents' level of education and their interest in their child's academic success appear to be important determinants of children's achievement level. These variables are not readily changeable. Is there an "easily manipulable" variable that will improve student achievement? It seems that increased study time shows a consistent effect on school achievement, as measured in the grades students receive in their classes. It appears that "the number of hours of homework per week is substantially related to achievement" (Wolf, 1979, p. 321). Futhermore, the amount of time spent studying has a significant effect on exam grades (Polachek, Kniessner, & Harwood, 1978). These researchers found that while ability did have an important effect on grades, so did the amount of time students spent studying. Students were able to compensate, in a single large class in economics, for a 100-point deficit in college board scores, with one and one-half additional hours of study time per week.

Keith's (1982) study also investigated the relationship between homework time and high school grades for a sample of 20,364 high school seniors. The analysis of the study confirms that an increase in time spent on homework had a positive effect on a student's grades, even after controlling for race, family background, ability, and the student's study program (general/vocational or college prep).

As can be seen from the graph, average grades and homework time have a strikingly linear relationship for all levels of ability. For example, students of high ability who studied 1 hour a week received mostly Bs and Cs, whereas students of comparable ability who studied 10 hours a week received mostly As and Bs. Homework time (the amount of time and effort one is willing to put in on studies), regardless of particular ability level, increases one's level of achievement based on grades received.

mance in school had begun to affect children's achievement-related expectations—a time when children are beginning to think of ability as a stable trait unaffected by effort.

Three additional studies have examined the power of beliefs about ability (stable trait or influence by effort) and its association with behavior and academic performance report findings consistent with the Stipek and Hoffman (1980) study (Chapman & Skinner, 1989; Chapman, Skinner, & Baltes, 1990; Skinner, 1990). In all three studies, when children associated ability with effort, chil-

dren's motivation levels and academic performance exceeded those who associated ability as a stable trait. All three studies reported, however, that children begin to think of ability as a stable trait at about age 11 or 12.

The results of these studies suggest that teachers must begin to use techniques that encourage children to attribute their failures to factors over which they have some control, such as effort, before self-defeating attributions occur. Heckhausen (1982) has found that when teachers are instructed to give children explanations that attribute their

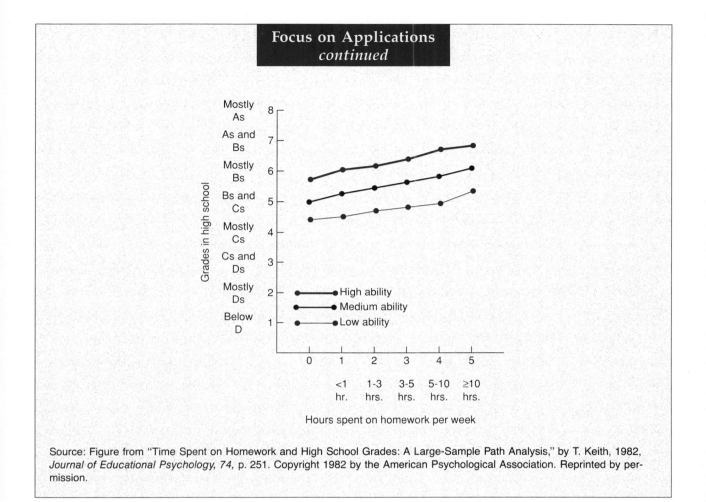

Hours spent on homework per week

Source: Figure from "Time Spent on Homework and High School Grades: A Large-Sample Path Analysis," by T. Keith, 1982, *Journal of Educational Psychology, 74*, p. 251. Copyright 1982 by the American Psychological Association. Reprinted by permission.

task failures to lack of effort rather than ability, the children's levels of achievement increase.

Recent studies have shown that when children "try harder" by doing their homework, they are more effective achievers. "Focus on Applications" reports these recent findings.

Social Comparisons When children "revise" their views of intelligence, it sharply increases children's use of social comparison to evaluate their competence. For example, Ruble, Feldman, and Boggiano (1976) found that 5-year-olds made social

comparisons, but they did not use this information to increase their own performance. In the experiment, by pushing a button, 5-year-olds could see their competitor on a monitor. The competitor was always ahead in filling out the coloring book, but this didn't seem to faze the 5-year-old. Children did not increase their efforts to finish the task first by coloring faster. At age 7, however, children did use social comparison information. As a result of seeing the competitor, 7-year-olds evaluated their performance in a more negative fashion.

Adult Evaluations   Finally, evaluations by others may cause achievement motivation to diminish in older, as compared to younger, children. Prior to attending school, children's experience with sustained effort and concentration has been centered primarily on physical skills. With school, there comes for many children the first major experience of deliberate, sustained, and required effort at the acquisition of intellectual skills. With physical tasks, compared to intellectual tasks, children can more easily begin, monitor, and guide the acquisition process and judge their own successes and failures. Children can observe the outcomes of their physical acts—they can successfully (or unsuccessfully) tie their shoes or ride their bikes. But, as Dweck and Elliott (1983) point out, "in the intellectual domain (for example, solving math problems) the problem-solving process requires a planned, covert sequence of skills. Further, the process yields an answer ("4") whose quality or correctness is not self-evident from inspections but must be subject to further evaluation" (p. 677). As a result, children may need an adult to teach the process, judge the products, and monitor the results. Thus, as children grapple with new kinds of tasks, they become more dependent on adults' evaluations, and these evaluations, particularly if they are negative, can diminish children's motivation to achieve.

Locus of Control   Another motivational factor that affects children's learning and performance is their beliefs about the outcomes they might experience on academic tasks, which tend to guide their subsequent behavior in that and analogous situations. This approach to studying achievement motivation is based on attribution theories, which analyze the cause to which one attributes successes or failures. Individuals tend to attribute achievement outcomes to either internal or external causes. Rotter (1966) has labeled the former group of individuals as having an **internal locus of control.** These children tend to perceive a causal relationship between their personal actions in an academic situation and the resultant events. They might comment, "I know I can do well on the test if I study very hard." Children who attribute their

successes and failures to factors that are beyond their control have an **external locus of control.** These children believe they lack the ability to do the task ("I can't do this, because I am no good at it.") If they achieve success in a certain task, they often attribute it to luck or some external circumstance over which they have little or no control. Furthermore, these children will devalue the success they achieved on a certain task and will feel that this certainly will not continue. In contrast, children with an internal locus of control often credit themselves when they achieve. Those attributing events of their lives as being beyond their control usually achieve less.

Kourilsky and Keislar (1983) conducted an experiment with 1,853 third- and sixth-graders. The program involved a social studies project in which considerable autonomy was granted to the children while they were engaged in their various projects. They found that students who perceived personal control over their own academic successes and failures (judged by their scores on the Intellectual Achievement Responsibility Questionnaire, an index of children's locus of control) showed significantly larger achievement gains. Further, they had a more favorable attitude toward learning (judged by the Attitude Toward Learning Test). Children with an external locus of control did not show significant gains in achievement and had a less favorable attitude toward learning.

Findley and Cooper (1983) concluded from a synthesis of 98 studies on achievement motivation involving students ranging from first grade through college that those students who had an internal locus of control had higher levels of achievement. Similarly, Walden and Ramey (1983) reported that an experimental group of socially disadvantaged children who had participated in a 5-year preschool educational day-care program had perceptions of control over academic successes equal to those of the middle-class comparison group. Control beliefs predicted achievement for the experimental and middle-class comparison children but were unrelated to achievement for the socially disadvantaged children who had not had the benefits of preschool intervention.

Academic Failure Children who experience failure are particularly likely to develop warrantedly low expectations for success on academic tasks. That is, they are likely to develop expectations, or levels of aspiration, that are consistent with their past performances. Children exposed to frequent failure either set goals for learning that are so low they can attain them effortlessly, or they set ridiculously unobtainable goals. (Failing on an extremely difficult task has more face-saving potential then failing on an easy task.) Figure 3.5 shows children's level of aspiration after successfully completing a task and after unsuccessfully completing a task. When children have experienced failure, their expectations of themselves as achievers are lowered, and they are not inspired to work to their fullest abilities.

Moreover, when children are exposed to frequent failures, they may develop a feeling of **learned helplessness.** These children tend to feel they are unable to handle certain tasks; they perceive themselves as unable to surmount failure. They often put themselves down when they fail, yet when they succeed they are likely to say it was just luck. Children view failure experiences as indicative of their ability, and as more failure experiences occur this "lack-of-ability" feeling is continually reinforced.

Learned helplessness represents a focus on avoidance of task situations that produce negative self-judgments. Covington (1985) holds that achievement behavior of children exhibiting learned helplessness can be understood largely in terms of their attempts to maintain a positive self-image of ability and competence. Covington maintains that children's conceptions of intelligence are a pivotal factor in explaining their "no effort" strategies. As noted previously, younger children tend to think that effort is the key to academic success; older children tend to think that innate ability determines their level of academic performance. In Covington's Self-Worth Theory, Covington (1988) maintains that young children measure their worth primarily in terms of effort, whereas older children measure their worth in terms of ability. As Covington and Beery (1976) note, "The individual's sense of self-worth is threatened by the belief

FIGURE 3.5   Aspiration Levels

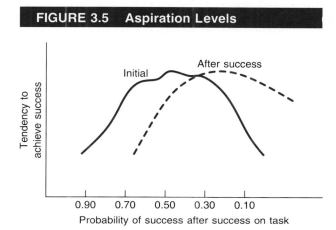

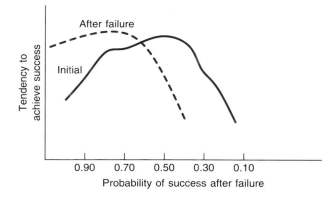

Success produces an increase in the probability of success at the same and similar tasks and raises the child's level of aspiration. Change in level of aspiration after failure. Failure produces a decrease in probability of success at the same and similar tasks. The change in motivation following failure favors a lowering of the level of aspiration.

Source: From *Personality, Motivation and Achievement* (p. 28) by J. W. Atkinson and Joel O. Raynor, 1978, Bristol, PA: Hemisphere Publishing Corp.

that his value as a person depends on his ability to achieve" (p. 6). High-achieving children gain their self-esteem from recognition and praise for their academic performance. In contrast, children who are not doing well academically are confronted with frequent failures and must attempt to protect their self-esteem through alternative modes of behavior. For example, they may resort to cheating or to failure-avoidance strategies (low effort or procrastination, because failure without effort is viewed as "failure with honor"), or they may attempt to gain self-esteem through acting out in class, thereby earning admiration from their peers. By their actions, these children are increasing the likelihood that they will continue to fail. In short, the need to avoid failure in order to protect self-esteem is one of the main obstacles to school achievement.

Teachers Behaviors, Expectations, and Relationships   Although this research has a number of methodological and conceptual weaknesses, it continues to be an important line of investigation. Studies in the 1960s and 1970s (Rist, 1970; Rosenthal & Jacobson, 1968) suggest that teacher behaviors and expectations have an important influence on children's academic achievement. More recent studies suggest that teachers expect certain kinds of behavior from high achievers and different behavior from low achievers; they treat each differently and thereby sustain the patterns (Cooper, 1979; Good, 1980). High achievers are given more opportunities to participate in class and more time to respond. They receive more praise for giving the right answers and less criticism than low achievers. Low achievers are expected not to know and not to participate and are given less opportunity and encouragement for doing so. Cooper (1979) also posits that students for whom teachers have high expectations are criticized when the teacher thinks they have not tried and praised when they do try, while students for whom the teacher has low expectations are treated less logically. They are less often praised and are both praised and criticized for reasons irrelevant to their effort.

Research on the effects of classroom climate indicates that the quality of the student/teacher relationship is associated with students' achievement motivations and attitudes toward school (Berndt & Hawkins, 1988). Vernoff (1983) suggests that adolescent girls have a greater need than boys for affiliation and social connectedness and may be more sensitive to teacher support or the lack of it in a classroom. Successful teachers are energetic, self-

What motivates children to learn is dependent on more than just their IQ.

confident, concerned, humanitarian, innovative, warm, friendly, and emotionally involved with their students (Midgley, Feldlaufer, & Eccles, 1989), and these teacher behaviors tend to motivate children to achieve (see "Studying Children").

CULTURAL CONTEXTS OF DEVELOPMENT

In order to examine the impact that culture has on children's behavior, look at one of the most extensively studied countries: Japan. It will be interest-

STUDYING CHILDREN

MOTIVATED TO LEARN

Interview several children at various grade levels, and ask them what their teachers can do, or do now, to make learning an exciting experience. Do they think it is fun to learn? If so, why? If not, why?

ing to compare and contrast children in Japan to children in the United States. In this way you will be able to see how different cultural contexts influence children's development. One significant reason why Japan has been studied so extensively is that Japanese students are consistently among the top performers in international studies of achievement in both math and science.

Each culture can be thought of as setting priorities for behavioral development that guide socializing agents (parents, teachers, peers) to select some of children's potentials for realization and neglect others. That is, socialization goals of every culture are translated into creating environments for children so they will acquire the behaviors that are perceived as being valuable in a particular culture.

Perhaps the main distinction between Japan and the United States, which colors the way in which the two countries socialize their children and influence their educational practices, is Japan's belief in **collectiveness** and the United States's belief in **individualism.** Collectiveness emphasizes the interconnectedness of persons. Japanese society places a high value on harmony in interpersonal relations and the ability to cooperate with others. In Japan, the social, the collective, and the group are valued over the personal, the familial, and the individual. Individualism, the cornerstone of the U.S. society, emphasizes traits such as self-reliance, independence, and freedom. Patience, persistence, and accommodation are virtues promoted among Japanese schoolchildren, whereas originality, exploration, and self-assertion are characteristics encouraged among U.S. children. It will become apparent to you that these beliefs and needs of a particular culture strongly influence so-

cialization practices and subsequently children's behavior.

FAMILIES IN JAPAN

In Japan, being a mother and homemaker is thought of as a highly prestigious profession. As such, mothers hold a strong position in the family; it is believed to be their domain and fathers are discouraged from interfering. Children are a mother's first priority. Japanese mothers are always held responsible for their children's unhappiness, whether it is expressed in sickness, fussing, crying, sadness, or doing poorly in school. To avoid criticism from husbands and neighbors, Japanese mothers do whatever is possible to keep their children calm and happy (Sasaki, 1985).

Mothers' major goal is to make sure that their children are doing well in school. In fact, the community's perception of women's success as mothers depends in large part on how well their children perform in the academic setting. Children's goals are clear: success in entrance exams and getting into a good school (Stevenson & Lee, 1990).

Ideally mothers should be working full time in the home. The Japanese still adhere tenaciously to the idea that male heads of household should be the sole breadwinners, and that mothers should stay home and devote themselves to the care of the household and children (Imamura, 1987). This belief is held much more emphatically in Japan than in the United States. However, financial demands make it more difficult for Japanese women to conceive of mothering as a full-time, lifetime job. While it is unlikely that individual women will have successful careers, the number of mothers working in Japan is rising. A working mother, however, still connotes economic misfortune.

Baby-sitting for children so that mothers can have some time off—perhaps to pursue personal interests—is unheard of in Japan. American parents don't doubt their right to enjoy themselves away from their children. In Japan, leaving children with outsiders, for such frivolous reasons, would be frowned on.

In many Japanese families, the position of the father is peripheral. The formal head of the family

To Japanese mothers, children are the first priority.

is accorded respect; however, in reality he doesn't exert much control. Fathers are treated in many ways like high-status guests in the home, friendly and even jovial guests, but ones who stand on the periphery of the intimate relationship between mothers and children (Vogel, 1963). It is still often said, "A great husband is one who is healthy, and stays out of the home." Or put differently by one Japanese mother, "A woman does not need a husband except as a supplier of money" (Lebra, 1984).

Goals of Child Rearing   Early training instills in children a deep sense of responsibility to their mothers and the family. Patterns of socialization seem to foster politeness, attentiveness to others, and a strong sense of family and group identity. A basic concept in understanding Japanese interpersonal relationships is **amae.** Amae is a feeling of dependency coupled with the expectation of indulgence (Lebra, 1984). It is mothers' indulgence that encourages children's strong sense of dependence on them. Children sense what pleases their mothers and behave accordingly (Azuma, 1986). In a sense, mothers establish their control over their children through devotion and indulgence; the sequence seems to work like this: indulgence—dependence—identification—controllability.

Protecting feelings of closeness is an important goal of Japanese mothers. This excessive closeness is taught through practices such as prolonged breast-feeding, cobathing, and cosleeping. Moreover, if the child is obstinate, mothers will give in rather than injure the relationship. For example, if a child does not like what her mother has prepared for dinner, and refuses to eat, the mother will simply clear away the plate and prepare the child's preferred dish. This is obviously different from what U.S. mothers would do, and what they have been told to do. American mothers are told to be consistent, not lose battles with their children, and to be firm and follow through with their requests.

Children's understanding often takes priority over compliance in Japanese families. To the Japanese, children are inherently good. Every child is born with potential for five virtues: humaneness, righteousness, decorum, wisdom, and sincerity. A good child is one who is mild, gentle, obedient, cooperative, and smart. These qualities, however, would remain unactualized without the assistance of learning. An incident in one report shows how a teacher seemed to view the gaining of children's understanding, and not their compliance, as the goal of intervention (White & Levine, 1986). Boys in one classroom were dropping clay "bombs" on the fish in an aquarium. The teacher explained that the clay could hurt the fish, but she did not specifically tell the boys to stop (nor did they). In her announcements to the whole class at the end of the school day, the teacher explained that some boys in the class thought they were "helping" the fish by throwing in clay "food," but that the boys were really harming the fish. When one of the authors in this study interviewed the teacher about the incident, the exchange was as follows:

INTERVIEWER: Did you really think the children were trying to help the fish by throwing the clay pellets?

TEACHER: Yes.

INTERVIEWER: Don't you think the boys understood they might hurt the fish by throwing the clay pellets?

TEACHER: If they understood it was wrong, they wouldn't do it. (p. 60)

With regard to compliance, the most important concern of Japanese mothers is not absolute obedience, but rather the preservation of closeness between mother and child. Although U.S. parents value compliance, their emphasis is on independence and personal freedom. In fact, U.S. mothers may discourage compliance that is seemingly unfair or unreasonable.

Disciplining Techniques Disciplining techniques are also designed to bring about children's dependency on their mothers. Mothers frequently appeal to their children's sense of empathy, presenting themselves as victims of ridicule and humiliation if their children misbehave or do poorly in school (Kobayashi-Winata & Power, 1989).

Japanese mothers communicate to their children (from an early age) a fear of the world, particularly strangers. At the same time, they demonstrate to their children that they will be there to comfort them—thereby encouraging children to remain close and dependent. Japanese mothers tend to rely more on teasing, shame, and ridicule. They appeal to children's duties and responsibilities, along with guilt. Mothers control their children's behavior calmly and without anger. In this way, they are making sure that children do not develop feelings of resentment that might weaken the bonds of love and filial gratitude.

STUDYING CHILDREN

GOALS OF CHILD REARING

Interview parents and ask them to list the behaviors they want their children to exhibit as adults. Are these behaviors consonant with the individualism philosophy?

SCHOOLS IN JAPAN

Ninety-five percent of all 4-year-olds in Japan are enrolled in nursery schools (Tobin, Wu, & Davidson, 1989). The *yochien* serves children of blue-collar, working mothers, while the *hoikoen* serves wealthier, nonworking mothers. One of the major reasons Japanese mothers send their children to preschool is for them to learn perseverance, concentration, and the ability to function effectively in group situations. Japanese mothers are not particularly concerned about academic achievement, which they tend to see as inappropriate and counterproductive for these young children. Instead, they are concerned that their children will develop positive attitudes toward school and cultivate the skills in thinking, studying, and getting along with others that will promote educational success later on.

In the formal school setting, Japanese students attend 7 hours of classes every weekday and a half day on Saturday for 240 days a year. U.S. children attend classes 174 days a year, 5 days a week. Twice a year Japanese children must take examinations in order to be promoted to the next grade. Each lesson taught in the Japanese schools lasts around 40 to 45 minutes; a 10- to 15-minute recess time follows each lesson. (The ability of Japanese children to focus so closely on academic activities may be due to the opportunities for vigorous play provided in between classes.)

U.S. students spend about 3 hours a week on math; Japanese spend twice that. U.S. students tend to spend more time on reading and social studies. As Stevenson and Lee (1990) point out, "It seems quite likely to us that the poor performance of U.S. children in math may be traced, in part, to this large difference in time in which they were engaged in activities related to math" (p. 133). Moreover, moral development plays a fundamental role in the Japanese curriculum. Through lessons and activities, skills such as cooperation, thoughtfulness, hard work, endurance, fairness, trust, and harmony with others are taught.

The Japanese children spend 4 times as much time each day doing homework as do U.S. children. U.S. children tend to spend fewer hours in school and devote less time in school and after

school to academic activities than Japanese children (Garden, 1987). Chen and Stevenson (1989) report that Japanese parents, teachers, and children tend to perceive homework as extremely useful and important in promoting academic achievement.

Only 9% of Japanese children do chores around the house; older children do not work. The most common reason for not assigning chores or engaging in outside employment is that these activities divert children from schoolwork (Stevenson & Lee, 1990).

The Importance of Group Identity   The Japanese believe that being a well-organized and tightly knit group that works hard toward common goals is a natural and pleasurable human experience. Schools reflect this cultural priority. Classroom activities are structured to encourage or require participation in group activities and to emphasize the responsibility of individual students to the class as a group and to the school as a whole. Motivation through group activity is accomplished by promoting a strong sense of shared identity and by allowing individuals opportunities to influence group goals and activities.

Learning group skills in the United States means learning to "stand out," that is, to make one's individuality salient. In Japan, by contrast, one learns to "stand in," that is, to become so identified with the group that one's individuality will not be noticed.

Within each classroom, students are organized in small, mixed ability groups called *han*. (In Japan students are not grouped according to ability, and there is an absence of special teachers for children with learning problems, emotional disturbance, or mild forms of mental retardation.) These groups of four to six children are cooperative study and work units. Teachers frequently ask the class to divide into han to work on special assignments and have them report the results to the class. The han is also the primary unit for discipline, chores, and other classroom activities. Through the use of han, teachers delegate much responsibility for classroom management and discipline to the students themselves. To illustrate, rather than calling inattentive children by name, and encouraging them to hurry, the teacher typically remarks that a particular han is not ready, and allows the children to exert peer pressure to encourage these children to complete the necessary action. There is a lower incidence of irrelevant activities in Japan (talking to peers, walking around the classroom). Japanese teachers spend very little time on disciplining (as compared with U.S. teachers), and Japanese students are more compliant and ready to undertake the tasks the teachers offer.

Juku Japanese children are required to take entrance exams in order to be admitted into the best high schools, which then enables them to continue on to the university. Juku schools are a large and diverse group of private, profit-making tutorial enrichment/remedial preparatory or cram schools designed to help students pass those important admission exams. Currently, juku institutions have reached the 800-billion-yen level annually (about $5 billion U.S.) and are still growing. Approximately 16% of the primary school-age children, and 45% of junior high school students attend juku. Students attend juku after school and on weekends.

Explanations for Japanese Superiority in School
Many hypotheses have been advanced to account for the high levels of achievement of children from families of Asian cultures, including the possibility that the cognitive abilities of these children exceed those of U.S. children. Stevenson and Lee (1990), however, found no support for the argument that there are differences in the general cognitive functioning of Chinese, Japanese, and U.S. children, nor for the contention (Lynn, 1982) that the superiority of Japanese children in mathematics and science is due to a generally higher level of cognitive functioning than is found in U.S. children.

In a recent study (Stevenson et al. 1990), 10 cognitive tasks and tests of achievement in reading and math were given to 240 children. In each grade from one through five, from Minneapolis (Minnesota), Taipei (China), and Sendai (Japan), similarities were found in level, variability, and structure of cognitive abilities. The authors conclude:

Positing general differences in cognitive functioning of Japanese and Chinese children is an appealing hypothesis for those who seek to explain the superiority of Japanese and Chinese children's scholastic achievement, but it appears from the present data that it will be necessary to seek other explanations for their success. (p. 733)

While it seems unlikely that cross-cultural differences in academic achievement among Japanese and U.S. students can be accounted for by differences in general intelligence, there are several factors that may account for these differences: (a) a more egalitarian educational philosophy, (b) a more academically demanding classroom, and (c) higher parental expectations.

In the Japanese society, parents and teachers place a great deal of value on equality—children have the potential to master the work they are given. Potential success or failure has to do with effort, not with raw inborn ability. The Japanese are consistent advocates of equal opportunity and consistent supporters of social and educational egalitarianism. They see an injustice in providing children with unequal educational beginnings. The Japanese believe that all children have the ability to learn well and to master the regular school curriculum. Differences in student achievement are thought to result largely from the level of effort, perseverance, and self-discipline, not from differences in individual ability.

Teachers try to speed up and encourage slow learners, and at times to slow down more talented members of the class. Teachers do not see this as a disservice to the brighter children because they believe that students benefit in the long run by developing an increased sensitivity to the needs of others and a sense of security that comes from being a member of the group.

Japanese parents hold higher academic expectations for their children than U.S. parents. Stevenson and Lee (1990) suggest that two factors that work strongly against high achievement by U.S. children are the low academic standards held by parents and the overestimations that parents make of their children's abilities. A significantly higher percentage of U.S. parents, as compared with Japanese parents, believed their children were doing well in school and were meeting the expectations of parents and teachers (see Figure 3.6).

Cross-national differences are even more dramatic when only the "very satisfied" mothers are considered. Less than 5% of the Japanese mothers, but over 40% of the U.S. mothers, said that they were very satisfied with their child's performance. It was also evident that the Japanese mothers were more likely than U.S. mothers to adopt successively higher criteria for their children's academic performance as their children became older. Perhaps these very high parental perceptions and high confidence that their children were meeting their educational expectations prevent U.S. children from acknowledging the need to work hard. If parents believe that their children are doing well in school and convey this impression to their children, children may see no purpose in studying harder.

Several studies (Lee, 1987; Yao, 1985) have examined other family characteristics in attempting to understand successfully achieving Asians. The family backgrounds of 15 successful Chinese, Japanese, and Korean high school and college students in Boston were examined in one study (Mordkowitz & Ginsburg, 1987). Structured interviews began with an open-ended question on the individual's memories of learning. A strong home environment (e.g., strict monitoring of children's free time, investment in educational opportunities) and parental emphasis on respect for education and expectation of achievement were factors the students had in common. The students also held a strong belief that effort would be rewarded, and they had been taught to respect teacher authority and avoid peer conflict. The authors concluded that the common socialization patterns were due to ethnicity and that this accounted for achievement. A summary of cross-cultural child-rearing beliefs and strategies and school philosophy between Japan and the United States is presented in Table 3.4.

FIGURE 3.6   Mothers' Degree of Satisfaction with Their Children's Performance

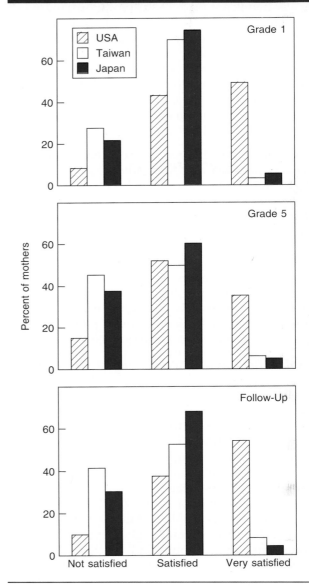

Source: From "Contexts of Achievement" by H. Stevenson and S. Lee, 1990, *Monographs of the Society of Research in Child Development, no. 221,* vol. 55, nos. 1–2, p. 77. © The Society for Research in Child Development, Inc. Reprinted by permission.

Parental involvement in children's schoolwork is an important determinant of children's academic performance.

PRACTICAL IMPLICATIONS: ENHANCING U.S. STUDENTS' ACADEMIC PERFORMANCE— LESSONS FROM JAPAN

There are some aspects of the Japanese school system that should be emulated by the United States. Japan's educational philosophy emphasizes effort as a key determinant of children's academic success. Ability is not differentiated from effort. Similarly, children's academic limitations are attributed to lack of effort on their part. Teachers, parents, and children in Japan hold the sincere belief that everyone is capable of mastering the curriculum, and that academic success is within the grasp of all children if they apply themselves wholeheartedly to their school work (Stevenson & Lee, 1990). Results of several studies (Ruble et al., 1976; Harter, 1983; Stevenson & Lee, 1990) suggest that children's perceptions of the cause of past performance mediates their expectations for future success. Children who attribute poor performance to effort, rather than ability, have higher levels of achievement.

This is in marked contrast to the U.S. culture, which holds the stronger nativistic view that not all children are capable of the same levels of achievement, no matter how hard they try. In the United States, older students tend to think of intelligence or ability as concrete and innate, causing them to feel that there is very little they can do if they are not doing well in school. As a result, many children who have been exposed to academic failure learn to do just that—nothing.

The United States could profit from having a "curriculum for caring," in which children were encouraged to think of others and treat others kindly and fairly. The Japanese also emphasize

TABLE 3.4	Cross-Cultural Similarities and Differences: United States and Japan	
	JAPAN	**UNITED STATES**
FAMILIES:	Mother: homemaker very prestigious profession children first priority totally responsible for children's happiness	Mother: homemaker role not as prestigious, children are top priority, but mother's personal needs also considered to be important, mother partially responsible for children's happiness
	Father: breadwinner little control in the home	Father: role may be as breadwinner, but expected to engage in child-rearing chores ideally participation for two-wage-earner families should be a 50–50 situation
GOALS OF CHILD REARING:	foster responsibility to mother politeness, attentiveness to others dependency group identity doing well in school	responsibility to self assertiveness independence individuality
CHILD-REARING TECHNIQUES:	amae: feeling of dependency, coupled with expectation of indulgence children's understanding takes priority over compliance appeal to child's sense of empathy with mother as victim of humiliation if child does not do well love withdrawal, cobathing, cosleeping	reasoning with child compliance
SCHOOL:	major emphasis on group skills/learning to "stand in" academic success results from children's effort no ability grouping major emphasis on math/science more time on-task in classroom belief in usefulness of homework parents hold higher academic expectations for children	emphasis on developmental individual skills "stand out" academic success innate ability ability grouping major emphasis on reading/social science less time on-task in classroom lower parental, academic expectations

concentrated learning time, followed every 45 minutes by a 10- to 15-minute vigorous break. Having one or two recess periods, as we do in the United States, may be one reason why restless students can be discipline problems.

High parental expectations and involvement are other positive factors of the Japanese culture. While U.S. parents are involved with helping their children, they do tend to place more responsibility on the teachers and the schools in helping their children achieve certain academic standards.

Another high mark goes to Japan for emphasizing that preschools need to help children learn how to get along with others and develop a love for learning. In the United States there appears to be quite a rush to put very young children into structured, "academic" environments. More and more children are attending cognitively oriented preschools in which they are taught how to count, read, write, and so forth. (This is thought to be a necessity by some who live in school districts in which children have to know these things in order to pass the kindergarten screening test.) Developing curiosity and a love for learning will have a much greater effect on promoting educational success later on.

Developing children's natural curiosity by exposing them to varied and stimulating environments is important to later academic achievement.

There are some definite drawbacks to the Japanese school system. One cannot ignore, for example, the toll this system exacts on its children (and mothers) in terms of their committing suicide when they have failed the rigorous exams for getting into prestigious schools. One also cannot ignore the positive aspects of the Japanese school system which, if adopted by U.S. schools, may enhance our children's learning potential.

REVIEW OF KEY POINTS

Currently there are 10.5 million preschoolers who have mothers in the labor force. A significant percentage of these children are in day care. In terms of the effect of day care on cognitive development, available evidence indicates that for middle-class children, day care has neither a beneficial nor an adverse effect. For economically disadvantaged children, day care may have positive effects. Research suggests that economically disadvantaged children in day care do better on achievement tests than their home-reared, disadvantaged counterparts.

Day care seems to have both positive and negative effects on social development. On the positive side, day-care children are more socially competent and show more prosocial behaviors; on the negative side, they are more aggressive, assertive, impulsive, and noncooperative. Some research indicates that the quality of day care is the salient factor in influencing children's social development. Children enrolled in good-quality day care tend to exhibit positive social qualities, not negative ones.

It appears that peers are a highly influential socialization force. The importance of the peer group and the way in which children at various ages interact with their peers were discussed. Conformity to peers tends to reach its peak between the ages of 11 and 14 years, and then subsides.

Another important context of development is television. Some children watch an inordinate amount of television, a pattern that is believed to be established in early childhood. Television is likely to increase both prosocial and aggressive behavior, perpetuates stereotypic notions about social groups, and is persuasive in influencing children's food, toy, and clothing preferences.

In the social context of the school, children's achievement motivation (the energizing force that stimulates children to do well academically) is influenced by children's conceptions of intelligence (innate or influenced by effort), their locus of control (external versus internal), their experiences with failure, teachers' behavior, expectations, and relationships, and parental styles.

In the cultural context of development, child-rearing practices and the educational system and the effects these socializing forces have on the behavior of children in Japan and in the United States were examined. The priorities set by the culture guide parents and teachers to select certain behaviors, while neglecting others, so that children will acquire the behaviors valued and needed by the particular culture. For Japan, the behaviors that are valued center on a collectivist philosophy: cooperation, interrelatedness with others, group orientation, and loyalty first to mother, then gradually moving to peers, company, and country. In the United States, an individualistic philosophy influences socialization practices toward raising autonomous, self-reliant, independent individuals.

ENHANCING YOUR CRITICAL THINKING

Broadening Your Knowledge

Japan

Stevenson, H., Azuma, H., & Hakuta, K. (Eds.). (1986). *Child development in Japan.* New York: Freeman.

This book will help students understand Japan's collective philosophical outlook and how this affects parental socialization practices and subsequently child development outcomes. Azuma's chapter, "Why study child development in Japan" (pp. 3–13) is a good place to begin.

Critical Thinking

Supplemental Care

Belsky, J. (1988). The "effects" of infant day care reconsidered. *Early Childhood Research Quarterly, 3,* 234–272.

Clarke-Stewart, K. A. (1989). Day care: Maligned or malignant. *American Psychologist, 44,* 266–273.

As noted in the text, considerable attention is being given to the relationship between mothers' working and the effects of day care on infants in their first year of life. Belsky (1988) offers a review of the research and his interpretation of the findings. Clarke-Stewart (1989) does not agree with Belsky's conclusion. After reading the two articles, whom are you inclined to believe and why?

Personal Growth

Achievement Motivation

Findley, M., & Cooper, H. (1983). Locus of control and academic achievement: A literature review. *Journal of Personality and Social Psychology, 44,* 419–427.

An important motivational factor that affects learning and performance is an individual's locus of control. Findley and Cooper present a state-of-the-art review on this topic and its relationship to achievement outcomes. Before reading the article, think about these questions: Do you tend to feel in control of events in your life? Or, do you believe what you do has little effect on what happens to you? Do different situations (academic or social, for example) affect your locus of control status?

The In Utero, Physical, and Perceptual World of the Child and Adolescent

PART II

The Beginning of Life

CHILDREN'S THOUGHTS

On "How do you think babies are begun?" . . .

I don't know, I never saw. Jesus makes them in a factory.
North American girl, age 5

By eating good food. She swallows it and it grows into a baby, if its good food.
English boy, age 7

The mother always had it there. (Where?) In the tummy. Ever since she was a little girl. All little girls have them, lots of tiny seeds. Then they grow. (What starts them to grow?) Dunno.
Australian girl, age 5

The doctor gives an injection and that starts it to grow. From the seed, it's kind of a tube that grows and grows until it becomes a baby.
English girl, age 9

It's because you're married. That's when you have children. People have children if they get married. They sleep together and cuddle. The baby just grows from the food mother eats. Father warms her tummy in bed and it grows.
North American boy, age 11

CHAPTER OUTLINE

LIFE BEGINS

The Male Reproductive System
The Female Reproductive System
Fertilization

GENETIC TRANSMISSION

Autosomes
Sex Chromosomes
Genes
Deoxyribonucleic Acid (DNA)
Principles of Cell Division: Mitosis and Meiosis

PRENATAL PERIODS OF DEVELOPMENT

Germinal
Embryonic
Fetal

HEREDITARY INFLUENCES ON PRENATAL DEVELOPMENT

Down Syndrome
Turner's Syndrome
Kleinfelter's Syndrome
Phenylketonuria (PKU)
Diagnosing Developmental Defects

ENVIRONMENTAL INFLUENCES ON PRENATAL DEVELOPMENT

Diseases of the Mother
Pediatric Acquired Immunodeficiency Syndrome (AIDS)
Mothers' Age
Fathers' Age
Radiation
Immunological Effects
Mothers' Diet
Caffeine
Aspirin
Mothers' Emotions
Alcohol
Cigarettes
Marijuana
Drugs

THE BIRTH PROCESS

Labor
Delivery
Afterbirth
Neonatal Assessment Techniques
Preterm Births
Appearance of the Newborn

PRACTICAL IMPLICATIONS: PREPARED CHILDBIRTH

KEY TERMS

Testes
Testosterone
Ovum
Ovulation
Fallopian tubes
Zygote
Chromosomes
Homologous
Autosomes
Locus
Sex chromosomes
Sex-linked characteristics
Genes
Homozygous
Heterozygous
Alleles
Genotype
Phenotype
Deoxyribonucleic acid (DNA)
Ribonucleic acid (RNA)
Somatic cells
Gametes
Blastocyst
Implantation
Endometrium
Chorion
Amnion
Placenta
Umbilical cord
Ossification
Down syndrome
Turner's sydrome
Kleinfelter's syndrome
Phenylketonuria (PKU)
Amniocentesis
Teratogen
Acquired immunodeficiency syndrome (AIDS)
Fetal alcohol syndrome (FAS)

FOCUS ON ISSUES

Artificial Fertilization

It has been estimated that there are over 300,000 infertile couples who desire to have children. Although there are numerous causes of sterility, the two most common causes of infertility in women are reduced egg production and blocked fallopian tubes. In order to correct blocked fallopian tubes, delicate microsurgery is necessary. Unfortunately, it is successful only about 50% of the time. Women can be treated with fertility drugs for low egg production. In men, infertility may be caused by a low sperm count. In this case, sperm may be collected, concentrated, and frozen in sperm banks to be used later for artificial insemination.

Artificial fertilization reflects the advances that have been made in our knowledge of human fertility, genetics, and understanding of prenatal development. In July 1978, Patrick Steptoe and Robert Edwards topped decades of work by delivering by Caesarean section 5-pound 12-ounce Louise Joy Brown, the first test-tube baby to be carried to term. Human reproduction has been changed forever. Since Baby Louise, about 15,000 babies have been born by artificial fertilization. Other artificial fertilization means include intrauterine insemination, gamete intra-fallopian transfer and zygote intra-fallopian transfer.

Recently, however, artificial fertilization has leaped forward to the most astounding development of all: *preimplantation genetics.* Preimplantation genetics is a fledgling science that can determine the health of egg and sperm before mating, supervise fertilization, and then double-check the fitness of an early embryo before it implants itself in the uterus and starts pregnancy. In the reduction-division process by which the egg prepares itself for fertilization, the cell's original second set of 23 maternal chromosomes is discarded in the polar body. An egg can carry either a deleterious gene for a particular disease or the normal gene, but not both. By examining the chromosomes in the polar body, the health of the egg can be deduced. For example, if doctors are dealing with a woman who may be a carrier of a deadly disease, such as cystic fibrosis, and if the polar body carries the gene for cystic fibrosis, doctors know, by process of elimination, that the egg is healthy, and it can then be fertilized and implanted.

Goldman and Goldman (1982) asked over 800 children, ages 5 to 15, from Australia, North America, England, and Sweden how they thought babies were begun. The children's responses offer some refreshing new insights into the origins of babies. Do you remember as a child your theory as to how babies were made? You eventually sorted out the facts of life—perhaps with the help of Walt Disney movies in health classes, your parents, or an older, "sophisticated" friend armed with an arsenal of information and misinformation.

Conception requires the union of a sperm cell and an egg cell, a process that generally requires the physical union of the bearers of the sex cells (see "Focus on Issues"). This chapter will look at the growth and development of this single, fertilized cell, the developmental milestones that take place during gestation, hereditary and environmental influences on the unborn child, prepared childbirth, and the birth process.

LIFE BEGINS

The prenatal period of development is unique in a number of ways. Although it is the shortest stage of growth in the life cycle (approximately 266 days from conception to birth), the individual develops from one cell to several hundred billion cells. During the average gestation period, the biological foundations that will influence developmental potential are established. For these reasons, many experts consider this stage in the life cycle to be the most important stage in development.

THE MALE REPRODUCTIVE SYSTEM

The main parts of the male reproductive system are the **testes,** which produce the hormones **testosterone** and androsterone. These hormones are responsible for the development at puberty of secondary sex characteristics: lowering of the voice, facial and pubic hair, and thick muscles. The testes also produce millions of sperm cells. These individual sperm are small, approximately 1/500 of an inch from head to tail. Spermatozoa, when combined with secretions from other internal organs, form semen, which is ejaculated by the penis during intercourse. The sperm cell, with its long tail and pointed head, swims 6 or 7 inches on its journey to reach the ovum.

THE FEMALE REPRODUCTIVE SYSTEM

The sex cell of the female is called an **ovum,** or egg, and is one of the largest cells in the human body. It is around 0.15 millimeter or 1/175 of an inch in diameter—smaller than the dot over an "i." The ova are produced by two oval-shaped ovaries that are located in the pelvic cavity. Approximately once a month, a healthy female releases a mature ovum. The ejection of the egg is called **ovulation**. After ovulation, the egg travels from the ovary to the **fallopian tubes;** each tube is 4 inches long and no wider than a human hair.

FERTILIZATION

Fertilization may occur any time up to 24 hours following ovulation. If conception does not occur, the ovum disintegrates and the possibility of conception ceases until the next ovulation. However, if in the ovum's journey down the fallopian tube it encounters healthy spermatozoa and one of the sperm manages to penetrate the wall of the egg, life processes begin (see Figure 4.1).

Occasionally two ova are released during ovulation instead of one. If both are fertilized, fraternal or dizygotic twins result. Each will have an independent placenta and umbilical cord. Such twins are no more alike genetically than other siblings of different ages. Brother and sister twins are always dizygotic. Occasionally, a fertilized egg will split and two separate embryos will develop. Since they originated from the same zygote, they have the same genetic structure and are called identical or monozygotic twins. Triplets, quadruplets, and quintuplets may be identical or fraternal or a combination.

The chances of having twins are 1 in 96. The chances of having triplets are 1 in 9,216, quadruplets 1 in 900,000 and quintuplets 1 in 85 million (Tortora & Anagnostakos, 1984). Giving birth to more than one child depends on many factors: mother's age, history of multiple births in the family, and the use of fertility drugs. Fertility drugs are generally administered to stimulate egg production in infertile females with reduced egg production; they may stimulate ovulation to cause superovulation. This occurs when a woman releases several ova rather than just one, resulting in multiple births (see Figure 4.2).

Generally about 300 to 500 million sperm are released in a single ejaculation. Although that number seems large, it appears to be a necessary one, for only a few hundred sperm are able to reach the fallopian tube, which harbors the ovum. The sperm, on penetrating the ovum, releases a substance that makes the surface of the egg impermeable to other sperm. After penetrating the egg, the sperm loses its tail, and the head becomes a cell nucleus. Typically, conception takes place in the fallopian tube, from which the fertilized egg, or **zygote,** travels down into the uterus and implants in the lining of the uterus. The nucleus from the egg and the nucleus from the sperm lose their nuclear membranes and unite into a single set of 23 pairs of chromosomes (46). A new life begins.

Prospective parents may be wondering a number of things about their unborn child. Perhaps the most common question is whether it will be a boy or girl. Gynosperm, bearing the X chromosome, and androsperm, bearing the Y chromosome, have

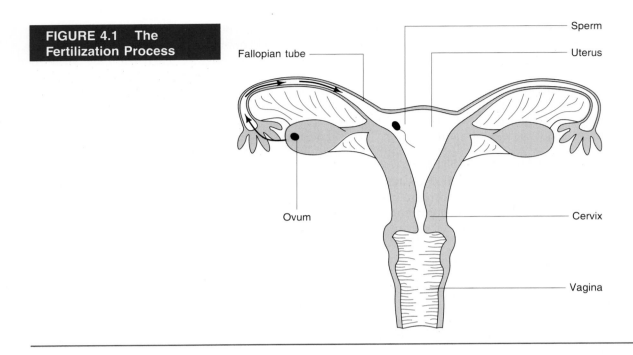

FIGURE 4.1 The Fertilization Process

different physical and behavioral characteristics. Androsperm are more streamlined, faster, less sensitive to acidity, and shorter-lived than gynosperm. Intercourse at the time of ovulation after the female uses a baking soda douche (which reduces the acidity of the uterus) increases the chances of conceiving a boy from about 53% to as much as 65% to 68%. Similarly, the chances of conceiving a girl increase from about 47% to 55% if intercourse precedes ovulation by 1 day, and if the acidity of the uterus has been increased through a vinegar and water douche.

Advanced technology has made it possible to increase the odds of having a boy or girl when using artificial human fertilization. Paul Dmowski at the Family Fertility Center at Grant Hospital in Chicago has developed a technique of sex preselection through sperm isolation, which was invented in the early 1970s by fertility specialist Ronald Ericsson. By placing sperm in a test tube over layers of a bovine blood protein, serum albumin, Ericsson discovered that whole legions of Y-bearing sperm (about 85%) will determinedly swim down through the serum to the bottom, where they may be collected. In turn, Dmowski discovered that X, or female-bearing sperm, will just as stubbornly swim up to the top of the solution. The sperm that are found there are at least 70% female-bearing sperm.

Sperm are then collected from the male and soaked, cleansed, and spun around in a centrifuge to concentrate them in a small pellet. They are then put into the chemical solution that would allow the Y sperm, for example, to gang up, which are then used to fertilize the egg. Dmowski has thus been able to change the odds for a boy to about 80 to 20, and for a girl to about 70 to 30.

GENETIC TRANSMISSION

The fertilized egg contains an individual's genetic endowment, which is represented by 46 elongated, threadlike bodies called **chromosomes.** In Greek, *chromo* means color and *soma* refers to body. These structures were so named because when a

FIGURE 4.2 Multiple Births

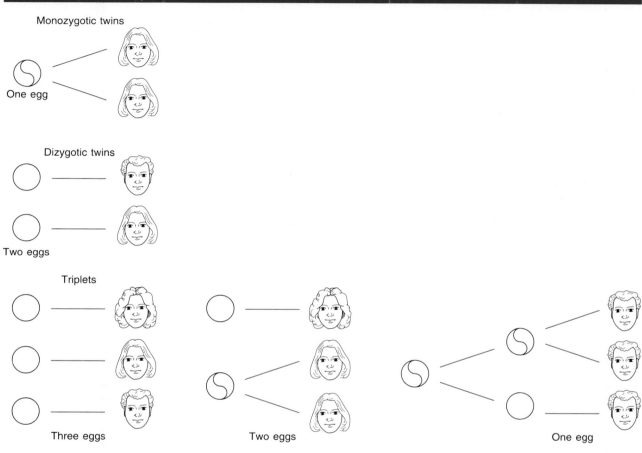

Monozygotic twins

One egg

Dizygotic twins

Two eggs

Triplets

Three eggs

Two eggs

One egg

cell is stained with certain drugs, the chromosomes take on a deep color.

A human being is a diploid organism, which means that chromosomes occur in pairs. This does not mean that they physically exist in pairs, for in appearance they seem to be randomly placed in the nucleus of the cell. Nonetheless, as can be seen in Figure 4.3, for each sperm chromosome there is a corresponding egg chromosome that is closely related functionally. The two chromosomes of each pair, one having come from the male and the other from the female, are called **homologous** because of their similar sizes and shapes.

AUTOSOMES

Of the 23 pairs of chromosomes in the nucleus of the cell, 22 are called **autosomes.** In the autosomes, each member of a pair perfectly complements the other member; that is, each member carries the same gene types in the same position, or **locus,** on the chromosome. In other words, the genetic material is organized in a specific order along the chromosome, and a given gene always occurs in the same place on the chromosome. For example, the eye-color genes on the bottom segment of the chromosome complement each other. One chromosome may favor blue eyes, the other brown;

FIGURE 4.3   Chromosomes Under a Microscope

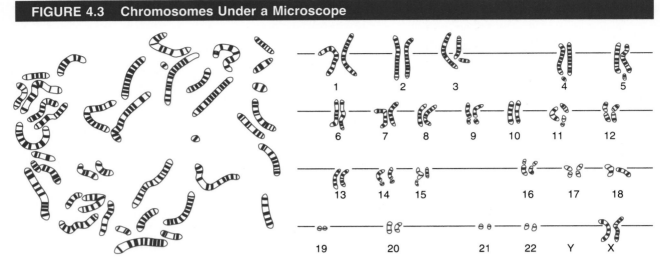

Chromosomes seen under a microscope have been cut from a photograph and arranged artificially so that members of each pair are together.

that is, eye-color instructions may differ, but the basic function of each—eye color—is the same. The vast majority of inherited traits are carried on the autosomes.

SEX CHROMOSOMES

The 23rd pair of chromosomes is responsible for gender determination; its chromosomes, the X and the Y, are appropriately referred to as the **sex chromosomes.** The genetic constitutions of the X and Y chromosome differ. The X is relatively large and contains many loci of known function; the Y chromosome is smaller than the X and contains no loci that have been identified by precise function (Scarr & Kidd, 1983).

Some characteristics depend on genes carried in the twenty-third pair of chromosomes and are called **sex-linked characteristics.** Hemophilia, color blindness, and some forms of baldness are examples of sex-linked characteristics. These chromosomal abnormalities appear primarily in males. Why is this so?

Hemophilia, for example, is caused by a recessive gene that appears only in the X chromosome. The female has two X genes, and so is protected from having this disorder by the fact that she has a normal gene on the homologous chromosome. She must have two recessive genes for that trait to appear. The male has only one X chromosome, and instead of a second X chromosome, has a Y. The loci on the X chromosome are present only in single copy in males and consequently show a different pattern of inheritance. If the male receives the gene for hemophilia X', he has no corresponding gene on the other X chromosome because he has a Y—thus the disorder appears in the male. The characteristics coded by genes on the X chromosome do not have a second X chromosome to override them and are passed from mother to son (see Figure 4.4).

GENES

Chromosomes serve as the carriers of the actual units of genetic transmission, **genes.** Genes con-

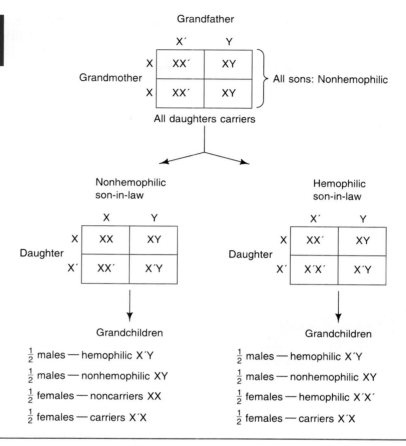

FIGURE 4.4 Sex-linked Transmission of Hemophilia

Source: From *Developmental Psychology* by M. Fitzgerald. © 1982 by The Dorsey Press. Reprinted by permission of Brooks/Cole Publishing Company, Pacific Grove, CA 93950.

tain the "instructions" that govern biological development. Each chromosome consists of roughly 20,000 genes. It is important to note that a gene is not defined by any externally observable, physical quality but rather by its effect on development. Through careful observation, scientists have determined that the chemical instructions contained in particular portions of a chromosome have specific and distinct developmental effects. A gene, then, is simply a particular segment of the chromosome made up of specific chemical instructions.

Genes direct the process by which some cells of the body grow into skin and others into nerves or muscles; they also control the process by which cells become grouped into organs such as the heart, liver, or stomach. They are responsible for such aspects of development as the color of eyes and the length of bones. Each gene is believed to be responsible for some particular phase of development by itself, but more often in combination with other genes (Schneider & Tarshis, 1975). Most traits are polygenic, which means that most traits do not usually result from a single gene pair, but from a combination of many genes that interact in a number of ways.

Just as each chromosome is paired, so is each gene. When the paired genes are identical, for example, when both code for brown eyes, the individual is **homozygous** for that trait. When paired genes have contrasting traits—one *gene* for blue eyes and one *gene* for brown eyes—the individual is **heterozygous** for that trait. The genes that have contrasting effects on an homologuous chromosome are called **alleles.** With regard to height, for instance, T (representing the gene for tall) is an allele of t (representing the gene for short).

When genes have a contrasting effect on the homologous chromosome, there are several possible outcomes. One is that the *dominant gene* will be expressed. Dominance, a principle observed by Gregor Mendel, means that one gene may prevent the expression of another gene on an allele. It does not mean that it is a superior trait, or even the one that will always be transmitted. It refers to the relationship between alleles. To illustrate, a child re-

ceives one gene for curly hair and one gene for straight hair. Curly hair is dominant and straight hair is recessive (nondominant). When the dominant allele is placed in a combination with a recessive allele, the dominant allele has a greater impact in determining what a person will inherit. This child will have curly hair. The influence of a *recessive gene* cannot be observed unless the person is homozygous for that trait, that is, has two recessive genes paired at the same locus on the chromosome. Thanks to Mendel, we can explain how this works (see Figure 4.5).

Alleles form a genetic combination called a **genotype.** A person's genotype refers to the actual genetic composition of the organism, whether it is directly observable or not. **Phenotype** refers to the organism's observable traits. For example, three of

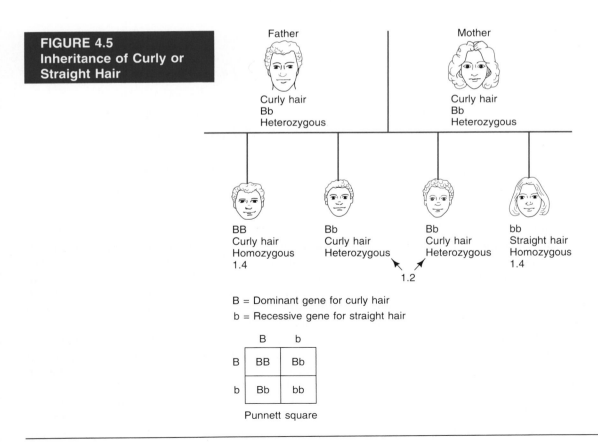

**FIGURE 4.5
Inheritance of Curly or
Straight Hair**

Father

Curly hair
Bb
Heterozygous

Mother

Curly hair
Bb
Heterozygous

BB
Curly hair
Homozygous
1.4

Bb
Curly hair
Heterozygous

1.2

Bb
Curly hair
Heterozygous

bb
Straight hair
Homozygous
1.4

B = Dominant gene for curly hair
b = Recessive gene for straight hair

	B	b
B	BB	Bb
b	Bb	bb

Punnett square

STUDYING CHILDREN

GENOTYPES AND PHENOTYPES

How can we figure out what the offspring of two parents will look like? By knowing the parents' genotype we can figure out the phenotypic ratio of their offspring. To illustrate, let's say that T is the dominant gene for tallness and t is the recessive gene for shortness. If the father is homozygous for tallness, his genotype is TT. If the mother is heterozygous for that trait, her genotype is Tt. By using the Punnett square, we can figure out the probabilities of what their offspring's phenotype will be.

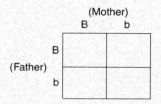

Figure out the phenotypic ratio for the offspring of a father and mother who are heterozygous for brown eyes (Bb). B is dominant for brown eyes, and b is recessive for blue eyes (see Figure 4.5).

the four children in the previous example have curly hair (phenotype); however, genetic compositions (genotype) are different. The recessive trait (b) recedes or is masked in the heterozygote. Try our "Studying Children" experiment.

DEOXYRIBONUCLEIC ACID (DNA)

Each gene is actually a single but unique molecule of **deoxyribonucleic acid (DNA)**. Two British scientists, Watson and Crick (1953), astounded the world by describing the functions and structure of the DNA molecule.

The DNA that forms the genes consists of two long strands of alternating phosphates and sugars held together by cross-links of four different kinds of compounds that pair together. Thus, DNA resembles a spiral staircase or twisted rope ladder. The arrangement of these four compounds forms the genetic code that provides the pattern for the development of the fertilized egg.

One of DNA's unique properties is that it can reproduce, or copy, itself. As shown in Figure 4.6, during cell division, the DNA molecule "unzips" along the weak-paired hydrogen bonds. Then, each half duplicates itself by attracting new material from the cell to synthesize a second chain and form a new DNA molecule.

When the DNA molecule unzips, it creates a second type of nucleic acid, **ribonucleic acid (RNA)**. Although DNA contains the complete blueprint of the living organism, it cannot move out of the nucleus of the cell. But RNA, which acts as a messenger to carry out the instructions of the DNA, can. DNA directs the functions of RNA.

The remarkable duplicating ability of DNA makes it possible for the genetic code of each of the parents to be passed on to their offspring, thus creating a unique individual. The transmission of this genetic code from one cell to the next in the developing organism allows it to develop from a *single cell* into the roughly *60 trillion* cells that comprise the human body.

PRINCIPLES OF CELL DIVISION: MITOSIS AND MEIOSIS

Sometime between 24 and 60 hours after conception, the first cell begins to divide. Gradually, as the process continues, the resulting cells begin to assume special functions. Human beings and other higher organisms have two kinds of cells: **somatic cells** and sex cells, also called *germ cells* or **gametes.** Somatic cells comprise the various organs and body systems (digestive, respiratory) and carry on life-giving processes: They carry the oxygen, rebuild the tissue, feed cells, and so on. The gametes carry on the equally vital task of reproduction and transmission of human characteristics.

The somatic cells divide to produce new cells via a process known as *mitosis*. In mitotic cell division, an identical copy of the original zygote is reproduced. After the process is complete, the resulting daughter cells have the same material and genetic potential as the parent cell. Mitosis occurs in a series of stages such as those seen in Figure 4.7.

FIGURE 4.6   DNA Replication

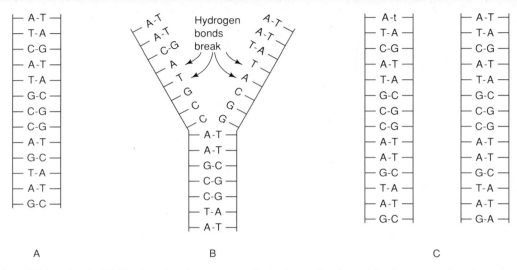

A   B   C

(A) Portion of one DNA molecule. (B) The two strands separate at the hydrogen bonds, and free bases attach to the appropriate base in the original strand. (C) Two new DNA molecules, each identical to the original molecule.

Source: From *Understanding Inherited Disorders* (p. 19) by L. F. Whaley, 1974, St. Louis: Mosby.

The second type of cells, the germ cells, divide in number as do the somatic cells during mitosis, but they divide in chromosome content via meiosis, a process of chromosome division unique to germ cells. *Meiosis* means to make smaller, that is, the developing sperm or ovum relinquishes its duplicate set of chromosomes so that the mature gamete has 23 pairs of chromosomes. Figure 4.8 summarizes the steps in meiotic cell division.

PRENATAL PERIODS OF DEVELOPMENT

The 9 months during which the fertilized cell develops from a microscopic entity to a highly developed 7- to 8-pound baby is one of the most dynamic of the human developmental periods. Prenatal life has been divided into three phases. The first phase of development, germinal, lasts from fertilization until the time the zygote is firmly implanted in the wall of the uterus, a process that takes between 10 and 14 days. This phase of development is followed by the embryonic period, which begins in the second week in utero and lasts until the eighth week. The fetal period lasts from the eighth week until delivery.

GERMINAL

The process of cell division begins a few hours after fertilization of the ovum, and produces two cells. In some cases, the first division of the zygote produces two identical cells, which then separate and develop into two individuals (monozygotic twins). The zygote wanders through a fallopian tube and the uterus for up to 8 days. As it free-floats, its cells divide until it becomes a 200- to-300-cell mass called a **blastocyst,** a hollow ball of cells. During the formation of the blastocyst, the cells begin the process of differentiation; they separate into groups according to their future function. The blastocyst influences a woman's body by secreting

FIGURE 4.7 Mitosis

1. A somatic cell with chromosomes exists.

2. Each of the 46 chromosomes duplicates itself by splitting along its length, and forming two new chromosomes, called chromotids.

3. Chromotid pairs are pulled to opposite sides of the cell by tiny fibers.

4. The cell starts pinching apart into two cells near the midline.

5. The nuclear membrane draws around and encloses the two daughter cells. Two cells now exist where one existed before. Each daughter cell has identical sets of genetic material.

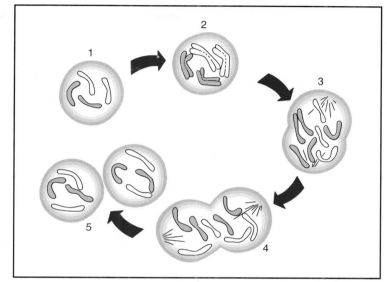

FIGURE 4.8 Meiosis

1. Sex cells originate from a cell with 46 chromosomes (23 pairs) (only two single chromosomes are shown here).

2. Each chromosome duplicates itself.

3. The duplicate halves of the chromosomes (chromotids) split. Members of the chromotid pairs are pulled to opposite sides of the cell by tiny fibers.

4. The cell begins to divide, resulting in two cells with the same number of chromosomes as the original cell.

5. Each of these cells divides.

6. There are now four cells, each with half as many chromosomes (23) as the original cell.

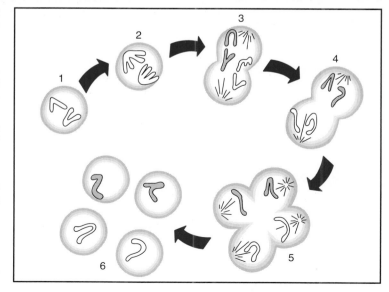

a hormone that inhibits menstruation, allowing the blastocyst to continue to grow.

As the blastocyst enters into the uterine cavity, fluid seeps in between the cells, causing them to separate into two parts. As can be seen in Figure 4.9, a small cavity is formed within the mass of cells, which results in an outer and inner cluster of cells. The outer layer, called the trophoblast (trophe, from the Greek, means ''to nourish''), will ultimately develop accessory tissues that will form the placenta and protective membranes. The inner cluster of cells, the embryonic disk, will become the embryo.

At about the fourth day after conception, the two cell layers of the blastocyst separate further to form a cavity. **Implantation,** the major developmental task of this period, can now begin (see Figure 4.10). The colony of cells does not simply attach itself to the uterine wall, but actually digs into it. Small, rootlike extensions have begun to grow outside the trophoblast, and it is by means of these tendrils that the ovum will rupture the small blood vessels of the uterine wall in order to obtain nourishment. At the time of implantation, the zygote is about the size of a pinhead and has several dozen cells. Implantation enables the blastocyst to absorb nutrients from the blood vessels of the **endometrium,** which is the inner, mucous membrane of the uterus, for its subsequent growth and development.

The process of implantation is difficult; half or more of the blastocysts never become implanted (Roberts & Lowe, 1975), usually because they are abnormal in some way. The zygote that fails to implant is lost in the normal menstrual cycle. If implantation is successful, growth continues, with the trophoblast forming protective membranes.

The yolk sac produces blood cells until the embryo's liver, spleen, and bone marrow develop enough to do that job, whereupon the yolk sac partly develops into the digestive tract, urinary system, and lungs. The rest of the yolk sac disappears by the second month of pregnancy. Another membrane forms the umbilical cord and the blood vessels in the placenta. The outer layers of the blastocyst give rise to two fetal membranes: the **chorion,** the lining of the placenta, and the **amnion,** which is a flexible sac filled with a watery medium, the amniotic fluid. Acting as a buffer, the amniotic fluid protects the embryo from shocks experienced by the mother and helps provide a constant temperature for the embryo (see Figure 4.11).

The **placenta** is a truly amazing organ that makes it possible for the embryo (and later, the fetus) to receive nutrients and oxygen from the mother. It is important to note that the mother and child do not actually share the same blood system and that the exchange of nutritive and waste materials occurs across cell membranes in the placenta. These semipermeable membranes keep bloodstreams separate and selectively allow certain substances such as oxygen, salts, drugs, vitamins, some nutrients (protein and sugar), and other substances of small molecular size to pass through to nourish the embryo. Blood cells are too large to pass through these membranes, so there is no direct link between the circulatory system of the mother and that of the embryo. Bodies carrying

FIGURE 4.9   Blastocyst Stage

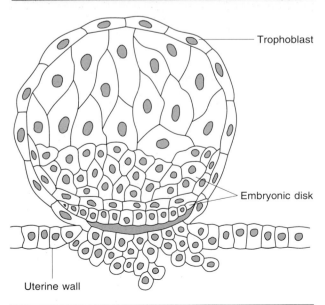

Trophoblast

Embryonic disk

Uterine wall

FIGURE 4.10   Implantation

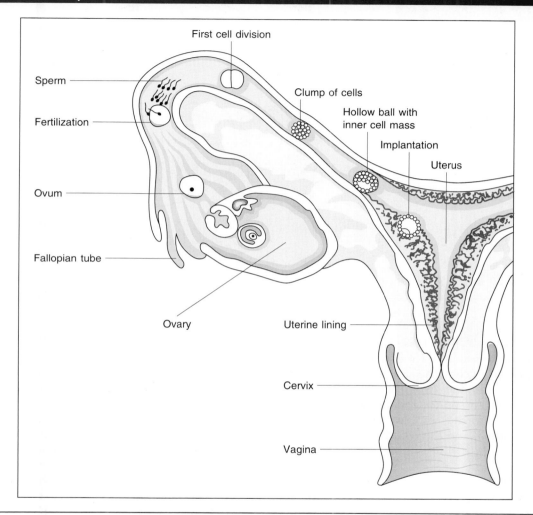

Source: Adapted figure from "Prenatal Life and the Pregnant Woman" by David W. Smith and Morton A. Stenchever in *The Biological Ages of Man: From Conception Through Old Age*, Second Edition, by David W. Smith, Edwin L Bierman, and Nancy M. Robinson, copyright © 1978 by Saunders College Publishing, reprinted by permission of the publisher.

immunity also pass through the membranes from the mother to the fetus, thus giving the child some protection for several months after birth from diseases to which the mother is immune. The placenta is connected to the embryo by the **umbilical cord.**

The umbilical cord is roughly three quarters of an inch wide and between 10 and 20 inches long. This vital connection between the embryo and its placenta has two arteries and one vein that carry as much as 300 quarts of blood per day flowing at the rate of about 4 miles per hour. Since the cord is

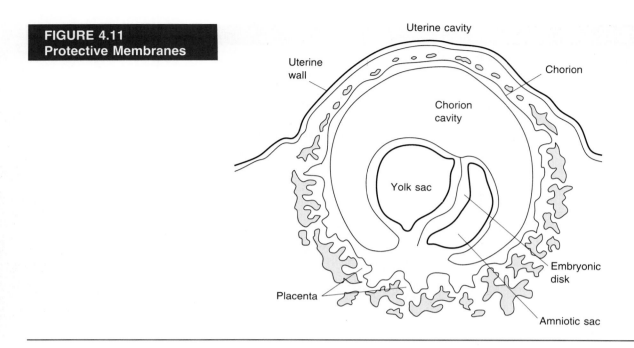

**FIGURE 4.11
Protective Membranes**

under this kind of pressure, it will not knot or tangle around the embryo (or fetus) no matter how many flip-flops occur. The one fetal vein carries nourishment, and the two fetal arteries remove waste products. As soon as the infant takes its first breath after birth, the complex umbilical circulation system stops, and the blood is oxygenated by the lungs.

EMBRYONIC

After the zygote successfully attaches itself to the uterine wall, development enters the embryonic period. The growing organism is no longer called a blastocyst, but an embryo. The prominent task of this period is differentiation and development of organs. By the end of this period, differentiation has been completed, but organ development has not. Cells become so rapidly differentiated that the organism's features have become distinctly human. Differentiation of body structures is now 95% complete. The tiny being has the rudimentary beginnings of arms, legs, fingers, toes, a heart that beats, a brain, a liver that secretes bile, lungs, and

all the other major organs—all of this before many mothers even know they are pregnant! The organism, however, could not survive outside the womb because it still lacks the ability to breathe.

Some 16 days after fertilization, the embryo develops into three distinct germ layers from which all tissues and organs of the body develop. The *ectoderm*, or outer layer, will become the outer layer of skin, hair, nails, skin glands, teeth, brain and spinal cord, and sensory cells. The *mesoderm* will become the inner layer of skin, skeleton, muscles, and circulatory and excretory systems. From the *endoderm*, or inner layer, the lining of the entire digestive tract, thymus, Eustachian tubes, pancreas, thyroid, trachea, bronchia, lungs, and liver will emerge. The process of cell-layer differentiation is completed by the third week.

By 18 days, the embryo has already taken some shape. By the third week, a primitive heart has developed and has begun to beat. (The heart is one of the larger organs of the body.) By the end of the fourth week, the embryo is 0.6 cm (3/16 in). As can be seen in Figure 4.12, the embryo does not look

FIGURE 4.12 Embryo at 1 Month

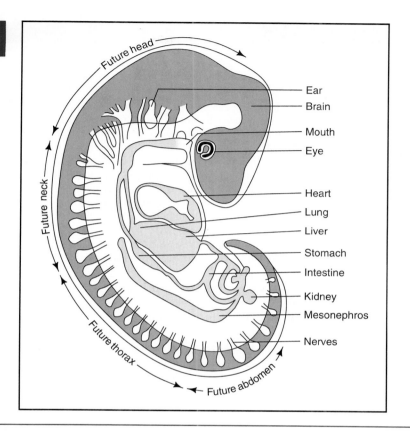

Future head

Ear
Brain
Mouth
Eye
Heart
Lung
Liver
Stomach
Intestine
Kidney
Mesonephros
Nerves

Future neck

Future thorax

Future abdomen

Source: After *Biography of the Unborn* by M. S. Gilbert, 1938, Baltimore: Williams and Wilkins. Reprinted by permission.

human. However, the head region becomes more clearly differentiated and the tail regresses to be enveloped, leaving a trace of bones at the base of the spine. The embryo begins to give more promise of the infant that will emerge at birth. A system for digesting food has begun to form and the first series of kidneylike structures emerge.

At the end of 2 months, the embryo is approximately 3 cm (1¼ in) and weighs 1g (1/30 oz). Mouth, eyes, and ears have begun to take on a fairly well-defined form and have assumed their correct position. Hands and feet with stubby fingers and toes become distinct. Development of muscle and cartilage also begins. Intestines, liver, pancreas, lungs, and kidneys take on definite shape and assume some degree of function. Up to

this point the embryo's skeleton has been formed of flexible cartilage. Sometime during the eighth or ninth week, bone cells begin to replace the cartilage cells, a process called **ossification.** In this period there is an extremely rapid development of the nervous system, which makes it particularly vulnerable to injury. Mechanical or chemical interference with development is more likely to cause permanent nervous system damage (Moore, 1983).

FETAL

The period of the fetus is marked by continued elaboration and growth of the basic systems and ossification. Growth proceeds in two directions: *cephalo-caudal* (head to tail) and *proximal-distal*

TABLE 4.1   Milestones in Fetal Development

END OF 3RD MONTH	7.5 cm (3 in); 28 g (1 oz). Head is one third of body size. First external sign of gender differentiation becomes apparent: the penis and scrotum in the male and the beginning of the labia in the female. Small buds for teeth form. Nose bridge develops. Ossification continues. Able to move spontaneously.
END OF 4TH MONTH	18 cm (6½–7 in); 113 g (4 oz). At the beginning of the 4th month, fetus weighed 1 oz and was roughly 3½ inches tall; no other month shows a comparable growth rate. Physician can detect heartbeat (120 to 160 beats per minute). Although eyes fused shut, blinking occurs. Hands become capable of gripping.
END OF 5TH MONTH	25–30 cm (10–12 in); 227–454 g (½–1 lb). Fetus increases the amount of force of its movement; mother will be able to feel an elbow, foot, or head. Sleep–wake cycle organizes, as do reflexes for swallowing and hiccupping. Eyelashes and eyebrows appear. Soft hair—lanugo—grows over body. Fetus undergoes process of skin-cell replacement. Skin cells mix with fatty substance from oil glands to form white, cheesy coating called vernix, which helps prevent the skin from hardening in the mineral-laden amniotic fluid.
END OF 6TH MONTH	25–35 cm (10–14 in); 567–681 g (1¼–1½ lb). Ossification is still taking place. Head becomes less disproportionate to rest of the body. Eyelids separate. Skin is wrinkled and pink.
END OF 7TH MONTH	325–425 cm (13–17 in); 1135–1362 g (2½–3 lb). Age of viability; when fetus is born, has reasonable chance to survive, although special care is required. Premature infants born at this stage still have poorly developed sleep–wake cycles, and breathing is irregular.
END OF 8TH MONTH	41–45 cm (16½–18 in); 2043–2270 g (4½–5 lb). Skin is less wrinkled. Bones of head are soft. Subcutaneous fat is deposited. Chances of survival are 70%.
END OF 9TH MONTH	50 cm (20 in); 3178–3405 g (7–7½ lb). Additional subcutaneous fat accumulates. Lanugo hair is shed. Antibodies are received from mother's blood. Movement is quite restricted. Fetus begins to turn to a head-down position in preparation for birth.

(spine to extremities). At birth the head will make up 22% of the infant's height, a proportion that changes dramatically with age. The fetus increases in size and maturation so that it begins to show some independent functioning. Organs, limbs, and muscles become functional. Even with eyes sealed shut, the fetus can frown and squint. It is able to open and close its mouth and by doing so swallow a few small gulps of amniotic fluid. Table 4.1 summarizes the development of the fetus.

HEREDITARY INFLUENCES ON PRENATAL DEVELOPMENT

Each of us carries some defective genes. Fortunately, in most situations, two parents do not carry the same faulty genes. Consequently, the healthy gene is dominant over the faulty gene. Yet, abnormalities do occur, and they cause great concern.

DOWN SYNDROME

The child with **Down syndrome** has distinctive facial features: large, protruding tongue, broad skull, and slanting eyes. After birth, the rate of growth continues to be slow, with shortness of stature common. These infants generally show poor balance. Sexual maturity is rarely attained. Individuals with this disorder usually have 47 chromosomes instead of 46. The extra chromosome is responsible for the syndrome. All the chromosomes of a Down syndrome child are in pairs except the 21st pair—represented in triplicate and known as Trisomy 21. Having an extra chromosome 21 affects many aspects of development, the most salient of which is a decreased rate of intellectual development. Physical abnormalities, such as heart and intestinal defects, cause an increased mortality rate (20% to 30%) during the first few years of life, and about 1% of children with Down syndrome develop leukemia.

Children with Down syndrome often exhibit physical characteristics such as eyelid folds, round, flattened heads, short necks, small noses, and protruding tongues.

Down syndrome caused by mosaicism accounts for less than 5% of the cases. The complement of the chromosome is normal when the egg is fertilized. During the second or subsequent cell division, an error produces one cell with 47 chromosomes (3 chromosomes on the 21st chromosome) and one cell with 45 chromosomes (1 chromosome on the 21st chromosome). The cell with 45 chromosomes dies, and the cell with 47 chromosomes continues to reproduce itself as do the remaining normal cells with 46 chromosomes. The result is an individual whose body contains a mixture of normal and abnormal cells. Physical signs and mental retardation are less severe in persons with mosaicism.

TURNER'S SYNDROME

In **Turner's syndrome,** the sperm cell fails to produce sex chromosomes, and the resulting zygote becomes a female who has one instead of two X chromosomes, giving a total of 45 chromosomes. Turner's syndrome results in higher rates (about 20%) of mild retardation and is strongly associated with substantial space-form perceptual deficiencies. Many are not diagnosed until adolescence, when sex development fails to occur and short stature is noted. Others are diagnosed at birth when certain physical abnormalities, such as webbing of the neck, are noted. Although women are sterile because they lack functional ovaries, development of secondary sex characteristics is possible with the administration of female hormones.

KLEINFELTER'S SYNDROME

Kleinfelter's syndrome is another chromosome abnormality that occurs when a normal ovum is fertilized by a sperm that has both an X and a Y chromosome instead of having only an X or Y. This produces a zygote with an extra X chromosome (XXY). Their appearance is unequivocally male. There are approximately two cases per 1,000 males with a 47-XXY chromosome. Often having small testes and prostates, these men also have diminished body and facial hair. Some breast development may also show at puberty, but the men are frequently infertile. Mental retardation occurs in 25% to 50% of the cases, but it is usually mild with no outstanding deficits.

Rare cases of individuals with several other kinds of sex chromosomes have been found including XXX, XXXX, XXXY. Little is known about these disorders; however, the XYY pattern found in males has been associated with a tendency to be muscular and taller than average, but otherwise display no specific physical anomalies.

PHENYLKETONURIA (PKU)

Phenylketonuria (PKU) is a well-known genetic cause of mental retardation, affecting 1 in 10,000 to 20,000 live births (Benson & Fensom, 1985). The disorder is the consequence of mutations in the gene that codes for the enzyme phenylalanine hydroxylase (DiLella, Marvit, Lidsky, Guttler, & Woo, 1986). Children with PKU fail to produce a liver enzyme that converts phenylalanine, an amino acid, into tryosine, another amino acid. In the absence of this enzyme, excess phenylalanine from protein in the diet is not utilized and accumulates in the body. Excess phenylalanine produces toxic by-products that are detrimental to the development and growth of the central nervous system. High concentrations of phenylalanine and other chemical by-products result in reduced brain development and irreversible mental retardation.

Screening newborns for PKU is inexpensive and is now widespread in the United States; such screening has significantly reduced this kind of retardation. Formerly, PKU was responsible for about 1% of the population of institutionalized mentally retarded individuals, but now early detection and dietary intervention has virtually eliminated PKU as a cause of severe retardation (Plomin, 1990). Even with early treatment, however, it is possible that PKU may cause subtle, specific cognitive deficits (Welsh, Pennington, Ozonoff, Rouse, & McCabe, 1990). The main effects on cognition in PKU are caused specifically by dopamine depletion, which is hypothesized to impair prefrontal functioning and result in deficits in executive function. *Executive function* is defined as the ability to maintain an appropriate problem-solving set for attainment of a future goal. Appropriate set maintenance allows for strategic planning, impulse control, organized search, and flexibility of thought and action. Patients with conditions associated with dopamine deficiency (e.g., Parkinson's disease, attention deficit disorder) also display impairment in executive functioning skills (Weinberger, Berman, & Chase, 1987).

The treatment for PKU is simple: almost completely eliminating the intake of phenylalanine. Milk, for example, has high levels of phenylala-nine; thus, its intake must be curtailed. The diet prescribed by a physician must be appropriate for the child and thus needs to be monitored carefully in the first few years of life. Too high a level of phenylalanine in the system and mental retardation occurs; too low a level and lethargy and poor physical growth may result. In general, studies of treated PKU children indicate that early dietary restrictions alter the biochemical abnormality and result in the attainment of at least average intellectual abilities (Schneider & Tarshis, 1975). Dietary restrictions generally continue only through the early school years. After the brain is sufficiently developed, excess phenylalanine will not hurt it (Plomin, 1990).

DIAGNOSING DEVELOPMENTAL DEFECTS

Many genetic problems can be avoided with genetic counseling and testing. Couples, particularly those who already have a child with a condition that might be genetic, or who have relatives who have genetic problems, or who have had several miscarriages, should be aware of the importance of consulting a genetic specialist. Once he knows the couple's personal and family histories, the specialist may then accurately diagnose the risk of conceiving an affected child. The genetic counselor's ultimate responsibility is to help prospective parents digest the information about genetic disorders and help them to make the right decisions for themselves.

For a woman who is already expecting a child, an ultrasound test may be performed to detect placental difficulty, gross structural anomalies such as missing or deformed limbs, implantation in the fallopian tube instead of the uterus, and multiple fetuses. High-frequency sound waves directed toward the fetus bounce off its contours, and a transducer transforms them into a fairly detailed picture. Locating the position of the fetus by means of ultrasound enables the doctor to perform a diagnostic test.

Over 50 biochemical, inherited disorders and close to 300 chromosomal disorders can be detected through **amniocentesis,** a technique of withdrawing some of the amniotic fluid that bathes the developing fetus to diagnose disorders. The amniotic fluid is obtained by inserting a hollow needle through the mother's abdominal wall and into the

The genetic counselor's ultimate responsibility is to help prospective parents digest the information about genetic disorders and help them make the right decision about having children.

FIGURE 4.13   Amniocentesis

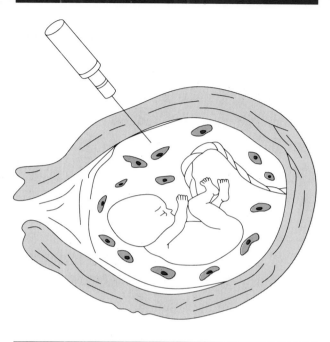

amniotic sac (see Figure 4.13). Amniocentesis usually is performed between the 14th to 16th week of gestation (the volume of amniotic fluid is insufficient before this time), and results are not available for 3 to 4 weeks.

Chorionic villus sampling can be performed early, in weeks 8 to 12, and is an important alternative to amniocentesis. Cells can be suctioned from the developing placenta via a small tube passed through the vagina and cervix. These cells then can be analyzed to determine the fetus's genetic makeup.

ENVIRONMENTAL INFLUENCES ON PRENATAL DEVELOPMENT

The idea that some specific experience that occurs at one time during the life span will affect the development of an organism more than it would at other times has been around for a long time. This concept led to a branch of study called teratology—a **teratogen** is anything that causes birth defects. There are hundreds of known teratogens that affect embryonic/fetal development during some prenatal periods to produce an irrevocable result. While all 9 months of prenatal development may be critical periods in some respect, much of the damage produced by various teratogens have their maximum impact during the germinal and embryonic periods. During the germinal period, teratogens may affect the number and differentiation of cells. During the embryonic period, the formation of body parts and organs is taking place (organogenesis). Because these body parts and organs are undergoing a rapid state of development, they are particularly vulnerable to insult. Critical periods in the development of primary organs during the prenatal period of development are shown in Figure 4.14.

FIGURE 4.14 Critical Periods in the Prenatal Development of the Body Organs

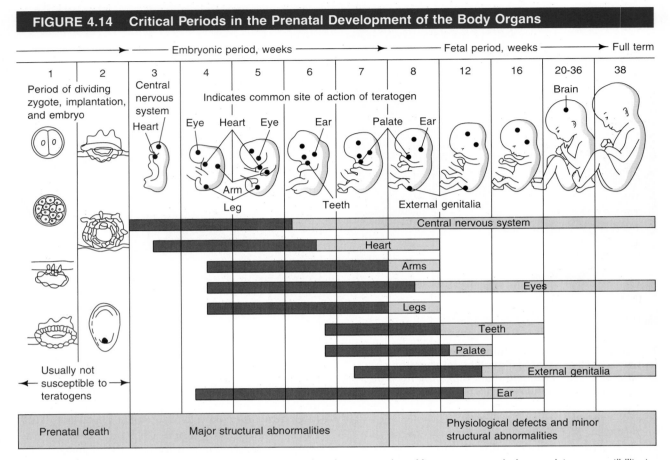

Sensitivity to teratogens reaches its peak at roughly 4 weeks after conception. After organogenesis is complete, susceptibility to anatomical defects diminishes (light color).

Source: Figure from *Before We Are Born: Basic Embryology and Birth Defects* by Keith L. Moore, copyright © 1983 by Saunders College Publishing, reprinted by permission of the publisher.

A terrible illustration of the damage that can occur during the rapid development of certain body parts and organs occurred in the 1960s, when a drug called thalidomide was given to pregnant women, notably in Germany, to relieve morning sickness. If the drug was taken during the 34th to 38th day after conception, a time when ears develop, the child was born without ears. If the drug was taken during the 38th to 46th day after conception, a time when the arms are forming, the child was born without arms or with deformed arms. If the drug was taken during the 40th to 46th day after conception, when the legs are forming, the child was born with deformed legs or no legs at all. If taken after the 50th day, the child was normal. Over 10,000 babies (5,000 of whom would survive until adulthood) were born before thalidomide was discovered as being the teratogen responsible for causing these abnormalities.

While the majority of infants develop into healthy infants, others are born with serious defects that could in many cases have been prevented with proper prenatal care. As you will see, the intrauterine environment is a delicate one.

DISEASES OF THE MOTHER

Viral diseases such as German measles (rubella), mumps, herpes, and influenza can affect the fetus during early stages of pregnancy. Rubella is one of the best-known examples of viral disease. Depending on when the virus enters the mother's body, rubella infants may be born deaf or blind, have heart defects, central nervous system damage, or mild retardation. With rubella, the chances of deformity are 70% in the first trimester, 50% in the second trimester, and drops to zero percent in the last trimester. Fortunately, a vaccination for rubella, given before pregnancy, prevents the disease.

PEDIATRIC ACQUIRED IMMUNODEFICIENCY SYNDROME (AIDS)

Recently the acquisition of human immunodeficiency virus (HIV), the virus associated with the pathogenesis of **acquired immunodeficiency syndrome (AIDS),** among infants has received considerable attention. The first cases of pediatric AIDS were seen in the United States as early as 1979, although an official case definition to include criteria for diagnosing children was not developed by the Centers for Disease Control (CDC) until seven years later. The CDC reported a total of 1230 cases of pediatric AIDS (diagnosed between birth and 12 years of age).

Pediatric cases constitute less than 2% of the total reported AIDS cases in the United States, however 46% of the known pediatric AIDS cases have been reported in the last year (Rich, 1989). The National Academy of Sciences' report, *Confronting AIDS* (1986) projected an almost 10-fold increase in the number of pediatric cases from 1986 to 1991, with 3,000 cumulative cases of pediatric AIDS expected by the end of 1991. An estimated 10,000 additional children will be HIV infected, but not diagnosed with AIDS, by the end of 1991.

Minority children are disproportionally affected, with African Americans constituting 53% of the pediatric cases of AIDS, and Hispanics, 23%. Although more than half the cases have been re-

ported from only three states (New York, New Jersey, and Florida), the epidemic among children is spreading geographically (Arenson & Finnegan, 1989).

Nineteen percent of the CDC-reported cases of pediatric AIDS have resulted from transfusions with HIV-contaminated blood and blood products. With screening of blood supply and heat treatment of blood products, however, this mode of infection is now virtually eliminated. Seventy-eight percent of the cases involve perinatal transmission from an infected mother to her child. This is based on the presence of HIV in cord blood in fetuses in early or mid-trimester abortions, and infected infants from Caesarean section deliveries.

A significant number of women, however, are infected through heterosexual contacts with HIV-positive sexual partners. In some cases, the child's father is the index case, and the mother is an asymptomatic carrier. The population of women infected in such a manner is steadily increasing. Whether infection can occur in addition by exposure to HIV known to be present in the blood and secretions in the birth canal in a vaginal delivery is a matter for speculation until more definitive data are available. At present, the data do not support routine Caesarean deliveries. In the majority of cases, the mother's infection can be linked to her own or her sexual partner's use of intravenous drugs.

One problem confounding the diagnosis of HIV infection in infants is the presence of maternal antibodies in the fetal circulation. If a mother is infected with HIV, then her HIV antibodies will usually cross the placenta and be detected in the umbilical cord blood at birth. These antibodies usually persist for several months in the infants' circulation, whether or not the child is infected. On occasion, they can be detected as late as 18 months of age. Therefore, in the absence of other supportive data (clinical signs and symptoms), a child cannot be considered definitely HIV-positive until after 15 or 18 months of age.

Some children infected perinatally, however, develop symptoms within the first 12 months of life, including recurrent bacterial infections, swollen lymph glands, failure to thrive, neurological impairment, and delayed development. Some HIV-infected infants exhibit distinct facial features, such as widespread eyes, small head circumference, and protruding forehead (Cole, 1991). The developmental progress for babies infected or at risk for AIDS is very chaotic, and they do not respond well to the medication used for detoxification; indeed, this symptom may be one of the first markers that the infant has AIDS (Cole, 1991). The infants show abnormal posturing, fluctuating tone, undulating, uncontrolled movement patterns, and very flat affect (unanimated facial expression). They do not present much positive feedback for their caregivers.

A frequently posed but as yet unanswered question is the risk that an infected woman has of giving birth to an HIV-infected child. The few limited studies reported to date show a wide range of figures. In one study of 92 pregnant intravenous drug-using women, 56% tested HIV positive and 35% of this group gave birth to an infected infant (Norwick, 1989). Certainly what is needed are more studies that define the risk of transplacental transmission more clearly and identify factors predictive of fetal infection.

Treatment of HIV infection in children with antiviral drugs is still in early trial stages. Management of the secondary infections resulting from the immune deficiency has been more successful, and early recognition and treatment of the symptoms may prolong life. However, with no cure or vaccine likely in the near future, the disease will be a major and growing public health problem in children for many years.

Parents' fearful responses to the placement of HIV-infected children in their child's school suggests lack of knowledge about modes of HIV transmission. The disease is transmitted through the exchange of body fluids, primarily blood/blood exchange, or through semen/blood exchange. Accordingly, transmission occurs mainly through anal intercourse (because of the thinness of rectal tissues, which frequently tear during intercourse), through blood transfusions involving infected blood, and through communal use of hypodermic syringes. In all the studies of households where infected children have lived with uninfected children and adults, there is no evidence of horizontal transmission of the virus (Lifson, 1988; Norwick, 1989).

The only means to prevent further spread of the virus to children is through education and counseling sexually active women of childbearing age and their partners. In particular, women who use or have used intravenous drugs, or have partners who use or have used intravenous drugs, wives of infected hemophiliacs, and women with multiple sexual partners living in regions of the country with a high incidence of HIV infection should be targeted.

MOTHERS' AGE

Women under the age of 18 and older than 35 have a higher probability of experiencing a high-risk pregnancy. The optimal age for childbirth appears to be 20 to 29. The most consistent findings for pregnant teens is that they are more likely to experience labor complications, have a higher prematurity rate, and bear babies with low birth weight. The fetal mortality rate is nearly 2½ times higher than that for babies of mothers in their early 20s. Their immature reproductive apparatus, lifestyle, and nutritional status, combined with inadequate prenatal care and psychological factors, are commonly mentioned as the risk causes.

As age increases, so does the risk of an infant's developing abnormalities, or the mother's having stillborns, miscarriages, and complications in pregnancy. For example, women over 40 have twice the fetal mortality of women between the ages of 20 and 35. The chances of having a Down syndrome child is highest in women over 40. The chances of having fraternal twins, which may be regarded as good by some and not desirable by others, increases with age. As women get older and their ovulation becomes more irregular, they may be more likely to produce no egg one month and two the next.

FATHERS' AGE

All the ova in women are formed before birth, and the final stages of meiotic cell division occurs at ovulation. You might expect higher-risk pregnancies to result from "old eggs." Since the male is not born with sperm already formed, but rather forms them daily, birth disorders cannot be attributed to old sperm. The frequency of chromosomal disorders, however, increases as the male reproductive system ages (Money & Ehrhardt, 1972). Thus, a real possibility exists that older men may produce a higher percentage of defective sperm.

Research has also shown that chromosomal disorders may also be due to fathers being exposed to certain drugs. It has been found, for example, that wives of men who worked as operating-room personnel and who were exposed to anesthetic gases had higher rates of spontaneous abortions (Kolata, 1978). Moreover, the babies born to these mothers and fathers were more likely to have congenital defects than the offspring of unexposed men. Recent findings have suggested that abnormalities of the sperm occur when the father is exposed to lead, marijuana, radiation, and pesticides (Fried & Watkinson, 1990).

Fathers' attitudes toward their wives' pregnancy have an indirect bearing on the developing fetus. How mothers take care of themselves and how they view the pregnancy may be related to how supportive the fathers are. Mothers' positive attitudes toward pregnancy and birth are fostered when fathers are active and concerned partners and coaches. Fathers' positive attitudes toward their wives' pregnancy and subsequent birth of their children may be related to their degree of involvement (taking educational classes, witnessing and participating in prepared childbirth, feeding and cuddling the newborn child). It is generally agreed that the earlier fathers get involved in pregnancy and delivery, the better for family development. Try the "Studying Children" experiment.

RADIATION

People are constantly exposed to low levels of radiation from television sets, microwave ovens, and X rays to name a few. The period of greatest danger to radiation exposure comes between the second and sixth week after conception. Exposure to radiation in utero is likely to cause malformation, retarded growth, and increase the risk of developing malignant tumors and leukemia. The potential

---

STUDYING CHILDREN

FATHERS' ROLE

How do young men today feel about their role as fathers? Ask several of your male classmates to tell you what they perceive their role to be during their wives' pregnancy, delivery, and child care. Do they plan to take classes? Do they plan to observe the delivery of the child? What kind of child care chores will they do? Are our "future fathers" more involved than fathers a decade ago?

---

dangers of radiation is not limited to the period of pregnancy. Radiation is a major cause of gene mutations in the sex cells of mature gametes. For this reason X rays, particularly of the lower abdomen and pelvis, should be avoided. The "safe" period for X rays appears to be during the first 2 weeks after a normal menstrual period.

IMMUNOLOGICAL EFFECTS

During the final weeks of pregnancy, the mother transfers to the fetus immunities to such diseases as polio, chicken pox, measles, hepatitis, and diphtheria. The antibodies for such diseases cross the placenta and immunize the child for several months after birth. Other antibodies can cause serious problems, however.

The most common problem is Rh disease. The Rh factor is a protein substance in the red blood cells of about 85% of the population. It is a genetically dominant blood trait so named for the rhesus monkey who is always positive for this trait.

When an Rh-positive father and an Rh-negative mother have a child who is Rh positive, the child's blood is incompatible with the mother's. If this is the woman's first pregnancy there is rarely a problem. However, subsequent children may be in danger. With the birth of the first child (or miscarriage), some of the fetus's blood may mingle with the mother's when the membranes of the placenta are ruptured. Because the fetus's blood is incompatible with the mother's, the mother's body starts producing antibodies to combat the foreign blood of the fetus. These antibodies continue to exist through subsequent pregnancies. If subsequent pregnancies produce another Rh-positive infant, the mother's antibodies attack the red corpuscles in the blood of the fetus, causing erythroblastosis fetales, or Rh disease. Possible outcomes of Rh incompatibility are fetal anemia, fluid retention in the fetus, brain damage, nutrition deficiencies, and death. Rh disease poses no threat to the mother.

Several years ago, Rh disease was treated by monitoring the antibody count in the developing fetus. If the count became dangerously high, and the infant was old enough to survive outside the womb, labor was induced. On delivery, the infant would be given a complete blood transfusion. If the infant was too young to survive, a fetal transfusion, which replenished the fetal red blood cells, was given directly to the fetus through the uterus every 10 to 14 days. Today, an anti-D globulin, Rhogam, is given to the mother within 72 hours after every delivery or miscarriage (or in the seventh month of pregnancy with the first child). Rhogam is usually effective in reducing the buildup of antibodies so that other children can then be carried by the mother with little risk of fetal erythroblastosis. Rhogam is Rh-negative blood that already has antibodies, which eventually dissipate and which prevent the formation of additional antibodies.

MOTHERS' DIET

Eating well during pregnancy makes good sense. After all, the growing fetus's food comes from the mother's blood stream via semipermeable membranes of the umbilical cord and placenta. Both the amount of food a pregnant woman eats and the vitamin balance are important. The fetus stores none of the necessary substances except iron. Proteins provide for the growth and maintenance of body tissue and are vital during pregnancy. A pregnant woman needs at least 100 grams of protein per day to promote the normal growth of the baby and maintain the mother's health as well. The most complete protein foods are meat, fish, eggs, and cheese. "Focus on Applications" discusses mothers' nutritional needs during pregnancy.

CAFFEINE

The consequences of caffeine consumption to the development of the immature organism are of particular interest, given the fact that caffeine can cross the placenta and reach the fetus. Research findings that directly link caffeine to teratogenic effects in humans is limited, but some evidence exists. An increased incidence of spontaneous abortions, stillbirths, and premature births has been associated with maternal consumption of more than 500 mg of caffeine per day, approximately eight cups of coffee (Weathersbee, Olsen, & Lodge, 1977). However, these findings have not been replicated with larger samples.

Other studies have found no relationship between low birth weight, gestation, or malformations and drinking four cups of coffee per day (Linn, Schoenbaum, Monson, Rosner, Stubblefield, & Ryan, 1982). However, the researchers did not consider other sources of caffeine, such as cola or tea, and they did not control for changes in behavior during pregnancy.

It should be noted that the half-life of caffeine triples during the third trimester of pregnancy (Aldridge, Bailey, & Neims, 1981). Consequently, the same amount of caffeine results in much higher blood levels during the last trimester. Some of the more common sources of caffeine, the general average content of caffeine for each of these sources, and their approximate ranges are noted in Table 4.2. Note that the content of caffeine listed in the table is based on 5 ounces of coffee, tea, or cocoa, 12 ounces of soft drink, and 1 ounce of chocolate.

ASPIRIN

Aspirin use during the first half of pregnancy has been associated with as much as a 10-point decrement in IQ of the offspring at 4 years of age (Streissguth, Treder, Barr, Shepard, Bleyer, Sampson, & Martin, 1987). Aspirin, but not acetaminophen, use during the first half of pregnancy was also associated with poorer balance and fine motor unsteadiness in the offspring of aspirin-using mothers (Streissguth, Martin, Martin, & Barr, 1981). Klebanoff and Berendes (1988), however, found no adverse effect of aspirin exposure on IQ.

Nutritional Needs During Pregnancy

Many problems, including premature birth, stillbirth, prolonged labor, and greater susceptibility to disease, can be caused by poor nutrition. Malnutrition may take its greatest toll during the first 3 months of pregnancy when the cells are rapidly increasing and differentiating into specific cells and brain cells are rapidly growing. In the last trimester, the fetus gains three fourths of its birth weight (Tanner, 1978).

Between 10 and 15 years ago, women were urged to restrict their weight gain to 10 or 15 pounds. Recent studies show that a weight gain of 24–30 pounds increases the infant's chance of survival (Brazelton, 1981). Nearly half of that weight gain will be the fetus, placenta, amniotic fluid; the rest is mainly the calorie bank that the mother will draw on for lactation and increased postpartum activity.

The pregnant woman has three basic and complementary dietary obligations. Her first duty is to consume about 150 extra calories a day in the first trimester; 300 extra calories a day in the second trimester; and 400 extra calories a day during the third trimester—approximately 80,000 additional food calories over the nine-month period. Second, the future mother needs to obtain sufficient amounts of selected nutrients needed for fetal development. Her third obligation is to meet the body's increased need for iron, which may have to be met by an iron supplement. The table listed below provides a nutrition guide for pregnant women.

Nutritional Needs During Pregnancy and Breastfeeding	Daily Amount	Protein for tissue, growth	Calcium and Phosphorus for bones and teeth	Vitamin C	Vitamin D	Iron for blood, cells*	Vitamin A for growth, vision	B Vitamins (thiamin, riboflavin, niacin)	Iodine	Energy
Foods										
Milk (fortified), cheese, yogurt	4–6 cups	40%	100%	10%	100%	—	24%	10%		640
Meat, fish, poultry, liver once a week	4 oz	40%	—	—	—	10%	—	50%		420
Eggs	3–4 week	10%	—	—	—	—	16%	—		80
Vegetables:										
dark, leafy green,	1 cup									
deep-yellow, other	2 cups	10%	10%	100%	—	—	200%	10%		100
Potato with skin	1 medium	5%	—	40%	—	—	—	13%		75
Citrus or tomato	2									
Other fruit	2	5%	10%	100%	—	—	16%	1.6%		320
Grains, cereals, legumes	4–5 servings	10%	10%	—	—	30%	—	21%		540
Fats, oils	2 tbsp	—	—	—	—	—	16%	—		200
Salt, iodized		—	—	—	—	—	—	—	100%	—
Liquids in addition to a quart of milk	6–8 cups for energy									
Custards, puddings		10%	14%	—	—	—	9%	2%		200
										2,375/ 2,500

Folacin: increased need for folacin (for cell growth and protein synthesis) is 400 micrograms.

Source: From *Eat Better, Live Better.* Copyright © 1982 The Reader's Digest Association, Inc. Reprinted by permission.
*30–60 mg supplement is recommended

TABLE 4.2 Common Sources of Caffeine

Type of Product	Average mg Caffeine	Range
Coffee (5 oz)		
Brewed	98	40–180
Instant	65	30–120
Decaffeinated	3	1–5
Tea (5 oz)		
Brewed	50	20–110
Instant/Iced	30	25–76
Cocoa beverage (5 oz)	4	2–26
Chocolate (1 oz)	14	1–35
Soft drink (12 oz)	40	1–59
Prescription drugs	51	32–100
Nonprescription drugs		
Weight-control aids	170	100–200
Alertness tablets	150	100–200
Analgesic/pain relief	41	32–65
Diuretics	167	100–200
Cold/allergy remedies	27	16–30

MOTHERS' EMOTIONS

Although the nervous system of the mother and fetus are not connected, it is quite probable that maternal emotions affect the fetus. During a strong emotional state, the endocrine system releases the hormones epinephrine and norepinephrine into the bloodstream; these hormones can then pass through the placenta into the bloodstream of the fetus. Such endocrine changes may alter the fetal environment by producing a more rapid heart rate, constriction of the blood vessels, and increased uterine contractions as well as restlessness, sleeplessness, and indigestion in the mother. It has also been found that the effects of prolonged chronic anxiety, upset, and unhappiness with pregnancy has been linked with hyperactivity, irritability, crying, feeding difficulties, and sleeping problems in offspring.

ALCOHOL

Alcohol, like many other drugs, passes freely across the placental barrier and enters the fetal circulatory system. Blood ethanol levels in the fetus are compatible with those of the mother (Weathersbee & Lodge, 1978). However, it may stay in the fetus's system longer than the mother's system because the immature liver of the fetus is only half as effective in breaking alcohol down. Of course, the degree to which intrauterine exposure to any drug affects the fetus will depend on the type of drug injected, the amount consumed, and individual or genetic factors in mother and fetus. The type of teratogenic effects on the developing organism can range from death to malformation, growth deficiency, and behavioral abnormalities. Research has indicated that varying levels of alcohol use during pregnancy have been associated with a variety of fetal problems, such as an increased incidence of stillbirths, midtrimester abortions, congenital abnormalities, growth retardation, and delayed physical and mental development (Streissguth, Barr, & Martin, 1983).

The term **fetal alcohol syndrome (FAS)** has been suggested for the symptoms observed in infants subjected to high levels of alcohol in utero. It is now well established that heavy alcohol consumption during pregnancy (over 8 units a day) (a unit of alcohol is equivalent to half a pint of ordinary lager, beer, or cider, a single measure of spirits, or a single glass of wine) can result in a child being born with FAS (Streissguth & Little, 1985).

It has been estimated that of the known causes of child handicap, alcohol is the third most common in the United States (Waterson & Murray-Lyon, 1990). The Department of Health and Human Services now estimates that between 1,800 and 2,400 infants are born with FAS every year in the United States, and that a further 36,000 pregnancies are affected by Fetal Alcohol Effects (FAE). Other estimates of the incidence of FAS vary from 1 in 1,000 live births in France (Dehane, Samaille-Villette, & Samaille, 1977), and 1 in 600 births in Sweden (Olegard, Sabel, Aronsson, Sandin, Johansson, Larlsson, Kyllerman, Iveson, & Harben, 1979).

FAS is a birth defect consisting of three types of features: growth deficiency, dysmorphic characteristics, and central nervous system manifestations. The growth deficiency is of prenatal origin for height and/or weight, and continues postnatally. The dysmorphic characteristics include flat mid-

The best advice is to abstain from drinking while pregnant.

face, thin upper lip, and/or small chin. The central nervous system characteristics include small head, tremulousness, seizures, slow development, hyperactivity, learning problems, attentional deficits, and/or memory problems (Streissguth, Sampson, & Barr, 1989). To be diagnosed FAS, it is necessary to have some manifestations from each of the three categories and a history of heavy in utero exposure to alcohol. Children who do not have enough characteristics for a diagnosis of FAS are often called possible FAS, or FAE.

The effects of maternal alcoholism during pregnancy go beyond birth. At 7 years of age, children born with FAS exhibit signs of borderline retardation or are frankly mentally retarded (Streissguth, 1978). In addition, the children tend to have poor social relationships, are dependent, and display frequent temper tantrums. Barr, Streissguth, Darby, and Sampson (1990) found that young children with FAS showed the following signs of motor dysfunction: tremors, motor incoordination, weak grasp, difficulty with eye-hand coordination, and low motor performance time. Thus, the future mental and physical defects of infants born to alcoholic mothers are as much of a concern as the effects noted at birth.

Mothers need not be alcoholics; infants born to social drinkers have been found to have low birth weights, abnormal heart rates, and lower IQs (Streissguth et al., 1983). Women who consume 2 to 4 ounces of hard liquor daily have a 10% chance of producing a child with FAS; the percentage increases to 50% if the woman consumes 10 ounces or more of whiskey or a six-pack of beer. Eight drinks a day will produce the full FAS syndrome for most babies (Barr et al., 1990). In a study of more than 9,000 pregnant women, investigators found increased stillbirths, low birth weight infants, and lower placental weights for infants born to mothers who consumed in excess of 1.6 oz of absolute alcohol per day (Randall, Taylor, & Walker, 1977). The risk for these deleterious effects remained even after controlling for other risk factors such as smoking. The highest risk was associated with beer, rather than wine or liquor, despite the lower actual absolute alcohol content of beer (Kaminski, Rumeau, & Schwartz, 1978). Although eight drinks per day constitute a major risk, no safe levels of alcohol ingestion have been established. Perhaps it is best to abstain from drinking, period. Damage caused by alcohol seems to be permanent.

CIGARETTES

Smoking cigarettes has been related to lower average birth size (Aaronson & Macnee, 1989). Smoking is a contributing factor in 20% to 40% of the cases of low birth weight infants in the United States, and in general is associated with a 150 to 200 gram reduction in infant birth weight (Fielding, 1978). One study (Mochizuki, Maruo, Masuko, & Ohtsu, 1984) found that infants born to women who smoked more than 20 cigarettes per day weighed on the average 290 grams less than infants of nonsmokers. Further, smoking outcomes are dose-related. The odds of a woman delivering an infant weighing less than 5½ pounds increases by 26% for every five cigarettes she smokes per day (Kleinman & Matans, 1985). Smoking may be especially harmful during the last 3 months (particularly the last month) when the fetus normally gains weight (Tanner, 1978). Specifically, smoking may affect birth weight by direct interference with nutrition through the physiologic depression of maternal weight gain or indirect interference through decreased maternal nutritional intake. Diebel (1980) suggests that smoking causes inadequate nutrition directly through difficulties in absorption and/or metabolism of calcium, vitamin B12, and vitamin C. Diebel proposed that the fetus may be compromised from poor nutrient assimilation rather than from the toxic effects of tobacco alone.

Whereas smoking clearly is implicated as a contributor to low birth weight, other effects of smoking on the outcomes of pregnancy are less clear. In a review of the effects of smoking on 28 pregnancy outcome variables such as bleeding, premature rupture of membranes, and stillbirths, McIntosh (1984) found a "remarkable" conformity of relative risk factors and concluded that 15% to 45% of unfavorable pregnancy outcomes may be caused by smoking. Chronic smokers have a 30% higher rate of stillbirths and twice the number of premature births than nonsmokers (Aaronson & Macnee, 1989).

In addition, smoking may increase the chance of the placenta's separating from the womb too soon, causing a miscarriage. Babies born to smoking mothers are twice as likely to have heart anomalies (Christianson, 1980). Smoking increases the carbon monoxide level in the blood, which slows blood flow through the placenta, in turn causing the blood to absorb less oxygen. Smokers thus may be linked to impaired brain development. Nicotine, a powerful stimulant, appears to restrict blood vessels in the placenta. Fried and Watkinson (1990) found in examining 133 36-month- and 48-month-old children for whom prenatal exposure to cigarettes had been previously ascertained that exposure to cigarette smoking was significantly associated with poorer language development and lower cognitive scores at both 36 and 48 months.

While the long-term effects of smoking have not been established conclusively, it must be concluded that smoking is harmful to fetal development. Despite the fact that the nicotine and tar content of cigarettes has decreased, there does not seem to be a significant beneficial effect on birth weight or perinatal mortality (Naeye, 1988). Protection of the fetus can come about only by quitting.

MARIJUANA

Perhaps the only definitive statement to be made about marijuana use during pregnancy and its consequences on offspring is that there is a surprising paucity of objective data. Marijuana is not a drug that has just arrived on the scene. Abel's (1980) title of his engaging book says everything: *Marijuana: The First 12,000 Years*. The lack of studies served as an impetus for the Ottawa Prenatal Prospective Study in which pregnancy data was collected on 700 women between 1979 and 1985 (Fried, 1989). Data revealed no difference between marijuana users and control subjects who were matched in terms of alcohol consumption, cigarette use, and family income on outcome measures: type of presentation at birth, Apgar status, and the frequency of complications, or major physical anomalies at birth. Other studies have shown that marijuana use during pregnancy is associated with a variety of adverse outcomes including prematurity, low birth weight, decreased maternal weight gain, complications of pregnancy, difficult labor, increased stillbirth, and perinatal mortality (Richardson, Day, & Taylor, 1989).

DRUGS

Drug abuse among young women of childbearing age is a recognized sociocultural problem (Cole, 1991). Drug levels that may not be considered harmful in adults may have serious toxicological effects on newborns. Heroin, lysergic acid diethylamide (LSD), and tranquilizers may cause deafness, heart defects, and malformed limbs, as well as behavioral disorders and neurological defects (Wilson, 1989). It has been established that infants born to narcotic-addicted mothers are, on the average, small for gestational age, with approximately 50% below 5½ pounds at birth (Fricker & Segal, 1978).

Evidence of intrauterine stress on the developing fetus comes in the reports of violent kicking of the fetus when the mother is denied narcotics (Desmond & Wilson, 1975). The fetus may be undergoing periodic withdrawal *in utero,* as this kicking subsides when the mother is given the proper dose of the narcotic. While the data are inconclusive, it has been suggested that these repeated withdrawals could create a risk of cerebral anoxia that may result in brain damage or neurological impairment (Householder, Hatcher, Burns, & Chasnoff, 1982).

Although the majority of narcotic-addicted infants are born with normal Apgar scores (a behavioral assessment test described later), signs of withdrawal develop within 24 to 72 hours after delivery. It has been estimated that between 70% to 90% of the infants born to narcotic-addicted mothers undergo some degree of withdrawal (Householder et al., 1982). Narcotic withdrawal is manifested by a number of symptoms: most frequently of the central nervous system (irritability, that is, restlessness; incessant, shrill crying; inability to sleep; and breathing difficulties), decreased muscle tone, hyperactive reflexes, tremors, and in severe cases generalized convulsions. The severity of the symptoms is directly related to the drug dosage taken by the mother. Gastrointestinal symptoms are frequent. The infants may frantically mouth

their hands as if in extreme hunger, yet feedings are taken poorly, and vomiting, diarrhea, and progressive weight loss are common. Other symptoms include yawning, sneezing, stretching, sweating, nasal stuffiness, and skin pallor. Poor temperature regulation and fever tend to signify severe withdrawal symptoms. Infants exposed to heroin, or methadone, are significantly smaller at birth, and have higher incidence of intrauterine growth retardation than infants born to drug-free controls (Wilson, 1989).

For over 20 years the treatment of choice in the United States for heroin abuse has been methadone maintenance (a synthetic opioid drug). Hans (1989) found that in the first week after birth, most opioid infants show a well-documented neonatal abstinence syndrome that includes a variety of behaviors associated with central and autonomic nervous system hyperarousal, such as tremors, hyperactive reflexes, high-pitched crying, poor sleeping and feeding, and fewer and rapid respiration. These signs attenuate dramatically during the first month of life. By 1 month of age, only subtle differences can be observed between methadone-exposed infants and unexposed infants. Hans further found that there were no direct effects on mental development. However, methadone-exposed infants reared in extremely poor environmental circumstances showed very delayed mental development. They function more poorly than nonexposed infants reared in poor environmental circumstances. This finding is important because it suggests that in the cognitive domain, methadone may not cause a behavioral deficit, but instead create a vulnerability in these children that then makes them more susceptible to impoverished environments.

Some addicts switch from other drugs to cocaine when pregnant, believing cocaine will be less harmful to the fetus (Cole, 1991). In fact, the alarming rise in the use of cocaine by pregnant women has led to increased concern about the potential deleterious effects of in utero cocaine exposure on the infant (Lester et al., 1991). Actually, cocaine is a most insidious drug. It is now believed to be more harmful to the fetus than any other drug, heroin included, and irrevocably affects the infant's brain chemistry, altering neurochemical transmitters in the brain and putting infants at terrible risk for their lives and developmental outcomes (Mirochnick, Meyer, Cole, & Zuckerman, 1990).

Chasnoff and Griffith (1989) studied the effects of cocaine on the newborn and found that mothers who used cocaine had higher rates of spontaneous abortions, abruptio placentae (separation of the placenta from the uterine wall prior to delivery), and neonatal neurobehavioral deficiencies. They also suffered from a higher rate of premature labor and delivery, intrauterine growth retardation, and sudden infant death syndrome (SIDS) (Fulroth, Phillips, & Durant, 1989). Cocaine use during pregnancy has been related to reductions in infant birth weight, length, and head circumference (Bingol, Fuchs, Diaz, Stone, & Gromisch, 1987).

Chasnoff (1989) studied 70 infants born to cocaine-using women. Each of these women used cocaine intranasally, intravenously, or by freebasing in the first trimester of pregnancy, and 60% of the women continued to use cocaine throughout the pregnancy. For evaluation of outcome of the cocaine-exposed infants, a drug-free comparison group (N = 70) was selected. The cocaine-using women had a higher rate of complications of labor and delivery than the control women. Problems at delivery were reflected in the high rate of fetal distress noted in the cocaine-exposed infants. These infants also experienced deficiencies in their ability to move adaptively through the various states of arousal in response to the demands of the Brazelton Test and in their ability to attend to and actively engage auditory and/or visual stimuli.

Unlike narcotic exposure, cocaine does not cause addiction in the infant. Similarly, only a small percentage of cocaine-exposed infants experience withdrawal symptoms. Two studies (Bingol et al., 1987; Doberczak, Shanzer, Senie, & Kandall, 1988) have reported signs of mild withdrawal (irritability, crying, and vigorous sucks) in 10% of exposed infants. However, no evidence of symptomatology was reported in five studies (Dixon &

Bejar, 1989; Hadeed & Siegel, 1989; Livesay, Ehrlich, & Finnegan, 1987; Madden, Payne, & Miller, 1986; Ryan, Ehrlich, & Finnegan, 1987).

Cocaine does depress the central nervous system of the infant, and causes a drowsy "shutdown" behavior, sometimes described as hypersomnolence. Cocaine-exposed infants' responses to stimuli are delayed, then once the stimulus breaks through the infants' hypersomnolent state, they are difficult to console. Although irritable, these infants rarely become aroused enough to sustain a vigorous cry, the result of a depressed central nervous system.

The majority of cocaine-exposed infants can be classified as "fragile" infants who are easily overloaded by environmental stimuli (Kramer, Locke, Ogunyemi, & Nelson, 1990). The cocaine-exposed infants have very few self-protective mechanisms for avoiding overstimulation and require considerable assistance from caretakers in order to maintain control of their hyperexcitable nervous systems. When using the Brazelton Neonatal Test shortly after birth, cocaine-exposed newborns often made abrupt state changes that were inappropriate for the level of stimulation being presented. One pattern that was quite common in these newborns was the inability to sleep or cry to shut themselves off from external stimulation.

In Chasnoff (1989), cocaine-addicted mothers had a high rate of infectious disease complications, especially hepatitis (24%) and venereal disease (10.5%). There was an increase in complications of labor and delivery in cocaine-using women as compared to drug-free women (see Table 4.3). There was an increased incidence of premature labor among cocaine-complicated pregnancy, and mean gestational age was reduced for the cocaine group of infants. Many of these infants displayed a number of abnormal reflexes as well as unbalance in muscle tone. The difficulties have been shown to persist through at least 4 months of age (Schneider & Chasnoff, 1987). The data further suggest that the number of women experiencing abruptio placentae did not decrease for women that ceased using cocaine after the first trimester. This suggests that induced damage to the placenta occurs early

TABLE 4.3	Complications of Labor and Delivery*			
	Cocaine		Drug Free	
	N	%	N	%
Premature labor	17	24	2	3.0
Precipitous labor	7	10	2	3.0
Abruptio placentae	12	17	1	1.0
Fetal monitor abnormality	7	10	4	5.0

*x^2 analysis, $p < .05$ for all results

Source: From "Cocaine, Pregnancy, and the Neonate" by I. Chasnoff, 1989, *Women and Health, 15*, p. 28. Copyright 1989 by The Haworth Press, Inc., Binghampton, New York. Reprinted by permission.

in pregnancy and places women at risk for abruptio placentae even if cocaine use ceases.

PCP ("angel dust") has become another favorite street drug (Schwartz, Hoffmann, Smith, Hayden, & Riddile, 1987). Children with fetal exposure to PCP appear extremely tremulous, are sensitive to touch and environmental sounds, and show increased muscle tone and abnormal eye movements. PCP exposure during gestation has been shown to adversely affect motor and language development (Van Dyke & Fox, 1990).

Some conflicting evidence has been presented in researching environmental teratogens, which may be due to problems inherent in this type of research. For example, it is difficult to control for confounding variables. That is, women who use one substance are likely to use others as well. Miller, Gold, Belkin, and Klahr (1989) found that there was a high prevalence of alcohol and marijuana dependency in 150 patients with cocaine dependency. The question then is, Which drug is doing the damage? Moreover, women who use drugs differ in life-style variables from women who do not use drugs. Further, the age of the infant at time of study has varied. The time of assessment has ranged from 27 hours to 3 to 6 days. Because neonatal behavior is variable during the postpartum period, an assessment at one time cannot readily be compared with one at a different time. Finally,

different levels of consumption of the drugs has not always been considered when conducting research, and this could have an important bearing on the results.

THE BIRTH PROCESS

The 266-day gestation period is nearly over and the excitement builds as the parents await the arrival of their child. The needs of individuals who will shortly be going through childbirth vary greatly. For some couples, a hospital delivery, with complete medical back-up systems, seems optimal. Others, however, may desire the hominess and safety of an out-of-hospital birth center. Others may feel that home is the best place to deliver their child.

The overwhelming benefit of a hospital birth is the security of having medical help in the event of birth complications. Some women, however, have complained of the "dehumanizing" atmosphere. Often confined to a bed during labor, subject to an overenthusiastic use of medication, and being routinely separated from families, women are opting for a more humanistic environment. Several hospitals have created rooming-in facilities in which the mother and newborn are together continuously. In addition, some hospitals have birthing rooms, which are decorated to resemble more homelike settings. There are also homelike birthing centers located outside the hospital. In many of these settings a nurse/midwife is in attendance.

A nurse/midwife's training generally entails a course of study of 1 to 2 years after the nursing degree. During training, the midwife will attend approximately 150 births. Midwives do not practice independently, but rather are found on the staff of a clinic, health center, maternity center, or hospital. They are always members of a health-care team.

For some women, their own home seems the best place to give birth to their child. The home birth provides the least disruption of family life and the maximum opportunity for intimacy with the newborn. The greatest risk is the absence of

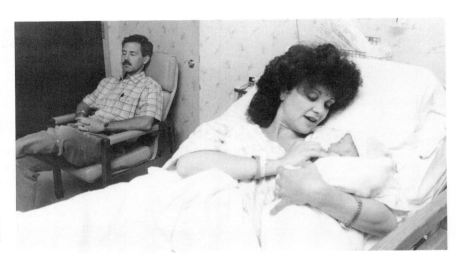

Some hospitals have birthing rooms, delivery rooms with a homelike atmosphere.

emergency equipment, however. Therefore, in describing a low-risk candidate for home birth, one stipulation is being 10 miles or less from the hospital. In addition, it is recommended that the mother has no evidence of hypertension, epilepsy, RH problem, severe anemia, diabetes, history of multiple births, or a previous Caesarean section. Table 4.4 provides a summary of the alternate forms of maternal care.

LABOR

During the last month, the fetus drops down into the lower part of the abdomen. During the last few weeks of pregnancy, women sometimes experience mild muscular contractions that may be mistaken for labor. They are Braxton Hicks contractions, or false labor, that are felt as the uterus enlarges to accommodate the increasing size of the fetus. Birth of the child is not far off. The birth process is divided into three stages: labor, delivery, and afterbirth.

The precise cause of the onset of true labor is not known. Labor involves the gradual opening of the cervix to allow the baby to pass from the uterus and through the vagina. The beginning of labor often is announced by the release of the mucous plug, the material that has sealed off the cervical opening throughout pregnancy. Then, the amniotic sac that enclosed the fetus may break and

some amniotic fluid may escape. The first contractions begin about 15 to 20 minutes apart and last 1 or 2 minutes. (A contraction is the involuntary narrowing and lengthening of the uterine cavity.) The mother cannot initiate or control the onset, regularity, or the intensity of the contractions—except perhaps through relaxation. As labor proceeds, contractions become more intense and appear more frequently. The uterus works hard to expand the cervix to its full 8 to 10 centimeter diameter.

DELIVERY

The explusion, or delivery stage, includes the time from full dilation of the cervix to the birth of the child, and lasts between 1 and 2 hours for first births and between a few minutes to a half hour for subsequent births. In Figure 4.15 we can see that the baby is pushed by the uterus through the cervix and down the birth canal. As the head passes through the pelvis, a curvy, bony passageway, it rotates, helping to protect the baby's head from being injured. The baby's head crowns (becomes visible) at the vaginal opening, and the mother experiences an incredible urge to push and bear down. The baby is born in a face-down position. Once the head appears, shoulders and then trunk and legs follow quickly (see Figure 4.15). The average first labor and delivery is about 14 hours.

TABLE 4.4   Alternate Maternal Care Facilities

Arrangement	Suitability	Description
Nonprofessionally supervised home birth	Questionably suitable	Includes do-it-yourself and unprepared or informally apprenticed lay-midwifery care. Prenatal care may or may not be carried out, and a backup with the hospital system may or may not be available.
Professionally supervised home birth	Suitable for normal or low-risk births	Includes care supervised by a formally prepared practitioner duly licensed to provide maternity services, i.e., a physician (specialist or nonspecialist), nurse-midwife, or in some states lay-midwife. Prenatal care and postpartum follow-up are provided by the practitioner, and there are appropriate links to consultation and care within the hospital system.
Birth and childbearing centers	Suitable for normal or low-risk births	Include independent and system-sponsored homelike settings away from, near, or within hospital, but with autonomous policies. Aspects of home birth are included, such as presence of family members, flexible routines, nonseparation of infant and parents, inclusion of family in decision making, and early discharge with follow-up. Care is provided by all levels of licensed practitioners with some technological supports available in the event of emergency. Effective linkage to the system and specialist consultation are available.
Humanized hospital birth	Suitable for "at-risk" or "complicated" births. May or may not be satisfactory for normal and uncomplicated births	Includes birth rooms within labor–delivery suites, childbirth education, and rooming-in. Somewhat flexible care dominated by obstetrical practitioners with nurse support. May, but usually does not, include nurse-midwives or nonspecialist physicians. Priorities generally those of staff, based on institutional needs and student physician teaching requirements rather than consumer's requests. Technology in selective, rather than generalized, use.
Conventional hospital birth	Considered suitable for "at-risk" or "complicated" births. Low or no priority given to satisfaction	Specialist-dominated birth with routine interventions such as amniotomy, use of ultrasound and electronic monitors, pitocin induction of labor, analgesia, regional and general anesthesia, lithotomy position for birth, separation of family members, de-emphasis of childbirth education and breastfeeding. High value placed on "benefits" of Caesarean section and emphasis on consumer "inability" and "lack of desire" to participate in decision making. Neonatal period also liable to be technologically conducted.

Source: From "Alternate Maternity Care," by R. W. Lubic, in Shelly Romalis (Ed.), *Childbirth.* (Austin: University of Texas Press, 1981), p. 221.

In some cases, the mother has to undergo a surgical childbirth. A Caesarean section is performed for the following reasons: The baby's head is larger than the mother's pelvis can accommodate, breech birth (child's head emerges last), rupture of the placenta or cord collapse, prolonged labor, and severe fetal distress. In this operation, done under a general or local anesthetic, the obstetrician cuts through the layers of the abdomen, into the uterus, and lifts the baby out. Recently, there has been a rise in the use of regional (spinal) anesthetic for Caesareans, which allows the mother to see her infant immediately. In any case, it is major abdominal surgery, requiring intensive postoperative care.

FIGURE 4.15   Birth of the Baby

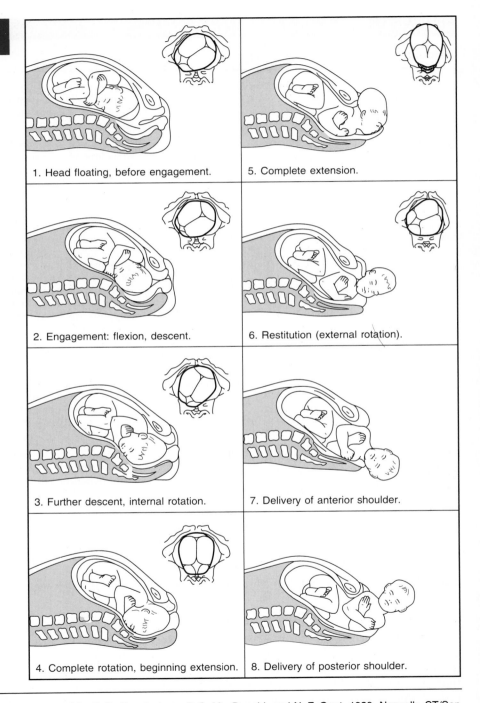

1. Head floating, before engagement.

2. Engagement: flexion, descent.

3. Further descent, internal rotation.

4. Complete rotation, beginning extension.

5. Complete extension.

6. Restitution (external rotation).

7. Delivery of anterior shoulder.

8. Delivery of posterior shoulder.

Source: From *Williams Obstetrics* (18th ed.) (p. 228) by F. G. Cunningham, P. C. MacDonald, and N. F. Gant, 1989, Norwalk, CT/San Mateo, CA: Appleton & Lange.

AFTERBIRTH

About 10 minutes after the birth of the baby, the uterus contracts once again and the placenta and membranes as well as any remaining amniotic fluid is expelled. This stage is painless and generally lasts 10 to 20 minutes.

At the time of birth, the umbilical cord contains as much as 100cc of blood, about one half the total blood supply of the newborn. Postponing the clamping and cutting of the cord for a few minutes allows this blood to drain into the baby's system and helps prevent anemia in the newborn. Complete drainage of the cord's arterial blood into the baby requires perhaps 7 minutes at the most (Parfitt, 1977).

NEONATAL ASSESSMENT TECHNIQUES

Clinical testing of nervous functions at birth is standard practice in all obstetrical hospitals. The recognition of injury to the nervous system at this time depends mainly on the demonstrations of disorders of responsiveness, instability of temperature, respiration, and blood pressure, all of which are under the control of the brain stem and spinal mechanisms.

Neonatal assessment is done for a variety of reasons, but perhaps the most important one is to guide practitioners in assessing the status of the infant and in making some decision concerning treatment or special care for the infant. Often neurological assessments are done that make extensive use of the infant's reflexes. Responsiveness to stimulation is examined, as well as muscle tone, physical condition, and general state. From evaluation of the infant's behavior, state, and responsiveness, a diagnosis is typically made about the maturity and functioning of the infant's central nervous system and sensory functioning. Sometimes various tests are given, the most widely used ones in the United States being the Apgar Scale, The Gesell Developmental Schedules, the Bayley Scales of Infant Development, and the Brazelton Neonatal Behavioral Assessment Scale.

The Apgar Scale is given to the infant 60 seconds after birth and then again at 5 and 10 minutes after birth. The infant is rated for five signs: heart rate, respiratory effort, muscle tone, reflex irritability, and color. A score of 2 is given if the infant is in the best possible condition for a particular sign; a 0 is given if the sign is not present and a 1 is given for all conditions between 0 and 2. Thus, the optimal score an infant can obtain is 10 (see Table 4.5).

TABLE 4.5 The Apgar Scale

Characteristic	0	1	2
Heart rate	Not detectable	Slow—below 100 beats/minute	100–140 beats/minute
Respiratory effort	Infant is apneic	Shallow breathing	Regular breathing; lusty crying
Muscle tone	Completely flaccid infant	Weak, inactive	Flexed arms and legs; resists extension
Reflex irritability: (stimulation of soles of feet)	No reaction	Grimace	Cry
Color	Blue, pale	Body pink; extremities blue	Entirely pink

Source: From "A Proposal for a New Method of Evaluation of the Newborn Infant" by Virginia Apgar, 1953, *Current Research in Anesthesia and Analgesia, 32,* p. 262. Copyright 1953 by the International Anesthesia Research Society. Reprinted by permission.

The Brazelton Scale (NBAS) was developed to assess the dynamic processes of behavioral organization and development in the neonate. It is a psychological scale for the neonate and views the infant as part of a reciprocal, interactive feedback system between infant and caregiver. While the exam includes the assessment of reflex responses, it focuses on the infant's capability to respond to the kind of stimuli that caregivers present in an interactive process. The scale assesses 16 reflexes and 26 behavioral items that are shown in Table 4.6. The examiner plays the role of the caregiver and systematically manipulates the baby from sleep to alert to crying states and back down to quiet states, bringing the infant through an entire range of situations that captures the baby's coping and adaptive strategies.

PRETERM BIRTHS

A full definition of prematurity would include gestation length (less than 37 weeks), weight (less than 2,500 grams), body length (less than 47 centimeters), and head circumference (less than 33 centimeters). In most cases, gestation length and body weight are the main factors to consider.

Infants' prematurity is reflected immediately after birth in that they have a greater difficulty making adjustments to their extrauterine world. They have underdeveloped sucking and swallowing mechanisms. Because premature infants have very few fat cells, they maintain poor body heat. Preterm infants, as a result of their physiological immaturity, are more susceptible to a variety of respiratory, metabolic, and other disorders. A preterm infant has a less well-developed muscula-

TABLE 4.6 Behavioral Items on the Brazelton Neonatal Behavioral Assessment Scale	
	1. Response decrement to repeated visual stimuli (2,3)*
	2. Response decrement to rattle (2,3)
	3. Response decrement to bell (2,3)
	4. Response decrement to pinprick (1,2,3)
	5. Orienting response to inanimate visual stimuli (4 only)
	6. Orienting response to inanimate auditory stimuli (4,5)
	7. Orienting response to animate visual stimuli—examiner's face (4 only)
	8. Orienting response to animate auditory stimuli—examiner's voice (4 only)
	9. Orienting responses to animate visual and auditory stimuli (4 only)
	10. Quality and duration of alert periods (4 only)
	11. General muscle tone—in resting and in response to being handled—passive and active (4,5)
	12. Motor activity (4,5)
	13. Traction responses as he is pulled to sit (3,5)
	14. Cuddliness—responses to being cuddled by examiner (4,5)
	15. Defensive movements—reactions to a cloth over his face (4)
	16. Consolability with intervention by examiner (6 to 5,4,3,2)
	17. Peak of excitement and capacity to control himself (6)
	18. Rapidity of buildup to crying state (from 1,2 to 6)
	19. Irritability during the examination (3,4,5)
	20. General assessment of kind and degree of activity (alert states)
	21. Tremulousness (all states)
	22. Amount of startling (3,4,5,6)
	23. Lability of skin color—measuring autonomic lability (from 1 to 6)
	24. Lability of states during entire examination (all states)
	25. Self-quieting activity—attempts to console self and control state (6,4,3,2,1)
	26. Hand-to-mouth activity (all states)

*Numbers in parentheses refer to optimal state for assessment.

Source: From *Neonatal Behavioral Assessment Scale* (p. 115) by T. B. Brazelton, 1984, Philadelphia: Spastics International. Reprinted with permission from Brazelton (1984), Spastics International Medical Publications, London.

ture and less well-developed brain (Landry & Chapieski, 1988).

Because of a fragile central nervous system, preterm infants often can deal with only one sensory modality at a time (Cole, 1991). They may be able to look at a visual stimulus, but if an auditory component is added (for example, a voice), it becomes too stimulating and can cause distress. The infants will either go to sleep or become very agitated. This behavior can continue until term age and can be very difficult for parents unless they understand the infant's behavior, realizing that this is the way such infants communicate signs of overstimulation.

Preterm infants progress from visual gazing at a black and white decal, to gazing at a mobile, and then finally interacting with the caregiver. This developmental sequence needs to be adhered to, otherwise the infants are constantly overstimulated, which can deplete their energies as well as affect other developing systems (Turkewirtz & Kenny, 1985). Parents and other caregivers need to read the infant's behavioral signs of overstimulation and to provide a more modulated approach. Once parents realize that turning away (visual or auditory averting) is a coping strategy that infants use when overstimulated, they begin to see this behavior as a strength and not a deficit.

Finally, preterm infants differ in their environment from full-term babies in that they are usually put in incubators after delivery to protect them from harmful microorganisms. They usually experience a prolonged hospitalization: The average length of hospitalization for preterm infants is about 28 days with a range from a few days to several months. Even when leaving the hospital, preterm infants differ from full-term infants at the time of their discharge. Differences occur in areas of interactive processes (they show less responsivity) and motoric processes (preterm infants show less motor maturity and more deviant reflexes) (Als & Brazelton, 1981).

The exact causes of preterm birth, in many cases, are unclear, although numerous factors have been implicated. Included among them are maternal health and nutritional status prior to and during pregnancy, smoking, use of drugs, uterine problems, lack of prenatal care, diabetes, multiple births, and urogenital infection. It is evident that many conditions are linked directly and indirectly to adverse social and economic conditions, thus it is not surprising to find higher rates of preterm birth among women who are disadvantaged.

It used to be believed that premature babies were more likely to have learning difficulties. However, recent research has found that unless they are brain damaged, premature babies are just as capable as their full-term contemporaries from the same social class (Landry, Chapieski, Richardson, Palmer, & Hall, 1990). Those that are born with loving, nurturing parents show little long-range handicaps.

APPEARANCE OF THE NEWBORN

Compared to the rest of the body, the newborn's head is quite large. The important bones of the baby's head are separated by sutures, membranous spaces that feel soft to the touch. The space where several sutures meet is called a fontanelle. The newborn's skin is soft and wrinkly and covered with the vernix, a light cheesy coating that disappears after a few baths. Their arms and bowed, little legs move in quick, jerky movements. Their minute hands with tiny little fingernails can grasp with decisive firmness.

Prior to birth, the right and left ventricles of the heart have an opening between them that keeps the blood from flowing into the dysfunctioning lungs. This opening between the ventricles closes at birth, and the heart begins its normal functioning. Most newborns breathe spontaneously at birth. Their breathing, however, is irregular, shallow, rapid, and punctuated frequently with coughs and sneezes in order to clear the air passages and lungs. After birth, blood begins to flow into the lungs and oxygenation begins. The newborn also changes from taking in nutrients through the placenta to ingesting food into its mouth and stomach, and eliminating wastes through its own elimination system.

Newborns are self-regulatory organisms from birth onward, and even before. This means that their behavior processes tend to minimize deprivations, defend against the intrusion of noxious

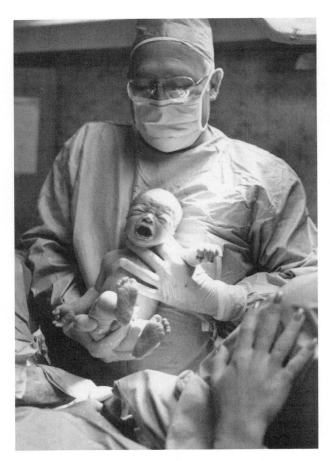

After 40 weeks, the neonate greets the world.

stimulation, correct imbalances, thwart disturbances, and otherwise perpetuate life, protect limbs, and protect against extremes of emotional excitement.

PRACTICAL IMPLICATIONS: PREPARED CHILDBIRTH

Although relatively little about the management of childbirth has changed in U.S. hospitals in the past 50 years, what has changed significantly is the patient. The modern expectant mother, and father, are now frequently prepared; the mother knows what to expect and tends to accept the course of labor and delivery as normal and natural. The term *natural childbirth* has been applied with considerable variation. Most recently it has come to mean the use of breathing or relaxation techniques during labor and delivery to provide the mother with psychological/physical tools for dealing with pain. Because these breathing and relaxation techniques require concentrated effort and hard work on the part of the parents, perhaps *prepared* or *educated* childbirth are more accurate terms.

Since the 1940s, various techniques of prepared childbirth have been introduced into the United States. In particular, three European obstetricians, Grantly Dick-Read, Fernand Lamaze, and Frederic Leboyer have contributed major theories about childbirth and have developed specific techniques to their ideas.

Dick-Read (1959) observed as an obstetrician that some women suffered horribly during labor and birth, while others experienced very little pain. What distinguished the relatively painless labors, he came to realize, was that these mothers were calm and relaxed. Fear and expectation of pain, Dick-Read pointed out, cause the body to become tense, and that tension increases and emphasizes the pain response. Dick-Read maintained that a program of education with breathing and relaxation exercises would eliminate or greatly reduce the needs for drugs during labor and delivery. While this advice may not be particularly earth-shaking today, it was in the 1940s when he made these statements. At that time, the trend was to administer general anesthesia in labor to the "grateful" mother in order to obliterate sensation entirely.

The best-known and most widely used system of precise breathing and relaxation exercises is the *Lamaze Method*. These exercises teach a precise set of breathing techniques associated to the various stages of labor. Lamaze, like Dick-Read, also stresses the importance of factual education in preparation for childbirth. The father plays a crucial role in this program as the exercise coach, timer of contractions, and major support.

The effectiveness of the Lamaze Method has been supported by a variety of research studies. These suggest that women who attend classes

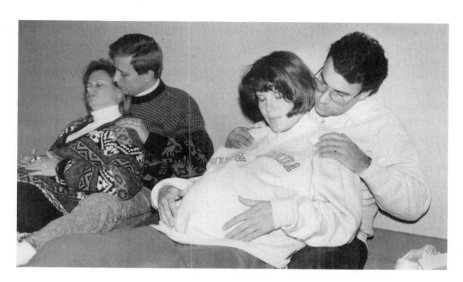

Working together on Lamaze exercises.

tend to have shorter labors, fewer complications, less anxiety, less medication, and healthier babies than other motivated women who do not take classes (Hughey, McElin, & Young, 1988). One criticism of the Lamaze training, however, is that the issue of medication is barely treated. The mother and father are encouraged to have strong, positive thoughts about labor and delivery and learn to envision an easygoing time. What happens, then, to those mothers who may lose control, or decide they need some relief from the pain? Will they emerge from this experience with a sense of failure?

After the birth of the child, the new father, if present, beams with delight at the little bundle, and the mother smiles in a satisfied, relieved way; the attending physician proudly holds the tiny baby. The only one in this quartet who does not seem to be relaxed and contented is the newborn. Leboyer (1975) has been delivering calm and con-

tented babies for the past quarter-century. He maintains that birth is a violent, painful, and traumatic experience for the newborn. The task of obstetrics, therefore, according to Leboyer, is to impose fewer demands on the baby. Rather than thrust the newborn into a brightly, fluorescent-lighted room, the baby should be delivered in a darkened room. The delivery room should be as quiet as possible. The newborn should be placed on the mother's abdomen before the cord is cut, and then given a bath as a first independent experience.

The bath experience has received the most criticism. Some say it puts too heavy a demand on the temperature-regulating system of the newborn. Others point out that rather than being reassuring to the newborn, it may be sensorily confusing once the transition out of the wet, warm uterus has already been accomplished.

REVIEW OF KEY POINTS

Life processes begin with the union of a sperm cell and an egg cell. The 23 pairs of chromosomes, one set from each parent, unite and the biological inheritance of the child begins to unfold.

Genes are the basic transmitters of heredity. Each gene has a partner gene, or allele. If the alleles have contrasting effects, the individual is said to be heterozygous for that trait. If the genes have the same trait, the individual is said to be homozygous for that trait. Genes are composed of a complex chemical called deoxyribonucleic acid (DNA). While DNA contains the complete blueprint of the living organism and the genetic code to regulate the functioning and development of the organism, it cannot move out of the nucleus into the cytoplasm. RNA can, however, and acts as a messenger to carry out the instructions of DNA to the cytoplasm; it thus guides the synthesis of thousands of proteins needed to create and sustain life processes in a cell or organ. Human beings have two kinds of cells: somatic (body cells) and gametes (germ or sex cells). Both types of cells reproduce in number via mitosis, which results in an identical copy of the parent cells. Gametes divide in chromosome content via meiosis, in which the duplicate set of chromosomes is relinquished, resulting in a mature gamete with 23 single chromosomes.

The prenatal periods of development are the germinal period, the embryonic period, and the fetal period. As the zygote makes its descent down the fallopian tube, it continues to divide and enters the uterus as a hollow ball of cells called the blastocyst. The blastocyst separates into two parts: the trophoblast (eventually forms the placenta and protective membranes) and the embryonic disk, which will become the embryo. The placenta is a disk-shaped organ in which the blood vessels of the fetus and those of the mother come together without joining. Nutrients, oxygen, hormones, and waste products are exchanged by diffusing from one blood-vessel system to another. The vital connection between the placenta and the embryo is the umbilical cord. It consists of two arteries and one vein that carry nourishments from the mother and remove waste products from the fetus. During the embryonic period, germ layers form and differentiation of body parts is almost complete. The fetal period is marked by continued elaboration and growth of basic systems.

Down syndrome, Klinefelter's syndrome, and Turner's syndrome were discussed. The environmental influences on neonatal development reviewed the effects of various teratogens. When organs are undergoing rapid development, they are particularly sensitive to various teratogens such as viral diseases, radiation, alcohol, tobacco, narcotics, and lack of proper nourishment. It was pointed out that prolonged stress during pregnancy may affect the development of the fetus. Many of the problems discussed in this section can be prevented if mothers are aware of the harmful effects of these teratogens and abstain from use of alcohol, narcotics, smoking, and so forth.

The last section discussed labor, delivery, and afterbirth. In order to assess their health and developmental status, newborns are given a neurological exam, and quite commonly the Apgar Scale or the Brazelton Scale is administered.

ENHANCING YOUR CRITICAL THINKING

Firsthand Experiences

Down Syndrome

Trainer, M. (1991). *Differences in common: Straight talk on mental retardation, Down syndrome, and life.* Kensington, MD: Woodbine House.

Although the text gives a description of the physical characteristics and causes of Down syndrome, this book will help students develop an understanding of the psychological effects of Down syndrome on children and their families. If you have a special interest in this topic, visit a center for mentally handicapped children; observe and talk with these children, their teachers, and parents.

Teratogens

Lester, B. M., Corwin, M. J., Sepkoski, C., Seifer, R., Peucker, M., McLaughlin, S., & Golub, H. I. (1991). Neurobehavioral syndromes in cocaine-exposed newborn infants. *Child Development, 62,* 694–705.

As noted in the text, there has been an alarming rise in the use of cocaine by pregnant women, which has led to increased research on the deleterious effects of this drug. Lester et al.'s article will broaden students' understanding of the indirect effects of this drug on the newborn. A valuable but sobering experience is to visit the newborn intensive care unit. Observe the infants who are being treated for drug addiction.

Newborns

White, B. L. (1988). *Educating the infant and toddler.* Lexington, MA: Lexington Books.

Although all the chapters in this book are worthwhile reading, Chapter 10, "The Amazing Newborn" (pp. 63–68), discusses the newborn capabilities based on well-founded studies. On the same day that you visit the intensive care unit, visit the regular nursery as well. In what ways do these infants differ from those in intensive care?

CHAPTER 5

Physical, Motor, Sensory, and Perceptual Development

CHILDREN'S THOUGHTS

On "What makes our bodies grow?" . . .

Our bodies need lots of food and energy to help them grow. We need vegetables and fruits and food from the meat group.
Amy, age 7

You need to eat nutritious foods. Our bodies grow for 24 hours straight. Your body eventually stops growing about age 29. But sometimes you don't know you stopped growing until age 30.
Matt, age 8

Vitamins help you get bigger. We grow from about 5 inches when we are born to 5 feet when we are old. Here is a picture of me when I was just little and how I look now. I'm big because I eat vitamins.
Ricky, age 7

THE DEVELOPMENT OF THE BRAIN

The many aspects of physical development discussed in this chapter involve visible changes in children's size, shape, and motor and perceptual skills. Less visible changes, however, are also occurring in a very complicated structure, the brain. Because the development of the brain is so integral in studying not only children's physical development but also their overall development, it is vital to understand its structures, development, and functions. The purpose of this discussion is not to go over the brain in technical detail or to focus on one tiny area or function at a time; but rather to present a broader, holistic picture of the brain as it relates to children's development.

PHYSICAL STRUCTURE

Within 2 weeks after conception, a slender, tube-like structure becomes differentiated. This tubelike structure will enlarge and develop into the brain (see Figure 5.1). The most recognizable form of the adult brain is noticeable by the 9th or 10th week of gestation. However, the convolutions or folds on the surface of the brain, which enormously increase its area and volume, do not begin to appear until the eighth month of gestation. At birth, the brain is about 350 grams or 12 ounces in weight.

BRAIN-BODY RATIO

At maturity, the adult brain weighs 1,450 grams or roughly 3 pounds. Individual brains vary considerably but, within a normal range, variation in size does not directly signify greater or lesser ability. On a species basis, size does tend to be significant. Among mammals, for example, humans have by far the largest brains except for porpoises, whales, and some other heavy animals, which there is no reason yet to believe surpass us in mental capacities. The ratio of brain

FIGURE 5.1 Embryonic and Fetal Brain Development

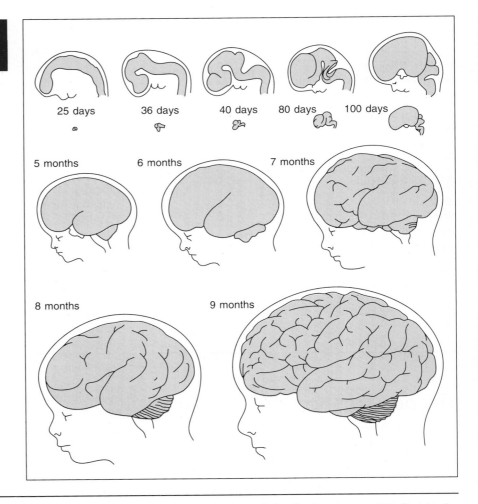

Source: From "The Development of the Brain" by W. Maxwell Cowan, September, 1979, *Scientific American*, p. 116. Drawing by T. Prentess. Copyright 1979 by Scientific American. Reprinted by permission.

to total body weight appears to be a key factor in determining mental ability.

If we consider the average weight of a human being as 150 pounds and the average weight of the human brain as 3¼ pounds, then the brain-body ratio is 1:50. Each pound of brain is in charge of (so to speak) 50 pounds of body, a most unusual situation. Compare it with the apes, for example, our closest competitor. A pound of chimpanzee brain is in charge of 150 pounds of chimpanzee body (differently expressed, the body-brain ratio is 1:150).

THE TRIUNE BRAIN

The human brain is a product of hundreds of millions of years of evolution. MacLean (1978) has given a very useful simplification of the overall structure of the brain based on a great deal of knowledge of how animal brains have developed over approximately the last 250 million years or so. As can be seen in Figure 5.2, the brain consists of three brains, each of which was formed at different times in our evolutionary history. The oldest brain, or the **reptilian brain,** is around 200 million years old. It may be compared to the kind of brain possessed by agile reptiles that became ancestors of mammals. The reptilian brain in humans is the control site of the elemental requirements for life: heartbeat, respiration, reflexes. The second brain, the **old mammalian brain,** or the paleomammalian brain, is many 10's of millions of years newer. It is common to all mammals because most reptiles of the dinosaur age became extinct about 60 million years ago. The old mammalian brain in humans appears to be involved in emotional and motivation functions.

The lower-right bulge in Figure 5.2 represents the cerebellum, which is a specialized structure that coordinates physical movement. The large, top bulge is the **cerebrum,** or the **new mammalian brain.** It has been around so few millions of years that in evolutionary terms it may be considered, especially in humans, as brand new.

The **cerebrum,** a layer of gray matter overlying the entire brain, accounts for almost 85% of the entire brain. It contains billions of brain cells that are responsible for higher order thinking. All the

FIGURE 5.2 The Triune Brain

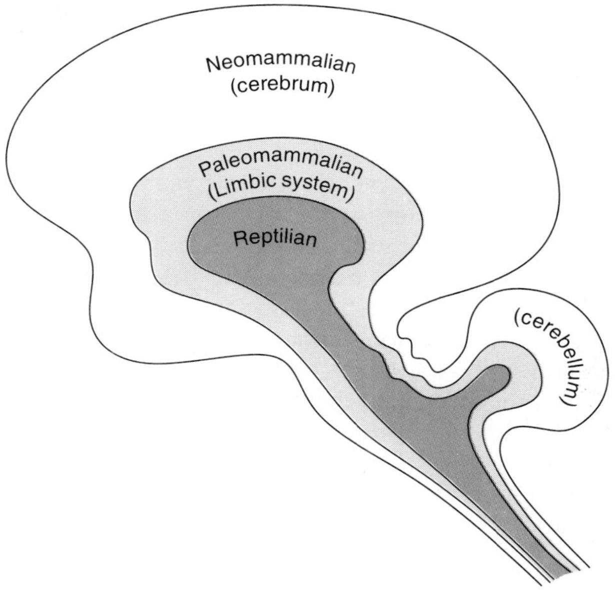

Source: From "A Mind of Three Minds: Educating the Triune Brain" by Paul D. MacLean, in Jeanne Chall and Allan Minsky (Eds.), *The Seventy-seventh Yearbook of the National Society for the Study of Education* (p. 32), 1978, Chicago: University of Chicago Press. Reprinted by permission of the National Society for the Study of Education.

language and symbols that people use, written and oral, along with the ability to act and plan and think abstractly stem from the newest brain. The cerebrum consists of two hemispheres, which are roughly (but not exactly) mirror images. The main connection between the hemispheres is a bridge called the **corpus callosum.** This band of more than 200 million nerve fibers is the communication link between the two hemispheres, allowing them to function as a single unit. In the newborn, old brain structures dominate. The behavioral capabilities of the newborn are largely reflexive in nature. As the new brain continues to develop its powers, however, the two older parts of the brain come under its control. As a result, the infant exhibits more advanced and voluntarily controlled motor behavior.

An interesting aspect in studying the development of the cerebrum is that its regions do not develop at the same rate. Some regions complete their development and become functional before others do. Initially, motor areas are more advanced, followed in descending order by sensory, visual, and auditory areas. Last to mature are the association areas of the cerebrum. It is not until the child has reached the age of 4 to 7 years that these areas become prepared finally for action (Luria, 1975). They will continue to grow and develop for a number of years, usually until the early teens. The development of the association areas enables children to perform higher order thinking, look ahead, and make plans and stick to them in spite of distractions. As these association areas are brought to use, the child will make tremendous strides in using more effective thinking strategies, setting more distant goals, and carrying through a chain of activities.

NEURONS

The basic unit of the central nervous system that is responsible for transmitting messages to and from the brain is the **neuron.** It is said that by the 20th to 24th week of fetal life, the main cell masses of the brain have acquired their full quota of neurons, variously established at 16 to 22 billion. Each neuron may have 10,000 connections with other neurons that are feeding it impulses. The communication network that results means that the possible pathways soar up into the trillions and above (Cowan, 1979).

As can be seen in Figure 5.3, each neuron consists of a **soma,** or cell body, which ranges in size from about 5 to 100 micrometers. Extending from the cell body are neural processes: dendrites and the axon. **Dendrites** are fine, wirelike processes that receive messages from adjacent cells and conduct them to the cell body. The **axon** is the long extension from the cell body that transmits messages away from the cell body to other neurons, across the **synapse,** the small space existing between neurons. All neurons have the same structural components but vary in size and shape.

MAJOR EVENTS IN BRAIN GROWTH

People are born with a full complement of neurons; no new neurons grow after birth. In favorable conditions, the actual physical growth of neurons continues as they build a vast number of neuronal connections. Much as a tree sends out more and more branches and twigs, the neurons send out their processes. Figure 5.4 shows a section of the cerebrum for a 6-month-old and an 8-month-old child. Notice how these neurons have increased their processes. Increase in brain size and brain weight comes in part from this kind of development (Cowan, 1979).

It is thought that the most important clue to the functional capacity of a brain is the "connectivity" of its neurons, that is, the number of connections each cell makes with the others. The importance of these connections to the early development and later functioning of the brain is seen in the fact that deficits or abnormalities in forming these connections seem to be the underlying problem in many kinds of mental deficiencies in humans (Purpura, 1977). One possible explanation for retardation is that the connections between the neurons in the cerebrum have been greatly reduced or that for some reason cortical neurons become connected during development into "incorrect" neural circuits. The effectiveness of communication between neurons, and thus among the widespread parts of the nervous system, depends on the number and individual strength of connections formed during development (Cragg, 1974). The more communication and connections that exist among pathways, the more potential there is, in principal, for highly sophisticated mental activity. Connectivity of the neurons is the first critical area of brain development; the second involves **myelination.**

MYELINATION

Neurons are not tightly packed together like cells in most other tissues; there are narrow gaps between each, filled with tissue fluid. The microscopic gap (about $\frac{1}{1,000,000}$ of an inch wide) is known as the synapse. The connection with other cells is made through branches of an axon coming into close proximity with the dendrites of other cells. Messages are

FIGURE 5.3   Parts of the Neuron

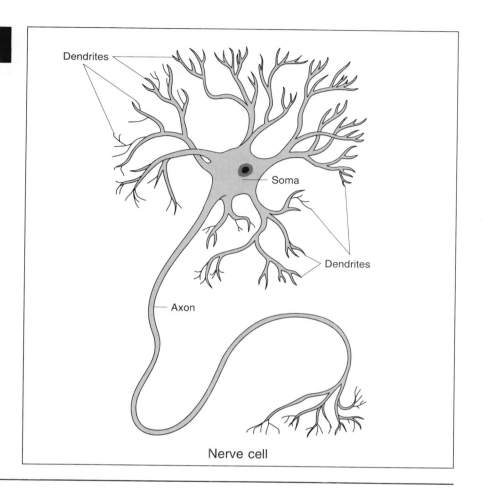

passed across the tiny gaps by chemicals (neuro-transmitters) released at the nerve endings.

Most of the fast-conducting pathways of the central nervous system are myelinated; that is, during the process of myelination, they develop a protein covering called a **myelin sheath** that helps to preserve energy in nerve-impulse conduction and to maintain a nerve-impulse conduction velocity (Schulte, 1974). Thus, myelin serves to keep nerve-impulse conduction velocity fast in spite of the increasing distances that impulses must travel as the body continues to grow.

Although it seems reasonable to assume that myelination of certain sets of neurons is the one factor relating to corresponding functions becoming more proficient, it must be kept in mind that the brain is highly complex. Many facets of brain development are occurring simultaneously, including maturity of structure of the neurons, number of connections between axons and dendrites, and development of synapses. Throughout brain growth from early fetal life, the appearance of function is related to all these factors (Dickerson & McGurk, 1982). However, the presence of myelin in axonal tracts is one factor, and an essential one, that is implicated in the development of function. That is, various functions do not develop until corresponding nerves are myelinated. For example,

FIGURE 5.4   Development of Axons and Dendrites in Neurons

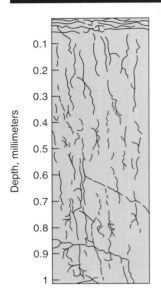

Myelination is a major factor relating to the increasing proficiency of corresponding functions within the body. The child, for example, cannot walk until the nerves connecting the leg muscles become myelinated.

the nerves connecting the muscles of the baby's leg are not myelinated at birth. The child must wait almost a year before myelination is complete, thus enabling the child to take those first, few, wobbly steps.

Research has shown that there is an order in which neurons are myelinated. Myelin formation begins in the spinal cord during midfetal life and continues through postnatal years. At about the fourth to fifth year the rate of myelination slows down but continues into adolescence. In general, motor roots are the first parts of the central nervous system to develop myelin, a process that begins about the fourth fetal month.

The major motor pathways from the cortex undergo rapid myelination during the last month of gestation and show rather complete myelination at 2 years. If you observe the motions of a baby's arms and hands over the first few weeks, you can note the progress from random movements and jerks to controlled and purposeful actions. Myelination is one factor in brain development that accounts for this sophistication and progression in motor skills. As neural pathways between the brain and the skeletal muscles myelinate, the child becomes capable of increasingly complex motor activities, such as lifting head and chest, reaching with arms, rolling over, sitting, standing, and eventually walking and running. Voluntary motor pathways seem to be functionally mature at about 2 years (Parmelee & Sigman, 1983). At birth, or shortly thereafter, the pathways between the sense organs and the brain are reasonably well myelinated. As a result, the neonate's sensory equipment is in good working order.

A major period of growth in the visual area is between birth and 5 to 6 months of age (Morse, 1979). At 6 months, myelin growth in the visual system is nearly functionally complete. Increased growth in myelin in the auditory pathways begins about the time of birth and continues into early childhood (approximately 4 years of age). While fibers of the sound-receiving system begin to myelinate as early as the sixth fetal month, they complete the process gradually, continuing until the fourth year. In contrast, the neurons associated with vision begin to myelinate only just before birth, but then complete the process very rapidly. Vision is ahead of hearing, which suggests that there is more discriminative ability in vision than in hearing (Javel, 1980).

Finally, the fibers that link the cerebellum to the cerebral cortex, and which are necessary to the fine motor control of voluntary movement, only begin to myelinate after birth and do not have their full complement of myelin until about age 4. Thus, fine motor coordination is difficult or impossible for most children before they are 4 years of age, regardless of experience or practice. But once fine motor coordination is physically possible, it may be exercised and developed in many forms. The very rapid development of skills and abilities, which is a hallmark of the school years, may very well depend on this neurophysiological structural development. The axons of the neurons in the reticular formation, which allow us to concentrate on one stimulus (reading a book) while ignoring irrelevant ones (listening to the radio) are not completely myelinated until mid- to late teens.

Many experts maintain that fully effective functioning of nerve cells is not possible until these cells have been myelinated. Although behavior cannot appear until the neurophysicological structure has developed, structural maturation does not guarantee that the behavior it makes possible will appear. Such factors as experience, motivation, and practice determine whether and how a child will use available structures behaviorally.

BRAIN GROWTH SPURT

The brain growth spurt is a period of time during which there are large increases in brain weight and during which the number of other processes, including myelination and dendritic and synaptic growth, proceed at a very rapid rate. It is now known that the brain growth spurt is predetermined to occur at a given chronological age, even when conditions are not favorable for its support. Restrictions during this developmental growth spurt universally result in a permanent and irreconcilable reduction, not simply a delay, in the extent of brain growth. Since the brain has a "once only" opportunity for laying down its foundation for optimum development, the brain growth spurt represents a period of great vulnerability for elaboration of neural processes and potential brain function (Dobbing, 1976).

When does this growth spurt occur? Dobbing and Sands (1970) studied the development of the human brain by collecting human fetuses resulting from therapeutic abortions, stillbirths, and perinatal deaths and then measuring the amount of DNA content of the brain at different periods of pregnancy. They concluded that there are two major periods of growth spurt involving cell multiplication in the human brain: The first occurs between the 15th and 20th weeks of pregnancy, a period of time when the number of neurons increase dramatically. The second begins about the 25th week and continues until the second year after birth. During this time there is an explosive increase in dendritic complexity with establishment of synaptic connections. This component may be as important in the development of brain function as the neuronal cell number.

BRAIN WEIGHT

One measure of brain growth is weight gain. From early fetal life onward, the brain, in terms of its gross weight, is nearer to its adult value than any other organ of the body, except the eyes. In this sense it develops earlier than the rest of the body. The brain grows rapidly during the early postnatal period, increasing nearly 200% in weight during the first 3 years after birth. During the next 10 years, the additional weight gain is only about 35%. At birth, the brain is about 25% of its adult weight; at 6 months, nearly 50%; at 1 year, 60%; at 2 ½ , 75%; at 5 years, 90%; and at 10 years, 95% (Tanner, 1978). This contrasts with the weight of the whole body, which at birth is about 5% of the young adult weight and at 10 years about 50%. The weight of the brain during the course of development is presented in Table 5.1. Increase in total brain weight results from an increase in cell size, further differentiation of cells, or increase in extracellular substance.

Although the rate of growth is greatest before birth, the major increase in the size of the human brain occurs soon after birth. The brain nearly triples in size during the first year of life, a growth rate that is not shared by any other animal and that is a direct result of our placental origins. An infant with a full-sized brain could not be delivered through the female pelvic canal, and yet without a fully developed brain, the human race could probably not have survived as a species. The evolutionary solution to this problem was to delay a major part of the brain development until the period immediately following birth.

This solution, however, created a new problem. Rapid postnatal growth of the brain requires a sus-tained supply of appropriate nutrients in adequate quantity, without which normal brain development would be jeopardized. No other organism shares this vulnerability to the same degree.

BRAIN DYSFUNCTION

Brain damage may occur on different levels ranging from obvious gross destruction of brain matter (cerebral palsy) to an environmental or emotional damping effect that influences behavior and learning in a more tenuous manner. There are several reasons why damage to the brain occurs. Brain development can be affected by conditions that affect the availability of oxygen to the cells. The degree of brain damage or behavioral deficits that result when there is deprivation of oxygen is directly related to the length of time the organism is exposed to reduced or restricted supplies of oxygen.

Why should brain function fail when the brain is deprived of oxygen? The brain has a relatively low energy reserve of oxygen while having a relatively high metabolic rate. As adults, even though the brain represents about 2% of our total body weight, it requires about 25% of all the oxygen in the blood at all times. The young brain has an even greater rate of consumption of oxygen and cerebral blood flow. Thus, when the much-needed supply of oxygen is eliminated or greatly reduced, energy sources for brain functioning are quickly depleted and brain function is affected (Dobbing, 1976).

Undernutrition has also been implicated in brain dysfunction. The development of the brain may be particularly vulnerable while the child is in utero. Intrauterine undernutrition is usually the result of placental insufficiency and the consequent decrease in the flow of nutrients to the fetus. A malnourished mother, for example, may be unable to contribute adequately to her placental development. Fetal growth is affected, because a deficient placenta may be unable to keep up with the fetal demands for essential nutrients. Stephan and Chow (1969), of Johns Hopkins University School of Medicine, and Winick (1970), of Cornell University Medical College, demonstrated with pregnant rats that malnourished mothers produced smaller and lighter placentas than adequately fed mothers.

TABLE 5.1. Weight of Human Brain		
Newborn	340	grams (11.9 oz)
Age 6 months	750	grams (26.25 oz)
Age 1	970	grams (2.12 lb)
Age 2	1,150	grams (2.52 lb)
Age 3	1,200	grams (2.63 lb)
Age 6	1,250	grams (2.72 lb)
Age 9	1,300	grams (2.84 lb)
Age 12	1,350	grams (2.95 lb)
Age 20	1,400	grams (3.06 lb)

The most striking finding by this research group was that newborn animals from deficient placentas also had fewer brain cells. Therefore, placental inadequacy resulted in inadequate nutrition of the fetus, which affected brain development during its growth spurt.

It has also been shown that undernutrition during early brain development, particularly during the brain growth spurt, results in maturational deficits in brain size, in number of cells formed, and in the amount of myelin development (Dobbing & Smart, 1974).

It appears that nutrition can and does have an important and long-lasting effect on brain growth and development in both animals and humans. The long-lasting effects may be seen in permanent deficits in motor, intellectual, and emotional growth, as well as in the underlying neural mechanisms that support such behavior.

BRAIN PLASTICITY

Research has pointed out that there is room for modification in the brain. The fact that adults are continually learning new and complex tasks shows that even in the mature brain, modifiability exists. However, research also points out that the power of adaptive *plasticity* of the brain is greatest during the developmental years up to age 8 or 9 (Williams, 1983). The general consensus among experts in the field is that injury to the brain results in fewer and less effects on behavior when that injury occurs in infancy and early childhood as compared to maturity.

Brain plasticity, or recovery of function, involves a number of factors. The growth of new dendrites, known as sprouting, is a factor. Newly sprouting fibers "rearrange" neural circuits and thus have important functional properties. Another factor involved in the brain's plasticity is the redundancy of neuronal connections. It appears that neurons have many pathways by which they can communicate with other neurons—actually more than they need to carry on normal functions. If some of these communicative pathways are damaged, connections not previously used may take over and thus behavior will be spared. Finally,

some researchers believe that recovery from cerebral damage essentially represents a recovery from *diaschisis*, a shock or depression of neuronal functioning. When damage occurs to the brain, immediately after and often for long periods of time, the neurons near to and distant from the injury site decrease in their response function. This decreased responsivity is thought to be caused by an active inhibitory mechanism in the brain. With time, this inhibitory process is reduced, and normal functioning is again attained. "Focus on Issues" gives further insight to the brain's adaptability.

INFANCY

Excluding prenatal development, the two periods of greatest physical growth and development are infancy and adolescence. In fact, children's physical development in infancy happens so rapidly that their size and skills appear to change daily. One way of noting the rapid sequence of physical development is by looking at their changing height and weight.

HEIGHT AND WEIGHT

During the infancy period (birth to age 2) the child grows from about 20 inches to 34 inches in length and from a birth weight of 7 to 8 pounds to a full 28 pounds. Weight changes are much more dramatic than height changes during the first year after birth. The human baby doubles in weight during the first 3 months of life and almost triples his or her weight in the first year. From birth to 6 months of age, babies increase in weight about 2 grams (less than 1/10 oz) every 24 hours. From 6 months to 3 years, the daily increase averages about .35 grams (about 1/100 oz), and from 3 to 6 years about .15 grams (about 1/200 oz) per day. The growth rate is faster in the first 6 months of life than it will ever be again (Tanner, 1978).

Growth is not steady or constant in all areas. From birth to 1 year, the trunk is the fastest-growing portion, accounting for about 60% of the total increase in body length during this time.

FOCUS ON ISSUES

How Adaptable Is the Human Brain?

The brain is an adaptable organ. The degree of plasticity for recovery, however, is dependent on a variety of factors including age and the extent and location of damage to the brain. Research (Cragg, 1974) suggests the following about cerebral plasticity in the form of recovery. If cerebral injury occurs during the developmental years, impairment of function generally happens, but in milder form; if such injury occurs during the first year of life, little or no deficit in behavior may be detectable. Recovery from cerebral injury depends not only on the age at which the injury occurred but also on the locus of the damage. Recovery of function also depends on the functional maturity of the other brain structures that remain intact after the injury and that are related to or associated with the damaged area. Functional recovery occurs most commonly with those behaviors that have a high level of automatization before injury (for example, behaviors that are well learned by and/or are of "second nature" to the individual). Finally, recovery of language function is possible if injury occurs early in life; however, this recovery may come at the expense of a somewhat lowered general level of intellectual functioning due to "crowding" of functions in one hemisphere.

From age 1 to the onset of adolescence, legs grow the fastest, accounting for 66% of the total increase in height during this period. During adolescence, the trunk once again becomes the fastest growing portion, accounting for 60% of adolescent height increase (Tanner, 1978). As you can see in Figure 5.5, changing proportions are perhaps more dramatic than total growth. During the first year, the head is disproportionately large. The pot-bellied look is normal and has nothing to do with overfeeding or malnutrition in healthy babies. The infant's liver is relatively large at this age, and the immature abdominal muscles lack the strength to hold in the abdominal contents.

Although growth rates are relatively stable, dietary deficiencies can affect them and cause a temporary slowing. If the child suffers an illness or does not eat properly, the velocity of growth development slows down. Physical retardation due to malnutrition is partially self-correcting, however. If the debilitating cause does not last over a certain length of time, the organism velocity of growth accelerates until normal height has been attained. This period of growth is known as **catch-up growth.** Once the projected height is reached, the velocity returns to normal. That is, the organism continues to grow at its original rate.

UNDERNUTRITION

Undernutrition is the most serious obstacle to adequate growth throughout the world. Recent World Health Organization statistics indicate that 40% to 60% of the world's children suffer from mild to moderate undernutrition and 3% to 7% are severely malnourished in some parts of the world (Lozoff, 1989). While undernutrition is more prevalent in developing nations, it does exist in affluent countries such as the United States as well. In the United States undernutrition is most prevalent among ethnic minorities from low socioeconomic levels.

Children under 1 year of age who are severely deprived of necessary proteins and calories suffer from a form of starvation called **marasmus.** In its primary form it results from too little food of any kind being offered to the young child. The main clinical features include wasting of muscles, diarrhea, and anemia. The weight of the child is often

FIGURE 5.5 Changing Proportions of the Human Being

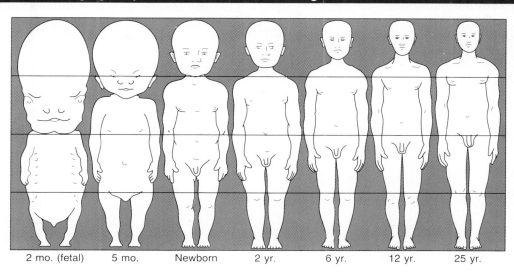

| 2 mo. (fetal) | 5 mo. | Newborn | 2 yr. | 6 yr. | 12 yr. | 25 yr. |

Source: From "Some Aspects of Form and Growth" by C. M. Jackson, in W. J. Robbins, S. Brody, A. F. Hogan, C. M. Jackson, and C. W. Green (Eds.), *Growth*, 1929, New Haven: Yale University Press.

less than 60% of that considered normal for the child's chronological age. Marasmic infants gain very little or no weight, hardly grow, and, if they survive, remain unresponsive.

Children between the ages of 2 to 4 whose diet consists of carbohydrates and little or no protein may suffer from **kwashiorkor.** The word is derived from a tribe in Ghana; literally translated, it means "the sickness that the older child gets when the next baby is born." The condition often develops when the child is taken from the breast and placed on a starchy diet. Kwashiorkor manifests itself by growth failure, muscle wasting, edema of the legs or any part of the body, and mental changes, such as apathy and irritability. The mental changes may lead to alterations in the attitude of the mother to her child and may reduce her responsiveness and warmth.

A study done in Barbados (Salt, Galler, & Ramsey, 1988) identified important functional consequences of early undernutrition. In this longitudinal study, the researchers compared the behavior

and development of 129 school-aged children who suffered from severe protein-energy undernutrition in the 1st year of life (a critical time for human brain growth) with 129 classmates of similar social backgrounds who had no history of undernutrition. Although undernourished during infancy, children in the undernutrition group had been born at term with no perinatal complications or other medical problems that might adversely affect development. They had been protected against recurrences of undernutrition through the activities of health visitors and nutrition counselors. The IQ scores of children in the early undernutrition group averaged 12 points lower than those of control-group children.

One of the most interesting findings was that children who had been undernourished in infancy showed a fourfold increase in symptoms of attention deficit disorder, that is, impaired attention, poor school performance, poor memory, and easy distractibility. Fully 60% of the children in the early undernutrition group were diagnosed with atten-

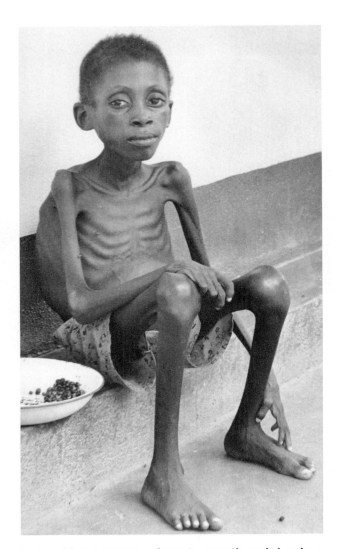

Malnutrition prevents adequate growth and development.

tion deficit disorder. Further, when these children were later retested—up to 18 years of age—increased distractibility and attentional problems persisted and were significantly associated with compromised school performance and high school dropout rates. Current environmental factors were not found to account for their poor cognitive performance.

MOTOR DEVELOPMENT

Physical growth, as was mentioned in Chapter 4, develops in two directions simultaneously: from head to tail—cephalo-caudal, and from spine to extremities—proximal-distal. The development of motor abilities proceeds in the same fashion. For example, cephalo-caudal development may be observed by noting that infants' head turning and eye movements develop first, followed by hand and arm movements, and then crawling. Similarly, in proximal-distal development, larger movements close to the trunk precede the finer movements of the wrist and hand.

Much of the complex motor behavior children use later on is anticipated in early infancy in the form of **reflexes,** unlearned responses that involve a partial reaction of an organism to a specific, eliciting stimulus. Involuntary, autonomic responses are the building blocks of later motor behavior.

Reflexes: The Beginning   Newborns are capable of an amazingly complex series of reflex activities. These early reflexes are slow, generalized, patterned movements of head, trunk, and extremities. For example, if you press your finger against the palm of an infant's hand, the infant's fingers will close over your finger; this is known as the *palmar reflex.* In fact, the infant's grip is so strong that his head and chest can be lifted completely off the ground as you gently pull.

The *rooting reflex* occurs when one of the infant's cheeks is stroked gently; the infant will root or move her mouth toward the stimulus. This reflex disappears at about 3 or 4 months. At birth the infant exhibits a *sucking reflex,* which means that the child will make sucking motions when lips are touched or something is inserted into the mouth.

If young infants are held up and their feet are on a flat surface, they will stiffen their legs and trunk in an attempt to support themselves. Held in this standing position, the newborn will gradually pick up one foot in the air, then put it down again to lift the other foot. "Walking" in this rhythmic, patterned way is the precursor of the voluntary walking pattern that newborns develop much later in

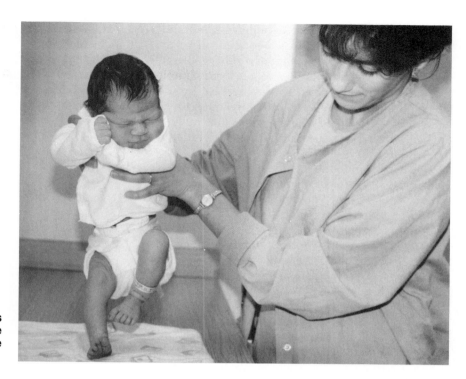

If a newborn is held up with his feet placed on a flat surface, he will first lift one foot and then the other as though walking.

the first year. At about 8 weeks, infants lose this *stepping reflex.*

The *Moro reflex* is set off whenever the baby's head drops backward suddenly. As part of a massive startle, the baby will throw out the arms and legs in extension, then follow with a hugging movement, flexing them back toward the torso. This reflex disappears at about 3 months of age. The *startle reflex,* often confused with the Moro reflex, is elicited by loud noises or unexpected stimuli. The response is similar.

When babies' heads are turned to one side, they react by extending the arms and legs on that side and flexing the arms and legs on the other side as if in a fencing position. This *tonic-neck reflex* abates by 20 weeks of age. When the sole of a baby's foot is stimulated, the toes will spread apart and then curl in. This is known as the *Babinski reflex.* In the *plantar reflex,* older infants just curl their toes in response to a stimulus. The *swimming reflex* occurs

when infants are lying on their stomachs. In this position they will make characteristic swimming movements. This response disappears at around 6 months.

What purposes do these reflexes have? It may be that the reflexes occur because the cerebrum has little involvement in behavior. The pathways of the central nervous system and brain may be inadequately myelinated to provide the integration of actions required by the more mature responses. Primitive reflexes governed by the older structures of the brain drop out or disappear when the cerebrum begins to dominate. If primitive reflexes are still present later on, it may indicate that something has gone wrong with the development of the cerebrum and may demonstrate brain damage.

Changing Reflexes to Voluntary Behavior Reflexes, which appear in newborns and in early infancy, disappear, only to reappear later as voluntary behavior. As the reflexive motor abilities come under voluntary control, they are elaborated on to produce new, more sophisticated and effective motor skills. The increasing ability to perform complex motor functions is linked to the increase in body size, brain growth, development, and to the growth of various body parts, bones and muscles, and maturation of neuronal pathways. The infant masters an impressive array of motor feats.

There is some disagreement as to what role learning and maturation play in development of motor skills. Some maintain that motor skills should be taught, and, in this way, have their development accelerated. Others say the development of motor skills, such as standing alone and walking, occur naturally and that practice plays only a small role in their development. Evidence exists on both sides of the maturation-versus-learning controversy.

In general, these studies have used twins to determine the role of learning in motor skills. In each case, one of the twins receives a great deal of training in a particular skill such as walking upstairs. The other twin is not given such extensive training, but rather is given only a brief period of practice later in development. The results of these studies have shown that both of the twins perform equally well. No matter how much training the first twin receives, she will not learn the particular skill until the muscles, bones, and central nervous system have developed sufficiently. Once that point is reached, as long as the child is given some opportunity to move about and to explore the environment, the development of a particular motor activity occurs on schedule.

While motor skills such as standing or walking seem to appear naturally without practice or learning, some motor skills are strongly influenced by learning and motivation. Certain skills, such as hitting a baseball, are more dependent on receiving appropriate instruction and a chance to practice that skill.

Locomotive Skills   Children are active little beings, with an insatiable urge to explore. It isn't long before they have mastered the art of navigating in, under, around, and through their environment. Young children invent all sorts of strategies to get that sought-after toy or just to see what there is to see. Some children roll over and over, some do the old Marine crawl, some scoot on their seats—but all these methods of locomotion serve the same purpose. By 40 weeks, children begin

creeping on their hands and knees, which involves the coordination of arms and legs. Some creep as early as 5 months, others not until 12 months, and others not at all.

Somewhere between 36 and 40 weeks, children are able to pull themselves up on the furniture and stand for a few shaky moments, which helps them learn the fine art of balancing. At 48 weeks they can stand alone, usually followed shortly thereafter by walking. Walking is quite a feat as the onlookers give their ohs and ahs, and the child beams with delight in taking those first jerky, unstable, flat-footed steps. Although the onset of walking generally occurs around 13 to 15 months, it is not until around age 4 that the child assumes the adultlike walk with the smooth, rhythmical transfer of weight from heel-to-toe and the rhythmical swing of the arms in opposition to leg action (Espenschade & Eckert, 1980).

At 18 months, children can walk upstairs in a "mark-time" pattern, that is, the lead foot steps up, followed by the other foot, which is placed beside it. The alternating foot pattern does not occur until around age 3. Going upstairs is easier than coming down. Children generally are unable to descend stairs using the alternating foot pattern without support until age 4, perhaps 5. Two-year-olds can climb, run forward and backward, and seemingly have unlimited powers in order to get where they want to go. Figure 5.6 shows the sequence of motor events leading to the walking stage. Note that the average age at which a child masters a certain task has a wide range.

Manipulative Skills   Early motor development is largely concerned with reaching, grasping, and manipulating objects. Hands provide a rich sensory input from the environment. Young children show a great deal of reaching and grasping behaviors, which initially are done in a random and pur-

---

FIGURE 5.6   Sequence of Motor Development Leading to Walking

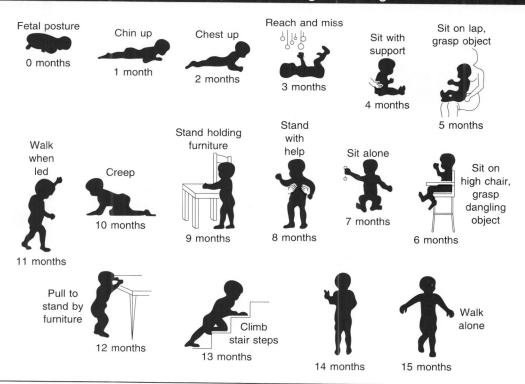

Source: From *The First Two Years*, Institute of Child Welfare Monograph, No. 7 by M. M. Shirley. © 1933, renewed 1961. Reprinted by permission of the University of Minnesota Press.

poseless fashion. At 1 month, babies will stare at an object in their fields of vision. At a little over 2 months, they will make swiping motions at it. By 4 months, children can glance at the object and their hands and then perhaps touch the object. (What sometimes happens, however, is that babies get so absorbed in staring at their hands that they forget about the object!) By 5 months or so, children can reach for the object and contact it efficiently. Children at this age begin to intentionally reach, grasp, and hold onto an object. One problem exists, however: children don't know how to let go. Usually what happens is that they eventually lose interest, their hands relax, and the object, unnoticed by the infants, drops. By 6 months, most children are able to intentionally release an object. Figure 5.7 shows the development of manipulative skills.

Cross-Cultural Differences in Motor Capabilities
In a pioneering study Caudill and Weinstein (1969) observed Japanese and U.S. infants interacting with one another. The researchers concluded that American babies were more motorically active than were Japanese babies. In another study (Shand & Kosawa, 1985) American and Japanese babies were observed when 3 hours, 1 month, and 3 months old. Contrary to the Caudill and Weinstein study, Shand and Kosawa (1985) concluded that Japanese babies were more motorically active than were American babies.

While disagreeing on activity level, all the authors of these studies concurred that American and Japanese babies behave equivalently in the sphere of biological function, such as time spent sucking, eating, and sleeping. All of the investigators found that American babies vocalized nondistress more often than Japanese babies.

Many observers have reported that African and Asian infants deviate from established European norms with respect to the timing of motor development. Indeed, the findings of some 50 studies point to a generalized accelerated pace of motor

**FIGURE 5.7
Development of
Grasping Skills**

No contact
16 weeks

Contact only
20 weeks

Primitive squeeze
20 weeks

Squeeze grasp
7 months

Hand grasp
7 months

Palm grasp
7 months

Superior palm grasp
32 weeks

Inferior-forefinger grasp
36 weeks

Forefinger grasp
52 weeks

Superior-forefinger grasp
52 weeks

Source: From "An Experimental Study of Prehension in Infants by Means of Systematic Cinema Records" by H. M. Halverson, 1931, in *Genetic Psychological Monographs, 10,* pp. 212–215. Reprinted with permission of The Helen Dwight Reid Educational Foundation. Published by Heldref Publications, 1319 Eighteenth St., N.W., Washington, DC 20036-1802. Copyright © 1931.

Genetics and environment combine to affect the development of children.

development among non-Western infants (Werner, 1972; Super, 1976). Ghanda infants, for example, are reputedly more advanced in motor functioning than Causasian age norms would predict (Geber, 1958). Ghanda infants showed remarkable control over motor reactions. They were able to be pulled to sit by extended arms; they not only maintained excellent head control in bringing their heads up parallel to their bodies, but also turned their heads to look around the room as they sat.

A study by Hopkins and Westra (1989) was conducted with 124 Jamaican, Hindi-speaking Indian, and English mothers and their firstborn infants. The Jamaican mothers' expectation of when their infants would achieve sitting and walking alone was significantly earlier than both their English and Indian counterparts, and, indeed, the Jamaican infants achieved these skills at strikingly earlier ages than the English and Indian infants. The

authors concluded that cultural differences may be related to different expectations for the attainment of milestones between non-Western mothers and European or American counterparts.

It appears, then, that cross-cultural differences in motoric behavior exist early in life (Bornstein, 1989). Are these differences attributed to culturally different child-rearing practices, or do these differences reflect genetic dispositions of a group? Caudill and Weinstein (1969) argue that essentially no meaningful biological differences distinguish Japanese and American babies, and that a culture–mother–infant chain of cause and effect best explicates the relation between culture and individual behavior. That is, infant activities develop under maternal influences, which are in turn guided to conform to culturally preferred patterns. In specific, Caudill and Weinstein contended that activity level is plastic to experience and that maternal behavior, which reflects expectations and patterns of the larger culture, molds infant activity, and that, indeed, the goal of American culture is an active, individualistic, assertive baby, whereas the goal of the Japanese culture is a passive, accommodative, placid baby.

In support of this cultural-learning view, Caudill and Weinstein (1969) found that American mothers stimulated (e.g., talked to and looked at) their babies more than Japanese mothers did theirs. The authors concluded that maternal activity can exert a significant (and lasting) influence over infant activity even at a very early age. Super (1976) found advanced sitting, standing, and walking among Kenyan Kipsigis babies, but he also found retarded head lifting, crawling, and turning over. In the absence of "generalized precocity" among Kipsigis infants, Super was led to study their mothers, the vast majority of whom deliberately taught their infants to sit, stand, and walk. Caudill's data and subsequent replications (Bornstein & Tamis-LeMonda, 1988) lend support to a model of culture and mother as the primary causal influences over individual differences in infant activity.

By contrast, Shand and Kosawa (1985) argue that biological differences probably do distinguish Japanese and American babies, and that a genes–infant–mother–culture direction of causality underpins the relation between culture and individual behavior. They propose that differences in motor activity level between culture and individual behavior reflect "biologically related (and possibly genetic) constitutional factors" (p. 227) in origin, and that these differences (among others) are so thoroughgoing and impressive as actually to promote distinctiveness between cultures. In their words, "culture differences in behavior are at least in part a matter of variable genetic predispositions and genetically differentiated predispositions for behavioral epigenesis" (Shand & Kosawa, 1985, p. 225). In essence, this model specifies that the individual genotype is central in determining initial behavioral and temperamental differences, in that it governs spontaneous activity and individual responsiveness to various aspects of the environment, which in turn may modify traits within the individual. On this basis, the model proposes that infants are "prompted" by their unique genetic endowments to evoke, selectively experience, and thence shape the environments they encounter.

Of course, one data set cannot address a question so large and unwieldly as the origins and maintenance of culture, or genetic versus experiential determinants of infant motor capabilities. Neither the empiricist view of Caudill and Weinstein nor the nativist view of Shand and Kosawa can be wholly determinative. Two investigators (Goldsmith & Gottesman, 1981) identified at least a moderate genetic component in activity level, 35% of the variance, when they found that pairs of identical 8-month-old twins were more alike than fraternal twins on a cluster of Bayley Scale items all having to do with motor activity level. Goldsmith and Gottesman's heritability estimate for activity leaves as much as 65% of the variance to be accounted for by other, presumably environmental influences. Consonant with this view, motor activity level is acknowledged to be influenced in part by genetic endowment, but it also is responsive to environmental inputs.

SENSORY AND PERCEPTUAL DEVELOPMENT

In the past few years, infant research has advanced considerably in many areas of sensation and perception. Today we have a better, though certainly not complete, understanding of a variety of sensory abilities and functions near the beginning of life. **Sensation** is the ability of the sense receptors to detect a particular stimulus in the environment. **Perception** is the process of organizing and interpreting these physical sensations. Pulsating air transmitted to the cochlear nerve of the ear (sensation) is interpreted as a dog barking (perception). While it takes some time for children to acquire skills that enable them to make sense of the information carried via the senses, most researchers are in agreement that at birth an infant's senses of sight, sound, touch, taste, and smell are nearly complete and improve rather rapidly in the first 6 months of life.

A common technique for studying children's sensory capabilities is known as *habituation*, which is the most primitive kind of learning. Habituation involves getting used to a sound, sight, or other stimulus, which results in a lowered intensity of response to that stimulus. For example, if an infant is presented with a change in an ongoing stimulus, the alert infant responds to that change. With repeated exposure to the same stimulus, the child will stop responding. Studies of habituation show us how well babies can see and hear, and how much they remember.

What are the sensory capabilities of the young child? It used to be thought that the behavior of newborns was entirely reflexive and that they lived in a world of confusing smells, sounds, and shifting shadows. As a case in point, it was not discovered until recently that babies could see at all because it had not been realized that infants have a fairly rigid distance of focus—approximately 9 inches. "Studying Children" offers some activities that will help you to discover how capable the newborn child is. Ingenious experiments, which we shall discuss, have been performed that show just how talented young infants are.

Vision Because vision is the dominant sensory system in humans and the major modality for interacting with the environment, it has been studied more extensively than touch, taste, smell, or hearing. Because of the absence of light in utero, vision does not function prenatally. Newborns can perceive light, as demonstrated by the pupillary reflex (constriction of the pupil to bright light and dilation to low levels of illumination). However, accommodation, or focusing of the lens, is relatively poor at birth. Research indicates, however, that accommodation is adultlike by as early as 2 months of age, with many younger infants displaying good accommodative ability. Convergence refers to both eyes looking at the same object, an ability not possessed by newborns. Convergence and coordination (both eyes following a moving stimulus in a coordinated fashion) improve over the first months of life and are adultlike by 6 months. Research assessing the visual acuity in the newborn, or the ability to see clearly, has yielded mixed results. With normal acuity for adults being 20/20, estimates of newborn acuity range from 20/400 to 20/600 (Cole, 1991), making the neonate legally blind in most states. Acuity improves over the next several months. This slow process of the development of the visual system helps protect the infant from too much stimulation. Visual acuity reaches adult levels by 6 months (Haith, 1980). Researchers have also studied other aspects of vision, notably children's perception of form, color, and depth.

STUDYING CHILDREN

THE AMAZING NEWBORN

It is truly amazing to discover how capable newborn infants are. In a quiet, not too brightly lit room you can perform various activities with the infant and discover her extraordinary abilities for yourself. Putting your index finger in the palm of her hand, the small infant will grasp it with surprising determination and strength. When the infant is lying on his back, pull him up by his arms, and he will try to maintain his head upright. A little boy will look intently at a red or soft yellow object dangled before him; he will even follow it with his eyes, turning his head when the object is moved slowly from side to side and up and down. A little girl will exhibit a quieting and alerting to a soft, high-pitched voice. Sometimes you are able to produce fleeting smiles in the newborn by making soft noises.

Form Perception Before infants can actively explore their environment with their hands and feet, they are busy exploring with their eyes. When they encounter an interesting stimulus, newborns appear to explore the areas of greatest contrast. Salapatek and Kessen (1966) studied newborns who were 4 to 7 days old. Each of the infants was shown an 8-inch, equilateral, black triangle at a distance of 9 inches. The ocular movements of the eyes were photographed by using infrared lights placed behind the triangle permitting the experimenter to get a precise reading of what the infant was looking at. As can be seen in Figure 5.8, newborns seemed to be more sensitive to contrasting edges and contours, for example, the edge of a black line on a white background. Similarly, 1-month-old children, when viewing a human face, scanned the areas of most contrast: the hair-

FIGURE 5.8 Visual Scanning in Infants

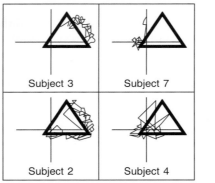

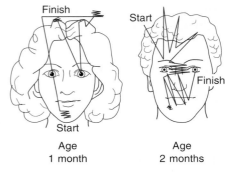

Source: Triangle scanning from "Visual Scanning of Triangles by the Human Newborn" by P. Salapatek and W. Kessen, 1966, in *Journal of Experimental Child Psychology*, 3, p. 161. Copyright 1966 by Academic Press. Reprinted by permission. Face scanning from "Developmental Changes in Scanning of Faces by Young Infants" by D. Maurer and P. Salapatek, 1975, *Child Development, 47*, p. 525. © The Society for Research in Child Development, Inc. Reprinted by permission.

line of the face, angles, and edges. The experimenters concluded that young infants do not respond to or perceive total form, but instead respond to some feature of the stimulus. At 2 months of age, children track an individual trait of the face: a bright red mouth, or shiny eyes.

The study of the development of form perception received its contemporary impetus from the work of Robert Fantz, which began in the 1960s (Fantz, 1961; Fantz, Fagan, & Miranda, 1975). Fantz's studies demonstrated that infants prefer rather complex patterns. Monitoring infants' attention to two paired stimuli, he assumed that if infants look at the stimuli for the same amount of time either they cannot tell the difference between them or they do not prefer one over the other. If, however, infants stare at one stimulus longer than the other, they do notice the difference or prefer one over the other.

In one experiment, infants were presented with six test objects, all flat disks, 6 inches in diameter. As can be seen in Figure 5.9, three of the disks are patterned: a face, a bull's-eye, and a patch of printed matter. The other three disks are plain but brightly colored: red, fluorescent yellow, and white. These disks are presented one at a time in varied sequence, and the length of the first glance

at each is timed. The face pattern is overwhelmingly the most interesting to infants, followed by the printing and the bull's eye. The three brightly colored plain circles trail far behind and receive no first choices.

Fantz (1961) also showed a series of babies three flat, face-shaped objects, such as those seen in Figure 5.10. On the first, a stylized face is printed in black on a pink background; the second has the same features as the first, but scrambled; the third has a solid black patch at one end equal in area to the features of the first two.

All the babies looked most at the stylized face, somewhat less at the scrambled face, and least at the third oval. In fact, infants seem to have an innate interest in looking at the human face—both real and stylized. Infants will stare as long as 20 minutes at the stylized face. However, if presented with a real face, newborns appear surprised, look back at the schematic face, frown, and return to look at the real face. When the real face continues to stare fixedly, the newborn looks worried, frowns, and turns away. Even at birth it appears that newborns seem not only to prefer looking at human faces, but also have an expectation for interaction with it. The nonhuman or schematic face attracts the baby, but does not carry this kind of

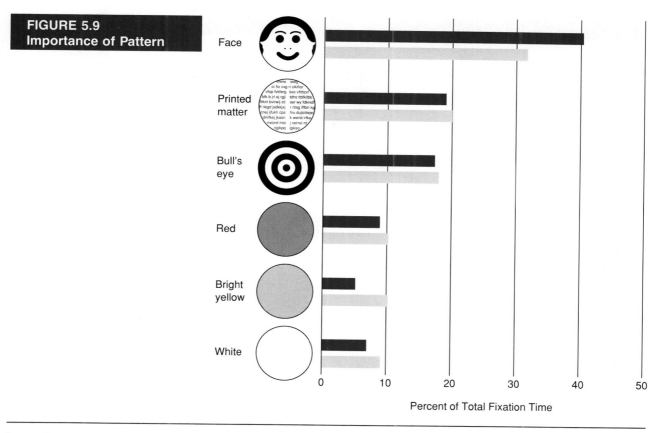

FIGURE 5.9
Importance of Pattern

Face

Printed matter

Bull's eye

Red

Bright yellow

White

Percent of Total Fixation Time

Source: From "The Origin of Form Perception" by R. L. Fantz, May, 1961, *Scientific American*, p. 72. Drawing by A. Semenoick. Copyright 1961 by *Scientific American*. Reprinted by permission.

expectation with it; newborns, therefore, will stare at it for longer periods of time.

How soon does the baby recognize the mother's face? The developmental time course of visual recognition is somewhat ambiguous. When tested with photographs of a female's face, 3-month-old infants recognize their mother's face (Barrera & Maurer, 1981). More recent experiments have revealed that 22- to 93-hour-old infants respond preferentially to the silent faces of their mother over the faces of unfamiliar women (Field, Cohen, Garcia, & Greenberg, 1984).

Langlois and her colleagues (Langlois, Roggman, Casey, Ritter, Rieser-Danner, & Jenkins, 1987; Langlois & Roggman, 1990) have shown that young infants visually discriminate among adult female faces based on the adult-judged attractiveness of the faces and that infants exhibit both visual and behavioral preferences for attractive compared with unattractive female faces. Moreover, the generality of these preferences has been shown across different types of faces (Langlois, Ritter, Roggman, & Vaughn, 1991). Sixty 6-month-old infants were exposed to male faces, African American adult female faces, and faces of other young infants. As in her previous studies, the slides were selected for high and low attractiveness as rated by 40 graduate students. The results of her study show that 6-month-old infants can discriminate attractive from unattractive faces and that they visu-

FIGURE 5.10   Fantz's Faces

The results charted here show the average time scores for infants at various ages when presented with the three face-shaped objects.

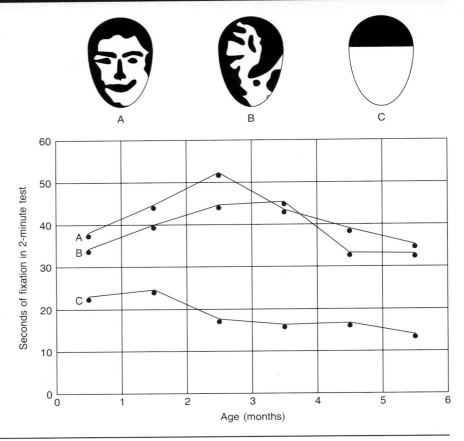

Source: From "The Origin of Form Perception" by R. L. Fantz, May, 1961, *Scientific American*, p. 72. Drawing by A. Semenoick. Copyright 1961 by *Scientific American*. Reprinted by permission.

ally prefer attractive faces of diverse types. Langlois et al. (1991) conclude that preferences for attractiveness are either innate or acquired with only minimal experience with faces in the environment.

Research has also shown that older infants (12 to 18 months old) are capable of discriminating gender in faces and that infants display same-sex preferences when presented with photographs of male and female same-age infants (Lewis & Brooks-Gunn, 1979).

Color Perception   Newborns do not see colors but rather perceive their world in black, white, and gray. At birth, infants can see the difference between darkness and brightness (Bornstein, 1985). Researchers have cited the physiological evidence of changes in breathing, heartbeat, or galvanic skin response, and data showing that the infant stares longer at one colored card over another at approximately 2 weeks. Such preference suggests that the first color infants see is blue, followed by red, yellow, and green (Bornstein, 1976). By 6 months, infants' color perception equals that of an adult.

Depth Perception   Experiments done by Gibson and Walk (1960) demonstrate that most infants can discriminate depth as soon as they can crawl. In their "visual cliff" experiment, a child crawls onto a checkerboard pattern stretched out from a table. One area of the checkerboard is optically distorted so that the squares appear smaller, thus creating the illusion of being further away. The infant, perceiving the illusion as true depth, will not crawl over the "cliff." While some infants patted the glass on the deep side, they nevertheless refused to cross, even with this tactile assurance of solidity.

The visual cliff experiment does not prove that human infants' perception and avoidance of the cliff are innate. However, such an interpretation is supported by experiments done with nonhuman young. Performed with kittens, turtles, lambs, and dogs, studies by Gibson and Walk (1960) found that in young animals the awareness of the difference between height of the table and the floor was generally enough to make them refuse to travel over the cliff, even when they were only 1 day old. (Only turtles were somewhat inaccurate in their perception of the depth cues.)

Campos, Langer, and Krowitz (1970) tested infants in the pre-crawling stage to see if depth perception develops before babies crawl. Infants were placed on the "deep" side of the cliff, directly on the protective glass. In measuring heart rates they found that 8-month-olds showed a rapid increase in heart rate; infants younger than 8 months showed a decrease in heart rate. What do these differences mean? Although infants younger than 8 months did notice the deep side and paid attention to it (heartbeats tend to slow down when an infant is attentive to something), they were essentially fearless. More than likely, perception and cognitive maturation are necessary to know what the edge of the cliff means. Perhaps, too, babies have to fall or nearly fall before fear develops.

Hearing   The auditory system of the infant is fully functional from 5 months gestational age onward, which means the infant has the ability to hear in utero. This system, however, is also protected from overstimulation, and newborn infants have a high threshold for sound, which decreases gradually over the first year of life (Klaus & Klaus, 1986). For the first few days after birth, hearing is probably diminished because the middle part of the ear behind the eardrum is still full of amniotic fluid, which will gradually be absorbed or evaporate. At around 4 days, babies are able to localize sounds (Javel, 1980). For example, babies can turn their heads toward the sound of a bell. Even with a deeply sleeping baby, you may see a slight stir to a quiet voice near the baby's ear. The infant's breath-

Eleanor Gibson and Richard Walk, in performing their "visual cliff" experiment, discovered that most infants will not crawl over the cliff even after they pat the solid, clear covering.

ing will change, she may open her eyes slightly, or she may even slightly smile in response. If the soft-spoken voice continues, she will gradually begin to stir and awaken. The softest sound that a newborn can hear is 10 to 20 decibels, approximately the amount you hear when you have a head cold (Trehub, Schneider, Thorpe, & Judge, 1991). Infants have anywhere from 10 and 30 decibels less sensitivity to sound than adults (Schneider, Trehub, Morrongiello, & Thorpe, 1986). One possible basis for poorer sensitivity is that although the middle and inner ear are about the same size as those of adults, myelination is not complete at birth. Table 5.2 shows some common sound levels in decibels.

Hearing can be investigated by recording changes in heart rates, sucking rates, or brain-wave patterns when a sound is presented. Researchers, using these techniques, have found that 1- to 2-week-old infants can discriminate between loud and soft sounds and high and low ones. Young infants can even hear contrasts in a foreign language that adults who do not speak the language cannot hear. For example, Japanese babies have no trouble with the L/R distinction that their parents find difficult. Adults apparently have had long practice at learning not to hear many sounds that are not significant in their own language. This effect sets in early. Even at 1 year of age, infants have more trouble than they did earlier distinguishing sounds that are not used in their own language.

In utero, the baby is exposed to the loud rhythmical sounds of the mother's heartbeat and blood flowing through the uterine wall. It seems from this that patterned, rhythmic sounds produce more response than pure continuous tones in young infants. The most effective sound of all is one that includes the fundamental frequencies found in the human voice. Infants seem to prefer a high-pitched voice. (Perhaps this justifies the high-pitched baby talk that many of us use when "conversing" with infants.)

Additional research has shown that it doesn't take a particularly loud sound to penetrate the womb and amniotic sac. Other than loud noises, the fetus may hear normal conversational sounds. Without being aware of it, parents may begin to sensitize the child to their voices even before a child is born. Perhaps this explains why babies recognize their parents' voices as familiar sounds once they are born (Rivlin & Gravell, 1984).

Evidence further suggests that this preference for a familiar voice may have its origins before birth (DeCasper & Spence, 1986). Pregnant women read aloud one of three passages twice a day during the last six weeks of their pregnancy. Shortly after birth, the neonates were tested for which passages, if any, would have more reinforcing values. Headphones were placed over babies' ears, and various passages were played to the infants. Nonnutritive sucking was assessed as a function of what passage was being played. The general finding was that the familiar passage was more reinforcing than the novel passage. Infants were more likely to alter their sucking rate to hear the familiar passage than to hear the novel passage. Furthermore, the reinforcing value of the story was independent of who recited it, an infant's mother or another woman. These findings indicate not only that the auditory system in newborns is working well but also that babies are "learning" some things about the outside world while still in utero.

It has also been demonstrated in other experiments that infants can learn to change their sucking patterns to produce a reward. In this experiment, young infants were taught to modify their sucking frequencies to hear their mothers. Equipped with microphones, the infants sucked on a pacifier that held a pressure sensitive elec-

TABLE 5.2 Some Common Sound Levels in Decibels

Sound	dB
Barely audible sound (threshold)	0
Leaves rustling	20
Quiet residential community	40
Average speaking voice	60
Loud voices	80
Subway	100
Rock band	120
Jet engine at takeoff	140

tronic device. Five infants heard (a) their mothers' voices when they sucked faster on the pacifier and (b) a stranger's voice when they sucked slower. The other five infants heard (a) their mothers' voices when they sucked slower and (b) a stranger's voice when they sucked faster. Eight out of the 10 infants changed their sucking patterns to hear their mother's voice (DeCasper & Fifer, 1980).

Smell Smell is another way newborns gather information about their environment. That very young babies can smell has been shown in a study at Brown University (Lipsitt, Engen, & Kaye, 1963). These researchers observed the activity, heart rate, and breathing patterns of twenty 2-day-old babies. Each baby was presented with two of four smells: anise oil, asafetida (similar to garlic), acetic acid (vinegar), and phenyl alcohol. When a smell is first presented to the baby, her heart rate, activity level, and breathing pattern change. If the smell continues, the baby gradually learns to take no notice of it. If the smell changes, however, up goes the activity level—heart rate and breathing changes again—and the infant recognizes the smell as being different from the one to which she had become accustomed.

Young infants have the ability to detect **pheromones,** chemical signals given off by others of the same species that communicate various messages such as fear, identification, and so forth. Within 2 weeks of birth, sleeping children will turn instinctively toward the breast pads of their own mother or a strange mother—food, any food, is essential. At six weeks, breast-fed infants show a strong preference for their own mother's breast pads rather than those of another woman's (MacFarlane, 1977).

Since MacFarlane's original study, there have been additional corroborating reports of infants responding selectively to their nursing mothers' breast odor. Six-week-old babies reacted with sucking and orienting movements when presented with a breast pad worn by their mother, but not to pads from a strange mother or treated with cow's milk (Schaal, 1986). Similarly, reduced head and arm movements were observed in breast-fed infants when their nose came into contact with a breast pad worn by their mother (Schaal, Montagner, Hertling, Bolzoni, Moyse, & Quichon, 1980). This calming effect did not occur in response to odors from unfamiliar control mothers.

The "security blanket" is a real phenomenon by which the young child marks and recognizes his own environment by its scent signals, allowing the environment to be transported away from home with the favorite object.

One researcher (Steiner, 1977) suggests that infants may be especially sensitive to food-related chemical stimuli. Prior to their first feeding, neonates were presented with (artificial) odors of butter, bananas, vanilla, shrimp, and rotten eggs, and their facial expressions were photographed. Photographs were then classified by judges as expressing acceptance (the baby liked the odor), indifference, or rejection (the baby disliked the odor). Overall, expressions presumed to be indicative of acceptance were elicited by butter, bananas, and (to a lesser extent) vanilla. Shrimp and rotten-egg odors tended to evoke rejection expressions, with 100% of the infants reacting with aversion to rotten eggs. On the basis of these data, Steiner concluded that infants are able to discriminate odors of fresh and valuable nutrients from those of food that would be ''instinctively'' rejected by adults.

Taste Taste is a relatively simple sense in human beings, and the fine discriminations that you think you can make by taste alone, you actually smell. An observation indicates that babies inside the uterus are able to taste. Surrounded by amniotic fluid, babies swallow it and then eliminate it continually. In certain pregnancies too much fluid accumulates too quickly. Forty years ago, a physician developed a novel way of treating this. By sweetening the amniotic fluid surrounding the baby with an injection of saccharine, he discovered he could reduce the amount of fluid, possibly because the baby was encouraged to swallow more. Another doctor found that injecting an opaque substance that had an unpleasant taste decreased the swallowing. This was clear from the x-ray pictures of the substance being swallowed by the child (Steiner, 1977).

The neonate's sense of taste is reasonably well developed. Newborns display different facial expressions, tongue movements, and physiological responses for each of the 4 basic tastes of sweet, sour, salty, and bitter, and show a preference for sweet substances. Lipsitt (1969), in working with babies 2 to 3 days old, arranged a system by which each time babies sucked, they got a tiny amount of sugar water. He found that the more sugar, the slower the baby sucked and the more their heart rates increased. Why did they suck slower? Wouldn't you think they would suck faster? Perhaps babies suck slower in order to savor the sweeter liquid, and perhaps the excitement of tasting it increases the heart rate. Then again, perhaps the answer is not that simple.

Pain and Touch Little research has been done on the baby's perception of pain—after all, no one wants to hurt tiny newborns. However, if you have ever observed an infant's reaction to a blood test (usually done by pricking the baby's heel with a small stylette), you would assume, as he jerks back his foot and wails with anguish, that he is aware of pain. Similarly, after circumcision a newborn's sleeping patterns are often disturbed, and there is a prolonged period of fussiness (Gunnar & Malone, 1985). We know that babies are sensitive to touch because most of the early reflexes are triggered by touching various parts of the body.

EARLY AND MIDDLE CHILDHOOD

In early and middle childhood, spanning the years from 3 to 12, children's arms and legs grow longer; they lose their baby fat; stomachs become flat; and they grow proportionally thinner as they grow taller. In short, they take on a more adultlike appearance. Muscles grow in size and strength, but they are still immature in function compared with during adolescence. Children improve to a marked degree in their ability to move and to manipulate objects in their environment. Development of motor skills is the hallmark of children during this period.

HEIGHT AND WEIGHT
The growth rates for height decelerate slowly during early and middle childhood. From age 3 to 12 children grow between 2 and 2½ inches per year. In early childhood, ages 3 to 7, the child's weight more than doubles, from roughly 25 lbs to 65 lbs, which is about one third to one half of adult weight. The child between 6 and 12 years generally gains about 5 pounds per year. Most of the in-

crease in weight is due to muscle growth. The average height of a 6-year-old is 3½ feet; the average height of a 12-year-old is 5 feet. At age 12 children have reached 90% of their adult height.

Inches and pounds tell us children are growing; however, the best measures of establishing a child's level of physical maturation is to x-ray the child's wrist or hand. The X ray shows the number of bones and the extent of their ossification (skeletal age), as can be seen in Figure 5.11. X rays tell us the maturity of the child's skeleton and show how fully the immature central cartilage cells have broken down and hardened into bone.

Girls grow up faster than boys. Girls reach 50% of their adult height at an earlier age (on average at 1¾ years compared with 2 years in boys), enter puberty earlier, and cease earlier to grow (Tanner, 1978). Boys and girls differ in maturation. Boys have more muscles per pound of body weight and more bone than girls. Baby fat disappears sooner, giving boys a leaner look throughout childhood. Girls have more fatty tissue.

FIGURE 5.11

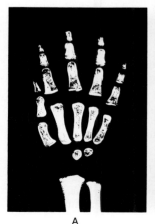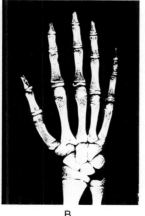

A   B

X rays showing the amount of skeletal development seen in (A) the hand of an average male infant at 12 months or an average female infant at 10 months and (B) the hand of an average 13-year-old male or an average 10½-year-old female.

STUDYING CHILDREN

PHYSICAL SELVES

Select two or three children who are between 5 and 7 years old. Have each child draw a picture of him- or herself. Encourage them to take their time and include as much detail as possible. Do their drawings reveal anything about how children view their physical selves? What features are included in their drawings? Do children draw body parts in order of importance to them? For example, 5-year-olds generally omit the trunk of the body but often include legs and feet. Perhaps they do so because their trunks are not active like legs and feet.

Boys are better at throwing a ball, jumping, and going up and down ladders; girls are more coordinated, and can balance and hop better than boys. Girls tend to have more mature fine motor skills than boys; thus, they do better than boys at tasks such as writing, drawing, and cutting out. Girls tend to be slightly shorter and lighter than boys. There appears to be little difference in strength between boys and girls until the age of 6, when boys generally become stronger than girls.

Growth occurs in legs and trunk (leg growth accounts for 66% of the height increases that occur from age 1 to the onset of adolescence). By 5½ years of age, the body-fat layer is half as thick as it was at 9 months. The body systems slow down and stabilize during early childhood. The child's metabolic rate, heart rate, respiration rate, and blood pressure all are slower than in infancy. By age 3, the respiratory system has matured to permit adultlike chest and abdominal breathing movements.

How do children during this developmental period perceive their "physical selves"? What physical features seem important to them? The activity suggested in "Studying Children" may provide the answer.

MOTOR DEVELOPMENT

In the years of early and middle childhood, basic skills are expanded and refined. By the end of middle childhood, children move with considerable agility; they become quite proficient at balancing, locomotion, and manipulative abilities.

Large muscles develop before small muscles; therefore, children generally become more skillful in activities that involve *gross motor* movements than in those that require *fine motor* movements. For example, preschoolers use their whole bodies and arms to catch a ball, not hands, fingers, and wrists. Catching is merely the passive acceptance of an object. Greater levels of overall body coordination and dexterity and general body awareness contribute to the development and refinement of motor skills. Table 5.3 notes the gross-motor skill development of preschoolers.

Motor development in middle childhood is summarized in Table 5.4. Children can discriminate left from right in their own bodies by age 7.

Handedness is well established by age 6, and fine muscle ability improves steadily from then until age 12. At age 12, children have developed about 90% of their potential mobility and speed of reaction. Balance, speed, strength, and coordination seem to improve with time and practice.

In a study done in the 1960s, it was reported that left-handed children tend to be more clumsy, poorly coordinated, and poor at making smooth and efficient motor movements (Flick, 1966). Tan (1985) investigated whether handedness is related to motor competence. From a population of 512 4-year-olds attending preschool, 41 children were identified as left-handed and 23 were identified as lacking hand preference. These children's motor abilities were compared with right-handed children who were matched for age and sex. Results indicate that there is no difference in motor abili-

TABLE 5.3   Motor Skill Development of Preschoolers

	SKILL CHARACTERISTICS		
Motor Pattern	3-Year-Old	4-Year-Old	5-Year-Old
Walking/running	Run is smoother; stride more even. Cannot turn or stop quickly. Can take walking and running steps on the toes.	Run improves in form and power. Greater control, stopping, starting, and turning. In general, greater mobility than at age 3.	Has adult manner of running. Can use this effectively in games. Runs 35-yard dash in less than 10 seconds.
Jumping	42% rated as jumping well. Can jump down from 8-inch elevation. Leaps off floor with both feet.	72% skilled in jumping. Jumps down from 28 inch height with feet together. Standing broad jump of 8 to 10 inches.	80% have mastered the skill of jumping. Makes running broad jump of 28 to 35 inches.
Climbing	Ascends stairway unaided, alternating feet. Ascends small ladder, alternating feet.	Descends long stairway by alternating feet, if supported. Descends small ladder, alternating feet.	Descends long stairway or large ladder, alternating feet. Further increase in overall proficiency.
Throwing	Throws without losing balance. Throws approximately 3 feet; uses two-hand throw. Body remains fixed during throw.	20% are proficient throwers. Distance of throw increases. Begins to assume adult stance in throwing.	74% are proficient throwers. Introduction of weight transfer; right-foot-step-forward throw. Assumes adult posture in throwing.
Catching	Catches large ball with arms extended forward stiffly. Makes little or no adjustment of arms to receive ball.	29% are proficient in catching. Catches large ball with arms flexed at elbows.	56% are proficient in catching. Catches small ball; uses hands more than arms.

Source: Adapted with permission from Charles B. Corbin, *A Textbook of Motor Development*. Copyright © 1973 Wm. C. Brown Publishers, Dubuque, Iowa. All Rights Reserved.

TABLE 5.4 Motor Development in Middle Childhood	**Age**	**Selected Behaviors**
	6	Girls are superior in movement accuracy; boys are superior in forceful, less complex acts.
		Skipping is possible.
		Can throw with proper weight shift and step.
	7	One-footed balancing without looking becomes possible.
		Can walk 2-inch-wide balance beams.
		Can hop and jump accurately into small squares.
		Can execute accurate jumping-jack exercise.
	8	Have 12-pound pressure on grip strength.
		Number of games participated in by both sexes is greatest at this age.
		Can engage in alternate rhythmic hopping in a 2-2, 2-3, or 3-3 pattern.
		Girls can throw a small ball 40 feet.
	9	Girls can vertical-jump 8½ inches, and boys 10 inches, over their standing height plus reach.
		Boys can run 16½ feet per second.
		Boys can throw a small ball 70 feet.
	10	Can judge and intercept pathways of small balls thrown from a distance.
		Girls can run 17 feet per second.
	11	Standing broad jump of 5 feet is possible for boys; 6 inches less for girls.
	12	Standing high jump of 3 feet is possible for boys and girls.

Source: From *Perceptual and Motor Development in Infants and Children* (p. 222) by B. J. Cratty, 1979, Englewood Cliffs, NJ: Prentice-Hall.

ties between left-handed and right-handed children. Tan points out that perhaps left-handed children are judged less skillful because their mode of action looks different from that of the right-handed majority. Tan did, however, find that children who were lacking hand preference obtained significantly lower scores on the tests of motor ability administered to these children. Tan (1985) suggests, "The lack of hand preference may serve as a marker indicating children who need special assistance with the development of motor skills. These children should receive direct training in motor skills to improve their motor coordination" (p. 123).

EATING PATTERNS

Overnutrition is a significant problem in physical development. Being overweight is likely to be a tremendous handicap to children, considering all that is said about thinness in our society. **Obesity** is defined as body weight greater than 20% of normal for height and weight. What causes obesity?

Heredity and environment both play a role. Heredity determines our body type, including the distribution of fat. Genes may have a direct effect on the metabolic rate (how fast we burn food calories into energy). However, the environment determines the amount of physical activity (inactive people are likely to burn fewer calories), types of food we eat, and the quantity of food we consume.

The prevalence of obesity has increased by more than 50% in the past 15 to 20 years and even more so for African American children (Dietz, 1986). The older the child, the stronger the relationship to subsequent weight. For example, Epstein and Cluss (1986) found that 40% of the children who were obese at age 7 became obese adults.

The effect of television on this process is worthy of particular attention. Many youngsters spend large amounts of their time in front of television sets and consume large quantities of food while doing so. This led some researchers to suggest that watching television may be causally related to the obesity that is increasingly afflicting young people.

In the past 15 years, obesity has increased 54% among 6- to 11-year-olds and 39% between 12- to 17-year-olds (Erickson, 1988). Among one group studied, the prevalence of obesity was found to increase 2% for each hour increase in the amount of television watched (Kolata, 1986). Another study of children's programs revealed that 68.5% of the commercial messages were for food, of which 25% were for cereal, 25% were for candy and sweets, 8% snacks and other foods, and 10% for fast-food eating places. Children between the ages of 5 and 10 have been noted to attend more closely to commercials than older children and less likely to question commercial content (Ward, Levinson, & Wackman, 1972). Children do attempt to influence parental buying practices on the basis of what they see on television, and mothers are more likely to honor requests for food than for other products. In one study (Select Panel for Promotion of Child Health, 1988) mothers bought the foods their 8- to 10-year-olds liked more than 90% of the time.

Fat infants, those above the 85% mark on weight charts, may become fat adults who gain weight more easily because of the greater number of fat cells present and waiting to soak up more calories. Fetal fat does not appear until quite late in gestation (30 weeks) and then increases quite rapidly. During the first year of life, fat increases from 40% to 53%. In fact, 67% of weight gain during the first 4 postnatal months is **adipose tissue,** or fat cells. During the years between 2 and 10, there is little or no increase in the number of adipose tissue, whereas at pubescence there is another increase in fat cells.

If the mother overeats during the last trimester, or if the infant is overfed in the first few years or during pubescence, the number of fat cells increases. Overfeeding produces an abundance of fat cells. With the exception of these growth periods, the number of fat cells in the body remains the same through life, no matter how much a person does or doesn't eat. People become thinner because each fat cell becomes emptier, not because fat cells are lost; people become fatter because each fat cell becomes fuller. It has been found that obese children of all ages had a greater amount of adipose tissue than did children of normal weight who served as controls, and this differential was not removed by weight loss (Brasel, 1978). These observations suggest that overeating while expecting, particularly in the last trimester, or overfeeding during early infancy or pubescence, may be an important etiologic factor in some forms of obesity.

Psychological factors in food consumption are also important in a discussion of overnutrition. In some families, food is used as a reward or as a punishment. Food is also used as a compensation for lack of success or lack of companionship. Children need to learn to deal with problems and needs in a direct, constructive way; anger, boredom, and frustration are not relieved by eating chocolate chip cookies.

Because our society places such a stigma on fatness, and because children's general health may suffer as a result of their obesity, every effort should be made to control children's weight. Further, there is some evidence that peers view obesity more negatively than physical handicaps, and it is reasonable to infer that ridicule and social isolation contribute significantly to obese children's problems. Physical activity and exercise should be encouraged.

PERCEPTUAL SKILLS

During early and middle childhood, there is a shift from primary reliance on tactual-kinesthetic (touch and sense of one's body movement) sensory systems to primary reliance on visual systems for regulation of behavior. Although 3- and 4-year-olds prefer to explore unfamiliar objects by touch, 5- and 6-year-olds rely on vision. There is an increase in intersensory functioning, enabling children to interrelate information received from many sensory systems. For example, they can match up what they see with what they hear. By age 5 or 6, children are as skilled as adults at coordinating the senses of touch, vision, and hearing. The normal farsightedness of preschool children becomes 20/20 vision between the ages of 9 and 10.

Attention span, or the amount of time children focus on an activity, grows longer during the preschool period as a result of their increasing ability to direct and control their own attention. Children are able to focus on important features of a problem and successfully avoid distracting, irrelevant parts. To illustrate, Neisser (1979) showed first- and fourth-graders a film of a ball game. The children were to monitor critical events in the playing of the game. During the film, a woman with an umbrella walks across the playing field (a totally irrelevant event in the film). Neisser found that 75% of the first-graders noticed her, whereas only 22% of the fourth-graders noticed her. Incidentally, when adults participated in this experiment, they did not notice the woman at all.

Young children are highly inaccurate in copying geometric figures. However, they can discriminate between different shapes, even if they cannot copy them correctly. Perhaps this is so because the motor skills of a young child are inadequate for drawing shape characteristics with precision. There seems to be a rapid improvement in copying shapes when children are between the ages of 5 and 6.

Very young children have difficulty discriminating an upright figure from the same figure turned upside down, but their accuracy on these tasks increases rapidly as they grow older. However, reversals from left to right are a much more frequent cause of difficulty (Vernon, 1976). Thus even a 6-year-old has difficulty telling a *b* from a *d*.

Constancy means that observers see that properties of objects stay the same, or are constant, even though they view them in different conditions. Adults are very accurate on constancy tasks. For example, if a stick 1 meter high (slightly over 1 yard) is placed 30 meters (99 feet) away, adults adjust the height of the comparison stick so that it is approximately 1 meter high. Adults acknowledge that the size of the stick remains the same, even though the distance changes. In general, children show fairly good constancy up to a distance of about 3 meters (9 feet). When objects are moved farther away, however, children show less constancy. To children, a distant figure seems to look smaller.

As children grow older, they pay attention to different aspects of an object. For example, kinder-

gartners pay attention to shape and color, and they ignore the number of items in a picture. Sixth-graders pay relatively less attention to shape and color, and the number of items is now almost as noticeable. Moreover, older children can adjust their attention to meet the demands of the task. In one study (Hale & Taweel, 1974), it was found that 8-year-old children paid attention to two features of a stimulus (color and shape) when this was a useful strategy. However, they paid attention to only one feature (shape) when this was a useful strategy. In other words, 8-year-olds can be flexible about what they attend to, whereas 5-year-olds did not show this kind of flexible strategy of attention.

Children grow perceptually as they change from focusing on one aspect of an event or situation (part perception) to exploring systematically the entire field, focusing on more than one dimension at a time (whole perception). Elkind, Koegler, and Koegler (1964) presented children with two-dimensional pictures such as those shown in Figure 5.12 in their investigation of part and whole perception. It was found that 4- and 5-year-olds would report perceiving only the parts from which the total drawings were constructed; they might say, for example, "I see vegetables." By the age of 7, however, children would seem to alternate in their organization of the interesting figures; they would say, for example, "I see candy" and, while still looking at the same picture, would state "It is a scooter," and so on. By the age of 8, however, 60% of the children, and by 9 years 78%, would apparently perceive both the wholes and parts at the same time, as evident in their statements: "It is a person made of vegetables," or "It is a heart formed by giraffes' necks," and so forth.

ADOLESCENCE

The onset of adolescence is usually associated with **puberty,** a period of rapid change to biological, sexual maturity. Within a few years, 4 on the average, the child is transformed into an adult, at least in physical appearance. Changes at puberty are grouped into two classes: those related to the

FIGURE 5.12   Illustrations Used to Evaluate Whole versus Part Perception

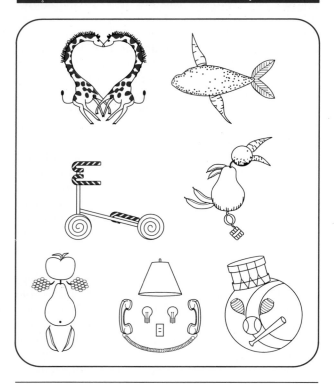

Source: From "Studies in Perceptual Development: II. Part-Whole Perception" by D. Elkind, R. R. Koegler, and E. G. Koegler, 1964, *Child Development, 35*, p. 84. © The Society for Research in Child Development, Inc. Reprinted by permission.

development of male or female sexual characteristics and those related to overall physical growth, known as the growth spurt.

SEXUAL MATURITY

Puberty begins with a complex series of hormonal changes. Hormones are powerful and highly specialized chemical substances that interact with cells. The entire process of maturing sexually begins when hormones of the hypothalamus trigger hormones from the pituitary gland. The anterior pituitary, lying just beneath the base of the brain in approximately the geometric center of the head, secretes *gonadotrophic* hormones. The gonadotrophic hormones stimulate the gonads, the ovaries in the female, and the testes in the male, which in turn secrete their own hormones. When the testis is stimulated by the gonadotrophic hormones, it secretes **testosterone;** when the ovary is stimulated, it secretes **estrogens,** female hormones of which the chief one is **estradiol.**

Testosterone in boys is responsible for the growth of testes, penis, first pubic hair, capacity for ejaculation, growth spurt, voice changes, beard development, and completion of pubic hair. In girls, estrogen causes the beginning of breast development, first pubic hair, widening of hips, growth spurt, menarche, and completion of breast and pubic hair growth. The sequence of these developments is quite similar, although there is great variation in the age at which each starts.

Girls' first external sign of puberty is elevation of the breasts. Growth of the uterus and vagina occurs simultaneously with breast development. The labia and clitoris also enlarge. Menarche almost invariably occurs after the growth spurt has begun to slow. Figure 5.13 represents a diagram of the sequence of events at puberty in boys and girls. A glance will suffice to show how very large the growth ranges are.

The first sign of puberty in boys is the increase in the rate of growth of the testes and scrotum; beginning of growth of pubic hair occurs at about the same time. Approximately a year later, an acceleration in growth of the penis accompanies the beginning of the growth spurt in height. Body hair and facial hair usually make their first appearance about 2 years after the beginning of pubic hair growth. The most obvious aspect of development is perhaps the lowering of the voice, which occurs late in puberty. The larynx enlarges and the vocal cords double in length. This lengthening of the vocal cords results in a drop in pitch of about an octave.

GROWTH SPURT

Another fundamental hormone that affects the adolescent is the **growth hormone.** This hormone is

FIGURE 5.13   Sequence of Events at Adolescence in Males and Females

The lines and bars of these diagrams give the sequence and duration of physical events at puberty for girls (top) and boys (bottom). The range of ages at which each change may begin and conclude is indicated by the figures directly below the average start and finish points.

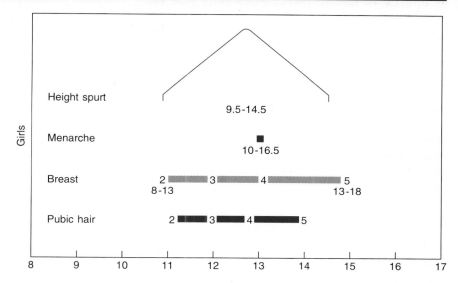

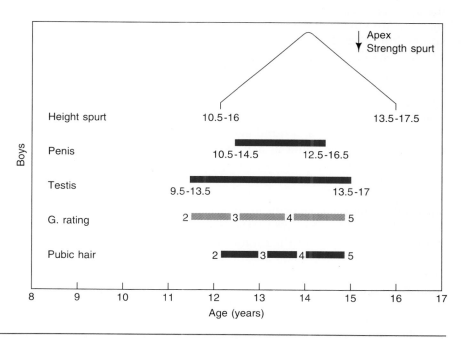

Source: From "Variations in the Pattern of Pubertal Changes in Boys" by W. A. Marshall and J. M. Tanner, 1970, *Archives of Disease in Childhood, 45*, p. 13. Copyright 1970 by the British Medical Association. Reprinted by permission.

produced throughout life in varying amounts and is directly related to increases in body size and weight. Children who have a deficiency of the growth hormone are of normal size at birth but grow very slowly, and by 2 years of age have usually fallen below the normal levels for height. One of the great advances in pediatrics has been the successful treatment of this disorder. The growth hormone must be obtained from autopsied human corpses (the animal growth hormone is not effective in human beings). Treatment continues throughout childhood and adolescence. Provided the child is diagnosed and treated early, normal stature is almost always achieved (Tanner, 1978). The growth hormone is also responsible for the growth spurt.

There is a fairly regular order in which the dimensions accelerate; leg length as a rule reaches its peak first, followed a few months later by shoulder width, and a year later by trunk length. Most of the spurt in height is due to trunk growth rather than leg growth. The muscles appear to have their spurt a little after the last skeletal peak (Marshall & Tanner, 1970).

In girls, the growth spurt begins about age 10 or 11, reaches its peak about 12, and decreases at age 13, with slow continual growth for several additional years. Boys begin their growth spurt later than girls, beginning at around age 13, reaching a peak at 14, and declining at age 15½. In normal girls the age range is 9½ to 14½; in boys the range is 10½ to as late as 16 (Dorn, Susman, Nottelmann, Inoff-Germain, & Chrousos, 1990). Figure 5.14 shows that the peak velocity in growth occurs at about 12 years for girls and at about 14 years for boys. Girls reach 98% of their adult height at 16¼ years; boys reach 98% of their adult height at 17¾ years (Tanner, 1971). The growth in height results from the final stages of bone maturation. It is in puberty that the epiphyses—the parts of the long bones made of cartilage—finally turn to bone. The muscles, too, lengthen and strengthen. A similar spurt in growth at adolescence can be shown for weight, muscle size, head and face growth, and especially for reproductive organs. In fact, "every muscular and skeletal dimension of the body

seems to take part in the adolescent's growth spurt" (Tanner, 1962, p. 10).

Over the past century, puberty and adult height have been achieved earlier. This change has been called the **secular trend.** For example, the onset of menarche today is, on the average, 12.3; in the early 1800s, girls' first menstruations occurred at age 17. In addition, boys and girls are taller and heavier before and at the end of adolescence than they were a few generations ago. The average boy is 5½ inches taller than a boy the same age in the late 1800s. These trends have resulted from a combination of genetic and environmental factors (better nutrition and health care, for example) that have allowed human stature to approach the maximum of its reaction range. There are some signs that the secular trend involving earlier sexual maturation and greater height is coming to an end. The onset of menarche, for example, has not changed over the past 30 years.

PRACTICAL IMPLICATIONS: THE ADOLESCENT AND THE "IDEAL BODY"

In an earlier section, puberty was discussed in terms of objective biological data; however, you also need to be aware that biological and sexual maturation has a profound effect on adolescents psychologically as well as socially. Their physical appearance is so important that their feelings about themselves are directly related to their body images. Early or late physical maturation is one factor that appears to relate to the adolescent's self-esteem. Early-maturing individuals tend to have a more intense adolescent growth spurt than do late-maturing individuals (see Figure 5.15). Tanner (1978) suggests that "in early maturers, the whole process goes more quickly, and also more intensely, so that a great total result is achieved despite the small amount of time taken" (p. 94).

EARLY- AND LATE-MATURING MALES
In a pioneering longitudinal study, The Oakland Growth Study, (Jones & Bayley, 1950) on the psy-

FIGURE 5.14   Body Growth and Development from 10 to 18 Years

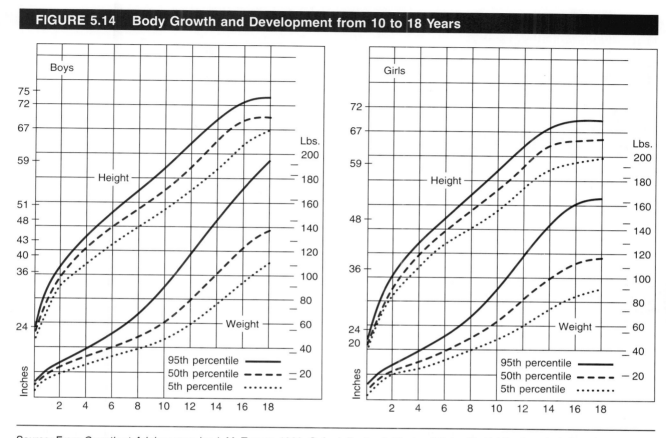

Source: From *Growth at Adolescence* by J. M. Tanner, 1962, Oxford, England: Blackwell Scientific Publications Ltd. Copyright 1962 by Blackwell Scientific Publications. Reprinted by permission.

chological effects of early or late maturation, 16 early-maturing and 16 late-maturing boys from a public school were studied from the prepubescent period to age 40. Early-maturing males are large for their age, more muscular, and better coordinated than late-maturing males, so they enjoy a considerable athletic advantage. They also enjoy considerable social advantages in relation to peers. Early-maturing males tend to have a more positive self-image.

Adults tend to rate early-maturing males as more physically attractive, more masculine, and more relaxed than late-maturing males. Adults tend to expect more of early-maturing males and

expect adult behavior and responsibility. Thus, early-maturing males may have less time to enjoy the freedom that comes with childhood. Another disadvantage is that early-maturing males may be more likely to get involved in problem or deviant activities (Duncan, Ritter, Dornbusch, Gross, & Carlsmith, 1985).

Late-maturing males may suffer socially induced inferiority because of their delayed growth and development (Peskin, 1967). At age 15, the late-maturing male may be 8 inches shorter and 30 pounds lighter than his early-maturing counterpart. Accompanying this size difference are marked differences in body build, strength, motor

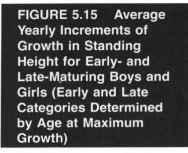

FIGURE 5.15   Average Yearly Increments of Growth in Standing Height for Early- and Late-Maturing Boys and Girls (Early and Late Categories Determined by Age at Maximum Growth)

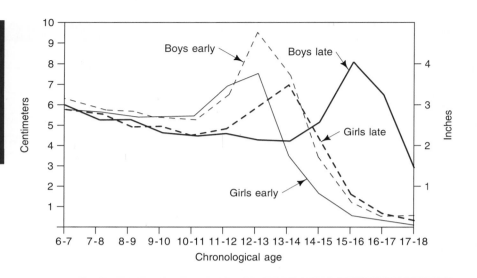

Source: From *The Psychology of Adolescence* by J. Horrocks, 1962, Boston: Houghton Mifflin. With permission of author and the Society for Research in Child Development. Adapted from F. K. Shuttleworth. "The Physical and Mental Growth of Girls and Boys Age Six Through Nineteen in Relation to Age of Maximum Growth" by F. K. Shuttleworth, 1939, *Monographs of the Society for Research in Child Development, 4*, pp. 245–247.

performance, and coordination. Because late-maturing males tend to be shorter and physically weaker, they are less apt to become outstanding athletes.

Late-maturing males are seen by their peers as more childish; they were less popular and less likely to show leadership positions. On personality measures, late-maturing males exhibited stronger feelings of inadequacy, higher needs for autonomy, more negative conceptions of self, less control, and less self-assurance.

EARLY- AND LATE-MATURING FEMALES

Although early maturation tends to be a plus for boys, it is generally not so for girls. It appears that early maturation has a negative effect during the elementary school years. A physically mature 5th- or 6th-grader is at some disadvantage because she is out of phase with the majority of her classmates. Early-maturing girls often find themselves towering over others, and many assume a slouching posture to conceal their height. Their advanced breast development seems to violate others' expectations of petiteness and femininity. Since girls ma-

ture about 2 years earlier than boys, the early-maturing girl is not only more physically advanced than her female agemates but far more advanced than nearly all her male classmates as well. By junior high, however, the early maturing female comes into her own, socially. She begins to look more like a grown-up woman, is envied by the other girls, begins to attract the attention of older boys, and starts dating. The girl, however, may find herself emotionally unequipped to deal with sophisticated social activities and sexual enticements.

Slow-maturing girls tend to worry that they are not physically normal. During the early teen years, most adolescents want to be like their peers. While these concerns may seem trivial to some, they are very real and disturbing to the child who desperately wants to be grown up but whose body is just not cooperating, as the following quote suggests:

Are you there, God? It's me, Margaret.
Gretchen, my friend, got her period. I'm so jealous, God. I hate myself for being so jealous, but I am. I wish you'd help me just a little. Nancy's sure she's going to get it soon, too. And if I'm

late I don't know what I'll do. Oh, please God, I just want to be normal. (Blume, 1990, p. 100)

The subjects in the Oakland Growth Study were contacted again at about the age of 30. At that time, there were few differences between the early and late maturers. The two groups did not differ in attractiveness, grooming, marital status, family size, or educational level. The early-maturing males, however, did show earlier patterns of job success and scored higher on a test designed to measure the ability to make a good impression on others. They were self-confident, responsible, co-operative, and sociable. They were also rigid, mor-alistic, humorless, and conforming. Late-maturing males were impulsive and assertive but also in-sightful, perceptive, creatively playful, and able to cope with new situations. Early-maturing females appeared self-possessed, self-directed, able to cope, and exhibited high ratings of overall psycho-logical health. Late-maturing females were likely to experience difficulty adapting to stress and were more likely to score low in ratings of overall psy-chological health.

THE IDEAL MALE PHYSIQUE

Another factor that psychologically affects adoles-cents is physical attractiveness. Most adolescents desire to be physically attractive, to have the "ideal body." In our culture "the ideal" most often means tall and muscular for boys, and tall and slender for girls.

In order to get bigger muscles, boys may inject themselves with steroids. Today an estimated 10% of high school students—overwhelmingly adoles-cent boys—either take or have taken steroids. Many teenage boys say they take steroids not so much for improved athletic performance as for cos-metic purposes: to make them more muscular. An-abolic steroids come in many chemical structures, but essentially they are forms of testosterone, the chief male hormone. Some steroids may be taken orally in tablet form, but injection is actually pre-ferred because it lessens the drugs' harmful effects on the liver.

Potentially severe side effects—the possibility of liver dysfunction, cancer, damage to the reproduc-tive system—may result from long-term use or

Our society puts a great deal of emphasis on the "ideal" body--tall and muscular for males and tall and thin for females.

such practices as "stacking"—taking 2 or 3 types of steroids simultaneously. Short-term effects are hair loss, severe acne, and high blood pressure as well as shrunken testicles and low sperm production. (Women users may find masculine characteristics such as growth of facial hair and male pattern bald-ness; these effects tend to be irreversible.)

Steroids may have a profound effect on behav-ior. Increased aggressiveness, known as "roid rages," often leads to violent, destructive behavior. Recovering steroid users can become extremely de-pressed when they try to give up the drug, which, in some cases, has led to suicide.

THE IDEAL FEMALE PHYSIQUE

The importance of physical attractiveness in West-ern society is undeniable. Pressure is brought to bear particularly on the female in the form of slimness. New diets proliferate for that segment of the population that wants to lose a few extra pounds. This turns out to be a large market, for it appears that the majority of young women are unhappy with their weight and want to be thinner (Levenkron, 1982).

Some researchers regard the cultural heritage, particularly for women, that "thin is chic" to be directly responsible for the eating disorders of anorexia nervosa and bulimia.

Anorexia Nervosa   Anorectics use two different means of achieving thinness. The first group relies on strict dieting—restricters. The second group alternates between dieting and binge eating followed by self-induced purging and vomiting—bulimics. The central psychopathologic feature of anorexia nervosa and bulimia is an extreme fear of fatness. **Anorexia nervosa** is a disorder generally found in adolescent women but can also be seen in older women as well as men. It is characterized by self-induced starvation (intake of 300 to 600 calories a day), fear of fatness, amenorrhea (absence of menstruation) in women, and diminished sexual drive in men.

Estimates of the incidence of anorexia nervosa range from 1% to 3% (Lucas, 1981), which is roughly 1 out of every 250 adolescent girls. The patients are predominately females; only 10% are men; and the common age of onset is between 13 and 22 years of age (Levenkron, 1982).

The highest probability of development of anorexia nervosa is found in a female who is highly perfectionistic and self-critical. Restricters tend to be conforming, reliable, insecure, socially obsessional, and inflexible in their thinking. Anorectics typically go on a diet during their early teenage years to lose 5 to 20 pounds. Many of these individuals come from a family of upper or middle socioeconomic status. Exhibiting obsessional thinking about food and liquid intake, they are likely to have feelings of inferiority about their personality and appearance. They tend to show a disinterest in sexuality or fear physical and emotional intimacy. Delusional thinking develops, especially with regard to body size and quantities of food

ingested. Paranoid fears of criticism from others are often experienced, especially with respect to being seen as "too fat." Anxiety is alleviated only by weight loss and fasting. Anorectics generally tend to deny their emaciated appearance, viewing others who are substantially heavier as thinner than themselves. Such individuals have a history of high achievement at school and are compliant and cooperative both in school and at home. They are often considered to be "model children" without associated behavioral abnormalities.

Bulimia   **Bulimia** describes an eating disorder that occurs when an individual binges (engaging in the rapid ingestion of a large quantity of food) and then attempts to avoid weight gain through self-induced vomiting. An anorectic eating pattern between binges is common. Some individuals starve all day only to eat for hours at night. Preferred foods are usually high in sugar and carbohydrates. Although some individuals alternate overeating with extended fasting, most relieve it by vomiting. The typical bulimic is a white female who begins overeating at about 18 years of age and begins purging by vomiting a year later.

Bulimia has been noted in one study to occur in 19% of college women and 5% of college men (Halmi, Falk, & Schwartz, 1981). Studies at the University of Chicago and Ohio State University have indicated that between 25% and 33% of entering freshmen use some degree of self-induced vomiting to control their weight.

Bulimics are more extroverted and sociable but more unstable and tend to have problems with impulse control such as stealing and substance abuse. While socially more skillful than restricters, their relations tend to be brief, superficial, and troubled. Their families tend to be more unstable than those of restricters; there is more discord, maternal and paternal depression, and impulsivity and substance abuse (Yates, 1989). Etringer, Altmaier, and Bowers (1989) found that bulimic females have lower self-appraised problem-solving ability, lower sense of personal efficacy in successful performance of life tasks and a tendency to attribute positive events to external, global factors. Jacobson and Robins (1989) found that bulimic females were characterized by a high degree of social dependency on men and low levels of social support (from men).

Many factors have been cited as probable causes for the development of these eating disorders. Among those most frequently cited are factors related to family interaction pathologies: overprotectiveness, rigidity masking unconscious hostilities, parental occupation with appearance and success, and poor conflict resolution (Minuchin, Rosman, & Baker, 1978). It has been maintained by others that these eating disorders represent a struggle for a self-respecting identity that takes the form of willful starvation (Bruch, 1981). Pallazzoli (1978) describes the mother-daughter relationship as being riddled with guilt, anger, and overprotectiveness (by both toward each other) and characterized by mutual clinging that is devoid of trust.

In families showing children with eating disorders, the father has been described as nondemonstrative. Some maintain that fear of growing up and assuming adult responsibility is highly characteristic of anorectics. Failure to accept a more adult-looking body (that is, to be more separate from parents) leads the individual to diet as a means of gaining control over fears of inadequacy, rejection by others, and unidentifiable fears.

Bulik, Sullivan, and Rorty (1989) studied the family environment and psychiatric histories of 35 bulimic women. The study revealed that 12 of the 35 subjects had been sexually abused. Bulimic females from families in which sexual abuse occurred were more likely than bulimic subjects with no personal or family history of sexual abuse to have had a personal history of dependence. The authors suggest that the presence of bulimia should alert clinicians to screen for concomitant depression, suicidality, and substance abuse as well as the possibility of severe, if hidden, familial pathology, including sexual abuse.

Although it is possible that these eating disorders have a single discrete cause, it is more prob-able that complex chains interact to precipitate these illnesses.

In treating these disorders, there must be simultaneous improvement in weight and the eating abnormalities, along with fundamental therapeutic attempts to uncover the underlying psychological conflicts and reverse the maturational arrests. Strict attempts of getting these patients to eat their way out of the hospital are not successful unless one deals with the underlying causes of the pathology as well. Achieving a true recovery from these eating disorders means that the patient understands and appreciates her complexity, and relinquishes the need to retreat to obsessive simplification of emotional conflict. Approximately 40% of anorectics totally recover, 30% considerably improve, and 20% remain unimproved or seriously impaired by depression (Silber, 1986). Early onset (before the age of 6) is associated with a favorable prognosis while chronicity, pronounced family difficulties and poor vocational adjustment are associated with poor outcome.

The treatment of bulimia is less clearly defined than that of anorexia. Hospitalization is less likely but may be necessary because of fluid and electrolyte imbalance, severe depression, the threat of suicide, or resistance to intensive outpatient treatment (Yates, 1989). Impatient treatment involves monitoring intake and purging behaviors and some combination of supportive, behavioral, group, individual, and family therapies.

Because of their extreme concern about fatness, all patients should be given the reassurance that they will not be allowed to gain too much weight (Andersen, 1983). Otherwise, they may return to their rituals to bring about relief from unresolved fears.

A major focus of treatment is the gradual identification by patients of uncomfortable mood states that trigger unconscious transformation of anxiety into abnormal weight control or an abnormal eating pattern. Families of these patients need to be involved in therapy as well. Additional suggestions for helping the anorectic individual at home are offered in "Focus on Applications."

FOCUS ON APPLICATIONS

Dealing with the Anorectic Child at Home

To deal with the anorectic child, Levenkron (1982) offers the following suggestions:

1. Demand less decision making from the anorectic.
2. Offer her fewer choices and less responsibility. She should not have to decide what the family eats for dinner or where to take its vacations.
3. In conflicts about decisions, do not retreat from your own positions as parents out of fear your daughter will become increasingly ill.
4. Maintain a supportively confident posture when dealing with your daughter. This is not to suggest, however, that harshness, rigidity, or anger be employed in the maintenance of an authoritative posture.
5. Express honest affection toward the child or adolescent. Verbal and physical expression of this affection is necessary.
6. Develop a parent-child dialogue on personal issues other than food and weight.
7. Do not demand weight gain or berate your daughter for having anorexia nervosa.
8. Do not make nondifferentiating statements such as, "Your illness is ruining the whole family." "Why did this happen to me?" "I can't take much more of this." These statements put the anorectic in charge of the family's well-being and are received by her as dependent remarks. This throws her deeper into weight loss and illness.
9. Try to avoid abandoning statements such as, "Help me to help you!" "What can I do for you?" These statements request that the anorectic take charge of the family's behavior toward her. Because she doesn't know the answer to these questions, she feels like more of a failure. These statements are often made in frustration and even rage on the parents' part, but they should be eliminated.
10. Do not become directly involved with the child's weight once she is in therapy and under a physician's care. If you see a change in appearance that indicates weight loss, call her physician.
11. Do not demand that she eat with you, but do not allow her eating problem to dominate the family's eating schedule or use of the kitchen.
12. Do not allow her to shop for or cook for the family. This puts her in a nurturing role and allows her to deny her own need for food by feeding others (pp. 169–170).

REVIEW OF KEY POINTS

Because the development of the brain is so integral to the child's overall development, a special section on the structures of the brain and the ways the structures develop in utero and in early childhood were discussed. The brain is composed of billions of neurons that transmit messages. People are born with their full complement of neurons, or brain cells; when the cells die, they cannot be replaced.

Myelin, a fatty protein, coats the axons of the neurons and aids in quickening the velocity of nerve impulses. Motor pathways become myelinated first before sensory or association pathways. The brain undergoes a rapid growth spurt during the 15th and 20th weeks of gestation, and again at the 25th week to 2 years of age. The first growth period involves the growth in number of neurons and the second involves an explosive increase in dendritic complexity. Then the effects of malnutrition and lack of oxygen on the developing brain were discussed. The brain is an adaptable organ and is capable of modification. After injury to the brain, subsequent recovery of function is dependent on the organism's age and the extent and location of damage.

The period of infancy is a time of rapid physical growth and development. In a short 2 years, the average child grows some 14 inches and gains roughly 20 pounds. The child's motor behavior, which initially consisted of numerous uncoordinated and reflexive movements, changes to the voluntary, coordinated motor behavior of reaching, grasping, and manipulating objects. Children become highly mobile as they explore their environment. The neonate has a number of sensory and perceptual capabilities that develop rapidly over the first 6 months. Newborns appear to be more attentive to contrasting edges and contours, and prefer complex patterns and the human face. In addition, experiments have shown that most infants can discriminate depth as soon as they can crawl. Young infants are able to localize sounds and prefer high-pitched voices. They have the ability to smell and detect pheromones. Infants are able to taste the differences between various substances and to react to pain.

Proportionally, children in the developmental period of early and middle childhood lose their babyish appearance by developing long legs and flat stomachs. Growth slows to about 2½ inches a year. Children learn to master many motor skills and become quite agile. In early and middle childhood, children develop proficient perceptual skills in terms of organizing data and noticing more than one dimension in a situation at a time.

Puberty signals the onset of adolescence, a time of sexual maturity and physical growth. Gonadotrophic hormones stimulate the gonads (ovaries in females, testes in males). The hormone testosterone causes the growth of testes, penis, pubic hair, as well as the growth spurt and voice changes. Estrogen, the female hormone, causes breast development, growth of pubic hair, widening of hips, the growth spurt, and menarche. While the progression of events leading to sexual maturity in males and females is similar for all adolescents, there is a tremendous variation in the age at which it starts. Puberty also signals the beginning of the growth spurt, for girls around ages 10 to 11; for boys, around age 13.

Some adolescents intent on developing the "ideal body" resort to drastic measures. Males, in search of the muscular physique, use steroids. Short- and long-term effects of using this chemical were noted. Females appear to believe that being thin is the ideal body type. An extreme fear of fatness may be one factor in producing the pathological eating disorders known as anorexia nervosa and bulimia. Anxiety caused by feeling too fat is alleviated by fasting and weight loss for the anorectic, and binge eating followed by vomiting for the bulimic adolescent.

ENHANCING YOUR CRITICAL THINKING

Broadening Your Knowledge

Firsthand Experiences

The Brain

Ornstein, R., & Thompson, R. F. (1991). *The amazing brain*. Boston: Houghton Mifflin.

For students who wish to get a more detailed discussion of the brain in readable, understandable, "user-friendly" language.

Anorexia Nervosa

Palmer, R. L. (1988). *Anorexia nervosa: A guide for sufferers and their families*. New York: Penguin Books.

The book provides a good description of how an anorectic feels and thinks. In addition, it offers practical information on how to deal with individuals who are anorectic. An interesting experience would be to visit a clinic that deals with eating disorders and discuss anorexia and bulimia with a knowledgeable staff member.

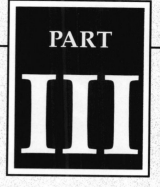

PART
III

The World of the Child's and Adolescent's Mind

Views of Cognition: Jean Piaget

CHILDREN'S THOUGHTS

On what they will be doing at age 70 . . .

I'll go to work everyday. I'll be a doctor. My grandmother is the oldest person I know. She's 32. For fun she takes naps and goes to the bank. I'll probably live until I'm 10.

child, age 5

I'll get my mail. That's what granny does. She also pulls the string on my doll then laughs and spits in your face. Granny is the oldest person I know. She's 2.

child, age 4
PhotOpinion (1979)

On their favorite recipes . . .

Chops

Some chops that are enough to fill up your pan
Fresh salt and pepper
Fresh flour
1 ball of salad lettuce
1 sponge cake with ice cream

Put the chops in the bag and shake them for 5 hours—and the flour too. Put them in a skillet pan on the biggest black circle on the roof of your stove. Cook them for plenty of time. Fringe up the lettuce in little heaps in all the bowls. Go on the porch and bring the high chair and have your supper everybody! Note: But stoves really is dangerous—and you shouldn't go near one till you get married.

Martel (1974)

CHAPTER OUTLINE

THE PIAGETIAN MIND

THE MECHANISMS OF COGNITIVE DEVELOPMENT

Schemes
Logical Structures of Thought
Sensorimotor Period
Preoperational Period
Concrete Operational Period
Formal Operational Period
Organization and Adaptation
Assimilation and Accommodation
Equilibrium and Equilibration
Interrelatedness of Piagetian Concepts

STAGES OF COGNITIVE DEVELOPMENT

Sensorimotor Period (Birth to Age 2)
Preoperational Period (2 to 7 years)
Concrete Operational Period (7 to 11 Years)
Formal Operational Period (11 to 15 Years)

PRACTICAL IMPLICATIONS: ENHANCING CHILDREN'S COGNITIVE GROWTH

Infancy: Birth to Age 2
Early Childhood: 2 to 7 Years
Middle Childhood: 7 to 11 Years
Adolescence: 11 to 15 Years

KEY TERMS

Cognition
Schemes
Logical structures
Functional invariants
Organization
Adaptation
Assimilation
Accommodation
Equilibrium
Equilibration
Sensorimotor period
Object permanence
Operations
Preoperational period
Reversibility
Symbolic functioning
Centration
Transductive reasoning
Concrete operational period
Conservation
Formal operational period
Hypothetical-deductive reasoning
Combinatorial analysis

How fascinating it is to try to understand children's thought processes. Generally, investigators of cognitive development have taken one of three approaches: the developmental theory of Jean Piaget, information-processing theory and the psychometric theory. Although researchers of each of these approaches study different aspects of children's cognitive development, they nevertheless would find these children's themes on time and quantity interesting examples of how children think. Our young theme-writing thinkers show an uncertainty of time (grandmothers who are 2 years old, shaking chops and flour for 5 hours).

The qualitative approach of Jean Piaget is concerned with how children's thinking strategies change over time. Piaget's landmark theory fo-

cuses on discovering qualitative developmental changes in the ways children perceive, understand, and operate in their environments. Viewing intelligence as a particular instance of biological adaptation, Piagetians have attempted to establish universal regularities in the child's progression through hierarchical stages of intellectual development. According to Piaget, cognitive processes emerge as a result of a developmental reorganization of logical structures resulting from the individual's interactions with the environment.

In contrast to Piagetians, information-processing theorists are interested in how the processing system actually operates in a particular problem-solving situation. The information-processing approach to understanding intelligence is a detailed, step-by-step analysis of cognitive processes. It describes how people gather and use information to solve problems and to acquire knowledge. Information processing theory will be discussed in Chapter 7.

The major approach to the study of individual differences in intelligence is known as the psychometric theory. Psychometric researchers take a more quantitative approach, examining how much one knows or is capable of knowing in relation to others of the same age. This approach allows us to compare the abilities of individuals and groups of individuals, as you will see in Chapter 8.

Many of the theories presented in these chapters take as their starting point the observations and assumptions laid down by Piaget. While the three approaches are quite different, they do converge on two basic Piagetian assumptions: that cognitive development results from an interaction between biological and environmental factors, and that children play an active role in their own cognitive development. Rather than reviewing these theories as radical departures from Piaget's, it is more appropriate to view them as extensions of his approach.

No single approach can give you enough information to understand the nature of children's thinking processes and skills, but through a combination of these approaches, you will receive a rich base for understanding children's cognitive development. Not all theories are neo-Piagetian, but few ignore him. Therefore, understanding Piaget is a necessary beginning in order to appreciate new theories of cognitive development.

Piaget was interested in studying children's thinking from birth to adolescence. As you shall see, he spent his life researching the developmental transitions between different levels of children's thinking so that he could understand the entire developmental sequence of children's thought processes. His research has resulted in valuable insights as to how children think, reason, and perceive the world—all those mental activities that are labeled **cognition.**

Piaget was a pragmatist; he believed that knowledge has a purpose. Human cognition is to aid adaptation to the puzzles encountered in the world. Thought is to serve action. Hence, Piaget concentrated on the cognitive processes that are activated when the child is solving problems.

THE PIAGETIAN MIND

The cognitive system Piaget envisaged is an extremely active one. That is, it actively selects and interprets environmental information in the construction of its own knowledge rather than passively copying information just as it is presented to the senses. Children do not merely incorporate the already developed knowledge of the world, but reconstrue and reinterpret the environment to make it fit in with their own existing mental framework. Children are cognitively active and inventive; they acquire knowledge initially through manipulation of objects, and later ideas. They are always trying to construct a more coherent understanding of events by continually integrating what they know and making sense out of discrepant experiences. The view that cognitive development proceeds as the child actively constructs a system of knowledge during the course of interaction with the environment is a pivotal Piagetian contribution in explaining children's cognitive development.

THE MECHANISMS OF COGNITIVE DEVELOPMENT

Piaget was not concerned with the accumulation of static knowledge contained in rules or categories; he was concerned with process. How do children think? How does the relationship between the knower and the known change with the passage of time? To discover children's ways of thinking, Piaget began to analyze the similarity of the incorrect responses made by children of the same age and how their responses differed from the responses of older and younger children.

SCHEMES

When discussing a particular system reflecting some specific knowledge, Piaget used the term *scheme.* **Schemes** reflect a particular way of interacting with the environment. They reflect children's knowledge at all stages of development—their "old ideas" or what they know. For Piaget, a scheme is whatever is generalizable and repeatable in an action. A scheme may be as simple as how to pick up a chess piece, or as complex as a strategy for beating a particular chess opponent. Piaget was not concerned with the particular set of schemes children had, but rather the types of *schematic organization* available to them. Schemes are interrelated to form an organized whole. The mind is not a grab bag of facts. It is a coherent view of the world.

LOGICAL STRUCTURES OF THOUGHT

Logical structures, according to Piaget, are organizational properties of thinking. Logical structures refer to a set of capabilities that fit together to explain why a certain content (what a child says or does in various learning situations) has emerged rather than some other content. Structures are thinking strategies and as such underlie or determine overt behavior. Another way of saying this is that children's actions and thoughts are directed by their structures; they determine what children are capable or incapable of doing. Structures determine the extent and limits of the child's power to solve problems.

Piagetian structures are very abstract ideas, not tangible entities that can be seen or directly measured. Their presence, therefore, must be inferred from children's content—their words and actions.

Piaget suggested that similar understandings tend to be acquired at about the same age across a wide variety of domains because these understandings all require the same underlying logical structures. Logical structures are the source of stagelike phenomena that are observed in intellectual development. Each stage of cognitive development is characterized by qualitatively different sets of logical structures. Piaget has conceptually partitioned the types of schematic organization available to the child into qualitatively different stages: sensorimotor (birth to age 2), preoperational (ages 2 to 7), concrete operational (ages 7 to 11), and formal operational (ages 11 to 15).

Children's stage of cognitive development defines the limits and kinds of experience that can be processed. Each stage has a more or less unified cognitive system with its own unique form and rules. However, the child is constantly encountering new information, and old logical structures change, giving away to new ones. It is this orderly progression of logical structures that creates the stages that are important feature of Piaget's theory.

In discussing the logical structures characterizing the stages of cognitive development, it will become apparent to you that the thinking patterns at each stage can be categorized by the refinement and transformation of logical structures, which enable children to achieve a higher level of adaptation to their environment. However, due to a lack of appropriate logical structures, they also become ensnared in a certain type of embeddedness that puts limits on their problem-solving abilities. In other words, while each new stage of cognitive development represents a more sophisticated adjustment to the world, there are limitations in thinking abilities in the new, more advanced stage. Given the parallel development in understanding across so many domains and the role of logical structures in producing this development, Piaget felt it important to characterize the nature of logical structures in detail.

Sensorimotor Period   In the sensorimotor period, logical structures in young children are physical. They involve something a child does, such as reaching, looking, grasping, and sucking. Logical structures in the sensorimotor period afford the child increasing coherence and stability in their world of objects.

Preoperational Period   With each progressive increase in schematic organization, children's understanding of their world in the preoperational period becomes greater. Just as the world of objects took on an increasing coherence and stability during the first cognitive stage, the world that depends on symbolic representation—the world of socially shared meaning, categories, and relations—begins to take on a greater coherence and stability during the second stage of their lives. Although children's earliest structures involve an activity, as they get older they gradually are able to free their thought processes from motor activities and are able to interiorize actions; knowledge becomes a mental activity. Older children learn increasingly to represent the world mentally by means of memories, imagery, language, or symbols. Thus, there is a qualitative change when children move from logical structures based on actions in the sensorimotor period to logical structures based on mental representation in the preschool years.

Representational thought has some obvious advantages over sensorimotor thought: It is faster and more mobile; it can deal with the past, present, and future; and it can create ideas that refer to nothing in reality (for example, monsters that go bump in the night). However, preoperational children's thinking is embedded in their perceptions. These children are unable to separate themselves from their perceptions; they cannot distinguish between how something appears to them and how something is. For example, the young preoperational child is presented with two boards, about 2 feet square, covered with a green cloth (see Figure 6.1). On each board there are sev-

eral barns and a cow. The child is asked to pretend that this is a countryside and to indicate which cow has more grass to eat.

Interestingly enough, when the barns on both fields are solidly packed in one corner, the child answers, "The cows have the same amount to eat in each field." If, however, you spread out the barns on one field in various locations and leave the barns on the other field grouped together, the child indicates that the cow on the field with the barns in various locations has less to eat than the one in the field where the barns are closely grouped.

Young children answer the way they do because their thinking is perception bound. "Distinguishing between how something appears and how something is, is just what the child cannot do when he is subject to his perceptions" (Kegan, 1982, p. 29). Preoperational children's structures are limited in the sense that they cause children to overattend to the thing that strikes them first and most vividly. The preoperational child is unduly influenced by perception rather than logic of quantity, and errs accordingly.

FIGURE 6.1

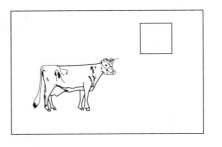

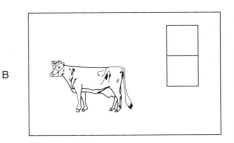

A

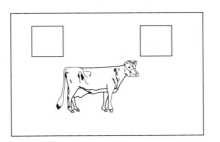

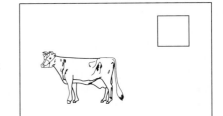

B

FOCUS ON ISSUES

How Do Children at Each Stage of Cognitive Development Solve Problems?

Give a child at each stage of cognitive development a specific problem. What would happen, for example, if you gave a child a tub of water and various small objects of differing densities, weights, shapes, sizes, and colors? The sensorimotor infant would probably splash, throw the objects, and attempt to eat them. A preoperational child might imagine that the objects are boats or fish. This child would probably notice that some objects float and that others sink, but the child would be content to give differing reasons as to why this is so. He might claim, for example, that one object floats because it is little, another because it is dry, another because it is a boat, and so on. The concrete operational thinker would be bothered by inconsistencies that some small objects sink while some small objects do not (the preoperational thinker would not be bothered). The concrete thinker makes comparisons between objects, but they are neither systematic nor exhaustive. She does not hold their amounts constant, for example, while varying their weights. She does, however, develop several categories of "sinkability" (always floats—lightweight; always sinks—heavy). The formal-thinking adolescent has both a plan and the necessary operations to solve the problem. She systematically varies the factors to determine their influence and uses the results to test her hypotheses. She knows that density is the proportion of weight to volume and that the relative density of the object to the water is the critical factor.

Concrete Operational Period Building from the logical structures in the preoperational period, concrete operational thinkers acquire new logical structures that enable them to extract higher concepts or quantitative invariants. Mental operations are applied to objects and events. These children classify objects and events, order them, and reverse them. The essential characteristic of this period has been designated as "conservation." The central definition of the attainment of conservation is that the child understands that certain properties remain invariant in spite of substantial perceptual transformations.

Concrete thinkers can easily solve the problem in Figure 6.1, for they realize that the amount of grass to eat remains the same if the only change is in the arrangement of the barns. However, lack of appropriate structures limits children's problem-solving abilities to that which they can concretely imagine or manipulate. They cannot reason in the abstract.

By the time children reach the end of this period, they understand that quantities obey laws that are independent of any perceptual state. Once

they have obtained this understanding, they are ready to combine these laws into theoretical systems in a fashion that is at a higher level of understanding. In Piaget's terminology, they are ready for the transition to formal operational thinking.

Formal Operational Period During the formal operational period, the acquisition of logical structures enables children to perform higher-order operations or operations on operations, which enables them to construct invariants of a higher order still. As a consequence, another qualitative change takes place in their intellectual functioning. They now begin to show an aptitude for, and an interest in, systems for relating variables, that is, abstract theories. With this interest comes the capacity for operating in a hypothetical-deductive fashion: for seeing specific events as an example of general principles, and for arranging events such that these principles can be identified. In general, the adolescent's thought comes to take on a far more abstract, systematic, and scientific quality. "Focus on Issues" discusses children's problem-

Knowledge is a product of the child's active mind interacting within a complex and changing world.

solving abilities as they relate to their logical structures at each stage of cognitive development.

In sum then, Piaget sees children as ever-evolving organisms passing through stages, each of which is relevant to earlier and later development. Fundamental to Piaget's developmental theory is the view that cognitive development is not merely an additive process but a continual reconstruction of existing schemes and logical structures. Piaget believed that children play active roles in constructing a system of understanding the world during the course of interaction with the environment. This belief is shared by most cognitive development researchers. In fact, many believe it is one of Piaget's most significant contributions to the field of cognitive psychology.

To Piaget, cognitive development is the elaboration of logical structures that children use to construct and interpret the environment. The primary requirement of Piaget's model is that each of the stages of cognitive development represents logical structures that apply, not only to cognitive skills, but to all cognitive functions demonstrating synchrony across domains. When a logical structure emerges, it catalyzes change in most or all of children's schemes.

Piaget's model conjures an image of children as young scientists building successfully more sophisticated conceptions of the world by the application of more sophisticated logical structures. What children learn is based on some property inherent in the functioning (or logic) of the structures that children use to represent the world. Each stage of cognitive development can be categorized by the logical structures that are available to children for understanding their world. Thus, the major periods differ from one another in the kinds of logical structures that children will use to solve problems.

According to Piaget, logical structures in each stage of cognitive development determine how children attack a specific problem.

ORGANIZATION AND ADAPTATION

Logical structures are said to grow and change as a result of two immutable laws of development: organization and adaptation, which are so important that Piaget called them **functional invariants.** These processes are characteristic of all children (and adults) and are rooted in some innate or inborn mechanism.

Within children's biological selves, a process of **organization** operates to ensure that all schemes are properly interrelated and adjusted to each other to form an integrated person. For example, infants have several schemes, such as grasping or looking, that at first function independently. Infants grasp objects placed in their palms. They will look at objects that appear in front of their eyes. Infants who have not yet organized these two schemes, however, will not perform the two behaviors simultaneously. With development (that is, with maturation and exercise of the two schemes of grasping and looking), infants come to look at things they grasp and grasp at things they see.

The purpose of all behavior or thought, according to Piaget, is to enable people to adapt to their environments in ever more satisfactory ways. **Adaptation**—the most important principle of human functioning—is the continuous process of applying and revising the internal representation of the world so that it accurately represents the outside world. Adaptation has a dual nature; it consists of two processes: assimilation and accommodation.

ASSIMILATION AND ACCOMMODATION

Piaget (1952) describes the adaptive nature of knowing, through assimilation and accommodation. Although it is convenient to talk about them as if they were distinct and separate cognitive activities, it must be kept in mind that Piaget conceived of them as two undissociable aspects of the same basic adaptation process. **Assimilation** is the process of taking in new information and fitting it into an already existing notion about objects of the world. In this sense, to assimilate is to use what you already know how to do in order to do something new. An example of incorporation of reality (sights, sounds, events) into existing schemes can be observed in young infants who grasp everything. Children's grasping scheme seems to press them to search for items that can be readily assimilated. Thus, children compulsively grasp and manipulate toys, blankets, and so on.

What happens when something is encountered in the environment that does not readily fit available schemes? One of two consequences can be expected: The first is that the event is not assimilated at all; it is ignored or passed by. Such may be the case when children do not experience any discrepancy in what they know and the new experience they encounter. Three-year-old Ryan may be perfectly content to call all things that fly "birds" and does not try to assimilate other flying objects. It is only when he realizes that his present way of organizing the world is inadequate that he may try to create new schemes to accommodate new classifications for things that fly.

The second possibility is not outright rejection, but dissatisfaction and continued efforts to achieve a match. Schemes, under pressure from perceived realities of the environment, are altered in form or multiplied to accommodate for lack of an adequate match. Piaget used the word **accommodation** to identify this process. If there are repeated experiences in which reality doesn't fit, then schemes have to change. The person accommodates to reality by changing the internal structure of schemes. As can be seen in Figure 6.2, a young child's scheme of things that fly contains only "birds" and "butterflies." When the child points to something flying in the sky and says "bird," the mother may say, "No, that's an airplane." Mother goes on to describe an airplane. The next time mother and child are out for a walk, the child may point to a bird and say "bird" and point to an airplane and say "airplane." Thus, the scheme of "things that fly" has been modified.

EQUILIBRIUM AND EQUILIBRATION

Equilibrium is a relatively stable state of some scheme that can be adapted to varied input without any essential change. It is a state of cognitive balance between assimilation and accommodation. According to Piaget, cognitive balance is a condition toward which the individual is continually striving. You achieve a state of equilibrium when you have figured out the solution to a difficult math problem, or are finally able to understand a new concept. You experience a feeling of relief, a "Eureka, I understand it!" state of affairs.

**FIGURE 6.2
Assimilation and
Accommodation**

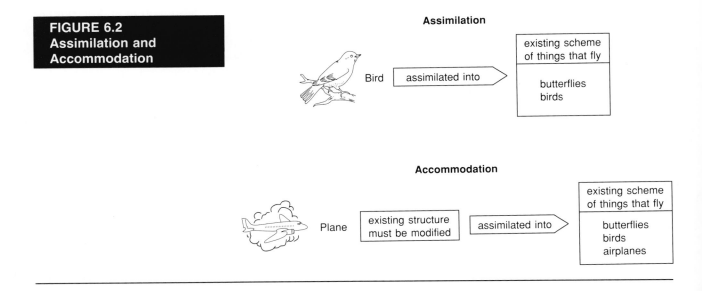

Because equilibrium is neither perfect nor permanent, eventually some input will defeat the assimilation and accommodation powers so far developed by the existing scheme. For example, when children hear contradictory or challenging statements, or encounter something in their environment that does not fit into their present schemes, their equilibrium is disturbed. They then set out in search of an answer that enables them to achieve a new and higher equilibrium.

One of Piaget's students coined the term *cognitive conflict* for these stages of disturbed equilibrium. This nonbalance produces the driving force of development; without it, knowledge remains static. The key tension in every problem is the initial preference for using knowledge and abilities that have worked in the past, pitted against the recognition that old schemes are not adequate and must be altered. It is this period of searching for new and better adjustments, of striving to achieve a balance between past experiences and present uncertainties, that leads to cognitive progress, to further structural development. When people are thrown into a state of cognitive conflict, they search for a solution. It is the search for equilibrium, for answers that satisfy, that spurs the mind on to higher levels of thought.

The process of seeking mental equilibrium, of restoring harmony between the world and the individual's view of the world, is known as **equilibration.** Equilibration, in Piaget's view, is the principal motive responsible for cognitive development. It is a self-regulatory motivational process in which the individual initiates new assimilations and accommodations in order to reduce the unpleasant feelings associated with disequilibrium. New forms of experience that disturb the individual's equilibrium at one level of structuring initiate the compensatory process of equilibration that terminates in a new level of structuring (Piaget, 1950b). Intellectual behavior thus consists of the resolution of conflict between using old responses for new situations and acquiring new (or changing old) responses to fit new realities.

Probably the most fascinating thing about reading Piaget is that he makes you aware of the rhythm inherent in the process of cognitive growth. Beginning with the refinement of reflexes in the sensorimotor period and continuing through the entire cycle of development to the adolescent's abstract reasoning, you see how children's minds seek to understand and to explain at all levels. When equilibrium is established in one area, the restless individual begins to explore in another.

INTERRELATEDNESS OF PIAGETIAN CONCEPTS

Say you have a child named Sarah who is 18 months old—in the sensorimotor level of thinking. Sarah is sitting on a blanket surrounded by a few of her favorite things: a trumpet, an apple, some blocks, and a Tonka truck. Now hand Sarah a magnet. She has never seen one before. At first, she just ignores it (refuses to assimilate it), but soon it gains her interest. What will Sarah do? She will try to assimilate this new object. Credit her with having a certain organized body of knowledge and certain activities concerning the concrete functional properties of the main entities in this situation (schemes). She knows about apples; apples are good to eat. She knows about trumpets; they make noise. Initially, objects encountered for the first time are not viewed as truly novel but are treated as new examples of things already known. So when you observe Sarah trying to eat the magnet or blow into it, you are observing the process of assimilation—using old ideas to meet new situations.

The magnet does not taste as good as an apple, and it makes no sound. As Sarah goes through her repertoire of old ideas (none of which seem to be working) she feels "tense" or "uncomfortable." She has encountered a new object in her environment that calls for intellectual behavior that goes beyond the scope of her present schemes and a state of cognitive conflict results. It is this state of imbalance that propels Sarah to seek a state of equilibrium. She is moved to make meaning or resolve discrepancy and establish meaning in her present reality (process of equilibration).

Suppose that she discovers that this new object can pick up and hold her Tonka truck. When you

The process of using old ideas to meet new situations is known as assimilation. Sarah knows that apples are good to eat. She will use this information in trying to understand the new object, the magnet.

give Sarah the magnet again and she puts the magnet to the truck, you may assume that she has accommodated this new object into her existing sensorimotor schemes. Sarah then modifies her conception of the world (accommodates), which now allows her to handle information that was beyond her scope. Of course, the accommodation is very rudimentary; she will elaborate and sophisticate this accommodation.

Each time children accommodate a new event or problem their intellectual growth is nudged closer to maturity. New, more precise schemes are created from their more primitive predecessors. Figure 6.3 summarizes the important Piagetian concepts and shows how they are interrelated.

STAGES OF COGNITIVE DEVELOPMENT

As you trace children's progress through the stages, you will see them grow from being self-centered infants with no knowledge of their environment to become adolescents who employ logic and language with facility to intellectually manipulate the environment and thus comprehend, ever more realistically, how the world functions.

SENSORIMOTOR PERIOD (BIRTH TO AGE 2)

Piaget (1950a) and his wife, Valentine, spent considerable time observing their three children—Jacqueline, Lucienne, and Laurent—and keeping detailed records of their behavior. The result of their research was the theory of sensorimotor intelligence, which described the spontaneous development of a practical intelligence.

During the **sensorimotor period,** infants move from a neonatal, reflexive level marked by a complete lack of self-world differentiation (children do not distinguish between themselves and the rest of the world) to relatively coherent organisms capable of sensorimotor actions within their environment. Children's organization of their environment involves simple motor and perceptual adjustments to environmental phenomena rather than symbolic manipulations. Sensorimotor thinking is unreflective, practical, a perceiving-and-doing sort of intelligence, not the conceptual, symbol-producing kind that words like cognition and thought usually connote. Piaget describes six major substages of this period, which are summarized in Table 6.1.

Dawn of the Object World The "objectless" world of the young infant gradually becomes a world in which physical objects, as well as the primary caregiver, become separate from the child. The child is able to differentiate between "me" and "not me." Second, children gradually develop the ability to know that objects in their environment continue to exist even when they cannot see them (Piaget, 1973). This is known as **object permanence.** In the earliest stages of development of ob-

FIGURE 6.3   Summary of Basic Piagetian Concepts and Their Relatedness

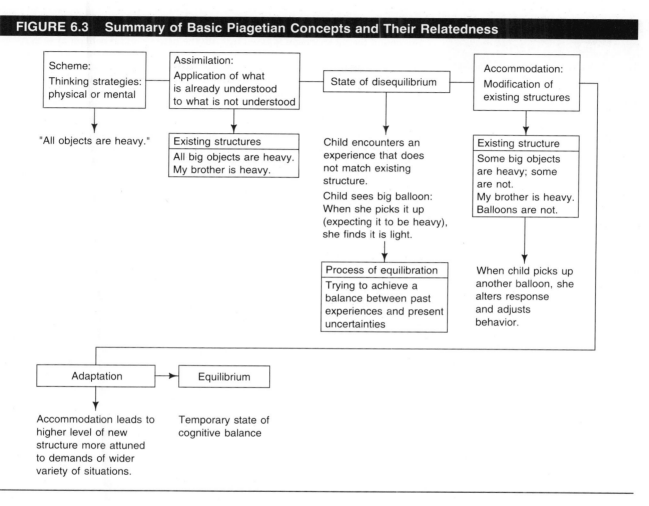

ject permanence, children do not respond to an object once it is removed from sight. They then progress through a series of stages in which they search for an object but only where they last saw it. Finally, they achieve a complete realization of object permanence in a variety of places after hidden displacements. These transformations do not take place over a weekend; rather, the process is a gradual one described in the six substages summarized in Table 6.2.

Current Research on the Sensorimotor Period
Some researchers contend that babies younger

than Piaget's stage 4 may understand that objects are permanent. When testing infants' object permanence, Piaget gave them a choice of two locations in which they could search for a hidden object. One location was where the object was hidden first (A), and the other was where the object was hidden second and remained (B). Piaget demonstrated that infants would search for objects in the A position, not B, which is known as the AB error.

It is contended that infants may make this error not because they do not understand object permanence but, rather, because they may lack the skills

TABLE 6.1   Piaget's Six Stages of the Sensorimotor Period

SUBSTAGE 1: REFLEXIVE STAGE (BIRTH TO 1 MONTH)
The first of the six substages is taken up with the practice and repetition of such reflexes as grasping, sucking, gazing, and listening. Children's days are spent trying to fit the world into their limited repertoire of reflexes. It is important to note that one of Piaget's primary considerations of reflexive behavior at this stage is that even these basic types of adaptations are not evoked merely by direct external stimulation; infants are active, not passive, creatures and often initiate reflexive activity.

SUBSTAGE 2: PRIMARY CIRCULAR REACTIONS (1 TO 4 MONTHS)
In the second substage, infants engage in nonintentional, spontaneous actions that center about their bodies (thus these actions are termed primary), and they are repeated over and over (circular) until the adaptation becomes strengthened and established. Actions are nonpurposeful and are repeated for their own sake. Examples of such actions are thumb sucking or fingering a blanket. The remaining four stages of the sensorimotor period are marked by an ever-increasing intentionality on the part of children.

SUBSTAGE 3: SECONDARY CIRCULAR REACTIONS (4 TO 8 MONTHS)
Infants' attention now turns to the manipulation of objects, rather than their bodies. Hence, the actions are termed secondary. Infants now strike, swing, and shake objects with intense interest in their sights and sounds. Infants repeat these actions because of the interesting stimulus effect created by the particular activity. The activity of infants is intentional, but still occurs only after events have first occurred by chance.

SUBSTAGE 4: COMBINATION OF SECONDARY SCHEMES (8 TO 12 MONTHS)
For the first time, infants' behavior is truly intentional in nature, and children begin to solve simple problems. For example, if Eric wants a toy and an object is in his way, he is able to inaugurate a successful means-end series, if the response is already in his repertoire of sensorimotor schemes. In this case, Eric may combine the schemes of reaching and grasping to obtain the toy. He has begun to comprehend cause and effect. That is, certain acts will bring about predictable results. To Piaget, this is the beginning of practical intelligence.

SUBSTAGE 5: TERTIARY CIRCULAR REACTIONS (12 TO 18 MONTHS)
Children begin to vary their actions to see their effects. Their intelligence is now indicated by tertiary circular reactions—repeating actions, but modifying them slightly each time to test the effect of modification. Toddlers now perform experiments in order to see what happens. Children in this stage can solve problems that demand new and unfamiliar means. They combine habitual grasping and reaching schemes and may create new ones. If unable to reach the ball under the chair, substage-5 children can combine habitual schemes (reaching and grasping), but can also create a new scheme (using a stick) to get the sought-after toy. All children's sensorimotor coordinations are visible; they actively seek and experiment with novel means of attaining a particular end.

SUBSTAGE 6: BEGINNING OF REPRESENTATION (18 MONTHS TO 2 YEARS)
In this stage you see the beginnings of thought; children are beginning to use symbolic representations. Children no longer have to experiment with objects themselves to solve problems; they can represent them mentally. They can carry on "internal experimentations." They can picture and follow a series of events in their minds. Instead of fumbling for a solution by a series of overt and visible sensorimotor explorations (as in substage 5), substage-6 children can invent one through covert processes. For example, a child at this stage sees a toy outside her playpen, out of reach. She can combine schemes, as well as invent new ones, but she can now do this covertly. She can mentally preplan her actions and is not bothered with the cumbersome trial-and-error behavior we saw in substage-5 children.

TABLE 6.2 Six Stages in the Acquisition of Object Permanence	Approximate Ages	Principal Characteristics
	Substage 1: birth to 1 month	Infants do not know that objects exist even when they do not see them.
	Substage 2: 1 to 4 months	Infants prolong images by staring at where last seen. If the mother's face suddenly appears in infants' field of vision, then disappears, infants will continue to stare at place where face was last seen.
	Substage 3: 4 to 8 months	Infants search for partially covered objects.
	Substage 4: 8 to 12 months	Infants search for completely covered objects, but only in a special place: the first place it was hidden. If an object is hidden under blanket A, children will find it. If, before their eyes, you take that object from under blanket A and hide it under blanket B, children will look for it under blanket A.
	Substage 5: 12 to 18 months	Infants search after visible displacements. If you move an object behind screen A, then behind screen B, and finally behind screen C, children will follow these visible displacements and look for the object behind screen C.
	Substage 6: 18 to 24 months	Infants search after hidden displacements. If you put a penny in your hand, put your hand under the blanket and leave the penny there, children, seeing that the penny is no longer in your hand, will look under the blanket.

either to determine where an object is or to carry out an effective search. Finding a hidden object requires two things: (a) mentally representing the hidden object and (b) figuring out where it might be. Piaget did not allow for the possibility that an infant might be capable of the first but not the second, that an infant might know that an object exists without being able to find it.

Bower (1977) believes that one reason for very young infants' failures at object permanence tasks is their poor memories. Bower suggests that infants during the first 2 months of life have some notion of constancy of objects but "forget" them shortly after they are hidden. Out of sight may be out of mind, but it is because of poor memory and not because of a lack of object permanence.

The role of memory in object permanence in AB tasks was assessed in a longitudinal study (Diamond, 1985). Twenty-five infants were tested beginning at about 7 months and continuing until 12 months of age. Diamond reported that the delay between hiding and searching that was necessary to produce the AB error increased with age at a rate of about 2 seconds per month. That is, 7½-month-old infants would search for the hidden object at the erroneous A position following only a 2-second delay. By 12 months of age, infants made the error only if approximately 10 seconds transpired between the hiding of the object and the beginning of the search. Diamond's results are graphically displayed in Figure 6.4. Such findings clearly implicate changes in infants' memories as an important factor in the development of object permanence during this period.

PREOPERATIONAL PERIOD (2 TO 7 YEARS)

As the names of the stages denote, each is characterized by **operations** or, in the case of the **preoperational stage,** the lack of them. Operations are particular types of cognitive schemes, and they de-

This 6-month-old infant stops looking at a toy when it is no longer visible. The process of knowing that an object exists when not visually present—object permanence—develops gradually during the first 2 years of life.

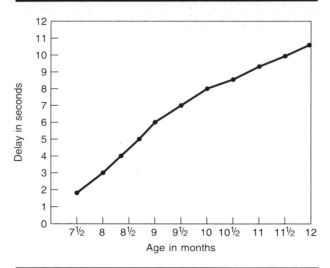

FIGURE 6.4 The Delay Between Hiding of an Object and Infants' Searching for It at Which the Infants Made the AB Error, by Age

Source: Adapted from "Development of the Ability to Use Recall to Guide Action, as Indicated by Infants' Performance of AB" by A. Diamond, 1985, *Child Development, 56*, p. 876. © The Society for Research in Child Development, Inc. Reprinted by permission.

scribe ways in which children act on their world. To be classified as operations, actions must be internalizable, reversible, and coordinated into systems that have laws that apply to the entire system and not just to a single operation.

By *internalizable* Piaget means the action can be carried out in thought "without losing their original character of actions" (1950b, p. 8). Piaget characterized operations as being mental, and thus requiring the use of symbols. The three periods that follow sensorimotor are similar in that children have symbolic representational abilities.

Operations are logical, in that they follow a system of rules, the most critical of which is **reversibility.** Reversibility comes in two types: negation (or inversion) and compensation (or reciprocity). The negation rule states that an operation can always be negated, or inverted. In arithmetic, for example, subtraction is the inverse of addition. If 5 plus 2 equals 7, then 7 minus 2 equals 5. The second type of reversibility states that for any operation there exists another operation that compensates for the effects of the first. If water is poured from a short, wide glass into a tall, thin glass, the increased height of the water level in the second glass is compensated for by a decrease in the breadth of the water. Preoperational thinkers are unable to reverse thought. They are unaware that an operation exists that will restore the original situation. The following dialogue (Phillips, 1975) between an adult and a male child is typical of their inability to reverse thinking.

ADULT: Do you have a brother?
CHILD: Yes.
ADULT: What's his name?
CHILD: Jim.
ADULT: Does Jim have a brother?
CHILD: No.

Here the child's thought processes can go from himself to his brother, but he is unable to reverse them to go from his brother back to himself.

The third requirement for operational thinking is coordinating actions into systems that apply to an entire system. An example of this capability may be best illustrated through an example involving the displacement of volume. When preoperational children are asked what will happen if a stone is dropped into the water, children say the water will rise because the "stone is heavy." When asked if the pebble hanging from a piece of thread will make the water rise, children tend to respond, "No, because it is not heavy enough." In contrast, concrete operational thinkers say that the water will rise when the pebble hanging from a string is put into the water. When asked why, they tend to reply that it will do so because "the pebble takes up space." When asked which would make the water rise the most—a small, heavy pebble or a large, light piece of wood—they tend to answer, "The wood takes up more space; it will make the water rise most." Thus, these children demonstrate that they are capable of coordinating actions that apply to an entire system of laws.

During the preoperational stage, children evolve from those who function primarily in a sensorimotor mode, and whose thinking are through actions, into those who function increasingly in a conceptual and representational mode. Children become increasingly able to represent events internally and become less dependent on their current sensorimotor actions for direction of behavior. The

STUDYING CHILDREN

PREOPERATIONAL THINKING

With modeling clay, make two round balls of clay of equal size. Ask children (aged 2 to 7 years) if the two balls are of equal size, and if they don't think so, work with the clay until they agree that they're the same. Then roll one of the balls into a cylinder or flatten it. Ask the children if the new shape has more clay, the same amount of clay, or less clay than the ball of clay. Ask also why that is. Tell the children, "The other day a little girl told me that there was more in the rolled out clay. How would you prove that she was right or wrong?" (Sund, 1976)

logical structures of thought in preoperational children are so organized that they overattend to the appearance of things; they lack a need to reconcile opposing impressions (Piaget, 1970). Preoperational children's structures are limited in the sense that they cause children to overattend to the thing that strikes them first and most vividly. A single, isolated cognition of this sort, with little or no systematic reference to other cognitions, is the hallmark of the preoperational child (see "Studying Children").

Piaget's genius is never more apparent than in his analysis of young children's ways of thinking. Piaget tried to understand not only what children were saying but why they were saying it. After interviewing hundreds of children between the ages of 4 and 9 at the Maison des Petits in Geneva, Switzerland, Piaget discovered many things about the preoperational thinker (Piaget, 1952). All too often, preoperational children's thinking is described in terms of a dreary litany of their wrong answers to concrete-operational tests. The positive intellectual accomplishments of this period as well as those cognitive features that are destined for development should be stressed. Some important dimensions of preoperational thought are representational or symbolic thinking, centered thinking (centration), transductive reasoning, immanent justice, animism, and egocentrism.

Representation The major development during the preoperational stage is the ability to represent objects and events. Several kinds of representation are apparent: deferred imitation, symbolic play, mental imagery, and spoken language. Each is a form of representation in the sense that something other than objects and events (a signifier) is used to represent them. Piaget referred to this as **symbolic functioning**: the ability to use symbols or signs to represent objects and experiences.

Deferred imitation is the imitation of objects and events that have not been present for some time. Children who play peek-a-boo by themselves, imitating an earlier session with their parents, are engaging in deferred imitation. The significance of deferred imitation is that it implies that children have developed the ability to mentally represent (remember) the behavior imitated. Without representation, deferred imitation would not be possible.

Make-believe play is important because through it the child is assimilating the activities, roles, and ideas of the world.

The second form of representation is *symbolic play:* a form of self-expression with only the self as the intended audience. Symbolic play is a game of pretending. The young child, for example, plays with a block of wood as though it were a car. Piaget felt that the make-believe play of this period is very important because through it children are assimilating symbolically the activities, roles, and ideas of the world. At the same time, assimilation is balanced by accommodation, which Piaget describes as being the primary function of imitation. By imitating the speech, the behaviors, and the activities of others, children learn to adjust to new situations in their world.

The single most evident development during the preoperational period is of *spoken language.* During the sensorimotor period, children had to carry out actions in order to "think"—movement produced thought. With the development of spoken language, thinking can occur in part through representations of actions, rather than actions alone. The ability to use words and to understand their symbolic meanings gives children's surroundings a whole new meaning and significance. Moreover, it enables children to engage in socialized verbal interchange with others.

Symbolic manipulations and language free children's thinking from the immediately perceptible and permit children to create thoughts out of their imaginations. Preschoolers have marvelous imaginations. For example, 5-year-old Gordon came into the den where 3-year-old Eric and their mother were sitting. Gordon was carrying a small box and carefully put it on the floor. The conversation went something like this:

GORDON: Eric, do you have any pennies?
  ERIC: Yep.
GORDON: Come here and see what I have in this box. (Eric looked into the empty box.) Be careful now. These are baby alligators. Want to buy one?
  ERIC: Yep.
GORDON: Go and get some pennies.

Eric ran to his room and returned with some pennies, which he gave to Gordon. Gordon then carefully handed Eric his baby alligator. Eric, now walking slowly and carefully, hands cupped to hold his baby alligator, left the room, presumably to find a suitable home for his new pet. As he was leaving Gordon said, "Eric, do you have more pennies?" "Yep," Eric replied. Then Gordon said, "Do you want to buy a leash?"

Centration Preoperational children are only capable of focusing on one dimension of a situation at a time, known as **centration.** For example, in one of Piaget's experiments, children are shown two identical, tall, linear beakers that contain the same amount of liquid. The children agree that the amount of liquid is the same in both beakers. Then the experimenter pours the content from one of the tall beakers into a shallow, wide beaker. The children, when asked if the beakers now have the same amount of liquid, reply that the tall, linear beaker has more liquid. They are able to focus on one dimension at a time—in this case, the volume level of the liquid.

Preoperational thinkers seem unable to "explore" all aspects of the stimulus, or decenter the visual inspection. As a result, children, when centering, tend to assimilate only limited aspects of an event.

Transductive Reasoning **Transductive reasoning** involves reasoning from one particular instance to another particular instance without reference to the general (Ginsburg & Opper, 1979). Although preoperational children are beginning to understand cause and effect, their grasp of this concept is somewhat shaky, as the following example illustrates. In 1965, a massive power failure blacked out most of upstate New York. The *New York Times* reported a story about a 5-year-old boy who ran his tricycle into an electric pole at the exact moment of the power failure. The little boy saw the lights go out and believed that he caused the blackout. He was fully expecting to be punished for having broken the power system.

Immanent Justice To many preschoolers, the world is equipped with a built-in justice system. They tend to believe that they will be punished,

regardless if the parents witness this misdeed or not, if they do something wrong, something they were told not to do by their parents. If a child stumbles and falls, she may reason that this occurred because she is not supposed to run fast.

Animism Piaget asserted that younger preoperational thinkers attribute animistic (particularly, human) characteristics to all objects. Later, they attribute life only to those objects that move spontaneously. Finally they distinguish between biologically animate and inanimate objects. Movement or action seems to be the criterion in young children's determination of whether an object is alive. This way of thinking is illustrated in an excerpt from Piaget's (1969) interview with Kenn, age 7, and Vel, age 8:

KENN: Is water alive?—Yes.—Why?—It moves. . . . Is fire alive?—Yes, it moves. . . .

VEL: Is the sun alive?—Yes.—Why?—It gives light.—Is a candle alive?—No.—Why not?—(Yes.) Because it gives light. It is alive when it is giving light, but it isn't alive when it is not giving light.—Is a bicycle alive?—No, when it doesn't go it isn't alive. When it goes it is alive. (p. 196)

Egocentrism Preoperational children are delightfully egocentric in their thinking. They are the *raison d'ête* of the universe. The egocentrism of these young children leads them to assume that everyone thinks as they do, and that the whole world shares their feelings and desires. This sense of oneness with the world leads naturally to their assumptions of magic omnipotence. The world is not only created for them, but they can control it. The sun and the moon must follow them when they go for a walk; they can make it snow by frantically dancing around in circles. They do not feel that they need to justify their own statements. Why should they, when all the world shares their thoughts and feelings?

Piaget and Inhelder (1969) demonstrated that children are egocentric perspective takers. In their experiment, a doll was placed at various positions

Egocentric preoperational think-ers believe they have magic pow-ers. If you wish something very hard, you can make it happen.

around three mountains. Children were asked to tell the experimenter how the mountains would appear to the doll at each position. The children tended to chose the picture that reflected their own perspective rather than the doll's.

Current Research on the Preoperational Period It appears that preschool children are not as animis-tic, intuitive, illogical, or egocentric as Piaget sug-gested. Research subsequent to Piaget's initial ob-servations have failed to find any significant degree of animism in young children (Bullock, 1985). In Bullock's (1985) study 3-, 4-, and 5-year-old children and adults were shown separate vid-eotapes of four objects, two animate (a 2-year-old and a rabbit) and two inanimate (a plastic wind-up worm and a set of wooden blocks). The subjects were asked a series of questions concerning the type of attributes each object possessed. Some at-tributes were appropriate for animate objects (for example, "Does X have a brain?") and others were appropriate for inanimate objects (for example, "If X breaks, can we fix it with glue?"). The judgments

of 4- and 5-year-olds were similar to those of the adults.

The judgments of 3-year-olds seemed to reflect a "general uncertainty about the precise properties of many objects" rather than judgments of ani-mateness (p. 224). The 3-year-olds were just as likely to attribute inanimate characteristics to ani-mate objects as they were to attribute animate characteristics to nonliving objects. These findings suggest that children's decisions about what is alive and what is not are a function of their degree of knowledge about objects.

Similarly, in a study done by Flavell (1977), it was demonstrated that children are less egocentric than Piaget indicated. It appears that young chil-dren have some ability to understand that other people see things differently from what they see. Three-year-olds were shown a card with a picture of a dog on one side and a picture of a cat on the other. The card was then held vertically between the child (who could see the dog) and the experi-menter (who could see the cat), and the child was asked which animal the experimenter could see.

The flawless performance of the 3-year-olds indicated that they could assume the experimenter's perspective. The age at which nonegocentric perspective taking occurs appears to depend on the nature of display and the type of response required.

CONCRETE OPERATIONAL PERIOD (7 TO 11 YEARS)

Children in the **concrete operational period** reach a higher level of equilibrium; they are no longer dependent on immediate visual circumstances. They can go beyond perception and conceptualize the world in terms of mental actions. The concrete operational thinker makes cognitive and logical decisions as opposed to perceptual decisions. Kegan (1982) relates a story told to him by a friend, which illustrates how concrete children are no longer embedded in their perceptions as preoperational children are. Two boys were overheard at the top of the Empire State Building. Both boys looked down at the sidewalk and exclaimed simultaneously, "Look at the people. They're tiny ants!" (younger boy); "Look at the people. They look like tiny ants!" (older boy). Whether the younger boy actually thought the people had become tiny ants isn't known. What is known is that the older boy could take a perspective on his own perceptions. He said, "They *look* like tiny ants." His statement is as much about his looking at his perception as it is about looking at the people.

Although advancements have occurred in children's thinking in the concrete stage (they comprehend that quantity remains invariant despite perceptual transformations, their thinking is characterized by the deployment of reverse operations, and they become less egocentric), their thinking is bound to concrete things and the immediate present (Piaget, 1972). Consideration of potentiality (the manner in which events may occur) or reference to future events or situations is limited in scope.

Their thinking in this period is dominated by and therefore limited by what they know from their perceptions to be true about the world. Their thinking, although not limited by immediate perceptions, is, nevertheless, tied to what is concrete and active. Kagan's (1972) favorite syllogism illustrates the concrete-bound thinking of the 7- to 11-year-old compared with the formal operational thinker. Suppose you were to ask a concrete operational thinker the following: "All purple snakes have four legs. I am hiding a purple snake. How many legs does it have?" The child is likely to stare at you the way you might stare at something stirring in your wastepaper basket and is likely to argue with the very idea of a purple or four-legged snake. Such snakes are not found in the concrete world and therefore reasoning about them is problematic. The adolescent, however, can transcend the particular givens and see that conclusions can be drawn from the propositions themselves. Incidentally, the preoperational child is also unaffected by purple or leggy snakes, but is likely to say something totally unrelated to what you have asked, such as, "I knew a kid that had a purple snake!" (Kagan, 1972).

Thus, the term *concrete* means that the problems involve identifiable objects that are either directly perceived or imagined. In the formal operational period, children are able to move ahead to deal with problems that do not concern particular objects. To illustrate this difference, consider the following two items, the first suitable for the concrete operational child, the second for the more advanced formal operational child or adolescent:

> Concrete: If Alice has two apples and Caroline gives her three more, how many apples will Alice have all together?
>
> Formal: Imagine that there are two quantities that together make up a whole. If you increase the first quantity but the whole remains the same, what has happened to the second quantity? (Thomas, 1979, p. 313)

Concrete operational thinking is also characterized by other advancements over preoperational thinking: classification, class inclusion, and conservation.

Classification   The primary task of the 7- to 11-year-old appears to be organizing and ordering what is immediately present. Classification involves the ability to group objects according to common attributes. Children learn to classify things during this stage, which enables them to put their world in order and simplify it. Concrete children are engaged in collecting, keeping records, memorizing baseball statistics—in short, they are healthy obsessive-compulsive creatures. Piaget believed that classification, like conservation, was central to development of concrete operations (Inhelder & Piaget, 1958).

Class Inclusion   Children's knowledge that a superordinate class (flowers) is always larger than any of its subordinate classes (tulips, daffodils) is considered to be a concrete-operational thought. Children are able to reason simultaneously about the part and the whole. If a child is given 5 daffodils and 3 tulips, and asked whether there are more daffodils or more flowers, the mastery of class inclusion is shown when the youngster claims to have more flowers than daffodils. One researcher (Winer, 1980) found that most children were 10 years of age before they could successfully solve class inclusion problems of this kind. Siegler (1978), on the other hand, thought part of the problem may lie in the way the experimenter verbally expressed the problem. When the question was rephrased by deleting the words "more" and "less," even preoperational children did well on class inclusion problems. When the children in his study were shown three M & Ms and two jelly beans and asked, "Do you want to eat the M & Ms or the candy?", most children showed some understanding of class inclusion by gulping down all the candy.

Conservation   Children in the concrete stage of operations practice **conservation;** they achieve the understanding that the quantity is the same despite a change in its appearance. Although most children acquire conservation skills in about the same sequence, the ages at which these abilities appear can vary. A 4-year longitudinal study (Tomlinson-Keasey, Eisert, Kahle, Hardy-Brown, & Keasey, 1979) gives evidence of asynchronous development of conservation skills. Fifty-six kindergarten children were followed through three testing phases over 2 years; 38 were tested in an additional 2 years. The tests assessed conservation of number, substance, length, area, weight, and volume. The study demonstrated that children master number around 6 or 7 years of age, followed by conservation of substance and length (ages 7 and 8), area and weight (ages 9 and 10) (see "Studying Children"), and finally volume (age 12). Further, the authors point out that children who are slower in developing simple conservation skills are slower in developing more complex conservation skills such as weight and volume. Inhelder and Piaget (1958) called the developmental inconsistencies in conservation skills *decalage* from the French *decaler* meaning lag or gap. Although Piaget's theory provides a descriptive label for differing levels of awareness or understanding in conservation tasks, Piaget gives no further explanation. Table 6.3 shows various conservation skills and the approximate ages of achieving them.

Current Research on the Concrete Operational Period   One of the major criticisms concerns the notion of logical structure. As noted in the conservation section, certain tasks, which appeared to share the same logical structure, were found to be passed at widely different ages. This phenomenon is difficult to explain because, according to Piaget's theory, the only mental requirement for passing such tasks was the availability of a general logical structure. This unevenness in development is

---

STUDYING CHILDREN

CONCRETE OPERATIONS

Use eight square rubber erasers. Place four of the erasers in a square figure, and make a straight row out of the other four. Ask children if it is farther around the square or the long row. Ask how they figured it out.

Note: By the age of 8 or 10, children will usually conserve area, but will think that if the area is the same the perimeter must be the same. If children cannot figure it out, have them count the sides and ask the questions again (Sund, 1976).

TABLE 6.3 Conservation Tasks

Type of Conservation	Basic Principles	Child Sees Step 1	Child Sees Step 2	Child Asked
Number (ages 6-7)	The number of units remains the same even though they are reorganized in space.	A ○○○○○ B ○○○○○	A ○○○○○ B ○○ ○○ ○	Which row has more beads? Pre-Cons: "Row B." Cons: "Same"
Substance (ages 7-8)	The amount of clay remains the same, regardless of the shape it assumes.	A B Two clay balls, same size	A B One ball is flattened out.	Are the clay balls the same? Pre-Cons: "B is bigger." Cons: "Same"
Length (ages 7-8)	The length of a line from one end to the other remains unchanged, regardless of how it is arranged in space or changed in shape.	A B	A B	Which stick is longer? Pre-Cons: "Stick B." Cons: "Same"
Area (ages 8-9)	The total amount of surface covered by a set of plane figures remains unchanged, regardless of the position of the figures.	A	B	Which picture has more surface area? Pre-Cons: "B" Cons: "Same"
Weight (ages 9-10)	The heaviness of the object remains unchanged, regardless of the shape it assumes.	A Units placed on top of each other	B Units placed side by side	Which weighs more? Pre-Cons: "A" Cons: "Same"
Volume (ages 12-13 — formal)	The volume of the water is changed if something is added to it, regardless of the way it appears.	A B Two balls of clay placed in two beakers containing equal amounts of water; child sees water level rise equally in both beakers	A B Clay ball B is molded into a different shape and held above the beaker.	When clay ball B is placed in a beaker, will the water level be higher, lower, or the same as in A? Pre-Cons: "Lower, because the ball flattened out" Cons: "Same. Nothing has changed."

problematic for a strong stage notion because the mental operations underlying concept should be content-free, so that the theory applies across a variety of problem-solving situations.

The second problematic finding is that the correlations among conservational development tasks are often low and insignificant. For example, children who are first in their classes to pass the number conservation problem are rarely the first to pass all the others as well. This phenomenon poses a difficulty for Piaget's theory for the same reason as the first. The theory assumes that the primary determinant of children's success on conservation developmental tasks is whether or not they possessed the appropriate logical structure.

FORMAL OPERATIONAL PERIOD (11 TO 15 YEARS)

Just as the development from preoperational to concrete-operational thinking is marked by movement from fantasy to reality, development from concrete-operational thinking to formal-operational thinking is marked by movement from reality to possibility. Adolescents in the **formal operational period** are no longer exclusively preoccupied with systematizing and organizing what comes to their senses, as were concrete children. At the formal level, concrete props and points of reference are no longer needed. "The adolescent has the potentiality of imagining all that might be, both the very obvious and the very subtle, and thereby of much better ensuring the finding of all that is there" (Flavell, 1963, p. 205). To Piaget, this suggests that intelligence has moved from the realm of "things" to that of "ideas." Adolescents are thus freed from their embeddedness in the concrete and can now construe the world abstractly, hypothetically, and inferentially. Their thinking, however, tends to be rather idealistic and egocentric, as you can see from reading "Focus on Applications." In the concrete operational stage, what is—the actual—was everything. A cognitive shift during adolescence enables the 11- to 15-year-old to think not only about what is but also about what might be. This rebalancing, the hallmark of formal operations, unhinges the concrete world. The actual becomes one instance of the infinite array of the possible.

Several characteristics of formal thought are implied by this new orientation to the realm of ideas. Among these are hypothetical-deductive reasoning and combinatorial analysis. To understand the cognitive achievements of the formal period, specific Piagetian experimental situations will be discussed, which are of a physical and logical-mathematical nature used to assess formal operational thinking. These experiments have been designed to reveal the qualitative way in which formal thinking differs from the thinking of children in middle childhood.

The Pendulum Problem and Hypothetical-Deductive Reasoning **Hypothetical-deductive reasoning** involves identifying all the various alternative explanations or hypotheses, and then testing them in a systematic way. It entails reasoning from the general to specific. Inhelder and Piaget (1958) used a series of tasks to assess this scientific reasoning, one of which, the pendulum problem, is briefly discussed.

The apparatus for this experiment (see Figure 6.5) consists of three strings of different lengths (S1 < S2 < S3) and three pieces of metal of different weights (W1 < W2 < W3). Each piece of string can be tied to the center of a stick. If one of the weights is tied to the other end of the string, the string may be swung freely back and forth. Sometimes the string swings more rapidly than at other times. The experimenter demonstrates this fact to the subject. For example, string S1 is attached to the stick, with weight W3 suspended from its other end. The string is then given a push and allowed to swing freely back and forth. Next, the same procedure is repeated with string S3 and weight W1.

The experimenter calls the subject's attention to the fact that the string swings more rapidly in the former case than in the latter. The experimenter may repeat this demonstration with other pairs of strings and weights. After the demonstration is completed, the problem is posed. What exactly is it that makes the string swing more rapidly on some occasions than on others?

Adolescents, like scientists, begin by formulating hypotheses about what specific factors might possibly influence the speed of the string's oscilla-

FOCUS ON APPLICATIONS

Understanding Egocentrism in Adolescence

Elkind (1990) provides some interesting insights into adolescent egocentricity. Adolescents fail to differentiate between what others are thinking about and their own mental preoccupations. They assume that other people are as obsessed with their behavior and appearance as they are themselves. It is this belief that constitutes the egocentrism of adolescence. In a sense, adolescents are continually constructing or reacting to an imaginary audience. It is an audience because adolescents believe that they will be the focus of attention, and it is imaginary because in actual social situations this is not the case. The adolescent's desire for privacy may be a reaction to the feeling of being under the constant scrutiny of other people.

A second personality correlate of egocentrism is the experience of the *personal fable*. Elkind uses this term to refer to adolescents' notions that their feelings and experiences are unique. It seems impossible to them that an adult might know what they are experiencing or feeling. What looks like defiance or negativism in an early adolescent may often be the result of such an adherence to a personal fable. One consequence of the egocentrism may be unrealistic idealism. Piaget states that "the adolescent not only tries to adapt his ego to his social environment, but just as emphatically tries to adjust the environment to his ego" (Inhelder & Piaget, 1958, p. 343). Thus, the adolescent may be highly interested in politics, religion, or educational reform and may develop ideas of an egocentric nature as solutions to problems in these areas. Adolescents feel that the world should submit itself to idealistic structures rather than systems of reality. Young adolescents do not understand that the world is not always rationally ordered, as they think it should be.

As the egocentrism of other periods gradually diminishes, so does the egocentrism of adolescence. When adolescents learn to use their logic effectively in relation to the reality of life, and not only in relation to life as they think it should be, egocentrism diminishes. Secondly,

Once young people can see themselves in a more realistic light as a function of having adjusted their imaginary audience to the real one, they can establish true rather than self-interested interpersonal relationships. Once relations of mutuality are established and confidences are shared, young people discover that others have feelings similar to their own and have suffered and been enraptured in the same way. (Elkind, 1980, p. 86)

tions. They begin solving this problem by trying to envisage all the possible relations revealed in the data: length of string, weight of swinging object, height from which the weight is dropped, and the push given to the object. The fact that they can generate correct tests and recognize their necessity indicates that formal reasoning has transpired. Then, they attempt to find out which of these relations, in fact, hold true. They start with the variable that they believe will have the greatest potential for influencing oscillation, though they carefully test out all the variables before finishing.

The 11- to 15-year-old's experimental behavior, directed by hypotheses that are based on more or less refined causal models, is exemplified in the pendulum problem in which formal thinkers are able to construct hypotheses to account for particular phenomena. That is, instead of focusing on the facts that are immediately before them, they seem to generate hypotheses about what may be going on. The capacity to reason in terms of verbally stated hypotheses and no longer merely in terms of concrete objects and their manipulation, to reason hypothetically and deduce the conse-

FIGURE 6.5 The Pendulum Problem

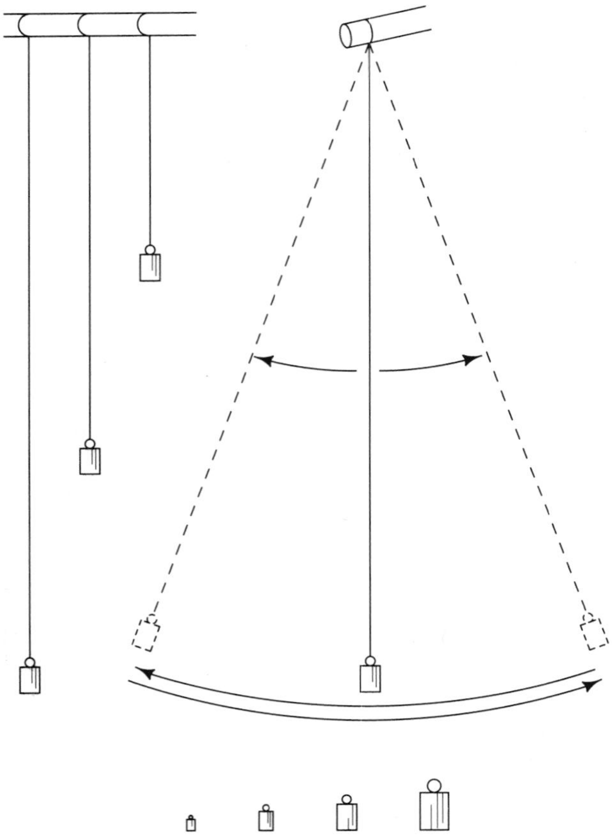

Children are to determine what factor or combination of factors is responsible for the rate at which the pendulum oscillates.

Source: From *The Growth of Logical Thinking* by B. Inhelder and J. Piaget. Copyright © 1958 by Basic Books, Inc. Reprinted by permission of Basic Books, a division of HarperCollins Publishers.

STUDYING CHILDREN

FORMAL OPERATIONS

Materials: string and modeling clay.

Put some clay on the end of the string and hold it to form a pendulum with a length of about 3 feet. Ask the child to figure out how to change the speed at which the pendulum swings.

Success on this task is achieved by figuring out that the one variable that changes the speed of the pendulum is the length of the string. The child's justification must include the idea of holding the other variables (weight of clay, height of drop) constant, while altering the string length. Formal thinking involves separating and controlling one variable at a time in solving the problem. Preoperational children will play with the apparatus, but will not produce a plan of approach to the problem. Concrete-operational-level children may come up with the correct answer, but will not separate and control the variables systematically (Sund, 1976).

through the method of holding all of the factors constant except one, is presented by Piaget as another clear sign of the presence of the formal operational system. Formal operational thinkers subject all the variables to a **combinatorial analysis,** a method that nicely guarantees that the possible will be exhaustively inventoried. Formal operational thinkers hold all but one variable constant and test one variable at a time as compared with the concrete operational thinker who haphazardly tests variables in a random order.

The capacity to think using combinatorial analysis is best illustrated by the problem of the colorless liquids (see Figure 6.6). The subject is exposed to five colorless, odorless bottles of liquids. The bottles, labeled 1, 2, 3, 4, and g, contain diluted sulfuric acid, water, oxygenated water, and thiosulfate. The subject does not know the chemical elements in the flasks. While the subject is watching, the contents of three of these containers are mixed and a yellowish liquid is produced. Adding the contents of a fourth container returns the liquid to its original colorless state. The subject's problem is first to reproduce the yellow, using any

quences that the hypotheses necessarily imply, is a formal operational reasoning process. Test the hypothetical-deductive reasoning of an adolescent by performing the problem found in "Studying Children."

Combinatorial Analysis and the Problem of Colorless Liquids The ability to separate the effects of several variables in an experimental situation,

FIGURE 6.6 All Possible Combinations of the Four Test Tubes to Which the Fifth Can Be Added

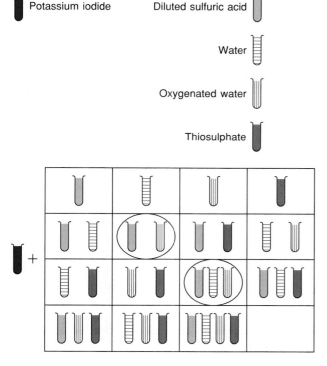

Potassium iodide

Diluted sulfuric acid

Water

Oxygenated water

Thiosulphate

The experiment requires the subject to discover the combination(s) that yields a yellow liquid when potassium iodide is added. The correct solutions are circled.

Source: From *The Growth of Logical Thinking* by B. Inhelder and J. Piaget. Copyright © 1958 by Basic Books, Inc. Reprinted by permission of Basic Books, a division of HarperCollins Publishers.

combination of the bottles 1, 2, 3, 4, and *g*, and then to return the liquid to its colorless state.

The approaches of concrete operational children are characterized by two forms of behavior: First, they systematically add *g* to all the liquids because this is what they saw the experimenter do; second, they appear to think that color is attributed to only one of the elements, which reveals the difference between a noncombinatorial and a combinatorial

structure of intelligence. Those with formal reasoning accomplish this in a coordinated manner and can determine the effect of one, all, or some combination of variables. The relationships among variables must be constructed through reasoning and verified through systematic experimentation. Some children in the concrete stage come on the correct combination through luck and experimental prodding. Once they hit on it, however, they cannot remember how they achieved it!

The adolescent shows an understanding that the color results from the combinations of elements. The final phase occurs when a youngster establishes that the color is due to a combination of 1, 3, and *g*, and then experiments with 2 and 4 to verify which one will bleach out the color. This systematic structuring of formal thought provides the adolescent with the necessary tools for separating out the variables that might be causal, holding one factor constant in order to determine the causal action of another, and so on.

Problem-finding Thinkers   Although not all adolescents attain formal operations during early adolescence, there is evidence that some older adolescents may go beyond formal operations. This phase has been called *problem finding* in contrast to the problem solving that typically characterizes formal operations. The thinking of some older adolescents might be characterized as *divergent* (moving toward new or creative solutions or the identification of problems) rather than *convergent* (moving toward known or accepted solutions to problems). This second phase of formal operations is identified by the quality of the questions asked rather than arrival at known conclusions. The problem-finding thinker is able to rethink or reorganize existing knowledge and then to ask important questions or define totally new problems.

Adolescent and Adult Thinking   In the formal operational period, the qualitative development of logical structures is presumed to be complete. That is, after this stage there are no further logical structural improvements. The adolescent has the mental apparatus required to solve problems logically, as does the adult. This does not mean, however, that adolescent thought is necessarily "as good as" adult thought, only that the attainment of formal operations means a new potentiality has been achieved. Assimilation and accommodation continue throughout life to produce changes in thought. From the end of the period of formal operations, changes in thought abilities are quantitative and no longer qualitative with respect to logical operations and structures. Structures of intelligence do not improve after this period. This is not meant to imply that the use of thought cannot or does not improve after adolescence. The content of thought is free to vary and improve after this period, which helps to explain in part some of the classical differences between adolescent and adult thought.

Current Research on the Formal Operational Period
Cross-cultural studies have demonstrated that cognitive development through concrete operations is universal except for the mentally retarded. There is considerable evidence that not all adolescents use formal operational thinking. In one study, for example, only 32% of 15-year-olds and 34% of 18-year-olds were even beginning to use formal operations (Epstein, 1979). Although many adolescents may have the capacity for formal operational thinking, whether they actually use it depends on their experience and their education—particularly in math and science courses. Environmental conditions may have a great deal to do with achieving formal operational thinking.

Moreover, the types of tests used by Piaget to assess formal operational thinking are extremely difficult, and in many cases, unclear. The tasks are classics of physics: balance scales, pendulums, projections of shadows, falling bodies, and so on. The intellectual attributes assessed by these tests are designed for discovering the ideal scientist—one that has the ability to engage in purely abstract thought, to reason both inductively and deductively, to consider all possible outcomes, and to recognize and admit when the evidence is insufficient to reach any conclusion. Individuals from technologically underdeveloped countries, for ex-

ample, where there is little emphasis on science, certainly would not fare well on these tests. Flavell (1982) found, however, that Kalahari bushmen showed remarkable inferential and analytical skills when tracking animals, where they had to make inferences and hypothesize about probable animal behavior. Thus, as Ginsburg and Opper (1969) relate, "One cannot infer the lack of competence from a subject's failure at some conventional tasks which are inappropriate to his interests or culture" (1969, p. 202). A summary of the thinking patterns at each of the four stages of cognitive development is found in Table 6.4.

PRACTICAL IMPLICATIONS: ENHANCING CHILDREN'S COGNITIVE GROWTH

Now that you have seen the theoretical dimensions of Piaget's theory, look at some implications. As future parents or teachers, what can you expect at each level of development and how can you enhance children's cognitive growth?

INFANCY: BIRTH TO AGE 2
Granted, most parents define significant milestones in this early period of development in terms of their children taking their first steps and uttering their first words. You do not often observe a parent exclaiming to a friend, "My child can now combine secondary schemes!" The six Piagetian substages of this period, however, are major achievements. As parents and teachers, you should now be aware that infants are active, curious creatures and should be given opportunities to actively explore their environment. You should also expect active children to find it difficult to make fine distinctions in what they can or cannot do. Remember that very young children are continually repeating their newly acquired schemes on every object available. Therefore, they delight in pulling the cord on their "Speak and Say" and see very little difference between that and pulling on the cord to the television set.

TABLE 6.4 Summary of Thinking Patterns at Each Stage of Cognitive Development	**SENSORIMOTOR (BIRTH TO 2 YEARS)**
	Action-oriented thinking not capable of representation thinking, perceiving and doing sort of intelligence
	Develops *object permanence*
	
	PREOPERATIONAL (2 TO 7 YEARS)
	Development of language skills enables children to internalize words in the form of thoughts and internalize action so child does not have to depend on physical actions to solve problems: *representational thinking*
	    Large portion of child's talking and listening is *egocentric* (sees things from one's own point of view)
	    Reasoning abilities are influenced by immediate perception (problem solving based heavily on what they see and hear directly)
	    Thought is *centered:* (unable to see that more than one factor at a time influences an event)
	    Unable to *reverse* thoughts
	    Reasons are one particular instance to another without reference to the general (transductive reasoning)
	
	CONCRETE OPERATIONS (7 TO 11 YEARS)
	Capable of reasoning only about identifiable objects that are either directly perceived or imagined
	Gains greater command of the notions of *conservation* and *reversibility*
	Capable of *decentering* their attention (of recognizing 2 or more dimensions of an event interact to produce a given result)
	
	FORMAL (11 TO 15 YEARS)
	Can now imagine the conditions of a problem—past, present, future—and develop hypotheses about what might logically occur under different combinations of factors
	Can engage in pure thought that is independent of action (abstract reasoning)
	Scientific thinker: capable of hypothetical–deductive reasoning (identifying alternative explanations or hypotheses and test them systematically)

Piaget believed that children actively construct their world views, therefore, children should be given extensive opportunities to engage in discovery learning. Children should be given the chance to manipulate objects, so that they can learn through direct experience how objects function in their environment. Spontaneous interactions with the environment are critical to children's progress toward a more accurate view of the world.

EARLY CHILDHOOD: 2 TO 7 YEARS

During infancy, children's curiosity is expressed motorically as they physically explore their environment. A 2- to 7-year-old's curiosity is expressed in asking why. Granted, their "whys" can go on *ad infinitum*, but be patient and do the best you can.

Children in early childhood are egocentric; they simply believe that everyone sees the world in exactly the same way they do. Sometime it's very frustrating to them that parents or teachers do not understand them. A short section from St. Exupery's *The Little Prince* may help you understand their egocentrism and the frustration they feel when adults don't understand them.

The little boy draws a wonderful picture, something like this:

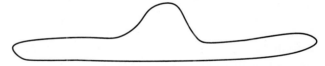

I showed my masterpiece to the grown-ups and asked them whether the drawing frightened them. But they answered "Frighten? Why should anyone be frightened by a hat?"

My drawing was not a picture of a hat. It was a picture of a boa constrictor digesting an elephant. I made another drawing. I drew the inside of the boa constrictor so that the grown-ups could see it clearly. They always need to have things explained.

Grown-ups never understand anything by themselves, and it is tiresome for children to always and forever explain things to them.

Nursery school children should have extensive play areas with large toys in which children learn to control their actions and to obtain a working knowledge of spatial relationships. A diversity of smaller toys and apparatus for construction or for use in imaginative play is important. Clothes for "acting" encourage imitation and playing of roles. Parents and teachers who are aware of the memory capacity of young children will make their list of directives to children short, and not expect them to concentrate for long periods of time.

MIDDLE CHILDHOOD: 7 TO 11 YEARS

Many 7- to 11-year-olds will be great collectors of such significant paraphenalia as beer cans, bottle caps, and stickers. At times, these collections may seem trivial to adults. Having their own collectibles, however, not only helps in their ability to organize and categorize, but has social benefits as well: prestige among peers and pride of ownership to name two.

In middle childhood, a large part of children's thinking proceeds at the intuitive level. The danger is still very great that learning will be conducted purely on a verbal plane. Verbal explanations can be effective only after a basis in concrete activity has been established. If concrete activity has not been established, children will fail to become attached to the activity, which is essential if it is to have meaning.

It is important for teachers to remember that these children cannot think abstractly. During the middle grades and junior high, children are exposed to a number of abstract terms. For example, in history or social studies, there are a number of concepts (individual rights, government, compromise, environment) that require more than verbal definitions to help students grasp their meaning. Merely memorizing these definitions will not indicate understanding or the ability to apply them to other situations or different contexts. In one study (Bull & Wittrock, 1973), a group of fifth-grade children were presented with new vocabulary words such as brain, truth, liberty, and the like. Half of the children were told to read the definition of the word and then draw a picture of the concept. The other half were told to write the definition over and over again. On a multiple-choice test given 1 week later, the picture-drawing group received a significantly higher number of correct responses than the control group. Drawing pictures, participating in simulation games, and creating charts or maps may help students to recognize objects that represent or illustrate important concepts.

Social interactions among peers through group discussions in the classroom can aid in cognitive development. When children talk to other children, they come to realize that theirs is not the only way of viewing things and that other people do not necessarily share their opinions. Interactions inevitably lead to conflict and arguments. Children's views are questioned, and they must defend their views and justify their opinions. In doing this they are forced to clarify their own thoughts. If they want to convince others of the validity of their views, their ideas must be expressed clearly and logically.

It appears that children profit when their attention is called to the "right" things to study in a textbook. In one experiment (Crouse, 1974), students were allowed to read the assigned chapters until they felt they were ready to take a test. They could repeat the study-test cycle up to five times. The students showed virtually no improvement; they did not benefit much from repeatedly reading

Jean Piaget believed that social interaction in the form of classroom group discussions can aid in cognitive development.

assigned chapters when studying for a test. Perhaps, then, by calling attention to boldface printed words, chapter summaries, section titles, and other important cues found in most books, children will be able to study the correct material.

ADOLESCENCE: 11 TO 15 YEARS

In many ways, adolescents are idealists. They feel that the world should submit itself to idealistic structures rather than systems of reality. They do not understand that the world is not always rationally ordered as they think it should be. Therefore, you may expect adolescents to be rather argumentative. When answering their questions, it's best to give a response that is as detailed and as factual as you can make it.

Piaget places the full development of the capacity to deal with formal abstract thinking at about 15 years. During the first 2 years of secondary school, programs should be suitable for adolescents who think in concrete terms. When beginning a new topic, learning should be based on concrete experience or on the adolescent's own experiences, even in the case of the most able students.

Social interaction is also important at this level. It can be a fruitful means of stimulating cognitive conflicts that can generate accommodation to the views of others. Proposing general hypotheses that help adolescents come up with their own conclusions through active scientific experimentation aids in formal development.

Using imagery may help adolescents to memorize material more effectively. The imagery technique has been examined in a study, in which adolescents who were learning to speak Russian were asked to associate the spoken Russian word with an English word that sounded like it or part of it (Atkinson & Raugh, 1975). For example, the Russian word *zvonok*, meaning bell, is pronounced something like "zvahn-oak." The subject was told to form a mental image of the spoken word interacting with its English translation. The subject might imagine a large oak tree with little brass bells for acorns. While the method may seem somewhat awkward at first, it was found in this study that the technique is quite effective. The test score for those using imagery was 72%, while the control group who did not use imagery received a test score of 42%.

REVIEW OF KEY POINTS

Piaget believed that logical structures within the child underlie intelligence and that cognitive development is the development of these structures. He viewed children as being intrinsically active and thus responsible, to a large extent, for their own development.

Infants and very young children come to know their world through direct sensory and motor experiences. Children's earliest schemes are organized action patterns, such as grasping, reaching, looking, and sucking. As children get older, they are able to interiorize thought. Throughout cognitive development, you may observe that as structures qualitatively change, more sophisticated reasoning strategies evolve. Piaget has categorized four different stages: sensorimotor, preoperational, concrete, and formal. To say that a child has entered a new stage of cognitive development is to say that qualitative changes in structures have occurred.

When children are confronted with something new, they will try to take in or modify the stimuli (assimilation); when children acquire a new way of doing things, when they revise existing schemes, they have accommodated the new stimuli. Two inherent tendencies that govern how children interact with their environment are organization and adaptation. The process of organization operates to ensure that all schemes are interrelated. The purpose of all thought and behavior is to adapt to our environment.

Piaget described the intelligence of human infants as sensorimotor in nature, in that infants, through the first 2 years of life, understand the world mostly in terms of their actions on it. Piaget divided the sensorimotor period into six stages. A major accomplishment of the sensorimotor period is the development of object permanence, the knowledge that an object has an existence independent of one's perceptions of or actions on that object.

Piaget described the thought of preoperational children as intuitive, egocentric, and illogical. The thought of preoperational children was said to lack reversibility, the benchmark of operations. Piaget described the perception of preoperational children as centered on the most salient aspects of a perceptual array.

Concrete operational thinkers are conservers; that is, they realize that quantity remains the same despite perceptual transformations. Concrete thinkers are able to classify objects, and know that a superordinate class is always larger than any of its subordinate classes.

Formal operational thinkers are abstract thinkers who are capable of solving complex math and science problems in which they must generate hypotheses, hold variables constant, and create solutions.

ENHANCING YOUR CRITICAL THINKING

Broadening Your Knowledge

The Sensorimotor Period

Wadsworth, B. J. (1989). *Piaget's theory of cognitive and affective development.* New York: Longman.

Chapter 3 offers a detailed account of children's mental development in the six substages of the sensorimotor period.

Critical Thinking

Piagetian Tasks

Sprinthall, N. A., & Sprinthall, R. C. (1989). *Educational psychology: A developmental approach* (pp. 128–132). New York: McGraw-Hill.

While the text offers activities in "Studying Children" that are based on Piaget's actual tasks, you may like to examine the actual tasks used by Piaget. Do you feel that these tests represent good ways to measure intelligence? What aspects of intelligence are these tests measuring?

Personal Growth

Piaget for Educators

The following sources are recommended for those students who are majoring in education and may wish more information on applying Piagetian principles in the classroom:

Furth, H. (1970). *Piaget for teachers.* Englewood Cliffs, NJ: Prentice-Hall.

Pulaski, M. (1980). *Understanding Piaget.* New York: Harper & Row.

Wadsworth, B. J. (1980). *Piaget for classroom teachers.* New York: Longman.

Views of Cognition: Information-Processing Theory

CHILDREN'S THOUGHTS

On "How do you remember things?"

If you want to remember something in your mind, you have to say it over and over, or two times.
Ronnie, age 5

If I have a lot of things to remember, I write them down on a list. But, sometimes, I lose the list. Really my mom helps me to remember the things I need to.
Lynne, age 8

Actually, it depends on what it is I'm trying to remember. If I am studying for an exam—I do lots of different things. I say things out-loud; I write stuff down. I have my dad quiz me to see if I've remembered everything. I even made up a song once to remember things for my history exam.
Larry, age 13

CHAPTER OUTLINE

KEY TERMS

Executive processing space
Automaticity
Control structures
Sensory register
Iconic memory
Echoic memory
Attention
Perception
Short-term memory
Long-term memory
Memory strategies
Rehearsal
Organization
Elaboration
Retrieval
Recognition
Recall
Encoding
Knowledge base
Metamemory

Partly in response to criticisms of Piagetian theory, some developmental psychologists began to adopt a different perspective on the nature of cognitive development. Piaget and information-processing viewpoints are quite different. Unlike Piaget's theory, which is derived from one man's astute observations of children, the information-processing approach is the accumulation of the work of many investigators. While Piaget postulates that all cognitive growth is organized around coordinated principles or logical structures that set limits on children's problem-solving abilities, information-processing theorists view the mind as a diverse collection of individual processes that do not necessarily follow the same rules and are not under the control of an underlying logical structure. Information-processing theory may thus be more sensitive to diversities found in children's thinking and abilities.

In this approach, the human mind is conceived of as a complex cognitive system, analogous to a digital computer. Its primary objective is to provide an explicit, detailed understanding of what the subject's cognitive system actually does when dealing with a task or problem.

Information-processing theorists define intelligence as the ability to solve problems and adapt effectively to the environment. They are interested in studying the nature of information that children pick up from the vast amount of stimuli that bombard their senses and the series of stages through which they pass as they absorb and transform this information. The method refers to the *processes* by which people take in, analyze, store, and retrieve various types of things they have perceived or that have happened to them—*information.*

Some investigators like Robbie Case have attempted to modify Piagetian theory so as to take into account information-processing considerations. Thus, one sees "neo-Piagetian" theories with an information-processing look about them. Other theorists, notably Robert Siegler, have restudied cognitive-developmental phenomena initially discovered by Piaget but using concepts and methods in the information-processing tradition. Siegler's investigations using his rule-assessment approach represents a good example of how cognitive growth can be profitably studied from an information-processing approach.

In addition to studying these information-processing theories, this chapter will focus on the basic information-processing skills involved in acquiring information from the environment and the way that information is manipulated, processed, and organized into memory, in particular, the structure of memory, the development of memory strategies, and factors that influence children's use of memory strategies. As revealed in the children's themes, the sophistication and effectiveness of children's memory strategies increases with age. Thus, as development proceeds, children become more effective information processors.

ROBBIE CASE'S INFORMATION-PROCESSING THEORY

Robbie Case sees his work as emerging from Piaget's. Because he preserves so much of Piaget's theory—exemplified by his belief in stages, sequences, and structural change—many would classify him as a neo-Piagetian. However, because of his inclusion of new constructs such as skills,

rules, limited memory capacity, and automaticity, many classify him as an information-processing theorist. Actually, his theory is an attempt to synthesize Piaget into information-processing perspectives.

In contrast to Piaget's domain-general classification of logical structures, Case (1985) focuses on domain-specific concepts that pertain only to a particular area or areas. He shows how limits in processing capacity limit logical reasoning and constrain what children can learn at any developmental level. Similarly, increases in capacity create a new opportunity for the further development of logical thinking. Case organizes his theory around four developmental stages and four universal substages in each of these stages, the role of automatization in the growth of working memory capacity, and the effects of automatization on specific experiences.

EXECUTIVE PROCESSING SPACE

Case's work presents an important new working memory theory. His term for working memory (our active, temporary, conscious memory) is **executive processing space,** which refers to the maximum number of schemes children can activate at any one time while working at a goal about which some executive decision must be made. There is one central working memory, which can serve as a space for storing information, or for operating on it.

The functional capacity of the executive processing space increases due to increases in **automaticity** with which operations are executed on the content characteristic of the stage. The term *automatization* captures the movement from laborious execution of a skill to execution that is smooth and without deliberation. As each operation is executed more efficiently, executive processing space is freed for additional operations.

Case maintains that children's thinking has a common general pattern across various domains at the same age. The reason for this, in Case's view, is not that they have (or have not) acquired certain logical structures as Piaget would maintain, rather, their thinking is subject to a common quantitative constraint: a limited executive processing space. It is this constraint that guarantees that development will proceed at a relatively slow pace through identifiable stages. Case maintains that the executive processing space does not increase with age; however, the operating space, that portion of space used for actually processing information, decreases with age.

When conceptualizing memory processes, Case distinguishes between operating space and storage space. Storage space refers to the hypothetical amount of space that children have available for storing information. Operating space is the amount of mental space that can be allocated to the execution of intellectual operations. Case proposed that there is a developmental decrease in the amount of operating space required for the execution of cognitive processes with a concomitant increase in operational efficiency. Developmental changes in operating and storage space are displayed in Figure 7.1.

To illustrate, Case, Kurland, and Goldberg (1982) assessed the independent contributions of storage space and operating efficiency to memory performance in children ranging in age from 3 to 6

years. Storage space was measured by counting the number of items that children recalled under conditions that minimized the effects of memory strategies. Operating efficiency was measured by the speed with which a set of cognitive operations, such as identifying items, could be performed. The study showed that there was a relationship between operational efficiency (as reflected by speed of identification) and storage space (as reflected by how much was remembered). Children who were slow in identifying items (thus requiring substantial amounts of operating space) realized lower levels of memory performance for those items (see Figure 7.2).

What factors are responsible for increasing operational efficiency? The first factor is experience.

FIGURE 7.2   The Relationship Between Word Span and Speed of Word Repetition at Age Levels from 3 to 6 Years and Adulthood

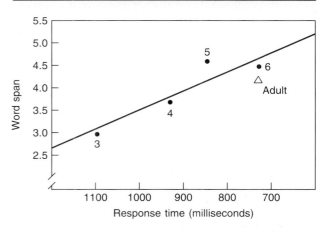

Younger children were generally slower to identify words and had shorter word spans than older children. When the identification times of adults were slowed to levels comparable to those of 6-year-olds, they showed a corresponding deficit in word span.

FIGURE 7.1   With Age, Children Process Information More Efficiently, Requiring Less Operating Space and Leaving More Storage Space

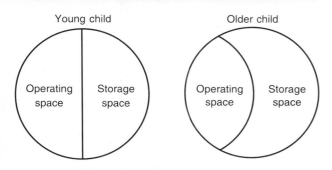

Source: From *Children's Thinking: Developmental Function and Individual Differences*, by David F. Bjorklund. Copyright © 1989 by Wadsworth, Inc. Reprinted by permission of Brooks/Cole Publishing Company, Pacific Grove, CA 93950.

Source: From "Operational Efficiency and the Growth of Short-term Memory Span" by R. Case, M. Kurland, and J. Goldberg, 1982, *Journal of Experimental Child Psychology, 33*, p. 386. Reprinted by permission of Academic Press.

As children practice encoding numbers, for example, the automaticity of their encoding increases. Maturation is another factor. Case hypothesizes that increased myelination (lipoprotein covering the axons of neurons) during development increases the efficiency of the conduction of neural impulses. Perhaps the increased automaticity of sensorimotor operations requires maturation on the part of the brain that directs motor activity.

CONTROL STRUCTURES AND STAGES OF DEVELOPMENT

As working memory increases, it becomes easier to acquire and utilize more elaborate **control structures.** Each major stage is characterized by different domain-specific control structures, which involve qualitatively distinct underlying operations. Executive control structures involve procedural knowledge that children acquire about how to reach certain classes of goals. The operations of any given stage must be assembled in working memory from the components available at a previous stage. It follows that the transition to any given stage depends on the attainment of a certain degree of automaticity during the previous stage.

Case organized his theory around four developmental stages: sensorimotor (birth to 1½ years), relational (1½ to 5 years), dimensional (5 to 11 years), and vector (11 to 18 years). The difference between the stages of development lies in the nature of the operations that form the basic units of thought. Each stage has different executive control structures. Operations that are characteristic of each general stage are noted in Table 7.1.

The basic units of thought in the first stage, sensorimotor, are sensory objects and motor actions. The infant's control structures are limited to physical movements, which enable young children to explore their visual and physical world. In the second stage, relational, the basic units of thought become relationships between such objects and actions. Children detect and coordinate relations among objects, events, or people. In the next stage, dimensional, the basic units of thought become quantitative dimensions on which children focus. Although preschoolers can focus on weight

or number, children in this stage extract the dimensions of significance in their physical and social world. They learn to compare two dimensions such as height and width in a logical quantity task, in a quantitative way. In the final stage, vectorial, the basic units of thought become abstract dimensions. In effect, children are no longer focusing on either of the two concrete dimensions separately; rather, they are focusing on a more abstract dimension: the vector that results from their opposition. Case refers to these second-order dimensional operations as vectorial operations.

While the stages and structures portion of Case's theory is similar to Piaget's, Case clarifies and refines the notion of stages by attempting to differentiate domain-specific achievements. Within each of the four major stages a universal is a sequence of substages: unifocal, unifocal coordination, bifocal coordination, and elaborated coordination. These operations, also noted in Table 7.1, specify the way in which children's mental processes are structured at each stage. Unifocal operations restrict children to performing single actions in infancy, single relationships in early childhood, single dimensions in middle childhood, and single vectorial operations in adolescence. Bifocal operations enable children to carry out related actions in infancy, related relationships in early childhood, related dimensions in middle childhood, and related vectorial operations in adolescence. Elaborated operations allow children to coordinate several actions, relationships, quantitative dimensions, and qualitative dimensions, respectively.

If children have the necessary processing capacity, they can use their innate processing abilities to take advantage of their experiences to construct more advanced executive control structures. Consequently, as Case points out, the problem of children showing unevenness in problem-solving abilities, which is contrary to Piaget's logical structure premise, can be explained by pointing out that different forms of the same logical insight may require executive control structures of differing complexity. Conservation of number can be acquired by counting each of the two transformed arrays and making a determination of the relative number. This requires a unidimensional control structure, acquired at age 5 or 6. By contrast, conservation of liquid volume cannot be acquired unless children make a quantification along two dimensions. This insight requires a bidimensional control structure, and is not acquired until age 7 or 8. Although logically equivalent, then, the two forms of conservation are not psychologically equivalent. That they are not acquired at the same point in time ceases to be a problem in Case's theory.

EVALUATION OF CASE'S THEORY

Case's theory presents a view of global organization or structure of children's mental activity at successive points in time, and provides a glimpse of the more detailed processes, which occur at each successive point in time. It is an ambitious and venturesome theory of cognitive development. As with all theories, however, it has been subject to some criticism. In particular, John Flavell criticizes Case's working-memory notion and the four-step developmental sequence proposed for each major stage.

In regard to the first criticism, Flavell (1985) asks,

> How are we to decide, in a consistent fashion, exactly what constitutes an "item" in working memory for any given problem-solving strategy, and hence, how are we to decide exactly how much memory load the use of that strategy imposes? Or phrased differently, how can we guarantee good inter-psychologist reliability in assigning memory-demand numbers to execute strategies or other cognitive episodes? (p. 100)

Flavell's second criticism bears on Case's ideas about developmental sequences. The form is a four-step developmental sequence in which each step has characteristic properties. The first step is always unifocal. Flavell (1985) comments that Case has not "formally defined it [or any of his four steps] or carefully explained what all instances of it have in common" (p. 101). Finally, further supportive evidence of the role of myelination for increasing mental efficiency is needed.

ROBERT SIEGLER'S INFORMATION-PROCESSING THEORY

Robert Siegler (1978, 1986) believes that much of cognitive growth can be usefully characterized as the sequential acquisition of increasingly powerful rules for solving problems. He begins by predicting the different problem-solving rules that children of different developmental levels might use. These hypotheses about the developmental ordering or sequence of rules are usually based, in part at least, on prior research findings by Piaget. It is in this sense that Siegler's work can be said to build on and extend Piaget's.

RULE-ASSESSMENT APPROACH

Siegler's model of cognitive development portrays children as qualitative information processors. The picture drawn by him is that children are rule governed. Typically, a rule refers to a mental procedure whose operation affects performance on many problems within a task domain. The concept of rule provides a tool for describing change and continuity in cognitive organization. Changes in performance are typically explained in terms of modifications, additions, or deletions of particular rules.

Siegler formulated his precise description of the rules that children develop at different ages by using a balance beam and asking children how it operates. Siegler emphasized what children of different ages are able to encode and distinguished different rules for processing information about a balance scale, such as the one shown in Figure 7.3.

On each side of the fulcrum are four pegs on which metal weights can be placed. The arms of the balance could tip left or right or remain level, depending on how the weights are arranged. A lever, however, is set to hold the arm motionless. The task is to predict which, if either side, would go down if the lever were released. Siegler proposed that children develop one of four possible strategies or rules based on the information of the number of weights and the distance of the weights from the fulcrum.

TABLE 7.1   Development of Control Structures

Sensorimotor

Substage 0 Unifocal	(1 to 4 months) Children execute single movements. For example, small object in reach; children make contact with object.
Substage 1 Unifocal Coordination	(4 to 8 months) Children coordinate two forms of activity or two distinct precursor structures—for example, reaching and visual tracking. Children see interesting, moving object and visually track and reach for it.
Substage 2 Bifocal Coordination	(8 to 12 months) Children capable of insightful solutions to problems. Children push down arm of balance beam and realize that this motoric action is responsible for ringing the bell placed above the arm of the balance beam. They are able to insightfully connect the first action to the final outcome. It is this grasping of the overall problem that is the prominent feature of bifocal coordination.
Substage 3 Elaborated Coordination	(1 to 1½ years) In the balance beam problem, the bell is placed below the arm of the balance beam. The experimenter shows how the bell can be rung by reversing earlier actions (lifting the arm instead of pushing it down). Children at this stage not only understand that an action produces a reaction, but also understand that the particular nature of their action must be tailored to the particular nature of the effect that is desired. In order to arrive at this insight, they must assemble a more complex or elaborated control structure.

Relational

Substage 0 Unifocal	(1 to 1½ years) Children understand a single relationship. For example, children push down on balance beam and the other end goes up. Children understand inverse relationship between action at one end of the lever and the action at the other end.
Substage 1 Unifocal Coordination	(1½ to 2 years) Children can combine two different kinds of relationships. In the balance beam problem, supports had to be removed before the balance arm was pushed or pulled. Success at this task requires children to focus on two different types of relationships: (a) the instrumental relationship between their actions on one end of the beam and the reaction at the other and (b) the preventative relationship between the blocks and the beam.
Substage 2 Bifocal Coordination	(2 to 3½ years) Children's focus expands to include two systematic interrelationships rather than one. Balance beam set in front of children with supports in place; then a peg is placed in the slot on the opposite arm of balance from the bells. A heavy weight is placed on the arm causing the arm to move sharply down when the supports are removed, thus ringing the bells. The position of the bells is changed on every trial. Children have to select which side of balance arm to place weight in order to ring bells.
Substage 3 Elaborated Coordination	(3½ to 5 years) In previous experiment, children could succeed by placing light or heavy pegs on arm. In this experiment, children are given light and heavy weights. Children have to place the light weight on the side of the beam they wish to go up, not down. They then have to place the heavier of the two weights on the opposite side, which they wish to go down. Children apprehend the relationship between heavy and light weights to each other, and coordinating the action of the arm once the supports are removed.

TABLE 7.1 *continued*	
	Dimensional
Substage 0	(3½ to 5 years)
Unifocal	Children focus on single concrete dimension: weight. Children look at balance beam and predict that the one that looks heavy will go down, the light one up.
Substage 1	(5 to 7 years)
Unifocal Coordination	Children can focus on weight or number in situations in which only one of these dimensions is of importance. They can focus on both dimensions or use one as a means to drawing a conclusion about the other.
Substage 2	(7 to 9 years)
Bifocal Coordination	Children begin to focus on a second quantitative dimension. On the balance beam, this may be seen in the situation in which an equal number of weights is placed on each side of the balance. Children decenter and compute the distance from the fulcrum of each weight. They predict that the weight that is at a greater distance from the fulcrum will go down.
Substage 3	(9 to 11 years)
Elaborated Coordination	On problems in which there is a difference both in weight and distance from the fulcrum, children must choose between the two. Children do not base their decisions strictly on weight when the two are in conflict. Children add the number of weight and distance units on each side, and pick the one with the greater total value as the one that will go down.
	Vectorial
Substage 0	(9 to 11 years)
Unifocal	Children execute single vectorial operations. Children compare weight difference to distance difference and pick the larger as more potent.
Substage 1	(11 to 13 years)
Unifocal Coordination	Faced with a problem in which two weights on the left are opposed by one weight on the right, while two distance pegs on the left are opposed by four distance pegs on the right, children no longer note that the left side has only one more weight than the right, whereas the right side has two more distance pegs than the left. Thus, they no longer predict that the right side will go down. Instead, they note that there are twice as many distance pegs on the left or "two for one," and that there are twice as many distance pegs on the right as well. They, therefore, conclude that the two sides will balance.
Substage 2	(13 to 15 years)
Bifocal Coordination	Children are capable of taking a second division operation into account. They can solve the problem in which the distances on the two sides are 5 and 2 and the weights are 2 and 1. Children take the quantity that is "left over" after 2 is divided by 5 (i.e., 1) and divide it up as well. They end up comparing the unit ratio of the weights that is given (2:1) with the unit ratio in the distances that they have computed (2½:1).
Substage 3	(15 to 18 years)
Elaborated Coordination	The particular set of operations that were used to adjust one of the dimensions into a new ratio at previous substages can now be executed for the second dimension as well. Children can now deal with a problem in which neither quantity is stated in unit form, and in which neither set of quantities can be transformed in any fashion into a ratio that is directly comparable to the other. For a problem involving seven weights and three weights, at distances of two units and five units, they may therefore reason that two distance pegs and five distance pegs is the same as 1 for 2⅓, while three weights and seven weights is the same as 1 for 2. Thus the weight factor should predominate.

FIGURE 7.3   A Balance-Scale Apparatus

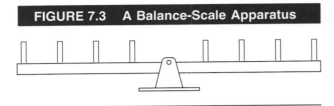

Source: From *Children's Thinking: What Develops?* by R. S. Siegler, 1978, Hillsdale, NJ: Lawrence Erlbaum Associates. Copyright 1978 Lawrence Erlbaum Associates. Reprinted by permission.

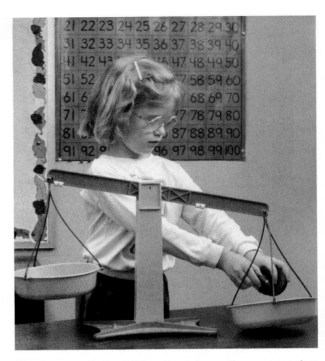

Siegler studied children's information-processing skills by asking them to solve problems on a balance scale.

Rule 1: Using rule 1 reflects the typical performance of preschoolers. Children using this rule attend to only the number of weights on each side of the fulcrum. If they are the same, the children predict balance, otherwise, they predict that the side with the greater amount of weights will go down.

Rule 2: Some children first apply rule 1, but if the weights are equal, they predict that the side with the weights farther from the fulcrum is heavier. The side with the weights that are a greater distance from the fulcrum will go down. Children using rule 2 are more advanced in that they consider distance of the weights from the fulcrum.

Rule 3: Some children consider both weight and distance, but do not fully understand the relationship between the two (e.g., if one side has more weights whereas the other side has fewer weights but the weights are farther from the fulcrum, children become confused and guess what will happen).

Rule 4: Some children attend to both weight and distance, and understand the relationship between the two. This rule represents mature knowledge of the task because it includes torque calculation; children using it always make the correct prediction.

Siegler then constructed six types of problems that would differentiate children at the different levels of sophistication. Thus, it is possible to determine which, if any, of these rule models accurately characterizes children's knowledge about the balance scale by examining correct answers and errors on these six types of problems:

1. Balance problems: The same configuration of weights on pegs on each side of fulcrum

2. Weight problems: Unequal amounts of weight equidistant from the fulcrum

3. Distance problems: Equal amounts of weight different distances from the fulcrum

4. Conflict-weight problems: One side with more weight, the other side with its weight farther from the fulcrum, and the side with more weight going down

5. Conflict-distance problems: One side with more weight, the other side with more distance, and the side with more distance going down

6. Conflict-balance problems: The usual conflict between weight and distance cues and the two sides balancing

As shown in Table 7.2, children who use different rules produce different response patterns on these problems. Those using Rule I predict correctly on balance, weight, and conflict-weight problems but never predict correctly on the other three problem types. Children using Rule II be-

TABLE 7.2 Problems Used to Assess Understanding of the Balance Scale

Problem-type	Rule			
	I	II	III	IV
Balance	100	100	100	100
Weight	100	100	100	100
Distance	0 (Should say "Balance")	100	100	100
Conflict-Weight	100	100	33 (Chance Responding)	100
Conflict-Distance	0 (Should say "Right Down")	0 (Should say "Right Down")	33 (Chance responding)	100
Conflict-Balance	0 (Should say "Right Down")	0 (Should say "Right Down")	33 (Chance Responding)	100

Source: From *Children's Thinking: What Develops?* by R. S. Siegler, 1978, Hillsdale, NJ: Lawrence Erlbaum Associates. Copyright 1978 Lawrence Erlbaum Associates. Reprinted by permission.

have similarly except that they also solve distance problems. Those adopting Rule III invariably are correct on all three types of nonconflict problems and perform at chance level on the three types of conflict problems. Those using Rule IV solve all problems.

Siegler (1978) examined 5-, 9-, 13-, and 17-year-olds' existing knowledge about balance scales. The rule models fit the predictions of 90% of the children at all age levels. Five-year-olds used Rule I; 9-year-olds used Rule II or III; 13- and 17-year-olds used Rule III. Few children of any age used Rule IV (see Table 7.3).

Siegler maintains that the ability to learn a new rule depends not just on children's current rule but on their ability to encode relevant information. For example, Siegler tried to teach 5- and 8-year-olds who were using Rule I to use Rule II. His efforts to help them were more successful with older children, despite the fact that the older children were initially at the same level of understanding as the younger children. The key difference between the two ages was encoding. Although all children were solving the balance scale problems on the basis of weight alone, it seemed that the older children were at least aware of distance information

TABLE 7.3   Modal Course of Development on Balance Scale Task

| Age | ASPECT OF DEVELOPMENT | | | |
	Existing Knowledge	Encoding	Response to Feedback	Supplements That Aid Response to Feedback
3 years	No rule	Neither weight nor distance	Does not learn rule 1 from weight and balance problems	50% learn rule 1 if given weight-encoding training before feedback
4 years	50% rule 1 50% no rule	Weight	Learns rule 1 from weight and balance problems	—
5 years	rule 1	Weight	Does not learn rule 3 or 4 from conflict problems	Learns rule 3 if given weight and distance encoding training before feedback
8 years	50% rule 2 50% rule 1	Weight and distance	Learns rule 3 from conflict problems	—
13 years	rule 3	Weight and distance	Does not learn rule 4 from conflict problems	50% learn rule 4 if given both quantitative encoding instructions and external memory aids along with feedback
17 years	rule 3	Weight and distance	Does not learn rule 4 from conflict problems	Learns rule 4 if given either quantitative encoding instructions or external memory aids along with feedback

Source: From *Children's Thinking: What Develops?* by R. S. Siegler, 1978, Hillsdale, NJ: Lawrence Erlbaum Associates. Copyright 1978 Lawrence Erlbaum Associates. Reprinted by permission.

and were thus able to profit from new experience involving it. The younger children appeared to ignore such information entirely.

EVALUATION OF SIEGLER'S THEORY

Siegler's work represents an interesting, well-articulated example of information-processing approaches to cognitive growth. He avoids postulation of global, vague, and cognitive metamorphoses. His theory, however, is in danger of treating children too narrowly. The simple set of rules developed by Siegler is an appealing model of development, yet this simplicity has been the focus of criticism. How much of children's knowledge and thinking can be adequately expressed or captured in rules, whether of the type that Siegler posits or of any other type? It has been suggested (Bjorklund, 1989) that these simple rules emerged because Siegler's methodology restricts children to them. Presenting the same task in an open-ended rather than forced-choice manner may produce more complex reasoning.

At first glance, Siegler's theory seems remarkably similar to Piaget's work on age differences in problem solving. However, the critical difference is that Siegler's rule-assessment approach allows the investigator to specify exactly how children are processing (or failing to process) relevant information, and thus indicate why they fail to solve a particular problem or set of related problems. The rule-assessment approach is more precise than Piaget's theory of predicting why a child's thinking takes the form it does and specifying the information that the child must now consider in order to move from one level of understanding to the next.

THE STRUCTURE OF MEMORY

Information-processing theorists are concerned with the fundamental processes that underlie thinking. They believe that it is more useful to describe intelligent individuals, for instance, as those who encode information more rapidly than others, store material more durably, or retrieve it with greater efficiency. Similarly, they believe that a measurement of intelligence that assesses an individual's impairment (lack of rehearsal strategies, poor retrieval strategies) may have greater value as an educational tool than the quantitative estimates of ability intelligence tests provide.

In this model, the learning-process flow of information is analyzed as it moves from a transitory to a relatively permanent store. By following the flow of information from the point of sensory stimulation to your response, you can gain insight into the fundamental operations of the cognitive system.

Processing of information is postulated to occur in a sequence of layers, starting with an environmental stimulus impinging on your senses and continuing on to "deeper" processes, eventually leading to a response. Figure 7.4 shows the layers through which information is passed. Each layer receives information from the preceding layer, performs its unique function, and then the information is passed on to another level for further processing.

Researchers study the various processes involved in the transfer, expecting that an understanding of these mechanisms increase understanding of cognition. The detection of sensory signals is the initial step in processing information.

SENSORY REGISTER

You see, hear, smell, taste, and feel the phenomena of the world as the first link in the chain of processing information. The **sensory register,** sometimes called the *sensory store,* permits the effect of a stimulus on a sensory system to persist briefly (250 milliseconds) after the stimulus itself has been removed. The sensory register is a sort of

photographic memory that is rather primitive in that it will record faithfully, but decays quickly. Unless information from the sensory register enters the short-term memory, it is lost completely. The material in the sensory register is unprocessed information, which basically means that the material has not yet been interpreted.

The vast bulk of information about the sensory register concerns vision and hearing. Unfortunately, not enough data have been collected on taste, olfaction, or touch to report on. Neisser (1979) used the term **iconic memory** to describe visual sensory memory, or the brief persistence of visual impressions.

Visual Memory George Sperling's studies done in the 1960s show the existence of a sensory register. In one of his studies (Sperling, 1960), three rows of letters, each four letters long, were briefly presented to his sample of college students.

X B D F
M D Z G
L C N H

His subjects were then asked to report as many of the letters as they could remember. The subjects typically reported four or five—roughly 40% of the list. Then Sperling changed the procedure. The subjects were now told that they would have to report one row of the three-row array. The row that they were to report would be signaled by a tone. A high-pitched tone meant they would report the top row, a medium-pitched tone the middle row and a tone of low pitch for the bottom row. The tone was presented either simultaneously with the letters or else delayed by a fraction of a

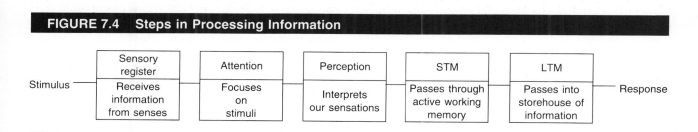

FIGURE 7.4 Steps in Processing Information

	Sensory register	Attention	Perception	STM	LTM	
Stimulus	Receives information from senses	Focuses on stimuli	Interprets our sensations	Passes through active working memory	Passes into storehouse of information	Response

second. Sperling found, as can be seen in Figure 7.5, that when the tone was presented simultaneously with the letters, the subjects could report 80% of the letters in the row. When the tone was delayed by 300 milliseconds, recall declined to 55%, and when it was delayed by 1 second, performance declined to the original 40%. These data are taken as support for the existence of a rapidly decaying memory—the sensory register.

Auditory Memory **Echoic memory** is the name given to brief auditory impressions that persist after the sound itself has disappeared. In one experiment (Massaro, 1972), one tone is presented to a subject and another tone is presented less than a second later. The second tone often masks or prevents the perception of the first tone. It was concluded from this experiment that echoic memory lasts about 1/4 second.

Children's and Adults' Sensory Registers Research has shown that children may be deficient relative to adults in the nature and operation of the sensory register. An experiment conducted with 5-year-old children and adults found that while adults could remember up to four geometric forms accurately, 5-year-olds could not remember more than two (Haith, Morrison, Rheingold, & Mindes, 1970). It appears that adults remember more because they are using more effective strategies for encoding the items before they decay from the sensory register. They are able to interpret a stimulus and store a representation of that interpretation in memory before the information is lost. Children are not as effective in executing this strategy, and hence not as much information is remembered.

FIGURE 7.5 Sperling's Experiment

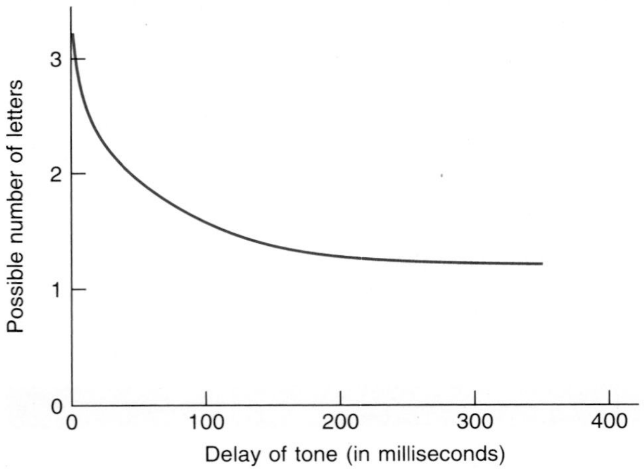

Accuracy was plotted as function of the delay of the tone.

Source: From "The Information Available in Brief Visual Presentations" by G. Sperling, 1960, *Psychological Monographs, 74.* Copyright 1960 by the American Psychological Association.

ATTENTION

According to information-processing theorists, cognition really subsumes a large number of individual processes such as attention and perception. Although people are information-gathering creatures, it is evident that under normal circumstances they are highly selective in the amount and type of information they attend to. The first critical determinant of information processing is **attention,** which, according to William James (1890/1907) "is the taking possession by the mind, in clear and vivid form, of one out of what seem several simultaneously possible objects or trains of thoughts. Focalization, concentration and consciousness are of its essence. It implies withdrawal from some things in order to deal effectively with others" (pp. 403–404).

One aspect of attention then is *selectivity.* The ability to screen out distractions and concentrate on a particular stimulus while ignoring others improves steadily during childhood (Pearson & Lane, 1990). Young children, it appears, are somewhat less able to control their attentional process (Enns & Akhtar, 1989). They are more distractible and less flexible in deploying attention among relevant and irrelevant information. The ability to attend selectively to relevant stimuli and ignore irrelevant stimuli improves developmentally from childhood to adolescence. For example, in one study (Pick, Christy, & Frankel, 1972), second-grade and sixth-grade children were asked to make judgments about some aspect of two colored wooden animals—whether they were the same color or the same shape. Efficient performance of this task requires focusing on the relevant aspect and ignoring the irrelevant aspects. The older children responded more quickly than did the younger children.

The improvement with age in children's ability to attend to relevant stimuli has been shown to be related to a developmental increase in children's ability to follow instructions (Vlietstra, 1982) and to allocate attention in accordance with task demands (Gibson & Rader, 1979). In an experiment done by Schiff and Knopf (1985), 20 9-year-olds and 20 13-year-olds were asked to monitor and respond to two sets of stimuli that were presented simultaneously. The children were instructed to press a button when they saw a star, which would always appear at the center of the monitor. Then they

Children's ability to attend to relevant stimuli increases with age.

were instructed to remember the letters that would then appear in the corner of the screen. The 13-year-olds were able to focus their attention in accordance with the experimenter's task demands and thus made significantly more correct responses and recalled significantly more letters than 9-year-olds. In examining the eye-movement data, it was found that the older children fixated at the center of the screen until the star appeared. After responding, they briefly fixated on the corner letters and then returned to fixating on the center of the display. By contrast, the 9-year-olds fixated on the corners and blank areas of the screen for long periods of time throughout the task and fixated on the center at intervals that were not related to the appearance of the star. This study demonstrated that as children get older they become better able to allocate their attention in accordance with task demands.

Controlled attention improves as an individual develops. In one experiment, subjects were shown a series of pictures and asked to learn the location of each picture in the series. Each picture also happened to have a different-colored background, but nothing was said about this. Research shows that older children regularly remember more of the intentional material than younger children, but there are no clear age differences in memory for incidental material (Pick, Frankel, & Hess, 1975). These findings suggest that older children are better able to direct their attention toward the material the researcher wants them to remember (and on which they will be tested).

With increasing age, children can more easily adapt their attention strategies to the demands of specific tasks and situations. There is no one attentional strategy that is appropriate to all situations or problems. Older children are more flexible than younger children in modifying their attention in accordance with the requirement of the task (Pick, 1980). Eight-year-olds focus on multiple aspects of a stimulus more frequently than 5-year-olds, when the stimulus is adaptive in problem solving, and on a single dimension of a stimulus, when the stimulus has functional value (Hale & Taweel, 1974).

Enns and Akhtar (1989) demonstrated that visual selection often breaks down for children because of the intrusion of task-irrelevant information into the processing of task relevant information. The subjects, ranging in age from 5 to 19 years old, participated in a selective-attention task. The results revealed that older observers are better able to inhibit the processing of distractors than younger children. The authors concluded that the subject's ability to skillfully allocate cognitive resources to the relevant task components determines performance.

PERCEPTION

Once children attend to a particular stimulus, it must be interpreted perceptually. **Perception** may be defined as "the process by which the child extracts meaningful information from the meaningless mosaic of physical stimulation" (Mussen, Conger, & Kagan, 1984, p. 278). When you smell cologne, taste caviar, listen to a concert, you experience more than the immediate sensory stimulation.

Young children appear to have a slower rate of perceptual processing than do older children for both visual and auditory information (Massaro & Burke, 1991). Consistent with age-related improvements in the rate of perceptual processing is that less perceptual information is needed in order to perceive events as children get older. Often young children need to have a lot of information presented before they are able to interpret perceptually an object or event. In contrast, older children and adults can recognize events with incomplete information. For example, in Figure 7.6, the older child is likely to recognize the stimulus as a chair in drawing A. The younger child, however, must see more of the stimulus to recognize it such as seen in drawing B.

Perception becomes more differentiated as children get older (Gibson, 1969). Practice or prior experiences teach the child which features or patterns of features are distinctive and critical for identification. For example, if we presented young children with four letters, *b*, *d*, *p*, and *q*, they may

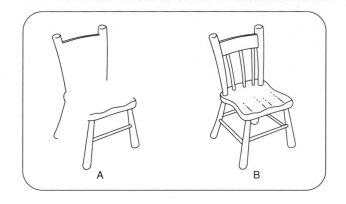

FIGURE 7.6   Partially Completed Drawings of a Chair

A   B

think that the line and the loop are distinctive features. Because these two characteristics are irrelevant to this discrimination, the four letters would not be distinguished. With more experience, the loop's position (at top or bottom of the line) and the left-right orientation of the loop are noted and the four letters are distinguished (Ault, 1977). Older children are also able to ignore irrelevant information. With experience, they can ignore such unnecessary details as the size and color of the letter.

The perceptual process does not function in isolation from other thought processes. Perceptions are stored in memory, where information is recalled to help interpret incoming perceptions. You need to examine memory as the next process of thinking.

SHORT-TERM MEMORY

Information that is attended to and perceptually interpreted enters the **short-term memory.** It is temporary, active, conscious—your attention span or working memory. Short-term memory is the central processing unit, where information from the immediate environment, as well as information from long-term memory, are combined to per-

---

FOCUS ON ISSUES

Templates or Feature Analysis

Sensory registers are just the first step in the processing of information. To make sense of the jumbled data, the information in the sensory registers must be processed for meaning. Only when new input information is matched with information in long-term memory will it be recognized. How does this initial processing happen?

One explanation is that we match the incoming information to a set of templates stored in our long-term memory. When a match is found, the information is assigned the meaning that is associated with the template. To illustrate, the pattern recognition now used at many major food stores provides an analogy as to how template matching works. As the clerk pulls the item across the beam, the computer identifies the special numbers on the product by scanning each character and comparing it to the list of digit representations stored in the computer's memory. The digit representations in the computer's memory function as templates.

There are a few difficulties with this approach. First, can you imagine the gigantic number of templates you would have to have in order to encode the stimuli in your environment? Second, many stimuli vary so widely from instance to instance that recognition by template matching seems all but impossible.

Another explanation, feature analysis, seems to be a better way of explaining how you match up new stimuli with information in our long-term memory. Let's say you are trying to build a model car. You begin by building a rough model or close approximation of the finished product—a prototype. Some information-processing theorists suggest that long-term memory does not contain exact detailed templates, but rather, contains rough prototypes that identify new information and give it meaning. In other words, you break down incoming stimuli into *features* or key elements, which are then matched with a list of features stored in long-term memory. When a match is found, you recognize the stimulus, and it has meaning.

---

form whatever calculations are necessary (Atkinson & Shiffrin, 1968).

Some of this information from the sensory store is matched up with what you already know (long-term memory), and as a result you recognize the new information. Once it has been recognized, you become aware of it (short-term memory). To illustrate, you are walking to class oblivious to the sea of faces passing by you. One of these faces (your good friend Joe), however, is picked up by the sensory register and matched up with long-term memory—you recognize Joe (short-term memory). As can be seen in "Focus on Issues,"

some theorists believe that you can recognize Joe through template matching; others suggest that feature analysis brings about recognition.

There are several types of limits on operations of the short-term memory. One of these involves its capacity: the number of symbols it can hold at one time. Memory-span experiments show that people have a capacity of seven + or − two items or "chunks" of information at a time (Miller, 1956). A chunk can be defined circularly as a stimulus pattern or sequence that the perceptual system recognizes as a familiar single unit. Chunking refers to grouping items together in a more inclusive category. For example, look at these letters for a few seconds and then try to repeat them:

IBMFBICIATV

Rather difficult to do, right? It has 11 letters and is thus beyond the span of short-term memory for letters. But if we chunk them together like this

IBM FBI CIA TV

you'll probably remember them. The capacity constraint, then, is a function of the number of chunks rather than the number of physical units. Chunking information into larger and larger units greatly increases the scope of the short-term memory by providing an organized method for remembering.

The other limitation of the short-term memory is the rate of decay of information. Generally, material in the store is lost in a half minute or so. For example, you and your roommate are planning a party, and you are in charge of buying the food. After class, on your way to the store, you fumble through your pockets to find that the all-important list is gone. You telephone your roommate to get the list: hot dogs, buns, ketchup, onions, beer, pickles, potato chips, and cupcakes. On to the store. Upon your return your roommate grumbles, "You forgot the ketchup, onions and pickles!" What has happened not only shows that information quickly fades in your short-term memory but also demonstrates the primacy and recency effect. You remember the items at the beginning of the list, because they have a better chance of getting into our long-term memory, since you are paying more attention to them. Items at the end of the list tend to stay in our short-term memory. The ones in the middle are forgotten. Figure 7.7 shows the percent of accuracy in retention as a function of the serial position of the item in a list. When people are asked to memorize a list of words, the words memorized first and last are remembered best; those in the middle are recalled least efficiently. Why was the beer remembered? Well, sometimes if something is personally important or specially significant, even though it appears in the middle of the list, it will be remembered.

You must organize and encode material in the long-term memory or it is lost and gone forever. When you have encoded material, you have added more information to your permanent storehouse of information: your long-term memory. The memory

Information in short-term memory only lasts about 30 seconds. That's why we forget a telephone number that we have just looked up if we wait too long before dialing.

FIGURE 7.7 Primacy and Recency Effects

Accuracy of remembering item in a 17-item list

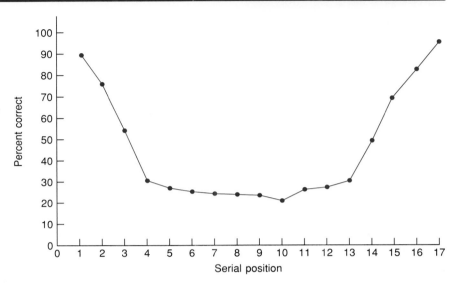

process from sensory to short-term to long-term memory is graphically demonstrated in Figure 7.8.

LONG-TERM MEMORY

Long-term memory is the repository of our more permanent knowledge and skills. Basically, it includes all things that have been coded in memory that are not being currently used. Fergus Craik (1979) provided evidence that there is a short-term and a long-term memory. In the first part of his experiment, he presented college students with 10 lists, each having 10 words. After each list, the students were asked to recall the 10 words. Then Craik asked the students to recall all 100 of the words that had been presented. That changed the task from a test of short-term memory to a test of long-term memory, because the list presentation had lasted several minutes.

In the first part of the experiment, Craik observed elevated remembering at the beginning of the list (primacy effect) and at the end of the list (recency effect). In the second part of the experiment, the primacy effect remained but the recency effect disappeared. The probability of recall actually was lower for the last words in each list than for any other of the 10 positions. The results suggested that primacy effects reflect long-term memory whereas recency effects reflect short-term memory.

Researchers have concluded that long-term retention is a developmental constant (Lehman, Mikesell, & Doherty, 1985). In general, the argument is that storage in long-term memory is permanent; that is, previously stored information does not decay, nor is it obliterated by intervening events. Information stored in long-term memory, however, is continually reorganized in memory. Because memory is updated by new information and is restructured to accommodate more sophisticated knowledge, it is likely that information in long-term memory is altered, transformed, and distorted. Whenever some new information is reg-

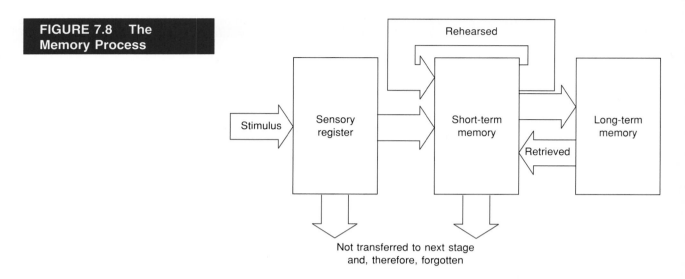

FIGURE 7.8 The Memory Process

Source: From E. Loftus, *Memory*, © 1980, by Addison-Wesley Publishing Company, Inc. Reprinted with permission of the publisher.

istered in long-term memory, it is possible that previous memories are reactivated to assimilate the new information and are modified in the process (Howe & Brainerd, 1989; Loftus, 1980).

If information is permanent or even if it is modified in some way, why can't you remember everything you learn? Inability to recall is due either to structural interference from other contents in long-term memory or to difficulties in accessing the material. Let's make a general comparison to a computer. To retrieve a fact from a computer, you have to know how to locate it. If you don't know the name of the program, it may as well not exist. The program is still in the computer, but because you don't know how it's been classified and labeled, it is unavailable to you. Granted, human beings have numerous starting points and a vast number of routes for getting to long-term memory, and much information is recalled effortlessly. What is your name? What is your address? What is your Social Security number? Other information may be available, but you do not have access to it.

Have you ever dodged someone at a party, because you couldn't remember her name? It's right on the tip of your tongue. The person is now making her way toward you. Frantically you start searching for *cues*. Cues help us check different parts of long-term memory to see if any of them contain the fact you are looking for. You begin to go through the alphabet. Does her name begin with A? B? C? (You certainly hope her name is not Zelda, for she is getting closer.) "Diane, how good to see you!" When you fail to retrieve the right information, you have forgotten. Not all information in long-term memory is accessible at any given time, though apparently most of it is always available, which is why long-term memory is considered relatively permanent.

Developmental Changes in Long-term Memory
There are some aspects of the information processing system that do not change with age. To illustrate, children, like adults, have sensory registers, short-term memory, and long-term memory. Once something is locked in the long-term memory, the young child remembers it quite readily. In fact, earlier research showed that younger children remember information in long-term memory better than older children. To illustrate, in one study (Walen, 1970) fifth-graders and college students

learned high- and medium-frequency word lists to a criterion of 80% correct responding using free recall. Half of the subjects received an immediate (30 second) retention test while the other subjects received a delayed (7-day) retention test. There were no age differences on the immediate test, but the children showed better recall than the college students on the delayed test. These data would seem to suggest that when recall tests are used, retention is inversely related to age. These studies, unfortunately, failed to equate learning during the initial memorization phase. It has been pointed out that the absence of controls for level of learning poses serious difficulties for the interpretation of retention data.

There are some recent studies that have challenged the finding that younger children's retention rate is greater than that of older children and adults (Brainerd & Reyna, 1988a, 1988b; Howe, 1987). Brainerd, Kingma, and Howe (1986) used recall tests and stringent acquisition criteria to study retention rates in 7- to 17-year-olds. In using categorized and uncategorized items and a 1-week retention interval, they found that consistent improvements in retention occurred from the early-elementary school years to adolescence. Retention was better in 17-year-olds than in 11-year-olds, and it was better in 11-year-olds than in 7-year-olds. Similarly, using picture-word pairs and a 2-week retention interval, Howe (1987) found better retention for sixth-grade than second-grade children. So, it would appear that there are developmental improvements in long-term memory retention.

THE DEVELOPMENT OF MEMORY STRATEGIES

Children gradually discover that they can take deliberate actions to help them remember things. Techniques that improve memory are called **memory strategies,** which generally refer to voluntary, purposeful plans adopted to enhance performance and are subject to conscious evaluation. Four of the most investigated memory strategies in develop-

mental psychology are *rehearsal,* in which children repeat the target information; *organization,* in which children combine different items into categories, themes, or other units; *retrieval,* the process of accessing information and entering it into consciousness; and *elaboration,* in which material is extended or added to in order to make it more memorable.

REHEARSAL

A large part of all the changes that take place in children's intellective processes during their development appear to be describable as change in the strategies children carry around with them (Brown, Bransford, Ferrara, & Campione, 1983). There is now abundant evidence that young children are less likely than older children to practice **rehearsal** (repeating material silently or outloud), and as a result hold verbal material in short-term memory less effectively than adults.

Among the best replicated findings in developmental psychology is that younger children are less likely than older children to rehearse material that they are trying to memorize. In one study (Flavell, Beach, & Chinsky, 1966), kindergartners, second-, and fifth-graders were shown a set of pictures that they were asked to remember. Following the presentation, there was a 15-second delay during which the children could prepare for the recall test. An experimenter, who was trained to identify lip movements corresponding to the words the children were trying to remember, watched the subjects' mouths. Flavell and his associates reported age-related increases in recall with corresponding increases in the amount of rehearsal. Eighty-five percent of the fifth-graders displayed evidence of some spontaneous rehearsal, whereas only 10% of the kindergarten children did so. Furthermore, within a grade level, children who had rehearsed more recalled more, on average, than children who had rehearsed less. These findings led the researchers to conclude that rehearsal is a powerful mnemonic device that increases with age.

A subsequent experiment (Keeney, Cannizzo, & Flavell, 1967) used the same procedure with a group of first-graders, a transitional age when

Children who rehearse the material they are trying to remember, such as these pictures, have better recall than children who do not.

some children would be expected to have developed a tendency to rehearse and some would not. There were four major findings. First, children who spontaneously rehearsed the picture names, according to lip-reading evidence, recalled the sequences of pictures better than those who did not. Second, the nonrehearsers were quite capable of rehearsing and could be gotten to do so with only minimal instruction and demonstration by the experimenter. Third, once induced to rehearse, their recall rose to the level of that of spontaneous rehearsers. Fourth, when subsequently given the option on later trials of rehearsing or not rehearsing, more than half of them abandoned the strategy, thereby reverting to their original, preexperimental status as nonrehearsers.

The rehearsal of older and younger children differs in quality as well as in probability of occurrence. Younger children, when they do rehearse, use strategies that are not as effective as older chil-

dren. To illustrate, Cox, Ornstein, Naus, Maxfield, and Zimler (1989) and Ornstein, Naus, and Liberty (1975) found that older children rehearsed the material to be remembered more effectively. The researchers asked 8-, 11-, and 13-year-old children to rehearse outloud after the presentation of each word in a list. The children were to memorize the entire list of 10 words. For example, if the series "yard, cat, man, dog" was presented to a younger child, a typical rehearsal pattern after the presentation of dog would be to say the word over and over again: "dog, dog, dog." The 13-year-olds, however, combined the newly presented word with those that preceded it. They would say "yard, cat, man, dog." The older child is more likely to rehearse and to construct larger chunks by using a cumulative rehearsal strategy.

Although younger children use less efficient rehearsal strategies when they do rehearse, it has been found that they can be taught to use more successful ones (Seamon, 1980). Third-graders, who typically rehearse only one or two items at a time, were trained to rehearse in the more active, organized fashion of older children. That is, they were taught to rehearse three items together—the word presented and the two words preceding it. The young children, when so trained, rehearsed more actively, and memory performance increased. The study also showed that third-graders could utilize the more mature rehearsal pattern, but only when prompted or instructed to do so. When these children were presented with a new problem, they failed to use the more sophisticated rehearsal strategies.

ORGANIZATION

Organization consists of children's attempts to bring order and pattern to the material to be learned. Organization in memory refers to the structure discovered or imposed on a set of items that is used to guide subsequent performance. Evidence suggests that younger children tend to organize items to be remembered according to sound or rhyming patterns whereas older children use concepts or associations based on meanings of words. Moreover, younger children tend to use simple associations (hat/coat) more often than older children, who tend to use specific categorization (clothing: hat/coat).

There is a developmental trend toward deliberate use of organization (Andreassen & Waters, 1989). If allowed to manipulate a randomly arranged but potentially categorizable set of object pictures during a study period, for example, older children are likelier than younger ones to adopt the strategy of physically segregating the pictures into groups by category and then studying same-category items together.

This organizational pattern has been referred to as *chunking.* Older children and adults are likely to seek out structural relations existing among the words in the list. That is, they are trying to construct chunks containing several words each. Forming multiple-word chunks facilitates recall of the list because in a sense fewer "things" have to be remembered. For example, if asked to remember a list of several words, older children group these words into categorized lists. Words such as horse, cow, dog are grouped under animal names; bed, table, lamp, chair are grouped under articles of furniture; and so forth.

Younger children are not likely to use this grouping strategy. When children in kindergarten, first, third, and fifth grades were asked to recall the names of pictures they were shown, very few of the first- and third-graders grouped the pictures by category. In contrast, 60% of the fifth-graders did so, and consequently were able to recall more items than their younger counterparts (Moely, Olson, Halwes, & Flavell, 1969). "Studying Children" provides you with an experiment that will enable you to test children's organizational strategies.

ELABORATION

Related to organization is the third memory strategy: **elaboration.** Both organization and elaboration strategies are not spontaneously used until adolescence (Pressley, 1982). Elaboration strategies add meaning to what is presented. An example of elaboration would be the construction of a vivid verbal image linking two normally unrelated objects that are supposed to be remembered together as in a paired-association task. To illustrate, if the child is to remember "lifeguard/hammock," the child may form a mental image of a lifeguard relaxing in a hammock.

Not only are older children more likely to use elaboration strategies, they are also more likely to use elaborations that involve active interactions. Older children's elaborations may be particularly meaningful to them, thus leading to superior recall, whereas the elaborations of younger children may be obscure or unmemorable, thus producing inferior recall.

RETRIEVAL

So far, only storage strategies have been discussed—getting things into memory. The ability to retain material, **retrieval,** is equally important. Retrieval refers to the resourceful moves an individual may make when actively trying to recover things from memory storage. Development here consists of an increasing ability to search memory intelligently, efficiently, flexibly, systematically, and selectively, in whatever manner the specific retrieval problems at hand requires. The available evidence indicates that this ability develops relatively late—during middle childhood and adolescence rather than during infancy and early childhood (Howe & Brainerd, 1989).

However, given the vast amount of learning that infants acquire in the first year of life, it is apparent that they must have efficient but elementary means by which to code and retrieve information. Work by Rovee-Collier and her colleagues (Borovsky & Rovee-Collier, 1990; Rovee-Collier & Fagen, 1981; Vander Linde, Morrongiello, & Rovee-Collier, 1985) demonstrate that 3-month-old infants can retain and retrieve information over relatively long periods of time.

In the researchers' procedure, a ribbon is tied to an infant's ankle and connected to a mobile that is suspended over the crib. Infants quickly learn that when they kick their feet, the mobile moves, and they soon make repeated kicks, controlling the movement of the mobile overhead. In a typical experiment, during the first 3 minutes the ribbon is

---

STUDYING CHILDREN

ORGANIZATIONAL STRATEGIES

Make a photocopy of the pictures on this page and use scissors to cut them apart. In this experiment (Matlin, 1983, p. 328) you will test a child between the ages of 4 and 8; ideally, it would be interesting to test children of several different ages. Arrange these pictures in random order in a circle facing your subject. Instruct the child to study the pictures so that they can be remembered later. Mention that the pictures can be rearranged in any order. After a 2-minute study period, remove the pictures and ask the child to list as many items as possible. Notice two things in this demonstration: First, does the child rearrange the items at all during the study period? Second, does the child show clustering during recall, with similar items appearing together?

Source: Demonstration from *Cognition* by Margaret Matlin, copyright ©1983 by Holt, Rinehart and Winston, Inc., reprinted by permission of the publisher.

---

not connected to the mobile, so that kicks do not cause it to move (baseline nonreinforcement period). This period is followed by a 9-minute reinforcement period in which the ribbon and mobile are connected, and infants quickly learn to kick to make the mobile move.

What happens, however, when the infants are hooked up to the apparatus days later? Six to 8 days later, these infants showed they remembered what they had previously learned by starting to kick when their memory was reactivated by showing them the mobile the day before testing. Not showing them the mobile, however, resulted in

significantly impaired retrieval of the forgotten memory. Thus, these studies demonstrate that by 3 months infants encode information about the physical setting in which an event occurs, and that this information, in turn, is an important source of retrieval cues for the memory of that event, particularly after longer retention intervals.

In older children, most recognition procedures involve the presentation of a set of stimuli (pictures, words, or letters). Flavell (1985), for example, gave individuals in first, third, and seventh grade and college students an incidental memory problem. The experimenter named a letter of the

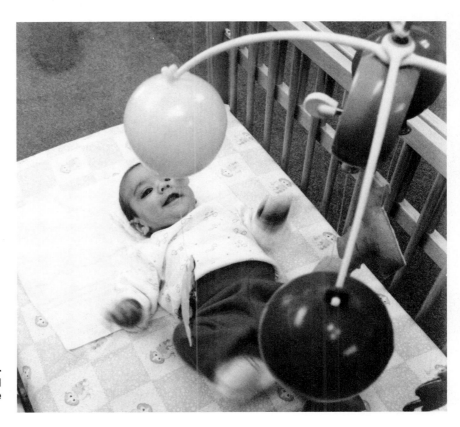

A baby's memory has to be triggered by some kind of perceptual reminder, for example, the mobile in Rovee-Collier's experiment.

alphabet, the subject wrote it on a card, the experimenter removed the card and randomly named another letter, the subject wrote that letter on a new card. This process continued until 20 letters had been written. The subjects were then asked to write down each letter that they had written on the other cards. An effective retrieval strategy in this situation is to go through the entire alphabet in your mind and write down each letter that is recognized as having recently been seen and written out. It is easy for the experimenter to recognize when this strategy has been used because the retrieved target letters are in alphabetical order.

The younger children did not use the alphabet strategy and their inability to recall the letters seen and written reflected this. In contrast, older subjects (seventh-graders and college students) were able to spontaneously use the alphabet strategy during retrieval and accurately recalled the letters they had previously seen and written. The research indicates that young children have much to learn about what retrieval cues are and about how to use them effectively. Beal (1985) found that 5- and 6-year-old children often feel they can remember or relocate an object without retrieval cues. Thus, younger children also have not acquired detailed knowledge about exactly how retrieval cues can help them remember.

Older children tend to use more superior coding strategies than younger children. That is, they engage in active, systematic rehearsal, process information more deeply, organize it more richly, and store more relevant features in long-term memory, and thus, can more easily retrieve material (List, Keating, & Merriman, 1985). They tend to spontaneously use such strategies as visualization and perseverance, which aid in retrieval of information (Hall & Tinzmann, 1989). For example, if an older child has lost his math book, he may visualize what he had done that day and where he had gone. Picturing these steps may help him "see" where he left his book. Perseverance is simply "sticking to" solving the problem. The child continues to try to remember where he left his book.

Recognition and Recall   Two kinds of retrieval are commonly distinguished: recognition and recall. For **recognition,** the task is usually easy, with the original stimulus prompting the retrieval of the memory representation. **Recall** is not so simple. In recall, the familiar something is not initially present in conscious thought or perception. Rather, *recall* is the term used for the very process of retrieving a representation of it from memory.

Recognition is among the basic information processes that seem to be present from early life (Nelson & Collins, 1991). Much of what we know about infants' recognition comes from experiments using the habituation design. The first part of this paradigm is the familiarization phase, in which infants are repeatedly exposed to a stimulus. Then a new stimulus is introduced, either together with the familiar one or alone. Infants' attention to a stimulus declines as a result of repeated presentation of that stimulus (habituation) but returns to previously high levels when a new stimulus is presented (dishabituation). Differential attention to the novel stimulus is taken to indicate recognition of the familiar one. Thus, babies display recognition by attending more to a previously unseen stimulus than to a familiar one; that is, they recognize it as different from something they have seen before (Nelson & Collins, 1991). Such a finding not only indicates that infants can discriminate between the two stimuli, but also implicates visual recognition memory in that the discrimination is being made between one stimulus that is physically present and another that is present only in memory.

Perhaps the most influential work demonstrating visual recognition memory in infants by using the preference for novelty design is that of Fagan (1973, 1974). Five-month-olds who were exposed

to a photograph of a face for 5 to 10 seconds showed evidence of recognizing it as long as 2 weeks later.

Adults' recognition is exceptional. In one study (Shepard, 1967), it was demonstrated that adults recognized 90% of over 600 photos they had seen 1 week earlier. Research with children (Brown & Scott, 1971) has shown similarly high levels of performance for 3- to 5-year-old children. Children shown 100 pictures displayed remarkably high levels of recognition over delays that ranged from 1 to 28 days.

Some researchers have reported that age differences emerge on recognition tasks only under certain conditions (Mandler & Robinson, 1978). These researchers showed pictures to children in first, third, and fifth grades and later showed them variants of those pictures, some of which were identical to the originals and others of which had been changed in some way. Half of the children at each grade level were shown organized scenes, in which sets of objects were placed in juxtaposition to one another so that they formed a coherent picture, such as a living room. The remaining children were shown the same sets of objects but with no coherent arrangement to them (unorganized scenes) (see Figure 7.9).

The results, shown in Figure 7.10, revealed that no age differences were found for the unorganized scenes, with performance being generally poor. However, performance increased with age for the organized scenes. Thus, older children are more likely than younger ones to use what they know about the world to guide their recognition.

Recall represents a more complex demonstration of memory. It is dependent on mental imagery and the ability to retrieve information from long-term memory. A common example would be an essay exam.

In general, children have excellent recognition memory but poor recall memory (Kail, 1979; Tinzmann & Hall, 1989). Perlmutter (1980) performed a series of studies to test children's recall and recognition skills. In one study, to test recognition, 2- and 4-year-old children were shown 18 unrelated objects. Then the children were presented with 36

Source: From "Developmental Changes in Picture Recognition" by J. M. Mandler and C. A. Robinson, 1978, *Journal of Experimental Child Psychology, 26*, pp. 122–136. Copyright 1978 by Academic Press. Reprinted by permission.

FIGURE 7.10   Children's Recognition Performance for Organized and Unorganized Scenes

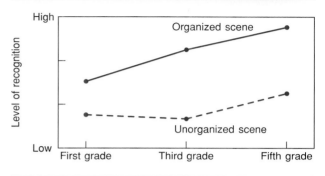

Source: Adapted from "Developmental Changes in Picture Recognition" by J. M. Mandler and C. A. Robinson, 1978, *Journal of Experimental Child Psychology, 26*, pp. 122–136. Copyright 1978 by Academic Press. Adapted by permission.

items, including the 18 objects presented earlier and 18 new objects. As you can see in Figure 7.11, children of both ages were quite accurate.

Perlmutter also tested recall in another group of children who saw nine unrelated objects from the recognition task. After the experimenter presented each item and named it, the children were told that they could keep all the objects that they could successfully recall. Despite this tempting reward, recall, as can be seen from Figure 7.10, was quite poor. Perhaps this is so because recall, unlike recognition, requires more active rehearsal strategies and a more thorough search in memory in order to retrieve the right cues.

Leal, Crays, and Moely (1985) found that self-monitoring or self-testing increases children's recall of information. In studying 48 third-grade children, Leal et al. found that they did not spontaneously engage in self-testing or looking away from the material and trying to reproduce the items from memory. Half of the children, comprising the experimental group, were taught how to self-test. The control group of the remaining

children were not taught to self-test, but were given an equivalent amount of time to try to memorize an array of stimuli. The results showed that the experimental group showed superior recall, compared with the control group. Moreover, the researchers found in a follow-up study done 9 months later that the self-testing technique was being applied in other academic situations.

Research on recall typically presents children with a list of items at a relatively slow rate (for example, one item every 5 seconds), and then they are asked to remember as many items as they can in any order they wish. A general finding is that the amount recalled increases with age. McGilly and Siegler (1989) studied the recall performance in kindergartners, first- and third-graders. Each child received some lists with three numbers and others with five, some with delays of 5 seconds between presentation of the list and the time of recall, and others with a delay period of 15 seconds. It was found that between kindergarten and third grade, children's recall becomes increasingly accurate. Moreover, third-graders were more likely to use memory strategies such as rehearsal. The role of memory strategies, particularly as they re-

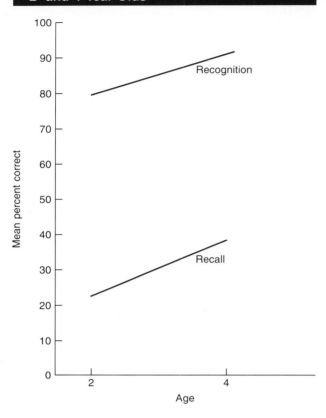

FIGURE 7.11 Recognition and Recall for 2- and 4-Year-Olds

Source: Based on *Children's Memory: New Directions for Child Development* by M. Perlmutter (Ed.), 1980, San Francisco: Jossey-Bass. Copyright 1980 by Jossey-Bass Inc., Publishers. Adapted by permission.

late to recall, indicates that improvement in recall relates to children's ability to use more efficient memory strategies (Bjorklund & Muir, 1988).

FACTORS THAT INFLUENCE CHILDREN'S AND ADOLESCENTS' USE OF MEMORY STRATEGIES

The sophistication and effectiveness of children's memory strategies increase with age. Some of the factors that influence children's strategic functioning are encoding, knowledge base, and metamemory.

ENCODING

Encoding is a dynamic process wherein incoming information is integrated with current schemes in a child's knowledge base (Bjorklund, 1987). In encoding individual words, for example, research has shown that younger children tend to use fewer features to represent the words than older children (Ackerman, 1984). In one study (Ceci, 1980) 4-, 6-, and 9-year-olds were given intensive training for sets of words that they would be asked to remember. They were told about common characteristics of animals (their diet and habitat). The more children were told about the items, the greater their subsequent recall. The younger children, however, relied more on the externally provided information than older children. This suggests that older children spontaneously encode words with more features and, as a result, remember more efficiently.

Older children often know and use a variety of strategies for encoding information. In a serial recall experiment done by McGilly and Siegler (1990) 5-, 7-, and 9-year-olds were given lists of numbers to remember. Children encountered three types of lists: ascending, contiguous lists (e.g., 3, 4, 5, 6, 7); descending, contiguous lists (e.g., 7, 6, 5, 4, 3); and random lists (e.g., 5, 7, 3, 4, 6). The results showed that 9-year-olds chose encoding strategies adaptively; that is, as opposed to their younger counterparts, these children were more likely to use repeated rehearsal on random lists and less likely to use it on contiguous ones.

KNOWLEDGE BASE

An additional factor that contributes to improved memory of school-age children is that they know more things than younger children. In recent years, several investigators have postulated that, to a large extent, age differences in what children know, or their **knowledge base,** is responsible for corresponding differences in memory performance. Basically, when children are very knowledgeable about a particular subject, they process information from that domain rapidly and display enhanced levels of memory performance.

What children know (memory in the wider sense) greatly influences what they learn and remember (memory in the strict sense). Developmental changes in knowledge should lead to developmental changes in what is stored and retrieved. For example, people who are very knowledgeable about chess can remember chessboard arrangements better than those who are less knowledgeable.

Chi (1978) has provided the most dramatic demonstration to date of the impact of the knowledge base. She compared the memorial performance of 10-year-olds and adults on two tasks: a standard digit span task and a chess memory task. The 10-year-olds were skilled chess players, whereas the adults were novices at the game. The primary chess memory task involved displaying on a board for 10 seconds an organized arrangement of pieces. Then the experimenter covered the pieces and asked the child or adult to reproduce the arrangement on a second chess board.

Children's reproductions of the chess boards were more accurate than those of adults (see Figure 7.12). The finding was not attributable to the children being generally smarter or possessing better memories. On the standard digit span task, adults showed the usual superiority of recall. Thus, Chi concluded, differences in knowledge can outweigh all other memorial differences between children and adults.

METAMEMORY

If young children are capable of utilizing memory strategies such as rehearsal and organization, why do they fail to do so spontaneously? Flavell (1985) has suggested that children fail to utilize or generalize these strategies because they do not possess knowledge of memory skills or of when it is most appropriate to use these strategies. This has been called **metamemory.** Young children often do not "know what to do" when they have to remember something and thus cannot employ effective strategies. Older children, however, are more aware of how memory works. For example, they know that

Differences in an individual's knowledge base are responsible for differences in memory performance.

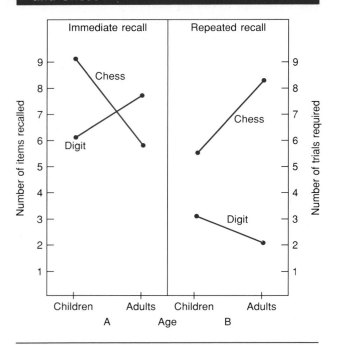

FIGURE 7.12 Predictions for Repeated Recall by Children and Adults for Digits and Chess

Source: From *Children's Thinking: What Develops?* by R. S. Siegler, 1978, Hillsdale, NJ: Lawrence Erlbaum Associates. Copyright 1978 by Lawrence Erlbaum Associates. Reprinted by permission.

saying things out loud, writing things down, and grouping similar items all help them remember (Kreutzer, Leonard, & Flavell, 1975), and, more so than younger children, use these strategies in memory tasks.

Although young children do not spontaneously engage in elaborate rehearsal techniques or organization strategies, they do engage in some rudimentary forms of these skills (Diamond, 1985). Children's developing understanding of cognitive cueing has been studied as an important aspect of metamemory development. Research by DeLoache (1986) shows that in simple tests, even 2-year-olds can exploit cues as sources of knowledge about the location of a hidden object. In one experiment, children watched while the experimenter hid a small Snoopy toy. After a prescribed delay interval, children were allowed to retrieve the toy. During the delay interval, they visually rehearsed. That is, from time to time, they looked at the place where the toy was hidden and then nodded their heads affirmatively. Some children walked over to the hiding place. Therefore, young children do engage in simple behavioral strategies, which correlate positively with memory performance. Children who produced more memory strategies tended to achieve higher retrieval scores (DeLoache, Cassidy, & Brown, 1985).

The early development of children's metamemory concerning cueing strategies may proceed in two steps: First, children begin to realize that cues may be helpful in remembering. This idea may emerge from firsthand experiences such as realizing that putting things where they belong is generally better than putting them in arbitrary places. Second, around the age of 6, children begin to understand the causal relation between the presence of a cue and the acquisition or retrieval of a certain piece of information (Sodian & Schneider, 1990).

Children are using metamemory skills when they have knowledge about memory and memory processes, when they think about the need to remember, and how to go about remembering. In addition, metamemory entails the ability to monitor their own memory performance in a given situation. Among the processes that are said to indicate metamemory knowledge are predicting, checking, monitoring, reality testing, and coordination and control of deliberate attempts to learn and solve problems (Brown, Bransford, Ferrara, & Campione, 1983).

Flavell (1985) has argued that the beginnings of metamemory occur during the preschool years and several studies demonstrate the metacognitive skills of preschoolers. For example, Wellman (1977) found that 3-year-olds know that more items are harder to remember than a few, and that distracting noise interferes with remembering. By age 5, most children also understand that memory is facilitated by drawn or written reminders, increasing age, help from others, longer study time, a short time between encoding and recall, and external cues (Wellman, 1977, 1978). Preschoolers also are beginning to understand the utility of various cues for recall.

Three- and 4-year-olds understand that children who are motivated (like the activity) or are in a quiet rather than a noisy room are more able to write numbers and listen to their mothers' instructions (Miller & Zalenski, 1982). When the two variables were pitted against each other, interested children in a noisy room were chosen over uninterested children in a quiet room on 84% of the trials. Similarly, in another study, older preschoolers could take both effort and number of objects into account when predicting memory performance and, of the two, considered effort more important (Wellman, Collins, & Glieberman, 1981).

There is evidence that older children tend to have a more realistic and accurate picture of their own memory abilities and limitations than younger ones do. For example, when preschoolers and school-age children were asked how many of 10 pictures they thought that they could remember, school-age children realized that they would not be able to remember all of them. Preschoolers, on the other hand, said they could perform this feat (Flavell, Friedrichs, & Hoyt, 1970).

Young children are often unaware of strategies such as rehearsal and organization, or at least they are not conscious that these and related techniques may be useful when they are given a specific memory task (Justice, 1985). Younger children are also unaware of how a particular strategy works to improve memory. Fabricius and Cavalier (1989) found that having a conception of how a strategy works, in terms of its relations with other strategies or memory processes, might be an important aspect in children using such memory strategies. Those who understood how labeling pictures works used this strategy more often than children who did not understand how this strategy works. For example, 6-year-olds who said that saying the names helps them keep "pictures in their minds" used this strategy more often than 6-year-olds who did not understand how labeling works.

EVALUATION OF INFORMATION-PROCESSING THEORY

The information-processing approach receives good marks for its careful, refined descriptions of the memory system at various cognitive levels. An exception is that there is little work on information processing in infancy. The relative neglect of infancy is unfortunate because, to be a viable developmental theory, the information-processing approach must describe preverbal, cognitively immature infants. It is important to know, for example, what kinds of nonverbal representations infants are capable of and why their recognition memory is so advanced.

As you have seen, information-processing theorists focus intently on specific cognitive processes and view cognitive development as the acquisition of problem-solving strategies in many different domains. The specificity of the information-processing approach can be viewed as a strength and a weakness. On the negative side, their demands for specificity conjures an image of the child as a "rational, decontextualized isolated mind, with limited knowledge, without interests, without feelings, attitudes, or views of the world" (Sigel, 1985, p. 99). The information-processing approach has focused on which processing mechanism a child brings to a task or setting and on the task parameters more than the interplay between the demands or possibilities of the larger setting and the needs, goals, and abilities of the person.

However, on the positive side, because of its focus on task demands for specificity, clarity, and fine-grained analysis in the account of behavior, information-processing theory possesses considerable promise in making specific predictions about children's problem-solving abilities.

In the early years of developmental psychology, theories were all-encompassing—reflecting an "everything you ever wanted to know" approach. Certainly, the advantages of these types of theories were in terms of their breadth and scope in the questions they attempted to answer. The extreme disadvantage is that these theories often depended on the correctness of the main structure of the theory. If weaknesses were found in the main struc-

Young children are often unaware of how memory strategies can help them remember information and thus use these strategies infrequently.

ture, the theory crumbled. In the 1990s, theories tend to deal with finite aspects of not only cognitive development, but also personality, social, and moral development as well. While the disadvantage is that more limited theories may be fragmented or limited in scope and breadth, the advantage is they are less susceptible to toppling down.

PRACTICAL IMPLICATIONS: IMPROVING MEMORY SKILLS

People forget things they have learned, which is frustrating. Incidentally, verbal material is forgotten much more readily than motor skills. If you haven't ice-skated for years, after a few whirls around the pond you are less shaky, and while you may not look like a gold medalist, you're able to stiffly glide along. Your only consolation may be that once you have learned something and have "forgotten" the material, you can relearn it again more readily.

If you forget a good deal of what you learn, are there some helpful hints that will improve your

memory? Probably the most important thing that you can do is *pay attention.* Attention is the set of processes that filters information and determines what small part of it will occupy the central processor (short-term memory) at any given time. What is deceiving is that at times you may feel you are paying attention, but in actuality you are not. Surely this has happened to you: You are sitting at your desk reading your textbook, your eyes are focusing on the words as you skim over the sentences. After turning three or four pages, you realize that you have not read or comprehended anything at all! Or, you are in the classroom and suddenly the professor calls your name and you realize at that moment you were in never-never land and haven't heard a word she was saying. Your brain was taking a micro-mini nap. When attention wanders, memory suffers.

It used to be believed that memory was located in one particular area of the brain and this particular area was right behind the eyes. People with huge, bulging eyes were thought to have fantastic memories. Now it is known that memory is diffuse (spread throughout) the entire brain. Different senses record different aspects in a learning situa-

Verbally discussing material can help one retain and retrieve the information more readily.

tion. Therefore, the more senses you can incorporate in learning, the more ways you have to index a piece of information or the more associations you have with it, thus it is easier to remember.

Sometimes if you don't understand a concept, you simply memorize a definition so you can write it on an exam and get a good grade. The word's definition is quickly forgotten because it never made any sense to you in the first place. A certain amount of rote memorization is necessary in some learning situations, but whenever possible, if you are to retain the material, it must mean something to you; it must make sense. You need to use logic, see relationships, see patterns, see its applicability, and think autonomously if you are going to remember it (see "Focus on Applications").

A stimulus must stand out if it is going to register in sensory store, short-term, and long-term memory. Let's say you are reading a book and come across a word you are not familiar with. It is late and you are too lazy to check *Webster's* so you sort of guess what it means. You have not learned the word and obviously you won't remember it. As a result it will not become a distinctive stimulus, and you may pass it by on another occasion.

One extremely important benefit from all your course work is that more stimuli in your environment should become more distinctive. For example, after taking a course in introduction to psychology, you notice an article entitled "The Libido and Sexual Energies." If you hadn't been exposed to Freud you perhaps would not have even noticed the article, let alone read it. It's like when you buy a new car—an orange Volvo. You have never noticed orange Volvos on the road before, but now that you own one, you notice them all the time. Education should help us to be more aware of various stimuli and help them to become more distinct.

Mnemonic devices can help us remember some types of material. "Every good boy does fine" (lines on treble clef). Can you name the colors of the rainbow? You can by remembering Roy (red, orange, yellow) G. (green) Biv (blue, indigo, violet). These are all memory devices to remember certain things.

Finally, you have a better chance of coding and retrieving information if you rehearse it either silently or vocally. Discussions with classmates will help you remember.

To Think Is to Invent

Kamii (1984), in her article "Autonomy: The Aim of Education Envisaged by Piaget," states that autonomy means being governed by oneself. The antithesis of this term would be heteronomy, which means governed by someone else. Unfortunately, Kamii maintains, schools do not encourage children to think autonomously. This is shown in several ways. For example, children are sanctioned when they give the "right" answers, and it is the teacher who has the right answers. This becomes very apparent if you just walk around a first-grade class. Stop and ask a child who is working on a science or math worksheet, "How did you come up with that answer?" The child, in all probability, will frantically search for an eraser and immediately try to blot out what he has written, even if the answer is correct! Already they distrust their own thinking.

Kamii offers the suggestion that teachers, rather than always marking an answer wrong, from time to time question how the child comes up with a certain answer. If one child's answer differs from that of another, perhaps these children can be encouraged to explain their thinking to each other. Children can often correct themselves autonomously as they try to explain their reasoning to someone else. While trying to coordinate their point of view with another point of view, they often realize their own mistakes.

Less emphasis should be put on memorization. Certainly you have experienced the feeling of exuberance when you feel free to forget the things you memorized in order to pass an exam. Answers that are memorized from the "correct" textbook or teacher have no or very little personal meaning. Once again, heteronomous children are being trained—children who depend on others to come up with the correct answer.

Interactions with peers is of paramount importance in producing autonomous thinking. Social interaction should play a significant role in the classroom. It's hard to see why schools force children to be quiet when results seem to be only an authoritarian situation and extreme boredom. "Let us restrict the view of silence to selected orders of monks and nuns" (Ginsburg & Opper, 1969, p. 225).

Educators should stimulate children's thinking by bringing different points of view into confrontation, because the exchange of points of view contributes to children's intellectual, social, and affective development. Interaction with peers is of paramount importance in producing autonomous thinking. It encourages children to think critically by putting different opinions into perspective, and to modify old ideas autonomously when *they* are convinced that a new idea is better. Children acquire knowledge by construction from within, through interactions with the environment. Social interactions are essential for this construction to take place. The honest exchange of ideas is bound to lead to autonomy in the long run.

Autonomous thinking can be encouraged in various subjects. In literature, for example, you can ask for different interpretations of a poem or personal reactions to a novel. So often teachers will insist that their interpretation (or the manual's) is the only correct one. Science teachers can suggest projects aimed at producing certain effects, such as making cars for a soapbox derby. To produce the desired effect, children have to understand the relevance of such factors as gravity, friction, and so on.

Many have not been taught to think for themselves; even at the college level you are sometimes "coerced" into writing an answer you know will be appreciated by the professor (after all, it was mentioned in lecture). Autonomous thinking should be the goal of education at every level from nursery school on up. It is in this way that you can build individuals capable of inventive thought rather than individuals with conforming, unquestioning minds that keep them to the already mapped outpaths of accepted truths.

REVIEW OF KEY POINTS

Information processing refers to the *processes* by which you take in, analyze, store, and retrieve various types of things you have perceived or that have happened to you, called *information.* Two current information-processing theories were discussed. Robbie Case's theory focuses on children's working memory, known as executive processing space. The functional capacity of working memory depends on the automaticity with which operations are executed. As working memory increases, it becomes easier to acquire more elaborate control structures, which determine the problem-solving strategies available to children at the various four stages of cognitive development. Each stage of cognitive development has a universal sequence of substages: unifocal, biofocal, and elaborative. Robert Siegler suggests that children's cognitive development is rule-governed. Siegler proposed that children will develop one of four possible rules, which they will use when attempting to solve various balance-scale problems.

Information-processing theorists see cognitive development as a flow of information through various processes, each with its unique capacity and function. On presentation of a stimulus, the sensory register receives all sensory information for fractions of a second. Certain stimuli are selected and perceptually interpreted. At the next level, information is passed for further processing to the short-term memory, where information is retained for somewhat longer periods of time. It is then either encoded into long-term memory, your permanent storehouse of information, or it is lost and forgotten.

The development of memory strategies has been found to be of critical importance to age changes in children's memory. The most frequently studied memory strategies are rehearsal, organization, retrieval, and elaboration. Several trends emerged in this discussion of the contributions of memorial strategies to information-processing skills. The use of such strategies becomes more frequent with age, particularly between ages 5 and 10, and children adjust the strategies increasingly finely to task demands. Children who use the strategies remember more than those who do not. Young children can be taught to use memory strategies, but the instruction often fails to generalize over time and to new tasks. A number of factors influence developmental differences in children's use of strategies and memory performance, including encoding, knowledge base, and metamemory (children's knowledge of how memory works).

ENHANCING YOUR CRITICAL THINKING

Personal Growth

Information Processing Theory

Royer, J. M., & Allan, R. G. (1978). *Psychology of learning: Educational applications.* New York: Wiley.

To check your understanding of information processing theories, read this useful text. It provides

basic information and asks questions that require written responses and provides feedback.

Memory

Lorayne, H., & Lucas, J. (1974). *The memory book.* New York: Ballantine Books.

For students who wish to improve their memory skills, read this book, one of the most useful on the subject. The book offers various mnemonic techniques for remembering factual material for academic purposes as well as everyday material (remembering names and faces) for social purposes.

CHAPTER 8

Views of Cognition: Psychometrics

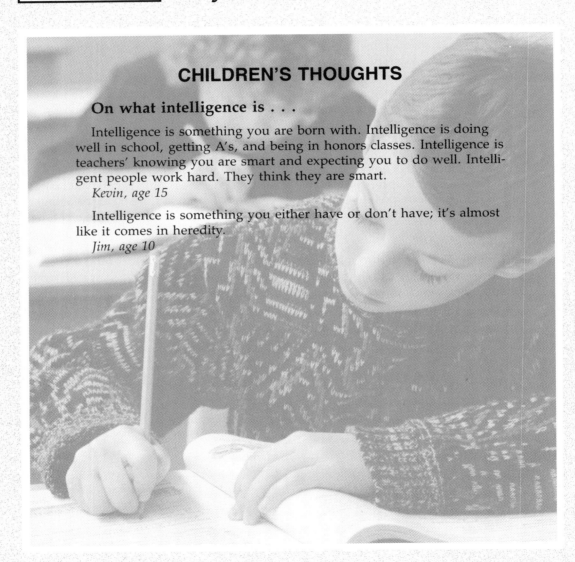

CHILDREN'S THOUGHTS

On what intelligence is . . .

Intelligence is something you are born with. Intelligence is doing well in school, getting A's, and being in honors classes. Intelligence is teachers' knowing you are smart and expecting you to do well. Intelligent people work hard. They think they are smart.
Kevin, age 15

Intelligence is something you either have or don't have; it's almost like it comes in heredity.
Jim, age 10

CHAPTER OUTLINE

KEY TERMS

An interesting aspect of children's definitions of intelligence is that they are surprisingly similar. The majority of the responses to the question, "What is intelligence?" are similar to those cited. With few exceptions, intelligence, to many children, is viewed as a fixed entity, an inherited phenomenon, and equated with teachers' thinking that you are smart, getting good grades, and being in accelerated classes.

Experts, too, have their own conceptions of intelligence. The opening section of this chapter discusses the various definitions and views of intelligence of the theorists representing the psychometric tradition, which describes intelligence in terms of test performance. Unlike Piaget and the information-processing theorists, who are inter-ested in finding out how thinking changes over time, psychometric theorists are interested in studying how children of the same age differ in their thinking skills and how such differences can be measured. These theorists generally define intelligence as information a child has at a given point in time. They are interested in quantifying intelligence, which usually means producing a number, an IQ, to describe a child's current level of intelligence.

DEFINITIONS AND VIEWS OF INTELLIGENCE

Each of the theorists discussed in this section conceives of intelligence in a slightly different way, which has a direct bearing on the types of tests they devise to measure it. Psychometric theory and research seem to have evolved along three interrelated lines: the unitary, the two-factor, and the multiple-factor theories of intelligence.

UNITARY THEORY OF ALFRED BINET

Binet's (1916a) **unitary theory** and research grew out of practical educational concerns. In 1904, the Parisian minister of public instruction named a commission whose task was to create tests that would ensure that mentally retarded children received an adequate education. Binet was appointed to that commission.

Devising a test to accomplish this purpose had to begin with some preconceived notion of what intelligence was. Binet and his coworker Theophile Simon defined **intelligence** as judgment, otherwise called good sense, practical sense, initiative, the faculty of adapting one's self to circumstances. "To judge well, to comprehend well, to reason well, these are the essential activities of intelligence" (Binet & Simon, 1905, pp. 42–43). Intelligence to Binet and Simon is conceived of as being a unitary trait: a general capacity to learn, which is applicable in all kinds of learning situations. This factor of general capacity to learn, according to these authors, was abstract reasoning: the effective use of concepts and verbal and numerical symbols in solving problems. The items in Binet's test reflect these beliefs. As you can see in Table 8.1, the items are grouped according to age levels. Here, they are selected and placed at a certain age level if a specific percentage of, for example, 7-year-old children passed all of these items.

Stern (1924) developed the concept of **intelligence quotient,** which is a ratio of children's **mental age** (MA) divided by their chronological age (CA); the result is multiplied by 100 to eliminate the decimal. Mental age is a measure of intelligence test performance, a child's degree of brightness. A 6-year-old scoring a mental age of 9 years would have an IQ of 9/6 × 100, or 1.5, or 150. A 5-year-old child who passes all the items at the 5-year-old level, and none at the 6-year-old level, would have an IQ of 100. The more items passed beyond the

TABLE 8.1	The 1908 Binet-Simon Scale

AGE 7
1. perceives what is missing in unfinished pictures
2. knows number of fingers on each hand and on both hands without counting
3. copies a model
4. copies a diamond
5. describes presented pictures
6. repeats five digits
7. counts 13 coins
8. identifies by name four common coins

AGE 8
1. reads a passage and remembers two items
2. adds up the value of five coins
3. names four colors: red, yellow, blue, green
4. counts backward from 20 to zero
5. writes short sentence from dictation
6. gives differences between two objects

Source: From *The Development of Intelligence in Children* by A. Binet (E. S. Kite, Trans.), 1916, Baltimore: Williams and Wilkins.

child's chronological age, the higher the IQ. People with low to average IQs have mental ages that are not as high as their chronological age.

The Stanford-Binet test was revised in 1960, and again in 1985. The 1960 version used a different method of computing IQ, a method previously used by David Wechsler and called the *deviation IQ.* The problem with the original method of calculating IQ was that by age 13 the ratio began to break down. The mental age of teenagers no longer continues to increase as it did when they were young. Nor do adults add to their mental age from year to year. Thus, the ratio of mental-to-chronological age could be used only with fairly young children unless statistical corrections were added in. The deviation IQ avoids this problem by using the percentage of cases in each age group achieving a given score. Thus, a 17-year-old scoring at the 84th percentile for that age group (that is, equaling or exceeding 84% of all 17-year-olds taking the tests) would have a Stanford-Binet IQ of 116. This is because the Stanford-Binet has a standard deviation of 16 points. Statistical tables are used to find what percentages of cases fall below the various standard deviation unit points.

To Binet, intelligence is not a fixed thing; he tried to assess IQ at a given point in time. He argued that a child's intelligence is a product of experience and can be modified. The Binet-Simon method of assessing intelligence was the first tool that enabled others to study children's cognitive development and to translate cognitive events into quantifiable units.

The Americanization of the Binet Scale Terman (Terman & Merrill, 1960), a psychologist at Stanford University, revised and "Americanized" the Binet-Simon Scales. The Americanized version, which became known as the Stanford-Binet IQ Test, measures one general factor of intelligence: abstract reasoning.

The Wechsler Intelligence Scale A psychologist working at New York's Bellevue Hospital, Wechsler (1974) felt that the Binet Scale was too verbal to adequately assess his patients: criminals, neurotics, and psychotics. Wechsler defined intelligence as the ability to adapt to changing conditions, the capacity to learn and to profit from one's experiences. The Wechsler tests mark a rather significant departure from the Binet tests. Wechsler contended that intelligence, which he viewed as a global concept composed of interdependent elements, consists of two large group factors that are relatively independent of each other—verbal and performance. His tests—the Wechsler Preschool and Primary Scale of Intelligence (WPPSI), designed for children ages 4 to 6½ years; the Wechsler Intelligence Scale for Children–Revised (WISC–R), designed for ages 6 to 16 years; and the Wechsler Adult Intelligence Scale–Revised (WAIS–R), designed for people 16 and older—produce three deviation IQ scores: a score for verbal skills, another for performance skills, and a composite score for these two areas.

The verbal IQ on the WAIS-R is calculated on the basis of six subtests:

1. Information: Twenty-nine items that test the subject's general storehouse of information about the world.

2. Comprehension: Fourteen questions that evaluate the individual's level of practical information and general ability to utilize past experience.

3. Arithmetic: Fourteen questions that test the individual's powers of arithmetical reasoning.

4. Digit span: A test of short-term memory in which the examiner reads a series of digits and asks the subject to repeat them.

5. Similarities: Thirteen items for which the subject attempts to discover in what way two things are alike. This test appears to measure an individual's ability to think in abstract terms.

6. Forty words that attempt to predict the size of the person's vocabulary.

The performance score is based on five subtests:

1. Picture arrangement: Seven pictures that, when arranged properly, tell a logical story. This is an attempt to measure an individual's ability to size up and understand a total situation.

2. Picture completion: The subject is shown a set of incomplete pictures and is asked to name the missing part. This is a test of visual recognition.

3. Block design: The subject is given a number of small wooden blocks that must be put together to form a number of patterns. This is a test of perceptual analysis and visual-motor coordination.

4. Digit symbol: The subject must associate certain symbols with certain digits and then be able to write the appropriate symbol in squares containing the associated digit. This is a test of speed of movement and memory.

and

5. Object assembly: The subject must arrange various puzzle parts to form a certain object. This is a test of manual dexterity and powers of recognition.

The Goodenough Draw-a-Person Test Another performance test used to assess IQ is Goodenough's Draw-a-Person test (1926). This test is based on the assumption that the ability to form concepts is the major sign of intelligence. The way children draw a familiar object will reveal the child's conception of that object. Thus, the more complex the concept demonstrated (in this case drawing a person) the higher the child's IQ. "Studying Children" provides more information on this test and how to administer it to children.

STUDYING CHILDREN

DRAW-A-PERSON

Have three children of different ages draw a picture of a person for you. Tell them to take their time and to do their very best, but do not give them "hints" such as "Your person has no arms. Do you want to draw them?" If the child rushes through the drawing, you can say, "Could you draw another person for me and try your best?" The drawing will show ability to perceive likenesses and differences, ability to abstract or to classify and generalize. Thus, the more complex the concept demonstrated—in this case drawing a person—the higher the intellectual development.

The child is given one point for every item that is included in the drawing and mentioned on the test. For example, one point is given if the child has drawn a head, another for legs, arms, trunk, shoulders, neck, eyes, nose, mouth, nostrils, hair, clothing, and so forth. Using the Goodenough point scale, you can assess the child's mental age (MA). Once we know the child's mental age and chronological age (CA), you can determine the child's IQ. Even without the actual scoring of this test, it is interesting to note how children's drawings become increasingly detailed and complex.

Below are a drawing done by a 9-year-old child and the number of points she received on the Goodenough test. These data can then be converted into a mental age score. You can then derive an IQ score.

Barret Q.
9 years

CA = 9 years, 4 months
MA = 12 years, 3 months — 37 points
IQ = 135

TWO-FACTOR THEORY OF CHARLES SPEARMAN

Spearman (1927) agreed with Binet that there is a factor of general intelligence, which Spearman called g, and that it involved seeing and manipulating the relationship between bits of information. The **g factor** contains our basic skills and general strategies for solving a problem. All intellectual activity is dependent on and is an expression of g, according to Spearman. It is possessed by all individuals, but of course in various degrees, because individuals differ in mental ability. Intelligence is viewed as existing on a single dimension and not being some multifaceted phenomenon. People who behave intelligently in one situation should behave intelligently in other situations.

Spearman also postulated the existence of specific factors called **s factors,** each of which is specific to a particular type of activity; hence, his theory is sometimes referred to as the **two-factor theory** of intelligence. He proposed that there are numerous special abilities, such as reading comprehension, manual dexterity, speed of decision making, and others. In some types of problems the g factor will be relatively high; in others, relatively low. For example, in solving a math problem, a child has to grasp the relationships between the data presented, organize them with reference to the propositions given in the problem, and deduce the correct answer. The g content in this task is high. By way of contrast, if the child merely has to repeat a table of multiplications or add a few numbers—both of which can be learned by rote memorization—no insights are necessary, and no relationships need to be grasped. In these tasks, the amount of g involved is very small.

Spearman concluded that the principal distinguishing characteristic of tests highly loaded with g is that they require insight into relationships. A test conforming to this theory would contain items saturated with the general factor, so that measurement by it would cause the child's g factor to emerge, while the effects of specific factors would be canceled out.

MULTIPLE-FACTOR THEORY OF GUILFORD, THURSTONE, AND CATTELL

Over the years, the number of abilities thought to comprise intelligence has ranged from Spearman's two (*g* and *s*) to Guilford's (1967, 1971) 150. According to Guilford, every mental task requires three kinds of intellectual abilities: operations, contents, and products. *Operations* refer to the kinds of thinking an individual employs and consist of cognition (discovery, recognition), memory (retaining information), divergent thinking (generating new ideas), convergent thinking (looking for correct answers), and evaluation (was your thinking right or wrong?). *Contents* refer to the types of materials people use when thinking, such as figural information (concrete materials), symbolic information (letters and numbers), semantic information (meanings of words), and behavior information (social relations). *Products* describe the form in which information occurs. It includes units (nouns, such as *house* or *dog*), classes (several grouped items with something in common), relations (connections between two items), systems (organization of items), transformations (changes or modifications), and implications (what you can expect from certain information). Because the subcategories are independently defined they are multiplicative; so there are $5 \times 5 \times 6 = 150$ different mental abilities. There are five kinds of contents: visual, auditory, symbolic, semantic, and behavioral, and there are six kinds of products: units, classes, relations, systems, transformations, and implications.

Between the extremes of Spearman and Guilford lie theories such as Thurstone's (1938), which includes seven "primary mental abilities." Thurstone dismissed the notion of a general factor of intelligence. Just because someone is smart in one area doesn't mean she will be smart in all areas. Thurstone's view of intelligence stresses that there are a specific number of factors that make up intelligence. To determine what these specific factors are, Thurstone used **factor analysis,** a statistical technique of analyzing experimental results by correlating (comparing) scores in a variety of tests. It is assumed that strong correlations between scores indicate a specific (common) factor.

Thurstone gave his subjects many intelligence tests that tapped different abilities. He then began to analyze what psychological functions the various types of items had in common. By taking all the different abilities tested in intelligence tests and correlating them with one another he found positive correlations between some abilities. Some factors were found so frequently in his studies that he eventually decided that intelligence comprises seven primary mental abilities: spatial, perceptual speed, numerical ability, verbal comprehension, memory, word frequency, and reasoning.

Cattell's (1971) theory recognizes both a general intellectual factor similar to Spearman's *g* and two second-order factors that he called *fluid* and *crystallized abilities.* Basically, fluid intelligence is proposed to be biologically determined and is reflected in tests of memory span and most tests of spatial thinking. In contrast, crystallized intelligence is best reflected in tests of verbal comprehension or social relations, skills that are more highly dependent on cultural context and experience.

HOWARD GARDNER'S THEORY

Gardner (1983), an associate professor at the Boston University School of Medicine, objects to assessing intelligence in only two dimensions: linguistic and logical-mathematical abilities. His concept also includes the following dimensions:

Spatial intelligence: The ability to form spatial images and to find one's way around in an environment.

Musical intelligence: The ability to perceive and create pitch and rhythmic patterns.

Body-kinesthetic intelligence: The gift of fine motor movement.

Interpersonal intelligence: The ability to understand others, how they feel, what motivates them, and how they interact.

Intrapersonal intelligence: The ability to know oneself and to develop a sense of identity.

Gardner has suggested stopping measuring people according to some unitary dimension called *in-*

telligence and beginning to think in terms of individual strengths.

STERNBERG'S TRIARCHIC THEORY

A recent theory of intelligence that has received substantial attention is Sternberg's (1985) triarchic theory. Sternberg's major criticism of psychometric theorists is that they estimate individuals' intelligence from the quality or correctness of their answers, while completely ignoring how they produce intellectual responses. Psychometric theories, according to Sternberg, are generally based on kinds of tasks whose relevance to the world is, at best, slight. There seems to be a substantial gap between the kinds of real world adaptation required for everyday functioning and the kinds of adaptations required for taking tests well.

Sternberg's theory on cognitive processes, capacity, and the time course of thinking, along with careful task analyses, are in the tradition of the information-processing approach. The concern with individual differences reflects the psychometric approach. Finally, his interest in cognitive development and logical structures shows the influence of Piaget. Sternberg suggests that people are governed by three aspects of intelligence: componential, contextual, and experiential. Each of these aspects of intelligence is described in a subtheory.

The *componential subtheory* is Sternberg's information-processing model of cognition (Sternberg & Okagaki, 1989). He proposed three general types of information-processing components: metacomponents, performance components, and knowledge-acquisition components.

Metacomponents refer to metacognitive abilities and involve the monitoring of task performance and the allocation of attentional resources. Metacomponents play an executive, decision-making role in cognition. Examples of metacomponents are defining the nature of a problem, setting up a strategy to solve the problem, allocating attentional resources to various aspects of the problem as well as to other things going on simultaneously, and monitoring your problem solving as you are proceeding through the solution of a problem. *Performance components* include encoding, mental comparison, and retrieval of information. For example, you may need to infer certain things or compare possible solutions or justify one solution as best. *Knowledge-acquisition components* are the processes involved in gaining new knowledge and selectively acting on recently encoded information and information in your long-term memory. Three such components are *selective encoding* (deciding what information is relevant for learning about something), *selective comparison* (deciding how this information is relevant to what you already know), and *selective combination* (putting together seemingly disparate pieces of information in an organized and unified way). A child who receives high test scores and is a whiz at test taking and analytical thinking exemplifies the componential subtheory.

The *contextual subtheory* holds that intelligence must be viewed in the context in which it occurs. Intelligent behaviors for the middle-class American schoolchild may not be considered intelligent behaviors for the ghetto dropout. Sternberg (1985) defines intelligence as "mental activity directed toward purposive adaptation to, and selection and shaping of, real-world environments relevant to one's life" (p. 45). By defining intelligence in terms of real-world environments, he stresses the importance of the external as well as the internal world to intelligence.

From this definition, Sternberg proposes three processes of contextual intelligence: adaptation, selection, and shaping. *Adaptation* refers to adjusting your behavior to achieve a good fit with your environment. When adaptation is not possible or desirable, you may *select* an alternative environment in which you can adapt well. A child, for example, may find it difficult to get along with children in the neighborhood and instead becomes friendly with other children from school who do not live close by. If for some reason a new environment cannot be selected, however, you may attempt to *shape* the environment. A child may try to alter the behavior of his neighborhood peers by inviting only one child over to play rather than the entire group. Basically, the contextual subtheory is one of cultural relativism. Intellectual skills that are critical for survival in one culture may not be so important in another. A child who is "street smart," who has learned how to play the game and how to manipulate the environment, exemplifies Sternberg's contextual intelligence.

The *experiential subtheory* is concerned with how prior knowledge influences performance on certain cognitive tasks. More specifically, the subtheory examines the ability to deal with *novelty* and the degree to which processing is *automatized* (that is, made to involve relatively little mental effort). Both skills are highly dependent on experience. The experiential subtheory suggests what tasks are good indicators of intelligence—namely, those that involve dealing with novelty or automatic processing for their successful completion. A child who does not receive the best test scores but who is a creative thinker combining disparate experiences in insightful ways is an example of the experiential subtheory. Thus, there are three ways to be smart, but ultimately what you want to do is take the components of (a) intelligence, apply them to your (b) experience and use them to (c) adapt to, select, and shape your environment. This is the Triarchic theory of intelligence.

Sternberg is currently working on an IQ test, the Sternberg Multidimensionality Abilities Test, which is based on his theory. The test will measure intelligence in a broader way than traditional IQ tests currently do. Rather than giving a child an IQ number, this test will be used as a basis for diagnosing a child's strengths and weaknesses.

Sternberg's theory is an attempt to go beyond earlier, single theories. The three subtheories provide a framework for understanding intelligence and its development that, in many ways, is more inclusive than earlier theories.

QUANTITATIVE CHARACTERISTICS OF IQ SCORES

The quantitative characteristics of intelligence test scores discussed in this section are the distribution of scores for the population as a whole and the stability found in IQ scores over a period of time. The section addresses the critical question, Do scores on IQ tests predict anything useful?

DISTRIBUTION OF ABILITY

Figure 8.1 shows the IQ ranges and the theoretical distributions of IQ scores. It should be pointed out here that intelligence is not your IQ; your IQ is an outcome of a test and only a partial reflection of intelligence. In looking at the bell-shaped curve, the large bulge you see at the center is where the IQ scores of most people fall. This section of the distribution would then be considered average.

Mental Retardation Infrequent and below-average performances are on the left side of the curve. **Mental retardation** is a label that describes a child's position in relation to other children on the basis of some standard or standards of performance—usually an IQ test. Major changes in

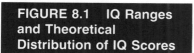

FIGURE 8.1 IQ Ranges and Theoretical Distribution of IQ Scores

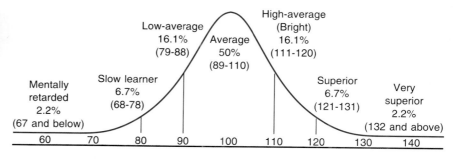

Source: From *Stanford-Binet Intelligence Scale:* Fourth Edition, Copyright, 1986 by The Riverside Publishing Company, 8420 W. Bryn Mawr Avenue, Chicago, Illinois 60631. Reproduced by permission of the publisher.

defining mental retardation have occurred recently. These changes include (a) incorporating the concept of adaptive behavior as part of the definition; (b) lowering the IQ cutoff, such that a child must perform at least two standard deviations below the mean on a test of general intelligence with concurrent deficits in adaptive behavior (thus eliminating from services children with IQs between 70 and 85); (c) extending the upper age limit for initial diagnosis (primarily to offer services to a large number of late adolescents and young adults who have severe neurological impairment secondary to vehicle and sports injuries and drug abuse); and (d) dropping lifelong permanence as part of the concept.

A diagnosis of mental retardation on the basis of the two most widely used tests, the Stanford-Binet and the Wechsler, is made when a child receives an IQ score of 67 or 69, respectively. Within the group of people who are mentally retarded, four levels of classification are recognized. These levels and their corresponding IQ score ranges are shown in Table 8.2.

Adaptive behavior is defined as the effectiveness or degree with which the individual meets the standards of personal independence and social responsibility expected of the individual's age and cultural group. The former includes the ability to meet basic physical needs such as eating, toileting, and dressing, and the ability to function as an in-

TABLE 8.2 Characteristics of Children Who Are Mentally Retarded		
Category	**IQ Range**	**Characteristics**
MILD RETARDATION (89% of retardates)	55–69	From birth to age 5, child can develop social and communication skills, often not distinguished from normal until older. From ages 6 to 20, child can learn academic skills up to approximately sixth-grade level by late teens; can be guided toward social conformity. From age 21 and older, the individual can learn adequate social and vocational skills for minimum self-support, but may need guidance and assistance when under unusual social or economic stress.
MODERATE RETARDATION (6% of retardates)	40–54	From birth to age 5, child can talk or learn to communicate; poor social awareness, fair motor development; benefits from training in self-help; can be managed with moderate supervision. From ages 6 to 20, the individual can profit from training in social and occupational skills; unlikely to progress beyond second-grade level in academic subjects; may learn to travel alone to familiar places. From age 21 and older, the individual may be able to support self in unskilled or semiskilled work under sheltered conditions; needs supervision and guidance when under mild social stress.
SEVERE RETARDATION (3½% of retardates)	25–39	From birth to age 5, child has poor motor development; minimal speech; generally unable to benefit from self-help training; little or no communication skills. From ages 6 to 20, individual can talk or communicate; can be trained in simple health habits; benefits from systematic habit training. From age 21 on, individual may contribute in part to self-support under complete supervision.
PROFOUND RETARDATION (1½% retardates)	below 25	From birth to age 5, child shows gross retardation; minimal capacity for functioning in sensory-motor areas; needs nursing care. From ages 6 to 20 there is some motor development; may respond to minimal or limited training in self-help. From age 21 on there is some motor and speech development; may learn a little self-care; requires nursing care.

Source: From "A Manual on Terminology and Classification in Mental Retardation" by R. Heber (Ed.), 1959, in *American Journal of Mental Deficiency Monograph Supplement, 64,* pp. 56–72. Copyright 1959 by the American Association on Mental Retardation. Used by permission.

tegral member of the community in terms of communicating adequately, handling money, traveling, and so forth. The latter includes participating in group activities, helping others, and so forth. Because these expectations vary for different age groups, deficits in adaptive behavior vary with different ages.

The data about the effectiveness of these changes are quite discouraging. Initial referrals and diagnostic workups continue to reflect inadequately acknowledged cultural attitudes and pressures. For example, white middle-class children are more likely to be classified as learning disabled (which results in more intensive and integrated special education services, as well as more sophisticated clinical evaluations) than are minority and lower class children who show similar cognitive and behavioral profiles, but are labeled mentally retarded (Ysseldyke, 1985).

What causes mental retardation? The most current classification distinguishes between **organic causes of retardation** and **cultural-familial causes of retardation.** In cultural-familial retardation, there are no obvious biological abnormalities, but there is a history of one or both parents being retarded. It is not yet known whether familial retardation is due primarily to genetic factors or to the experience of being reared by retarded parents.

In organic mental retardation, there is damage to the brain, which may occur during either prenatal or postnatal development. An example of prenatal damage to the brain, caused by an abnormal chromosome distribution, is Down syndrome. Although over 100 rare single-gene mutations that involve mental retardation have been identified (McKusick, 1986), chromosomal abnormalities represent the single most important class of genetic causes of retardation.

A chromosomal condition that has been the focus of research recently is called *Fragile X syndrome* because a certain part of the X chromosome tends to break during preparation of cell cultures. The significance of Fragile X is that it is inherited as a recessive trait and appears to be a major reason for the excess of mild mental retardation in males (Nussbaum & Ledbetter, 1988). Because females

receive two X chromosomes and one of these is inactivated, they are somewhat buffered against the effects of having one Fragile X chromosome. It has been estimated that Fragile X chromosome is the second-most common chromosomal cause of mental retardation, exceeded only by Down syndrome (Nussbaum & Ledbetter, 1988).

The prevalence of Fragile X syndrome in the general population ranges from 1.9% to 5.9% (Blomquist, Gustavson, Holmgren, Nordenson, & Palsson-Strade, 1983). The syndrome is associated with variable clinical characteristics, which include a set of facial features (a thin, elongated facial contour, a prominent mandible, enlarged, poorly developed ears). Impairments in cognitive and language functioning are common (Bregman, Leckman, & Ort, 1988).

Unlike Down syndrome, which has specific abnormal physical features, patients affected with Fragile X syndrome may have very subtle features. Fragile X patients undergo changes in appearance from childhood through adult years. The adult male patient typically has a long face, large ears, prominent forehead, and a prominent jaw. Facial features among the Fragile X females are exceedingly variable and do not serve as an aid in diagnosis.

Intellectual problems are the most significant factors affecting lifetime functioning and may be a better aid to diagnosis than are physical findings. It appears that there is a slowly progressive neurological degeneration (Simensen & Rogers, 1989). To illustrate in one study (Lachiewicz, Guillion, Spiridigliozzi, & Aylsworth, 1987), longitudinal intellectual data on 21 Fragile X males were analyzed. A significant decrease in IQ during childhood was noted. The initial evaluation of the young child might be indicative of a learning disability, whereas subsequent evaluations might be consistent with mental retardation. Among females, it is more common to find patients with learning disabilities and/or mild mental retardation.

Other prenatal damage to the brain may be linked to the pregnancy of the mother. For example, overdoses of radiation, contraction of syphilis, an accidental fall by the mother, or inadequate protein intake may cause damage to the fetus's brain. Postnatally, anoxia, an inadequate supply of oxygen to the brain that occurs when there are difficulties in getting the newborn to start breathing, may cause brain damage.

Gifted Children   Above-average performances are on the right side of the curve. Children in this category are often described as **gifted children**—those who are generally in the top 3% to 5% of their class academically and have an IQ of 130 or above. The identification of gifted children has also changed in recent years. Research shows that the limits of standardized testing and IQ tests with specific cutoff scores are not the only tools for identifying students. A multiple criteria approach is now used to gather as much information as possible about the child from a variety of sources.

Sternberg (1985) argues that *insight skills* form a particularly important criteria for identifying intellectual giftedness. Significant and exceptional intellectual accomplishments—for example, major scientific discoveries, new and important inventions, and new and significant understandings of major literary, philosophical, and similar works—almost always involve major intellectual insights. The thinkers' gifts seem directly to lie in their insight abilities and abilities to do nonentrenched

thinking rather than in their IQ-like abilities or their mere abilities to process information rapidly (Sternberg, 1985).

Second, the gifted should be expected to be superior in dealing with novel kinds of tasks and situations in general. Third, the gifted should be able to automatize highly practiced performances to a greater extent than the nongifted, as well as being more adept at automatization in general than are others. Fourth, Sternberg comments that gifted individuals should be particularly adept at applying their intellectual skills to the task or situational environment in which they display their gifts.

Odom and Shaughnessy (1989) reported that when gifted boys and girls are screened separately according to personality factors, certain differences between gifted and nongifted children seem to emerge. The most prominent differences are that boys show more dominance, more individualism, and less group dependency than the norm for their age and sex. Girls seem to be more outgoing, more conscientious, more forthright, and natural than the norms for their age. "Focus on Applications" offers further guidelines in recognizing the gifted child.

A classic study done by Terman and Merrill (1960) has given a great deal of insight into what gifted children are like. The 1,500 gifted individuals comprising Terman's group appeared to be well

According to Sternberg, gifted children have superior insight skills that enable them to achieve exceptional intellectual accomplishments.

FOCUS ON APPLICATIONS

Recognizing the Gifted Child

Perino and Perino (1981) have pointed out some characteristics of gifted children. Gifted children, even as young infants, tend to be very alert and observant. They appear to be more involved than usual in what is going on around them. Many gifted youngsters are precocious talkers. They use complex phrases and sentences and possess a quick and thorough grasp of abstract concepts. Along with manipulating abstract concepts, many verbally gifted children often exhibit advanced vocabulary. Children whose strong skills are in nonverbal areas are often early walkers. They are able to grasp and hold objects accurately, while other infants will not even make an effort to do so. Although precocious academic skills do not necessarily single out the gifted child, it is estimated that many gifted children read before coming to school. In most instances, the parents had done little formal instruction other than pointing out the letters of the alphabet. Basic arithmetic skills also appear at an early juncture. Many gifted children seem to possess remarkable memories. Gifted preschoolers are very curious creatures and ask endless questions. They almost appear driven to explore their environment.

adjusted as children and seemed to turn into well-adjusted, successful adults. Of the 800 males, 125 had earned Ph.D.s or M.D.s, 85 had law degrees, and 100 were engineers. The men and women together had published over 90 books and written 350 short stories and plays.

STABILITY OF IQ SCORES

A considerable amount of research has dealt with the extent to which IQ scores are constant over a person's life. Such research generally focuses on obtaining correlations between test scores gathered from an individual at successive ages. The Berkeley Growth Study has provided the most systematic evidence relating to the stability of IQ scores. It is a longitudinal study involving 61 children born between 1928 and 1929 who were tested repeatedly from infancy to adulthood.

The results of the study indicate that there is no relationship between tests given at 6 months of life and IQ at 18 years. It is not until the 18- to 24-month period that any appreciable degree of predictability can be achieved. A relatively high degree of predictability is achieved by IQ tests given

between ages 5 and 7, at the very beginning of formal education. They predict IQ at the end of the high school period. The correlation is 0.86 between IQ at ages 5, 6, and 7 and at 17 and 18 years of age.

Although the degree of consistency is relatively high, a number of qualifications should be made. The sample from this study is small and slightly biased; it consisted of "normal," white subjects from an above-average socioeconomic class. It would be difficult, then, to generalize the findings of this study to nonwhites and children from lower socioeconomic levels.

While the correlation of IQs at 5 and 18 years is quite high, indicating a considerable degree of stability in IQ scores, many children do show large changes in IQ scores. In a study done by McCall, Appelbaum, and Hogarty (1973), 140 children's test scores from the ages of 2½ to 17 were carefully examined. The test scores over the years fell into five different groups, each with a characteristic pattern of change. While the children in group 1, representing 45% of the group, had test scores that remained the same, children in the other groups showed significant changes in IQ scores. Some children showed shifts of 20 to 30 points over the age span studied, and 15% of the children showed shifts of 40 points.

Although many IQ scores remain stable, others may go up and down and changes may continue in later life. Moreover, different dimensions of intelligence may remain stable, decline, or improve. One must conclude from this research that intellectual performance as measured by IQ tests is neither constant nor fixed.

THE SPECIAL CASE OF INFANT INTELLIGENCE

As noted earlier, there is relatively little relationship between scores on infant tests of intelligence and subsequent tests of intelligence. The correlation between infant intelligence scores and preschool intelligence measures is quite low (see Figure 8.2). One reason for this lack of predictability between infancy and later childhood may lie in the types of tests that are used in the infancy and postinfancy periods. Intelligence tests for infants are designed for use with children who have not developed language. They deal with attending to objects, visual following, and simple motor tasks. Later tests, even so-called nonverbal tests, assume that the person being tested understands language. The aspects of intelligence tested during infancy (sensorimotor) are not the same aspects of intelligence tested during later childhood (verbal). For example, the Bayley Scales tap sensory and motor capacities such as reaching, grasping, and orienting, which bear little conceptual relation to measures included in traditional psychometric tests of intelligence administered in childhood. The lack of consistency between infancy and later childhood measurements may be explained by differences in tests rather than differences in ability.

The problem seems to be finding some aspect or aspects of intelligence that are present in both infants and older people and that can be measured in both.

Recently, infant research into attention and information processing has shown that individual differences in infancy can predict later IQ. Bornstein (1989) demonstrates that habituation, the

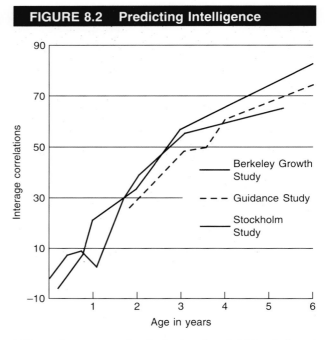

FIGURE 8.2   Predicting Intelligence

Evidence from separate longitudinal studies of children indicated a negative correlation between infant intelligence scores and scores on the Stanford-Binet test at 8 years of age.

Source: From "Measuring Abilities in Infancy: The Value and Limitations" by M. P. Honzik, 1983, in M. Lewis (Ed.), *Origins of Intelligence in Infancy and Early Childhood*, New York: Plenum. Copyright 1983 by Plenum Publishing Corporation. Reprinted by permission.

decrement in attention an infant pays to a familiar stimulus, is significantly, if moderately, related to mental status later in development. Habituation, according to Bornstein, signifies the infant's processing of information about the stimulus. More mature babies, for example, habituate more efficiently than less mature babies; simpler stimuli provoke more rapid habituation than do more complex stimuli; and infants habituated to one stimulus later distinguish a second, novel stimulus from their internal representation of the first. Relatively greater decrements, quicker decays, or lesser amounts of cumulative looking, which are generally interpreted as more efficient styles of information processing in habituation in infancy, are related to better intellectual performance in childhood.

In addition, Bornstein and Sigman (1986) demonstrate that infants who more efficiently encode visual stimuli or more efficiently recollect visual or auditory stimuli tend to perform more proficiently on traditional psychometric assessments of intelligence during childhood. Relatively greater amounts of looking at novel stimuli or reciprocally lesser amounts of looking at familiar stimuli, are generally interpreted as more efficient information processing. Thus, two attentional processes, attention decrement (or habituation) and recovery of attention (or novelty preferences), appear to be central to infant cognition and underlie those measures that are predictive of later intelligence.

These newer, predictive skills have in common a response to novelty. Some recent research has shown that the infant's attitude toward and performance of novel tasks may be one aspect of intelligence that is stable between infancy and later childhood (Sternberg & Gastel, 1989). Fagan and McGrath (1981) showed 7-month-old infants pictures of two identical faces. After 40 seconds, these pictures were taken away, and the infant was shown a picture with the familiar face and one new one. Some infants looked longer at the new face, indicating that they had remembered or recognized the familiar one and preferred to look at the novel face. Fagan and McGrath gave these same children IQ tests when they were 7 years old. They found that the children who as infants had shown a greater interest in looking at the novel faces had higher IQs. Thus, infants' visual preferences for novel targets in recognition memory at 7 months predicted later performance on IQ tests at 7 years.

In a related study, it was also found that visual novelty scores at 6 months of age predicted the cognitive status of the child at 6 years of age (Rose & Wallace, 1985). Thompson and Fagan (1991) administered a test of visual novelty preference to a group of 113 full-term infants at 5 and 7 months of age. The infants were followed longitudinally. The Bayley Scales were administered at 12 and 24 months and the Stanford-Binet and the Colorado

Specific Cognitive Abilities tests at 36 months. The Specific Cognitive Abilities test consists of eight subtests for verbal ability, spatial ability, perceptual speed, and memory. Novelty preference correlated significantly with 36-month Binet IQ; all of the specific abilities were significantly related to novelty preference. Overall, the results indicate that novelty preference during the first year of life not only predicts later IQ but also reflects specific cognitive processes.

The results of another study (DiLalla, Thompson, Plomin, Phillips, Fagan, & Haith, 1990) further contribute to the growing evidence of stability in intellectual development from infancy. The study used 208 pairs of same-sex infant twins and demonstrated that infant measures of attention, novelty preference, and reaction rate can predict later IQ longitudinally up to 3 years of age. Thus, evidence is emerging that the part of the intellect that involves seeking, finding, learning, and solving novel problems may be an important part of intelligence that is stable across the remainder of the life span.

These results seem to argue for a "continuous" as opposed to a "discontinuous" point of view about IQ, at least with respect to the relation between scores on infant tests and scores on tests given in later childhood. *Continuity* in cognitive performance has to do with the smoothness of the IQ-growth curve and to the constancy of the rank orders of individual differences across ages. *Discontinuity* has to do with the lack of smoothness of the IQ-growth curve and to the lack of constancy of the rank orders of individual differences across ages. As Sternberg and Okagaki (1989) point out,

> The question of whether a correlational continuity exists between infant and later tests depends largely on how one defines intelligence for the infants. If one defines intelligence in a way that emphasizes skills such as coping with novelty then continuity will be seen as predominant. But if one defines intelligence in infants in a way that emphasizes perceptual-motor skills (as has been done traditionally), discontinuity will be seen as predominant. . . . At times, knowledge acquisition may be smooth and largely continuous, and at other times it may move ahead in

fits and starts. Development is simultaneously both continuous and discontinuous depending upon the particular locus of intellectual development being examined. (pp. 164–165)

WHAT IQ TEST SCORES PREDICT

In general, IQ tests are fairly good predictors of a child's success in school, with the correlation figure at 0.70 (McClelland, 1973). You can hardly be surprised, since from the very beginning the tests were validated by school success. That is, questions that seemed to pick out good students were considered good test questions and those that did not were dropped. Are IQ tests useful, however, for predicting anything else—for example, success in later life?

Apparently not. Jencks (1972) of Harvard University and a group of his colleagues surveyed most of the available information about intelligence testing, education, and social and economic status in the United States. Jencks's unexpected conclusion was that "scores on the tests show remarkably little relation to performance in most adult roles. People with high scores do a little better in most jobs than people with low scores, and they earn somewhat more money, but the differences are surprisingly small" (p. 13).

Thus IQ tests may be a useful tool for obtaining a fairly accurate picture of the scholastic potential of a child—at least of a middle-class child. They do not, however, measure the great number of abilities that might be included under intelligence. Because they are relatively good predictors of success in school, IQ tests may be a beneficial tool in locating children who may have learning deficits and as such require special attention. They have also identified the exceptionally gifted child.

There are some negative things about IQ tests, as well. The terrible harm that children can suffer—and often do—from unintelligent interpretation of intelligence testing can make them out to be psychological and statistical monstrosities. For example, Hoffman (1978) tells of a young girl in a big city public school who had been working very nicely in "slow regular" classes in the third and fourth grades. In the fifth grade she was at the top

IQ tests may be a useful tool in judging a child's scholastic potential, but they do not measure his or her occupational success.

of her class. Then a school psychologist discovered that her IQ was below 70. A rule clearly stated: IQ less than 70, class for the mentally retarded. The girl was transferred. There are many other examples.

Moreover, the first question teachers will often ask about their students is, What are their IQ scores? The answer determines the posture of some, if not all, of the teachers toward their students.

GROUP DIFFERENCES IN INTELLIGENCE TEST SCORES

This section focuses on the differences in intelligence test scores for groups of individuals, particularly the five major variables that appear to be related to intelligence test scores: race, culture, social class, family size, and birth order. It is important to note that these factors are intimately related.

RACE, CULTURE, AND INTELLIGENCE

In 1969, Jensen wrote an article entitled "How much can we boost IQ and scholastic achievement?" The answer to this question, according to Jensen, was "not much." Jensen went on to discuss why the average African-American's score on IQ tests is 15 points below the average white's score. It should be pointed out that there is complete agreement in accepting the empirical finding of an African-American–white difference of 15 points on intelligence test scores. How you interpret this finding, however, can vary.

The "culture-as-social-class" model, for example, attributes the differences between African-Americans and whites to social and economic disadvantages, leading to African-Americans' poorer performance in school and on IQ tests. More African-Americans than whites are being raised in single-parent homes. Of children under 18 years of age in the United States today, about 1 in 5 lives in a home that is below the federally defined poverty line; of African-American children, however, almost half live in poverty (Slaughter-Defoe, Nakagawa, Takanishi, & Johnson, 1990). From this standpoint, poverty is the most important variable accounting for observed differences in the functioning between African-American and white children. This perspective suggests that discrimination and economic inequities suffered by African-Americans result in their increased likelihood of living in poverty and that problems engendered by economic stress have a negative impact on a child's competence at school. If their families were provided with equal economic circumstances and compensation for past inequities, African-American children would be expected to perform as well at school and on IQ tests as white children (Edelman, 1987).

The problems engendered by poverty for the African-American child growing up in low-income, mother-headed, single-parent homes are: (a) absence of the father, which is thought to undermine boys' gender-role identity; (b) absence of a male presence, which could reduce exposure to analytical thinking; and (c) lack of parental supervision—a single parent has less time to spend with

children than do two parents (or two adults) (Slaughter-Defoe et al., 1990).

African-American girls are generally perceived or shown to fare better in school (Solomon & Houlihan, 1972). It is the African-American male who is perceived as being particularly vulnerable to the single-parent living conditions (Spencer, 1988). Being male, of minority ethnic status, and growing up in low-income, single-parent homes have all been identified as heightening the risk of poor academic performance in school and poor performance on IQ tests (Patterson, Kupersmidt, & Vaden, 1990).

The theoretical perspectives of Ogbu (1988) and Bronfenbrenner (1986) emphasize that although the family is clearly most central to childhood achievement socialization and development, the way in which both the family as a group and as a collection of individuals interacts with other cultural groups and institutions will significantly influence human adaptation to and development in schools.

Jensen (1969) suggests that, perhaps, the differences between African-Americans' and whites' performance in school and on IQ tests are innate. He argues that they are due to genetic factors. IQ "heritability" is the extent to which IQ differences are due to genetic differences. Jensen argues that IQ has a heritability of 80%—only 20% of IQ differences being due to differences in the environment.

Jensen proposes that there are two levels of innate types of learning. Level one, known as *associative learning,* basically involves simply associations, short-term memory, and rote memorization. By contrast, level two, *cognitive learning,* involves more complex abstract reasoning skills. Most IQ tests stress the latter level of learning. It is this level, maintains Jensen, in which African-Americans are innately at a disadvantage, as compared with whites.

Jensen believes that the difference between African Americans and whites in intelligence test scores is too large to be accounted for by environmental factors. It has been found, however, that environmental factors can produce change in IQ scores, change in the magnitude of the present difference between African-Americans' and whites' scores. A classic study done by Skodak and Skeels (1949) attained IQ scores for 63 mothers. Their average IQ score was 86. The researchers, on the basis of the fact that all the fathers were semiskilled or unskilled laborers, estimated their IQs to be around 86 as well. The children of these mothers and fathers had all been adopted by parents with normal IQs. The average IQ of these children was 106—approximately 13 points higher than would be predicted on the basis of the biological parents' IQ scores. The study demonstrates that a 15-point increment in intelligence test scores is a reasonable expectation of the expected influence of a middle-class environment on children with lower-class genotypes for intelligence.

Scarr and Weinberg (1976) also studied African-American children raised in white middle– and upper–middle-class families. The average IQ for these children was 110 — 15% higher than the average score of U.S. African-American children reared by their own parents. It was also pointed out in this study that the younger the children were at the time of adoption, the closer they came to the white IQ averages.

There are still other interpretations of the African-American–white differences in IQ test performance. The kinds of observations made by Jensen were not new. H. H. Goddard, the psychologist who brought the Binet test to the United States, tested immigrants at Ellis Island, the immigrant receiving station for New York. He concluded that 83% of the Jews, 80% of the Hungarians, 79% of the Italians, and 87% of the Russians were "feebleminded" (Kamin, 1974). Congress was informed of this influx of the feebleminded, and new immigration quotas were established— many of which are still in effect today.

Goddard took a strong genetic stance on IQ, and because of his influence, IQ test scores were interpreted from his viewpoint. Today, however, it is recognized that the tests the immigrants took were culturally biased. That is, in order to do well on these tests, immigrants needed to have a good knowledge of the middle-class U.S. culture. It was not that these people were feebleminded, but

rather that they were unaware, unfamiliar with the context of these culturally biased questions. This same sort of cultural bias may be another reason that African-Americans do not score as well as whites.

Furthermore, experts in heredity do not agree with Jensen (see chapter 2). They recognize that IQ is influenced by both heredity and environment. When you think about it, how can you discount the influence of environment when the test is designed to measure the influence of environment?

Jensen's work has failed to provide clear evidence to support his genetic hypothesis. Although the point spread between African-Americans and whites is undeniable, the reasons for it—indeed, the value of the IQ test itself—are debatable. As Jencks (1972) points out:

> IQ, whatever its origin, plays a relatively modest role in determining a man's life chances. Otis Dudley Ducan has shown, for example, that blacks with high IQs are almost as disadvantaged economically as those with low IQs. . . . Low IQs are not the cause of America's racial problems and higher IQs would not solve these problems. Any white reader who doubts this should simply ask himself whether he would trade the genes which make his skin white for genes which would raise his IQ 15 points. (p. 15)

SOCIAL CLASS AND INTELLIGENCE

Differences in IQ scores may be more closely related to social class than to racial factors. When tests are given to children in areas where everyone is white, those from the middle and upper classes score well while those from lower social classes tend to do poorly. Thus, even among whites, social class is related to IQ test performance.

For the first 18 months of life, white, African-American, lower- and middle-class babies all score about the same on infant intelligence tests. After 18 months, differences in social class begin to appear. There may be something about the intellectual quality of the environment of lower-class families, compared with middle-class families, that lead to the differences in IQ scores among socioeconomic classes. For example, children from lower-class homes tend to encounter sterile learning environments; they are restricted in their

Children from different cultural backgrounds may not do as well on culturally biased IQ tests.

movement and freedom; their diet is poor; their home environment is more disorganized and unpredictable; and their mothers tend to spend little time interacting with their children (Bradley & Caldwell, 1976).

Early Intervention Programs Because it is difficult to separate the specific environmental conditions that are associated with low socioeconomic classes and IQ, researchers have turned to intervention programs to determine if IQ test scores and school performance will improve for children at an increased risk for lower cognitive performance. Children who grow up in poverty are at increased risk for lower cognitive performance, and their performance is frequently associated with later school failure (Lazar, Darlington, Murray, Royce, & Snipper, 1982). The Head Start program, which began in the late 1960s, was designed to help preschool children from low socioeconomic classes improve their academic skills and performance. Children in the program showed an initial increase of 10 to 15 IQ points, but when the program was terminated and these children entered the formal education setting, it was found that their IQs dropped and continued to drop, so later

there were no measurable effects of the Head Start experience.

Heber (1959) and Garber and Heber (1981) have stated that four fifths of the mentally retarded population in the United States do not suffer from any organic difficulties. Heber felt that through adequate training, these children could overcome their "sociocultural mental retardation." Forty children born to low-class, low-IQ mothers were selected for study. Twenty of these children comprised the control group and the other 20 formed the experimental group. The mothers and infants of the experimental group received training in various skills. The mothers were given vocational training and help in child-care skills. The infants were given training in perceptual-motor skills and when they were older, they received more formal instruction in language, reading, and math.

The differences in the IQs of the experimental and control group are rather impressive. For example, at 36 months the children in the experimental group had an average IQ of 124; the control group's average IQ was 94. At 6 years of age, the average IQ for the experimental group was 121, compared with an average of 87 for the control group. The results point to a very large potential

Intervention-program studies show that involving parents can increase their effectiveness in raising academic performances of high-risk children.

impact of rearing conditions on the child's cognitive development. Unfortunately, however, when children in the experimental group entered school their IQs dropped.

Some intervention-program studies have shown that while experimental group children enter school with considerably higher IQs than control group children, they have not shown commensurately better school performance (Garber & Heber, 1981).

In reviewing preschools, it has been noted that the most effective programs have been those that actively involved the parents (Gray & Wandersman, 1980). It seems logical to explore the consequences of increasing parental involvement (Prov-

ence & Naylor, 1983). Bronfenbrenner (1974) reviewed the existing intervention programs and concluded that

> the family seems to be the most effective and economical system for fostering and sustaining the child's development. Without family involvement, intervention is likely to be unsuccessful, and what few effects are achieved are likely to disappear once the intervention is discontinued. (p. 300)

Wasik, Ramey, Bryant, and Sparling (1990) studied 65 families at risk for cognitive difficulties. The Bayley Scales of Infant Development were administered when the children were 6, 12, and 18 months; the Stanford-Binet Intelligence Tests at 24, 36, and 48 months; and the McCarthy Scales of Children's Abilities at 30, 42, and 54 months. Each of the families was randomly assigned to one of three groups: an educational day-care program with a family education component, a family education-only program, and a control group. Families participating in the family education program were provided general family support, including helping parents learn effective problem-solving strategies and specific knowledge and skills related to positive child development. Results indicated that children participating in an educational day-care program supplemented with a family education program responded significantly better on measures of cognitive performance than other intervention children. Educational day-care and family education programs appear to be two effective components in helping children at risk for low academic success.

FAMILY SIZE, BIRTH ORDER, AND INTELLIGENCE

It has long been known that children from large families tend to score lower on intelligence tests than do children from smaller families (Anastasi, 1956). The reasons for this are speculative. It may be possible that the more children there are in the family, the less likely it will be that all the children will receive equal parental attention. As a result, these children are more likely to experience an environment that is not conducive to intellectual development. There is also the speculation that mothers provide an increasingly inadequate prenatal environment with successive births.

In addition to the influence of family size, there is evidence suggesting that birth order influences intellectual development (Zajonc, 1983). As can be seen in Figure 8.3 within each family size, children born earlier tend to score higher on IQ tests than later-born children (Zajonc & Markus, 1975).

Zajonc (1976) has interpreted these findings in the following way. He suggests that children's intellectual development is determined by the overall intellectual quality and climate of the home environment. The intellectual quality of the home is determined by the average intellectual ability of all family members. A family's intellectual environment is never stable, but changes over time. The arrival of infants and the departure of older siblings and adults can worsen a family's intellectual environment by lowering the average intellectual ability of its members. For example, when a child is born into a family with many closely spaced siblings, the availability of intellectual resources is greatly diminished. In this type of environment, the child receives fewer exchanges with knowledgeable parents and a larger number of exchanges with unknowledgeable siblings. Thus, later-born children, according to Zajonc, have lower IQs.

Zajonc does point out, however, that when there is adequate spacing between children the intellectual level of the family is raised and allows each new member of the family to have more exchanges with advanced siblings and parents. Zajonc's theory predicts that the early-born children should have the highest level of intellectual competence of any birth position because these children encounter a high-intellectual-level environment. That is, they have a greater opportunity to interact with their parents who function at a higher cognitive level. Early-born children may also have another advantage of playing the role of tutor to younger brothers and sisters, which may enhance the child's cognitive development.

Although Zajonc's theory neatly explains the effects of birth order and family size on intelligence, the crucial test of the theory has yet to be performed (McCall, 1985). Zajonc's theory that the spacing of children is a critical determinant in birth-order effect has not been tested. If predictions about spacing are supported by research, then belief in the validity of his theory will be substantially increased (Rodgers, 1984).

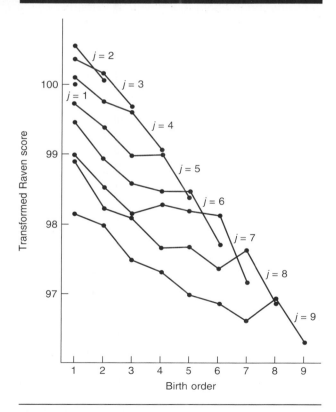

FIGURE 8.3   Birth Order

Source: From "Birth Order and Intellectual Development" by R. B. Zajonc and G. B. Markus, 1975, in *Psychological Review*, *82*, p. 75. Copyright 1975 by the American Psychological Association. Reprinted by permission.

CREATIVITY

One aspect of intelligence that has been generally ignored by the psychometric approach is **creativity**—an area that traditional intelligence testing barely touches. New theories of cognitive

FOCUS ON ISSUES

Do Creative Children Have High IQs?

Although creative persons are intelligent, an exceptionally high IQ does not appear to be a prerequisite to creativity; however, a basic intelligence is needed for creativity to be useful. This "basic" IQ has been estimated at 110+ (Renzullit & Hartman, 1971).

Getzels and Jackson (1962) made a careful study of creativity and intelligence in children. Children from the sixth grade up through the senior year in high school (N = 292 boys and 241 girls) were given creativity tests and IQ tests. The researchers concluded that they could identify two groups of students. One group exhibited high intelligence, but not concomitantly high creativity. This group had an IQ average of 150. The second group scored high on creativity and had an average IQ of 127. An interesting point, however, is that despite the difference of 23 IQ points between the groups, there was no measurable difference in their scores on achievement tests, which measure how much has been learned at a given point in time. The implication is that creativity makes up for lower IQs. That is, a combination of intelligence and creativity brings about much higher academic achievement than either alone. Torrance (1962, 1964) has replicated the Getzels and Jackson studies and six of the eight replications yielded almost identical results.

development have encouraged researchers to examine this important component of intelligence.

Creative thinking is divergent thinking of a kind that produces many different answers or solutions to a problem or situation and generates clever ideas. Creative children have a way of going beyond set limits in thinking. They seem to be saying, "What if?" They like to be originators and developers of ideas and are not put off by the unorthodox (Feldman, 1989).

Besides divergent thinking, there are other aspects of creative thinking, one of which is fluency. (Williams, 1979). Fluency suggests the idea of quantity, and it involves the number of relevant ideas presented to a child—for example, the responses to instructions to list all the alternative sites for the town's power plant. Another aspect of creativity is original thinking, which is identical to the concept of uniqueness and closely akin to divergence. It implies rareness or novelty. Originality is the ability to come up with unusual solutions. Creative thinking is also flexible thinking. Creative children have the ability to make

shifts in their methods of analysis—the opposite of the rigid approach to tasks. The flexible thinker can shift information from one category to another and is willing to accept and utilize new information on a subject when it suddenly appears on the scene.

Three factors acting in concert contribute to the development of persistent motivation that is typical of productive creators: (a) values relating to intellectual achievement; (b) precocious development of a basic ability in a relevant domain; and (c) stress (Ochse, 1989). These influences apparently cause a tendency to engage in independent intellectual pursuits, which offer palliation, afford a sense of control, build a wider repertoire of skill and knowledge than is usually gained through adherence to a curriculum, and establish a habit of working alone. Thus, creative children's thinking is divergent and fluid. Are these children above average in IQ? How do these children do on intelligence tests? Is there a relationship between IQ and creativity? "Focus on Issues" discusses creativity and intelligence.

TESTS OF CREATIVITY

In assessing creativity in children, various types of tests can be given. For example, in one test, children are presented with various kinds of pictures of rather common scenes and asked to tell a story about what is happening in each picture. One picture is of a man sitting in an airplane. In the stories below, it is rather obvious that one child's response diverges from the expected, is more original and novel, and thus is considered to be more creative.

Child number one responds:

> Mr. Smith is on his way home from a successful business trip. He is very happy and he is thinking about his wonderful family and how glad he will be to see them again. He can picture it, about an hour from now—his plane landing at the airport and Mrs. Smith and their three children all there welcoming him home again.

Child number two relates:

> This man is flying back from Reno where he just won a divorce from his wife. He couldn't stand to live with her anymore, he told the judge, because she wore so much cold cream on her face at night that her head would skid across the pillow and hit him in the head. He is now contemplating a new skidproof face cream. (Getzels & Jackson, 1962)

There are other tests that differentiate creative from less creative children. Like the test above, these tests measure a child's ability to diverge from the expected—give unusual, unexpected responses. "Studying Children" discusses another example of a creativity test.

CHARACTERISTICS OF CREATIVE INDIVIDUALS

Torrance (1962) surveyed a number of studies and compiled no fewer than 84 characteristics that identified creative individuals. He proceeded to list them in alphabetical order, from "accepts disorder" to "withdrawn." Some of the other characteristics cited in between were "altruistic," "industrious," "assertive," and "versatile"—characteristics most of us desire. There were also entries on the list for attraction to the mysterious, independence in judgment, and defiance of con-

Creative responses to viewing this picture tend to show divergent, unexpected, and unusual themes.

STUDYING CHILDREN

CREATIVITY

Have children tell you what each of these drawings could be.

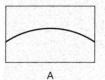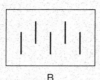

A   B   C

Some particularly creative responses given by children: For drawing A, "This is a fisherman's line. You can't see him nor the fish, but he's on the left pulling in a big one." For B, "These are worms hanging." For C, "It's a foot with toes." What kind of responses do you receive from children? Another type of test is the Use of Things test (Getzels & Jackson, 1962). Have children tell you all the ways they can think of for using a brick, clip, or pencil. How many original responses do your subjects mention?

ventions. Other traits are more negative, such as "discontented," "disturbs organization," "is stubborn and temperamental."

It appears that creative individuals are more observant (Barron, 1969). That is, they are more open to relevant experiences and are able to see both what others see and what others do not see. They seem able to cope with difficulties, inconsistencies, and contradictions rather than being immobilized by them. They appear to be very involved in their work and engage in more fantasies than noncreative individuals.

Creative children possess a good sense of humor (Bleedorn, 1982); in fact, it has been argued that incorporating humor in the classroom is one method of recognizing and developing creative talent. Creative children are self-starters, with lots of energy, a high degree of independence, and a great deal of initiative.

These children seem to arrive almost spontaneously at their unique and divergent responses to situations and problems. There appear, however, to be various stages involved in the creative thinking process, pointed out in Table 8.3.

FAMILIES OF CREATIVE CHILDREN

A sizable body of literature relates children's degree of creativity to the degree of autonomy they receive in the home—for example, that greater freedom is related to higher levels of creativity in children (Domino, 1979). The research data on this matter, however, are quite inconsistent. Some studies have found that restrictive practices tend to be positively related to creativity (Orinstein, 1962), and some studies have found no relationship between autonomy and creativity (Reid, 1972). Despite these mixed findings, it seems to make sense that a somewhat permissive family structure, which allows the child a certain degree of freedom, would be more conducive to producing a creative child than an autocratic or inflexible one. After all, freedom is based on the nature of creativity itself, because it involves producing something that is new and different.

Parents who have been described as moderately affectionate, nonrejecting, and encouraging produce more creative children (Silverberg, 1971). Here again, however, no consistent pattern of results has emerged from research on this question. These mixed results may indicate that there is no relationship between creativity and parental warmth.

The research in this area has been less than helpful. Although it is assumed that parental behavior influences a child's creativity, none of the research reviewed sheds light on what these influences might be. What is needed, perhaps, are more precise definitions of freedom—is it greater independence or is it ideational playfulness? In addition, new research should examine which particular aspects of parental behaviors influence specific types of creativity and how these variables interact with each other and with the characteristics children bring to their life situations (Rejskind, 1982). There is also a great deal of disagreement about what creativity is and how to measure it. It is no wonder there would be inconsistent results if studies have differing definitions of creativity and different tests as well.

THE KINDS OF SCHOOL SITUATIONS THAT PRODUCE CREATIVE CHILDREN

Torrance (1962) sets forth five principles that teachers should follow to reward creative thinking:

TABLE 8.3 Stages of Creative Thinking	Stage	Characteristics
	Insight	In this initial stage, you realize that there is a problem that needs to be solved or an activity you want to engage in, such as writing a story or painting a landscape. It is the stage in which the germinal idea is conceived. James Watson, for example, concentrated on discovering the structure of DNA, because he believed that the solution to this problem would reveal the mechanism of genetic transmission.
	Preparation	In the second stage, information is assembled. This is a time for reading, talking to others, exploring, familiarizing yourself with the ideas of others, which all form a springboard for launching your own imaginations. This almost always involves an extended period of time. To illustrate, James Watson and Francis Crick spent 1½ years trying to discover the structure of DNA before developing the model that won them a Nobel prize. Einstein spent 7 years working on the problem of the velocity of light before he developed his theory of relativity.
	Incubation	As the word suggests, incubation means that something is gradually developing. In this stage, you may occasionally think about the problem, but you are not really "pressured" to solve it. It is a time of temporary relaxation; a time of turning the matter over to the subconscious.
	Illumination	Some highly creative individuals have reported suddenly hitting on a solution after having put the problem aside for a time. Suddenly everything falls into place in a brief moment of insight.
	Evaluation	The final stage involves testing of the completed process or product. The time spent on these processes may vary. Some may be relatively short. For example, it took Einstein only 5 weeks to develop his theory of relativity after his initial insight into the meaning of time and simultaneity. Some may spend much more time testing their hunches. This was the case with Madame Curie, who spent 4 years trying to isolate radium, after she had tentatively identified it as a new element.

(a) treat unusual questions with respect; (b) treat unusual ideas with respect; (c) provide opportunities for self-initiated learning and give credit for it; (d) show children that their ideas have value; and (e) provide periods of nonevaluated practice or learning. In addition, work and play should not be thought of as opposite sides of the coin. School work can be joyful too, and play may be very constructive and instructive.

By way of contrast, creativity suffers when the school is oriented solely toward success rather than achievement for its own sake. Teachers discourage creativity when they recognize and reward only convergent thinking (searching for the one right answer to a question or problem), when memory processes are emphasized, when anxiety is aggravated, and when the text, rather than the child's thoughts and ideas, becomes the only authority.

By the same token, peers, with their emphasis on immediate action, compliance, and conformity, can thwart creativity in children. For example, Torrance (1962) has postulated that the decline in creativity that occurs at the ages of 9, 13, and 17 is caused by children's needs for peer approval and identification with peers, which results in conforming types of behaving and thinking.

PRACTICAL IMPLICATIONS: FAMILY FACTORS THAT PROMOTE CHILDREN'S ACADEMIC ACHIEVEMENT

The nurture position holds that mental abilities (intelligence) are greatly influenced by the experiences of the individual (the environment) within some loosely set limits imposed by genetic endowment. By way of contrast, the nature position specifies that genetic endowment is the single most important factor in determining intelligence in any individual, while experience plays little, if any, role in determining mental abilities. Because of the complex nature of the controversy, no answer is likely to be acceptable to all members of the scientific community until heredity and environment can be absolutely separated in development and their interactions controlled.

Experience is a powerful component in the development of mental abilities. Children can be provided with experiences that will allow them to maximize their potential levels of abilities. In this sense, heredity and environments are floors, not ceilings.

In this section family factors that influence children's performance in the academic setting will be discussed. An overview of the ways in which parents can enhance children's innate potential and improve their academic performance would require volumes of books; here, the surface is merely scratched.

CREATING A STIMULATING ENVIRONMENT

Bloom (1974) has suggested that interventions designed to increase IQ by providing a stimulating environment are more effective when presented at an earlier rather than later age. If early intellectual ability is a precursor of the ability to develop further skills, then early interventions might have widespread effects that would influence subsequent learning.

It has been found that young children's mental abilities are enhanced in a home environment in which the parents provide rich sensory experiences and encourage the child's active exploration

Parents who take an active role in helping their children with homework find that they do better academically.

of the sights, sounds, and objects in the environment (Kelly & Worell, 1977). Provision of appropriate play material geared to the child's developmental level and the mother's involvement with the child also appear to be important in the development of children's thinking abilities (Dweck & Elliott, 1983).

PARENTING STYLES

Some studies have examined the relationship between parenting style and adolescent school performance (Dornbusch, Ritter, Leiderman, Roberts, & Fraleigh, 1987). The results of this study indicate that authoritative parenting (parents are warm but firm, place high value on the development of child's autonomy and self-direction) is positively related to adolescent school performance, whereas authoritarian (parents tend to favor more punitive, absolute, and forceful disciplinary measures and place a high value on conformity and obedience) and permissive parenting (parents more passive in matters of discipline and give the child a high degree of freedom) are negatively so. More specifically, adolescents who describe their parents as behaving more democratically, more warmly, and more encouraging earn higher grades in school than their peers. This finding is consistent with an extensive literature linking authoritative parenting practices to children's psychosocial competence and well-being, virtually however indexed (Maccoby & Martin, 1983).

The purpose of another study (Steinberg, Elmen, & Mounts, 1989) was to "unpack" authoritativeness into its constituent components—acceptance, psychological autonomy, and behavioral control—and examine the independent contributions of these components to adolescent school performance. The sample for the study was composed of 120 families with a firstborn child between the ages of 11 and 16. The results indicated that aspects of authoritative child rearing, including parental warmth and acceptance, made both direct and indirect contributions to the child's academic achievement over time. This parenting style affects children's academic achievement primarily through the development of "psychosocial maturity" (e.g., aspirations for performing competent work, experiencing pleasure in one's work, and development of initiative and a sense of control over events). The development of these intrapersonal qualities might enhance the child's academic achievement over time as academic demands become more challenging and success experiences accumulate.

Grolnick and Ryan (1989) sought to identify relevant dimensions of parent styles believed to be associated with children's competence in school. The study involved children, parents, and teachers in 20 classrooms, third through sixth grades. It was found that children's academic performance is enhanced when parents hold reasonable expectations for their children, offer general, facilitating assistance, and expect and accept independent behavior when the child is ready.

Some studies (Dweck & Elliott, 1983; Teevan & McGhee, 1972) emphasize that the timing of independence training (too early, too late, or optimal) covaries with orientation for academic success or failure. High school boys are more likely to be failure oriented if they are trained too early to be independent, and late independence training was related to high test anxiety (Teevan & McGhee, 1972). It appears that if children are confronted with requirements to be independent before they have developed the prerequisites for solving the tasks, frequent failures become inevitable. Children, because they cannot identify the relationship between effort and outcome, attribute their failure experiences to lack of ability and subsequently develop a strong need to avoid failure. When independence training is optimal, however—that is, the child has developed the prerequisite cognitive and motor abilities—a high personal aptitude is developed.

MOTHERS' AND FATHERS' WARMTH

There is some evidence that a mother's support and affection for her children as shown in her physical and verbal responses to them and her positive regard for herself and her children seem to have a good influence on children's level of achievement (Dornbusch et al., 1987; Dweck & Elliott, 1983). These supportive attitudes tend to release the child's ability to concentrate on mastery of learning tasks.

Similarly, children who perform well academically appear to value their fathers' companionship. The children perceive themselves as similar to their fathers; fathers of high achievers are more accessible to their children and are democratic in dealing with their children (Osofsky, 1979). More often than not, paternal nurturance has been found to be positively related to high child achievement. High-achieving college students, for example, reported that their fathers were more accepting and somewhat less controlling than fathers described by low achievers (Cross & Allen, 1969). Another study (Teahan, 1963) administered a questionnaire to low-achieving college freshman males (who had previously done well in school) and their parents. These sons had fathers who felt that children should make only minor decisions, they should always believe their parents, they should be under their parents' complete control, and it was wicked to disobey parents. The picture emerged of a clash between a domineering, punitive, overprotective father and his underachieving son.

It is possible that the relationship among the variables of paternal nurturance, high academic expectations, sex-role attitudes, quality of cognitive facilitation, and marital congruence with spouse may interact in subtle and complex ways to foster a child's intellectual competence.

REVIEW OF KEY POINTS

Four ways of viewing intelligence were discussed: unitary theory, two-factor, multiple-factor theory, and Sternberg's triarchic theory. One group of researchers supports the theory that states that intelligence is a unitary trait. Simply put, you have a general functional level: If you are bright in one area, you will do magnificently in other areas. The other side of cognitive research represents those who feel that intelligence is not based on a general factor or trait but on a specific number of abilities that are not necessarily dependent on or correlated with each other. Sternberg's theory includes three subtheories:

1. Contextual—Intelligence must be viewed in the context in which it occurs. What is intelligent in one environment may be irrelevant in another. Thus, the ability to adapt to one's environment is no small part of intelligence.

2. Experiential—Intelligence is purposeful, goal-oriented, relevant behavior consisting of two general skills: the ability to deal with novelty and the degree to which processing is automatized; that is, the ability to learn from experience to perform mental tasks effortlessly or automatically.

3. Componential—Intelligence depends on acquiring information-processing skills and strategies, which involve metacomponents, performance, and knowledge-acquisition components. The theorists' conceptual models of intelligence will, of course, be reflected in the form and content of their intelligence tests.

The next section noted the range and distribution of IQ scores. Mental retardation and gifted children were discussed. The stability of IQ scores was questioned and the possibility that IQ cannot be thought of as a stable and fixed entity was raised. It was noted that there is no correlation between infant IQ scores and scores received on tests given later in childhood. Part of this is due to the fact that infancy tests and tests given later measure different things. One research group has found that interest in novel things is one aspect of intelligence found in infants and is predictive of IQ in later childhood. IQ tests are generally good predictors of children's success in school. It needs to be remembered, however, that IQ tests measure only one aspect of intelligence.

The major variables related to intelligence test scores appear to be race, culture, social class, family size, and birth order. While African Americans score approximately 15 points lower than whites on IQ tests, the factors responsible for this spread are still debatable. The culture-as-social-class model attributes African-Americans' poorer performance in school and on IQ tests to social and economic disadvantages. Jensen (1969) has taken the stand that the difference is too large to be attributable to environmental factors, yet studies have shown that environment can account for changes of this magnitude. Moreover, social class is related to IQ performance; lower-class whites, for example, score lower than middle-class whites. In early intervention programs designed to help lower-class children from poor socioeconomic classes, it has been found that although IQ increases occur while children are in these programs, the changes are not lasting. Once the child leaves the program, IQ drops, and the IQ points gained are lost again. In addition to race and social class, family size and birth order are related to IQ scores. Zajonc (1983) has maintained that the intellectual level of the family environment is an important element in explaining the different IQ levels of children from varying family sizes and different birth order positions.

One important component of intelligence is creativity. Creative children are capable of divergent thinking that goes beyond set limits. Studies have shown that to some extent affectionate, nonrejecting parents who allow their children a certain degree of independence and freedom tend to produce more creative children. In school, teachers can help promote creativity by providing nonevaluated learning periods, treating children's ideas respectfully, and recognizing and rewarding divergent thinking.

Research seems to confirm that children's intelligence and performance are stimulated when parents provide a supportive environment that offers a variety of objects and materials for the child to explore and manipulate, when independent behavior is expected and encouraged (when the child is ready), when discipline is firm but fair, and when mother and father offer affection, interest, and support to their children.

ENHANCING YOUR CRITICAL THINKING

Broadening Your Knowledge

Critical Evaluation of Tests

Cronbach, L. J. (1984). *Essentials of testing.* New York: Harper & Row.

In order to understand the potentialities and limitations of various tests, you need to understand two important concepts: validity and reliability. Cronbach does an excellent job explaining these concepts in his text.

Firsthand Experiences

Evaluating Standardized Tests

Conoley, J. C., & Kramer, J. J. (Eds.). (1989). *The 10th Mental Measurements Yearbook.* Lincoln: The University of Nebraska Press.

In this book you'll find out everything you might ever want to know about the positive and negative points of most published tests. Look up *The Wechsler Intelligence Scale for Children* (p. 385) and the *Stanford Binet* (p. 342) to see how these tests are evaluated.

Critical Thinking

Evaluating IQ Tests

Hoffman, B. (1978). *The tyranny of testing.* Westport, CT: Greenwood.

Many of us regard intelligence testing as a necessary tool in assessing students' capabilities. Students of developmental psychology, however, need to be aware that these tests have been interpreted in ways that are detrimental to children. This book is an excellent one to read in order to develop insights into some of the potential negative effects of IQ testing. It also enables you to make your own intelligent interpretation of IQ tests.

CHILDREN'S THOUGHTS

Some typical utterances made by Eric . . .

At 13 months:

"More" (reaching for a cookie)
"No" (resisting having his shoes put on)

At 19 months:

"Allgone daddy" (as his father leaves the house for work)
"More read" (holding up a book)

At 2 years:

"Mom that on" (wanting the light turned on)
"Where go car?" (looking for missing toy car)

By 2½:

"What he can ride in?"
"I want to open it."

At 3 years, 4 months, Eric talks to his friend John while playing with a few small pieces of clay:

ERIC: Don't crush mines up!
JOHN: Did you make something?
ERIC: An animal what gots two feets. Dis is mines.
JOHN: Dat's yours.
ERIC: Dis is mines. . . . You stealed some more!
JOHN: I dint.

CHAPTER OUTLINE

KEY TERMS

Children's language is always fascinating. What is truly amazing about analyzing children's speech is that despite the complexity of language—any language—children master many of its intricacies in a very short period of time. How do they master language? What accounts for this tremendous feat, especially because a young child rarely receives a great deal of formal language instruction?

In many ways language is the most vital function a child develops—verified, perhaps, by the enormous amount of work in progress on the study of children's acquisition of language. Some of the important areas of language research center on these questions: How do children learn various rules that make communication possible? What stages do children pass through in learning to speak? What kinds of experiences promote or enhance a child's language development? Before these questions can be answered, it is necessary to first understand what language is.

LANGUAGE: WHAT IS IT?

Language is an ordered system of rules that people comprehend in speaking, listening, and writing. The key words in this definition are "ordered system of rules." Children tend to learn language in a very methodic, rule-governed way.

The rules children learn are **implicit rules,** which means that they cannot be formulated or expressed. For example, look at these two sentences:

1. The boy aggravates his father.
2. The aggravates boy his father.

Sentence 2 is obviously wrong. Because the words are out of order, it makes little sense. You notice this right away, even though you may not be able to explain why—you know it implicitly. You know this is wrong because you never say sentences like 2. A collection of these implicit rules is termed a **grammar of language.** Not until children are in school and study grammar do they learn **explicit rules**—rules that help them to learn (among other things) the eight parts of speech and then to jumble these words into a grammatically correct sentence.

Implicit rules are learned in early childhood. Within a short period of time and with almost no direct instruction children will analyze language completely. As Slobin (1971) points out:

> A child's mind is somehow "set" in a predetermined way to process the sorts of structures which characterize human language. This is not to say that the grammatical system itself is given as innate knowledge, but that the child has innate means of processing information and forming internal structures, and that, when these ca-

pacities are applied to the speech he hears, he succeeds in constructing a grammar of his native language. (p. 56)

There are rules to deal with the three main branches of grammar: **phonology,** the study of sounds and their structure, **syntax,** the way words come together to form sentences, and **semantics,** the meaning of words and sentences. Taken together, the rules form a complex system that ideally captures all aspects of language structure. How children go about learning the "elements of language," or the phonological, syntactic, and semantic rules that make communication possible has always fascinated psycholinguists as well as parents. Developmental **psycholinguistics** is the interdisciplinary field that studies how children acquire grammatical rules. The term underscores the fact that the two disciplines of psychology and linguistics now work together to further understanding of children's language development.

Most of the time astounding language achievements are taken for granted. Just think, however, how difficult and frustrating life would be if you were unable to communicate such simple thoughts as, "Pass a piece of the pepperoni pizza" or "I love your hazel eyes." The gift of language, for many generations, was assumed to be unique to humans alone. For a further discussion of this issue see "Focus on Issues."

THEORIES OF LANGUAGE ACQUISITION

How do children learn language? Numerous theories have been proposed to account for the normal development and use of language. The three major theorists are B. F. Skinner, Noam Chomsky, and Dan Slobin. Skinner maintains that language is learned entirely from experience. Chomsky is the leading proponent of the theory that states that environment plays a limited role in the acquisition of language. According to him, children are born with an innate capacity to acquire language. Slobin's theory conceptualizes language development in terms of both environmental and biological factors.

FOCUS ON ISSUES

Chimps and Language

Can animals use language? Gardner and Gardner (1969) are the pioneers in animal language research. They raised a baby chimp, Washoe, in their home and communicated with it, using the symbols of American Sign Language. American Sign Language uses signs to represent objects or concepts—for example, rubbing the first finger against the teeth for "toothbrush," tapping the head for "hat," or tapping the thigh for "dog." Washoe picked up the vocabulary easily and quickly. After 4 years of teaching, she used a vocabulary of about 150 signs. She also learned to use combinations of two or three signs together quite often.

Terrace (Terrace, Petitto, Sanders, & Bever, 1979) raised a chimp named Nim in his home. For the 4 years that Nim lived there, he was taught, like Washoe, to communicate using American Sign Language. Terrace, however, videotaped more than 20,000 sign utterances and was able to analyze Nim's ability to create new signs and combine symbols. He found no evidence that Nim could combine symbols to create new meanings, despite his ability to learn a vocabulary.

There also is a computer-communicating monkey, Lana (Rumbaugh & Gill, 1976). Lana types messages on a keyboard and receives visual symbols back via a console above the keyboard situated in her room at the Yerkes Primate Research Center. The benevolent computer also delivers candy, fruit, and other items requested by Lana. Lana simply types, "Please machine give me movie." She is then shown a 30-second segment from the film *A Gorilla's First Year.* Another command from Lana, "Please machine give me tickle," and one of Lana's trainers comes into Lana's cage and tickles her.

Washoe, Nim, and Lana have led us to believe that chimpanzees can perform varieties of linguistic tasks. However, Terrace noted that while Nim had learned new vocabulary words, and his utterances became longer and longer, they did not increase in complexity. The following utterance by Nim exemplifies this point: "Give orange me, give eat orange me, eat orange give me eat orange give me you." This does not represent an increase in grammatical complexity compared to Nim's shorter utterances. These research studies on language acquisition in chimpanzees tell us that while these chimps do communicate, they are not quite as facile language users as the human child. Terrace concludes:

For the moment, our detailed investigation suggests that an ape's language learning is severely restricted. Apes can learn many isolated symbols . . . but they show no unequivocal evidence of mastering the conversational, semantic, or syntactic organization of language. (Terrace et al., p. 899)

As you shall see, unlike chimpanzees, children do master the phonological, semantic, and syntactic organization of language development. Children don't just acquire words, but instead acquire a basic rule system that makes it possible for them to understand and generate an infinite array of complex sentences.

B. F. SKINNER'S BEHAVIORISTIC THEORY

Little Henry, lying in his crib, is contentedly babbling away in what sounds like a language from some remote country. He blurts out a sound that resembles "mama." Mother, near at hand and unable to suppress her joy, picks Henry up and hugs and kisses him. "You said 'Mama!' " she coos with glee. Just to make sure Henry doesn't forget, his mother repeats "mama" a few dozen times, interspersing the repetitions with more kisses and hugs. If surprised little Henry responds with a meaningless babble, he does not receive such a positive response from his mother.

Learning theorists, particularly Skinner (1972), believe that language occurs through the action of the environment shaping the individual's behavior. In particular, learning a language comes about through reinforcement as well as by imitation. Although babies may be born with the tendency to babble, these early sounds are gradually shaped into meaningful language by the way in which those around them respond to the sounds babies make. Sounds that are not reinforced eventually are extinguished. Thus, children come to use language by operant conditioning and imitation. Their attempts to say "mama" (and, of course, other words) are being reinforced and the strength of the reinforcement lends them the motivation to try. Children understand language by a classical conditioning process such that by endless repetition they come to associate "mama" with their mother. Eventually, the word sound comes to evoke the same behavior as the sight impression.

The behavioristic approach is somewhat simplistic and general. It is difficult, for example, to account for the uniformity of language acquisition throughout the human species. Virtually all children acquire a language, and they do so in some strikingly similar ways. If language acquisition were simply a matter of environment shaping the child's language, the resulting shapes and sequences and processes leading to those resulting shapes would be far more diverse than they in fact are.

Second, there is the other side of the "uniform" argument, the individually diverse argument.

Learning theory fails to explain children's use of novel sentences and words ("I doos it").

Adhering to the learning theory approach as the sole explanation for language acquisition presents further difficulties. For example, young children understand more language than they can use (receptive language). Learning theory has no explanation for the child's understanding of various words and phrases. Furthermore, reinforcement and imitation cannot account for the extraordinary rapidity with which children learn the language once they have begun to speak.

Moreover, adults tend to reinforce the content of speech, even though the phrases or sentences test grammatical limits. Brown, Cazden, and Bellugi (1968) compared the correctness of children's utterances that were followed by signs of approval from parents with those children's utterances that were followed by signs of disapproval. In the majority of instances, the grounds on which an utterance was approved or disapproved were not linguistic at all, but rather were based on the correspondence between utterance and reality—that is, the truth of the sentence. Thus, if the child says, "I drinked all my milk," the adult is likely to reinforce by saying, "Good, I'm proud of you." By the same token, the adult is likely to fail to reward a grammatically correct sentence if the sentence is untrue: "I am asleep." "No, you're not."

Children are exposed to many sentences, yet what they learn is not those specific sentences, but the organizational principles underlying them. What young children say is in the main not sentences that are repetitious of those they have heard, but rather sentences they have created according to their own rule system. It is difficult to see in what sense the young child is being—or could be—reinforced here. In light of these criticisms, it is probably best to think that reinforcement and imitation are two strategies by which children learn language, but not the only ones.

NOAM CHOMSKY'S NATIVISTIC THEORY

Chomsky and Lenneberg find the learning model naive and untenable. To Lenneberg (1967), the emergence of speech is under strict maturational control. He discusses several universals in language development to underscore the innate maturational phenomena of language development:

1. The onset of language regularly occurs between the 2nd and 3rd years of life.
2. Language emerges before it is of any immediate use to children.
3. Early vocalizations, such as cooing and babbling, do not represent practice or learning requirements for later language acquisition.

Chomsky (1968, 1986) also believes that language development is primarily a matter of maturation and that the environment is of little importance. The only environmental factor necessary for the child to learn to speak is exposure to some language. In other words, knowledge of language rules—rules of how words are combined into meaningful phrases and sentences (syntax)—is biologically based.

The Language Acquisition Device   According to Chomsky, every human being is born with a highly specialized innate capacity to acquire language, which he calls a **language acquisition device (LAD).** Every child is born with a universal linguistic structure, which guides a child's efforts to grasp underlying rules of grammar. The brain's language acquisition device allows a young child to deduce the basic rule system just by listening to language without being taught. Children discover abstract regularities in the speech they hear, analyze these patterns, and reproduce the results of this analysis in their own language.

LAD accounts for the fact that all children proceed through the same stages of language acquisition despite great differences in their vocabulary or native language. It also accounts for children's commonly made errors in forming plurals ("feets"), past tense ("goed"), and negatives ("no go bed"), which they could not possibly have heard and thus imitated.

Chomsky suggests that the speech heard by the child enters the LAD, and by the processing that goes on there, unconsciously creates ideas about language rules. The inborn rules that make up the LAD and the special acquired rules of a specific language constitute the grammar for that language—its system of rules.

It should be pointed out that there are special language areas in the brain, the principal one referred to as *Broca's area,* so named after Pierre-Paul Broca. Broca did extensive research on this area of the brain and discovered that when damage occurred, *aphasia* was frequently the result. Children and adults suffering from aphasia are often unable to name objects or unable to produce words at all. Another area in the brain that is implicated in speech is *Wernicke's area.* Damage to this area of the brain may result in inability to process auditory statements or follow simple instructions ("Put the book on the kitchen table."). The existence of LAD, however, has not been empirically verified (or disproved, for that matter).

Surface and Deep Structure   Part of the child's ability to learn language is an inborn understanding of the basic structure of language, which Chomsky calls **deep structure.** The deep structure represents the meaning or idea behind the words in a sentence. The other level of understanding that takes time to learn is the **surface structure,** which is the sentence you see going from one word to the next across the page.

The following sentences will help to illustrate the differences between these two levels of understanding.

The girl swung the hammer.

The hammer was swung by the girl.

These two sentences have different surface structures, yet they mean the same thing. Both are talking about a girl who is swinging a hammer. So the deep structure is the same. The same trick works the other way.

The shooting of the hunters was terrible.

This sentence has only one surface structure, but two plausible meanings: (a) hunters were shooting badly and (b) hunters were being shot. In this case, there are two deep structures and one surface structure. The deep structure is transformed or translated into a surface structure by applying a set of rules. These rules are called transformational rules, and Chomsky's theory is called a theory of **transformational grammar.**

One difficulty with Chomsky's theory is that it does not give a great deal of attention to semantic development. Many consider this to be a major deficiency. Furthermore, it is rather difficult to make statements about a possible LAD. No one has verified or disproved that the brain actually contains this special language device. Because of a general lack of empirical nutrition, Chomsky's theory is gradually expiring.

DAN SLOBIN'S LINGUISTIC THEORY

Slobin (1971, 1973, 1988) attempts to establish a compromise between these two extremes. His theory assumes that biological factors influence the course of language acquisition, but he insists that interaction between children and adults is absolutely necessary if language skills are to develop. Innate mechanisms alone cannot explain the child's mastery of language, and that mastery involves more than conditioning and imitation.

Slobin agrees with Chomsky that there is a special, innate capacity for language in humans. Special features of the brain and articulatory apparatus make it clear that language capacity has a distinct biological foundation. Species-specific behavior and distinct neural and anatomical structures are good evidence for the special evolution of those capacities, preserved in the genetic code, which make us mature into speaking creatures. The uniquely human biological foundations of language thus support the theoretical and empirical arguments for inborn language capacities in human beings.

Slobin is not debating an innate capacity in humans that enables almost all members of the species to be successful in this incredible feat of learning a language. Rather, his argument centers on the nature of this innate ability. Is it some sort of advanced knowledge that is activated by language exposure? Is it processing abilities?

Slobin suggests that the special capacity of children for acquiring language may be special processing strategies or operating principles that enable children to figure out how language works. In Slobin's (1971) words, "A child is not born with a set of linguistic categories but with some sort of

process mechanisms—a set of procedures and inference rules, if you will—that he uses to process linguistic data. The linguistic universals, then, are the result of an innate cognitive competence" (p. 114). He suggests that every child begins life with some initial procedures for perceiving, storing, and analyzing linguistic experience, and for making use of capacities and accumulated knowledge for producing and interpreting utterances.

Moreover, although Skinner and Chomsky see children as passive participants in learning language, Slobin suggests an active, curious child. Slobin (1985) remarks that, "in one way or another, every modern approach to language acquisition deals with the fact that language is constructed anew by each child, making use of innate capacities of some sort, in interaction with experiences of the physical and social worlds" (pp. 1158–1159). Recent investigations are revealing children as active language learners who are constantly analyzing what they hear, and then proceeding in a methodical, predictable way to put together the jigsaw puzzle of language (Moskowitz, 1978). "Linguistic competence is not intuitive but the fruit of some long and dramatic performances nurtured by prelinguistic characteristics at the start and spurred to full flower through the child's cognitive contact with a speaking environment" (Reynolds & Flagg, 1977, p. 365).

It is apparent from our review of the principal theories of language development that the literature is complex and controversial. The debate goes on; however, it does not center on whether or not there is an innate capacity in humans that enables learning to speak. Rather, the debate centers on the nature of this innate ability. There is also an ongoing debate about the role that language plays in thinking. Does thought influence language or does language influence thought?

THOUGHT AND LANGUAGE

Thought and language appear to travel independent courses that intersect during the second year of life. Before that time you can observe vocalization without meaning (cooing and babbling), as well as action patterns without verbal labels (reaching and grasping). The first stage of the integration of language and thought involves the naming of objects.

JEAN PIAGET'S VIEW

Piaget (1955) suggests that the rudiments of intelligence evolve before language develops. That is, cognitive development comes first, which in turn makes language development possible. He does not believe that language is entirely necessary for cognitive development. Piaget contends that the emergence of internal representation (of which language is one form) increases the powers of thought in range and speed. Children can have thoughts about objects before they can name them; thus, not having a language does not prevent the individual from thinking. To Piaget, then, language is not the cause of intellectual advancement, but merely a tool used in operational thinking.

Piaget argued that language is a reflection of cognition, rather than being independent from cognition or a shaper of it. Children begin with a sensorimotor understanding of the world and then try to find linguistic ways to express that knowledge. Sensorimotor knowledge determines the forms language takes. Development of cognition takes precedence over the acquisition of language. Language allows the child to describe or make public a system that would otherwise remain private.

JEROME BRUNER'S AND LEV VYGOTSKY'S VIEW

Bruner (1964) disagrees with Piaget. He believes that language ability affects almost every aspect of the child's thought. Language is a potent instrument in structuring thought and regulating cognitive behavior. Therefore, thinking would not be possible without language. Bruner is suggesting an idea that was first suggested by Russian psychologists Lev Vygotsky and A. R. Luria over 50 years ago.

Vygotsky (English edition, 1962) believes that when children are young, speech does not involve

thought (babbling), and thought does not involve speech. At some point in the maturational cycle (generally around age 2), speech and thought combine forces. When this occurs, they begin to mutually influence one another: Thought takes on some verbal characteristics and speech becomes rational as the expressive outlet for thought. As Vygotsky (1962) states, "Speech begins to serve intellect and thoughts begin to be spoken" (p. 43). Children's thoughts are initially directed by the child saying things out loud. Gradually, however, the child's language becomes internalized—that is, the child engages in an internal dialogue. This inner speech comes to help the child solve complex problems. While Piaget felt that language was not necessary for thinking, Vygotsky saw it as constantly interacting with thought.

Vygotsky was particularly interested in the role of egocentric speech in affecting children's thought. Egocentric speech, or private speech, as it is commonly referred to, can be thought of as speech for self. To illustrate, a young child may give a running commentary of describing her actions as she washes her baby doll, "Now I am going to wash her hair and I have to be careful not to get soap in her eyes." Such overt speech is carried out with apparent satisfaction even though it does not function to communicate.

Vygotsky believed private speech plays a specific role in affecting children's thoughts and problem solving. Language can serve to guide children's behavior (and thus their thoughts), but young children cannot yet use language covertly, "in their heads." With development, the self-regulating function of language changes so that children can direct their behavior using inner speech. In other words, private speech serves as a cognitive self-guidance system, and then goes underground as covert verbal thought.

Piaget believed that the egocentric speech of preschoolers reflects their general egocentric perspective of the world. What Piaget is talking about when he uses the term *egocentric* is what he sees as children's inability to differentiate between themselves and the world around them. According to Piaget, there is an early period of development in

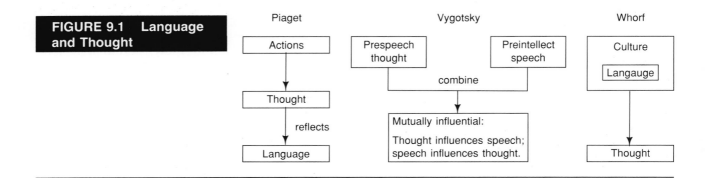

FIGURE 9.1   Language and Thought

children's lives when they cannot distinguish be-tween themselves and the object world. They cannot make generalizations and they cannot look at what they see from someone else's perspective. Children's point of view is limited, not because they are egotistical but because they do not yet have the capacity for reversibility, for seeing or imagining the world from more than one point of view. As they become increasingly able to de-center their cognition and perception and see the point of view of others, private speech decreases. For Piaget, private speech plays no functional role in cognitive development but is merely symptom-atic of ongoing mental activity. Most recent re-search suggests that Vygotsky was closer to the truth than Piaget, suggesting that most private speech has a cognitive self-guidance function.

BENJAMIN WHORF'S VIEW

If language has an impact on thought, does it also influence the way our world is perceived and structured? Whorf (1956) believes that language af-fects thought. He suggests that the form of a par-ticular language affects an individual's perception of the world. He points out that languages differ drastically; therefore, the world is experienced dif-ferently by speakers of different languages. For ex-ample, since Eskimos have a greater number of categories to describe snow, Whorf hypothesizes that they will have a greater ability to see different kinds of snow compared with others whose lan-guage has fewer categories. There is a problem

with Whorf's theory, similar to the chicken-and-egg concept. Does the difference in language lead to different perceptions or do different perceptions lead to different word categorizations? Figure 9.1 summarizes how these theorists depict the role of language in thought.

ELEMENTS OF LANGUAGE

One important way of studying the development of language in children is to describe their progress in learning the basic rules in phonological, syntac-tic, and semantic development. With the exception of many subtle refinements, children have com-pleted the greater part of the language process by the age of 5 (Moskowitz, 1978). By that age, chil-dren have discovered the rules for combining sounds into words; they will have discovered the meaning of words and the rules for combining them into meaningful sentences; and they will know the intricate uses of language and its social requirements.

PHONOLOGICAL DEVELOPMENT

The study of how children go about learning the rules for combining basic sound patterns, or **pho-nemes,** is known as *phonology*. Table 9.1 lists the phonemes of American English. It is from these 34 basic sounds that all words in the English language are formed.

It appears that the child has the ability to pro-duce a vast number of phonemes, including those

Benjamin Whorf believed that a particular language affects the individual's perception of the world. Because Eskimos have many words to describe snow, Whorf hypothesized that they have a greater capacity to see different kinds of snow compared to others who have few words to describe snow.

TABLE 9.1   Common Phonemes for the English Language

CONSONANT PHONEMES

p	(pass)	δ	(this)	n	(no)
b	(but)	s	(so)	nj	(ring)
t	(to)	z	(zero, boys)	l	(love)
d	(do)	š	(should)	w	(wish)
k	(kiss, calm)	ž	(azure)	hw	(when)
g	(go)	č	(church)	y	(yes)
f	(for)	J	(Jim)	r	(run)
v	(value)	m	(more)	h	(how)
θ	(thing)				

VOWEL PHONEMES

i	(bi t)	e	(bet)	ae	(map)
i	(chi ldren)	ə	(above)	a	(not)
u	(put)	o	(boat)	c	(law)

Source: From *The Psychology of Speech and Language* (p. 72) by J. DeVito, 1970, New York: McGraw Hill, Inc.

that are not a part of the English language. Most research has lent credence to the idea that infants start out ready to learn any language and only gradually narrow down their learning to their native tongue (Moskowitz, 1978). Because certain sounds which are not indigenous to English are generally not reinforced, they are dropped from the child's repertoire. For a child who grows up learning only one language, the movement of the muscles of the vocal tract ultimately become so overpracticed that eventually it is difficult to pronounce those that have not been rehearsed. On the other hand, children who learn at least two languages appear to retain a greater flexibility of vocal musculature (Moskowitz, 1978). Figure 9.2 lists the common phonemes for American English and the age level for the acquisition of these speech sounds.

FIGURE 9.2   The Acquisition of Speech Sounds

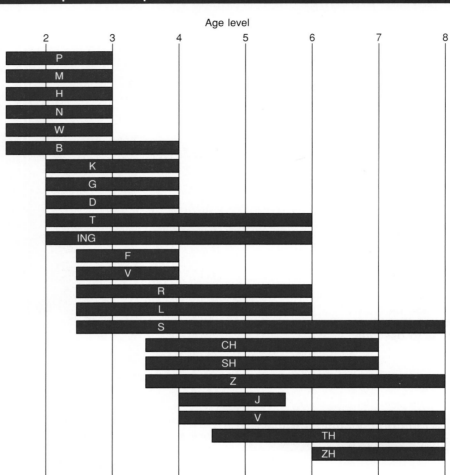

Source: From "When Are Speech Sounds Learned?" by E. Sanders, 1972, in *Journal of Speech and Hearing Disorders, 37,* p. 62. Copyright 1972 by the American Speech Language Hearing Association. Reprinted by permission.

SYNTACTIC DEVELOPMENT

Syntactic rules govern the ordering of words in a sentence. Initially the very general rules are hypothesized, and gradually they are narrowed down by the addition of more precise rules, which apply to a more restricted set of sentences. That is, children are continually revising and refining the rules of their internal grammar, learning increasingly detailed subrules, until they achieve a set of rules that enable them to create the full array of complex, adult sentences. Children acquire the details of the syntactic system in a systematic and orderly way.

SEMANTIC DEVELOPMENT

Semantics refers to the rules governing the meaning of sentences and words, or **morphemes.** When phonemes are combined so that they express meaning, they are called morphemes. For example, if the phonemes "k," "a," and "t" were combined they would form a morpheme, "cat." Not all morphemes are words; some are word fragments. For example, the prefixes (pre-, re-, ex-, con-), the suffixes (-tion, -est, -ic, -ly), and the verb tense markers (-ing, -ed) are also morphemes.

One component of semantics is how the child uses words to refer to objects and events. There have been two contrasting explanations offered by investigators to explain how children initially attach meanings to words. Clark (1975, 1983) of Stanford University re-examined old diary studies in which parents recorded their children's early communication attempts. She noticed that the development of words during the first several months of the one-word stage seemed to follow a basic pattern. Her theory is known as the **semantic feature hypothesis**. The meaning of a word is composed of semantic features associated with a particular object or event. Children tend to notice features that are directly perceived through their senses and apply the word when one or more of these features are present. That is, children learn that words have very concrete, perceptual features or attributes (a dog is four-legged, barks, has a tail). The meaning of a word is to be understood as specifiable in terms of a set of perceptual features.

Nelson (1973, 1979) suggests that children may initially learn the meaning of words by attending to their function. Word meaning may not exist apart from the context in which the words are used. This theory is known as the **functional core hypothesis**. Nelson believes that meanings are attached to words on the basis of the functions of the objects named by the words. To illustrate, children first encounter a ball. They form a scheme of the representation of the situations in which they have encountered the ball: mother throws, picks up, holds; I throw, pick up, hold. The ball bounces and rolls. Children encounter the ball again, and certain functional features of the ball are noted again (throw, catch, bounce, roll). Development of meaning involves the children's acquisition of experiences with a ball leading to a matching of common functional experiences between the first and

second experiences. It is in this way that children learn the meaning of certain words.

Superficially, there appears to be disagreement about exactly what kinds of early experiences lead to the meanings children express in their earliest words. Clark appears to be saying that reception of sensory input from hearing, seeing, feeling, and tasting is enough to provide children with data to organize into categories. Nelson holds that active experience with the environment, such as movement and participation, provides the bases for early categorization. Both viewpoints, however, place the locus of meaning in children's early experience with the environment before any language has been learned or any attempts to teach them language have occurred.

INFANCY AND EARLY CHILDHOOD

Understanding the fundamental insights into the nature of children's linguistic abilities in phonological, syntactic, and semantic areas helps us to understand the process of language development. As children gradually form more specific and sophisticated rules, language development proceeds through various stages of development.

Language development is divided into two periods: prelinguistic and linguistic. Before infants speak their first intelligible words, they are called **prelinguistic**. They communicate to us initially through their crying, cooing, and babbling. The **linguistic** period begins when children utter their first words, followed by the two-word stage, and then simple sentences known as telegraphic speech. Thus, as Table 9.2 shows, the acquisition of language is hierarchically organized.

PRELINGUISTIC DEVELOPMENT

Crying At the beginning, an infant has no language other than crying. Although the newborn behaves in ways that can be very informative to the skilled observer or parent, there is no intention to transmit information and no expectation of any effect on the world as a result of this behavior (Shatz, 1983). Obviously, the infant's cry may have a communicative value, but it appears that in the

TABLE 9.2 The Acquisition of Language	Item	Age at Which Produced
	Single sound—for example, "ma," "da"	6 months
	Repetition of single sound—for example, "ba, ba, ba"	8 months
	One-word stage—for example, "mama"	12 months
	Two-word stage, for example, "red truck"	24 months
	Sentences produced, for example, "Mama give me car"	30 months

Language development mirrors this sequential organization. The production of sounds precedes the production of single words, the production of single words precedes the production of sentences, and so on.

first 9 months, this behavior is, from the infant's point of view, merely a built-in reaction to an internal state. Although cries may not be purposeful, behavioral expressions of internal states may still be necessary to the establishment of later intentional communication systems. Adults recognize the internal states for which these behavioral expressions stand. Infants cry, or reach toward their goals, and the adult interprets their desires and intervenes to meet them. Children, however, do not realize when they emit their signals that they will serve a communicative purpose.

A number of investigators suggest that the onset of communicative intentions and conventional signaling occurs around 9 to 10 months of age for most infants. Before that time, intentional communication does not take place. In the latter half of the first year of life, a major cognitive milestone is reached, which facilitates the process of effective communication. Children develop the capacity to behave intentionally. Children, for example, are able to inaugurate a successful means-end series of actions in order to solve a problem such as getting a desired toy (Piaget, 1955).

Bates (1979a) has underscored the importance of the 9- to 13-month period for the emergence of intentional communication. As can be seen in Figure 9.3, an infant is placed at point A, facing the goal out of reach at point B. The adult who will eventually obtain the goal for the child is placed at right angles at point C.

Before 8 or 9 months, children will reach, fuss, and perhaps cry in the direction of B (goal). If they are sufficiently unhappy, they may cease their efforts altogether and turn to C (adult) for comfort.

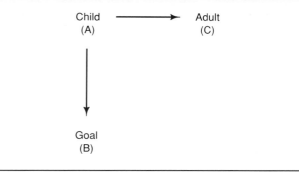

FIGURE 9.3   Schema for Testing the Emergence of Intentional Communication

Typically, they do not, while reaching toward the goal, turn to look at the adult. Around 9 months of age, this pattern changes. Infants begin to interrupt their goal behaviors to look toward the adult, and their eye contact shifts back and forth from point C to point B. Furthermore, if the adult does not move toward the goal, the child may vocalize more loudly and substitute or add different signals. Hence, the child's signaling behavior now appears to be contingent on the actions of the adult, rather than on the position of the goal itself. From this sort of evidence, it is inferred that the child now has intentional control over his communicative behaviors as signaling devices, rather than as reactions to internal states. Try the experiment in "Studying Children."

Cooing and Babbling   Children typically do not say their first words until approximately 10 to 12 months of age, but these words are preceded by a history of vocalization. By 2 months, infants have developed the musculature to produce certain sounds basic to language. With increased control of the tongue and mouth, a baby progresses to babbling, which is largely controlled by maturational factors rather than inputs from the environment. Even deaf babies babble around 4 months of age, and the babbles of French, Chinese, and American babies are indistinguishable at 5 months (Nakazima, 1962). The babbling sounds become differentiated beginning at around 6 months when infants begin taking on the characteristics of the language that surrounds them.

Babbling involves the prolonged production of a wide variety of speech sounds. Infants are busy working on disassembling the language to find the separate sounds that comprise that language. At 3 to 4 months, most infants' vocalizing consists of open vowel sounds. They say "aaa" and "ooo." Often they are described as **cooing.** Although all infants increase and diversify their vocalizations during these months, there are marked differences in the number of different sounds made and the richness of their use. Highly stimulated infants are far more vocal than less stimulated ones. A substantial amount of evidence points to the important role the baby's surroundings play in influencing these early vocalizations. Babies will vocalize

more when they are touched and when sounds are greeted by a response that enables them to interact with people around them.

Conversing with Others "Conversations" between parent and child consist of facial expressions, gestures, and movements, as well as sounds. The definite intent is to communicate. Parents and babies communicating in this way fall into a conversational rhythm such that, although either partner may initiate the interaction, they then take turns, so that the vocalizations, smiles, expressions, and movement of each mesh into those of the other as if they danced together to the same tune (Kaye, 1982).

Once children begin to utter words, their turn taking is suddenly nearly perfect. Interruptions drop to only a small percentage of all turns. It is interesting to note that turn taking is not so easy for sign-language-using apes to learn to do. They are terrible about interrupting. In fact, Terrace et al. (1979) argue that this is the major reason for the meagerness of their linguistic accomplishments, compared to humans. They have acquired surprisingly large vocabularies, but have not progressed to producing long sequences of signs. This may be because as soon as they recognize a sign or two they respond, and as soon as they produce one they expect a response. Children, on the other hand, expect their turns to be monitored and responded to as a whole, and expect to monitor and respond to the whole turn of their partner.

Progression in Babbling As babies continue to make more varied sounds, they begin, by the fifth or sixth month, to combine them into a series of sounds resembling language, which we call **babbling.** Although the age at which infants start babbling varies widely, most infants do so by the time they are 6 months of age. By 6 months, infants engage in a variety of sounds, including those of consonants, and will carry on long babble conversations with their parent.

At 7 months, the infant's babble becomes enriched by two-syllable "words." The syllables are quite distinct; they are not lifted subjectively out of a blur of sound, but can be written down phonetically, as they are uttered, with a high degree of

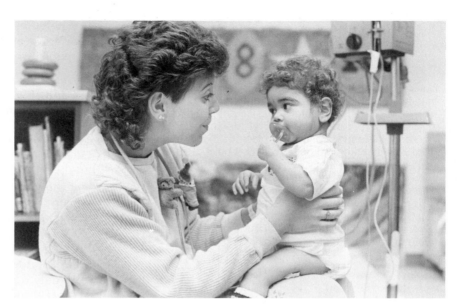

While infants are considered to be prelinguistic, infants and their mothers do engage in an intricate prototype of human communication.

agreement between one listener and another. (Try the "Studying Children" experiment.) The infant says words like "mimi," "ippi," "aja," and so forth. By late infancy, babbling begins to take on the intonations and rhythms of the baby's native tongue.

By the eighth month, most infants have learned to listen to and try to join conversations that are not directly aimed at them. If mother and father are talking, and the infant is sitting between them, his head will turn from one adult to the other and back again, as if closely watching a tennis match. Soon children learn how to interrupt; they develop a shout for attention (Rubin & Fisher, 1982; Rubin, Fisher, & Doering, 1980).

STUDYING CHILDREN

BABBLING

Spend some time with a 6-month-old child to listen carefully to her babbling sounds. Can you phonetically write the sounds down (aaa, ooo, di, and so on), or does it appear to be a blur of sounds? What vowels are repeated more frequently? What consonants?

Toward the end of the eighth month, and in the ninth, the repetitive babbling syllables are strung together into long, drawn-out phrases of four or more syllables, such as "loo-loo-loo-loo." Sometimes infants repeat a sound over and over again; sometimes they have more variety—"ah-dee-dah-dah."

Phonological Achievements Recognizing different speech sounds is the beginning of understanding a language and learning to use it. Almost from the moment of birth a baby pays special attention to the sounds of speech—a skill basic to learning to talk. Infants have receptive abilities, enabling them to hear sounds, discriminate among different sounds, and interpret them. For example, research shows that young infants turn their heads toward the sound of someone talking more than toward any other sound. By the end of the first month, infants discriminate the human voice from other sounds and can be quieted by soft, high-pitched talking.

Thus, it appears that infants tend to find language sounds especially interesting. Eisenberg (1979) found that newborns consistently showed distinctive overt reactions (e.g., visual fixation, increased motor activity) when hearing complex auditory stimuli such as speech sounds and tone sequences, while they showed little overt response to other sounds, such as pure tones or noise bands.

It appears that infants can discriminate basic phonemes shortly after birth. It has been found, for example, that 1-month-old babies can hear the small but important differences between such similar speech sounds as "pa" and "ba." The way scientists discovered that babies can hear these sounds is an interesting story.

Researchers observed that babies who are sucking from a bottle will suck more quickly when they hear a new sound. The infants sucked on a pacifier that held a pressure-sensitive electronic device. Measuring the rate of their sucking showed that when babies hear a new speech sound—"ba," for example—they suck very rapidly. After the sound is repeated several times, their sucking rate decreases to a steady level—they're getting used to the sound. However, when a new sound is introduced, such as "pa," their sucking rate increases once again and stays there until they become accustomed to that sound (Eimas, Sigueland, Jusczyk, & Vigorito, 1971). These findings suggest that either babies are born with the ability to recognize the subtle differences in speech sounds, or that they learn this ability very early in life.

Other studies have shown that infants can make discriminations among speech sounds that are *not* found in their native tongues and that their parents cannot make (Werker, Gilbert, Humphrey, & Tees, 1981). English-speaking adults have a difficult time discriminating phonetic contrasts that occur in Czech but that are not found in English. Yet, babies from English-speaking homes have little difficulty with these contrasts, suggesting that they were born with the ability (Trehub, 1976). Some discriminations, however, are made only with experience. In a study of 6- to 8-month-old infants (Eilers, Gavin, & Wilson, 1979), it was found that infants from English-speaking homes were unable to discriminate some phonetic contrasts that are found in Spanish but not in English. Babies from homes where Spanish was spoken had no trouble with such contrasts.

Similarly, some scientists used to believe that infants begin by babbling all the different speech sounds found in all human language. Later on, through differential social reinforcement or some similar mechanism, they gradually stop producing those speech sounds they do not hear in their speech communities and continue and practice those they do hear. Research evidence now suggests, however, that infants do not even come close to babbling all the world's speech sounds. This naturally implies that there will normally be a good number of speech sounds in whatever specific language they do learn that they will never have practiced during the babbling period.

What these and other data suggest is that the process of acquiring the basic sounds of one's language is, at least, a two-way street. Babies can make some sound discriminations that adult speakers of their language communities cannot make; with time, they lose the ability to make these contrasts, because they rarely hear them. There are other sound discriminations, however, that infants cannot make that adults of their language cultures can. The development of perceiving (and producing) language sounds involves a loss and acquisition of some discriminations.

LINGUISTIC DEVELOPMENT

One-Word Stage The babbling stage ends when infants utter their first words marking the transition from prelinguistic to linguistic development. Generally first words appear at 1 year of age. Children typically produce their first 30 words at a rate of three to five new words per month. The same children learn their next 30,000 words at a rate of 10 to 20 new words per day (Jones, Smith, & Landau, 1991). Children understand more language than they can speak but productive speech (what they actually produce, or say) is limited to single words at a time. Yet, children's one-word utterances carry more meaning than might be expected from their brevity. The term **holophrastic** speech has been used to describe the notion that toddlers' words sometimes serve as entire sentences. For example, if the child says "cookie," it is taken to mean that the child is expressing "I want a cookie." Bloom (1973, 1974) argues, however, for a more skeptical interpretation of one-word utterances. She believes that there is no evidence that the child understands anything about syntax. Our problem in evaluating these differing hypotheses is that we are attempting to read the mind of the child who is providing us with only the barest of clues, a single word.

No one knows for sure how words grow out of babbling. Sometimes it appears that children learn them overnight, but the process is a continuous one. One thing that is known is that first words incorporate the various speech sounds babies have been practicing while babbling. In fact, the resemblance between babbling and real words is so close that parents often mistake babbling sounds for real

While children speak in one-word utterances, they convey more meaning than can be expected from their brevity.

words before children have actually attached any meaning to them. Perhaps another reason why parents believe that infants' babbles are speech is the variation in intonation patterns.

It is so readily accepted that speech begins with single words that the question why infants should choose to begin in this way is seldom asked. Why does their speech not begin with the phrases that they hear repeated quite often, such as "night-night" or "upsadaisy"? If they are going to begin with single words, why do they choose certain words? We do not know. Some researchers speculate that infants may be able to store in their memories only a single word at this stage, not a word sequence. Perhaps they subjectively perceive certain isolated words, or the first or last or most stressed words of a sentence. These words may stand out from what is otherwise still a blur of talk. These "topic" words may be repeated more often. They learn the word "bottle" because the bottle is important to them, and because whatever is said about the bottle, that word is the one consistent sound in a vast complexity of other sounds they often hear: "Do you want your bottle?" "Here's your bottle of juice." "Let's get your bottle and have a nap." Moreover, some words may be used by some children because they are easy to pronounce—"mama," for example.

A Word Is a Word Is a Word First words are sometimes standard ones, correct copies of the adult word; more often, they are approximations. With such a variety of possible sounds, it is sometimes difficult to recognize a word as a word. It is probably safe to call a sound a word when the infant uses it consistently and exclusively for a single object or class of objects. "Caw" is a word if it always represents a certain object, such as a ball, and never anything other than a ball.

What do children talk about first? They talk about the objects around them and, in general, they show considerable agreement in their first words. Animals, food, and toys are the most frequently mentioned first words (Nelson, 1973). When children have a vocabulary of about 50 words, most of them use words for food, body parts, clothing, animals, household items, cars, and people. The words in these categories that occur most frequently are "juice," "milk," and "cookie" for food; "ear," "eye," and "nose" for body parts; "shoe," "hat," and "sock" for clothing; "ball" and "block" for toys; and "mama" and "dada" and "baby" for people. Relational words (big, little, short, more) appear quite early, but are not used in all their complexity. For example, a child may say "more milk," but it is not until much later that a child will use "more" in a relational sense (He got more candy than I did). No abstract nouns, those describing groups or concepts such as size, weight, or measure, appear before 2 years (Rubin & Fisher, 1982).

Phonological Achievement   Although children in the first stages of word formation may be able to articulate as many as eight consonants properly, they never use more than one in any individual word. This phenomenon can be seen clearly in one of Franke's (1912) examples of children's pronunciations of the German word *baum* (tree). Of the three children observed, one said "mau mau," one said "bau," and one said "maum." Although each of the three is different from the others, they have in common the fact that a word with two consonants was changed to a one-consonant form by dropping one consonant or substituting another for it. This may explain why young children produce "word distortions" when they try to say certain words. For example, "cup" may become "pup" or "cuc," elephant may become "ef," or telephone may become "te" or "fo."

While some children may not be able to pronounce certain phonemes, it is apparent that they know these sounds exist for certain words. Brown (1973) had what has become a classic conversation with a child who referred to a "fis." Brown repeated "fis," and the child indignantly corrected him, saying "fis." After several such exchanges Brown tried "fish," and the child replied, "Yes, fis!" It is clear that although the child was still unable to make the vocal distinction between the sounds "s" and "sh," he knew such a systematic phonological distinction existed.

Syntactic Achievement   Prior to the one-word stage, very little can be inferred about children's knowledge of syntax and semantics. The place to begin asking about syntactic and semantic knowledge is when they utter their first words. Early syntactic development, when the child communicates in one-word utterances, is not just a time for learning the meaning of words. In that period, a child is developing hypotheses about putting words together in sentences, and is already putting sentences together in meaningful groups. Scollon (1976) of the University of Hawaii observed that 19-month-old Brenda was able to use a series of one-word sentences to express what an adult might say with a construction of a multiword sentence. Brenda's pronunciation, which is represented phonetically below, was imperfect, and Scollon did not understand her words at the time. Later, when he transcribed the tape of their conversation, he heard the sound of a passing car immediately preceding the conversation and was able to identify Brenda's words as follows:

BRENDA: "Car (pronounced 'ka'). Car. Car. Car."
SCOLLON: "What?"
BRENDA: "Go. Go."
SCOLLON: (Undecipherable.)
BRENDA: "Bus (pronounced 'baish'). Bus. Bus. Bus. Bus. Bus. Bus. Bus. Bus."
SCOLLON: "What? Oh, bicycle? Is that what you said?"
BRENDA: "Not ('na')."
SCOLLON: "No?"
BRENDA: "Not."
SCOLLON: "No. I got it wrong."

Brenda was not able to combine two words syntactically to express "Hearing that car reminds me that we went on the bus yesterday. No, not on a bicycle." She could express that concept, however, by combining words sequentially.

Children's Semantic Achievement   In studying children's semantic knowledge, Bloom (1973) has observed that the words children use are more than just labels for things. Observations of infants suggest that these first words have a more complex communicative purpose. Infants do not simply state, "dog" as if to say, "That is a dog." Sometimes they use the word as an emphatic "Dog!" expressing surprise, annoyance, or delight at the dog's arrival. They use the word as a question, too. "Dog?" they ask, perhaps looking at an animal, perhaps hearing a noise outside. In the early stages of language development, children use words to serve different functions: as a statement, a negative, a request, or a demand. For example, a young child may use the word "push" in several ways.

STATEMENT: Push. (I push the car.)
  NEGATIVE: No push.
   REQUEST: [Will Daddy] push?
    DEMAND: Push!

Children are able to separate the different functions that are indicated by a word by applying their semantic knowledge of stress and pitch.

Another area of interest in semantic development is vocabulary development. Most infants will say three words by the end of the 12th month, whether these are standard, approximations, or self-words. Four or five words will be clear by the 15th month and six or seven by the 17th month. During the next 3 years, children will acquire over 1,800 words. Most agree that new words come very slowly at the beginning, so that the child·may acquire only one to three words a month between, say, 11 and 15 months. Most researchers also agree that there is a tremendous spurt in word acquisition during the 18- to 24-month range (Waxman & Kosowski, 1990), during which time the average toddler learns about 250 new words (see Table 9.3).

In early semantic development, it is not uncommon for children in the one-word stage to overextend the meanings of words used as nouns. **Overextension** refers to the tendency to generalize a word, based on some feature of the original object, and use it to refer to many other objects. For example, a child named Hildegard first used "ticktock" as the name for her father's watch, but she quickly broadened the meaning of the word: first, to include all clocks, then all watches, then a gas meter, then a firehose wound on a spool, and then

TABLE 9.3   Children's Average Vocabulary Size

Age (years; months)	Number of Words	Increment
0;8	0	
0;10	1	1
1;0	3	2
1;3	19	16
1;6	22	3
1;9	118	96
2;0	272	154
2;6	446	174
3;0	896	450
3;6	1222	326
4;0	1540	318
4;6	1870	330
5;0	2072	202
5;6	2289	217
6;0	2562	273

Source: From "The Development of Language in Children" by Roger Brown, 1973, in George A. Miller (Ed.), *Communication, Language, and Meaning* (p. 55), New York: Basic Books.

a bathroom scale with a round dial (Clark, 1975). Her generalizations appear to be based on her observation of common features of shape, roundness, dials, and so on.

According to Clark, a word's meaning for adults is made up of a set of component features or properties that serve to distinguish its meaning from other words. For example, "cat" comprises the features of four-legged animal, soft fur, whiskers, and so forth. When children first start trying to learn how to apply this word, they are apt to notice only a small subset of the adult set of features. For example, they may only notice that it applies to animals with four legs, and hence they overextend it to other animals besides cats. With subsequent experience, they add the missing features and thereby achieve the adult meaning of the term.

In general, children overextend meanings based on similarities of movement, texture, size, and most frequently, shape. The tendency to overextend word meanings can be amusing and perhaps on some occasions slightly embarrassing—as when your little girl happily greets every man she meets as "daddy." If children tend to overextend the meaning of a word, does this mean that they cannot tell the difference between the things they call by the same name? Perhaps not. Try the experiment in "Studying Children."

Children may also use a word within a smaller range than is used in adult language. This is known as **underextension.** For example, children may initially apply "cat" only to cats seen out the window, rather than to all cats. That child's problem is to get rid of an unneeded semantic feature (seen out the window) rather than, as Clark's theory would have it, to accumulate needed ones.

Two-Word Stage Between 18 and 24 months, two-word utterances appear. In this stage, children put together nouns, which started their naming, with main verbs and principal adjectives. They use their new "second word" to amplify what they used to communicate with one word by intonation and inflection only. Earlier they might watch the family cat depart through the backyard and say "Cat!" in tones of shock. Now they say, "Cat gone!" When two-word sentences first begin to appear, they are primarily of the following forms: subject-noun ("Mommy go"), verb and object ("Read it"), and verb or noun and location ("Bring home").

Two-word phrases allow the child to communicate more accurately. In one-word communication, a child may say "bikkit" just after consuming a biscuit. The mother may misunderstand and think the child has just made a comment about the biscuit he just ate. When, however, he says "more bikkit," he is less likely to be misunderstood and get his "bikkit" more quickly and efficiently.

Phonological Achievement The development of the sound system is a long process; it is generally not completed until age 7. Some sounds are more difficult to produce than others. At age 4, for example, children are still learning consonants such as "s" (as in ship), "v," and "z." Even though they can produce a large range of sounds, it does not mean that they will be able to use the sound in combination with other sounds. Three- and 4-year-olds have trouble with words like macaroni and ravioli. They also have trouble with double consonants such as "st," "dr," and "sm." Children often drop the first consonant—steak becomes take, for example.

Syntactic Achievement Syntactic knowledge advances, as the child is now able to express a primitive sense of property. Certain objects and spaces seem to be assigned to particular family members. Children's possessives always omit the possessive inflection, and they come out simply with "daddy chair" or "mommy dress" (Brown, 1973).

Children produce two or three words in succession and intend to express certain relations between ideas. They demonstrate that they have already learned the basic rules of grammar and syntax in their language. They invariably get the sequence of words right in the context of what they are trying to say. For example, if Sally saw a cat bite a dog, she might say, "Cat bite dog" or "Cat bite"—the word order being appropriate to the reference setting. It is this kind of discrimination with respect to order that shows that the child has in mind not only certain animals, persons, things, qualities, and actions, but definite structural relations among them.

Braine (1963) studied children's early syntactic development. He found that when an analysis was conducted on children's speech, at least two classes of words appeared. One contained a small number of words, each used frequently, known as the pivot class. The other contains more words, each infrequently used, known as the open class.

For example a child might say, "Allgone sticky," "Allgone shoe," "Allgone lettuce," "Allgone outside." Here "allgone" is the pivot word, and it occurs in the first position. A pivot word may occur in the first or second position, but each pivot word has its own fixed position. Moreover, pivot words never occur by themselves, or with other pivot words. Table 9.4 shows the pivot and open classes of three children studied by Brown and Bellugi (1964) and Braine (1963). Just a portion of each open class is represented; however, the pivot class is included in its entirety.

Research has raised some questions about the adequacy of the theory to explain syntactic development. Bowerman (1974) has shown that children may have words that satisfy one or two of the pivot-word criteria, but rarely do they meet them all. "No," for example, often occurs by itself (pivot words do not occur by themselves). Children may say, "Tommy bye-bye" and "bye-bye doggie" (pivot words occur in fixed positions). Finally, it has been shown that pivot words do occur with other pivot words—"allgone bye-bye." In brief, pivot grammar is too restrictive; children's language is rarely as simple as that.

Clark (1983) points out that children as young as 2 years of age commonly coin words when they need names for objects they are talking about. Among these are numerous compound nouns constructed of two nouns combined, as in "fire dog," for a large dog found at the site of a fire. Heavier stress is placed on the modifier, "fire," than on the second noun, "dog." The head noun, dog, picks out the category being talked about and the modifer, fire, identifies the subcategory by virtue of its bearing some relationship to fires. Moreover, in studying 96 2-year-old children, Clark, Gelman, and Lane (1985) found that children comprehend the relationship between the head noun and the modifier noun. That is, in using a compound word such as "apple knife," children were aware that this is a kind of knife connected with apples.

Semantic Achievement In studying children's semantic development, Nelson (1973) found that children's words tend to be referential (naming objects) or expressive (expressing wants or social in-

TABLE 9.4 Open and Pivot Classes

Braine		Brown	
P	O	P	O
			Adam
	boy		Becky
	sock	my	boot
allgone	boat	that	coat
byebye	fan	two	coffee
big	milk	a	knee
more	plane	the	man
pretty	shoe	big	mommy
my	vitamins	green	nut
see	hot	poor	sock
night-	mommy	wet	stool
night	daddy	dirty	Tinker
hi		fresh	Toy

Source: From "The Ontogeny of English Phrase Structure: The First Phase" by M. Braine, 1963, in *Language, 39*, p. 5. Copyright 1963 by the Linguistic Society of America. Reprinted by permission.

teractions). **Referential children** were most concerned with labeling, while **expressive children** used language for social purposes. Expressive children used words that were primarily personal-social, such as "bye-bye," "more," and "naughty." Referential children employed words that named objects, such as "doggie," "penny," and "moo" (for cow). In part, these differences seemed to reflect differences in child-rearing style on the part of the mothers. Referential children had parents who were object oriented and frequently named things. Expressive children had parents who focused on the child and social behaviors. The first-word combinations of a high-referential and a high-expressive child, each 16 months old, are listed below:

Child R	Child E
Daddy all gone	I do
Daddy shoe	You do
Daddy milk	I want it
Mommy bite	I don't want it
Mommy cookie	Do it
Coat on	Don't do it
Meat bite	I love you
Spoon milk	I don't know
Blanket dirt	What d'you want
Coat wet	Go away

Children often coin their own words. One child, whose father called a pumpkin a jack-o'-lantern and whose mother called it a pumpkin, coined his own term, punk-a-leeter.

Telegraphic Speech By the age of 3½, most children have learned the essential elements of language and use them creatively. They continue further learning of the sound system, better understanding of the grammar of language, vocabulary growth, and more sophisticated conversational skills.

There is no three-word stage in child language. Instead, following the two-word stage, children spend the next few years creating short sentences. Early **telegraphic speech** is characterized by multiple-word utterances. These communiques are short, simple sentences made up primarily of content words. These are words that are rich in semantic content, usually nouns and verbs. Speech is called telegraphic, because the sentences lack function words, tense endings on verbs, and plural endings on nouns: "Daddy go bye-bye car"; "Me want this story." As the telegraphic speech stage progresses, function words are gradually added to sentences.

Why do children typically omit low-information words and include high-information words, such as nouns and verbs? The explanations offered are that the child's memory span is too short to include more than just high-information words and

that their vocabulary is too limited to copy adult kinds of sentences.

Semantic and Syntactic Achievement As children's semantic knowledge expands, they begin to understand and appreciate relational contrasts. Words that specify relations among people, objects, and events occur quite early in language, although young children do not fully appreciate the meaning of many of these terms. The word "more," for example, is often one of the child's first words. Generally, it is a request for some kind of a repetition ("more tickle"). Yet, it is not until they are 3½ that children use this relational term in its full comparative sense to specify relations (She has more than I do). Understanding "less" does not occur until 4½ or 5. Relational words such as "big/little" are usually the first spatial adjectives to appear, followed by "short/tall" and "in/on" (deVilliers & deVilliers, 1979). Children hear these adjectives more than others and generally pay more attention to heights and lengths than to widths and thicknesses.

Children continue to make some semantic errors. For example, they frequently misinterpret passive constructions such as "The boy was hit by

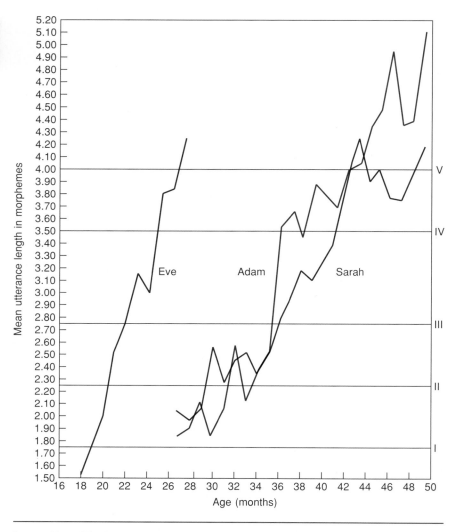

FIGURE 9.4   Mean Length Utterance for Three Children

Source: From "The Development of Language in Children" by R. Brown, 1973, in G. A. Miller (Ed.), *Communication, Language, and Meaning* (p. 55), New York: Basic Books.

the girl." They more readily understand the active version "The girl hit the boy" (Lempert, 1989). Children younger than 5 or 6 years tend to interpret passive construction as if it were an active sentence. One exception to this rule is passive sentences that make little sense. For example, even a 3-year-old would correctly interpret "The candy was eaten by the girl" because it is nonsense to assume that the candy was the agent doing the eating.

Most preschoolers have more than one category label for certain things (Au, 1990). For instance, they may know that their pet is an animal as well as a dog; that their toy train is a toy as well as a train. That is, they begin to learn that objects can be categorized at multiple levels. There is some evidence that even 2- and 3-year-olds can learn a new subordinate label, such as "terrier" and "mutt," for an object that they already have a basic label for, such as "dog" (Taylor & Gelman, 1989).

Brown (1973, 1977, 1988) has examined syntactic development during the telegraphic phase of language development. The result is a series of stages that describe different rule systems. Brown does not assign particular ages to these stages of syntactic development, but believes that children's **mean length utterance (MLU),** the number of words used in a sentence, is a more useful benchmark of children's syntactic sophistication than their age. Figure 9.4, for example, shows the relationship between chronological age and mean length utterance for three children: Eve, Adam, and Sarah. Note that while Eve is younger than Adam and Sarah, she progressed at almost twice their rate, showing a higher level of grammar sophistication.

In studying syntactic development, Brown noticed several types of errors that children make in forming the past tense of verbs and pluralizing nouns, which occur when children's MLU is 4 to 5 words. When forming the past tense of verbs, children learn a rule and then how to apply that rule. Initially, they may use irregular verb forms such as "came," "saw," and "went," but once they have formulated a rule for saying verbs in the past tense, they add the "ed" sound to all past-tense verbs, so that they say "goed" and "comed," as well as "jumped" and "laughed." They use this form even after they have heard the correct usage and after they have used correct forms. Once again, the child proves to be a sensible linguist by learning the "ed" tense that exhibits the least variation in form.

Parents sometimes become alarmed after their children discover the "ed" rule and continually say things like "I breaked it," "Mommy goed." This, however, is a normal phenomenon in language development, called *overregulation*—making the language more regular than it is. Similarly, children often overregularize the format of plurals.

When plurals begin to appear regularly, the child forms them according to the most general rule: Add the "s" or "z" sound to the end of the word to make it plural. At this point it is the child's overgeneralization of the rule that results in words such as "mans," "foots," or "feets," "sheeps," and "gooses." The grammatical mistakes the child makes are both logical (in the sense that they are wrong but logical deductions) and consistent from child to child.

Gleason (1958) invented a production test, known as the "wug test," to see whether children have mastered the English rules for making plurals. In one case they are shown a funny birdlike creature, such as seen in Figure 9.5, and are told, "This is a wug. Now there's another one. There are two . . . ?" If they correctly answer "wugs," one can be sure that they know how to make plurals because they could never have heard that word from anyone else.

FIGURE 9.5   An Example from Jean Berko Gleason's Wug Test

This is a wug.

Now there is another one.
There are two of them.
There are two _____ .

Source: From "The Child's Learning of English Morphology" by J. Berko, 1958, *Word, 14*, pp. 50–177. Copyright 1958 by the International Linguistics Association. Reprinted by permission.

TABLE 9.5   Three Stages in the Acquisition of Negative Sentences

STAGE 1	No . . . wipe finger. No a boy bed. No the sun shining. No money. No sit there. No play that. Not a teddy bear. Wear mitten no.
STAGE 2	I can't catch you. We can't talk. You can't dance. I don't like him. No pinch me. Don't bite me yet. He not little, he big. That no mommy. There no squirrels. He no bit you. I no taste them.
STAGE 3	I don't want cover on it. It's not cold. I didn't did it. I didn't see something. I isn't . . . I not sad. This no good. I not crying.

Source: From "Syntactic Regularities in the Speech of Children" by E. S. Klima and U. Bellugi, 1966, in J. Lyons and R. J. Wales (Eds.), *Psycholinguistic Papers* (p. 196), Edinburgh: Edinburgh University Press. Copyright 1966 by Edinburgh University Press. Reprinted by permission.

Studying the way children use negative forms in a sentence is another way to analyze children's syntactic structures. As you can see by examining Table 9.5, children acquire negative structures in a systematic, orderly, rule-governed way. Initially, children make a sentence negative by simply attaching "no" or "not" to the beginning of a declarative statement ("No singing song"; "No sun shining."). Negative words do not appear inside the sentence (Akiyama, 1984). In the next stage, children incorporate into their grammars more complex rules that generate sentences including the negatives "no," "not," "can't," and "don't" after the subject ("I don't want it"; "He not little; he big."). Sometimes they go overboard: "No, I don't not have none." In the third stage of acquiring negatives, many more details are incorporated. The main thing that still needs to be worked out is the use of pronouns: "I didn't see something"; "I don't want somebody to wake me up." (Moskowitz, 1978).

Each of these stages has brought about significant advances in language development. A summary of the milestones in language development may be found in Table 9.6.

MIDDLE CHILDHOOD

REFINEMENTS IN LANGUAGE DEVELOPMENT

By 6 years of age, children's language is well established; there are few deviations from the adult norms. Such deviations tend to be more in style than in grammar. Children in middle childhood have mastered the syntax of their language and have a rather extensive vocabulary. Around this age, children begin to use inflections in their speech. They may say, "He *broke* my toy." They also begin to build their auxiliary verb system: "Daddy go" becomes "Daddy has gone." Children master a number of rules for morphemes in language. They pluralize nouns, specify verb tense, include prepositions like "on" and "in," and insert articles "a" and "the." Vocabulary continues to grow as their experience continues and expands; by age 6, children have a vocabulary arsenal of between 8,000 and 14,000 words. These children seem to be in love with words—rhyming words, using words in an unusual way in order to form a secret code, and impressing others with their big words are exciting things for them.

The process of language refinement continues until the age of 10 and probably considerably longer for most children. By the time children are 6 or 7, however, the changes in language development may be so subtle and sophisticated that they go unnoticed. Learning about grammar continues until adolescence in two areas: (a) comprehension of increasingly complex grammatical structures us-

TABLE 9.6   Milestones in Language Development

At the Completion of:	Vocalization and Language
12 weeks	Markedly less crying than at 8 weeks; when talked to and nodded at, smiles, followed by squealing-gurgling sounds usually called cooing, that is vowel-like in character and pitch-modulated; sustains cooing for 15–20 seconds.
16 weeks	Responds to human sounds more definitely; turns head; eyes seem to search for speaker; occasionally some chuckling sounds.
20 weeks	The vowel-like cooing sounds begin to be interspersed with more consonantal sounds; acoustically, all vocalizations are very different from the sounds of the mature language of the environment.
6 months	Cooing changing into babbling resembling one-syllable utterances; neither vowels nor consonants have very fixed recurrences; most common utterances sound somewhat like *ma, mu, da,* or *di.*
8 months	Reduplication (or more continuous repetitions) becomes frequent; intonation patterns become distinct; utterances can signal emphasis and emotions.
10 months	Vocalizations are mixed with sound-play such as gurgling or bubble-blowing; appears to wish to imitate sounds, but the imitations are never quite successful; beginning to differentiate between words heard by making differential adjustment.
12 months	Identical sound sequences are replicated with higher relative frequency of occurrence and words (*mamma* or *dadda*) are emerging; definite signs of understanding some words and simple commands (Show me your eyes).
18 months	Has a definite repertoire of words—more than 3 but less than 50; still much babbling but now of several syllables with intricate intonation pattern; no attempt at communicating information and no frustration for not being understood; words may include items such as *thank you* or *come here,* but there is little ability to join any of the lexical items into spontaneous two-item phrases; understanding is progressing rapidly.
24 months	Vocabulary of more than 50 items (some children seem to be able to name everything in environment); begins spontaneously to join vocabulary items into two-word phrases; all phrases appear to be own creations; definite increase in communicative behavior and interest in language.
30 months	Fastest increase in vocabulary with many new additions every day; no babbling at all; utterances have communicative intent; frustrated if not understood by adults; utterances consist of at least two words, many have three or even five words; sentences and phrases have characteristic child grammar, that is, they are rarely verbatim repetitions of an adult utterance; intelligibility is not very good yet, though there is great variation among children; seem to understand everything that is said to them.
3 years	Vocabulary of some 1,000 words; about 80% of utterances are intelligible even to strangers; grammatical complexity of utterances is roughly that of colloquial adult language, although mistakes still occur.
4 years	Language is well-established; deviations from the adult norm tend to be more in style than in grammar.

Source: From *Biological Foundations of Language* (pp. 128–130) by E. H. Lenneberg, 1967, New York: Wiley.

ing conjunctions (although, since, unless), and (b) those in which some sentence elements are embedded, such as "The lady *who came to sing* was funny." Average children's use of these constructions may begin at an early age, but full control may not be apparent until children are 11 or 12.

Moreover, children use such words as "because," "so," and "but" to signal subordinate clauses. This kind of language use is indicative of the presence of complex syntactic rules, and it is not fully developed until adolescence, although its beginnings can be seen in 3-year-olds.

Despite these tremendous advances over a few short years, children in middle childhood do have some language limitations. For example, they take all statements literally and tend not to understand figures of speech. If we say something like "The cat's got her tongue," the child may think that the cat is literally holding the child's tongue.

Nor do they always understand sarcasm. A remark that may be obvious to you from the speaker's voice as not necessarily what he means is not so for younger children. A complete understanding of sarcasm actually requires several quite complex ideas. First, children would have to understand that the speaker did not intend what was said literally, but rather intended to convey a meaning quite different (often opposite to) the literal meaning. In addition, children need to understand that the speaker knew that children knew that the speaker did not mean to be taken literally—otherwise, children might think that the speaker was lying. Some studies (Winner, Kaplan, & Rosenblatt, 1989; Winner, Windmueller, Rosenblatt, Bosco, Best, & Gardner, 1987) have shown that by the age of 8, children are able to understand the intended meaning in sarcastic utterances in at least some cases. Capelli, Nakagawa, and Madden (1990) have shown that children tend to rely on intonation, not context cues, when interpreting sarcastic remarks, which may account for their less than 100% accuracy in identifying sarcastic speech. Adults tend to use both cues. For example, adults sometimes use context cues. You and your roommate oversleep and are late for class; you arrive at class and find that you'll be taking a pop quiz, and after class a friend informs you that he could not get the tickets for a rock concert. Your roommate then turns to you and says, "This is turning out to be a great day." The second important cue is intonation. When someone makes a sarcastic remark it is generally said in a characteristically mocking intonation. In Capelli et al.'s (1990) study, 32 third-graders and 32 sixth-graders were exposed to tape-recorded stories. Some of the stories involved contextual cues and others involved intonation cues to sarcasm. The results indicated that both age groups relied more heavily on intonation than context to help them infer the intent of the speaker.

A knowledge of phonology, semantics, and syntax enables children to produce grammatically correct sentences, but there is no guarantee that the speech they generate is appropriate for the setting in which they find themselves. Children in middle childhood are becoming increasingly aware of the **pragmatics** of language, the rules specifying when to say what to whom in order to communicate effectively. In middle childhood, there is a greater use of gestures, pauses, and facial expressions. In addition, there is greater facility in adapting information to fit the listener's needs and adopting the listener's point of view if the situation warrants it. Pragmatic abilities and social editing skills evolve rather gradually over the course of childhood as new social contexts are encountered. Children continue to become more adept at varying their way of talking to teachers, peers, and parents.

SENSE OF HUMOR

Due to an increased knowledge base, communication skills, and more advanced abilities to process information, children in middle childhood develop a rather sophisticated sense of humor. Younger children, for example, 2-year-olds, think it is funny when they call something by its wrong name. They find great mirth in pointing to a dog and calling it a "cat." Three-year-olds overrely on appearance; a picture of an elephant in a tree is very amusing. Children in middle childhood become capable of understanding more abstract and implied incongruities and not just those that can be immediately perceived (McGhee, 1979).

During middle childhood, children become capable of understanding verbal humor based on the double meaning of a word, which not only involves the knowledge of both meanings of that word, but also the ability to keep one meaning in mind while shifting to the other. Puns begin to appear. The discovery of ambiguity of words is also linked to the enjoyment of riddles and jokes, which are based on double meanings. In the elementary school years, the child is able to understand not only more complex cartoons, but also comic strips.

Children in early middle childhood, age 6 or 7, may not find incongruities particularly funny. For example, when presented with a drawing in which a horse is seen walking away in the distance with a series of human footprints trailing behind it, some children may say, "Here are a man's footprints, and here is a horse; the horse can't have made these footprints" (Bariaud, 1983). Such reac-

Children in middle childhood find incongruities in pictures to be highly humorous.

tions indicate that the child has not yet mastered the convention according to which such a cartoon purposefully distorts things in order to be funny. Children's realistic attitudes interfere with the tendency to see incongruities as humorous. Not all 6- and 7-year-olds manifest this type of refusal to playfully accept the incongruity, but those that do not refuse do so for all impossible events that they see. With increasing age, this rejection of incongruity because of its incompatibility with reality disappears. Ten- or 11-year-olds, because of their greater mastery of humor conventions and their better understanding of others' expectations in humorous situations, are able to enjoy incongruities.

ADOLESCENCE

REFINED UNDERSTANDING OF LANGUAGE

Although language acquisition is basically complete by the beginning of adolescence, important refinements continue. There is greater precision in speaking, sophistication in writing, and better comprehension in reading. Eleven- and 12-year-olds no longer focus on the literal meanings of metaphors, parables, and proverbs (Winner, 1988). For example, in interpreting the proverb, "People in glass houses shouldn't throw stones," a 5-year-old commented, "Because it breaks the glass."; a 7-year-old related, "You know people don't live in glass houses. I don't see no glass houses."; a 9-year-old said, "If you buy a glass house, expect to have a window broken."; however, an 11-year-old said, "If you hurt people, you may get hurt yourself." Eleven-year-olds were able to escape the literal interpretation and were able to realize that words can have symbolic meaning beyond their reference to physical objects.

Adolescents continue to increase their vocabulary and refine their understandings of word meanings as well. Their definitions are more abstract, and they often include the superordinate category to which the object belongs. An adolescent, for example, might define a chair as a piece of furniture on which people sit. A younger child would indicate that a chair is for sitting but wouldn't mention the class of things—furniture—to which it belongs.

COMMUNICATING WITH ADOLESCENTS

The most important aspect of language is communication, an interaction between two or more people that involves an exchange of information. Every time you talk with or to children and adolescents, you are adding another brick to define your relationship. Most of us tend to take communication for granted; it isn't until we experience some problem that we may begin to wonder how we can be more effective communicators. Parents sometimes remark that their teenagers just "clam up and don't say anything to us anymore." Adolescents may remark, "Teachers boss too much"; "My Mom is always telling me what to do"; "Sometimes I want to plug up my ears when she opens her mouth." (Many do.) In this section, how parents and teachers can communicate more effectively with adolescents is discussed. It needs to be stressed that the points mentioned in this section are equally applicable to individuals of any age.

Typical Ways of Responding   Gordon (1970) has pointed out typical ways in which adults respond to adolescents and the subsequent feelings they arouse in them. Often adults simply order or command: "As long as you live in this house, you will do as you are told to do." Many adults moralize or preach: "When I was your age, my parents didn't help me with my homework. It was up to me to finish it." They judge and criticize: "You are such a messy kid; your room looks like the city dump." They advise and give solutions: "Listen to me; I know what's best. If I were you I would spend more time studying." These kinds of communiques close the door to effective communication. They communicate unacceptance of the individual, produce fear of the parent's or teacher's power, cause feelings of guilt, and make the adolescent feel inadequate and inferior.

The typical ways of responding are often used to send what Gordon (1970) called a solution-type message to the adolescent. For example, adults may not wait for the adolescent to initiate appropriate behavior; they simply blurt out what the adolescent must, ought, or should do. As Gordon relates, suppose a friend is visiting your house and he happens to put his feet on the rungs of one of your new dining room chairs. You certainly would not say to him, "Get your feet off my chair this minute!" This sounds ridiculous in a situation involving a friend, because most people treat friends with more respect. Most likely the chair owner would send some message, such as, "I am really worried that my new chair might get scratched by your feet." Adults send this type of message to friends but seldom to adolescents.

Similarly, adults tend to send put-down messages: "You lose everything; you're so irresponsible." "John, you are never prepared for your math work; why don't you wake up!" It seems that most parents and educators do not use these put-downs to intentionally wound adolescents and destroy their self-esteem; the statements are made with the hopeful expectation that they will somehow change the adolescent for the better. If adults could really understand just how devastating these comments can be, they might consider some other form of verbal message in an attempt to change negative behavior.

Effective Communication   There are a number of techniques that adults can use to increase their effectiveness as communicators with children and adolescents (as well as with other adults). Being a good listener, engaging in active listening, and sending I-messages are important techniques that will help to establish a positive relationship between adult and adolescent and open the door to further communication.

Being a Good Listener   There are two aspects to communication: One is output—the speaking and writing; the other is listening. Being a good listener is an integral part of effective communication. Be sure that you are really listening to the adolescent and not thinking, instead, of your own incredibly important chores or pressing concerns. When you are really listening, you are trying to make an honest effort to understand the adolescents' feelings and thoughts from their point of view.

Active Listening   One of the most effective and constructive ways of responding to adolescents is to offer them an invitation to say more and to share their own judgments, ideas, and feelings by giving responses that reflect their thoughts (Roberts & Patterson, 1983), a technique known as **active listening.** Listeners restate, in their own words, the message the speaker has just sent. It involves paraphrasing the speaker's words, not parroting them. If the message is simply repeated verbatim, there is still a great chance that listeners might be misunderstanding what's been said. Amazingly enough, simply feeding back a person's ideas often helps in sorting out and solving the problem.

In many cases you need to go beyond reflecting thoughts and rephrase also the often unspoken emotions that accompany the verbal message. For example, in response to a person who has just discussed a work situation, you may respond, "When you talk about all the petty tasks your boss gives you, I hear you saying that you're hurt and disappointed that she hasn't given you more responsibility." These comments are phrased tentatively, not dogmatically. You are sharing an interpretation and allowing the speaker to decide whether it is correct. Active listening is a great way to get through the layers of hidden meanings.

Active listening is not used in all situations. Sometimes adolescents are just looking for information and not trying to work out their feelings.

At times like these, active listening would be out of place. In addition, active listening takes a great deal of time. Therefore, if you're in a hurry and don't have time to listen, it is wise to avoid starting a conversation that you will not be able to finish.

Sending I-Messages   I-messages are critical, because adolescents need to know how the adult feels. They are essential in keeping communication lines open and for establishing healthy relationships (Lytton, 1980). Sometimes when communicating with teenagers, people send you-messages, which imply sending a judgment. "You are always picking on your younger brother." "You are being inconsiderate when you blast your stereo like that." Try to rephrase these sentences to begin with an "I" plus a description of your feelings. "I get upset with all this fighting." "I cannot think straight when the music is being played so loudly." You simply say how the adolescent's behavior is making you feel. You take responsibility for and acknowledge ownership of your thoughts, opinions, and feelings. The message focuses on you, not on the adolescent. It does not blame. The tone of voice is important. An I-message delivered in anger becomes a you-message conveying hostility.

Effective communication involves active listening in which the adult reflects the thoughts and feelings that the child is expressing.

PRACTICAL IMPLICATIONS: ENHANCING CHILDREN'S LANGUAGE DEVELOPMENT

This chapter focused on how children and adolescents' language complexity grows and examined some of the paths they follow in trying to approximate adult language. This section focuses on certain social experiences in children's and adolescents' lives and the effect they may have on communicative and linguistic growth.

EMOTIONAL CONTACT

Many researchers believe that in order for speech to develop, children must receive warm emotional and physical contact with the caregiver. It is in this way that children are motivated to coo, babble, and finally make the transition to meaningful speech. The reasons, then, that children learn to speak are social. They are ultimately tied up with their attachment to the parents or surrogate and the pleasure and affection infants get from them (Mowrer, 1960).

McCarthy (1954) cited the case of one little girl who, unknown to her parents, had a hearing loss such that she could not hear gentle, affectionate, conversational tones. The only sounds that she could hear were loud and explosive sounds when her parents spoke harshly in anger. This child developed no language on her own until the hearing loss was detected and a hearing aid enabled her to pick up the missing range of gentle speech. Recent research has confirmed and extended the idea that pleasure and affectionate relationships are vital in early speech development (Schantz, 1983). Moreover, because many adults and older children express their pleasure at a baby's communication by smiling at, stroking, or talking to the baby, we can presume that these positive personal responses to vocalization have an important effect on children's progress.

Moreover, early babbling and later sound making almost always occur when infants are pleased. When they are angry or distressed they do not "talk." It certainly seems that the precursors of language are related to pleasant emotions, not to unpleasant ones.

VERBALLY INTERACTING WITH OTHERS

A child who hears no language learns no language. Most infants coo and babble, but deaf infants cease babbling after 6 months, whereas normal infants continue. Children with a minimal hearing loss also have difficulties acquiring language.

A child does not learn language, however, by simply hearing it spoken. A boy with normal hearing but with deaf parents who communicated by the American Sign Language was exposed to television every day, so that he could learn English. Because the child was asthmatic and was confined to his home, he interacted only with people at home, where his family and visitors communicated in sign language. By age 3, he was fluent in sign language but neither understood nor spoke English. It appears that in order to learn a language, a child must also be able to interact with real people in that language. Snow (1981) reported that young Dutch children who watched German television every day did not acquire any German. Children, then, can develop language only if there is language in their environment and if they can employ that language to communicate with other people in the immediate environment.

CONTINGENT RESPONDING

The young infant gazes at the mother's eyes, the mother smiles and says, "Good morning," the child responds with "Goo," and mother smiles and says, "How are you this morning?" In this type of experience, when the adult responds to the child's cues, the infant begins to gain a sense of cause-and-effect relationships. When children begin to notice that their behaviors have a predictable effect on their world, they can then develop the notion of **signal,** which is the first stage in developing the ability to communicate (Snow, 1979).

A signal is defined as "a behavior of a more or less constant form produced with the expectation that it will have some predictable effect in a certain class of receivers. Learning to signal involves learning that certain behaviors are responded to predictably by certain people, and intentionally applying that knowledge" (Snow, 1981, p. 198). For example, the child eventually is able to gaze at the mother's eyes and smile and know that because of these signs, the mother will respond with soft words and smiles.

Studies of mother-infant interaction have shown that the most frequent caregiver behaviors to young infants are touching, vocalizing, and smiling, and that these behaviors are often, although not always, done in response to infant behaviors (Snow, deBlauw, & van Roosmalen, 1979). Learning to signal depends on having experienced these and other contingent responses (Barton & Tomasello, 1991).

CAREGIVER SPEECH

One of the most important ways in which adults can promote effective communication is by considering the child capable of communication and behaving as though the child, from the very beginning, is a partner in the communicative exchange. Most middle-class parents do (Hoff-Ginsberg, 1991). Moreover, the adult often acts as a second participant for the child. Thus, the caregiver provides, in advance, sensitive and significant actions that the child still does not possess. For example, the young child may hiccup, and the adult responds, "My goodness, what happened?" In conversations, the adult often fills in for the child (Snow, 1977).

Mother	Baby
	Smiles
Oh, what a nice little smile!	
Yes, isn't that pretty?	
There now.	
There's a nice little smile.	
Yes!	
There's a nice voice.	

In this exchange the baby's smiles and coos are responded to by the mother as "turns" in a conversation.

Caregivers' language styles when talking with children differ from those they use with adults. Adults don't complain to children about the difficulties in obtaining a bank loan. Or, if they do, they don't expect them to understand. They don't expect them to follow long explanations, so they frequently check to make sure that the children understand them. People often comment, some-

times in exaggerated ways, on their pleasure or disgust in children's actions.

Moreover, people simplify language when speaking to children. In a study done by Snow (1972), mothers were asked to play with 2-year-old and 10-year-old children in three conditions: telling a story to the child about a picture, sorting some toys, and explaining some physical phenomenon. When addressing 2-year-olds, mothers used more repetitions ("Get the red block. The red block. Not the green block. Can you find the red block?"), exaggerated intonation, fewer pronouns, higher pitch, and fewer endings (for example, plural *s* or possessive *s*).

MOTHERESE

Other studies have shown that mothers speak to children in short, simple sentences; to 2-year-olds, the average sentence length is four words, compared with eight- or nine-word sentences used when communicating with adults (Phillips, 1973). In addition, when communicating with children, mothers tend to talk in the "here and now," usually about whatever is directly in front of the child's eyes. These differences in the nature of speech have been called **motherese,** or child-directed speech, and include fewer words per utterance, more repetitions and expansion, better articulation, and decreased structural complexity. Paralinguistic (or prosodic) modifications differ dramatically from those of adult conversation as well (Fernald, 1989). Even with newborns, people use higher overall pitch, wider pitch excursions, more distinctive pitch contours, slower tempo, longer pauses, and increased emphatic stress (Hoff-Ginsberg, 1990).

Infant-directed speech has been observed in the interactions between infants and their parents in French, Italian, German, Japanese, Chinese, and British homes. In one representative study (Fernald, Taeschner, Dunn, Papousek, de Boysson-Bardies, & Fukui, 1989), the speech of eight Mandarin Chinese mothers speaking to their infants found that even in this tonal language (where pitch changes are used to signal phonemic distinctions) mothers alter their prosodic features when talking to infants. Moreover, infant-directed speech has been observed in the speech of males when speaking to young infants (Jacobson, Boersma, Fields, & Olson, 1983).

It is interesting to note that not only do mothers and fathers adjust their speech when speaking to their infants, but also that young children do so as well. For example, 4-year-olds raise their pitch and shorten their sentences when speaking to younger children (Sachs & Devin, 1976). Children's conversational interactions with younger children, as compared with mothers', tend to be shorter and contain fewer of the conversational devices (repetition and attentional devices such as "look" or "hey") used to maintain a dialogue (Tomasello & Mannle, 1985). Infant-directed speech appears to be a prevalent form of language input to infants across a variety of ages and cultures.

What is the significance of these modifications in adult speech? Is it at least plausible that simplification is an aid to learning language? The most general feature of parental speech—simple, short sentences—is likely to be helpful to language-learning children and it has been shown to be most likely to produce a response (Glanzer & Dodd, 1975)—that children may not respond at all if the input is too complex (Shipley, Smith, & Gleitman, 1969).

Although these general features do help language-learning children, there are no clear demonstrations that motherese contributes to children's linguistic success. Although research has found no direct relation between mothers' usage of child-directed speech and objective measures of children's language development (Gleitman, Newport, & Gleitman, 1984), it is generally believed that successful language learning depends on a positive, interactive verbal environment between child and caretaker (Gottfried & Gottfried, 1984). In one study (Werker & McLeod, 1989), it was reported that both 4- and 5-month-olds and 7- to 9-month-olds who were watching videotapes of a female talking to an infant and talking to an adult

Young children also adjust their speech when talking to infants in a way that is very similar to the way adults adjust their speech.

demonstrated more positive affect while watching the infant-directed speech tape, and the magnitude of this effect was greater in the younger infants.

The majority of these studies focus on studying children between 4 and 12 months old. Cooper and Aslin (1990) wanted to see if younger infants showed a preference for infant-directed speech. In this experiment the newborns and 1-month-old infants could activate either a recording of infant-directed or adult-directed speech by looking at a visual stimulus. The amount of time these babies spent looking at the visual stimulus while listening to different auditory stimuli was the dependent measure. In these experiments, speech preference was operationally defined as longer average looking times to the visual stimulus when looking was associated with a particular kind of speech. As can be seen in Figures 9.6 and 9.7, newborns and 1-month-old infants looked longer when the infant-directed speech was presented. The available data appear to indicate that infant-directed speech is a prevalent form of language input to infants and that it may serve important social, attentional, and language-related functions in early development.

IMITATION

It is commonly believed that imitation plays an important role in children's language development. It is one characteristic of children's speech that most everyone notices. This imitation typically assumes the form of telegraphic speech. For example, the adult may say, "There is a big truck," and the child responds, "Big truck." Brown and Bellugi (1964) called this "imitation with reduction" and theorized that it was important to grammar learning.

Bloom, Hood, and Lightbown (1974) studied children in homes in natural conversational settings and noted that children vary in their tendency to imitate. One child, Allison, never produced imitations at a rate greater than 6%. For another child, Peter, the imitations made up about one third of his total responses.

McNeill (1970) provides an example of how difficult it may be to teach a child via imitation:

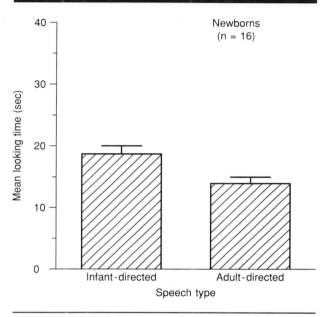

FIGURE 9.6   Mean Looking Times (in Sec) of Newborn Subjects from Experiment 2 (Including Standard Errors); ID = Infant-Directed and AD = Adult-Directed.

Source: "Preference for Infant-Directed Speech in the First Month after Birth" by R. P. Cooper and R. N. Aslin, 1990, *Child Development, 61*, 1584–1595. © The Society for Research in Child Development, Inc. Reprinted by permission.

CHILD: Nobody don't like me.
ADULT: No, say "Nobody likes me."
CHILD: Nobody don't like me.
    (Eight repetitions of this dialogue)
ADULT: No, now listen carefully; say, "Nobody likes me."
CHILD: Oh! Nobody don't likes me. (pp. 106–107)

The child finally partially corrected his utterance, so it is possible to teach through imitation, but in this case, at least, the process hardly seems very efficient. The major importance of imitation to communicative development might be in learning the individual sounds and words of language.

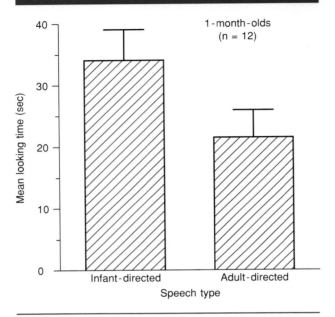

FIGURE 9.7 Mean Looking Times (in Sec) of 1-month-old Subjects from Experiment 1 (Including Standard Errors); ID = Infant-Directed and AD = Adult-Directed.

Source: "Preference for Infant-Directed Speech in the First Month after Birth" by R. P. Cooper and R. N. Aslin, 1990, *Child Development, 61*, 1584–1595. © The Society for Research in Child Development, Inc. Reprinted by permission.

LABELING

People seeking to explain language acquisition have assumed that ostensive definition, such as pointing to an object and labeling, plays a critical role in helping children's language proficiency (Baldwin & Markman, 1989). Tomasello, Mannle, and Kruger (1986) recorded and analyzed linguistic interactions between 24 mothers and their infants when they were 15 and 21 months old. They found that very general measures of the mothers' speech to their infants (such as total amount of speech and speech complexity) did not predict the infants' language proficiency or language development. Yet, more specific measures, the extent to which mothers spoke about objects to which they and their infants were jointly attending (such as toys they were sharing), were a strong predictor of early language. The mothers who referred to such objects the most had children with the largest productive vocabularies.

TELEVISION VIEWING

Research has shown that mere exposure to television does not result in normal acquisition of language, apparently because its dynamic linguistic stimulation is provided without the benefit of social interaction. While social interaction is important in the acquisition of language, Rice, Huston, Truglio, and Wright (1990) did find that children's vocabulary does increase when viewing television. Three- to 5-year-olds viewed animated programs that introduced unfamiliar words in a story context. The study showed that 5-year-olds learned five new words and 3-year-olds learned two new words after two viewings. In a 2-year longitudinal study (Huston, Wright, Eakins, Kerkman, Pinion, Rosenkoetter, & Truglio, 1985), 326 3- and 5-year-old children were given a vocabulary test at the beginning and end of the two-year period. Positive viewing effect on vocabulary development was reported.

In summary, it appears from the studies cited that one of the most important factors in influencing children's language development is the extent to which adults are sensitive to their children's linguistic attempts. Adults need to respond to children's communications with an act that is meaningful and relevant in the context of the ongoing situation. One way of developing a sensitivity to children's communiques is by really trying to listen to what the child is saying. It takes two to make a conversation, however, and much of the smoothness of the interaction depends also on the child's own contribution. Children's characteristic styles of interaction may well limit or increase the amount of useful input they can elicit.

Available evidence does suggest an answer to any adult who wishes to know how to facilitate a

Sensitivity to children's linguistic attempts facilitates language development.

child's language development; it is aptly expressed by Brown (1977):

> Believe that your child can understand more than he can say, and seek, above all, to communicate. To understand and be understood. To keep your minds on the same target. . . . There is no set of rules of how to talk to a child that can even approach what you unconsciously know. If you concentrate on communicating, everything else will follow. (p. 28)

REVIEW OF KEY POINTS

Language is an ordered system of rules that is understood when speaking, listening, and writing. A collection of these implicit rules is known as the grammar of language. There are rules for the three main branches of grammar: phonology, syntax, and semantics.

Three principal theories of language acquisition were presented. Skinner's theory, which stresses the importance of the environment in language learning, was discussed. Children learn to say certain words because they are reinforced (operant conditioning), and they learn to understand the meaning of words via classical conditioning.

Children utter sounds that are reinforced or shaped by their environment and gradually learn to make distinguishable sounds to form correct sentences.

Chomsky believes that children learn language via a language acquisition device in the brain. This device allows children to deduce basic rules of language or the grammar of language just by listening to language without being taught. Chomsky believes that grammars are composed of two types of syntactic structure: surface structure and deep structure. Chomsky's theory is called transformational grammar because rules of transformation are applied to change deep sentence structures into surface structures.

Slobin proposes that every child possesses a basic language-making capacity made up of a set of fundamental information-processing strategies, and sees the child as an active participant in deciphering the operating principles or rules of language acquisition.

Piaget believes that language does not structure thought. Language is primarily a reflection of children's intellectual abilities. In contrast to Piaget, Bruner and Vygotsky consider logical thought and language, at around 2 years of age, to be inseparable. Whorf suggests that the forms of a particular language affect the individual's perception of the world.

Children do not just learn words but acquire a basic rule system that makes it possible for them to create complex sentences. They learn grammatical rules for phonological development (study of sounds and their structure), syntactic development (study of how words come together to form sentences), and semantics (meaning of words and sentences). The grammar of language is its rules or principles for organizing the sounds into meaningful units.

One cannot help but reflect on how relatively easy it is for children (with almost no help from adults) to master such a complex task as learning to speak a language. As the rules children apply in phonological, syntactic, and semantic areas of development differentiate and become more finite,

children become more sophisticated in their speech. From their prelinguistic beginnings, when communications consisted of crying, cooing, and babbling, children advance into the linguistic period, beginning with one-word utterances, followed by two-word utterances, telegraphic speech, and finally the ability to communicate using complex sentences.

The way adults communicate with children and adolescents determines to a large extent the type of relationship that will be built with them. Parents and educators need to be aware of the typical ways in which they respond to children and how these responses make children feel. Constructive ways of responding to children and adolescents offer them an invitation to say more, to share their feelings by reflecting the feelings they are experiencing back to them. It involves sending I-messages that communicate how the adolescent's behavior is making you feel.

The implications section focused on various social experiences and how these experiences might affect children's communicative and linguistic growth. It appears that the following factors play an important role in enhancing language learning in children: emotional and physical contact, contingency responding, playing games, simple, short sentences, responding in rich and varied ways to children's utterances, and communicating in ways that are meaningful and relevant to the context of the child's speech.

ENHANCING YOUR CRITICAL THINKING

Broadening Your Knowledge

Factors Influencing Language Acquisition

Hoff-Ginsberg, E. (1991). Mother-child conversation in different social classes and communicative settings. *Child Development, 62,* 782–796.

Many of the characteristics of maternal speech that are associated with child language development have been found to vary as a function of social class. Hoff-Ginsburg investigated the dyadic interactions of working-class and upper-middle-class mothers and their infants. Significant social class differences in the mothers' child-directed speech were then noted. According to the findings of this study, what factors are the most important influences on children's linguistic development?

Critical Thinking

Language Acquisition Theory

Slobin, D. I. (1988, April). Confessions of a way-ward Chomskyan. *Papers and Reports on Child Language Development* (Vol. 27) (pp. 131–138). Proceedings of the Annual Language Research Forum, Stanford University, Palo Alto, CA.

Slobin proposes that, in contrast to Chomsky's argument, it is possible to arrive at an empirically grounded definition of innate linguistic competence that guides children in the construction of grammar, particularly when this process is viewed as developmental. The article enables you to analyze how Slobin's theory differs from Chomsky's.

Personal Growth

Communication

Gordon, T. (1970). *Parent effectiveness training: The tested new way to raise responsible children.* New York: David McKay.

This text discusses ways of responding that close and open the door to communicating effectively with others. Gordon's book provides various exercises you can perform to practice effective communication techniques. Because communication is the cornerstone of all relationships, this reading is well worth your while. Try to analyze your conversations with friends and family. Notice how many times that you begin a statement with the "accusative *you.*" Try to rephrase these questions with an "I" plus a statement of your feelings. When you do this, are your thoughts and feelings communicated more effectively? Does it open the door to communication with your friends and family?

PART

IV

The Psychosocial World of the Child and Adolescent

CHAPTER 10

Social Cognition

CHILDREN'S THOUGHTS

On "Who are you?"

I am a person. A person who deserves rights. I get pretty good grades and I'm an O.K. athlete. Even though I can lead my life maybe a little better if I try harder, I'm proud of myself.

Michael, age 11

I am a person who has few friends and has many problems. My friends never really like me a lot so I have many hobbies. I'm not good at sports. No one sits next to me at lunch. Everyday I go to school thinking something bad is going to happen. Someday, I'll be that person that I want to be.

Eric, age 11

On "What is a friend?"

A friend is someone who likes you and you like her. You play together and have fun. But when you fight she is no longer your friend.

Sally, age 8

A friend is a person that you can confide in and know they will not tell someone else. I guess you could say they are dependable, trustworthy, and loyal.

Tom, age 14

CHAPTER OUTLINE

KEY TERMS

Self
Self-as-subject
Self-as-object
Self-concept
Self-schemata
Self-esteem
Significant others
Introspection
Identity crisis
Identity foreclosure
Moratorium
Identity achievers
Identity diffusion
Inclusion
Distinctiveness

This chapter deals with social cognition—children's knowledge and thinking about psychological events that occur in themselves as well as in others. With respect to knowledge of others, this chapter will focus on children's conceptions of social relationships. Issues such as concepts of friendship, fairness, and authority will be addressed. In the realm of knowledge of self, attention will center on the development of children's notions of themselves as distinct from others and on the growth of an image of self: the self-concept and self-esteem. Developmental social cognition, then, has to do with the way in which knowledge of self and others develops.

The discussion of developmental social cognition begins with a look at the development of self and self systems, followed by consideration of the development of knowledge of social relationships.

Part of infant social cognition can be characterized as a process of differentiation of self. One of the major developmental tasks in this area is the gradual evolution of a sense of self as a distinct and separate entity. Before discussing the emerging sense of self, a few terms need to be defined.

DEFINING THE SELF AND SELF SYSTEM

The **self** is defined as the part of people of which they are consciously aware (Rosenberg, 1986). William James studied the development of the self, and even though his significant publications appeared before the turn of the century, his definition of self is still popular and remarkably contemporary. In his *Principles of Psychology* (1890/1950),

FIGURE 10.1   Structure of Self-Concept

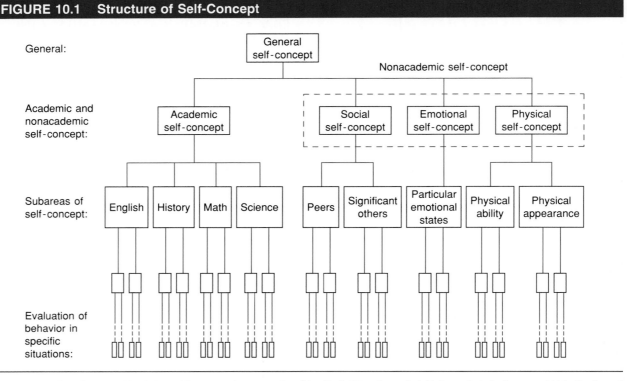

Source: From "Self-Concept: Validation of Construct Interpretations" by R. J. Shavelson, J. J. Hubner, & J. C. Stanton, 1976, *Review of Educational Research, 46*, pp. 407–441. Copyright 1976 by the American Educational Research Foundation. Reprinted by permission of the publisher.

James describes the self as being composed of two distinct components: the "I" and the "Me."

SELF-AS-SUBJECT

The "I" is the **self-as-subject,** the self-as-knower; it organizes and interprets experience in a purely subjective manner. With the emergence of "I," individuals realize they are separate from other objects and persons in the world. The "I" represents the feelings of individuality or distinctiveness as well as the sense of volition, of being an active processor of experiences.

SELF-CONCEPT

The "Me" is the person's self-perception as an object or entity. "Me," as James points out, is the **self-as-object,** the self-as-known. Your **self-concept** is your personal representation of "Me." Out of your awareness of yourself grows ideas (concepts) of the kind of person you see yourself to be (Kihlstrom, Cantor, Albright, Chew, Klein, & Niedenthal, 1988). Your self-concept is an organized cognitive structure derived from the experiences you have had. It consists of well-differentiated ideas, **self-schemata,** (Markus, 1977; Markus & Sentis, 1980) of the kind of person you are with respect to a variety of areas.

Recent theoretical accounts of self-concept emphasize its multidimensional nature. Although earlier definitions and empirical studies thought of self-concept as a global, general phenomenon (Coopersmith, 1967), today it is viewed and studied as being hierarchically organized and com-

---

FOCUS ON ISSUES

Is Self-Esteem a Global Concept?

Charles Cooley (1909) and William James (1890/1950) maintained that the sum total of one's pleasures (or pains) and successes (or failures) is synonymous with one's pride (or mortification). Coopersmith and Gilberts (1982) were also proponents of global self-esteem. In analyzing data from a sample of 56 10- to 12-year-old boys, they found that children make very little distinction about their worthiness in different areas of experience, or if such distinctions are made, they are within the context of the overall general appraisal of worthiness that children have already made.

Your own common sense, however, tells you that there is an inconsistency between diverse aspects of your self-esteem. For example, you may feel that you are a good student, but not very good in social situations. Confidence (or lack of it) in one area does not necessarily mean we feel totally positive (or negative) about ourselves in all areas. Harter (1982) tested children in three specific competence domains: cognitive, physical, and social. Also included in her test was a general-worth scale, which intended to tap the degree to which children like themselves and feel they are good persons. While there were moderate correlations among the cognitive, physical, and social scales, a large portion of the variance of the general-worth scale was unaccounted for by the other three scales.

Wegner and Vallacher (1980), Yawkey (1980), and Harter (1983) say this: Young children may have a global feeling of self, which may be applied to all situations. As children get older, however, self-esteem undergoes increasing differentiation from global to rather specific components, including the physical, intellectual, social, and emotional domains. The young child may think, "I am a good boy," but the older child would be more inclined to recognize differentiated abilities: "I am good at sports and terrible in math."

---

posed of a general component as well as domain-specific components. Shavelson, Hubner, and Stanton (1976) and Marsh, Byrne, and Shavelson (1988) propose that a general self-concept is at the apex of the hierarchy that is divided into academic and nonacademic self-concepts; academic self-concept is further divided into subject-specific facets of self (e.g., English and mathematics); non-academic self-concept is divided into social, emotional, and physical self-concepts that are further divided into more specific components (e.g., physical self-concept into physical ability and physical appearance). Marsh (1989) has concluded that self-concept cannot be adequately understood if this multidimensionality is ignored (see Figure 10.1).

SELF-ESTEEM

As the self-concept becomes better known and articulated, children begin to formulate values for themselves and to make value judgments about themselves. **Self-esteem** refers to how the "I" evaluates the components as well as the totality of "Me." Whereas the self-concept is the cognitive part of the self, you might view self-esteem as the affective portion of the self (Blyth & Traeger, 1991). Self-esteem refers quite literally to the extent to which people admire or value the self. Are self-evaluations global or do people evaluate themselves differently in different contexts (see "Focus on Issues")?

In summary, the self is what you know about yourself and comprises the "I" and the "Me." The

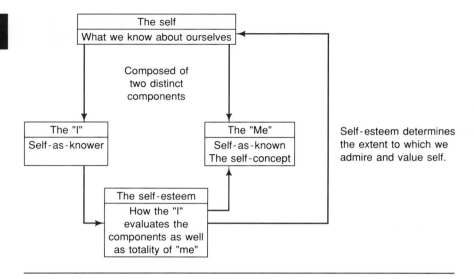

FIGURE 10.2 The Self and Self Systems

"Me," known as your self-concept, is what you *think* about yourself, and self-esteem is what you *feel* about yourself. Self-esteem determines the extent to which you admire and value the self (see Figure 10.2).

INFANCY

During infancy, the child's major task, in terms of self-development, is to learn to differentiate self from others and come to see self as an active, independent, causal agent. The self-as-subject develops as children meet with the experiences of life.

DEVELOPMENTAL PROGRESSION OF THE EMERGING SELF

At first, infants have a simple, poorly defined image of themselves and the world. Cooley (1909) believed that the very young infant is not conscious of the self or the "I." The infant experiences a simple "stream of impressions"—impressions that gradually become discriminated as the child differentiates self or "I" from "not I." With the passage of time, children show increasing signs of being able to distinguish between people and things and between themselves and others. They begin to acquire an increased awareness of their personal identity and resources. Children notice that things from the outside world act on them, and they in turn act on and influence objects and people in their environment.

Mahler, Pine, and Bergman's (1975) theory addresses the organization and emergence of a sense of self, an awareness that the self exists as a separate being. Mahler et al. suggest that infants are born with no sense of identity. Their sense of self is totally fused with that of their caregivers, and it is only in the course of development that children develop a sense of their own boundaries and of their own identities.

Development begins with the state of *normal autism* (birth to 1 month). The baby lacks an awareness of a mothering agent. During this phase, physiological process dominates and there is a minimal responsivity to external stimulation. The second phase, *symbiosis* (2 to 4 months), signals a beginning awareness of a need-satisfying object. This phase describes a state of undifferentiation, of fusion with the caregiver. Infants, however, cannot maintain this state of symbiotic fu-

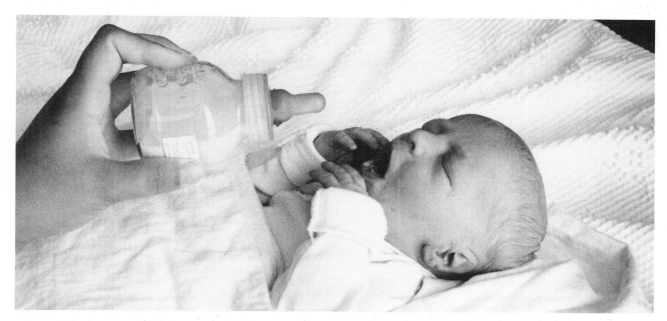

Parents who provide reliable responses to their infants' needs help them to become sensitive to the cause-effect relationship between their own actions and their effect on the environment.

sion with their caregivers if a sense of self is to be achieved.

The third phase is a rather lengthy phase known as *separation and individuation.* The first subphase is *differentiation* (5 to 9 months). During this phase, children slowly begin to differentiate as they hatch out of their symbiotic union with their caregivers. As infants separate from their caregivers, they simultaneously begin to organize a sense of being. From Mahler's perspective this is not a sense of "who I am" but a sense of "that I am"—that I exist as a separate, distinct entity. Key signs of this differentiation are infants' staring at their body parts, such as a hand. Infants seem mesmerized as they watch their hand open and close and their fingers wiggle. (They are only dimly aware that they are producing these actions.) Some infants stare for a long time to contemplate these newly discovered bits of self.

Subphase 2, *practicing* (10 to 15 months), comes at about the time children begin to walk. During this subphase, they learn to distance from the per-

son to whom they are attached. A critical subphase, the *rapprochement phase* (15 to 22 months), is next. Here children essentially play at a game in which they practice moving away from their caregivers in the context of an insurance that the caregivers will be there when they return for refueling. The game of being chased and of being playfully pursued is paradigmatic of this phase. Finally, in subphase 4, *consolidation* (22 to 36 months), children move on to the resolution of the separation-/individuation process. Through the achievement of complex cognitive factors, ego differentiation, and the realization of object constancy, children attain a distinct sense of individuality. They are now ready to organize a sense of self-identity and self-concept.

EXPERIENCES CONTRIBUTING TO THE EMERGING SELF

Several experiential and cognitive achievements contribute to the emergence of self. One key to developing a sense of "I" lies in the infants' expe-

The infant who is just getting his teeth may emit a pained scream when he bites his foot—obviously he had no idea that he was about to nibble part of himself.

riences of regular and consistent feedback between their actions and the outcomes they produce. As Lewis and Brooks-Gunn point out (1981), "It is our strong belief that the first definition or feature of self is the simultaneity and identity of action and outcome. Self is defined from action and reflects the identity of action and outcome in a specific locus of space" (p. 224). In other words, infants learn cause and effect—that if they do something, a certain consequence or action will follow. Thus, they begin to realize that they are causal agents. Regular and consistent feedback provides the basis for establishing general expectancies about infants' world and their control of it. Such expectancies should help infants differentiate their actions from the actions of others.

Initially, kinesthetic feedback (the sensations perceived through the muscles of the body) produced by the infant's own actions forms the basis for development of "I." For example, each time a certain set of muscles operates (infant closes eyes), it becomes black (infant cannot see). These kinesthetic systems provide immediate action-outcome pairings.

Moreover, infants develop their concept of self-as-subject when they become more active participants in their environment; subsequently, they become sensitive to events that occur as a direct result of their own actions. For example, the infant strikes at the mobile hanging over the crib and gradually learns that the action of striking the object causes it to swing back and forth.

In addition, social stimuli (especially the caregiver) provide extensive feedback and form the basis for the development of "I." Indeed, feedback provided by the social world is more critical to the development of "I" than feedback from inanimate objects. Thus, the social world plays a greater role in establishment of self than the nonsocial world (Lewis & Brooks-Gunn, 1981). The first social distinction of "I" and "not I" probably involves the mother or caregiver.

The feedback given by the mother provides for infants' generalized expectancies about control of their world. Infants cry and their caregivers respond by picking them up and cuddling them. Gradually, children learn that crying brings their caregivers. Such expectancies also help infants differentiate their actions from those of others. The consistency, timing, and quality of the caregiver's responsiveness to the infant's cues create powerful expectancies for the infant about her control of and competence in the social environment (Hales, 1990).

The development of self-as-subject may also be related to the general issue of permanence. Permanence deals with the recognition that objects and people exist even when perceptually absent. With a fully elaborated sense of object permanence, children begin constructing the self as a permanent object with enduring qualities. Bertenthal and Fischer (1978) tested 6- to 24-month-old infants' self-recognition and object-permanence skills. As can be seen in Figure 10.3, the researchers found that the differentiation of self and other takes place at the same time the child is acquiring object permanence. This is not to say that object-permanence skills are a prerequisite for the development of self-

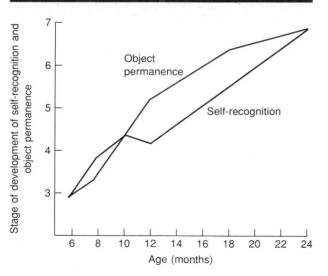

FIGURE 10.3   Object Permanence and Self-Recognition

Source: From "Development of Self-Recognition in the Infant" by B. I. Bertenthal and K. W. Fischer, 1978, *Developmental Psychology, 14*, p. 49. Copyright 1978 by the American Psychological Association. Reprinted by permission.

recognition; however, the parallel between the development of these two skills is interesting.

VISUAL RECOGNITION OF SELF

Empirical efforts to study the emergence of the "I" in early infancy have focused primarily on the visual recognition of self, because verbal behavior is a late-emerging skill. Some rather ingenious tests have been used, the majority of which have relied on showing infants images of themselves in mirrors, pictures, and other visual media. In a series of experiments, Lewis and Brooks-Gunn (1981) observed infants' (ranging in age from 9 to 36 months) responses to their images reflected in mirrors, videotapes, and pictorial representations. Mirror images always move contingently, which means the child looking in a mirror sees an image that moves immediately in tandem with the child's own physiological sensations of movement. Photographed images never do and videotape images can be either contingent (children watching themselves on a television monitor as they actually perform) or noncontingent (children watching themselves on a prerecorded videotape). The results of the study confirm that as early as 9 months of age the infant recognizes the self through contingency cues.

Lewis and Brooks-Gunn also found that children between 18 and 24 months are capable of recognizing their own pictures, using only perceptual feature differences. For example, 22-month-olds smile and look more at their own pictures than at pictures of same-age babies. (Try the experiment in "Studying Children.") The authors speculate that infants are able to distinguish their own images from the images of other babies by referring to differences in the facial features of the two. Self-recognition thus is postulated to pass through two phases: first recognizing the self through contingency cues, followed by recognition during the second year based solely on static perceptual features.

In another study, Lewis and Brooks-Gunn (1981) also observed infants' responses to mirror images prior to having their noses surreptitiously dabbed with rouge and after their noses were

STUDYING CHILDREN

SELF-RECOGNITION

According to Lewis and Brooks-Gunn (1981), children in their second year of life are capable of recognizing certain self-features. That is, they can recognize themselves in pictures and prefer to look at pictures of themselves rather than at pictures of other same-age, same-sex infants. How do 2½-year-olds react to seeing themselves in pictures? Do they look longer, react more intently, smile more frequently at their own pictures? Show two or three 2½-year-old children a picture of a same-sex, same-age child and then a picture of themselves. How do your young subjects respond to these pictures?

marked. The assumption is that children's ability to locate a red spot on the face shows that they associate their own faces with the face in the mirror. The results showed that no babies under a year

seemed to recognize that the smudged nose in the mirror belonged to them.

Children between 9 and 12 months did smile at their mirror images, which demonstrates that they did notice the mark to some degree (see Figure 10.4); however, none of the children showed self-recognition in directing their actions toward the mark. Among babies 15 to 18 months, 25% immediately touched their noses and among those between 21 and 24 months, 75% grabbed for their noses as soon as they looked in the mirror.

Based on the results of their studies, Lewis and Brooks-Gunn postulate that there are four major advances in infants' self-knowledge during the first 2 years of life. The first major advance in self-knowledge, occurring from birth to 3 months of age, is an unlearned attraction to the images of other people and especially to the images of young babies. This attraction shows up in a young infant's fascination with mirror images, drawings, and pictures of faces, especially when the face is

Marked-directed behavior (touching the spot on the nose) during the mirror-rouge episode has been found to be the most reliable indicator of self-recognition.

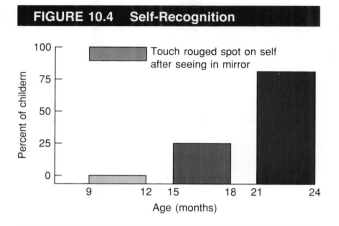

FIGURE 10.4   Self-Recognition

Touch rouged spot on self after seeing in mirror

Source: From *Social Cognition and the Acquisition of Self* (p. 41) by M. Lewis and J. Brooks-Gunn (Eds.), 1981, New York: Plenum. Copyright 1981 by Plenum Publishing Corp. Reprinted by permission.

that of the self or of another young infant. Second, between 3 and 8 months of age, infants begin to recognize the self through contingency cues. The third advance, between the ages of 8 and 12 months, is the association of certain stable categorical features with the self. The infant now can go beyond recognizing the self merely as the origin of paired causes and effects in the world and can begin constructing the self as a permanent object with enduring qualities. In this manner, the permanence of the self is realized and becomes an important organizing principle for the infant's knowledge of both self-as-subject and self-as-object. Finally, the fourth infancy advance, which occurs throughout the second year of life, is the defining of self through categorical features alone, independent of any contingency knowledge that the subject may have.

Lewis and Brooks-Gunn have further concluded that "age or developmental status is the single most important determinant of self-recognition" (1981, p. 17). Perhaps age differences may be related to social and cognitive factors, since self-recognition is both a social and a cognitive skill. In the social realm, Gallup (1977, 1979) has reported that chimpanzees that have been reared as social isolates do not exhibit marked recognition, even

after extensive exposure to mirrors. Perhaps differential social experience also affects the acquisition of self-knowledge in man. In the cognitive realm, a similar study with mentally retarded children found that they were nearly 3 years old before they reached for their noses (Mans, Cicchetti, & Sroufe, 1978). This delay in self-recognition indicates that self-awareness may be closely linked to the child's level of cognitive development.

UNDERSTANDING OTHERS

According to some researchers, it is friends, those with whom people share an affective bond and relationship charged with positive feelings, and not merely any peer, who play a significant role in social development (Miller & Aloise, 1989). Sullivan (1953) proposes that friendship contributes to the child's social development in two important ways: It broadens the child's understanding of social reality by providing new possibilities for social exchange and it expands the child's self-understanding by providing a sense of mutuality with others. Children begin to develop a real sensitivity to what matters to the other person.

During the first year of life, the infant makes major strides in the acquisition of knowledge about the social world. Behavior such as fear of strangers, formation of specific attachments, and the onset of communicative skills are all reflections of this. Although you would not say that young infants have friends in the usual sense of the term, it is interesting to note that play between familiar babies (those who have had regular contact with each other) is more interactive and their social behaviors more synchronized than between unfamiliar infants (Hartup, 1989). These babies, however, have not chosen each other, and friendship overtures may be in the eye of the mother rather than in the activities of the babies.

EARLY CHILDHOOD

The emergence of self continues to develop during early childhood. According to James (1890/1950), children are aware of the "I" through two types of experiences: volition (one's motivation or "free will") and distinctiveness (how people differ from others). One's sense of one's self as a person derives from the twin experiences of self-sameness over time and of being a unique individual. It appears that these dimensions of self do not develop in a series of qualitatively distinct levels but rather appear in some rudimentary form in the youngest children. As the child gets older there is a gradual emergence of some new notion in both of these dimensions (Damon, 1983).

EMERGENCE OF SELF-CONCEPT

Neisser (1988) indicates that awareness of separateness from another has emerged by the middle of the second year and prepares the child for the second major feature of self development: the acquisition of categories that define the self. Work by Stipek, Gralenski, and Kopp (1990) has shown that only toddlers who have achieved an understanding of themselves as separate entities were able to use self-referential terms (e.g., their name or personal pronouns) and applied descriptive and evaluative terms to themselves. Thus, the self-concept evolves from a recognition of the self as physically distinct and recognizable to a representation of self as an entity with distinguishing, verbally representable characteristics.

Thus, a second source of evidence for the development of the self-system comes from speech during the second and third years. Children begin to use their name or self-related terms such as *I* and *me* (van der Meulen, 1987), refer to themselves as the agents of everyday speech, increasingly acknowledge others as independent agents, begin to refer to internal states, and identify objects as belonging to themselves (Levine, 1983).

A third source of information concerning the self-system is toddlers' increasing self-involvement during acting. Examples are children's refusal of help, especially on challenging tasks (Geppert & Kuster, 1983; emotional reactions to potential failure (Kagan, 1981); embarrassment in social interactions (Lewis, Sullivan, Stanger, & Weiss, 1989); and negativistic reactions; each of which emerge during the second year. The infer-

ence from such reactions is that the self ("I") has a separate psychological status because the child acts differently depending on whether or not the self is engaged. An example is a positive emotional reaction to self-produced, but not other-produced, outcomes (Bullock & Lutkenhaus, 1988).

Once the "I" emerges, then children begin to recognize those particular features, characteristics, and categories that define the self-as-object. It is around the age of 15 to 18 months that children acquire the ability to recognize and respond to self, independent of contingency. This advancement represents an important developmental milestone in self-recognition, for it heralds the emergence of the "me" or self-concept. When the self-as-object emerges, children gradually develop categories by which to define themselves vis-à-vis the external environment. This acquisition requires an appreciation of which characteristics are distinct or unique to the self.

Cognition and Development of Self-Concept   Self-concept is seen as a cognitive structure or set of structures that organize, modify, and integrate behavior. Viewing self-concept as a set of cognitive structures that have an extremely important powerful role in organizing an individual's experiences provides an understanding of the differences between younger and older children, as well as characterization of the similarities among same-aged children.

Self-conceptions appear to undergo developmental transformations. The content of the self-concept and the way in which children process information depends on the level of cognitive development of the child (Lynch, Norem-Hebeisen, & Gergen, 1981). For example, children in early childhood (ages 2 to 7) are in the stage of preoperational thinking, according to Piaget (1965). It is the emergence of representational thought and the acquisition of language that enable children to form more elaborate, sophisticated thinking or reasoning strategies (logical structures, to use Piaget's term), which govern cognitive processes, resulting in a rapid growth of the self-concept. Thus, you would anticipate a proliferation of categories the child can use to define the self.

Eder (1989) suggests that self-concept is organized in the same manner as other concepts in memory. If so, age-related changes observed in memory should also be reflected in the development of self-concept. Information about personal events can be represented in two ways, either as *specific* memories for details of events (e.g., I played on the jungle gym with Susie today), or *general* memories (I usually play with friends). General memories are present by 3 years of age; stability to access specific memories emerges at about 4 or 5 years. This same developmental pattern was observed for children's self-concepts. General memories about one's self dominate the responses of 3½ year olds; specific memories increased substantially from 3½ to 5½. Thus, age-related changes that occur in memory also occur for self-concept.

Distinguishing Features of Self-Concept When young children begin to distinguish themselves from others on the basis of noncontingency cues, they are particularly attuned to physical features. In particular, when they begin constructing the self-as-object, children focus on facial features associated with sex and age (Bullock & Lutkenhaus, 1990). That is, they find it especially easy to tell themselves apart from opposite-sex children and from older persons.

Another element in the development of self-concept of children is the beginning of a capacity to scan and respond to inner states. Toddlers, for example, can identify mood states and changes in mood (Heckhausen, 1988). They occasionally share a memory or report a nightmare, all of which are examples of the toddler's awareness of mental activity and support the view of the toddler's self-concept as including a private inner world. Distinguishing an inner self from the bodily self or outer self emerges between 3 and 4 years of age (Pennebaker, 1980). After they have developed an understanding that they have private selves, children then set about the task of defining the characteristics of those private selves.

Young children generally attend to the overt, exterior, public aspects when categorizing the self, rather than to underlying qualities or feelings. Children between the ages of 2 and 3 are likely to organize their self-concepts around physical features and motor performance ("I have big feet. I can run fast."). Children between the ages of 3 and 5 tend to categorize their selves in terms of bodily activity rather than in terms of body parts. When children between the ages of 3 and 5 were asked to say things spontaneously about themselves, 50% of their responses were action statements: "I play baseball"; "I walk to school." (Keller, Ford, & Meacham, 1978).

Similarly, young children do not differentiate themselves from their physical surroundings. That is, they are, in an important sense, what they own, where they live. They do not differentiate the outward, observable aspects of the person from the inward, covert aspects (Bullock & Lutkenhaus, 1990). People are how they look and behave.

In early childhood, youngsters do not differentiate traits about themselves. For example, when trait labels such as good or bad first become available to children, they describe themselves as "all good" or "all bad" (Harter, 1982); they do not believe they can be both at the same time. Young children are better at describing themselves than they are at describing others, perhaps on account of their egocentric outlook.

Research has addressed the question as to whether young children organize their behaviors and internal states into meaningful and consistent self-conceptions. Eder (1990) found that when 61 3½-year-olds and 61 5½-year-olds were presented with a set of statements representing several personality dimensions in random order, children do select statements as being self-descriptive in a nonrandom fashion. The types of statements presented to the children are listed in Table 10.1. Eder suggests that young children possess an elaborate self-concept enabling them to recognize behaviors and emotions as being consistent or inconsistent with their self-concepts.

DEVELOPMENT OF SELF-ESTEEM

Self-esteem is essentially a social structure; it arises in social experiences. The origin of self-esteem lies

Typical 3- to 5-year-olds tend to describe themselves in terms of action statements. "I can ride my bike very fast."

in the complex interrelationships between children and others who comprise their environment. As such, self-esteem reflects the responses and appraisals of others. People come to evaluate themselves from the "reflected appraisals" of others. This is known as the outer source of self-esteem. Children more or less see themselves the way others see them. This contention has been empirically supported in a number of studies. In one study,

195 subjects were divided into 10 groups (Miyamoto & Dornbusch, 1956). The subjects were volunteering members of two fraternities and two sororities. Each member had lived in his or her own house for at least three months. Subjects were asked to rate themselves on a 5-point scale with regard to four characteristics: intelligence, self-confidence, physical attractiveness, and likableness. Using the same 5-point scale, each person rated every other member of the group on the same characteristics. Each subject then predicted how every other member of the group would rate him or her on the four scales. The specific test of the principle of direct reflection was whether those who rated themselves favorably were more likely to be rated favorably by others. The data clearly show that individuals tend to see themselves as they are seen by others.

Parents provide the atmosphere in which most children have their first experience as social beings and are considered to be significant sources in the development of children's self-esteem (Hales, 1990). Because the home remains the child's chief environment for so long, it tends to become inextricably part of the child before the world outside has any consistent chance to exert an influence.

The process by which an awareness of personal attributes is translated into a self-esteem may be diagrammed as follows:

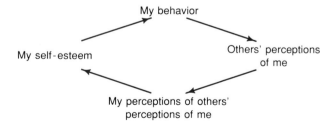

It logically begins with "others' perceptions of me," for children's self-esteem is gradually abstracted from the ways other people have reacted to them. Children evaluate and value themselves in congruence with the general reactions of others toward them. The conditions in the affective, interpersonal environment, which cause children to know success or failure, triumph or humiliation,

TABLE 10.1 Definitions and Examples of Statements for the 10 Dimension Categories

Dimension	Definition	High Statement	Low Statement
Achievement	Works hard; enjoys demanding activities; is a perfectionist.	I mostly do things that are hard.	I mostly do things that are easy.
Aggression	Will hurt others; is physically assertive; tries to frighten others.	When I get angry, I feel like hitting someone.	When I get angry, I feel like being quiet.
Alienation	Believes others wish him/her harm; feels unlucky; feels left out and alone.	No one cares what happens to me.	People care what happens to me.
Harm-Avoidance	Avoids possibility of physical danger; seeks physical safety.	I don't climb things that are high.	I climb really high things.
Control	Does not do things on the spur of the moment; is planful; does not begin one activity without finishing previous one.	When I color, I try to stay inside the lines.	When I color, I don't try to stay inside the lines.
Social Closeness	Friendship dimension: seeks intimacy; loves people; helps.	It's more fun to do things with other people than by myself.	It's more fun to do things by myself than with other people.
Social Potency	Leadership dimension: likes to stand out, influence people, be the center of attention.	I tell my friends what to do.	My friends tell me what to do.
Stress Reaction	Is upset, scared, angry.	I get mad a lot.	I don't usually get mad.
Traditionalism	Authority dimension: cares about manners, being polite.	I usually do what Mommy or my teacher says.	Sometimes I don't do what Mommy or my teacher says.
Well-Being	Happiness dimension: is joyful; is content; degree of comfort; shows silliness, enthusiasm.	I like myself.	I sometimes don't like myself.

Source: From "Uncovering Young Children's Psychological Selves: Individual and Developmental Differences" by R. A. Eder, 1990, *Child Development, 61*, p. 853. © The Society for Research in Child Development, Inc. Reprinted by permission.

acceptance or rejection, are important determinants of their self-esteem. From personal experiences and the quality of those experiences with the significant others in the environment, children mentally begin to construct evaluations of self.

Evaluative feedback from others is a powerful determinant of self-esteem, but it is not the only factor. As James (1890/1950) noted a century ago, self-perceived competencies provide an important basis for self-esteem. Perceived competence reflects children's beliefs about their ability to succeed at particular tasks; it results from being able to act effectively and master their environment. This is known as the inner source of self-esteem. Thus, positive self-esteem is *earned* through one's own competent actions (Hales, 1990). High self-esteem comes to be based on children's developing actual intellectual and physical competencies and social skills, which produce positive evaluations from self and others.

Thus, self-perceived competencies in areas that are valued by the person provide an important basis for self-esteem (Hales, 1990). The importance of personally valued competencies was underscored by William James (1890/1950).

I, who for the time have staked my all on being a psychologist, am mortified if others know much more psychology than I. But I am contented to wallow in the grossest ignorance of Greek. My deficiencies there give me no sense of personal humiliation at all. Had I "pretensions" to be a linguist, it would have been just the reverse. . . . So our self-feeling in this world depends entirely on what we back ourselves to be or do. (p. 310)

TABLE 10.2   Self-Estimate as Likable and Global Self-Esteem

GLOBAL SELF-ESTEEM	CARE A GREAT DEAL ABOUT BEING LIKABLE SELF-ESTIMATE (PERCENT)			CARE SOMEWHAT, A LITTLE, OR NOT AT ALL ABOUT BEING LIKABLE SELF-ESTIMATE (PERCENT)		
	Very	Fairly	Not Very or Not at All	Very	Fairly	Not Very or Not at All
High	54	45	17	46	49	31
Medium	39	42	33	39	43	50
Low	7	13	50	15	8	19
	(N = 345)	(N = 569)	(N = 52)	(N = 41)	(N = 133)	(N = 134)

Source: Adapted from "Psychological Selectivity in Self-Esteem Formation" by M. Rosenberg and F. Rosenberg, 1982, in M. Rosenberg and H. Kaplan (Eds.), *Social Psychology of the Self-Concept* (p. 536), Arlington Heights, IL: Harlan Davidson.

Rosenberg (1986) has conducted research that supports James's contention that traits valued by individuals are important in influencing self-esteem. Consider the statement, "I am a likable person." Rosenberg found that those who considered themselves likable and felt that this was an important trait to them had higher global self-esteem. As Table 10.2 shows, the strength of the relationships depends on the importance attached to being likable. Only 19% of the students who said they were not very or not at all likable, and really did not care if they were or not, had low self-esteem. Fully 50% of the students who cared a great deal about being likable and said they were not had low self-esteem.

Rosenberg then chose 16 qualities in his study that were most highly valued by his subjects. He discovered that those who cared about the qualities and felt they did not have these qualities had a low self-esteem. The results of his study are presented in Table 10.3. To know that people consider themselves deficient with regard to a particular quality is plainly an inadequate indication of what they think of themselves. You must also know how much they value this quality.

Seeing yourself through the subjectively perceived reflected appraisals of others develops gradually. Suls and Mullen (1982) found in their research that 3-year-old children tend to evaluate their abilities in a very direct way. Because motor accomplishments predominate children's activities, competence is defined by the direct feedback of obvious successes or failures. Objective standards and physical reality dominate children's world and cognition.

Therefore, children's self-esteem tends to derive from what they observe about themselves: their physical characteristics (strong/weak), social identity (boy/girl), and specific actions and abilities (can pull a wagon, cross the street). Their self-evaluations are not stable or enduring. At this moment, a child may say, "I am smart" because she can tell you how old she is. Tomorrow she may say, "I am not smart" because she can't tell you when her birthday is. Young children's self-esteem relates to that which they observe about themselves and requires no probing or sophisticated analysis on their part.

Similarly, social comparisons will not be used by young children in evaluation of self because they are egocentric in orientation and preoccupied with their own point of view rather than that of others. Moreover, children live within a limited social environment that does not yet foster appreciation of social standards. Ruble (1983) conducted two studies in which children of different ages performed against same-aged peers. The results consistently indicated that younger children's self-evaluations were little affected by relative comparisons.

TABLE 10.3 Low Self-Estimates and Low Self-Esteem According to Importance of Qualities Rated	CARE ABOUT QUALITIES LISTED (PERCENT WITH LOW SELF-ESTEEM)	
	Great Deal	**Little or Not at All**
Rate Self Poor on Qualities Below		
Good student in school	32	18
Likable	50	19
Dependable and reliable	36	23
Intelligent, good mind	34	26
Clear-thinking, clever	34	22
Rate Self Poor on Qualities Below		
Hardworking, conscientious	28	17
Easy to get along with	38	23
Realistic, able to face facts	30	17
Friendly, sociable, pleasant	29	24
Honest, law-abiding	42	21
Mature, not childish	29	31
Good sense, sound judgment	33	26
Kind and considerate	28	22
Get along well	39	21
Well-liked by many different people	35	23
Stand up for rights	27	26
Moral and ethical	32	25

Source: From "Psychological Selectivity in Self-Esteem Formation" by M. Rosenberg and F. Rosenberg, 1982, in M. Rosenberg and H. Kaplan (Eds.), *Social Psychology of the Self-Concept* (p. 537), Arlington Heights, IL: Harlan Davidson.

Children less than 7 years of age based their self-evaluations on the "absolute standard" of whether they completed the tasks. As greater cognitive sophistication develops (increased memory skills, appreciation of past, present, and future, being able to take the perspective of others), social comparison becomes possible. Ruble found that children older than 7 years compared their performances against those of others and based their self-evaluations on such social comparisons.

While Ruble states that social comparisons begin as early as 7 years, other researchers maintain that they take place somewhat later. Aboud (1985), for example, found that it is not until children are 9 years old that they begin to evaluate their ability relative to peers' performance.

Gradually, children begin to place more emphasis on the evaluations of the significant others who comprise their environment. **Significant others,** a term coined by Sullivan (1953), refers to those per-sons who are important or who have significance to children by reason of sensing their ability to allay insecurity or intensify it, increase or decrease children's sense of helplessness, and promote or diminish children's sense of well-being.

With the lessening of egocentrism and the development of perspective-taking skills, children have the ability to imagine what significant others think of them. The term *self-consciousness* captures the process whereby one is conscious of being judged by others, which in turn causes one to be conscious of the self that is being evaluated. You might explain this phenomenon as indicating that these children have reached the Piagetian stage of reciprocity and cooperation; they are obliged to take the viewpoint of others into account, and as a result they become more self-conscious.

In summary, there are two sources of self-esteem: perceived evaluations from others (outer source of self-esteem) and actually developing your own competencies in valued contexts of action (inner source of self-esteem). Thus, significant others have two socialization goals: responding positively to children and helping them develop more competent behaviors.

UNDERSTANDING OTHERS: EGOCENTRIC ROLE TAKING

In early childhood, most of the social exchanges in peer groups occur in the setting of play, which generally involves engaging in a nonserious activity for the sheer satisfaction it brings. Most children spend countless hours at play, reveling in being silly and gleeful and in just plain having fun.

Play is more important, however, than just being silly or having fun. Many theorists, researchers, and educators adhere to the belief that play causes growth in a variety of developmental domains (Smith & Vollstedt, 1985). During the toddler and preschool years, many of children's attempts to gain effective control of the environment and autonomy occur in the context of social interaction with peers. Play facilitates the development of competence and autonomy and helps children to achieve a balance between independence and dependence. Through active involvement with the environment, play stimulates cognitive growth. Moreover, play facilitates language development; during play, children are stimulated to use language to ask questions, talk about their experiences, solve problems, and direct activities. Simply put, play can be one of the major ways in which children experiment with social relations and develop their social skills.

The earliest form of play is sensorimotor manipulation, also called *functional play.* Functional play consists of simple, repetitive movements, with or without objects, that seemingly have no intent or end goal in mind. Piaget (1962) has mentioned that functional play is engaged in simply for the pure pleasure of exercising existing schemes without efforts of adaptation. It is the primary way children between 14 and 30 months spend their free time (Sponseller & Jaworski, 1979). Infants' first attempts at play include finger staring, mouthing objects, banging blocks, and repetitious behaviors

such as hitting a string to watch it swing. Later, as motor activities come increasingly under children's own control, children begin to manipulate and explore in a playful way. Some functional play—like peek-a-boo, and this little piggy—have a clear, gamelike quality. Still later, children like to run through the house or spend a considerable amount of time pushing and pounding clay with no purpose to construct with it. After a while, functional play declines in frequency, dropping to only 17% of free time in 5-year-olds (Howes, Unger, & Seidner, 1989).

As opposed to play dominated by sensorimotor schemes (banging, mouthing, striking objects) in infancy, play in early childhood shifts to activities that are generated from the child's own fantasies and delights (Fenson & Ramsay, 1980). *Symbolic,* or *pretend, play* offers children an avenue for assimilating novel experiences into familiar schemes. There is also some empirical evidence that the opportunity to develop symbolic play fosters the development of social skills. To illustrate, 40 hours of training in sociodramatic play were given to African-American children in low-economic kindergartens (Rosen, 1974). Training sessions included role playing and creating fantasy themes. Compared with the control group who had not received training, the children in the experimental group helped each other more, interrelated with each other more, and worked more cooperatively.

In addition to fantasy play, 4-, 5-, and 6-year-olds engage in *constructive play.* That is, they like to manipulate objects in order to construct or to create. Hetherington (1979) observed that children at these age levels spend 51% of their free activity time in constructive play. In addition, as children get older, they engage in more interactive and cooperative play. It appears that children who have had experience in playing with peers engage in more interactive and cooperative play than children who are inexperienced in playing with peers (Harper & Huie, 1985). "Studying Children" offers an activity that will help you learn more about preschoolers' play patterns.

Physical objects or toys seem to be central in early peer action (Mueller & Vandell, 1979). For

STUDYING CHILDREN

PRESCHOOLERS' PLAY

Observe at a nursery school and note the types of play activities (solitary, parallel, and so on) in which the children are engaging. What type of play activity pattern occurs most frequently?

---

toddlers, physical objects seem so important that when all objects are removed from the room, they take off their shoes to create toys! Toddler sociability seems to revolve around doing some things together, and toys are the prime currency of social exchange. Object-centered contacts are the initial basis of sustained social interactions among young children. Toys that are easily manipulated (flexible and wiggly) and make noises seem to be especially attractive to toddlers (McCall, 1974).

Sharing of toys first appears toward the end of the first year and increases markedly between 18 and 24 months (Hay, 1979). This is not to imply that toddlers are always generous little souls; often 2- and 3-year-olds seem to perceive toys as an extension of self rather than as existing independently of the self. Therefore, toddlers may be reluctant to share a favorite toy.

Selman (1980) studied children's friendships and has given us a great deal of information as to how children's understanding of interpersonal relationships changes over time. He suggests that children's development of social ideas depends on systematic developmental shifts in role-taking skills. Selman presented stories to children in which two individuals were in conflict. He then questioned the children about what might be happening to the participants in the dilemma. One dilemma, for example, involves a girl, Holly, who is the best tree climber in the neighborhood. One day she falls from a tree and her father says no more tree climbing. A few days later she sees her friend's kitten caught up in a tree and only she can get it down. In particular, Selman asked children how they would resolve these conflicts; how they would define friendship; and what trust in a rela-

tionship meant. He noted that developmental change in interpersonal understanding is defined as an orderly progression through a series of five hierarchically organized stages or levels. Table 10.4 lists the five stages; each stage will be discussed in more detail in their appropriate age-related sections.

Selman's first (level 0; 3 to 6) is known as *egocentric role taking*. Preschoolers' definitions of friends give no indication of a lasting relationship. These children are unable to define friendship beyond the momentary or repeated incidents of interaction between two persons who come together to play. Thus, friendships at this level are based on where you live and with whom you are playing at the moment. Even though friendships are not associated with well-articulated expectations, they can be quite intense, but also may be short-lived. Parents sometimes express surprise at the number and frequency of changes among young friends. It is not uncommon for children to announce that someone they just met and talked with briefly is a friend. It is not uncommon for young children to drop friends of long standing because they have had a fight.

According to Selman, preschoolers' friends are people who are nice; those who are mean are not friends. Trust is limited to faith in a friend's physical ability. That is, trust in a friend is knowing that she can play with your toys without breaking them.

Previous research has indicated that preschoolers' psychological statements pertaining to inner states and emotions about friends are entirely absent from their descriptions about friends. In asking 3½- and 5½-year-old children about their best friends, Eder (1990) reported that these children do have a rudimentary understanding of the internal states and emotions of others. For example, in asking a 3½-year-old to tell about a friend's day at school, the child responded by saying, "He didn't feel very good. He was naughty today and got a time out." Children frequently justified their responses by referring to a belief or attitude: "I don't feel that good with grownups 'cause I don't like grownups."

TABLE 10.4   Selman's Five Levels of Role Taking

LEVEL 0: EGOCENTRIC ROLE TAKING (3 TO 5):	Children's response to the dilemma: Father would be pleased if Holly saved the kitten; Holly sees the importance of it so surely will her father. At this level, there is no role taking because children do not realize that others have different psychological perspectives. Children understand thoughts and emotions of others by projecting their own perspective onto others.
LEVEL 1: SOCIAL INFORMATION ROLE TAKING (6 TO 8):	Children's response to the dilemma: Children may focus on Holly's promise to her father not to climb trees anymore, or they may focus on the importance of saving the kitten. At this level, children are capable of noticing the conflict; they are aware of the different perspectives that can lead to different actions. Despite this ability, children have great difficulty keeping both viewpoints in mind at once, and are likely to focus on one perspective at the expense of the other.
LEVEL 2: SELF-REFLECTIVE ROLE TAKING (8 TO 10):	Children's response to the dilemma: Holly should save the kitten because her friend will be grateful, or Holly should obey her father and not climb the tree because if she does her father will be angry with her. Children at this level begin to realize that other people can evaluate their actions. They understand that their own perspective is not the only valid one, and they begin to evaluate themselves in terms of how others will view them.
LEVEL 3: MUTUAL ROLE TAKING (10 TO 12):	Children's response to the dilemma: Children realize that Holly's father might not agree with her about her climbing the tree to save the kitten; however, they believe that Holly's father would be able to understand if she did save the kitten. Children in Level 3 can simultaneously consider the viewpoints of both participants in the conflict as well as by a third party.
LEVEL 4: SOCIAL AND CONVENTIONAL SYSTEM ROLE TAKING (12 TO 15):	Adolescents' response to the dilemma: Holly should save the kitten; it is the humanitarian thing to do. Adolescents are able to take a detached view of the dyadic relationship and view it from the perspective of a third person (peer, teacher, or society). Adolescents begin to compare their own views with those of society at large and realize that the social system in which they operate is a product of the shared views of the members of society.

Source: Based on *The Growth of Interpersonal Understanding* by R. Selman, 1980, New York: Academic Press.

MIDDLE CHILDHOOD

Broughton (1978) noted that children in middle childhood are aware that they are distinct or different from others, not just because of physical differences, but because they have different thoughts and feelings. The self is now defined internally rather than externally. As one 10-year-old responded, "There could be a person who looks like me and talks like me, but no one who has every single detail like I have. Never a person who thinks exactly like me" (Broughton, 1978, p. 86).

Children now begin to understand the mental and volitional aspects of self on their own terms, removed from direct links to any particular body parts. In other words, children now begin to distinguish mind and body, although this distinction is not as finely articulated as it will be in adolescence (Damon, 1983). They now see that the self can monitor its own thoughts. "I can do well in math if I really try."

CONCRETE CONCEPTIONS OF SELF

Many changes take place as children enter school. A combination of physical growth and cognitive maturity enables them to undertake tasks that require manual dexterity, self-control, peer cooperation, planning, and prolonged concentration. New intellectual competencies give children tools for self-conceptualization.

Concrete operational thinkers are busy classifying and systematically organizing the concrete experiences and objects in their lives. Perhaps, too, classifying and organizing characteristics of the self in a systematic way occurs during this time. Because children are not capable of reasoning abstractly, you would also expect their concept of self to revolve around concrete, observable traits.

Children's descriptions of self become more coherent, more complex, better organized, and more selectively focused (Rosenberg & Rosenberg, 1981). Global evaluations of self and others ("all smart" or "all dumb") are replaced by differential evaluations ("smart in English" "dumb in math") (Harter, 1983). With increasing age, portrayals of self shift from emphasis on superficial, concrete qualities in middle childhood to more ephemeral and abstract features in adolescence.

During middle childhood (ages 7–11), children's breadth of self-description increases from a few physical qualities, motor skills, sex type, and age, which are the hallmarks of young children's self-concept, to a number of new categories centering primarily on concrete and observable characteristics. In a study done by Montemayor and Eisen (1977), 136 males and 126 females from grades 4 through 12 were given the "twenty statements test." In the test, the children were given 12 minutes to write 20 answers to the question, "Who am I?" As can be seen in Figure 10.5, younger children tended to view themselves in terms of specific features—how they look, what activities they enjoy, and possessions. Children in middle childhood tended to conceptualize self in more dispositional terms.

Consider the following self-descriptions (Livesley & Bromley, 1973) reported by a girl aged 7 and a boy aged 9.

> I am 7 years old. I have one sister. Next year I will be eight. I like colouring. The game I like is hide the thimble. I go riding every Wednesday. I have lots of toys. My flowers are a rose, and a buttercup and a daisy. I like milk to drink and lemon. I like meat to eat and potatoes as well as meat.
>
> I have dark brown hair, brown eyes, and a fair face. I am a quick worker, but am often lazy. I am good but often cheeky and naughty. My character is sometimes funny and sometimes serious. My behaviour is sometimes silly and stu-

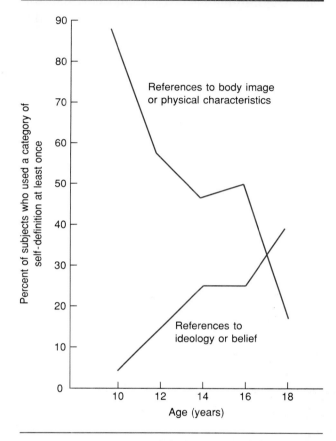

FIGURE 10.5   References to Body Image and Ideologies or Beliefs

Source: Adapted from "The Development of Self-Conceptions from Childhood to Adolescence" by R. Montemayor and M. Eisen, 1977, *Developmental Psychology, 13*, p. 316. Copyright 1977 by the American Psychological Association. Reprinted by permission.

pid and often good. It is often funny my daddy thinks. (p. 238)

According to Livesley and Bromley these descriptions can be categorized into "peripheral" statements; which refer to appearance, identity information (such as name or age), routine activities or habits, possessions, details of life events, likes and dislikes, social roles, and kinship relations; and "dispositional" statements; which include personality traits, general trends in behavior (such as "always hits people"), motives, needs values, and finally attitudinal orientation. Consistent with self-descriptions of this younger child and this older child, Livesley and Bromley found a clear increase with age in the use of disposition statements to describe the self and other persons. Moreover, the most pronounced change occurred between the ages of 7 and 8.

In another study done by McGuire and Padawer-Swinger (1976), 252 sixth-graders were given the "tell us about yourself test." The children were given a booklet headed with this question and were asked to write for 7 minutes. Twenty-five percent of all the responses fell in the categories of habitual activities (recreations, daily routines) and physical attributes (I have blond hair; I am tall).

The investigators also found that subjects most frequently chose characteristics of self that were uncommon in relation to other children. For instance, children who were 6 or more months older or younger than the model age for their class were more likely to mention their age. Similarly, foreign-born children mentioned their birthplace. Children reported hair color, eye color, and weight much more frequently if their own versions of these were distinct from their classmates. Apparently, then, older children are very sensitive to even small quantitative differences in the commonness of particular characteristics. This research suggests that children often define the self by characteristics that they sense will distinguish them clearly from others.

It is interesting to note that even though the children were told not to write their names on the test, 19% did so. (Perhaps a larger percentage think their names are an important part of their self-concept and would have included this information if they had not been given the inhibitory instructions that stressed anonymity.) On the other hand, they were instructed to write down anything that came to their minds. Thus, names appear to be a salient part of children's self-concepts.

Moreover, children tend to describe themselves in terms of their active abilities relative to others, such as, "I can ride a bike better than my brother." This indicates that children are now distinguishing

Children in middle childhood tend to describe themselves in terms of characteristics that are uncommon to their classmates or that set them apart from others, such as being the tallest in the class.

themselves in terms of their active abilities in comparison to others rather than in absolute terms, as they did in early childhood. As children progress through the elementary grades, evaluation is increasingly based on normative criteria, and children begin to define competence in terms of social comparison.

Social self-conceptions make their appearance during the school-age years. Who they are becomes intimately tied to the many other people around them; that is, children define the self in terms of traits they usually exhibit in their dealings with others: kind, friendly, tough, shy, and so on. Similarly, children refer to social group memberships in their self-descriptions. A child might say, for example, that he is a Boy Scout or a Catholic. This suggests that although the social self does not seem to be as predominant during early middle childhood as either the active or the physical self, it is occasionally present in the self-awareness of children (Damon, 1983).

Consistency of Self-Concept Although self-concepts continually grow and change, children are beginning to solidify them and resist any changes that disturb the self-system. Children in middle childhood move from a definition of "me" in terms of transient actions and emotions to a definition of "me" in terms of stable personality traits (Beane, 1983). Sometime between the ages of 5 and 8, children develop a relatively stable view of their capacities in all perspectives of self (Rotenberg, 1982). Once children's self-concepts begin to jell, they tend to behave in accordance with their preconceived impressions regarding themselves (Epstein, 1981). Their biased evaluations of themselves become the core element in structuring their behavior. This means that children try to protect and preserve the concepts they hold of themselves; a need for internal consistency pushes them to resist and reject anything incompatible with their evaluation. Behavior must always be appropriate to the self (Beane & Lipka, 1980). Most ways of behaving that are adopted by children are those that are consistent with the self-concept. How do children in middle childhood manage to keep consistency in their self-systems?

Markus (1977, 1982) has provided a developmental framework for viewing the self-concept as a set of cognitive structures for processing information, known as self-schemata, that in turn regulates behavior. In Markus's (1982) words, "Self-schemata are cognitive generalizations about the self, derived from past experiences, that organize and guide the processing of self-related information contained in the individual's social experience (p. 50)."

Self-schemata become the central cognitive units in the human information-processing system. Over the course of their lives, children become increasingly aware of the distinctive characteristics of their personality: appearance, temperament, abilities, and so on. As they gather knowledge about themselves, they proceed through life behaving according to their self-schemata. Self-schemata provide the individual with a point of view, an anchor, a frame of reference. As mechanisms of selectivity, they guide the individual in choosing the aspects of social behavior to be regarded as relevant and function as interpretive frameworks for understanding behavior.

Children search for information that is congruent with their self-schemata. As Markus (1977) points out, "Once established, self-schemata serve as selected devices that determine whether information is attended to, how it is structured, how much importance is attached to it and what happens to it subsequently (p. 64)." Self-schemata can shape children's interactions in their environment by influencing how information is handled (that is, encoded, monitored, retrieved, stored, and evaluated). They also determine the type and nature of information about the self that will be managed and presented to others in the course of an interaction.

Thus, people are motivated to act in accordance with the self-schemata to which they have become committed. Once a particular self-schema is well established—that is, formed, used continually, and supported by data—it becomes increasingly resistant to contradictory information. People tend to notice behaviors that support that construct and interpret behaviors in its light.

One of Markus's (1977) studies examined the impact of self-schemata on the selection and processing of information about the self. The procedure of the first part of her study was to select a dimension of behavior, identify individuals with or without schemata on this dimension, and compare the subjects' performances on a variety of cognitive tasks.

To gain a preliminary idea of each subject's self-schemata on various dimensions, a number of self-rating scales were administered in introductory psychology classes. The most appropriate pattern of variation in self-ratings was found on the independent/dependent dimension, and that dimension was selected for further study. Forty-eight students who thought of themselves as either dependent or independent were selected to participate individually in laboratory sessions.

Markus found that when the group of individuals who thought of themselves as independent were given a list of a number of trait adjectives associated with independence and dependence, these individuals endorsed significantly more adjectives associated with the concept of independence than did those individuals who did not characterize themselves in this way. In addition, when subjects who thought of themselves as independent were asked to select trait adjectives and cite instances from their own past behavior to support their endorsement of a particular adjective as self-descriptive, they were able to supply examples of independent behavior. A parallel pattern of results was found with those individuals who thought of themselves as dependent.

A month later, 47 of these same students participated in another phase of the experiment. They were given the QPAT Suggestibility Test, which actually was a fictitious test prepared especially so that the experimenter could provide feedback not congruent with the subjects' self-schemata. Markus found that the subjects were not willing to accept information incongruent with their self-schemata. These studies, then, provide evidence for the concept of self-schemata, cognitive generalizations about self, which tend to organize, summarize, and explain behavior along a particular dimension.

Self-schemata tend to select what stimuli will be acted on by the individual and to screen out those that are out-of-tune with the present rhythm of the individual's self-development. The self-concept,

then, is seen as a perceptual phenomenon; it is a set of rules (or self-schemata) for processing information. The self-concept plays a central role as the "meaning-maker" (Kegan, 1982) in perceptual-processing activities. As such, it provides a frame of reference that instigates, maintains, and directs behavior.

Seeing What You Subjectively Think You See   Children's self-concepts tend to become more selective as to which features of their experiences are assumed to be self-referring. If an attitude or value seems to fit in, people are likely to adopt it. If it is inconsistent with self-schemata, people are likely to ignore or reject it. As Schlenker (1980) describes the situation, children erect a perceptual barrier around themselves. Events that confirm the already developed self or that are new readily gain admittance; others are denied or discouraged.

For example, if one of your self-schemata is that you are a poor speller, and you receive a good grade on your spelling test, you may resort to a number of things to "reject" this information, which is inconsistent with that particular self-schema. You may say that the words on this test were so easy that anybody could get a good grade, or that you were just lucky this time, and so on. Children will twist and cram new experiences into preconceived slots in an attempt to maintain consistency of self. Any value entering the self-system that is inconsistent with individuals' evaluation of themselves will not be assimilated (Epstein, 1981).

Because people have a strong tendency to defend their self-concept, they are apt to blot out any positive messages about their own competence, if such messages are in conflict with an unfavorable picture of self (Bannister & Agnew, 1977). Children, for example, who believe that they are weak or stupid will cling to perceptions that bolster this unflattering picture and reject any suggestions that they may be strong or bright. To protect a good self-concept, children will strive hard or will select behaviors that preserve or enhance it. Children generally solve any dissonance between evidence about themselves and their judgment of a situation in which they are involved by retaining their customary judgment of themselves.

Behaving Consistently   Even as socialization processes are helping to form self-concept, self-concept, in turn, is influencing socialization. It becomes strong enough to help dictate behavior, and thus becomes an agent of socialization as well as a product of it. To illustrate, children with negative self-schemata seem to want others to think as poorly of them as they do of themselves (Markus, 1982). They attempt to produce in others the response they expect. In accordance with this explanation, children who feel academically inadequate see themselves as unable to achieve and therefore behave in such a way that they really do fail to attain academic superiority. Such children *have* to make poor grades in order to be true to themselves, for it would be just as wrong for children who believe themselves to be dumb in their studies to make good grades as it would for children who define themselves as honest to steal.

Lecky (1945), a pioneer in research on the self, studied children who were relatively bright, but atrociously bad in spelling. He found that tutoring these children was of little avail. Further, Lecky discovered that these children made approximately the same number of errors per page. Consciously or perhaps unconsciously, they were maintaining their poor-speller construct. Apparently their behavior was consistent with their self-schemata. Whatever children tend to expect, their own perceptions and behaviors tend to fulfill. Once children have definite self-schemata, they *create* experiences to fortify those constructs. For example, a boy says that no one sits next to him at lunch. Perhaps it is possible that he may choose a seat in the cafeteria that is in the corner away from most of the students. Thus, every day, by isolating himself, he creates a condition under which no one will sit next to him.

PEERS AS SOURCES OF SELF-ESTEEM

With increasing age, children in middle childhood assimilate into their picture of self the recognition or feedback received from their peers as well as teachers and other people in authority. Children begin to judge themselves through many experiences and interactions, gradually attaching more importance to their peers' evaluations of them.

Several studies have shown that between the fourth and eighth grade, children's gradual integration into the peer group is accompanied by a shift from their reliance on parents for evaluations of their selves to that of a reliance on peers (Harter, 1983; Kizziar & Hagedorn, 1979; Wylie, 1979). Further, these studies have shown that 12- and 13-year-olds are the most conforming, reflecting the importance of peers. The proposition that the peer

By isolating himself from others at recess time, this child is creating a condition that reinforces his image of self as one who has no friends.

group becomes the predominant reference group for the child may be measured by the degree to which the child conforms to group norms. In other words, with children's increasing integration into the peer group between early childhood and late childhood, they grow to value it with increasing positiveness.

It should be pointed out that while peers and family influences play a significant role in determining children's level of self-esteem, peers tend to be less influential than family influences (Harter, 1983). This is so because when children begin to incorporate nonfamily influences into their self-pictures, they are at a more cognitively advanced and therefore less helpless age. That is, the evaluations and standards of nonfamily agents are more amenable to scrutiny by children's higher intellectual faculties. By contrast, the evaluations and standards of the child's family, incorporated at an earlier, less advanced age, tend to be accepted without critical judgment.

UNDERSTANDING OTHERS: MUTUAL ROLE TAKING

Around the ages of 6 to 8 children are at Selman's level 1: *social information role taking*. In this stage children define friends as those individuals who share their worldly goods, act nice, and are fun to be with. The relationship is seen as momentary and transient, with little individuality associated with a friend; that is, "all friends are the same." Children focus on specific acts performed by the friend that meet the self's wishes. Friends are important because they perform something you want done ("You need a friend because you want to play games"). A close friend is one who is known better than others and knowing someone better means knowing his or her likes or dislikes, which children feel is necessary before making friends.

Selman's level 2, known as *self-reflective role taking*, occurs around 8 to 10 years of age. Friends are described as people who help one another either spontaneously or in response to an expression of need. The two most central features of this level are trust and reliability. In this stage, children can take a relativistic perspective and see that each

party has a set of likes and dislikes that need to be coordinated. Conflicts occur between parties, rather than being caused by one person. Both parties must engage in resolution. The basic limitation, however, is that children still feel that the solution to the problem should be self-serving. Friends are important because everyone needs a companion. Trust implies someone you can tell a secret to and it will be safely stored away.

Level 3, *mutual role taking,* occurs between the ages of 10 and 12. Children at this level are able to simultaneously consider the viewpoints of both the participants in a conflict. Children are aware of their own unique feelings but also recognize that others may have unique feelings. Social facts and interpersonal relationships have a shared nature.

Gender concordance marks children's friendships at all ages during middle childhood. Cross-sex friendships are relatively rare in middle childhood; in most studies, they account for about 5% of the friendships. Both boys and girls describe loyalty as a major element in friendships. Friends are expected to stick up for and be loyal to each other. Finally, children are aware of differences in degrees of friendship—for example, between their very closest friends and their other friends (Berndt, 1989; Berndt & Hawkins, 1987); yet they normally think of friendships not just as relationships between pairs of children but as sets of relationships among small groups of children who frequently interact with one another.

ADOLESCENCE

There is noteworthy convergence in findings that adolescent's self-understanding shows increasing use of psychological and social relational concepts from describing the "me," a more prominent belief in the "I's" agency and volitional power, and a tendency toward integration of the disparate aspects of self into an internally consistent construct system. Adolescents, in the formal operational stage of thinking, are capable of abstract thinking, so you may anticipate the emergence of new constructs in theorizing about the self and one's "personality." The emergence of abstract thinking also enables adolescents to think abstractly about their attributes, behaviors, emotions, and motives.

ABSTRACT CONCEPTIONS OF SELF

The shift from physical, concrete conceptions of self to abstract, psychological conceptions that occurs during adolescence reflects cognitive advances in thinking and reasoning (Dusek & Flaherty, 1981). Adolescents are able to think abstractly, reason about the hypothetical, and introspect. The emergence of formal operational thinking substantially affects adolescents' self-concept.

Older children (13–18) begin to describe themselves more in terms of psychological traits (their feelings, personality traits, and their relations with others) reflecting on an inner world of thoughts and feelings (Montemayor & Eisen, 1977). "I get along well with others because I am basically a friendly person." Thus, with increasing age an individual's self-concept becomes more abstract. Adolescents no longer describe themselves in terms of specific acts and qualities; they describe themselves in terms of abstractions and general evaluations. In short, the self becomes less a pure perceptual object and more and more a conceptual trait system.

Why do older children, as compared with younger children, conceptualize the self and others in terms of a psychological interior (an inner world of thought and feeling)? The basic explanation of the age differences is to be found in the different cognitive processes of children and adolescents. Rosenberg (1986) suggests that **introspection** (looking into your own mind and inspecting your own feelings) is a critical process that differentiates children and adolescents and contributes to self-concept differences. Unlike young children, mature individuals are alert and responsive to their own thought processes.

Examples are common: Older children think of an idea and dismiss it as stupid; they laugh at their own jokes, argue with their own conclusions. In order for introspection to occur, thought must first become conscious of itself. Young children are less likely to see themselves in terms of a psychological interior, because they haven't developed the ability to introspect.

In addition to the increased use of abstract psychological terms, the descriptions of early and late adolescents are more likely than those of young children to be integrated coherently and to include explanations for and qualifications of the descriptions offered. ("He's not very smart, but then again, he doesn't study.") (Barenboim, 1977). Such descriptions are indicative of both a greater ability to organize your thoughts and a greater recognition of the multidimensional nature of personality.

Whereas younger children invariably describe themselves in terms of the immediate present, adolescents describe themselves in terms of their past and future. In addition, some researchers have reported features of adolescent thinking that are not always apparent in every study. One prominent example is the adolescent's growing awareness of self-reflection (another "I" conception).

Older adolescents are capable of acknowledging that the self can be characterized by traits and qualities that are opposites, for example, that one can be smart and dumb at different times. When Harter (1985) asked students in grades 7, 9, and 11 to describe themselves in four social contexts (with family, with friends, in school, in romantic relationships) she found that there was a dramatic increase between 7th and 9th grades in the use of the number of paired oppositions. This suggests that conflicting traits are recognized in early adolescence.

Another difference between children's and adolescents' self-concepts is to be found in the locus of self-knowledge. In children's view, the truth about the self tends to be vested in an external authority. The perceived locus of self-knowledge shifts from the other (especially the parent) to the self in adolescence. Adolescents now feel that they know themselves better than others do (Lackovic-Grgin & Dekovic, 1990). These changes represent a qualitative shift in the structure of thoughts about self and others. Try the experiment in "Studying Children" to see if older children tend to describe themselves in terms of psychological concepts.

STUDYING CHILDREN

WHO AM I?

Ask four or five children between the ages of 7 and 11 and an equal number of adolescents (14–17) to write down 20 words that answer the question, "Who am I?" Do children in middle childhood define the self in terms of concrete, observable traits? Do adolescents tend to describe themselves in more abstract terms?

Sex Differences in Self-Concept   Marsh (1989) used 12,266 responses to self-description questionnaires and found that sex differences in self-concept were consistent with sex stereotypes. Boys had higher self-concepts in achievement/leadership than girls, girls had higher self-concepts in congeniality/sociability. Boys tend to describe themselves as more self-sufficient and achievement oriented; girls describe themselves as more sociable and help-seeking. Another study (Boersma & Chapman, 1979) found significant differences favoring girls in school satisfaction, reading, spelling, penmanship, and neatness; no significant differences for general ability and confidence were found. Marsh et al. (1988) reported that boys had higher math self-concepts and girls had higher verbal self-concepts.

A greater portion of males than females mention the athletic abilities and professional athlete categories, while females tend to mention physical appearance. Koff, Rierdan, and Stubbs (1990) have shown that appearance is more integral to self-identity for females than for males. Their sample, consisting of 92 males (age 14) and 77 females (age 14), completed a packet of questionnaires assessing various aspects of body satisfaction, body experience (clean/dirty, sick/healthy), self-esteem, and self-awareness. The results indicated that males were more satisfied with their bodies and experienced them more positively than females. Males were concerned more with task mastery and instrumental effectiveness than with physical appearance. Valuation of the body was more closely associated with the self-concept of females than of

males (Bybee, Glick, & Zigler, 1990). Females are more concerned with physical attractiveness than males. Desires for social acceptance are more prevalent among girls.

Gender differences in the domain of family are also consistent with the tendency of females to emphasize relationship, connection, and expressive function as compared with the male preference for agency and autonomy.

Moreover, the establishment of a separate sense of self seems to be more easily achieved by men than by women (Olver, Aries, & Batgos, 1990). As with most sex differences, what is referred to here is not an absolute difference between males and females; rather, females on the average have more difficulty than males in experiencing an autonomous sense of self. Self-definition for adult women has been characterized as being embedded in relationships and the emotional responses of others, whereas self-definition for adult men has been characterized as having more distinct boundaries between self and others. The research indicates that women defer to the wishes of others (Butler, 1981), take on the interests and orientations of others (Gutmann, 1965), and experience greater difficulty than men in knowing their own needs or what they genuinely want or feel apart from what others expect or approve. Women's identity is anchored more deeply in relationships (Jordan, 1986). In addition, women are more in need of affirmation from others, and their assessment of their abilities is more vulnerable to criticism by others.

Some provocative arguments have been put forward that this sex difference in the experience of a separate sense of self has its origins in the mother-infant relationship. There is more difference and separateness between mother and son than between mother and daughter. As a result, boys are pushed out and encouraged to separate and individuate and develop a more defensive firming of ego boundaries. Separation from the mother and assertion of difference are crucial for the development of masculinity. Girls, however, are encouraged to remain in a matrix of emotional connectedness.

In partial support for this hypothesis Olver et al. (1990) gave 120 college-age men and 182 college-

TABLE 10.5   Self–Other Differentiation Scale

1. If someone close to me finds fault with what I do, I find my self-evaluation lowered.
2. I find myself becoming depressed or anxious if a close friend is feeling that way.
3. I find it hard to decide how I feel about something until I've discussed it with those close to me.
4. I tend to be uncertain how good my ideas are until someone else approves of them.
5. I find it difficult to feel good about myself when I don't get affirmation from other people.
6. A chance criticism from a friend will deeply upset me.
7. When my mother criticizes my decisions, I become uncertain of them.
8. I find it hard to make a separate judgment in the face of a strong opinion expressed by a friend.
9. I feel very vulnerable to the criticism of others.
10. I feel uncomfortable if my best friend disagrees with an action I take.
11. If my parents don't approve of a decision I've made, I question my competence in making the decision.

True responses are scored as 0; false responses are scored as 1.

Source: "Self-Other Differentiation and the Mother-Child Relationship: The Effects of Sex and Birth Order" by R. R. Olver, E. Aries, and J. Batgos, 1990, *Journal of Genetic Psychology, 150,* p. 319. Reprinted with permission of the Helen Dwight Reid Educational Foundation. Published by Heldref Publications, 1319 Eighteenth St., N.W., Washington, D.C. 20036-1802. Copyright © 1990.

TABLE 10.6   Permeability of Boundaries Scale

1. My mother expresses concern about my weight.
2. My mother asks to read papers I have written for school.
3. My mother enters my room without knocking.
4. My mother makes comments about how to change my room.
5. My mother goes through my bureau drawers at home.
6. My mother buys things for me without consulting me.
7. My mother reads my personal papers.
8. My mother likes to spend time with my friends.
9. My mother gives unsolicited advice about my relationships.
10. My mother inquires about my bodily functions.
11. My mother confides in me about her personal life.
12. My mother tells me how I feel about things before I have said anything on the topic.
13. My mother inquires about what I am thinking and feeling.
14. My mother comments critically about the clothes I wear.
15. My mother worries about the food I eat.
16. My mother inquires about my personal relationships.
17. My mother gives advice about how to improve my looks.

Source: "Self-Other Differentiation and the Mother-Child Relationship: The Effects of Sex and Birth Order" by R. R. Olver, E. Aries, and J. Batgos, 1990, *Journal of Genetic Psychology, 150,* p. 320. Reprinted with permission of the Helen Dwight Reid Educational Foundation. Published by Heldref Publications, 1319 Eighteenth St., N.W., Washington, D.C. 20036-1802. Copyright © 1990.

age women the self-other differentiation scale (see Table 10.5). In addition, a questionnaire that assessed the degree of maternal involvement and intrusiveness, with higher scores indicating more permeable boundaries between mother and child, was administered (see Table 10.6). The data indicated that men showed a more separate sense of self than women. There was also clear support that mothers were more highly involved and intrusive in their relationships with their daughters' lives than in their sons' lives.

Self-Concept and Identity Status   Erikson's (1968) theory of the identity crisis represents the most comprehensive analysis of the development of self-concept during adolescence. According to

Erikson, adolescents engage in an active search in trying to achieve a new understanding of self. This search has been referred to as the **identity crisis:** a sense of confusion about who one is and what one wants out of life. An important developmental task for adolescents is to bring together all the things adolescents have learned about themselves as students, sons, daughters, friends, workers, and so on and begin to develop a sense of what they are and where they are going—an *identity.* As a psychosocial task, striving for a sense of unification and cohesiveness in the self provides meaning and direction and purpose while also serving a critical function for the individual's manifest competence and adaptive function (Allen & Majidi-Ali, 1989).

Marcia's (1980) interviews with adolescents have revealed four possible identity statuses. An individual's position on these tasks can be described along two dimensions: commitment and crises. Commitment refers to a stable investment in one's beliefs with supportive activity. Crises refers to the examination of alternatives with an intention to establish a firm commitment. Four identity statuses are derived from combinations of these two dimensions:

Identity foreclosure exists when individuals have not actively questioned alternatives, but they have made a commitment. This commitment is typically an extension of the values or expectations of significant others, which the adolescent has accepted without consideration of alternatives. Hence, foreclosed commitments may be labeled premature and deemed developmentally unsophisticated.

Moratorium exists when individuals are in the process of selecting among alternatives, actively seeking information, and looking to make a decision. They are in crisis. The moratorium status is seen as an antecedent to the most sophisticated decision-making mode, identity achievement.

Identity achievers refers to those adolescents who experience an optimal sense of identity. The most obvious concomitants of achieving a sense of identity are feeling at home in your body, a sense of knowing where you are going, and an inner assuredness of anticipated recognition from those who count. If an adolescent is to function satisfactorily as an adult, a conception of "my way of life" or a sense of personal identity must be achieved. Recognition of continuity and sameness in your personality, even when in different situations and when reacted to by different individuals, leads to identity.

Your self-concept must be fairly consistent, or the personality will be fragmented and you will suffer from **identity diffusion.** This is the least sophisticated status. Individuals in this status have

An important developmental task in adolescence, according to Erik Erikson, is to establish a sense of identity—a feeling of knowing who one is and where one is going.

made no commitment nor are they attempting to arrive at a commitment in a given content area. According to Erikson, failure to accept your self, crystallize your goals, receive recognition from those who count, experiment with various roles may lead to delayed commitment, prolonged adolescence, negative identity, or adjustment problems of varying degrees of severity. The identity diffusion status is characterized by the absence of any commitment to a system of values, by a reluctance to accept the explanations, and by a tendency to challenge authority.

> The loss of a sense of identity is often expressed in a scornful and snobbish hostility toward the roles offered as proper and desirable in one's family or immediate community. Any aspect of the required role, or all of it—be it masculinity or femininity, nationality, or class membership—can become the main focus of the young person's acid disdain. (Erikson, 1968, p. 173)

An adolescent boy, for example, whose parents have constantly stressed how important it is for him to do well in school so that he will be admitted to a prestigious college, may deliberately do poorly in school or quit school entirely. Table 10.7 summarizes the four identity statuses.

Although identity researchers have acknowledged the need for subcategories of identity statuses (Adams, 1988), to date there have been few systematic attempts to delineate subcategories within any of the statuses (Archer & Waterman, 1990). The most comprehensive system for the identity diffusion status was advanced by Marcia (1988). He distinguished four types of identity diffusions: (a) the "disturbed" diffusion, a person who evidenced pathology in the manner in which the identity task was approached; (b) the "carefree" diffusion, a person who is something of a free spirit, untroubled by the absence of commitments; (c) the "culturally adaptive" diffusion, a person who is responsive to social expectations to avoid commitments; and (d) the "developmental" diffusion, a person who has not as yet addressed identity questions but who may be expected to deal with the task at such a time as it is situationally appropriate.

There has been some research carried out with American minority adolescents based on Marcia's (1980) identity status model. It has been reported in these studies that minority adolescents tend to score higher in foreclosure than white adolescents. In examining ethnicity as a variable in a study of ego identity (Streitmatter, 1988), it was found in a sample comprising 367 white, Hispanic, African-American, American Indian, Asian, and other persons that white adolescents scored significantly lower than the minority adolescents on foreclosure in both interpersonal and ideological components of identity.

Spencer and Markstrom-Adams (1990) have addressed the factors that interfere with the identity formation of minority youth. The authors cited several factors that represent important impeding factors: value conflicts that exist between cultures, the lack of identity-achieved adult role models, and the lack of culture-focused specific guidance from the family. The preponderance of negative stereotypes about minorities in general is also counterproductive to acquiring a solid sense of self.

The development of an integrated sense of self-identity is a complex and difficult task. Adolescents are expected to master many different roles. It is the rare, perhaps even nonexistent, adolescent who doesn't experience serious doubts about her capabilities in handling at least some of these roles competently.

Successful completion of the identity is important because it allows young adults to develop mature relations with members of the opposite sex. They can then convey love and emotional security to them. If the identity crisis is not successfully resolved, the adolescent is faced with a sense of identity diffusion and an inability to cope with the demands of adulthood. Identity achievers have the highest conceptions of self, followed by those in the moratorium status, followed by foreclosure, and last, identity diffusion. The adolescent's self-concept, then, is crucial in the development of an integrated personality.

Two ingredients are necessary to consolidate an optimal sense of personal identity: (a) adolescents

TABLE 10.7 Summary of Research Findings on Marcia's Four Identity Statuses

Status 1. Identity Confusion*

Individuals in the state of identity confusion

1. may be the "playboy" type; don't care what others do as long as they are allowed to do what they want.
2. may avoid crises and confrontation by escaping through drugs and self-delusion.
3. may be the "personality disintegration" type; become so disoriented that they may fall into schizophrenia or attempt suicide.
4. tend to be opportunists.
5. are extremely interested in what others think and will adopt the attitude of those they are currently impressed by. Frequently have deep feelings of guilt and rejection.
6. are too willing to change their opinions about themselves. Found to be the most willing to accept incorrect personality sketches about themselves.
7. have the most problems with interpersonal relationships.
8. tend to enroll in the easiest college majors, even though they are as intelligent as others.
9. are the most likely to role play in different situations.
10. have fathers who are more controlling than those in any of the three other categories.
11. demonstrate the least amount of basic trust.

Status 2. Foreclosure

Individuals in the state of foreclosure

1. appear superficially like the identity-achieved person (status 4).
2. have not really considered other goals and values, accepting the ones that were given to them.
3. frequently explain their choices on the basis that they will be pleasing to their parents.
4. take great satisfaction in pleasing others, especially those they look up to.
5. have the most rigid personality.
6. have the greatest interest in maintaining traditions.
7. are most bound by their habits.
8. carefully avoid conflict situations.
9. show the greatest respect for authority and enjoy being told precisely what to do.
10. may have the highest level of aspiration, even in the face of failures.
11. evaluate themselves most critically.
12. are least flexible in their judgments.
13. have the lowest ratings in anxiety.
14. have the highest self-esteem ratings, if female.
15. have the most favorable attitude toward education.
16. have fathers who are neither too harsh nor too lenient, but very effective at control.
17. are most likely to set unrealistic goals for themselves.
18. overidentify with their peer group and heroes.

Status 3. Moratorium

Individuals in the state of moratorium

1. have many unresolved questions.
2. "play the field" with the opposite sex.
3. are very much experimentalists.
4. frequently change their minds about values.
5. like to be an extremist, at least temporarily.
6. frequently are concerned about their own mental health.
7. tend to become involved in "changing the system."
8. often think of themselves as phonies because they are aware of their conflicts.
9. are the least willing to be influenced or controlled by others.
10. are the least cooperative with those who would give them help.
11. are the least predictable in their activities.
12. score the highest on anxiety tests.
13. are the least confident in their choice of a college major, the least confident in the use of education in general.
14. have parents who are the most permissive.
15. are the most critical of society.

Status 4. Identity Achievement

Individuals in the state of identity achievement

1. have the strongest ego.
2. are the most stable and mature in their behavior.
3. are most accepting of themselves.
4. may or may not have values similar to their parents, but whatever values they have are strongly held.
5. have a stable self-definition.
6. are the most willing to act on the basis of their values.
7. are capable of real intimacy with others.
8. are the most aware and accepting of their own limitations.
9. score the highest when given tasks under stress.
10. set more realistic goals for themselves than others.
11. are the best able to evaluate themselves.
12. are the most flexible when interacting with others.
13. are the most consistent in judgment, regardless of the opinions of others involved.
14. rate lowest in discrepancy between self-perception and the perception others have of them.
15. are most effective in interpersonal interaction.
16. have fathers who tend to be relaxed and encouraging rather than controlling.

*Research findings here are somewhat contradictory.

Source: Adapted from *Adolescent Behavior and Society* by R. E. Muuss, 1975, New York: Random House. Reprinted with permission of McGraw-Hill, Inc.

must carry forward from middle childhood an inner confidence about their competence and ability to master new tasks and (b) adolescents must have ample opportunity to experiment with new roles both in fantasy and practice and they must get support in this effort from parents and adults (Fillmore & Britsch, 1988).

Moreover, the strength young people find in adults at this time, adults' willingness to let teenagers experience life, adults' eagerness to confirm adolescents at their best, adults' consistency in correcting adolescents' excesses, and the guidance they give adolescents will codetermine whether adolescents eventually make sense or order out of their necessary inner confusion (Hauser, Powers, Noam, Jacobson, Weiss, & Follansbee, 1984).

Similarly, encouraging adolescents to express their own opinions and ideas, allowing them to take an active role in decision making in the family context, tolerating the adolescents' assertiveness, and allowing them to consider various alternative solutions to a problem are important ways in which adults help adolescents achieve identity formation during the late high school years (Grotevant & Cooper, 1985).

The journey toward self-identity is not an easy one; small progressions may be followed by regressions. There will be times when adolescents vacillate between the world of their childhood and the world of adulthood. Adolescents at times enjoy the safety and protection of home; at other times, they want to be free-spirited and independent.

REORGANIZATION OF SELF-ESTEEM

Some theorists suggest that because of cognitive, physical, and social changes during adolescence, a considerable amount of reorganization and reorientation of self takes place (Blyth & Traeger, 1990).

In the cognitive realm, there is a movement to formal operational thinking. In addition, there are social changes (need to be independent from parents, more sophisticated heterosexual relationships, increasing need for acceptance by peers) that may also contribute to an unstable self-picture. And, because of a number of physical changes (the onset of puberty, the growth spurt) that occur, the adolescent must come to terms with

a "new body" and perhaps update their body image. As a result, self-esteem may be subject to a period of reorganization.

Does research support the premise that there is reorientation, reorganization, and disturbance in self-esteem? Several studies identify early adolescence as an apparently disturbing period (Hartup, 1983; Simmons, Blyth, Van Cleave, & Bush, 1979). Disturbance is not meant to connote psychopathology, but rather any change in a direction presumed to be uncomfortable for the adolescent. Not all studies report a decline in self-esteem during adolescence; none, however have reported an increase. Most available evidence suggests that adolescents' self-esteem becomes less stable and more negative in early adolescence (roughly the junior high years) compared with earlier and later periods (Marsh, Smith, Marsh, & Owens, 1988; Wylie, 1979).

On the basis of scores on various psychological scales, Simmons et al. (1979) concluded that the largest negative change seemed to occur among 12-year-olds. The first purpose of their study was to investigate whether the movement from childhood into early adolescence is stressful, specifically in terms of self-esteem. Second, they wanted to find out which types of children are most vulnerable in this regard, and third, what specific impact pubertal development, environmental change, and social behaviors have on the self-esteem of early adolescents.

The 798 subjects participating in the experiment came from 18 public schools (grades 3–12) in the Milwaukee area. Each child was given a self-esteem inventory. Pubertal development for boys was determined by their height; for girls, by the onset of menstruation. Social behaviors referred to whether the child had begun dating.

The data suggested that girls who demonstrated the lowest self-esteem were the ones who had experienced change in three major areas earlier than their peers (see Figure 10.6). Girls who had reached puberty earlier, those who had embarked early on the new social behavior of dating, and those who had experienced a major environmental change by moving into a junior high setting were a particularly vulnerable group.

FIGURE 10.6   Self-Esteem Levels

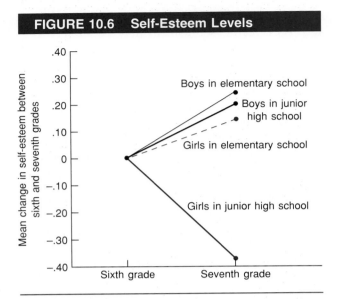

Source: From "Entry into Early Adolescence: The Impact of School Structure, Puberty, and Early Dating on Self-Esteem" by R. G. Simmons, D. A. Blyth, E. F. Van Cleave, and D. M. Bush, 1979, *American Sociological Review, 44*, p. 956. Copyright 1979 by the American Sociological Association. Reprinted by permission.

The pattern of environmental change, early development, and dating, although a disadvantage for girls, appears to be an advantage for boys. The boys who were maturing faster, dating earlier, and entering junior high demonstrated higher self-esteem than their late maturing, nondating, no-school-change counterparts.

Why is it that boys and girls react quite differently to the transition into early adolescence in terms of their self-esteem? Simmons et al. make the following conjectures. It may be that the sexes develop different value systems at this age. Girls have a tendency to value sociability or popularity and appearance. For example, when subjects in the study were asked to rank popularity, competency (being the best), and independence, girls ranked popularity first, while the boys rated competency as most important. As a result, "Staking oneself on others' opinions of oneself, as popularity assumes great importance, would appear to

provide the student with an especially unstable reference point, particularly if one is in a new school where the peers who are doing the evaluating are less well known" (Simmons et al., 1979, p. 966). Therefore, because girls place a higher value on popularity than boys, they will feel more vulnerable in junior high. Also, placing value on your appearance or looks may also place your self-picture in jeopardy, particularly where physical changes are more dramatic in the case of girls as compared with boys, who are becoming more muscular looking.

Similar findings were also found by Rosenberg (1979). When studying 1,917 boys and girls, in grades 3 through 12 in the Baltimore area, he found that early adolescents (12–14) showed a higher level of self-consciousness, greater instability of self-concept, slightly lower global self-esteem, and less favorable judgments of valued self-components. Further, Rosenberg reported that this change occurs rather suddenly. The movement from the 11-year-old group to the 12-year-old group was the only one-year period in which children showed an increase in disturbance in all of these areas, but these changes leveled off in later adolescence. Rosenberg concludes, "Self-concept disturbances appear to be most acute during early adolescence, around the ages of 12 to 14. This is not true of all self-concept dimensions but it appears to be true of most of them" (1985, p. 241).

UNDERSTANDING OTHERS: SOCIAL AND CONVENTIONAL ROLE TAKING

Selman's last stage of understanding others (level 4: *social and conventional system role taking*) occurs between the ages of 12 and 15. Children are able to take a detached view of the dyadic relationship and view it from the perspective of a third person (peer, teacher, or society). Adolescents begin to compare their own views with those of society at large, and they realize that the social system in which they operate is a product of the shared views of the members of society. Friendships are seen as open relationship systems subject to change, flexibility, and growth. Trust is knowing that each partner helps the other and allows the other to develop independent relations. True close friends attend to the deeper psychological needs of each other.

During adolescence, there is a change from defining friendship as a concrete, behavioral, surface relationship of playing together and giving goods to a more abstract, internal dispositional relationship, of caring for one another, sharing one's thoughts and feelings, and comforting each other (Shantz, 1983). There is a greater emotional investment with peers during adolescence—evidenced, perhaps, by the increase in the amount of time that is spent with friends. Friendships no longer need to be so exclusive, as pairs of friends accept each others' need to establish relationships with other people. Whereas younger children tend to express their feelings toward others in vague, global, and nonspecific ways ("nice," "kind," "good," "bad"), with increasing age, descriptions become more precise and differentiated ("cheerful," "generous," "considerate of others").

Girls tend to develop considerably more sensitivity to trust and emotional intensity, and appear to be more capable of intimacy in their friendships than boys. Intimacy has most often been equated with the depth and breadth of self-disclosure as well as the feelings of being understood, validated, and cared for that accompany self-disclosure. Buhrmester (1990) found in studying 102 10- to 13-year-olds and 70 13- to 16-year-olds that the ability to establish close, intimate friendships becomes increasingly important during early adolescence. Girls tend to have more intimate relationships with friends than boys. Moreover, he found that adolescents whose friendships were rated (by both self- and friend reports) as companionate, disclosing, and satisfying were more competent, more sociable, less hostile, less anxious/depressed, and had higher self-esteem compared with peers involved in less intimate friendships. Jones and Dembo (1989) found when studying 217 children, aged 8 to 14, that only boys who were highly stereotypically masculine were significantly lower than girls in intimacy. Boys who were less stereotypic in their gender-role behavior tended to report intimacy levels with friends that were as high as those reported by females.

STUDYING CHILDREN

FRIENDSHIP

Select two or three children between the ages of 7 and 9 and record their responses to the following questions: "Tell me about your friend." "Why is he or she your friend?" In answering the first question, do children tend to describe their friends in terms of observable traits? "She's got brown hair." "He is tall." In responding to the second question, do they view friendship as unidirectional—a friend is someone who "lets me play with his toys"? Or do they view friendship as reciprocal—"We have fun together."?

Research seems to indicate that friendship conceptions undergo a great deal of change, with the major changes appearing to be these:

1. From defining friendships in a rather superficial way, as concrete, behavioral, surface relationships, to having more abstract, internal dispositional relationships in adolescence shown by caring for one another, sharing thoughts and feelings, and comforting each other.

2. With increasing age, a shift from self-centered orientation of the friend satisfying your wants and needs to a mutually satisfying relationship.

3. A change from momentary or transient relationships to ones that endure over time and despite occasional conflict.

"Studying Children" provides an activity for learning more about changes in children's conceptions of friends.

PRACTICAL IMPLICATIONS: ENHANCING CHILDREN'S SELF-ESTEEM

Building a positive self-concept and healthy self-esteem is an important developmental task for children (Coopersmith & Gilberts, 1982; Gecas, 1982; Rogers, 1961). The fact that children's self-concepts and self-esteem are not innate or predetermined underscores the importance of helping children develop positive pictures of themselves.

If, as parents or professional persons, you have a basic understanding of how a healthy self develops and the conditions and the interpersonal relations that nurture it, you are then in a position to move actively in the direction of creating those conditions.

The self, it should be pointed out, is not formed by any one particular experience, but is based on continual repetition. Each positive experience, each life situation that enables children to feel more personally valuable adds to their feelings of self-worth. An isolated episode can rarely change a child's image without additional support. Continued, persistent, positive or negative treatment is required to produce long-term positive or negative self-evaluations (Fahey & Phillips, 1981).

BUILDING SELF-CONCEPT AND SELF-ESTEEM IN THE FAMILY SETTING

The amount and quality of acceptance manifested by parental attention and approval determine to a large extent children's picture of themselves (Squyres, 1979). Children tend to perceive their parents' approval and attention as indications of their significance. Basking in these signs of their personal importance, they learn to think of themselves in a positive way.

Parental interest is positively related to children's self-concepts. This finding of a positive relationship between parental support/affection and a child's self-concept is one of the most consistent in the family research on self-concept formation (Hales, 1990).

In interviewing parents of children with high self-esteem, Coopersmith and Gilberts (1982) found that these parents are generally more accepting of others and are inclined to lead active personal lives. Mothers are acceptant of their roles and are more calm and poised in dealing with their children.

Boys with positive self-esteem have close relationships with their fathers, who take an active and supportive role in child rearing. Many studies highlight the significance of close, supportive parent-child relationships, not only in developing high self-esteem, but also in enabling children to develop healthy personal outcomes in adulthood.

The quality of earlier relationships in the family is outstanding in its predictive power (Mortimer & Lorence, 1981; Offer & Offer, 1975).

Parents of high self-esteem children expect them to strive and comply with the standards they establish. They have established clear lines of authority and responsibility, but children are encouraged to present their own ideas for discussion.

Discipline   Dobbins (1978) found that reward as a disciplinary technique had a significant, positive influence on children's developing sense of self, while coercive power had a significant negative influence. When punishment is required in homes that are nurturing of good self-esteem, it is geared to managing undesirable behavior rather than to harsh treatment or loss of love. Harsh, rejecting judgments prevent children from accepting themselves. Moreover, parents who do not resort to harsh or frequent evaluation comparisons enable children to know and accept themselves (Anderson & Hughes, 1990). Positive relationships have been shown between high self-esteem and the degree to which children rated mothers as likely to explain reasons for disciplining them and being clear in their expectations of them (Enright & Ruzicka, 1989). High self-esteem has also been associated with children's perceptions of fathers as more likely to take away privileges than in using other forms of punishment (Drummond & Gilkison, 1989). When parents are strict in the sense of imposing many restrictions, their children's self-esteem tends to be low. When parents are strict in the sense of exercising firm control—monitoring their children's behavior and following through on requirements—children's self-esteem tends to be high. The critical factor appears to be whether parental strictness is accompanied by emotional support, commitment to the child's welfare, and an open interchange of ideas between parent and child (Loeb, Horst, & Horton, 1980).

Rejecting Parents   Just as loving, accepting parents enhance their children's self-esteem, rejecting, nonloving parents thwart the growth of a healthy self-system. If children live in an environment in which they are rejected, denied the free-

Boys with positive self-esteem appear to have close relationships with their fathers.

dom to explore, and cannot identify with nurturing parents, they will begin at an early age to develop the kind of behavior that we find in children who perceive themselves as unworthy. They will feel hostile and probably will project their hostility onto others (Clemes & Bean, 1981).

Overprotective Parents Overprotection, domination, and neglect are three common causes of a negative self-concept (Yawkey, 1980). When parents try to direct the children's actions, rush to their assistance when children are trying to solve a problem, make all the decisions for them, continually do for their children what they can do for themselves, they communicate to their children that *they* are the competent ones. In addition, an overabundance of put-downs, a string of failures,

demands that border on requiring perfection, and unfavorable comparisons can lead to negative self-concepts and low self-esteem.

Children's Basic Yearnings Kegan (1982) points out that a positive self-concept and high self-esteem occur when children's two basic "yearnings" are met at each stage of development. The first basic yearning is for **inclusion** (to be connected, held, welcomed, a part of) and the second yearning is for **distinctiveness** (to be autonomous, independent, to have self-chosen purposes).

In meeting children's needs for inclusiveness and distinctiveness, parents can assist in the following ways. In infancy, children's need for inclusiveness is met when strong emotional bonds are formed between children and caregivers. Caregivers must constantly give children confirmation and recognition by providing for their physical and psychological needs. At the same time, parents need to help children develop their distinctiveness by "letting go." In the infancy period, they must assist in the differentiation process by not giving in to children's every need, by acknowledging children's display of independence, and by helping children to see themselves as separate, causal agents.

Between the ages of 2 and 7 years, inclusive needs are met when parents can accept children's intense attachments and their psychological dependence. Letting go takes the form of holding children responsible for their actions, helping them meet responsibilities at home and school, and recognizing their self-sufficiency.

Children's needs for inclusiveness during middle childhood are met when the parents continually let children know that they are praiseworthy and competent. Their needs for distinctiveness are met by respecting their privacy and space in the home and by giving them control over their actions: an allowance, or, perhaps, permitting them to choose their own clothes.

The best way to meet adolescents' needs for inclusiveness, maintains Kegan, is to avoid criticism and negative value judgments. Furthermore, it is important at this time to share the child's internal subjective states, moods, and innermost feelings. By the same token, parents need to allow children to assume responsibility for their initiatives and for their own psychological definition. By meeting children's needs of inclusiveness and distinctiveness, adults can provide the psychological support needed to nourish and enhance children's sense of self at each of the developmental stages.

BUILDING SELF-CONCEPT AND SELF-ESTEEM IN THE SCHOOL SETTING

Children entering school bring with them the attitudes and concepts of self established through their home experiences. Thus, no teacher is completely free of children's prior concepts about themselves. Children's self-concepts and self-esteem are still developing, however, and the school can exert a powerful influence. Although the impressions of early childhood are important, you should not write off the impact that the long succession of weeks, months, and years spent in school may have. For many children, school is second only to the home as an institution that determines their self-image.

Building Competencies Evaluative feedback from others is a powerful determinant of self-esteem, but it is not the only factor. High self-esteem is based on more than just a blind acceptance of self-worth. In order to develop positive self-esteem, children need to develop competencies in valued contexts of action. Self-esteem is not given to children; it must be earned by them through their competent actions. Thus, not only do children need positive feedback from teachers, they need to learn to develop competencies as well.

Harter (1983) proposes a model of how children perceive themselves that defines discrete domains of self-evaluation: cognitive (academic), social (competence in relation to peers), and physical (mostly sports related), as well as an overall, general self-esteem (the degree to which you like yourself as a person). Harter has designed the Perceived Competence Scale for Children (PCSC), a scale that taps these separate domains as well as the overall picture of self. She has found a consistent relationship between children's judgments of their perceived competence (as measured by the PCSC cognitive scale) and their self-esteem.

Thus, teachers and parents need to create environments that encourage the development of skills necessary to earn (through recognition of real accomplishments) both the positive evaluations of others and their own positive evaluations. High self-esteem comes to be based on intellectual and physical competence and social skills. Therefore, children need to develop qualities that justify positive conceptions.

As children perceive themselves gaining competence, in a gradually widening sphere, they begin to see themselves as causal agents, and are able to feel that they have greater ability to control more of their environment. This feeling is often referred to as an internal locus of control.

Internal Locus of Control It has been noted that a positive self-concept and high self-esteem are significantly related to a child's sense of efficacy and active control (Prawat, Grissom, & Parish, 1979). Helping children with low self-concepts feel that they are active, causal agents will assist in enhancing their self-pictures. Helping children feel that they can make things happen according to their intentions and wishes, that they can effectively deal with environmental and interpersonal demands, will ultimately translate into self-confidence in their capacity to realize personal strivings and accomplish valued goals.

Children's perceived control can serve to foster or hinder their effective regulation of effort, actions, and emotions, or how they cope with challenges, frustration, and failure. Research reveals that children's reports of an internal sense of control is linked with higher levels of performance and psychological functioning, starting in kindergarten (Skinner, 1990).

As parents or teachers, you can help children develop a sense of control by answering their questions promptly, involving them in decision making, setting clearly defined rules (which contribute to a predictable environment), letting them make choices, and communicating to them that their opinions are worthy.

Feeling Positive about Students If, as teachers, you want your students to feel positive about themselves, then you must feel positive about your students. Davidson and Lange (1970) found a significant correlation (+ 0.82) between children's perceptions of their teachers' feelings toward them and children's perceptions of self. A positive appraisal by the teacher serves as a catalyst for growth in all areas of children's development.

A worthwhile task for teachers at the start of the school year is to attempt to determine each student's greatest asset. By looking into the child's accumulative folder, conferring with the child's previous teacher, meeting with the parents, or questioning the child directly, teachers can discover what each child in the classroom likes most and is most successful in doing. On the basis of this information, teachers can capitalize on the child's strengths. By focusing on the positive rather than the negative, teachers allow their own

faith and confidence to strengthen the child's self-concept. If teachers make their evaluations of children salient, such as pointing out the children's best work, children's self-evaluations can show some consistency with those of the teacher (Stipek & Daniels, 1988).

Effectively using praise and criticism appears to be situation specific. To suggest that teachers should avoid criticism or give praise more freely overlooks the power of the context in determining the meaning of any message. A well-chosen criticism can convey as much positive information as a praise; abundant or indiscriminate praise can be meaningless; insincere praise, which does not covary with the teacher's expectations for the students, can have detrimental effects on many students. Praise is positively related to self-esteem only when it conveys information about the teacher's expectations. It is the informative value of praise and criticism with regard to the teacher's expectations that is critical.

Avoiding Negative Labels Avoiding negative labeling will help enhance children's self-concepts and self-esteem. Children's behavior directly coincides with the labels that are attached to them (Harter, 1983). Negative labels are incorporated into children's self-images and help to confirm negative views of self, leading to further maladaptive behavior. If a word or label is attached to children long enough, they tend to become that type of person; the labels are verified by children developing that behavior, attitude, or feeling. Stressing the negative and labeling the mistaken behavior keeps the idea going and tends to "stamp in" the inappropriate actions. Thus, many children think of themselves as uncooperative, sloppy, careless, and so on because they are told time and time again that they are that kind of person. Positive labels (hardworking, responsible, friendly, smart) are also incorporated in the self, and children learn to produce behavior that reflects these labels.

Helping children to succeed in their academic work, to experience more success than failure, is vital to developing a positive conception of self in the academic setting. (The importance of success and the drawbacks of failure were discussed in Chapter 8.)

CHANGING INADEQUATE SELF-CONCEPT AND SELF-ESTEEM

Before discussing how you can change a child's inadequate self-systems, you might ask, How do I know if children have adequate or inadequate images of themselves? Table 10.8 points out some of the characteristics of children with high as well as low self-esteem.

In addition, observing children's behavior at home or school may offer some clues to their self systems. In order to determine a child's level of self-esteem there are several questions that you might ask: Does she like herself? Who is his best friend? (Often children's pictures of themselves are similar to those of their best friends.) What does she think about herself in general? How does

he get along with his peers? His teachers? Are her feelings easily hurt? Does he feel everyone is against him? Is she negativistic—an "I won't" type of attitude—or pessimistic—an "I can't" type of attitude? "Focus on Applications" offers a number of other questions that can be used to obtain an informal assessment of children's self-esteem.

Is it possible to help children change their negative conceptions of self? Some psychologists feel that the self is highly responsive to change throughout life, because it is continually being subjected to new social pressures and experiences (Fischer & Lazerson, 1983). Others maintain that the self-concept is difficult to change because the main contours of self are set by the end of childhood (Kagan & Moss, 1983). A low self-concept is relatively stable and quite difficult to change (Brockner, 1979).

The stability of the self-concept of 442 males at the University of Michigan over two periods—freshman

TABLE 10.8 Characteristics of Children with High and Low Self-Esteem		
HIGH SELF-ESTEEM		
Proud of accomplishments		"Look at this; I really like this picture I made."
Acts independently		"I made my own lunch."
Assumes responsibility		"I'll water the plants."
Tolerates frustration		"This is hard, but I think I can do it."
Approaches new challenges with enthusiasm		"Our teacher said we were going to begin long division tomorrow. That's neat."
Feels capable of influencing others		"Let me show you how you can learn this new game."
Exhibits a broad range of feelings and emotions		"I feel so good when dad is home; and sad when he's gone."
LOW SELF-ESTEEM		
Avoids situations that provoke anxiety		"I'm not going to school today; there's a hard math test."
Demeans own talents		"Nothing I draw looks good."
Feels unvalued by others		"They never want to play with me."
Blames others		"You didn't tell me where the broom was, so I couldn't clean up the mess."
Feels powerless		"I'll never finish this project."
Defensive and easily frustrated		"This kite will never fly, so I'm going to smash it up."

Source: From *Your Child's Self-Esteem* by Dorothy Corkille Briggs. Copyright © 1970 by Dorothy Corkille Briggs. Used by permission of Doubleday, a division of Bantam Doubleday Dell Publishing Group, Inc.

FOCUS ON APPLICATIONS

Assessing Children's Self-Esteem

Informal assessment can be accomplished by observing the child in daily interactions and by answering the following questions with "always," "usually," "sometimes," "seldom," or "never."

1. Does this child adapt easily to new situations?
2. Does this child hesitate to express himself?
3. Does this child become upset by failures or stressful situations?
4. Do other children seek this child out to engage in activities?
5. Does this child become alarmed or frightened easily?
6. When this child is scolded or criticized, does she become either aggressive or withdrawn?
7. Does this child indicate frequently that he does not do as well as others expect or as well as he expects of himself?
8. Does this child tend to dominate or bully other children?
9. Does this child continually seek attention by speaking out of turn, boasting, making unnecessary noises, or by displaying other inappropriate behaviors?
10. Does this child appear to accept the appearance and performance of her body?

If "always" or "usually" is the answer to questions 2, 3, 5, 6, 7, 8, or 9, and "seldom" or "never" to questions 1, 4, or 10, these items can be identified as goals to help improve the child's self-concept.

Source: "Enhancing a Child's Positive Self-Concept" by K. A. McDonald, 1980, in T. Yawkey (Ed.), *The Self-Concept of the Young Child* (pp. 53–54), Provo, UT: Brigham Young University.

---

year in college to graduation and from graduation to 10 years after graduation—was examined in one study (Mortimer & Lorence, 1981). The self-concept was measured along five dimensions: perception of self as happy, relaxed, and confident; interpersonal qualities (social, interested in others, open, warm); competence; unconventionality (independent from social practices); and self-doubts (perception of self as hypersensitive, unable to concentrate).

Results demonstrate a striking stability of the five dimensions of the self-concept over the 14-year period. The researchers therefore support the widely held view that the development of identity occurs prior to adulthood—that is, in adolescence or childhood—and thereafter remains quite stable over time.

Although estimates of self-concept stability within phases of the life course do indicate a high degree of persistence, they leave substantial proportions of the variance unexplained, indicating the potential for change and responsiveness to external influence. The self is not a fixed entity, and if conditions are right, the self will respond to change.

Subjectivity in Perception   In changing children's perceptions, your first goal is to grasp the essence of how they compose their private realities. The best vantage point from which to understand children's behavior is from the internal reference of the children themselves. How they subjectively view themselves is a matter of great importance, for children function according to this image, even though others may not see a situation in the same way at all (Eato & Lerner, 1981).

Being aware of new developmental cycles, such as entering the world of reading, and helping children feel positive about themselves in these new situations will help to enhance children's conception of self.

Often a parent, teacher, or outsider does not share the same beliefs as the children. For example, an educator may feel that a child is progressing at a level commensurate with her ability and therefore is doing well academically. The child, however, may see herself as not working up to a desired standard of performance and may feel academically inferior.

Parents, teachers, and concerned adults need to become aware of how children perceive themselves in their relationship to the environment, because children function on the basis of their convictions regardless of the relationship of these convictions to reality. Because all behavior is viewed from a personal context, you need to try to view children's behavior on the basis of their own biased perceptions. You have to acquire this sensitivity if you are to help children modify an inadequate self-concept.

New Experiences   If the self is allowed to grow through positive experiences, it will gradually assimilate modifications about itself. Even though the self is a stable entity, it can still be affected by new experiences. When children are exposed to new opportunities for success, they change their

inadequate self-concept. The self-concept may thus be regarded not as an enduring substratum of experience, but as being linked to the social context and fully dependent on it for its strength. An effective technique, then, is to counteract old negative experiences that have led to the formation of an inadequate self-concept by exposing the child to new, positive experiences. For example, if children feel they have no friends, you should try to help them see themselves as people who get along with others. Perhaps, you could start by having these children work with younger children in school, tutoring them in areas in which the young children need help.

Developmental Cycles   Many self-theorists tell us that a shift in the self-concept can occur rather readily in children at certain stages in their development. When children begin a new cycle in their lives or start an important activity for the first time, new images of self are formed. For example, when children enter school, begin to read, or earn a weekly allowance, their self is particularly vulnerable to change. It is important to be aware of new phases in development and help children feel positive about themselves in these new situations.

REVIEW OF KEY POINTS

The self is synonymous with personality and consists of two categories—the "I" and "me." As the "I" emerges, children realize that they exist as a separate and distinct person. The "I" is the self-as-doer in the sense that it includes active processes such as thinking, remembering, and perceiving. The "me," or self-concept, is an abstraction that individuals develop about the attributes, capacities, and objects they possess. Self-esteem is how children evaluate their self-concept, which in turn influences their overall evaluation of self.

During infancy, the self-as-subject gradually emerges as children learn that they are active, causal agents separate and distinct from others. The self-as-subject is fully elaborated at around 2 years of age. Once the self-as-subject is formed, children begin to form conceptions of self. Children's fear of strangers, formation of attachment bonds, and communicative skills reflect infants' knowledge of their social world.

In early childhood children conceive of the self in terms of specific body parts and attribute the "I's" volitional power to those body parts. Their sense of individuality is also based on how they physically differ from others. Children in early childhood tend to organize their self-concepts in terms of physical characteristics and physical actions. Children's self-esteem is initially based on what they directly observe about themselves: their successes and failures in accomplishing various activities and skills. They tend to evaluate themselves in absolute terms and do not compare their performances with those of other children. Children understand others by projecting their own perspective onto others. Friendships tend to be fleeting and unstable.

In middle childhood, children see themselves as distinct from others because they think and feel differently from others. They feel more in control of their thoughts and actions. Middle childhood is a time when the self-concept is expanding to incorporate new dimensions of self in myriad domains and from many sources (peers, teachers, other authority figures). But it is also a time for solidifying self-schemata. The self that was so changeable in early childhood becomes more concrete during middle childhood. Once children have achieved various stable self-schemata, they tend to process information received from their environment in congruence with their self-schemata. Your self-concept, composed of various self-schemata, provides the frame of reference, which instigates, maintains, and directs your behavior. Gradually, children begin to place more emphasis on the evaluations of the significant others in their environments. Parents are considered to play a major role in the development of children's self-esteem. With increasing age, peers, teachers, and other authority figures play an influential role in determining a child's level of self-esteem. Children between the ages of 6 and 8, Selman's level 1, define friends as those who share their worldly goods, act nice, and are fun to be with. Although children can consider two conflicting views when analyzing social dilemmas, they cannot keep both viewpoints in mind at once, and are likely to focus on one perspective at the expense of the other. Children at Selman's level 2, ages 8 to 10, describe friends as those who help one another and are reliable and trustworthy. They understand that their own perspective is not the only valid one, and begin to evaluate themselves in terms of how others view them. At level 3, ages 10 to 12, children are able to simultaneously consider the viewpoints of both participants in a conflict.

In adolescence, there is a more prominent belief in the "I's" volitional power, and distinctiveness from others is based on the privacy of your thoughts and experiences. Adolescents tend to describe the self in terms of social and psychological constructs. This shift in ways of conceiving the self reflects greater cognitive abstractness as well as a search for a new understanding of the self. It is during adolescence that individuals search for a sense of identity—a feeling of continuity and stability in one's personality. During adolescence, there is a reorganization of the self. Studies seem to indicate that in early adolescence, self-esteem becomes less stable and more negative. Selman indicates that adolescents, ages 12 to 15 (level 4), are able to take a detached view of the dyadic relationship and view it from a perspective of a third person. Friends are defined as relationships in which people care for each other, share thoughts and feelings, and comfort each other.

Helping children develop competencies in social, physical, and academic domains enables children to earn positive evaluations from self and others. Helping them feel they are in control of their actions is important in developing positive pictures of self. Recognizing children's needs for inclusion and distinctiveness, building a strong affectional bond with children, and being an

appropriate model for children are also ways to help build a positive self-concept and high self-esteem. Although the self is seen as a relatively stable entity, there are indications that it is responsive to external influence, and thus will respond to change. If children are induced to do something contrary to a negative self-construct, they will alter this conception of self in the direction of the spoken opinion or overt action. If children receive positive labels, they may learn to produce behavior that reflects these labels. When children are exposed to new, positive experiences that counteract old, negative experiences, their inadequate self-concepts may be subject to revision. Being aware of new developmental cycles and helping children experience success when beginning a new cycle in their lives will help children feel positive about themselves in these new situations.

ENHANCING YOUR CRITICAL THINKING

Broadening Your Knowledge

Identity Statuses in Adolescence

Archer, S. L., & Waterman, A. S. (1990). Varieties of identity diffusions and foreclosures: An exploration of subcategories of the identity statuses. *Journal of Adolescent Research, 5,* 96–111.

This article suggests, based on empirical evidence, that identity diffusion and foreclosure statuses are too broad and need to be differentiated into subcategories.

Critical Thinking

Inner and Outer Sources of Self-Esteem

Cooley, C. H. (1909). *Social organization.* New York: Schocken Books.

Cooley emphasizes an outer source of self-esteem (the looking-glass self), but also discusses an equally important source of information about self—that which is active and is based on developing competencies—an inner source of self-esteem.

CHAPTER 11

Social Development

CHILDREN'S THOUGHTS

On how children learn to behave in socially acceptable ways . . .

Children learn to behave in socially accepted ways from many different people. From the time a child is old enough to talk, his parents teach him manners and ways to behave. Teachers and friends also teach a child. If the child constantly sees his friends acting in a certain way, chances are, he will too.

Christy, age 13

Everyone wants to be accepted. There is nothing worse than not fitting in. Learning to behave is a very important part of growing up. Your parents teach you when you are very young certain rules you are to follow. "Don't swear." "Respect your elders." "Never call up boys." "Don't brag; no one likes a bragger." Teachers also give you rules to follow in the classroom. Children are like a marionette—someone is always pulling their strings so they learn how to behave.

Jennifer, age 13

CHAPTER OUTLINE

KEY TERMS

People are a social species; most happiness and fulfillment rests in the ability to relate effectively to other humans. Thus, another important aspect in studying children and adolescents is their social development. The word *social* refers to children's interactions with others in their environment. Young children engage in social behavior when they begin to respond to others (initially the parents) in a predictable and consistent way that shows that the parents are meaningful stimuli to them. Our first area to study is the emotional tie between infant and caregiver, conceptualized in terms of the attachment relationship, which figures prominently in most writings concerning infant social development. The quality of this relationship, particularly in terms of the security it affords the developing child, affects children's future development.

Early childhood focuses on the development of social control in children. **Socialization** is the process by which children learn to acquire the habits, expectations, skills, and standards that the family and social group value for adulthood. This discussion of socialization centers on the people, the

social agents, who influence children's social development. In general, the principal and most influential agents are the children's parents. Understandably, then, they have been the most thoroughly studied socializing agents. Parents provide many different kinds of rules and dicta so that children learn the "right" way of behaving.

The second section deals with how parents socialize their children to behave in socially approved ways. Although socialization forces may begin in the home, during middle childhood they widen to include forces outside the family—the society of children. In the society of peers, children are assigned a certain status, which strongly affects the course of children's socialization. Those children at the bottom of the social system experience the world very differently from those who are accepted.

During adolescence, many teenagers begin to work part-time. What are the benefits and drawbacks of working? In addition to entering the world of work, many adolescents develop an interest in the opposite sex. Their social world of dating opens up exciting and wonderful experiences. There are, however, some important and compelling issues regarding teenage sexuality that are addressed in this section—namely, teenage pregnancy and adolescent AIDS. The Implications section discusses socially rejected children and how concerned adults can help these children become socially competent individuals.

INFANCY: ATTACHMENT

The investigation of social development in infancy now claims the most eager and extensive attention. In particular, the development of **attachment** has been the subject of a great deal of empirical investigation. Generally speaking, when the affectional ties between infant and caregiver are strong, the infant happily greets the caregiver after a brief separation, and is able to use her as a secure base from which to explore the new surroundings; these infants are classified as securely attached. By contrast, when the physical and emotional bond between infant and caregiver is weak or nonexistent, the infant shows ambivalent responses to the caregiver after a brief separation (momentarily clinging, then pulling away or ignoring him on his return) and does not actively explore in a novel surrounding; these infants are classified as insecurely attached. An important part of attachment research has centered on the quality of children's attachment to their caregivers, which has been related to various aspects of children's functioning, including sociability and cognitive abilities.

DEVELOPMENTAL SIGNIFICANCE OF ATTACHMENT

According to Bowlby (1980), the first important function of attachment between caregiver and infant is that it is crucial to the infant's survival. So important is this bond, Bowlby maintains, that situations that endanger the bond elicit actions on the part of the organism to preserve it. When these efforts are successful, the bond is restored. When they are not, sooner or later the effort wanes. For example, Spitz (1945) observed infants in institutions. Although these infants were physically taken care of—diapered and fed—they did not have affectionate interactions with the caregivers. Some of these infants became very apathetic, showed an unsmiling, waxy gaze, and withdrew. In these extreme kinds of conditions, when young children are not exposed to consistent, loving treatment (are not held, touched, or caressed), when they exist in an impoverished, unstimulating, dull, affectionless world, they may fail to develop, may sicken, or even die. Bowlby maintains, then, that the basic importance of attachment is to keep children alive.

Social Development Important as its protective function is, attachment works in other ways to help children develop essential social and cognitive skills. Their many differences notwithstanding, most of the major theorists approve of Freud's (1938) dictum that "the mother-infant relationship is unique, without parallel, established unalterably as the prototype of all later love relations" (p. 45).

All of their later choices in the realms of friendship and love follow on the basis of memory traces left behind by these prototypes. Ainsworth (1973) concurs by saying that children who do not form bonding ties as infants may suffer from a lifelong inability to "establish and maintain deep significant interpersonal relations" (p. 53).

Bowlby (1980) suggests that infants and young children develop an *inner working model* of self and others. This is more than the learning of roles; rather, children internalize the very nature of relationships themselves. Thus, in experiencing sensitive caregiving, the securely attached child not only learns to expect care, but also more generally learns that when a person is in need, another responds empathically. The inner working model that is formed during early childhood serves as the basis for the construction of subsequent relationships. The insecurely attached child develops a working model of parents as rejecting or inconsistently responsive. Either of these consequences could have deleterious consequences for children's social relationships with peers. Children who do not develop secure attachment relationships tend to see themselves as unlovable and others as rejecting and unresponsive. Insecure children will each reenact aspects of their nonnurturant caregiver role in their interactions with each other (Teti & Ablard, 1989).

In contrast, children who develop secure attachments are able to develop a sense of trust in themselves and others. Impressions of the infant, gained both from informal observation and empirical research, suggest that this trust emerges through numerous interactional activities between the caregiver and the child. As infants learn that parents are reliable and predictable, the sense of trust generalizes to other people and helps determine the quality of future interactions with others. Learning that certain others can be relied on is portrayed by students of infant social development as perhaps the most elementary and important social concept (Erikson, 1950).

Sroufe (1983) and Pianta, Sroufe, and Egeland (1989) have provided extensive evidence of a vital link between quality of children's attachment to caregivers and developmental outcomes in social areas. Sroufe (1979), for example, found that 3½-year-olds who had developed a secure attachment relationship with their caregivers during infancy were more socially active, were sought after by other children, exhibited more leadership qualities, and were more sympathetic to other children than were same-age children who had not developed a secure attachment relationship with their caregivers.

Brody and Axelrod (1978) noted that children labeled securely attached as infants were "more satisfied, more resourceful, more able to be occupied when alone, had better relationships with people and were more capable of age adequate behavior" at ages 3 to 7 (p. 243). Lieberman (1977) reported that 3-year-olds with secure attachments to their mothers played more harmoniously with peers than insecurely attached toddlers. The securely attached children were less likely to fight and more likely to share with others (Belsky, Lerner, & Spanier, 1984). Children with secure attachment histories tend to have many friends, more often select as partners other children with secure attachment histories, and experience deeper friendships.

Other researchers have reported that insecurely attached children are less competent, less sympathetic in interaction with their peers (Matas, Arend, & Sroufe, 1978), more fearful of strangers, and more prone to behavior problems, including social withdrawal and being more dependent on adults (Radke-Yarrow, Cummings, Kuczynski, & Chapman, 1985). Infants classified as insecure have been rated by preschool teachers as less empathic, less compliant, less cooperative, and exhibiting more negative affect and less self-control than securely attached agemates (Erickson, Egland, & Sroufe, 1985; Sroufe, Schork, Motti, Lawroski, & La Frenier, 1984). Cohn (1990) reported that first-grade boys classified as insecurely attached were seen by both peers and teachers as being less socially competent (more aggressive, showing more behavior problems) than were securely attached children.

In a longitudinal study done by Bates, Maslin, and Frankel (1985), no relation between attach-

Securely attached children tend to be more socially active than insecurely attached children.

ment classification and problem behaviors during preschool was found in their sample of 6-year-olds. This study may indicate that infants are neither made invulnerable by secure attachment nor are they doomed by insecure attachment to later psychopathology.

The attachment classification of insecure-avoidant has been discussed most often as a predictor of future problems. Avoidance is assumed to reflect some doubt on the part of the infant with respect to availability and responsiveness of the mother (Sroufe & Fleeson, 1986). The child who uses avoidance to cope with stress is assumed to be masking anger (Main & Weston, 1978). Belsky (1988) suggests that this lack of trust in the attachment figure and the anger of the child in the insecure-avoidant class place children at risk for subsequent social difficulties, with lack of compliance, lack of cooperation, and increased aggressiveness. The empirical evidence supporting Belsky is not as striking and the theoretical implications are not explicit enough to be testable.

Cognitive Abilities   Empirical work has demonstrated the importance of the attachment relationship to children's exploratory behavior (Cassidy, 1988). Attachment to the caregiver is seen as pro-

viding a secure and safe base from which the infant can move in order to explore the environment. Wariness provides the motivation to terminate exploration and seek proximity to the attachment figure when the environment is seen as threatening (Caruso, 1989). Infants designated as secure differ significantly from nonsecure infants in their ability to use caregivers as a secure base from which to explore in the home (Vaughn & Waters, 1990). Additional evidence concerning the interrelationship between attachment and exploration is provided by findings that infants move and explore more freely and exhibit less negative affect in a novel environment when in the presence of the attachment figure (Waters, Kondo-Ikemura, Posada, & Richters, 1990).

Infants who are securely attached are more independent than insecurely attached infants and thus are more likely to leave their mothers' sides and explore the environment. This increased exploration, in turn, produces a more intelligent child. To summarize, Ainsworth (1973) proposed: Mothers' sensitivity to infants' signals reflected secure attachment, increased exploration, and greater cognitive competence.

Research also points out that children who have developed strong bonds with caregivers are more curious during the preschool years than those children who have not developed such bonds (Arend, Gove, & Sroufe, 1979). It has also been found that 2-year-old children who have developed solid bonds with their caregivers tend to be happier and more enthusiastic and less likely to give up when engaging in problem-solving tasks (Matas et al., 1978). At age 5 the same children are described by their teachers as being resourceful, curious, self-reliant, and confident. Insecurely attached children are less effective in eliciting and accepting help in problem-solving situations (Frodi, Bridges, & Grolnick, 1985).

Secure attachment has been associated with patterns of cognitive functioning that suggest effective internalization of regulating and monitoring mechanisms (Hartup, 1989). For example, at 18 months of age, securely attached toddlers more often engage in symbolic play, are more enthusiastic and teachable in simple tasks, exhibit few frustration-related behaviors, and are more sophisticated in negotiating coordinated problem-solving with caregivers than insecurely attached toddlers. Hartup (1989) suggests that these cognitive differences remain into the fourth year in exploratory tasks requiring social coordinations with caregivers and in ''academic'' tasks in which the caregiver teaches the child a simple skill.

In other research, 3-year-olds who had been classified as securely attached at 18 months showed increased effort during a competitive game with an adult (building a tower) following failure feedback (the adult's tower was bigger than the child's). In contrast, 3-year-olds who had been classified as insecurely attached at 18 months showed a corresponding decrease in effort as a result of failure feedback (Lutkenhaus, Grossmann, & Grossmann, 1985). Further evidence also links the quality of the attachment between children and caregivers among 6-year-olds to the children's estimations of their own cognitive competence (Cassidy, 1988).

Evidence is not entirely clear concerning the mechanism through which affective relationships influence cognitive functioning. Although the results point to a relationship between quality of attachment and later cognitive competence, you must be cautious in interpreting this relationship. It is unlikely that being securely attached *causes* children to be more intellectually advanced; rather, securely attached children may have some other factors in common, namely, (a) mothers who have good relationships with their children may be especially encouraged to engage them and support them in solving problems; (b) children in these relationships may also be more competent and hence more willing to accept tutelage and maternal assistance; and (c) children use stable emotional relationships as a base for exploring the wider world.

Evidence is accumulating from dozens of reports on numerous samples that secure attachment between caregivers and children may be correlated with children's later social and cognitive behavior.

DEVELOPMENTAL PROGRESSION OF ATTACHMENT

Attachment between caregivers and children does not occur suddenly; rather, it develops gradually. It was Bowlby (1980) who first distinguished four phases of the development of attachment. Ainsworth (1973) elaborated on these developmental phases. The first phase, known as the *initial-preattachment phase,* occurs from birth to 3 months. The infant is attracted to all social objects and begins to prefer humans to inanimate objects. During the first 3 months of life, infants do not form specific attachments. Anyone's warm arms and cuddles are welcome. Around 3 or 4 months, the *attachment-in-the-making phase,* infants begin to discriminate among the adults with whom they come into contact. Children make a clear distinction between familiar and unfamiliar figures, smiling and vocalizing more to familiar figures than to strangers. In the third phase, the *clear-cut-attachment phase* that takes place around 6 or 7 months, children develop specific, intense attachments, usually, but not always, to their mothers. Strong indications of this attachment are the children's fear of strangers and separation anxiety.

Stranger Anxiety Beginning somewhere around 6 months, reaching a peak at 8 to 10 months, and generally disappearing around 15 months, many babies show a pronounced fear of unfamiliar people or **stranger anxiety.** Stranger anxiety develops gradually as one can see by examining Figure 11.1. At the approach of an unfamiliar person, infants are likely to scream, bury their faces in caregivers' laps, clutch dramatically at the caregiver, and so on. This is not a universal characteristic of infancy; its presence or absence is determined by a complex set of factors. Why are some children afraid of strangers and others are not? Caldwell (1963) proposed that those youngsters who had been exposed to only a very limited variety of caregivers were more likely to show stranger anxiety. Cosmopolitan children who had been close to a diversity of people were less likely to show stranger anxiety.

Separation Anxiety Not only do children cry when a strange person enters the room, they also become unhappy when a familiar person (mother or father) leaves the room. This desire for the familiar person to remain near makes its appearance at about 8 to 12 months and reaches its peak at about 2 years. This phenomenon has often been referred to as **separation anxiety.** Between the ages of 2 and 3 years, children generally become less fearful when their parents leave.

The intensity of separation anxiety is influenced by many factors. Young children are more likely to cry when left in an unfamiliar place, such as at a new baby-sitter's house. In addition, seeing mothers leave through an unfamiliar exit rather than a familiar one produces a more intense response (leaving via the patio door rather than the front door). Leaving children with someone familiar (Aunt Jane) produces less anxiety than leaving children with an unfamiliar person. It is generally not a good idea just to disappear without saying good-bye to children in order to avoid hearing their cries. Say good-bye, give a hug, and then leave. Separation anxiety is only temporary, but the anxiety produced by a parent vanishing without a word may not be.

Ainsworth (1973) labels the fourth phase in the development of attachment as *goal-directed partnership phase.* Children begin to understand caregivers' goals, feelings, and points of view, and are able to adjust their behaviors accordingly. In this phase, children become attached to more than one person. Multiple attachments occur as many young children show affectional bonds toward older brothers and sisters, grandparents, and regular baby-sitters. The developmental course of these attachments is presented in Figure 11.2.

CHILDREN'S CONTRIBUTIONS TO THE ATTACHMENT PROCESS

What pulls caregivers and infants together? This fascinating question can be answered by examining the interaction between them. Today, it is recognized that caregivers and infants engage in a constant two-way flow of influence, that the relationship is an interactive one. Harmony depends on the adaptive abilities of both caregivers and children. Caregivers must be sensitive to children's proximity-promoting behaviors, and infants must be socially responsive and provide feedback to the caregivers.

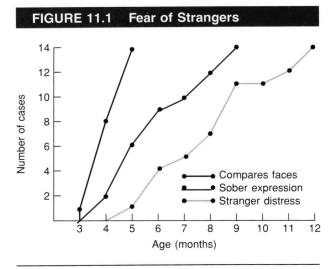

FIGURE 11.1   Fear of Strangers

Number of cases (y-axis) vs. Age (months) (x-axis)

- Compares faces
- Sober expression
- Stranger distress

Source: From "Emotional Expression in Infancy: A Biobehavioral Study" by R. M. Emde, T. Gaensbauer, and R. Harmon, 1976, *Psychological Issues, 10* (whole No. 1), p. 98. Copyright 1976 by International Universities Press, Inc. Publishers. Reprinted by permission.

Children in the clear-cut attachment phase may experience separation anxiety but, upon mother's return, are easily consoled.

Crying Infants' cries have a uniquely potent and predictable effect on adults. Crying may communicate salient messages to adult listeners, even in the absence of parental experience (Zeskind, 1983). On hearing infants cry, adults experience physiological arousal and usually translate this arousal into an attempt to relieve the infants' distress. Picking up infants usually terminates the crying, which helps caregivers feel competent in their role. The distress-relief situation facilitates the development of an affectively positive relationship and represents the origins of affective attachment bonds (Lamb & Sherrod, 1981).

Moreover, these early and simple interactions, centered on relief of infants' distress, appear destined to advance the developing sociability of infants. If the distress-relief sequence is sufficiently

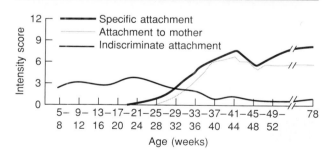

FIGURE 11.2   Developmental Course of Attachments

Source: From "The Development of Social Attachments in Infancy" by H. R. Schaffer and P. E. Emerson, 1964, *Monographs of the Society for Research in Child Development, 29,* p. 3.

predictable, infants may develop expectations concerning the probability of their caregivers' responses, permitting them to develop a sense of their own efficacy. Perceived control develops when infants recognize that they are able to elicit certain responses predictably from the environment.

Gazing   Mutual gaze emerges sometime between the third and sixth weeks, just prior to the first social smile. The visual system provides one of the most powerful networks for the mediation of caregiver attachment (Klaus & Kennell, 1982). This fact is emphasized by the work of Fraiberg (1974), who has described in detail the difficulties that mothers of blind infants have in feeling close to them. Without the affirmation of mutual gazing, mothers feel lost and like strangers to their babies until both learn to substitute other means of communication. Fraiberg did find, however, that the general sequence of attachment was the same for blind and sighted infants, although somewhat delayed for the former. Apparently, blind infants make use of other sensory modalities, especially auditory and tactile modalities, to organize early social relations.

There is no reason to believe that newborns look at caregivers because they are attached to them. But, infants' gazing does have an effect on the caregivers' attachment to the children. The responses of fixation and visual pursuit are present soon after birth and rapidly become important in the infant-caregiver tie. If children are unable to manage or maintain mutual gaze, caregivers are likely to feel estranged from them.

Communicating   From their numerous clinical experiences, Klaus and Kennell (1982) believe that an essential principle of attachment is that parents must receive some response or signal such as body or eye movements from their infants to form a close bond. Exciting observations reveal that newborns move in tune with the structure of adult speech. When caregivers and infants are observed "communicating" with each other, both the listeners and the speakers are moving in tune with the words of the speakers, creating a type of dance. As the speakers pause for a breath or accent a syllable,

infants almost imperceptibly raise an eyebrow or lower a foot. When infants are alert, they are ready to dance to mother's speech and movements.

Smiling   During the first few weeks of life, smiles are seen during light sleep and drowsiness, rarely when the baby is awake and alert. These are called **endogenous,** or spontaneous, **smiles** because they bear no relation to the external world (Sroufe, 1979). Smiles occur when babies are aroused and then relax. As the baby relaxes, facial muscles relax too and for a brief moment a contented little grin appears. During the second week of life, infants begin to smile when eyes are open, and by the fourth week, their smiles seem to be evoked by specific stimuli in the environment. The smile may be the sight of a toy or of a human face, familiar or strange. Smiling may serve to keep caregivers near infants; it is gratifying to the caregivers so they stay close, thereby ensuring that the infants receive the care they need.

Social smiling is established sometime between the second week and the second month of life. Smiles triggered by something in the external world are called **exogenous smiles.** At around 4 months, infants can distinguish between familiar and unfamiliar faces, smiling at the former and staring or frowning at the latter. This guarded reaction to unfamiliar faces, called *wariness* (Bronson & Pankey, 1977) and smiling at the familiar ones is a vital landmark in the development of attachment (perhaps more so for parents than for children). Not only are children's smiles produced by external stimuli, but for the first time they may be instrumental; that is, they are produced in order to get a smile back (Stern, 1974).

Locomotive Skills   Between 6 and 24 months and because of their increased locomotive skills, infants now actively seek proximity to their caregivers. They begin to make purposeful efforts to stay close. Young toddlers also seek proximity by calling to their caregivers from another room, requesting assistance and/or company.

It can be seen that infants engage in certain behaviors that help them secure contact with those persons in their environment who are necessary for providing protection, shelter, and food. The fact that such a small being can elicit positive (and negative) responses from parents tells us something about the role of infants in establishing attachment relationships.

CAREGIVERS' CONTRIBUTIONS TO THE ATTACHMENT PROCESS

Ainsworth (1973) pioneered the empirical study of individual differences in infants' quality of attachment to their caregivers. She bases her attachment theory on three premises: (a) Over the course of infants' first year of life, they develop an emotional tie with the person who provides primary care; (b) the quality of this relationship is significantly influenced by the nature of interactions between caregivers and infants; (c) the attachment relationships infants develop with caregivers provide them with a set of expectations (caregivers' availability and predictability) to social interactions that children carry forward and that is therefore likely to influence children's subsequent socioemotional functioning and development. She advanced the proposition that it is caregivers' consistent perceptions and accurate interpretations of as well as contingent and appropriate responses to infants' signals that are thought to nurture the development of security. *Synchrony* is a key word in capturing the type of relationship between caregivers and infants. Synchrony reflects an interactive experience between infants and caregivers; it reflects an appropriate fit of caregivers' and infants' behavior, presumed to derive from sensitive responsiveness and to foster a state of social harmony. Conversely, insecure attachments are thought to develop as a function of caregivers' inconsistent or negligent perceptions, interpretation, and responses to infants' signals (i.e., insensitivity). Maternal intrusiveness, unresponsiveness, and inconsistency characterize interaction of insecure dyads.

Ainsworth, Blehar, Waters, and Wall (1978) observed the interaction of mothers and their infants in their homes on several occasions during the infants' first year. Mothers were rated on four dimensions: sensitivity/insensitivity, acceptance/rejection, cooperation/interference, and accessibility/ignoring. Then, at 12 months, the infants and their mothers came to a laboratory where the nature of the infants' attachment was assessed through the **strange situation test.**

The Strange Situation Test   Briefly, the strange situation test is a structured observation involving a mother and infant (usually between the ages of 12 and 18 months) entering a small room. The mother interests the infant in some toys and allows it to explore or play freely. This is followed by a series of 3-minute periods of separations and reunions. First, an unfamiliar adult enters the room, talks to the mother, and interacts with the infant. Then, the mother leaves the room, often resulting in a distressed infant. The eight episodes in the strange situation test are summarized in Table 11.1.

The strange situation test is designed to assess infants' attachment using three criteria: (a) how well the infant can use the adult as a secure base for exploration; (b) how the infant reacts to strangers; and (c) how the infant reacts to separation from and reunion with mother. Ainsworth considers the attachment construct to be interrelated with separation anxiety, fear or wariness of strangers, and exploration of the environment.

In assessing the overall quality of the infant-parent attachment relationship, Ainsworth et al. utilized a configuration of infant behaviors. It is not so much the infant's crying on separation or even willingness to approach an unfamiliar other that reliably indexes differences in the security of the infant-mother attachment relationship, but rather the behavior that the toddler directs or fails to direct to the mother on reunion following separation. These behaviors include the extent to which the toddler seeks proximity and/or contact with the mother; strives to maintain contact with the mother; directs anger or resistant behavior toward the mother; and ignores or otherwise avoids mother's bid for interaction. On the basis of the behaviors exhibited by the infants, they are classified as secure, insecure-ambivalent, or insecure-avoidant.

Attachment Classifications   A central assumption made by attachment theorists (Ainsworth, 1982; Sroufe & Fleeson, 1986) is that attachment quality is the cumulative product of caregivers' responses to infants' signals for proximity and contact. The

TABLE 11.1 Eight Steps of the Strange Situation Test	Episodes	Participants	Duration	Behavior Highlighted
	1	Mother, baby, experimenter	30 sec	Introduction
	2	Mother, baby	3 min	Exploration of strange environment with mother present
	3	Stranger, mother, baby	3 min	Response to stranger with mother present
	4	Stranger, baby	3 min	Response to separation with stranger present
	5	Mother, baby	variable	Response to reunion with mother
	6	Baby	3 min	Response to separation when left alone
	7	Stranger, baby	3 min	Response to continuing separation, and to stranger after being left alone
	8	Mother, baby	variable	Response to second reunion with mother

Source: From *Patterns of Attachment* by M. Ainsworth, M. Blehar, E. Waters, and S. Wall, 1978, Hillsdale, NJ: Lawrence Erlbaum Associates. Copyright 1978 by Lawrence Erlbaum Associates. Reprinted by permission.

importance assigned to caregiver behavior has stimulated considerable research on the differences in care received by securely and insecurely attached infants. Indeed, the focus of much of Ainsworth's work has been the description of maternal behaviors that predict qualitative differences in attachment.

Ainsworth, Blehar, Waters, and Wall (1978) found that earlier in the infants' lives, the caregivers of securely attached infants with **secure attachment** (type B) responded sensitively (promptly and appropriately) to their infants' needs. These sensitive caregivers were able to perceive and accurately interpret their infants' communications and thus were more responsive to their infants' needs. They held their babies more tenderly and carefully and exhibited greater sensitivity in initiating and terminating feeding. These caregivers were tuned in to their infants' signals. Ainsworth surmised that the underlying characteristic related to infant security was the caregivers' ability to establish an atmosphere of harmony between themselves and their babies.

In the strange situation experiment, infants of sensitive mothers showed signs of positive attachment. They took pleasure in their mothers' presence and warmly greeted them after a brief absence. The mother was able to soothe the child, so that it returned to exploring the environment or even interacting with the stranger. Securely attached infants were able to use their mothers as secure bases from which to explore their novel surroundings. They cried less and generally seemed content.

By contrast, infants whose mothers had been insensitive behaved in one of two ways: insecure ambivalent or insecure avoidant. The group of infants labeled with **insecure-ambivalent attachment** (type C) had mothers who were relatively insensitive to their babies' cues. Mothers in this group, at times, responded to their infants' signals, but their responsiveness was not geared to the infants' ongoing needs. Rather, it was dependent on the changing moods of the mother. Insecure-ambivalent relationships tend to originate from depressed levels of maternal involvement and responsiveness.

The infant's open, rounded eyes and her alert, satisfied facial expression communicate important signals to the mother, eliciting caregiving and assurance.

These infants were unable to use their mothers as secure bases from which to explore assertively. They greeted their mothers with a mixed response, both approaching and turning and looking away. If picked up, the infants showed a mixed response also, momentarily clinging, but also squirming to get away. The behavior of these infants indicated either that the infants were uncertain about how their mothers would behave or that they were angry.

Mothers of infants in the third group, those with **insecure-avoidant attachment** (type A), were highly insensitive to their babies' signals. Belsky, Rovine, and Taylor (1984) and Isabella and Belsky (1991) found that mothers of avoidant infants displayed the highest and lowest levels, respectively, of reciprocal interaction and involvement. Mothers of avoidant infants tend to be more responsive to general infant behavior and facial emotions expression than mothers of nonavoidant infants (Lewis & Feiring, 1989). The evidence suggests that insecure-avoidant attachment has its origins in intrusive and hyper-responsive caregiving.

These infants were unable to develop a complete sense of trust and confidence in mothers' availability. They behaved independently in pre-

separation episodes. They failed to meet mothers on return or actually avoided interaction and/or contact by averting their gaze, ignoring their mothers' solicitations, or by actually moving away and turning their backs to their mothers. A summary of the patterns of attachment is provided in Table 11.2.

A fourth classification has been added (type D), although very little research has been done on these children, who are characterized as disorganized and disoriented. Some studies suggest that infants in this classification have mothers who are depressed, and it is speculated that their depression interferes with the capacity to relate in a way that promotes the development of a secure attachment (Main & Solomon, 1990). Depressed mothers may be perceived as inconsistent and unpredictable. The mother's inability to respond to affect and associated physical and emotional unavailability are likely to compound the child's difficulties in establishing a secure attachment relationship.

Thus, according to Ainsworth (1982), mothers play a crucial role in helping their infants develop a secure bond with them. Maternal characteristics that Ainsworth has identified as antecedents of se-

TABLE 11.2 Patterns of Attachment	
	SECURE ATTACHMENT (Type B)

SECURE ATTACHMENT (Type B)
1. Caregiver is a secure base for exploration.
   a. readily separate to explore toys
   b. affective sharing of play
   c. affiliative to stranger in mother's presence
   d. readily comforted when distressed (promoting a return to play)
2. Active in seeking contact or interaction on reunion
   a. if distressed
      a. immediately seek and maintain contact
      b. contact is effective in terminating distress
   b. if not distressed
      a. active greeting behavior (happy to see caregiver)
      b. strong initiation of interaction

AMBIVALENT ATTACHMENT (Type C)
1. Poverty of exploration
   a. difficulty separating to explore, may need contact even prior to separation
   b. wary of novel situations and people
2. Difficulty settling on reunion
   a. may mix contact seeking with contact resistance (hitting, kicking, squirming, rejecting toys)
   b. may simply continue to cry and fuss
   c. may show striking passivity

AVOIDANT ATTACHMENT (Type A)
1. Independent exploration
   a. readily separate to explore during preseparation
   b. little affective sharing
   c. affiliative to stranger, when caregiver absent (little preference)
2. Active avoidance on reunion
   a. turning away, looking away, moving away, ignoring
   b. may mix avoidance with proximity
   c. avoidance more extreme on second reunion
   d. no avoidance of stranger

Source: Adapted from *Patterns of Attachment* by M. Ainsworth, M. Blehar, E. Waters, and S. Wall, 1978, Hillsdale, NJ: Lawrence Erlbaum Associates. Copyright 1978 by Lawrence Erlbaum Associates. Reprinted by permission.

cure attachment during the child's first year include sensitivity, cooperation, acceptance, accessibility, sociability and displays of positive affect. Attachment theorists (Ainsworth, 1982; Pederson, Moran, Sitko, Campbell, Ghesquire, & Acton, 1990; Sroufe, 1985) make explicit assertions that maternal sensitivity is the major experiential antecedent to the development of a secure relationship. Factors that affect maternal sensitivity are discussed in "Focus on Applications."

Ainsworth's (1982) work may raise some questions. First, are the differences observed in children's classification patterns stable over a period of time? Second, is there a certain time period for establishing strong affectionate bonds between caregivers and children?

STABILITY OF SECURE AND INSECURE ATTACHMENTS

Research on parent-child attachment continues to flourish, with a particular emphasis on the predictive value of various types of attachment patterns. Do secure and insecure attachment patterns last?

Some studies have shown that there is stability in secure and insecure classification patterns, at least for short periods of time. Others, however,

Maternal Sensitivity

Parental sensitivity is important in that it reflects parents' accuracy in diagnosing children's signals and consequently how rewarding their reactions will be. Also, it reflects how close the linkage in time will be between children's signal and the parents' contingent response.

Parental differences in sensitivity are a product of the interrelations among several influences, notably the parents' personality traits, situational or attitudinal factors, and infant characteristics. Several personality traits appear to be especially relevant in producing sensitive parents. Self-centeredness affects the extent to which parents monitor infants' state and signals, as well as the evaluation and interpretation of infants' signal or need. Self-centeredness may lead to insensitivity when adults fail to put infants' needs before their own desires.

Adaptability may be reflected in the adults' ability to tolerate ambiguity of their infants' signals. In the first few months of life, in particular, it may be rather difficult to "read" infants' signals correctly. Parents who are able to tolerate this ambiguity are likely to be more sensitive. Persistence may be another personality trait that aids parents in becoming more sensitive. Persistence will undoubtedly affect how long parents attempt to soothe the distressed infant and how patient they are in trying alternative strategies.

Adults' perceptions of their effectiveness as parents may also be important in determining their degree of sensitivity. When parents can think of themselves as competent in their role, they are more likely to be sensitive and caring. The amount of time that parents have available to be with their children and the quality of their interactions have an important bearing on their sensitivity. Each parent can aid the other in trying to make sure that both of them have time to effectively interact with their children.

It also appears that the mother's emotional outlook is related to her ability to respond sensitively to her child's cues. It has been found, for example, that depressed mothers (sad affect, feeling of hopelessness, irritability) are more likely to express less positive emotion toward their children and to respond less frequently and less meaningfully to their infants' proximity-promoting behaviors (Radke-Yarrow et al., 1985). Depression seems to interfere with mothers' ability to relate to their children in ways that promote secure attachment.

While personality and attitudinal and situational factors are important and undoubtedly affect the degree of parental sensitivity, the characteristics of infants are also important: notably, the infants' temperament, responsivity, adaptability, and sociability, to name a few. Temperament refers to infants' relatively enduring style of responding to the world about them. It is no doubt easier to develop sensitivity to an infant who is happy, agreeable, and compliant than with a difficult, irritable, discontented infant. It has been found, for example, that mothers of difficult infants are less sensitive to changes in signals, compared with mothers of easy infants (Leavitt & Donovan, 1979). Moreover, if the mother feels a loss of control over her difficult infant (what she does makes no difference in the behavior of the child), this state of helplessness will be evidenced in reduced sensitivity to the child's needs (Donovan & Leavitt, 1985).

Infants' responsiveness refers to the extent and quality of infant responses to stimulation. If infants are unresponsive to parents' smiling and talking, it may influence the quality of the mother's responsiveness to her infant. Finally, readability refers to the definitiveness of infant behavioral signals. An easily read infant is one who produces unambiguous cues that allow caregivers to recognize infant states quickly and respond promptly and correctly.

have shown that substantial change in classification patterns does occur (Ainsworth, 1982; Pianta et al., 1989). For example, Egeland and Sroufe (1981) studied 31 infants with a history of extreme neglect and 33 infants with a history of excellent care. The neglected infants were characterized by a low proportion of secure attachment at 12 but not at 18 months. Fifty-two percent of the mistreated infants changed classification from insecure to secure attachment. Secure-attachment classification for the excellent care group remained stable between 12 and 18 months.

Some of the conditions that were associated with changing from an insecure- to a secure-attachment classification for the maltreated group included the presence of a supportive family member and a less stressful, chaotic life-style. The important implication of the study is that the quality of attachment can change even when early attachment is poor or nonexistent.

Seitz, Rosenbaum, and Apfel (1985) did a 10-year follow-up study of 17 children from impoverished families. These families had received a coordinated set of medical and social services, including day care for their children. The services began during the mothers' pregnancy and continued for 30 months postpartum. Seitz found that teachers, 10 years later, tended to rate these children, particularly boys, academically and socially better adjusted. The control group of children whose families had not received these services were rated as disobedient, usually to a serious degree. Seitz et al. suggest that the causal link between the intervention program and the children's better social and school adjustment is to be found in the greater parental nurturance brought about by the program. They concluded that a plausible assumption is that intervention strengthened the mother-child bond, which led to better emotional development and long-term behavioral differences now evident in these children.

In support of Seitz's suggestion, Jacobson and Frye (1991) studied the effects of maternal social support on the development of attachment. The sample consisted of 46 first-time mothers who were randomly assigned to an experimental group or a control group. The experimental group of mothers met with volunteer coaches who were trained to provide maternal support and information prenatally and during the first postpartum year. At 14 months, experimental infants scored higher on an attachment ratings cluster. These findings provide experimental evidence regarding the importance of social support on infant attachment.

Tizard, Philips, and Plewis (1976) found that children from orphanages who were adopted when they were 4 years old were able to develop close relationships with their adoptive parents. The results of these studies suggest that children display a certain resiliency; they can and do recover from insecure-attachment classification. How long they retain this resiliency is not known.

SENSITIVE PERIODS

Quite a number of studies have addressed the question of whether there is a sensitive period for parent-infant contact. A **sensitive period** denotes a particular interval of time in which certain physical and psychological growth (in this discussion, the development of attachment behaviors) must take place. After this time, so the theory goes, it is extremely difficult if not impossible for bonding to take place. Some researchers maintain that the first few minutes or hours of life are crucial in the development of attachment (Klaus & Kennell, 1982).

Emde and Robinson (1979) noted that the infant is in a quiet alert state for a period of 45 to 60 minutes immediately after birth. In this state infants' eyes are wide open and they are able to respond to their environment. They can see; they have visual preferences and will turn their heads toward sounds. After this hour, the exhausted newborn sleeps for 3 to 4 hours.

Does the bond begin then? Most probably it *begins* then, but it is not being implied that this hour is the only time for developing bonding behaviors. After all, it wasn't long ago that it was common hospital practice to give the mother a brief glance at her child and then whisk the baby off to be checked, washed, and clothed. If this is *the* time for bonding then many who were born when this was the usual hospital procedure wou..u nave been doomed as far as the formation of secure attachments is concerned. Of course, the same would be true for premature infants (see "Focus on Issues"). This is simply not the case. The attachment process is more complex and ongoing than that.

Some intriguing observations about the effect of early contact have been made by Klaus and Kennell (1982). They conducted a study that points out the importance of early and extended contact. Early contact refers to opportunities for contact in the delivery or recovery room. Extended contact refers to opportunities for additional contact during the remainder of the hospital stay. Fourteen mothers, comprising the control group, experienced the usual brief "hello" with their infants, no touching, only looking briefly. Fourteen mothers, comprising the experimental group, were allowed to experience immediate contact with their newborns.

In the experimental group, the naked infant was placed on the mother's abdomen immediately after birth; some 5 minutes later the infant was placed up toward the mother's breast and was helped to suckle. In addition, these women were with their infants 5 extra hours (compared with the control group) each afternoon during the 3 days after delivery.

In follow-up studies 1 month, 1 year, and 2 years after delivery, differences between the experimental and control groups were found in maternal attachment behavior. At 1 month, it was observed that mothers in the experimental group tended to be more likely to touch, comfort, and look at their infants than the control-group mothers. At follow-up sessions 1 and 2 years later, the mothers in the experimental group still displayed more interaction with their children than did the control group mothers.

In another study, socioeconomically disadvantaged mothers who had extra contact with their newborns were compared with socioeconomically disadvantaged mothers who did not (Siegel, Bauman, Schaefer, Sanders, & Ingram, 1980). It appears that socioeconomically disadvantaged mothers tend to be less emotionally responsive to their infants, more punitive, and less involved than socioeconomically advantaged mothers (Ramey & Farran, 1979; Ramey & Ramey, 1990). It also appears that lower-class mothers tend to show stronger or longer-lasting effects of early contact than middle-class mothers. Goldberg (1983) argues that middle-class mothers have fewer stresses and tend to engage in nurturing behavior that is close to the maximum possible, whether afforded opportunities for attachment or not. Among lower-class mothers, higher stress levels and fewer social supports can depress maternal affectionate behavior, allowing the effects of early and extended contact to be more readily demonstrable.

Mothers who were allowed extra contact with their infants in the Siegel et al. study showed significant increases in positive versus negative responses to their infants. They exhibited more touching and caressing behaviors, were more acceptant of their infants, and more consoling toward their crying infants. Socioeconomic class and educational level may be very difficult to change, but all mothers and fathers can be given the opportunity for early and extended contact with their infants, which may possibly start them off toward a positive relationship with their children.

Other investigators are questioning the contention that the close physical contact between mother and infant in the first few hours of life is necessary for parent-to-infant attachment (Grossman, Eichler, Winickoff, Anzalone, Gorseyeff, & Sargent, 1980; Svejda, Campos, & Emde, 1980). One group of researchers, for example, found no differences in the attachment classifications of prematurely born infants and infants who were not separated from their mothers at birth (Rode, Chang, Fisch, & Sroufe, 1981). The data from this study suggest that attachment patterns are influenced by mother-infant interaction over a period of time, and provide evidence of the resiliency of infants in their formation of attachment patterns.

Goldberg (1983) has argued convincingly that the concept of a sensitive period has not been adequately tested. Moreover, in her review of mother-infant bonding research, she maintains that the effects of early and extended contact have not been

FOCUS ON ISSUES

Premature Infants and Attachment

Are premature infants who are separated from their mothers immediately after birth able to form secure attachments with their mothers? Bonding may be more difficult, because premature infants need special care and monitoring. Consequently, parents are often unable to touch, hold, feed, or play with their newborns. Mothers are often forced into a supporting, peripheral position that makes bonding harder (Easterbrooks, 1989).

Malatesta, Culver, Tesman, and Shepard (1989) point out that in some cases of premature birth, there are difficulties in the formation of this bond because premature infants

> have been found to differ from full terms in many ways thought to have an effect on the mother's attempts to interact with her child. For example, premature babies tend to be more irritable than their full-term counterparts. They show a lag in social smiling, are less ready to withstand the stimulation that occurs in playful, face-to-face interaction, and show more gaze aversion. They also sleep a greater proportion of the time and are less alert and responsive when awake. Their motor organization is poorer, and their states of arousal are less well modulated. In sum, in the premature infant, the caregiver is faced with a less adept social partner, one at risk for subsequent interactive difficulty. (p. 24)

Another factor affecting bonding is that the mother of a premature infant looking at her forbiddingly small baby understandably may feel apprehensive about the child's survival. Fearing that she may lose the child, she may not want to feel close to her baby. Some parents of premature infants may not immediately name their children. Other emotions may enter in. For example, mothers may also feel guilty because they cannot care for their babies as well as the hospital staff.

What can be done to foster the development of the bond between premature infants and their parents? One suggestion consistently offered is that the parents of premature infants need to stimulate their child more often. One must be careful, however, about recommending increased stimulation. For example, it has been observed in spontaneous play situations that mothers of premature infants often overstimulate them, which results in the infants decreasing their gaze time (Mangelsdorf, Gunnar, Kestenbaum, Lang, & Andreas, 1990). Overstimulation in this sense means that mothers may continue to initiate interactions through talking, smiling, and touching their infants,

---

consistently demonstrated. This is not to say that early and extended contact is unimportant— overrated, perhaps, but not unimportant. Babies develop best when in their earliest contacts with their caregivers they are given loving, responsive care. The emphasis on early bonding, as Goldberg (1983) points out,

> may create an expectation on the part of many parents that if they do not have this experience they have somehow failed and will never be fine

parents. For all of those who cannot have these experiences, it is important to emphasize that the parent-infant relationship is a complex system with many fail-safe or alternative routes to the same outcomes. Its success or failure does not hinge on a few brief moments in time. (p. 1379)

FATHER-INFANT RELATIONS

Prior to the 1970s, only two studies considered father-infant relations; the bulk of the research

Focus on Issues
continued

even when the infant has turned away. In observations of premature infants, it has been noted that mothers were interacting up to 90% of the time, whereas the infant was only looking 30% of the time (Field, 1977). According to one study, mothers of preterm infants may be likely to initiate and continue interactions because they find it difficult to read and understand their infants' cues. As a result, they may try harder by more often leading the interaction (Lester, Hoffman, & Brazelton, 1985).

Maternal activity that is excessive or minimal results in nonoptimal interaction. Mothers may severely overload children with signals as they try to engage them in playful encounters. The child who is overloaded turns away and may resort to crying. If this overstimulation continues, the mother-child relationship may be seriously damaged. The fact that overstimulation may be damaging is often forgotten. Therefore, parents need to learn how to engage in continguent stimulation—that is, stimulation related to the cues from the infant. When the mother moves at her infant's pace, it aids the infant's development and enhances the bond between infant and parent.

Premature infants need to be touched, rocked, or cuddled daily during their hospital stay. Those who receive this special care by a consistent caregiver, according to Segall (1972), have fewer apneic periods (short interruptions in infant's breathing pattern), show increased weight gain, and show an advance in some areas of higher central nervous system functioning that persists for months after discharge from the hospital.

Parents need to know that despite their size, many premature infants are strong little ones. Parents also need an opportunity to discuss their fears and concerns. Hospital personnel need to recognize the needs of parents and premature infants and need to provide special attention to the parent-infant bonding. Flexible visiting policies, letting mother and father share responsibilities for the care of the infant, and offering not only advice for caring but emotional support are some of the ways that hospitals can help.

In concluding, the results from research can be interpreted as providing an optimistic perspective. When parents feel confident and competent, which enables them to establish a general caregiving atmosphere that is warm, consistent, and contingent on the needs of the infant, there is every reason to believe that preterm infants will develop a strong, secure attachment with their caregivers (Lyons-Ruth, Connell, Grunebaum, & Botein, 1990).

centered on mothers. One of these pioneering studies (Schaffer & Emerson, 1964) found that most of the infant subjects in the study were attached both to mothers and to fathers by 9 months of age, and by 18 months, 80% of the infants were attached to both parents. Pedersen and Robson (1969) noted that most infants were clearly delighted to see their fathers and warmly greeted them after a brief absence. Although the findings of these studies were revealing, some methodological problems existed. In both studies, the re-searchers did not observe or interview fathers directly, but relied on mothers as their primary source of information.

Current research points out the important role that fathers play in providing social support for their wives, which, in turn, positively affects mothers' attachment behaviors toward their infants (Hartup, 1989). It appears that fathers' ability to be supportive is influenced by the quality of the marital relationship. The impact of marriage on parenting may be greater for fathers than for mothers (Parke & Tinsley, 1987). Both the fathers' psychological adjustment and the close/confiding nature of the marriage make independent contributions to the prediction of the fathers' attitudes about their infants and their roles as parents. Unhappily married men not only give less social support to their wives but withdraw from them and also distance themselves from their children (Dickstein & Parke, 1988).

Early developmental researchers appeared to be content in assuming that the sole relationship enjoyed by young infants was that with their mothers. In addition, these early studies concentrated on infants who were 6 months of age or older, and very few systematic investigations were done on the behavior of the father before, during, and immediately after childbirth. Increasingly, there has been a developing interest in the earliest stages of interaction, with observations of the father often beginning during his wife's pregnancy.

The Prenatal Period The expectant father, like the mother-to-be, shows a wide variety of reactions during the pregnancy. The struggle for the expectant male during the prenatal period is to remain emotionally available to his wife and at the same time meet his own needs for feeling responsible and productive (Yogman, 1982). In this regard, Shereshefsky and Yarrow (1973) found an association between the husband's responsiveness to his wife's pregnancy and her successful adaptation to it, which may help the mother feel more positive toward her newborn child. Moreover, fathers who attend prenatal classes have been observed to be more comfortable in giving care to their infants (Greenberg & Morris, 1974).

Birth Attendance Fathers' potential role in childbirth has evolved "from one of an unnecessary source of infection to an essential source of affection for both mother and newborn" (Kunst-Wilson & Cronenwett, 1981, p. 362). Since the early 1980s, the concept of fathers' attending the birth of their children has gained wide acceptance, and popular beliefs indicate that birth attendance plays a significant role in the development of father-child attachment. No conclusive evidence has been reported that strongly suggests bonding as a result

of fathers' early history with their infants (Palkovitz, 1985). Palkovitz does point out that studies reporting positive findings for birth-attending versus nonattending fathers slightly outnumber studies finding no group differences. Early and extended contact studies are also inconclusive; there are as many studies that report positive results as there are that report negative results.

The first detailed account of birth attendance was done by Greenberg and Morris (1974). Thirty fathers responded to written questionnaires 48 to 72 hours after delivery. The researchers reported that fathers who attended their child's birth were more confident in their ability to identify their child and were more comfortable holding the child. Subsequent reports have cited this study as a classic in documenting the impact of birth experience on fathers. As noted by Palkovitz (1985), however, an important part of their report is often not cited. Greenberg and Morris (1974) note that "there were no significant differences in observations of engrossment [absorption, preoccupation, and interest in the infant] among fathers who saw their newborn's birth as opposed to those who did not" (p. 527). Results of this study are confounded with prebirth differences in the samples. Birth-attending fathers also attended more prenatal classes than non-birth-attending fathers. As a result, these fathers may have felt more prepared for parenthood, facilitating their ability to identify their child and greater comfort in holding the child.

In a longitudinal study, 46 families were followed from the sixth month of pregnancy until 6 months after the birth of the child (Peterson, Mehl, & Leiderman, 1979). It was found that the emotional quality of the birth experience was the most significant predictor of father's attachment to his infant. Fathers who had attended the birth *and* had experienced positive involvement and emotions during delivery received higher attachment scores when the child was 6 months old than a control group of fathers who had not attended birth or who had attended birth but experienced negative emotions. The authors concluded that "the birth experience acts as a powerful catalyst for nurturing behavior" (p. 337).

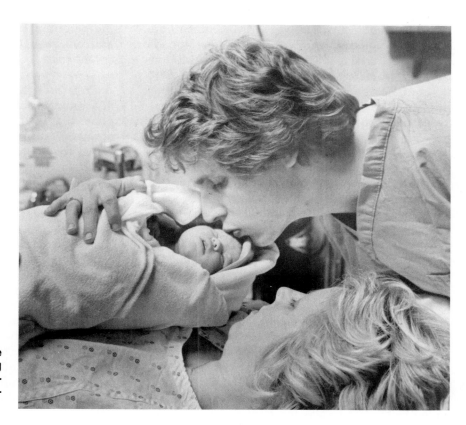

Fathers who experience positive involvement and emotions during delivery tend to have strong attachment bonds with their children.

Other studies have reported no significant differences between fathers who have attended their child's birth and those who have not (Nicholson, Gist, Klein, & Standley, 1983). Lozoff (1974), who studied fathers in 120 different cultures, concluded that there was "no increase . . . in paternal involvement when fathers were allowed at childbirth" (p. 599).

Early Contact   Parke (1979) believes that the father must have an extensive early exposure to the infant in the hospital where the parent-infant bond is initially formed. He maintains that there is a lot of learning that goes on between mother and child in the hospital from which the father is often excluded. The father must be included so that he will not only have the interest in and a feeling of closeness to his child, but also so that he can develop the kinds of skills that the mother develops.

Some studies of father-infant interaction suggest that fathers can become attached to their infants in the early period following delivery if they are allowed contact with them. For example, it was found that paternal caregiving in the first 3 months increased in Swedish fathers when they were asked to undress their infants twice each day and to establish eye-to-eye contact with their infants for 1 hour during the first 3 days of life (Lind, Vuorenkoski, & Wasz-Hockert, 1973).

Rodholm and Larson (1979) have observed father-infant interaction at the first contact after delivery. They filmed 15 fathers of full-term infants delivered by Caesarean section. The naked infant was presented to the father 15 minutes after birth and pictures were taken every second. They noted an orderly progression of behavior. The father began touching the infant's extremities first with his fingertips, then using his palms. An increase in eye-to-eye contact was also observed. Similar findings were noted when observing fathers immediately after birth in a homelike situation (McDonald, 1978).

Contrasting results were obtained in another study (Pannabecker, Emde, & Austin, 1982). These researchers studied the effect of granting fathers an extra hour of contact with their infants, distributed across two ½-hour sessions in the first 3 days following the infant's birth. During contact, the experimenters pointed out physical characteristics of the infants and demonstrated physical exercises. The control group received the same information from a videofilm of a typical newborn infant. The fathers' interactive behavior with their infants was videotaped during an office visit to the pediatrician 1 month later. The authors noted that there were only two behavioral differences between the experimental- and control-group fathers. The former patted their infants more and the latter group of fathers kissed their infants more. Thus, the experimenters concluded that early contact did not significantly affect the father's behavior 1 month later. Perhaps, as Palkovitz (1985) points out, the amount of additional contact provided in this study was too brief and rigidly controlled to make any long-term impact on the fathers' behavior.

Palkovitz's (1985) conclusions in summarizing the literature of father-infant bonding are quite similar to those of Goldberg (1983) regarding mother-infant bonding. Like Goldberg, Palkovitz is not saying that attending birth and early and extended contacts between father and children are unimportant. Rather, he tries to make the point that perhaps some researchers, medical personnel, and media have been too exuberant in their statements that birth attendance and early contact lead to strong attachments between fathers and their infants. Although such a belief creates no difficulty if it increases father involvement in child care and child rearing, it does create some problems if a high proportion of fathers feel guilty over missing their child's birth. Palkovitz calls for a more balanced approach—one in which fathers, in consultation with their partners, choose, in all stages of the parenting process, levels of involvement that are consistent with their skills, desires, and perceived roles.

A Preference for Father?   Studies of infant-father attachment parallel those of infant-mother attachment; that is, they investigate infants' reactions to strangers and separations. In order to learn something about the earliest phases of mother-infant and father-infant attachments, Lamb and Easterbrooks (1981) observed 20 infants (7 to 13 months) in their homes, when both parents and a female stranger were present. He found no consistent preference for either parent over the other in terms of the attachment behaviors studied (separation protest, directed crying, requests to be held, touching, and proximity). Thus, he concluded that in a stress-free home environment there is no indication that either parent could be described as a primary or preferred attachment figure.

Fourteen of the original 20 infants, as well as 6 additional subjects, were studied until they had reached their 2nd birthdays. Across the second year of life, significant preferences for fathers occurred among the boys. Girls were much less consistent—some preferred their mothers, some their fathers, some both or neither parent. The emergent preferences for fathers on the part of sons may be due partially to the tendency of fathers to be more attentive to their sons, especially immediately following birth and after their first birthday.

Bowlby (1980) and Ainsworth (1982) might quibble with Lamb's findings; they have argued that true preferences may be obscured in such secure surroundings. They maintain that when infants are distressed, they reduce the amount of interaction with the secondary attachment figure. Lamb investigated 8-, 12- and 18-month-old infants in laboratory settings under increasingly stressful circumstances. Another sample of 24-month-olds had been observed previously (Lamb, 1977). When both parents were available, 12- and 18-month-old infants sought comfort from their mothers preferentially. Interestingly, 8- and 24-month-old children did not show preferences for their mothers.

STUDYING CHILDREN

I WANT MY MOM!

Research shows that under stressful situations young children prefer their mothers to their fathers. See for yourself by conducting a study similar to Lamb's (1977) study. Observe a mother, father, and their 15- to 24-month-old child interacting in a normal play situation. Does the child seem to show any preference for his mother? His father? What happens when you present a toy that makes a noise? Does the child show preferences when he becomes stressed?

When moderately distressed, these infants increased the display of attachment behavior to the available parent—mother or father.

Lytton (1980) found in studying 2-year-old boys that about 70% of the children displayed more attachment behavior to their mothers and 30% to their fathers. It must be stressed, however, that almost all children showed some attachment behavior to both parents. It appears, however, that in stressful situations, when infants have a choice, they choose their mothers (Goossens & van Ijzendoorn, 1990). Try the experiment in "Studying Children." In the next chapter it will be shown that although mothers are preferred in anxiety-producing situations, fathers are preferred over mothers for affiliative interactions, especially play.

EARLY CHILDHOOD: SOCIALIZATION FORCES

Socialization is "an adult-initiated process by which developing children, through insight, training, and imitation, acquire the habits and values congruent with adaptation to their culture" (Baumrind, 1980, p. 640). A major part of children's socialization involves helping them to develop social controls, or, put somewhat differently, to adopt society's rules of behavior. In this sense, parents monitor their children's acts, offering approval or withholding it, in order to help shape children's future acts. While socialization does oc-cur in the child's first year, the onset of socialization pressure generally comes in the second year. At this time, parents make a more concerted effort to socialize their children to behave in socially approved ways.

Although socially approved ways of behaving vary according to the child's age and cultural milieu, in Western society this idea usually means helping children to establish meaningful and sustained relationships with others, to work cooperatively with others, and to play an active part in the social order. Through the use of various methods of control (reinforcement, disciplining and punishing techniques, establishment of rules and regulations) parents seek to mold, shape, and refine children's behavior.

PARENTS AS SOCIALIZING AGENTS

Fathers tend to place more emphasis on child protection, self-sufficiency, initiative, and competition, while mothers tend to focus on concern for others and self-sacrifice. In accomplishing these goals, fathers are apt to use forceful techniques such as parental power and authority, whereas mothers stress more interpersonally oriented techniques such as reasoning, nurturance, and praise. Power and Shanks (1989) found in studying mothers and fathers of 42 children that fathers emphasized instrumental behaviors and mothers emphasized communion. That is, fathers were more likely to report encouraging independence and assertiveness in their children, whereas mothers were more likely to report encouraging appropriate interpersonal behavior (manners and politeness). Fathers tended to use physical punishment and mothers relied more on material punishment. It was further noted that parents are more punishing and less rewarding with same-sexed children. For both mothers and fathers, reasoning and persuasion tends to increase as children get older.

The process of child rearing undergoes important changes as children develop. During each phase of children's development, different problems become foci for parental concern and subsequent action. Concerns in the infancy and toddlerhood period center on irritability, illness, sleeplessness, toilet training, disobedience, inability to play coop-eratively with others, and delayed verbal skills. Child-rearing concerns during the preschool years tend to focus on bedtime routines, control of tem-per tantrums, fighting with siblings or other chil-dren, eating and table manners, getting dressed by themselves, and attention seeking. Some of these is-sues carry over into school age, for example, fight-ing and children's reactions to discipline.

In middle childhood, parents tend to be con-cerned about standards of performance, encourag-ing children to entertain themselves, their chil-dren's relationships with peers, informing parents of where they are, dealing with problems at school, and children's achievement. During ado-lescence parents continue to be concerned about their children's social and academic performances, along with dating, sexual activities, and drugs.

A major influence regulating parenting behavior may be parents' beliefs and attitudes about chil-dren and children's behavior at different ages. That is, parents' disciplining techniques are apt to reflect their inferences about children's compe-tence and responsibility for misconduct. When parents think misdeeds reflect an absence of com-petence, they prefer calm induction more and power assertion less. The parental attitude toward 3-year-olds tends to be predominantly indulgent and protective, while much more is expected of older children who are thought to be capable of conforming to nearly adult norms of behavior (Mullis & Mullis, 1989).

Parents certainly recognize that enormous ad-vances in social skill occur across age and should therefore think that, in general, older children are more responsible (Dix, Ruble, & Zambarano, 1989). Studies suggest, at least in some respects, that transfer of power from parent to child occurs slowly with the major shift to genuine autonomy beginning to occur at about age 12. Parents tend to give children more responsibility for their behavior as they get older by replacing directive techniques such as forcing compliance and repetition of com-mands with less directive approaches involving reasoning and explanation (Smetana, 1989).

Ogbu (1988) provides useful theoretical frame-works to understand the development of caregiv-ing environments in different socioeconomic classes. He argues that child-rearing techniques depend to some extent on the nature of the instru-mental competences that adults are expected to have in a given population. Consciously or uncon-sciously, adults try to inculcate through various techniques cognitive, motivational, and social competencies that are considered relevant to their cultural milieu.

Thus, the parents' position in the social struc-ture has an impact on how they discipline chil-dren. Low socioeconomic-status parents tend to emphasize respect, obedience, neatness, and stay-ing out of trouble because those are the attributes that they view as critical for success in the blue-collar economy. Lower-class parents stress obedi-ence to external authority because this is adaptive in their existing social structure. Middle class par-ents tend to emphasize less power assertion and more democratic modes of discipline (Lytton, 1980). It has been suggested that middle class par-ents value curiosity, consideration for others, in-dependence, and self-control in their children be-cause they want to prepare them for positions, similar to their own, that require them to make decisions and take responsibility.

PARENTING STYLES

Over the years, researchers have examined many different kinds of parenting disciplining tech-niques. One prominent researcher, Baumrind (1971, 1989), has characterized two aspects of par-ents' behavior toward children: *parental responsive-ness* and *parental demandingness*. Responsiveness refers to the degree to which parents respond to children's needs in an accepting, supportive man-ner. Demandingness refers to the extent to which parents expect and demand mature, responsible behavior from children.

Because responsiveness and demandingness are more or less independent of each other, it is possible to look at various combinations of these two dimensions (see Figure 11.3). Labels have been given to the fourfold classification. A parent who is very responsive but not at all demanding is labeled *indulgent*, whereas one who is equally re-sponsive but also very demanding is labeled *au-*

FIGURE 11.3 A Scheme for Classifying Parenting Types

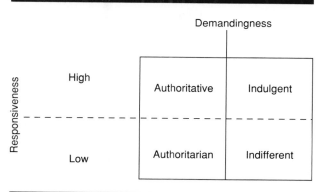

Source: Adapted from "Socialization, Personality, and Social Development" by E. E. Maccoby and J. A. Martin, 1983, in E. M. Hetherington (Ed.), *Handbook of Child Psychology:* Vol. IV (p. 39), New York: John Wiley & Sons.

thoritative. Parents who are very demanding but not responsive are *authoritarian;* parents who are neither demanding nor responsive are labeled *indifferent.* These four general patterns are described in Table 11.3.

The categorization proposed by Baumrind provides a useful way of summarizing and examining some of the relations between parenting practices and children's psychosocial development. She noted that children who were most responsible and mature tended to have parents who established consistent standards of behavior, negotiated with their children concerning those standards, used explanations, and had warm relationships with their children—**authoritative parents.** Generally speaking, children raised in authoritative households are more psychosocially competent than children raised in authoritarian, indulgent, or indifferent homes.

The authoritative parent expects mature behavior from the child. They exhibit a high level of demandingness and a high level of responsiveness to their children. Such parents encourage children to be independent, but still place limits, demands and control on their actions. Children from authoritative homes show greater social responsibility (achievement orientation, friendliness toward peers, cooperativeness toward adults) and independence (social dominance, nonconforming behavior, purposiveness).

Authoritarian parents exhibit high levels of demandingness and low levels of responsiveness to their children. Rules in these homes are not discussed in advance or arrived at by any consensus or bargaining process. They are decided upon by the parents. Parents attach strong value to the maintenance of their authority and suppress any efforts by their children to challenge it.

Baumrind makes a distinction between firm control of authoritative parents and restrictive, punitive control of authoritarian parents. Firm control "is not a measure of restrictiveness, punitive attitudes, or intrusiveness, but is a measure of strict discipline" (1971, p. 6). She notes that "it is not the exercise of firm control per se, however, but the arbitrary, harsh, and nonfunctional exercise of firm control that has negative consequences for child behavior" (Baumrind, 1989, p. 139).

Baumrind found that this type of discipline tends to produce children who display dependent, regressive behavior (crying and thumb sucking). Moreover, it seems that parents who are highly restrictive and follow an absolute standard of conduct and control are likely to have children who fail to initiate activities and are ineffective in social situations.

Whereas authoritarian parents make all the decisions, **permissive parents** allow children to make all the decisions; they do not feel in control and do not exert control. Little or no parental control is associated with impulsive behavior in children. In addition, these children tend to be immature, dependent, regressive, the least self-reliant, and the poorest in self-control.

Children raised by **indifferent parents** are often impulsive and more likely to be involved in delinquent behavior and in precocious experiments with sex, drugs, and alcohol. In general, the effects of indifference tend to be slightly worse among boys than girls.

To summarize, authoritative parents are controlling, but affectionate, and encourage autonomy in their children; authoritarian parents are controlling

TABLE 11.3   Parenting Styles

Authoritative parents are *warm but firm*. They set standards for the child's conduct but form expectations that are consistent with the child's developing needs and capabilities. They *place a high value on the development of autonomy and self-direction* but assume the ultimate responsibility for their child's behavior. Authoritative parents deal with their child in a rational, issue-oriented manner, frequently engaging in discussion and explanation with their children over matters of discipline.

Authoritarian parents place a high value on obedience and conformity. They tend to favor more punitive, absolute, and forceful disciplinary measures. Verbal give-and-take is not common in authoritarian households, because the underlying belief of authoritarian parents is that the child should accept without question the rules and standards established by the parents. They tend not to encourage independent behavior and, instead, place a good deal of importance on restricting the child's autonomy.

Indulgent parents behave in an accepting, benign, and somewhat more passive way in matters of discipline. They place relatively few demands on the child's behavior, giving the child a high degree of freedom to act as he or she wishes. Indulgent parents are more likely to believe that control is an infringement on the child's freedom that may interfere with the child's healthy development. Instead of actively shaping their child's behavior, indulgent parents are more likely to view themselves as resources that the child may or may not use.

Indifferent parents try to do whatever is necessary to minimize the time and energy that they must devote to interacting with their child. In extreme cases, indifferent parents may be neglectful. They know little about their child's activities and whereabouts, show little interest in their child's experiences at school or with friends, rarely converse with their child, and rarely consider their child's opinion when making decisions. Rather than raising their child according to a set of beliefs about what is good for the child's development (as do the other three parent types) indifferent parents are "parent-centered"—they structure their home life primarily around their own needs and interests.

Source: From "Current Patterns of Parental Authority" by D. Baumrind, 1971, *Developmental Psychological Monographs, 4* (1, Pt. 2).

but less affectionate; indulgent parents are minimally controlling but affectionate. Teachers who run their classrooms in an authoritarian, indulgent, or authoritative way may affect their students' behavior. Table 11.4 shows the three ways in which teachers may relate to their students and how their students' behavior is affected. After becoming familiar with the characteristics of authoritative, authoritarian, and permissive teachers, try the "Studying Children" activity.

On the basis of her findings, Baumrind conceptualizes parental discipline as being composed of two dimensions: warmth and control. Both dimensions are deemed essential for effective child management and children's acquisition of effective social skills. Firm parental control when coupled with parental warmth (an attitude, rather than a practice) promotes the development of such qualities as social responsibility, self-control, independence, and high self-esteem in children. In addition, children who describe their parents as warm, democratic, and firm are more likely than their peers to develop positive attitudes toward and be-

STUDYING CHILDREN

TEACHING STYLES AND CHILDREN'S BEHAVIOR

With one of your classmates, observe three or four different teachers and classify their teaching style according to Baumrind's classifications. Do you both agree on your classifications? Observe the children in the classroom. How do the children behave? Do your observations of the children's characteristics match what research has said?

TABLE 11.4 Methods of Teacher Discipline and Effects on Children	Ways of Relating	Effects on Children
	Authoritarian—domineering, uses coercive force, punishing, shows little respect for students, opposed to change, inclined to see things as right or wrong	Low in group morale, fearful, prone to cheat, rebellious, attention seeking, misbehave when teacher not present, lacking in self-direction and self-control; thinking will be memory oriented and convergent
	Permissive—unwilling to intercede, indifferent, no attempt to control children	Confused, unorganized, nonproductive; thinking will be disorganized and without direction
	Authoritative—respectful, values children's individuality, encouraging, atmosphere of approval, kind, a helper, a participant	Show personal initiative, enthusiastic, growing in self-control and self-initiative; thinking will be divergent, organized

Source: From *Educational Therapy in the Elementary School* by P. Ashlock and A. Stephen, 1966, Springfield, IL: Charles C Thomas. Copyright 1966 by Charles C Thomas, Publisher. Adapted by permission.

liefs about their achievement, and as a consequence they are likely to do better in school (Steinberg, Elmen, & Mounts, 1989).

Several studies have established that parental warmth is an important variable in the socialization process. The affectional tie between parents and children creates a powerful motive in children to please their parents. Moreover, when parents are highly involved with their children—that is, they frequently engage in joint task-related activities and high levels of playful, affectively positive interaction—children tend to be high in obedience (Martin, 1981).

NONCOMPLIANCE

The initial response of some children to parental requests or commands is often noncompliance. Noncompliance is conceptualized as a coercive response maintained by parents' unskillful management of their children's behavior (Patterson, 1982). Early noncompliance places children at risk for a chain of events including coercive family interactions, poor social relationships, poor academic performance, delinquency, and problems later in life (Patterson, DeBaryshe, & Ramsey, 1989). The function of nonproblematic levels of noncompliance is less understood, but it is clear that children in well-functioning families also engage in a considerable amount of noncompliance. Noncompliance rates of between 20% and 40% have been reported in different studies (Forehand, 1977).

Passive noncompliance involves children ignoring or not responding to a directive, and active forms of noncompliance involve signs of deliberate resistance (Kuczynski & Kochanska, 1990). Passive forms of noncompliance may have positive functions in children's development of autonomy and social skill (Kochanska, Kuczynski, Radke-Yarrow, & Darby-Welsch, 1987). Kuczynski and Kochanska (1990) found that indirect commands (suggestions, requests, polite commands) as a way of initiating requests to 5-year-old children and the use of feedback in the form of verbal reprimands for inappropriate behavior was associated with high levels of compliance. The use of positive reinforcement was also found to be associated with decreased use of passive noncompliance. Punishment, however, was associated with frequent passive and active forms of noncompliance.

PUNISHMENT

Punishment and discipline are not synonymous. The term *discipline* comes from the word *disciple*, meaning "one who gives instruction." Discipline goes beyond the confines of short-term, immediate behavioral gains. Discipline influences children's

When parents are warm, supportive, and accepting of and interested in their children, children
are more compliant and cooperative with their parents.

future behavior. Punishment, on the other hand, is causing children to pay some kind of price that is more painful than the forbidden behavior or activity in which they are engaging. The probability that that particular response will occur decreases. Patterson (1975) comments that parents erroneously think that punishment works and that its effects are long term.

No doubt, the immediate effects of punishment account for its popularity, but, as research points out, although it has an immediate effect of reducing a tendency to behave in a certain way, in the long run its effects are temporary and impermanent. Moreover, when punishment is consistently used, the punishing agent must be present in order for it to be effective. For example, in one study (Chapman, 1979) mothers were observed with their 4- to 6-year-old children in a lab setting. The mothers were asked to get their children to work on a task in order to raise money to send a child to summer camp. After a short while the mothers left the laboratory and the children were observed. It was found that the children of the mothers who had resorted to power-assertive disciplining tech-

niques such as punishment worked well while the mother was in the room, but did not continue to do so when she had left. Children whose mothers had explained the importance of the task and did not resort to punishment persistently worked on the task in mother's absence. In this experiment, punishment worked in the short run, but was not effective in the long run.

Temporary control may be obtained at a rather high price. Although there are many ways that children can learn to respond to punishment, in general, they try to avoid contact with the punishing agent, which gives the parent less opportunity to socialize the child. When children are physically punished for inappropriate behavior, they are hurt from the experience, frustrated at not being understood, resentful that no one will help, helpless to retaliate directly, and fearful of further punishment. The result of all this is further negative feelings.

Crockenberg and Litman (1990) found in studying 95 mothers and their 2-year-old children that deviant behavior (negativism for its own sake) was associated with parental control strategies that were highly power-assertive, such as maternal anger, harshness, and criticisms, and excessive control characterized in particular by physical punishment. The most effective strategies appear to combine firm control and guidance for eliciting compliance. When control is combined with guidance, it provides the child with clear information about what the parent wants, but at the same time it invites power sharing. These techniques are reminiscent of Baumrind's authoritative pattern of parenting: Authoritative parents exert firm parental control but they also listen to what their children have to say and could be influenced by them.

REINFORCEMENT

From the very beginning, parents train their children in the Skinnerian fashion of rewarding or reinforcing them for certain kinds of behavior. To illustrate, young children receive positive attention when they begin to share with others. Rewarded responses become stronger and increase in frequency. Negative behaviors are sometimes ignored or punished. Simply put, parents generally reward children when they behave in socially approved ways (sharing with others) and show disapproval when their behavior is socially unacceptable (kicking Stanley in the shins and grabbing his truck). When rewards are administered immediately, consistently, and genuinely, learning proceeds more rapidly than when reinforcement is delayed, inconsistent, and nongenuine.

Potential reinforcers may be *intrinsic* rewards such as verbal praise, a hug, or a pat on the back, or *extrinsic* rewards, such as candy, toys, or money. Children are more likely to respond to either of these rewards if they are prudently used (Maccoby & Martin, 1983). In other words, if parents praise children for every little thing they do, praise tends to become rather meaningless. When praise is used sparingly and in meaningful ways, it is more effective. Similar problems attend the use of extrinsic rewards. If they are given regularly, they come to be expected, their absence is experienced as punishment, and their presence may no longer stand out as rewarding.

Moreover, as you will see in the Chapter 14 on moral development, younger children tend to conceive right and wrong in terms of what they will be rewarded (and punished) for. With development, children shift away from this orientation. Therefore, rewards may be more effective in shaping the behavior of young children and not too effective with older children.

CONSISTENCY

Another important element in the socialization of children is consistency in disciplining. Most parents are familiar with the fact that if they follow through with predictable and reliable actions toward their children's behavior, the results will be effective. Most parents are also aware that this, at times, is difficult to do. There are times when various family situations, interruptions, and diversions prevent parents from following through. If, however, parents make threats (No television for a week!), they should follow through. If they do not, children learn very quickly not to believe in their parents' authority. The use of idle threats is associated with high levels of disobedience (Newson & Newson, 1968). In addition, if children encounter wide fluctuations in the type of discipline they encounter (parents are tyrants one day and Mr. and Mrs. Milquetoast the next), if some behaviors are punished one day and overlooked the next, children soon learn not to comply with parental requests.

Similarly, there should be a consistency in the number and type of rules. For example, in one study (Lytton, 1980), 136 boys aged 2½ and their parents were observed in their homes where the parent behavior and the children's compliance were recorded. It was found that consistent enforcement of rules was related to high levels of voluntary compliance by the children. Parents can become more consistent by not creating too many rules and demands. If parents have numerous rules, there are numerous areas of behavior that parents have to monitor, and they are liable to slip up and forget their own rules. Moreover, parental rules and requests need to be clearly stated and easy to remember and must deal with behaviors that can be regulated.

CHILDREN'S INFLUENCE ON PARENTS

Controlling children is not something parents do *to* or *for* their children, but *with* their children. Children play an active role in their own socialization. It is apparent that what parents do with their children is determined by several factors, some of which are children's temperament, degree of attractiveness, age, and birth order.

In one study on temperament, 168 mother-infant pairs were observed at 6, 13, and 24 months (Bates, 1980). Infants who displayed a high frequency of fussing and crying and were hard to soothe were classified as difficult infants. The authors found that mothers of these infants engaged in more behavior control, produced more conflict in control situations, and tended to use more power-assertive techniques than mothers of easy infants, who cried less and were easy to soothe.

Other studies have found that difficult temperaments in boys lead mothers, over a period of time, to reduce their socialization pressure. One researcher has reported that when boys had been hot-tempered and difficult to control in early childhood, their mothers tended, at a later time, to be somewhat permissive toward their children's aggression (Olweus, 1980). Exerting relatively little teaching pressure against their sons' aggression resulted in these children becoming more aggressive.

Parents tend to treat their pre-school-aged children who are independently rated as physically attractive quite differently from children who are rated as physically unattractive (Langlois & Sawin, 1981). Parents tend to resort to power-assertive techniques with unattractive children.

Children's birth order also tends to have an effect on parents. With their firstborns, parents are inclined to expect more mature behavior at an earlier age and impose higher demands, which results in firstborn children being more conscientious, independent, and serious. With later born children, parents tend to be more lax with their disciplinary efforts. These differences in ways of socializing firstborns and later borns may occur because parents are inexperienced novices with their firstborns and may be more idealistic; thus, they may try harder to do just the right thing. Second, they usually have more time to spend with their firstborns compared with later-born children.

MIDDLE CHILDHOOD: PEER STATUS

The peer group plays an important role in assigning status to its individual members, which strongly affects the course of children's socialization. Membership in a group seems to get structured into an hierarchical arrangement from those accorded the highest status to those at the bottom of the popularity poll. It appears that even first-graders are quite capable of rating the children in their classes as well as ranking their own position in the power hierarchy. In one study, for example, there was 62% to 73% agreement as to who was the toughest child in each of the classes from first through fourth grades (Edelman & Omark, 1973). In later grades children were able to differentially label children as nicest or smartest. These perceptions remain quite stable within and between years of school (Hartup, 1989).

What determines a child's status in the popularity poll? What determines a child's acceptance or rejection? The relevant literature consists almost entirely of correlational studies. That is, the typical research strategy has been to collect sociometric data (see Figure 11.4) on children's status in the peer group and then relate status data to the child's social interaction patterns in the group. The two sets of measures are then correlated. This methodology has yielded modest but statistically significant relationships between positive social behavior (helping, sharing) and sociometric acceptance, and between negative and antisocial behavior and sociometric rejection. Thus social acceptance and rejection are correlated with different child characteristics.

BEHAVIORS ASSOCIATED WITH POPULAR CHILDREN

Across all ages, social competence is related to the same general set of behaviors. Social popularity and peer acceptance have been found to be related

FIGURE 11.4 Sociometric Techniques

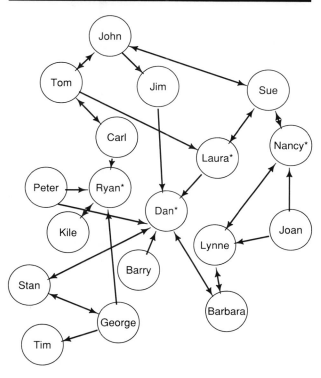

A common technique used in assessing a child's acceptability in a classroom setting is to have the child choose three classmates for each of these statements:

I would like best to work with these children.
I would like best to play with these children.
I would like to have these children sit near me.

This will give an indication of each child's acceptability or unacceptability by the other children in the room, but it does not show the patterning of friendships or choices the other children have made. A sociogram such as this one will provide this information.

The popular child is more sociocentric than egocentric. That is, popular children are thoughtful of others' feelings, accepting of others, and show concern and interest in others (Denham, McKinley, Couchoud, & Holt, 1990). They are sensitive not only to the feelings of others but also to the effect their behavior has on others. They can analyze their actions and communications and adjust them so as to interact in a positive manner (Asher, 1978). For example, Custrini and Feldman (1989) found in studying 9- and 12-year-olds with above- or below-average levels of social competence that children with high social competence were more accurate at encoding emotions of others (anger, disgust, happiness, and sadness) than less competent, same-sex peers. A high level of skill in understanding others' feelings is associated with social competence and, in turn, popularity (Edwards, Manstead, & McDonald, 1984). Thus, evidence supports the hypothesis that high-status children show greater discrimination of basic affective expressions; that is, children who can recognize the affective expression of others are better liked by their peers (Walden & Field, 1990). Similarly, responsiveness and relevance have been identified as among the key dimensions in the interaction style of socially competent children and appear to be lacking in the interactions of unpopular children.

BEHAVIORS ASSOCIATED WITH UNPOPULAR CHILDREN

Rejected children are actively disliked by their peers and may show symptoms of aggression or withdrawal (Hymel, Rubin, Rowden, & LeMare, 1990). Withdrawal is not defined here in terms of shyness or lack of social assertiveness but in terms of pulling back from peers and being shunned and ignored by peers. Rejected children tend to be conceited, disruptive, and silly. Additional attributes of the low-acceptance child are anxiety, excessive emotional dependence on adults, uncertainty, bitterness and sarcasm to others, withdrawal or aggression, and social indifference. Further, rejected children are more likely to be low achievers in school, to experience learning difficulties, or to

to athletic/extracurricular competencies and academic achievement. Personality traits such as extroversion, honesty, cheerfulness, and cooperation have been noted as desirable personality traits found in popular children (Tedesco & Gaier, 1988). Popular children are prosocial (rarely aggressive) and tend to help set up rules and norms for the group (Black & Hazen, 1990).

drop out of school than socially accepted peers (Asher & Gottman, 1981). In order for children to concentrate on their learning tasks and succeed in school, they need to feel some acceptance by peers.

Rejected children have great difficulty seeing a situation from another person's perspective (Bernstein, 1981). They have been shown to be deficient in a variety of social skills, such as communicating emotions and needs accurately or responding to peers with appropriate affection or help (Gottman, Gonso, & Rasmussen, 1975).

In contrast, neglected children who seldom interact garner very little in the way of liking or disliking in the peer group; they are simply "overlooked" by their peers. They have few friends but are not disliked by their peers. Neglected children tend to display less aggression (Coie and Kupersmidt, 1983) and engage in more solitary play (Coie, 1990). They tend to receive fewer social overtures from peers than more sociable children.

Neglected children tend to exhibit more egocentric speech and direct more of their utterances to imaginary companions or inanimate objects (Rubin, LeMare, & Lollis, 1990). They are less mature, less assertive, and more compliant or deferential.

Research seems to bear out the theory that rejected children present a more serious problem than neglected children. As one can see in Figure 11.5, children who are rejected in preadolescence tend to have more adjustment problems in adolescence, as measured by encounters with the police, truancy, dropping out of school, being retained or suspended in school, than neglected, popular, or average-status children (Kupersmidt & Coie, 1990).

Further support that rejected children have more adjustment difficulties than neglected children comes from a study done by French and Waas (1985) involving 401 second-grade and 469 fifth-grade children. Students in these grades were asked to write out the names of three students

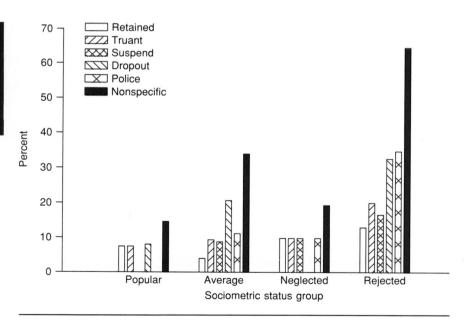

FIGURE 11.5   Percent of Adolescents Having a Negative Outcome as a Function of Preadolescent Sociometric Status Group

Source: "Preadolescent Peer Status, Aggression, and School Adjustment as Predictors of Externalizing Problems in Adolescence" by J. B. Kupersmidt and J. D. Coie, 1990, *Child Development, 61,* p. 1355.© The Society for Research in Child Development. Reprinted by permission.

with whom they would like to play and three students with whom they would not like to play. Children were classified into three groups on the basis of these data: popular, neglected, and rejected. The parents of these children were given a child behavior checklist and teachers were given a school behavior checklist to complete for the children in these groups. Both of these checklists include questions that indicate children's social competence as well as behavior problems. It was found that the neglected children were seen as exhibiting no more problem behavior than popular children and were scored as less deviant than rejected children. Rejected children, however, tended to exhibit a variety of problem behaviors both at school and at home. Longitudinal research suggests that these children continue to be rejected by peers over time (Asher & Coie, 1990) and are at risk for a variety of adolescent and adult adjustment problems.

Neglected children are more likely than rejected children to improve their status over time (Coie & Dodge, 1983) and there is little evidence that these children are at risk for later disorders. Children who are neglected by peers at one time in one context are not commonly neglected at other times in other contexts. Furthermore, even though neglected children receive few best friend nominations, they are as well liked by peers, on a rating scale measure, as average-status children (French & Waas, 1985). Together, this data concerning neglected versus rejected children suggest that it is having few friends in class *and* being widely disliked by the peer group that lead to behavior adjustment problems.

Rejected-Aggressive Children   A number of investigators have suggested the value of differentiating between rejected children who also show behavior problems such as aggression and rejected children who do not (Bouvin & Begin, 1989; French, 1988). Aggression appears to be the primary correlate of rejection (Coie, Dodge, Terry, & Wright, 1991). French (1990) collected data on 46 rejected and 20 popular children. The children who were consistently rejected by their peers were those who ex-

hibited high amounts of aggression. This group of rejected-aggressive children, as compared with rejected and popular children, displayed more adjustment problems evidenced by high levels of anxiety, and behavioral and academic difficulties. In contrast, those in the rejected-nonaggressive group exhibited social withdrawal but were otherwise indistinguishable from popular status children.

A study done by Patterson, Kupersmidt, and Griesler (1990) provides important information about differences in subjective experiences of self and of social relationships among rejected-aggressive children. The investigators studied five groups of children: 67 popular children, 82 average children, 66 rejected children, 26 neglected children, and 42 controversial children (did not fit any of the above categories). Rejected-aggressive chil-

Rejected-aggressive boys are at a greater risk for future adjustment problems than rejected-nonaggressive boys.

dren reported that they did experience conflict with peers. However, this was the only indication in the data that rejected-aggressive children acknowledged experiencing difficulties with peers.

Analysis of the subjective reports of rejected-aggressive children revealed that these children significantly overestimated both their social and behavior competence. No other group of children so consistently overestimated their own levels of competence relative to information from other sources. Overestimating their competence may help to create a protective defense against realities that are too painful for children to fully acknowledge.

Rejected-aggressive children report the least supportive relationship with their fathers of any group (Parke, MacDonald, Beitel, & Bhavnagri, 1988). They tend to report receiving less love and affection from their fathers than popular, average, and neglected children. Their reports of relationships with mothers and teachers did not differ from the other children. This finding fits well with other data showing tighter linkages between father-child relationships and peer acceptance than between mother-child relationships and peer acceptance (Coie, 1990).

Neglected children were more likely to report feeling lonely and socially dissatisfied than the other groups of children. They reported the least companionship from best friends and also reported the lowest perceived social competence. Neglected children tend to display a generally negative pattern of self-perception including low efficacy and low social expectations.

DETERMINANTS OF PEER STATUS

Because rejected children are by and large a heterogeneous group (French, 1990), there may be multiple pathways leading to being disliked by peers. Current evidence, however, suggests that aggressive and antisocial behavior arise early in coercive family interactions (Patterson & Bank, 1989). According to Patterson (1982) and Dishion, Patterson, Stoolmiller, and Skinner (1991), unpopular children are usually difficult to socialize and their parents are inept socializing agents, thus the two individuals become entrapped into reinforcing noxious behavior in the other. Subsequently, these children are impulsive, mean, and disruptive in their interactions with children outside the home. With time, these transactions limit the child's opportunities for constructive social involvement with other children. The children's social reputation is impaired and assortative processes occur so that the children's companions are more and more extreme in terms of their own social inadequacies and antisocial proclivities.

Parental Behaviors   Success or failure with peers is influenced within the family primarily through parent discipline practices. Putallaz and Sheppard (1990) reported that parental use of physical punishment was positively related to boys' aggression. Children of more power-assertive parents tended to be less competent with peers and more inclined to expect positive outcomes for unfriendly resolution of peer conflict. The association between boys' peer relations, their antisocial behavior, and family ecology was examined in another study using two cohorts of boys and their families who were interviewed, observed at home, and assessed at school. Mothers' aversive behavior (controlling, negative) correlated positively with children's aversive behavior with peers (Keane, Brown, & Crenshaw, 1990).

The parent-child relationship has been thought to be associated with children's peer status. Children's interactional history with their parents is shaped through their expectations of how others will behave. Children whose parents are rejective and inaccessible are more likely to approach peer interactions with a set of negative expectations and to anticipate negative responses from other children (Putallaz & Sheppard, 1990).

Russell and Finnie (1990) have commented that children could learn aspects of their social skills through their mothers' explicit teaching. Forty-nine mothers and their 4½-year-olds, who had been categorized as popular, rejected, or neglected children according to sociometric procedures carried out in their preschools, participated in the study. Each of the mothers and their children entered a room in which a small group of children were already engaging in play. The mothers were instructed to wait 5 minutes before letting their children join the group. They were told to use the 5-minute period to offer suggestions, ideas, and comments that would help their child successfully enter the play group. Mothers of popular children tended to be quite sensitive toward the group's needs; they explained to the children what the group was doing and offered suggestions as to how their child could help the play group. Rejected children received minimal preparation instructions from their mothers. Mothers of neglected children tended to use their authority to take charge of the play so as to obtain a role for their child. This take-charge type of behavior may explain why neglected children tend to be less assertive, to hover, and to play alone.

Keane et al. (1990) found that a relationship between maternal social behavior and children's sociometric status exists. Mothers viewed videotapes in which a confrontation occurred between two children. Mothers of popular and rejected children were found to differ in how they would resolve the provocation. Mothers of popular children provided more prosocial resolutions to conflict, whereas mothers of rejected children provided more hostile resolutions.

Children's Perceptions of Others   How children expect peers and adults to respond to them in social exchanges may further your understanding of the origins of peer relations difficulties. Rejected children tend to perceive peer behavior as hostile. Dodge, Murphy, and Buchsbaum (1984) showed children a series of videos in which a provocation occurs in typical peer interactions. A positive correlation between children's interpretations and their behavioral responses was found. Rejected children's interpretation of the ambiguous scenarios showed a hostile misattribution bias that lead to a subsequent maladaptive behavior response. Rejected children indicated that they would respond more aggressively to the provocation, whereas popular children provided more prosocial behavior responses. Rejected children were more

likely to think that unfriendly strategies (e.g., commanding a peer) would be instrumentally successful (would succeed in getting what they wanted) than did more popular peers.

Earn and Sobol (1990) examined children's attributions for social success and failure. The participants in this study were selected from a group of 262 fourth- and fifth-grade children who filled out a sociometric instrument. Each child was asked to nominate three children from their class whom they would choose to sit near, play with, not sit near, and not play with. The results of this study suggest a solid link between sociometric status and attributions. The sociometric groups differed in the categories that they used when explaining social success and failure. Popular children appear to employ a more sophisticated social analysis than the other sociometric groups and thus use different types of social explanations. One example of this tendency is that they used luck less and personality interaction more than did unpopular children when explaining social success and therefore appear to take more credit for success.

The popular children's approach to failure is also interesting in that they tend to externalize failure. That is, rather than primarily using luck to explain their failures, they are more likely to use external, but more sophisticated, reasons such as others' motives. The results tend to suggest that popular children use more controllable causes to explain social outcomes and see social/personality attributes as malleable qualities rather than fixed entities, as unpopular children tend to do.

Communication Skills   Various communication skills have been found to predict social acceptance in middle childhood, and training in communication skills has been used successfully as a means of bolstering peer acceptance in school-aged children. Three communication skills appear to be necessary to establish coherent discourse: (a) the ability to direct initiations clearly; (b) the ability to respond contingently to the initiations of others; and (c) the ability to reinitiate by providing responses that also serve as new initiations. Hazen and Black (1989) studied 54 children, age 5, and reported that liked children were more inclined to clearly direct their initiations to specific listeners, to speak to both interaction partners rather than just one, to respond contingently, and to acknowledge others. All of these skills contribute to coherent discourse and may be basic to successful social interaction and subsequently young children's peer acceptance.

Dodge has also shown that popular children are more capable of initiating and maintaining coherent discourse with others. Dodge (1983) and Pettit, Bakski, Dodge, and Coie (1990) formed play groups from 48 previously unacquainted second-grade boys. Children who became popular from the beginning responded positively to the initiations of others. They realized that going for a thing directly may not be the most effective way of attaining it. At first they waited in the new group and slowly increased their conversations over time. They tended to perceive a social situation accurately and then entered the group by contributing with relevant conversation. Unlike their popular counterparts, unpopular children tended to approach others quite frequently (and in an aggressive fashion) at first, but they were often rebuffed. These children showed ineptness in their initial approaches to others; that is, they introduced irrelevant conversations that tended to disrupt the ongoing interactions of the group.

Previous research has indicated that gaining successful entry into ongoing peer play is an important social skill (Putallaz & Wasserman, 1989). Black and Hazen (1990) found that high-status children were better able to adapt to the demands of the entry situation by exchanging information more and expressing their feelings less; in contrast, low-status children showed the opposite pattern in their communication.

Physical Attractiveness   Hartup (1989) has pointed out that physical attractiveness (facial attractiveness and body build) is correlated with social acceptance. Even young children (ages 3 and 5) manifest facial stereotypes that match those of adults when choosing the "prettier" or "cuter" of two photographs (Dion, 1973).

It has been found that children (and adults) have different expectations for attractive and unattractive children (Adams & Crane, 1980). There is now considerable evidence that both adults and children make inferences about the behavior of others on the basis of physical appearance; desirable traits are attributed to attractive individuals, while undesirable traits are attributed to unattractive persons. Unattractive children are perceived as dishonest, unpleasant, and chronically antisocial, compared with attractive children (Dion, 1972). Attractive children were rated by teachers as having greater academic ability, better social relations and adjustment, and as more likely to become successful in life than unattractive children (Lerner & Lerner, 1977). Attractive children are seen as having more pleasing personalities and are more desirable as prospective playmates (Styczynski & Langlois, 1980).

Do children react differentially to attractive and unattractive children because these children in fact behave differently? Langlois and Downs (1979) found in observing 64 children aged 3 and 5 that there were no behavioral differences (in terms of aggressiveness and affiliative behaviors) between unattractive and attractive 3-year-olds. They did observe, however, that unattractive 5-year-olds were more active with and aggressive toward their classmates. The researchers reasoned that the differential levels of activity and aggression in unattractive 5-year-olds, and the lack of such differences in 3-year-olds, suggest that expectations for attractive and unattractive children may set a self-fulfilling prophecy into motion. Unattractive children may be thought of and labeled as antisocial and as a result learn over time the behaviors that others associate with unattractiveness.

What's in a Name?   Asher, Oden, and Gottman (1977) have suggested that a number of personal characteristics may exert an influence on a child's subsequent peer relations. It appears, for example that the commonness of a child's first name bears a relationship to popularity, and that social risk seems to accompany uncommon names. To illustrate, four classes of 10- to 12-year-olds were asked to rate the attractiveness of a large group of first names, including the names of the children themselves (McDavid & Harari, 1966). Later, popularity ratings were obtained and a positive relation was found between the ratings of the names and the popularity of the children. Ratings of the names were also made by other children (who did not know the children studied), and these, too, were found to be positively correlated with the popularity ratings.

School Task Behavior Rejected children tend to not do well academically. The best evidence that low achievement is partly responsible for low social status is the fact that tutoring rejected children in school subjects is an even better way of enhancing their social competence than is training in social skills (Coie, 1990).

In the classroom setting, rejected children display fewer task-appropriate behaviors and more task inappropriate behaviors in contrast to popular children. They spend less time on assigned academic tasks and are observed to spend their time clowning around, daydreaming, or walking aimlessly around the room. These children quite frequently attempt to interact with other children during seat work periods. These attempts lead to high rates of rejection from the other children. Apparently, the rejected children's peers think that these approaches are inappropriate (Dodge, Coie, & Brakke, 1982).

Reputation and Expectations Dodge suggests a cyclical, self-perpetuating process for aggressive boys in which aggressive reputation leads to differential responding from peers, which elicits more aggression and in turn strengthens aggressive behavior. Thus, reputation and expectations within a peer group serve to maintain peer rejection. Studies have shown that peers become biased in their perceptions of a child and alter their behavior toward a child once they have identified that child as liked or disliked (Dodge & Frame, 1982). This behavior, in turn, may lead the child to respond in ways that perpetuate peers' perception. Coie and Kupersmidt (1983) observed popular, average, neglected, and rejected boys (as de-

termined by classroom peers) in play groups. The 10 play groups met once a week for 6 weeks. Each group was composed of a popular, an average, a neglected, and a rejected status boy. The authors noted that rejected and average status boys were the recipients of aversive behavior more often than were popular boys. Hymel (1986) examined attributional biases in children's interpretations of peer behavior as a function of prior affect (liking versus disliking) toward peers. Popular and unpopular 2nd-, 5th- and 10-graders were asked to explain why liked or disliked classmates performed actions that had either a positive or a negative outcome for the perceiver. Subjects varied their interpretations of peer behaviors as a function of both their affect toward the child (liked/disliked) and their reputations. Disliked children were held more accountable for negative behavior than were liked peers. Thus, social behavior tends to be perceived in a biased fashion as a function of prior attitudes and beliefs about the child.

CONSEQUENCES OF REJECTION

Research indicates that the consequences of peer rejection may be severe, resulting in mental health problems in later life (Cowen, Pederson, Babijian, Izzo, & Trost, 1973) or dropping out of school (Parker & Asher, 1987; East & Rook, 1992). Children's antisocial dispositions interfere with the learning experience conducive to development of academic skills (Patterson, Cohn, & Kao, 1989), interpersonal skills and work skills (Patterson, 1982). Caspi, Elder, and Bem (1987) showed that antisocial children's failure in childhood often translates to social failure in adulthood in terms of downward social drift, academic underachievement, and difficulty in marriage and family relationships. These outcomes are similar to those reported by Parker and Asher (1987) in their review of research on the long-term adjustment problems of socially rejected children.

Among elementary school children, peer acceptance has been identified as a most reliable predictor of later psychosocial adjustment. Negative peer status in childhood is predictive of maladaptive outcomes in adolescence and adulthood, including delinquency and mental-health referrals (Hymel et al., 1990; Roff, Sells, & Golden, 1972). For example, it has been found that poor peer relations in middle childhood are predictive of adult neurotic and psychotic disturbances (Roff, 1966). It would be quite inaccurate to assert that social inadequacy or social incompetency inevitably lead to some form of mental disorder. More modestly, it is reasonable to propose that the prognosis of many rejected children is based on processes that begin with parenting practices and that translate to problem behavior and skill deficits of children and later to the development of neurotic symptoms.

Children who are actively disliked or rejected by their peers seem to be at a heightened risk for a wide range of mental health difficulties (Asher, 1978; Kupersmidt et al., 1990). Although much more needs to be learned, the most clearly identified risk factors for psychopathology, delinquency, substance abuse, or all three appear to be: (a) antisocial, rebellious, and defiant behavior, (b) poor peer relations, (c) poor academic skills, and (d) low self-esteem (Guralnick & Groom, 1990). Rejected-aggressive children present a greater risk of disorders than other rejected children (Rubin, LeMare, & Lollis, 1990).

Children who are disliked by their peers are more likely to have emotional problems (Asher et al., 1977; Patterson et al., 1990). Asher, Parkhurst, Hymel, and Williams (1990) have shown that both loneliness and social anxiety are likely to be elevated among children who are low in peer acceptance, especially among rejected children. Crick and Ladd (1990) have also reported greater loneliness among rejected children. As you can see in Figure 11.6, rejected children report feeling significantly more lonely than children in other peer status classifications. It is possible that children's reports of loneliness are implicit calls for help. In admitting loneliness, children are saying that they are unhappy with their social situation and wish it were otherwise. Other investigators have reported an association between low peer status and depression (Strauss, Forehand, Frame, & Smith, 1984). The generally negative picture of unpopular children as anxious, lonely, and depressed sug-

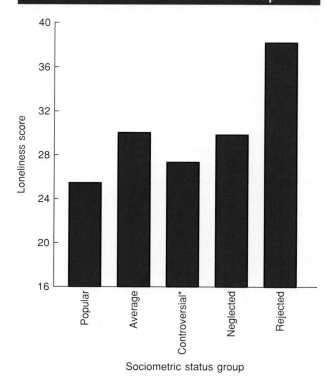

FIGURE 11.6 Loneliness Scores as a Function of Sociometric Status Group

*Did not fit into any of the other groups

Source: From "Children's Loneliness: A Comparison of Rejected and Neglected Peer States" by S. Asher and V. A. Wheeler, 1985, *Journal of Consulting and Clinical Psychology, 53*, pp. 500–505. Copyright 1985 by the American Psychological Association. Adapted by permission.

gests that these children may also be expected to report low self-esteem.

Another researcher (Johnson, 1981) points out children who for one reason or another are unable to establish acceptable relationships often develop considerable frustration and alienation. They often cling to unproductive and unskilled ways of reaching out to others. If they lack social acceptance, their lowered social status causes them to feel inadequate, helpless, and alone. Much of the anxiety and stress children feel is produced because they feel they don't belong (Boskoff, 1982). In fact, it is impossible to find one study to refute the statement that children's general emotional adjustment is related to their general acceptance by others. Data consistently show that the degree of emotional maladjustment is associated with the degree of social acceptance throughout the formative years (Asher et al., 1977; Asher & Coie, 1990).

Coie (1990) found a modest stability for popular and neglected children, but higher stability for rejected children. Stability was not simply due to the fact that the composition of the examined peer groups remained the same over time. Even in new groups with unfamiliar peers, children tended to retain their social rank. When unfamiliar boys of differing social status were brought together in play groups once a week for 6 weeks, within 3 weeks their social status in these new groups was very similar to their social status in their classrooms. Boys who were rejected in school were similarly shunned by their peers in their new setting. In a 5-year follow-up study of rejected children, Coie reported that 30% to 50% of the rejected children tended to remain that way. Therefore, it is important to identify children who persist at maladaptive behavior patterns, and help them develop more socially competent ways of behaving.

ADOLESCENCE: WORKING, DATING, AND TEENAGE SEXUALITY

Many adolescents engage in work outside the home while they are attending high school. Contrary to what you may think or have been told, part-time employment appears to have some beneficial effects, but it has some harmful effects on adolescents' social and psychological development as well.

ADOLESCENT EMPLOYMENT

In our society, adolescents spend a considerable amount of time providing labor for adults. Approximately 80% of high school youth have held or are holding part-time positions (see Figure 11.7).

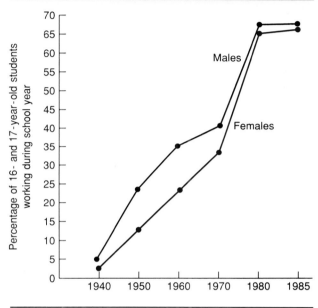

FIGURE 11.7   More U.S. High School Students Are Working During the School Year Now Than at Any Other Time in Recent History

Source: From *Adolescence* (p. 217) by L. Steinberg, 1989, New York: Knopf. Reprinted with permission of McGraw Hill, Inc.

In the United States, most adolescents begin working in a part-time job when they are 16 or 17 years old. In Japan, only 2% of the 16- and 17-year-olds are working while attending school.

Greenberger and Steinberg (1986) found that about 17% of U.S. high school students tend to work at fast-food restaurants and about 10% work in offices as clerical assistants. The remainder tend to work in retail stores as cashiers and sales clerks. Few of these jobs permit independent decision making or allow for the use of skills being taught in school, and rarely do adolescents receive any type of instruction from their supervisors. Most jobs held by teenagers are rather dreary, repetitive, monotonous, and not intellectually stimulating.

Although most people are aware of the nondemanding nature of teenagers' jobs, they tend to believe that working helps adolescents develop a sense of independence as well as teaches them important skills such as responsibility and how to manage money. Greenberger and Steinberg (1986) and Steinberg and Dornbusch (1990) bring into question some of these expectations.

Research tends to indicate that few adolescents exercise a great deal of judgment when it comes to managing money. Most youths who work spend their earnings in self-indulgent ways, such as buying designer clothing and personal entertainment. A fair proportion is spent on drugs and alcohol (Greenberger & Steinberg, 1986). Most teenagers do not put money aside for education, or for helping their parents with household expenses.

Steinberg and Dornbusch (1990) examined the relation between part-time employment and adolescent behavior and development in a multiethnic, multi-class sample of approximately 4,000 15- through 18-year-olds. The results indicated that long work hours (in excess of 15 to 20 hours) during the school year were associated with diminished investment in schooling and lowered school performance, increased psychological distress and somatic complaints, higher rates of drug and alcohol use, higher rates of delinquency, and greater autonomy from parental control. Workers did not have any advantages over nonworkers with respect to self-reliance, work orientation, or self-esteem. In no ethnic or socioeconomic group were the correlates of employment positive, either in terms of lower rates of dysfunctional behavior, better school performance, or enhanced psychosocial well-being.

Similarly, a recent review of the research on experiences outside of the classroom that may affect school achievement during the high school years was conducted (Steinberg, 1988). The review focused on family and peer influences as well as part-time employment of students and its relation to academic success. The studies on part-time employment and student achievement suggested that employment in excess of 15 hours per week during the school year may adversely affect high school students' school performance and investment in

school, especially among students who begin working when they are sophomores or juniors. These and similar findings from previous research suggest that parents and educational practitioners should monitor the number of weekly hours adolescents work during the school year.

On the positive side, research has noted that adolescents who work part-time, compared to those who do not, are more likely to grow in self-reliance (Steinberg, Greenberger, Garduque, Ruggiero, & Vaux, 1982). That is, they tend to develop a more mature "work orientation"—the ability to complete work tasks and take pride in doing so. In general, however, working does not enhance adolescents' feelings of social obligation, or being concerned for the well-being of others. In fact, working tends to make teenagers more cynical toward work. Thus, it appears that many of the assumptions about adolescents' working are not supported when they are examined scientifically.

DATING

Children begin dating a bit earlier than they begin working—around the age of 13. One major purpose of dating is to have fun and to get out and do things. Dating is also associated with gaining or improving one's status with peers. It provides a means of personal growth as males and females learn to know, understand, and get along with different types of people. Through dating, adolescents learn cooperation, consideration, responsibility, and matters of etiquette.

First dating experiences tend to be group dating, in which several boys and girls meet at prearranged places. There may or may not be couples involved at these encounters. The second stage consists of individual dating. Initially, adolescents tend to focus on physical appearance as the major criteria in choosing whom they will date. Older adolescents tend to focus on social sophistication and personality followed a bit later by focusing on deeper psychological traits when choosing their dates. About 30% of adolescents at any one time are going steady. Interest in the opposite sex, dating, and first loves can represent an exciting time for many adolescents, however, there are some compelling problems that beset some adolescents during this "young-love" period as well (Miller, 1990).

TEENAGE SEXUALITY

It is estimated that 12 million teenagers are currently sexually active in the United States; approximately 7 million males and 5 million females (Hechtman, 1989). A young couple's motivations for engaging in premarital sex include: purely for physical enjoyment, expression of love, maintaining a relationship, proving independence from parents, controlling one's partner, and affirmation of sexual identity (Hogan, Hao, & Parish, 1990). It appears that for females, love relationships provide an almost universal context for the first coital experience, while for males the reward is intrinsic to the act itself, or perhaps, for the recognition of the achievement by self and others. A significant percentage of males talk about their coital experience to a friend (Simon, Berger, & Gagnon, 1972). In contrast, most females engage in coitus to maintain an enduring dyadic relationship.

Many teens, however, do not consciously plan to become sexually active, and they often do not foresee their first sexual experience. As such, it frequently is not experienced as a decision but rather as something that "happened" (Chilman, 1983). Parental influences on sexual behavior are believed to be strong, although there is not much research on this topic. Adolescents who rate perceived communication with their parents as poor are more likely to initiate sex early (Ooms, 1981). Close relationships with parents as well as feelings of connectedness and supportiveness seem to be associated with later onset of intercourse (Binghma, Miller, & Adams, 1990). Perceptions about what one's peers are doing or what is normative in one's peer group are strongly associated with sexual behavior (Cvetkovich & Grote, 1980). Teenagers who are not doing well in school and have lower educational aspirations are more likely to have sex during adolescence than those faring better in school (Hofferth & Hayes, 1987). Some of the more undesirable consequences of sexual behavior are unwanted pregnancy and AIDS and other sexually transmitted diseases.

TEENAGE PREGNANCY

The average age at which females become sexually active is 16 with over one million of these sexually active women becoming pregnant each year. Longitudinal data suggests that the proportion of adolescents who are sexually active is increasing for all ages from 15 to 19 years, with the greatest increase observed for 16-year-old white females (DiClemente, 1990). Moreover, data have indicated that adolescents below the age of 14 show the greatest increase in rate of initiation of sexual activity relative to other ages (Centers for Disease Control, 1989). Two thirds of pregnant teens carry their pregnancy to term and one third opt for an abortion. Only 4% who carry their pregnancy to term give their infants up for adoption. Of the 96% of adolescents who decide to keep their babies, fewer than one-half are married (National Research Council, 1987).

The occurrence of pregnancy in the 12- to 19-year age group places this population and their offspring at risk, one of which is medical complications. When teenage mothers receive good prenatal care, they can have a healthy pregnancy. More often than not they do not receive good prenatal care. Excessive consumption of junk food and unbalanced crash diets damage the pregnant mother and her unborn child. Studies show that low birth weight babies are 2 to 6 times as common in adolescent mothers. Ehrenhaft, Wagner, and Herdman (1989) suggest that 85% of these low birth weight infants are premature, and 15% are small for gestational age. Stillbirths are twice as frequent in an adolescent pregnancy. Infants born to adolescent mothers are 2 to 3 times more likely to die within the first year of life than children born to women 20 to 30 years of age. Furthermore, infants born to these young mothers seem to experience long-term effects with regard to development. One report shows that 11% of children born to young moth-

One million teenagers become pregnant each year.

Other risks include financial disadvantage resulting from limited employment opportunities and social isolation of the parent, which might manifest itself in child abuse. Such risks are underscored by statistics that document at least one suicide attempt by 13% of all pregnant teens (Jaslow, 1982) and a death rate resulting from pregnancy and childbirth that is 60% higher for teenage mothers under 15 years than for females in their early 20s (Carey, McCane-Sanford, & Davidson, 1981).

The Teenage Father   There are very few studies of teenage fathers. Premarital pregnancy and childbearing are apparently considered to be female problems. Legally, it should be added, the father has no right to decide on an abortion or to have the baby—this decision is solely up to the female at present. Socially, people tend to look at the male as the bad guy, the one who caused this whole problem. Some fathers, however, do view the problem of pregnancy as a dual responsibility. In a study of 272 adolescent mothers and their partners, about one third of the men and women said that their partner was one of their two main sources of emotional support, even when they were married. The percentage was still lower for unmarried couples (Lamb, Elster, Peters, Kahn, & Tavare, 1986). The fact remains, however, that teenagers need to develop some foresight into the consequences of their sexual activities.

ers (under the age of 16) have scored less than 70 on intelligence tests at age 4, versus 2% of children in the normal population (Cohen, 1979). Many studies in the research literature document the fact that infants of adolescent mothers are more prone to be the victims of child abuse and neglect (Washington, 1982).

Another risk is the probability of an uncompleted education for the young mother. In one study, 8 out of 10 girls who gave birth at age 17 or less did not complete high school. For those who are 15 or younger at the time of their first delivery, the estimate is that 9 out of 10 will never complete high school, and 4 out of 10 will not get past eighth grade (Baum, 1980). Teenage mothers are more likely to drop out of high school, even when compared with women of similar socioeconomic backgrounds and academic aptitude who postpone childbearing (Mott & Marsiglio, 1985).

ALTERNATIVES FOR A YOUNG COUPLE EXPECTING A CHILD

One alternative in a pregnancy is abortion. Teens who decide to abort are more educationally ambitious, are more likely to be good students, are more likely to be from higher socioeconomic backgrounds, are from less religious families, have mothers and peers who have more positive attitudes toward abortion, and are less likely to have friends or relatives who are teenage single parents (Eisen, Zellman, Leibowitz, Chow, & Evans, 1983). Many teenagers, however, are rather far along in the pregnancy (beyond the first trimester) when they discover they are pregnant. Also, a young female is likely to suffer damage to the cervix during the abortion procedure, because the cervix is small and inelastic.

Adoption may be another recourse. Up to the 1970s, 80% of the unmarried girls who gave birth gave up their babies to adoptive parents and 20% were kept by the natural mothers (Ulvedal & Feeg, 1983). By the end of the decade, the statistics were reversed. Keeping and raising the child without adequate support from family is probably beyond what one can reasonably expect of most girls under the age of 16. Their emotional immaturity and inability to deal with frustration (often extreme frustration) may cause them undue hardship. Nor does it seem that marriage is the answer: The husband is likely to be young and equally emotionally immature. More likely than not, he is not through with school and therefore his job opportunities are limited. Furthermore, marriage does not protect them from both unhappiness and many practical problems. It appears to be a no-win situation all the way around. Obviously, the only reasonable policy is one of prevention.

Many experts say that sex education helps prevent unwanted pregnancies. No study, however, has ever borne out the prevalent notion among adults that sex education has any effect on students' rate of sexual activity. Sex education in many studies, however, has been finitely defined. It is more than just one parent-child talk about the facts of life, or a sixth-grade course in physical development, or a lecture on contraception and family planning. From infancy on, parents influence a child's attitudes toward sex in hundreds of ways. A loving, accepting family system, for example, is conducive to development of sex attitudes that will allow children to make future decisions regarding their own sexuality. It is in this context that something like prevention of pregnancy in lovemaking fits into the natural course of learning. In this type of environment, young people learn to understand that sexual conduct with another person involves a deep, emotional commitment, respect, and concern for the other's welfare. In addition, classes combined with school-based clinics offering contraceptives or information about birth control have been proven effective in delaying sex and lowering birth rates (Hofferth & Hayes, 1987). No study has shown that teaching adolescents about birth control encourages them to have sex.

SEXUALLY TRANSMITTED DISEASES

National data on the prevalence of gonorrhea among sexually active females show that those between the ages of 10 and 19 had the highest rates of infection compared with older age groups — approximately 3,500 cases per 100,000 (Hein, 1987). Similar data regarding syphilis and chlamydia reveal that the highest rates occur among adolescents, despite the impression that sexually transmitted diseases are a problem particularly endemic to the adult population (Hein, 1987). Minority adolescents have even higher rates for sexually transmitted diseases with rates for gonorrhea and syphilis substantially higher among African-American adolescents as compared with their white counterparts. The average age-adjusted gonorrhea rate in African-American males ages 15 to 19 is approximately 15 times greater than that of white males, and that of African-American females in the same age group, approximately 10 times that of white females (DiClemente, Forrest, & Mickler, 1989).

ADOLESCENT AIDS

Because of the high number of sexually active teens, the threat of their contracting AIDS is of major concern. Different subgroups of adolescents represent varying degrees of risk. Adolescents in general are at high risk for HIV infection because of the sexual and drug experimentation that is common in this age group. Two groups of highest risk for HIV infection are male homosexual adolescents and adolescent runaways who live on the street. Among 18- to 24-year-olds, 79% have reported to have contracted AIDS through homosexual activity (Hein, 1988). Because the symptoms of AIDS may not appear for 5 to 7 years after initial infection with HIV, these young adults may have been infected as younger adolescents (Centers for Disease Control, 1989). There are no reliable statistics on the rate of infection in adolescents who live on the streets. This group, however, is potentially at high risk because many may survive by engaging in prostitution and often use intravenous drugs. Specialized prevention programs need to be developed to reach both these groups.

Thurman and Franklin (1990) examined 294 college undergraduates about their knowledge about AIDS and their reactions to the health threat posed by it. Students were found to be reasonably well informed about AIDS, aware of recommended precautions for avoiding HIV infection, and fearful that the virus may spread within the student population. Data also showed, however, that these students would be reluctant to change their sexual behavior unless the threat of infection was personalized.

Similar data was generated from a sample of 300 high school students (Roscoe & Kruger, 1990), with 96% of them knowing about how one can contract AIDS. Yet one third of these teenagers continued to engage in risky behavior. The main change was in being "more selective" in choosing sexual partners. A major concern, however, is *how* young people are being more selective. Smilgis (1987) reported that some look for signs such as blisters or other physical manifestations, and if partners do not "look" like they have the disease, they believe they are safe. Others believe that if the sexual partners they are with are nice, they will not have AIDS. Such misconceptions could put individuals at risk no matter how selective they believe they are.

Surveys of adolescent knowledge about AIDS indicate that they are generally unaware of the risk. One study found that only 15% of sexually active adolescents had changed their behavior to avoid contracting AIDS (Strunin & Hingson, 1987). Of those who had changed their behavior, only 20% had adopted methods that were effective. Of sexually active adolescents, only 47% of females and 25% of males, respectively, report using condoms (Harris, 1986). Although adolescents may cognitively recognize the value of using condoms, they may not acknowledge a personal susceptibility to AIDS that would necessitate the use of them. The majority were "more careful" in selecting their

partners, perhaps believing they could readily identify HIV-infected individuals. Another survey found that 61% of adolescents believed that they were not the kind of person to get AIDS (DiClemente, Zorn, & Temoshok, 1986).

In another study (Kegeles, Adler, & Irwin, 1988), sexually active adolescents reported knowing that condoms can help prevent sexually transmitted diseases. Yet the females continued intending not to have their partners use condoms, and the males' intentions to use condoms decreased. Although this study was conducted in Florida, which has a high prevalence of AIDS, and media and school coverage of the epidemic was extensive, the sexually active adolescents in this study continued to have multiple sex partners and did not substantially increase their use of condoms, thus continuing to place themselves and their partners at possible risk for sexually transmitted diseases, including HIV infection. Females were mildly negative regarding their partners using condoms. Likewise, females were uncertain about males' desires regarding condom use when, in reality, males were quite positive about it. Interventions targeting such misperceptions might result in an increased ability among the females to request that their partners use condoms. Solely providing information to adolescents that condoms reduce the risk of contracting AIDS may be insufficient to cause an increase in condom use.

For younger children who need material on what HIV is and how it is transmitted, clear informational materials can be quite effective. However, for teenagers, information about AIDS is insufficient. The research evidence suggests that a substantial proportion of adolescents engage in high-risk behavior associated with the acquisition and transmission of sexually transmitted diseases, that is, engaging in unprotected sexual intercourse, even though they are well aware that sexual intercourse is a primary route of disease transmission. The alarmingly high rate of pregnancy and the fear of AIDS have opened up the debate over what to do about the precocious sexual activity of young people. In a two-volume report that reviewed the evidence on the efficacy of existing informational programs on AIDS, *Risking the Future* (Hayes, 1987), it was concluded that if people wish to lower the risk of adolescent AIDS priority must be given to improving contraceptive use among sexually active teens.

PRACTICAL IMPLICATIONS: DEVELOPING SOCIALLY COMPETENT CHILDREN

Interpersonal relationships are essential for personal well-being in many ways. Many higher level needs, those of status, respect, and self-expression, are satisfied by group recognition or thwarted by group denial. Progress in any area of endeavor is dependent on social stability. At any age level, a feeling of belonging is essential to functioning effectively, but interpersonal relations play such an important role in children's lives that they may be regarded as kind of a barometer of their level of adjustment to life in general.

Without intervention, rejected children stand a good chance of remaining outsiders. A child who is allowed to become socially inadequate in the nursery school years or primary grades is likely to remain so as an adult.

Research indicates that young children's social-emotional competence is in part dependent on maternal interaction behavior. The findings of Denham, Renwick, and Holt (1991) suggest that mothers' task orientation (i.e., ability to support the child and to create appropriate structure and limits), positive emotion (i.e., lack of hostility and confidence in successful interaction), and allowance of autonomy are predictive of children's social-emotional competence. In addition, parents and teachers can become coaches who verbally transmit rules of social behavior, a technique known as *coaching*.

COACHING

The coaching procedure consists of three basic components: verbal instruction of skill concepts, opportunity for skill rehearsal, and review of skill outcomes. Oden and Asher (1977) taught third-

and fourth-grade children how to begin playing a game, how to be attentive, how to share, how to follow rules, and so on. Then these children were given opportunities to practice these skills with other children in the class. They then met with their coaches to review the skills they had been taught. Training resulted in significant short-term and long-term gains in rejected and neglected children's classroom peer acceptance.

Mize and Ladd (1990) have developed interventions that are designed to teach children social skills that promote social acceptance in the peer group. Individual differences in social competence and peer acceptance begins to emerge in preschoolers (Howes, 1988). Thus, it should be possible to identify children in preschool classrooms who could benefit from social skill training. Another compelling reason for early intervention is that many children's social interaction difficulties in preschool tend to persist into elementary school (Ladd & Price, 1987).

Previous research indicated that asking questions of peers, leading peers (offering useful suggestions or directions), and offering supportive statements to peers are three skills that are correlated with peer acceptance in preschoolers (Ladd & Oden, 1979). Mize and Ladd (1990) tested 36 third-graders who were targeted as being deficient in these skills as well as lacking peer acceptance. The children were randomly assigned to one of three experimental conditions: skill training, attention control (receiving a similar amount of experimenter attention and experience with peers but no skill training), and nontreatment control.

The data support the conclusion that skills training had a beneficial and lasting effect on children's peer acceptance in the classroom. As expected, children in the second group did not change; peer acceptance cannot be attributed to effects of experimenter attention. Also, the absence of any form of intervention was associated with little or no change in behavior or sociometric measures. Apparently, social isolation or rejection at these ages is a relatively stable characteristic.

Modeling and coaching may be effective techniques for helping children to learn to engage in behaviors that are positively perceived by their peers. For example, interrupting others when they are engaged in seat work is a behavior that unpopular children engage in rather frequently. Children should be helped to learn that this kind of behavior is perceived in a negative way by others. In addition to interfering behaviors, rejected children should be helped to see that such behaviors as noncompliance, derogation, and aggression are inappropriate ways of interacting. By using the coaching technique, eight highly aggressive nursery school children were taught that aggression hurts others and makes them sad, that it really doesn't solve anything, and that sharing and taking turns is more fun (Zahavi & Asher, 1978). These eight children's aggressive behaviors decreased and positive behaviors such as cooperating increased.

AN AREA OF EXPERTISE

Parents can help find an area of expertise for rejected and neglected children. By capitalizing on their hobbies, collections, skills, and interests, parents can help to stimulate their children and positive recognition from other children.

INTERACTING WITH YOUNGER CHILDREN

Increasing social competency, particularly for the neglected child, may be assisted by providing opportunities for these children to interact with younger children. The idea comes from research done on monkeys reared in isolation (Suomi & Harlow, 1975). The researchers found that these monkeys, who wanted nothing to do with anyone, became almost completely rehabilitated by young monkeys. In this experiment, monkeys who were reared in total isolation for the first 6 months of their life were placed in cages with 3-month-old monkeys who still exhibited infants' clinging behaviors. These young monkeys were not aggressive nor had they developed complex social behaviors. The isolate huddled in a corner when the young monkey "therapist" was placed in the cage. The younger monkey approached and clung to the isolate. Within 2 weeks, the isolates were reciprocating the contact. By the end of the 6-month "therapy session," the isolates were engaging in

social play with the young monkeys and with the other isolates. Follow-up studies have shown that the isolates improved social behavior did not diminish over time.

THE ROLE OF TEACHERS

Teachers can help the rejected and neglected children in their classrooms. Respond positively to these children. When others in the class see that you like these children, they respond more positively to them. Some researchers have reported that when the quality and frequency of communication between the teacher and the rejected child increase, the social acceptance of these children increase (Leyser & Gottlieb, 1981).

Positive reinforcement by teachers in the form of verbal praise or approval in front of their peers is valuable in increasing the status of socially rejected children. Praise can be meaningless, how-

Teachers can help children learn social skills that will enable them to develop socially competent ways of behaving.

ever, if it is overused and insincere. It is particularly meaningful when it is informative, conveys information about the teacher's expectations, and, of course, is sincere.

Group activities may be another effective procedure for improving peer relationships (Denham et al., 1990). Socially unaccepted children can be placed with socially accepted students to work cooperatively on a class project. Two rejected students should not be put in the same group. Select group activities that promote cooperation—sharing of common goal creates interdependency among group members. Teachers should also encourage sharing of ideas and materials and explain that the goal to be met is a group goal, not an individual one. Perhaps children could work on a project to raise money for the school.

As a teacher, you should be particularly aware of personal criticisms. It is highly probable that in the course of your education you have encountered one or more insensitive, callous teachers who were prone to making comments about children that were highly unflattering. The other children most assuredly pick up these comments and, perhaps more importantly, the child who is the object of them may remember them for a long time.

No child wants to grow up to be self-centered, discontented, and disliked by others; no one would choose persistent endurance of negative behaviors if he felt there was an alternative way to get acceptance and recognition positively. These children need help and guidance in learning to act in socially approved ways; they cannot develop social competency by wishful thinking.

REVIEW OF KEY POINTS

Social development during infancy focused on the development of attachment between the caregiver and the infant. Through mutual interaction, the caregiver and infant (each bringing to the developing relationship unique characteristics and actions as well as degrees of responsiveness) establish a particular kind of attachment relationship. The importance of infants' developing a secure attachment to their caregivers was pointed out. Infants engage in various proximity-promoting behaviors that tend to pull caregiver and infant together, for example, crying, gazing, communicating, and smiling. Caregivers' sensitivity and responsiveness to their infants' proximity-promoting cues are important variables in securely attached infants' development. Fathers' roles in the attachment process have recently received considerable emphasis. It was pointed out that father-infant bonding may not be a result of the father's early history (attending the birth, early contact with his infant). Studies have reported inconclusive results. It was suggested that fathers, in consultation with their partners, should choose, in all stages of parenting, the level of involvement that is consistent with their skills and desires.

Parents as socializing agents were discussed. Through the use of various disciplining techniques, punishment, and establishing rules and regulations, parents play an important role in socializing children to behave in socially approved ways. It was pointed out that reinforcement is more effective when used sparingly and in meaningful ways. In regard to disciplining techniques, parents who are restrictive, punitive, unaffectionate, or authoritarian are likely to have children who fail to initiate activities and are ineffective in social interactions. Permissive parents who give considerable freedom to children to regulate their own behavior tend to have children who are immature, dependent, regressive, the least self-reliant, and the poorest in self-control. Authoritative parents encourage children to be independent, but still place limits, demands and controls on their actions. This type of parenting is associated with social competency and social responsibility. Punishment, another method of control, tends to have only short-term results. Children also influence parents through certain temperamental traits, attractiveness, and birth order.

During middle childhood, peers assign status to each other. Popular children tend to be friendly, outgoing, cheerful, and cooperative. Rejected children are egocentric, aggressive, and quarrelsome. Neglected children seldom interact with others and engage in more solitary play. It appears that rejected children are more at risk for future developmental problems than neglected children. In particular, rejected-aggressive children show signs of greater adjustment problems. Determinants of rejected peers status are related to parental use of punishment, poor parent-child relationships, hostile perception of the behavior of others, task-inappropriate behaviors, and poor interactive communication skills.

When discussing teenage employment it was noted that, on the positive side, those who work show gains in self-reliance and in their knowledge of practical information about the world of work. On the negative side, however, adolescents who work a great deal (15 to 20 hours or more a week) develop cynical attitudes about working; do less well in school; and become less involved in family and peer activities. Working does not appear to help teenagers become better money managers.

Many teenagers also enter the world of dating. Among those who date regularly, there are vast numbers who are sexually active, which can present problems such as unwanted pregnancies and contracting sexually transmitted diseases such as AIDS. Teenage pregnancy can be harmful to both the mother and her child. Teenagers are informed about how people contract AIDS, but they are not altering their sexual behavior. It was suggested that priority should be given to improving contraceptive use among sexually active teenagers.

Some of the ways in which parents and teachers may help children develop social competence—coaching, helping children find an area of expertise, sincere praise, working with popular peers, working with younger children—were pointed out.

ENHANCING YOUR CRITICAL THINKING

Firsthand Experiences

Peer Rejection

Asher, S. R., & Coie, J. D. (Eds.). (1990). *Peer rejection in childhood.* New York: Cambridge University Press.

A highly readable and interesting book for those students who wish to further explore this topic. A worthwhile experience is to visit an elementary school and observe the children at recess or at lunch time. Can you spot the rejected children? Do they tend to exhibit the characteristics cited by Asher and Coie?

AIDS

DiClemente, R. J., Zorn, J., Temoshok, L. (1986). Adolescence and AIDS: A survey of knowledge, attitudes, and beliefs about AIDS in San Francisco. *American Journal of Public Health, 76,* 1443–1445.

The authors asked teenagers various questions about their knowledge of AIDS and whether they have changed their sexual behavior as a result of the AIDS epidemic. Ask a group of your peers these same questions. Are the responses you receive similar to or different from the findings of this study?

Critical Thinking

Attachment

Teti, D. M., & Ablard, K. E. (1989). Security of attachment and infant sibling relationships: A laboratory study. *Child Development, 60,* 1519–1528.

Interesting study on attachment bonds between siblings. From your own experience and those of your friends, what are some other factors not cited in the article that can promote or thwart sibling bonding?

CHAPTER 12

Gender-Role Development

CHILDREN'S THOUGHTS

On "If you woke up tomorrow and discovered you were opposite of your own sex, how would your life be different?"

If I woke up and discovered I was a girl, it would be terrible! Girls have such a hard life. They have to make sure that their clothes are perfect and their hair looks good. As a woman, you wouldn't earn as much money as a man because you are a woman. There are not a lot of woman lawyers or doctors. So, I would probably be a nurse or flight attendant. In addition, as a woman you would have to clean the house and take care of the children. It would be a little hard to do all this, but it's their job. I just couldn't be a woman; I couldn't be non-aggressive and noncompetitive.

Gordon, age 15

If I woke up and discovered I was a boy, lots of things about my life would change. The first thing that comes to mind is that instead of wanting to be thin and small, I would want to be tall and muscular. Being tall and muscular is important so that I could be good in sports. Being a good athlete is important to boys. Looking pretty is important to girls. Inwardly I would change too. I would not want to be quiet but outgoing and dominant. I would be more assertive as a boy and wouldn't show my feelings. Thinking about the future, my life would be different. As a male I would expect to be the financial supporter of my family. So my career would be very important to me. I would probably choose a career in computers or engineering.

Sally, age 15

CHAPTER OUTLINE

CHILDREN'S GENDER-ROLE BEHAVIOR

THEORIES OF GENDER-ROLE DEVELOPMENT

Psychoanalytical Theory
Social Learning Theory
Cognitive Theory
Gender Schema Theory
Biological Theory

INFANCY AND EARLY CHILDHOOD

Parents as Socializing Agents
Gender-Socialization Roles of Mothers and Fathers

MIDDLE CHILDHOOD

Television
Teachers
Actual Sex Differences
Aggression

ADOLESCENCE

Masculinity and Femininity in Adolescence
Androgyny and Its Relation to Psychosocial Well-Being

PRACTICAL IMPLICATIONS: RAISING ANDROGYNOUS YOUTHS

Toward Raising More Independent, Achievement-Oriented Girls
Toward Raising More Expressive, Nurturant Boys
Speculations on the Future

KEY TERMS

Gender identity
Gender role
Gender-role stereotyping
Identification
Oedipal complex
Defensive identification
Anaclitic identification
Expressive behavior
Instrumental behavior
Androgyny

The Institute for Equality in Education conducted a survey (Papageorgiou, 1983), in which approximately 2,000 students in the 3rd to 12th grades in both large, metropolitan districts and in smaller, rural districts throughout Colorado participated. The students' responses to the gender-reversal question in "Children's Thoughts" indicated that an overwhelming majority of them saw their gender roles along very traditional lines.

Recently, approximately 150 students in grades 9 through 12 were asked the same gender-reversal question. Surely, adolescents today have more liberal and less-stereotyped notions of men and women. The responses were still quite traditional.

The majority of girls said that as males they would be the primary breadwinner. Boys noted that as girls they would be expected to get married rather than pursue a career: "Females work inside the house and depend on their husbands for support." Girls responded that as males they would start taking more math, science, and computer courses so they could pursue their "lifetime" career. Pilot, engineer, lawyer, doctor, and professional athlete were the most common careers mentioned by girls. Girls seemed to be saying that they would have more career choices and options as males. Boys had a tendency to list secretary, nurse, or teacher as the only occupational choices available to them as females. Boys also felt that most of the occupations open to women were inferior: "I'd hate to do something stupid like be a housewife!"

What about personality characteristics? As boys, girls mentioned they would have to be rowdy, aggressive, loud talking, independent, active, and "macho." As girls, boys said they would have to say nice things, be submissive, polite, talk softer, and be more friendly.

What about physical appearance? Many boys commented that as girls they would have to look pretty: "I'd have to spend more time fixing my hair and junk like that." In addition to the hours they would have to spend making themselves attractive, boys mentioned that as girls they would have to be small and petite "in order to be popular with boys." In reading the themes, you get the impression that boys would find these kinds of beautifying activities extremely bothersome.

Boys often pointed out that they would have to help around the house and do different kinds of chores, for example, vacuum and dust as opposed to taking out the garbage or mowing the lawn. Many girls said they would feel "liberated"—after all, many of these girls have learned firsthand by observing their "lazy brothers, who don't help at all!"

A majority of boys said that they would miss sports most of all. As females, they would not be able to play the rough games and would probably have to sit on the sidelines and watch sports, not join in them.

All in all, it seemed that girls wouldn't be too devastated if they discovered they were boys. In fact, some commented that their lives might even be better. Not one boy in my survey, however, said he'd be happy being a girl. Boys had a tendency to say it would be "disastrous," an "impossible nightmare," or as one boy put it, "If I woke up and discovered I was a girl, it would be just the pits!"

The responses from this informal survey conjured up a lot of questions. How do children develop what appear to be dichotomous ways of behaving? Why do they see themselves as playing different roles in society and displaying different personality characteristics? What parts do biology, children's cognitive development, and culture play in the acquisition of gender roles? In particular, what role do parents, teachers, peers, and children themselves play in the acquisition of gender-role behavior? The development of sex-typed behavior represents an important and obvious role in social development.

The word *gender* is used in this text to refer to your assignment as either female or male. The use of the word *sex* is considered by many to suggest biological explanations for male-female differences, while the term gender is considered to be more neutral. **Gender identity** is the awareness and acceptance of being male or female. The awareness of being male or female leads to **gender role,** which includes everything children do, say, feel, and think that indicates to the children as well as to others that they are male or female. Gender role involves a set of cultural and social expectations regarding sex-appropriate behaviors and attitudes and their integration into the individual's attitudes and behaviors. Gender role is the expression of gender identity.

In every society, children learn over time the behaviors and attitudes defined by their culture as being appropriate for their particular sex. **Gender-role stereotyping** applies to a set of beliefs or rigid conceptions of appropriate ways of behaving for males and females. For example, a stereotypic conception of males is: "Males are nonemotional, logical, and insensitive." Stereotypic notions of maleness and femaleness are not necessarily based on fact or experience.

CHILDREN'S GENDER-ROLE BEHAVIOR

From a very early age, children tend to act in stereotypic masculine and feminine ways. O'Brien and Huston (1985) demonstrated that, when given a choice, toddlers as young as 19 months selected gender-role "appropriate" toys over other toys. In a study done with 71 preschool children, it was noted that young children had already accepted and begun to incorporate into their response repertoire the gender-role differences frequently shown in the behavior of adults (Caldera, Huston, & O'Brien, 1989). In this study the children were allowed an average of 2 minutes to present toys and to interact with a 6- to 12-month-old infant. After, the child's picture was taken with the infant. In the next phase of the experiment, children were instructed to "dress up" in play clothes appropriate to gender and asked to pretend how mommy or daddy acts.

Girls stood closer to the infant and smiled at and touched the infant more than boys when presenting themselves for photos. Differences in responding to the infant indicated that girls were already aware of societal expectations of behavior considered appropriate for their gender. When they were asked to "act like mommy" they consistently stood closer to the infant than they did when they were asked to simply pose for a picture with the infant. In contrast, when boys were asked to play the role of the father, some actually stood further away from the baby. Girls smiled more in all conditions.

Ollison (1977) asked a group of kindergarten children from an inner-city school if they would rather be boys or girls. She found that 28 of the 29 boys said they would rather be boys; 6 of the girls wanted to be boys also. Further, when Ollison asked the children whether their mothers or their fathers were smarter, over half the girls and boys answered that their fathers were smarter. Such results may not necessarily mean that children think males are superior; a plausible explanation may be that these children perceive that it is a man's world and they want to be a part of that world. In questioning nursery school children (ages 3 to 5), it was found that a significant percentage of 3-year-olds identified various traits (owns big store, talks loudly, makes lots of rules) as masculine and other traits (fussy, afraid, weak, talkative) as feminine (Kuhn, Nash, & Brucken, 1978). They thought the former category of traits were better.

Matthews (1981) reports in an analysis of 4-year-olds' fantasy play that both boys and girls depicted the wife as a helpless individual, but a kind person. Boys, on the other hand, perceived the male to be the leader both as husband and father. Wives were seen by little boys as being dependent on the husband. It appears that for even very young children, masculine and feminine behaviors are thought to be mutually exclusive and masculine is better.

What about older children? Zuckerman and Sayre (1982) interviewed 60 middle-class children between the ages of 4 and 8 in order to determine the extent to which recently changing cultural mores have influenced children's gender-role concepts.

In particular, the children were asked about the careers they would choose if they were the opposite sex, the reasons why they like being a boy or girl, and their opinions regarding the appropriate behavior of men and women. The data suggest that children hold very stereotypic notions about their career choices and appropriate behaviors for males and females. For example, 83% of the boys and 68% of the girls chose careers in traditional fields (males—veterinarian, firefighter, police officer, and females—teacher, nurse, mother). Boys responded that they like being boys because they liked sports. Males were still supposed to work at a job outside the home and females were still supposed to wash dishes and sew.

The question that now needs to be addressed is, "How do children learn their gender roles?" Several theories have offered explanations. You have read in chapter 1 about a number of perspectives and theories of child development, which will be presented again with an eye toward what they have to say about the child's gender-role development. It should be kept in mind that no single approach is the best approach. Each theory contributes to the understanding of gender-role development, but none provide a perfect and complete picture. Development of gender roles is best thought of as an interaction of biological, social, cultural, and cognitive factors.

THEORIES OF GENDER-ROLE DEVELOPMENT

The means by which children learn to behave in socially acceptable ways and the means by which gender-type behavior is transmitted from parent to child has received considerable attention from social scientists. This learning is generally referred to as the identification process. Unfortunately, **identification** is a rather fuzzy term. Some writers suggest that it is simply the process by which children acquire their parents' attitudes, values, and behavior patterns (Bandura, 1977). Children become like their parents; they "take the role of the other," as Mead (1934) put it. This does not imply that children take the specific roles of their parents, but rather, that the boy, for example, learns to become *a* father and the girl learns to become *a* mother. When children identify with a parent, they internalize (incorporate) countless aspects of the parents' behavior and then they endeavor to mold their behavior after the parental model by imitating the parents' actions.

PSYCHOANALYTICAL THEORY

Freud (1940) is usually credited with the first detailed view of the child's identification with parents, from which subsequent theories have been partially derived. Identification with the mother or father is a process or state whose core elements are children's emotional attachment to their parents and the desire to be like them. During the first 6 years, the development of identification with the same-sex parent is crucial to the development of appropriate gender-role behavior.

According to Freud's theoretical speculations, during boys' early years, the development of gender roles or adoption of appropriate gender-type behaviors centers on the resolution of the **Oedipal complex** and boys' identification with their mothers. Some psychoanalysts believe that girls experience an Electra complex, the female counterpart of the Oedipal complex, but Freud (1931/1961) insisted, "it's only in the male child that we find the fateful combination of love for one parent and simultaneous hate for the other as a rival" (p. 229). As you will recall from Chapter 3, Freud was a stage theorist and explained that children pass through five psychosexual stages of development with the first three stages being the most influential. In the third stage, the phallic stage, 4- to 6-year-olds become aware of their genitals. This awareness leads to sexual fantasies toward the opposite-sex parent. While these sexual desires take place at the unconscious level, the child does feel an inner conflict and anxiety. To relieve this anxiety, children pattern their behavior after the same-sex parent. The process of identifying with the parent of the same sex forms the basis for appropriate gender-role behavior, with the parent also becoming the model for values that will be part of the child's adult personality.

Why do children give up their desire for the opposite-sex parent? The process proceeds differently for boys than for girls. A boy views his father as a competitor and he fears his powerful father will retaliate by castrating him. After all, the boy assumes, this is why little girls do not have penises. Out of fear and "castration anxiety," the little boy then represses his desire to possess his mother and at the same time begins to identify with his father. Freud referred to this as **defensive identification.** For the boy, it has the effect of making him more similar to his father, and the child expects that this similarity should decrease the possibility of his father harming him.

Little girls, when they discover that they do not possess the noticeable, external genitals of the male, blame their mothers for this loss. The little girl wants to have a penis and is greatly disturbed by her lack of such an impressive organ. She gradually turns away from her mother as an object of her sexual affection and begins to prefer her father who has the organ she is missing. Her love for her father is mixed with envy because he possesses something she does not have. This is known as *penis envy;* it is the feminine counterpart of the boy's castration anxiety. The little girl, however, failing to supplant her mother and fearing her mother's resentment and loss of her love, resolves the anxiety she feels by once more identifying with her mother. This is known as **anaclitic identification.**

By identifying with the same-sex parent, children incorporate the parents' standards and characteristics into their own personalities. Boys who successfully identify with their fathers develop "masculine" behavior, while girls who successfully identify with their mothers show "feminine" behavior. Although, according to Freud, a portion of identification is direct and self-conscious, much of children's behavioral patterns are acquired unconsciously.

The development of gender role, according to Freud, arises out of children's recognition of their own genitals. Freud saw gender identity as being intrinsically tied to the genitals: "I have a penis" means "I am a boy." "I do not have a penis" means "I am a girl" (Kessler & McKenna, 1978). Freud, however, fails to explain how children learn to see the genitals as the dichotomizing feature by which they distinguish all people and categorize self. Why not bigger muscles or shorter hair? Moreover, Freud's theory does not explain how some children have male gender identities even though they do not have penises (Money & Ehrhardt, 1972). Similarly, how can it be that blind children have stable gender identities, even though they cannot see genital differences?

SOCIAL LEARNING THEORY

Social learning theorists (e.g., Mischel, 1966) assume that no particular kind of knowledge about gender is required for the acquisition of sex-typed preferences. Instead, they emphasize that gender-role behaviors are acquired, maintained, and changed primarily through the learning process (Cairns, 1979). This view focuses particularly on learning by identification or imitation (a term more frequently used by social learning theorists) as well as reinforcement and punishment (Bandura, 1977). Social learning theorists maintain that from the very beginning of life, parents and other caregivers treat boys and girls differently. Little girls are rewarded for certain behaviors and punished for other behaviors, and these are not the same set of behaviors for which little boys are rewarded or punished. Children are also believed to choose to imitate models of the same sex. By and large, social learning theory depicts the child as a somewhat passive recipient of culturally transmitted information.

It is through observing and imitating parents that children first begin to flesh out the behavior categories outlined by a gender identity. When the child does imitate the behavior of the same-sexed parent, the reinforcement outcome (reward, neutral, or punishment) influences the probability of the child repeating the performance. For example, a young son and daughter are observing their mother putting on lipstick. When the little girl tries this, the parents may comment, "How cute," while the son is told disapprovingly, "Boys don't wear lipstick." Gradually, from this differential reinforcement from parents, teachers, peers, and others, children learn what they can or cannot do. Thus, according to social learning theory, in a

"typical" family the girl would be reinforced for imitating the behavior of the mother and the boy for imitating the masculine acts of the father. These behaviors, learned from the respective parents, are most often appropriate to the child's sex, and are the ones most likely to be rewarded. Males are generally rewarded for aggressive, independent behaviors and females are rewarded for nurturing, passive behaviors. Thus, according to this framework, children learn appropriate gender roles through observation of the rewards and punishments received by models. It is in this way that they learn to engage in the stereotypic behaviors rewarded in North American culture.

Some social learning theorists emphasize the importance of learning that takes place without explicit reinforcement or punishment, portraying *observational* or *vicarious learning* as a crucial process in gender-role development. If children see someone punished after engaging in a particular activity, or there is no particular result, it is less likely that they will imitate that behavior than if they see the person rewarded. When a little boy sees a classmate ridiculed for behaving like a sissy, or when a little girl observes another girl commended for her neat picture, these actions vicariously reinforce the child's understanding of appropriate sex-type behavior. Thus children learn appropriate gender-role behavior by imitating same-sex parents or models and being reinforced directly or indirectly for doing sex-appropriate things.

There is not nearly the exclusive identification with the same-sex parent in social learning theory that is expounded in psychoanalytical theory. Rather, children learn from various models. Social learning theory focuses on learning particularly through observation and imitation of others, rather than emphasizing the unconscious psychodynamics of Freudian theory.

The major problem with social learning theory is that the majority of the experiments have been conducted in a laboratory situation under controlled conditions. Very little research has been based on naturalistic observations in real-life settings. This criticism notwithstanding, the theory has cast considerable light on how children use role models to establish their gender roles.

According to social learning theorists, gender-role behaviors are learned through observation and imitation of the same-sex parent and other same-sex adults.

COGNITIVE THEORY

Psychoanalytical and social learning theories see children as first focusing on the same-sex parent, either on a psychodynamic or a reward-probability basis, and then acquiring behavior appropriate to their own sex. Kohlberg (1966) states that "the child's gender role concepts are the result of the child's active structuring of his own experience; they are not passive products of social training" (p. 85). Cognitive developmental theory places the identification with the same-sex parent at a much later stage in the process of gender-role learning. Kohlberg was one of the first people to postulate a cognitive basis for gender identification. He proposed that children's understanding of gender follows Piaget's model of cognitive development,

with children not having a mature notion of gender until the advent of concrete operational thinking, beginning about 7 years of age. Kohlberg argues that there is a sequential pattern in three stages in the development of gender roles. First, the child, around the age of 2, establishes *gender identity*—"I am a boy." Around the age of 3 or 4, the child can correctly label the sex of others, and gender is perceived as permanent. This is called *gender stability*. However, certain situations cause some confusion. Many young children believe that change in external features and/or age can result in change in gender. That is, if a female is wearing a man's suit and hat, for example, they may label the female as a male. At about 6 or 7, children recognize that gender is invariant over time *and* situations; Kohlberg refers to this as *gender consistency* or *constancy*. He suggests that children understand that gender does not change regardless of changes in appearance, clothing, or activities. Gender constancy, which is a kind of conservation, involves the recognition that people stay the same gender even though they may appear to change by wearing different clothes or having different hair length. This leads them to seek out same-sex models to observe and imitate. The sure knowledge that one's gender is unchangeable, believes Kohlberg, has a tremendous influence on the development of gender roles. Slaby and Frey (1975) have confirmed this three-stage sequence. These researchers reported an age-related developmental sequence with gender identity being acquired before gender stability and gender stability being acquired before gender consistency.

After becoming cognizant of and attached to the role of their sex, children begin to identify with people of the same sex, particularly the same-sex parent. Once children know their gender will never change, they decide they are happy with it. Kohlberg maintains that children's concept of their gender identity becomes the organizing force for future behaviors. They begin valuing same-sex behaviors and attitudes and devaluing opposite-sex ones. They believe the positive things they hear about their own sex and the negative things they hear about the opposite sex. Children's understanding of the unchangeability of gender is an essential element in gender-role acquisition. As Kohlberg states, "the growing cognitive constancy or irreversibility of gender identity in early childhood is the bedrock of later sexual and sex-role attitudes" (Kohlberg & Ullian, 1974, p. 210).

Martin, Wood, and Little (1990), however, in studying 61 4-year-olds, reported that gender-consistency understanding does not play a particularly critical role. Children need only a rudimentary understanding of gender for preferences and knowledge to be influenced. It appears that once children learn to label their own sex and that of others, they have a beginning gender concept. It is then that they show strong sex-typed toy and peer preferences and knowledge about gender differences in toys and clothing. More sophisticated levels of understanding may not be required to influence knowledge and preferences.

Thus, a criticism of Kohlberg's theory is his contention that it is only when children develop gender consistency or constancy, at around age 7, that they will identify with the parent of their own sex and seek out, from all available sources, the behavior and attitudes that go along with that gender. Research does not seem to support this contention. A summary of these theories is found in Table 12.1.

GENDER SCHEMA THEORY

Contemporary cognitive theories of gender identification since Kohlberg have been based on the tenets of information processing, particularly on the concept of schemas. A schema is a mentalistic structure consisting of a set of expectations and associations that guide processing with respect to a particular content. Schemas influence how children process information about gender and serve as a way for them to organize information about sex. Schemas develop primarily from observation. Gender is a salient characteristic in children's worlds, relating both to themselves and to others. It is thus used to organize information in a place that may be used by older and more knowledgeable children.

Martin and Halverson (1981, 1987) have proposed an information-processing model to explain how children learn "appropriate" masculine and feminine ways of behaving. They suggest that sex stereotypes serve as schemata to organize and structure social information. Young children form concepts of maleness and femaleness by age 2 or 3 and thus readily incorporate stereotyped views of play activities, roles, and behaviors that are appropriate to their gender. Sex stereotypes function at two levels. The first level is an overall "in-group/out group" schema, which consists of general information children need in order to categorize objects, behaviors, and roles as being feminine or masculine. Second, there is an "own sex" schema, a narrower, more detailed version of the first, consisting of information children have about objects, behavior, traits, and roles that characterize their own sex. Once gender schemata are formed they "structure" experience by providing an organization for processing social information.

TABLE 12.1   Theories of Gender-Role Development

FREUDIAN PSYCHOANALYTIC:	Own awareness of genitals → fantasy → identification → gender role (implicit: gender identity)
SOCIAL LEARNING:	Others' awareness of genitals → differential reinforcement → gender role $\nearrow$ identification (modeling) $\downarrow$ → gender identity
COGNITIVE DEVELOPMENTAL:	Others' awareness of genitals → labeling → gender identify → gender role → identification

Source: From *Gender—An Ethnomethodological Approach* (p. 88) by S. Kessler and W. McKenna, 1978, New York: John Wiley & Sons. Copyright 1978 by John Wiley & Sons. Adapted by permission.

The following example may help you understand the differences in the type of information found in each of these schemata. The overall schema guides behavior by giving information at the level of labels ("This is appropriate/inappropriate behavior for girls." "This is appropriate/inappropriate behavior for boys.") Boys should play with trucks; girls should not. Girls should play with dolls; boys should not. Thus, young children can identify their gender and reliably place themselves in the appropriate gender-related category (in-group) and not in the other (out-group).

Martin et al. (1990) suggest that children pass through a series of stages. Children in the first stage learn what kinds of things are directly associated with each sex, such as "girls play with dolls" and "boys play with trucks." Around the ages of 4 to 6 years, children move to the second stage when they begin to develop the more indirect and complex associations for information relevant to their own sex but have yet to learn the associations for information relevant to the opposite sex. By the time they are 8, children move to the third stage, where they have also learned the associations relevant to the opposite sex. These children have mastered the gender concepts of masculinity and femininity that link information within and between the various content domains.

In one experiment (Damon, 1977), it was found that the bases of children's evaluations of in-group/out-group undergo developmental changes. Two- to 4-year-olds tend to evaluate in-group behaviors in an egocentric way: "What I am doing is good for me and my sex." Five- to 7-year-olds evaluate in-group and out-group evaluations in terms of rule violations: "I know what's in-group for me and my sex because there is a rule that boys do this and girls do not." Seven to 10-year-olds' evaluations shift to a concern for social sanctions: "What's good for me is what others will not laugh at."

The own-sex schema consists of detailed plans of action necessary to carry out sex-appropriate behavior. For example, if a little girl's overall schema is that "girls sew," in order for her to act consistently with that schema she needs to learn how to sew. As children get older, they will tend to increase their knowledge of things "for me" (own-sex schema) by learning the sex-appropriate plans of action.

Information about in-group/out-group behavior is acquired by watching members of both genders. By observing same-sex models, children learn what in-group members do. Similarly, by observing opposite sex-models, children learn what in-group members do not do.

The schematic model differs from other cognitive theories in that attention is shifted from children simply learning categories of "male things" or "female things" to thinking about "things appropriate for me" "things not appropriate for me." Moreover, according to the schematic model, children do not simply learn behavior appropriate for gender; they learn concepts of both masculine and feminine behavior (Martin & Little, 1990).

The schematic model also differs from Freud's original identification theory on gender role development. Most theorists today do not emphasize that parents are the sole source in learning masculine and feminine ways of behaving. Parents are now seen as being just one socializing influence; children learn gender-role behavior through observation of many different models.

Not only has recent research deemphasized identification with the same-sex parent but it has also emphasized that the learning of gender role behaviors is an ongoing process with developmental changes occurring throughout the life span. Thus, the psychoanalytic premise that gender-role behavior is learned by 5 or 6 years of age is no longer tenable. Contemporary theories focus on active, constructive cognitive processes. Research today seems to be saying that children process information in terms of an evolving gender schema, and it is this gender-based schematic processing that constitutes the way in which children learn dichotomous gender behaviors.

BIOLOGICAL THEORY

Of the major theories detailing how children learn gender-role behaviors, only the biological theory stresses genetic and hormonal influences. It is difficult, however, to determine the extent to which a child's learning of gender-role behavior may be influenced by underlying biological predispositions, because from the moment of birth, the child's maleness or femaleness is constantly being shaped by environmental experiences. Biological theorists, although recognizing that environment is implicated in the development of gender roles, stress that the genetic makeup of the individual and the influence of hormones cannot be overlooked when studying gender-role development.

Evidence on the relation between hormones and behavior in humans is very meager. It should be pointed out that investigators manipulate neither chromosomes nor hormones, but merely examine the effects of accidental chromosomal or hormonal variations.

In examining the influence of genetic and environmental factors, it is reasonable to expect that masculine and feminine attributes might have etiologies similar to those found for other personality characteristics (see Chapter 2). In a joint analysis of data from two twin studies (Horn, Plomin, & Rosenman, 1976; Loehlin & Nichols, 1976) and one adoption study (Loehlin, Willerman, & Horn, 1982), Mitchell, Baker, and Jacklin (1989) reported that genetic factors accounted for 32% of the variance on the California Psychological Inventory feminine scale. From the same reanalysis, environmental factors shared by family members accounted for only 1% of the variance in this subscale. Thus, genetic factors and idiosyncratic experiences and other environmental factors specific to each individual appear most influential in determining masculinity and femininity, which is a consistent finding for other personality traits.

Basic Embryology   Before studies on the effects of hormones on the development of masculine and feminine ways of behaving are discussed, it would be best to review briefly some basic embryology. From the beginning as a single fertilized cell that multiplied rapidly, your cells soon clustered to form the rudimentary organs of an embryo. Sexually, it was an all-purpose embryo, with the growth buds (embryologists call them anlagen) of either male or female organs. As can be seen in Figure 12.1, first there is a pair of gonads, which develop into either testicles or ovaries. Then there are two sets of internal genital ducts or tubes, one of which is called the Wolffian, which develops into the seminal vesicles, the prostate gland, and the long tubes, one on each side, called the vasa deferentia, for the male. The other structure, called the Müllerian, develops into a uterus, fallopian tubes, and the upper vagina in the female (Tortora & Anagnostakos, 1984).

Until the sixth week of pregnancy, the external genitalia as well as the internal reproductive organs and tracts are in an undifferentiated or bipotential state. After the first 6 weeks of embryonic development, the internal reproductive organs (testes or ovaries) develop in response to the presence or absence of the Y chromosome. If the chromosomal pattern is XY (genetic male), the testes develop and begin to secrete male hormones. Androgens are male hormones and testosterone is a special type of androgen. These highly specialized chemical substances interact with cells that are able to receive the hormonal message and respond to it. The male external organs and the male ducts will develop and the female ducts will regress. If the chromosomal pattern is XX (genetic female), the embryo will not be exposed to sufficiently high concentrations of androgens; the genitalia will have the appearance of those of a normal female. At 3 to 4 months of prenatal development, testosterone secreted by the testes leads to the development of the penis and scrotum. If testes are absent, the female external genitalia will form. Thus, without specific instructions to become male, the embryo develops female organs.

It is not the Y chromosome per se that determines the sex of the child, but a precise bit of DNA that actually determines maleness, known as the testes-determining factor gene. (Kinoshita, 1991). To produce a male, all you need is that switch on the Y chromosome. Genetic screening has revealed that some rare males—1 in 20,000—have two Xs and no Y. The XX males, however, actually do have fragments of a Y that has somehow been shuffled onto one of their X chromosomes. In the case of an XY female, the tiny gene to make a male is missing.

°FIGURE 12.1   Development of Reproductive Organs

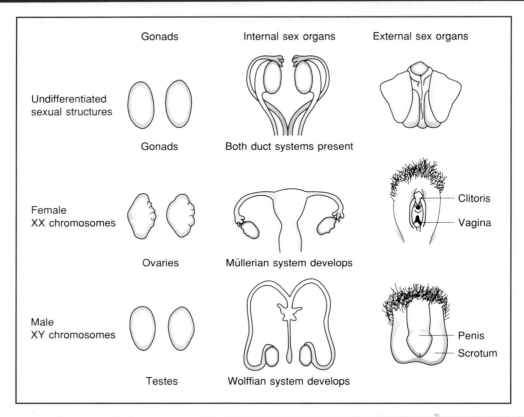

Source: From *Physiological Psychology* (p. 335) by Allen M. Schneider and B. Tarshis, 1975, New York: Random House. Reprinted with permission of McGraw Hill, Inc.

When testosterone is present during the prenatal period, the pituitary will function at puberty to cause a regular production of testosterone and sperm. When testosterone is absent during the prenatal period the pituitary will function at puberty to cause high levels of cyclical hormonal activity, which result in ovulation and menstruation. These differences in pattern of hormone production do not appear until the full functioning of the pituitary gland at puberty, yet the patterns seem to be set during the second or third month of gestation.

Some biological theorists believe that sex hormones in the developing embryo, in addition to controlling the growth of genitalia and directing pituitary activity at puberty, also throw a neural switch in the brain toward "male" and "female" behavior. Hormones seem to sensitize certain central nervous system structures to allow for differences in the appearance of dimorphic gender-role behavior patterns when proper stimulus situations are presented later in life (Levine, 1968). It is speculated that testosterone is related to making males more physically active and aggressive.

Androgenized Females   Is there any evidence to show how hormones affect behavior? The development of pregnancy hormones in the 1950s inadvertently led to a situation in which biological and environmental factors relating to sex differences could be examined separately. Women who wanted to prevent an unwanted, spontaneous abortion were given androgens during their pregnancy. It was discovered that women who received the androgens gave birth to masculinized daughters—that is, females in whom the influence of androgens caused the development of male sex organs. In several cases this condition was diagnosed at birth and the masculine sexual organs were surgically modified.

Money and Ehrhardt (1972) did research on such females; they found 25 androgenized girls ranging in age from 4 to 16 and matched them with 25 normal girls of the same race, socioeconomic background, and IQ. The androgenized girls showed more enthusiasm for vigorous kinds of activities; they enjoyed vigorous outdoor sports; they expressed an interest in a career over romance and marriage, should a choice be offered. The researchers hypothesized that masculinization in androgenized girls involves masculinization of the part of the brain that mediates "dominance assertion and manifests itself in competitive energy expenditure" (p. 103).

Money and Ehrhardt's findings should be viewed as suggestive rather than conclusive, since genital ambiguity was present in these girls at birth and was known by the parents. This knowledge could well have affected the parents' treatment of them. The parents, suggest Money and Ehrhardt, may have encouraged more masculine activity in these girls.

Androgen-Deficient Males Because androgen must be added for male development, the counterpart of a prenatally androgenized girl is a prenatally androgen-deficient boy. Among the prenatally underandrogenized boys are those whose body cells are unable to make full use of androgens (Masica, 1982). Because there is no way to correct this condition, androgen insensitivity continues throughout life.

It should be pointed out that in Money and Ehrhardt's study of androgenized females, a prenatal overdose of androgen did not interfere with the differentiation of female internal reproductive organs. The effect on external genitals ranged from zero through degrees of masculinization that were either negligible or easily corrected by postnatal surgery. None of the androgenized girls needed hormone therapy. Once the androgenization stopped, their bodies developed normally. Thus, there are no boys exactly comparable to the girls whose overandrogenization stopped when they were born. Nevertheless, the profile of the under-androgenized boy is pretty much the profile of the overandrogenized girl. The typical boy in this category is quieter than most boys and does not participate in competitive sports (Ehrhardt & Meyer-Bahlburg, 1981; Levine, 1967).

Prenatal Hormones and the Brain Is it to be assumed from these studies that androgens masculinize the brain, which lead to higher energy expenditures in boys? Or if the fetal brain is androgenized, masculine personality traits will appear? Basnow (1980) comments,

> At this time it appears that prenatal hormones, by affecting certain areas of the brain, may influence the ease with which certain behaviors are acquired. The behaviors would still be markedly affected by environmental factors. For example, prenatal exposure to androgen may predispose the individual to engage in more vigorous kinds of activities. Such a predisposition may increase sensitivity to certain stimuli such as large muscle movements, making them more rewarding and thus more likely to occur. (p. 24)

The "ease-of-learning" model (Hamburg & Lunde, 1966) attempts to account for sex differences as a result of the impact of androgens on the prenatal organization of cortical and subcortical pathways in the brain. Specifically, the model proposes that there are behavior patterns that are easier for males to learn and others that are easier for females to learn. It is hypothesized, for example, that a higher concentration of androgen in the system means that it takes *less* stimulation to evoke children's response as far as strenuous physical activity is concerned and *more* stimulation to evoke children's nurturing behavior.

The theory posits two types of effects: sensitization and activation. Sensitization is believed to

Sensitization to testosterone in utero may sensitize the brain, which may later influence behavior by making males more responsive to stimuli that activate aggressive ways of behaving.

occur during the prenatal period, when circulating hormones act to program the fetal brain in a number of ways. This early sensitization may itself affect later behavior. During and after puberty, circulating hormones then activate or interact with the sensitized brain to produce behavioral effects.

It is probable that prenatal hormones predispose children to certain kinds of behavior. Fetal exposure to androgens may result in a temperament inclination to the rough and tumble, aggressive kinds of activities. For that inclination to become manifest, however, the environment must be one that permits such play. As Spence and Helm-

reich (1978) state, "Even if genetic differences do exist, their effects appear to be exaggerated rather than minimized by the differential socialization practices that parents tend to employ with boys and girls" (p. 9).

Although Money and Ehrhardt (1972) are aware that biological factors influence sex-type behavior, they also maintain that environmental factors obviously influence the emergence of such forms of behavior. The researchers give a striking example. In the process of circumcision of identical twin boys, one boy's penis was severely injured. The parents and the doctor decided that the boy should be given an artificial vagina—a simpler operation—and should be raised as a girl. Follow-up studies at ages 5 and 6 showed the twins to be clearly differentiated in terms of activities, toy preferences, and mannerisms, as a result of different child-rearing practices. Money and Ehrhardt suggest that most gender-identity differentiation is learned by way of social transmission from those responsible for the daily practices of child rearing. Parents appear to play a major role in the socialization of "appropriate" gender-role behavior.

INFANCY AND EARLY CHILDHOOD

PARENTS AS SOCIALIZING AGENTS

In recent years, efforts to determine parents' roles in their children's acquisition of gender-role behavior have focused primarily on the issue of whether parents treat boys and girls differently, particularly in ways that would lead to sex-type differences in behavior. Do mothers and fathers differ in their reactions to children? Perhaps this question is too simplistic. Research has shown that there are some differences in parenting styles; for instance, fathers are more likely than mothers to engage in positive interaction (particularly play) with their children. Any statement comparing the roles of the mother and father, however, needs to specify the age of the children being considered. Most studies show parent treatment differences in the younger ages (Lytton & Romney, 1992).

Newborns enter a world in which there are well-developed belief systems with associated expectations, hopes, and desires on the part of their parents. Perhaps the most well-researched issue concerns the beliefs that parents hold in connection with the sex of the child. Studies have shown that, even from conception, the baby elicits stereotyped sex-related responses and treatment because of its gender (Stattin & Klackenberg-Larsson, 1990). Aspects that are perceived as more masculine (e.g., big, sturdy, hungry, curious, vigorous, irritated) are more often attributed to the baby if it is believed to be a boy, whereas "feminine" attributes (e.g., pretty, cute, little, fine-featured,

cuddly) are given to the baby if it is believed to be a girl (Rubin, Provenzano, & Luria, 1974). If the baby is active, it is believed to be a boy; if inactive, it is believed to be a girl.

Parents tend to respond differently toward their sons and daughters during infancy and toddlerhood. They tend to respond more quickly to a crying girl than a crying boy (Condry, Condry, & Pogatshnik, 1983), offer masculine toys for boys and feminine toys for girls (Eisenberg, Wolchik, Hernandez, & Pasternack, 1985; Sidorowicz & Lunney, 1980), and encourage more motor activity for boys and "nurturance play" for girls (Smith & Lloyd, 1978). Parents react more positively to "adult-oriented, independent behavior," when exhibited by boys, and more negatively to "active, large motor activities," when exhibited by girls (Fagot, 1982, p. 459).

Between 1½ and 3 years, children begin to show pronounced sex-typed behavior (Jacklin, 1989). During this period, children are likely to develop gender-specific behavior largely on the basis of parental beliefs and their subsequent behavior regarding sex-appropriate behavior (Bem, 1989). Extensive literature has documented the differential socialization practices, depending on the sex of the child, with regard to physical contact, communication style, amount and type of play, choice of toys, clothing, showing affection, and so forth (Honig, 1991; Stattin & Klackenberg-Larsson, 1991).

Activity, independence, and assertiveness are rewarded in boys, while passivity, cooperation, and compliance are required of girls by parents, teachers, and other adult models (Burns, Mitchell, & Obradovich, 1989). In interviewing 40 families with children between the ages of 24 to 33 months, McGuire (1988) reported that parents tend to associate physical ability or athletic skill as the most appropriate characteristic for boys—together with getting dirty, being rough, and taking interest in cars, trucks, and tools. Traits considered to be appropriate traits for girls were being gentle, being interested in clothes and makeup, and not being rough. Thus, these 2-year-old children are receiving some fairly clear information from parents on which to build bipolar gender schemes.

In examining the physical environment of 120 boys and girls, ages 5, 13, and 25 months, Pomerleau, Bolduc, Malcuit, and Cossette (1990) reported that parents still encourage sex-typed behavior through their selection of the quantity and types of toys, the colors and types of clothing, and the colors and motifs of children's rooms. Parents provide boys with more sports equipment, tools, and large and small vehicles. Girls are provided with dolls, fictional characters toys, child's furniture, and other toys for manipulation. They are given pink and multicolored clothes. Boys are given blue, red, and white clothing. The authors suggest that these differential environments have an effect on the development of dichotomous abilities and preferential activities for boys and girls.

Toys have properties that elicit particular types of behavior in children. Thus, play with sex-typed toys may be the source of some observed behavioral sex differences. For instance, masculine toys such as trucks and adventure figures promote motor activities. Caldera et al. (1989) found in studying 20 mothers and 20 fathers and their children, who ranged in age from 18 to 24 months, that sex-stereotyped toys had clear effects on the nature of the parent-child interaction. Masculine toys (trucks, cars) were associated with relatively low levels of questions and teaching with low proximity between parents and children. Parents tended to make animated sounds (beeps and whistles) rather than statements that conveyed or elicited information from the child. Play with feminine toys (dolls) elicited close physical proximity and more verbal interactions in the form of comments and questions. These patterns of interaction were evident for both boys and girls and fathers and mothers. These marked differences in children's and parents' behaviors associated with different toys give support to the hypothesis that sex differences in behavior arise partly from differences in the toys with which girls and boys are provided and with which they typically play.

McHale, Bartko, Crouter, and Perry-Jenkins (1990) reported that dichotomous socialization patterns continue into middle childhood. Their data indicate that boys and girls are assigned different chores by their parents. Nine- to 12-year-old girls tend to spend more time shopping, housecleaning, cooking, and dishwashing, while boys provide maintenance assistance (mowing the lawn, taking out the garbage). It was further noted that girls in dual–wage earner homes engaged in more domestic chores than did girls from single–wage earner homes. These findings suggest that sex-typing in household labor remains evident. The results further suggest that gender-role norms in the family may mediate the links between task performance and children's function.

GENDER-SOCIALIZATION ROLES OF MOTHERS AND FATHERS

Mothers, as compared with fathers, devote a greater proportion of their time to caregiving, and are more likely to engage in toy-mediated, non-physical, and verbal play. Fathers devote a greater proportion of their time to play interactions, especially the intense, physical stimulation type of play (Power & Parke, 1985).

Amount of Time Spent   One study (Lewis & Ban, 1977) reported that fathers of 12-month-olds spend an average of 15 minutes of play a day (ranging from zero to 2 hours.) It should be added, of course, that the amount of time adults spend with children is not linearly related, perhaps not related at all, to the amount of influence they have. Moreover, how much time a father spends with his children may be a less salient dimension of his influence than how he spends time with his children.

Ways in Which Time Is Spent   Homemakers spend seven times as much time as employed men in child-care activities, and employed women twice as much time. The mean amounts of time that mothers and fathers reported engaging in caregiving were an average of 0.8 hour per day for fathers and 2.1 hours per day for mothers. Although less than a tenth of women's child care is play, half of all men's child care is play.

In one study of 144 fathers with children from 4 to 12 months old, only 25% of the fathers reported that they had any regular caregiving activity (Kotelchuck, 1981). In another study of fathers and mothers of 2- to 3-year-old, middle-class children in large metropolitan areas, fathers reported spending only 15% of their total time in caregiving activities with their children, whereas mothers reportedly spent 25% of their total time caregiving (Weinraub, 1980).

There appear to be three major determinants of fathers' participation in child care: (a) the more resources a husband has relative to his wife, the less domestic labor he does; (b) the more traditional the husband's sex-role attitudes, the less domestic labor he performs; and (c) the more domestic task demands made on the husband and his capacity or available time to respond to them, the greater his participation in domestic labor (Coverman, 1985). Radin and Harold-Goldsmith (1989) found in studying 700 men that the last determinant, the demand-response situation, was most salient in influencing men's participation in child care. The variables of men having several children, employed wives, and jobs that did not require long hours accounted for 62% of the variance in fathers' participation in child-rearing and domestic chores.

Fathers' primary interaction with their offspring is play (Richards, Dunn, & Antonis, 1977). In fact, 90% of the fathers in this study played regularly with their infants, while less than half participated in child care. From infancy, fathers engage in physically stimulating and playful interactions with their children. From the first year onward, infants and young children appear to prefer playing with their fathers; young infants tend to respond more positively to paternal bids (Clarke-Stewart, 1980). Moreover, when fathers play with their sons, they are more physically rough, play more gross motor games, and use toys less than when they play with their daughters (Power & Parke, 1983). Fathers appear to encourage boys in active, gross motor, and manipulative play; they encourage girls in quiet, passive play. They may add a spatial dimension to children's experience by frequent and intense physical play interactions with them. In addition, they may influence cognitive development by acting in more task-oriented and informative ways, which they do particularly with their sons (Bornstein, 1989).

Mothers and fathers have different styles of interacting with their children. Play is the predominant mode of interaction between father and child. Mothers are primarily responsible for caregiving behaviors.

Expressive and Instrumental Role Differences Johnson (1982) describes mothers as having typically more **expressive behavior** (nurturant, empathic) in dealing with their children. Their role appears to be to give warmth and understanding. Mothers tend to keep the family subsystem functioning smoothly by performing the expressive, integrating, supportive functions (Orlofsky, 1983; Parsons, 1955). Mothers' responsibility is to care for the family members. Orlofsky (1983) found through his observations of parent-child interaction in laboratory situations that fathers were consistently likely to take an action-oriented role with their 5-year-olds whereas mothers more often provided emotional support and encouragement.

Mothers are less likely to make differentiations in their treatment of female and male children and are less likely to be concerned with sex-type behavior (Johnson, 1982; Lamb, 1981). This is not to say that mothers do not value or encourage sex-appropriate behavior. Mothers do share common cultural values with fathers concerning appropriate masculine and feminine behavior but they do not ordinarily make as sharp of a distinction in their attitudes toward their sons and daughters as fathers do (McHale & Huston, 1984).

While the mother has a primary expressive relationship with both boys and girls, the father rewards his male and female children differently. He encourages **instrumental behavior** (competence directed, achievement focused) in his son and expressive behavior in his daughter. For example, with his son the father plays roughly and invites aggression and assertive responses, whereas he is flirtatious and pampering with his daughter, encouraging her to be affectionate and docile (Lamb, 1981).

Fathers and Sex-Role Socialization It has been suggested that fathers may be the principal agents in gender-role socialization. Some studies have found a greater differentiation on the part of the father, even among parents who believe in nonsexist child rearing in which sex differences are minimized (Parke, 1981; Stattin & Klackenberg-Larsson, 1990). Fathers prefer that sex distinctions be easily recognized, so they exert a strong and dogged influence on their children's development (Fields, 1983). Other studies have found minimal support for the uniqueness of the father's role (Siegel, 1987). Although fathers in some studies played physically with boys more frequently than with girls and were more consistent in their encouragement of sex-typed toys, there was actually little support for a differential effect on other sex-role variables. Lytton and Romney (1992) completed a meta-analysis of 172 studies examining the socialization differences of boys and girls and found few consistent differences across studies. The studies reviewed, however, involved children of all ages. Research has shown, however, that younger children receive more gender-role socialization than older children (Fagot & Hagan, 1991).

Fathers want their daughters to be pretty and likeable and their sons to be achievement and competence directed. Fathers think their sons should show an ability to hold their own in a man's world. In each case, the father's reaction is representative of the gender-role demands that the world outside makes on his children. This pattern of fathers expressing affection for their daughters and stimulating their sons toward achievement may be the earliest form of gender-role learning.

To illustrate, Rubin et al. (1974) interviewed 3 first-time parents within 24 hours of their baby's

Fathers tend to engage in rough and tumble play with their sons and passive, nurturing activities with their daughters.

birth. Each baby had been routinely examined after birth by hospital personnel for physical and neurological characteristics such as muscle tone, reflexes, and irritability with no objective differences between males and females, even in size, being found. Yet, there were important differences in the way parents of girls described their newborns, compared with the way parents of boys described their infants. The parents of the girls rated their babies as softer, more finely featured, smaller, and more inattentive than did parents of boys. Fathers were particularly influenced by the gender of the child; they described their sons as firmer, larger featured, better coordinated, more alert, strong, and hardy. Men thought their daughters were more inattentive, weak, and delicate.

Block (1979), using information regarding child-rearing practices obtained from 696 mothers and 548 fathers, found that parents, but particularly fathers, socialize boys and girls differently. Gender-role socialization for girls emphasized communal aspects such as development and maintenance of close interpersonal relationships and expression of feelings. Girls were encouraged to show affection and give comfort to others. Boys, on the other hand, were encouraged to be active and dominant.

Radin (1981) reported that although fathers encouraged cognitive growth in both their sons and daughters, they focused their direct teaching on sons, not daughters. Block (1979) videotaped fathers interacting with their sons and daughters in a learning situation. It was observed that fathers set higher standards for their sons and placed greater emphasis on achievement. With their daughters, fathers focused more on interpersonal aspects of the teaching situation: encouraging, supporting, joking, and protecting. The father is more demanding with his sons, often playing the role of the mentor. "Studying Children" offers some activities for you to try to see if fathers do expect more from their sons than from their daughters.

One study examined high school boys' and girls' perceptions of treatment by their parents. High school boys perceived their fathers as being more concerned with gender-role enforcement

STUDYING CHILDREN

INDEPENDENCE AND ACHIEVEMENT

In order to determine, informally, whether fathers do pressure their sons for achievement and independence, ask three or four fathers the following questions:

At what age would you expect your son, your daughter to be able to do each of the following:

1. Ride a two-wheel bicycle by himself to a friend's house, where he would have to cross a relatively busy street.
2. Go to a sleep-away camp for a 2-week session.
3. Stay at the movies with other kids unaccompanied by an adult.
4. Travel by herself on a train to a nearby city to visit a relative or family friend.
5. Take a job as a baby-sitter on a weekend evening at a time when you will be home and can be reached if needed.

Then have the fathers rate on a scale of 1 to 4 (1 being not very important, 4 being very important) how important it is to have your preschool son, then your preschool daughter, do each of the following things:

1. Be a leader of other children
2. Excel in school work
3. Stand up for himself in children's groups
4. Come out on top in games and sports
5. Complete a college education
6. Be eager to compete
7. Be able to earn her own living (Barnett, 1981)

Did you find a difference in the ages at which fathers grant independence to their sons as compared with their daughters? Is there a difference in the score their daughters received, compared with their sons, on the achievement scale? Do fathers encourage boys and girls equally to be independent and achievement oriented?

than did high school girls, thus confirming a consistent finding with studies in which similar information was elicited from the parents themselves. The boys also reported that their fathers were stricter and more critical, less positive, and less protective than did the girls. Boys, in comparison with girls, indicated that their fathers were less affectionate and nurturant than their mothers (Hoffman & Saltzstein, 1967).

FOCUS ON ISSUES

Who's Socializing Whom?

The data cited thus far on direct influences of social agents in a child's life suggest genuine differences in the treatment of boys and girls. The difference may not be simply a unilateral tendency on the part of parents and other social agents to use differential socialization practices; male and female behavior may also contribute to the differences in socialization practices. For example, young boys have been observed to be more active and disruptive in their behavior than girls; they are more likely to show greater resistance to control and are less likely to be responsive to adult directives, both at home and at school, thereby more frequently eliciting critical, negative reactions from adult caregivers (Levinson, 1982).

A study by Snow, Jacklin, and Maccoby (1983) seems to suggest that the way fathers differentially treat their sons and daughters may be due to the children's behavior as much as to the fathers'. Snow et al.'s study was designed to examine differences in the behavior of fathers toward their 12-month-old sons and daughters. One hundred and seven fathers and their sons and/or daughters were observed in a "waiting room" (with a one-way mirror). The room had several tempting but potentially disaster-producing objects: a vase with flowers, a plastic pitcher filled with water, ashtrays filled with cigarettes. There were also some toys (two dolls, two trucks, a vacuum cleaner, and a shovel) placed on a shelf that was low enough for the children to see, but too high for them to reach.

Snow and her colleagues found that fathers were significantly more likely to use physical and verbal prohibitions with their sons than with their daughters. It was also the case, however, that boys were more likely than girls to touch tempting objects. The father-daughter interactions tended to include more holding and close proximity than father-son interactions. The close physical nature of father-daughter interaction actually prevented the girls from being as mischievous as the boys. Girls appeared more content when being held; boys were fussier and did not like being confined. When the fathers offered the toys to their children, girls played longer with them; the boys' attention span was shorter. After a short period of time, the boys were ready to explore the room once again.

Snow et al.'s study seems to say that it may not simply be fathers who display sex-type behaviors toward their children. It appears that boys and girls differ from one another in terms of the sex-type behavior they exhibit in the presence of their fathers, and this may play an integral role in the socialization practices used by their fathers.

It is difficult to determine how much of fathers' differential treatment of sons and daughters is a result of their own preconceived notions about how boys and girls should act, or whether children themselves through their behavior and attitudes socialize their fathers. "Focus on Issues" discusses the issue of who's socializing whom.

Father Absence   If fathers play a crucial role in the acquisition of gender-role behavior, what are the effects of their absence on daughters and sons? The issue is particularly important in light of the rising number of divorces and the increasing number of female-headed households. There are some reservations about these studies that should be noted.

The absence of the father may not be the only variable that can cause differences between children from father-absent and father-present homes. Other factors, such as the altered family structure and the qualitatively different maternal behavior vis-à-vis the child, can heighten or ameliorate the impact of father absence. The age of the child at the time of the father's departure, whether the child has opportunities for exposure to other male role models, length of the father's absence, ages and sex of siblings, and socioeconomic status of the family may operate singly or in concert with other factors. Thus, delineating the "true" causal agents on the child's development may be impossible.

Effects of Father Absence on Girls In girls, early father absence appears to be more disadvantageous, even though the effects may remain unobserved until adolescence. Hetherington (1972) found that working class adolescent girls who had lost their fathers before they were 5 seemed uncertain about their actions around males. Fatherless girls reported feeling anxious around males. Daughters of widows appeared shy and uncomfortable when around males and daughters of divorced mothers were more assertive around male peers and men, both initiating and responding more to them. When the girls were observed at a dance, for example, the daughters of widows stayed with the other girls and frequently hid behind other girls. Some even spent most of the evening hiding in the rest room. Daughters of divorcees behaved very differently, spending more time at the boys' end of the hall, more often initiating encounters, and asking male peers to dance.

Hetherington (1979) is still continuing to study these girls. She has pointed out that daughters of divorcees do tend to marry younger than daughters of widowed mothers. Daughters from father-absent homes have more marital adjustment problems than girls from intact homes. Daughters from intact homes seem more relaxed, more content, and competent in their roles as wives and mothers.

How can these patterns of behavior be accounted for? All of the mothers were equally "feminine" and reinforced their daughters for sex-appropriate behaviors. Hetherington suggests that daughters of divorced women may have viewed their mothers' lives as unsatisfying, and felt that for happiness it was essential to secure a man. In contrast, daughters of widows may have idealized their fathers and felt that few men could compare favorably with them, or alternatively may have regarded all men as superior and as objects of deference and apprehension.

One word of caution is in order when interpreting Hetherington's work. All of the girls in her study were deprived of contacts with males in general—not just fathers. None of the girls had brothers or stepfathers in their homes.

Levy-Shiff (1982) studied 40 nursery school children (ages 2 years, 6 months) from father-absent homes and compared them with 40 children from intact homes. Data about the children were gathered in interviews with the mothers of both father-absent and father-present homes. The girls from father-absent homes were more independent and more assertive in social situations than girls from intact families. The experimenter concludes:

> Father absence is highly associated with impaired development for boys and less so for girls. . . . Father-absent girls, unlike boys, still have a parent of their own sex as a model. Hence, although being negatively affected, the girls have less difficulty in continuing to progress toward psychological maturity. (p. 1402)

Effects of Father Absence on Boys For boys, Hetherington reasoned that the age at which separation from the father occurs could differentially affect the pattern of gender-role identification. Early separation could prevent masculine identification from occurring and could create a disruptive effect on learning masculine gender-role behaviors. Most evidence indicates that boys without adult male-role models demonstrate more feminine behavior. A variety of studies have shown that fathers' influence on children's gender-role development tends to be more traditional because, when compared with mothers, they more routinely differentiate between masculine and feminine behaviors and encourage greater conformity to conventional gender roles. Later separation may have little effect, or could result in an overemphasis on masculine behavior that was learned through identification with the father prior to his absence.

The dividing point between early and late separation is usually regarded as roughly 5 years of age, both in theoretical discussions of gender-role development and in a sizable number of studies that have explored the knowledge of children of various ages about the appropriateness of various kinds of behavior for males or females in general. Hetherington included 32 African-American and 32 white boys from a low socioeconomic-status area, all of whom were between 9 and 12 years of age and the firstborn in their family. Half of each group of boys were from father-absent homes and half from father-present homes. In half of each racial group, separation of the father had occurred at 4 or earlier; in the other half, separation occurred at age 6 or later. The causes of father separation specified were desertion, divorce, death, and illegitimacy. The boys were all participants at a recreation center, so their behavior was rated on 23 scales by recreation directors who had known the boys for at least 6 months.

Boys from father-absent homes were rated as significantly more dependent on peers. In ratings of aggression, boys from father-present homes and those who were separated from their fathers after the age of 6 were significantly more aggressive than those who were separated from their fathers earlier. In addition, it was found that the early-separation boys played fewer physical games involving contact (boxing, football) than did the late-separation or father-absent boys. The early-separated boys spent more time in nonphysical, noncompetitive activities (reading, working on puzzles) than boys from unbroken homes did. In general, Hetherington's study indicates that the boys who were separated from their fathers at the age of 4 or earlier were less masculine in some areas of their behavior, while boys who were separated after 6 were more similar to those from unbroken homes.

Results from the Levy-Shiff study (1982) showed that nursery school boys from father-absent homes were observed to be emotionally more dependent, showed more separation-anxiety behavior, and exhibited less autonomous achievement striving. The boys from father-absent homes were less socially adjusted and had more difficulties in peer interactions.

The effects of father absence on older boys is less clear. Some investigators find no difference between father-absent and father-present boys. Others find a pattern called *compensatory masculinity* in boys separated from their fathers. In this pattern, the boy displays excessive masculine bravado and at other times shows feminine behavior, such as dependency.

Children whose fathers are psychologically absent (present in the home, but distant and inaccessible) suffer consequences that are similar to—although not as extreme as—those suffered when fathers are physically absent (Hoffman, 1979).

MIDDLE CHILDHOOD

Parents are not the only people who are involved in the acquisition of children's gender-role behavior. Socialization forces outside the family—television, teachers, and peers—are other potent forces affecting the development of masculine and feminine ways of behaving.

TELEVISION

Television is imbedded in the cultural fabric and tends to reinforce the values, the approved sex-typed behavior of our society. It continues to present to the child the standardized version of male-female stereotyping. What does the television world convey about appropriate gender roles? The most widely researched aspect of the relationship among children, television, and gender-role stereotypes is the nature of gender roles in television material seen by children (Steenland, 1990). There are markedly more males than females on television. Males are seen as dominant, aggressive, get-the-job-done people. They are more active, autonomous, and problem solving (Signorielli, 1989). The roles they play are highly prestigious; they are usually doctors, lawyers, law-enforcement officials, and the like (Perloff, 1982). On prime time television 71% of the men are portrayed as professionals compared with 29% of prime time female characters.

Females are underrepresented in virtually every aspect of the television schedule and in every kind of programming seen by children (Lott, 1989). Women fill only about one third of the roles in prime time, and are most frequently seen as nurses, secretaries, or entertainers. In general, women are in marital, romantic, or family roles, and are portrayed as more attractive, sociable, and rule abiding. Women are usually younger than men. Among men on prime time television, 72% are middle-aged and 16% are young adults. Among women, 57% are middle-aged and 27% are young (Signorielli, 1989).

Content items relating to home, family, and romance are especially important to conceptions about gender roles and reveal very traditional and stereotypic portrayals. More women than men are likely to be romantically involved, performing homemaking activities for others, and engaging in child-care activities. Finally, family life is presented as more important for females than for male characters.

Lott (1989) and Lott and Lott (1985) conducted a series of investigations of sexism in face-to-face situations in which the behavior of men toward women was compared with behavior toward other men; similar comparisons were made for women. The behaviors conceptualized as discrimination in face-to-face situations were: (a) negative attitudes toward women (hostility, dislike), (b) negative, stereotypic beliefs about the nature of women (overemotional, submissive), and (c) exclusion, separation, avoidance, or distancing behaviors. Television characters were observed across a wide variety of situations. The findings were that men TV characters manifested distancing and separation significantly more often in their responses to women than in their responses to men.

Commercials are perhaps more biased. As Huston (1983) points out, commercials for boys are action packed, aggressive, and are narrated by males. Commercials aimed at girls are characterized by camera fades, soft background music, and have female narrators. These production features appear to mimic some of the culturally shared symbolic associations with masculinity (loud, fast, sharp) and femininity (gradual, soft, fuzzy). They may convey messages about sex typing at a level considerably more subtle and therefore more difficult to detect or alter than the content messages.

The primary focus of other studies is to show a relationship between the amount of television children watch, what they watch, and how it affects their attitudes and behavior. It appears that third- and fifth-graders who watch a lot of television are more likely to stereotype both gender-related activities and gender-related qualities along traditional lines (Rothschild, 1979). Beuf (1979) found that 76% of preschool heavy television watchers, compared with 50% of moderate viewers, expressed an interest in occupations traditional for their sex. The more time spent watching television, the more likely children's conceptions of social reality will reflect what is seen on television. Moreover, studies have shown that children have a better memory for stimuli that are consistent with societal stereotypes about males and females (Bigler & Liben, 1990).

Children's acceptance of televised stereotypic gender-role behavior has been explored (Freuh & McGhee, 1975). It was reasoned that if children accept television gender-role messages, frequent television viewers should have more stereotypic beliefs (for example, that girls should play with dolls, dishes, and dresses and boys should play with guns and trucks) than infrequent viewers. The experimenters did find that kindergarten, second-, fourth-, and sixth-grade boys and girls who were heavy television viewers were likely to identify more readily with gender-role stereotypes and exhibit more traditional gender-role preferences than moderate viewers. One may ask, however, what is the direction of the causation? Could it be that children with traditional gender-role attitudes prefer to watch more television than those with nontraditional gender roles?

What is the message children are likely to gather from television viewing? A male should be powerful and have a good job. In trying to reach these goals he should be aggressive, try to remain unemotional, and be smart. A female should strive for marriage; the jobs she is capable of performing are mediocre and pay poorly, so she needs the support of a man. In order to achieve this goal, she must

Television plays a major role in socializing children to behave in stereotypic masculine and feminine ways.

remain youthful looking, attractive, and be warm and sensitive. Being impressionable, watching massive doses of stereotypic models of masculinity and femininity, and not being exposed to many counterstereotypic examples may encourage children to internalize these stereotypes into their own attitude system and behave accordingly (Gross & Jeffries-Fox, 1978).

TEACHERS

Early differences in socialization are clearly seen by the time children enter school, with boys being more inquisitive and independent and girls more quiet and content. This behavior, however, is promoted in schools. Thus, it is important to examine

the influence of the school environment on the development of gender roles.

The Title IX law states that no person shall, on the basis of sex, be excluded from participation in, be denied the benefits of, or be subjected to discrimination under any education program or activity receiving federal financial assistance. Although school districts have taken certain important actions required by this law, the emphasis has been on those areas where the results are highly visible and easily verifiable—girls' participation in sports, for example.

More subtle yet powerful forms of differential treatment may occur in the classroom. Teachers, for example, represent an important gender-role

Teachers tend to interact more frequently and give more attention to high-achieving boys than to high-achieving girls.

socializing force in the school. In reviewing the literature about teachers, it appears that the educational system still supports a policy of training boys for individualistic behavior and girls for socially conforming behavior.

Research done in the classroom, which documents behaviors, attitudes, and expectancies of teachers, is critical in pinpointing those actions that distinguish between how girls are treated and how boys are treated. It has been said that teachers respond more positively to their preferred gender (Janman, 1989). If so, whom do they prefer? In general, it appears that female teachers prefer male students to female students (Etaugh & Harlow, 1975). Some have pointed out that males are more honest, more willing to exchange their ideas, more willing to try new things, and in general are easier

to talk with. The only reason mentioned for liking girls was that they are rule abiding and thus do not present disciplinary problems.

Although girls are rated by teachers as being more hardworking than boys, boys have the most interactions of all kinds with their teachers. In fact, it is the boys for whom the teacher has high expectations, who have the most favorable interactions with their teachers; low-expectancy boys are criticized the most, while girls of all achievement levels are treated similarly to one another.

In particular, teachers prefer high-achieving boys and will interact at a higher level and encourage continued responses from them (Weitzman, Birns, & Friend, 1985). High-achieving boys have been shown to receive more praise than high-achieving girls at the elementary and high school level (Parsons, 1982). Girls at all achievement levels were treated similarly to each other. As a consequence, the way teachers treat high-achieving girls may facilitate less achievement. Teachers prefer the dependent girl—the one who is attentive in class, does extra-credit assignments, follows directions, and obeys rules. Thus, the submissive kind of achieving girls and the high-achieving, outspoken boys are preferred, and their behavior is rewarded by their teachers (Hall, Braunwald, & Mroz, 1982).

Data from the classroom indicate that teachers are more apt to direct comments pertaining to the self's action (how well or poorly a problem was handled) to boys than to girls, while they are more apt to direct comments pertaining to the self (good or bad child) to girls than to boys (Cherry, 1975). The type of teacher responses associated with boys is likely to promote a mastery orientation.

Good, Sikes, and Brophy (1973) set out to compare the behavior of male and female teachers with that of boys and girls in 16 classes at the junior high level. Interaction analysis showed the expected sex difference: Boys were much more active and interacted more frequently with their teachers. Teachers were more apt to ask boys process questions ("What part of speech do you think this word is?") and to ask girls product or choice questions ("Is this word a noun or a verb?")

Teachers tend to pay more attention to boys and give them twice as much individual instruction on tasks as they gave girls (Kimball, 1989; Serbin & O'Leary, 1975). Boys were rewarded more for academic achievement, and girls were reinforced for being dependent and staying close to teachers. Boys were encouraged to be creative and independent in their activities, while teachers were more likely to take over and complete a task for a girl.

Teachers may encourage dependency in preschool girls by attending to them particularly when they are nearby. In contrast, boys receive directions and instructions when they solicit their teacher's attention. In one study, a proximity measure of interaction was used, from which it was learned that boys and girls receive equal amounts of attention only when they are very close to the teacher (Serbin & O'Leary, 1975). Boys received more attention than girls when they were out of the immediate vicinity of the teacher. This teacher behavior encouraged girls to stay near the teacher and emphasized all the supportive elements of physical contact, including nodding praise, slight helping, and eye contact. Boys who were at work in the classroom out of the teacher's reach still received encouragement and attention from the teacher, thus supporting their adventurous and independent activities.

Fagot, Hagan, Leinbach, and Kronsberg (1985) and Fagot and Leinbach (1989) have pointed out that teachers often use gender-role stereotypes to guide their reactions to younger children and thus may perpetuate stereotypic behavior. Fagot's research has discovered that a commonly held belief for many teachers is that boys are more physically assertive and girls talk a lot. In one study, 34 children who were 13 to 14 months of age were observed in a nursery school setting and were again observed 9 to 11 months later (Fagot & Hagan, 1985). Teachers of these young children tended to respond to boys when they were behaving aggressively, but tended to ignore girls when they were behaving in an aggressive manner. Furthermore, teachers tended to respond and attend to girls' low-intensity demands. All these responses give the child attention and teach boys that being phys-

---

STUDYING CHILDREN

TEACHERS AND THEIR STUDENTS

Conduct your own study by observing teachers' interactions with their students in any of the elementary grades. Do teachers praise high-achieving boys more often? Do they tend to interact more frequently with high-achieving boys? Do teachers tend to respond to girls when they are near them? Do they respond to boys when they are farther away? Do teachers tend to ask boys process questions (How do you think we can solve this problem?)? Do they tend to give girls the answers to their questions? Are there other behaviors that you observed that would lead to positive achievement in boys and mediocre achievement in girls?

---

ically assertive is okay and that girls get attention by talking. Thus, expectations can become self-fulfilling prophecies. Try the observational activities in "Studying Children" to see, informally, if teachers do interact differently with boys than they do with girls.

ACTUAL SEX DIFFERENCES

From the studies reported in this chapter, it appears that boys and girls engage in dichotomous, stereotypic masculine and feminine ways of behaving. Girls are frequently portrayed as empathic, socially attuned, and cooperative, whereas boys are depicted as impulsive, aggressive, and egocentric. Are there any psychological differences between males and females that may account for their differing constellations of behavior patterns? It should be pointed out that when discussing existing and documented sex differences it merely means that the average in a given attribute is higher for one sex than the other; however, there is always a large degree of overlap in the distribution of these traits. An exhaustive review of available literature on sex differences is provided by Maccoby and Jacklin (1974). In their review, the authors attempt to describe how boys and girls actually differ from one another. Table 12.2 summarizes the results of their work.

TABLE 12.2 Sex Differences	
	Verbal ability: From the age of 3 to the age of 11, sex differences are minimal; after that females excel in grammar and spelling.
	Quantitative ability: There are few sex differences in math ability until seventh grade; after that, boys move ahead.
	Visual-spatial abilities: Males excel after age 8 and maintain their advantage through old age. (These abilities refer to the visual perception of objects or figures in space and the way they relate to each other.)
	General intelligence: There are no known differences between males and females in overall intelligence.
	Physical abilities: Males are more muscular and larger. Females tend to have greater body fat to muscle ratio than do boys at all ages.
	Activity level: By preschool age, boys have higher activity levels and are often rated as more active. Boys are more physically aggressive than girls.
	Vulnerability: At every stage of life, males are more vulnerable to disease, physical disorders, and death.

Source: From *The Psychology of Sex Differences* by E. E. Maccoby and C. M. Jacklin, 1974, Palo Alto, CA: Stanford University Press. Copyright 1974 by Stanford University Press. Reprinted by permission.

AGGRESSION

Research findings suggest that gender differences are small (Cohn, 1991; Lytton & Romney, 1992). Males tend to be more active and more physically aggressive than females (Hyde, 1984; Jacklin, 1989). Hyde (1984) reviewed findings from 143 studies. As expected, males were significantly more aggressive than females. Eagly (1987) conducted a quantitative review of 63 studies of aggression (in subjects 14 years and older). Consistent with Hyde's (1984) review, males were found to be more aggressive than females. In Maccoby's (1980) words "The tendency of males to be more aggressive than females is perhaps the most firmly established sex difference and is a characteristic that transcends cultures" (p. 216).

Fagot et al. (1985) found that adults in general paid more attention to boys' negative behaviors. With small children, this meant that boys received more positive reactions when engaged in acting-out behaviors. Girls' negative behaviors were more likely to be ignored, which for the young child is a type of extinction paradigm. This early attention to aggression in boys and the ignoring of the same behaviors in girls may have important implications for the development of sex differences in aggression. Other gender differences cited in the Maccoby and Jacklin (1974) study are rather general cognitive abilities—verbal ability, spatial ability, and mathematical ability.

Verbal Behavior   Although Maccoby and Jacklin's review of studies comparing male and female performance on intellectual tasks found sex differences in verbal behavior, current research does not. Hyde and Linn (1988) compared the verbal ability scores of girls and boys in 165 studies reporting data on gender differences in verbal ability. They found that differences between the sexes has been reduced across the decades:

> Our meta-analysis provides strong evidence that the magnitude of the gender difference in verbal ability is so small that it can effectively be considered to be zero. A more detailed analysis of verbal ability (e.g., vocabulary, reading comprehension, and analogies) similarly yielded no evidence of a substantial gender difference. (p. 64)

Spatial Ability   Boys tend to perform better on spatial tasks than do girls. Sex differences in spatial ability are more specifically described by Linn

FIGURE 12.2   A Spatial Perception Item

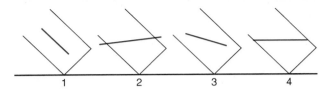

Source: From "Emergence and Characteristics of Sex Differences in Spatial Ability: A Meta-Analysis" by M. C. Linn and A. C. Petersen, 1985, *Child Development, 56*, p. 1482. © The Society for Research in Child Development. Reprinted by permission.

FIGURE 12.3   A Mental Rotation Item

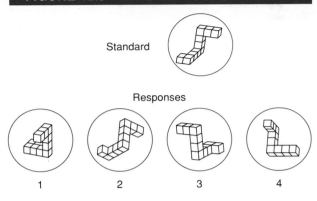

Source: From "Emergence and Characteristics of Sex Differences in Spatial Ability: A Meta-Analysis" by M. C. Linn and A. C. Petersen, 1985, *Child Development, 56*, p. 1483. © The Society for Research in Child Development. Reprinted by permission.

and Petersen (1986) in the categories of spatial perception, mental rotation, and spatial visualization. Spatial perception tests require the subject to determine spatial relationships with respect to the orientation of their own bodies, in spite of distracting information. One example is the water level test that requires subjects to draw or identify a horizontal line in a tilted bottle. An example of this test appears in Figure 12.2. The ability to rotate a two- or three-dimensional figure rapidly and accurately is known as mental rotation. An example on the Shepard-Metzler Mental Rotation Test appears in Figure 12.3. Spatial visualization involves hidden figures, paper folding, and block design (see Figure 12.4).

Linn and Petersen (1986) have concluded that the magnitude of gender differences varies with the type of spatial ability examined. In sex differences for spatial perception, emerging around 8 years of age, a medium magnitude of sex differences (favoring males) is observed. For mental rotation—detected whenever measurement is possible, generally around the age of 13—there are large gender differences (favoring males). For spatial visualization, there are no sex differences.

Mathematical Ability   Boys tend to have superior mathematical skills. For example, in the United States, males tend to perform better on the College Board's Scholastic Achievement Test (SAT) than do females. They score approximately 50 points

higher on a scale of 200 to 800. Gender differences reflecting male superiority on tests of achievement in mathematics has been found in Japan and China as well (Lummis & Stevenson, 1990).

Earlier studies speculated about the biological causes of males' superior mathematic performance. Geschwind and Behan (1984) reported that exposure to excessive testosterone during pregnancy may be a contributing factor in producing superior mathematic skills in males. Their sample of seventh- and eighth-grade math "whiz-kids" (scored 700 or above on the mathematic portion of the SATs) also tended to be left-handed and suffer from allergies, characteristics that have been linked to exposure to excessive testosterone in utero. Current research suggests that math anxiety, gender-stereotypic beliefs of parents, and the perceived value of math to the student account for the major portion of sex differences in mathematical achievement (Entwisle & Alexander, 1990; Stevenson & Lee, 1990).

Gender differences in children's mathematical performance are frequently seen in middle childhood and can be at least partly attributed to parent expectations. Mothers tend to think their sons will

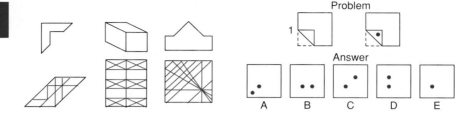

FIGURE 12.4   Spatial Visualization Items

Source: From "Emergence and Characteristics of Sex Differences in Spatial Ability: A Meta-Analysis" by M. C. Linn and A. C. Petersen, 1985, *Child Development, 56,* p. 1485. © The Society for Research in Child Development. Reprinted by permission.

do better in math than their daughters, and this apparently causes the sons to see themselves as better in math than daughters. Moreover, boys may be given more encouragement to develop mathematical skills, and as a result perform better on tests of mathematical knowledge. Entwisle and Baker (1983) studied 1,100 children from the beginning of first grade to the end of the third grade and found that boys developed higher expectations for their performance in math than did girls, apparently in response to differential expectations held by parents. The parents felt that boys would need mathematics training more than girls and encouraged them to do well in that subject. Parental expectations affect children's own expectations and can lead to differential mathematics performance. Moreover, it has been found that when parents have high expectations for their daughters to do well in mathematics and encourage their daughters to do well in mathematics, there are no sex differences in math ability at all grade levels through high school (Paulsen & Johnson, 1983).

When girls are encouraged to do well in mathematics, their achievement levels do not differ from that of boys.

ADOLESCENCE

According to a stage-sequence model of gender role development presented by Hefner, Rebecca, and Oleshansky (1975), children first hold notions of gender roles that are global and undifferentiated. In the second stage, children are taught sex-appropriate behavior and demonstrate polarization of their gender role stereotypes. Individuals tend to hold very rigid gender-role stereotypes: Males are masculine, females are feminine, and these stereotypes are applied to oneself as well as others. This stage is viewed as temporary and allows time for the organization of gender roles to occur. In the third stage, transcendence of gender role stereotypes occurs, and behavior is adopted

STUDYING CHILDREN

ADOLESCENTS AND STEREOTYPES

Ask three or four young adolescents (13 to 15 years) and three or four of your contemporaries the following questions:

- If you met the officers of the senior class and they were all the same sex, what sex would they be?
- If you walked into a classroom and 90% of the students were the same sex, what subject might that be?
- When you walk into a gymnasium and a group of the same sex is engaged in a lively game of basketball and a group of the same sex is watching on the sidelines, which sex is playing? Which sex is watching?

How do the students respond? Do young adolescents show more stereotypic notions than your classmates? Is there a difference in the way females and males respond to these questions? Do you see a shift from rigid conceptions of gender roles in early adolescence to a transcendence of stereotypic gender roles in later adolescence?

according to what is adaptive to the circumstance. Adolescence is regarded as a key time for transcendence in gender roles to occur. The central assertion of this model is that rigidity in gender roles diminishes throughout adolescence. Young adolescents, particularly males, tend to behave in stereotypic ways; older adolescents tend to transcend stereotypic ways of behaving (see "Studying Children").

MASCULINITY AND FEMININITY IN ADOLESCENCE

There is some support for the idea that young adolescents tend to engage in stereotypic gender-role behavior. The idea that gender-appropriate behaviors intensify during early adolescence has been called the *gender-intensification hypothesis* (Hill & Lynch, 1983). These researchers have noted, in support of this idea, that girls in early adolescence tend to become more self-conscious; achievement behavior becomes more stereotyped, with girls be-

ginning to excel in verbal skills and boys in spatial skills; and socially, girls invest more time than boys in forming intimate friendships.

The findings of Nelson and Keith's (1990) study of 146 males and 154 females in adolescence indicate that early adolescents (ages 13 to 15) did not dichotomize attributes by gender, but seemed to focus on the attribute as a desired quality for any person, regardless of gender. Male adolescents, however, were found to be more traditional than female adolescents. While attitudes expressed by adolescents in this study were somewhat liberating, the data revealed that there was little evidence that gender-role behaviors had changed very much. The moderate to high level of traditionalism found in this study in both male and female adolescent gender-role behaviors is consistent with other research findings (Martin et al., 1990).

Moreover, Galambos, Almeida, and Petersen (1990) support the idea that male and female adolescents tend to experience an intensification of stereotypic gender behavior. The results of their study indicated that during early adolescence a marked increase in stereotypic masculine and feminine ways of behaving occurred, with males exhibiting more independent behaviors and females more nurturing kinds of behavior. Higher levels of stereotypic behavior were found in males than in females. Because masculine behaviors, preferences, and interests are socially valued, it is not surprising that there is an escalation of masculinity among boys.

The results of a study by Fischer and Narus (1981) on a sample of 332 college undergraduates (18 to 25 years) support the view that transcendence from rigid, stereotypic gender roles is an emergent characteristic in later adolescence and/or early adulthood. Cross-sexed characteristics—femininity in men and masculinity in women—tended to increase with age. How androgynous are you? See "Focus on Applications."

ANDROGYNY AND ITS RELATION TO PSYCHOSOCIAL WELL-BEING

Do feminine girls and masculine boys feel better about themselves? Are they happier, healthier, and

Sample Questions from the Andro Scale

Answering T (for true) to the following sample items is indicative of a high score on the femininity scale: 1, 13, 14, 18, 20, 21, 23, 36, 37, 39, 41, 43, 44, and 45. Answering T to these items is indicative of a high score on the masculinity scale: 2, 4, 7, 8, 11, 12, 17, 25, 26, 27, 29, 30, 31, 33, 35, and 42.

	True	False
1. I like to be with people who assume a protective attitude with me.	_____	_____
2. I try to control others rather than permit them to control me.	_____	_____
4. If I have a problem I like to work it out alone.	_____	_____
7. I feel confident when directing the activities of others.	_____	_____
8. I will keep working on a problem after others have given up.	_____	_____
11. I don't care if my clothes are unstylish, as long as I like them.	_____	_____
12. When I see a new invention, I attempt to find out how it works.	_____	_____
13. People like to tell me their troubles because they know I will do everything I can to help them.	_____	_____
14. Sometimes I let people push me around so they can feel important.	_____	_____
17. I seek out positions of authority.	_____	_____
18. I believe in giving friends lots of help and advice.	_____	_____
20. I make certain that I speak softly when I am in a public place.	_____	_____
21. I am usually the first to offer a helping hand when it is needed.	_____	_____
23. I would prefer not being dependent on anyone for assistance.	_____	_____
25. When I am with someone else, I do most of the decision-making.	_____	_____
26. I don't mind being conspicuous.	_____	_____
27. I would never pass up something that sounded like fun just because it was a little hazardous.	_____	_____
29. When someone opposes me on an issue, I usually find myself taking an even stronger stand than I did at first.	_____	_____
30. When two persons are arguing, I often settle the argument for them.	_____	_____
31. I will not go out of my way to behave in an approved way.	_____	_____
33. If I were in politics, I would probably be seen as one of the forceful leaders of my party.	_____	_____
35. I prefer to face my problems by myself.	_____	_____
36. I try to get others to notice the way I dress.	_____	_____
37. When I see someone who looks confused, I usually ask if I can be of any assistance.	_____	_____
39. The good opinion of one's friends is one of the chief rewards for living a good life.	_____	_____
41. When I see a baby, I often ask to hold him.	_____	_____
42. I am quite good at keeping others in line.	_____	_____
43. I think it would be best to marry someone who is more mature and less dependent than I.	_____	_____
44. I don't want to be away from my family too much.	_____	_____
45. Once in a while I enjoy acting as if I were tipsy.	_____	_____

Source: From *The PRF Andro Scale User's Manual* by J. Berzins, M. Welling, and R. Wetter, 1975, Unpublished manuscript, University of Kentucky, Lexington.

more well-adjusted? Or, would they be better off being somewhat androgynous, as some psychologists suggest (Bem, 1983; Spence & Helmreich, 1978)? **Androgyny** is defined as the ability to behave in ways traditionally associated with both sexes. A male or female, for example, can be nurturant to a child, assertive with employees, and sympathetic with a friend.

In classifying adolescents into four gender-role orientations, that is, masculine, feminine, androgynous, and undifferentiated (low on both masculine and feminine characteristics), are androgynous adolescents characterized by greater psychosocial well-being and better adjustment than adolescents classified in the other gender-role orientations? It needs to be pointed out that masculinity and femininity are not viewed as end points of a bipolar unidimensional construct. Researchers have sug-

gested that traits of masculinity and femininity operate on two separate, independent dimensions (Constantinople, 1973). To be masculine does not compromise femininity, or vice versa.

In the studies to be reviewed, gender-role orientations were measured by the Bem Sex Role Inventory (Bem, 1972) or the Personal Attributes Questionnaire (Spence & Helmreich, 1978). Both instruments allow for the classification of an individual as masculine, feminine, androgynous, or undifferentiated.

According to Bem (1985), the combination of masculine and feminine characteristics is deemed to have desirable implications for an individual's behavior, regardless of sex. Androgynous adolescents are more likely to develop a firm self-confidence and a broad range of adaptive qualities that transcend narrowly defined gender-role stereotypes. Androgynous youth have a wider range of capabilities, and depending on what the situation requires, can show assertiveness and warmth and be equally effective in both situations.

Bem's work suggests that androgynous adolescents have personality characteristics that make them more adaptable to changing social conditions and situations. In a series of experimental studies on the flexibility of androgynous adolescents, it was found that androgynous males and females were capable of changing their behavior to suit the situation (Bem, 1975; Bem, Martyna, & Watson, 1976). These studies suggest that androgyny is a very flexible gender-role identity that allows fluidity in various social situations.

In Wells (1980), adolescents between the ages of 14 and 18 completed the Bem Sex Role Inventory and the Rosenberg Self-Esteem Scale. Androgynous subjects of both sexes had the highest superior adjustment and undifferentiated subjects had the poorest. In a study of 10th-, 11th-, and 12th-grade students, androgynous males were found to have higher self-esteem than masculine and undifferentiated males (Lamke, 1982). Androgynous and masculine females had higher self-esteem than undifferentiated females.

In contrast, Taylor and Hall (1982) analyzed a dozen studies and reported that androgynous peo-

Androgyny implies flexibility of gender roles.

ple do not consistently exhibit higher self-esteem or better adjustment. Rather, in both males and females, a positive self-concept was linked to masculine traits. Describing oneself as independent, assertive, and self-confident contributes to high scores on masculinity scales and self-esteem scales. Similar results were found in Massad (1981) on a sample of 8th- to 11th-graders. In particular, the study examined the relationship between adolescents' self-image, their acceptance by peers, and their scores on standardized measures of masculinity, femininity, and androgyny. Although androgynous girls felt better about themselves than either very masculine or very feminine girls, it was the masculine boys (not the androgynous boys) who showed the highest levels of self-acceptance and overall high peer acceptance.

The findings of these two studies suggest that it is easier for girls to behave, at times, in masculine ways during adolescence than it is for boys to act occasionally in feminine ways. Androgynous males may be more likely to be criticized, but their flexible and multiple interests and attitudes will also enable them to adapt to their surroundings. There may be a deeper message from these studies: Perhaps the culture values masculine traits more highly than feminine traits.

From the studies reviewed on the relation between gender-role orientation and aspects of psychosocial well-being in adolescence, androgyny has been found to be associated with high self-acceptance and high peer acceptance in females, better social relations and superior adjustment for both males and females, and high self-esteem in both males and females. Yet, masculinity, more than femininity, was associated with positive and psychological correlates. Masculinity has been found to be related to such positive attributes as high self-esteem in females, high peer acceptance and high self-acceptance in males. Androgynous adolescents are much like adolescents who score high in masculinity. These findings are interesting in that they suggest that it is more acceptable for women to adopt masculine traits than for men to adopt feminine traits. They also suggest that greater societal value is placed on masculine traits

than feminine traits. Masculinity, and perhaps the masculine component of androgyny, appears to be the gender role classification that is most associated with adolescents' psychosocial well-being.

PRACTICAL IMPLICATIONS: RAISING ANDROGYNOUS YOUTHS

Rigid sex typing is not regarded as the desirable outcome in gender-role development (Markstrom-Adams, 1989; Marsh & Jackson, 1986). Although rigid sex typing may facilitate the organization of gender roles, current research suggests that transcendence in gender roles is more desirable. An adult needs to be independent, assertive, and self-reliant as well as nurturant, sensitive, and concerned about the welfare of others. These are all commendable human qualities; however, as you will see in "Focus on Issues," traditional concepts of masculinity and femininity inhibit instrumental behaviors (competence-directed, achievement-oriented) in many women and expressive behaviors (nurturant, empathic) in many men.

Because males tend to be dominated by a sense of exhibiting instrumental behaviors and females by exhibiting expressive behaviors, the developmental task of each is different. Men and boys should learn to mitigate instrumental behaviors with expressive behaviors, and women and girls the reverse. Parents and other agents need to stop socializing children in ways that perpetuate these dichotomous areas of self-investment for boys and girls. Socializing agents can foster and help maintain expressive and instrumental behavior in boys and girls.

Perhaps the reason that we are not seeing educationally and occupationally liberated women and emotionally liberated men is that parents and other influential agents in children's worlds have a hard time overcoming their own socialization histories and continue to reinforce children's traditional masculine and feminine ways of behaving. Boys should be aggressive, are expected to do well in such subjects as mathematics, should be nonemotional, and are socialized to behave in this man-

FOCUS ON ISSUES

Are Men and Women Today Truly Liberated?

Research seems to be saying that men and women in contemporary Western society are moving away from traditional roles assigned on the basis of gender. More women are joining the work force and combining a career with homemaking activities. Men are becoming more involved with child-rearing tasks. Yet, the "liberation" of men and women from traditional roles doesn't seem to be reflected when you look at present conditions in society. Although stereotypic conceptions of men and women have been gradually crumbling over the years, they are by no means remnants from a distant past. First, consider women today. Most female workers remain segregated in relatively low-status, low-paying, female-dominated occupations.

A survey of the federal government's *Dictionary of Occupational Titles,* which rates the complexity of tasks in some 30,000 jobs (which has also influenced many public and private compensation plans), ranks foster mother, nursery school teacher, and practical nurse in the lowest category—all of these occupations were considered to be less demanding than that of a parking lot attendant (Steinberg & Haignere, 1987). Employed women are far more likely than men to be administrative support workers (a category that includes clerical workers) and service workers; in fact, almost half (46%) of all women can be found in jobs in these broad occupational groupings. Nonetheless, the occupational distribution of female workers has been changing. Just under 11% of all women are now managerial workers, more than double the percentage in 1972. Women in the 1990s are also slightly more likely to be professionals and less likely to be operatives than they were in the 1970s.

Some improvements have been made in formerly male-dominated professions such as law, medicine, and management, where women's representation ranged between 3% and 14% in the early 1960s and increased to levels of 20% to 40% in the late 1980s (U.S. Bureau of Labor Statistics, 1989). However, while female lawyers in the late 1980s comprised 25% of all associates, only 6% of female attorneys were partners in law firms (American Bar Association, 1988).

As of 1988, there were over 100,000 female physicians, or more than double the number in 1975. Women have a much higher representation in the teaching profession but only one quarter of all school principalships are held by women. According to the Census Bureau there were 2.9 million women-owned businesses in the U.S. in 1982, the latest year for which data is available. In business, it is still unusual to see women in the bastions of financial power. Only 1.7% of the executives in the top 500 American companies are women (Morrison & Von Glinow, 1990). "Virtually all the wealthiest women in our country got their money by marrying it or inheriting it, not by earning it" (Travis & Offir, 1977, p. 19).

In terms of salary, what is a woman worth? Among full-time workers, the average female college graduate still earns less than the average white male with a high school diploma. The average African-American female college graduate in a full-time position receives less than 90% of her white counterpart's salary (which is equal to the earnings of a white high school male dropout). In 1955, the

Focus on Issues
continued

median annual wages of full-time female workers were approximately 64% of the annual wages of males. Over the next several decades, that figure declined and then climbed back to 64% in 1986 and 65% in 1987 (National Committee on Pay Equity, 1989).

Given the low wages of women and barriers to advancement, it has been economically rational for working couples to give priority to the husband's career, to relocate in accordance with job prospects, and to assign a disproportionate share of domestic obligations to women. Wide disparities have persisted in the vocational status of men and women.

Most studies have concluded that characteristics such as education and experience cannot account for more than half of current gender disparities in earnings (Duncan, 1984). On the whole, women who make comparable investments in time, preparation, and experience still advance less far and less quickly than men (Ando, 1990). Society's commitment to equal opportunity has not extended to equal obligations in domestic spheres. Most contemporary studies have indicated that women still perform about 70% of the family tasks in an average household. Employed wives spend about twice as much time on homemaking tasks as employed husbands (Rhode, 1989).

Although women have made substantial inroads in a number of male-dominated occupations, it has been estimated that at current rates it would take between 75 and 100 years to achieve complete occupational integration in the work force (Rhode, 1990).

What about males? While physical and intellectual horizons may at present be broader for the male than for the female, some men who are caught up in the gray–flannel-suit rat race are not experiencing success, and a sense of self-inadequacy prevails. Even when men do achieve some degree of success, they must continue on the treadmill, continue to compete. After all, a man's worth is judged by his success in his job, success that is perhaps measured by the dollar amount on his paycheck.

Second, a man's emotional development may be stunted by rigid stereotypes. Starting in infancy, boys are taught to be independent, to explore, to conquer the world. For many males the necessity to curb gentleness, sentiment, and emotional feelings results in an unexpressive male. Men tend to bottle up their emotions and run on automatic pilot for years and years. It is paradoxical that little boys are raised to be emotionless automatons, only to be admonished later as boyfriends, husbands, and fathers for not being the emotional, caring, and understanding persons that girlfriends, wives, and children want them to be.

As Goldberg (1983) points out:

A man's psychological energy is used to defend *against,* rather to express what he really is. His efforts are directed at proving to himself and others what *he is not:* feminine, dependent, emotional, passive, afraid, helpless, a loser, a failure, impotent, and so on. . . . To his final day he is driven to project himself as "a man," whether on the battlefield, behind the desk, in lovemaking, on the hospital operating table, in a barroom, or even on his deathbed. And, when he fails, his self-hate and humiliation overwhelm him. (p. 91)

ner. Girls should be passive, nurturant, and sensitive. It is apparent that we need to remove the burden of these stereotypes and allow individuals to feel free to express the best traits of men and women (Bem, 1983). We need to overcome these traditional gender-role polarities to reach a new level of synthesis.

TOWARD RAISING MORE INDEPENDENT, ACHIEVEMENT-ORIENTED GIRLS

A problem parents face today is how to help their daughters develop a strong sense of self so that they don't grow up expecting to "lose themselves" in relationships with other people because they never "found themselves" in relationships with their mothers. Daughters can gain a stronger sense of self, of their individuality and independence, if they receive their mothers' support in learning that separation from them is all right.

There are indications that suggest that daughters stay close to their mothers' identities and that to some extent never achieve a clear sense of a separate self at all (Hock, McBride, & Ginezda, 1989). Respect for separateness of females has never been very great, and it may be that the most basic aspect of identity has not usually been encouraged in girls. Research has shown that young girls who experience symbiotic closeness with their mothers do not move to Mahler's differentiation stage and consequently, as older children and adults, continue to seek approval from others and to define the self in terms of others (Hock & Schirtzinger, 1992).

Hock and Schirtzinger (1992) noted in their study of 87 mothers of 6-year-old children that mothers high in "maternal separation anxiety" tended to prolong symbiotic closeness with their children. Maternal separation anxiety is defined by the authors as "an unpleasant emotional state evidenced by expressions of worry, sadness, or guilt" (p. 93). Bowlby (1980) suggested that high levels of separation anxiety when children are infants is adaptive, but after the age of 3, "healthy" separation anxiety should change from one of physical closeness and constant surveillance to one of rec-

ognition of age-appropriate needs for autonomy of a toddler. Mothers need to "let go" of their children in age-appropriate ways.

This diffuse personal identification of daughter with mother, this lack of encouragement by the mother to separate from her, encourages the merging of the self with the perspective of the other and a consequent diffidence about asserting one's own perspective. A girl's self-identity merges with that of others. Women have a tendency to live in and through other people—to behave as though there is no difference between self and other. Girls tend to rely more on their relationships with other people for a sense of safety and as a way of feeling they have an effect on the world.

A mother's role is a complicated one. She must be nurturing, but at the same time she must support her daughter's sense of autonomy. The mother needs to help her daughter grow and develop as an individual in her own right. This is what mothers do for their sons; it is important for them to do this for their daughters as well.

Daughters also need to receive support from parents in learning that roles labeled by society as masculine will not compromise their sense of themselves as women. The social definition of femininity must be broadened to include achievement and self-assertion (Fields, 1983).

Exposure to nontraditional models, such as a strong, intelligent, competent female friend, boss, or mother is another influential factor in promoting androgynous behavior in females. Daughters of working women, for example, conceive of the ideal woman in our society as being independent and active—adjectives traditionally associated with men (Fingerman, 1989).

Positive reinforcement from family and teachers for achieving intellectual behavior is perhaps the most significant factor in producing androgynous females (Olds, 1981). In the Olds study, half of the androgynous women described themselves as coming from high-achieving, academically oriented families. These women reported having fathers who pushed and rewarded achievement or assertiveness and mothers who encouraged them to be able to support themselves and advance in school. Daughters who identify with an affectionate and competent father tend to be more assertive and competent than daughters who do not (Crouch & Neilson, 1989).

TOWARD RAISING MORE EXPRESSIVE, NURTURANT BOYS

Expressive characteristics in males may be enhanced if social agents encourage boys to express their emotions more freely. Girls are given much more freedom in expressing emotional kinds of behavior, but boys, as though their tear ducts automatically stop functioning at the age of 6, are given strong messages to suppress feelings—to "take it like a man . . . big boys don't cry." Showing feelings is a mark of weakness and must be suppressed.

Males need to be socialized to express their innermost feelings. Male relationships are rather superficial as a result of not doing so. Rarely does a male confide his innermost feelings to another person. As a result, males do not receive the maximum benefits from friendships.

Boys should not have to walk such a rigid tightrope in order to conform to masculine roles. Parents, as we have seen, put much more emphasis on their sons' conformity to masculine roles than on their daughters' femininity. Inappropriate behavior for girls does not appear to carry with it the social stigma that inappropriate behavior for boys does.

One factor that stands out as being an overwhelming influence in producing androgynous males is the impact of key women in men's lives. Sensitivity toward gender-role equality appears to be influenced by exposure to competent, professional women, be it early in life with exposure to a mother figure or relative or in adolescence with a girlfriend.

SPECULATIONS ON THE FUTURE

Given the growing number of married women in paid employment and the decrease in the proportion of a woman's life devoted to child rearing, the expectation is that socialization of girls exclusively for motherhood will diminish in favor of socialization for motherhood and occupational endeavors. After all, in the United States, 60% of the mothers are in the marketplace. This represents a dramatic increase since the early 1980s and a doubling of the rate since 1965 (Hoffman, 1984; U.S. Bureau of The Census, 1983). The reality is that 90% of the girls in high school today can expect to be part of the labor force for an average of 25 years if they marry and an average of 45 years if they don't. Furthermore, 66% of the women who are currently employed are either the sole support for themselves and their families or are the major wage earner (Papageorgiou, 1983).

As productivity and material wealth increase, the work week may be shortened so that males will spend more time at home. Socialization of males exclusively for occupational endeavors may diminish in favor of socialization for occupational endeavors and fatherhood. The current possibility that fathers will assume more expressive tasks inside the boundaries of the family signals the cultural development of the "post-modern" family (Pleck, 1979). In order to raise children to adapt successfully to these life-styles, perhaps parents will need to adopt a nonsexist method of child rearing, one that focuses on the human being regardless of gender.

A change in the family structure may be required. The modern family, as Lamb (1981) notes,

> will reflect a developmental progression toward an increased integration of function; modern men are more affectively oriented when involved in family relations, formerly the sole province of women. Androgynous men and women are sensitive, forceful, and capable of task *and* affective orientations. (p. 102)

Thus, there may be an equal sharing between mothers and fathers in child rearing, homemaking, and breadwinning. Gender stereotypes of "if you are a man you will be . . ." or "if you are a woman you will be . . ." will be swept away as people learn to relate to each other as human beings.

REVIEW OF KEY POINTS

How do boys and girls develop behaviors and attitudes that are consistent with their gender roles? Psychoanalytical theorists maintain that identification with the same-sex parent is crucial to the development of masculine and feminine ways of behaving. Identification with the same-sex parent represents a resolution of the Oedipal and Electra relationships and a termination of the phallic period. For social learning theorists, the source of gender-role acquisition is to be found in cultural factors. Children will imitate the models in their particular society and emulate their behavior. Social learning theory and cognitive theory both involve rewards and reinforcement in gender-role development. Although social learning theorists suggest that rewards for sex-appropriate behavior lead to gender identity, Kohlberg (1966) argues that gender identity comes first, followed by sex-appropriate behavior, which is then rewarding and satisfying. Information-processing theorists suggest that children learn gender-role behavior by forming schemata about behaviors that are "appropriate/inappropriate for me and my gender."

Biological theory stresses genetic and hormonal influences in the development of masculine and feminine ways of behaving. These theorists maintain that hormones absorbed prenatally may contribute to differences in the behavior between the sexes—in particular, that the male hormone, androgen, may affect certain areas of the brain. Androgen makes males more susceptible to the stimuli in their environment that will evoke strenuous, physical ways of behaving. Although stressing biological influences, biological theorists also point out that environmental factors obviously influence the emergence of such forms of behavior.

Children in early childhood engage in stereotypic behaviors. This behavior can be explained, in part, by the fact that parents tend to hold stereotypical attitudes about appropriate sex-role behavior for their sons and daughters and engage in behaviors that tend to promote dichotomous ways of behaving in their children. Fathers and mothers differ in the ways in which they interact with their children and the types of behaviors they reinforce. From the empirical data presented, it appears that mothers spend more time with their children than fathers. Fathers engage in stimulating, playful activities, while mothers are primarily responsible for caregiving. The mother's role is one of giving nurturance and warmth in dealing with her children, while the father is described as being expressive with his daughter and instrumental with his son. Thus fathers, more so than mothers, appear to perpetuate dichotomous gender-role behavior in their children. Four ways fathers have been repeatedly found to treat sons and daughters differently are (a) by encouraging sex-appropriate play in the two sexes, (b) by being harder on boys or punishing them more than girls, (c) by being softer on girls or more acceptant of their dependent behavior, and (d) by demanding higher achievement in boys and actively encouraging high academic standards. The absence of a father, especially in the early years, is associated with low levels of masculine behavior for boys, and for girls a relative difficulty in interacting with males during adolescence.

In discussing socialization forces outside the family, it appears that the sexes are stereotypically portrayed. Peers, especially for boys, are potent forces in maintaining dichotomous ways of behaving for males and females. Biased messages from the media, teachers, and peers slowly alter children's perceptions until stereotypes and myths about men and women are accepted as reality.

From the studies reviewed on the relation between gender-role orientation and aspects of psychosocial well-being in adolescence, males who scored higher on masculinity and females who scored higher on androgyny (perhaps the masculine component of androgyny) have been found to be associated with positive psychological correlates.

While gender-role stereotypes for males and females may be slowly fading away, they do continue to exist. By rigidly defining what males do and how they should act and what females should do and how they should act, both society and its individuals suffer. Women have been limited in intellectual and occupational areas. Men's stereotypic behavior stunts their emotional growth and puts undue pressure on them to be competitive, independent, and successful wage earners.

The key factor that appears to promote androgynous behavior in girls is having a mother and a father who value and actively encourage their children's intellectual pursuits. The key factor in producing androgynous males is warm, nurturing parents and exposure to competent, achievement-oriented women. When examining current economic and technological trends, society appears to be moving toward a time when males and females will share equally in child rearing, homemaking, and breadwinning.

ENHANCING YOUR CRITICAL THINKING

Firsthand Experiences

Stereotypes

Martin, C. L., & Little, J. K. (1990). The relation of gender understanding to children's sex-typed preferences and gender stereotypes. *Child Development, 61,* 1427–1439.

An interesting study that analyzes children's stereotypic notions of gender role. Interview your family and friends at school. What are their beliefs about "appropriate" gender-role behavior for males and females? Are your family's beliefs similar or different from those of your friends?

Critical Thinking

Androgyny

Taylor, M., & Hall, J. A. (1982). Psychological androgyny: Theories, methods, conclusions. *Psychological Bulletin, 92,* 347–366.

Does culture tend to value masculine characteristics more highly than feminine characteristics? Is it the masculine component of androgyny that is most associated with adolescents' psychosocial well-being? Taylor and Hall analyzed a dozen studies and concluded that in both males and females, a positive self-concept was linked to masculine traits (independence, assertiveness, self-confidence). After reading the article, do you concur?

CHILDREN'S THOUGHTS

On what emotions are . . .

Emotions are feelings inside of you. Like anger. I am angry when my sister makes fun of me and when she turns on the radio in the car real loud.

Mona, age 8

Anger is an emotion. I get angry with my little brother. He is always trying to get me into trouble. He says things like, "Stop hitting me!" and my parents will come running, yelling, "Colleen, Stop it!" They never believe me. When I try to explain, they tell me to stop talking back.

Colleen, age 12

KEY TERMS

Emotion
Adrenaline
Noradrenaline
Temperament
Easy child
Difficult child
Slow-to-warm-up child
Goodness-of-fit
Poorness-of-fit
Fear
Anxiety
Phobia
Stress
Stressors
Eustress
Distress
General Adaptation Syndrome
Coping

What are emotions? Most commonly, children in second through eighth grades responded to this question with a simple one-word definition: feelings. Although they mentioned many different feelings, most chose to write about anger. Younger children frequently report that their brothers or sisters make them angry because they don't share or because they constantly "beat them up." Older children's angry feelings are caused by their friends (having fights with friends, friends "being mean") and their parents lecturing to them ("When I was your age, I used to walk 10 miles to school, through wind and rain with my brown-bag lunch—and you think you've got it tough!").

Generally, information about children's emotional development has been rather meager, thus underscoring the relatively minor role given to it (Lewis & Michaelson, 1983). Children grow as social, cognitive, and emotional beings. As such, their emotions cannot be overlooked if a total, integrative view of children is to be formed.

EMOTIONS: WHAT ARE THEY?

Most people think they understand what emotions are—at least until they attempt to define them, and then no one claims to understand them. Emotion means something different to everyone. To some, emotions are good feelings, a source of enrichment to their lives. Life and people would be dull and boring without emotions. Others see emotions as bad feelings, as sources of disruption to their lives, and the cause of illnesses, both physical and mental. Obviously defining emotion is not a simple phenomenon. Most experts would agree, however, that **emotion** is an arousal state that has cognitive and physiological components.

THE COGNITIVE COMPONENT

The cognitive component of emotion involves the central nervous system (brain and spinal cord) and constitutes the intellectual part of an emotion. It involves perception, awareness, knowledge, and feeling. Plutchik and Kellerman (1983) believe that emotion is a chain of events that begins with some stimulus and is followed by cognition, emotional state, and behavior. For example, a child sees a huge dog (stimulus incident) and then thinks, "This dog is dangerous. It could hurt me" (cognition). This decision causes a physiological response of fear, which motivates the child to run away.

The cognitive context is provided by external cues. From knowledge of the situation in which the arousal occurs, including the social behavior of other people, the individual creates the emotional experience. Thus, the individual comes to interpret, evaluate, and infer emotional states (that is, states characterized by such statements as "I am afraid.").

From Plutchik and Kellerman's perspective, emotions are viewed as a result of what you say to yourself rather than the direct, inevitable result of something that happens to you. They believe that your interpretation of the stimulus plays a critical role in determining the physiological arousal of the body, what you will do, how you will feel, and what you will express.

THE PHYSIOLOGICAL COMPONENT

Imagine that you are a volunteer for an experiment being conducted by your school (Ax, 1953). You are in the lab, wired to an electroencephalograph (EEG) that will measure your heart rate, blood pressure, face and hand temperature, skin conductance, and muscle tension. You haven't the foggiest notion as to what the researchers are trying to find out, but you are in a good mood and willing to go along with the experiment. After a few minutes, you feel an intermittent shock in your little finger, coming from the wire that is attached to it. It is noticeable, and you call the experimenter over. The wires are checked and he presses a button on the EEG machine. Suddenly, sparks start flying, and the experimenter shouts, "There is a dangerous high-voltage short circuit!" Wouldn't you be frightened? Eventually, the wire is fixed and things get back to normal.

About 15 minutes later, the polygraph operator enters. You can immediately see that this guy is a snobbish nerd. He criticizes you for moving, which threatens the outcome of the experiment, and comments how useless you are. Before you can punch this guy out for his rudeness, he leaves the room. Wouldn't you be angered by this treatment? You didn't know it, but you have just been measured for your physiological responses while you were afraid and then angry.

Two powerful hormones are secreted during emotions that are responsible for the physiological changes that occur during an emotional state. **Adrenaline** produces an increase in heart rate (in strong anger or fear, the heart rate may increase as much as 40 to 60 beats per minute), secretion of sweat glands, constriction of blood vessels, and the shutting off of digestion. (That is why, when you are excited, scared, or wildly in love you do not want to eat.)

Noradrenaline causes a decrease in heart rate, secretion of the salivary glands, dilation of blood vessels; it constricts the pupils of the eyes and facilitates digestion. These dramatic changes in body functions when experiencing various emotions suggest that virtually all of the neurophysiological systems and subsystems of the body are involved, to greater or lesser degrees, in emotional states.

It used to be believed that only adrenaline was produced during fear situations, and that noradrenaline was the only hormone that flooded our system in anger-response situations. New research has shown that adrenaline and noradrenaline are secreted into our systems in both fear- and anger-producing situations. In fear situations, however, there is a higher concentration of adrenaline in the system; when angry, there is a higher concentration of noradrenaline.

Emotions are classified as mild or strong, depending on the amount of adrenaline or noradrenaline that floods your system, which in turn determines the degree of physiological changes that take place in the body. Mild emotions give one a "pepped-up" and invigorating feeling. Mild emotions are a source of motivational energy. For example, the excitement the athlete may experience before the championship game, the flutters an actor may feel before opening night, or the mildly tense state a student may feel before taking an examination are all examples of experiencing a mild emotion, which tends to have a positive effect on performance.

With strong, active emotions, great quantities of adrenaline and noradrenaline are released into the system. The body is mobilized for immediate activity. There is a stepping up of all actions. A strong, emotional state may have a negative impact on a person's performance. In a high state of arousal, the athlete may not be able to recall the appropriate plays during the game, the actor may suffer from stage fright, and the student may draw a blank when trying to think of the correct answers for the exam.

Strong, depressive emotions, such as grief, failure, and self-pity, result in a reduction of energy output. Heart beat slows down, respiration lowers, and the rate of all processes is markedly decreased. The level of noradrenaline in the brain goes down, which brings on mental and physical immobility.

THEORIES OF EMOTIONAL DEVELOPMENT

There are three prominent theories about how emotional states develop in children: Sroufe's cognitive/constructivist theory, Izard's discrete emotions theory, and Bowlby's attachment theory.

SROUFE'S COGNITIVE/CONSTRUCTIVIST THEORY

Sroufe's (1979) theory advances a differentiation theory of emotion based on Bridges's (1932) observations of early infant affect. Based on daily observations of infants, ranging in age from less than 1 month to 24 months (N = 62), Bridges concluded, after 4 months of studying these infants, that emotions develop in a treelike fashion. A gradual evolution of emotions takes place, increasing in number and complexity as the child develops. According to Bridges, the newborn probably experiences one kind of emotion: a state of general excitement. The state of general excitement differentiates, at approximately 3 months, into distress and shortly thereafter, delight. As can be seen in Figure 13.1, at 6 months, distress differentiates into specific responses of fear, disgust, and anger; delight into elation and affection.

The way in which the general state of arousal develops into specific emotional states remains speculative. No theory has articulated precisely how differentiation occurs, although it is assumed to be associated with the biological maturation of the nervous system, social experience, changing adaptational needs, and increased cognitive capacities. Sroufe's (1979) theory emphasizes the cognitive factors that may underlie the unfolding of these emotions. Only with some development of causality, object permanence, intentionality, and meaning can children experience joy, anger, and fear. In Sroufe's view, affects begin as undifferentiated precursor states, distress and nondistress, and differentiate into specific emotions only gradually. Differentiation occurs in a stagelike way as a function of major developmental reorganizations. Cognition is an all-important variable in his devel-

FIGURE 13.1 The Approximate Ages of Differentiation of the Various Emotions During the First 2 Years of Life

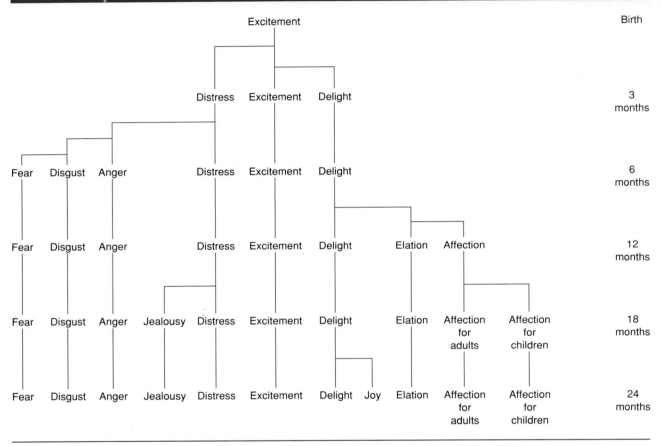

Source: From "Emotional Development in Early Infancy" by Katherine Bridges, 1932, *Child Development, 3*, p. 327. © The Society for Research in Child Development. Reprinted by permission.

opmental scheme and acts as a central mechanism in the growth, elaboration, and differentiation of the emotions.

He discounts the existence of discrete emotions during the opening weeks of life, instead referring to what appear to be emotional behavior as precursor affects. Differentiation does not begin until about 2 to 3 months of age; the emergence of "true" emotions requires the prior establishment of elementary forms of cognitive activity promoting consciousness. Other theorists whose work

falls within the cognitive/constructivist camp defer the emergence of feeling states until even later, into the second half of the first year of life and beyond (Kagan, 1984; Lewis & Brooks, 1978).

Certain emotions are said to be functionally present at birth whereas others require maturational and adaptational demands before they become manifest. Conscious voluntary control over affective expression is not expected until the second year when the child becomes capable of more intentional planning. Sroufe's work suggests that children are capable of expressing anger at around 12 months of age, but anger has its beginnings in early infancy in the form of rage. Rage seems to be a primitive response to prolonged periods of distress or disappointment—such as when an infant fails to reach a sought after toy. With cognitive advances, specific anger toward objects or people emerges out of rage in the second half-year. The infant can now perceive the *cause* of an interruption. In contrast with earlier rage, which builds from continued distress, anger reactions directly follow the unwanted event. Situations much more diverse and subtle than physical restraint or disruption of an ongoing action pattern can now produce anger.

The literature on positive emotions such as pleasure and joy is essentially a discourse on smiling and laughing, in the development of which cognitive factors play a role. Infants actively attend to stimuli in their environment, interpret their meaning, and develop a scheme of the stimulus. With the development of primitive recognition skills, coordination of schemes, and anticipation, the end result is smiling, which is associated with pleasure. Laughter, which appears about a month later, is held to indicate delight or joy.

Sroufe also maintains that the development of fear is dependent on qualitative cognitive changes. He hypothesized that the fear of strangers observed in infants cannot occur in the first few months of life, simply because the child has not developed a perceptual-cognitive capacity to discriminate familiar from unfamiliar faces. This ability emerges between roughly 6 and 9 months of age, and it is during this age span that most observers report occasional fear of strangers in infants.

Some caution is necessary in taking a purely cognitive interpretation of emotion. The occurrence of particular cognitive developments and the observed developments in the emotional domain have often rested on an apparent coincidence. That is, it has been observed that when children achieve object permanence, they experience distress when their mothers leave. This does not mean, however, that object permanence is a necessary prerequisite for children to experience separation anxiety. It should also be pointed out that emotions influence cognition. It is best to view cognition and affect as interdependent and as mutually influential. The result of cognitive functioning is equally a result of affective functioning (motivation, interest, expectancy).

To illustrate, in one study, 16-month-old infants were observed (Meng, Henderson, Campos, & Emde, 1983). These infants were divided into two groups; one underwent the stress of two maternal separations, and the other played joyfully with a series of puppets. After a brief interval, the infants were given a problem to solve. They had to rotate a bar away from them to bring toward them a toy on the other side of the bar. The results indicated that the greater the intensity of happiness in the puppet task, the better the performance up to a certain point, then performance decreased. On the other hand, the greater the intensity of distress elicited by the separation, the poorer the subsequent performance. Emotional intensity is related to performance; mild happiness leads to enhanced performance; more intense distress leads to a decrease in performance.

IZARD'S DISCRETE EMOTIONS THEORY

An alternative model is that emotional states are discrete states that are preprogrammed in some sense and need no further differentiation (Izard, 1978). Izard's theory is developmentally oriented toward a neo-Darwinian perspective, which emphasizes the innate aspects of emotion—their evolutionary, preadaptive nature. According to Izard, all emotions exist at birth, although they may not emerge until a later point in development. Specific emotional states emerge either as needed in the life of the infant or in some predetermined order.

Some investigators claim that infants do exhibit highly differentiated emotional states at birth or shortly after. Two separate studies involving interviews with mothers have revealed that mothers report many emotional expressions in their infants during the first 3 months of life. It was found that 84% of the mothers interviewed stated that their

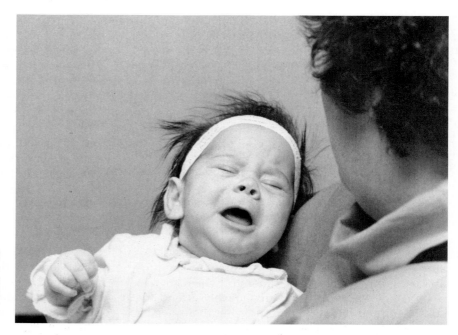

Contrary to Sroufe's theory that young infants experience a general state of excitement, many mothers report observing distinct emotions such as surprise, joy, or anger in their young infants.

babies, even at 1 month of age, expressed anger, 74% surprise, 95% joy, 58% fear, and 99% interest (Johnson, Emde, Pannabecker, Stenberg, & Davis, 1982).

Granted, maternal reports are subject to biases and "adultomorphising" (Murphy, 1983). Adults tend to interpret infants' general behaviors in accordance with how they themselves would have felt in a similar situation. When babies cry, it is assumed they feel bad, just as grown-ups feel bad (generally speaking) when they cry. When a small infant smiles and coos, the joy is recognized empathically. Perhaps, too, mothers who are more distressed, joyful, fearful, and so on are more likely to see these states in their children. Despite these problems, parents clearly expect to see a variety of emotions in infants quite a bit earlier than Sroufe's theory predicts.

Izard (1990) proposes that emotions are a function of naturally elicited facial expressions (determined by intrinsic processes in the somatic nervous system): sensory feedback from the face produces autonomic arousal and emotional experience and further suggests that differentiated fa-

cial expressions imply differentiated affect expression. Sroufe, however, maintains that emotional expressions are instigated by such cognitive factors as recognition and appraisal. Izard has examined the facial expressions of young infants by using an elaborate measurement system (Izard, 1982). He has demonstrated the existence of discrete emotional expressions of interest, joy, disgust, surprise, and distress in infants as young as 1 month. Other researchers (Hamilton, 1989; Weinberg, 1989) have identified facial expressions of sadness and anger in 3- to 6-month-old children. Inferring emotional states in young infants, however, presents some formidable problems (Ratner, 1989), as you will see in "Focus on Issues."

BOWLBY'S ATTACHMENT THEORY

John Bowlby's theory (1980) does not specifically address the question of whether there are innate, discrete expressions of emotions early in development. His theory does assume that infants are preadapted to display a number of differentiated signals that are activated by appropriate stimuli and that typically elicit different kinds of responses from caregivers. Three of these signals present at birth, or shortly after, are crying, orientation, and smiling.

Like the other theories of emotion, attachment theory is concerned with the organizational aspects of behavior and with the role of affect in the development of social relationships and personality. Attachment theory argues that individual differences in the development of personality are closely linked to the outcome of attachment. Individual differences in competence and styles of adaptation in later childhood are sequelae of the early affective bond that is established between caregivers and their infants. Research on attachment has documented that the manner in which caregivers respond to their infants' communications is associated with different emotional profiles and patterns of expressivity.

Attachment theory originated with Bowlby's attempt to synthesize principles from psychoanalysis and ethology in order to illuminate the nature of young children's attachment to their parents. Young children are said to be innately predisposed to engage in behavior strategies that ensure proximity to their caregivers. It is in this context of these early attachment behaviors and reciprocal interactions that children come to develop an attachment bond to caregivers.

At the emotional level, attachment connotes "felt security"; children discriminate their caregiver from others and prefer to be in this person's presence, especially under conditions of threat. Later, the focus of attachment shifts from maintenance of physical proximity to achieving a balance between attachment and exploratory needs and ultimately to an elaboration of an internal working model of that relationship and of interpersonal relationships in general.

The way in which the mother responds to her infant is crucial in producing attachment outcomes. In particular, Bowlby has noted three maternal difference variables thought to affect the development of attachment: the mother's degree of acceptance or rejection, her degree of cooperation or interference, and her accessibility or ignoring.

An accepting mother is characterized as having an open emotional awareness of both her positive and her negative feelings toward the infant and as having the ability to integrate these feelings so as not to suppress awareness of either. The cooperating mother possesses balanced attempts to guide rather than control her infants' behavior. The interfering mother has been described as trying to "train" her infant—to shape it to fit her own conception of a good infant. Although you cannot rule out the possibility that maternal patterns may be in part reactive to infant predispositions, the theoretical literature assigns an important role to maternal affective responses in altering the trajectory of children's expressive development. How mothers respond to the emotional signals of their infants early in life is a major influence on both the outcome of attachment and the infant's emotional expression.

Analysis of discrete emotions of infants furnishes evidence of different affect characteristics for securely and insecurely attached infants. In general, insecurely attached children are more emotionally negative than securely attached children (Thompson & Lamb, 1984). Malatesta, Culver, Tesman, and Shepard (1989) and Malatesta and Wilson (1988) found that insecure-avoidant babies tended to be rather fearful, showing a tendency to freeze under conditions of stress. Insecure-ambivalent children appeared to be organized around the emotion of anger in that they had a very low threshold for frustration and were set off by the slightest provocation or they exhibited an emotionally sad organization and tended to weep sadly and passively.

Gaensbauer, Harmon, Cytryn, and McKnew (1984) found that infants classified as insecure attached were rated as angrier, more fearful, less curious, and less happy than infants classified as securely attached. Insecure-avoidant children have been characterized as angry, vigilant, and emotionally controlled (Main, Kaplan, & Cassidy, 1985).

Many of the insecurely attached infants in these studies had interfering mothers who tended to be constantly doing something to their babies and in some cases overwhelmed them in a physical sense. Thus, infants of interfering mothers may experience these interactions as aversive and overstimulating. It seems likely that infants who experience

FOCUS ON ISSUES

How Can We Infer Emotional States in Infants?

Adults may assume that a particular emotion is experienced by an infant when the particular affective expression is first observed. Can you assume, when a child exhibits a certain facial expression, that in fact that child is experiencing anger? or happiness? Izard (1979) has done a great deal of research on facial patterning. The following illustrations are of the facial changes that characterize each of the basic emotions of anger—rage, interest—excitement, enjoyment—joy, fear—terror, sadness—dejection, and disgust. These illustrations are taken from Izard's Maximally Discriminative Facial Movement Scoring System (Izard, 1979, 1990).

As Campos, Barrett, Lamb, Goldsmith, and Stenberg (1983) point out, research on facial expressions of emotion in infancy is faced with some formidable problems. The first is accuracy. In studies of spontaneous expression of emotion, older children can simply tell you the emotion they are experiencing. In the case of infants, however, when emotional expressions are elicited by the presentation of various stimuli, what criterion of accuracy do you use? How can you know with certainty that infants are responding emotionally the way you think they should to that stimulus? Furthermore, the presentation of a stimulus may produce several emotions or a blend of emotions, not just one.

Moreover, researchers assume that the facial expressions and their accompanying affective states are the same in adults and infants and that the expressions will emerge in their most stereotyped and recognizable forms—assumptions that have not been verified by research (Sroufe, 1979).

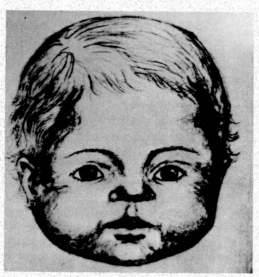 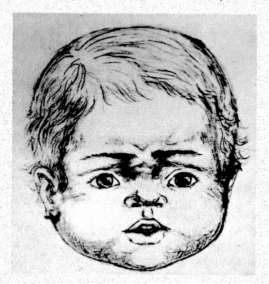

Another problem is that judgments of emotions are not always based on facial expressions per se. The experimenter, knowing the instigating stimuli (restraining the child's movements), may use the situational context as a primary clue in determining the emotion (anger). Experimenters must be presented with facial-expression recordings devoid of any suggestion of the context and eliciting stimuli.

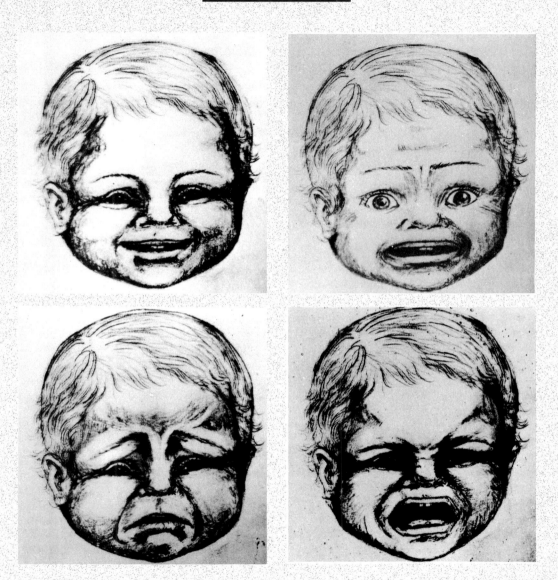

Although there has been compelling evidence that some emotions can be recognized in facial pattern (Izard, 1979), more empirical work needs to be done before it can be said with confidence that facial expressions provide reliable information about discrete emotions in infants.

Source: From "Social Emotional Development" by J. J. Campos, K. C. Barrett, M. E. Lamb, H. H. Goldsmith, and C. Stenberg, 1983, in P. H. Mussen (Ed.), *Handbook of Child Psychology*, 4th ed., V. 4 (pp. 792–797), New York: Wiley. Copyright © 1983 by John Wiley & Sons, Inc. Reprinted by permission of John Wiley & Sons, Inc.

such high facial contingency as overstimulating and aversive may develop defensive maneuvers of avoidance (turning away, escaping, becoming perceptually unavailable), which may then produce disengagement from the caregiver as a means of self-protection.

Whichever developmental model you prefer, there remain challenges: to specify the nature of early emotional life; to trace the increasing complexity of emotional life over time; and to determine the processes responsible for this increased complexity.

INFANCY

During the neonatal period, the affective expression of infants are immediate and unmodulated. Although socialization has played no role yet in the expression of affect, young infants have been neurally primed to be aware of and responsive to the emotional signals of their caregivers. In other words, infants are prepared to affectively respond to others. Tronick (1989) has shown, for example, that very young infants react in emotionally different ways to objects and people. He has demonstrated, for example, that when presented with an object 2-month-old, prereaching infants will look intently at it, sit up straight, remain relatively still, and punctuate their fixed gaze with swiping movements and brief glances away. When presented with people, infants' posture is more relaxed and their movements are smoother. They become active at a slower pace and then look away for longer periods of time than they do with objects. Furthermore, infants give full greeting responses to people but not to objects. Simply stated, infants communicate with people and act instrumentally on objects.

FACIAL EXPRESSIONS

Young infants can also discriminate the facial expressions of others (Malatesta & Izard, 1984). For example, infants look more at facial expressions of joy than anger (Ludemann, 1991). More significantly, it appears that the emotional content of dif-

ferent maternal emotional expressions are appreciated by infants (that is, they lead to different infant emotions). When newborns are in a quiet, alert state, looking at them and gently talking to them can produce a smile.

Recent research suggests that 10-week-old infants react to maternal facial and vocal displays of anger with anger but have fewer angry responses when their mothers pose sadness (Tronick, 1989). Moreover, infant reactions are even influenced by their appreciation of the context surrounding the event; for example, a mother wearing a mask elicits laughter, whereas a stranger wearing the same mask elicits distress and fear (Sroufe, 1979).

Data indicate detection of smiles and frowns by 3 months when a happy or sad expression is posed by a familiar person (Barrera & Maurer, 1979). Weinberg (1989) found that in normal interactions, specific facial expressions are related to specific behaviors. In 6-month-olds, for example, facial expressions of joy are more likely to occur when the infant is looking at the mother, positively vocalizing, and using gestural signals, whereas facial expressions of sadness occur when the infant is looking away and fussing, but not crying. These data demonstrate the organized quality of the infants' affective system.

Tronick (1989) and Cohn and Tronick (1989) found that 7-month-old infants of the most disengaged mothers show the greatest amounts of protest, that the infants of the most intrusive mothers look away the most, and the infants of the most positive mothers express the most positive affect. Similarly, Hamilton (1989) found that 3-month-old infants' affective expressions are strongly related to maternal reports of their own affect. Three-month-old infants whose mothers reported more anger expressed more anger, whereas infants of mothers who reported more sadness expressed more distress.

IMITATION

Recent studies of infants' abilities to imitate have some bearing on questions about the perception of affective expressions as well. Investigators have studied infants' emotional responses by observing their facial expressions. A particularly relevant finding is that neonates imitate others' facial responses and that individual differences in early expressivity seem to be partially inherited (Walden & Field, 1990). Although imitation of another's emotional reactions does not necessarily imply the internal experiencing of the other's emotion, it is possible that such imitation is a manifestation of emotional contagion (Walker-Andrews, 1988). Even if the infant's imitation does not involve any emotional component, it may reflect the infants' attempt to understand the other's emotional state.

Haviland and Lelwica (1987) recorded 10-week-old infant's responses to their mothers' happy, sad, and angry expressions during a play session. To the mothers' happy expressions, infants showed some imitative responses as well as an increase in the frequency of interest expressions. The infants frequently matched their mothers' angry expressions, while showing only chance levels of facial movements associated with joy and a decrease of interest expressions when anger was presented to them. The researchers concluded that infants can discriminate joy, anger, and sadness, that they can match joy and anger, and that they can both inhibit specific behaviors or show imitative responses to their mothers' facial expressions. As the mothers also accompanied their facial expressions with vocal expressions, it is possible that the infants responded to auditory information for emotion as well. It is unclear whether both auditory information and visual information are necessary for imitation to occur, or whether either one will suffice.

It has been suggested that maternal imitation of infant facial expressions and gestures serves a number of different functions, including increasing infants' gazing at their mothers, facilitating the infants' sense of control over the environment, encouraging infant imitation, and enhancing the attachment relationships between the infant and the mother. Mothers who do not imitate their infants' expressions may decrease their infants' sense of self-efficacy, bring about an insecure-attachment

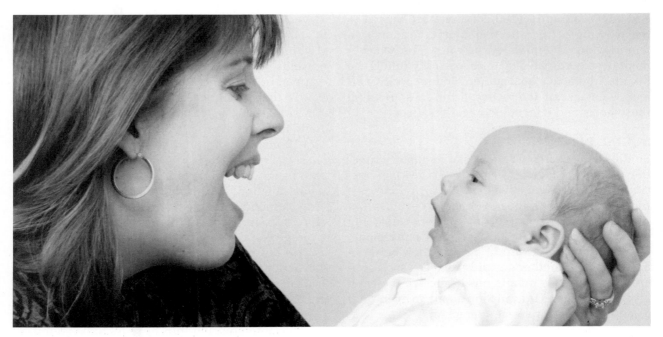

Infants imitate others' facial expressions.

relationship, or instill a negative emotional set in their children (Malatesta & Izard, 1984).

AFFECTIVE COMMUNICATION

Infant and adult communication capacities make possible mutually coordinated infant-adult interactions starting at 3 months. That is, infants modify their affective displays and behavior on the basis of their appreciation of their mothers' affective displays and behavior (Cohn & Tronick, 1987). Infant smiles and vocalizations are contingent on specific maternal affective turn-taking signals; adults make similar modifications. Good interaction is characterized by frequent moves from affectively positive, mutually coordinated states to affectively negative, miscoordinated states and back again on a frequent basis. Poor interactions are characterized by chronically experienced miscoordinated interactions and infrequent periods when the infant and mother are mutually positive; few of the interactions evidence any continqency. Tronick (1989) and Tronick and Cohn (1989) argue that different emotional outcomes observed in children—happy and curious children, sad and withdrawn children, and angry and unfocused children—are related to the working of the affective communication system in which the infant participates. The achievement of a coordinated state successfully fulfills the infants' interactive goal and engenders positive affect, whereas an interactive error fails to fulfill those goals and engenders negative affect.

SOCIAL REFERENCING

Studies have examined the social regulatory function of affect, which is called *social referencing*. Specifically, researchers have asked, Can infants use the affective expressions of others to evaluate an external event? To do so, infants must not only detect and discriminate facial or vocal expressions, but they must be aware of a connection between an event and another's expression. For social referencing to occur, infants must perceive the caregivers' message as information about an event, not as an invitation for social interaction.

In order to study social referencing, researchers have set up interesting events with ambiguous consequences and instructed the infants' mothers to respond to the event in a particular way (with a designated expression). Klinnert (1984) presented 12- and 18-month-olds with a set of novel, mobile toys and had their mothers pose either happy, fearful, or neutral expressions. At both ages, the infants came closer to the mother when she posed fear, stayed at a middle distance when she posed a neutral expression, and moved farthest away from the mother when the happy expression was shown. In a similar study, Campos, Bertenthal, and Caplovitz (1982) found that when 10-month-old infants were exploring the surface of the visual cliff that they looked to their mothers when they came to the "drop-off." If the apparent depth is ambiguous as to its "danger," infants will look at their mothers. When the mothers pose a fearful or angry face, most infants will not cross. Infants act similarly to maternal vocalizations conveying fear or joy. Campos et al. concludes that the infants' behaviors are not the result of passive processes such as mirroring, but rather the behavior results from the infants' active use of another's emotional expression in forming their appreciation of an event and using it to guide action.

Two studies have assessed social referencing with fathers (Dickstein & Parke, 1988; Hirshberg & Svejda, 1990). Both of these studies showed no apparent differences in infants' referencing looks or in their emotional and behavioral responses to maternal and paternal expressions of happiness and fear. Hirshberg (1990) studied the responses of 74 12-month olds and their mothers and fathers in a social referencing design with conflicting (happy and angry) signals given by each of the parents. In this situation, infants did not selectively or primarily respond emotionally or behaviorally to the expressed emotions of their mothers (as primary caregivers, or primary attachment or reference figures) but responded to both parental signals and experienced conflict. Infants tended to show agitated sucking, marked avoidant behavior, incomplete movements, and aimless or disoriented-appearing behavior.

Social referencing thus appears to be an important process by which infants gain information about how to deal with ambiguous events. It also seems to have unsuspectedly powerful consequences in regulating behavior. It is not yet clear by what process the emotional expressions of others affect the child. One possibility is that such expressions serve as mere cues—conditioned stimuli associated in the past with certain outcomes. Moreover, a positive message from the caregiver, for example, might lead to a positive evaluation of an event or object; or it could engender a more positive mood in the infant, resulting in friendlier or less fearful responses. Another possibility is that emotional expressions create a like emotional state in children and produce their behavioral consequences through an empathylike process unmediated by past social learning. Unfortunately, no one has been able to establish if an infant's response to mother or father is a demonstration of understanding or merely an imitative or reflexive act.

TEMPERAMENT

Individual differences in tendencies to express the primary emotions is referred to as **temperament** (Goldsmith & Campos, 1986). It is the apparently innate inclination toward a consistent style of emotional response in many different situations. Temperament refers to an early or stable pattern of emotional response, or to children's intensity of emotional response. Most researchers agree that temperament includes individual behavioral differences in affective expressiveness, motor activity, and stimulus sensitivity (Braungart, Plomin, De-Fries, & Fulker, 1992).

Many parents in the United States recognize temperamental differences in their children. Temperamental differences in children have been found cross-culturally as well. For example, Freedman (1969) has found that newborn Caucasian babies and Chinese babies display different ways of responding emotionally. Caucasian babies start to cry more easily, and once they have started, they are more difficult to console. Chinese babies adapt to almost any position in which they are placed. For example, when placed face down in their cribs, they tend to keep their faces buried in the sheets

rather than immediately turning to one side, as Caucasian babies do. Similarly, when a baby's nose is briefly pressed with a cloth, forcing him to breathe with his mouth, most Caucasian and African-American babies fight this maneuver by immediately turning away or swiping at the cloth with the hands. Chinese babies, however, simply lie on their backs, breathing from the mouth—"accepting" the cloth without a fight. Moreover, Freedman found that Chinese babies are less perturbable, less labile in terms of state, better able to soothe themselves, and quicker to habituate than their U.S. counterparts.

Freedman's research has been replicated and extended with Navajo newborns (Chisholm, 1983). Through the first 10 days of life, Navajo infants are slower to reach a crying state, less likely to respond to aversive stimuli with a cry, and more easily consoled if they do cry than other U.S. infants.

Dimensions of Temperament In the late 1960s Thomas, Chess, and Birch (1968) and Thomas and Chess (1977) began the New York Longitudinal Study (NYLS) in which they systematically studied infants' individual differences in behavioral styles. The experimenters began by asking parents to describe precisely how their 2-month-old infants behaved during specific daily routines, such as sleeping, bathing, feeding, and responding to people. The original research studied 80 children from predominantly middle and upper class white parents. A short while later, 95 children from Puerto Rican working class parents were added to the sample. Analysis of the data indicated nine dimensions of temperament, which are summarized in Table 13.1.

Easy, Difficult, and Slow-to-Warm-Up Children From the presence and rating of these characteristics, it was found that most children fell into one of three temperament clusters or categories, which Thomas et al. subsequently identified as the easy child, the difficult child, and the slow-to-warm-up child. **Easy children** are characterized by high rhythmicity, being usually positive in mood, low or mild in the intensity of their reactions, and usually positive in their approaches to new situations.

TABLE 13.1	Dimensions of Temperament	
Characteristic	**Definition**	**Illustration**
Activity level	Amount of motor activity	High: Always on the move Low: Doesn't move around much.
Rhythmicity	Regularity of repetitive biological functions, including waking, eating, and elimination	High: Eating, sleeping, active periods; bowel and bladder functions occur at predictable times. Low: Eating, sleeping, active periods; bowel and bladder functions irregular and unpredictable.
Approach-withdrawal	Characteristic initial response to a new situation	High: Approaches new situations, such as meeting people or starting school. Low: Hangs back or initially refuses to enter new situations, such as meeting people or starting school.
Adaptability	Ease with which child can change behavior to fit new situations, regardless of initial response	High: Readily adapts to change in schedule, even if there was initial resistance (withdrawal). Low: Actively resists changes in routines over continuing period of time.
Intensity of reaction	How much energy the child puts into responding	High: Reacts intensely—laughs and cries long and hard, resists with vigor. Low: Reacts mildly, smiles rather than laughs, cries softly, passive resistance.
Threshold of responsiveness	How strong external stimulation must be before child responds	High: Does not smile, cry, or get frightened easily. Low: Smiles readily, cries over minor events, is easily frightened.
Quality of mood	Amount of pleasant, friendly behavior compared with amount of unpleasant, unfriendly behavior	High: Characteristically outgoing, friendly; takes pleasure in activities. Low: Characteristically unfriendly; expresses displeasure or dislike of many activities.
Distractibility	Ease with which child can be distracted from ongoing activity, or interrupted	High: Does not concentrate well—other events disrupt activity. Low: Can concentrate on ongoing activity despite interruptions or distractions.
Persistence and attention span	Stick-to-itiveness maintaining an activity despite obstacles	High: Continues activity over time or until finished—a distractible persistent child may be distracted, but will continue to return to original activity until finished. Low: Gives up readily; short attention span.

Source: From *Temperament and Behavior Disorders in Children* by A. Thomas, S. Chess, and H. G. Birch, 1968, New York: New York University Press. Copyright 1968 by New York University Press. Adapted by permission.

The **difficult child** is characterized by the opposite pattern of behaving. Difficult children are moody and intense, react negatively to new people and situations, exhibit frequent expressions of negative moods, sleep poorly, cry often and loudly. **Slow-to-warm-up children** adapt slowly to new situations, are reluctant to participate in activities, and are negative in their moods. Unlike temper tantrum–prone, difficult children, slow-to-warm up children are reluctant to express themselves.

In a study done by Hubert and Wachs (1985), 96 mothers and 46 fathers were asked to temperamentally categorize their 6- to 13-month-old infants and explain why they labeled their children "easy" or "difficult." The parents associations with easiness were good health, normal rate of development, positive responses to stimuli, cuddliness, sociable responses to parents, acceptance of food, positive responses to bathing, cooperativeness, and patience. The opposites of these associations were used to define difficult infants.

Continuity of Infant Temperament Characteristics

The view that temperament is present at birth, rigidly stable across time, and invariant across situations is no longer accepted. Results tend to support a view of temperament as tendencies to show certain behavioral patterns; these tendencies are modulated by situations, occasions, and other dispositions (Goldsmith & Campos, 1990). The definition of temperament, however, implies that some temperament characteristics have a biological basis.

A genetic component for temperament has been observed for emotionality, activity, sociability, impulsivity, and inhibition in children (see Chapter 2). If so, then you would expect these characteristics to be relatively stable over specified developmental periods after their emergence. It should be pointed out that no clear pattern of genetic influence on temperament has been shown in the neonatal period. For the most part, expression of temperament does not become manifest until later in infancy. Genetic influences on temperament increase with increasing age from infancy to early childhood (Riese, 1990; Wilson & Matheny, 1986). Thomas and Chess's (1977) analysis of their data revealed that over the first 10 years of life a remarkable degree of stability in temperament profiles, first observed at 2 months, exists. (Try the "Studying Children" experiment.)

Researchers have found inhibition (tendency to withdraw or show fearfulness in presence of unfamiliar people or objects) to be an important dimension of temperament that is at least partly heritable (Buss & Plomin, 1984; Daniels & Plomin, 1985). Kagan and Moss (1962), found that children's inhibition to the unfamiliar was 1 of 15 infantile behaviors to predict later behavior. Children who were extremely inhibited at age 3 were easily dominated by their peers and were likely to withdraw from social interaction between 3 and 6 years

---

STUDYING CHILDREN

STABILITY IN TEMPERAMENT

Ask your parents how they would have labeled you as a newborn, using Chess's categories of easy, difficult, and slow-to-warm-up. What are their reasons for classifying you as they did? Do you see yourself today as being similar to the classification they gave you as a newborn? If not, why not? If so, in what ways?

---

of age. Between ages 6 and 10, they were still socially timid and, if boys, they avoided sports and other "masculine" activities as adolescents (Kagan, Reznick, Snidman, Gibbons, & Johnson, 1988).

Rothbart (1981) used parental questionnaires and interview methods and assessed parents' perception of their infants' temperament at 3, 6, 9, and 12 months and found a pattern indicating increasing stability of fearfulness, activity level, anger, and smiling and laughing.

Garcia-Coll (1981) filmed the reactions of 21-month-old children to various incentive situations designed to create uncertainty (encounter with stranger, exposure to a robot, separation from mother). Out of a larger sample, she selected 58 children who were either extremely inhibited (withdrawing, clinging to the mother) or extremely uninhibited when presented with these incentives, and had them return 1 month later to be retested in the same situations. The tendency toward inhibition or lack of inhibition was stable over this period.

In addition, 40 of these 58 children were visited at home when they were 31 months old. The children who had been inhibited in the laboratory at 21 months of age were less likely to interact with either of the two female visitors and stayed closer to their mothers during the period of observation. In addition, when observed with an unfamiliar child of the same age who had the opposite behavioral style, the inhibited children remained extremely inhibited with their less inhibited peer.

Broberg, Lamb, and Hwang (1990) examined the continuity of fearfulness in 144 Swedish children. Their results confirm that individual differences in inhibited behavior are stable across the toddler and preschool years. These data suggest that a dimension of extreme inhibition, or fearfulness, in an unfamiliar situation tends to be a salient and stable quality in children.

It is important to note that observed temperamental traits may be instigated by different situations and expressed in different ways as children get older. For example, a child's temperamental trait of fearfulness may be expressed as follows: The child may cry unconsolably when placed on the deep side of the visual cliff at 8 months, cling to mother at 18 months when a jack-in-the-box pops up, and scream on a roller coaster at 8 years. Both the events that elicit fearfulness and the behavior expressing fearfulness change at different points in development, but the child remains high in fearfulness, compared with others of the same age (McCall, 1979).

Activity level has widespread acceptance as a dimension of temperament (Gandour, 1989). A longitudinal study using maternal interviews to as-sess temperament in 137 pairs of twins (6 to 24 months old) found significant stability for activity level and sociability level (cuddling, accepting people, and smiling) (Matheny, Wilson, Dolan, & Krantz, 1981). Korner, Zeanah, Linden, Berkowitz, Kraemer, and Agras (1985) have also found that children's activity level shows a high degree of continuity. Fifty children whose activity level was monitored when they were newborns were monitored again by an ambulatory microcomputer when they were 4 and 8 years old. The researchers found that highly active babies tend to become very active children and inactive babies tend to become inactive children.

Thus, it appears from the research reviewed that some temperamental characteristics, most notably inhibition, fearfulness, activity level, and sociability level, do show some degree of inheritability and stability in children's behavioral actions.

Goodness- or Poorness-of-Fit   Temperamental traits are not immutable. The impact of temperament lies, according to the NYLS group, in whether a particular individual's repertoire provides a **goodness-** or **poorness-of-fit** with the characteris-

Activity level has widespread acceptance as a dimension of temperament and shows considerable stability over time.

tics of a specific context. In other words, the influence of temperament in shaping healthy or unhealthy development and functioning must consider the simultaneous effects of temperament and environment. Goodness-of-fit occurs when the demands and expectations of the environment are consonant with the individual's capacities and characteristics. When this is so, healthy psychological development and functioning is likely. Poorness of fit, on the other hand, results when the individual does not have the capacities or characteristics to cope adequately with environmental demands and expectations. When this is so, excessive stress is likely to occur, and the child or adult becomes at high risk for behavior problem development.

Thus, goodness-of-fit indicates that the meaning of temperament lies not in the child's possession of particular attributes per se, but rather in the extent to which the attributes coincide with contextual demands regarding behavioral style. The stability of temperament characteristics is not inevitable, but rather a function of interaction effects between temperament characteristics and environment. For example, Korn (1978) has presented data indicating that among lower class Puerto Ricans, arhythmicity, characterized by negative mood and high intensity reactions, is highly regarded. Because these temperamental characteristics are perhaps encouraged and reinforced, it is likely that children will exhibit these patterns of behavior and do so for a considerable period of time. These same kinds of behaviors do not fit in the environmental context of children in the white, middle class sample, and therefore may be modified to some extent.

This study also points out that children who have a "difficult" temperament are not necessarily at an elevated risk for later childhood problems. Temperament affects development only in interaction with environmental forces. If the fit between early infant behavior and parental values and expectations is a good one (Puerto Rican parents' positive reactions to "difficult" behavioral styles in their infants), infants are likely to experience optimal development. By contrast, if the parents' values and expectations do not coincide with an infant's temperament style, the child's development may not be optimal (Bates, 1980).

To illustrate, in a study done by Lee and Bates (1985), 111 mothers were asked to assess their infants' temperament at 6 and 13 months. When these children were 2 years old, the researchers observed mother and child interacting in the home setting. They found that mothers who had described their children as difficult were more likely to have conflictual interactions with their children. Mothers who described their children as difficult, compared with those who described their children as easy, tended to use more intrusive control strategies with their children. These 2-year-old difficult children were observed to be more negative or resistant to the mothers' control attempts. The mixed match of mother and infant temperament and a mother's negative perception of her child generates a vicious cycle of negative behavior—fortifying the mother's perception and in turn exacerbating the negative behavior in the child, which may lead to problem behavior at later ages.

Moreover, the degree of match or congruence between the behavioral characteristics of infants with their families may influence the nature of their interactions and the success of their mutual adaptation (Buss & Plomin, 1984). A study done by Sprunger, Boyce, and Gaines (1985) was designed to explore the notion of family-infant congruence using one construct of temperament, rhythmicity. Rhythmicity refers to the degree of predictable regularity in the ongoing daily life of the infant and family. It was found in studying 285 mothers who had infants between the ages of 2 and 13 months, and who had at least one other child, that when an incongruence existed it caused adjustment difficulties. That is, incongruence in rhythmicity (infant more rhythmic than family or family more rhythmic than infant) was a significant predictor of the families' and infants' overall adjustment. When a goodness-of-fit existed between infant and family, the authors reported a success in mutual adaptation between infant and family, mothers perceived their children as less difficult, they experienced a sense of competence, and older siblings were described as more content and happier.

Thus, an important factor contributing to goodness- or poorness-of-fit may be the parents' subjective perceptions, because how one perceives another seems likely to play a role in how one actually interacts with children.

EARLY CHILDHOOD

Interest, joy, physical distress, and disgust expressions appear to be present at or shortly after birth (Izard, 1978; Lewis, 1991). Although the sequence of emotions has yet to be fully articulated, it seems that by 12 months of age, all emotions have appeared. Anger appears at 4 months (Stenberg, Campos, & Emde, 1983). Prior to 4 months, the child is unable to understand the relationship between the cause of a frustration and the response needed to overcome it. For this reason, prior to 4 months frustration does not produce anger, but general distress. Surprise appears by 6 months (Charlesworth, 1969), and given the appropriate eliciting circumstances, surprise, fear, and sadness can be observed in 10-month-old infants (Sullivan & Lewis, 1989).

By the middle of the first year, the undifferentiated emotions that existed at birth have become differentiated. By this time, joy is seen under two conditions: (a) when the child comes in contact with a significant social other, such as the caretaker, mother, father, or other family members; and (b) when the child is able to demonstrate mastery over particular events.

It is not until the middle of the 2nd year that the secondary emotions are observed. These emotions are sometimes called *self-conscious emotions*, for their emergence is dependent on the development of a particular important cognitive capacity: self-awareness. This new class of emotions includes embarrassment, empathy, pride, shame, and envy. In order for these emotions to be felt, children must not only be self-aware, but also a standard of behavior against which the self can evaluate its own action must be understood.

Children reveal considerable growth in talking about emotions between 18 and 24 to 30 months (Bretherton, Fritz, Zahn-Waxler, & Ridgeway, 1986). For example, the findings in one study (Ridgeway, Waters, & Kuczaj, 1985) confirmed that 60% to 90% of 24-month-olds recognize the four basic emotion terms not expressions (happy, sad, mad, and scared), whereas 83% to 97% use them in their own speech by 36 months. Similar age trends would be expected in identifying actual expressions (Stifter & Fox, 1986). The expansion of children's emotion communications parallels the heightened displays of feelings that appear during the late toddler and early preschool period (Kopp, 1989). Temper tantrums are common. Negativism and resistance to adults seem to peak at age 4 (Wenar, 1982), whereas anger, competition, and rivalry increases with peers. Moreover, fears are commonplace at this age.

It appears that children come to understand emotions in the order that these emotions become adaptive in their lives (Izard, 1971). Denham and Couchoud (1990) found in studying 45 preschoolers (26 to 54 months old) that they were more adept at naming happy and sad faces. Distinguishing among negative emotions, especially correctly identifying anger and fear was most difficult for these children. Thus, negative emotions, compared with happiness, were difficult to differentiate at these age levels.

Inferring emotions from facial expressions becomes more differentiated during the preschool years, coming to include anger and surprise (Walden & Field, 1982) as well as excitement, disgust, calm, and sleepy (Russell & Bullock, 1986). Interestingly, young children can more accurately infer the causes of negative emotions than positive ones (Trabasso, Stein, & Johnson, 1981).

Preschool children find it more difficult, however, to combine various cues concerning another's emotional state. For example, their ability to infer emotions by resolving discrepant information from these cues is limited. Sometimes person cues such as facial expressions or behaviors conflict with situational cues (child frowning at a birthday party). In these cases preschoolers prefer person cues (Reichenbach & Masters, 1983).

Preschoolers not only differentiate emotions and have some knowledge about how they function, but they also organize them to some extent. They tend to organize them according to the same dimensions used by adults, that is, pleasure-displeasure and arousal-sleepiness. These categories become more specific and differentiated during later development.

Research has demonstrated that, with increasing age, children's emotional understanding deepens (Nannis, 1988), their lexicon of emotional terms expands, and they make more complex differentiations of the emotions appropriate to different situations (Russell, 1990). The emotions that appear at 5 and 6 years of age have as their immediate cause an evaluation of self. The products of that evaluation lead to emotional reactions to which names like insecurity, inferiority, humility, pride, and confidence are given.

LOVE

The developmental pattern of affection and love appears to follow sequential phases. The emotion of love is first centered on the parents or primary caregivers. Affection and love for parents becomes particularly strong between 9 and 12 months. At this stage, protection and preservation of self appear to be the basic components of children's affection and love. The quality of young children's affection and love is not the same as older children's and adult's love. Young children's love appears to be more demanding and less giving. It is built on the children's needs and the parent's ability to gratify these needs.

Children deprived of love are less able to relate to others; they may even be uncooperative and hostile toward others. Deprivation of love can have serious effects on children's total development. Persons suffering from an inability to give love are characterized as having an impoverished emotional range. They have difficulty experiencing joy, grief, and guilt (Williams & Stith, 1980).

Preschoolers may be quite demonstrative when expressing their affection and love. They jump up and down, clap their hands, give bear hugs, and passionate kisses. As with other emotions, as chil-

dren get older they are often socialized to control these outward manifestations of their affection and love. This may be more true for boys than for girls, for these types of emotional demonstrations may be thought babyish and effeminate.

School-aged children may consider overt expression of love childish and resort to other means of demonstrating affection and love to family and friends. Girls may express affection to friends by holding hands or walking with their arms around each other. Boys demonstrate the same emotion by friendly wrestling and punching each another.

As normal children mature, the second phrase of love appears. Children's affections extend to peers of the same sex and approximately the same age. Affection seems deeply related to children's need to feel a sense of belonging and being accepted by others. All children need love, and during the elementary school years, the need for affection (approval) is apparent. Expressions of affection for friends is evident in their desire to "always" be with their friends, in their secret notes of endearment, in the telephone calls, and so on.

Klein (1989) asked 200 2 1/2- to 6-year-old children whom they loved. Forty percent of the children between the ages of 2 and 3 said their friends; the majority of 3 1/2 to 5-year-olds mentioned names of other children as primary choices for targets of their love; and 55% of the 5- and 6-year-olds chose close friends. Approximately 30% of the children at each of the age levels chose their parents.

The third phase of love is extending affection to persons of the opposite sex. Romantic love differs from the attachment love of infancy and the belonging love of early and middle childhood. In adolescence and young adulthood, the emotion of love is characterized by sexual attraction, intimacy, and the need to be with a particular other. Adolescents commonly label this warm, tingling, exciting feeling they have for someone as love.

ANGER

Although the study of some emotions, such as distress and fear, has been widespread, the study of anger has not. It does seem paradoxical that anger research has been so minimal, because several researchers have reported that anger seems to occur more frequently among children than fear, jealousy, and other emotions (Fabes & Eisenberg, 1992; Izard, 1982). Stapley and Haviland (1989) interviewed 262 children between the ages of 5 and 11 and found that anger was the most commonly experienced negative emotion.

Experiencing anger in moderate and resolute form is not only normal, but also essential. Yet, it appears that early in life children are indoctrinated against being angry (Cummings, Vogel, Cummings, & El-Sheikh, 1989). When children complain of unhappiness or express a positive emotion, people encourage the child to communicate. When children express anger, that is, when they are responding assertively, adults often admonish them or reject them for doing so. Perhaps, anger is taboo in our society because people are afraid of these feelings that may ultimately lead to violence. Violence is anger that has gotten out of control and is expressed with the intent to physically hurt someone.

Causes of Anger   Shortly after the newborn period of infancy, head or limb restraint is apparently an adequate stimulus for extreme distress. The negative reaction comes from blocking the flow of behavior (Stenberg et al., 1983). As children grow older, increasing demands for independence, increasing limitations, and demands for delaying gratification may lead to angry feelings. Early anger reactions may be caused by objection to routine physical habits (dressing and eating), disagreement with peers over possession of toys, loss of possessions, minor physical discomfort, changes in routine, toilet training, arrival of a second baby, and conflict with parents over authority. Inanimate objects may also be elicitors of anger, as when a bottle of milk or a pacifier is situated immediately out of an infant's reach or when a mechanical toy fails to work as a child expects it to.

In younger children, anger is more likely to be reflected in expressions of protest and movement toward a stimulus, often in response to an interruption in an ongoing activity or a failure of events to conform to specific expectations. For example,

Anger seems to be one of the most frequently experienced emotions in children.

children may display anger by shoving a child who has grabbed a toy, or they may throw tantrums when their mother turns off the television, saying that it is time for bed.

A common stimulus to anger in older children is when one's aim or goal is blocked, or the child is restrained from achieving something that she intensely desires. The restraint may be in terms of physical barriers, rules and regulations, or one's own lack of capacity. Older children experience anger when they receive insults, encounter everyday frustrations that block their goal-oriented behavior, are taken advantage of, and are being compelled to do something that goes against their wishes.

Sheviakov (1969) cites the following factors that contribute to older children's anger: lack of love or lack of respect; rigid rules; overburdening the child by excessive demands; lack of informal, friendly communication with children, through which they can express their own true feelings; loneliness—not having a single friend; lying to children; lack of opportunity to experience success; living in fear of parents and teachers; and a grim home or school life that does not include occasional fun and laughter and having a good time with others.

Boys are more likely than girls to use aggressive retaliation and to vent their emotions in response to anger provocation. Girls use coping strategies that maintain social harmony (Fabes & Eisenberg, 1992). As both boys and girls get older, however, there is a shift from wholehearted and violent reactions to a more subdued response. With increasing maturity, children learn to express their anger verbally (Gherman, 1981). By the time children reach school age, most have learned to control overt reactions of anger. Older children's response may take the form of sulking, staring, swearing, and the old silent treatment.

FEAR

Fears come in all sizes, shapes, and intensities. Our responses to fear vary from being mildly timid to being wide-eyed and paralyzed with terror. Not all fears are bad; some fears are good in that they provide a safeguard against harm and disaster. Children's fears help them to be aware of possible dangers. Some fears are reasonable and justifiable within the limits of experience; other fears are unreasonable. Fear of walking across a bridge that looks decrepit and decayed is reasonable; fear of walking across a bridge that is solidly constructed is unreasonable. Fears can mobilize the body for action. Whether the action is purposeful or not depends on many factors, intensity of fear being one factor. Fear, unlike anger, has probably been the subject of scientific investigation more frequently than any other fundamental emotion.

Anxiety and Phobias   **Fear** has been defined as a legitimate response to a tangible threat or danger—a trip to the doctor for shots. It generally has a specific source. What is anxiety then? Although some writers have made no distinction between fear and anxiety (Nietzel & Bernstein, 1981),

others prefer to do so. **Anxiety** refers to a global, undifferentiated emotional reaction, which is brought about by a general situation.

Anxiety is a painful uneasiness of the mind concerning impending or anticipated ills or dangers. The apprehension of danger or disaster in anxiety arises from something within people, from their own conflicting drives and impulses and unresolved problems. Thus, anxiety is a response to a hidden and subjective danger; fear, to an obvious or objective danger (Barrios, Hartmann, & Shigetomi, 1981). Anxiety is closely related to fear, but it is a fear of a vague object or no object at all. Fears of insecurity, deprivation, neglect, or loss of affection may lead to an uneasy feeling—a tension state called anxiety.

Phobias have been regarded as a special form of fear that is out of proportion to the demands of the situation, cannot be reasoned away, is beyond voluntary control, and leads to avoidance of the feared situation (Knopf, 1979). Phobias disrupt a child's adjustment and go far beyond the potential harm or threat.

School phobia is the irrational dread of some aspect of the school situation accompanied by physiological symptoms of anxiety or panic when attendance is imminent, resulting in a partial or total inability to go to school. These children tend to have average IQs and perform satisfactorily in the academic setting. They are more dependent, anxious, immature, and depressed than nonphobic children. They also tend to have an increase in other behavior problems such as eating disorders, enuresis, anxious, or hysterical reactions.

The three most frequently mentioned etiologies for school phobia are: fear of separation from mother, lack of confidence, and an unrealistically high self-image that magnifies any threat of failure. Their own self-reports express frequent fears, such as that something will happen to their mothers while they are in school, being ridiculed by peers, and fear of failure in school. The prognosis is generally good; 83% of phobic children return to school. Many of these studies, however, fail to consider subsequent relapses or the appearance of other school problems.

What Causes Fear in Children? Anything that weakens children or lowers their self-confidence may make them more subject to fear. The tendency to be afraid may be increased by a weakened condition due to illness or being tired. Lack of familiarity, competition, or loss of affection may cause fear, in addition to many circumstances that belittle children, humiliate them, and make them feel guilty, worthless, or reprehensible. While still at an age when they are dependent on their parents, children may be troubled by any sign of fear or weakness their parents may show. Many of children's fears are the same as those of their parents.

Sudden, intense stimuli confronting children will produce a fear reaction. The cause of fear may be either the presence of something threatening or the absence of something that provides safety and security. The causes of fear are influenced by their contexts, by individual differences in temperament, and by experience, or person-environment interactions. The threshold of fear, like that of any other emotion, is influenced by biologically based individual differences, idiosyncratic experiences, and the total sociocultural context of the occasion. Being alone, strangeness, sudden approach, sudden change of stimuli, and pain are conditions that tend to increase the probability of fear. Finally, the causes of fear are, in part, a function of age or maturation (Bauer, 1976).

Developmental Sequence of Fears According to the research literature, incidences of fear are not widely observed in the first months of life, except for loss of support and loud noises. Fear reactions to masks make their first appearance during the last half of the 1st year of life. Scarr and Salapatek (1970) found that between 20% and 40% of infants younger than 7 months of age exhibited fear of masks. Separation anxiety emerges around 8 to 9 months, reaches a peak at the beginning of the 2nd year, and then gradually disappears toward the end of the 2nd year (Weinraub & Lewis, 1977). Fear of strangers emerges at around 6 to 12 months and expressions of fear in general increase steadily. Fear reactions have been observed in infants around 8 months of age when they were placed on the visual cliff (fear of depth).

Preschool children tend to fear animals, the dark, imaginary creatures, separation from parents, sudden, intense stimuli, and loud noises (Lewis, Sullivan, Stanger, & Weiss, 1989). Fear reactions appear to be limited to situations that threaten their immediate physical security. (Separation from mother is an important source of anxiety in the young child.)

Bowlby (1973) has cited four situations that can be observed to arouse fear in the first 5 years of life: noise and situations associated with noise, sudden change of illumination and sudden, unexpected movement, the approach of an object, and height; strange people and familiar people in strange guise, strange objects and strange places; animals; and darkness, especially being alone in the dark.

When children from 24 to 71 months were studied, it was found that they had an average of 4.6 fears (Jersild, 1968). As Table 13.2 shows, Jersild calculated the percentage of children who demonstrated specific fears within the experimental setting. The results show that some fears increase with age (fear of the dark, large dog, strange person) and some are highly variable (fear of snakes).

Because of their interactions in the expanding social world, children in this period have fears that relate to social stress: fear of school, fear of failure, fear of losing friends, fear of not being promoted. These fears seem to be associated with the development of understanding the idea of competition and standards set by others, and the growth of a capacity for self-criticism. Fears of imaginary creatures, "bogeymen," witches, the dark, and being alone are also common.

Adolescents tend to fear snakes, accidents, high places, being alone at home, the unknown, burglars, the future, the present-day world, hospitals, and what happens after death. Fears of physical harm, bodily danger, illness and disease, personal safety, and incapacity are fears that tend to increase or remain strong through the various age levels of adolescence (Morris & Kratochwill, 1983). Also fears related to social relations, reprobation, and ridicule remain strong in adolescence. And,

TABLE 13.2 Children's Fears in Various Experimental Situations	PERCENTAGE OF CHILDREN SHOWING FEAR			
Situation	24–35 Months	36–47 Months	48–59 Months	60–71 Months
Being left alone	12.1	15.6	7.0	0.0
Falling boards	24.2	8.9	0.0	0.0
Dark room	46.9	51.1	35.7	0.0
Strange person	31.3	22.2	7.1	0.0
High boards	35.5	35.6	7.1	0.0
Loud sound	22.6	20.0	14.3	0.0
Snake	34.8	55.6	42.9	30.8
Large dog	61.9	42.9	42.9	0.0

Source: Reprinted by permission of the publisher from Jersild, A., & Holmes, F.B., Children's Fears, *Child Development Monographs*, no. 20, 1935. (New York: Teachers College Press, © 1935 by Teachers College, Columbia University. All rights reserved.), 'An Experimental Study of the Fears of Young Children' p. 237.

fears related to economic and political matters (war, present-day situation) are common (Bamber, 1979). "Studying Children" offers an activity for helping you learn more about fears in middle childhood and adolescence.

JEALOUSY

Jealousy is a universal emotion and is thought to be unavoidable (Buhrmester & Furman, 1990). The origin and handling of this emotion bears mentioning. The discussion of jealousy will be primarily concerned with jealousy between siblings, which will be defined here as one sibling's resentful suspicion of another sibling or that sibling's influence.

Jealousy actually has two faces, one of which is a sign of love—a side of jealousy that is sometimes neglected, but is extremely important. It indicates that jealousy includes a positive evaluation of, an attachment, or commitment to the person one is jealous over or about. One can be jealous only of something that is highly valued. The second face of jealousy is fear of loss. In jealousy, there is always a rival, actual or imagined, and the loss of something is experienced as a loss *to* someone else. At the center of jealousy is fear of loss, fear of alienation of affections, and insecurity (Dunn & Kendrick, 1980).

Each child wants a good share of parental love, attention, and affection. It is not an unnatural reaction for children to want to be the most important, to be the best, and to come first. When children feel that they are not getting the lion's share of parental love and understanding, their disadvantaged feeling causes them to feel jealous.

The desire to be the mother's "one and only" is so strong that it tolerates no rivals. It hurts to share the mother's love. Sharing anything, to most children, simply means getting less of it, and is charged with feelings of resentment, jealousy, and love. Children cannot understand that their parents have enough love to encompass more than one child. The prospect of sharing is bad enough, but parental expectations that children should be happy and overjoyed at the arrival of a new sibling is beyond their logic. "Focus on Applications" discusses jealousy in firstborn, second, and middle children.

STUDYING CHILDREN

FEARS

How do children tend to deal with their fears? Is there a difference between the way children in middle childhood and adolescence cope with their fears? Choose two or three children between the ages of 8 and 11, and two or three adolescents and ask them some of their common fears and how they deal with them. Do fears tend to become less concrete and more abstract in adolescence?

FOCUS ON APPLICATIONS

Jealousy Between Siblings

As a general rule, jealousy exists more in firstborn children than in others that follow (Abramovitch, Corter, & Pepler, 1981). Perhaps this is because firstborns are the only ones to have had their parents' love and attention all to themselves for a period of time, and consequently it is more difficult for them to share these priceless possessions with other siblings. The beginning of jealousy feelings may occur when mother and father bring home the second child, the intruder.

The arrival of the second child means a lot of changes around the house. Dunn and Kendrick (1980) studied the interaction between mother and firstborn children in 41 families before and after the birth of a second child, using home observations and interview techniques. With the arrival of the sibling, most children in the sample studied experienced a decrease in maternal playful attention, an increase in confrontation, and a decrease in their mothers' initiating conversations with verbal games.

Parental expectations and demands toward the firstborn child are raised and increased, which brings about another problem older children face: losing their dependency. Parents generally begin to demand more independent behaviors and are a little less tolerant of their firstborn's dependency. Parents have a lot more to do after the arrival of the second child and simply don't have the time to be overly accommodating and indulgent. Jealousy arises out of this dependence and the feeling of being deprived by someone else. Younger children are always enjoying what older children have had to relinquish. Although they may recognize the advantages and privileges of being older, they also want the advantages and privileges of being "the baby." Firstborn children resent the loss of whatever helpless, baby behaviors they enjoyed and may attempt to hold on to these previous behavior patterns that they associate pleasantly with dependency.

Second-born children feel envious of the firstborn's skills. They encounter the situation of having a sibling who is always ahead of them. Sometimes they try to copy the firstborn, and if they cannot do as well, they tend to feel resentful, inferior, and defeated. More often than not, however, second-born children develop their competencies and skills in areas of achievement different from those of their older sibling. The second-born's personality tends to differ from the firstborn's. Second-borns often become what their older sibling is not; they may become bold or shy, authoritarian or submissive, good at sports or bookworms, neatniks, or careless.

Middle children occupy a more complicated position, for they do not carry the strength or privileges of the oldest child, nor do they reap the advantages of being the youngest. The second-born is likely to feel a rivalry with the older child, who has more privileges and freedom and is likely to be jealous of the younger sibling who has displaced him or her. Middle children's lack of status may cause them to feel neglected or squeezed out. The oldest child is praised for accomplishment and the baby is always stimulating ohs and ahs. Life is just unfair. They may maintain their middle-of-the-road status, or they may succeed in pushing both competitors down and gain superiority over both of them.

All people harbor some jealous feelings. A certain amount of jealousy is normal, but not in its extreme forms. It becomes debilitating when children are overloaded and constantly preoccupied with jealous feelings. As a result, they suffer from poor self-images, cannot form good peer relationships, and their school work is mediocre.

Jealousy Wears Many Masks Jealousy comes in a thousand assorted disguises. It may show itself indirectly in overly dependent behavior, regressive behavior, or in constant demands for material objects and possessions. Jealous children may try to degrade and tear down others with criticisms in order to elevate themselves. They may become energetically obstinate, try to spoil the fun of others, or restrict another's freedom (Stocker, Dunn, & Plomin, 1989). Jealous children may brood and build unhealthy feelings toward themselves and resentment, anger, and hostility toward others. Repressed feelings of jealousy may express themselves in physical disorders (skin rashes, chronic coughing, minor infections, frequent colds) or nervous habits (nail biting, pulling one's hair). An obvious form of jealousy is striving for power and superiority. Jealous children feel that they have to show everyone that they are terrific; they are constantly pushing themselves in competitive situations in their attempts to outdo others. Or, they may totally shun competition and continually take a submissive back seat.

MIDDLE CHILDHOOD

Another dimension of children's emotional development of concern that has recently received a great deal of empirical attention is the study of stress. **Stress** is a feeling of high emotional tension that individuals experience when they encounter an event or situation that is perceived by them as a threat to their existence and well-being. These environmental forces or events, called **stressors,** make individuals feel that they lack adequate coping strategies. They can be physical, such as walking on a long, hot road in the desert, or psycho-

logical, such as working for a temperamental boss. Stress has three components: the *reaction* to an *event* and the *perception* of the event. In other words, children and adults interpret the events and situations in their lives as good, bad, neutral, terrible, great (Armacost, 1989).

PERCEPTION OF STRESS

People's perception or cognitive appraisal of life events strongly influence their response (Lazarus & Launier, 1978). A particular event may be perceived by different individuals as irrelevant, benign, positive, or threatening and harmful. Hence, it is highly likely that children's primary cognitive appraisal of the positive or negative meaning of a particular life event will determine whether it is experienced as stressful. As Garmezy and Rutter (1983) say,

> The individual engages in cognitive appraisal of an event, interprets it as threatening or nonthreatening in terms of his or her capacity to deal with it and only when a disparity is found to exist between the demand of the situation and the individual's ability to meet that demand is the stress-induced response with its marked emotional component activated. (p. 47)

There is a hypothetical story involving two sons whose father was an alcoholic. One of the sons followed in his father's footsteps; the other never drank. When the sons were asked about their drinking habits, each replied, "With an old man like that, what do you expect!" This story may illustrate one of the more salient points that can be concluded from stress research. That is, it may not be *what* people face, but how they *interpret* what they face that really matters.

Pinpointing stress events in children's lives is difficult. You just can't say simply that negative things produce stress in children, for what you tend to think of as negative events or situations may not be perceived at all that way by children. It is possible, for example, that divorce, not making the team, or moving could be viewed by children as positive. (Not making the team may mean that a boy won't have to suffer the nightly harassments

It's difficult to pinpoint stressful events in children's lives. Moving, for example, may not be perceived by some children as stressful.

from his father for a poor performance in the game.) Therefore, you must keep in mind that children's perceptions of events determine whether situations are considered stressful or not.

CONSEQUENCES OF STRESS

Selye (1956/1976) defined stress as the "nonspecific response of the body in any demand," and drew a distinction between **eustress,** a positive force that is the equivalent of finding excitement and challenge in life, and **distress,** the destructive form of stress (p. 74). Many persons associate the term *stress* with *distress,* and think only of the negative consequences. Selye was one of the first to explore the physiological effects of negative stress. He points out that people react to stress in three stages: the alarm reaction, the stage of resistance and the stage of exhaustion. The three stages are called the **General Adaptation Syndrome,** or G.A.S.

The *alarm reaction,* the first stage, involves the organism's reaction when it is suddenly exposed to stimuli to which it is not adapted. It is the "call to arms" of the body's defenses. For example, in the case of a physical stressor, think of the shock you experience when you dive into a cold lake; or, in the case of a psychological stressor, the first day you meet your boss.

The *stage of resistance* is the period when the organism "adapts" to the stressor. After being in the lake for a few minutes, the water feels less cold. As soon as your body adjusts, you find the water to be quite refreshing. Likewise, the longer you work for your boss, the "easier" it seems to adjust to his tirades. Sufficient exposure to any noxious elements (severe cold of the lake water or nagging boss) leads to the third phase.

The third phase is the *stage of exhaustion,* which occurs when adaptive energies are depleted and physical breakdown occurs. Sooner or later your body feels cold again, and you begin to shiver; the stage of resistance is wearing off, and the stage of exhaustion is imminent. You now can no longer produce heat to offset its loss in the water; the wastes in the cells of your muscles are beginning to accumulate, resulting in muscle aches and tiredness. Or, in dealing with your tyrannical boss, each day that you go to work you may find that you have a headache or feel depressed and tired. You may be constantly suffering from some minor physical ailment, such as a cold or the flu.

ADAPTATION ENERGY

The body's adaptability, or one's *adaptation energy* is finite. That is, people are born with a limited amount of it. Experiments on animals have shown that exposure to stressors can be tolerated only so long. It still is not known precisely what is lost, but something must be, or else, given enough food, the body would be able to resist forever. Selye (1980) points out,

> After exhaustion from excessively stressful activity, sleep and rest can restore resistance and adaptability almost to previous levels, but the emphasis here is on *almost.* Just as any machine eventually wears out even if it has enough fuel, so the human body sooner or later becomes the victim of constant wear and tear. (p. 129)

Long-term exposure to a stressor, or not being able to cope adequately, depletes adaptive reserves and leads to physical dysfunction. When adaptive reserves are depleted, the organism enters a stage of exhaustion. At this point, resistance declines, physiological breakdown occurs, and the body becomes highly susceptible to disease.

STRESS AND ILLNESS

Unremitting stress can break down the body's protective mechanisms. Therefore, when people are run down, they are far more likely to catch an illness that, in peak condition, could usually be resisted. Potentially pathogenic microbes are in and around all the time; yet they cause no disease until people are exposed to stress. In this case, the illness is due neither to the microbe nor to the stress, but to the combined effect of both. In most instances, disease is not due to the germ itself or to our adaptive reactions, but to the inadequacy of reactions to the germ. No disease is caused merely by maladaptation to stress.

Similarly, many of you have probably read about Type A and Type B personality patterns, and that Type A behavior patterns are linked to coronary heart disease as an adult. Type A personalities are characterized by aggressiveness, easily aroused hostility, a sense of time urgency, and competitive achievement. In contrast, Type B personalities are noncompetitive, relaxed, easygoing, and enjoy leisure. Recent research has convincingly shown that Type A behavior per se does not lead to heart attacks, but rather, the crucial component in Type A personalities is negative emotions, especially the anger associated with aggressively reactive personalities (Friedman & Booth-Kewley, 1988; Matthews, 1988). Now that the association between adult Type A behavior and coronary heart disease has been documented, researchers have begun to turn their attention to the study of the developmental antecedents of the behavior pattern, with an eye toward understanding the childhood origins.

One line of research (Matthews, 1979; Matthews & Volkin, 1981) has demonstrated that children do exhibit Type A behavior patterns. Children categorized as Type A tend to exhibit competitive achievement striving; they tend to be impatient and easily aroused to anger. However, demonstrating that there exist Type A children is one thing, demonstrating that these children grow up to be Type A adults is another. Steinberg (1985b) examined the developmental antecedents of Type A behavior. In particular, he examined the role of early childhood temperament in the development of adult, Type A behaviors. The subjects of this study were drawn from a sample of 133 individuals, now young adults, who comprised the core sample of the ongoing NYLS. The sample consisted of white, middle and upper middle class children. The data presented in this report included measures of temperament derived from interviews conducted with children's mothers when the children were 3 and 4 years old and from measures of Type A behaviors derived from interviews with participants themselves as young adults (age

21 years). The results suggest that certain temperamental attributes, identifiable in early childhood, may predispose individuals toward the development of the Type A pattern.

Several specific dimensions of temperament stood out as being especially predictive of Type A behaviors: For both males and females, achievement striving was associated with high adaptability, negative mood, high approach, and low rhythmicity during early childhood. Impatience-anger in both genders, had as its antecedents low sensory threshold, low persistence, and low adaptability. It is easy to imagine youngsters who have a low threshold for stimulation, have difficulty being persistent, and adapt poorly to new situations as impatient, irritable, and easily angered adults. Some caution should be noted in generalizing these results because the sample was a very homogenous, middle and upper middle class group. Thus, the results may only be applicable to populations of individuals whose socioeconomic backgrounds are similar.

COMMON STRESSORS

What stress could children have? It is often assumed they couldn't possibly experience stress the same way adults do. How can you equate an adult's stress over divorcing a spouse with a child's stress over being shunned by an ex-best friend? Adults should not judge troubles by their size, but by the size of the pain they produce. These pains may be as great for children as the pains adults experience.

Holmes and Rahe (1967) focused their experimental investigations on stressors in adults. After having identified the common ones, they developed the *Social Readjustment Scale* to measure normal life stress. Their research found that anyone with a score of 300 or above on the stress scale is likely to get sick. Miller (1982) has revised the Holmes and Rahe scale to fit situations in the life of a child (see Table 13.3).

As Miller (1982) points out,

Totaling the score, you may be surprised to find how quickly an average child can reach the 300 level of severe stress potential. Changes occur rapidly in his life, far more rapidly than in the

---

STUDYING CHILDREN

STRESS

Choose four children between the ages of 8 and 12 and give them the following list of 20 items. Have the children rank these items from 1 to 20, 1 being the most stressful, 20 the least stressful. What items do children rank as the most stressful? When Medeiros, Porter, and Welch (1983) did this study, their subjects ranked the first in order of the most stressful event to the least, just the way that they are listed here. Mix the items around and present the list to the children. Do they tend to rank the items the same as Medeiros et al.'s subjects?

1. losing a parent
2. going blind
3. being held back a year in school
4. wetting your pants in school
5. hearing parents quarrel
6. being caught stealing
7. being suspected of lying
8. receiving a bad report card
9. being sent to the principal's office
10. having an operation
11. getting lost
12. being made fun of in class
13. moving to a new school
14. having a scary dream
15. not getting 100 on a test
16. being picked last for the team
17. losing in a game
18. going to the dentist
19. giving a report in class
20. acquiring a baby sibling

Source: Based on *Children under Stress* (pp. 11–12) by D. C. Medeiros, B. J. Porter, and L. D. Welch, 1983, Englewood Cliffs, NJ: Prentice-Hall.

---

life of his parents. Six hours of school alone subjects him to Life Events 8, 10, 15, 18, 22, 25, 27, 31, 33, 40, and 42 almost on a routine basis. In addition, the ups and downs of his social life add the stress of Life Events 13, 17, 32, 35, 36, 39, 41. He is far more susceptible to personal injury because of the high percentage of his time spent in physical activities. (p. 23)

Selye (1956/1976) lists 11 stress areas for adults: job, human relations, climate, crowding, boredom, loneliness, captivity, relocation, urbaniza-

TABLE 13.3 Childhood Stress	
Life Event	**Value**
1. Death of parent	100
2. Divorce of parents	73
3. Separation of parents	65
4. Parent's jail term	63
5. Death of close family member	63
6. Personal injury or illness	53
7. Parent's remarriage	50
8. Suspension or expulsion from school	47
9. Parents' reconciliation	45
10. Long vacation (summer)	45
11. Parent or sibling sickness	44
12. Mother's pregnancy	40
13. Anxiety over sex	39
14. Birth of new baby (or adoption)	39
15. New school or classroom	39
16. Money problems at home	38
17. Death (or moving away) of friend	37
18. Change in studies	36
19. More quarrels with parents	35
20. Not applicable to a child	
21. Not applicable to a child	
22. Change in school responsibilities	29
23. Sibling going away to school	29
24. Family arguments with grandparents	29
25. Winning school or community awards	28
26. Mother going to work or stopping work	26
27. School beginning or ending	26
28. Family's living standard changing	25
29. Change in personal habits—for example, bedtime, homework, and so on	24
30. Trouble with parents—lack of communication, hostility	23
31. Change in school hours, schedules	20
32. Family's moving	20
33. A new school	20
34. New sports, hobbies, family recreation activities	19
35. Change in church activities—more involved or less	19
36. Change in social activities—new friends, loss of old ones, peer pressure	18
37. Change in sleeping habits—staying up later, giving up nap, and so on	16
38. Change in number of family get-togethers	15
39. Change in eating habits—going on or off diet, new way of family cooking	15
40. Vacation	13
41. Christmas	12
42. Breaking home, school, or community rules	11

Source: From *Child-Stress* (pp. 22–23) by Mary Susan Miller, 1982, New York: Doubleday.

tion, catastrophe, and anxiety. In Table 13.4, these adult stress areas are applied to children.

What are some other common stressors for children? "Studying Children" discusses an activity that will help you learn more about what stresses children.

When children with just one stressor in their lives were studied they did not appear any different from children with no presumed stress in their lives (Garmezy & Rutter, 1983). When stressors increased to two, however, the risk of stress increased 4 times (Work, Parker, & Cowen, 1990).

TABLE 13.4   Children and Stress

JOB (SCHOOL FOR CHILDREN)
Lack of ability to read is a major stressor for children. School is also a place where test anxiety is learned. In a typical school day, the child experiences a great deal of stress in terms of academics, sports, peer relations, and teacher interactions.

HUMAN RELATIONS
Children have many relationships to juggle in the course of their day. Further, children take these relations intensely—running the gamut of love, hate, anger, and envy.

CLIMATE
Children, and adults react to changes in the weather. Teachers have reported that schools are louder on rainy days, that children are uncontrollable on gray and gloomy days, and that more work is completed on sunny days.

CROWDING
Children feel stress when they don't have any private space for themselves. As with adults, children need to be away from the crowd from time to time.

BOREDOM
"I have nothing to do. I'm bored." Is there a child who has never said that? Schools can be tedious and boring. Being at home with no one to play with is boring. Children do experience their share of boredom.

LONELINESS
The sense of not belonging, of being an outsider with no friends is a big source of stress to children.

RELOCATION
It isn't just moving that causes stress, but often children cannot do anything about it. Dad's new job means a new place to live, and the child must simply go along with the parent's decision. Relocation can also mean changing classrooms every period, having new teachers with every class change. This can produce stress in some children.

URBANIZATION
With increasing urbanization it may be more difficult for children to find a place to fly a kite or ride a bike.

CATASTROPHE
A failed test, the death of a pet, being ridiculed by a teacher can all be major catastrophes to a child.

ANXIETY OR UNCERTAINTY
The uncertainty of the future in a nuclear age, unsettled racial and religious wars, a struggling economy may all be potential stressors to children.

FAMILY SITUATION
Of course, the child's family may be a major stressor. Arguing parents, divorce, loss or separation from parents, rejection by parents, verbal and physical abuse are all major stressors.

Source: From "The Stress Concept Today" by H. Selye, 1980, in I. Kutash (Ed.), *Handbook on Stress and Anxiety.* San Francisco: Jossey-Bass.

The figures look like this: If children have zero or one stressor in their lives, then the chance of psychological problems is about 1%. If children have two stressors, then the chance of psychological problems increases to 5%. If children have four stressors, the chances of psychological problems increase to 20% (see Figure 13.2). One conclusion from this research is that whatever can be done to alleviate stress in children should be done.

dren learn to meet the demands of the outside world, can teach them how they must behave in order to be accepted by others, and can stimulate each child's creative interests. A little conflict helps children learn to share, compete, achieve, and respect the rights, privileges, and property of other people.

Some friction between siblings is common and natural. Gradually, the time will come when siblings will live together on better terms. Buhrmester and Furman (1990) found in studying 363 3rd- to 12th-graders that as children get older their relationships typically become less intense and less conflictual. In fact, many 12th-graders reported having a warm and close relationship with their older siblings.

Learning to get along with each other may be due, in part, to children's changing conception of

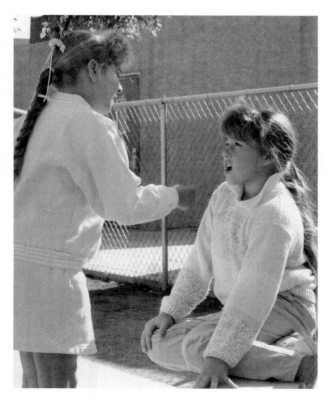

Friction between siblings is generally a big thorn in most parents' sides.

love. Younger children tend to have a quantum view of love, that is, the amount of love any individual has is limited. If someone you love also loves someone else, that must mean that there is less love for you. The love for another is given at our expense. This is the presumption of a jealous child (and adult). Gradually many children learn that parental love is not a quantity but a quality, and that the love they previously enjoyed is not taken away by the arrival of brothers and sisters. This is a difficult concept to learn, however, and often it is not mastered until late in childhood (Rorty, 1980). Thus, the following guidelines may help parents help their children to live together more harmoniously.

Focus on the Positive   It is necessary for parents to focus on the positive aspects of sibling relationships. By doing so, parents build strong emotional bonds between siblings. For example, older children, at times, may protect, teach, and be a companion to their younger siblings. Abramovitch, Corter, and Lando (1979) found when observing 36 pairs of mixed-sex siblings in their homes (younger siblings averaged 20 months of age and the interval between siblings was either large (2.5–3.5 years) or small (1–2 years), that older siblings initiated 65% of the prosocial behaviors (explaining, taking turns, offering a toy). So although it may seem that they are fighting all the time, siblings do have moments of playing well together. It is at these times that we should take notice.

Don't Be a Referee   In conflict situations between siblings, it is quite common for the youngest to flee to the parent for protection. When the second born comes to parents with cries of fright, parents may react by punishing the older child. After all, they are bigger, stronger, older, and should be able to control themselves. Eventually, in any situation in which an aggressive action takes place, parents punish their eldest and perhaps give a more lenient admonishment or do nothing at all to the younger child, the underdog.

Younger children, being smaller and more helpless, soon use these attributes to their advantage. They become the "subtle antagonist." They develop their own devices for getting back at their older sibling and do anything (just as long as what they do is not noticed by mother) to provoke their older sibling. Each child learns what irks the other child the most, and each delights in doing just those things.

To illustrate, in a study done by Dunn and Munn (1985), six families were observed when the second born was aged 14, 16, 18, 21, and 24 months. At each of these ages, two home observations of 1 hour were made 1 week apart. The experimenters observed that the younger children, with increasing frequency, showed pragmatic understanding of how to annoy the older siblings. As the authors point out,

> They not only perceived what would upset the sibling but also acted upon this understanding. The form of the teasing became more elaborate during the second year. At 16 and 18 months most instances of teasing involved removal of the older child's comfort object. By 24 months, however, one child was teasing her sibling by pretending to "be" her imaginary friend. (p. 485)

Although older children cannot be allowed to physically abuse a younger sibling, parents can try not to attack their personalities by labeling them as mean or bad people. Parents can still protect their younger children without giving the older children the feeling that they are not loved. Older children should be allowed to express their feelings, and adults should help their children feel that they understand these feelings.

As children get older, there is less need for parents to intervene. The older children should learn more control and resort less to physical attacks, and younger children become less helpless and more capable of protecting themselves. It is quite common that if parents are still playing the role of referee when their children are older, it is because children's fighting and quarreling behaviors serve a purpose, mainly to keep caregivers occupied with them. Fighting annoys caregivers and makes them stop whatever they are doing so that they can come in and settle matters. A good brawl always brings caregivers to the scene. It is a good, effective means of keeping their attention.

Whenever possible then, stay out of fights. Step out of children's problems. By being aware of this principle, caregivers will no longer feel compelled to be annoyed. When adults interfere, children learn nothing about how to resolve conflicts on their own. Whenever parents take sides, one child is the winner and the other becomes the loser. The loser then tries to get even with the winner. Thus, as soon as one fight is over, another is brewing.

Understand Your Own Feelings Adults can minimize their children's jealous feelings by taking a look at their own feelings about their children. Unwittingly, a parent's past experiences may influence how children are treated. Parents who were middle children, for example, and felt cheated out of parental privileges or indulgences, may show favoritism toward their middle child. If babies of the family shows certain characteristics that parents possess, they may be unconsciously overemphasizing these qualities. Danger develops when parents, as a result of their past experiences and present needs, give preferential or punishing treatment to one of their children.

Treat Children as Individuals Older and younger children should not be treated alike. Sometimes parents, in their zeal to be fair and just, forget that older children should be given privileges and responsibilities commensurate with their age. Older children should be allowed to stay up a little later, or ride their bike a little further from home, or receive a little more allowance than their younger siblings. These same privileges will be accorded the younger children when they get older. As a result, younger children will look forward to growing up.

Avoid Comparisons In some homes, children are constantly being judged and pushed by comparisons between siblings. "Why aren't you neat like your sister!" "I wish you would eat as well as your older brother." Comparisons of brothers and sisters is one of the most frequent causes of jealousy between siblings. It grows when favoritism, comparisons, or lack of respect for individuality are present.

Arrival of the Baby Although there are no studies that examine the value of preparing a child for the new arrival, it seems to make sense that such a preparation may help the child to be more accepting of and perhaps less jealous of the new baby. In announcing the arrival of the new baby, adults should tell the older child a short while in advance and avoid long, false explanations. No matter how well you prepare children for the arrival of the baby, however, and how clearly children seem to understand what the arrival will mean, as Anna Freud (1958) pointed out, children may easily be emotionally overwhelmed by the real event. You should recognize, after all, that even as adults you may be rationally prepared for a change, yet devastated by the experience of that change.

It is generally good advice to avoid saying that you will love both children equally. If adults say this, children will probably devote most of their time testing the parent's "equal love." More often than not, if their testing behaviors are negative (and they usually are), they will prove the parent wrong. It is better to explain to children that no one ever loves two people in the same way. We love people for different reasons. In this way, adults set the stage for explaining that their response to the new baby and to the older child will be different.

COPING WITH STRESS

Coping has been defined as "efforts to manage [that is, master, tolerate, reduce, minimize] environmental demands and conflicts that tax or exceed a person's resources" (Lazarus & Launier, 1978, p. 311). These researchers suggest that "the ways people cope with stress [may be] even more important to overall moral, social functioning and health/illness than the frequency and severity of episodes of stress themselves" (p. 308).

Most forms of stress do not constitute a short-term single stimulus but a rather complex set of changing conditions that have a past history and a future (Mechanic, 1978). Hence, adaptation or coping needs to be considered as a process extending over time.

Selye (1956/1976) has mentioned four ways in which individuals can learn to cope with stress: First, they can remove the stressor. A child who is stressed by the fifth-grade bully who is always beating him up may learn the "art of self-defense" and thus remove the stress of being victimized. Second, they can refuse to allow neutral situations to become stressors. A child who has a long term paper to write can plan ahead by deciding what steps need to be completed on a daily basis in order to get the paper competed on time. In this way,

By helping children develop a sense of control over events in their lives, such as preparing for a book report well in advance, we can help children deal more effectively with stress.

the child can keep a neutral event neutral and avoid the hysteria of having to write the paper in 2 days. Third, they can deal directly with the stress. A child can try to manipulate or alter his relationship to the stressful situation. The boy being victimized by the bully can think of different routes to and from school, so the bully is unable to find him. And finally, they can find ways of relaxing to ease the tension of stress. Children can ride bikes, climb trees, dance, exercise, and engage in various hobbies and sports to relieve stress.

You can help children learn to cope with stress by helping them develop their self-confidence, learn to delay gratification, see themselves as individuals and become feeling individuals—in touch with themselves and with others (Altshuler & Ruble, 1989). Moreover, you can help them to be more open to change and novelty (Garmezy & Tellegen, 1984). Encourage them to engage in as many different types of activities as possible; praise them in more than one area—school, friends, chores, sports, and so on. Children are better able to cope with stress when they feel that they have some control over their lives. Praise children for trying; give them tasks or chores that are commensurate with their abilities; allow them some choice in family decisions. As Selye (1980) said, "Though internal and external factors influence or even determine some responses, we do have control over ourselves. It is the exercise of this control, or lack of it, that can decide whether we are made or broken by the stress of life" (p. 143).

Faced with life stresses, many children develop psychological difficulties, while others function well. Children in the latter group have been labeled *resilient* or *stress resistant*, and defy expectation by developing into well-adapted individuals. The primary aim of a recent investigation by Luthar (1991) was to explore variables that promote resilience. The sample consisted of 144 inner-city ninth-grade students, with a mean age of 15.3 years. Stress was operationalized by scores on a negative life events scale. Personality variables explored in this study included intelligence, locus of control, and social skills (warmth, spontaneity, and expressiveness). Both locus of control and social skills were significant in protecting against stress. Intelligence, however, rather than being a protective in the face of stress was involved as a vulnerability mechanism. That is, at low levels of stress, intelligence was positively related to competence for school grades as well as classroom assertiveness. When stress was high, on the other hand, the intelligent children appeared to lose their advantage and demonstrated competence levels more similar to those of less intelligent children.

It has been suggested that more intelligent children tend to have higher levels of sensitivity to their environments. This greater sensitivity might account for the higher susceptibility to stressors of brighter children as compared with those who are less intelligent.

REVIEW OF KEY POINTS

Emotions are composed of cognitive interpretations and physiological changes. Many theorists today believe that your interpretation of the stimulus incident plays a critical role in determining how you physiologically react, what affective state you experience, and how you respond. Two powerful hormones are responsible for the physical changes you experience during emotions: Adrenaline causes the heart to beat faster, constricts the blood vessels, and shuts down the digestive system. Noradrenaline decreases heart beat, dilates blood vessels, and facilitates digestion.

Emotional development theories are similar in that they all point out that emotions develop from general reactions to specific reactions; later emotions develop from earlier precursors. There is an orderly unfolding of emotions and there is increasing patterning and flexibility of emotional reactions in the course of development. Sroufe's elaboration of Bridges' theory adds some insight into the cognitive achievements, which may explain the qualitative emotional changes we observe. The alternative model as to how discrete emotional states are developed is presented by Izard, who maintains that infants are endowed at birth with already differentiated, discrete emotional states. The timing of their appearance is related to the infant's social experience and the level of cognitive development. Bowlby's theory emphasizes the central role that attachment relationships play in the regulation of affect.

Young infants are able to react to human facial and vocal displays, imitate emotional expressions, and engage in affective communicate with their parents. At about 1 year of age, children use social referencing, which involves using the affective expressions of others to evaluate an external event. Social referencing appears to be an important source by which infants gain information about how to deal with ambiguous events. It also seems to have unsuspectedly powerful consequences in regulating behavior. It was pointed out when discussing temperament (relatively stable individual differences in arousal, a prevailing mood) that irritability, fearfulness, activity level, and sociability level show some degree of stability in children's personalities. Temperament characteristics in and of themselves are not pathological; rather they exist in the child and depending on the contextual features of the environment, there may be a conflictual, stressful interaction, a benign one, or a positively facilitating one.

In the section on emotional development in early childhood, emotions were separated into discrete and specific emotional states: love, anger, fear, and jealousy. It needs to be pointed out, however, that there is no such thing as a "pure" emotion. People experience a combination or blending of emotional feelings: Love is mixed with hate, anger with shame, and so on. Almost unlimited combinations of emotions are experienced when encountering various emotion-eliciting stimuli. The discussion began with the positive emotions of affection and love. The primary caregivers are children's first love objects. Children who are provided with love and affection manifest these in their behavior toward others. Anger is caused pri-

marily by being blocked from achieving a valued goal. It appears that children are indoctrinated at a very early age not to express anger. Fears, anxieties, and phobias and the subtle differences of each were discussed, and common fears at various development were noted. The last section discussed jealousy, the desire to be desired and noticed by valued people.

Stress is the perception of threat to physical or psychological well-being and the individual's reactions to that stress. Selye (1956/1976) has pointed out that there are three stages in the stress syndrome: the alarm stage, stage of resistance, and stage of exhaustion. If a stressor continues unabated for a long period of time, your adaptation energy is depleted, which may lead to various illnesses that, in peak condition, could have been resisted. Children do experience stress. Some of the common stressors to children were pointed out. The chance of psychological problems increases as children encounter more and more stress.

Adolescence has been characterized as a period of extreme emotionality; a period in which emotional states are more extreme, variable, and intense than earlier or later periods. Research seems to show that positive and negative affect does not increase during adolescence, which challenges the hypothesis of increased emotionality during this period. During adolescence, emotional autonomy emerges as adolescents become emotionally independent from parents. That is, throughout adolescence, you observe adolescent increases in accepting responsibility for their choices and actions, rather than depositing this responsibility on their parents' shoulders. Although emotional autonomy, or emotional separateness, emerges in adolescence, so does emotional connectedness, or intimacy. Intimacy is defined as developing close, trusting, self-disclosing relationships with peers. Although intimacy with peers increases, intimacy with parents does not decrease.

Various ways in which parents and teachers can help children deal effectively with anger, fear, and jealousy were pointed out. Children should be allowed to express their angry feelings, but firm limits should be set on the physical expression of these feelings. Parents and teachers who recognize their own anger, calming down before reacting in an anger situation and not carrying grudges, will help children learn to deal with their anger. In regard to fear, it was suggested that helping children feel more control over their fear, making pleasant associations with the feared object or situation, and gradually exposing them to the feared object or situation will be useful. Parents can help their children deal with their jealous feelings by noticing when the children are playing well together, not constantly becoming a referee, treating them as individuals, and avoiding comparisons. Parents and teachers can help children cope with stress by helping them develop their self-confidence, encouraging them to be open to change, and helping them to feel more in control of themselves in various situations.

ENHANCING YOUR CRITICAL THINKING

Broadening Your Knowledge

Social Referencing

Hirshberg, L. M. (1990). When infants look to their parents: Twelve-month-olds respond to conflicting emotional signals. *Child Development, 61*, 1187–1191.

Laurence Hirshberg studied 1-year-olds' responses when they received conflicting messages from their mothers and fathers (one happy; one angry). How does the infant act under these circumstances?

Critical Thinking

Stress

Armacost, R. L. (1989). Perceptions of stressors by high school students. *Journal of Adolescent Research, 4*, 443–461.

This article discusses the stressors that are most frequently experienced by high school students. Are these stressors different from or similar to the types of stressors college students experience? How would you explain the similarities and/or differences?

Personal Growth

Love

Fromm, E. (1989). *The art of loving*. New York: Harper Collins.

In order to gain a clear picture of mature love and how we need to work at the "art of loving," read this classic.

Moral Reasoning, Feelings, and Behavior

CHILDREN'S THOUGHTS

On the following dilemma . . .

You and your best friend are walking through a department store. You are both looking at an expensive Sony Walkman. Before you know it, your friend stuffs the Walkman into his (her) pocket. Your friend leaves the store. As you are about to leave, a few seconds later, the store detective stops you and says, "I know your friend stole the radio. Give me his (her) name, or I'll call your parents." What would you do?

I would tell the detective her name. It is Sally Marks with long black hair, blue eyes, about 4.6 (sic) inches. If the detective called my parents—Wow!
Nancy, age 8

The first few seconds of what's going through your mind would be unbearable. I would stay there and say call my parents. A best friend would mean a lot more to me than a phone call to my parents.
Rick, age 11

I would ask the guard if I could go and get it back. My parents wouldn't care and I am not in trouble so I have no liability. I would simply tell them that and say, here's my driver's license, I'll go and get the Walkman and bring it back to you. You'll get your radio back and I'll keep my loyalty to my friend. My way, all are happy. My parents would be pleased as I solved the situation effectively. Then when the radio is given back, I'll get my license back and leave.
Andre, age 17

What is **morality?** A somewhat simplistic definition is knowing right from wrong behavior and engaging in the former. Every day, you are faced with countless minor and sometimes major situations that awaken your inner voice and "test" your morality. "Should I cut my eight o'clock class and sleep an extra hour?" "Should I tell my parents about the low grade I'm receiving in history?" "Is it fair to keep dating Sheldon if I really don't care that much about him?" In each of these situations you try to determine what course of action would best fulfill a moral ideal—what *ought* to be done in the situation. But who or what determines what is right or wrong conduct? The "right" way to behave, by and large, is determined by your level of moral development (Rest, 1979).

According to cognitive-developmental theorists, morality develops in a sequential pattern, that is, the development of moral reasoning follows certain stages of development. Children and adults have a somewhat different conception of what

good behavior is and how they can best fulfill their moral ideal in each of these stages. Each successive stage is said to build and elaborate on the previous stage. A later stage is "higher" than an earlier one because it can more adequately organize the multiplicity of facts, interests, and possibilities life holds in store. Higher stages of moral reasoning are superior to lower stages because they show greater understanding about society and thus are more socially adaptive.

In this chapter the development of children's moral reasoning is examined by discussing three prominent theories: those of Piaget, Kohlberg, and information processing. Children's prosocial and antisocial ways of behaving during early and middle childhood are examined. Then adolescents' concepts of social convention, their value system, and illegal ways of behaving—juvenile delinquency—are explored. "Practical Implications" centers on how concerned adults can facilitate the development of moral reasoning in children.

THEORIES OF MORAL REASONING

Exposing children to various moral dilemmas reveals children's **moral reasoning:** how children think in certain situations involving moral conduct. Children's moral reasoning reflects their level or stage of moral development. For example, the children who were questioned about a friend stealing a Sony Walkman revealed various levels of thinking about what ought to be done.

The responses of the young children (around 5 and 6 years of age) reveal that they appear to believe that right and wrong are defined in terms of what one is told to do. Good behavior is what mom or dad say it is. Young children's moral reasoning, then, tends to focus on one perspective, that of authority. Children tend to decide on what is right on the basis of fear and the avoidance of punishment. The moral reasoning of 7- to 9-year-olds reflects pragmatic or selfish consequences. That is, what secures their own interests is good; what does not is wrong. Twelve- to 13-year-olds feel that the right behavior in the Sony Walkman stealing situation is to protect the friend. The desire to maintain established relationships appears to be their motivation for judgment. Older children appear to be able to survey with the mind's eye the whole scene and then decide what is best "from everyone's point of view." Cognitive-developmental theorists are interested not only in how children's moral reasoning develops but also in how and why their thinking changes over time.

JEAN PIAGET'S THEORY

Jean Piaget began researching the development of moral reasoning more than 60 years ago. Piaget (1932, 1963, 1965) was the first to investigate the cognitive aspects of moral development. He was concerned with the reasoning processes underlying moral concepts and focused on developmental changes in children's ways of thinking about their social world and about right and wrong.

Piaget tried to explain cognitive-developmental changes in moral reasoning in two areas: a child's respect for *social rules* and a child's *sense of justice.* His inquiries focused on the attitudes expressed by 4- to 13-year-old Swiss schoolchildren toward the origin and changeability of rules in a game of marbles, and on children's responses to stories concerning motives and justice.

After analyzing rules in children's games, Piaget went on to study the development of moral judgment in children. To investigate the child's developing sense of justice, Piaget started off in his usual creative way. He began by saying to the children that a lot of parents just don't know how to punish children fairly. Piaget then told stories to the children about people engaged in wrongdoing.

The stories were presented in pairs illustrating different degrees of responsibility for damage done. In one story, the central figure performed an act that unintentionally resulted in considerable damage; in the other, the child caused a negligible amount of damage as a result of a deliberate improper act. The child's task was to decide who was good and who was bad. For example, one story is about a child who accidentally knocks over a tray and breaks 15 cups. In its companion story, a boy climbing up to steal jam out of the kitchen cabinet, against his mother's orders, knocks over one cup, which falls on the floor and breaks. He then asked his listeners how they would have punished the young offender and analyzed the results. Even though younger children have learned many social norms, their answers to Piaget's questions display striking misunderstandings of the nature and function of social rules.

From his research, Piaget proposed two broad stages of moral development: **moral realism** or **heteronomous morality** and **moral relativism,** also known as *morality of reciprocity.*

Moral Realism—Age 7 and Younger Moral realism is characterized by the naive assumption, on the part of children, that rules are external, absolute, and unchanging. Children see themselves as inferior to adults, and from a mixture of fear, affection, and admiration, children adopt their parents' moral beliefs unquestioningly. They adopt an inflexible moral code based on obedience. Morality at this stage, then, is essentially conformity to social prescriptions.

STUDYING CHILDREN

RULES

Play a game with two 4- or 5-year-olds. As Piaget did, tell the children that you would like to play the game with them, but you need to have them explain the rules to you. Do they explain the rules clearly, so that you understand? (Sometimes they omit very important facts, because they egocentrically assume that you know as much about the game as they do.) Ask them why there are rules for games. Finally, ask them to explain how they know what the rules for the game are. Do children tend to follow their own egocentric system of "rules," as Piaget found in his research?

Rules   Before the age of 4, children have no sense of obligation to rules at all. Instead, they behave in a highly individualistic or egocentric way. They are unable to see a situation from any other perspective but their own, and they assume that everyone shares their thoughts and feelings. They do not know the rules, but may insist that they do. Preschool children of 4 or 5, Piaget reported, tended to imitate the rules for playing marbles by drawing a square in the ground, but would play in an egocentric way, either by themselves or with others. Their understanding of the rules consisted only of going through the accepted motions, with individual variations as their fancies dictated. Children may understand other children's rules, but in fact follow their own system of rules, which bear little relation to the other children's rules. Children often invent new rules of their own as they play the game, to accommodate their own needs. "Studying Children" offers an activity for learning more about children's conceptions of rules.

Around the age of 7 or 8, however, Piaget noted that children become increasingly aware of the rules of the game. These are regarded as sacred and unchangeable and, according to the children, are probably invented by parents (the ultimate authorities) or some divine source.

Punishment   The very youngest children decide rightness and wrongness of something by whether or not the person gets punished. They are punished when they are bad, and thus believe that the delivery of punishment means that some bad behavior must have occurred. Similarly, they feel that children who are punished are receiving their just reward. To illustrate, 4- and 7-year-olds were asked to judge whether the child in a story was good or bad. The child in the story was told to watch his baby brother while his mother was away. The child was described as being helpful and obedient; however, he received a spanking when his mother returned. Many 4-year-olds said the child was bad—after all, he was punished, right? Some young children even made up a misdeed in order to explain the child's punishment. It wasn't until age 7 that children said the child was good and unfairly punished.

The child's earliest concepts of punishment are based on retribution. The child who has misbehaved must be punished, and for many younger children, the fairest punishment is the most severe. It may be an arbitrary kind of punishment, which bears no relation to the misdeed. Piaget calls this **expiatory punishment,** because the child feels that painful punishment will expiate any guilt.

In studying children's attitudes toward justice, Piaget came across an interesting phenomenon. He found among young children the notion that justice is immanent in the natural order of things. **Immanent justice** is the belief that wrongdoing inevitably leads to punishment. Piaget told his subjects a story about a child who, in trying to cross a stream, steps on a rotten plank and falls into the water. He then asked, "Why did this happen?" An immanent-justice response typical of 6- and 7-year-olds is that the boy fell into the stream because he had disobeyed his mother. Thus, to a young child, things like rotten planks are the accomplices of grown-ups in making sure that a punishment is inflicted. Children, said Piaget, eventually realize that punishment is a socially mediated event that occurs only if a relevant person witnesses the wrongdoing, and even then punishment is not inevitable.

Intentions and Consequences   Children under the age of 7 tend to judge another child's behavior, as well as their own, in terms of actual consequences rather than in terms of good or bad intentions. Piaget (1965) told children two stories:

> A little boy who was called Augustus once noticed that his father's ink pot was empty. One day when his father was away he thought of filling the ink pot so as to help his father, and so that he should find it full when he came home. But while he was opening the ink bottle, he made a big blot on the tablecloth.

The corresponding story was as follows:

> There was a boy named Julian. His father had gone out and Julian thought it would be fun to play with his father's ink pot. First, he played with the pen and then he made a little blot on the tablecloth.

"Which child is naughtier?" Piaget asked. Most young children said the one who made the big blot. "Why?" Because it was big. When asked why the child made the blot, the children said because he was trying to be helpful and the one who made the small blot was not trying to be helpful. Nevertheless, the naughtier of the two was the one who made the big blot. It is evident that children are perfectly aware of the character's intentions, and yet ignore them. What determines guilt is not intention, but quantity of damage.

Piaget largely ignored the fact that parents may not be so inclined to inquire after their children's intentions. Whatever the circumstances, they may punish the child more severely for making the bigger blot ("I don't care what you were trying to do, look at the mess you've made!") than for the one making a smaller one. It is plausible that the child learns much about consequences and little about intentions. If adults punish according to the severity of the damage, regardless of the child's intentions (the greater the damage, the heavier the punishment), it is likely that children's moral judgments will be consequence based.

The shift from moral realism to moral relativism occurs primarily as a result of changes in cognitive ability as well as children's broadened social experience. As children become members of a group, their moral judgments may become less absolute

and authoritarian and more dependent on the needs and desires of the group; when that occurs moral relativism replaces moral realism.

Moral Relativism—Age 7 and Older   The second kind of morality, moral relativism, is a cognitively more mature stage. It is characterized by an understanding that morality depends on mutual respect, rather than on unquestioned obedience to authority. Children become better at understanding motives and feelings of others. Both these moralities can exist side by side. The child can apply a morality of realism in one situation and a morality of relativism in another. Piaget believed, however, that as children get older they tend to judge in terms of the morality of relativism.

Rules   Around 10 to 11 years of age, children alter rules to fit unusual situations and may invent new rules to cover special circumstances. Rules are seen as changeable; they are no longer seen as sacred laws laid down by adults. Rules are decisions made by the children who play the games; they can be changed at will, as long as everyone agrees. Because these children are no longer controlled by egocentrism, they can more easily consider and appreciate the viewpoint and feelings of a peer, which leads to genuine cooperation. Children learn that cooperative social arrangements can lead to mutually valued goals. In addition, they show a thorough mastery of the rules of a game, often delighting in a legalistic fascination with the rules. For these older children, rules are products of lawful convention and mutual respect among peers; they are not imposed by an external authority.

Punishment   At about age 10, children gradually lose their sense of objective responsibility (focusing on the obvious, concrete aspects of a situation) and begin to place more emphasis on subjective intentions (the individual's motives and the circumstances of the situation). Their notions of justice now include consideration of intention. To illustrate, in the example given previously, breaking 15 cups accidentally is not as bad as breaking one to take some forbidden jam. The child who did not mean to break the cups is now excused, while the one who deliberately disobeyed is guilty. As children grow older, they feel that the punishment should fit the crime, so that wrongdoers better appreciate the consequences of their acts.

Children in the moral realism stage tend to judge behavior in absolute terms: Behavior is totally right or totally wrong. Moreover, young children feel that *everyone* sees and judges the morality of people and behavior exactly the same way they do. In the moral relativism stage, children are aware that things are neither all bad or all good, but a mixture of both. As children come to notice the more subtle cues of intention, intention may be more regularly taken into account. Table 14.1 provides a summary of the stages of moral realism and moral relativism.

Evaluation of Piaget's Theory Piaget did not fully demonstrate that moral judgments elicited by his questioning on stories correspond to moral judgments in real life. Children's moral judgments do not necessarily determine their actual behavior. Just because children have notions of right and wrong that they can use to evaluate the behavior of others does not necessarily mean that they will make similar evaluations of their own behavior and then use these evaluations to guide their behavior.

Damon (1977), for example, asked young children how 10 candy bars ought to be distributed as rewards for making bracelets. In interviews, the children described various schemes for a fair distribution of rewards, explaining why they thought

TABLE 14.1 Moral Realism and Moral Relativism: Characteristics	Moral Realism (children under 7)	Moral Relativism (children over 7)
	Moral behavior based on specific rules	Moral behavior based on more general concepts of what is right and wrong
	Belief that rules are arbitrary, fixed, eternal	Belief that rules grow out of mutual consent
	Dependence on adults	Peer-group solidarity
	Morality of adult constraint	Morality of mutual cooperation
	Moral conduct in response to external demands: heteronomous	Moral conduct in response to internal standards, which are adopted as their own: autonomous
	Attention to objective responsibility only	Understanding of importance of subjective intentions
	Immanent justice; justice of expiation	Justice of reciprocity and equality
	Judgment of acts in terms of physical consequences	Judgment of acts in terms of intent to deceive or do harm
	Judgment of seriousness of act in terms of seriousness of punishment	Judgment of acts according to harm done or whether or not a rule was violated
	Necessity of judging acts of others according to inflexible standards	Ability to judge acts of others according to circumstances in which action occurred and underlying motivation
	Belief that an act is totally right or totally wrong; adult view is always right	Awareness of steps of rightness and wrongness; of differences in points of view; adult may be mistaken

Source: Adapted with permission of Macmillan Publishing Company from *Middle Childhood: Behavior and Development*, 2/e by Joyce W. Williams and Marjorie Stith. Copyright © 1974, 1980 by Macmillan Publishing Company.

STUDYING CHILDREN

GENEROSITY

Ask three children from a nursery school class to help you distribute some treats to the children because they played so well at recess time. Before giving them each a bag containing inexpensive party favors, have them verbally explain their distribution process. Then let them do whatever they want with the treats. Do they give any away? Do they give more than half away? Are there differences between the children? How do the other children respond to the children's generosity or selfishness? Finish the experiment by giving all the children an inexpensive treat.

Lawrence Kohlberg believes that moral development goes through six stages.

a particular distribution ought to be followed. When, however, these same children were actually given the 10 candy bars to distribute, they deviated from their espoused fairness schemes and instead gave themselves a disproportionate number. Although some researchers have found a modest relationship between moral reasoning and moral behavior, the results of most research thus far remains obscure. Therefore, you must question the extent to which children's ability to reason about the morality of the behavior of others influences the morality of their own behavior. "Studying Children" discusses an experiment similar to Damon's study.

Another criticism leveled at Piaget's stories is that the child had to remember and then compare two intents and two outcomes; the intentions of the actors are not always clearly stated and the outcome is always stated last. When the stories are simplified so that only one intent and one outcome have to be considered at a time, and both intent and outcome are explicitedly stated and systematically varied, young children show much more advanced reasoning than Piaget found. Young children not only can distinguish between accidental and intended actions and between good and bad intentions, they also can weigh both intention and consequence in making moral judgments (Surber, 1977).

LAWRENCE KOHLBERG'S THEORY

Kohlberg's (1978, 1981) approach to moral development is an elaboration of Piaget's with respect to both theory and method. Like Piaget, Kohlberg's original position was based on the responses of 7- to 17-year-old boys to brief stories depicting moral dilemmas. Typically, children have been asked to resolve moral dilemmas in which a story protagonist can assist another at a cost to the self. Table 14.2 provides you with one of Kohlberg's dilemmas, the story of Heinz.

Piaget was interested in asking children how bad a person is who acts in a certain way in a given situation. What matters in Kohlberg's model is not the nature of the solution a person offers to a moral dilemma; he does not consider any one choice better than another. Instead, the basis on which the

TABLE 14.2 The Heinz Dilemma

In Europe, a woman was near death from a special kind of cancer. There was one drug that the doctors thought might save her. It was a form of radium that a druggist in the same town had recently discovered. The drug was expensive to make, but the druggist was charging ten times what the drug cost him to make. He paid $200 for radium and charged $2,000 for a small dose of the drug. The sick woman's husband, Heinz, went to everyone he knew to borrow the money, but he could only get together about $1,000 which is half of what it cost. He told the druggist that his wife was dying, and asked him to sell it cheaper or let him pay later. But the druggist said, "No, I discovered the drug and I'm going to make money from it." So Heinz got desperate and broke into the man's store to steal the drug for his wife.

Source: From "Stage and Sequence: The Cognitive-Developmental Approach to Socialization" by L. Kohlberg, 1969, in D. Goslin (Ed.), *Handbook of Socialization Theory and Research* (p. 379), Chicago: Rand McNally. Reprinted by permission of the author.

person reasons in making a decision is deemed important. Kohlberg and his colleagues asked children to decide what an actor ought to do in a certain situation. The children must decide and justify a course of action for the actor and define the actor's rights and obligations. Kohlberg's interest focused on the quality of the individual's judgments, as indicated by the justifications they gave for their replies. The predominant stage orientation of an individual is assessed by analyzing the child's responses to a number of dilemmas.

Levels of Moral Reasoning As can be seen in Table 14.3, Kohlberg's theory suggests a culturally universal sequence of six developmental stages ordered into three levels of moral orientation. Also included in this table are some of the typical responses that children, at various levels of moral reasoning, gave to the Heinz dilemma. Note that the same stage of reasoning can underlie different judgments about whether Heinz should steal the drug, thus the pro and con responses. In Kohlberg's theory, moral judgments are made according to the stage of moral development. The notion implies that moral judgments across different moral domains show an underlying stage-based unity.

Kohlberg held that moral judgments progress through an unvarying series of stages. Although interactions with peers provide its impetus, the progression is irreversible, and not all people reach the highest stages of moral development. Kohlberg assessed moral development by having trained coders examine people's justifications for their decisions on a series of moral decisions. Should Heinz break into a drugstore to obtain expensive medicine that would ameliorate his wife's illness? By evaluating not the decision itself but the justifications behind it, Kohlbergians have seemed to assume that all moral decisions are equally amenable to justification.

The stages are arranged in ascending order of complexity, with each representing a more stable and logically powerful framework for resolving conflicts than the one before (Kohlberg, 1963). Each stage in the sequence is progressively more differentiated and integrated. With development, each new stage employs cognitive operations that are more reversible and equilibrated. Development, then, is essentially a change from global, diffuse, confused thinking to systematic, articulate, and hierarchical thinking. "Studying Children" offers an exercise that will help you to learn more about children's stages of moral reasoning.

It should be mentioned that Kohlberg now suggests that stage 6 is a theoretical construct suggested to him by the lives of extraordinary individuals like Martin Luther King or John F. Kennedy. It is not, maintains Kohlberg, verifiable empirically (Colby, Kohlberg, Gibbs, & Lieberman, 1983).

Kohlberg (1976) maintains that as children grow older, more of their judgments are made at higher levels of reasoning. In an early study involving boys between the ages of 7 and 16, he found that **preconventional morality** (avoiding punishment or gaining a fair exchange) was the dominant reason for children's moral decisions. Obeying society's rules or social approval responses **(conventional morality)** rose rapidly in middle childhood. **Postconventional morality** rose rapidly between the ages of 10 and 13 and accounted for about 20% of the judgments at age 16 (see Figure 14.1).

TABLE 14.3 Summary of Kohlberg's Stages of Moral Reasoning

Level and Stage	What Is Right?	Reasons for Doing Right	How People Answer the Heinz Dilemma PRO	CON

Level I: Preconventional Level: The child is responsive to cultural rules and labels of good and bad, right or wrong, but interprets these labels in terms of either the physical or the hedonistic consequences of action (punishment, reward, exchange of favors) or in terms of the physical power of those who enunciate the rules and labels.

Level and Stage	What Is Right?	Reasons for Doing Right	PRO	CON
Stage 1: Heteronomous morality	To avoid breaking rules that are backed by punishment; obedience for its own sake; avoiding physical damage to persons and property.	Avoidance of punishment; the superior power of authorities.	Heinz should steal the drug. It is not really bad to take it. It is not like he did not ask to pay for it first. The drug he would take is only worth $200; he is not really taking a $2000 drug.	Heinz shouldn't steal; he should buy the drug. If he steals the drug, he might get put in jail and have to put the drug back anyway.
Stage 2: Individualism, instrumental purpose, and exchange	Following rules only when it is to one's immediate interest; acting to meet one's own interests and needs and letting others do the same. Right is also what is fair, what is an equal exchange, a deal, an agreement.	To serve one's own needs or interests in a world where it is recognized that other people have their own interests too.	Heinz should steal the drug to save his wife's life. He might get sent to jail, but he'd still save his wife.	He should not steal it. The druggist is not wrong or bad; he just wants to make a profit. That is what you are in business for, to make money.

Level II: Conventional Level: Maintaining the expectations of the individual's family, group, or nation is perceived as valuable in its own right, regardless of immediate and obvious consequences. The attitude is not only one of conformity to personal expectations and social order, but of loyalty to it, of actively maintaining, supporting, and justifying the order, and of identifying with the people or group involved in it.

Level and Stage	What Is Right?	Reasons for Doing Right	PRO	CON
Stage 3: Mutual interpersonal expectations, relationships, and interpersonal conformity	Living up to what is expected by significant others or what is generally expected of people in the role of daughter, brother, friend, and so on; "being good" is important and means having good motives, showing concern about others; it also means keeping mutual relationships, such as trust, loyalty, respect, and gratitude.	The need to be a good person in one's own eyes and those of others; caring for others; belief in the Golden Rule; desire to maintain rules and authority that support stereotypical good behavior.	If I were Heinz, I would steal the drug for my wife. You can't put a price on love, no amount of gifts make love. You can't put a price on life either.	He should not steal. If his wife dies, he cannot be blamed. It is not because he is heartless or that he does not love her enough to do everything that he legally can. The druggist is the selfish or heartless one.

Source: From "Stage and Sequence: The Cognitive-Developmental Approach to Socialization" by L. Kohlberg, 1969, D. Goslin (Ed.), *Handbook of Socialization Theory and Research* (pp. 379–380), Chicago: Rand McNally. Adapted by permission of the author.

TABLE 14.3 *continued*

Level and Stage	What Is Right?	Reasons for Doing Right	How People Answer the Heinz Dilemma PRO	How People Answer the Heinz Dilemma CON
Stage 4: Social system and conscience	Fulfilling duties to which one has agreed; laws are to be upheld except in extreme cases in which they conflict with other fixed social duties; right also means contributing to society, the group, or institution.	To maintain the institution as a whole; to avoid the breakdown in the system that would happen "if everyone did it"; or the imperative of conscience to meet one's defined obligations (easily confused with Stage 3 belief in rules and authority).	When you get married, you take a vow to love and cherish your wife. Marriage is not only love, it's an obligation. Like a legal contract.	It is a natural thing for Heinz to want to save his wife, but it is still always wrong to steal. He still knows he is stealing and taking a valuable drug from the man who made it.

Level III: Postconventional, Autonomous, or Principled Level: There is a clear effort to define moral values and principles that have validity and application apart from the authority of the groups of people holding these principles and apart from the individual's own identification with these groups.

Level and Stage	What Is Right?	Reasons for Doing Right	How People Answer the Heinz Dilemma PRO	How People Answer the Heinz Dilemma CON
Stage 5: Social contract or utility and individual rights	Being aware that people hold a variety of values and opinions, that most values and rules are relative to the group; these rules, however, should usually be upheld, in the interest of impartiality and because they form the social contract; some nonrelative values and rights such as life and liberty, however, must be upheld in any society and regardless of majority opinion.	A sense of obligation to law because of the social contract to make and abide by laws for the welfare of all and for the protection of all people's rights; a feeling of contractual commitment, freely entered on, to family, friendship, trust, and work obligations; concern that laws and duties be based on rational calculation of overall utility; "the greatest good for the greatest number."	The law was not set up for these circumstances. Taking the drug in this situation is not really right, but it is justified to do it.	You cannot completely blame someone for stealing, but extreme circumstances do not really justify taking the law in your own hands. You cannot have everyone stealing whenever they get desperate. The end may be good, but the ends do not justify the means.
Stage 6: Universal ethical principles	Following self-chosen ethical principles; particular laws or social agreements are usually valid because they rest on such principles; when laws violate these principles, one acts in accordance with the universal principles of justice: the equality of human rights and respect for the dignity of human beings as individual persons.	The belief as a rational person in the validity of universal moral principles, and a sense of personal commitment to them.	This is a situation that forces him to choose between stealing and letting his wife die. In a situation where the choice must be made, it is morally right to steal. He has to act in terms of the principle of preserving and respecting life.	Heinz is faced with the decision of whether to consider the other people who need the drug just as badly as his wife. Heinz ought to act not according to his particular feelings toward his wife, but considering the value of all the lives involved.

STUDYING CHILDREN

MORAL REASONING

Choose a comfortable time for talking with a child. Begin in a casual way by saying, "Let me tell you a story and ask you what you think the child in the story should do."

Kenny's Dilemma

Kenny is walking to the store. It's his mother's birthday on Saturday. He's feeling bad because he hasn't been able to save up enough money to get her the present he'd like to give her. Then, on the sidewalk, he finds a wallet with $10 in it—just what he needs to buy the present! There's an identification card in the wallet, giving the name and address of the owner.

Questions

1. What should Kenny do? Why?
2. What would be a good reason for Kenny to return the wallet? Can you think of any other reasons?
3. Would it be stealing to keep the money? Why is it wrong to steal?

On the basis of the child's answers, try to figure out the child's stage of moral reasoning. Don't be discouraged if this is difficult to do. For one thing, children say things that don't always fit into a particular stage. For another, it takes practice to figure out a child's stage of moral reasoning.

Source: From "Building Moral Dilemma Activities" by D. Adams, 1977, *Learning, 5*, p. 44.

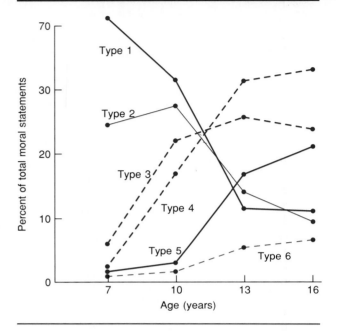

FIGURE 14.1 Use of Six Types of Moral Judgments at Four Ages

Source: From "The Development of Children's Orientations toward a Moral Order: I. Sequence in the Development of Moral Thought" by L. Kohlberg, 1963, *Vita Humana, 6*, p. 16. Reprinted by permission of S. Karger AG, Basel.

Evaluation of Kohlberg's Theory   Kohlberg's theory has stimulated a great deal of research that has been critically reviewed. Simpson (1974), for example, maintains that Kohlberg's model is culturally biased. It is based on the style of thinking and social organization peculiar to Western culture. Stage 5, as a case in point, makes sense only in a constitutional democracy.

Kohlberg has made some very bold claims about a subject's consistency in moral judgment across situations (Berling, 1981). He believes that each stage must be traversed in order, that order is never reversed, and that no stage can be skipped.

By and large, evidence supports sequentiality (Colby et al., 1983; White, Bushnell, & Regnemer, 1978), particularly for the early stages. Stages and substages at the postconventional or principled level do not always appear in Kohlberg's postulated order (Walker, 1982). For example, subjects tested in high school scored at stages 4 or 5, but as sophomores in college they scored at stage 2. Some subjects skipped from stage 3 to stage 5 (Kohlberg & Kramer, 1969).

Evidence suggests that the themes of some of the Kohlberg dilemmas often involve situations that are foreign to children and more likely to be faced in adulthood and thus, are not very representative of actual moral problems of children (Muuss, 1988; Rest, 1983). Therefore, you may question whether the exercise constitutes detached intellectual reasoning with a moral content or whether it really assesses a personal, existential moral judgment. Similarly, by not providing children with familiar material, Kohlberg may have underestimated children's moral capacities. Leming (1974) compared the responses of eighth- and 12th-graders on "classical" Kohlberg dilemmas and practical dilemmas, which were generated by the subjects themselves. Subjects' stage scores on the practical dilemmas were significantly higher than those on the Kohlberg ones. Similar results were found by Walker and Taylor (1991) when examining children's responses to Kohlberg's dilemmas and real-life dilemmas that had direct relevance to the children's lives. It is noteworthy, in this regard, that the Kohlbergian moral education paradigm has shifted from one entailing classroom discussion of hypothetical moral dilemmas to one involving resolution of real moral and political problems through student self-governance and community building (Power, Higgins, & Kohlberg, 1989).

Another criticism related to Kohlberg's stories is that they are open ended and the discussion can range over a large number of features and topics. Although the freedom of Kohlberg's stories has led to the identification of many new forms and features of thinking previously unnoticed (Turiel, 1990), the complexity and diversity of responses to Kohlberg's dilemmas have raised vexing problems in scoring such data.

Gilligan (1982) maintains that there are two different voices utilized by the majority of males and females. One of these voices, the one most commonly identified with the masculine world, speaks of preserving rights, exercising justice, obeying rules, and upholding principles; logical and individualistic, this male voice advocates equality, reciprocity, autonomy, and individuation; in short, this represents the justice orientation. The other voice, more dominant in women than in men, speaks of caring for others, sensitivity to others, concern for others, connectedness to others. It emphasizes responsibility to human beings rather than to abstract principles and advocates avoiding hurt and violence, maintaining relationships and attachments, even if self-sacrifice becomes necessary. In short, this female voice represents the "interpersonal network" or care orientation.

Gilligan has criticized Kohlberg's model for being insensitive to typically feminine concerns for welfare, caring, interpersonal obligations, and responsibility. These concerns are assigned to lower stages of moral reasoning—stage 3 with its orientation to the approval and feelings of others. Men, however, are more likely than women to appeal to abstract concepts such as justice and equity. Men tend to advocate equality, reciprocity, autonomy, and individuation, and thus, progress to stage 4 with its emphasis on the maintenance of social order. This sex difference has commonly been explained as a deficiency in the female's ability to advance to the principled level of moral judgment. Freud maintained, for example, that women have weaker superegos because of an incomplete resolution of the Oedipal complex.

Gilligan analyzed six studies including four longitudinal investigations and reported that 92% of the women included interpersonal or care orientation; 62% of the men included a justice orientation. Females at stage 3 used more empathic role-taking rationales than did males. No males, but 21% of the females, used interpersonal approval as a reason for choosing a particular course of action. This greater use of reasons related to conscience (or self-reward or self-punishment) by females, maintains Gilligan, is quite contrary to Freud's contention that females have weaker superegos than males.

There is no consistent evidence that morality in males is dominated by concerns with justice and rights and that for females it is dominated by concerns with care in interpersonal relationships. The vast majority of studies do not identify neat, consistent, unequivocal sex differences as Gilligan implies, and thus do not support her notion that males' moral judgments tend to be governed primarily by a principled justice organization with its focus on rights and duties, and that females' moral judgments show more empathy because of a focus on relationships, welfare, and caring.

Walker (1989), for example, found in his 2-year longitudinal study with a sample of 233 subjects of both sexes ranging in age from 5 to 63, a nonsignificant pattern of sex differences in levels of moral reasoning. Girls and women can and do use fairness and justice reasoning when the problem calls for it. Thus, the belief that women are less morally advanced than men, or that they are treated improperly in the Kohlbergian scheme, appears unjustified. Similarly, Smetana, Killen, and Turiel (1991) found, in two different studies, that concerns with justice and interpersonal relationships coexist in judgments of male and female children in third, sixth, and ninth grades. This evidence presents serious problems for Gilligan's criticisms. The ultimate contribution may lie in her broadening of assumptions about men's and women's moral reasonings and her redefining of the under-standing that the really moral person must integrate the concept of abstract justice and the concern for particular others.

Kohlberg maintained that moral development is dependent on cognitive development, and changes in moral judgment are dependent on changes in cognitive development. Many recent studies have maintained this orientation. Thus, there appears to be a dependence of certain sophisticated moral capacities on certain underlying cognitive capacities. Cognitive development alone, however, is insufficient to bring a child to make judgments at a particular level of moral development; peer interactional influences are likewise necessary to actualize the potential changes in moral perspective.

Cognitive-developmental theories have stimulated and redirected the focus of considerable research in the moral area. In addition, Kohlberg's theory has provided guidelines for major new efforts in moral education. He has made people aware of the highly complex nature of moral development and the cognitive dimensions that may be necessary in order to reach higher levels of moral reasoning.

INFORMATION PROCESSING THEORY

Information processing theory focuses on the specific principles individuals use to make specific moral judgments (for example, responsibility, blame, and punishment for moral transgressions) and on rules for the distribution of rewards. Information processing theorists are interested in determining the information and inference rules that individuals use in their judgments of wrongdoing. In contrast to Kohlberg's concentration of rationalization of past moral decisions, the emphasis here is on the use of rules of reasoning to process information.

The Schultz-Schleifer model (Shultz & Schleifer, 1983) focuses on cases in which a person may have done something to harm someone else. It specifies that major decisions in such cases focus on whether that person is the cause of harm, is morally responsible for the punishment, and is deserving of blame; a final decision concerns how much,

Empirical evidence does not support sex differences in moral reasoning in which females more so than males are thought to use concern for welfare, caring, and interpersonal obligations and men more so than women advocating obeying rules and exercising justice.

...ld be administered. Each ...e first makes use of infor-... ...ing previous major deci-...

...igure 14.2, the first informa-... ...is causation, which is deter-... ...ation of conditional informa-... ...n-causer is deemed morally ...a second set of information is ...ral responsibility of the harm-... ...on factors such as intention, ...egligence, and so forth are ana-... ...als can also be blamed for harm ...e caused indirectly. This is accom-... ...gh the mechanism of vicarious re-... ...After responsibility for wrongdoing ...analyzed, the issues of blame, based on

net harm, and finally the type of punishment deemed appropriate, are processed.

Research designed to test the Shultz-Schleifer model developmentally provides support for the view that children reason according to some aspects of the model, particularly in their use of necessity information to determine causation. Shultz and Schleifer (1983) have reported a fairly sophisticated use of a variety of the moral concepts by children from 5 years of age. Children revealed evidence of using information on intention and negligence to assign moral responsibility and information on restitution to assign punishment. Developmental trends in this experiment included an increasing sensitivity to these concepts, greater tolerance for harm-doing, and more emphasis on restitution rather than punishment with increasing age.

Zanna (1988) reported on cross-sectional and short-term longitudinal studies of the development of concepts of intention, foreseeability, and justification. His findings suggest that between the ages of 4 and 6, children come to distinguish between intentional and unintentional harm and then to distinguish simultaneously between foreseeable and unforeseeable harm, on the one hand, and justified and unjustified harm on the other.

Although Piaget maintained that there is an age-related shift from a focus on consequences to a consideration of intention, information-processing studies (Berndt & Berndt, 1975; Ferguson & Rule, 1983) have found that children as young as 6 or 7 view intentional harm as more blameworthy and more punishable than accidental harm.

There are major differences between the information processing approach and a Kohlbergian approach to moral reasoning. Kohlberg's primary interest was in the subject's justification for a prior moral judgment. In contrast, information processing researchers attempt to assess the rules used to make moral judgments. Kohlberg uses moral dilemmas, difficult questions without clear-cut moral answers. Information processing theorists use simpler, clearer cases to aid in the diagnosis of reasoning rules. In the information processing approach, use of a particular rule of reasoning is identified by

FIGURE 14.2 Overview of the Shultz-Schleifer Model

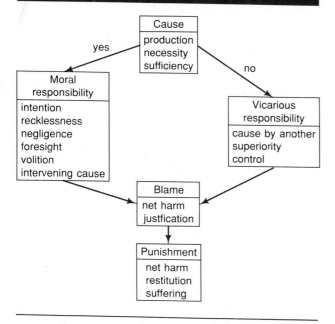

Source: From "Moral Rules: Their Content and Acquisition" by J. M. Darley and T. R. Schultz, 1990, *Annual Review of Psychology, 41*. Reproduced, with permission, from the *Annual Review of Psychology*, Volume 41, © 1990 by Annual Reviews Inc.

finding that differences in judgment are produced by manipulated differences in rule-relevant information presented to the subjects. Thus, while Kohlberg's approach requires subjects to have direct conscious access to the rules they use, the information processing approach does not (Darley & Shultz, 1990).

EARLY AND MIDDLE CHILDHOOD

PROSOCIAL WAYS OF BEHAVING: ALTRUISTIC BEHAVIOR

Behavior that has clear moral implications is a prosocial or altruistic way of behaving. **Prosocial behaviors** or **altruistic behaviors** are actions that aid or benefit another person or society. To this definition is sometimes added the condition that altruistic behavior carries with it no anticipation of external reward. The definition also implies that the beneficial act must be performed voluntarily, not as a result of external threat or enforcement. It is recognized, however, that an individual may feel an internal pressure or obligation that can lead to prosocial behavior.

It has frequently been reported that older children are more altruistic than younger children (Froming, Allen, & Jensen, 1985), and a number of social-cognitive and affective processes have been held to account for the observed age trends. Among these processes are children's increased ability to assume the perspective of another in need and children's enhanced moral reasoning capacities (Zarbatany, Hartmann, & Gelfand, 1985). The ability to empathize with another is also postulated as central in the development of a variety of prosocial behaviors: cooperation, friendliness, kindness, generosity, sharing, and so on (Hoffman, 1984; Kohlberg, 1969).

Empathy is frequently defined as a largely involuntary, vicarious response to the emotional cues from other people or their situations (Hoffman, 1982). Hoffman has written the largest body of work on the development of empathy, and maintains that when one empathizes with distress in others, the awareness of t_ state of empathic arousal that _ helping and comforting are car_ss leads to a reduce empathic distress. Affect_ng. Thus, tant role in the expression of en_g. _der to ways. Its source may lie in empat_ guilt over failure to live up to your sel_or- the pleasure of social interaction. En_ sympathy are not synonymous; symp_ emotional response stemming from _ emotional state or condition. It consists of _ or sorrow or concern for the other's welfare (_ berg & Strayer, 1987).

Cognitive-developmental theorists relate _ pathic behavior to decreasing egocentrism _ young children and to a developing sense of the "other." Empathic behavior is also dependent on the ability to discriminate and label emotional states in others (Eisenberg-Berg & Neal, 1979). It is now generally agreed that empathy is best understood as a construct involving complex interactions between cognitive and emotional components (Hoffman, 1984). Children's ability to infer what another is experiencing or thinking or to feel another's emotional state develops gradually.

The Development of Empathy: Jean Piaget According to Piaget, children are not capable of developing a concern for others until they are around 7 years old. Prior to that age, Piaget indicated that younger children's empathic abilities are limited and inconsistently applied. He maintained that young children do not have sufficient cognitive maturity to take another's point of view. Until the age of concrete operations (7 to 11 years), children cannot decenter—they can attend to only one dimension in a situation at a time and cannot consider other aspects involved in a problem or situation. Moreover, children before the age of 7 are too egocentric to see the situation from another person's perspective. Piaget demonstrated children's egocentric and centered thinking by performing his three-dimensional mountain experiment (see Figure 14.3). He found that children under the age of 7 could correctly describe a three-

FIGURE 14.3   Diagram of Mountain Scene in Space Projection Task

dimensional mountain scene on the table in front of them. They were unable, however, to describe how the doll sitting on the opposite side of the table facing them would view the mountain scene.

Further evidence for Piaget's postulation that truly empathic responses do not occur until around the age of 7 in most children comes from another study (Hughes, Tingle, & Sawin, 1981). These researchers concluded, after testing 48 kindergartners and second-graders, that children between the ages of 5 and 7 become increasingly aware of other persons' perspectives in emotion-eliciting situations. In general, the older children (second-graders) showed a better understanding of other children's emotional states than younger children; they were more adept at placing themselves cognitively and emotionally in the other's place. Older children's reasons for their own emotional reactions were more likely to focus on psychological processes within themselves, rather than exclusively on the situation of the story child, as was characteristic of younger children.

The Development of Empathy: Martin Hoffman
Hoffman (1982, 1984) believes that the roots of empathy may be observed earlier than age 7. Hoffman believes that children progress through four stages, gradually developing a more complete ability to reveal an interest in and reaction to the needs of others.

Empathic Distress   Hoffman argues that empathy is experienced in the 1st year of life as personal distress or as purely vicarious contagion. This is because the child is unclear as to who is experiencing the distress. In Hoffman's first stage, *empathic distress*, birth to age 2, infants begin to cry if another infant in the immediate vicinity cries. This is a kind of automatic matching of emotions, perhaps arising out of the infants' lack of a clear distinction between self and others. Infants' reaction to sounds of crying, which may be regarded as a form of primitive empathy, is not prosocial behavior, but it may be a rudimentary basis of empathic responsiveness that leads to prosocial behavior (Thompson, 1987).

Zahn-Waxler (1979) and Zahn-Waxler and Radke-Yarrow (1979) have provided some fascinating insights into the development of concern for others. By training mothers to report on the reactions of their children to distress in others, these investigators were able to establish that children as early as 10 months show signs of agitation and general disturbances to others' distress. The authors suggested, however, that these young children appear to be experiencing either emotional contagion or personal distress. Recent research indicates that children as young as 14 months show empathic and prosocial involvement in other people's distress (Zahn-Waxler, Robinson, & Emde, 1991). Girls showed more concern and reproduced or imitated the affective experience of others more often than did boys.

By the middle or end of the second year, prosocial interventions and imitation of others' emotions were typical reactions to another's distress. These prosocial interventions included physical contact, instrumental acts, and verbal concern. One child, for example, ran to her mother who was crying, patted her face, and then buried her face in her mother's lap—apparently both providing and requesting comfort. Not only are the beginnings of concern for others seen at an early age, but they also appear to provide the prototype for later altruism (Eisenberg, 1989). Two thirds of the children who exhibited prosocial behaviors observed at 2 years showed similar prosocial behaviors at 7 years. Children who were caring when young behaved in an analogous way in later childhood.

Prosocial behavior does occur in preschool-aged children as well (Caplan & Hay, 1989). To illustrate, Rheingold, Hay, and West (1976) reported that young children engage in several behaviors that they called sharing: showing or giving objects to others and partner play. Partner play involves giving someone else an object and then proceeding to play with it while the other person has possession of it. They found such behavior among 15-month-old children, and its frequency increased from 15 to 24 months. These behaviors indicate some role taking and the desire to share one's perspective or interest.

Zahn-Waxler, Radke-Yarrow, Wagner, and Chapman (1992) examined children between the ages of 1 and 2 years and their responses to distress they witnessed in others. The affective, behavioral, and cognitive components of children's responses to others' distress were explored. The findings indicate that during the second year of life, children develop a capacity to intervene on behalf of others. The prosocial interventions take a variety of forms, including sharing, helping, and comforting others in distress. The authors noted that during the second year of life there is a shift from self-concern to empathic concern for others. The researchers note that children as young as 2 years old have

(a) the cognitive capacity to interpret the physical and psychological states of others, (b) the emotional capacity to affectively experience others' states, and (c) the behavioral repertoire that permits the possibility of trying to alleviate discomfort in others. (p. 127)

Person Permanence   In the second stage, *person permanence*, ages 3 to 6, older children will know that someone is in distress and be able to locate that individual. Children, however, assume that the person in distress feels exactly as they do. Young children do not understand that the distressed person may have inner feelings different from their own. It has also been observed that 3-year-olds bring toys or objects to children who are distressed, give verbal sympathy, bring someone to help, and attempt to cheer up the distressed child (Radke-Yarrow, Zahn-Waxler, & Chapman, 1983). Children from ages 3 to 6 have been observed to help another in distress, protect and defend, warn of danger, and become visibly anxious.

Radke-Yarrow and Zahn-Waxler (1984) also examined individual differences in children's responding. Among 1- and 2-year-olds, some children responded to others' distress with prosocial behavior accompanied by affective arousal. In contrast, other children, who were equally effective in their prosocial interventions, were cognitively prosocial: They approached others' distress by inspecting, exploring, and asking questions. Yet other children either manifest an aggressive component (for example, hit the person who caused the distress) or shut out and retreated from others' signals of distress. These individual differences in predominant mode of reaction were stable over a period of approximately 5 years for two thirds of the children.

In another study (Sawin, 1980) of 3- and 7-year-old children's reactions to a distressed peer, observations were limited to instances when a child was crying very hard. The children closest to the crying child almost always showed some response (7% did not). Slightly less than half of the children showed a concerned facial expression, and 17% engaged in consoling-type behavior. Ten percent ran to get an adult and 5% threatened the child who caused the distress. Twelve percent of the children walked away, however, and 2% made overtly unsympathetic responses.

Whether preschool-aged children detect that another child is having trouble and consider help to be an appropriate response is influenced by the

While children as young as 3 years often help a distressed peer, they do not understand that the distressed child may have inner feelings different from their own.

explicitness of the cues in the distress situation and the explicitness of the cause of that distress. A study by Pearl (1985) found that when distress is expressed subtly, young children may simply not notice or understand that there is a problem. Moreover, unless the cause of the distress is also explicit, young children may not know quite how to help.

In Pearl's (1985) study, 64 4-year-old preschoolers and an equal number of third-graders (ages 8 and 9), observed videotapes of a child who was unable to open a cookie jar. Children were shown different versions of the videotape, varying the explicitness of the child's problems and distress. The children were then asked various questions to determine whether they detected the problem or thought that a "nice" child witnessing the scene would offer to help. Older children consistently recognized the problem and suggested appropriate actions whether the cues were subtle or explicit; however, the explicitness of the cues was an important influence on younger children, who tended to be aware that the child in the videotape was having a problem and to suggest a helpful response only when the cues indicating the distress and its cause were explicit. Only when the

child in the videotape gave up trying to open the cookie jar and said, "Rats, the top's stuck," were the younger children able to recognize the problem and respond with helpful comments. When the distress cues and causes were subtle (boy gives up and looks sadly at the cookie jar), these young children failed to respond with altruistic suggestions.

Role Taking   In the third stage, *role taking*, which occurs around the age of 7, children can pick up subtle cues regarding another person's feelings. They have developed an awareness that people may have responses to a situation that differ from their own. In cross-sectional and longitudinal research, investigators have noted decreases in reasoning reflecting hedonistic concerns from preschool to the middle elementary school years (Eisenberg, 1986), accompanied by an increase in reasoning reflecting an orientation toward others' needs (see Figure 14.4).

When children come to understand that the self and others are individuals with separate and different histories and identities and that people have feelings beyond the immediate situation, they can imagine the other's emotional state in the immediate context. They also may realize that others' dis-

FIGURE 14.4

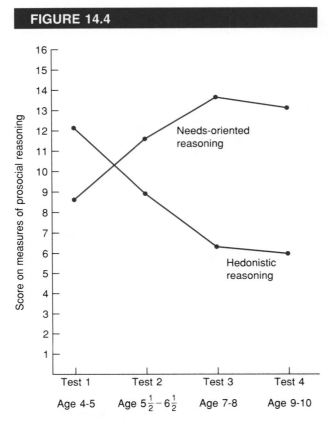

Over 5 years, Eisenberg repeatedly asked a group of children what a person should do when confronted with each of a series of dilemmas about doing good (such as helping someone who is hurt). The answers changed steadily with age. The minimum score on these measures is 4 and the maximum is 16. You can see that hedonistic reasoning (in which self-interest is placed first) drops to nearly minimum levels by age 7 or 8, while needs-oriented reasoning (such as "He needs help") rises to high levels at the same age.

Source: From *Altruistic Emotion, Cognition, and Behavior* (Table 7.7, p. 143) by N. Eisenberg, 1986, Hillsdale, NJ: Erlbaum. Copyright 1986 by Laurence Erlbaum Associates. Reprinted by permission.

tress is chronic rather than merely transitory. Seven-year-olds may realize that their mother is crying, not because she fell down and hurt herself, but because she is sad. It is not until middle child-

hood that children become adept at identifying the emotions of people unlike themselves in an unfamiliar situation.

The reason why children in middle childhood are more adept at identifying the emotions of other people than younger children is partially answered in a study by Hoffner and Badzinski (1989). In studying 83 children from preschool to fifth grade, the authors reported that younger children used only facial cues to identify emotional states of others, and sometimes were incorrect in labeling the emotion. Older children, around 8 or 9 years old, were more likely to use facial expression and situational cues to arrive at judgments of others' emotional states. As a result, they were much more accurate in correctly identifying feelings in others.

In middle or later childhood, use of reasoning reflecting stereotypic concepts of good and bad behavior, approval-oriented concerns, and self-reflective role taking as well as empathic responding increases. In late childhood and adolescence, children's use of reasoning reflecting internalized norms and values as well as affect related to such norms also increases, whereas stereotypic and approval-oriented reasoning declines (Eisenberg, 1986).

Comprehensive Empathy   In stage 4, *comprehensive empathy,* which begins in late childhood (around age 12), children develop an appreciation of others' feelings that goes beyond the immediate situation. An older child may collect money to contribute to some charitable organization to help needy children. A summary of Hoffman's stages of the development of empathy is found in Table 14.4.

Socialization of Empathy   Empathy shaped by parents and other important socializers is enhanced by a secure attachment between parent and child, by parental child-rearing practices, by being exposed to warm and empathic models, by inductive discipline, by communicating feelings to children, and by prosocial television episodes.

Attachment   It has been demonstrated that empathic, responsive preschoolers are more likely to have been securely attached infants (Darley &

TABLE 14.4 Hoffman's Stages in the Development of Empathy	Stage	Description	Example
	Stage 1: Empathic distress	Rudimentary form of empathy; child responds to another.	11-month-old sees another child crying.
	Stage 2: Person permanence	Child knows someone is in distress and can locate that child. Child does not realize that the other child may have feelings different from own.	18-month-old sees another child in distress, runs over, and tries to soothe child.
	Stage 3: Role taking	Children respond to another's distress because they are able to imagine themselves in the other's position.	Child pretends to like a present so as not to disappoint friend.
	Stage 4: Comprehensive empathy	Child becomes aware of distress within larger life.	12-year-old collects money for a charity.

Source: From "Affective and Cognitive Processes in Moral Internalization" by M. Hoffman, 1982, in E. T. Higgins, D. M. Ruble, and W. W. Hartup (Eds.), *Social Cognition and Social Behavior: Developmental Perspectives*, New York: Cambridge University Press. Copyright 1982 by Cambridge University Press. Reprinted by permission.

Shultz, 1990). In sharp contrast, children who show avoidant patterns of attachment are thought to have experienced repeated rejection in times of emotional need. They are overcontrolled as preschoolers (Arend, Gove, & Sroufe, 1979), and though they may become aroused to another's distress, they will have no framework for responding adequately. They may defend against the feelings that are aroused. Thus, avoidant children are most likely to appear unempathic, at times displaying attacking behavior. Children who have experienced insecure-avoidant attachment histories are thought to have experienced inconsistent care. In the face of strong feelings, they remain anxious, confused, and uncertain. They may show arousal and some responsivity, but because of their disorganization and anxiety, they have difficulty acting empathically. Due to problems in maintaining distance between themselves and others, they may be confused as to who is experiencing the distress.

Child-rearing Practices Baumrind (1975) reported that part of the pattern of child rearing by parents

of prosocial children was the assignment of household duties to their children. Mussen, Rutherford, Harris, and Keasey (1970) point out that encouragement of responsibility by mothers was associated with peers' perceptions of a child's helpfulness, particularly in boys. Whiting and Whiting (1975) examined behavior of children in six cultures and found that those who were more altruistic were the ones who were assigned responsibility that contributed to the maintenance of the family. The more the children had to tend animals, take care of younger siblings, and so on, the more altruistic their behavior.

Tompkins (1963) also suggested that when parents respond openly and nurturantly to their children's distress feelings, they not only learn that it is okay to express their feelings, but also learn to respond empathically to others.

Modeling The fact that mothers who were identified as providing empathic caregiving had more altruistic children suggests that these mothers were modeling, and their children were imitating sensitive reactions to need. Thus, teaching children to engage in prosocial behavior may be accomplished through other strategies such as modeling. If children learn by observing others, then prosocial behaviors could be learned via a socially empathic and socially effective model. Observing such a model may suggest to children that it is appropriate to help others and may lead to knowledge of how to help others. (Adults who verbally advocate nurturance and helpfulness, but do not practice what they preach, do not heighten children's helpfulness.) Children may also learn that helping acts result in beneficial consequences for the helper as well as for the recipient. Zahn-Waxler and Radke-Yarrow (1979) found that children whose mothers were rated as empathic were more empathic than children whose mothers were rated as nonempathic, which could indicate that these children were modeling their mothers' empathic or nonempathic behaviors.

Hay, Murray, Cecire, and Nash (1985) show that parents who consistently behave in a generous, caring manner with their children tend to have children who treat others in a similar fashion. Hoffman's (1984) work also suggests that prosocial behavior results from observing prosocial parental behavior.

Research has demonstrated that the effects of modeling show great durability (Grusec, 1981). The effects of modeling, however, do not generalize to situations different from the original training situation. For example, Grusec, Saas-Kortsaak, and Simutis (1978) found that children who had imitated a model who gave up game winnings to poor children in one experimental situation were not likely, in another experimental situation, to share with classmates pennies they had won.

One part of the research on modeling and altruism has focused on the role played by characteristics of the model. The two major characteristics that have been studied are nurturance (warmth, concern, interest) and power (prestige, control of resources) of the model. Both have been assumed to facilitate a child's willingness to emulate a model's altruism.

Modeling is not limited just to adults. For example, it has been found that children imitate their peers also (Hartup & Coates, 1967). In this study, nursery school children exposed to an altruistic peer model displayed significantly more altruism than children who were not exposed to the peer model.

Inductive Discipline   Hoffman's (1982) research suggests that prosocial behavior in children results from parental affection and the use of disciplinary techniques that emphasize the consequences of the children's behavior, known as **induction,** rather than techniques that represent power assertion. It appears that parents' use of reasoning techniques when disciplining (pointing out the harmful consequences of the children's behavior for others) helps children learn to consider the effects of their actions on others and to regulate their activities accordingly. This leads to an understanding of others' feelings and to attempts to help others (Knight, Kagan, & Raymond, 1982).

Moreover, a moral orientation characterized by independence of external sanctions and high guilt is associated with the mother's frequent use of inductive discipline. A moral orientation based on fear of external detection and punishment is associated with discipline techniques having high power-assertive components: physical force, material deprivation, or the threat of these.

Zahn-Waxler (1979) reported, however, that mothers' messages that proved effective in promoting prosocial behavior in toddlers were not calm, reasoned communications, but were charged with intense feeling and made statements of principle or of disappointment. These messages were "inductions," as they pointed out the effects of children's behavior, but they also contained both love withdrawal and power-assertive components. Zahn-Waxler concluded that the effective inductive technique is emotionally charged and forceful (e.g., "Look what you did? Don't you see you hurt Amy? Don't ever pull hair."). On the other hand, neutral explanations ("Tom's crying because you pushed him.") did not affect either reparations or prosocial behavior, although they were understood by these young children.

Communication   Another child-rearing technique that promotes prosocial behavior in children is

Explaining the possible consequences of a child's behavior is a disciplinary technique that is associated with facilitating higher levels of moral reasoning in children.

adults' verbal communications that suggest that children are indeed helpful, cooperative, sharing types of people. Jensen and Moore (1977) worked with 7- and 12-year-old behavior-problem boys. They found that positive attributions verbally expressed in a meaningful way ("It shows that you are really concerned about others." "You share well with others.") led these boys to engage in more cooperative and prosocial behaviors.

Furthermore, when social agents suggest that prosocial behaviors are part of the child's personality, these behaviors increase in frequency. In a representative study, 7- and 10-year-old children were induced to donate some of their winnings from a game to poor children (Grusec et al., 1978). One group of 14 children was told, "You share quite a bit." To this statement was added that they did so because they were the kind of people who liked to help others. Another group of 14 children were told that they shared quite a bit, but that they did so because the experimenter expected them to do so. The remaining 14 children were not pro-

vided with any explanation for their behavior. The children in the first group donated significantly more—an effect that endured when they were tested 2 weeks later. The results of this study suggest that socializing agents who attribute prosocial characteristics to children increase their helpfulness.

ANTISOCIAL WAYS OF BEHAVING: LYING, CHEATING, AND STEALING

Lying   Despite the centrality of lying and truthfulness to all major theories on morality (Freud, 1940/1964; Piaget, 1965), this aspect of morality has been largely neglected by developmental psychologists. Lying has been defined in terms of a statement that differs from reality, or a statement that fails to separate reality from fantasy (Paniagua, 1989). Piaget was perhaps the first researcher to study systematically young children's conceptions of lies. He asked children questions to determine their definitions of lying, and why people should not lie. It appears that before 6 or 7, a lie is conceptualized as something that is naughty. Children used punishment criterion to determine whether a lie is permissible: "One should not lie, because you get punished." Between the ages of 7 and 10, children define a lie as something that is not true, and maintain that it is wrong to lie even if you do not get punished. After the age of 10, children recognize that being truthful is necessary for social cooperation. Children come to oppose lying because truthfulness is necessary for cooperation and friendship.

Strichartz and Burton (1990) studied children's concepts of lies and truth in order to indicate some age trends. Their sample consisted of 150 subjects ranging in age from nursery-school children to adults. By age 4, children distinguish lies from truth on the basis of whether a statement is factual. Preschoolers, however, show no additive effect from the intent and belief systems of the speaker who may be doing the lying. Young children have to be able to factually verify in order to label a lie as a lie. That is, if Tommy says that he did not eat the cake, the child is able to label this a lie if he can observe that the cake is gone and Tommy has frosting on his face. Children rely on the simple matching rule that lying requires factuality, until sometime between 6 and 10 years old. During that time, children begin to place emphasis on the belief system of the speaker, and thus begin a modification of their reliance solely on factuality.

Similarly, lying has a reciprocal relationship to children's age, their awareness of reality, and the legitimacy of the goal they are seeking. Often the telling of tall tales by younger children is passed through without any serious results. As children gradually emerge into the world of reality they learn to keep their fantasy world separate from reality.

Bussey (1992) examined whether children could differentiate between lies and truthful statements and whether they could judge lies as more morally reprehensible than truthful statements on a sample of 72 preschoolers, second-graders, and fifth-graders. Her results indicate that even preschoolers could differentiate between lies and truthful statements about misdeeds. Truthful statements

were, however, not evaluated more favorably than misdeeds by preschoolers. Thus, although young children appreciated the naughtiness of lying, they failed to appreciate the value of truthfulness about misdeeds.

In accord with Piaget's (1965) theory, punishment affected the moral judgments of preschoolers, but not of the older children. Statements that led to punishment were evaluated by preschoolers more negatively than statements that did not lead to punishment. Thus, it appears that observable physical consequences are a major determinant of preschoolers' judgments of lies and truthful statements.

Lying is frequently judged by adults as a problem behavior. Data on child psychopathology and development support adults' concerns about lying in children. Researchers have found that children who lie at an earlier age might show high frequency of stealing, truancy, temper tantrums, aggression, and negativism at a later age (Achenbach & Edelbrock, 1984). In this study, the general conclusion was that lying by children could be a predictor of later maladjustment.

What are the conditions that lead to lying? Several home factors have been cited such as absence of parental warmth and honesty, parental and maternal rejection, lack of parental supervision, single and unhappy mothers, disharmonious homes, parental untruthfulness, and association with undesirable peers (Stouthamer-Loeber, 1986). Genuine lies are frequently born of a fear of punishment. Harsh reprisals for punishment only teach a child to be more skillful in lying. The defensive lie is a natural product of any situation in which children find themselves in danger of blame (Peterson, Peterson, & Seeto, 1983). Children generally do not deny an act unless they fear that their confession will result in punishment. Lying is a conscious defense against harsh repercussions from the environment. Thus, you might assume that punishment could also lead to an increase in the frequency of lying because the act of lying is, precisely, the condition necessary to avoid punishment. Punishment also teaches children what not to do; it does not teach children what to do (that is,

TABLE 14.5 Dealing with Children Who Lie

1. Explore and understand specific causes of lying incidents.
2. Establish a climate in which frankness is permissible and fostered.
3. Avoid harsh punishment and reduce the threat of punishment.
4. Ensure honest behavior in adult contacts inasmuch as imitation of adult behavior is common.
5. Plan so consequences of behavior give insight and stem naturally from act if possible.
6. Use children's imagination in socially approved channels.
7. Help children to understand it is to their advantage to tell truth because advantage rarely comes from lies.
8. Help children to develop appreciation of honesty through discussions of principles of stories.
9. Foster acceptance by classmates.
10. Establish avenues for obtaining social approval and recognition.

TABLE 14.6 Distribution of Cheating Ratios Among School Children

Cheating Ratio	Number	Percent*
1.00	78	3.2
.90	105	4.3
.80	178	7.3
.70	231	9.4
.60	252	10.3
.50	308	12.6
.40	310	12.7
.30	439	17.9
.20	231	9.4
.10	140	5.7
.00	171	7.0

*Percentages do not add to 100 because of rounding.

Source: Reprinted, with permission, from Hartshorne and May, *Studies in the Nature of Character*. Vol. 1, p. 379. © 1928–1930 by Macmillan Book Company.

an alternative and positive behavior). In this sense, punishment is not an educative procedure. Table 14.5 offers some possible actions to take with children who lie.

Cheating Psychologists have attempted to answer questions concerning honest actions. In a classic study on cheating (Hartshorne & May, 1928–1930), U.S. schoolchildren were given a variety of opportunities to lie, cheat, and steal. Children had a chance, for example, to cheat on tests in reading, math, and English. Children had 10 tests on which they could cheat. In a well-controlled tally of cheating behavior, the investigators computed a ratio between the number of times the child cheated and the number of chances to cheat.

A ratio of 1.0 meant that children with such a score cheated every chance they had. A ratio of 0.00 meant that children with such a score never cheated despite the opportunity to do so. Table 14.6 shows the distribution of cheating ratios among 2,443 school children. The table points out that 3.2% cheated all the time while 7.0% cheated none of the time. About half the children cheated

on between one third and two thirds of the chances they had and about 13% cheated half the time.

Impossible standards, fear of censure if standards are not met, humiliation, need for power, and a feeling of accomplishment are some of the factors that may cause children to cheat. Children's value systems may center around the improper assumption that acceptance only comes with the highest accomplishments. Cheating may be the only way some children can achieve these goals of excellence and consequently the recognition they crave.

Children need to be encouraged to accept standards and goals that are commensurate with their level of accomplishment. Children should learn that they cannot always get the highest marks; sometimes even the best of us may do poorly. Children need to learn that they cannot always win when playing a game but that, at times, everyone loses. It is better to lose than to cheat and win.

Stealing In order to understand children's dishonest behavior it is necessary to ascertain children's age, how long they have been stealing,

Whether we are talking about playing a game or taking a test, when the fear of losing or failure are too great, the problem of cheating may arise.

what they steal, and what they do with the stolen objects.

Very young children show a limited sense of property value. Often they take things that belong to others as an expression of their wishing to have the object. Primary grade children can take possessions of others because of their appeal without the knowledge that such an action is stealing or without distinct knowledge of the difference between borrowing and stealing. Sometimes children have to learn to do things the right way by doing them the wrong way first. Although many young children may steal something at one point in their lives, most learn to internalize standards of honesty. It takes time, however, for children to internalize moral and social values and standards.

Although the acceptance of the prohibition against taking what belongs to another may begin as a result of parental disapproval, it is strengthened as children come to value acceptance by their own peer group. Identification with the feelings that another experiences in losing a valued object is a later development in most children. As children develop a firm property sense, they enjoy the pleasurable feelings and approving responses of others for their honesty.

If children have been stealing on several occasions, it is obviously a more serious symptom. Persistent stealing over a period of time needs to be carefully analyzed.

Noticing what children take may indicate what they are lacking physically, materially, or psychologically. Children may steal food if they are constantly hungry. They may steal an article of clothing because they feel they are poorly dressed. Stealing, however, is not always the result of a need for material things. Stealing may also indicate that children's emotional and social needs are not being met. If children steal things they do not need, or destroy the things that they steal, several factors may be responsible. Comparatively meaningless objects or thefts that appear unintelligible suggest a symbolic theft indicative of frustration or tension in other areas, such as the need for affection, retaliation, relief of frustration from failure, and attempts to gain recognition from peers (Nettler, 1982). Stealing may represent a blind grasping for love and affection. In some homes, for example, parents may show caring by showering children with material gifts. Things become substitutes for love. Then when children need affection, they may resort to stealing. Young children tend to equate love with the number of gifts they are given. Stealing in these cases may represent stealing love.

Stealing may be prompted by children's need to establish a place within the peer group—to be recognized and accepted by others. Buying friends with stolen money may indicate a need for some kind of social recognition. Children who cannot release animosity directly may strike at parental values. If children learn that stealing upsets their parents, they may then use it as an unconscious weapon to punish them.

Parents should not be too deeply shocked, hurt, surprised, or emotionally overreact when stealing occurs. Nor should parents continually give moralizing lectures on dishonesty. It is best to downgrade the seriousness of the stealing incident. The stolen article should be returned or restitution made by the child. Downgrading the importance of stealing may be difficult for parents who think they have an obligation to teach their children. Parental scorn, criticisms, and punishment, however, may provide children with further ammunition and increased desire to do wrong for the sake of power and defeating their parents. Children do not need instruction; they know perfectly well that lying and stealing are wrong.

Actions taken to correct the problem need to be consistent with the causes indicated. If lacking necessary funds, children need an allowance that is ample enough to satisfy their needs. Children who steal to buy friends need help in satisfying their need for prestige in the group. If they steal as a result of lack of love, they need to be helped in correcting the assumption that they can retaliate against their lack of affection by stealing. It is important for adults to forget children's past stealing episodes, and not keep harping on their past mistakes. Adults need to show children that they have confidence in them that they will not steal again.

MORAL FEELINGS: GUILT

Most children experience some degree of guilt when they have lied, cheated, or stolen something. At an adaptive level, guilt promotes prosocial and inhibits antisocial behaviors (Ferguson, Stegge, & Damhuis, 1991). **Guilt** involves a sense of feeling responsible for your actions and an ability to sense that your actions have brought psychological or physical harm to another. It results from wrongdoing or from breaking a rule or violating your standards or beliefs. Guilt refers to your sense of wrongdoing, whether or not you are caught. Guilt feelings may be evoked by real or imagined wrongdoing. In order to experience guilt, several social and cognitive capacities are apparent.

Social and Cognitive Capacities In order to experience guilt, children need to be able to distinguish between self and not self. You may not expect any signs of guilt until children feel a sense of separateness, which is around 6 to 10 months of age. Children who are not aware of the self and others as separate entities may be uncertain as to who committed the harmful act—the victim or the self (Hoffman, 1977). Another minimal requirement for experiencing a feeling of guilt is that children have developed a sense of "self-as-causal-agent." That is, in order to experience guilt, children need to have developed an awareness of being the agent of harm. Children must be able to recognize the harmful effects of their behavior.

When children are able to recognize that their actions have brought harm to others, they experience guilt.

Moreover, children must realize that others have independent, internal states. In other words, children need to be aware that other people's thoughts may sometimes differ from their own and that others' perspectives may be based on their own interpretations of events (Hoffman, 1982). This generally occurs around 2 to 3 years of age. If children are unaware that others have feelings different from their own, they may not feel guilty over hurting another's feelings. A final cognitive dimension of guilt is the awareness that there exists a moral norm that does not sanction harming others and that actual or contemplated behavior is discrepant from that norm.

The Development of Guilt   Keeping in mind the social and cognitive capacities that are necessary in order to experience the feeling of guilt, Hoffman (1983) makes some speculations as to the kinds of situations that might make a child feel guilty. According to Hoffman, there appear to be distinct stages in the development of guilt that are dependent on the child's cognitive and social skills and experiences.

Empathic Distress Response   Once children have the capacity to recognize the consequences for others of their actions and to be aware that they have a choice and control over their own behavior, they have the necessary requisites for a self-critical and self-blaming response to their actions. It follows that if the cues in a situation—in which they respond empathically to someone in distress—indicate that they caused that distress, their response may then have both the affectively unpleasant and cognitive self-blaming component of the guilt experience.

Young children appear to experience a kind of *empathic distress*. That is, they become responsive to others' inner states. To illustrate, Zahn-Waxler (1979) trained parents to observe and record their children's behavior. These investigations described guiltlike behavior in a third of their sample of 15- to 18-month-old children in certain situations. For example, on seeing their mothers cry, the children would ask apologetically, "Did I make you sad?" or, "Sorry, I be nice." The experiment suggests that an early rudimentary tendency to feel guilty over harming others occurs in young children, which is perhaps a precursor of the more fully developed guilt response that comes later.

Guilt over Physically Harming Another   Perhaps the simplist case of feeling guilty occurs when children commit a physically harmful act. Because the consequences are immediate and observable, it is minimally demanding, cognitively speaking. In addition, a parent is usually around to point out the harmful effect of the children's act. Thus, the first rudimentary feelings of guilt occur when children believe that they have caused some kind of physical harm to another.

Guilt over Inaction   A second kind of guilt, *guilt over inaction*, becomes a possibility once children acquire the additional capacity to construct a mental representation of an event that might have occurred, but did not. Guilt over not taking any action (omission) is more demanding, cognitively speaking. In such a situation, children must be able to imagine something that might have happened, and to be aware of the consequences of not doing anything. Hoffman (1987) asked fifth- and seventh-graders to complete the following story:

> A child who is hurrying with a friend to an important sports event encounters a small child who seems lost. He suggests that they stop and help, but his friend talks him out of it. The next day he finds out that the small child, who had been left alone by an irresponsible babysitter, ran into the street and was killed by a car.

The transgression in this story was one of omission, not stopping to help. The protagonist actually did nothing wrong and there was no reason for him to anticipate the tragic consequences of inaction. Despite these reasons for deserving little blame, most of the children's responses indicated that they would feel very guilty in similar situations. Hoffman's findings suggest that children from about 10 years of age and older typically respond with guilt feelings when they believe they have harmed others by neglecting to take action. Try the experiment in "Studying Children."

Anticipatory Guilt   Even more demanding cognitively is guilt over contemplating a harmful act. In

STUDYING CHILDREN

GUILT

Choose two or three children between the ages of 8 and 12 and ask them how they would feel if they were Tom in the following story:

Tom is hurrying with his friend to an important sports event, when they encounter a small child who seems lost. Tom (Susan) suggests that they stop and help, but his (her) friend talks him (her) out of it. The next day he (she) finds out that the small child, who had been left alone by an irresponsible babysitter, ran into the street and was killed by a car.

Hoffman (1987) found in his research that children at around 10 years of age and older typically respond with guilt feelings when they believe they have harmed others by neglecting to take action. Do your subjects respond with guilt feelings over inaction?

order to experience *anticipatory guilt*, children must have the capacity to visualize not only an act that they have not performed (but may be contemplating), but also the other person's probable distress response as well. Children in middle childhood are generally able to experience anticipatory guilt. For example, a 12-year-old may experience anticipatory guilt when he thinks about stealing the social studies notes from another student. He realizes that if he does, the other student will not do well on the exam.

Survival Guilt   In adolescents and young adults, *survivor guilt* occurs when they have neither done nor contemplated doing anything wrong, but feel somehow to blame for a bad event, even though the circumstances were beyond their control. The experiencing of guilt, even when no wrong has been done is exemplified by an African American student at Harvard who wrote that he and others like him had to "wrestle with the keen sense of guilt they feel being here while their families still struggle in black ghettoes" (Hoffman, 1987, p. 301). Are these feelings of guilt a desirable phenomena? (See the "Focus on Issues.")

FOCUS ON ISSUES

Is Guilt Good or Bad?

On the negative side, guilt feelings can be highly deprecatory and threatening to children's self-image. An overdeveloped sense of guilt or too low a threshold of guilt may lead to serious adjustment problems. Excessive guilt may cause fears and anxieties that can, in turn, bring on a galaxy of illnesses, ranging from chronic fatigue to drug abuse.

Guilt may, however, be a desirable feeling in the sense that it makes you aware that you have done something wrong when you have violated your own conscience and the mores of your society. If children never felt guilt, they would not learn in school, obey rules, or live in harmony with one another. In short, guilt is society's regulator (David, 1981). There is also some empirical evidence that guilt may have a positive social value. Freedman, Wallington, and Bless (1967) asked college subjects to sit either at a wobbly table or at a stable table to do an experiment. Subjects at the wobbly table inevitably upset a graduate student's supposedly carefully arranged index cards. Of course, those at the stable table did not. Following this treatment condition, the experimenter asked the subjects to volunteer for an experiment by a graduate student—the same graduate student whose cards had been on the table. Seventy-five percent of the subjects who had upset the index cards complied with the request to participate, while only 39% of the control subjects complied.

ADOLESCENCE

During childhood, moral guidelines are seen as absolutes emanating from such authorities as parents or teachers; judgments of right and wrong are made according to concrete rules. During adolescence, however, such absolutes and rules come to be questioned, as the young person begins to see that moral standards are subjective and based on points of view that are subject to disagreement. Later in adolescence comes the emergence of reasoning that is based on such moral principles as equality, justice, or fairness—abstract guidelines that transcend concrete situations and can be applied across a variety of moral dilemmas (Kohlberg & Gilligan, 1972). The development of social conventions appears to follow a similar course (Geiger & Turiel, 1983).

Helwig, Tisak, and Turiel (1990) have demonstrated that young children and adolescents develop parallel and independent perspectives of two sorts of rules—*moral rules* and *social conventional rules*. A rule is a moral one if adherence to it is experienced as obligatory, if it applies to all people regardless of their attitude toward it, and if its force is impersonal and external. Moral rules involve intrinsic principles of justice, fairness, and the welfare of others. In contrast, the realm of social conventional rules includes those arbitrary social formulations whose validity is limited to the social systems in which they are constructed (Gabennesch, 1990). Recognizing that conventions lack inherent moral significance, children and adolescents do not regard them as sacred, obligatory, and absolute.

CONCEPTS OF SOCIAL CONVENTION

Social conventions are behavioral uniformities and shared rules that coordinate the stable interactions of individuals within a social system (Geiger & Turiel, 1983). Social conventions pertain to social norms such as modes of dress, forms of greeting, forms of address, and so forth that guide day-to-day behavior. The development of social conventions follows a stage sequence with seven levels of reasoning. These age-related changes in concepts of social convention are presented in Table 14.7.

TABLE 14.7 Levels of Social-Conventional Concepts	Ages*	Characteristics
		Level 1: Convention as descriptive of social uniformity
	6–7	Convention viewed as descriptive of uniformities in behavior. Convention is not conceived as part of structure or function of social interaction. Conventional uniformities are descriptive of what is assumed to exist. Convention maintained to avoid violation of empirical uniformities.
		Level 2: Negation of convention as descriptive social uniformity
	8–9	Empirical uniformity not a sufficient basis for maintaining conventions. Conventional acts regarded as arbitrary. Convention is not conceived as part of structure or function of social interaction.
		Level 3: Convention as affirmation of rule system; early concrete conception of social system
	10–11	Convention seen as arbitrary and changeable. Adherence to convention based on concrete rules and authoritative expectations. Conceptions of conventional acts not coordinated with conception of rule.
		Level 4: Negation of convention as part of rule system
	12–13	Convention now seen as arbitrary and changeable regardless of rule. Evaluation of rule pertaining to conventional act is coordinated with evaluation of the act. Conventions are "nothing but" social expectations.
		Level 5: Convention as mediated by social system
	14–16	The emergence of systematic concepts of social structure. Convention as normative regulation in system with uniformity, fixed roles, and static hierarchical organization.
		Level 6: Negation of convention as societal standards
	17–18	Convention regarded as codified societal standards. Uniformity in convention is not considered to serve the function of maintaining social system. Conventions are "nothing but" societal standards that exist through habitual use.
		Level 7: Convention as coordination of social interactions
	18–25	Conventions as uniformities that are functional in coordinating social interactions. Shared knowledge, in the form of conventions, among members of social groups facilitate interaction and operation of the system.

*Approximate.

Source: From "Disruptive School Behavior and Concepts of Social Convention in Early Adolescence" by K. M. Geiger and E. Turiel, 1983, *Journal of Educational Psychology, 75*, p. 679. Copyright 1983 by The American Psychological Association. Reprinted by permission.

At each level, judgments about social conventions stem from a conceptualization of social organization. During middle childhood, social conventions, such as waiting in line at McDonalds for a Big Mac, are seen as arbitrary and changeable, but adherence to them is not; compliance with such conventions is based on rules and dictates of authority. Thus, when you were 7 years old, you might not have seen why people wait in line to buy a hamburger, but your mother told you to wait in line—so you did. By early adolescence, conventions are seen as arbitrary and changeable in both their origins and their enforcement; conventions are merely social expectations. Adolescents realize that you wait in line because you are expected to, not because you are forced to. Adolescents see social conventions as a means by which society regulates behavior.

VALUES

Values are normative ideas that guide behavior and provide external and internal standards toward which people strive. Values provide the foundation for moral behavior. Studies of adolescent values reveal some very positive images. In a study of 200 college students (McFalls, Jones, Gallager, & Rivera, 1985), 65% anticipated that family life would be their major source of life satisfaction, followed by occupation as a second major source of life satisfaction. Simmons and Wade (1985) asked adolescents to complete the sentence, ''The sort of person I would like to be . . .'' Twenty percent of the youths surveyed indicated that they would not like to be anyone but themselves. Seventeen percent expressed that they would like to be friendly, courteous, or good humored. Eighteen percent wanted to be reliable, honest, industrious, and kind. The desire to fulfill oneself as a person and to have opportunity for self-expression—a freedom to be oneself—was valued quite strongly among many adolescents.

Peer-Approved versus Parent-Approved Values Are adolescents' values similar to parental values? Bachman, Johnston, and O'Malley (1987) found that the values of high school seniors appear to be in much closer agreement than many suppose, as you can see in Figure 14.5. Agreement, however, is greater on basic values (for example, the value of education) than on life-style (how to spend leisure time) choices.

Many adolescents place high values on physical well-being as evidenced in jogging, health programs, and concern for nutrition.

Association with antisocial peers is a salient factor in producing juvenile delinquency.

Thus, parents and peers occupy somewhat separate spheres of influence. Peers are likely to be more influential than parents in conflicts involving social activities and friendship choices. Adolescents tend to have values similar to their peers on issues relating to daily living and matters of taste, dress, speech, and social behavior, but do not change basic family values. Adolescents have values similar to their parents on basic values such as scholastic goals or future-oriented decisions and aspirations. Adolescents continue to side with parents on issues that relate to the larger society and ethical questions. Similarly, research by Sebald (1989) supports the Bachman et al. (1987) study. Sebald found, in questioning 570 high school students that the nature of the issue determined which reference group (parents or peers) was activated. Although education, career, and financial concerns were more parent oriented, almost all social activities were peer oriented.

What happens when peer values oppose parental values? In one study, 10- to 14-year-olds were

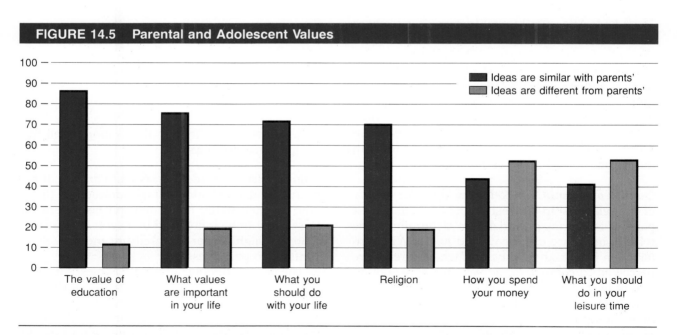

FIGURE 14.5   Parental and Adolescent Values

Legend:
- Ideas are similar with parents'
- Ideas are different from parents'

Categories (x-axis): The value of education | What values are important in your life | What you should do with your life | Religion | How you spend your money | What you should do in your leisure time

Source: From *Monitoring the Future, 1986: Questionnaire Responses from the Nation's High School Seniors* (pp. 170–171) by J. G. Bachman, L. D. Johnston, and P. M. O'Malley, 1987, Ann Arbor: Institute for Social Research, University of Michigan. Copyright 1987 by the Institute for Social Research. Reprinted by permission.

presented with the dilemmas test (Devereux, 1970). The test consists of hypothetical situations that involve moral dilemmas of conduct, pitting peer-approved values that deviate from parent-approved values. One question involves going to a movie with a group of friends who proposed that they should all lie about their age in order to ride on the bus at half-fare. It was found that those who spent the most time with peers and preferred gangs were more likely to go along with the crowd in such deviant acts than were children who did not spend as much time with peers and preferred to be with their best friends.

Such a conflict between adult and peer values may not be a general thrust throughout adolescence or for all adolescents. Recent research has shown that whether adolescents conform depends on their age and maturity, the quality of their relationship with their parents, and whether the adolescent or parents possess certain characteristics.

Children's Age   Children become more and more inclined to go along with peers between the ages of 11 and 14. After age 14, children are less likely to accede to deviant peer pressure. Berndt (1979), for example, found in studying 251 children in grades 3, 6, 9, 11, and 12, that conformity to parents in neutral and prosocial situations (involving questions about what to wear and when to be helpful) gradually decreased from third grade to high school. For anti-social norms, however, peer conformity increased progressively from third to ninth grade, but not beyond (see Figure 14.6).

Quality of Parent/Child Relationship   The quality of the relationship between adolescents and their parents is a primary variable in determining the relative influence of parents and peers. When interaction is of high quality, and when parents are perceived as competent, adolescents generally do not differ from parents on significant issues. Those who have a close relationship with their parents may choose peers with a similar rather than conflicting value system. Parents have more influence than peers when they have warm relationships

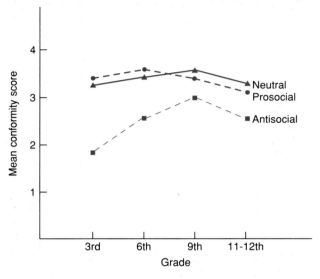

FIGURE 14.6   Mean Scores for Each Grade on Conformity to Peers for Different Types of Behaviors

Higher scores indicate greater conformity and the neutral point is 3.5.

Source: From "Developmental Changes in Conformity to Peers and Parents" by T. J. Berndt, 1979, *Developmental Psychology*, *15*, pp. 608–616. Copyright 1979 by the American Psychological Association. Reprinted by permission.

with adolescents, although this is more often true for girls than for boys.

Characteristics of Adolescents and Parents   It has been found that autonomous adolescents (those who are not highly dependent on peers) are the least likely to be influenced by peers. Adolescents who are highly peer oriented are more likely to conform to peer pressure.

The parents of nonconforming adolescents have moderate to high levels of support and nurturance for their sons and daughters. They are firm but not oppressive in their level of control. Moreover, these parents tend to demonstrate democratic decision making. In contrast, highly conforming adolescents tend to come from homes that are either high on permissiveness or high on punitiveness. They receive less support and less control from their parents.

Cross-Cultural Studies The nature and effects of peer groups are likely to be influenced by the culture in which the family resides. To illustrate, Bronfenbrenner (1970) conducted tests on 10- to 14-year-olds in the United States, Russia, England, and Germany. The test was administered in three separate conditions: *Scientific:* The subjects were told that the test was conducted for scientific reasons, and their answers would not be revealed to anyone. *Adult:* The subjects were told that the results would be shown to teachers and parents. *Peer:* The subjects were told that the results would be shown to their peers.

In all three conditions, adolescents from Russia were much less likely to engage in peer-endorsed deviant behavior than adolescents from the other countries. Girls, in all countries, were more adult conforming than were boys. In the peer condition, U.S. adolescents were more inclined to go along with peer-condoned misconduct. In contrast to the U.S. sample, Russian adolescents shifted toward greater adult conformity. Bronfenbrenner explains the reason for this cross-cultural difference. In Russia, the peer group is used as a transmitter and reinforcer of the Russian society's values. Russian children, for example, are expected by their teachers to take action against peers if they deviate from socially accepted norms. In the United States, peers represent values that are sometimes at variance to accepted parental norms. Peers in the United States tend to frown on a peer who "informs" on a fellow peer.

ADOLESCENT DELINQUENCY

Everyday, adolescents are faced with choices that involve doing the right thing versus engaging in unethical or illegal behaviors. Adolescents' ability to resist wrongdoing reflects socialization practices that stress the importance of subordinating the individual's impulses to the requirements of conventional authority or law. Although the majority of teenagers show a reasonable degree of adherence to moral principles, even under duress, others may yield to temptation or to group pressure to engage in illegal behavior.

Juvenile delinquency presents a serious moral topic of concern to society. More than 1.4 million juveniles are arrested each year for crimes such as vandalism, drug abuse, or running away, and almost 900,000 for crimes such as larceny-theft, robbery, or forcible rape (Federal Bureau of Investigation, 1987). Individuals under the age of 18 account for 17% of all crimes (see Figure 14.7). The United States spends more than 1 billion dollars per year to maintain the juvenile justice system. Of course, not all costs can be measured in terms of dollars and cents. These adolescents are likely to experience major adjustment problems in the areas of academic achievement and peer relations.

A juvenile delinquent refers to a young person, generally under the age of 18, who has been apprehended and convicted for transgression of established laws. Boys have a higher recorded delinquency incidence than do girls; however, there is an increasing number of females who are being arrested for a widening range of offenses (Patterson, DeBaryshe, & Ramsey, 1989). Offenses committed by males are more apt to involve burglary, auto theft, aggravated assault, and other aggressive behaviors. Girls, however, are more likely to commit such offenses as running away from home or illicit sexual behavior. For both boys and girls delinquency rates fall after age 16 (see Figure 14.8).

Factors Contributing to Juvenile Delinquency Researchers have extensively studied the variables that appear to predict the occurrence of juvenile delinquency. Although juvenile delinquency is a result of a number of complex factors with no single factor explaining its occurrence, high incidents of lying and stealing at an early age, poor relationships with parents, high marital discord in the family setting, dislike for school, and truancy are some of the more frequently cited factors.

Lying and Stealing Mitchell and Rosa (1981) found that those children who, according to their par-

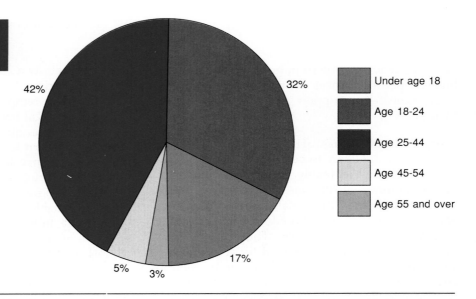

FIGURE 14.7   Age Distribution of All People Arrested, 1985

42%

32%

17%

5%   3%

Under age 18

Age 18-24

Age 25-44

Age 45-54

Age 55 and over

Source: From *Statistical Abstract of the United States, 1987* (table 279) by U.S. Bureau of the Census, Department of Commerce, 1987, Washington, DC: U.S. Government Printing Office.

FIGURE 14.8

In using the official arrest figures, the seriousness of delinquent acts appears to peak at about age 15. Boys commit more numerous and more serious delinquent acts than girls.

Delinquency and age

Source: From *The Future of Crime* by G. M. Sykes, 1980, National Institute of Mental Health, DHHS Publication No. ADM 80–912, Washington, DC: U.S. Government Printing Office.

ents, continually engaged in lying and stealing at an early age were more likely to engage in antisocial acts later on. Of the children engaging in frequent lying, 37.3% later committed at least one indictable offense. Only 8.3% of the children who were described by their parents as "always telling the truth" committed an indictable offense during adolescence. Of the children whose parents stated that they had stolen things on several occasions, 66.7% later committed at least one indictable offense, compared with 9.1% of those whose parents reported that their children never or rarely took anything that belonged to someone else.

Family Factors There is a long history of empirical studies that have identified family variables as consistent factors for early forms of antisocial behavior and for later delinquency (Loeber & Dishion, 1983; Synder & Patterson, 1986). A disproportionate number of juvenile delinquents come from families in which there is poor parental supervision, poor parental behavior, broken homes, and large families. Ensminger (1990) found in studying 1,242 adolescents from lower socioeconomic classes that the key difference between no-problem adolescents and those who had engaged in delinquent acts was that lack of parental supervision characterized the latter group. No-problem adolescents tended to have mothers who were aware of their children's behavior, exerted more parental control, and showed more parental concern for their adolescents.

In studying 500 delinquent and 500 nondelinquent children between the ages of 11 and 17, it was noted that parents of delinquent children were characterized as being unkind, inconsistent with discipline, and far more likely to use physical punishment. Other factors, such as parental rejection, discord between parents, lack of masculine identification in boys, low socioeconomic status of the family, and prolonged absence of a parent, tended to produce delinquent behavior in children (Glueck & Glueck, 1950).

Adolescents' feelings of alienation have been linked to juvenile delinquency, and, according to some psychologists, these feelings have their origins in the family (Bronfenbrenner, 1986). Alienation is defined as the individuals' sense of separation from work, themselves, or significant others (Erikson, 1980). Families characterized by disorganization and disintegration generated by external forces such as economic and social pressures, families in which the child is rejected, abused, and neglected nurture an environment that is conducive to the growth of alienation. Children and adolescents who are raised in this unstable environment frequently respond by exhibiting antisocial behaviors such as rebelling or withdrawing from society (Calabrese & Adams, 1990).

Peers Those who engage in juvenile delinquent acts as adolescents seem not to have been very popular in the early and middle elementary school grades. Several studies have shown that delinquent children are often described by their peers in the early elementary school grades as aggressive, unfriendly, and troublesome (Nelson, Smith, & Dodd, 1990; Osborne & West, 1978; Pulkkinin, 1982). Patterns of antisocial behavior emerge as salient predictors of juvenile delinquency.

Studies have shown that about half the antisocial children become adolescent delinquents, and roughly half to three quarters of the adolescent delinquents become adult offenders (Farrington, 1987). The association between antisocial behavior and rejection by the normal peer group has been well documented (Dodge, Coie, & Brakke, 1982; Roff & Wirt, 1984). Antisocial behavior and peer group rejection are important preludes to deviant peer group membership.

Recent studies have shown an impressive link between involvement with antisocial peers and juvenile delinquency (Dishion, Patterson, Stoolmiller, & Skinner, 1991; Dishion, Reid, & Patterson, 1988). A social interaction model has been developed by Patterson (1982) explaining how earlier social experiences contribute to children's gradually selected deviant peer relationships by the time they reach adolescence.

The first stage underlying child antisocial behavior begins with maladaptive parent-child interaction patterns that provide payoffs to children for coercive and antisocial behavior. The second stage

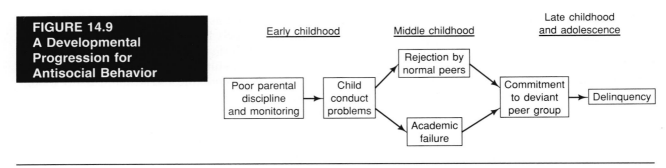

FIGURE 14.9
A Developmental
Progression for
Antisocial Behavior

Source: From "A Developmental Perspective on Antisocial Behavior" by G. R. Patterson, B. D. DeBaryshe, and E. Ramsey, 1989, *American Psychologist, 44*, p. 331. Copyright 1989 by the American Psychological Association. Reprinted by permission.

is failure in school and not being accepted by the conventional peer group. Studies have shown that poor academic performance and poor peer relationships are related to a higher frequency of delinquent behavior (Federal Bureau of Investigation, 1987). Poor academic performance results in being put in slower classes. Patterson points out that when students are tracked according to ability, potentially harmful consequences may result. Antisocial behavior may be molded and shaped as a result of constant exposure to peers with similar behavioral, social, and academic profiles. In these classroom settings, long-term friendships may emerge that support problem behavior and discourage academic engagement. Figure 14.9 graphically displays the developmental progression from poor parenting to rejection by peers and school failure, commitment to the deviant peer group, followed by delinquency.

Although adolescents can learn maladaptive or illegal behavior by imitating peers, it is interesting to note that children's relationship with their parents often determines whether they will imitate the negative behaviors of the peer group. In a study of 139 males between the ages of 14 and 17, it was found that when adolescents reported that their relationship with their parents was not very good, they were significantly more susceptible to becoming involved in delinquent acts through the influence of delinquent associates. Those adolescents who reported a good relationship with their parents were less likely to be negatively influenced by the peer group (Poole & Regoli, 1979).

School   Some researchers have discovered that a significant percentage of delinquent adolescents have IQs in the normal range, 95–105 (Adelson, 1980). Therefore, it appears that low intelligence is not a cause of delinquency. It has been discovered, however, that one outstanding trait of juvenile delinquent children is that they are "educationally retarded" (Magnusson, Stottin, & Duner, 1982). In other words, these children have a tendency, from an early age on, to repeat grades, hate school, want to leave school, are truant, and frequently misbehave in the classroom. It appears, then, that adjustment to school at an early age has a significant effect on adolescent adjustment.

Working with the Juvenile Delinquent   Treatment of antisocial youth tends to be most successful when the child is relatively young. If parents, teachers, and other adults are aware of the behavioral characteristics and the negative environmental influences that appear to lead to delinquent behavior, they can aid in the early identification of youths at risk of chronic juvenile delinquent behavior. By the same token, if children can realize that these inappropriate behaviors are learned and understand how they are learned, it becomes easier to teach them new and more adaptive responses.

PRACTICAL IMPLICATIONS: FACILITATING THE DEVELOPMENT OF CHILDREN'S MORAL REASONING

It was noted at the beginning of this chapter that children's level of moral reasoning is an important factor in determining how they will act in certain situations involving moral conduct. Higher levels of moral reasoning are superior to lower levels because children show a greater understanding about society and thus are more socially adaptive. How do children develop from a lower level of morality based on parental constraint to a higher one based on mutual cooperation? Or, phrased differently, how can you facilitate the development of moral reasoning? To cast light on these questions, several factors and their relationship to moral development have been studied.

FAMILY FACTORS

Both Piaget and Kohlberg relegated parents to a minimal and nonspecific role as agents in their children's moral development. The mechanism underlying development in each of their theories is cognitive disequilibrium. Such disequilibrium is engendered by exposure to higher-stage reasoning or by experiences of cognitive conflict. Such experiences challenge current ways of thinking, revealing their inadequacy, and thereby stimulate development toward a more equilibrated stage. There has been little research on the family as a context for moral reasoning development. Some studies, however, have characterized a positive influence of parents.

Walker and Taylor (1991) examined the relation between parents' and children's level of moral reasoning development and the level of moral reasoning used by parents when actually discussing two different types of moral problems with their child: a hypothetical moral dilemma and a real-life dilemma from the child's own experience. The sample consisted of 63 family triads (mother, father, and child) with children drawn from grades 1, 4, 7, and 10. The results indicated that parental discus-

sion style and level of moral reasoning were predictive of children's moral reasoning. The parental discussion style that predicted the greatest moral development in children included behaviors such as eliciting the child's opinion, asking clarifying questions, paraphrasing, and checking for understanding. The children of parents who relied on an informative discussion style—that is, directly challenging the child, critiquing the child's position, and lecturing—were associated with low levels of moral reasoning in children.

Other studies have indicated that children who exhibit higher levels of moral reasoning have parents who are verbal, rational people who encourage warm, close relations with their children. The parents tend to promote a democratic style of family life, with a fair consideration of everyone's point of view (Edwards, 1980). A democratic home requires more freedom of choice for the child and more time for the parent to discuss, when necessary, the choices made and to evaluate the consequences with the child.

By living in accordance with the same basic rules that are expected of the child, and by allowing the child a reasonable role in decision making, the parent can be an example of reciprocal morality (Thibault & McKee, 1982). Giving children opportunities to participate in decision making promotes a higher level of moral reasoning (see "Focus on Applications").

The father appears to play a special role in moral development, particularly for boys. In a study of father absence, seventh-grade boys who had been without their fathers for at least 6 months prior to the study obtained significantly lower scores on three of four moral internalization indexes (guilt, internal moral judgment, confession) than a group of boys (controlled for IQ and social class) who had fathers (Hoffman, 1971). Some studies have shown a possible relationship between children's levels of moral reasoning and various disciplining techniques. Hoffman (1977, 1984) has shown, for example, that a possible relationship between moral development and three types of disciplining techniques. The three broad types of discipline studied were: *power-assertive techniques* (physical force, dep-

---

FOCUS ON APPLICATIONS

Autonomous Moral Thinking

Ideally, as children get older, they become more autonomous and less heteronomous. That is, children are governed less by others and become more capable of governing themselves. The important question for parents and educators is, What makes children autonomous? One factor that appears to stimulate the development of autonomy is the exchange of points of view between adults and children. To illustrate, Holstein (1968) found that the moral judgment of 13-year-olds was related to the extent to which parents encouraged them to participate in discussions and the resolution of differences in moral opinions and hypothetical situations among mothers, fathers, and children. The children of parents who encouraged their children to participate and were rated as taking their children's opinions seriously tended to exhibit more autonomous behavior (70%) than did those whose parents did not encourage their children in this manner (30%).

In the light of this evidence, discussing moral issues at home and school appears to be a worthwhile activity. In addition, instead of simply punishing children for their misdemeanors and leaving it at that (thus promoting heteronomous behavior), discussion about the consequences of the children's behavior is important in promoting autonomous behavior.

---

rivation of material objects or privileges); *induction* (explaining the possible consequences of the child's behavior) and *love withdrawal* (ignoring child, threatening to leave child, explicitly stating dislike for child). Power-assertive techniques were associated with lower levels of moral reasoning in children, while induction was associated with higher levels. Love withdrawal is rather ambiguous, perhaps because the anxiety it induces can operate in two ways. It can lead a child to conform in order to please the parent and maintain emotional harmony, or to refuse to conform in order to annoy the parent. In either case, it is not a good method.

PEERS

Piaget's and Kohlberg's writings make it clear that interaction with peers promotes the development of moral reasoning. According to Piaget, moral development cannot take place under heteronomous conditions—that is, when parent-children relations are one-sided and authoritarian, adults over children. Piaget believed that children cannot de-

velop a true sense of justice when adults are strong and demanding and children feel weak and inferior. In these kinds of situations, children know what they are supposed to do and supposed not to do, but the rationale for conformity is often not understood, nor is there the sense of working out some arrangement for mutual benefit. Hence, interaction with adults short-circuits the process of building a deeper understanding of cooperative arrangements (Youniss, 1980).

As children get older, however, and attain a relative equality with adults and older children, they gain the confidence to participate with peers in decisions about applying and changing rules on the basis of reciprocity. The mutual give and take, which occurs among peers who have equal status, fosters a reciprocity of cooperation (each child has the freedom to enter into cooperative agreements and each must be satisfied with the agreement for it to be effective). Peer-group experiences help move children away from moral realism, in which rules are seen as external, constraining forces arbitrarily imposed by powerful adult authority figures, and toward the notion of morality based on principles of cooperation and mutual consent (Blatt & Kohlberg, 1975). Morality, then, develops from acquisition of autonomy, emerging from the need to get along with others.

Furthermore, exposure to other children's moral-reasoning strategies may produce a challenge, because they contradict expectations and thus may produce a state of cognitive disequilibrium. Disequilibrium (uncertainty) may motivate children to think through and question their earlier beliefs and make the kinds of moral discriminations and judgments essential to the development of autonomous moral reasoning. Children employ new cognitive skills as they try to resolve inconsistencies between their experiences and expectations. It is through this effort that preexisting patterns of moral reasoning are reorganized.

Kohlberg also makes the assumption that members of the peer group who initially operate at low moral levels of moral reasoning will be positively affected by exposure to other members who function at higher levels. The latter will not be adversely affected by the former.

Empirical support for Kohlberg's assumption comes from a series of studies by Turiel (1966, 1972). He found that children are most likely to advance in their moral reasoning abilities when they are exposed to arguments one stage above their own reasoning (+1 condition) than by either two stages above (+2 reasoning) or one stage below (−1 reasoning). In the −1 condition, children are unimpressed with arguments less adequate than their own, and in the +2 condition reasoning is too advanced to be understood and assimilated.

Social participation in groups appears to be another way to advance children's level of moral reasoning. In one investigation, fourth- and fifth-grade boys and girls who were leaders and members of extracurricular groups or activities, such as Boy Scouts, Girl Scouts, or athletic teams, responded with more advanced moral judgments than those who were not members of organized groups (Harris, Mussen, & Rutherford, 1976).

Piaget and Kohlberg maintain that peer interactions that pose cognitive conflict are most effective in facilitating moral change, but others (e.g., Youniss, 1980) emphasize the importance of coopera-

Teachers may enhance children's level of moral reasoning by involving them in discussions about various moral issues.

tion and communication with peers. Nor should the role of parent teaching be ignored. It is highly likely that children themselves generalize from their experiences with parent discipline and reasoning, deriving for themselves conceptions of morality that are based on, and expanded from, the material with which they are confronted.

TEACHERS

It has been pointed out that children at the preconventional level of moral reasoning tend to be oriented toward satisfying their needs, with little regard for others. Their viewpoints are egocentric and hedonistic. By way of contrast, children who reason at the conventional level believe that group interests, rules, and expectations are often more important than the instrumental desires of the individual. These children are oriented to please and help others to maintain social order. Are these differing levels of moral reasoning reflected in children's classroom behavior? Is the conventional-reasoning child likely to exhibit more adaptive behavior than others who reason at a lower level?

The relationship between moral reasoning and classroom behavior was studied by Bear and Richards (1981). Sixty-six children from two elementary schools in Iowa were presented with three of Kohlberg's moral dilemmas. The responses were scored and each was placed in one of Kohlberg's developmental levels. In addition, conduct ratings of the children were made by the classroom teacher, using a behavioral checklist.

Frequent conduct problems were found to be associated with the preconventional moral reasoning level. Moreover, Bear and Richards' research showed that conduct problems decline with advancing stages of moral development. To illustrate graphically the variability as well as the decrease in conduct problems with increasing moral maturity, Figure 14.10 gives each student's conduct problem score and moral maturity rank, individually plotted. As can be seen, conduct becomes increasing uniform as moral maturity advances. These findings suggest that it may be a worthwhile activity for teachers to help children advance to higher stages of moral reasoning.

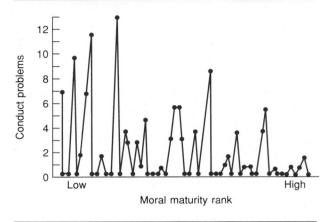

FIGURE 14.10   Conduct Problem Rating as a Function of Moral Maturity, Showing Rank Plotted for Each Student

Source: From "Moral Reasoning and Conduct Problems in the Classroom" by George Bear and Herbert C. Richards, 1981, *Journal of Educational Psychology, 73* (5), p. 668. Copyright 1981 by the American Psychological Association. Reprinted by permission.

Role-taking sessions are another worthwhile classroom activity (Ianotti, 1978). Role taking involves the ability to understand what another person feels, thinks, sees, and intends; it is almost universally viewed as having a necessary relationship to moral reasoning. Role-taking experiences provide children with different perspectives and thus may instigate cognitive conflict and its resolution through modification of previous (more primitive) ways of thinking. One way that teachers can enhance children's moral reasoning is by providing experiences in role-taking activities, in which children act out various problems, concerns, or dilemmas.

For example, a student at the stage 3 level of development may argue that it is morally permissible to steal from a local store, because "everybody does it."

Allowing such students to play the role of a storekeeper who needs his profits to feed his own children may help those students arrive through empathy and group discussion at a stage 4 appreciation for "law and order" in society. Actual experience in assuming another person's role may be an important concrete link between the child's world and the world of others (Munsey, 1980).

Teachers may also help to facilitate the development of moral reasoning in children by involving them in theoretical discussions about various moral issues. The issues should be seen as important to the students, thus encouraging their active involvement in the discussion. The teacher's role is first to ensure that students understand the moral dilemma or problem in question, and second to elicit students' rationale for their judgments. In addition, students with different rationales should be encouraged to interact with one another. The teacher deals with students' responses collectively and works toward a general analysis in class discussion, rather than insisting on individual analysis. The aim of moral education is not the inculcation of accepted values and standards, but rather to help students develop their abilities to think about their own values.

Although theoretical discussions are important, children's actual involvement in moral activities is important as well. Projects that may benefit the school and/or the community are worthwhile endeavors for all concerned.

REVIEW OF KEY POINTS

According to Piaget's theory, a young child in the stage of moral realism feels an obligation to comply with rules because they are sacred and unalterable. Whether an action is judged to be right or wrong depends on the magnitude of its consequences, the extent to which it conforms to established rules, and whether it is punished. Children believe in expiatory punishment (misbehavior must be punished and the more severe, the better) and immanent justice (automatic punishment emanates directly from objects). Children in the second, more cognitively mature stage (middle or late childhood)—moral realism—now believe that rules are established and maintained through reciprocal agreement and thus are subject to modification. Punishment should be related to the misdeed. These children now note the intention of the wrongdoer and take that into account when judging behavior.

Kohlberg has suggested that there are three levels of moral development, each having two substages. At the preconventional level, morality is externally determined by the avoidance of punishment and deference to those with superior power (stage 1) and by hedonistic emphasis on personal gain (stage 2). The conventional level stresses conformity and loyalty to the family and the priority of interpersonal relationships (stage 3). It also stresses conformity and loyalty to the larger society, the fulfillment of duties, and unquestioning obedience to the law (stage 4). The postconventional or principled level involves an emphasis on basic nonrelative values. These include liberty, the belief that laws are a service to society and subject to change (stage 5), the preeminence of self-chosen ethical principles, and the domination of conscience in making moral decisions (stage 6). The principled moral level is considered to be a more sophisticated and mature moral orientation. Over time, children generally change in the direction of making moral judgments on the basis of a better understanding of social relationships. These shifts reflect new cognitive abilities.

Information processing theory focuses on specific principles that individuals use to make specific moral judgments. In contrast to Kohlberg's concentration on children's justification for moral judgments, information processing theorists emphasize the use of rules of reasoning to process information. Initially, children will focus on whether the harm-doer was directly or indirectly responsible for the wrongdoing. If deserving of blame, a final decision of how much, if any, punishment should be administered is made.

Moral behavior and feelings during early and middle childhood focused on prosocial or altruistic behaviors—those that aid or benefit another person. Children's ability to empathize with another (to infer what the other person is thinking, feeling, or intending) is closely associated with the development of prosocial behaviors: cooperation, friendliness, sharing, and so on. Ways of promoting prosocial behaviors—helping children understand their own emotional reactions in various situations, being empathic and socially effective role models, using disciplinary techniques that emphasize the consequences of the child's behavior, responding openly and nurturantly to children's distress feelings—were pointed out.

Antisocial behaviors such as stealing, lying, and cheating were also discussed. The reasons why children engage in these behaviors and how adults can help them engage in honest behavior were discussed. Most children experience some feelings of guilt when they lie, cheat, or steal. Children first experience a rudimentary form of guilt over their wrongdoings, called empathic distress, when they respond to the inner states of others. The beginning of guilt feelings generally occurs in situations in which the child has physically harmed another child. With further cognitive and social advancements, children begin to feel guilt over inaction, because they are aware that they could have done something to prevent a bad situation or consequence, but did not. Children in middle childhood experience guilt even though they may not have actually carried out a harmful deed (anticipatory guilt). Finally, children in late childhood and early adolescence begin to feel guilty over their harmful actions (or inactions) beyond their immediate situations. This is known as survivor guilt.

During adolescence moral reasoning tends to be based on abstract guidelines that transcend concrete situations and can be applied across a variety of moral situations. The development of social conventions (behavioral uniformities that coordinate the stable interactions of individuals within a social system) appear to follow a similar course of development. Although children in middle childhood and adolescence view social conventional rules as arbitrary and changeable, the former follows conventions because they are forced to; adolescents, however, recognize that you are expected to as a means by which society regulates behavior. Adolescent values are surprisingly similar to parental values in terms of basic values (the value of education). Adolescent values on life-style, however, are more similar to their peers. When there is a conflict between adolescent values and parental values, whether adolescents go against parental values depends on the adolescents' age, the quality of their relationship with their parents, and whether the adolescents or parents possess certain characteristics. Adolescent delinquency is a result of complex factors, however. Family factors, a sense of alienation, antisocial behavior, poor academic performance, rejection by the conventional peer group, and association with antisocial peers are salient factors that lead to committing delinquent acts.

Ways in which parents, peers, and teachers can help to promote the development of moral reasoning in children were pointed out. A democratic home in which the child has some freedom of choice and plays a reasonable role in decision making facilitates moral development. Children's moral development is a product of social relationships and peer interactions are of major importance in developing moral reasoning. Teachers also can play a crucial role in developing higher moral reasoning skills in children. Group discussions and allowing children to engage in role-taking activities are two effective ways of developing children's moral reasoning skills.

ENHANCING YOUR CRITICAL THINKING

Firsthand Experiences

Lying

Paniagua, F. A. (1989). Lying by children: Why children say one thing, do another? *Psychological Reports, 64,* 971–984.

Interesting analysis of why children lie. Survey a few teachers in an elementary school or junior high and ask them how common lying is and why they think children lie. Do their responses concur with what Paniagua says?

Critical Thinking

Moral Reasoning

Walker, L. J. (1989). A longitudinal study of moral reasoning. *Child Development, 60,* 157–186.

One of the few longitudinal studies on children's moral reasoning. What kind of information does this type of study (conducted over a period of time) afford that you could not have learned about moral reasoning from a short-term study?

Empathy

Eisenberg, N., & Strayer, J. (1987). Critical issues in the study of empathy. In N. Eisenberg & J. Strayer (Eds.). *Empathy and its development.* New York: Cambridge University Press.

What pertinent methodological problems and issues that need to be addressed in studying empathy are noted in this chapter? Are these applicable to other areas of research?

Juvenile Delinquency

Guerra, N. G. (1989). Consequential thinking and self-reported delinquency in high school students. *Criminal Justice and Behavior, 16,* 440–454.

The study examines different thinking patterns between delinquents and nondelinquents. As you read the article, note the cognitive reasoning patterns typical of delinquent and nondelinquent adolescents. Delineate similarities and differences of the thinking patterns in these two groups.

Developmental Problems and Trends in the World of the Child and Adolescent

Disorders and Problems in Development

CHILDREN'S THOUGHTS

On "Why are some children shy?"

I'm shy. I guess I am shy because people make me nervous. I get scared that I'll say or do the wrong thing. I feel uncomfortable around people. I would rather not be around them. I feel better when I'm by myself. Then I can think of good things and feel good.

Martha, age 11

On "Why do kids use drugs?"

I think there are two main reasons—one would be to be mature or make themselves think they are mature. "Gosh, I'm drinking a beer— you have to be 21 to drink. It's like I'm 21." Also, peer pressure is everything. Just think of this situation. You are at a party with 20 other people and someone hands you a beer and you say, "No." And, they all laugh. So, you eventually have a beer, 'cause everyone else is.

Georges, age 15

KEY TERMS

Infantile autism
Childhood schizophrenia
Sudden Infant Death Syndrome
Attention-deficit hyperactive disorder
Shy children
Antisocial aggression

Developmental psychopathology is a special discipline within developmental psychology, and is distinguished from this larger field in its emphasis on studying developmental challenges and vulnerabilities in childhood and adolescence (Sroufe & Rutter, 1984). This chapter explores the basic concepts and findings in the field of developmental psychopathology. In the infancy and early childhood period, the focus is on autism, childhood schizophrenia, Sudden Infant Death Syndrome, and attention-deficit hyperactivity disorder. In middle childhood, the first topic of concern is overinhibited children who are shy, withdrawn, submissive, and seclusive. Unlike aggressive children, who tend to bulldoze their way through life and combat whatever it is that is threatening them, withdrawn children tend to ward off frightening stimuli in their environment by building a wall of noninvolvement around themselves. The next focus is on the aggressive child.

For the adolescent years, such problems as teenage suicide, drug abuse, and runaways are discussed. All these problems are on a sharp statistical rise. In the case of drug abuse, wanting to feel mature and wanting to be like everyone else may be important reasons why children and adolescents are using drugs.

INFANCY

You are a clinical psychologist observing children during recess time at the Playtime Nursery School. You notice a little boy playing in the sandbox. As you walk up to greet the child, you notice his pensive facial expression. The child does not look at you, nor does he turn away. It seems as though he is looking right through you—almost as though you do not exist. If you were to pick up the child and put him on your lap, his body does not accommodate to yours. He remains rigidly stiff and would sit as if you were a chair. This is an example of a child who has received a diagnosis of early childhood autism.

AUTISM

Infantile autism was first described as a syndrome (a group of behavior characteristics that describe a particular disorder) by Kanner (1943). In his first paper, Kanner presented 11 autistic children, 8 boys and 3 girls (a sex distribution fairly typical of the child population seen in clinics and hospitals).

Describing the Autistic Child The American Psychiatric Association's *Diagnosis and Statistical Manual of Mental Disorders* (American Psychiatric Association, 1987), better known as DSM-III-R, has listed broad categories of disorders, with infantile autism classified as a pervasive developmental disorder. Table 15.1 describes the diagnostic criteria for infantile autism.

There is considerable controversy regarding age of onset, which was previously specified to be before 30 to 36 months of age, but which is no longer included among the essential and necessary criteria. The reasons for no longer including age as an essential criteria is that age is not a behavioral criterion; classic autism can have its onset even long after age 2 to 3 years (Gillberg, 1986); and there is sometimes considerable problems in obtaining reliable medical histories when children are seen long after 3 years of age. This is not to suggest that age of onset is irrelevant, but that the diagnosis of autism is allowed in any child with the triad of severe and typical impairments.

There has been some debate as to whether it is possible to identify valid subtypes of pervasive developmental disorder. Subsequently, some researchers have pointed out a need to investigate disorders on the "boundary" of autism to see whether they should be considered as valid subtypes of autism. Wing (1990) has recently drawn attention to a pervasive developmental disorder known as Asperger syndrome, a condition outlined by Asperger in 1944. Asperger syndrome is considered by some researchers as a mild variant of autism (Gillberg & Svendsen, 1987; Gillberg, 1990). The researchers have outlined research diagnostic criteria for Asperger syndrome that are intended to make it possible to study Asperger syndrome according to specific criteria on one hand and "high level autism" on the other. Asperger children differ from the majority of autistic children, who are usually mentally retarded, without communicative language, and have a poor prognosis. Most Asperger children do not have these characteristics. The clinical features of Asperger syndrome are outlined in Table 15.2.

Studies indicate that the basic deficits are the same or similar in Asperger syndrome and high-level autism and thus, it lacks true diagnostic validity (Szatmari, Bartolucci, & Bremner, 1989; Wing, 1990). Therefore, it may be best to think of Asperger syndrome as a mild form of autism.

TABLE 15.1   Diagnostic Criteria for Infantile Autism

Pervasive lack of responsiveness to other people

Gross deficits in language development

If speech is present, peculiar speech patterns such as immediate or delayed echolalia, metaphorical language, pronomial reversal

Bizarre responses to various aspects of the environment, for example, resistance to change, peculiar interest in or attachments to animate or inanimate objects

---

TABLE 15.2   Clinical Features of Asperger's Syndrome

Solitary
　No close friends
　Avoids others
　No interest in making friends
　Is a loner

Impaired social interaction
　Approaches others only to have own needs met
　Clumsy social approach
　One-sided responses to peers
　Difficulty sensing feelings of others
　Detached from feelings of others

Impaired nonverbal communication
　Limited facial expression
　Unable to read emotion from facial expression of child
　Unable to give message with eyes
　Does not look at others
　Does not use hands to express oneself
　Gestures are large and clumsy
　Comes too close to others

Odd speech
　Abnormalities in inflection
　Talks too much
　Talks too little
　Lack of cohesion in conversation
　Idiosyncratic use of words
　Repetitive patterns of speech

Source: From "Asperger's Syndrome and Autism: Comparison of Early History and Outcome" by P. Szatmari, G. Bartolucci, and R. Bremner, 1989, *Developmental Medicine and Child Neurology*, 31. Copyright 1989 by Mac Keith Press. Reprinted by permission.

Recent estimates suggest that there are from 5,000 to 10,000 children nationwide between the ages of 2 and 5 years with the diagnosis of autism (Rogers & Lewis, 1989). A number of recent investigations now confirm that autism prevalence is probably higher than suggested by earlier studies. Gillberg (1990) and Steffenburg and Gillberg (1990) found 6.6 per 10,000 children with autism. Two thirds were said to be typical Kanner autism cases. Such children demonstrate significant social/emotional, communicative, and cognitive impairments (Hertzig, Snow, New, & Shapiro, 1990) that present a complex challenge to the psychotherapist, parent, and teacher.

Social/emotional impairments are reflected in the autistic child's *extreme isolation* and an inability to relate to people in ordinary ways (Schopler & Mesibov, 1984, 1988). For example, as infants, these children often fail to respond with an anticipatory posture in preparation for being picked up. At 2 to 4 months, they do not smile. Some children fail to form emotional attachments to significant people in their environment—for example, they do not show distress when mother leaves the room (McAdoo & DeMyer, 1978).

Ozonoff, Pennington, and Rogers (1990) tested the hypothesis that young autistic children are selectively impaired in one domain of social and affective development, emotion perception. Two groups of children participated, an autistic group (N = 14) and a control group of normal children (N = 14). The children's ability to identify the emotion (happy or sad) displayed in various photographs was assessed. Results provide strong support for specific deficits in the emotion perceptions of autistic children.

The second impairment is a pathological *need for sameness*. This need applies both to children's own behavior and to the environment. Often children's activities are simple, such as sitting on the floor and rocking back and forth for long periods of time. The need for environmental sameness can be expressed in wanting to wear the same article of clothing or in having the same type of food at each meal. The intensity of this need is evidenced by children's panic and rage when attempts are made to alter the environment, even in minor ways.

The third characteristic of autism is either *mutism or noncommunicative speech*. Almost half of the population of autistic children never acquire functional language (Paul, 1987). From the earliest stages in communication development, autistic children show profound problems with key aspects of intentional communication, especially

While the inability to relate to other people is a predominant characteristic of autistic children, it is interesting to note that they have a skillful, even affectionate relationship to objects.

those that are exclusively social-interactive, such as establishing joint attention, informing, and initiating.

The determination of many of these children not to communicate is impressive; it is so intense that these children may punish themselves severely—biting, hitting their heads against the wall—when the first desire and attempt to communicate arise in conflict with the earlier determination not to. Some children show great anxiety when addressed, putting their fingers in their ears, whispering to themselves, and repeating words. Others show echolalia, repeating phrases or conversations previously heard, without any indication that the words convey meaning. Speech is parrotlike; it is not symbolic.

In addition, some autistic children show apparent sensory dysfunction. That is, they tend not to respond to the sights and sounds in their environment. Because of this lack of response to external stimuli, or irregularity in their response to sensory stimuli (exhibiting extreme sensitivity or underresponsiveness to touch, light, sound, pain), they often are diagnosed as deaf or blind. Furthermore, these children show inappropriate emotional affect. They may, for example, fail to exhibit fear in a dangerous situation, or may not display appropriate facial expressions, or may laugh and giggle uncontrollably without eliciting stimuli.

Autistic children are described as having an undifferentiated sense of self; that is, they lack self-awareness and fail to distinguish self from nonself (Ferrari & Matthews, 1983). Such behaviors include failure to gaze at caregivers, absence of personal pronouns in speech, and lack of ability to comprehend references to the self (Fay, 1979).

Intellectually, autistic children generally have a below-average IQ. Only one fifth to one quarter of autistic children have normal to borderline intelligence; the majority are moderately to severely retarded (Bailey, 1989). A small percentage of autistic children, however, may have isolated aptitudes for high-level functioning in such areas as mechanics, mathematics, or music.

Causes of Autism   No single etiological factor is known to be responsible for this disorder. A num-

ber of etiological theories, however, have been advanced. Kanner (1943), basing his inferences on clinical interviews, initially suggested that the children suffered from innate inabilities, which might have been made worse by their parents who were described as cold, intelligent, detached, and emotionally unresponsive. Most professionals in the 1940s and 1950s focused on the parental personality factor of Kanner's hypothesis. Bettelheim (1977) placed emphasis on a hypothesized abnormal mother-child bond. The mothers of autistic children supposedly were inadequate in displaying care and responsiveness, which resulted in rage, hostility, and autistic withdrawal by their children.

Empirical research, however, has produced no evidence that autistic children have been rejected by cold, hostile parents. In fact, the once popular notion that parents are the primary causative factors in autism is on the wane. Several studies suggest that the cause of the disorder is probably unrelated to the psychological characteristics of the parents. In a representative study, Koegel, Schreibman, O'Neal, and Burke (1983), studied 49 parents of autistic children and found them to be very similar to other parents in their personality characteristics, marital adjustment, and family interactions.

Accumulating evidence suggests that autism is now regarded as a behaviorally defined syndrome of neurological impairment with a wide variety of underlying medical etiologies (Bryson, Smith, & Eastwood, 1988; Volkmar & Nelson, 1990). Several investigators report that pre-, peri-, and neonatal complications (which are known to cause such damage) appear with increased frequency in the histories of autistic children (Rogers & Lewis, 1989). To date, however, these data do not permit firm conclusions regarding the relationship between obstetrical complications and autism.

Recent studies of autistic patients in which magnetic resonance imaging (MRI) was used have implicated brain systems that are subserved by brainstem structures (Garber, Ritvo, Chiu, Griswold, Kashanian, Freeman, & Oldendorf, 1989). Perhaps the most consistent recent finding of all in the study of autism neurobiology has been that associated with brainstem pathology are enlarged fourth ventricle (Gillberg & Svendsen, 1987; Herold, Frackowiak, Le Couteur, Rutter & Howlin, 1988); prolongation of brainstem transmission time; and Moebius syndrome, which involves damage to brainstem nerve nuclei (Fernell, Gillberg & von Wendt, 1990).

Studies in the clinical field have made it clear that a number of identifiable medical conditions can occur in conjunction with autism (Gillberg, 1990). The most important of these seem to be the fragile X syndrome (Hagerman, 1990). Fragile X syndrome is a recently described X-linked disorder that is surpassed only by Down syndrome as the most prevalent form of mental retardation of genetic origin.

Rutter (1983) has suggested that social abnormalities in autistic children stem from a basic cognitive deficit in the field of dealing with social and emotional cues. That is, these children show a specific difficulty in dealing with stimuli that carry emotional or social meaning. Along these lines, the results of Hobson (1988) indicates that autistic children cannot perceive other people's mental states as reflected in their bodily expressions.

Diagnosis and Prognosis   Autistic children are an extremely heterogeneous population. Investigators have found no shared uniquely neural deficit, no shared cognitive functional deficit, no distinct shared behavior pattern, no shared specific life course, and no shared response to drug treatment. Studies typically find that only some (usually between 10% and 40%) of sampled individuals diagnosed as autistic exhibit any particular marker under study. There is wide variability in cognitive functioning and in language skills. For example, they may exhibit the general characteristics relating to the language disorder, yet differ in specific behavior; one child may be mute and another exhibit echolalic speech.

Even the autistic aloofness in social functioning, which is identified as the hallmark of the syndrome and is used as a diagnostic feature in all systems of diagnosis, is quite variable and may change with increasing age and in different environments (Wing & Attwood, 1987). Thus, the label *autism* does little to communicate the specific characteristics or abilities of any individual child. These factors may contribute to the relatively low reliability among professionals in diagnosing a given child as autistic.

Prognosis is always tentative. In summarizing eight follow-up studies of 474 autistic children, it was found that between two thirds and three quarters had poor outcomes in that they continued to be severely disturbed, roughly 40% of whom were institutionalized (Lotter, 1978). Speech, IQ scores, and severity of disturbance are the most potent predictors of future development. Children who have not developed communicative speech by 5 years of age, who are untestable or have an IQ score below 60, and who are evaluated as being severely disturbed will remain severely handicapped through life; those who achieve communicative speech and have average intelligence stand only a 50-50 chance of making an adequate social adjustment as adults (Rutter, 1988).

Konstantareas, Zajdeman, Homatidis, and McCabe (1988) examined the relationship between 10 higher functioning verbal and 10 lower functioning nonverbal autistic children and maternal speech. The results revealed that mothers of the higher functioning verbal children asked more questions, used more language modeling, gave more reinforcement for language, and answered more children-initiated questions than did mothers of lower functioning children. Mothers of lower functioning autistic children employed more directives, used shorter mean lengths of utterance, and reinforced their children's motoric rather than spoken behavior. You might assume that mothers of lower functioning nonverbal children are responsible for their child's linguistic impairment. You cannot, however, assume causation from correlational findings. Second, although more questions, answers, prompts, and reinforcement for speech were used by mothers of verbal children, at least two categories, questions and prompts, were also employed by the mothers of nonverbal children. Finally, it is understandable that the verbally higher functioning children, by being more verbal, have reinforced their parents' language-oriented speech. Far from being poor models for linguistic behavior, mothers of autistic children appear, therefore, to be quite responsive to their children's relative capabilities.

Treatment Just as there is no one etiologic key to understanding such a pervasive disturbance as autism, there is no one kind of therapy that should be regarded as a treatment of choice. For overall goals of therapy, Rutter (1988) lists the following.

1. Fostering normal cognitive, language, and social development
2. Promoting learning
3. Reducing rigidity and stereotypes
4. Eliminating nonspecific maladaptive behaviors such as tantrums and self-injurious behavior
5. Alleviating family distress

Some types of therapy focus on particular goals such as improving language skills. One of the most impressive language training programs has been conducted by Lovaas (1987). The meaningful use of language is accomplished by rewarding the child for making a verbal response to an object, such as correctly labeling a cup when it is presented or correctly responding to "Give me the cup." Lovaas (1987) has reported the results of a long-term experiment with autistic children who received 40 hours of one-to-one therapy for at least 2 years. Mean age at entry into the program was under 3 years. Eight of the 19 children in the program made significant intellectual and educational gains, permitting them to succeed in the first grade.

Criticism of this study, however, has focused on the low age of the children at entry and hence the possibility that developmental tests may have yielded too negative results at first evaluation (Schopler & Mesibov, 1988). In addition, the children constituted a biased sample in that they had IQs in the mildly retarded and normal ranges and all already, at a very early age, had some expressive language skills. Such a group of children with autism has a relatively fair prognosis anyway. Nevertheless, the control group did not seem to do as well as the intensely treated group.

Other remedial programs, such as TEACCH, which stands for Treatment and Education of Autistic and related Communication-Handicapped Children focus on whatever behavioral problems are considered most serious by the child's parents. Schopler and Mesibov (1988) have been working with autistic children and their parents in North Carolina for a number of years. Parents become the therapists in working with their autistic children, and use a variety of different types of techniques, such as behavior modification, in which the parent is taught how to ignore the child's inappropriate behavior and reward appropriate behavior. Language therapy, group therapy, and therapy for parents are also used. The program has reported considerable success with a number of children. Questionnaires returned by 348 families who participated in the program gave it an average "helpfulness rating" of 4.6 on a scale of 1 to 5. Areas in which the parents rated the program as most effective included managing the child's behavior, understanding the child, teaching the child, feeling competent as parents, and enjoying the child. Thus, some positive things have been achieved by treatment, but there is no cure in sight. One cure seems highly unlikely for that matter. Multiple etiologies will probably call for multiple treatments.

CHILDHOOD SCHIZOPHRENIA

Approximately 1 child out of 1,000 may be afflicted with a severe emotional disturbance known as **childhood schizophrenia** (Achenbach, 1982). The clinical picture for childhood schizophrenia and autism differs. Although both autistic and schizophrenic children exhibit impaired interpersonal relationships (are aloof and withdrawn), childhood schizophrenia is marked by a significant decline in contact with reality and social adjustment. Autism lacks the mood disturbances that characterize schizophrenia. The autistic child is highly ritualized; the schizophrenic child's behavior is excessive and bizarre. In their developmental courses, schizophrenia is marked by progressions and regressions, while autism is highly stable. Parents of autistic children tend to have average or above average intelligence and do not come from any one socioeconomic group, while parents of schizophrenic children tend to have below average intelligence and come from a low socioeconomic stratum. Table 15.3 summarizes the differences between childhood schizophrenia and autism.

Children with childhood schizophrenia exhibit a preservation of sameness (that is, they tend to resist change and prefer familiar routines), act in self-injurious ways, may sit and rock for long periods of time, and have problems eating and sleeping. They may exhibit disturbances in motor behavior and postural responses. Toddlers and preschoolers are awkward and insecure in mastering the many motor skills of the period, from walking and climbing stairs to using swings and tricycles. Frequently, there is extensive retardation. Finally, there are a variety of thought and language disturbances. They may be mute during the first few years of life. If schizophrenia occurs later, children's language may be fragmented, dissociated, and bizarre.

Although the pervasiveness of schizophrenia is apparent from this list, an individual child is not equally damaged in all areas. It is this unevenness of development—the juxtaposition of adequate and primitive functioning, of immaturity and precocity—that is so devastating because it prevents such children from making coherent sense of themselves and their environment.

The causes of childhood schizophrenia are difficult to pinpoint. Several theorists feel that it is caused by biological predispositions, such as a poorly controlled and hyperresponsive central nervous system. These conditions make the child less able to cope with a deleterious environment, for example, living in a disorganized family setting (Ross & Ross, 1982). This combination of genetic and environmental factors is believed to cause at least some types of schizophrenia. Although there has been some promising work done with therapeutic interventions, the prognosis for these disturbed children is not encouraging.

SUDDEN INFANT DEATH SYNDROME (SIDS)

A sleep-related disorder with traumatic consequences has been labeled **Sudden Infant Death Syndrome (SIDS):** the death of an infant with no clear indication of the cause, even after a thorough investigation, usually including an autopsy. Every year 8,000 to 10,000 babies in the United States alone die of this unexplained disorder, sometimes

TABLE 15.3 Similarities and Differences Between Autism and Childhood Schizophrenia	Childhood Schizophrenia	Autism
Onset	Normal appearance at birth; gradual onset between 5 and 12	Signs present at birth; easily apparent prior to 30 months of age
Health	Poor health at birth	Normal health at birth
Prevalence	Slightly more common than autism	1 out of every 2000 births
Responsivity	Impaired relations with others; regression to withdrawal.	Withdrawal and indifference from birth
Motor skills	Poor coordination; frequent self-injurious behavior; awkward repetitive movements	Better motor skills; head banging and body rocking; preoccupation with inanimate objects
Speech	Mutism or immature and meaningless speech; language ability characterized by thought disorder	Mutism or echolalia; absence of personal pronouns
Intelligence	Below-average IQ	Low IQ, but good intellectual potential
Prognosis	Not encouraging	Not encouraging

referred to as crib death; the incidence is 2 to 3 per thousand live births. Ninety percent of these deaths occur before 6 months of age, with 2 to 4 months being the peak ages (Field, Dempsey, & Schuman, 1979).

There is a higher incidence of deaths among African Americans, poor families, and babies born to teenagers (Lipsitt, 1982). Deaths most often occur in the winter and spring. Colds and sniffles have been observed in deceased infants in the few days prior to death. Most deaths occur when the infant is sleeping, usually between midnight and 9:00 A.M. Death occurs rapidly and the child turns blue and limp. There is usually no evidence of any agonal experience, no sign of pain or struggle (DeFrain, Taylor, & Ernst, 1982).

Causes of SIDS   The cause remains unknown. Studies, however, have demonstrated a consistent pattern of risk factors: low socioeconomic status, young maternal age, high parity, multiple birth, short interval between births, being a male child, being an African American or Native American, and low birth weight (Grether & Schulman, 1989).

Lipsitt (1982, 1990) has identified other risk factors. Lipsitt did an extensive study of the perinatal and pediatric records of 15 crib death cases. Then he selected two control groups: one consisting of the very next births of the same sex and the other of the very next births of the same sex and race in the same hospital. The SIDS victims proved to vary from the controls in several ways. It was found, for example, that respiratory difficulties occurred more frequently in the SIDS infants, compared with the control groups. The SIDS infants had lower Apgar test scorings (measurement of vital signs) at 1, 2, and 5 minutes after birth. The SIDS infants required more intensive care, were hospitalized longer, and required more resuscitative measures than the controls.

One may be tempted to conclude that there are pathological precursors in SIDS infants, but these infants do survive the neonatal period and seem quite well at birth, as well as immediately preceding death. Moreover, many infants with similar symptoms survive.

Lipsitt (1990) suggests that crib death may be a developmental disability involving a learning deficit, which jeopardizes infants' ability to defend themselves with appropriate behavioral adjustments when they have difficulty breathing or during apneatic episodes (cessation of breathing). He points out that many of the unconditioned reflexes that infants have at birth undergo marked changes between 2 and 4 months of age. Involuntary reflexive functioning is slowly superseded by slower, more voluntary, learned patterns of behavior, mediated by higher centers of the brain. This transitory period, which is characterized by disorganized behavior, occurs at 100 to 150 days old—just the age period when infants are most at risk of crib death.

To illustrate, an innate respiratory defense system is available at birth. That is, it appears that newborns are biologically equipped to engage in certain vital responses to respiratory occlusion. When a newborn's face is covered with a cloth, the infant reacts with an almost enraged response, which escalates as the stimulus is prolonged. The response culminates in crying, which frees the respiratory passages. The behavioral pattern is essentially fail-safe. This innate respiratory defense system will, however, diminish with the passage of time and is gradually supplanted by a slower, more deliberate, cortically mediated response pattern. It may be possible that the SIDS infant has not adequately learned to respond to respiratory difficulties when the unlearned protective reflexes have diminished.

Using a Monitor   In some cases, the use of a monitor is recommended for infants who have been diagnosed as at risk for apneatic episodes, but there is much controversy about that use. Physically, it is quite simple: Electrodes are placed on the baby's diaphram. This monitors the baby's breathing and will signal with an alarm if the baby ceases to breathe for longer than 20 seconds. There are some difficulties surrounding the use of a monitor: First, it has not been proved that apnea or cessation of breathing is the single cause of SIDS, and second there is no 100% guarantee that the infant will not succumb to SIDS, even with a monitor. For example, in one study of 35 infants that had been identified as at high risk of apneatic episodes, four deaths occurred despite the monitoring (Stark, Mandell, & Taeusch, 1978). As yet, there are no definite answers as to the exact cause of SIDS.

EARLY CHILDHOOD

ATTENTION-DEFICIT HYPERACTIVITY DISORDER (ADHD)

Attention-Deficit Hyperactivity Disorder (ADHD), as diagnosed by the American Psychiatric Association (1987), is characterized by lack of attention, impulsivity, and hyperactivity. The *inattention* component is typically characterized by a developmentally inappropriate attention span, difficulty concentrating, difficulty in sustaining attention, and distractibility (Carlson & Rapport, 1989; Seidel & Joschko, 1990).

Impulsivity refers to the lack of control ADHD children exhibit by acting without thinking of the consequences of their behavior and by starting a task before they have been given full instructions. They are unable to anticipate and work for long-term goals and appear unable to learn from past experiences or remember general rules (Henker & Whalen, 1989). They may blurt out incorrect answers in class or have difficulty taking turns in organized play, again because of a weakened ability to control the impulse to action.

Hyperactivity has been defined as "a constant high level of activity in situations where it is clearly inappropriate. Hyperactivity is coupled with an inability to inhibit activity on demand" (Ross & Ross, 1979, p. 288). Indeed, in hyperactive children, something is always moving. They are incessantly pulling, twisting, bending, and manipulating. They never appear to run out of energy. They seem compelled to react to all stimuli and are unable to respond only to appropriate stimuli. They appear to be distracted by sights, sounds, or ideas that are interesting and significant for them, but irrelevant to the main objective of the moment.

Overactive behavior in young children is sometimes difficult to diagnose. There is no test or cutoff point to determine whether a child is hyperactive; you can only compare the standard of behavior of the other children in a particular setting. Even then, observers are not always in agreement. Try the experiment in "Studying Children."

In hyperactivity, behavior is stimulus-bound. What children do is bound to what they see, hear, or feel. These children are unable to prevent themselves from reacting to sights and sounds in the environment. Behavior is shifting; attention span is very low. If there is anything within range that can be touched, pulled, bent, twisted, opened, or turned, the children will do it. The most severely hyperactive children are called *ricocheting children.* Every object in a room will be examined by these children; they will be in constant movement, and those around them are in constant ferment.

Some may not be afflicted with motor restlessness; hyperactivity may manifest itself in talking. The behavior here is the overflow of words in children who cannot control their verbal communication. These children are almost constantly talking, even to themselves. They continually blurt out answers out of turn and frequently interrupt others.

Later on, when these children enter school, they are often a disruptive element in the classroom. They are unable to sit still; they incessantly talk to their neighbors. They are constantly walking around, asking questions, wiggling, squirming— never relaxed or quiet. They drum their fingers on the desk, hum to themselves, pop up to sharpen

---

STUDYING CHILDREN

HYPERACTIVITY

With another classmate, observe children for 15 minutes in a free-play situation in a nursery school setting. Are there any children who you feel are particularly active—so much so that you would label them as hyperactive? Write down your reasons for this labeling. Does your colleague agree with you? If so, what behavioral characteristics did you agree on? If not, why? Is it easy to identify a hyperactive child?

Hyperactive children flit from one activity to another. They are in constant motion.

their pencils, and always manage to bump into someone on their way back to their desks. Academically, these children perform rather poorly and tend to have inadequate social relationships with their classmates (Hechtman & Weiss, 1983). The American Psychiatric Association's *Diagnostic and Statistical Manual of Mental Disorders* (DSM-III-R) (1987) indicates that a child given the diagnosis of ADHD must display eight of the characteristics cited in Table 15.4.

Causes of ADHD   Although the etiology of ADHD is unknown, it is not due to food additives, sugar, intolerant societies, or perinatal difficulty (Zamet-

kin, 1989). Zametkin states, "a set of well-established findings and observations taken together point toward a dysfunction of the central nervous system" (p. 584). One of the most frequently cited pieces of evidence for an organic etiology for ADHD is the response to stimulant medication, which has the paradoxical effect of increasing attention and task orientation.

Stimulants are the treatment of choice for ADHD children; the three major groups are amphetamines, methylphenidate (Ritalin), and pemoline. The overall effect of the drugs is one of making behavior more appropriate to the situation. Lambert, Sandoval, and Sassone (1979) report that

TABLE 15.4 Characteristics of ADHD

1. Fidgets, squirms, or seems restless
2. Has difficulty remaining seated when required to do so
3. Is easily distracted by extraneous stimuli
4. Has difficulty awaiting turn in group situations
5. Blurts out answers to questions before they have been completed
6. Has difficulty following verbal instructions
7. Has difficulty sustaining attention in tasks or play activities
8. Shifts from one uncompleted task to another
9. Has difficulty playing quietly
10. Often talks excessively
11. Often interrupts or intrudes on others
12. Often does not seem to listen
13. Often loses things necessary for tasks
14. Frequently engages in dangerous actions without considering possible consequences

Source: From *Diagnostic and Statistical Manual of Mental Disorders* (3rd ed. rev.) by American Psychiatric Association, 1987, Washington, DC: American Psychiatric Association.

86% of all children identified as ADHD will be given drugs at some time during the course of their treatment. In spite of their widespread use, however, the effectiveness of drug therapy for these children continues to be debated. Studies indicate that while various drugs are effective in reducing hyperactive behavior, they do not appreciably improve academic performance (Rapport, Quinn, DuPaul, Quinn, & Kelly, 1989). Other studies have indicated some side effects of drug use such as growth depression, insomnia, and weight loss (O'Leary, Pelham, Rosenbaum, & Price, 1976).

Other factors point to a neurobiological basis for ADHD. Research using positron emission tomography (PET) indicates that brain glucose metabolism differs in children with ADHD from that in normal children. Another indication that ADHD has a neurobiological cause is its apparent heritability. Thirty percent of biological parents of children with ADHD either had or have ADHD (Zametkin, 1989). This finding calls into question that the cause is sociological, or related to a specific setting, such as school.

Treatment Stimulant medication is not only the most prevalent therapy for ADHD, but also the most carefully studied treatment modality across the entire spectrum of childhood behavior problems. The most salient changes appear to be decreases in demanding, disruptive, and noncompliant behaviors in family and peer cultures, accompanied by welcome improvements in interpersonal responsiveness and in goal-directed efforts in the classroom.

In terms of a more traditional approach, counseling and psychotherapy are still rather prevalent, despite only scattered evidence of efficacy. Behavioral strategies have enjoyed greater success to date, both in family and school settings. For example, in one study (Gittelman, Abikoff, Pollack, Klein, Katz, & Mattes, 1980), 61 ADHD children were divided into three groups. The first group received the drug Ritalin and behavior-modification therapy, the second group received behavior-modification therapy and a placebo (a pill containing no medicine, used for its psychological effect). The third group of children just received Ritalin. Evaluations of children's behavior included assessments by parents as well as objective observations made by the researchers. The children in the first group, who had received Ritalin and behavior-modification therapy, improved the most.

Alternatively, cognitive-behavioral approaches appear to optimize the match between the problem and the treatment by focusing on enhancing the child's ability to monitor and regulate their own behavior and outcomes. To date, however, cognitive-behavioral treatments have not been as effective as stimulant medication in the short term, and no information is available about relative long-term efficacy.

CHILD ABUSE

Child abuse is characterized by most experts as producing problematic behavior patterns in children (Simons, Whitbeck, Conger, & Chyi-In, 1991). These include antisocial aggression (Bousha & Twentyman, 1984), troubled peer relationships, impaired social cognitions, lack of empathy, depression (Kazdin, Moser, Colbus, & Bell, 1985). As a group, abused children of all ages have been found to have a variety of psychological difficulties in comparison to nonabused children.

Kempe, Silverman, Steele, Droegemueller, and Silver (1962) first coined the term *battered child syndrome*. According to them, the major feature of this syndrome is the presence of an intentionally inflicted physical injury to the child, often a bone fracture and/or multiple soft tissue injuries. Prior to 1962, there was literally no public awareness of the problem of child abuse. This is certainly not the case today. The sheer repugnance of the concept of child abuse has drawn deeply on the compassion of sensitive people. Researchers and policymakers have recognized the extent and severity of violence toward children. Despite the flurry of research, however, there is still disagreement about its development, the consequences for victims, and the most effective avenues for intervention.

It is recognized today that child abuse is confined not only to children who are physically harmed by their parents, but also other forms of child maltreatment, child neglect and sexual abuse. Physical child abuse involves acts of *commission* by the parent, characterized by overt physical violence, beating, or excessive punishment. The use of physical punishment against children seems to reflect a mixture of positive belief in force as a tool for shaping behavior, lack of effective alternatives to force, and emotional tension in the parent. Child neglect involves maltreatment due to acts of *omission*, when the parent fails to meet a child's physical, nutritional, medical, emotional, and other needs (Friedman, Sandler, Hernandez, and Wolfe, 1981). Emotional abuse has been defined as the parents' failure to encourage normal development by assurance of love and acceptance. It involves verbal putdowns, labeling, humiliation, and unrealistic expectations. Sexual abuse in families, or incest, has been defined as "the involvement of dependent, developmentally immature children and adolescents in sexual activities they do not fully comprehend which violates the social taboos of family roles" (Schechter & Roberge, 1976).

Incidence of Child Abuse According to one estimate, there are approximately 1 million abused

and neglected children in the United States (American Medical Association, 1985). Of these, each year 100,000 to 200,000 are physically abused and 60,000 to 100,000 are sexually abused, and the remaining 700,000 to 840,000 are neglected. Sexual maltreatment has shown the greatest increase in reported cases relative to all other types of abuse and neglect (American Medical Association, 1985).

The overwhelming majority of abused children, however, never come to the attention of child protection agencies (Femina, Yeager, & Lewis, 1990). Explanations for the failure of many abused children to report their experiences have included (a) a tendency for severely abused children to interpret abusive treatment as deserved punishment (Amsterdam, Brill, Weisberg Bell, & Edwards, 1979), and (b) an effort to use "selective inattention" by suppressing the awareness of abuse and attending only to positive aspects of an experience (Herzberger & Tennen, 1983).

Characteristics of Abusive and Neglecting Parents If anything conclusive can be said about child abuse research it is that the psychopathological model does not apply to the great majority of abusive parents. No "abusive personality" has been identified. Although abusers cannot be distinguished from nonabusers by individual psychological factors or by clusters of factors measurable by psychological testing, a number of characteristics are reported in the literature as being found more frequently in parents who abuse their children than in parents who do not.

Mothers who abuse their children are more anxious, more suspicious of others, more dependent, less able to seek support from significant others, less nurturing, less understanding of how to be a parent, and interact less with their children than a group of mothers matched for high stress who do not abuse their children (Thompson & Gongla, 1983). Abusive and neglecting parents show decreased self-esteem and lower satisfaction with family life (Polansky, Chalmers, Buttenweiser, & Williams, 1979). Abusers tend to be of lower intelligence and demonstrate aggressiveness, impulsiveness, immaturity, and self-centeredness (Hotaling, Finkelhor, Kirkpatrick, & Straus, 1988).

Abusive families are often characterized by deficient social skills, low social desirability, high anxiety, and lack of receptiveness and support-seeking behavior (Egeland, Breitenbucher, & Rosenberg, 1980). Abusive families tend to score higher on certain child-rearing factors, such as authoritarian control and lack of encouragement of autonomy, and family climate factors, such as conflict and lack of cohesion (Trickett, Aber, Carlson, & Cicchetti, 1991).

In three separate samples Crittenden (1985) has shown that abusive mothers tend to be controlling, interfering, and either covertly or overtly hostile. Neglecting mothers are unresponsive in that they tend neither to initiate interaction nor to respond to their infants' initiatives. Crittenden notes that infants of abusive mothers tend to be difficult and infants of neglecting mothers tend to be passive.

Abusive parents are said to interpret certain age-appropriate behavior in children as "willful disobedience" or intentional misbehavior when the children's actions do not conform to parents' commands (Trickett & Susman, 1988). Moreover, abusive parents tend to interpret noncompliant behavior as an indication of the child's "bad" disposition, often using such descriptors as "stubborn" "unloving," and "spoiled" as explanations of contrary behavior (Rosenberg & Reppucci, 1983).

In another study (Plotkin & Twentyman, 1982), abusive mothers responded to vignettes in which their child behaved in ways that might be considered provoking. Results indicated that the abusive mothers not only reported that they would administer greater levels of punishment in these situations but also reported that their child was misbehaving to annoy them more frequently than did control mothers.

One of the most frequently cited characteristic of abusive parents is they, as children, were targets of violence from their own parents (Egeland, Jacobivitz, & Papatola, 1987). Klimes-Dougan and Kistner (1990) point out that existing research suggests that some intergeneration associations between being abused as a child and being an abusive parent does exist. These researchers have noted that parents abused as children do not necessarily become abusive; however, they do tend to adopt behavior patterns similar to those of their abusive parents such as prosocial skill deficits, social isolation, and deviant responses to stress. Milner, Robertson, and Rogers (1990) have noted that a childhood history of physical abuse was significantly related to adult potential for abusing children; as chronicity increased, so did abuse potential. The experience of abuse before puberty produced higher abuse rates than the experience of abuse after puberty.

Simons, et al. (1991) examined the parenting practices across generations while controlling for the social class of the adult. Analysis of the results revealed that grandparents who had engaged in aggressive parenting produced present-day parents who were likely to use similar parenting practices. Four avenues of transmission were identified:

1. Persons exposed to high rates of aggressive discipline may develop a parenting philosophy that favors strict, physical discipline as an approach to child rearing.

2. Harsh parenting may foster hostile personalities that lead to aggressive behavior toward others, including the person's own children.

3. Rather than promoting parenting beliefs favoring physical discipline, harsh parenting might result in the person learning a set of aggressive disciplinary behaviors that are used in a reflexive, rather unthinking way.

4. Harsh discipline is passed from one generation to the next because adult children tend to inherit the social class of their parents with its accompanying stressors and life-style.

A large number of investigators have proposed a relationship between socioeconomic disadvantage and patterns of child abuse and neglect (Gil, 1975; Trickett et al., 1991). It has been argued that the deprivations caused by poverty, including high-density living in deteriorating housing, limited financial resources, large numbers of children, absence of child-care alternatives, and inadequate support services create chronic stress and frustration. This level of pervasive life-style frustration creates a "triggering context" in which violence or neglect toward children is more likely to occur.

Social isolation of the parent (few close friends, no interpersonal sources of emotional support, loneliness) is another frequently cited characteristic of child-abusive families (Polansky et al., 1979). The picture described in research studies suggests a parent with few social gratifications, which leads to the feeling of being trapped alone at home with the child.

Characteristics of Abused and Neglected Children

The study of child abuse and neglect has shifted toward a greater consideration of the child's role in the abusive process (Frodi, 1981). Recent findings have led investigators to reconceptualize child-abusive behavior and neglect in terms of aversive interactions between parents and children rather than adult psychopathology alone. For example, many abused and neglected children are born prematurely and with a low birth weight. These children may be especially at risk for abuse or neglect, due, in part, to the extra child-rearing burden.

Other researchers have noted such differences between abused and nonabused children as psychomotor retardation, physical defects, colic, irritability, and hyperactivity (Kinard, 1980). In a study of the recorded social interactions of 10 1- to 3-year-old abused toddlers and 10 controls from families experiencing stress, it was observed that abused children were more likely to assault or threaten their own caregivers (George & Main, 1979). These researchers also found significant differences between abused and nonabused children in terms of their interactions with adults; friendly overtures and gestures from adults produced an apprehensive pattern of cautious approach-avoidance in abused preschoolers.

It has been noted that abused children show no concern when witnessing distress such as crying in toddlers. When they do respond, it is often in terms of fear, anger, or attack. These children have been described as joyless and hypervigilant (Camras, Ribordy, Hill, Martino, Sachs, Spaccarelli & Stefani, 1990).

In one study, 43% of the abused and neglected children had IQs in the mentally retarded range. Because 89% of these children were thought to have been retarded before the abuse or neglect, the stresses placed on parents by their children's limited cognitive functioning were thought to be an important contributor to violence and neglect (Morse, Sahler, & Friedman, 1970).

Other studies have reported on the role of the child's temperament in contributing to the likelihood of abuse and neglect. Two thirds of the mothers in a sample of 24 abused and neglected children complained that their children could not be cuddled (Ounsted, Oppenheimer, & Lindsay 1974). Such findings suggest that children with slow-to-warm-up or difficult temperaments may be more at risk for abuse and neglect than children with less stressful temperaments.

In contrast to the above findings, Burgess and Conger (1978) conducted a controlled comparison study in which recordings of parent/child interactions in the homes of 17 abusive, 17 neglectful, and 19 control families were obtained. Their conclusions on the behavior of abused and neglected children stressed that although these children displayed high rates of negative behavior, they did not appear to behave in a fashion remarkably different from that of the controls.

Effects of Abuse and Neglect on Children

Children who have been abused exhibit a diverse set of problems. These include antisocial aggression (Bousha & Twentyman, 1984), troubled peer relationships, impaired social cognitions, lack of empathy, and depression (Kazdin et al, 1985). As a group, abused children of all ages have been found to have a variety of psychological difficulties in comparison to nonabused children. Van Dalen (1989) asserts that the emotional impact of physical abuse of young children is predictable and occurs in a relatively orderly sequence, which comprises nine incremental steps that naturally group themselves into three levels of severity:

1. Conscious responses, including cognitive confusions; an intense search for an explanation; children's conclusion that they caused the abuse by their badness; and anger.

2. Unconscious responses, including repression of anger, guilt, punishment-seeking behavior, and gratification in punishment.

3. Denial and resignation, in which children attempt to elicit positive responses from the abuser.

Incest Family Dynamics The father-daughter dyad is used in discussing sexual abuse because it constitutes 70% of all reported cases (Coleman & Collins, 1990). Daughters are frequently the dominant female figures in incestuous households. There is often a role reversal, with the daughter assuming a role of equal power to that of the mother. Both the incidence and type of abuse seem to change as the child matures. As a child, contact is often limited to genital stimulation. As a girl grows older, the chances of intercourse increase. The average incestuous affair lasts about 3½ years, ending when the daughter struggles to establish autonomy from the family. Instead of reporting sexual abuse, more daughters choose to leave home as soon as possible through early marriage or running away.

The mother is thought to condone her daughter's sexual role with her father. Such women may have a history of emotional deprivation and be ill-equipped to protect their daughters. It appears that relatively few women actually take assertive action to protect their daughters once they find out (Coleman, 1987). However, the realistic nature of the fears that inhibit action, such as retribution by the husband and public humiliation, should make it somewhat understandable.

More is known about the father than is about the daughter in incest families. Many of these fathers are angry at their wives or women in general; they lack internal controls to respect the incest taboo; they have a marked history of emotional maladjustment; and they are not retarded, psychotic, or pedophiliac (Coleman & Collins, 1990). There is often marital discord in incestuous families and sexual incompatibility between the spouses (Mitnick, 1983). The father, however, is reluctant to seek a partner outside the family. The cognitions of men who have had sexual contact with children are more permissive and accepting of this behavior than normal men. They see more benefits resulting from sexual contact, greater complicity on the child's part, and less responsibility on the adults' part (Sternac & Segal, 1990). These factors, coupled with fears that the family will disintegrate, lead to incest, which paradoxically is seen as serving to keep the family together (O'Brien, 1980).

Effects of Incest on the Child Adams-Tucker (1982) studied 22 girls and 6 boys ranging in age from 2½ to 15½ years and found that these sexually abused children were depressed and withdrawn. They often engaged in fantasy and baby-like behavior. They often had poor relationships with other children and were unwilling to participate in physical activities. At times, the sexually abused child engaged in delinquent acts or ran away from home. Short-term effects of incest include regression to earlier behaviors, such as thumb sucking, eating disorders, sleep disorders, bed wetting, tics, or excessive fears. Caffaro-Rouget, Long, & Van Santen (1989) compared 240 sexual abused victims (aged 11–18 years) with 57 nonabused, matched controls. It was found that 49% of abused subjects showed no evident sign of emotional or mental trauma on pediatric examination. However, the longer the duration of abuse, the greater the likelihood of negative effects in the form of emotional and behavioral trauma and school problems in the victims. It is difficult to disentangle the effects of sexual abuse from those of the disturbed environment in which it occurs. In general, the closer the relationship between the aggressor and victim, the more damaging the abuse. Other considerations include the age and developmental status of the child, the use of force, the degree of shame or guilt the child feels, and reaction of parents.

MIDDLE CHILDHOOD

Children in middle childhood extend their mastery of various social and academic skills. As they leave home and begin school, they enter the world of peers and formal education. Some children encounter difficulties in this new social world. Some of these children have been labeled as shy and withdrawn, others as physically and verbally aggressive.

SOCIALLY WITHDRAWN CHILDREN

There are children who are outwardly submissive, never show signs of anger, have few friends, and

---

FOCUS ON APPLICATIONS

Is This Child Too Shy?

An inventory of the questions that follow may help to determine whether children are truly isolated, whether they are living too much within themselves.

1. Do the children always play alone or stay by themselves both at home and at school? Do they go home from school day after day and stay by themselves, reading or playing with toys in a solitary manner?
2. Do they have any friends—even one or two?
3. What are their interests?
4. What community activities to they participate in?
5. Do the children have many fears? (Because all children have fears, you would need to know their degree and extent.)
6. Do the children take part in school activities? Do they volunteer to recite in class or serve on a committee? Do they play games with other children, and if so, do they initiate the game or follow others' suggestions?
7. Do the children seem to be lost in daydreams much of the time?
8. Do they live in a make-believe world much of the time?
9. Are they learning what is expected of children their age?
10. Do they seem happy most of the time?

A child—of any age—who has no friends, never plays with others in school or at home, never volunteers to recite in class or to serve on committees, daydreams excessively, or has too many fears is indeed withdrawn and needs help. Some children are quiet and more gentle than others, and this may be in keeping with their normal temperament. All children—even quiet, gentle ones—should have friends and play with others.

Source: Adapted from *Meeting Children's Emotional Needs: A Guide for Teachers* by Katherine D'Evelyn, 1970, Englewood Cliffs, NJ: Prentice-Hall.

---

appear lost in a nonreal world. Not all shy children are "disturbed" and headed for disaster. "Focus on Applications" points out some ways in which you can identify the shy-withdrawn child who is in need of help.

Just as your body, if threatened, fights for life, so does your ego, if threatened, fight for survival. Aggressive children are willing to fight the forces around them with which they cannot come to an agreement on their own terms. Solitary children, however, appear to have given up the effort to adjust to the world of reality. They "adjust" by isolating themselves and thus blot out the annoying tensions of the world. In their world of fantasy, they are strong and loved. They experience no failure or disapproval and can achieve all their goals. The higher their level of anxiety becomes, the more they use fantasy as a protective device (Zimbardo, 1978). The longer this process continues, the more difficult it becomes for them to cope with the realities of life.

Shy children avoid participation with others; they compensate for their inability to find a place among their peers by remaining on the fringes.

Some children, who have difficulty in adjusting to their social world, isolate themselves from others, while other children tend to engage in combative relationships.

Shy children don't initiate, complain, demand their fair share, or stand up for their rights. They play by themselves, keep in the background, and try to remain inconspicuous.

Shy children avoid other children by taking refuge perhaps in watching television, reading, or devoting their free time to developing special skills or hobbies. For example, they may spend an inordinate amount of time making complex and intricate drawings, building models, or working on a stereo set. Such activities, whatever they may be, further isolate them. Withdrawing children usually reject attempts on the part of a well-meaning adult to get them more socially involved. Some children are prevented from entering into activities because they lack social know-how and have a fear of failure. Shy children are described as higher in anxiety and lower in self-esteem than unshy people (Peck, 1981).

Causes of Withdrawal   Children who avoid normal social contacts do so for many reasons. Some are motivated by physical weaknesses. Frail children with poor physical stamina may resist at-

tempts to push them into active participation with others. In such cases, shyness is a defense mechanism; it helps them avoid strenuous activities that they feel unable to undertake. Sometimes physical factors, such as braces or being overweight, can cause feelings of shyness.

Shyness in the United States may be a result of cultural norms that overemphasize competition, individual success, and personal responsibility. Parents may encourage shyness in their children by adhering to these traditional values of individual achievement, aspiration, and social approval as the primary measures of self-worth. These pressures for individual achievement may be greater for firstborn children. If so, do firstborn children tend to be more shy than later-born children? See "Focus on Issues."

Zimbardo (1978) believed that shyness is not something that children are born with, but rather, that it is a learned phenomenon. Some of the factors that may cause shyness in children are difficulties in school; unfavorable comparisons with older siblings, relatives, or peers; loss of usual social supports that result from frequent family

---

FOCUS ON ISSUES

Are Firstborn Children More Shy than Later-born Children?

Zimbardo (1990) has done extensive research on the shy child and has concluded that firstborn children tend to be more shy than later-born children. In his own words, these are his reasons for his conclusions:

Parents are more anxious and concerned about the health and future of first borns than they are of their later-born children (they mellow out as they become old hands at being parents). They set higher ideals for first borns than they do for the younger children and, consequently, place more demands on them. If the first born has the stuff (competence, skills, intelligence), then this greater parental push will pay off in terms of social and vocational success. They are likely to try harder, go for more prizes, and succeed. But if they don't have the talent and still experience those same pressures, inadequacy and low self-esteem follow. It is likely, then, that an awful lot of first borns feel they have not measured up to the goals set by Mom and Dad. If first borns feel inadequate, then perhaps more first borns are more shy than are later borns.

  Another way to look at the relationship between birth order and shyness is in terms of the power disadvantage of later-born children. Later-born children may learn to develop more effective interpersonal skills (negotiation, ingratiation, persuasion, compromise, for example) because they can't rely on the kinds of power their older siblings enjoy. If so, then later-born children should be both more popular and more liked by their age mates. Convincing support for this line of reasoning comes from a study done in southern California. Among a large sample of 1,750 grade-school children, later borns were found to be more popular than first borns. These findings point to another possible explanation for the development of shyness in first-born children. They are less popular because they have not developed their social skills to the same extent as later borns. Later borns do so as a matter of social survival, having to interact with their siblings who are initially bigger, smarter and tougher. They learn to use social finesse instead of raw power to achieve their ends. Less popular first borns are more likely to label themselves as shy, because they accurately perceive themselves as unpopular.

Source: From Philip Zimbardo, *Shyness*, ©1990, by Philip G. Zimbardo, Inc. Reprinted with permission of Addison-Wesley Publishing Company.

---

moves out of the neighborhood or from sudden changes in social bonding due to divorce, death, or going to a new school; and lack of experience in social settings.

Some shy children may be overwhelmed by all kinds of fears: of school, of failure, or rejection from their peers, and a general fear of the future. They may decide, as a result, to give up trying to master their environment by retreating into a pleasant world of make-believe. Such children often feel inferior to others, and their withdrawal is a method of avoiding painful situations in which their awkward behavior becomes clearly visible.

Not surprisingly, shy children often develop feelings of anger and resentment. Unlike aggres-

sive youngsters, they cannot relieve such tensions, which remain repressed within their minds. When a large amount of hostility builds up within them, it may explode one day. As Zimbardo (1978) related,

Typically, the sudden murderer is a young man who has been unobtrusive, shy, quiet, and an obedient good citizen before lashing out in the frenzy of violence. By being extremely overcontrolled in the expression of all strong feelings, including anger, the person has no outlets available. It is all bottled up inside. . . . This anger smolders until one day it is released in uncontrollable rage. (pp. 109–110)

Some cases of excessive shyness can be traced to problems within the home. A common reason for shyness in children is that they are simply copying their parents' shyness (Honig, 1987). The two extremes of rejection and overprotection by parents lead to unfortunate developments in their children. Unloved youngsters who live in an atmosphere of turmoil and verbal abuse may grow up either introverted or excessively aggressive. Similarly, overprotected children become clinging, dependent personalities. Often, their mothers try to anticipate their every need, to fight their every battle, and to suffer their every pain, thus robbing them of the freedom to develop their own emotional strength.

In searching for physiological correlates of shyness, infants' urinary cortisol excretion was measured on an ordinary day, and under two different stressful events—when mother left the house for an hour and when a stranger interacted with the child at home (Tennes, Downey, & Vernadakis, 1977). Infants who were more fearful with the unfamiliar adult had higher cortisol levels (indicative of high stress) under all conditions. Other research has concluded that biological factors predispose infants to display either shy or uninhibited behaviors (Garcia-Coll, Kagan, and Reznick, 1984). In this study, 31-month-old infants were exposed to four specific social situations (episodes of free play; stranger modeling of doll activities; exposure to a talking robot; brief separation from mother) to index inhibition. Extremely shy children had significantly lower heart rate variabilities and higher, more stable heart rates than uninhibited children. Kagan (1989) and Kagan, Reznick, and Snidman (1988) examined 40 shy preschoolers in a laboratory play situation with an unfamiliar, uninhibited peer. The shy preschoolers were dominated by the nonshy peers and tended to retreat to their mothers and become very quiet. In addition, Kagan reports that shy children had higher levels of central norepinephrine that amplify uncertainty and the excitability of the stress circuit as a result of unfamiliarity, unpredictability, or challenge. Robert Plomin and his associates (Plomin, 1990; Plomin & Daniels, 1987) assert that "heredity plays a larger role in shyness than in other personality traits in infancy" (1986, p. 63). Surveying 18 twin studies, strong correlations of shyness in monozygotic

twins compared with much lower correlations for dizygotic twins were reported.

Persistence of Shyness   What are the life-course consequences of childhood shyness? Caspi, Elder, and Bem (1988) examined the persistence of shyness using archival data from the Berkeley Guidance Study (Macfarland 1964). The authors identified individuals who were shy and reserved in childhood and traced the continuities and consequences of this behavioral style across the subsequent 30 years of their lives. Shy boys were more likely than their peers to delay entry into marriage, parenthood, and stable careers; to attain less occupational achievement and stability; and to experience marital instability. Shy girls were more likely than their peers to follow a conventional pattern of marriage, childbearing, and homemaking.

AGGRESSIVE CHILDREN

At some point in their lives, all children display aggression. This definition of aggression concerns children who deliberately seek to harm or injure others and who frequently resort to these kinds of behavior in different situations. **Antisocial aggression** has been characterized as one of the most prevalent, stable, socially transmitable, personally destructive, and clinically problematic behavior patterns (Guerra & Slaby, 1990).

Aggression can take various forms depending on the needs, goals, and emotions associated with it. Physically aggressive children meet others head on with their tactics of pushing, pulling, punching, and kicking. Or, their aggressions may be directed toward property such as destroying a book or carving designs on the furniture. Hard-boiled youngsters, commonly known as bullies, are examples of children who are expressing their aggression physically.

Verbally aggressive children often resort to name calling and making abusive statements to their peers. Physical aggression is not their style. Unlike bullies, children who tease other children usually do not have any intention of doing physical harm. Instead, they make their classmates feel uncomfortable by taunting them in malicious ways.

Concerned adults may want to know the origins of aggression in children. Is aggressive behavior innate or learned? Although the research on both sides has been impressive, the final answer has not been given. It appears, however, that the research is suggesting that biological-genetic factors, environment-situational factors, and cognitive-emotional factors all play important roles in shaping the development of aggression.

Biological-Genetic Factors   The relationship between hormones and aggressive behavior in humans is complex. The relationship is more apparent in lower animals; for example, it has been found that when female monkeys are given the male hormone testosterone, they become more aggressive (fighting behavior increases). Moreover, when male monkeys are given the female hormone estrogen, fighting behavior is reduced (Tieger, 1980).

While the relationship between hormones and aggressiveness in lower animals has been rather clearly stated, this is not the case for humans. Research pertaining to the relationship between testosterone levels and aggression has yielded conflicting results. For example, Olweus (1979) found a significant relationship between plasma testosterone levels in 16-year-old Swedish boys and self-reports of physical and verbal aggression. Moreover, boys with higher testosterone levels tended to be more impatient and irritable than boys with lower levels. Other studies have failed to show a positive relationship between aggression and testosterone levels. One group of investigators, for example, failed to show a significant relationship of high testosterone levels in prisoners convicted of violent crimes (Kreuz & Rose, 1972).

There does not appear to be a direct linear relationship between testosterone and aggressive behavior. If there is a systematic relationship between these two variables, it is more likely to be of a complex and indirect nature (Simon, 1983).

It seems that all that can be concluded from contemporary research is that biological factors interact with environmental factors in determining the extent to which aggression occurs. Hormones, then, should be viewed as part of a combination of determinants of aggression, rather than as definite causes of aggression.

Environment-Situational Factors   Parents can contribute, in many ways, to building aggressive behavior in their children. Perhaps unknowingly, they (and other authority figures) may provide clear-cut models of the very kind of behavior from which they want the child to refrain. For example, they may teach a child to become aggressive by being aggressive themselves. Children learn by identifying with their parents and imitating them. Perhaps, then, the children cannot always be blamed for their raging, hostile actions, but rather the models these children are attempting to emulate.

Studies have indicated that parents of aggressive children reason less with their offspring and use physical punishment more than do parents of nonaggressive children. Punishing a child by physical means may bring results opposite to those intended, as exemplified by the poem written by B. D. Grossman:

> My son is very aggressive
> He's always hitting other children
> I don't understand why . . .
> I hit him everytime he does it.

Patterson (1982) and Patterson, DeBaryshe, and Ramsey (1989) have studied parent-child and sibling interaction in the families of aggressive boys. They observe that in these families there is a high incidence of aggressive or coercive behavior on the part both of parents (threats, scolding, hitting) and of children (yelling, hitting, defiance). Both mothers and fathers are much more likely to initiate conflict—that is, to launch unprovoked attacks—with their aggressive children than are parents of normal controls. Moreover, aggressive children are more likely to counterattack than normal children. Aggressive exchanges continue for a longer time and more frequently in aggressive families than in normal families; they also tend to escalate in intensity.

Parents in aggressive families tend to be inconsistent in their use of punishment, which simply teaches children to be more persistent in their responding because they have learned that eventually the parent will give in to their wishes. In addition, parents in aggressive families are more likely to label neutral events as antisocial than prosocial, so that they may have more occasions to perceive as warranting negative reaction. On the child's side, Patterson et al. find that aggressive children are less responsive to social stimuli, including social reinforcement and social punishment (threats, scolding). The great virtue of Patterson et al.'s work is that it nicely demonstrates the interactive nature of parent and child in the development of aggression.

Recent studies have tentatively shown that an important variable between physical punishment and aggressiveness in children may be related to the intensity of the punishment received by the children. For example, it was found, after observing children in home settings, that abused children showed significantly higher rates of aggressiveness than nonabused children (Reid, Taplin, & Lorber, 1981). Moreover, it appears that abused children frequently strike out at others with hitting, kicking, and punching behaviors (George & Main, 1979). One caveat is in order: Abusive parents differ in a number of ways from nonabusive parents; thus, you cannot conclude from these studies that aggression is evident at levels of extreme physical punishment.

It has also been found that when parents tend to disagree about disciplining techniques, children tend to be more aggressive (Bandura & Walters, 1959). Parental disagreement about child-rearing values may be associated with the development of ego control, which in turn may mediate aggression (Block, Block, & Morrison, 1981).

Increasingly, researchers are beginning to study multivariate (a combination of) factors rather than single factors of aggression. For example, it was found that a high degree of parental punitiveness, in combination with such other parental characteristics as low acceptance and low use of reasoning, is related to children's aggressiveness (Martin, 1975).

Peers and Aggression Peers also play an important role in the development, maintenance, and modification of aggression. It has been shown, for example, that children will imitate aggressive peer models (Bandura, 1977). In fact, children may imitate aggressive behavior more often than passive behavior (Hall, 1973). In addition, it appears that nonaggressive children may learn to become aggressive in a peer setting. To illustrate, a child who is constantly the victim of physical attacks from others, may, in order to avoid being picked on, lash out at others in an aggressive manner (Patterson, 1982).

Certain subcultures, because of the greater status given to highly aggressive children, may promote this type of antisocial behavior (Parke & Slaby, 1983). It appears that aggressive, antisocial actions are more highly valued by the lower class. By way of contrast, aggressive children who pick fights and tease other children in higher socioeconomic levels both absorb and generate negative responses from others. Aggressive behavior signifies almost total isolation from peer-group involvement. Thus, in some groups, particularly those that give status to aggressive kinds of behaviors, children may be reinforced for their aggressions, which may tend to increase in frequency. Other groups, however, may function to inhibit aggressive behavior by punishing or ignoring those children whose behaviors violate the group norms.

Aggressive children do not distribute their aggression evenly across all available peer targets but instead selectively direct their attacks toward a minority of peers who serve consistently in the role of victim (Perry, Kusel, & Perry, 1988). Studies have shown that children who are victims of aggression from others are likely to reward their attackers with tangible resources and signs of distress and are unlikely to punish their attackers with retaliation (Patterson, Littman, & Bricker, 1967; Perry, Williard, & Perry, 1990). Teaching victimized children to respond to verbal and physical attacks in ways that aggressors do not find reinforcing (for example, to respond to teasing with humor or assertion rather than overt distress) may reduce their being targeted for abuse.

Cognitive and Emotional Factors A different approach to the analysis of aggression from a cognitive perspective is taken by Dodge (1986) and

Aggressive children tend to selectively choose their victims because these children tend to reinforce their aggression through their submissiveness.

Dodge, Coie, Pettit, and Price (1990), who have proposed a model focused on a more precise elaboration of the sequence of skills involved in the processing of social information and have formulated a five-step sequential model whereby individuals must encode social cues, interpret those cues, search for responses, decide on a response, and enact the response. Dodge (1986) notes that processing and interpretation of information at each of these steps will determine the nature of childrens' responding.

Initially, the appropriate cues must be the object of attention. If bias is operating at this point (information suggesting that an aggressive act might have been accidental is ignored, for example) or the child has cognitive deficits (for example, younger children may be more inclined to attend to specific behaviors and concrete features of the environment), then deviant behavior would result.

The next step in Dodge's model requires the child to interpret social cues. Was the peer acting benignly or was he intentionally trying to cause harm? At this point, cognitive deficits and attribu-

tional biases can get the observer into trouble. Aggressive children, for example, are much more likely to attribute hostility to the provocative act of a peer than are nonaggressive children, and are therefore more likely to respond with retaliatory aggression.

Next comes the generation of possible responses to the actor's behavior. Should I hit back? Should I go to an adult for help? Aggressive boys, asked to generate possible responses to aggressive provocation, initially give competent ones, but their subsequent responses are less so compared with those of nonaggressive boys. Aggressive boys are less able to recognize the inadequacy of certain potential responses than are nonaggressive boys (Dodge, 1986). Moreover, aggressive children expect more positive outcomes and fewer negative outcomes for aggressing than nonaggressive children (Boldizar, Perry, & Perry, 1989). Aggressive children also expect less guilt and less parental disapproval for their aggression than nonaggressive children (Dodge et al., 1990). The last step requires the ability to carry out the response adequately. It does not help to decide to respond to aggression with a verbal thrust and clever repartee if this is beyond the individual's capabilities.

Helping Shy and Aggressive Children Shy children, who are uncomfortable and miserable because of their shyness, and children who have no friends whatsoever, would definitely profit from some help in overcoming their intense shyness. These children need to be helped to feel more secure and to join in social activities (Ladd & Keeney, 1983). They should not, however, be pushed or forced into doing something they feel uncomfortable in doing. Shy children's anxieties increase under pressure. Pressure for standards out of their range of capability may lead to further feelings of inadequacy and further withdrawal.

Various kinds of guidance, modeling, and practice in social skills seem to bolster the morale and self-confidence of people who think of themselves as shy (Asher & Renshaw, 1981). Individual children need to know about and be able to perform successfully a range of behaviors that are necessary for initiating and maintaining positive social interactions.

It is best not to start a campaign against children's daydreaming. For many children, this is their only release, their only way of arranging their environment to receive some pleasure. If at all possible, these children need to be helped to receive in reality the pleasure, the joys that they are vainly seeking in their imaginary activities. By encouraging these children to talk about things and experiences in their imaginary world, concerned adults can perhaps help them channel some of these fantasies into real creative effort.

When disciplinary action is required, it is generally wise not to rush in and completely overwhelm the child. Quiet children are usually quite aware of what they're supposed to be doing and what the rules are. Furthermore, quiet children are very sensitive to negative appraisal and evaluation by others. A firm, but gentle reminder is usually all these children need.

Perhaps it would be a good idea for the parents of shy children to visit the children's teacher and become familiar with what the children are doing and learning at school. Familiarize the children, when possible, with these skills and learning tasks at home. Perhaps, then, when these skills are introduced in school, the children will feel more comfortable and more confident in what they are learning in the classroom.

Parents can ask their children's teacher to give them the names of other children in the class who are also rather timid and shy. This will give the children more equal companionship (Ladd & Mize, 1983). It is especially helpful to do this if shy children seem to be dominated by an older, more aggressive sibling or neighborhood playmate.

Controlling Aggression Unfortunately, when children behave aggressively, their behavior is often met with counteraggressive behavior by adults. In this situation, neither party reduces tension and neither learns to understand the other or solve the problem. The more adults deal with aggressive children in negative ways, the more aggressive the children become. Children disciplined by adults with punitive tactics are more likely to use these same tactics in dealing with other children (Gelfand, Hartman, Lamb, Smith, Mahan, & Paul, 1974). No amount of punishment seems effective with these children. In fact, what you usually consider punishment for normal children usually turns out to be a reward for aggressive children. The more you punish aggressive children, the more you reinforce this behavior (Risley & Baer, 1973).

These children usually have had their share of punishment; they don't need any more. Rather, they need firm help in controlling and channeling their aggressive tendencies. They need to realize that there are other ways to solve their problems than by bulldozing their way through life. When children behave aggressively in an abusive way, they must be shown that they are using their strength in misguided ways.

Sears, Maccoby, and Levin (1957) suggest, on the basis of their research findings, that the way for parents to help aggressive children is to make it abundantly clear that aggression is frowned on, to stop it when it occurs, but not to punish the children physically for that aggression. Although physical punishment may stop a particular form of aggression temporarily, it appears to generate a great deal of hostility in children, which leads to further aggressive outbursts at another time and place. Sears et al. comment that the most peaceful home is the one in which mothers will not tolerate aggression, especially toward themselves. In addition, mothers tend to rely mainly on nonpunitive forms of control. The homes in which children frequently show angry, aggressive outbursts are likely to be homes in which the parents have a relatively tolerant attitude toward aggression, or where they administer severe punishment for it, or both.

In the classroom setting, it has been found that an effective way to reduce aggression in children is by ignoring the transgressor (Brown & Elliott, 1965). For example, if two children are fighting, the teacher steps in between them, pays attention to the victim (gives the child something interesting to do, or comforts the child), and pays no attention to the aggressor. In this way, aggressive children do not receive reinforcement for the aggressive act: The teacher does not pay any attention to the child, nor does the victim submit to the aggressor.

It is best, whenever possible, not only to ignore aggressors when they are victimizing others but also to attend to them when they are displaying cooperative behavior. Patterson's (1982) program illustrates the value of accentuating the positive, as well as the value of using nonpunitive procedures for socializing children's deviant behaviors. The parents of children who behaved aggressively (27 couples) were taught about the principles of reinforcement, shaping, extinction, and generalization. Next, they were taught how to target deviant and prosocial behaviors: ignoring the former and rewarding the latter. Patterson found significant decreases in the children's aggressive behaviors, which were relatively stable over a year's period of time.

Another promising approach to treatment of antisocial aggression is based on a social-cognitive development model. This approach focuses on identifying and fostering children's cognitive resources for controlling aggression. Recent research has identified a broad range of social problem-solving skill deficits that have been linked to childhood aggression, such as cognitive skill deficits in searching for relevant social cues, generating non-aggressive alternative solutions, and generating consequences to aggressive responses (Guerra, 1989; Guerra & Slaby, 1989). Furthermore, as was pointed out earlier, aggressive children overattribute hostile intentions to others in ambiguous social situations, hold beliefs supporting the use of aggression, including the beliefs that aggression will lead to positive outcomes and will reduce aversive treatment by others. Guerra and Slaby (1990) designed a 12-session intervention program based on the social-cognitive model to remediate cognitive factors identified as correlates of aggression. Children ranging in age from 5 to 18 years who had been incarcerated for aggression offenses participated in either the social-cognitive program, an attention control group, or a no-treatment group. Compared with subjects in both control groups, subjects in the intervention treatment group showed increased skills in solving social problems, decreased endorsement of beliefs supporting aggression, and decreased aggressive, impulsive, and inflexible behaviors as rated by staff. What appears to be unique to the social-cognitive program is its emphasis on adaptive thinking processes as opposed to the training of specific behaviors.

ADOLESCENCE

The great majority of adolescents report feeling globally happy with their lives (Larson & Lampman-Petraitis, 1989; Offer, Ostrov, & Howard, 1981). Some adolescents, however, experience depressive illnesses. Hersch (1977) says, "At this time, neither social nor our health care system recognizes the existence of depression in the prepubescent child" (p. 11).

Helping children generate nonaggressive alternative solutions to conflict in social situations helps to decrease their aggressive behavior.

DEPRESSION

There is now compelling evidence from a diversity of studies that school-aged children and adolescents do experience depression, whether it is defined as a minor disorder, a painful emotion, or negative mood or as a major disorder that impairs adolescents' functioning with associated complaints of hopelessness, worthlessness, suicidal wishes, and lethargy (Kovacs, 1990).

Two essential symptoms must be present if the diagnosis of depression is to be considered: pervasive loss of interest or pleasure and persistent anxiety and dissatisfaction. Qualifying symptoms, such as sleep disturbance, excessive fatigue, feelings of worthlessness or guilt, and cognitive impairment (diminished ability to think or concentrate, increasingly poor school performance) are associated with the depressive syndrome but not necessarily specific to depression. Masked symptoms of depression may be use of drugs and sexual promiscuity, as well as such problem behavior as acting out, stealing, and lying (Rosenblatt, 1981). Although these behaviors may indicate depression, many parents, teachers, doctors, and others tend to see them as merely symptomatic of the adolescent period (Kovacs & Gatsonis, 1989). For example, fatigue may be explained as stemming from rapid growth and difficulty in concentrating because of adolescents' general disinterest.

In adolescence, depressive disorders and suicidal behavior generally go hand in hand, which further underscores the seriousness of depressive disorders (Brent et al., 1989).

SUICIDE

No single fact about adolescents has aroused more attention than the dramatic rise in their suicide rate over the past 25 years. The increase has been over 250% for young women (ages 15–24) and over 300% for young men (Bolger, Downey, Walker, & Steininger, 1989). Our country is not alone. Japan and Germany have suicide rates among their youth that far surpass ours (Konopka, 1983).

Young people of both sexes in the 15- to 24-year-old age group now constitute one fifth of the suicides in the United States each year—over 5,000, an average of 13 a day (Hendrin, 1982). Similarly, suicides in the 10- to 14-year-old age group have increased 32% since 1968—the third leading cause of death, behind accidents and homicide (Jerome, 1979). Studies have found about 1 in 200 to be successful among those who actually attempt to kill themselves (Curran, 1987), with firearms, by hanging, and other very serious methods leading to completion. Poisoning via overdose, the single greatest method used by adolescent female attempters, is serious but rarely lethal (Curran, 1987).

Moreover, thoughts of committing suicide increase rapidly during adolescence. Bolger, Downey, Walker, and Steininger (1989) reported that of the 364 college students who anonymously responded to their suicide ideation questionnaire over 75% had contemplated suicide at one point in their lives. As can be seen in Figure 15.1, the risk of suicidal thoughts increases sharply in adolescence relative to preadolescence.

It should be added that the statistics on actual suicides may not be totally adequate. There has always been a stigma attached to suicide—a sense of family disgrace. As a result, a suicide may be concealed and not accurately reported. For example, in upper and middle class families, a death may be reported as an accident, when in fact a suicide has occurred. For this reason, suicidal statistics may be higher than actually reported.

Accurate or not, however, the figures provide compelling reasons for attempting to understand the nature of suicidal behavior in adolescents. It is important for parents, teachers, counselors, and all persons who have influence on young people to understand this tragic waste of life.

Symptoms of Suicide   The most prevalent symptom of suicide is depression. Ritter (1990) studied 70 adolescent suicide attempters and found that both boys and girls demonstrated clinical levels of depressed behavior. High-risk adolescents exhibited a profile of behavior that incorporated very elevated depressed and self-destructive behavior symptoms.

Not all suicidal adolescents, however, manifest depressive symptoms. Some exhibit highly aggressive behavior. Others may seem happier than they have been in weeks and may display an overall calmness (Peck, 1984). This is a much more dangerous situation because it could mean that the young person has come to terms with death and is ready to take his or her life. This temporary exhilaration is what is known as the presuicidal mood. Another signal that needs immediate attention is the unexplained setting of the teenagers' affairs in order. Adolescents may give away prized possessions such as their stereo, record, and tape collections. They may make out a will. These actions could indicate impending death (Ray & Johnson, 1983). Relatively few suicides, however, show evidence of long-term advance planning or even precautions against being stopped or discovered at the time of the act. In addition, many adolescents are intoxicated before death, which suggests a mental state of impaired judgment and raises the question about the capacity for these young people to make rational judgments about their current life circumstances (Hoberman & Garfinkel, 1988). It is also possible that intoxication may in some cases

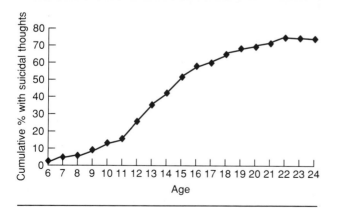

FIGURE 15.1   Cumulative Percentage Having Experienced Suicidal Thoughts by Age

Source: From "The Onset of Suicidal Ideation in Childhood and Adolescence" by N. Bolger, G. Downey, E. Walker, and P. Steininger, 1989, *Journal of Youth and Adolescence, 18,* pp. 175–188. Copyright 1989 by Sage Publications, Inc. Reprinted by permission.

indicate an attempt at disinhibition in order to commit suicide.

Causes of Suicide When young people kill themselves one question always surfaces: Why? Suicide is as varied in its dynamics as people are variable, but research has identified some common reasons for suicide in young people, including relief from an intolerable state of mind or escape from an impossible situation, making people understand how desperate they feel, making people worry for the way they have been treated or getting back at someone, trying to influence someone to change his or her mind, showing how much they loved someone or finding out whether someone really loved them, and seeking help (Dickstra, 1989). Often several reasons were given rather than a single one.

Jacobs (1981) investigated 50 14- to 16-year-olds who attempted suicide. A control population of 31 subjects, matched for age, race, sex, and level of mother's education was obtained from a local high school. Through an intensive investigation, Jacobs was able to reconstruct a five-step model of factors that may lead an adolescent to attempt suicide.

1. Long-standing history of problems from early childhood to the onset of adolescence. Such problems included parental divorce, death of a family member, serious illness, and school failure.

2. An acceleration of problems in adolescence. Far more important than earlier childhood problems was the frequency of distressing events occurring within the last 5 years; for example, termination of a serious romance was common, as were arrests and jail sentences.

3. The progressive failure to cope with the increase in problems leading to isolation from meaningful social relationships.

4. A dissolution of social relationships in the days and weeks preceding the attempt, leading to the feeling of hopelessness.

5. A justification of the suicidal act, giving the adolescent permission to make the attempt. This justification came in the form of suicidal notes stating that the problems were not of the adolescent's making but were long-standing and insolvable so that death was the only solution. The adolescents also tended to state that they knew what they were doing, were

sorry for their act, and begged indulgence. The motif of isolation and subsequent hopelessness is obvious.

Parental Effect Some researchers have observed that family situations of disorganization, parental disharmony, and rejection of the child are related to suicidal behavior in that they breed feelings of inadequacy and low self-esteem. Child maltreatment is another important precursor to attempted suicide. Pfeffer, Plutchik, and Mizruchi (1983) report that severe physical punishment in childhood can lead to suicidal behavior in adolescence. Children learn to treat themselves as they have been treated in the past by their parents. Kosky (1983) found that two thirds of suicidal children had witnessed arguments between their parents involving physical violence, and two thirds of the children themselves had been the target of physical abuse.

Tishler, McKenry, and Morgan (1981) studied 108 adolescents (average age was 15 years) who attempted suicide. The criterion for the label "attempted suicide" was treatment in a children's hospital emergency room. The majority of the adolescents were depressed. Over half (52%) identified parental problems as the reason for their depression and subsequent suicide attempt. Problems with the opposite sex and school problems were the next two reasons cited. Twenty-two percent had been exposed to recent suicidal behavior in a family member, and 20% had experienced a recent death of a friend or relative.

Loss of a parent through death, separation, or divorce is a very strong determinant in many suicide cases (Holinger & Luke, 1984). In fact, suicidal children have experienced a high incidence of losses (parent, friend, beloved pet), indicating that mourning in children may take a pathological turn. A literature review (Lloyd, 1980) provides support for this proposition: 10 out of 11 studies reviewed found elevated rates of adolescent bereavement among suicide attempters.

Previous research has shown that children of suicidal parents are more likely to engage in suicidal behavior themselves (Mann, 1987). In the case of parental death due to suicide, the possibility exists that genetic similarities for depression and suicidal tendencies may underlie any association with subsequent suicidal behavior (Plomin, 1986).

Academic Failure The United States is an achievement-oriented, highly competitive society, and children learn to be competitive very early. Failure to achieve may be extremely painful, and many youths choose social isolation or in extreme cases commit suicide as the only way out (de Cantanzaro, 1981). There is considerable emphasis on the fact that the suicide rate among college students is significantly higher than among youths not in college. With regard to those in college, the assumption has been made that academic pressures reflecting familial and cultural demands for achievement are primarily responsible (Schotte & Clum, 1982).

Suicidal Personality Although generalizations can be dangerous, there appears to be a picture of the kind of young people who are likely to commit suicide that emerges from the research studies. Suicidal children seem unhappy and dissatisfied with their lives. They appear to be unable to cope with the pain of living. They are children who have experienced significant losses. Their family life is marked by disintegration. These children seem to think in cognitively rigid ways (Zenmore & Rinholm, 1989). For example, they cannot think of alternative solutions necessary for coping with the stressors in their lives. The only way to relieve these stressors, they have decided, is by taking their own lives. Suicidal children may be the ones who experience an inordinant amount of failure, academically and socially. They have a history of problems—problems that appear to intensify in adolescence. Many of these children are quiet and well behaved.

Danger Signals of Suicide Verbal statements, such as, "I want to die," "How does one go about donating organs to science?" should not be overlooked as empty threats. They may be a danger signal. Many people mistakenly believe that individuals who talk about committing suicide don't do it. This is not true. Table 15.5 points out other common myths about suicide.

Such behavioral clues as previous attempts to commit suicide should be considered serious; a history of suicidal thinking, gestures, or attempts represent high risk. Situational cues are important, with family and relationship problems being most common. Dominant among the situational incidents that point toward suicide is one in which the youth is involved in family strife. As mentioned before, loss of a parent, alienation from family, and problems brought about by sudden change within the nuclear family may be key indicators of high risk.

Prevention What can be done to prevent suicide? When a parent or teacher becomes aware of warning signals from a child, the most critical preventive measure is to notify the appropriate mental health authorities so that the child can receive counseling. Parents and teachers can also play a vital role by listening to the child. Communication may play a larger role in preventing suicide among younger people than it does among older people. In adults, suicidal behavior more frequently represents a wish to die, whereas in younger people the suicidal behavior tends to reflect a wish to bring about changes in how others treat them (Adelson, 1980). The way in which you respond to suicidal adolescents, then, is of extreme importance. It is best not to belittle their comments, but to take them seriously. Don't say, "You're being silly." "You're just kidding; I know." "Everybody says that they want to die." If you act in a concerned manner and show that you really want to help them, there is a much better chance that they will not commit suicide.

Several studies have shown that a contract between a counselor and a potentially suicidal person is an effective method of stalling or preventing an attempt (Kosky, 1983). Contracting means an agreement between the suicidal individual and the concerned adult, that the former will not take the final step of suicide while the counselor interacts with the youth.

Most of the etiologic factors are not unique to adolescence; family dissolution and disharmony, loss of love, failure in school, and so on happen at all ages and take their toll on children's adjust-

TABLE 15.5 Suicide Myths

1. *"People who talk about committing suicide never do it."* One of the most tragically misinterpreted statements about all suicide victims, including adolescents, expresses the belief that as long as one threatens suicide, there is no danger of follow-through. Approximately 70% to 80% of suicides gave warning signals 3 months prior to the act. Any verbal threat is a cry for help. The reason troubled youths talk about suicide is that they are desperately hoping for someone mature and concerned to intervene before it is too late. The problem too often results in completed suicide, as the cry for help goes unheeded. Because of the unpredictable outcome, no threat should be taken lightly (Ray & Johnson, 1983).

2. *"There is a suicidal type of person."* That suicide is common only to people who are rich or poor, or that suicide "runs in the family," are misconceptions. Suicide knows no class or distinction. All kinds of people end their own lives regardless of age, sex, race, economic background, and mental or physical state. Prior suicide or suicidal behavior of a family member, however, can increase the likelihood of children becoming suicidal (Ray & Johnson, 1983).

3. *"Suicidal people are determined to die."* Most suicidal people are undecided about living or dying, and they "gamble with death," leaving it to others to save them. Very few people commit suicide without letting others know how they are feeling.

4. *"All suicidal individuals are mentally ill, and suicide always is the act of a psychotic person."* Studies of hundreds of genuine suicide notes indicate that although suicidal people are extremely unhappy, they are not necessarily mentally ill (Shneidman, Farberow, & Litman, 1976, p. 130).

5. *"Suicides are impulsive reactions to immediate distress such as failing an exam or breaking up with a boyfriend or girlfriend."* Although current disappointments and frustrations may be the last straw in precipitating a suicide or suicide attempt, suicidal behavior has been conclusively demonstrated to have more complex origins than these. Adolescents who attempt suicide have typically been wrestling for some time with conflicts and concerns they cannot resolve.

ment. Yet, it is in adolescence that suicide becomes a relatively frequent response. Research needs to address why this is so.

DRUG ABUSE

A major problem facing many teenagers is drug abuse. The United States still has the highest rate of illicit drug use of any industrial nation (Johnston, O'Malley & Bachman, 1987). According to Steeles and Josephs (1990) a drug is any substance, other than food, that by its chemical nature affects the structure or function of the living organism. Drug abuse is using a drug(s) to such an extent that everyday functioning is impaired.

Drugs are classified according to the type of effect they have on the human body. Four major types of drugs can be distinguished: central nervous system depressants, central nervous system stimulants, hallucinogens, and narcotics. *Central nervous system depressants* depress or slow down the activity of the central nervous system. Examples are alcohol, inhalants (anesthetics and solvents), tranquilizers (Librium and Valium), and sedatives (barbiturates, Quaaludes, and PCP). *Central nervous system stimulants* are used to stimulate activity, suppress the appetite, and ameliorate emotional depression. The stimulants include the legal drugs, caffeine and nicotine, as well as the legal and illegal amphetamines and the illegal methadrine and cocaine. *Hallucinogens* are mind-distorters. They create altered perceptions and have no medical uses. Marijuana, mescaline, and lysergic acid diethylamide (LSD) are the most commonly used hallucinogens. *Narcotics* have an analgesic effect. They are used to relieve physical and mental pain, reduce frequency of coughing, stop diarrhea, and induce sleep or stupor. Most narcotics are derived from the opium poppy (morphine, codeine, heroin), but can also be produced synthetically (methadone). All drugs are *psychoactive* in that they affect the central nervous system in such a way as to produce alterations in subjective feeling states. The coverage of drugs will be selective—focusing on drugs commonly used by the teenage population.

Alcohol, nicotine (tobacco), marijuana, and cocaine are the drugs most frequently used by young people. The statistics on regular drug use by adolescents are alcohol, 37.2%; smoking, 35%; marijuana, 16.7%; cocaine, .5%; sedatives and other drugs, 6.5% (Fishburne & Cisin, 1980). Cocaine use is the fastest growing drug problem in the United States. Most alarming is the recent availability of cocaine in a cheap but potent form called crack or rock. Crack is a purified form of cocaine that is smoked.

Drugs vary in psychological and physical dependence potential, narcotics, barbiturates, and alcohol being high on both, marijuana and hallucinogens being moderate to low on psychological dependence. In addition, physical tolerance affects the course of drug taking; the body seems to become sensitized to marijuana so that the individual requires less of the drug to achieve a high with time, while narcotics produce high tolerance resulting in an ever-increasing need for larger quantities.

Alcohol By the time adolescents reach 12th grade, over 92% have at least tried alcohol (Brooke & Whiteman, 1983). Five percent of high school seniors are daily drinkers and 37.5% have on at least one occasion in the past month drunk heavily—more than five drinks in a row (Noll, Zucker, & Greenberg, 1990). It appears that more youngsters are drinking to get high, rather than to show their "adult status" as they did a few years ago (Carman, Fitzgerald, & Holmgren, 1983). One reason for the increase in use of alcohol is that it is easy to get, not too expensive (compared with other drugs), and both teenagers and many parents feel that beer and wine are less dangerous

---

STUDYING CHILDREN

LET'S DRINK!

Interview three or four high school students and ask them the following questions:

1. Is drinking beer or wine less dangerous than taking other drugs?
   a. yes
   b. no

   (Experts say that one reason why alcohol is the drug of choice for most adolescents is that they—as well as their parents—believe that it is less dangerous. Do your subjects tend to agree?)

2. Why do most kids drink?
   a. to show their adult status
   b. to get drunk

   (Statistics show that most kids today drink to get drunk. Do your students' responses tend to agree with this statistic?)

3. Most kids who drink have parents who drink heavily.
   a. yes
   b. no

   (According to your sample, do adolescents tend to follow their parents' drinking examples? According to Jules Saltman [1977], they do.)

4. What is the most prevalent drug used by teenagers today?
   a. alcohol
   b. marijuana
   c. hard drugs

   (Statistics say alcohol; what do your teenage subjects say?)

---

than hard alcohol or drugs. Try the experiment in "Studying Children."

Smoking Smoking among young people, particularly girls, is increasing (Murray, Swan, Johnson, & Bewley, 1983). Because of availability, experimental use of tobacco products has the widest prevalence during preadolescence. A substantial portion of children at least experiment with puffing cigarettes by age 9, and in a new and disturbing trend, a small but significant portion (13% of third-grade boys in one Oklahoma survey) use smokeless tobacco (Newcomb & Bentler, 1989). Students continue to smoke despite the health hazards of increasing heart rate, shortness of breath, constriction of blood vessels, irritation of the throat, and deposits of foreign matter into sensitive lungs.

Van Roosmalen and McDaniel (1989) analyzed 1,689 eighth-graders to ascertain possible patterns of indirect influence by friends and acquaintances in initiating smoking. It was found that peer groups are crucially important in influencing starting smoking, especially with girls. Girls are also more likely than boys to continue smoking, once they have begun. Today, tobacco smoking may be superceded by marijuana smoking (Bailey, 1989).

Marijuana   Marijuana is most commonly used in the 10- to 15-year-old range (Bry, 1983). The older the adolescent, the more likely it is that he has tried marijuana: 6% of the 12- to 13-year-olds have used marijuana, 22% of the 14- to 15-year-old age group, 39% of those 16 to 17 years old, and 53% of the 18- to 24-year-old group (National Institute on Drug Abuse, 1987).

Marijuana produces an active resin known as tetrahydrocannabinol (THC) that is capable of effecting hallucinatory states within the user. Generally, marijuana tends to break down inhibitions; its usual effect is giggling and laughter and a distorted sense of time and space. For numerous adolescents, the subtle change from conforming, achievement-oriented behavior to a state of relaxed drifting has been attributed to the use of significant amounts of marijuana (Kizziar & Hagedorn, 1979).

Cocaine   There are now indications that the use of cocaine has increased dramatically among high school populations. It is most often used as a solid substance, called crack or rock. Crack is easily manufactured by cooking down ordinary powdered cocaine with bicarbonate of soda. Small pieces of the resulting solid are then smoked, usually in a waterpipe. The euphoric effect occurs within approximately 5 to 10 seconds, and is far more intense than that associated with inhaling ordinary cocaine.

Cocaine stimulates the central nervous system. Its immediate effects include dilated pupils and elevated blood pressure, heart rate, respiratory rate, and body temperature. Cocaine is extremely addictive; its use can cause death by disrupting the brain's control of the heart and respiration.

Reasons for Using Drugs   Early adolescence has been noted to be a period in which experimentation with various substances, such as tobacco and alcohol, occur (Bettes, Dusenbury, Kerner, James-Ortiz, & Botvin, 1990). Consequently, a great deal of research has been conducted examining factors that influence substance-use initiation in this age group. Two general classes of variables have been identified as critical in substance-use initiation in early adolescence: social factors, such as peer and parental influence, and intraindividual factors. Most use of drugs occurs as a result of social influences, whereas abuse of drugs is more strongly tied to internal psychological processes (for example, self-medication against emotional distress). The profile of the adolescent at risk for substance use includes low self-esteem, psychological distress, and a tendency to risk taking.

There are probably as many combinations of reasons for drug abuse, however, as there are drug abusers. The reasons most commonly cited in research are as follows:

Escape   There appears to be a correlation between drug use (and abuse) and escapism (Hollister, 1983). Escape from what? Parents, pressure, school, grades, responsibility, shortcomings, life? Although some adolescents may initially use drugs to escape reality, once they become acquainted with drugs, they may come to depend on them.

Peer Group Pressure   Many start smoking or drinking in order to maintain (or acquire) status in the peer group, or to be accepted by a peer group.

Low Self-Esteem   Inadequate feelings about self, feelings of low personal competence, and low sense of social responsibility are related to drug use (Smith & Fogg, 1978).

"Just Say No" campaigns seem to have the most impact on deterring cigarette smoking.

Unconventionality Some researchers have concluded that the extent to which young people seek varied and unusual experiences—their tolerance for deviance—best explains drug use (Jessor & Jessor, 1978; Segal, Huba, & Singer, 1980).

Personality Factors Kellam (1982) studied 1,200 youngsters, beginning in first grade and then observed them again in adolescence. More than one third of the students fell into one of the three personality categories below, and their use of drugs was significantly higher than that of the other children used as controls. *Passive-aggressive* children sat alone and didn't participate in the classroom work; they tended to be loners. These children, however, were also very aggressive. They tended to beat up other children and break school rules. Out of this group, 45% smoked marijuana, 60% were heavy cigarette smokers, 18% drank hard liquor, and 60% drank beer and wine. The second most likely candidates to use drugs were the *aggressive children* who were boisterous, misbehaved in the classroom, refused to follow directions and beat up on other children. Of this group, 35% smoked marijuana, 40% smoked tobacco, 18%

drank hard alcohol, and 38% drank beer and wine. In the third group, composed of *shy children*, 10% smoked marijuana, 5% smoked tobacco, none drank hard liquor, and 20% drank beer and wine.

Research suggests that there are two distinct subtypes of adolescent problem drinkers (Windle, Miller-Tutzauer, Barnes, & Welte, 1991). One subtype has been characterized as more influenced by peers. These teenagers tend to be nonconventional, rebellious, and aggressive. A second subtype is characterized as more socially isolated, possibly rejected by peers and others due to high levels of aggression ("bully") or to extreme shyness or withdrawal.

Parents It has been maintained that adolescent substance abusers may be viewed as never having fully achieved separation and individuation from parents; they are still in a dependent and symbiotic relationship (Weidman, 1983). Some studies have found that over two thirds of adult addicts still lived with their mothers (Stanton et al., 1978).

Stress Some researchers maintain that a child's likelihood of using drugs is dependent on how much (rather than exactly what) an individual has to cope with (Bry, 1983). When stress becomes too great to handle, the individual will employ coping mechanisms. Drug use is one of them.

Treatment   There is no definitive treatment for either substance misuse or chemical dependency, yet there are multiple treatment philosophies and modalities. Finding the most appropriate treatment for a specific child or adolescent is a difficult task. A recent publication entitled *Adolescent Drug Abuse: Analysis of Treatment Research* (Rahdert & Grabowski, 1988) suggests that dividing substance-abusing patients into homogeneous subgroups with common treatment problems would allow for better and more cost-efficient treatment. The Addiction Severity Index was developed to achieve such a patient-treatment match. Although this type of therapy has been shown to be reliable with adult substance abusers, it has not yet been tested on children and adolescents.

Until more effective means of selecting treatment approaches become available, parents must choose from four general categories: outpatient, inpatient, aftercare, and residential/therapeutic communities.

Most young substance abusers are treated as outpatients. Outpatient treatment is a generic mixture of resources available in a particular community, such as hotlines, drug and alcohol counseling and information centers, specialized staff in emergency rooms, half-way houses, self-help groups, and community mental health centers. Inpatient treatment involves a structured, time-limited inpatient stay in a treatment center. Treatment stresses an ongoing commitment to an Alcoholic Anonymous-like 12-step recovery program with considerable emphasis on educating the youth and the family about chemical dependency and the goal of exploring and developing alternatives to chemical use. Aftercare involves intensive, partial day-programs, weekly aftercare meetings, or both. The need for follow-up or aftercare is critical because the adolescent faces the greatest temptations in maintaining abstinence once returned to the home environment (Bailey, 1989). Residential treatment is generally indicated for substance-abusing youth

with additional psychiatric behavior (generally antisocial or family problems), and who have been unsuccessful following an inpatient stay.

According to a growing body of outcome research, family therapy appears to be a viable treatment alternative for families that have substance-abusing adolescents (Lewis, Piercy, Sprenkle, & Trepper, 1990). In contrast, if adolescents are treated individually (without their families) and their family systems have not changed, the adolescents may return home to play out the same roles that earlier had fostered their addictive behaviors. Furthermore, family system approaches view an adolescent's addiction as possibly serving a functional role in the psychosocial dynamics of the family. For example, adolescents may use drugs to gain their parents' attention and to get them to stop fighting. Lewis et al. (1990) found in treating 84 drug-abusing teenagers that family-focused drug interventions were significantly more effective than individual therapy in decreasing drug dependence.

RUNAWAYS

One out of every 10 American youths between the ages of 12 and 15 years of age runaway from home (Windle, 1989). Many are gone less than a week and travel less than 10 miles away from home; however, 25% are nonreturners. Janus, McCormack, Burgess, and Hartman (1987) estimate an incidence rate per year of between three quarters of a million and two million runaways and of about a half million homeless youth in the United States. These children break away from home and become a part of the street scene. Living on the street means survival through being pornography models, engaging in prostitution, dealing drugs, and other crimes such as robbery.

A number of studies of runaway youth have shown that they come from all socioeconomic strata, racial and ethnic groups, and kinds of families. They come from families that are intact, adoptive, male- or female-headed one-parent, or reconstituted families. They come from families with only one child, with just a few children, or with large numbers of children, although children from large, reconstituted families seem to be over-

Many runaway adolescents experience various forms of abuse in their homes.

represented among the homeless (Kufeldt & Nimmo, 1987). One problem that has been related to the displacement of youth is the abuse, neglect, and rejection of the young person by one or both of the parents.

Powers, Eckenrode, and Jaklitsch (1990) reported that 60% in a sample of 223 adolescents who sought services from runaway and homeless youth programs in New York State had experienced physical abuse, 42% emotional abuse, 48% neglect, and 21% sexual abuse. Neglect typically involved inadequate guardianship, abandonment, lack of supervision, or failure to provide adequate food, clothing, and medical care. A particular form of neglect was being "pushed out" of their homes, which occurred in one third of the sample. "Throwaways" are young people who do not willingly choose to leave home but are forced to leave by their parents with the intention that they not

return. Physical abuse typically involved long and severe beatings with objects (chains, belt buckles, broom sticks), being kicked, slapped, punched, and generally beaten up. Figure 15.2 shows the type of maltreatment experienced by the female and male youth in this study.

Repeat runaways report engaging in higher levels of substance use and abuse than never and one-time runaways (Windle, 1989). Female repeat runaways are particularly susceptible to abusing illicit drugs (not alcohol), whereas male repeat runaways are more susceptible to abusing alcohol, cigarettes, marijuana, and other illicit drugs.

Chronic runaways often find themselves involved in the juvenile and criminal justice systems. These systems are typically overwhelmed and risk exposing victimized youth to those involved in more serious criminal behavior. Although federal and state legislation have attempted to address this issue by instituting policies that separate minors from adult criminals, many youth continue to be inappropriately served. A number of programs have been and are being developed in this country that attempt to meet the needs of at-risk families and their children. The programs vary widely, but they indicate a recognition of the problems discussed here.

PRACTICAL IMPLICATIONS: DEALING WITH DRUG ABUSE

Major emphasis in dealing with drug abuse is directed at preventing its initiation. The abstinence or "Just Say No" model, however, shows only minimal effectiveness (Botvin, 1987). The better results come from programs aimed at cigarette smoking; however, the efficacy beyond 2 years has not been demonstrated. A second approach is called personal and social skills training. Although the content of individual programs may vary, all programs encompass two or more of the following: problem-solving and decision-making skills; cognitive skills for resisting social pressures; self-control and self-esteem enhancement skills; learning nondrug-using coping alternatives; enhancement

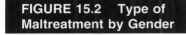

FIGURE 15.2   Type of Maltreatment by Gender

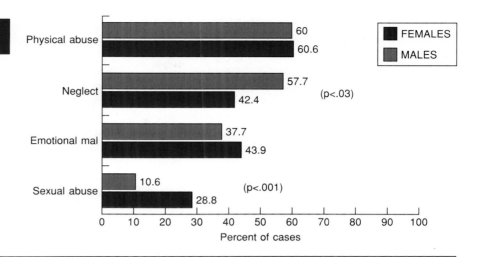

Percent of cases

Source: From Status of Child Protective Services in the United States: An Analysis of Issues and Practice by L. Brown, in *Child Abuse and Neglect: Research and Innovation* by J. E. Leavitt (Ed.), 1983. Boston: Martinus Nijhoff. Copyright 1983 by Mac Keith Press, London. Reprinted by permission.

of interpersonal skills; and assertiveness training. These are taught through instruction, demonstration, reinforcement, behavioral rehearsal, and "homework" assignments. All follow-up studies up to 1 year report significant efficacy of the personal and social skills training (Bailey, 1989).

The answer for parents and others concerned about drug abuse is not easy to find. Alcohol prohibition by law was a historic failure, and more likely than not, parental prohibition of drugs will have the same outcome. This is not saying that parents should acquiesce or condone the use of drugs. Parents must teach by example and by their own life-style. Of course, solving social problems, such as poverty, family disruption, use of drugs by parents, and so on is a tremendously good way to solve the problem of youth drug abuse, but unfortunately, it is unrealistic to think that much can be done in these areas.

In dealing with drinking, it might be useful to help children develop appropriate attitudes. Children in our society tend to observe adults who drink quickly, in solitary and uncomfortable conditions, without food. Often intoxication is tolerated. In societies in which the incidence of problem drinking is low, alcoholic beverages are sipped slowly, consumed with food, partaken in the company of others in relaxed and comfortable circumstances; drinking is given no special significance, no positive sanction is given for prowess in amounts consumed, and drunkenness is condemned. Do not drink quickly, or alone, or in anger.

REVIEW OF KEY POINTS

A pervasive developmental disorder known as infantile autism was discussed. Autistic children fail to display warm, affectionate behavior toward other people. Language is meaningless—if they learn to talk at all. The prognosis for these children is poor; roughly two thirds of all autistic children remain institutionalized for life. Childhood schizophrenia is another serious emotional disorder that emerges later in childhood. Although at birth these children may appear normal, they gradually retreat to their own private world. SIDS is a label applied to an infant's death when a satisfactory explanation for that death cannot be found. These infants appear to have a fragile beginning that, when compounded with experiential conditions, may make them especially vulnerable.

Children with attention-deficit hyperactive disorder are characterized by lack of attention, impulsivity, and hyperactivity. Although the etiology of this disorder is unknown, findings from research suggest a dysfunction of the central nervous system.

Physical abuse is characterized by overt physical violence to the child. Neglect is defined as the failure of the parent to properly provide an atmosphere in which the child has responsible safeguards for physical health, safety, and general well-being. Emotional abuse is failing to provide the love and acceptance needed for healthy adjustment. Sexual abuse, or incest, is the involvement of a developmentally immature child or adolescent and his or her parent in sexual activities that violate the social mores of family roles. The characteristics of abusive and neglectful parents and of abused and neglected children were discussed. Ways in which child abuse and neglect can be prevented, such as parental education programs and helping abused and neglected children to feel a sense of competency, were pointed out.

The section on middle childhood focused on shy, withdrawn children. Children in need of help are those who have no friends and tend to live in a world of fantasy and make-believe. Some of the factors that may cause shyness in children are physical frailty, frequent moves, lack of experience in a social setting, and inadequate self-esteem. Although shy children tend to build a wall of noninvolvement with others, aggressive children tend to behave in ways that deliberately harm or injure another person or animal. Certain biological factors (hormones), situation-environmental factors (parents and peers), and cognitive factors (how children encode, interpret, and decide on a response) play an important role in the development of aggression.

In the last section some of the problems common to adolescents were reviewed, such as drug abuse and running away from home. Clinical depression is characterized by a pervasive loss of interest or pleasure and persistent anxiety or dissatisfaction. Why youths take their own lives has been related to a number of causes: relief from an intolerable situation or state of mind, an attempt to make others understand how desperate they feel, getting back at loved ones for the hurt they have caused, family disorganization, family disharmony, and academic failures. Myths and danger signals were pointed out. Drugs may be classified as central nervous system depressants (alcohol), central nervous system stimulants (cocaine), hallucinogens (LSD), and narcotics (heroin). The four most common drugs used by adolescents are alcohol, tobacco, marijuana, and cocaine. All drugs are psychoactive, meaning that they affect the central nervous system in such a way as to produce alterations in subjective feeling states. Social factors, such as peer and parental influence, and intraindividual factors, such as self-medication against emotional distress, are critical factors in substance-use initiation. Four types of treatment currently available to adolescent drug users are inpatient care, outpatient care, aftercare, and residential treatment.

The problem of teenage runaways and homeless was then discussed. Research seems to indicate that many of these adolescents are the victim of abuse from parents, which appears to be the precipitating factor in their running away.

ENHANCING YOUR CRITICAL THINKING

Broadening Your Knowledge

Drugs

Lewis, R. A., Piercy, F. P., Sprenkle, D. H., Trepper, T. S. (1990). Family-based interventions for helping drug-abusing adolescents. *Journal of Adolescent Research, 5,* 82–95.

An in-depth look at how family-based interventions work and the effectiveness of these types of approaches in treating drug-abusing teenagers.

Firsthand Experiences

Autism

Gillberg, C. (Ed.). (1990). *Autism: Diagnosis and treatment.* New York: Plenum Press.

For those who are interested in knowing more about autism, this is an excellent source. A very worthwhile experience would be for you to visit a clinic for autistic children. If possible, spend some time interacting with these children. This will give you an idea of how autistic children vary in the characteristics and symptoms they express.

CHAPTER 16

Developmental Trends

This chapter is not like the other chapters. First, it differs in its style of presentation. This chapter does not contain new material; it is a review of the material in earlier chapters. Moreover, the material will be summarized in a number of tables and charts, so that you can better grasp the interrelatedness of these areas of development. Each of the important developmental areas of concern—physical, motor, and perceptual development; cognitive and language development; self- and social development; and emotional and moral development—are discussed during infancy and toddlerhood, early childhood, middle childhood, and adolescence.

PHYSICAL, MOTOR, AND PERCEPTUAL DEVELOPMENT

INFANCY AND TODDLERHOOD

In the first month of life, infants cry in response to distress because of hunger, pain, cold, or loud noises. They make small throaty sounds. They use sucking, rooting, grasping, cuddling, and visual tracking to maintain closeness to the caregiver. Some basic perceptual skills are present from birth: infants'

looking, listening, and to some extent their feeding, smelling, and tasting are inherently coordinated for obtaining information from their environment.

At birth the average child weighs around 7 1/2 pounds and is roughly 20 inches in length. Children double their weight during the first 3 months and almost triple it in the first year. By the time children are 2 years of age, they will have gained approximately 17 pounds and will have grown some 14 inches. Girls grow faster than boys, reaching 50% of their adult height at 1.75 years. Boys reach 50% of their adult height at 2 years of age.

In the first month of life, infants attain a working physiological adjustment to their postnatal environment. They now breathe regularly and calmly, and their heart has steadied. The most adaptive muscles are those of the eyes and mouth. A slight touch on the mouth and they will purse their lips and make sucking motions.

Newborns move around a lot—they kick, lift and turn their heads, and wave their arms in thrashing, uncoordinated ways. By 8 months, children crawl, stand with help, use the thumb in grasping, and are able to pick up small objects. By 36 to 40 weeks, children can pull themselves up on furniture; by 48 weeks many children can stand alone, which is followed shortly thereafter by walking.

At 52 weeks, the rate of growth slows down, but motor development continues to develop rapidly. Some 1-year-olds have acquired a few independent behaviors such as feeding themselves and cooperating for dressing.

Fifteen-month-olds are happy in the playpen for only a short period of time—approximately as long as it takes to throw out the toys that are contained therein. Some children have given up the bottle and can awkwardly hold a cup.

By 18 months, the child can walk steadily and may run with a stiff, propulsive, flat gait. These children tend to fall suddenly, often looking as though they have just collapsed. At 2 years of age, children run freely. They can stop and start well, but have difficulty making turns. Physically, the protruding

Young children have limitless energy—they get over, under, in, around, and through everything imaginable.

STUDYING CHILDREN

TWO-YEAR-OLDS

Frankenberg and Dodds (1967) studied 1,036 children and established developmental norms for gross motor (large muscle) activity, fine motor (small muscle) activity, language, and personal/social behavior between the ages of 1 month and 6 years. According to the results of that study, 90% of the 2-year-olds studied could do the following in each of the above areas:

Gross Motor Activity
Kick ball forward
Throw ball overhand
Walk backward

Fine Motor Activity
Scribble spontaneously
Build tower of four cubes
Dump raisin in bottle

Language
Combine two different
  words
Point to one named
  body part
Follow two or
  three directions

Personal/Social Behavior
Wash and dry hands
Remove garment

Test two or three 2-year-old children to see if they also can perform these tasks. Do your data agree with those of Frankenberg and Dodds?

stomachs, chubby cheeks, and double chins (all those endearing things that grandmothers love) disappear. Try the experiment in "Studying Children" to determine what 2-year-olds are capable of doing.

Perceptually, newborns seem to be sensitive to contrasting edges and contours. Similarly, 1-month-olds scan areas of most contrast, for example, the hairline of the face. Infants tend to prefer rather complex patterns. They also seem to have an innate interest in looking at the human face, real or stylized. Infants cannot discriminate colors until they are around 6 months old. The visual cliff experiments of Gibson and Walk (1960) demonstrated that most infants can discriminate depth as soon as they can crawl.

When infants are 4 days old, they can localize sound. For example, they can turn their heads toward the sound of a bell. Research also shows that infants soon after birth begin to recognize and prefer their mother's voice. The senses of smell, taste, and pain are fairly well developed at birth. Table 16.1 summarizes physical, motor, and perceptual development in infancy and toddlerhood.

EARLY CHILDHOOD

Early childhood is a time of growing sophistication in the physical/motor area. The body becomes more agile and controlled, and gross and fine motor development improves rapidly. Because of their increased motor control and muscle development, children in early childhood master a rather impressive number of skills. Large muscle development is more advanced than small-muscle de-

velopment, and thus these children love games with lots of movement and rigorous physical activity. Children are, however, becoming more nimble with their hands, exemplified by their drawings and their interest in finer manipulation of play materials. As one can see in Table 16.2, as children go through this period they get stronger, more skillful, and more coordinated.

MIDDLE CHILDHOOD

Between the ages of 7 and 11, height increases by 5% to 6%. There is a steady, regular improvement in coordination and performance. Middle childhood is characterized by the rapid development of long bones. Children generally exhibit a strong desire to engage in vigorous physical activities,

TABLE 16.1 Physical and Motor Development in Infancy and Toddlerhood	Age	Physical and Motor Development
	0–1 month	Establishing some regularity in physiological cycles; thrashing, uncoordinated body gestures.
	1–4 months	At 2 months, holds head erect when held; when lying on back can lift shoulders and chest off ground. At 3 months, "steps" when held erect, supports own head and upper back, reaches for objects but misses them, turns from side to back, hands mostly open, no grasp. Average nonfeeding alert periods of 90 minutes, in comparison to an average of about 5 minutes in the newborn. At 4 months, learns to roll over from back to side, sits with support, stares at and shakes rattle held in hand.
	5–8 months	Sits on another's lap, rolls from back to side, may, momentarily, keep both head and bottom up, thus being in crawling position; true crawling unusual at this age. At 7 months, sits with support, attempts to crawl, rolls from back to stomach. At 8 months, stands with help, crawls, uses thumb in grasping, picks up small objects with thumb and fingers.
	9–11 months	At 9 months, stands with support. At 10 months, creeps efficiently. May cruise along sides of playpen while holding on.
	12–18 months	At 12 months, walks when held by hand, actively manipulates objects in environment—opens latches and cabinets, pulls toys. Can throw or push objects away. The drive to pull oneself up, and if possible take a few steps, supersedes all other activity. Hands now more skillful in their manipulation of objects. At 18 months, grasps objects accurately, walks steadily, and may run. Loves to climb on large chairs. Gross motor activity still dominant over fine motor activity.
	19–35 months	Runs, good eye-hand coordination, builds tower of 6 cubes, walks upstairs, kicks large ball, puts simple geometric shapes into correct holes, holds glass in one hand.

TABLE 16.2 Physical and Motor Development in Early Childhood	Age	Physical and Motor Development
	3–4 years	Growth rate decelerates slowly during this period. Threes can stand on one foot, hop on both feet, catch a ball; can run smoothly, can decelerate and accelerate, negotiate sharp and fast curves, jump 12 inches, wash and dry hands. Fours can pedal tricycle, gallop, skip, jump over rope, hop on one foot, walk line, do stunts on tricycle, partially dress themselves, catch small ball, button and unbutton. Hand preference established.
	5–6 years	Fives can walk downstairs, alternating feet; march in rhythm, use pencil with correct grip, catch ball with elbows by side; copy letters, numbers, triangles, squares, draw recognizable person; likes large puzzles. Fives have advanced considerably in poise, coordination, and muscular skill. Sixes can skip, hop, jump, climb, run smoothly and quickly; sixes stronger and more skillful, but still have trouble with games and activities that demand more skillful coordination. Each child matures at own rate, as is apparent from the wide differences in height, weight, coordination, and general physical structures observed in sixes.

TABLE 16.3 Physical and Motor Development in Middle Childhood	Age	Physical and Motor Development
	7–8 years	Time of great motor development; tendency to have good body balance. Have developed hand preference in sports; high interest in sports activities; apparently unlimited energy supply.
	9–10 years	Ready for loosely organized games; tend to become somewhat compulsive about perfecting sport skills; may practice over and over again until satisfied with performance. Growth steady and slow at these ages; eyes almost adult size; children ready for more concentrated close work with less strain.
	11 years	Increased gains in motor control and coordination; increase in manual dexterity and accuracy of movements; increase in ability to display rhythm; girls may surpass boys. Boys can run faster, throw farther, and jump farther; girls have greater ratio of body fat to muscle; opposite true for males. Girls may begin to develop secondary sex characteristics; many of them on the brink of showing rapid growth in height. Boys have a more solid look than they did a year ago; no visual traces of sexual maturation, except in a small percentage.

which reflects their increasing size and strength of muscles (see Table 16.3).

ADOLESCENCE

The growth spurt begins around 10 or 11 years of age and reaches a peak at 13 years old in girls; it begins at 13 and reaches a peak at 14 or 15 years old in boys. Leg length reaches its growth peak first, followed by the body breadth, and a year later by trunk length. Rate of development is not uniform, fixed, and strictly predictable. There is no one pattern of development for all. During the growth spurt, girls will grow about 5 inches; boys will grow about 7 inches. Weight gain for girls is about 30 pounds and for boys 45 pounds over a 3- to 4-year period. Table 16.4 highlights the physical and motor achievements during adolescence.

Children in middle childhood sometimes appear awkward because of their long arms and legs.

TABLE 16.4 Physical Development in Adolescence	Age	Physical Development
	12–13 years	As children approach the junior high school years, it is difficult to describe physical characteristics in separate age levels, because of the wide disparity in growth patterns. In some children secondary sex characteristics are already developed; some are just beginning to develop, and others are still at the starting gate. Twelves and thirteens may act restless, lazy, and appear awkward as a result of rapid and uneven growth.
	14–15 years	Agility, control, and balance have greatly improved. Acne frequently appears. Voice lowers with growth of larynx. Boys' throwing, kicking, and catching exceeds girls'. Many boys at 15 have reached 95% of their height.
	16 years	Boys' physical strength is double what it was at 12.

COGNITIVE AND LANGUAGE DEVELOPMENT

INFANCY AND TODDLERHOOD

From birth to 2 years, children make great cognitive strides in adapting to their environment. They move from a neonatal reflexive level to become relatively coherent individuals, capable of sensorimotor actions within the environment. Initially, children's random movements in their environment are unintentional and they have no sense of cause and effect. Gradually (around 9 to 11 months), children begin to understand cause-and-effect relationships (kicking the feet makes the mobile swing) and they intentionally try to produce this result.

Although previous research has shown little correlation between infant intelligence and later intelligence, new research indicates that the part of the intellect that involves curiosity, learning and solving novel problems, and novelty preference does predict later intelligence.

Babies display recognition by attending more to a previously unseen stimulus than to a familiar one (they recognized it as different from something they have seen before). This indicates that infants can discriminate between the two stimuli, but also shows visual recognition memory.

During this 2-year period, children develop from activity-oriented thinking to symbol-oriented thinking. During the sensorimotor period, children's organization of their environment involves simple motor and perceptual adjustments to environmental phenomena rather than symbolic manipulations. Things are done, not thought about. Between 18 and 24 months, children can carry on "internal experimentation": thinking prior to acting.

The understanding that things and people continue to exist even when they are not present or when children cannot see them (object permanence) develops gradually during the sensorimotor period. At 6 months, for example, children will search for a toy that is half hidden, but give up this search if the toy is totally covered. It isn't until 9 months of age that children begin to get the idea that even if the toy is hidden, it is still there. They will search for the toy that is completely hidden, only if they see it being hidden. By 24 months children have developed a fully elaborated sense of object permanence.

The same orderly progression observed in the development of children's thinking is also apparent in the development of their language skills. At birth, children are able only to cry and grunt and occasionally sigh in order to communicate their needs. Infants, before they speak their first intelligible words, are known as prelinguistic. During the first year of life, young children are busy working on disassembling the language to find the separate sounds that comprise it. By 6 months of age, infants engage in a variety of sounds including consonants, and will carry on long babble conversations with caregivers. The babbling stage ends when infants utter their first words, marking the transition from prelinguistic to linguistic development. Generally, first words appear at 1 year of age. Two-year-olds have quite a range of words, accompanied by the appropriate gestures and facial expressions to communicate their needs.

Newborns consistently show distinctive overt reactions to human speech sounds such as visual fixation and increased motor activity. They show little response to other sounds, however, such as pure tones or noise bands. Thus, it appears that infants tend to find language sounds especially interesting.

Although children adopt their own timetable in learning language skills, most children follow the same sequence of development. They generally begin with vowel-like cooing at around 2 months of age, followed by babbling (5–6 months), one-word phrases (12–18 months), two-word phrases (2 years) and will produce multiword sentences by age 4. A summary of cognitive and language development during infancy is given in Table 16.5.

EARLY CHILDHOOD

Children between the ages of 3 and 6 are curious and inquisitive; they have so much to learn, and most do not waste any time in learning as much as they can. During this age period, children make the transition from sensorimotor thinking to pre-

TABLE 16.5	**Cognitive and Language Development in Infancy and Toddlerhood**	
Age	**Cognitive Development**	**Language Development**
0–1 month	Random reflex action: Reflexes become efficient and are replaced by more voluntary movements. Objects have no independent existence. No sense of cause and effect.	Cries, makes various grunting and humming noises.
1–4 months	Primary circular reactions: nonintentional, spontaneous actions that center around child's body. Infant prolongs image by staring at place where last seen.	At end of 2 months, crying decreases markedly; sustained, vowel-like cooing begins. At 3 months, makes throaty noises; gurgles and chuckles. At 4 months, turns head in response to human sounds; eyes seek speaker. Pitch becomes modulated; begins to produce consonantlike sounds.
5–8 months	Secondary circular reactions: repetition of interesting external events. Activity of the infant intentional, but still only occurs after having occurred by chance.	Cooing sounds change to babbling by introduction of consonantlike sounds. Makes string of noises, waits for reply, then makes another series of noises; one-syllable babbling. At 6 months, syllables are quite distinct. At 8 months, two-syllable babbling occurs; baby says "words" like "lala", "ama"; displays adult intonation in babbling; more continuous repetition.
9–11 months	Coordination of secondary reactions: Combines schemes to obtain goals; searches for partially covered objects. Understands means-ends relationships.	Repetitive babbling; syllables are strung in long, drawn-out series, "la-la-la-la." Shortly thereafter, combines vowels and consonants: "la-do-di-da." Inflections become so marked that it sounds like talking fluently in another language. Appears to want to imitate new sounds.
12–18 months	Tertiary circular reactions: Varying repetition for novelty. Children can combine habitual schemes, and they can create new ones. Child searches after visible displacement.	At 12 months, says "mama" and "dada"; has several other words; uses holophrases (words with many different meanings). At 15 months, language increases to perhaps a dozen words; may be able to imitate new words. At 18 months, can use two-word sentences: "All gone"; carries out simple errands: "Bring mommy the book." More intricate intonation patterns. Telegraphic speech: "Me go," "Daddy home."
19–35 months	Beginning of representation: Children can now carry on "internal representation"—think prior to acting. Child searches after invisible displacement of object. Infers causes from effects and effects from causes.	At 20 months, begins to use 2–3 word sentences. At 24 months uses 5 word sentences. Definite increase in communicative behavior and interest in language. Vocabulary 50 to 400 words.

operational thinking, which is signaled by several significant achievements.

The transition to preoperational thought, occurring around age 2 and lasting until roughly age 7, is signaled by several significant achievements. One is clearly the appearance of language, which dominates this period. Symbolic play, deferred or delayed imitation, and a fully elaborated object permanence also mark the transition. The salient feature among these phenomena is the ability to represent an absent object or event, which requires symbolic thought. Thought at this cognitive level is highly dependent on immediate, visual circumstances.

Children between the ages of 3 and 6 are curious and inquisitive; they have so much to learn and don't waste any time in learning as much as they can.

Several developmental patterns can be observed in preschool children. The beginning of metamemory occurs during this period. Three-year-olds, for example, know that more items are harder to remember than a few and that distracting noise interferes with remembering. Five-year-olds understand that memory is facilitated by written reminders and a short time between encoding and recall. A small percentage of preschoolers do show some signs of rehearsal but the majority of children are not likely to repeat material in order to remember it more efficiently. At school, kindergartners have short attention spans and for that reason cannot concentrate for a long period of time on one structured activity. Young children are less able to control attention, more distractible, and less flexible in deploying attention. Six-year-olds begin to show a new understanding in causal re-

lations. There is a deepening of purpose and persistence, which makes it possible to plan a program with more intellectual content and greater developmental sequence.

Children from the ages of 3 to 6 are rather proficient in their language skills. The average 3-year-old has a vocabulary that ranges from 850 to 1,000 words. Their typical sentence length is four to five words. Children's pronunciation of words is generally good, except perhaps for *l*s and *r*s and hissing sounds. They love new words like "surprise," "different," or "big," which are often good motivational tools. Four-year-olds have a vocabulary of roughly 1,500 words and their average sentence length is five to six words. They can use conjunctions (for example, "but" and "because"), and understand and react to prepositions ("Put the book under the table."). With their vocabulary arsenal

TABLE 16.6   Cognitive and Language Development in Early Childhood

Age	Cognitive Development	Language Development
3–4 years	Significant achievements: appearance of language, delayed imitation, and object permanence. Salient feature among these latter phenomena is ability to represent absent object or event, which requires symbolic thought. Thought at this cognitive level highly dependent on immediate, visual circumstances. At 3, beginning to understand conservation of amount.	Vocabulary 850 to 1000 words; uses past tense; enjoys verbal jokes; uses plurals correctly. At 4, vocabulary about 1,500 words; average sentence length, five to six words; language well established; deviations from adult norm tend to be more in style than in grammar; begins to use future tense; uses prepositions; can understand and react to "on," "in," "in front of"; expresses two or more ideas in compound sentence; names and counts several objects.
5–6 years	Fives beginning to understand conservation of number; classify objects largely on basis of color; short attention span; may reverse letters; thinking still egocentric. Sixes' classification largely on basis of shape.	Vocabulary around 2,100–2,300 words; language increasingly resembles adult models; ask meaning of words; generally love to talk; like new and big words. Sixes use more complex sentences.

(approximately 2,300 words), 5- and 6-year-olds use rather complex sentences ("I can play with you tomorrow, but I can't play with you today.") They can speak and understand sentences they have never used or heard before. These children love to talk, and their questions about the meaning of words appear to be endless. A summary of cognitive and language development in early childhood is found in Table 16.6.

MIDDLE CHILDHOOD

Children in the concrete stage of thinking reach a higher level of equilibrium; they are no longer dependent upon immediate visual circumstances, as are preoperational thinkers. They go beyond perception and conceptualize the world in terms of mental actions. They can classify and conserve number, substance, length, and weight. They can reverse thinking, appreciate the perspective of another person, and decenter. They are, however, able to reason only about phenomena that can be manipulated or concretely imagined. They have little capacity for abstract thinking.

Moreover, children between the ages of 7 and 11 are better information processors than younger children. It appears that changes in the short-term memory, where information is temporarily stored, and long-term memory, the permanent storehouse of in-

formation, account for this fact. The changes in short-term memory involve rehearsal, metamemory, and levels of processing. It seems that young children are less likely to rehearse (repeat material silently or outloud), and as a result retain verbal material less effectively than older children. Older children are more aware of how memory works, have metamemory, and are more likely to write things down, group similar items, and say things out loud.

Younger children tend to process information at a shallow level. Older children tend to process information more intricately, symbolically, and elaborately. They are more likely to rehearse in an active, organized fashion and to construct larger chunks of information by using a cumulative rehearsal strategy. For example, young children told to remember the word "horse" may do so by simply thinking of a rhyming word. Older children tend to think of words associated with the animal ("domesticated," "runs fast") and thus are able to process information at a deeper level, which aids in retention of the material.

Finally, older children tend to be better able to retrieve information from long-term memory than younger children. They tend to spontaneously use such strategies as mental visualization and to persevere in their task of trying to remember. For ex-

TABLE 16.7	Cognitive and Language Development in Middle Childhood	
Age	**Cognitive Development**	**Language Development**
7–8 years	Can conserve number, length, weight; can reverse thinking and decenter.	Sevens' vocabulary, 2,300 words; eights, 2,500 words. Have mastered syntax of language. Able to use language effectively in organizing, directing thought.
9–10 years	Discernible improvement in memorizing. Children able to analyze, compare, classify experiences, events, and objects. Can understand conservation of area. Firm grasp on cause-effect relationships. Preoccupation with classification continues. At 10, understanding of the conservation of substances acquired.	Child acquires average of 5,000 words between ages 9 and 10. Knowledge of syntax fully developed. Understands and uses comparatives—"wider," "longer," and so on.
11 years	Can find similarities among three things: rose, tree, potato.	Extensive vocabulary, which frequently includes slang expressions, used in the peer group.

ample, a boy who loses his book may try to visualize the last time he saw it and retrace his steps. Moreover, older children are more likely to stick to the task until the book is found. Self-monitoring or self-testing increases children's recall of information.

The process of language refinement continues during middle childhood. Learning about grammar continues in comprehending increasingly complex grammatical structures. They have mastered the syntax of language and have a rather extensive vocabulary, including their own special slang words. By the time children are 9 or 10 years old, they have acquired an average vocabulary of 5,000 words. They can pronounce most phonemes. Some children, however, may have trouble pronouncing such sounds as *s, r, l, ch, sh, z, th, st, sp* and *bl*. Some words are mispronounced because they contain so many syllables. Table 16.7 lists the cognitive and language achievements in middle childhood.

ADOLESCENCE

Formal operational thinkers are no longer preoccupied with trying to stabilize and organize what comes to their senses, as were concrete operational thinkers. At the formal level, concrete props and points of reference are no longer needed. This suggests that intelligence has moved from the realm of things to the realm of ideas. Adolescents are able to construe the world abstractly, hypothetically, and inferentially. They can think not only about what is but also about what might be. Formal operational thinkers can generate hypotheses, reach logical conclusions, and solve complex abstract problems.

Adolescents tend to use vivid verbal images, metaphors, elaboration, and organization memory strategies and thus recall material more efficiently. Moreover, they have a more realistic and accurate picture of their own memory ability.

In school, some 15- and 16-year-olds lack the spark of motivation to do well—commonly known as the "sophomore slump." Usually, in the junior year, they become more motivated to do well. Sixteen also represents the age when adolescents can legally drop out of school. Some teachers see dropouts as lazy, unmotivated individuals. See "Focus on Issues" for another look at the individual who drops out of school.

Adolescents continue to increase their vocabulary, particularly abstract terms. They no longer focus on literal meanings of metaphors, parables, and proverbs. Table 16.8 summarizes cognitive and language development during adolescence.

The formal operational thinker contemplates rather idealistic solutions to problems in politics, world affairs, and educational reforms.

TABLE 16.8	Cognitive and Language Development in Adolescence	
Age	**Cognitive Development**	**Language Development**
12–13 years	Able to think ahead or plan strategies in order to achieve a correct solution. For some children, beginning of formal operational period; move from realm of things to realm of ideas; can now construe the world abstractly, hypothetically, and inferentially; can generate hypotheses, reach logical conclusions, and solve complex abstract problems.	Vocabulary increases to about 50,000 words.
14–15 years	Understanding of conservation of volume. Greater meta-cognitive sophistication. Marked increase in introspection (probing own internal cognitive and emotional states). Issues such as society, religion, friendship, identity contemplated with high emotion, as well as increased cognitive ability.	
16 years	Able to shift category criteria flexibly and can use abstract as well as perceptual categories.	Vocabulary continues to increase: average 80,500 words. More abstract concepts used when defining words.

FOCUS ON ISSUES

Dropping Out of School

Statistics indicate that the current rate of youths who leave high school without a degree or diploma is 35% (Wilson, 1987), but the rates vary profoundly according to social class, race, and gender. In one study, for example, none of the students from the highest social class dropped out, whereas 71.4% of the lowest social class did (Bronfenbrenner & Crouter, 1983). It has been reported that 13.9% of white males, 12.8% of white females, 19.4% of African-American males, 20% of African-American females, 31.5% Hispanic males, and 34.2% Hispanic females drop out of school (U.S. Bureau of Census, 1987). A variety of contradictory views exist on who the dropouts are. Some researchers and educators portray these individuals as helpless and inadequate, hopeless individuals. However, Fine and Rosenberg (1983) have found that many dropouts are above-average intellectually and are keenly aware of the race/class/gender discrimination in school. Cairns, Cairns, and Neckerman (1989) studied a sample of 248 girls and 227 boys and found that students most vulnerable to dropping out of school had high levels of aggressive behavior and low levels of academic performance. Over 80% of the boys and 47% of the girls who fit this statistical cluster dropped out before completing grade 11.

What happens to these dropouts? Dropping out does intensify income and employment problems. According to Fine and Rosenberg (1983), however, a high school diploma does not reverse the effects of race/class/gender discriminations. African-American and Hispanic youths, particularly females, face bleak employment and income prospects whether they hold a high school degree or not (Young, 1982). It is a false assumption that a high school diploma is the path to equal opportunity. African-American teens with high school diplomas suffer 54% unemployment; African-American women with some college live beneath the poverty line.

Perhaps, instead of seeing dropouts as lazy, unmotivated, inadequate individuals, you should see them as individuals who are aware of the race/class/gender discrimination both in school and out of school in the market force. This is not to say that these individuals do not need a high school diploma but, rather, as Fine and Rosenberg (1983) point out, "Dropping out of high school needs to be recognized not as aberrant and not as giving up. Often it voices a critique of educational and economic systems promising opportunity and mobility, delivering neither" (p. 270).

SELF- AND SOCIAL DEVELOPMENT

INFANCY AND TODDLERHOOD

During infancy, children's sense of self develops from an apparent lack of self-awareness at birth to a rudimentary self-identity, which becomes the nucleus of a growing sense of personality. From the standpoint of self-development, children's primary task is to develop a sense of self that is separate from others. Children learn to see the self as an active, causal, separate agent. Once children see themselves as separate and distinct from others, they will begin to develop ways of categorizing that self, which is known as the self-concept. The developmental progression appears to follow this timetable: From birth to 3 months, the self is relatively undifferentiated from others. During this period, there is a general learning of co-occurrence, in which action and response connections are being formed. In other words, children

In the second year of life, social interaction becomes more common, coordinated, and complex.

learn that performing a particular action, crying, for example, will result in a particular response: their mother giving them food. From 4 to approximately 8 or 9 months, the capacity to differentiate self from others begins to emerge. Between 9 and 12 months, children can distinguish between "I" and "not I." Twelve to 18 months marks the continued consolidation and development of the third period. Beginning around 18 months, children are capable, through advanced symbolic behavior, of articulating an elaborate self-concept.

The infant makes major strides in the acquisition of knowledge about the social world. Behavior such as fear of strangers, formation of special attachments, the onset of communicative skills are all reflections of this. The newborn's responsiveness consists of silent gestures, rooting, sucking, crying, and cuddling—all of which help to maintain closeness with the caregiver. Between birth and 3 months of age, infants are attracted to all

social objects. They begin to prefer humans to inanimate objects, but do not form specific attachments; this is known as the initial preattachment phase. Around 3 and 4 months, young children can make clear distinctions between familiar and unfamiliar adults, and tend to smile and vocalize more to the former; this is known as the attachment in making phase. Around 6 to 7 months, children develop intense specific attachments usually, but not always, to their mothers; this is known as the clear-cut attachment phase. Finally, in the fourth phase, goal-directed partnership, children understand their caregivers' feelings and are able to adjust their behavior accordingly. They also form multiple attachment relationships.

At around 3 or 4 months, young children look, touch, and reach toward other young children. At 6 months they interact with other young children by smiling and vocalizing. Around 9 or 10 months, they begin to imitate others. Sociable 1-year-olds

TABLE 16.9 Self- and Social Development in Infancy and Toddlerhood		
Age	**Self-Development**	**Social Development**
0–1 month	Shows no body awareness.	Uses reflexes—sucking, rooting, cuddling—to maintain closeness with caregiver.
1–4 months	"Discovers" hands when they move into line of vision. At 3 months, scarcely perceives that hands and feet belong to same body.	At 3–4 months, infants show some social responsivity to other infants, first looking, then reaching and touching.
5–8 months	Watches self intently in mirror. No evidence that self is perceived as causal agent.	At 6 months, prefers people to objects; specific attachments begin; seeks out mother and reacts especially to her; smiles or "talks" more to mother, father; "greets" them excitedly. At 5 to 10 months, stranger anxiety occurs. Tries to initiate social interaction by smiling and talking to mother.
9–11 months	Self-as-subject (self as active agent or "I") emerges; beginning of self-other differentiation. Baby continues to sort out and classify world into me and not me, mother and not mother. Responds to own name.	Begins to fear strangers. Mother is central figure; infant seeks close proximity with mother. Enjoys social give and take; repeats performances that are laughed at; enjoys games with people, especially "Gonna get you" and "Peek-a-boo."
12–18 months	Self-conscious behavior emerges; acts silly, coy, or fearful when viewing self. Verbal labeling of self begins. With development of object permanence, begins to realize that other people exist; can name other family members.	Children do not stay too long at any particular activity. At 14–30 months, engages in functional play; (simple repetitive movements with or without objects—has no intent or end goal in mind). Because of locomotive skills (crawling and walking), now actively seeks proximity with mother. Just prior to 15 months, child experiences separation anxiety. Sharing toys first appears at end of first year; increases between 18 and 24 months.
19–35 months	Able to point to pictures of self. Development of "me" or self-as-object emerges. Labels self, using own name.	Engages in variety of behaviors in order to satisfy closeness to caregiver—asks to have story read, rub back, bandage knee. In second year of life, social interaction becomes more common, coordinated, and complex. Sustained social exchanges occur during this time; no evidence, however, that children are sought out as social agents nor that they serve necessary or unique functions in socialization. Toddlers engage in object-related social acts. Twos have learned gender label, but correct use does not always extend beyond themselves.

love to play and be played with. They are especially fond of giving command performances for their appreciative relatives and friends. In the second year of life, children engage in such activities as exchanging toys, chasing and being chased, leading and following. Table 16.9 summarizes self- and social development during infancy and toddlerhood.

EARLY CHILDHOOD

With the acquisition of language, 3- and 4-year-olds form more elaborate, sophisticated self-schemata. They are likely to organize these schemata around physical and motor features ("I am handsome/pretty." "I am good at playing baseball.") Evaluations of self tend to be simplistic, all-or-nothing beliefs. Children believe they are "all

	TABLE 16.10 Self- and Social Development in Early Childhood	
Age	**Self-Development**	**Social Development**
3–4 years	More elaborate and sophisticated self-constructs. Extension of body boundaries to include material possessions—"This is my toy; that is yours."	Ability to pretend during play; engage in solitary and onlooker play. Like to cooperate; for the most part easy to get along with. Fours interact with others verbally, rather than with objects. True mutual give-and-take behavior begins; enjoy inviting others to their house.
5–6 years	Fives understand self is part of interrelated group of others—family, friends; understand self as initiator of novel and creative behavior. Sixes become aware of other children's appraisal of them and the effect of their actions and behaviors on others; begin to make evaluations of self—good/bad, pretty/ugly; beginning to understand group structure and their place in that structure.	Fives are social people; moving from self-centered to other-centered; realize that sex does not change, and can correctly label sex of others; begin to conform to expectations; engage in associative and cooperative play; first friendships made; relationships with siblings may be improving. Sixes eager to become part of social group.

good" or "all bad." They understand self as an initiator of novel and creative behavior. Sixes become aware of other children's appraisal of them and the effect of their actions and behaviors on other children. Moreover, they are beginning to understand group structure and their place in that hierarchical structure of "top dog" to "underdog."

In general, 2-year-olds have learned their gender label, but the correct use of gender labels does not extend beyond themselves. Erika may say she is a girl, but may not be able to apply the same label to other girls and women she sees. Three- and 4-year-olds can label the sex of others, but occasionally make a mistake. They do not grasp the consistency of gender; that is, they do not realize that as boys they will not grow up to be mothers, or that as girls they will not grow up to be fathers. Gradually, children realize, around the age of 5, that gender does not change, and they can correctly label the sex of others. Very young children tend to be very stereotypic in their notions of maleness and femaleness.

Socially, children become more and more involved with their peers. Although they may initially play in a solitary fashion (child plays alone with toys other than those used by peers) or engage in onlooker play (child watches other children play), by the end of early childhood they interact cooperatively with other children in play situations. With their increased verbal abilities, threes and fours interact verbally, rather than with objects. True mutual give-and-take behavior begins. Four-year-olds tend to enjoy playing in one activity for a period of time, rather than cover lots of ground in a rather meaningless fashion, as they did when they were younger. Younger children tend to move quickly from one toy or piece of equipment to another.

Fives and sixes tend to be very social creatures. Many have special friends in kindergarten and first grade, although special friends tend to change rather quickly. Friendships tend to be based on where one lives and with whom one is playing at the moment. Fives and sixes seem to be eager to become a part of the social group. The milestones in children's self- and social development may be found in Table 16.10.

MIDDLE CHILDHOOD
Children's descriptions of self become more coherent, more complex, better organized, and more selectively focused. Global evaluations of self and others (smart in everything) are replaced by differentiated evaluations (smart in math and not so smart in English).

During middle childhood, the self-concept broadens to include a number of new categories centered primarily on children's concrete and observable characteristics. Although children's self-concepts are continually growing and changing, they are, at the same time, beginning to solidify. Thus, children's self-concepts are becoming more resistant to inconsistent information. Children, then, have a tendency not to readily assimilate information that is not consistent with their preconceived notions of self.

Social self-conceptions make their appearance during middle childhood. Children tend to define the self in terms of traits they usually exhibit in their relationships with others—kind, friendly, shy, and so on. In evaluating the self, 7- to 11-year-olds gradually attach increasing importance to their peer reference group. They show increasing sensitivity to and awareness of evaluations by others. They become conscious of the ways in which they differ from others. During middle childhood, children tend to classify their positive and negative points and arrive at an overall evaluation of their worth.

Socially, much of children's earlier interest with adults and parents subside, as they withdraw their emotional energy from adults and begin to unite with their society of peers. Middle childhood is characterized by a shift from egocentrism to a socio-centrism, a shift from initial awareness of self to an awareness of others, and by a shift from self-satisfaction to concern for the satisfaction of others. Six- and 8-year-olds define friends as those individuals who share their worldly goods, are nice, and fun to be with. Between the ages of 8 and 10, trust and reliability become salient characteristics of friends. In later middle childhood, loyalty is seen as a major element in friendships.

There is an overwhelming importance of doing what the gang does, of being competent, of being liked by the rest of the class. Children are busy with the process of blending into the social fabric. Their self-identities are based on the reflections they perceive from their peer group. The adequacy of their self-images is dependent on how well they master the specific skills and academic and social accomplishments required in school, at home, and in the peer group.

Their "Keep out!" signs reveal their need for privacy and their identity with the gang. They are seeking ways of expressing their individuality, independence, separateness, and need to escape from the adult world. Shifting from a dependent role to a more independent one is a gradual process, and children often vacillate between the two. At times, they may attempt to assert their inde-

During middle childhood, there is an overwhelming desire to do what the gang does, to be competent, and to be liked by the rest of the class.

TABLE 16.11 Self- and Social Development in Middle Childhood

Age	Self-Development	Social Development
7–8 years	Sevens: tendency to introspection; tend to be highly critical of self. Eights' world appears a little brighter; tend to see themselves fairly clearly: "I am shy." "I am not afraid of many things." Increasing signs of sensitivity to and awareness of evaluations by others; awareness that others are appraising the self.	Peers assume strong socialization role. Children evaluated by people outside the family. During beginning of period, boys show little interest in girls. Boys and girls have own interests; practically no crossing of the line. Engage in cooperative and constructive play. Peer relations now central to child's social world. Less time spent with parents. Less egocentric; more apt to share and cooperate.
9–10 years	Academic achievement of prime importance because it is one of the major ways child is evaluated. Improvement in ability to evaluate self, based on perceived evaluations from others.	Give impression of steadfastness and responsibility. Increased awareness of sex-appropriate behavior. Peers promote conformity to sex-role orientation. Sex differences in friendship patterns emerging; active participation in organized group activities; group membership more highly structured.
11 years	Children may become very critical of self as well as parents.	Friendships formed around mutual interests and temperament. More definite interest in opposite sex; however, may alternate between affection and hostility.

pendence by resisting adult control, being negativistic toward rules and regulations, or accusing their parents of treating them like babies. At other times, they may want to slip back into a more comfortable, dependent role.

During middle childhood children are developing a spirit of group mindedness and social consciousness. Children become quite concerned over what others think of them. Seven- to 11-year-olds develop an awareness of the feelings of others.

Ten- and 11-year-old girls tend to prefer small, intimate groups of friends; boys tend to prefer larger groups. These groups are usually fluid and a child may move freely between one group and another. Boys candidly, but not too strongly, express their disinterest in girls. Elevens tend to have a keen interest in their status in their peer group. Most hate to be alone. Friendships are formed around interests and temperament. At 11, there is a more definite interest in the opposite sex; emotions may fluctuate, however, between affection one minute and hostility the next. Table 16.11 provides a summary of the developmental changes in self and social development.

ADOLESCENCE

During adolescence, descriptions of self shift from physical, concrete conceptions to abstract, psychological conceptions. Adolescents tend to describe the self in terms of psychological traits (feelings, relationships with others) and are likely to include explanations for and qualifications of the descriptions offered. During adolescence there is a loosening of the consistency of self that was observed in middle childhood. A considerable amount of reorganization and reorientation of self takes place. Adolescents tend to spend a great deal of time thinking about their glowing qualities and disastrous traits.

Self-concept development in adolescence has been studied most cogently by Erikson (1968), who stated that adolescence is a time of searching for one's self-identity and ideally of attaining a realistic inner sense of what you are. Various stages of the search for one's identity have been pointed out by Marcia (1980). Adolescents who have made a commitment, but have not actively questioned alternatives, are in the identity foreclosure stage. These individuals typically select the values of the

TABLE 16.12 Self- and Social Development in Adolescence		
Age	**Self-Development**	**Social Development**
12–13 years	Likely to be quite critical of themselves as they analyze their own strengths and weaknesses.	Shift from single-sex group to a mixed-sex group. Members of clique—usually consisting of 3–4 members of the same sex. May also be member of crowd—10 to 20 members. Establish more mature relations with others of same age and both sexes.
14–15 years	Evaluation of concept of physical appearance based on the culture's "body ideal." Fifteens show heightened insecurity and decreased confidence in self.	Girls (14–15) and boys (15–16) begin to date. Peer group has begun to displace parents as models to emulate. Increase in dating by girls. Failure to differentiate between what others are thinking about and their own mental preoccupations; assumption that others are as obsessed with their behavior and appearance as they are themselves. Continually constructing and reacting to imaginary audience.
16 years	Gaining more confidence in self.	Age of social and political ideals, which are born of dissatisfaction with current existing conditions. Feeling of being able to contribute to making a happier world, an ideal that previous generations have failed to achieve.

significant others in their lives. The moratorium period is one in which the adolescent is in the process of selecting among alternatives. Erikson sees this stage as an antecedent to the identity achievement status. Identity achievers have achieved a sense of being at home in their bodies and a sense of knowing where they are going. Individuals who have made no commitment, and are not attempting to, are in the identity confusion stage. Thus, it is seen that the individual's self-concept must be fairly consistent or the personality will suffer from identity confusion.

The peer group, as before, is a highly influential agent. Many 12-, 13- and 14-year olds prefer to follow the code of their peer group and make a distinction between "their" world of friends and the adult world. Boys have an interest in girls, if sufficiently mature. During adolescence, a shift from a single-sex group to a mixed-sex group is common. Friends are chosen on the basis of mutual interest in activities, sports, or special undertakings.

Over the developmental stages, you can observe how children and adolescents' conceptions of friends change. Initially, young children define friendships in a rather superficial way, as concrete, behavioral, surface relationships ("He is my friend because we play together."). There is a more abstract, internal, dispositional relationship in adolescence of caring for one another, sharing one's thoughts and feelings, and comforting each other. With increasing age, children shift from a rather self-centered orientation toward the friend satisfying wants and needs to a mutually satisfying relation. Finally, relationships change from momentary or transient to long-lasting, with occasional conflict (see Table 16.12).

EMOTIONAL AND MORAL DEVELOPMENT

INFANCY AND TODDLERHOOD

Young infants can discriminate facial expressions of anger and joy, can imitate others' facial responses, modify their affective displays and behavior on the basis of their appreciation of mothers' affective displays and behavior. Pleasure, rage, startlement, and distress appear in the first 3 months. The social smile, appearing at 3 months,

TABLE 16.13 Emotional Development in Infancy and Toddlerhood	Age	Emotional Development
	0–1 month	Pleasure, rage, startlement, and distress appear in first 3 months.
	1–4 months	At 3 months, social smile may indicate pleasure; laughter, it is suggested, may indicate joy. At 4 months, child capable of forming representations of prior experience and of detecting discrepancies; wariness becomes possible.
	5–11 months	Fear, disgust, anger, surprise follow some time in course of first year.
	12–18 months	Shame is experienced; shyness and guilt (self-conscious reactions), as well as defiance and affection, emerge.
	19–35 months	Purposeful anger; self-affection; can experience full range of emotions.

may indicate pleasure, and laughter, appearing 1 month later, is thought to indicate delight. Affection and love for parents becomes particularly strong between 9 and 12 months. Fear, in the first months of life, is caused by loss of support (falling) and loud noises. Stranger anxiety, pronounced fear of unfamiliar people, begins at around 5 months, reaches a peak between 8 and 10 months and disappears at around 15 months. Separation anxiety, fear of the mother leaving, appears around 8 to 12 months and reaches its peak at around 2 years of age.

Rage or distress, the precursor of anger, in young infants is caused by head or limb restraint. Anger in toddlers may be produced by increasing demands for independence, increasing limitations, demands for delaying gratification, disagreement with peers over possession of toys, and changes in routine. Some developmental theorists maintain that these increasing demands for independence and increasing limitations, particularly on the 2-year-old, are some of the reasons why this age group has been described as the terrible twos. This is the topic of discussion in "Focus on Applications." At 2 years of age, children can experience the full range of emotions including guilt, shame, and embarrassment. Table 16.13 provides a summary of emotional development.

EARLY CHILDHOOD
Three- to 6-year-olds tend to display fluctuating emotional states. In anger, children may say "I hate you" and then return in a few minutes bright-eyed and ready for fun. They may be laughing and happy one minute and crying and miserable the next. Moreover, children tend to focus on one feeling at a time. For example, they are either "all loving" or all "nonloving."

Children in this period of development are in the stage of moral realism, according to Piaget. Their moral behavior is based on specific, unchanging rules that they believe to be fixed and eternal. These children believe in expiatory punishment (punishment based on retribution). The child who misbehaves, these children reason, must be punished and the fairest punishment is the most severe. They also believe in immanent justice—that wrongdoing inevitably leads to punishment. Their evaluations of whether another's behavior is right or wrong, good or bad, are made in terms of the physical consequences of the act (breaking 15 cups accidentally is worse than breaking one cup accidentally.) Table 16.14 gives a summary of children's emotional and moral development.

MIDDLE CHILDHOOD
Children tend to worry about their grades, passing to the next class, and what other people think about them. Ten- and 11-year-old girls tend to worry more about being popular. Seven- to 11-year-olds express their emotions differently. It is relatively common, for example, for 10-year-olds to suddenly explode into unmistakable anger: stomp to their rooms, scream and yell, and slam

FOCUS ON APPLICATIONS

The Terrible Twos

Developmental norms provide broad descriptions of what is considered typical behavior at a given age, and are a rough guide to what we can expect from children as they develop. These norms are determined through statistical evaluations of large numbers of individuals. The age descriptions, then, paint a behavioral picture of the "average" child—the way most or many children behave at a particular age. Chief among the researchers who have studied behavior at various age levels is Gesell (1972).

Gesell (1972) suggests from his observations of and interviews with children that just as a child's body grows in a reasonably patterned manner, so also does the child's behavior. He proposed that the better or worse phases appear in recurring cycles and are essentially the same for all children, or for nearly all. He notes that children experience periods of equilibrium in which they appear to be in

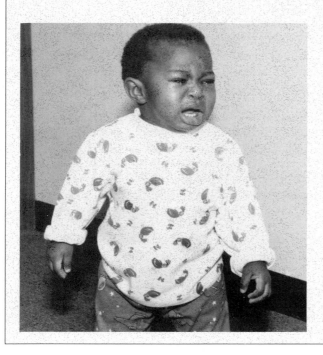

At 2½, children may not be as easy to get along with as they were a few short months earlier.

the door. Eleven-year-olds prefer a more "sophisticated" approach: to give the old silent treatment and quickly (with their best pout face) retire to the seclusion of their rooms.

Children in middle childhood usually accept the family climate of opinion regarding moral values.

Parents expect children to be responsible for their behavior. Children clearly show an awareness of right and wrong and generally are able to follow the straight and narrow. Many children do not understand and are shocked by white lies, injustice, and the many inconsistencies of adults who may

Focus on Applications
continued

good adjustment or in good balance, both within themselves and with the people in their world. These periods are followed by stages of disequilibrium, when children are unhappy and confused within themselves and at odds with their social and physical environments.

Typically, 2½-year-olds are in a state of disequilibrium. They tend to be domineering, demanding, explosive, rebellious, tense, and rigid. They like to engage in ritualistic behaviors. That is, there is a certain way to do things and they do not like to deviate from that pattern. They like taking the same route to a familiar destination, or having the same stories read over and over again. Trouble brews when someone interferes with their ritualistic procedures. Generally, these children have a hard time waiting for anything. Three-year-olds tend to be more easygoing and cooperative. They are no longer quite as ritualistic and demanding.

These types of descriptions of children are quite interesting and many parents have found reading books on the 1-year-old to the 16-year-old quite valuable. Parents and teachers should be aware, however, of some of the problems with developmental descriptions of behavior at various levels. It needs to be remembered that because children are composites of many forces, they are bound to deviate in behavioral growth rate as well as in physical and intellectual equipment. It must be remembered, also, that children add their own special twist on individuality to each of these developmental descriptions. Because children have their own special norms, developmental norms should not be used as absolute scales of judgment. In other words, the developmental data should not create a slavery to standards—"My child is so wonderful, he walked at 12½ months just as the book said." People should remember, too, that changes take place in a movement of constant fluctuation with a forward trend, and not in a fixed, straight, immutable line. Finally, it must be pointed out that descriptions of various age levels are oversimplified and often do not portray children as the complicated beings that they really are. On the positive side, if you keep these cautionary notes in mind, developmental norms may help you to see the "child" in children. That is, it may help the concerned adult to see that some of the annoying, disturbing behavior is normal for a child rather than a deviation. Thus, the behavioral descriptions at various age levels may help parents and teachers to relate to children, even in their "terrible twos," in a more positive way.

demand a standard of behavior from the child that they do not practice themselves. The world of middle childhood is black and white. Children are both bewildered and resentful when parents or other adults try to introduce shades of gray into their standards of values or behavior. Children seven and older are in the stage called moral relativism. Development of causality, declining egocentrism, decentering, and social experience lead to refinements in moral thinking. Table 16.15 shows the refinements in moral development as well as those of emotional development.

TABLE 16.14	Emotional and Moral Development in Early Childhood	
Age	**Emotional Development**	**Moral Development**
3–4 years	Emotional outbursts perhaps common at age 3, but tend to be brief. Fours tend to be prone to unreasonable fears; can remember emotions for longer period of time; experience feelings of sympathy toward others.	Moral realism; moral behavior based on specific rules that are fixed; dependence on adults—moral conduct in response to external demands. Child avoids breaking rules backed by punishment; immanent justice; expiatory justice; judgment of acts in terms of physical consequences.
5–6 years	Fives, tendency to be easy-going emotionally; at 5½ may become more tense. Display fewer fears—although still fear doctors who give shots, the dark, and evil goblins. Sixes, tendency to exhibit more fears; tendency to fear change; prefer sticking to known and safe ground; tendency to worry. Emotions tend to be fleeting; moods not retained for long periods of time.	

TABLE 16.15	Emotional and Moral Development in Middle Childhood	
Age	**Emotional Development**	**Moral Development**
7–8 years	Sevens tend to be pensive, moody, and quite sensitive. Eights tend to be more outgoing and less sensitive. Ages 7–11 show integration and coordination of others' feelings. Increasing ability to coordinate social perspective may accompany increased ability to be empathic. Develop feelings of justice and honesty. Sevens and eights can define certain emotions, but tend to focus on how others would be "ashamed" or "proud" of them: "Mom was proud that I took out the garbage." Sevens and eights can describe how they can be proud or ashamed of themselves—indicating that children can experience these feelings in the absence of observation or surveillance by others.	Period of moral relativism; moral behavior based on more general concepts of what is right or wrong. Morality of mutual cooperation. Moral conduct in response to internal standards that are adopted on their own. Understands importance of subjective intentions.
9 years	Can conceptualize the simultaneity of two emotions.	
10 years	Fears and anxieties tend to be minimal at this age. Emotional mood is one of contentment.	
11 years	Fears and worries of failure in school.	
12 years	Emotionally content; exhibit fewer fears.	

ADOLESCENCE

During adolescence, there is a heightening of emotionality, demonstrated by outbursts of anger, pouty behavior, and crying. Try the "Studying Children" experiment in order to test adolescents' emotional reactions.

At this age level, maintaining the expectations of the individual's family, group, or nation is perceived as morally valuable in its own right, regardless of immediate and obvious consequences. The attitude is not only one of conformity to personal expectations and social order but of loyalty to that

TABLE 16.16	Emotional and Moral Development in Adolescence	
Age	Emotional Development	Moral Development
12–13 years	Twelves appear calm emotionally; thirteens show heightened emotionality, demonstrated by outbursts of anger, pouty behavior, and crying; become preoccupied with own inner needs.	Belief that rules grow out of mutual consent—morality of mutual cooperation. Able to judge acts according to harm done or whether a rule was violated. Awareness that people hold a variety of values and opinions, and that most values and rules are relative to the group.
14–15 years	Coordination of feelings about others, themselves, and the world in general. At 14, tendency to be more controlled in emotional situations. Happy moods more common than unhappy moods. At 15, emotional ups and downs (mostly downs); in emotional situations, do not fly off the handle, but retreat to their rooms.	
16 years	Feelings of fear, guilt, and embarrassment about sexuality acquired in the prepubertal period slowly overcome. Relative freedom from fear of sexuality is one of the tasks of adolescence. Emotionally, sixteens are apt to be more content. They have a tendency to take life as it comes.	Beginning to understand social contracts, that is, rules in society for benefit of all and established by mutual agreement (postconventional morality). Cognitive skills characteristic of the formal operational period needed to reach this level of morality.

STUDYING CHILDREN

EMOTIONAL REACTIONS

Ask as many adolescents as you can how they react when they are angry. Categorize their responses by their age level. Is there an age-level consistency in their responses? Are twelves more easygoing? Do thirteens tend to explode in angry outbursts? Are fourteens more controlled in emotional situations? Do fifteens fly off the handle and retreat to their rooms? Do sixteens tend to be more content and take anger in their stride?

order of actively maintaining, supporting, and justifying it, and of identifying with the people or group involved in it. Table 16.16 summarizes emotional and moral development during adolescence.

PRACTICAL IMPLICATIONS: DISCIPLINING CHILDREN

Is there one right way to bring up children? Unfortunately, no. There are no glib answers, or easy-to-follow formulas, no simplified rules, or pat advice. There are some sound guidelines, however, that will give parents effective methods of training their children to become accepted members of society. This final section discusses some guidelines in disciplining children.

AUTHORITATIVE PARENTING

In Chapter 11 three ways in which parents may choose to discipline their children were discussed. The authoritarian parent is the dictator; rules and regulations are decided by the parent. Children exert little if any control or power. In contrast, the child is the supreme ruler with the permissive parent. In noting how these types of disciplining influence children's social development, it was mentioned that the authoritative method of disciplining was the best method. In this democratic atmosphere, children are given considerable freedom, within reasonable limits. Authoritative parents do set limits on behavior and do establish rules and regulations in areas in which they have greater insight or knowledge. Authoritative parents tend to be "authorities" in the sense that when they tell children to do something; they make sure, calmly and nonemotionally, that the children do what they have been asked to do.

Many parents and teachers fall into the habit of being verbally active and physically lazy. They thunder out orders throughout the day to their children or students: "Be quiet." "Stop fighting." "Do your homework." Parents and teachers know (from the children's nonresponsiveness to these demands and parents' and teachers' repetitions of "How many times do I have to tell you!") that these verbal barrages are not extremely effective. Parents and teachers need to establish themselves as authorities by providing lessons accompanied by words and communicated by action. For example, if Mary is hitting her younger sister, the parent would say, "Mary, stop hitting your sister." If she doesn't stop, Mary should be taken by the hand (avoid lectures), and removed from the room. Calmly make and follow through the request to the child.

It is best to begin with commands that you can enforce. Start when the child is very young to say something only once and then back it up with physical action. Just as some children learn that they don't have to mind unless their parents get to their full-volume yell, they will learn to obey the first command, if they know it will be followed by action without being repeated. Tell the child once, and then follow through firmly. Don't use unenforceable commands, such as "Go to sleep." "Eat your vegetables." until you have established yourself as an authority.

When children are told to do something by an adult in an official position, they will do it, because they have been trained to do it. They regard their parents as reliable authority figures—as people who mean what they say. Moreover, parents and teachers need to follow through *consistently*.

NATURAL CONSEQUENCES

Dreikurs and Soltz (1964) suggest that children are taught that the world responds in an orderly fashion to their actions. Ideally, the disciplining experiences of children should follow as a natural result of their behavior. Parents and teachers can allow children to experience the natural consequences of

their acts, which will provide an honest and real learning situation.

Natural consequences are those that occur when adults do not interfere at all, and at times it is possible to let that happen. Natural consequences represent the pressure of reality without any specific action by adults and are always effective. It is most important to use words that convey to children that they have it in their power to take care of their problems and not that they must do what we decide.

For example, say that a child refuses to eat. In the past, the parent has tried everything: reasoning, threatening, or bribing. What would happen if you let the child assume the responsibility for eating dinner? What would be the natural consequence of not eating? Going hungry. The child won't keep this behavior up for long, if you act genuinely unconcerned. Serve the dinner, for example, and make no comments. When everyone in the family is through eating, remove the plates and again say nothing. Do not serve the child food until the next meal. If the child starts to groan and moan from hunger pains a few hours later, calmly and pleasantly tell the child you are sorry that she is hungry and that the next meal will be served in a few hours.

LOGICAL CONSEQUENCES

Logical consequences are those that you may structure to fit a situation, when natural consequences are not immediately available or when they prove to be disastrous, such as in life-threatening situations. Adults need to structure events that logically follow the misdeed. If logical consequences are used as a threat or imposed in anger, they cease to be consequences and become punishments. The secret of effectiveness lies in the manner of application. It comprises a judicial withdrawal on the part of the adult that allows room for the logical sequence of events to take place.

Many times a logical consequence to fit the act will occur to a parent or teacher after a little thought. Parents and teachers merely need to ask themselves, "What would happen if I didn't interfere?" Toys destroyed are gone and not replaced.

Clothes not put in the hamper don't get washed. If a child has not finished his math by the time the baseball team gathers, it is quite logical that he cannot join the play until he does finish it. Children who constantly run out into the street and are totally oblivious to the danger of cars must play inside or in the backyard until they learn to stay out of the street.

BUILDING A POSITIVE RELATIONSHIP

Sometimes parents get so involved in "training" their children to behave appropriately that they overlook the most significant influence on the development of their children—the relationship they have with them. Some parents become so critical, so negative, so faultfinding that their relationships with their children are very poor.

By constantly responding to children's negative behavior, whatever it may be, you encourage it. The more fuss you make, the worse they get. The more you punish, the more children retaliate, and the worse your relationship with them becomes. Build on the positive. Reinforce your children when they act independently, creatively, lovingly.

REVIEW OF KEY POINTS

The greatest developmental physical transformations (with the exception of the gestation period) occur during the period of infancy and toddlerhood—birth to age 2. Early childhood is a time of growing sophistication in the physical/motor area. The body becomes more agile and controlled; gross and fine motor development improve rapidly. During middle childhood, height increases by 5% to 6%; growth is steady and there is a regular improvement in coordination and performance. The slow steady growth of middle childhood gives way to a period of rapid physical growth and development, which propels the adolescent to biological and sexual maturity.

Cognitively speaking, toward the end of the sensorimotor period, children have developed object permanence and causality and are beginning to move into the world of symbolic thought. The period of middle childhood, in all areas of development, is characterized by concreteness: cognitively, children's reasoning is locked into reasoning about things that can be concretely manipulated or imagined. Children seem extremely busy in categorizing and classifying everything into distinct and separate groups. The concreteness that you observed in cognitive, emotional, social, and moral development in middle childhood becomes more flexible as children approach adolescence. Adolescents' world is marked by a movement toward independence and autonomy. Adolescents are emerging from concrete operation thinking to formal operational thinking, based on abstract reasoning independent of specific experiences.

Children, in early childhood, become aware of the self as an initiator of creative and novel behavior and become aware of others' appraisals of them. They branch out socially as they learn to adapt to ever-widening social networks. Children, in middle childhood, are "classifying" their own positive and negative self-attributes in order to arrive at a general overall feeling about themselves. Friends, which tend to be so fleeting in early childhood, are now becoming more enduring. During adolescence, there is a social shift in interpersonal relationships, marked by more independence and autonomy. The adolescent strives for emancipation from parental control and influence. Group relations become of major importance.

Morally, young children learn to distinguish right from wrong and to live with parental restrictions. During middle childhood, morality is viewed from a black-and-white perspective, and gray areas are not tolerated. Emotionally, life is viewed rather realistically, rather than from a more fanciful perspective observed in early childhood. Adolescents tend to be morally idealistic; you observe a heightening of emotionality.

ENHANCING YOUR CRITICAL THINKING

Broadening Your Knowledge

Firsthand Experiences

How to Discipline Children

Bean, R., & Clemes, H. (1990). *How to discipline children without feeling guilty.* Los Angeles: Price Sterns.

A very well-done book that offers effective disciplining techniques that will help you in working with children.

Disciplining Techniques

Gordon, T. (1991). *Discipline that works: Promoting self-discipline in children at home and at school.* New York: Dutton.

The end goal in guiding children is to promote self-discipline, that is, children who have learned how to manage and control their own behavior. Several interesting exercises are offered by Gordon. Try one of his techniques with a child and see how effective it is in promoting self-discipline.

Glossary

Accommodation: Process of adjusting to new experiences or objects by revising old schemes to fit new information; involves modifying some elements of an old scheme or learning a new scheme that is more appropriate for the new object.

Achievement motivation: The energizing force that stimulates children to act and determines the vigor and persistence of their action.

Acquired immunodeficiency syndrome (AIDS): A virus that causes the immune system to cease functioning.

Active listening: The process of releasing a child's feelings by giving responses that reflect those feelings.

Adaptation: Continuous process of using the environment to learn and thus adjusting more effectively to that environment; involves the processes of assimilation and accommodation.

Adipose tissue: Fat cells.

Adrenaline: Powerful hormone released in emotional response; causes increased sympathetic nervous system activity, which results in increase in heart rate, secretion of the sweat glands, constriction of blood vessels, and shutting off digestion; also known as epinephrine.

Alleles: Pairs of related genes (such as those determining eye color); one allele is usually dominant and the other is recessive.

Altruistic behavior: Actions that aid another person or society and that are carried out without an expectation for a reward.

Amae: Japanese term that expresses disciplining procedures that focus on feelings of dependence coupled with the expectation of indulgence.

Amniocenteses: Removal of amniotic fluid by inserting a needle into the amniotic cavity in order to diagnose genetic and biochemical disorders.

Amnion: The inner of the fetal membranes. A thin, transparent sac that holds the fetus suspended in amniotic fluid.

Anaclitic identification: Girls, fearing their mothers' resentment, resolve their anxiety by giving up fantasies for their fathers and identifying with their mothers.

Androgyny: Individual is able to integrate male (instrumental) and female (expressive) characteristics.

Animism: Attribution of consciousness to inanimate objects.

Anorexia nervosa: Severe eating disorder in which the individual eats very little and loses 25% or more of original body weight.

Antisocial aggression: Behavior that is aimed at harming or injuring another person or persons.

Anxiety: A global, undifferentiated emotional reaction that is brought on by a general situation.

Assimilation: Process of gathering ideas, information, perceptions, and experiences into existing schemes; involves the process of applying old schemes to new objects.

Association areas: Regions in the cerebrum that are related to higher-order thinking.

Attachment: Strong, physical and emotional bond that exists between child and caregiver.

Attention: Process of taking in and focusing on a particular stimulus or set of stimuli.

Attention-deficit hyperactivity disorder (ADHD): Characterized by lack of attention, impulsivity, and hyperactivity.

Authoritarian parents: Parents who own all the power, make all the rules, and are highly inflexible.

Authoritative parents: Parents who believe in reasoning when disciplining the child. Flexible yet firm with the child.

Automaticity: Case's term for movement from laborious execution of a skill to execution that is smooth and without deliberation.

Autosomes: The 22 pairs of chromosomes other than the sex hormones.

Axon: Long extension from the cell body of a neuron that transmits messages away from the cell body to other neurons.

Babbling: At 5 to 6 months of age, infants make vowel-like and consonantlike sounds that resemble language.

Behavioral genetics: The study of the role played by genetic factors in promoting behavioral development.

Behaviorism: A school of psychology, first proposed by Watson, that emphasizes the study of observable behavior.

Blastocyst: Many-celled zygote.

Bulimia: A severe eating disorder in which the individual engages in episodic eating binges generally followed by vomiting.

Canalized: Referring to characteristics that are highly resistant to change by environmental factors.

Case study: The intensive study of a single subject.

Catch-up growth: After a period of illness or not eating properly, the velocity of growth accelerates until normal height for the individual has been attained.

Catharsis myth: Theory that states that children who watch violence on television will experience an emotional release, and thus not resort to behaving aggressively.

Centration: The focusing on one aspect or dimension of an object at a time and failing to take in other aspects or dimensions.

Cerebellum: A brain structure that extends out of the back of the skull; responsible for physical coordination.

Cerebrum: Portion of the brain consisting of two hemispheres implicated in higher-order thinking.

Childhood schizophrenia: Severe emotional disturbance characterized by impaired interpersonal relationships and excessive and bizarre behavior.

Chorion: Lining of the placenta.

Chromosomes: Threadlike structures consisting mainly of protein and DNA found in the nucleus of every cell.

Classical conditioning: A passive form of learning in which two stimuli (the unconditioned stimulus and the conditioned stimulus) are presented in close temporal proximity. Eventually, the subject responds to the conditioned stimulus in a manner similar to the response given to the unconditioned stimulus.

Classification: Grouping of objects by their similar properties.

Clique: A small and exclusive group of individuals with similar interests.

Cognition: Mental activities such as thinking, reasoning, remembering, and perceiving. The process by which the seemingly random information presented by the environment and social stimuli around a person is organized into meaningful units for memory and ultimate action.

Cohort: A group of individuals who were born at the same time.

Collectiveness: A philosophy that emphasizes the interconnectedness of persons puts high value on harmony and interpersonal relationships.

Combinatorial analysis: In Piaget's theory, a form of problem solving characterized by the ability to separate the effects of several variables in a problem-solving situation by holding all the factors constant except one.

Concordance: In studying environmental and hereditary influences, psychologists study the similarity or concordance on some variable such as intelligence with twins, siblings, or parents. The correlational coefficient is an estimate of the direction and magnitude of the similarity.

Concrete operations: Children ages 7 to 11 can understand logical principles that apply to the concrete world of reality.

Confounding variables: Any variable that may influence the dependent variable.

Conservation: Children achieve the understanding that a quantity stays the same despite a change in appearance.

Control group: In an experiment, this group does not receive the independent variable and thus serves as a comparison for evaluating the effect of the treatment.

Control structures: Case's term for the basic units of thought involving procedural knowledge that children acquire about how to solve certain problems.

Conventional morality: Kohlberg's second level of moral reasoning in which the child or adult conforms out of actively supporting the law and social order.

Convergent thinking: Finding the one best or correct answer to a problem.

Cooing: At 3 to 4 months, infants vocalize in open, vowel-like sounds.

Coping: Efforts to manage environmental and internal demands and conflict that tax or exceed a person's resources.

Corpus callosum: Band of neural fibers that transmit messages between the two hemispheres of the cerebrum.

Correlational method: Research method that allows researchers to measure the relationship between two or more variables.

Creativity: Child's responses to problems and situations are divergent, novel, and original.

Cross-sectional study: A research design in which different samples are observed at different ages in order to assess differences in behavior associated with each age group.

Crowd: A larger, more impersonal peer group generally consisting of 10 to 20 members who share common interests in social activities.

Cultural-familial causes of retardation: One or both the parents are retarded; it is not yet known whether familial retardation is due primarily to genetic factors or the experience of being reared by retarded parents.

Deep structure: The general idea or underlying meaning of a sentence.

Defensive identification: Out of fear and because of "castration anxiety," a boy gives up his sexual desires for his mother and begins to identify with his father.

Dendrite: Neural process extending from the cell body of the neuron; receives messages from adjacent cells and conducts them to the cell body.

Deoxyribonucleic acid (DNA): A group of nucleic acids found in nucleus of cell; contains genetic code to regulate the functioning and development of the organism.

Dependent variable: The variable that is measured in an experimental study in order to see the effects of the independent variable; usually the behavior or performance of the subjects in the experiment.

Difficult child: Thomas and Chess's temperamental classification for a child who exhibits frequent expression of negative moods, sleeps poorly, cries often, and takes some time to adjust to new situations.

Distinctiveness: A child's basic need to be independent and autonomous from parents; exists simultaneously with child's need for inclusiveness.

Distress: Negative stress; leads to physical and psychological damage.

Divergent thinking: Examining many different solutions to problems.

Down syndrome: A condition causing mental retardation and associated with physical disorders.

Easy child: Thomas and Chess's temperamental classification for a child who is usually positive in mood, has low intensity of reaction, and is usually positive in approaches to new situations.

Echoic memory: Brief persistence of auditory sensations.

Ego (Freud): The conscious mind, governed by the reality principle; operates to balance the demands of the id and superego.

Elaboration: A mnemonic device in which meaning is added to the material that is to be remembered; an example would be visual imagery.

Embryo: The early developmental stage of an organism that occurs between 2 weeks and 8 weeks after conception.

Emotion: A response of the whole organism involving physical arousal and cognitive components (perception, awareness, knowledge, and feeling).

Empathy: Vicarious response to the emotional cues from other people or their situations.

Encoding: A dynamic process in which incoming information is integrated with children's current schemes.

Endogenous smiles: Reflexive smiles, not produced by external stimuli.

Endometrium: The inner mucous membrane of the uterus.

Epigenetic principle (Erikson): Refers to the observation that anything that grows has a ground plan.

Equilibration: A self-regulating process of seeking mental equilibrium.

Equilibrium: A state of cognitive balance between assimilation and accommodation; a relatively stable state of some scheme such that it can adapt to varied output without any essential change.

Estrodiol: A substance that stimulates the development of secondary female characteristics; female hormones.

Estrogens: Female hormones responsible for the development of secondary sex characteristics in females.

Eustress: Pleasant or curative stress that does not produce harmful physical or psychological damage.

Executive processes space: Case's term for the maximum number of schemes a child can activate at any one time while working on a problem-solving task.

Exogenous smiles: Smiles that are produced by external stimuli.

Expectancy formation: Individual expectations for success (or failure) in achievement tasks.

Experimental group: Subjects in this group are exposed to the treatment, the independent variable.

Experimental method: A research method in which treatment is done in a controlled setting.

Explicit rules: Formal grammar rules taught in school.

Expressive behavior: Nurturant and empathic behavior.

Expressive children: When learning first words, these children use words that are primarily personal-social.

Extensive friendships: A child's tendency to have three or four friends.

External locus of control: Children who do not feel they have any control over their environment.

Factor analysis: A statistical technique of analyzing experimental results by correlating (comparing) scores on a variety of tests. It is assumed that strong correlations between scores indicate a common factor.

Fallopian tube: Either of a pair of tubes that transport the egg from the ovary to the uterus.

Fear: Immediate negative reaction to a threatening or sudden event.

Fetal alcohol syndrome (FAS): Physical and cognitive abnormalities in children caused by a pregnant woman's heavy drinking.

Fixation: According to Freud, excessive or insufficient gratification of needs in any of the first three psychosexual stages could cause a resistance to transferring libidinal energy to a new psychosexual stage, which could predispose a child toward specific psychological symptoms as an adult.

Formal operations: Stage at which thinking is no longer constrained to the concrete world. Children can think abstractly, can generate hypotheses, reach logical conclusions, and systematically solve problems.

Functional core hypothesis: Meanings are attached to words on the basis of the functions of the object.

Functional invariants: Two immutable laws of development—organization and adaptation.

Gamete: A sexual reproductive cell (sperm or egg) that unites with another cell, forming a zygote.

Gang: A relatively stable or enduring group of individuals who interact and share common goals and values.

Gender constancy: Child realizes permanency of sex across time and situations.

Gender identity: Awareness and acceptance of being male or female.

Gender role: Includes everything you feel, think, do, and say that indicates to yourself as well as others that you are a male or female.

Gender-role stereotyping: Relatively rigid conceptions individuals hold about behaviors that are "typical" for males and females.

Gender stability: Children realize permanency of sex but get confused in certain situations; for example, they may label a female as a male if she is dressed in masculine suit and tie.

General adaptation syndrome: Selye's concept of the body's response to stress, composed of three stages: alarm, resistance, and exhaustion.

Generalizability: Also known as external validity, generalizability refers to the extent to which research findings may be applied to broader populations or settings.

Genes: A unit in the chromosome that carries hereditary traits.

Genotype: Actual genetic composition of the individual.

g factor: Refers to general intelligence—the ability to see relationships between bits of information.

Gifted children: Children who show exceptional ability or potential in the general academic area, specific academic areas, visual and performing arts, and athletics.

Gonadotrophic hormones: Substances secreted by the anterior pituitary to stimulate the gonads (ovaries in females and testes in males), which, in turn, secrete their hormones.

Goodness-of-fit: Development of any temperamental characteristic depends on the degree to which that particular factor is supported and maintained by the environment.

Grammar of language: Implicit rules children apply in phonological, syntactic, and semantic structuring of language.

Group-factor theory: Thurstone's theory that intelligence is made up of seven primary mental abilities.

Growth hormone: Substance that is responsible for increases in body height.

Guilt: Involves a sense of feeling responsible for your actions and an ability to sense that your actions have brought psychological or physical harm to another.

Heteronomous morality: Children's moral behavior directed by external controls such as authority figures; children act in morally correct ways to avoid punishment.

Heterozygous: Referring to two alleles that are different for a particular trait.

Holophrastic: The one-word stage so named because the whole phrase or sentence is expressed in one word.

Homologous: Referring to the pair of chromosomes that have similar size and shape; one is from the mother and one is from the father.

Homozygous: Referring to two alleles that are the same for a particular trait.

Hypothesis: A specific prediction of behavior that can be tested.

Hypothetical-deductive reasoning: In Piaget's theory, a form of problem solving characterized by the ability to generate hypotheses and to draw logical conclusions.

Iconic memory: Brief persistence of visual images in memory.

Id (Freud): The unconscious mind—seat of all energy, motives, emotions, and drives; operates on the pleasure-seeking principle.

Identification: Process by which children acquire parents' and significant others' attitudes, values, and behavioral patterns.

Identity achievement (Erikson): These individuals have experienced moratorium and have made a commitment to occupational goals and personal values. They have established a sense of social connectedness that will allow them to function effectively in society.

Identity confusion (Erikson): These individuals have not developed a sense of who they are and where they are going. Individuals in this status of development have made no commitment.

Identity crisis: According to Erikson, adolescents engage in an active search in trying to achieve an understanding of self.

Identity diffusion: Individuals in this identity status have made no commitment nor are they attempting to arrive at a commitment in a given content area.

Identity foreclosure (Erikson): Identity status of those individuals who have not actively questioned alternatives, but who have made a commitment.

Imitation (Bandura): Emulation of the behavior of others.

Immanent justice: Term coined by Piaget conveying the concept that wicked deeds inevitably bring punishment.

Implantation: The attachment of the blastula to the lining of the uterus.

Implicit rules: Grammatical rules that cannot be formulated or expressed.

Inclusion: A child's basic need to be a part of, dependent on, and loved and respected by parents; this need exists simultaneously with the child's need for distinctiveness.

Independent variable: The variable that is manipulated in an experimental study in order to see what changes then occur in the subjects' behavior, the dependent variable.

Indifferent parents: Parents who do whatever is necessary to minimize the time and energy they must devote to interacting with their children.

Individualism: A philosophy that emphasizes self-reliance, independence, and self-assertiveness.

Induction: Disciplining technique in which the consequences of children's behavior are explained to them.

Infanticide: The deliberate murdering of infants particularly those of evident birth defects and excess progeny, especially females.

Infantile autism: Term used to characterize children who are unable to relate themselves in appropriate ways to other people, have an obsessive desire for sameness, and engage in nonsymbolic speech.

Insecure-ambivalent attachment: Infants momentarily cling and then push away from their mothers after brief separation; they do not actively explore in their environment.

Insecure-avoidant attachment: Infants actively resist contact with their mothers after a brief separation; they do not actively explore in their environment.

Instrumental behavior: Competence-directed and achievement-focused behavior.

Intelligence: The ability to reason abstractly, learn, and adapt.

Intelligence quotient: The ratio of mental age to chronological age multiplied by 100.

Intensive friendships: A child's tendency to have only one or two friends.

Internal locus of control: Children who perceive a causal relationship between their personal actions and resultant events.

Introspection: Looking into your own mind and inspecting your own feelings.

Kleinfelter's syndrome: A hereditary disorder in which the ovum is fertilized by XY sperm producing a zygote with an extra X chromosome (XXY).

Knowledge base: What children already know, which helps contribute to the new material they can learn and remember.

Kwashiorkor: Form of starvation that occurs in children (ages 2 to 4) whose diet consists of carbohydrates and little or no protein.

Language: An ordered system of rules that apply in speaking, listening, and writing.

Language acquisition device (LAD): Chomsky's term for a special structure in the brain that enables children to deduce the basic rule system of language.

Learned helplessness: The passive resignation learned when an individual is unable to avoid failure.

Level of aspiration: Involves both the difficulty of the learning tasks children are willing to undertake and the amount of work they are willing to try to do on them in a given time.

Limbic system: Part of the brain that is implicated in emotional and motivational functions.

Linguistic: Period begins when children utter their first intelligent words, around 1 year of age.

Locus: The fixed location of each gene on the chromosome.

Logical structure: Organizational properties of thinking that children and adults use to solve problems. Structures determine the extent and limits of the child's power to solve problems.

Longitudinal study: Same subjects observed over an extended period of time.

Long-term memory: Permanent storehouse of information.

Marasmus: Form of starvation in children under 1 year of age due to deprivation of necessary proteins and calories.

Mean length of utterance (MLU): The number of words child uses in a sentence; thought to be a good measure of vocabulary and grammar sophistication.

Memory strategies: Voluntary, deliberate techniques used to improve memory, such as rehearsal and organization.

Mental age: A measure of intelligence test performance; a child's degree of brightness.

Mental retardation: A condition of limited mental ability as indicated by score on IQ test.

Metamemory: Knowledge of memory skills and how memory works.

Morality: Knowing right from wrong behavior and engaging in the former.

Moral realism: Piagetian stage of moral reasoning: Rules are seen as being external, absolute, unchanging. Child adopts parents' moral beliefs unquestionably.

Moral reasoning: Ways in which children think in certain situations involving moral conduct.

Moral relativism: A cognitively more mature Piagetian stage of moral reasoning than moral realism: Rules determined by reciprocal agreements; morality depends on mutual respect rather than unquestioned obedience to authority.

Moratorium: Active searching and experimenting with various personal, vocational, and social roles.

Morphemes: Words and word fragments such as prefixes and suffixes.

Morphology: Study of rules used to combine phonemes to form words.

Motherese: The way mothers talk to young children: higher pitch, exaggerated intonation, short, simple sentences, omission of pronouns.

Multiple-factor theory: Thorndike's theory that intelligence is constructed from a multitude of separate factors or elements.

Multivariate analysis: Term used to categorize a family of analytic methods whose chief characteristic is the simultaneous analysis of one or more independent variables and one or more dependent variables.

Myelination: Process by which nerve fibers become enclosed by the myelin sheath.

Myelin sheath: Fatty substance that coats the axons of the neuron.

Naturalistic observation: Subjects observed in their natural environment.

Negative reinforcer: Any action that results in the removal of an unpleasant situation.

Neuron: Brain cell.

New mammalian brain: Layer of gray matter overlying the entire brain; implicated in higher-order thinking. Also known as the cerebrum and cerebral cortex.

Nonshared family environment: Experiences that are unique to each individual.

Noradrenaline: Hormone that causes an increased parasympathetic activity that results in decrease in heart rate, secretion of the salivary glands, dilation of blood vessels, facilitation of digestion, and constriction of the pupils of the eyes; also known as norepinephrine.

Obesity: Characteristic of children who fall at the 85% mark on weight charts or more are considered to be overweight or obese.

Object permanence: Children's ability in the sensorimotor period to know that objects in their environment continue to exist even when they cannot see them.

Oedipal complex: According to Freud, a young boy's sexual desires toward his mother and feelings of hatred and jealousy toward his father.

Old mammalian brain: Type of brain that evolved roughly 60 million years ago; in humans appears to be concerned with emotional and motivational functions of the limbic system.

Operant conditioning: A form of learning in which the child is more likely to behave in a certain way because those behaviors have been rewarded or have brought about a satisfying state of affairs.

Operations: Particular types of cognitive schemes; actions that are internalizable and reversible. Because operations do not exist in isolation, they are in the form of structured wholes.

Organic causes of retardation: Damage to the central nervous system, in particular the brain, which leads to a retarded level of cognitive functioning.

Organization (information processing term): A mnemonic device involving the categorization of items to be remembered (e.g., objects or words) by a common attribute (e.g., color, size, shape, or use).

Organization (Piagetian term): Process that ensures that all structures are properly interrelated; innate ability to integrate/combine schemes. As a result, schemes combine into a higher order.

Ossification: Process involves the replacement of soft and relatively pliable cartilagenous tissue with bone tissue.

Overextension: Child generalizes a word based on some feature of the original objects and uses it to refer to many other objects.

Ovulation: Ejection of the ovum into the fallopian tube.

Ovum: A female gamete or mature egg.

Peer group: A small cluster of friends.

Perception: Process of organizing and interpreting physical sensations.

Perfection principle (Freud): The guiding principle of the superego that seeks to encourage socially desirable behavior.

Permissive parents: Parents who behave in an accepting and somewhat passive way in matters of discipline.

Phenotype: The individual's observable or measurable characteristics.

Phenylketonuria (PKU): A hereditary disorder in which the child fails to produce an enzyme that converts phenylalanine into tryosine. If untreated, the affected child will suffer from moderate or severe mental retardation.

Pheromones: Chemical signals given off by others of the same species that communicate various messages such as fear and identification.

Phobia: Uncontrollable fear.

Phonemes: Smallest basic sound units.

Phonology: Describes how sounds (phonemes) are put together to form words.

Placenta: Disk-shaped organ in which the blood vessels of the fetus and those of the mother come together without joining. Nutrients, oxygen, hormones, and waste products are exchanged by diffusing from one blood-vessel system to another.

Pleasure principle (Freud): The id is guided by the pleasure principle, which seeks to obtain gratification and avoid pain.

Poorness-of-fit: Occurs when the demands and expectations of the environment are not consonant with the child's capacities and characteristics.

Positive reinforcer: Something pleasurable such as a reward that increases probability that behavior will occur.

Postconventional morality: Kohlberg's third level of moral reasoning in which older children and adults define moral values apart from authority of groups of people.

Pragmatics: Rules specifying when to say what to whom in order to communicate effectively.

Preconscious: Level of personality containing information that can be recalled with little effort.

Preconventional morality: Kohlberg's first level of moral reasoning in which child is responsive to cultural rules and labels such as good, bad, right, or wrong; child interprets these labels in terms of either punishment or hedonistic consequences.

Prelinguistic: Before infants speak their first intelligent words. During this period, the infant cries, coos, and babbles.

Preoperational: Piaget's second stage of cognitive development, lasting from about age 2 to age 7, when children are thinking at a symbolic level but are not yet using cognitive operations.

Prosocial behavior: Acting in ways that will benefit others or society.

Psycholinguistics: The disciplines of psychology and linguistics work together to study language development.

Psychosexual stages (Freud): Steps in the child's development in which sexual instincts are associated with changing erogenous zones.

Psychosocial stages (Erikson): Personality is formed as the ego progresses through a series of interrelated stages. Emphasis is on how the individual's social environment influences behavior.

Puberty: Complex series of hormonal changes resulting in physical growth and sexual maturation.

Random sampling: Each person in a population has an equal chance of being chosen as a subject for an experiment.

Reaction range: Range of possibilities for a certain trait or characteristic that the genetic code allows.

Reality principle: Ego operates on reality principle that attempts to reduce the id's needs through rational analysis of reality.

Recall: One kind of retrieval that is dependent on a minimal number of cues; an example would be an essay exam.

Recognition: One kind of retrieval in which the individual is able to recognize the correct object or answer; an example would be a multiple-choice test.

Referential children: When learning first words, these children are concerned with labeling things encountered in their environment.

Reflexes: Unlearned, involuntary responses to stimuli.

Rehearsal: A mnemonic device involving actively processing material by saying it out loud or silently.

Reptilian brain: The type of brain that evolved around 200 million years ago; site of elemental requirements for life: breathing, heartbeat, reflexes.

Retrieval: The ability to search for and obtain information from memory.

Reversibility: Process by which the child is able to reverse the direction of thought; for example, the child can now add and subtract.

Ribonucleic acid (RNA): Group of nucleic acids that carry genetic information.

Schemes: Reflect specific knowledge; they are generalizable and repeatable.

Scientific method: A procedure for studying children's development. It involves careful observation, formulating a hypothesis, testing the hypothesis, and analyzing and reporting the results.

Secular trend: Pattern of physical maturation happening earlier and of people growing taller and heavier over successive generations.

Secure attachment: Infants respond quickly and positively in greeting their mothers after a brief separation; after being comforted by their mothers, they explore their environment.

Self: A set of cognitive structures that organize, modify, and integrate the individual's inner psychological traits (personality).

Self-as-object: The "me" or self-as-known; synonymous with the self-concept.

Self-as-subject: The "I" or self-as-knower; child gradually sees the self as a causal agent that is separate and distinct from others.

Self-concept: Organization of qualities that the individual attributes to self.

Self-esteem: Affective or evaluative judgment children make about their own self-concepts.

Self-schemata: Cognitive generalizations about the self derived from past experiences that organize and guide the processing of self-related information contained in the individual's social experience.

Semantic feature hypothesis: Clark's theory that perceptual features give the meaning of the words and provide necessary and sufficient conditions for the applications of a word to an instance.

Semantics: Aspect of language development that is concerned with the meaning of words and sentences.

Sensation: Ability of the sense receptors to detect a particular stimulus in the environment.

Sense of identity: Being at home with one's self; a sense of unity and oneness with self that, according to Erikson, must be achieved during the adolescent years.

Sensitive period: A particular interval of time in which certain physical and psychological growth must take place; after this time it will be extremely difficult or impossible for growth to take place.

Sensorimotor period: In Piaget's theory, the stage (birth to 2 years) during which infants know their world through motoric actions and sensory impressions.

Sensory register: Receives information from the senses.

Separation anxiety: Fear expressed by child when familiar person, such as a parent, leaves.

Sex chromosomes: The 23rd pair of chromosomes (X and Y) that is responsible for sex determination.

Sex-linked characteristics: Characteristics that depend on genes carried by sex chromosomes.

s factors (Spearman's theory): Specific abilities individuals may possess such as reading comprehension and manual dexterity.

Shared family environment: Commonly shared experiences in a family such as socioeconomic class.

Short-term memory: Active, conscious memory in which information lasts for only a short period of time.

Shy children: Children who have few friends and are extremely anxious when interacting with others.

Signal: Behavior performed with the expectation that it will have some predictable effect on a group of receivers.

Significant others: Individuals in child's environment who are respected by the child and have a profound effect on the child's developing self.

Slow-to-warm-up child: Thomas and Chess's temperamental classification for the child who is reluctant to participate in activities and is negative in mood.

Social agents: Those who influence the social development of the child.

Socialization: Lifelong, complex process of learning to behave in socially acceptable ways.

Soma: Cell body of neuron.

Somatic cells: One of the cells of the body that compose the tissues, organs, and parts of the individual other than germ cells.

Stranger anxiety: Fear of person who violates child's scheme or concept of caretaker's face.

Strange Situation Test: Structured observation involving two brief separations and reunions between a child and a parent in an unfamiliar laboratory setting.

Stress: Nonspecific response of the body to any demand placed on it.

Stressors: Environmental forces or events that produce stress.

Sudden Infant Death Syndrome: Death of infant coupled by no clear indication of the cause of death.

Superego: According to Freud, it is a voice of conscience; its sole focus is how one ought to behave.

Surface structure: The linear arrangement of sounds, words, phrases, and clauses that actually specify what is spoken.

Survey: Research designed to gather information from a large sample of people via questionnaires and interviews.

Symbolic functioning: The ability to use symbols (for example, words and images) to represent objects and experiences.

Synapse: Microscopic gap that exists between neurons.

Syntax: Describes how words and morphemes are organized into understandable and acceptable phrases or sentences.

Tabula rasa: Locke's term meaning blank slate—children's personalities are determined by the experiences they encounter in their environment.

Telegraphic speech: Only high-information words are expressed ("Daddy go.") Low-information words are not expressed—just like in a telegram.

Temperament: Stable individual differences in arousal or level of liveliness in responding; the characteristic inclination or mode of emotion response to stimuli that is idiosyncratic to an individual.

Teratogen: A substance capable of causing damage to developing embryo/fetus.

Testes: The male sperm-producing glands.

Testosterone: Male hormone responsible for the development of secondary sex characteristics.

Theory: Formulation of principles of certain observed phenomena that have been verified to some degree.

Transductive reasoning: Reasoning from the particular to the particular, so that events that occur together are assumed to be causally related.

Transformational grammar: Chomsky's theory of the process by which implicit rules are used to transform the deep structure of a sentence into surface structure.

Turner's syndrome: A hereditary disorder in which a sperm cell fails to produce sex chromosome, resulting in a female with only one X chromosome.

Two-factor theory: Spearman's theory that intelligence is comprised of g and s factors.

Umbilical cord: Vital connection between the embryo and its placenta; has two arteries and one vein that carry nourishment and remove waste products.

Unconscious mind: Level of personality that contains information that cannot be recalled at will.

Underextension: Child uses a word within a smaller range that is used in adult language. For example, "dog" refers only to child's dog, not to other dogs that may be encountered.

Undernutrition: Condition characterized by an insufficient amount of nourishing foods; lack of quantity and quality of food detrimental to healthy growth and development.

Unitary theory: Intelligence is viewed as being a general capacity to learn. If, for example, a person is bright in one area, that individual will be bright in all areas.

Variable: A factor that is controlled and measured in an experiment.

Variance: A percentage that explains the individual differences found in a certain trait that are accounted for by another factor(s).

Vicarious learning: Children learn behavior by observing another person being reinforced or punished for a certain behavior. In vicarious learning, children are not directly reinforced or punished.

Zygote: Fertilized egg.

References

Chapter 1

American Psychological Association. (1968). *Newsletter*, 1–3.

Aries, P. (1962). *Centuries of childhood*. New York: Knopf.

Baltes, P. B., Reese, H. W., & Nesselroade, J. R. (1977). *Life-span developmental psychology: Introduction to research methods*. Monterey, CA: Brooks/Cole.

Bandura, A. (1977). *Social learning theory*. Englewood Cliffs, NJ: Prentice-Hall.

Bandura, A. (1991). Social cognitive theory of moral thought and action. In W. M. Kurtines and J. W. Gewirtz (Eds.), *Handbook of moral behavior and development* (pp. 45–103). Hillsdale, NJ: Erlbaum.

Beekman, D. (1977). *The mechanical baby*. Westport, CT: Lawrence Hills.

Bell, R. Q. (1979). Parent-child and reciprocal influences. *American Psychologist, 34*, 821–826.

Bettelheim, B. (1983). *Freud and man's soul*. New York: Knopf.

Borstelmann, L. J. (1983). Children before psychology: Ideas about children from antiquity to the late 1800s. In P. H. Mussen (Ed.), *Child psychology handbook*. New York: Wiley.

Bronfenbrenner, U. (1979). *The ecology of human development*. Cambridge, MA: Harvard University Press.

Buhler, C., & Massarik, M. (Eds.). (1968). *The course of human life*. New York: Springer.

Cable, M. (1972). *The little darlings*. New York: Charles Scribner's Sons.

Cairns, R. B. (1990). Multiple metaphors for a single idea. *Developmental Psychology, 27*, 23–26.

Charlesworth, W. R. (1992). Darwin and developmental psychology: Past and present. *Developmental Psychology, 28*, 5–16.

Cohen, D. (1979). *J. B. Watson: The founder of behaviorism*. London: Routledge and Kegan Paul.

Darwin, C. (1962). *On the origin of the species*. New York: Macmillan. (Original work published in 1859)

de Mause, L. (1974). *The history of childhood*. New York: Peter Bedrick Books.

Dennis, W. (1935). The effect of restricted practice upon the reaching, sitting, and standing of two infants. *Journal of Genetic Psychology, 47*, 17–32.

Despert, J. L. (1965). *The emotionally disturbed child*. New York: Doubleday.

Elkind, D. (1981a, November/December). All grown up and no place to go. *Childhood Education, 58*, 69–72.

Elkind, D. (1981b). *The hurried child*. Reading, MA: Addison-Wesley.

Elkind, D. (1988). *The hurried child: Growing up too fast, too soon*. Reading, MA: Addison-Wesley.

Erikson, E. (1959). Identity and the life cycle: Selected papers. *Psychological Issues, 1 (Monograph 1)*.

Erikson, E. (1968). *Identity: Youth in adolescence and crisis*. New York: W. W. Norton.

Erikson, E. (1975). *Life history and the historical moment*. New York: W. W. Norton.

Erikson, E. (1980). *Identity and the life cycle*. New York: W. W. Norton.

Fine, R. (1979). *A history of psychoanalysis*. New York: Columbia University Press.

Foss, B. (1975). *New perspectives in child development*. Edmonton, Canada: Penguin.

Fraser, A. (1966). *A history of toys*. London: George Werdenfield and Nicolson.

French, V. (1977). History of the child's influence: Ancient mediterranean civilizations. In R. Q. Bell and L. V. Harper (Eds.), *Child effects on adults*. Hillsdale, NJ: Erlbaum.

Freud, A. (1974). *The writings of Anna Freud*. New York: International Universities Press.

Freud, S. (1900/1953). The interpretation of dreams. In J. Strachey (Ed.), *The standard edition of the complete psychological works of Sigmund Freud* (Vol. 16). London: Hogarth.

Freud, S. (1953). Three essays on the theory of sexuality. In J. Strachey (Ed.), *The standard edition of the complete psychological works of Sigmund Freud* (Vol. 7). London: Hogarth. (Original work published 1905)

Freud, S. (1957). Beyond the pleasure principle. In J. Strachey (Ed.), *The standard edition of the complete psy-*

chological works of Sigmund Freud (Vol. 18). London: Hogarth. (Original work published in 1920)

Freud, S. (1973). *An outline of psychoanalysis.* London: Hogarth. (Original work published in 1938)

Freud, S. (1974). *The ego and the id.* London: Hogarth. (Original work published in 1923)

Fromm, E. (1980). *Greatness and limitations of Freud's thought.* New York: New American Library.

Gay, P. (1988). *A life for our time.* New York: W. W. Norton.

Greenleaf, B. (1978). *Children through the ages: A history of childhood.* New York: Barnes and Noble Books.

Jones, E. (1953). *The life and work of Sigmund Freud.* New York: Basic Books.

Kacerguis, M. A., & Adams, G. R. (1980). Erikson state resolution: The relationship between identity and intimacy. *Journal of Youth and Adolescence, 9,* 117–126.

Kerlinger, F. N. (1986). *Behavioral research: A conceptual approach.* New York: Holt.

Kessen, W. (1965). *The child.* New York: Wiley.

Kiester, E., Jr., & Cudhea, D. (1974). Albert Bandura: A very modern model. *Human Behavior, 17,* 27–31.

Krauthammer, C. (1984, December 3). The using of Baby Fae. *Time* magazine, pp. 87–88.

Locke, J. (1964). *Some thoughts concerning education.* F. W. Garforth (Ed.). Woodbury, NY: Barron's Educational Series. (Original work published in 1693)

Marcia, J. E. (1980). Identity in adolescence. In J. Adelson (Ed.), *Handbook of adolescent psychology.* New York: Wiley.

Masson, J. (1984). *The assault on truth: Freud's suppression of seduction theory.* New York: Farrar, Straus, & Giroux.

Misiak, H. K. (1966). *History of psychology.* New York: Grune and Stratton.

Natenberg, M. (1955). *The case history of Sigmund Freud.* Chicago: Regent House.

Nelson, B. (1961). *Freud and the twentieth century.* New York: The World Publishing Co.

Orne, M. (1962). On the social psychology of the psychological experiment. *American Psychologist, 17,* 776–783.

Pervin, L. A. (1970). *Personality: Theory, assessment, and research.* New York: Wiley.

Rappaport, H., & Enrich, K. (1982). Ego identity and temporality: Psychoanalytical and existential perspectives. *Journal of Humanistic Psychology, 22,* 4, 53–70.

Rieff, P. (1961). *Freud: The mind of the moralist.* New York: Doubleday.

Roethlisberger, F. J., & Dickson, W. J. (1939). *Management and the worker.* Cambridge, MA: Harvard University Press.

Rousseau, J. (1911). *Emile, or on education* (B. Foxley, Trans.). London: Dent. (Original work published in 1762)

Scarr, S. (1992). Developmental theories for the 1990s: Developmental and individual differences. *Child Development, 63,* 1–19.

Schorsch, A. (1979). *Images of childhood.* New York: Mayflower Books.

Schur, M. (1972). *Freud, living and dying.* New York: International Universities Press.

Shaffer, J. B. (1978). *Humanistic psychology.* Englewood Cliffs, NJ: Prentice-Hall.

Skinner, B. F. (1972). (Ed.). *Cumulative record: A selection of papers* (3rd ed.). New York: Appleton.

Skinner, B. F. (1974). *About behaviorism.* New York: Knopf.

Skinner, B. F. (1981). Are theories of learning necessary? *Psychological Review, 57,* 193–216.

Skinner, B. F. (1983). *A matter of consequences.* New York: Knopf.

Stevenson, H. (1983). How children learn—The quest for a theory. In P. H. Mussen (Ed.), *Handbook of child psychology.* New York: Wiley.

Thomas, R. M. (1979). *Comparing theories of child development.* Belmont, CA: Wadsworth.

Tucker, M. J. (1974). The child as beginning and end. In L. de Mause (Ed.), *The history of childhood.* New York: Peter Bedrick Books.

Walker, E., & Emory, E. (1985). Commentary: Interpretive bias and behavioral genetic research. *Child Development, 56,* 775–778.

Watson, J. B. (1914). *Behavior: An introduction to comparative psychology.* New York: Holt.

Watson, J. B. (1919). *Psychology from the standpoint of a behaviorist.* Philadelphia: Lippincott.

Watson, J. B. (1928). *Psychological care of infant and child.* New York: W. W. Norton.

Watson, R. (1971). *The great psychologists.* New York: Lippincott.

Winn, M. (1983, October). The loss of childhood. *Forecast for Home Economics,* 38–46.

Wright, H. F. (1960). Observational child study. In P. H. Mussen (Ed.), *Handbook of research methods* (pp. 92–104). New York: Wiley.

Chapter 2

Allison, P. D., & Furstenberg, F. (1989). How marital dissolution affects children: Variations by age and sex. *Developmental Psychology, 25,* 540–549.

Alvarez, W. F. (1985). The meaning of maternal employment for mothers and their perceptions of their three-year-old children. *Child Development, 56,* 350–360.

Anastasi, A. (1958). Heredity, environment, and the question of "how?" *Psychological Review, 65,* 197–208.

Anthony, K. H., Weidemann, S., & Chin, Y. (1990). Housing perceptions of low-income single parents. *Environment and Behavior, 22,* 2, 147–182.

Armistead, L., Wierson, M., & Forehand, R. (1990). Adolescents and maternal employment: Is it harmful for a young adolescent to have an employed mother? *Journal of Early Adolescence, 10,* 260–278.

Ash, P., & Guyer, M. J. (1986). *A followup of children in contested custody evaluations.* Paper presented at the 17th annual meeting of the American Academy of Psychiatry and the Law, Philadelphia.

Barglow, P., Vaughn, B. E., & Molitor, N. (1987). Effects of maternal absence due to employment on the quality of infant-mother attachment in a low-risk sample. *Child Development, 58,* 4, 945–954.

Baruch, G. K., & Barnett, R. C. (1983). *Correlates of fathers' participation in family work: A technical report* (Working Paper #106). Wellesley, MA: Center for Research on Women, Wellesley College.

Belsky, J. (1988). The "effects" of infant day care reconsidered. *Early Childhood Research Quarterly, 3,* 234–272.

Belsky, J., & Braungart, J. M. (1991). Are insecure-avoidant infants with extensive day-care experience less stressed by and more independent in the strange situation? *Child Development, 62,* 567–571.

Birnbaum, J. A. (1975). Life patterns and self-esteem in gifted family-oriented and career-committed women. In M. S. Mednick, S. S. Tangri, and L. W. Hoffman (Eds.), *Women and achievement.* Washington, DC: Hemisphere.

Block, J. H. (1983). Differential premises arising from differential socialization of the sexes: Some conjectures. *Child Development, 54,* 1335–1354.

Block, J. H., Block, J., & Gjerde, P. (1986). The personality of children prior to divorce: A prospective study. *Child Development, 57,* 827–840.

Bohman, M., Sigvardsson, S., & Cloninger, C. R. (1982). Maternal inheritance of alcohol abuse: Cross-fostering analysis of adopted women. *Archives of General Psychiatry, 38,* 965–969.

Bouchard, T. J. (1990). Sources of human psychological differences: The Minnesota study of twins reared apart. *Science, 250,* 223–228.

Bouchard, T. J., & McGue, M. (1981). Familial studies of intelligence. *Science, 212,* 1055–1059.

Bouchard, T. J., Scarr, S., & Weinberg, R. A. (1991). *Vocational interests among relatives of varying genetic relatedness.* Unpublished manuscript.

Bowlby, J. (1973). *Separation.* New York: Basic Books.

Bowlby, J. (1980). *Attachment and loss: Vol. 3. Loss.* New York: Basic Books.

Brand, E., Clingempeel, W. E., & Bowen-Woodward, K. (1988). Family relationships and children's psychological adjustment in stepmother and stepfather families: Findings and conclusions from the Philadelphia Stepfamily Research Project. In E. M. Hetherington and J. D. Arasteh (Eds.), *Impact of divorce, single-parenting, and stepparenting on children* (pp. 299–324). Hillsdale, NJ: Erlbaum.

Braungart, J. M., Plomin, R., DeFries, J. C., & Fulker, D. W. (1992). Genetic influence on tester-rated infant temperament as assessed by Bayley's Infant Behavior Record: Nonadoptive and adoptive siblings and twins. *Developmental Psychology, 28,* 40–47.

Bray, J. H. (1988). Children's development during early remarriage. In E. M. Hetherington and J. D. Arasteh (Eds.), *Impact of divorce, single-parenting, and stepparenting on children* (pp. 279–298). Hillsdale, NJ: Erlbaum.

Bronfenbrenner, U. (1986). Ecology of the family as a context for human development: Research perspectives. *Developmental Psychology, 22,* 723–742.

Bronfenbrenner, U., Alvarez, W., & Henderson, C. R., Jr. (1984). Working and watching: Maternal employment status and parents' perceptions of their three-year-old children. *Child Development, 55,* 1362–1378.

Brown, E., & Hobart, C. (in press). Effects of prior marriage children on adjustment in remarriages. *Journal of Comparative Family Studies.*

Bureau of the Census. (1988). *Statistical abstract of the United States, 1988.* Washington, DC: U.S. Government Printing Office.

Camara, K. A., & Resnick, G. (1988). Interparental conflict and cooperation: Factors moderating children's post-divorce adjustment. In E. M. Hetherington and J. D. Arasteh (Eds.), *Impact of divorce, single-parenting, and stepparenting on children* (pp. 169–195). Hillsdale, NJ: Erlbaum.

Chase-Lansdale, L., & Owen, M. T. (1988). Maternal employment in a family context: Effects on infant-mother and infant-father attachments. *Child Development, 58,* 1505–1512.

Clarke-Stewart, K. A. (1989). Day care: Maligned or malignant? *American Psychologist, 44,* 266–273.

Cohn, J. F., & Tronick, E. Z. (1983). Three-month-old infants' reaction to simulated maternal depression. *Child Development, 54,* 185–193.

Crosbie-Burnett, M. (1983). *Step-families.* Unpublished Ph. D. dissertation. Stanford University, Palo Alto, CA.

Crouter, A. C., & Crowley, M. S. (1990). School-age children's time alone with fathers in single- and dual-earner families. *Journal of Early Adolescence, 10,* 296–312.

Crouter, A. C., MacDermid, S. M., McHale, S. M., & Perry-Jenkins, M. (1990). Parental monitoring and perceptions of children's school performance and conduct in dual- and single-earner families. *Developmental Psychology, 26,* 4, 649–657.

Cummings, E. M., Iannotti, R. J., & Zahn-Waxler, C. (1985). Influences of conflict between adults on the emotions and aggression of young children. *Developmental Psychology, 21,* 495–507.

Cummings, J. S., Pellegrini, D. S., Notarius, C. I., & Cummings, M. (1989). Children's responses to angry adult behavior as a function of marital distress and history of interparent hostility. *Child Development, 60,* 1035–1043.

Cyphers, L. H., Fulker, D. W., Plomin, R., & DeFries, J. C. (1989). Cognitive abilities in the early school years: No effects of shared environment between parents and offspring. *Intelligence, 13,* 369–386.

Daly, M., & Wilson, M. (1985). Child abuse and other risks of not living with both parents. *Enthology and Sociology, 6,* 197–210.

Daniels, D., Dunn, J., Furstenberg, F., & Plomin, R. (1985). Environmental differences within the family and adjustment differences within pairs of adolescent siblings. *Child Development, 56,* 764–774.

Doherty, W. J., & Needle, R. H. (1991). Psychological adjustment and substance use among adolescents before and after a parental divorce. *Child Development, 62,* 328–337.

Dornbusch, S. M., Carlsmith, J. M., Bushwall, S. J., Ritter, P. L., Leiderman, H., Hastorf, A. H., & Gross, R. (1985). Single parents, extended households, and the control of adolescents. *Child Development, 56,* 326–341.

Dreman, S., Orr, E., & Aldor, R. (1990). Sense of competence, time perspective, and state-anxiety of separated versus divorced mothers. *American Journal of Orthopsychiatry, 60,* 1, 77–85.

Duncan, G., & Rodgers, W. (1987). Single-parent families: Are their economic problems transitory or persistent? *Family Planning Perspectives, 19,* 171–178.

Dunn, J., & Plomin, R. (1990). *Separate lives: Why are siblings so different?* New York: Basic Books.

Dusek, J. B., & Litovsky, V. G. (1988, March). *Maternal employment and adolescent adjustment and perceptions of child rearing.* Paper presented at the Second Biennial Meetings of the Society for Research on Adolescence, Alexandria, VA.

Easterbrooks, M. A., & Goldberg, W. A. (1985). Effects of early maternal employment on toddlers, mothers, and fathers. *Developmental Psychology, 21,* 774–783.

Eaves, L. J., Eysenck, H. J., & Martin, N. G. (1989). *Genes, culture and personality.* New York: Academic Press.

Emery, R. E. (1988). *Marriage, divorce, and children's adjustment.* Newbury Park, CA: Sage.

Emery, R. E. (1989). Family violence. *American Psychologist, 44,* 321–328.

Erlenmeyer-Kimling, L., & Jarvik, L. F. (1963). Genetics and intelligence: A review. *Science, 142,* 1477–1479.

Fauber, R., Forehand, R., Thomas, A., & Wierson, M. (1990). A mediational model of the impact of marital conflict on adolescent adjustment in intact and divorced families: The role of disrupted parenting. *Child Development, 61,* 1112–1123.

Field, T. M. (1991). Young children's adaptations to repeated separations from their mothers. *Child Development, 62,* 539–547.

Floderus-Myhred, B., Pedersen, N. L., & Rasmusson, I. (1980). Assessment of heritability for personality based on a short form of the Eysenck Personality Inventory: A study of 12,898 twin pairs. *Behavior Genetics, 10,* 153–162.

Forehand, R., Long, N., & Brody, G. (1988). Divorce and marital conflict: Relationship to adolescent competence and adjustment in early adolescence. In E. M. Hetherington and J. Arasteh (Eds.), *Impact of a divorce, single-parenting, and stepparenting on children* (pp. 155–167). Hillsdale, NJ: Erlbaum.

Friedman, D. E. (1988). *Families and work: Managing related issues.* New York: The Conference Board.

Gelles, R. J. (1989). Child abuse and violence in single-parent families: Parent absence and economic deprivation. *American Journal of Orthopsychiatry, 59,* 4, 492–501.

Gold, D., & Andres, D. (1978). Developmental comparisons between 10-year-old children with employed and nonemployed mothers. *Child Development, 49,* 75–84.

Goldsmith, H. H. (1983). Genetic influence on personality from infancy to adulthood. *Child Development, 54,* 331–355.

Goldsmith, H. H., & Campos, J. J. (1990). The structure of temperamental fear and pleasure in infants: A psychometric perspective. *Child Development, 61,* 1944–1964.

Gottesman, I. I., & Shield, J. (1982). *Schizophrenia: The epigentic puzzle.* New York: Cambridge University Press.

Gottfried, A. E., & Gottfried, A. W. (1988). Maternal employment, family environment and children's development: Infancy through the school years. In A. E. Gottfried and A. W. Gottfried (Eds.), *Maternal employment and children's development: Longitudinal research* (pp. 11–58). New York: Plenum.

Gottlieb, G. (1991). Experiential canalization of behavioral development: Theory. *Developmental Psychology, 27,* 4–13.

Gottman, J. M., & Katz, L. F. (1989). Effects of marital discord on young children's peer interaction and health. *Developmental Psychology, 25,* 373–381.

Grossman, F. K., Pollack, W. S., & Golding, E. (1988). Fathers and children: Predicting the quality and quantity of fathering. *Developmental Psychology, 24,* 82–91.

Henderson, N. D. (1982). Human behavior genetics. *Annual Review of Psychology, 33,* 403–440.

Herz Brown, F. (1988). The postdivorce family. In E. A. Carter and M. McGoldrick (Eds.), *The changing family life cycle: A framework for family therapy* (pp. 371–398). New York: Gardner Press.

Hess, R. D., & Camara, K. A. (1979). Post-divorce family relationships as mediating factors in the consequences of divorce for children. *Journal of Social Issues, 4,* 79–95.

Hetherington, E. M. (1987). Family relations six years after divorce. In K. Pasley and M. Ihinger-Tollman (Eds.), *Remarriage and stepparenting today: Current research and theory* (pp. 185–205). New York: Guilford Press.

Hetherington, E. M. (1989). Coping with family transitions: Winners, losers, and survivors. *Child Development, 60,* 1–14.

Hetherington, E. M. (in press). The role of individual differences and family relations in coping with divorce and remarriage. In P. Cowan and E. M. Hetherington (Eds.), *Advances in family research: Vol. 2. Family transitions.* Hillsdale, NJ: Erlbaum.

Hetherington, E. M., & Clingempeel, W. G. (1988, March). *Coping with remarriage: The first two years.* Symposium presented at the Southeastern Conference on Human Development, Charleston, SC.

Hetherington, E. M., Cox, M., & Cox, R. (1978). *Family interaction and the social, emotional, and cognitive development of children following divorce.* Paper presented at the Symposium on the Family Sponsored by Johnson & Johnson, Washington, DC.

Hetherington, E. M., Stanley-Hagan, M., & Anderson, E. R. (1989). Marital transitions: A child's perspective. *American Psychologist, 44,* 2, 303–312.

Hock, E. (1980). Working and nonworking mothers and their infants: A comparative study of maternal caregiving characteristics and infants' social behavior. *Merrill-Palmer Quarterly, 46,* 79–101.

Hock, E., & DeMeis, D. K. (1990). Depression in mothers of infants: The role of maternal employment. *Developmental Psychology, 26,* 2, 285–291.

Hofferth, S. L., & Phillips, D. A. (1989). Childcare in the United States: 1970 to 1995. *Journal of Marriage and the Family, 49,* 559–571.

Hoffman, L. (1986). Work, family, and the child. In M. S. Pallak and R. O. Perloff (Eds.), *Psychology and work: Productivity, change, and employment* (pp. 173–220). Washington, DC: American Psychological Association.

Hoffman, L. (1989). Effects of maternal employment in the two-parent family. *American Psychologist, 44,* 283–292.

Horn, J. M. (1983). The Texas Adoption Project: Adopted children and their intellectual resemblance to biological and adoptive parents. *Child Development, 54,* 268–275.

Horn, J. M., Loehlin, J. C., & Willerman, L. (1979). Intellectual resemblance among adoptive and biological relatives: The Texas Adoption Project. *Behavioral Genetics, 9,* 177–207.

Hotaling, G. T., Finkelhor, D., Kirkpatrick, J. T., & Straus, M. A. (Eds.). (1988). *Family abuse and its consequences: New directions in research.* Newbury Park, CA: Sage.

Howes, P., & Markman, H. J. (1989). Marital quality and child functioning: A longitudinal investigation. *Child Development, 60,* 1044–1051.

Husen, T. (1959). *Psychological twin research: A methodological study.* Stockholm: Almqvist & Wiksell.

Johnston, J. R., Kline, M., & Tschann, J. M. (1989). Ongoing postdivorce conflict: Effects on children of joint custody and frequent access. *American Journal of Orthopsychiatry, 59,* 576–592.

Jordan, P. L. (1990). Laboring for relevance: Expectant and new fatherhood. *Nursing Research, 39,* 11–16.

Jouriles, E. N., Pfiffner, L. J., & O'Leary, S. G. (1988). Marital conflict, parenting, and toddler conduct problems. *Journal of Abnormal Child Psychology, 16,* 197–206.

Kagan, J. (1980). Four questions in psychological development. *International Journal of Behavioral Development, 3,* 231–241.

Kagan, J., Reznick, G. S., Clarke, C., Snidman, N., & Garcia-Coll, C. (1984). Behavioral inhibition to the unfamiliar. *Child Development, 55,* 2212–2225.

Kashiwagi, K. (1986). Personality development in adolescence. In H. Stevenson, H. Azuma, and K. Hakuta (Eds.), *Child development in Japan* (pp. 167–185). New York: Freeman.

Kazdin, A. E., Moser, J., Colbus, D., & Bell, R. (1985). Depressive symptoms among physically abused and psychiatrically disturbed children. *Journal of Abnormal Psychology, 94,* 298–307.

Keith, J. G., Nelson, C. S., Schlabach, J. H., & Thompson, C. J. (1990). The relationship between parental employment and three measures of early adolescent responsibility: Family-related, personal, and social. *Journal of Early Adolescence, 10,* 399–415.

Kline, M., Tschann, J. M., Johnston, J. R., & Wallerstein, J. S. (1989). Children's adjustment in joint and sole physical custody families. *Developmental Psychology, 25,* 430–438.

Kuczynski, P. A., & Cummings, M. (1989). Responding to anger in aggressive and nonaggressive boys: A research note. *Journal of Child Psychology and Psychiatry, 50,* 2, 309–314.

Kurdeck, L. (1981). An integrative perspective on children's divorce adjustment. *American Psychologist, 36,* 856–866.

Lamb, M. (1984). Fathers, mothers and childcare in the 1980s: Family influences on child development. In K. Borman, D. Quarm, and S. Gideouse (Eds.), *Women in the workplace* (pp. 61–88). Norwood, NJ: Ablex.

Lamb, M. E., & Oppenheim, D. (1989). Fatherhood and father-child relationships: Five years of research. In S. Cath, A. Gurwitt, and L. Gunsberg. (Eds.), *Fathers and their families* (pp. 11–26). Hillsdale, NJ: Analytic Press.

Loehlin, J. C., Horn, J. M., & Willerman, L. (1989). Modeling IQ change: Evidence from the Texas Adoption Project. *Child Development, 60,* 993–1004.

Loehlin, J. C., & Nichols, R. C. (1976). *Heredity, environment, and personality.* Austin: University of Texas Press.

Long, N., Forehand, R., Fauber, R., & Brody, G. (1987). Self-perceived and independently observed competence of young adolescents as a function of parental marital conflict and recent divorce. *Journal of Abnormal Child Psychology, 15,* 15–27.

Long, N., & Slater, E. (1988). Continued high or reduced interparental conflict following divorce: Relation to young adolescent adjustment. *Journal of Consulting and Clinical Psychology, 56,* 467–469.

Lytton, H., Watts D., & Dunn, B. E. (1988). The stability of genetic determinism from age 2 to age 9: A longitudinal study. *Social Biology, 11,* 12–21.

McCombs, A., & Forehand, R. (1989). Adolescent school performance following parental divorce: Are there family factors that can enhance success? *Adolescence, XXIV,* 96, 414–421.

McGue, M., & Bouchard, T. J. (1989). Genetics. In R. J. Sternberg (Ed.), *Advances in psychology of human intelligence.* Hillsdale, NJ: Erlbaum.

Medeiros, D., Porter, B., & Welch, D. (1983). *Children under stress* (pp. 86–87). Englewood Cliffs, NJ: Prentice-Hall.

Moen, P. (1989). *Working parents.* Madison: University of Wisconsin Press.

Montemayor, R., & Clayton, M. D. (1983). Maternal employment and adolescent development. *Theory into Practice, 22,* 112–118.

Moore, T. W. (1975). Exclusive early mothering and its alternatives. *Scandinavian Journal of Psychology, 16,* 256–272.

Morgan, P. S., Lye, D. N., & Condron, G. A. (in press). Sons, daughters, and divorce: Does the sex of the children affect the risk of marital disruption? *American Journal of Psychology.*

Neal, J. H. (1983). Children's understanding of their parents' divorces. *New Directions For Child Development, 19,* 3–14.

Nichols, R. C. (1978). Twin studies of ability, personality and interests. *Homo, 29,* 158–173.

Novak, M. A., O'Neill, P. L., Beckley, S., & Suomi, S. J. (in press). Naturalistic environments for captive primates. In E. Gibbons, E. Wyers, and E. Waters (Eds.), *Naturalistic habitats in captivity.* New York: Academic Press.

Owen, M. T., & Cox, M. J. (1988). Maternal employment and the transition to parenthood. In A. E. Gottfried and A. W. Gottfried (Eds.), *Maternal employment and children's development: Longitudinal research* (pp. 85–119). New York: Plenum Press.

Packard, V. (1983). *Our endangered children.* Boston: Little, Brown.

Patterson, G. R., & Forgatch, M. (1987). *Parents and adolescents living together.* Eugene, OR: Castalia.

Paulson, S. E., Koman, J. J., & Hill, J. P. (1990) . Maternal employment and parent-child relations in families of seventh graders. *Journal of Early Adolescence, 10,* 279–295.

Plomin, R. (1986). *Development, genetics, and psychology.* Hillsdale, NJ: Erlbaum.

Plomin, R. (1990). *Nature and nurture: An introduction to behavioral genetics.* Pacific Grove, CA: Brooks/Cole.

Rebelsky, F. (1972). First discussant's comments: Cross-cultural studies of mother-infant interaction—description and consequence. *Human Development, 15,* 128–130.

Reid, W. J., & Crisafulli, A. (1990). Marital discord and child behavior problems: A meta-analysis. *Journal of Abnormal Child Psychology, 18,* 1, 105–117.

Rowland, G. L. (1964). *The effects of total social isolation on learning and social behavior in rhesus monkeys.* Ph.D. dissertation, The University of Wisconsin, Madison.

Rushton, J. P., Fulker, D. W., Neale, M. C., Nias, D. K. B., & Eysenck, H. J. (1986). Altruism and aggression: To what extent are individual differences inherited? *Journal of Personality and Social Psychology, 50,* 1192–1198.

Santrock, J. W., & Warshak, R. A. (1979). Children's and parents' observed social behavior in stepfather families. *Child Development, 53,* 472–480.

Scarr, S., & Weinberg, R. A. (1977). The influence of family background on intellectual attainment. *American Sociology Review, 43,* 674–692.

Scarr, S., & Weinberg, R. A. (1983). The Minnesota Adoption Studies: Genetic differences and malleability. *Child Development, 54,* 260–267.

Segal, N. L. (1990). The importance of twin studies for individual differences in research. *Journal of Counseling and Development, 68,* 612–622.

Shaw, O. S., & Emery, R. E. (1987). Parental conflict and other correlates of the adjustment of school-age children whose parents have separated. *Journal of Abnormal Child Psychology, 25,* 269–281.

Simons, R. L., Whitbeck, L. B., Conger, R. D., & Conger, K. J. (1990). *Parenting factors, social skills, and value commitments as precursors to school failure, involvement with deviant peers and delinquent behavior.* Unpublished manuscript.

Skodak, M., & Skeels, H. (1949). A final follow-up of one hundred adopted children. *Journal of Genetic Psychology, 73,* 85–125.

Social Indicators III. (1980). Washington, DC: U.S. Department of Commerce.

Spitz, R. (1945). Hospitalism: An inquiry into the genesis of psychiatric conditions in early childhood. *Psychoanalytic Study of the Child, 1,* 53–74.

Sroufe, L. A., Egeland, B., & Kreutzer, T. (1990). The fate of early experience following developmental change: Longitudinal approaches to individual adaptation in childhood. *Child Development, 61,* 1363–1373.

Sroufe, L. A., & Fleeson, J. (1988). The coherence of family relationships. In R. A. Hinde and J. Stevenson-Hinde (Eds.), *Relationships within families: Mutual influences* (pp. 27–47). Oxford: Oxford University Press.

Stevens, G., & Boyd, M. (1980). The importance of mother: Labor force participation and intergenerational mobility of women. *Social Forces, 59,* 186–199.

Stevenson, H. W., & Lee, S. (1990). Contexts of achievement. *Monographs of the Society for Research in Child Development, 55,* nos. 1–2.

Stuckey, M. F., McGhee, P. E., & Bell, M. J. (1982). Parent-child interaction: The influence of maternal employment. *Developmental Psychology, 18,* 635–644.

Suomi, S. J. (1976). *Early experiences and social development in Rhesus monkeys.* Unpublished manuscript, University of Wisconsin, Madison.

Taubin, S., & Mudd, E. (1983). *Contemporary families and alternate lifestyles.* Beverly Hills, CA: Sage.

Teasdale, T. W., & Owen, D. R. (1984). Heredity and familial environment in intelligence and educational level: A sibling study. *Nature, 309,* 620–622.

Tellegen, A., Lykken, D. T., Bouchard, T. J., Wilcox, K., Segal, N. L., & Rich, S. (1988). Personality similarity in twins reared apart and together. *Journal of Social and Personality Psychology, 54,* 1031–1039.

Thomas, R. M. (1979). *Comparing theories of child development.* Belmont, CA: Wadsworth.

U.S. Bureau of Labor Statistics. (1985, June). *Handbook of labor statistics.* Washington, DC: U.S. Government Printing Office.

U.S. Bureau of Labor Statistics. (1989, January). *Employment and earnings.* Washington, DC: U.S. Government Printing Office.

Waddington, C. H. (1968). *Principles of development and differentiation.* New York: Macmillan.

Wallerstein, J. S., Corbin, S. G., & Lewis, J. M. (1988). Children of divorce: A ten-year study. In E. M. Hetherington and J. Arasteh (Eds.), *Impact of divorce, single-parenting and stepparenting on children* (pp. 198–214). Hillsdale, NJ: Erlbaum.

Wallerstein, J. S., & Kelly, J. B. (1980). *Surviving the breakup: How children and parents cope with divorce.* New York: Basic Books.

Weinraub, M., Jaeger, E., & Hoffman, L. W. (1988). Predicting infant outcomes in families of employed and non-employed mothers. *Early Childhood Research Quarterly, 3,* 361–378.

Weiss, R. S. (1979). Growing up a little faster: The experience of growing up in a single-parent household. *Journal of Social Issues, 35,* 97–111.

Whitehead, L. (1979). Sex differences in children's responses to family stress: A re-evaluation. *Journal of Child Psychology and Psychiatry, 20,* 247–254.

Wierson, M., Forehand, R., Fauber, R., & McCombs, A. (1989). Buffering young male adolescents against negative parental divorce influences: The role of good parent-adolescent relations. *Child Study Journal, 19,* 2, 101–112.

Wilson, R. S. (1983). The Louisville Twin Study: Developmental synchronies in behavior. *Child Development, 54,* 298–316.

Wilson, R. S., & Matheny, A. P. (1986). Behavior-genetics research in infant temperament: The Louisville Twin Study. In R. Plomin and J. Dunn (Eds.), *The study of temperament: Changes, continuities and challenges.* Hillsdale, NJ: Erlbaum.

Wolchik, S. A., Ruehlman, L. S., Braver, S. L., & Sandler, I. N. (1989). Social support of children of divorce: Direct and stress buffering effects. *American Journal of Community Psychology, 17,* 485–501.

Wolfe, D. A. (1987). *Child abuse: Implications for child development and psychopathology.* Beverly Hills: Sage.

Woods, M. B. (1972). The unsupervised child of the working mother. *Developmental Psychology, 6,* 14–25.

Yogev, S. (1983). Dual-career couples: Conflicts and treatment. *American Journal of Family Therapy, 11,* 38–45.

Zahn-Waxler, C., Radke-Yarrow, M., & King, R. A. (1979). Child rearing and children's prosocial initiations towards victims in distress. *Child Development, 50,* 319–330.

Zaslow, M. J. (1988). Sex differences in children's response to parental divorce: 1. Research methodology and postdivorce family forms. *American Journal of Orthopsychiatry, 58,* 355–378.

Zaslow, M. J. (1989). Sex differences in children's response to parental divorce: 2. Samples, variables, ages, and sources. *American Journal of Orthopsychiatry, 59,* 118–140.

Zaslow, M. J., Pedersen, F. A., Suwalsky, J. D., Cain, R. L., & Fivel, M. (1985). The early resumption of employment by mothers: Implications for parent-infant interaction. *Journal of Applied Developmental Psychology, 6,* 1–16.

Zaslow, M. J., Pedersen, F. A., Suwalsky, J. D., & Rabinovich, B. A. (1989). Maternal employment and parent-infant interaction at one year. *Early Childhood Research Quarterly, 4,* 459–478.

Zill, N. (1978, February). *Divorce, marital happiness and the mental health of children: Findings from the FCD National Survey of Children.* Paper presented at the meeting of the National Institute of Mental Health, Bethesda, MD.

Zill, N. (1988). Behavior, achievement, and health problems among children in stepfamilies: Findings from a national survey of child health. In E. M. Hetherington and J. D. Arasteh (Eds.), *Impact of divorce, single-parenting and stepparenting on children* (pp. 325–368). Hillsdale, NJ: Erlbaum.

Chapter 3

A. C. Nielson Co. (1988). *1988 Nielsen report on television.* Northbrook, IL: Author.

American Psychological Association. (1985). *Violence on television.* Washington: DC: APA Board of Ethical and Social Responsibility for Psychology.

Anderson, D. R., Field, D. E., Collins, P. A., Lorch, E. P., & Nathan, J. G. (1985). Estimates of young children's time with television: A methodological comparison of parent reports with time-lapse video home observation. *Child Development, 56,* 1335–1357.

Anderson, D. R., Lorch, E. P., Field, D. E., Collins, P. A., & Nathan, J. G. (1986). Television viewing at home: Age trends in visual attention and time with TV. *Child Development, 57,* 1024–1033.

Andersson, B. (1989). Effects of public day care: A longitudinal study. *Child Development, 60,* 857–866.

Andersson, B. (1992). Effects of day care on cognitive and socioemotional competence of thirteen-year-old Swedish school children. *Child Development, 63,* 20–36.

Atkinson, J. W., & Raynor, J. O. (1978). *Personality, motivation and achievement.* New York: Wiley.

Azuma, H. (1986). Why study child development in Japan. In H. Stevenson, H. Azuma, and K. Hakuta (Eds.), *Child development in Japan* (pp. 3–13). New York: Freeman.

Ball, S., & Bogartz, G. A. (1970). *The first year of Sesame Street: An evaluation*. Princeton, NJ: Educational Testing Service.

Baran, S. J., Lawrence, J. C., Courtright, J. A. (1979). Television drama as a facilitator of prosocial behaviors: The Waltons. *Journal of Broadcasting, 23,* 277–283.

Belsky, J. (1988). The "effects" of infant day care reconsidered. *Early Childhood Research Quarterly, 3,* 234–272.

Belsky, J., & Steinberg, L. (1982). The effects of day care: A critical review. *Child Development, 49,* 929–949.

Beneson, J., & Dweck, C. S. (1986). The development of trait explanations and self-evaluations in the academic and social domains. *Child Development, 57,* 1179–1187.

Berndt, T. J. (1979). Developmental changes in conformity to peers and parents. *Developmental Psychology, 15,* 608–616.

Berndt, T. J. (1982). The features and effects of friendship in early adolescence. *Child Development, 51,* 1447–1460.

Berndt, T. J., & Hawkins, J. A. (1988). *Adjustment following the transition to junior high school*. Manuscript submitted for publication.

Bronfenbrenner, U. (1967). Response to pressure from peers versus adults among Soviet and American school children. *International Journal of Psychology, 2,* 199–207.

Bronfenbrenner, U. (1974). Developmental research and public policy. In J. Romanshyn (Ed.), *Social science and social welfare* (pp. 159–182). New York: Council on Social Work Education.

Brown, B. B., Eicher, S. A., & Petrie, S. (1986). The multidimensionality of peer pressure in adolescence. *Journal of Youth and Adolescence, 9,* 73–96.

Buhler, C. (1927). Die ersten sozialen verhaltungsweisen des kindes. In C. Buhler, H. Hertzer, and B. Tudorhart (Eds.), *Soziologische und psychologische studiend über das erst lebensjahr*. Jena, Germany: Gustav Fischer.

Burchinal, M., Lee, M., & Ramey, C. T. (1989). Type of day care and preschool intellectual development in disadvantaged children. *Child Development, 60,* 128–137.

Chao, P. (1983). *Chinese kinship*. London: Kegan Paul International.

Chapman, M., & Skinner, E. A. (1989). Children's agency beliefs, cognitive performance, and conceptions of effort and ability: Interaction of individual and developmental differences. *Child Development, 60,* 1229–1238.

Chapman, M., Skinner, E. A., & Baltes, P. B. (1990). Interpreting correlations between children's perceived control and cognitive performance: Control, agency, or means-ends beliefs? *Developmental Psychology, 23,* 246–253.

Chen, C., & Stevenson, H. W. (1989). Homework: A cross-cultural examination. *Child Development, 60,* 551–561.

Clarke-Stewart, K. A. (1989). Infant day care. *American Psychologist, 44,* 266–273.

Coleman, J. S. (1981). *The adolescent society*. New York: Free Press.

Collins, W. A., & Getz, S. K. (1976). Children's social responses following modeled reactions to provocations: Prosocial effects of a television drama. *Journal of Personality, 44,* 488–500.

Columbia Broadcasting System. (1979) *Communicating with children through television: Studies of messages and other impressions conveyed by five children's programs.* New York: CBS.

Comstock, G., Chaffee, S., Katzman, N., McCombs, M., & Roberts, D. (1978). *Television and human behavior.* New York: Columbia University Press.

Condry, J., Bence, P., & Scheibe, C. (1987). The nonprogram content of children's television. *Journal of Broadcasting and Electronic Media, 32,* 255–270.

Connell, J. (1985). A new multidimensional measure of children's perceptions of control. *Child Development, 56,* 1018–1041.

Cook, T. D., Appleton, H., Conner, R. F., Shaffer, A., Tamkin, G., & Weber, S. J. (1975). *Sesame Street revisited*. New York: Russell Sage.

Cooper, H. M. (1979). Pygmalion grows up: A model for teacher expectation, communication, and performance influence. *Review of Educational Research, 49,* 389–410.

Covington, M. V. (1985). The role of self-processes in applied social psychology. *Journal for the Theory of Social Behaviour, 15,* 355–392.

Covington, M. V., & Beery, R. G., (1976). *Self-worth and school learning*. New York: Holt, Rinehart and Winston.

Devereux, E. C. (1970). The role of peer-group experience in moral development. In J. P. Hill (Ed.), *Minnesota Symposia on Child Psychology* (pp. 94–140). Minneapolis: University of Minnesota Press.

Dornbusch, S. M., Ritter, P. L., Leiderman, P. H., Roberts, D. F., & Fraleigh, M. J. (1987). The relation of parenting style to adolescent school performance. *Child Development, 58,* 1244–1257.

Dunphy, D. C. (1963). The social structure of urban adolescent peer groups. *Sociometry, 26,* 230–246.

Dweck, C. S., & Elliott, E. S. (1983). Achievement motivation. In E. M. Hetherington (Ed.), *Handbook of child psychology.* New York: Wiley.

Engel, J. F., Blackwell, R. D., & Miniard, P. W. (1986). *Consumer behavior* (5th ed.). Hinsdale, IL: Dryden Press.

Erikson, E. H. (1968). *Identity: Youth and crisis.* New York: Norton.

Eron, L. D. (1982). Parent-child interaction: Television, violence, and aggression in children. *American Psychologist, 37,* 197–211.

Eron, L. D., Walder, L. O., and Lefkowitz, M. M. (1971). *Learning aggression in children.* Boston: Little, Brown.

Field, T. (1991). Quality infant day care and grade school behavior and performance. *Child Development, 62,* 863–870.

Field, T., Masi, W., Goldstein, D., Perry, S., & Parl, S. (1988). Infant day care facilitates preschool behavior. *Early Childhood Research Quarterly, 3,* 341–359.

Findley, M., & Cooper, H. (1983). Locus of control and academic achievement: A literature review. *Journal of Personality and Social Psychology, 44,* 419–427.

Friedrich, L. D., & Stein, A. H. (1975). Prosocial television and young children: The effects of verbal labeling and role playing on learning and behavior. *Child Development, 46,* 27–38.

Garden, R. A. (1987). The second IEA mathematics study. *Comparative Education Review, 31,* 47–68.

Gavin, L. A., & Furman, W. (1989). Age differences in adolescents' perceptions of their peer groups. *Developmental Psychology, 25,* 827–834.

Glover, J. A. (1979). *A parents' guide to intellectual testing.* Chicago: Nelson-Hall.

Golden, M., Rosenbluth, L., Grossie, M., Policare, H., Freeman, H., & Brownlee, E. (1978). *The New York City infant day care study.* New York: Medical and Health Research Association of New York City.

Good, T. L. (1980). *Teacher expectations, teacher behavior, student perception, and student behavior: A decade of research.* Paper presented at the meetings of the American Education Research Association.

Graves, S. (1976). *Content attended to in evaluating television's credibility.* Paper presented at the American Psychological Association, Washington, DC.

Greenberg, B. S. (1986). Minorities and the mass media. In J. Bryant and D. Zillman (Eds.), *Perspectives on mass media effects* (pp. 165–188). Hillsdale, NJ: Erlbaum.

Grolnick, W. S., & Ryan, R. M. (1989). Parent styles associated with children's self-regulation and competence in school. *Journal of Educational Psychology, 81,* 143–154.

Hallinan, M. T. (1980). Patterns of cliquing among youth. In H. C. Foote, A. J. Chapman, and J. R. Smith (Eds.), *Friendship and social relations in children* (pp. 321–342). New York: Wiley.

Hartee, S., Whitesell, N., & Kowalski, P. (1987). *The effects of educational transitions on children's perception of competence and motivation orientation.* Manuscript submitted for publication.

Harter, S. (1983). Developmental perspectives on self-esteem. In E. M. Hetherington (Ed.), *Handbook of child psychology.* New York: Wiley.

Hartup, W. W. (1983). Peer relations. In E. M. Hetherington (Ed.), *Handbook of child psychology.* New York: Wiley.

Heckhausen, H. (1982). The development of achievement motivation. In W. W. Hartup (Ed.), *Review of child development research.* Chicago: University of Chicago Press.

Hedin, D. (1987). Students as teachers: A tool for improving school climate and productivity. *Social Policy, 17,* 42–47.

Hofferth, S. L. (1989). What is the demand for and supply of child care in the United States? *Young Children, 4,* 28–33.

Hofferth, S. L., & Phillips, D. A. (1987). Child care in the United States, 1970 to 1995. *Journal of Marriage and the Family, 49,* 559–571.

Howes, C. (1983). Caregiver behavior in center and family day care. *Journal of Applied Developmental Psychology, 4,* 99–107.

Howes, C. (1988). Peer interaction of young children. *Monographs of the Society for Research in Child Development, 1* (Serial No. 217).

Howes, C. (1990). Can the age of entry into child care and the quality of child care predict adjustment in kindergarten? *Developmental Psychology, 26,* 292–303.

Howes, C., & Stewart, P. (1987). Child's play with adults, toys, and peers: An examination of family and child-care influences. *Developmental Psychology, 23,* 423–430.

Howes, C., & Unger, O. A. (1989). Play with peers in child care settings. In M. Bloch & A. Pellergrini (Eds.), *The ecology of child's play* (pp. 104–119). Norwood, NJ: Ablex.

Hui, C. H., & Villareal, M. J. (1989). Individualism-collectivism and psychological needs: Their relationship in two cultures. *Journal of Cross-Cultural Psychology, 20,* 310–323.

Huston, A. C., Watkins, B. A., & Kunkel, D. (1989). Public policy and children's television. *American Psychologist, 44,* 424–433.

Huston, A. C., Wright, J. C., Rice, M. L., Kerkman, D., & St. Peters, M. (1990). Development of television viewing patterns in early childhood: A longitudinal investigation. *Developmental Psychology, 26,* 409–420.

Imamura, A. E. (1987). *Urban Japanese housewives: At home and in the community.* Honolulu: University of Hawaii Press.

Johnston, J., & Ettema, J. S. (1982). *Positive images: Breaking stereotypes with children's television.* Beverly Hills, CA: Sage.

Keith, T. (1982). Time spent on homework and high school grades: A large-sample panel analysis. *Journal of Educational Psychology, 74,* 248–252.

Kobayashi-Winata, H., & Power, T. G. (1989). Child rearing and compliance. *Journal of Cross-Cultural Psychology, 20,* 333–356.

Kourilsky, M., & Keislar, E. (1983). The effect of the success-oriented teachers on pupils' perceived personal control and attitude toward learning. *Contemporary Educational Psychology, 8,* 158–167.

Kunkel, D. (1988). From a raised eyebrow to a turned back: Regulatory factors influencing the growth of children's product-related programming. *Journal of Communication, 38,* 90–108.

Kunkel, D. (1988, September). Testimony at *Commercialization guidelines for children's television.* Washington, D.C.: Hearings before the U.S. House of Representatives Subcommittee on Telecommunications and Finance.

Lally, R. (1974). *The Family Development Research Program* (Mimeograph). Syracuse, NY: Syracuse University.

Lawrence, F. C., & Wozniak, P. H. (1989). Children's television viewing with family members. *Psychological Reports, 65,* 395–400.

Lebra, T. (1984). *The Japanese woman.* Honolulu: University of Hawaii Press.

Lee, Y. (1987). *Academic success of East Asian Americans: An ethnographic comparative study of East Asian Americans and Anglo Americans' academic achievement.* Seoul: American Studies Institute, Seoul National University Press.

Lefkowitz, M. M. (1972). Television violence and child aggression: A follow-up study. In G. A. Comstock and E. A. Rubinstein (Eds.), *Television and adolescent aggression. Television and social behavior* (pp. 35–135). Washington, DC: U.S. Government Printing Office.

Lefkowitz, M. M., Eron, L. D., Walder, L. E., & Huesmann, L. R. (1977). *Growing up to be violent: A longitudinal study of the development of aggression.* New York: Pergamon Press.

Liebert, R. M., & Sprafkin, J. M. (1988). *The early window: Effects of television on children and youth* (3rd ed.). New York: Pergamon Press.

Lynn, R. (1982). IQ in Japan and the United States shows a growing disparity. *Nature, 297,* 222–223.

Lynn, R., Hampson, S., & Aga, E. (1989). Television violence and aggression: A genotype-environment, correlation, and interaction theory. *Social Behavior and Personality, 17,* 143–164.

Maccoby, E. E. (1951). Television: Its impact on school children. *Public Opinion Quarterly, 15,* 421–444.

Maccoby, E. E., & Jacklin, C. N. (1978). *The psychology of sex differences.* Palo Alto, CA: Stanford University Press.

Midgley, C., Feldlaufer, E., & Eccles, J. (1989). Student/teacher relations and attitudes toward mathematics before and after the transition to junior high school. *Child Development, 60,* 981–992.

Miller, A. (1985). A developmental study of the cognitive basis of performance impairment after failure. *Journal of Personality and Social Psychology, 49,* 529–538.

Mordkowitz, E. R., & Ginsburg, H. P. (1987, April). *The academic socialization of successful Asian-American college students.* Paper presented at the Annual Meeting of the American Educational Research Association, San Francisco.

National Issues Forum. (1989). The day care dilemma. Dubuque, IA: Kendall/Hunt.

Nichols, R. C. (1979). Heredity and environment: Major findings from twin studies of ability, personality, and interests. *Homo, 29,* 158–173.

Parke, R. D., & Slaby, R. G. (1983). The development of aggression. In E. M. Hetherington (Ed.), *Handbook of child psychology.* New York: Wiley.

Parsons, J. E. (1978). *The development of attributions, expectations, and persistence.* Unpublished manuscript, University of Michigan, Ann Arbor.

Piaget, J. (1962). *Play, dreams and imitation in childhood.* New York: Norton.

Polacheck, S. W., Kniessner, T. J., and Harwood, H. J. (1978). Educational production functions. *Journal of Educational Statistics, 3,* 209–231.

Polansky, N., Chalmers, M., Buttenweiser, C., & Williams, D. (1979). The isolation of the neglectful family. *American Journal of Orthopsychiatry, 49,* 149–152.

Presser, H. B., & Cain, V. S. (1983). Shift work among dual-earner couples with children. *Science, 219,* 876–879.

Rhodes, W. A., Blackwell, J., Jordan, C., & Walters, C. (1980). A developmental study of learned helplessness. *Developmental Psychology, 16,* 616–624.

Rice, M. L., Huston, A. C., Truglio, R. T., & Wright, J. C. (1987). *Words from Sesame Street: Learning vocabulary while viewing.* Unpublished manuscript, University of Kansas, Lawrence.

Rist, R. C. (1970). Student social class and teacher expectations: The self-fulfilling prophecy in education. *Harvard Educational Review, 40,* 411–451.

Rosenthal, R., & Jacobson, L. (1968). *Pygmalion in the classroom.* New York: Holt, Rinehart and Winston.

Rotter, J. (1966). Generalized expectancies for internal versus external locus of control of reinforcement. *Psychological Monographs: General and Applied, 80,* 1–28.

Ruble, D. N., Boggiano, A. K., Feldman, U. S., & Loehl, J. (1980). A developmental analysis of the role of social comparison in self-evaluation. *Developmental Psychology, 16,* 105–115.

Ruble, D. N., Feldman, U. S., & Boggiano, A. K. (1976). Young children in achievement situations. *Developmental Psychology, 12,* 192–197.

Rutter, M. (1981). Social-emotional consequences of day care for preschool children. *American Journal of Orthopsychiatry, 51,* 1174–1181.

Sasaki, K. (1985). *Hahaoya to Nippon-jin* (Mother and the Japanese). Tokyo: Bungei Shunju-sha.

Savin-Williams, R. C. (1976). An ethological study of dominance formation and maintenance in a group of human adolescents. *Child Development, 47,* 972–979.

Savitsky, J. C., & Watson, M. J. (1975). Patterns of proxemic behavior among preschool children. *Representative Research in Social Psychology, 6,* 109–113.

Sebald, H. (1989). Adolescents' peer orientation: Changes in the support system during the past three decades. *Adolescence, 24,* 937–946.

Siegal, M., & Storey, R. (1985). Day care and children's conceptions of moral and social rules. *Child Development, 56,* 1001–1009.

Sigel, I. E. (1988). Commentary: Cross-cultural studies of parental influence on children's achievement. *Human Development, 31,* 384–390.

Singer, J. L., & Singer, D. G. (1980, September). *Imaginative play in preschoolers: Some research and theoretical implications.* Paper presented at the meeting of the American Psychological Association, Montreal.

Skinner, E. A. (1990). Age differences in the dimensions of perceived control during middle childhood: Implications for developmental conceptualizations and research. *Child Development, 61,* 1882–1890.

Stein, A. H., & Friedrich, L. D. (1975). Impact of television on children and youth. In E. M. Hetherington (Ed.), *Review of child development research* (pp. 183–356). Chicago: University of Chicago Press.

Stevenson, H., Azuma, H., & Hakuta, K. (Eds.). (1986). *Child development in Japan.* New York: Freeman.

Stevenson, H. W., & Lee, S. (1990). Contexts of achievement. *Monographs of the Society for Research in Child Development, 55,* Nos. 1–2.

Stevenson, H., Lee, S., Chen, C., Lummis, M., Stigler, J., Fan, L., & Ge, F. (1990). Mathematics achievement of children in China and the United States. *Child Development, 61,* 1053–1066.

Stipek, D. J. (1981). *Children's use of past performance information in ability and expectancy judgments for self and other.* Paper presented at the Meeting of the International Society for the Study of Behavioral Development, Toronto.

Stipek, D. J., and Hoffman, J. M. (1980). Children's achievement-related expectancies as a function of academic performance histories and sex. *Journal of Educational Psychology, 72,* 861–865.

Stipek, D. J., & MacIver, D. (1989). Developmental change in children's assessment of intellectual competence. *Child Development, 60,* 520–538.

Stipek, D. J., & Tannatt, L. (1984). Children's judgements of their own and their peers' academic competence. *Journal of Education Psychology, 76,* 75–84.

Sullivan, H. S. (1953). *The interpersonal theory of psychiatry.* New York: Norton.

Teevan, R. L., & McGhee, P. E. (1972). Childhood development of fear of failure motivation. *Journal of Personality and Social Psychology, 21,* 345–348.

Thomas, M. H., Horton, R. W., Lippincott, E. C., & Drabman, R. S. (1977). Desensitization to portrayals of real-life aggression as a function of exposure to television violence. *Journal of Personality and Social Psychology, 35,* 450–458.

Tobin, J. J., Wu, D., & Davidson, D. (1989). *Preschools in three cultures.* New Haven, CT: Yale University Press.

U.S. Bureau of the Census. (1990). *Who's minding the kids?* (series p-70, no. 20). Washington, DC: U.S. Government Printing Office.

U.S. Bureau of Labor Statistics. (1988, September 7). Labor force participation unchanged among mothers with young children. *News, 3,* 1–8.

Vandell, D. L. (1980). Peer interaction in the first year of life. *Child Development, 51,* 1203–1214.

Vandell, D. L., & Corasaniti, M. A. (1990). *Variations in early child care: Do they predict subsequent social, emotional, and cognitive differences?* Unpublished manuscript, University of Wisconsin, Madison.

Vandell, D. L., & Mueller, E. C. (1980). Peer play and friendships during the first two years of life. In H. C. Foot, J. Chapman, and J. R. Smith (Eds.), *Friendship and social relations in children.* New York: Wiley.

Vernoff, J. (1983). Contextual determinants of personality. *Personality and Social Psychology Bulletin, 9,* 331–343.

Vlietstra, A. (1982). Children's responses to talk instructions: Age changes and training efforts. *Child Development, 53,* 534–542.

Vogel, E. (1963). *Japan's new middle class.* Berkeley: University of California Press.

Walden, T. A., & Ramey, C. T. (1983). Locus of control and academic achievement: Results from a preschool intervention program. *Journal of Educational Psychology, 75,* 347–358.

White, M. I., Levine, R. A. (1986). What is an li ko (good child)? In H. Stevenson, H. Azuma, and K. Hakuta (Eds.), *Child development in Japan* (pp. 55–62). New York: Freeman.

Wingert, P., & Kantrowitz, B. (1991). The day-care generation. In N. Lauter-Klatell (Ed.), *Readings in child development* (pp. 70–74). Mountain View, CA: Mayfield.

Wolf, R. M. (1979). Achievement in the United States. In H. J. Walberg (Ed.), *Educational environments and effects: Evaluation, policy and productivity.* Berkeley, CA: McCutcheon.

Wroblewski, R., & Huston, A. C. (1988). Televised occupational stereotypes and their effects on early adolescents: Are they changing? *Journal of Early Adolescence, 7,* 282–298.

Yao, E. L. (1985). A comparison of family characteristics of Asian-American and Anglo-American high achievers. *International Journal of Comparative Sociology, 26,* 3–4, 198–208.

Zarbatany, L., Hartmann, D. P., & Rankin, D. B. (1990). The psychological functions preadolescent peer activities. *Child Development, 61,* 1067–1080.

Zill, N. (1988). *Basic facts about the use of childcare and preschool services in the U.S.* Washington, DC: Child Trends.

Chapter 4

Aaronson, L. S., & Macnee, C. L. (1989). Tobacco, alcohol, and caffeine use during pregnancy. *JOGNN, 22,* 279–286.

Abel, E. (1980). *Marijuana: The first 12,000 years* (p. 266). New York: Plenum Press.

Aldridge, A., Bailey, J., & Neims, A. H. (1981). The disposition of caffeine during and after pregnancy. *Seminars in Perinatology, 5,* 310–314.

Als, H., & Brazelton, T. B. (1981). A new model of assessing the behavioral organization in preterm and full-term infants. *Journal of the American Academy of Child Psychiatry, 20,* 239–263.

Anastasi, A. (1958). Heredity, environment, and the question of how? *Psychological Review, 65,* 197–208.

Apgar, V. (1953). A proposal for a new method of evaluation of the newborn infant. *Current Research in Anesthesia and Analgesia, 32,* 260–267.

Arenson, C., & Finnegan, L. P. (1989). Women at risk for AIDS and the effect of educational efforts. In D. E. Hutchings (Ed.), *Prenatal abuse of licit and illicit drugs* (Vol. 562) (pp. 363–364). New York: Annals of the New York Academy of Sciences.

Barr, H. M., Streissguth, A., Darby, B., & Sampson, P. (1990). Prenatal exposure to alcohol, caffeine, tobacco, and aspirin: Effects on fine and gross motor performance in 4-year-old children. *Developmental Psychology, 26,* 339–348.

Bayley, N. (1970). Development of mental abilities. In P. H. Mussen (Ed.), *Carmichael's manual of child psychology.* New York: Wiley.

Benson, P. F., & Fensom, A. H. (1985). *Genetic biochemical disorders.* Oxford: Oxford University Press.

Berg, W. K., & Berg, K. M. (1979). Psychophysiological development in infancy: State, sensory function, and attention. In J. D. Osofsky (Ed.), *Handbook on infant development.* New York: Wiley.

Bingol, N., Fuchs, M., Diaz, V., Stone, R. X., & Gromisch, D. S. (1987). Maternal cocaine use: Neonatal outcome. In H. Fitzgerald, B. M. Lester, & M. Yogman (Eds.), *Theory and research in behavioral pediatrics* (Vol. 5). New York: Plenum.

Brazelton, T. B. (1981). *On becoming a family.* New York: Delacorte Press.

Brazelton, T. B. (1984). *Neonatal behavioral assessment scale.* Philadelphia: Spastics International.

Butler, N., & Goldstein, H. (1974). Smoking in pregnancy and subsequent child development. *British Journal of Medicine, 4,* 573–75.

Chasnoff, I. (1989). Cocaine, pregnancy, and the neonate. *Women and Health, 15,* 23–35.

Chasnoff, I., & Griffith, D. (1989). Cocaine: Clinical studies of pregnancy and the newborn. In D. E. Hutchings (Ed.), *Prenatal abuse of licit and illicit drugs* (Vol. 562) (pp. 260–266). New York: Annals of the New York Academy of Sciences.

Christianson, R. E. (1980). The relationship between maternal smoking and the incidence of congential anomalies. *American Journal of Epidemiology, 112,* 684–695.

Cole, J. G. (1991). High-risk infants: Prenatal drug exposure (PDE), prematurity, and AIDS. In N. Lauter-Klatell (Ed.), *Readings in child development* (pp. 36–42). Mountain View, CA: Mayfield.

Cooper, H. M. (1979). Pygmalion grows up: A model for teacher expectation, communication and performance influence. *Review of Educational Research, 49,* 389–410.

Dehane, P., Samaille-Villette, C., & Samaille, P. P. (1977). Le syndrome d'alcoholisme foetal dans le nord de la France. *Revue Alcool, 23,* 145–158.

Desmond, M. M., & Wilson, G. S. (1975). Neonatal abstinence syndrome: Recognition and diagnosis. *Addictive Diseases: An International Journal, 2,* 113–121.

Dick-Read, G. (1959). *Childbirth without fear: The principles and practice of natural childbirth* (2nd ed.). New York: Harper & Row.

Diebel, P. (1980). Effects of cigarette smoking on maternal nutrition and the fetus. *Journal of Obstetrics Gynecology Neonatal Nursing, 9,* 333–336.

DiLella, A. G., Marvit, J., Lidsky, A. S., Guttler, F., & Woo, S. L. C. (1986). Tight linkage between a splicing mutation and a specific DNA haplotype in phenylketonuria. *Nature, 322,* 799–803.

Dixon, S. D., & Bejar, R. (1989). Echoencephalographic findings in neonates associated with maternal cocaine methamphetamine use: Incidents and clinical correlates. *Journal of Pediatrics, 115,* 1770–1778.

Doberczak, T. M., Shanzer, S., Senie, R. T., & Kandall, S. R. (1988). Neonatal neurologic and electroencephalographic effects of intrauterine cocaine exposure. *Journal of Pediatrics, 113,* 354–358.

Dunn, H., McBurner, S., Ingram, S., & Hunter, C. (1977). Maternal cigarette smoking during pregnancy and the child's subsequent development. *Canadian Journal of Public Health, 68,* 43–50.

Eat better, live better (1982). *Reader's Digest.* Pleasantville, NY.

Fielding, J. E. (1978). Smoking and pregnancy. *New England Journal of Medicine, 798,* 337–339.

Fitzgerald, H., Strommen, E. A., & McKinney, J. P. (1982). *Development psychology: The infant and young child.* Homewood, IL: Dorsey Press.

Fricker, H. S., & Segal, S. (1978). Narcotic addiction, pregnancy, and the newborn. *American Journal of Diseases of Children, 132,* 360–366.

Fried, P. (1989). Postnatal consequences of maternal marijuana use in humans. In D. E. Hutchings (Ed.), *Prenatal abuse of licit and illicit drugs* (Vol. 562) (pp. 123–132). New York: Annals of the New York Academy of Sciences.

Fried, P., & Watkinson, B. (1990). 36- and 48-month neurobehavioral follow-up of children prenatally exposed to marijuana, cigarettes, and alcohol. *Developmental and Behavioral Pediatrics, 11,* 49–58.

Fulroth, R. F., Phillips, B., & Durant, D. J. (1989). Perinatal outcome of infants exposed to cocaine and/or heroin in utero. *American Journal of Diseases in Children, 143,* 905–910.

Gilbert, M. S. (1938). *Biography of the unborn.* Baltimore: Williams and Wilkins.

Goldman, R. J., & Goldman, J. (1982). How children perceive the origin of babies and the roles of mothers and fathers in procreation: A cross-national study. *Child Development, 53,* 491–504.

Good, T. L. (1980). *Teacher expectations, teacher behavior, student perceptions and student behavior: A decade of research.* Paper presented at the meetings of the American Educational Research Association.

Grobstein, E. (1979). External human fertilization. *Scientific American, 240,* 57–68.

Hadeed, A. J., & Siegel, S. R. (1989). Maternal cocaine use during pregnancy: Effect on newborn/ infant. *Pediatrics, 84,* 205–210.

Haith, M. (1980). *Rules that babies look by.* Hillsdale, NJ: Erlbaum.

Hans, S. (1989). Developmental consequences of prenatal exposure of Methadone. In D. E. Hutchings (Ed.), *Prenatal abuse of licit and illicit drugs* (Vol. 562) (pp. 195–297). New York: Annals of the New York Academy of Sciences.

Hedin, D. (1987). Students as teachers: A tool for improving school climate and productivity. *Social Policy, 17,* 42–47.

Hollestedt, C. L., Dahlgren, R., & Rydbert, U. (1983). Outcome of pregnancy in women treated at an alcohol clinic. *Acta Psychiatrica Scandanavia, 67,* 236-248.

Holmes, D. L., Nagy, J., Slaymaker, F., Sosnowki, R. J., Prinz, S., & Pasternak, J. (1982). Early influences of prematurity, illness and prolonged hospitalization on infant behavior. *Developmental Psychology, 18,* 744–750.

Horn, J. M. (1979). Intellectual resemblance among adoptive and biological relatives: The Texas Adoption Study. *Behavior Genetics, 9,* 177–207.

Householder, J., Hatcher, R., Burns, W., & Chasnoff, I. (1982). Infants born to narcotic-addicted mothers. *Psychological Bulletin, 92,* 453–468.

Hughey, M. J., McElin, T., & Young, T. (1988). Maternal and fetal outcome of Lamaze-prepared patients. *Journal of Obstetrics and Gynecology, 5,* 643–647.

Kaminski, M., Rumeau, C., & Schwartz, D. (1978). Alcohol consumption, pregnant women and the outcome of pregnancy. *Alcoholism: Clinical & Experimental Research, 2,* 155–163.

Klaus, M., & Klaus, P. (1986). *The amazing newborn.* Reading, MA: Addison-Wesley.

Klebanoff, M. A., & Berendes, H. W. (1988). Aspirin exposure during the first 20 weeks of gestation and IQ at four years of age. *Teratology, 37,* 249–255.

Kleinman, J. C., & Matans, J. H. (1985). A clinical trial of change in maternal smoking and its effect on birth weight. *Journal of the American Medical Association, 251,* 911–915.

Kolata, G. B. (1978). Behavioral teratology: Birth defects of the mind. *Science, 202,* 732–734.

Kopp, C. B. (1990). Risks in infancy: Appraising the research. *Merrill-Palmer Quarterly, 36,* 117–140.

Kramer, L., Locke, G., Ogunyemi, A., & Nelson, L. (1990). Neonatal cocaine-related seizures. *Journal of Child Neurology, 5,* 60–64.

Landry, S., & Chapieski, L. (1988). Visual attention skills and preterm infant risk. *Infant Behavior and Development, 11,* 177–185.

Landry, S., Chapieski, L., Richardson, M. A., Palmer, J., & Hall, S. (1990). The social competence of children born prematurely: Effects of medical complications and parent behaviors. *Child Development, 61,* 1605–1616.

Leboyer, F. (1975). *Birth without violence.* New York: Knopf.

Lester, B. M., Corwin, M. J., Sepkoski, C., Seifer, R., Peucker, M., McLaughlin, S., & Golub, H. I. (1991). Neurobehavioral syndromes in cocaine-exposed newborn infants. *Child Development, 62,* 694–705.

Lester, B. M., & Dreher, M. (1989). Effects of marijuana use during pregnancy on newborn cry. *Child Development, 60,* 765–771.

Lifson, A. R. (1988). Do alternate modes of transmission of human immunodeficiency virus exist: A review. *Journal of the American Medical Association, 259,* 1353–1356.

Linn, S., Schoenbaum, S. C., Monson, R. R., Rosner, B., Stubblefield, P. G., & Ryan, K. J. (1982). No association between coffee consumption and adverse outcomes of pregnancy. *New England Journal of Medicine, 306,* 141–145.

Livesay, S., Ehrlich, S., & Finnegan, L. P. (1987). Cocaine and pregnancy: Maternal and infant outcomes. *Pediatric Research, 21,* 238A.

Lubic, R. W. (1981). Alternate maternity care. In S. Romalis (Ed.), *Childbirth.* Austin: University of Texas Press.

Lynn, R., Hampson, S., & Aga, E. (1989). Television violence and aggression: A genotype-environment, correlation, and interaction theory. *Social Behavior and Personality, 17,* 143–164.

Madden, J. D., Payne, R. F., & Miller, S. (1986). Maternal cocaine abuse and effect on the newborn. *Pediatrics, 77,* 209–211.

Matheny, A. P., Jr., & Dolan, A. B. (1975). Persons, situations and time: A genetic view of behavioral change in children. *Journal of Personality and Psychology, 32,* 1106–1110.

McIntosh, I.D. (1984). Smoking and pregnancy: Attributable risks and public health implications. *Canadian Journal of Public Health, 75,* 141–148.

Miller, N. S., Gold, M., Belkin, B., & Klahr, A. (1989). The diagnosis of alcohol and cannabis dependence in cocaine dependents and alcohol dependence in their families. *British Journal of Addiction, 84,* 1491–1498.

Mirochnick, M., Meyer, J., Cole, J. G., & Zuckerman, B. (1991). *Circulating catecholamine in cocaine-exposed neonates.* Boston: Boston City Hospital.

Mochizuki, M., Maruo, T., Masuko, K., & Ohtsu, T. (1984). Effects of smoking on fetoplacental-maternal system during pregnancy. *American Journal of Obstetrics and Gynecology, 149,* 413–420.

Moltz, H. (1973). Some implications of the critical period hypothesis. *Annals of the New York Academy of Sciences, 223,* 144–146.

Money, J., & Ehrhardt, A. A. (1972). *Man and woman, boy and girl: The differentiation and dimorphism of gender identity from conception to maturity.* Baltimore: The Johns Hopkins University Press.

Moore, J. K. (1983). *Before we were born* (2nd ed.). New York: Saunders.

Moore, K. L. (1988). *The developing human: Clinically oriented embryology* (4th ed.). Philadelphia: W. B. Saunders.

Naeye, K. L. (1988). Fetal complications of maternal heroin addiction: Abnormal growth, infections, and episodes of stress. *Journal of Pediatrics, 83,* 1055–1061.

National Academy of Sciences. (1986).*Confronting AIDS: Directions for public health, health care, and research.* Washington, DC: National Academy Press.

Nichols, R. C. (1978). Heredity and environment: Major findings from twin studies of ability, personality, and interests. *Homo, 29,* 158–173.

Norwick, B. (1989). Pediatric AIDS: A medical overview. In J. M. Seibert and R. A. Olson (Eds.), *Children, adolescents and AIDS.* Lincoln: University of Nebraska Press.

Olegard, R. K. (1979). Effects on the child of alcohol abuse during pregnancy. *Acta Paediatrics Scandinavia, 275,* 112–121.

Olegard, R. K., Sabel, K. G., Arronsson, M., Sandin, B., Johansson, P. R., Larlsson, C., Kyllerman, M., Iveson, H., & Harben, A. (1979). Effects on the child of alcohol abuse during pregnancy. *Acta Paediatrics Scandinavia, 1,* 117–121.

Parfitt, R. (1977). *The birth primer.* New York: Facts on File.

Plomin, R. (1990). *Development, genetics, and psychology.* Pacific Grove, CA: Brooks/Cole.

Pritchard, F. A., & MacDonald, P. C. (1976). *William's obstetrics* (15th ed.). New York: Appleton-Century-Crofts.

Randall, C. L., Taylor, W. J., & Walker, D. W. (1977). Ethanol-induced malformations in mice. *Alcoholism: Clinical & Experimental Research, 1,* 219–224.

Rich, K. (1989). Maternal AIDS: Effects on mother and infant. In D. E. Hutchings (Ed.), *Prenatal abuse of licit and illicit drugs* (Vol. 562) (pp. 241–247). New York: Annals of the New York Academy of Sciences.

Richardson, G. A., Day, N. L., & Taylor, P. M. (1989). The effect of prenatal alcohol, marijuana, and tobacco exposure on neonatal behavior. *Infant Behavior and Development, 12,* 199–209.

Roberts, C. J., & Lowe, C. R. (1975). Where have all the conceptions gone? *Lancet, 2,* 498–499.

Rosen, R., & Pippenger, C. (1976). Pharmacologic observations on the neonatal withdrawal syndrome. *Journal of Pediatrics, 88,* 1044–1048.

Rosett, H. L., & Sander, L. W. (1979). Effects of maternal drinking on neonatal morphology and state regulation. In J. D. Osofsky (Ed.), *Handbook on infant development.* New York: Wiley.

Ross, G. (1985). Use of Bayley scales to characterize abilities of premature infants. *Child Development, 56,* 835–842.

Ryan, L., Ehrlich, S., & Finnegan, L. P. (1987). Cocaine abuse during pregnancy: Effects on the fetus and newborn. *Neurotoxicology Teratology, 9,* 295–299.

Scarr, S., & Kenneth, K. (1983). Developmental behavioral genetics. In P. H. Mussen (Ed.), *Handbook of child psychology.* New York: Wiley.

Scarr, S., & Kidd, K. (1983). Developmental behavioral genetics. In P. H. Mussen (Ed.), *Handbook of child psychology.* New York: Wiley.

Schneider, A. M., & Tarshis, B. (1975). *Physiological psychology.* New York: Random House.

Schneider, J. W., & Chasnoff, I. (1987). Cocaine abuse during pregnancy: Its effects on infant motor development—A clinical perspective. *Topics in Acute Care and Trauma Rehabilitation, 2,* 59.

Schwartz, R. H., Hoffmann, N. G., Smith, D., Hayden, G. F., & Riddile, M. (1987). Use of phenylcyclidine among adolescents attending a suburban drug treatment facility. *Journal of Pediatrics, 110,* 322–324.

Smith, D. W. (1978). Prenatal life. In D. W. Smith, E. L. Bierman, & N. M. Robinson (Eds.), *The biological ages of man* (2nd ed.). (p. 43). Philadelphia: Saunders.

Steinhausen, H., Nestler, V., & Huth, H. (1982). Psychopathology and mental functions in the offspring of alcoholic and epileptic mothers. *Journal of the American Academy of Child Psychiatry, 21,* 268–273.

Steinhausen, H., Nestler, V., & Spohr, H. L. (1983). Development and psychopathology of children with the fetal alcohol syndrome. *Journal of Developmental Behavior Pediatrics, 12,* 550–562.

Streissguth, A. (1978). Fetal alcohol syndrome: An epidemiologic perspective. *American Journal of Epidemiology, 107,* 467–478.

Streissguth, A., Barr, H. M., & Martin, D. C. (1983). Maternal alcohol use and neonatal habituation assessed with the Brazelton scale. *Child Development, 54,* 1109–1118.

Streissguth, A., Barr, H. M., Martin, D. C., & Herman, C. S. (1980). Effects of maternal alcohol, nicotine and caffeine use during pregnancy on infant mental and motor development at 8 months. *Alcoholism: Clinical and Experimental Research, 4,* 152–164.

Streissguth, A., Barr, H. M., Sampson, P. D., Darby, B. L., & Martin, D. C. (1989). IQ at age 4 in relation to maternal alcohol use and smoking during pregnancy. *Developmental Psychology, 25,* 3–11.

Streissguth, A., Herman, C. S., & Smith, D. W. (1982). Intelligence, behavior and dysmorphogenesis in the fetal alcohol syndrome: A report on 20 patients. *Journal of Pediatrics, 92,* 363–367.

Streissguth, A., & Little, R. E. (1985). Alcohol-related morbidity and mortality in offspring of drinking women: Methodological issues and a review of pertinent studies. In M. A. Schukit (Ed.), *Alcohol patterns and problems.* New Brunswick, NJ: Rutgers University Press.

Streissguth, A., Martin, D. C., Martin, J. C., & Barr, H. M. (1981). The Seattle Longitudinal Prospective Study on Alcohol and Pregnancy. *Neurobehavioral Toxicology and Teratology, 3,* 223–233.

Streissguth, A., Sampson, P. D., & Barr, H. (1989). Neurobehavioral dose-response effects of prenatal alcohol exposure in humans from infancy to adulthood. In D. E. Hutchings (Ed.), *Prenatal abuse of licit and illicit drugs* (pp. 145-158). (Vol. 562). New York: Annals of the New York Academy of Sciences.

Streissguth, A., Treder, R. P., Barr, H. M., Shepard, T. H., Bleyer, W. A., Sampson, P. D., & Martin, D. C. (1987). Aspirin and acetaminophen used by pregnant women and subsequent child IQ and attention decrements. *Teratology, 35,* 211–219.

Tanner, J. M. (1978). *Education and physical growth.* London: Hoddler and Stoughton.

Task Force on Pediatric AIDS. American Psychological Association. (1989). Pediatric AIDS and Human Immunodeficiency Virus infection. *American Psychologist, 44,* 256–264.

Tortora, G. J., & Anagnostakos, N. P. (1984). *Principles of anatomy and physiology* (4th ed.). New York: Harper & Row.

Trainer, M. (1991). *Differences in common: Straight talk on mental retardation, Down Syndrome, and life.* Kensington, MD: Woodbine House.

Turkewirtz, G., & Kenny, P. (1985). The role of developmental limitation of sensory input on sensory/perception organization. *Journal of Developmental Behavioral Pediatrics, 6,* 302–306.

Van Dyke, D. C., & Fox, A. A. (1990). Fetal drug exposure and its possible implications for learning in the preschool and school-age population. *Journal of Learning Disabilities, 23,* 160–163.

Waterson, E. J., & Murray-Lyon, I. M. (1990). Preventing alcohol related birth damage: A review. *Social Science Medicine, 30,* 349–364.

Watson, J., & Crick, F. H. (1953). Molecular structure of nucleic acids: A structure for deoxyribonucleic acid. *Nature, 171,* 737–738.

Weathersbee, P. S., & Lodge, J. R. (1978). Review of ethanol's effects on the reproductive process. *Journal of Reproductive Medicine, 21,* 2, 63–78.

Weathersbee, P. S., Olsen, J. R., & Lodge, J. R. (1977). Caffeine and pregnancy: A retrospective survey. *Postgraduate Medicine, 62,* 64–69.

Weinberger, D. R., Berman, K. F., & Chase, T. N. (1987). Prefrontal CBF during specific cognitive activation: Studies of Huntington's and Parkinson's diseases. *Journal of Clinical and Experimental Neuropsychology, 9,* 47.

Welsh, M. C., Pennington, B. F., Ozonoff, S., Rouse, B., & McCabe E. R. B. (1990). Neuropsychology of early-treated phenylketonuria: Specific executive function deficits. *Child Development, 61,* 1697–1713.

Whaley, L. F. (1974). *Understanding inherited disorders.* St. Louis: Mosby.

White, B. L. (1988). *Educating the infant and toddler.* Lexington, MA: Lexington Books.

Wilson, G. S. (1989). Clinical studies of infants exposed prenatally to heroin. In D. E. Hutchings (Ed.), *Prenatal abuse of licit and illicit drugs* (pp. 183–194). (Vol. 562). New York: Annals of the New York Academy of Sciences.

Wingert, P., & Kantrowitz, B. (1991). The day-care generation. In N. Lauter-Klatell (Ed.), *Readings in child development* (pp. 70–74). Mountain View, CA: Mayfield.

Zelson, C. (1975). Acute management of neonatal addiction. *Addictive Diseases: An International Journal, 2,* 159–168.

Chapter 5

Adelson, J. (1980). *Handbook of adolescent psychology.* New York: Wiley.

Anastasi, A. (1958). Heredity, environment, and the question of "how?" *Psychological Review, 65,* 197–208.

Andersen, A. E. (1983). Anorexia nervosa and bulimia: A spectrum of eating disorders. *Journal of Adolescent Health Care, 4,* 15–21.

Apgar, V. (1953). A proposal for a new method of evaluation of the newborn infant. *Current Researches in Anesthesia and Analgesia, 32,* 260–267.

Badr, F. M., & Badr, R. S. (1975). Induction of dominant, lethal mutation in male mice by ethyl alcohol. *Nature, 253,* 134–136.

Barrera, M. E., & Maurer, D. (1981). Recognition of mother's photographed face by the three-month-old infant. *Child Development, 52,* 714–718.

Bayley, N. (1970). Development of mental abilities. In P.H. Mussen (Ed.), *Carmichael's manual of child psychology.* New York: Wiley.

Bereson, G., Frank, G., Hunter, S., Srinivasan, S., Voors, A., & Webber, L. (1982). Cardiovascular risk factors in children. Should they concern the pediatrician? *American Journal of Diseases of Children, 136,* 855–862.

Berg, W. K., & Berg, K. M. (1979). Psychophysiological development in infancy: State, sensory function, and attention. In J. D. Osofsky (Ed.), *Handbook on infant development.* New York: Wiley.

Blume, J. (1990). *Are you there, God? It's me, Margaret.* New York: Bradbury Press/Macmillan Child Group.

Bornstein, M. H. (1976). Infants' recognition memory for hue. *Developmental Psychology, 12,* 185–192.

Bornstein, M. H. (1985). Human infant color vision and color perception. *Infant Behavior and Development, 8,* 109–113.

Bornstein, M. H. (1989). Cross-cultural developmental comparisons: The case of Japanese-American infant and mother activities and interactions. What we know, what we need to know, and why we need to know it. *Developmental Review, 9,* 171–204.

Bornstein, M. H., & Tamis-LeMonda, C. S. (1988). *Activities and interactions of mothers and their firstborn infants in the first six months of life: Reliability, stability, continuity, covariation, correspondence, and prediction.* Unpublished manuscript, National Institute of Child Health and Human Development.

Bower, T. G. R. (1966). The visual world of infants. *Scientific American, 215,* 80–92.

Brasel, J. (1978). Infantile obesity. *Dialogues in infant nutrition, 4,* 1–4.

Brazelton, T. B. (1973). *Neonatal behavioral assessment scale.* Philadelphia: Lippincott.

Brazelton, T. B. (1981). *On becoming a family.* New York: Delacorte Press.

Bruch, H. (1977). Psychological antecedents of anorexia nervosa. In R. A. Vigersky (Ed.), *Anorexia nervosa.* New York: Raven Press.

Bruch, H. (1981). Psychological antecedents of anorexia nervosa. In R. A. Vigersky (Ed.), *Anorexia Nervosa.* New York: Raven Press.

Bulik, C., Sullivan, P., & Rorty, M. (1989). Childhood sexual abuse in women with bulimia. *Journal of Clinical Psychiatry, 50,* 460–464.

Butler, N., & Goldstein, H. (1974). Smoking in pregnancy and subsequent child development. *British Journal of Medicine, 4,* 23–28.

Campos, J. J., Langer, A., & Krowitz, A. (1970). Cardiac responses on the visual cliff in prelocomotor human infants. *Science, 170,* 196–197.

Caudill, W. A., & Weinstein, H. (1969). Maternal care and infant behavior in Japan and America. *Psychiatry, 32,* 12–43.

Chase, H. (1973). The effects of intrauterine and postnatal under-nutrition on normal brain development. *Annals of the New York Academy of Sciences, 205,* 231–244.

Cole, J. G. (1991). High-risk infants: Prenatal drug exposure (PDE), prematurity, and AIDS. In N. Lauter-Klatell (Ed.), *Readings in child development* (pp. 36–42). Mountain View, CA: Mayfield.

Corbin, C. B. (1980). *A textbook of motor development.* Dubuque, IA: Wm. C. Brown.

Cowan, W. (1978). Aspects of neural development. In T. Porter (Ed.), *Neurophysiology.* Baltimore: University Park Press.

Cowan, W. (1979). *Annual review of neuroscience* Vol. 2. Palo Alto, CA: Annual Reviews.

Cragg, B. (1974). Plasticity of synapses. *British Medical Bulletin, 30,* 141–144.

Cratty, B. J. (1979). *Perceptual and motor development in infants and children.* Englewood Cliffs, NJ: Prentice-Hall.

Davie, R., Butler, N., & Goldstein, H. (1972). *From birth to seven.* London: William Clowes.

DeCasper, A. J., & Fifer, W. P. (1980). Of human bonding: Newborns prefer their mothers' voices. *Science, 208,* 1174–1176.

DeCasper, A. J., & Spence, M. J. (1986). Prenatal maternal speech patterns on newborns' perception of speech sounds. *Infant Behavior and Development, 9,* 133–150.

Desmond, M. M., & Wilson, G. S. (1975). Neonatal abstinence syndrome: Recognition and diagnosis. *Addictive Diseases: An International Journal, 2,* 113–121.

Dickerson, J. W. T., & McGurk, H. (1982). *Brain and behavioural development.* London: Surrey University Press.

Dietz, W. H. (1986). An adoption study of human obesity. *New England Journal of Medicine, 315,* 128–129.

Dobbing, J. (1976). Vulnerable periods of brain development. In W. Roberts and S. Thomson (Eds.), *The biology of human fetal growth.* New York: Halsted Press.

Dobbing, J., & Sands, J. (1970). Timing of neuroblast multiplication in developing human brain. *Nature, 122,* 639.

Dobbing, J., & Smart, J. (1974). Vulnerability of developing brain and behaviour. *British Medical Bulletin, 30,* 164–168.

Dorn, L. D., Susman, E. J., Nottelmann, E. D., Inoff-Germain, G., & Chrousos, G. P. (1990). Perceptions of puberty: Adolescent, parent, and health care personnel. *Developmental Psychology, 26,* 322–329.

Duncan, P., Ritter, P. L., Dornbusch, S., Gross, R., & Carlsmith, J. (1985). The effects of pubertal timing on body image, school behavior and deviance. *Journal of Youth and Adolescence, 14,* 227–236.

Eat better, live better. (1982). *Reader's Digest.* Pleasantville, NY.

Eichorn, D. H. (1979). Physical development: Current foci of research. In J. D. Osofsky (Ed.), *Handbook on infant development.* New York: Wiley.

Elkind, D., Koegler, R. R., & Koegler, E. G. (1964). Studies in perceptual development: II. Part-whole perception. *Child Development, 35,* 81–90.

Engen, T., Lewis, L., & Kaye, L. (1963). Olfactory responses and adaptation in the human neonate. *Journal of Comparative and Physiological Psychology, 56,* 73–77.

Epstein, L. H., & Cluss, P. A. (1986). Behavior genetics of childhood obesity. *Behavior Therapy, 17,* 324–334.

Erickson, J. (1988). Real American children: The challenge for after-school programs. *Child & Youth Care Quarterly, 17,* 86–90.

Espenschade, A. S., & Eckert, H. M. (1980). *Motor development.* Columbus, OH: Merrill.

Etringer, B., Altmaier, E., & Bowers, W. (1989). An investigation into the cognitive functioning of bulimic women. *Journal of Counseling and Development, 68,* 216–219.

Fantz, R. (1961). The origin of form perception. *Scientific American, 204,* 5, 66–72.

Fantz, R., Fagan, J. F., & Miranda, S. (1975). Early visual selectivity. In L. Cohen and P. Salapatek (Eds.), *Infant perception: From sensation to cognition* (Vol. 1: Basic visual processes). New York: Academic Press.

Field, T. M., Cohen, D., Garcia, R., & Greenberg, R. (1984). Mother-stranger face discrimination by the newborn. *Infant Behavior and Development, 7,* 19–25.

Flick, G. L. (1966). Sinistrality revisited: A perceptual-motor approach. *Child Development, 37,* 612–622.

Geber, M. (1958). The psycho-motor development of African children in the first year, and the influence of maternal behavior. *Journal of Social Psychology, 47,* 185–195.

Gesell, A. (1972). *The embryology of behavior: The beginnings of the human mind.* Westport, CT: Greenwood.

Gibson, E. J., & Walk, R. D. (1960). The visual cliff. *Scientific American, 202,* 64–71.

Gilbert, M. S. (1938). *Biography of the unborn.* Baltimore: Williams and Wilkins.

Goldsmith, H. H., & Gottesman, I. I. (1981). Origin of variation in behavioral styles: A longitudinal study of temperament in young twins. *Child Development, 52,* 91–103.

Gottesman, I. I. (1963). Heritability of personality: A demonstration. *Psychological Monographs, 77,* No. 572.

Grobstein, E. (1979). External human fertilization. *Scientific American, 240,* 66.

Gunnar, M., & Malone, S. (1985). Coping with aversive stimulation in the neonatal period: Quiet sleep and plasm cortisol levels during recovery from circumcision. *Child Development, 56,* 824–834.

Haith, M. M. (1980). *Rules that babies look by.* Hillsdale, NJ: Erlbaum.

Hale, G. A., & Taweel, S. S. (1974). Age differences in children's performance on measures of component selection and incidental learning. *Journal of Experimental Child Psychology, 18,* 107–116.

Halmi, K. A., Falk, J. R., & Schwartz, E. (1981). Binge-eating and vomiting: A survey of a college population. *Psychological Medicine, 11,* 697–706.

Halverson, H. M. (1931). An experimental study of prehension in infants by means of systematic cinema records. *Genetic Psychological Monographs, 10,* 107–286.

Hamill, P. V. V. (1977). *NCHS growth curves for children—Birth–18 years.* Vital and health statistics: Series 11, Data from the National Health Survey, No. 165. (DHEW Publication No. PHS 78–1650.) Washington, DC: U.S. Government Printing Office.

Heber, R. (1959). A manual on terminology and classification in mental retardation. *American Journal of Mental Deficiency Monograph Supplement, 64,* no. 2.

Hetherington, E. M., & Parke, R. D. (1981). *Contemporary readings in child development.* New York: McGraw-Hill.

Holmes, D. L. (1982). Early influences of prematurity, illness and prolonged hospitalization on infant behavior. *Developmental Psychology, 18,* 744–750.

Hopkins, B., & Westra, T. (1989). Maternal expectations of their infants' development: Some cultural differences. *Developmental Medicine and Child Neurology, 31,* 384–390.

Horrocks, J. (1962). *The psychology of adolescence.* Boston: Houghton Mifflin.

Jackson, C. M. (1929). Some aspects of form and growth. In W. J. Robbins, S. Brody, A. F. Hogan, C. M. Jackson, and C. W. Green (Eds.), *Growth.* New Haven: Yale University Press.

Jacobson, R., & Robins, C. (1989). Social dependence and social support in bulimic and nonbulimic women. *International Journal of Eating Disorders, 8,* 665–670.

Javel, E. (1980). Neurophysiological correlates of auditory maturation. *Annals of Otology, Rhinology, and Laryngology, 74,* 103–113. (Supplement).

Jones, M. (1957). The later careers of boys who were early or late maturing. *Child Development, 28,* 113–128.

Jones, M., & Bayley, N. (1950). Physical maturing among boys as related to behavior. *Journal of Educational Psychology, 41,* 129–148.

Klaus, M., & Klaus, P. (1986). *The amazing newborn.* Reading, MA: Addison-Wesley.

Kolata, G. B. (1978). Behavioral teratology: Birth defects of the mind. *Science, 202,* 732–734.

Kolata, G. B. (1986, April 4). Obese children: A growing problem. *Science, 232,* 20–21.

Langlois, J. H., Ritter, J. M., Roggman, L. A., & Vaughn, L. S. (1991). Facial diversity and infant preferences for attractive faces. *Developmental Psychology, 27,* 79–84.

Langlois, J. H., & Roggman, L. A. (1990). Attractive faces are only average. *Psychological Science, 1,* 115–121.

Langlois, J. H., Roggman, L. A., Casey, R. J., Ritter, J. M., Rieser-Danner, L. A., & Jenkins, V. Y. (1987). Infants' differential social responses to attractive and unattractive faces. *Developmental Psychology, 26,* 153–159.

Levenkron, S. (1982). *Treating and overcoming anorexia nervosa.* New York: Scribner's Sons.

Lewis, M., & Brooks-Gunn, J. (1979). *Social cognition and the acquisition of self.* New York: Plenum Press.

Lipsitt, L. P. (1969). Learning capacities in the human infant. In R. J. Robinson (Ed.), *Brain and early behavior.* New York: Academic Press.

Lipsitt, L. P., Engen, R., & Kaye, H. (1963). Developmental changes in the olfactory threshold of the neonate. *Child Development, 34,* 371–376.

Lozoff, B. (1989). Nutrition and behavior. *American Psychologist, 44,* 231–236.

Lucas, A. R. (1981). Toward understanding of anorexia nervosa as a disease entity. *Mayo Clinic Proc., 56,* 254–64.

Luria, A. R. (1975). *The working brain.* New York: Basic Books.

MacFarlane, A. (1977). *The psychology of childbirth.* Cambridge, MA: Harvard University Press.

MacLean, P. (1978). A mind of three minds: Educating the triune brain. In J. Chall and A. Minsky (Eds.), *The*

Seventy-seventh Yearbook of the National Society for the Study of Education.* Chicago: University of Chicago Press.

Marshall, W. A., & Tanner, J. M. (1970). Variation in the pattern of pubertal changes in boys. *Archive of Disease in Childhood, 44,* 291–303.

Maurer, D., & Salapatek, P. (1976). Developmental changes in the scanning of faces by young infants. *Child Development, 47,* 523–527.

Meltzoff, A. N., & Moore, M. K. (1977). Imitation of facial and manual gestures by human neonates. *Science, 198,* 75–78.

Minuchin, S., Rosman, B. L., & Baker, L. (1978). *Psychosomatic families: Anorexia nervosa in context.* Cambridge, MA: Harvard University Press.

Moore, J. K. (1983). *Before we were born* (2nd ed.). New York: Saunders.

Morse, P. A. (1979). The infancy of infant perception: The first decade of research. *Brain, behavior, and evolution, 16,* 351–373.

Neisser, U. (1979). The control of information pickup in selective looking. In A. D. Pick (Ed.), *Perception and its development: A tribute to Eleanore J. Gibson.* Hillsdale, NJ: Erlbaum.

Ornstein, R., & Thompson, R. F. (1991). *The amazing brain.* Boston: Houghton Mifflin.

Pallazzoli, M. S. (1978). *Self starvation.* New York: Aronson.

Palmer, R. L. (1988). *Anorexia nervosa: A guide for sufferers and their families.* New York: Penguin Books.

Parmelee, A., & Sigman, M. D. (1983). Perinatal brain development and behavior. In P. H. Mussen (Ed.), *Handbook of child psychology.* New York: Wiley.

Peskin, H. (1967). Pubertal onset and ego functioning. *Journal of Abnormal Psychology, 72,* 1–15.

Petersen, A. C., & Taylor, B. (1980). The biological approach to adolescence: Biological change and psychological adaptation. In Joseph Adelson (Ed.), *Handbook of adolescent psychology.* New York: Wiley.

Pollitt, E., & Thomson, C. (1988). Protein-calorie malnutrition and behavior: A review from psychology. In R. J. Wurtman and J. J. Wurtman (Eds.), *Nutrition and the brain* (pp. 261–306). New York: Raven Press.

Purpura, D. (1977). Factors contributing to abnormal neuronal development in cerebral cortex of human infant. In J. Berenberg (Ed.), *Brain fetal and infant development* (pp. 54–78). The Hague: Martinus Nijhoff Medical Division.

Richards, M. H., Boxer, A. M., Petersen, A. C., & Albrecht, R. (1990). Relation of weight to body image in pubertal girls and boys from two communities. *Development Psychology, 26,* 313–321.

Richardson, S. A. (1976). The influence of severe malnutrition in infancy on the intelligence of children at school age: An ecological perspective. In R. N. Walsh and W. T. Greenough (Eds.), *Environments as therapy for brain dysfunctions.* New York: Plenum Press.

Rivlin, R., & Gravell, K. (1984). *Deciphering the senses.* New York: Simon and Schuster.

Rodier, R. P. (1980). Chronology of neuron development: Animal studies and their clinical implications. *Developmental Medicine and Child Neurology, 22,* 525–545.

Sahler, O., & McAnamey, E. R. (1981). *The Child Between 3 to 18.* St. Louis: Mosby.

Salapatek, P., & Kessen, W. (1966). Visual scanning of triangles by the human newborn. *Journal of Experimental Child Psychology, 3,* 155–167.

Salt, P., Galler, J. R., & Ramsey, F. C. (1988). The influence of early malnutrition on subsequent behavioral development: The effects of maternal depressive symptoms. *Developmental and Behavioral Pediatrics, 9,* 1–5.

Scarr, S., & Kidd, K. (1983). Developmental behavioral genetics. In Paul H. Mussen (Ed.), *Handbook of child psychology.* New York: Wiley.

Schaal, B. (1986). Presumed olfactory exchanges between mother and neonate in humans. In J. LeCamus and R. Campan (Eds.), *Ethologie et Psychologie de l'Enfant* (pp. 100–110). Toulouse: Prival.

Schaal, B., Montagner, H., Hertling, E., Bolzoni, D., Moyse, A., & Quichon, R. (1980). Les stimulations olfactives dans les relations entre l'enfant et la mere (Reproduction). *Nutrition et Development, 20,* 843–858.

Schneider, B. A., Trehub, S. E., Morrongiello, B. A., & Thorpe, L. A. (1986). Auditory sensitivity in preschool children. *Journal of the Acoustical Society of America, 79,* 447–452.

Schulte, F. (1974). Nerve conduction velocity. In J. Berenberg, W. Caniaris, and R. Mosse (Eds.), *Pre- and postnatal development of the human brain.* New York: S. Karger.

Select Panel for the Promotion of Child Health. (1988). *Better health for children: A National Strategy.* (DHHS PHS Publication No. 79–55071). Washington, DC: U.S. Department of Health and Human Services.

Shand, N., & Kosawa, Y. (1985). Japanese and American behavior types at three months: Infants and infant-mother dyads. *Infant Behavior and Development, 17,* 225–240.

Shirley, M. M. (1961). *The first two years.* Minneapolis: University of Minneapolis Press.

Shuttleworth, F. K. (1939). The physical and mental growth of girls and boys age six through nineteen in relation to age of maximum growth. *Monographs of the Society for Research in Child Development, 4,* 245–247.

Silber, T. J. (1986). Approaching the adolescent patient: Pitfalls and solutions. *Journal of Adolescent Health Care, 7,* 31–40.

Smart, J. L. (1977). Early life malnutrition and later learning ability: A critical analysis. In A. Oliverio (Ed.), *Genetics, environment and intelligence* (215–235). Elsevier/North Holland: Amsterdam.

Steiner, J. E. (1977). Facial expressions of the neonate infant indicating the hedonics of food-related chemical stimuli. In J. M. Weiffenbach (Ed.), *Taste and development: The genesis of sweet preference.* Washington, DC: U.S. Government Printing Office.

Stephan, J. K., & Chow, B. F. (1969). The fetus and placenta in maternal dietary restriction. *Federation Proceedings, 28,* 915.

Super, C. (1976). Environmental effects on motor development: The case of "African infant precocity." *Developmental Medicine and Child Neurology, 18,* 561–567.

Tan, L. (1985). Laterality and motor skills in four-year-olds. *Child Development, 56,* 119–124.

Tanner, J. M. (1962). *Growth at adolescence* (2nd ed.). Oxford, England: Blackwell Scientific Publications.

Tanner, J. M. (1970). Physical growth. In P. Mussen (Ed.), *Carmichael's manual of child psychology* (Vol. 1) (pp. 77–155). New York: Wiley.

Tanner, J. M. (1971). Sequence, tempo, and individual variation in the growth and development of boys and girls aged twelve to sixteen. *Daedalus, 100,* 907–930.

Tanner, J. M. (1978). *Education and physical growth.* London: Hoddler and Stoughton.

Trehub, S. E., Schneider, B. A., Thorpe, L. A., & Judge, P. (1991). Observational measures of auditory sensitivity in early infancy. *Developmental Psychology, 27,* 40–49.

Vernon, M. D. (1976). Development of perception of form. In V. Hamilton and M. D. Vernon (Eds.), *The development of cognitive processes.* London: Academic Press.

Ward, S., Levinson, D., & Wackman, D. (1972). Children's attention to television commercials. In E. Rubinstein, G. Comstock, and J. Murray (Eds.), *Television and social behavior. 4, Television in day-to-day life: Patterns of use.* Washington, DC: U.S. Government Printing Office.

Werner, E. E. (1972). Infants around the world: Cross-cultural studies of psychomotor development from birth to two years. *Journal of Cross-Cultural Psychology, 3,* 111–134.

Whaley, L. F. (1974). *Understanding inherited disorders.* St. Louis: Mosby,

Williams, H. (1983). *Perceptual and motor development.* Englewood Cliffs, NJ: Prentice-Hall.

Windle, W. (1969). Brain damage by asphyxia at birth. *Scientific American, 221,* 77–84.

Winick, M. (1970). Cellular growth in intrauterine malnutrition. *Pediatric Clinics of North America, 17,* 69–77.

Winick, M., Meyer, K. K., & Harris, R. C. (1975). Malnutrition and environmental enrichment by early adoption. *Science, 190,* 1173–1175.

Winick, M., & Noble, A. (1966). Cellular response in rats during malnutrition at various ages. *Journal of Nutrition, 89,* 300–306.

Winick, M., & Rosso, P. (1969). Head circumference and cellular growth of the brain in normal and marasmic children. *Journal of Pediatrics, 74,* 774–778.

Yates, A. (1989). Current perspectives on the eating disorders: II. Treatment, outcome, and research directions. *Journal of the American Academy of Child/Adolescent Psychiatry, 29,* 1–9.

Zamenhof, S., Gravel, L., & van Marthens, E. (1971). Study of possible correlations between prenatal brain development and placenta weight. *Biology of the Neonate, 14,* 33–36.

Zamenhof, S., van Marthens, E., & Margolis, F. L. (1968). DNA (cell number) and protein in neonatal brain: Alteration by maternal dietary protein restriction. *Science, 160,* 322–323.

Chapter 6

Arlin, P. K. (1975). Cognitive development in adulthood: A fifth stage? *Developmental Psychology, 11,* 602–606.

Atkinson, R. C., & Raugh, M. R. (1975). An application of the mnemonic keyword method to the acquisition of a Russian vocabulary. *Journal of Experimental Psychology: Human Learning and Memory, 104,* 126–133.

Ault, R. (1977). *Children's cognitive development.* New York: Oxford University Press.

Azima, K. (1980). *Teaching students to reason: An application of Piaget.* East Lansing, MI: Michigan State University Learning and Evaluation Service.

Beilin, H. (1980). Piaget's theory: Refinement, revision, or rejection? In R. H. Kluwe and H. Spada (Eds.),

Developmental models of thinking. New York: Academic Press.

Block, J. (1982). Assimilation, accommodation, and the dynamics of personality development. *Child Development, 53,* 2, 283–295.

Bower, T. G. R. (1977). The object world of the infant. *Scientific American, 238,* 80–92.

Brainerd, C. J. (1978). *Piaget's theory on intelligence.* Englewood Cliffs, NJ: Prentice-Hall.

Brown, A. L., Bransford, J. D., Ferrara, R. A., & Campione, J. C. (1983). Learning, remembering and understanding. In J. H. Flavell and E. M. Markman (Eds.), *Handbook of child psychology.* New York: Wiley.

Bull, B. L., & Wittrock, M. C. (1973). Imagery in the learning of verbal definitions. *British Journal of Educational Psychology, 43,* 289–293.

Bullock, M. (1985). Causal reasoning and developmental changes over the preschool years. *Human Development, 28,* 169–191.

Chiappetta, E. L. (1975, March). *A perspective in formal thought development.* Paper presented at the National Association for Research in Science Teaching, Los Angeles.

Craik, F. I. M. (1979). Human memory. *Annual Review of Psychology* Vol. 30. Palo Alto, CA: Annual Reviews.

Crouse, J. H. (1974). Acquisition of college course material under conditions of repeated testing. *Journal of Educational Psychology, 66,* 367–372.

Diamond, A. (1985). Development of the ability to use recall to guide action, as indicated by infants' performance on AB. *Child Development, 56,* 868–883.

Donaldson, M. (1979). *Children's minds.* New York: Norton.

Elkind, D. (1966). Conceptual orientation shifts in children and adolescents. *Child Development, 37,* 493–498.

Elkind, D. (1971). Early childhood education: A Piagetian perspective. *The Principal, 6,* 48–65.

Elkind, D. (1980). Cognition in adolescence. In R. E. Muuss (Ed.), *Adolescent behavior and society.* New York: Random House.

Elkind, D. (1981). Adolescent thinking and the curriculum. *New York University Quarterly, Winter, XII,* 18–24.

Elkind, D. (1990). Cognition in adolescence. In R. E. Muuss (Ed.), *Adolescent behavior and society: A book of readings* (3rd ed.). New York: McGraw-Hill.

Epstein, H. T. (1979). Correlated brain and intelligence development in humans. In M. E. Hahn, C. Jensen, and B. C. Dudek (Eds.), *Development and evolution of brain size: Behavioral implications.* New York: Academic Press.

Epstein, H. T. (1980). Some biological bases of cognitive development. *Bulletin of the Orton Society, 30,* 56–62.

Flavell, J. H. (1963). *The developmental psychology of Jean Piaget.* Princeton, NJ: D. Van Nostrand.

Flavell, J. H. (1977). *Cognitive development.* Englewood Cliffs, NJ: Prentice-Hall.

Flavell, J. H. (1982). On cognitive development. *Child Development, 53,* 1–10.

Furth, H. (1970). *Piaget for teachers.* Englewood Cliffs, NJ: Prentice-Hall.

Gabel, K. (1980, September). Learning and development: Perspective studies. *Science Education, 64,* 4, 23–27.

Gelman, R., & Baillargeon, R. (1983). A review of some Piagetian concepts. In P. H. Mussen (Ed.), *Handbook of child psychology.* New York: Wiley.

Ginsburg, H., & Opper, S. (1969). *Piaget's theory of intellectual development.* Englewood Cliffs, NJ: Prentice-Hall.

Hobson, R. P. (1980). The question of egocentrism: The young child's competence in the coordination of perspectives. *Journal of Child Psychology and Psychiatry and Allied Sciences, 21,* 4, 325–331.

Inhelder, B., & Piaget, J. (1958). *The growth of logical thinking from childhood to adolescence.* New York: Basic Books.

Kagan, J. (1972). A conception of early adolescence. In J. Kagan, *Twelve to sixteen: Early adolescence.* New York: Norton.

Kail, R. V. (1979). *The development of memory in children.* San Francisco: W. H. Freeman.

Kamii, C. (1982). *Autonomy: The aim of education.* Unpublished manuscript.

Kamii, C., & DeVries, R. (1977). Piaget for early education. In M. C. Day and R. K. Parker (Eds.), *The preschool in action: Exploring early childhood programs.* Boston: Allyn and Bacon.

Kegan, R. (1982). *The evolving self.* Cambridge, MA: Harvard University Press.

Kuhn, D. (1979). The application of Piaget's theory of cognitive development to education. *Harvard Educational Review, 49,* 3, 18–23.

Labouvie-Vief, G. (1980). Beyond formal operations: Uses and limits of pure logic in life-span development. *Human Development, 23,* 141–161.

Levin, D. E., & Feldman, D. H. (1979, September 1–5). *Peer interactions as a source of cognitive development.* Pa-

per presented at the Annual Meeting of the American Psychological Association, New York.

Martel, J. (1974). *Smashed potatoes: A kid's eye view of the kitchen.* Boston: Houghton Mifflin.

Matlin, M. (1983). *Cognition.* New York: Holt, Rinehart and Winston.

Medin, D. L., & Ross, B. H. (1989). The specific character of abstract thought: Categorization, problem solving, and induction. In R. Sternberg (Ed.), *Advances in the psychology of human intelligence* (pp. 189–221). Hillsdale, NJ: Erlbaum.

Neimark, E. D. (1975). Intellectual development during adolescence. In J. D. Horowitz (Ed.), *Review of child development research* Vol. 4. Chicago: University of Chicago Press.

Neimark, E. D. (1979). Current status of formal operations research. *Human Development, 22,* 60–67.

Neisser, U. (1979). The concept of intelligence. In R. J. Sternberg and D. K. Detterman (Eds.), *Human intelligence: Perspectives on its theory and measurement.* Norwood, N.J.: Ablex.

Phillips, J. L. (1975). *The origins of intellect: Piaget's theory.* San Francisco: W. H. Freeman.

Phillips, J. L. (1982). Do children think as we do? *Improving College and University Teaching, 30,* 4, 142–158.

PhotOpinion. (1979, March 27). *Chicago Sun-Times,* p. 34.

Piaget, J. (1950a). *The psychology of intelligence.* (M. Piercy and D. E. Berlyne, Trans.). New York: Harcourt, Brace & Co.

Piaget, J. (1950b). *The origins of intelligence.* (M. Piercy and D. E. Berlyne, Trans.). New York: Harcourt, Brace & Co.

Piaget, J. (1952). Autobiography. In E. G. Boring (Ed.), *A history of psychology in autobiography* Vol. 4. New York: Russell and Russell.

Piaget, J. (1954). *The construction of reality in children.* (M. Cook, Trans.). New York: International University Press.

Piaget, J. (1965). *The moral judgment of the child.* New York: Free Press. (Original work published in 1932)

Piaget, J. (1967). *Six psychological studies.* New York: Random House.

Piaget, J. (1969). *The mechanisms of perception.* New York: Basic Books. (Original work published in 1930)

Piaget, J. (1970). *Science of education and psychology of the child.* New York: Orion Press.

Piaget, J. (1972). *Psychology and epistemology.* London: Penguin.

Piaget, J. (1973). *The child and reality*. New York: Viking Press.

Piaget, J. (1975). *The development of thought*. (A. Rosin, Trans.). New York: Viking Press.

Piaget, J., & Inhelder, B. (1969). *The psychology of the child*. New York: Basic Books.

Piaget, J., Jonckheere, A., & Mandebrot, B. (1958). La lecture de l'Experience. *Etudes d'Epistemologie Genetique V*. Paris: Presses Universitaires de France.

Prazdny, S. (1980). A computational study of a period of infant-object concept development. *Perception, 9*, 125–150.

Pulaski, M. (1980). *Understanding Piaget*. New York: Harper & Row.

Roberge, J. J., & Flexer, B. K. (1979). Further examination of formal operation reasoning abilities. *Child Development, 50*, 478–484.

Ross, R. J. (1975). The development of formal thinking for high and average achieving adolescents. In G. I. Lubin (Ed.), *Piagetian theory and the helping profession*. Los Angeles: Publication Department Bookstores, U.S.C.

Scholnick, E. K. (1983). Why are new trends in conceptual representation a challenge to Piaget's theory? In E. K. Scholnick (Ed.), *New trends in conceptual representation: Challenges to Piaget's theory*. Hillsdale, NJ: Erlbaum.

Siegler, R. S. (1978). The origins of scientific reasoning. In R. S. Siegler (Ed.), *Children's thinking: What develops?* Hillsdale, NJ: Erlbaum.

Sprinthall, N. A., & Sprinthall, R. C. (1989). *Educational psychology: A developmental approach* (pp. 128–132). New York: McGraw-Hill.

Sternberg, R. J., & Powell, J. S. (1983). The development of intelligence. In J. H. Flavell and E. M. Markman (Eds.), *Handbook of child psychology Vol. 3*. New York: Wiley and Sons.

Sund, R. B. (1976). *Piaget for teachers*. Columbus, OH: Merrill/Macmillan.

Thomas, R. M. (1979). *Comparing theories of child development*. Belmont, CA: Wadsworth.

Tomlinson-Keasey, C., Eisert, D. C., Kahle, L. R., Hardy-Brown, K., & Keasey, B. (1979). The structure of concrete operational thought. *Child Development, 50*, 1153–1163.

Valler, T. (1981). *Using Piagetian tasks in assessing levels of cognitive development in children*. Unpublished manuscript.

Vlietstra, A. (1982). Children's responses to talk instructions: Age changes and training efforts. *Child Development, 53*, 534–542.

Wadsworth, B. J. (1980). *Piaget for classroom teachers*. New York: Longman.

Wadsworth, B. J. (1981). Misinterpretations of Piaget's theory. *The Educational Digest, 47*, 56–60.

Wadsworth, B. J. (1989). *Piaget's theory of cognitive and affective development*. New York: Longman.

Winer, G. A. (1980). Class-inclusion reasoning in children: A review of the empirical literature. *Child Development, 51*, 309–328.

Chapter 7

Ackerman, B. P. (1984). Item specific and relational encoding effects in children's recall and recognition in memory for words. *Journal of Experimental Child Psychology, 37*, 426–450.

Andreassen, C., & Waters, H. S. (1989). Organization during study: Relationships between metamemory, strategy use, and performance. *Journal of Educational Psychology, 2*, 190–195.

Atkinson, R. C., & Raugh, M. R. (1975). An application of the mnemonic keyword method to the acquisition of a Russian vocabulary. *Journal of Experimental Psychology: Human Learning and Memory, 104*, 126–133.

Atkinson, R. C., & Shiffrin, R. M. (1968). Human memory: A proposed system and its control processes. In K. W. Spence and J. T. Spence (Eds.), *The psychology of learning and motivation: Advances in research and theory* Vol. 2. New York: Academic Press.

Ault, R. (1977). *Children's cognitive development*. New York: Oxford University Press.

Beal, C. (1985). Development of knowledge about the use of cues to aid prospective retrieval. *Child Development, 56*, 631–642.

Bjorklund, D. F. (1987). How age changes in knowledge base contribute to the development of children's memory: An interpretive review. *Developmental Review, 7*, 86–92.

Bjorklund, D. F. (1989). *Children's thinking: Developmental function and individual differences*. Pacific Grove, CA: Brooks/Cole.

Bjorklund, D. F., & Muir, J. E. (1988). Children's development of free recall memory: Remembering on their own. In R. Vasta (Ed.), *Annals of child development* (Vol. 5). Greenwich, CN: JAI Press.

Borovsky, D., & Rovee-Collier, C. (1990). Contextual constraints on memory retrieval at six months. *Child Development, 61*, 1569–1583.

Brainerd, C. J., Kingma, J., & Howe, M. L. (1986). Spread of encoding and the development of organization in memory. *Canadian Journal of Psychology, 40,* 203–223.

Brainerd, C. J., & Reyna, V. F. (1988a). *Can memorability gradients explain the development of forgetting?* Manuscript submitted for publication.

Brainerd, C. J., & Reyna, V. F. (1988b). *Development of retention: Amnesia, hyperamnesia, forgetting, and reminiscence.* Manuscript submitted for publication.

Brown, A. L., Bransford, J. D., Ferrara, R. A., & Campione, J. C. (1983). Learning, remembering and understanding. In J. H. Flavell and E. M. Markman (Eds.), *Handbook of child psychology.* New York: Wiley.

Brown, A. L., & Scott, M. S. (1971). Recognition memory for pictures in preschool children. *Journal of Experimental Child Psychology, 11,* 401–412.

Bull, B. L., & Wittrock, M. C. (1973). Imagery in the learning of verbal definitions. *British Journal of Educational Psychology, 43,* 289–293.

Case, R. (1985). *Intellectual development: Birth to adulthood.* New York: Academic Press.

Case, R., Kurland, M., & Goldberg, J. (1982). Operational efficiency and the growth of short-term memory span. *Journal of Experimental Child Psychology, 33,* 386–404.

Ceci, S. J. (1980). A developmental study of multiple encoding and its relationship to age-related changes in free recall. *Child Development, 51,* 892–895.

Chi, M. T. H. (1978). Knowledge structure and memory development. In R. S. Siegler (Ed.), *Children's thinking: What develops?* Hillsdale, NJ: Erlbaum.

Cox, B. D., Ornstein, P. A., Naus, M. J., Maxfield, D., & Zimler, J. (1989). Children's concurrent use of rehearsal and organizational strategies. *Developmental Psychology, 25,* 619–627.

Craik, F. I. M. (1979). Human memory. *Annual Review of Psychology* Vol. 30. Palo Alto, CA: Annual Reviews.

DeLoache, J. (1984). Oh where, oh where: Memory-based searching by very young children. In C. Sophian (Ed.), *Origins of cognitive skills.* Hillsdale, NJ: Erlbaum.

DeLoache, J. (1986). Memory in very young children: Exploitation of cues to the location of a hidden object. *Cognitive Development, 1,* 123–138.

DeLoache, J., Cassidy, D., & Brown, A. (1985). Precursors of mnemonic strategies in very young children's memory. *Child Development, 56,* 125–137.

Diamond, A. (1985). Development of the ability to use recall to guide action, as indicated by infants' performance on AB. *Child Development, 56,* 868–883.

Donaldson, M. (1979). *Children's minds.* New York: W. W. Norton.

Enns, J. T., & Akhtar, N. (1989). A developmental study of filtering in visual attention. *Child Development, 60,* 1188–1199.

Epstein, H. (1980). Some biological bases of cognitive development. *Bulletin of the Orton Society, 30,* 56–62.

Fabricius, W. V., & Cavalier, L. (1989). The role of causal theories about memory in young children's memory strategy choice. *Child Development, 60,* 298–308.

Fagan, J. F., III (1973). Infants' delayed recognition memory and forgetting. *Journal of Experimental Child Psychology, 16,* 424–450.

Fagan, J. F., III (1974). Infant recognition memory: The effects of length of familiarization and type of discrimination task. *Child Development, 47,* 527–638.

Flavell, J. H. (1985). *Cognitive development* (2nd ed.). Englewood Cliffs, NJ: Prentice-Hall.

Flavell, J. H., Beach, D. R., & Chinsky, J. H. (1966). Spontaneous verbal rehearsal in a memory task as a function of age. *Child Development, 37,* 283–299.

Flavell, J. H., Friedrichs, A. G., & Hoyt, J. D. (1970). Developmental changes in memorization processes. *Cognitive Psychology, 1,* 324–340.

Gabel, K. (1980, September). Learning and development: Perspective studies. *Science Education, 64,* 23–27.

Gibson, E. J. (1969). *Principles of perceptual learning and development.* Englewood Cliffs, NJ: Prentice-Hall.

Gibson, E. J., & Rader, N. (1979). Attention: The perceiver as performer. In G. Hale and M. Lewis (Eds.), *Attention and cognitive development.* New York: Plenum.

Ginsburg, H., & Oper, S. (1969). *Piaget's theory of intellectual development.* Englewood Cliffs, NJ: Prentice-Hall.

Haith, M. M., Morrison, F. J., Rheingold, K., & Mindes, P. (1970). Short-term memory for visual information in children and adults. *Journal of Experimental Child Psychology, 9,* 454–469.

Hale, G. A., & Taweel, S. S. (1974). Age differences in children's performance on measures of component selection and incidental learning. *Journal of Experimental Child Psychology, 18,* 107–116.

Hall, J. W., & Tinzmann, M. B. (1989). Sources of improved recall during the school years. *Bulletin of the Psychonomic Society, 27,* 315–316.

Howe, M. L. (1987). *The development of forgetting in childhood.* Paper presented at the biennial meeting of the Society for Research in Child Development, Baltimore.

Howe, M. L., & Brainerd, C. J. (1989). Development of children's long-term retention. *Developmental Review, 9,* 301–340.

James, W. (1907). *The principles of psychology.* New York: Henry Holt. (Original work published 1890)

Justice, E. M. (1985). Categorization as a preferred memory strategy: Developmental changes during elementary school. *Developmental Psychology, 21,* 1105–1110.

Kail, R. V. (1979). *The development of memory in children.* San Francisco: Freeman.

Kamii, C. (1984). Autonomy: The aim of education envisaged by Piaget. *Phi Delta Kappan, 65,* 410–415.

Karplus, R. (1975). *Proportional resources and control of variables in seven countries.* Unpublished manuscript.

Keeney, T. J., Cannizzo, S. R., & Flavell, J. H. (1967). Spontaneous and induced verbal rehearsal in a recall task. *Child Development, 38,* 953–966.

Kegan, R. (1982). *The evolving self.* Cambridge, MA: Harvard University Press.

Kellas, G., McCauley, C., & McFarland, C. E. (1975). Developmental aspects of storage and retrieval. *Journal of Experimental Child Psychology, 19,* 51–62.

Keniston, H. H., & Flavell, J. H. (1979). A developmental study of intelligent retrieval. *Child Development, 50,* 1144–1152.

Knopf, I. J. (1979). *Childhood psychopathology.* Englewood Cliffs, NJ: Prentice-Hall.

Kreutzer, M. A., Leonard, C., & Flavell, J. H. (1975). An interview study of children's knowledge about memory. *Monographs of the Society for Research in Child Development, 3,* 590–598.

Leal, L., Crays, N., & Moely, B. E. (1985). Training children to use a self-monitoring study strategy in preparation for recall: Maintenance and generalization effects. *Child Development, 56,* 643–653.

Lehman, E. B., Mikesell, J. W., & Doherty, S. C. (1985). Long-term retention of information about presentation modality by children and adults. *Memory and Cognition, 13,* 21–28.

List, J., Keating, D. P., & Merriman, W. E. (1985). Differences in memory retrieval: A construct validity investigation. *Child Development, 56,* 138–151.

Loftus, E. (1980). *Memory.* Reading, MA: Addison-Wesley.

Mandler, J. M., & Robinson, C. A. (1978). Developmental changes in picture recognition. *Journal of Experimental Child Psychology, 26,* 122–136.

Masankay, Z. S., McCluskey, K. A., McIntyre, C. W., Sims-Knight, J., Vaughn, B. E., & Flavell, J. (1974). The early development of inferences about the visual percepts of others. *Child Development, 45,* 357–366.

Massaro, D. W. (1972). Perceptual images, processing time, and perceptual units in auditory perception. *Psychological Review, 79,* 124–145.

Massaro, D. W., & Burke, D. (1991). Perceptual development and auditory backward recognition masking. *Developmental Psychology, 27,* 85–96.

Matlin, M. (1983). *Cognition.* New York: Holt, Rinehart and Winston.

McGilly, K., & Siegler, R. S. (1989). How children choose among serial recall strategies. *Child Development, 60,* 172–182.

McGilly, K., & Siegler, R. S. (1990). The influence of encoding and strategic knowledge on children's choices among serial recall strategies. *Developmental Psychology, 26,* 931–941.

Miller, G. A. (1956). The magical number seven, plus or minus two: Some limits on our capacity for processing information. *Psychological Review, 63,* 81–97.

Miller, P. H., & Zalenski, R. (1982). Preschoolers' knowledge about attention. *Developmental Psychology, 18,* 871–875.

Moely, B. E., Olson, F. A., Halwes, T. G., & Flavell, J. (1969). Production deficiency in young children's clustered recall. *Developmental Psychology, 1,* 26–34.

Mussen, P. H., Conger, J., & Kagan, J. (1984). *Child development and personality.* New York: Harper & Row.

Naus, M. J., Ornstein, P. A., & Aivano, S. (1977). Developmental changes in memory: The effects of processing time and rehearsal instructions. *Journal of Experimental Child Psychology, 23,* 237–251.

Neimark, E. D. (1975). Intellectual development during adolescence. In J. D. Horowitz (Ed.), *Review of child development research* Vol. 4. Chicago: University of Chicago Press.

Neimark, E. D. (1979). Current status of formal operations research. *Human Development, 22,* 60–67.

Neisser, U. (1979). The concept of intelligence. In R. J. Sternberg and D. K. Detterman (Eds.), *Human intelligence: Perspectives on its theory and measurement.* Norwood, NJ: Ablex.

Nelson, C. A., & Collins, P. F. (1991). Event-related potential and looking-time analysis of infants' responses to familiar and novel events: Implications for visual recognition memory. *Developmental Psychology, 27,* 50–58.

Ornstein, P. A., Medlin, R. G., Stone, B. P., & Naus, M. J. (1985). Retrieving for rehearsal: An integrative analysis of active rehearsal in children's memory. *Developmental Psychology, 21,* 633–641.

Ornstein, P. A., Naus, M. J., & Liberty, C. (1975). Rehearsal and organizational processes in children's memory. *Child Development, 26,* 818–830.

Pearson, D. A., & Lane, D. M. (1990). Visual attention movements: A developmental study. *Child Development, 61,* 1779–1795.

Perlmutter, M. (Ed.). (1980). *Children's memory: New directions for child development.* San Francisco: Jossey-Bass.

Perret-Clarmont, A. N. (1980). *Social interaction and cognitive development in children.* London: Academic Press.

Pick, A. D. (1980). Cognition: Psychological perspectives. In H. C. Triandis and W. Lonner (Eds.), *Handbook of cross-cultural psychology* Vol. 3. Boston: Allyn and Bacon.

Pick, A. D., Christy, M. D., & Frankel, G. W. (1972). A developmental study of visual selective attention. *Journal of Experimental Child Psychology, 14,* 165–175.

Pick, A. D., Frankel, D. G., & Hess, V. L. (1975). Children's attention: The development of selectivity. In E. M. Hetherington (Ed.), *Review of child development research.* Chicago: University of Chicago Press.

Prazdny, S. (1980). A computational study of a period of infant-object concept development. *Perception, 9,* 125–150.

Pressley, M. (1982). Elaboration and memory development. *Child Development, 53,* 296–309.

Roberge, J. J. (1980). Control of variables and proportional reasoning in early adolescence. *The Journal of General Psychology, 3,* 57–63.

Rovee-Collier, C., & Fagen, J. W. (1981). The retrieval of memory in early infancy. In L. P. Lipsitt (Ed.), *Advances in infancy research* (pp. 226–254). Norwood, NJ: Ablex.

Schiff, A. R., & Knopf, I. J. (1985). The effect of task demands on attention allocation in children of different ages. *Child Development, 56,* 621–630.

Seamon, J. G. (1980). *Memory and cognition.* New York: Oxford University Press.

Shepard, R. N. (1967). Recognition memory for words, sentences, and pictures. *Journal of Verbal Learning and Verbal Behavior, 6,* 156–163.

Siegler, R. S. (1978). The origins of scientific reasoning. In R. S. Siegler (Ed.), *Children's thinking: What develops?* Hillsdale, NJ: Erlbaum.

Siegler, R. S. (1983). Information-processing approaches to development. In P. H. Mussen (Ed.), *Handbook of child psychology* (Vol. 1) (4th ed.). In W. Kessen (Ed.), *History, theory, and methods.* New York: Wiley.

Siegler, R. S. (1986). *Children's thinking: What develops?* Englewood Cliffs, NJ: Prentice-Hall.

Sigel, I. E. (1985). *Parent belief systems.* Hillsdale, NJ: Erlbaum.

Sodian, B., & Schneider, W. (1990). Children's understanding of cognitive cuing: How to manipulate cues to fool a competitor. *Child Development, 61,* 697–704.

Sperling, G. (1960). The information available in brief visual presentations. *Psychological Monographs, 74* (whole issue).

Sternberg, R. J., & Powell, J. S. (1983). The development of intelligence. In J. H. Flavell and E. M. Markman (Eds.), *Handbook of child psychology* (Vol. 3). New York: Wiley.

Tinzmann, M. B., & Hall, J. W. (1989). Nonstrategic factors underlie improvements in free recall during middle childhood. *Bulletin of the Psychonomic Society, 27,* 317–319.

Tomlinson-Keasey, C., Eisert, D. C., Kahle, L. R., Hardy-Brown, K., & Keasey, B. (1978). The structure of concrete operational thought. *Child Development, 50,* 1153–1163.

Vander Linde, E., Morrongiello, B. A., & Rovee-Collier, C. (1985). Determinants of retention in 8-week-old infants. *Developmental Psychology, 21,* 601–613.

Vlietstra, A. (1982). Children's responses to talk instructions: Age changes and training efforts. *Child Development, 53,* 534–542.

Walen, S. R. (1970). Recall in children and adults. *Journal of Verbal Learning and Verbal Behavior, 9,* 94–98.

Weikart, D. P. (1973). *Development of effective preschool programs: A report on the results of the high/scope Ypsilanti preschool projects.* Paper presented at the High/Scope Educational Research Foundation Conference, Ann Arbor, MI.

Wellman, H. W. (1977). Preschoolers' understanding of memory-related variables. *Child Development, 48,* 1720–1723.

Wellman, H. W. (1978). Knowledge of the interaction of memory variables: A developmental study of metamemory. *Developmental Psychology, 14,* 24–29.

Wellman, H. W., Collins, J., & Glieberman, J. (1981). Understanding the combination of memory variables: Developing conceptions of memory limitations. *Child Development, 32,* 1313–1317.

Chapter 8

Anastasi, A. (1956). Intelligence and family size. *Psychological Bulletin, 53,* 187–209.

Andrews, G. R., & Debus, R. L. (1978). Persistence and the causal perception of failure: Modifying cognitive attributions. *Journal of Educational Psychology, 70,* 154–166.

Atkinson, J. W., & Raynor, J. O. (1978). *Personality, motivation and achievement.* New York: Wiley.

Barron, F. (1969). *Creative person and creative process.* New York: Holt, Rinehart and Winston.

Beane, J. A. (1983, May). Self-concept and self-esteem in the middle school. *NASSP Bulletin, 63–69.*

Beneson, J., & Dweck, C. (1986). The development of trait explanations and self-evaluations in the academic and social domains. *Child Development, 57,* 1179–1187.

Binet, A. (1916a). *The development of intelligence in children.* (E. S. Kite, Trans.). Baltimore: Williams & Wilkins.

Binet, A. (1916b). *The intelligence of the feeble-minded.* (E. S. Kite, Trans.). Baltimore: Williams & Wilkins.

Binet, A., & Simon, T. (1905). Application des methodes norvelles au diagnostic du nuveau intellectuel chez des enfants normaux et anormaus d'hospice d'ecole primarire. *L'Anne Psychologique, 11,* 245–336.

Bleedorn, B. B. (1982, April–May). Humor as an indicator of giftedness. *Roeper Review, 4,* 4, 33–34.

Blomquist, H., Gustavson, H. H., Holmgren, G., Nordenson, I., & Palsson-Strade, U. (1983). Fragile X syndrome in mildly mentally retarded children in a northern Swedish county: A prevalence study. *Clinical Genetics, 24,* 393–398.

Bloom, B. S. (1974). Time and learning. *American Psychologist, 29,* 682–688.

Bogen, J. E. (1975). Some educational aspects of hemispheric specialization. *UCLA Educator, 17,* 24–32.

Bornstein, M. (1989). Information processing (habituation) in infancy and stability in cognitive development. *Human Development, 32,* 129–136.

Bornstein, M., & Sigman, M. D. (1986). Continuity in mental development from infancy. *Child Development, 57,* 251–274.

Bradley, R. H., & Caldwell, B. M. (1976). The relation of infants' home environment to mental test performance at fifty-four months: A follow-up study. *Child Development, 47,* 1172–1174.

Bradley, R. H., Caldwell, B. M., & Elardo, R. (1977). Home environment, social status, and mental test performance. *Journal of Educational Psychology, 69,* 697.

Bregman, J. D., Leckman, J. F., & Ort, S. I. (1988). Fragile X syndrome: Genetic predisposition to psychopathology. *Journal of Autism and Developmental Disorders, 18,* 343–354.

Bronfenbrenner, U. (1974). Is early intervention effective? *Columbia Teachers College Record, 76,* 279–303.

Bronfenbrenner, U. (1986). Ecology of the family as a context for human development: Research perspectives. *Developmental Psychology, 22,* 723–742.

Brooker, W., & Passalacqua, J. (1981). Comparison of aggregate self-concepts for populations with different reference groups. In M. Lynch (Ed.), *Self-concept: Advances in theory and research.* Cambridge, MA: Ballinger.

Cameron, J., Livson, N., & Bayley, N. (1967). Infant socializations and their relationships to mature intelligence. *Science, 157,* 331–333.

Cattell, R. B. (1971). *Abilities: Their structure, growth, and action.* Boston: Houghton-Mifflin.

Chapman, M., & Skinner, E. A. (1989). Children's agency beliefs, cognitive performance and conceptions of effort and ability: Interaction of individual and developmental differences. *Child Development, 60,* 1229–1238.

Chapman, M., & Skinner, E. A., & Baltes, P. B. (1990). Interpreting correlations between children's perceived control and cognitive performance: Control, agency, or means-ends beliefs? *Developmental Psychology, 23,* 246–253.

Chechile, R. A., Richman, C. L., Topinka, C., & Ehrensbeck, K. (1981). A developmental study of the storage and retrieval of information. *Child Development, 52,* 251–259.

Clark, J. W., & Clark, J. S. (1979). The art of soaring. *Journal of Creative Behavior, 13,* 110–117.

Connell, J. (1985). A new multidimensional measure of children's perceptions of control. *Child Development, 56,* 1018–1041.

Conoley, J. C., & Kramer, J. J. (Eds.). (1989). *The 10th mental measurements yearbook.* Lincoln: The University of Nebraska Press.

Cronbach, L. J. (1984). *Essentials of testing.* New York: Harper & Row.

Cross, H. J., & Allen, J. (1969). *Relationship between memories of parental behavior and academic achievement motivation.* Proceedings of the 77th Annual Convention, American Psychological Association, Washington, DC.

Deci, E. L., & Ryan, R. M. (1985). *Intrinsic motivation and self-determination in human behavior.* New York: Plenum.

DiLalla, L. F., Thompson, L. A., Plomin, R., Phillips, K., Fagan, J. F., & Haith, M. M. (1990). Infant predictors of preschool and adult IQ: A study of infant twins and their parents. *Developmental Psychology, 26,* 759–769.

Domino, G. (1979). Creativity and the home environment. *Gifted Child Quarterly, 23,* 45–67.

Dornbusch, S. M., Ritter, P. L., Leiderman, P. H., Roberts, D. F., & Fraleigh, M. J. (1987). The relation of parenting style in adolescent school performance. *Child Development, 58,* 1244–1257.

Dweck, C. S. (1975). The role of expectations and attributions in the alleviation of learned helplessness. *Journal of Personality and Social Psychology, 31,* 674–685.

Dweck, C. S. (1983). Achievement motivation. In P. H. Mussen (Ed.), *Handbook of child psychology.* New York: Wiley.

Dweck, C. S., & Elliott, E. S. (1983). *A model of achievement motivation: A theory of its origins, and a framework for motivational development.* Unpublished manuscript, Harvard University, Cambridge, MA. Reported in P. H. Mussen (Ed.), *Handbook of child psychology.* New York: Wiley.

Edelman, M. W. (1987). *Families in peril: An agenda for social change.* Cambridge, MA: Harvard University Press.

Fagan, J. F., III, & McGrath, S. K. (1981). Infant recognition memory and later intelligence. *Intelligence, 5,* 121–130.

Feldman, D. H. (1989). Creativity: Proof that development occurs. In W. Damon (Ed.), *Child development: Today and tomorrow* (pp. 240–255). San Francisco: Jossey-Bass.

Feldman, N. S., & Ruble, D. N. (1977). Awareness of social comparison interest and motivations: A developmental study. *Journal of Educational Psychology, 69,* 579–585.

Garber, H. L., & Heber, R. (1981). The efficacy of early intervention with family rehabilitation. In M. J. Begab, H. C. Haywood, and H. L. Garber (Eds.), *Psychosocial influences in retarded performance: Vol. 2. Strategies for improving competence* (pp. 71–88). Baltimore: University Park Press.

Gardner, H. (1983). *Frames of mind: The theory of multiple intelligences.* New York: Basic Books.

Getzels, J. S., & Jackson, P. W. (1962). *Creativity and intelligence.* New York: Wiley.

Ghiselin, B. (1955). *The creative process.* New York: Mentor.

Glover, J. A. (1979). *A parents' guide to intellectual testing.* Chicago: Nelson-Hall.

Goodenough, F. L. (1926). *Measurement of intelligence by drawings.* New York: World Book.

Gray, W. Q., & Wandersman, L. P. (1980). The methodology of home-based intervention studies: Problems and promising strategies. *Child Development, 51,* 993–1009.

Grolnick, W. S., & Ryan, R. M. (1989). Parent styles associated with children's self-regulation and competence in school. *Journal of Educational Psychology, 81,* 143–154.

Guilford, J. P. (1967). *The nature of human intelligence.* New York: McGraw-Hill.

Guilford, J. P. (1971). *The analysis of intelligence.* New York: McGraw-Hill.

Haber, R. N. (1970). How we remember what we see. *Scientific American, 222,* 5, 104–12.

Hadamard, J. (1945). *The psychology of invention in the mathematical field.* New York: Dover.

Hagerman, R. J., Kemper, M. G., & Hudson, M. (1985). Learning disabilities and attention problems in boys with fragile X syndrome. *American Journal of Diseases of Children, 139,* 674–678.

Hamachek, D. E. (1978). *Encounters with the self.* New York: Holt.

Harter, S. (1983). Developmental perspectives on the self-system. In E. M. Hetherington (Ed.), *Handbook of child psychology: Vol. 4. Socialization, personality, and social development* 4th ed. (pp. 275–386). New York: Wiley.

Harter, S., Whitesell, N., & Kowalski, P. (1987). *The effects of educational transitions on children's perception of competence and motivation orientation.* Manuscript submitted for publication.

Heber, R. (Ed.). (1959). A manual on terminology and classification in mental retardation. *American Journal of Mental Deficiency Monograph Supplement, 64,* 56–72.

Heckhausen, H. (1982). The development of achievement motivation. In W. W. Hartup (Ed.), *Review of child development research.* Chicago: University of Chicago Press.

Hoffman, B. (1978). *The tyranny of testing.* Westport, CT: Greenwood.

Honzik, M. P. (1983). Measuring mental abilities in infancy: The value and limitations. In M. Lewis (Ed.), *Origins of intelligence in infancy and early childhood.* New York: Plenum.

Jencks, C. (1972). *Inequality: A reassessment of the effect of family and schooling in America.* New York: Basic Books.

Jensen, A. R. (1969). How much can we boost IQ and scholastic achievement? *Harvard Educational Review, 39,* 1–123.

Kamin, L. J. (1974). *The science of politics of IQ.* Hillsdale, NJ: Erlbaum.

Kelly, J. A., & Worrell, L. (1977). The joint and differential perceived contribution of parents to adolescents' cognitive functioning. *Developmental Psychology, 13,* 282–283.

Kourilsky, M., & Keislar, E. (1983, April). The effect of the success-oriented teachers on pupils' perceived personal control and attitude toward learning. *Contemporary Educational Psychology, 8,* 2, 158–167.

LaBoeuf, M. (1980). *Imagineering.* New York: McGraw-Hill.

Lachiewicz, A. M., Guillion, C. M., Spiridigliozzi, G. A., & Aylsworth, A. S. (1987). Declining IQs of young males with fragile X syndrome. *American Journal on Mental Retardation, 92,* 272–278.

Landesman, S., & Ramey, C. (1989). Developmental psychology and mental retardation. *American Psychologist, 44,* 409–415.

Lazar, I., Darlington, R., Murray, H., Royce, J., & Snipper, A. (1982). Lasting effects of early education: A report from the Consortium for Longitudinal Studies. *Monographs of the Society for Research in Child Development, 47* (2–3, Serial No. 195).

Lee, Y. (1987). *Academic success of East Asian Americans: An ethnographic comparative study of East Asian Americans and Anglo Americans academic achievement.* Seoul: American Studies Institute, Seoul National University Press.

Licht, B. G. (1980). *Determinants of academic achievement: The interaction of children's achievement orientations with task requirements.* Unpublished doctoral dissertation, University of Illinois, Urbana.

Lynn, R. (1977). The intelligence of the Japanese. *Bulletin of the British Psychological Society, 30,* 69–72.

Lynn, R. (1982). IQ in Japan and the United States shows a growing disparity. *Nature, 297,* 222–223.

Maccoby, E. E., & Martin, J. A. (1983). Socialization in the context of the family: Parent-child interaction. In E. M. Hetherington (Ed.), *Handbook of child psychology.* New York: Wiley.

Mansfield, R. S., & Busse, T. V. (1981). *The psychology of creativity and discovery.* Chicago: Nelson-Hall.

Markman, E. M. (1977). Realizing that you don't understand: A preliminary investigation. *Child Development, 48,* 986–992.

McCall, R. B. (1985). The confluence model and theory. *Child Development, 56,* 217–218.

McCall, R. B., Appelbaum, M. I., & Hogarty, P. S. (1973). Developmental changes in mental performance. *Monographs of the Society for Research in Child Development, 38,* (3, Serial No. 150).

McClelland, D. C. (1973). Testing for competence rather than intelligence. *American Psychologist, 28,* 1–14.

McKusick, V. A. (1986). *Mendelian inheritance in man.* Baltimore: Johns Hopkins University Press.

Miller, A. (1985). A developmental study of the cognitive basis of performance impairment after failure. *Journal of Personality and Social Psychology, 49,* 529–538.

Motamedi, K. D. (1982). Extending the concept of creativity. *Journal of Creative Behavior, 16,* 2, 75–88.

Nicholls, J. G. (1978). The development of the concepts of effort and ability, perception of academic attainment, and the understanding that difficult tasks require more ability. *Child Development, 49,* 800–814.

Nicholls, J. G. (1979). Development of perception of own attainment and causal attributions for success and failure in reading. *Journal of Educational Psychology, 71,* 94–99.

Nussbaum, R. L., & Ledbetter, D. H. (1988). Fragile X syndrome: A unique mutation in man. *Annual Review of Genetics, 20,* 109–145.

Ochse, R. (1989). Toward a prediction and stimulation of creativity. *South African Journal of Psychology, 19,* 113–121.

Odom, J., & Shaughnessy, M. (1989). Personality and mathematical achievement. *Psychological Reports, 63,* 1195–1201.

Ogbu, J. (1988). Black education: A cultural-ecological perspective. In H. P. McAdoo (Ed.), *Black families* (pp. 169–186). Beverly Hills: Sage.

Orinstein, A. S. (1962). An investigation of parental child-rearing attitudes and creativity in children. *Dissertation Abstracts, 22,* 4085–4086.

Osofsky, J. E. (Ed.). (1979). *Handbook on infant development.* New York: Wiley.

Parsons, J. E. (1978). *The development of attributions, expectancies, and persistence.* Unpublished manuscript, University of Michigan, Lansing.

Parsons, J. E., & Ruble, D. N. (1972). Attributional processes related to the development of achievement-related affect and expectancy. *American Psychological Association Proceedings, 80th Annual Convention,* 105–106.

Parsons, J. E., & Ruble, D. N. (1977). The development of achievement-related expectancies. *Child Development, 48,* 1075–1079.

Patterson, C. J., Kupersmidt, J. B., & Vaden, N. A. (1990). Income level, gender, ethnicity, and household composition as predictors of children's school-based competence. *Child Development, 61,* 485–494.

Peak, L. (1989, April). Who teaches Taro to behave at school?: Training classroom conduct in Japanese preschools and elementary school. In H. Ginsburg (Chair), *Academic socialization in ethnic groups*. Symposium conducted at the biennial meeting of the Society for Research in Child Development, Kansas City, MO.

Penfield, W. (1975). *The mystery of the mind*. Princeton: Princeton University Press.

Perino, S., & Perino, J. (1981). *Parenting the gifted: Developing the promise*. New York: Bowker.

Perkins, D. N. (1981). *The mind's best work*. Cambridge, MA: Harvard University Press.

Polachek, S. W., Kniesner, T. J., & Harwood, H. J. (1978). Educational production functions. *Journal of Educational Statistics, 3*, 209–231.

Provence, S., & Naylor, A. (1983). *Working with disadvantaged parents and children: Scientific issues and practice*. New Haven, CT: Yale University Press.

Reid, I. F. (1972). An exploratory study of the relationship between selected environmental variables and a measure of creativity in children. *Dissertation Abstracts International, 32*, 5619A.

Rejskind, F. G. (1982). Autonomy and creativity in children. *Journal of Creative Behavior, 16*, 1, 58–67.

Renzullit, J. S., & Hartman, R. K. (1971). Scale for rating behavioral characteristics of superior students. *Exceptional Children, 38*, 243–248.

Rhodes, W. A. (1977). *Generalization of attribution retaining*. Unpublished doctoral dissertation, University of Illinois, Urbana.

Rhodes, W. A., Blackwell, J., Jordan, C., & Walters, C. (1980). A developmental study of learned helplessness. *Developmental Psychology, 16*, 616–624.

Rodgers, J. L. (1984). Confluence effects: Not here, not now! *Developmental Psychology, 20*, 321–328.

Rose, S., & Wallace, I. (1985). Visual recognition memory: A predictor of later cognitive functioning in preterms. *Child Development, 56*, 843–852.

Ruble, D., Boggiano, A. K., Feldman, N. S., & Loebl, J. H. (1980). Developmental analysis of the role of social comparison in self-evaluation. *Developmental Psychology, 16*, 105–115.

Ruble, D., Feldman, N. S., & Boggiano, A. G. (1976). Social comparison between young children in achievement situations. *Developmental Psychology, 12*, 192–197.

Scarr, S., & Weinberg, R. A. (1976). IQ test performance of black children adopted by white families. *American Psychologist, 31*, 726–739.

Silverberg, R. A. (1971). The relationship of children's perceptions of parental behavior to the creativity of their children. *Dissertation Abstracts International, 31*, 6413–6414A.

Simensen, R. J., & Rogers, R. C. (1989). School psychology and medical diagnosis: The fragile X syndrome. *Psychology in the Schools, 26*, 380–389.

Simon, H. A. (1972). On the development of the processor. In S. Farnham-Diggory (Ed.), *Information processing in children*. New York: Academic Press.

Skinner, E. A. (1990). Age differences in the dimensions of perceived control during middle childhood: Implications for developmental conceptualizations and research. *Child Development, 61*, 1882–1890.

Skinner, E. A., & Chapman, M. (1987). Resolution of a developmental paradox: How can perceived internality increase, decrease, and remain the same across middle childhood? *Developmental Psychology, 23*, 44–48.

Skodak, M., & Skeels, H. M. (1949). A final follow-up study of one hundred adopted children. *Journal of Genetic Psychology, 75*, 85–125.

Slaughter-Defoe, D. T., Nakagawa, K., Takanishi, R., & Johnson, D. J. (1990). Toward cultural/ecological perspectives on schooling and achievement in African- and Asian-American children. *Child Development, 61*, 363–383.

Solomon, D., & Houlihan, K. (1972). Relationships of parental behavior to "disadvantaged" children intrinsic-extrinsic motivation for task striving. *Journal of Genetic Psychology, 120*, 257–274.

Spearman, C. (1904). General intelligence: Objectively determined and measured. *American Journal of Psychology, 15*, 201–293.

Spearman, C. (1923). *The nature of "intelligence" and the principles of cognition*. London: Macmillan.

Spearman, C. (1927). *The abilities of man*. New York: Macmillan.

Spearman, C., Conway, B. E., Ketron, J. L., & Bernstein, M. (1981). People's conceptions of intelligence. *Journal of Personality and Social Psychology, 41*, 37–55.

Spencer, M. B. (1988). Self-concept development. In D. T. Slaughter (Ed.), *Perspectives on black child development: New directions for child development*. San Francisco: Jossey-Bass.

Steinberg, L., Elmen, J. D., & Mounts, N. S. (1989). Authoritative parenting, psychosocial maturity, and academic success among adolescents. *Child Development, 60*, 1424–1436.

Stern, W. (1924). *Psychology of early childhood up to the sixth year of age*. New York: Holt, Rinehart and Winston.

Sternberg, R. (1985). *Beyond IQ: A triarchic theory of human intelligence*. New York: Cambridge University Press.

Sternberg, R., & Detterman, D. K. (1986). *What is intelligence?* Norwood, NJ: Ablex.

Sternberg, R., & Gastel, J. (1989). Coping with novelty in human intelligence: An empirical investigation. *Intelligence, 13,* 187–197.

Sternberg, R., & Okagaki, L. (1989). Continuity and discontinuity in intellectual development are not a matter of "either-or." *Human Development, 32,* 158–166.

Stevenson, H., & Lee, S. (1990). Contexts of achievement. *Monographs for the Society for Research in Child Development, 55,* Nos. 1–2.

Stevenson, H., Lee, S., Chen, C., Lummis, M., Stigler, J., Fan, L., & Ge, F. (1990). Mathematics achievement of children in China and the United States. *Child Development, 61,* 1053–1066.

Stevenson, H., Stigler, J., Lee, S., Lucker, G. W., Kitamura, S., & Hsu, C. (1985). Cognitive performance and academic achievement of Japanese, Chinese, and American children. *Child Development, 56,* 718–734.

Stipek, D. J. (1981, August). *Children's use of past performance information in ability and expectancy judgments for self and other.* Paper presented by the Meeting of the International Society for the Study of Behavioral Development, Toronto.

Stipek, D. J., & Hoffman, J. M. (1980). Children's achievement related expectancies as a function of academic performance histories and sex. *Journal of Educational Psychology, 72,* 861–865.

Stipek, D. J., & MacIver, D. (1989). Developmental change in children's assessment of intellectual competence. *Child Development, 60,* 520–538.

Stipek, D. J., & Tannatt, L. (1984). Children's judgements of their own and their peers' academic competence. *Journal of Educational Psychology, 76,* 75–84.

Teahan, J. E. (1963). Parental attitudes and college success. *Journal of Educational Psychology, 54,* 104–109.

Teevan, R. L., & McGhee, P. E. (1972). Childhood development of fear of failure motivation. *Journal of Personality and Social Psychology, 21,* 345–348.

Terman, L. M., & Merrill, M. A. (1960). *Stanford-Binet intelligence Scale: Manual for third revision, form L-M.* Boston: Houghton-Mifflin.

Thompson, L. A., & Fagan, J. F. (1991). Longitudinal prediction of specific cognitive abilities from infant novelty preference. *Child Development, 62,* 530–538.

Thorndike, E. L., Bregman, E. O., Cobb, M. V., & Woodyard, E. I. (1926). *The measurement of intelligence.* New York: Columbia University Teachers College.

Thurstone, L. L. (1924). *The nature of intelligence.* New York: Harcourt, Brace.

Thurstone, L. L. (1938). *Primary mental abilities.* Chicago: University of Chicago Press.

Torrance, E. P. (1962). *Guiding creative talent.* Englewood Cliffs, NJ: Prentice-Hall.

Torrance, E. P. (1964). Education and creativity. In C. W. Taylor (Ed.), *Creativity: Progress and potential.* New York: McGraw-Hill.

Wallach, M. A., & Kogan, N. (1965). *Modes of thinking in young children.* New York: Holt, Rinehart and Winston.

Wasik, B. H., Ramey, C. T., Bryant, D. M., & Sparling, J. J. (1990). A longitudinal study of two early intervention strategies: Project CARE. *Child Development, 61,* 1682–1696.

Wechsler, D. (1974). *Manual for the Wechsler intelligence scale for children–revised.* New York: Psychological Corp.

Wiener, B., Russell, D., & Lerman, D. (1979). The cognitive-emotion process in achievement-related contexts. *Journal of Personality and Social Psychology, 15,* 1–20.

Williams, F. E. (1979). Assessing creativity across Williams' cube model. *Gifted Child Quarterly, 23,* 4, 748–756.

Wittrock, M. D. (1977). *The human brain.* Englewood Cliffs, NJ: Prentice-Hall.

Wolf, R. M. (1979). Achievement in the United States. In H. J. Walberg (Ed.), *Educational environments and effects: Evaluation, policy and productivity.* Berkeley, CA: McCutchan.

Worden, P. E. (1975). Effects of sorting on subsequent recall of unrelated items: A development study. *Child Development, 46,* 687–695.

Wylie, R. (1979). *The self-concept* Vol. 2. *Theory and research on selected topics.* Lincoln: University of Nebraska Press.

Yao, E. L. (1985). A comparison of family characteristics of Asian-American and Anglo-American high achievers. *International Journal of Comparative Sociology, 26(3–4),* 198–208.

Ysseldyke, J. E. (1985). Basic achievement skills: Individual screener. *Journal of Counseling and Development, 64,* 90–91.

Zajonc, R. B. (1976). Family configuration and intelligence. *Science, 192,* 227–236.

Zajonc, R. B. (1983). Validating the confluence model. *Psychological Bulletin, 93,* 457–480.

Zajonc, R. B., & Markus, G. (1975). Birth order and intellectual development. *Psychological Review, 82,* 74–88.

Chapter 9

Akiyama, M. M. (1984). Are language acquisition strategies universal? *Developmental Psychology, 20,* 219–228.

Atkinson, M. (1982). *Explanations in the study of language development.* New York: Cambridge University Press.

Au, T. K. (1990). Children's use of information in word learning. *Journal of Child Language, 17,* 393–416.

Baldwin, D. A., & Markman, E. M. (1989). Establishing word-object relations: A first step. *Child Development, 60,* 381–398.

Bariaud, F. (1983). *La genese de l'humour ches l'enfant.* Paris: P.U.F.

Barton, M. E., & Tomasello, M. (1991). Joint attention and conversation in mother-infant-sibling triads. *Child Development, 62,* 517–529.

Bates, E. (1979a). *The emergence of symbols.* New York: Academic Press.

Bates, E. (1979b). The emergence of symbols: Ontogeny and phylogeny. In W. A. Collins (Ed.), *Children's language and communication.* Hillsdale, NJ: Erlbaum.

Berthoud, I. (1980). *La reflexion metalinguistique ches l'enfant.* Doctoral thesis, University of Geneva.

Bloom, L. (1971). Why not pivot grammars? *Journal of Speech and Hearing Disorders, 36,* 40–50.

Bloom, L. (1973). *One word at a time: The use of single word utterances before syntax.* The Hague: Moulton.

Bloom, L. (1974). Talking, understanding, and thinking. In R. L. Schiefelbusch and L. L. Lloyd (Eds.), *Language perspectives: Acquisition, retardation, and intervention.* Baltimore: University Park Press.

Bloom, L., Hood, C., & Lightbown, P. (1974). Imitation in language development: If, when and why. *Cognitive Psychology, 6,* 380–420.

Bowerman, M. (1974). Discussion summary: Development of concepts underlying language. In R. L. Schiefelbusch and L. L. Lloyd (Eds.), *Language perspective: Acquisition, retardation, and intervention.* Baltimore: University Park Press.

Braine, M. (1963). The ontogeny of English phrase structure: The first phase. *Language, 39,* 1–13.

Bretherton, I., & Bates, E. (1979). The emergence of intentional communication. *New Directions for Child Development, 4,* 81–100.

Brown, R. (1973). The development of language in children. In G. A. Miller (Ed.), *Communication, language and meaning.* New York: Basic Books.

Brown, R. (1977). Introduction. In C. A. Snow and C. Ferguson (Eds.), *Talking to children.* New York: Cambridge University Press.

Brown, R. (1988). Roger Brown: An autobiography in the third person. In F. S. Kessel (Ed.), *The development of language and language researchers: Essays in honor of Roger Brown* (pp. 395–404). Hillsdale, NJ: Erlbaum.

Brown, R., & Bellugi, U. (1964). Three processes in the child's acquisition of syntax. *Harvard Educational Review, 34,* 133–151.

Brown, R., Cazden, C., & Bellugi, U. (1968). The child's grammar from I to III. In J. R. Hill (Ed.), *Minnesota symposium on child psychology* Vol. 2 (pp. 28–73). Minneapolis: University of Minnesota Press.

Brown, R., & Hanlon, C. (1970). Derivational complexity and order of acquisition in child speech. In J. R. Hayes (Ed.), *Cognition and the development of language.* New York: Wiley.

Bruner, J. S. (1964). The course of cognitive growth. *American Psychologist, 19,* 1–15.

Cadzen, C. (1965). *Environmental assistance to the child's acquisition of grammar.* Unpublished Ph.D. dissertation. Harvard University, Graduate School of Education, Cambridge, MA.

Cadzen, C. (1970). The neglected situation in child language research and education. In F. Williams (Ed.), *Language and poverty.* Chicago: Markham.

Capelli, C. A., Nakagawa, N., & Madden, C. M. (1990). How children understand sarcasm: The role of context and intonation. *Child Development, 61,* 1824–1841.

Chomsky, N. (1968). *Language and mind.* New York: Harcourt Brace Jovanovich.

Chomsky, N. (1986). *Knowledge of language: Its nature, origin, and use.* New York: Praeger.

Clark, E. V. (1975). Knowledge, context, and strategy in the acquisition of meaning. In D. Dato (Ed.), *Proceedings of the 26th annual Georgetown University round table: Developmental psycholinguistics: Theory and application.* Washington, DC: Georgetown University Press.

Clark, E. V. (1983). Meanings and concepts. In J. H. Flavell and E. M. Markman (Eds.), *Handbook of child psychology.* New York: Wiley.

Clark, E. V., Gelman, S. A., & Lane, N. (1985). Compound nouns and category structure in young children. *Child Development, 56,* 84–94.

Cooper, R. P., & Aslin, R. N. (1990). Preference for infant-directed speech in the first month after birth. *Child Development, 61,* 1584–1595.

Dale, P. S. (1976). *Language development: Structure and function* (2nd ed.). New York: Holt, Rinehart and Winston.

Dale, P. S., & Ingram, D. (Eds.). (1981). *Child language: An international perspective.* Baltimore: University Park Press.

deVilliers, J. G., & deVilliers, F. A. (1978). *Language acquisition*. Cambridge, MA: Harvard University Press.

deVilliers, J. G., & deVilliers, F. A. (1979). *Early language*. Cambridge, MA: Harvard University Press.

DeVito, J. (1970). *The psychology of speech and language*. New York: Random House.

Eilers, R. E., Gavin, W. J., & Wilson, W. R. (1979). Linguistic experience and phonemic perception in infancy: A cross-linguistic study. *Child Development, 50*, 14–18.

Eimas, P., Sigueland, E. R., Jusczyk, P., & Vigorito, J. (1971). Speech perception in infants. *Science, 71*, 303–306.

Eisenberg, R. B. (1979). Stimulus significance as a determininant of infant responses to sound. In E. B. Thoman (Ed.), *Origins of the infant's social responsiveness* (pp. 1–32). Hillsdale, NJ: Erlbaum.

Fernald, A. (1989). Intonation and communicative intent in mothers' speech to infants: Is melody the message? *Child Development, 60*, 1497–1510.

Fernald, A., Taeschner, T., Dunn, J., Papousek, M., de Boysson-Bardies, B., & Fukui, I. (1989). A cross-language study of prosodic modifications in mothers' and fathers' speech to preverbal infants. *Journal of Child Language, 16*, 477–501.

Flavell, J. H. (1977). *Cognitive development*. Englewood Cliffs, NJ: Prentice-Hall.

Franke, C. (1912). Über die erste laustufe der Kinder. *Anthropos, 5*, 663–676.

Gardner, R. A., & Gardner, B. (1969). Teaching sign language to a chimpanzee. *Science, 165*, 664–672.

Gelman, S. A., & Taylor, M. (1984). How two-year-old children interpret proper and common names for unfamiliar objects. *Child Development, 55*, 1535–1540.

Glanzer, P. D., & Dodd, D. H. (1975). *Developmental changes in the language spoken to children*. Paper presented to the Biennial Conference of the Society for Research in Child Development, Denver.

Gleason, J. B. (1958). The child's learning of English morphology. *Word, 14*, 150–177.

Gleitman, L. R., Newport, E. L., & Gleitman, H. (1984). The current status of the motherese hypothesis. *Journal of Child Language, 11*, 43–79.

Gordon, P. (1987). *Determiner and adjective categories in children's grammars*. Paper presented at the biennial meeting of the Society for Research in Child Development, Baltimore.

Gordon, T. (1970). *Parent effectiveness training: The tested new way to raise responsible children*. New York: David McKay.

Gottfried, H. W., & Gottfried, A. E. (1984). Home environment and cognitive development in young children of middle-socioeconomic-status families. In H. W. Gottfried (Ed.), *Home environment and early cognitive development: Longitudinal research* (pp. 329–342). Orlando, FL: Academic Press.

Hoff-Ginsberg, E. (1990). Maternal speech and the child's development of syntax: A further look. *Journal of Child Language, 17*, 85–99.

Hoff-Ginsberg, E. (1991). Mother-child conversation in different social classes and communicative settings. *Child Development, 62*, 782–796.

Huston, A. C., Wright, J. C., Eakins, D., Kerkman, D., Pinion, M., Rosenkoetter, I., & Truglio, R. T. (1985). *Age changes in "Sesame Street" viewing: A report to Children's Television Workshop*. Lawrence: University of Kansas, Center for Research on the Influence of Television on Children.

Jacobson, J. L., Boersma, D. C., Fields, R. B., & Olson, K. L. (1983). Paralinguistic features of adult speech to infants and small children. *Child Development, 54*, 436–442.

Jones, S. S., Smith, L. B., & Landau, B. (1991). Object properties and knowledge in early lexical learning. *Child Development, 62*, 499–516.

Kaye, K. (1982). *The mental and social life of babies*. Chicago: University of Chicago Press.

Klima, E. S., & Bullugi, U. (1966). Syntactic regularities in the speech of children. In J. Lyons and R. J. Wales (Eds.), *Psycholinguistic papers*. Edinburgh: Edinburgh University Press.

Lempert, H. (1989). Animacy constraints on preschool children's acquisition of syntax. *Child Development, 60*, 237–245.

Lenneberg, E. H. (1967). *Biological foundations of language*. New York: Wiley.

Lieberman, P. (1967). *Intonation, perception, and language*. Cambridge, MA: MIT Press.

Lisina, M. I. (1982). The development of interaction in the first seven years of life. In W. W. Hartup (Ed.), *Review of child development research*. Chicago: University of Chicago Press.

Lytton, H. (1980). *Parent-child interaction*. New York: Plenum.

McCarthy, D. (1954). Language development in children. In L. Carmichael (Ed.), *Manual of child psychology* (2nd ed.). New York: Wiley.

McDevitt, T. M., Spivey, N., Sheehan, E. P., Lennon, R., & Story, R. (1990). Children's beliefs about listening: Is it enough to be still and quiet? *Child Development, 61,* 713–721.

McGhee, P. E. (1979). *Humor: Its origin and development.* San Francisco: W. H. Freeman.

McNeill, D. (1970). *The acquisition of language.* New York: Harper & Row.

Moskowitz, B. A. (1978). The acquisition of language. *Scientific American, 239,* 92–108.

Mowrer, O. H. (1960). *Learning theory and symbolic processes.* New York: Wiley.

Nakazima, S. (1962). A comparative study of the speech developments of Japanese and American English in children. *Studies in Phonology, 2,* 27–39.

Nelson, K. (1973). Structure and strategy in learning to talk. *Monographs of the Society for Research in Child Development, 38,* 149, 1–2.

Nelson, K. (1979). Features, contrasts and the FCH: Some comments on Barrett's lexical developmental hypothesis. *Journal of Child Language, 6,* 139–146.

Phillips, J. R. (1973). Syntax and vocabulary of mother's speech to young children: Age and sex comparisons. *Child Development, 44,* 182–185.

Piaget, J. (1955). *The language and thought of the child.* New York: Meridian Books.

Premack, A. J., & Premack, D. (1972). Teaching language to an ape. *Scientific American, 227,* 92–99.

Premack, D. (1971). Language in chimpanzees? *Science, 169,* 808–822.

Reynolds, A. G., & Flagg, P. W. (1977). *Cognitive psychology.* Cambridge, MA: Winthrop.

Rice, M. L., Huston, A. C., Truglio, R., & Wright, J. C. (1990). Words from "Sesame Street": Learning vocabulary while viewing. *Developmental Psychology, 26,* 421–428.

Roberts, R., & Patterson, C. J. (1983). Perspective taking and referential communication: The question of correspondence reconsidered. *Child Development, 54,* 1005–1014.

Rubin, R. R., & Fisher, J. J. (1982). *Ages 3 and 4: Your preschooler.* New York: Macmillan.

Rubin, R. R., Fisher, J. J., & Doering, S. G. (1980). *Your toddler.* New York: Macmillan.

Rumbaugh, D. M., & Gill, T. V. (1976). Language and the acquisition of language-type skills by a chimpanzee. *Annual New York Academy Science, 270,* 90–135.

Sachs, J., & Devin, J. (1976). Young children's use of age-appropriate speech styles in social interaction and role playing. *Journal of Child Language, 3,* 82–98.

Sanders, E. (1972). When are speech sounds learned? *Journal of Speech and Hearing Disorders, 37,* 62.

Schantz, M. (1983). Communication. In J. Flavell and E. M. Markman (Eds.), *Handbook of child psychology.* New York: Wiley.

Scollon, R. (1976). *Conversations with a one-year-old: A case study of the developmental foundation of syntax.* Honolulu: University Press of Hawaii.

Shatz, M. (1983). Communication. In J. H. Flavell and E. M. Markman (Eds.), *Cognitive development: Vol. 3.* P. H. Mussen (Gen. Ed.), *Handbook of child psychology.* New York: Wiley.

Shatz, M., & Gelman, R. (1973). The development of communication skills: Modifications in the speech of young children as a function of listener. *Monographs of the Society for Research in Child Development, 38,* 77–82.

Shipley, E. S., Smith, C. S., & Gleitman, L. R. (1969). A study in the acquisition of language: Free responses to commands. *Language, 45,* 322–342.

Skinner, B. F. (Ed.). (1972). *Cumulative record: A selection of papers* (3rd ed.). New York: Appleton.

Slobin, D. I. (1971). *Psycholinguistics.* Glenview, IL: Scott, Foresman.

Slobin, D. I. (1973). Cognitive perspectives for the development of grammar. In C. A. Ferguson and D. I. Slobin (Eds.), *Studies of child language development* (pp. 175–208). New York: Holt, Rinehart and Winston.

Slobin, D. I. (1985). Crosslinguistic evidence of the language-making capacity. In D. I. Slobin (Ed.), *The crosslinguistic study of language acquisition.* Vol. 2. *Theoretical issues* (pp. 1157–1256). Hillsdale, NJ: Erlbaum.

Slobin, D. I. (1988, April). Confessions of a wayward Chomskyan. *Papers and Reports on Child Language Development* (Vol. 27) (pp. 131–138). Proceedings of the Annual Language Research Forum, Stanford University, Palo Alto, CA.

Smith, M. E. (1926). An investigation of the development of the sentence and the extent of vocabulary in young children. *University of Iowa Studies in Child Welfare.*

Snow, C. (1972). Mothers' speech to children learning language. *Child Development, 43,* 549–565.

Snow, C. (1977). Mothers' speech research: From input to interaction. In C. Snow and C. Ferguson (Eds.), *Talking to children.* New York: Cambridge University Press.

Snow, C. (1979). The role of social interaction in language acquisition. In A. Collins (Ed.), *Children's language and communication.* Hillsdale, NJ: Erlbaum.

Snow, C. (1981). Social interactions and language acquisition. In P. S. Dale and D. Ingram (Eds.), *Child lan-*

guage: An international perspective. Baltimore: University of Baltimore Press.

Snow, C., deBlauw, A., & van Roosmalen, G. (1979). Talking and playing with babies. In M. Bullow (Ed.), *Before speech.* New York: Cambridge University Press.

Taylor, M., & Gelman, S. A. (1989). Incorporating new words into the lexicon: Preliminary evidence for language hierarchies in two-year-old children. *Child Development, 60,* 625–636.

Templin, M. C. (1957). *Certain language skills in children: Their development and interrelationships.* Minneapolis: University of Minnesota Press.

Terrace, H., Petitto, L., Sanders, R., & Bever, T. (1979). Can an ape create a sentence? *Science, 206,* 891–899.

Tomasello, M., & Mannle, S. (1985). Pragmatics of sibling speech to one-year-olds. *Child Development, 56,* 911–917.

Tomasello, M., Mannle, S., & Kruger, C. (1986). Linguistic environment of 1- to 2-year-old twins. *Developmental Psychology, 22,* 169–176.

Trehub, S. E. (1976). The discrimination of foreign speech contrasts by infants and adults. *Child Development, 47,* 466–472.

Vygotsky, L. S. (1962). *Thought and language.* (E. Hanfmann and G. Vakar, Trans.). Cambridge, MA: MIT Press.

Waxman, S. R., & Kosowski, T. D. (1990). Nouns mark category relations: Toddlers' and preschoolers' word-learning biases. *Child Development, 61,* 1461–1473.

Werker, J. F., Gilbert, J. H. V., Humphrey, K., & Tees, R. C. (1981). Developmental aspects of cross-language speech perception. *Child Development, 52,* 349–355.

Werker, J. F., & McLeod, P. J. (1989). Infant preference for both male and female infant-directed talk: A developmental study of attentional and affective responsiveness. *Canadian Journal of Psychology, 43,* 230–246.

Whorf, B. L. (1956). *Language, thought, and reality.* Cambridge, MA: MIT Press.

Winner, E. (1988). *The point of words: Children's understanding of metaphor and irony.* Cambridge, MA: Harvard University Press.

Winner, E., Kaplan, J., & Rosenblatt, E. (1989, April). *Discrimination and interpretation of metaphor and irony: Evidence for a dissociation.* Paper presented at the meeting of the Society for Research in Child Development, Kansas City, MO.

Winner, E., Windmueller, G., Rosenblatt, E., Bosco, L., Best, E., & Gardner, H. (1987). Making sense of literal and nonliteral falsehood. *Metaphor and Symbolic Activity, 2,* 13–32.

Chapter 10

Aboud, F. (1985). Children's application of attribution principles to social comparisons. *Child Development, 56,* 682–688.

Adams, G. R. (1988, June). *Identity formation: Theoretical and empirical issues.* Conference held at Utah State University, Logan.

Allen, L., & Majidi-Ali, S. (1989). Black American children. In J. T. Giggs and L. N. Huang (Eds.), *Children of Color* (pp. 148–178). San Francisco: Jossey-Bass.

Amsterdam, B. K. (1972). Mirror self-image reactions before age two. *Developmental Psychology, 5,* 297–305.

Anderson, L. W. (1981). An examination of the nature of change in academic self-concept. In M. Lynch, A. Norem-Hebeisen, and J. K. Gergen (Eds.), *Self-concept: Advances in theory and research.* Cambridge, MA: Ballinger.

Anderson, M., & Hughes, H. M. (1990). Parenting attitudes and the self-esteem of young children. *Journal of Genetic Psychology, 150,* 463–465.

Archer, S. L., & Waterman, A. S. (1990). Varieties of identity diffusions and foreclosures: An exploration of subcategories of the identity statuses. *Journal of Adolescent Research, 5,* 96–111.

Bachman, J. G., & O'Malley, P. M. (1977). Self-esteem in young men: A longitudinal analysis of the impact of educational and occupations attainment. *Journal of Personality and Social Psychology, 35,* 365–380.

Balif, B. L. (1981). The significance of the self-concept in the knowledge society. In M. Lynch, A. Norem-Hebeisen, and J. K. Gergen (Eds.), *Self-concept: Advances in theory and research.* Cambridge, MA: Ballinger.

Bannister, D., & Agnew, J. (1977). The child's construing of self. In J. Cole (Ed.), *Nebraska symposium on motivation.* Lincoln: University of Nebraska Press.

Barenboim, C. (1977). Developmental changes in the interpersonal cognitive system from middle childhood to adolescence. *Child Development, 48,* 1467–1474.

Beane, J. A. (1983, May). Self-concept and self-esteem in the middle school. *NASSP Bulletin,* 63–67.

Beane, J. A., & Lipka, R. P. (1980). Self-concept and self-esteem: A construct differentiation. *Child Study Journal, 10,* 1–13.

Beneson, J., & Dweck, C. (1986). The development of trait explanations and self-evaluations in the academic and social domains. *Child Development, 57,* 1179–1187.

Berndt, T. J. (1989). Friendships in childhood and adolescence. In W. Damon (Ed.), *Child development today and tomorrow* (pp. 332–353). San Francisco: Jossey-Bass.

Berndt, T. J., & Hawkins, J. A. (1987). *The contribution of supportive friendships to adjustment after the transition to junior high school.* Unpublished manuscript, Department of Psychological Sciences, Purdue University, West Lafayette, Indiana.

Bertenthal, B. I., & Fischer, K. W. (1978). Development of self-recognition in the infant. *Developmental Psychology, 14,* 44–50.

Blyth, D., & Traeger, C. (1991). The self-concept and self-esteem of early adolescents. In N. Lauter-Klatell (Ed.), *Readings in child development* (pp. 130–135). Mountain View, CA: Mayfield.

Boersma, F. J., & Chapman, J. W. (1979). *Student's perception of ability scale manual.* Edmonton, Alberta, Canada: University of Alberta.

Briggs, D. (1970). *Your child's self-esteem.* New York: Doubleday.

Brockner, J. (1979). The effects of self-esteem, success-failure, and self-consciousness on task performance. *Journal of Personality and Social Psychology, 37,* 1847–1854.

Brody, S., & Axelrad, S. (1970). *Anxiety and ego formation in infancy.* New York: International University Press.

Brooker, W. (1969). *Self-concept of ability and school achievement.* In W. Thomas, *The Thomas self-concept values test.* Washington, DC: U.S. Office of Education.

Brookover, W., & Passalacqua, J. (1981). Comparison of aggregate and self-concepts for populations with different reference groups. In M. Lynch, A. Norem-Hebeisen, and J. K. Gergen (Eds.), *Self-concept: Advances in theory and research.* Cambridge, MA: Ballinger.

Broughton, J. M. (1978). Development of concepts of self, mind, reality, and knowledge. *New Directions for Child Development, 1,* 75–100.

Broughton, J. M. (1981). The divided self in adolescence. *Human Development, 24,* 13–32.

Brown, J. D., Collins, R. I., & Schmidt, G. W. (1988). Self-esteem and direct versus indirect forms of self-enhancement. *Journal of Personality and Social Psychology, 55,* 445–453.

Buhrmester, D. (1990). Intimacy of friendship, interpersonal competence, and adjustment during preadolescence and adolescence. *Child Development, 61,* 1101–1111.

Bullock, M., & Lutkenhaus, P. (1988). The development of volitional behavior in the toddler years. *Child Development, 59,* 664–674.

Bullock, M., & Lutkenhaus, P. (1990). Who am I? Self-understanding in toddlers. *Merrill-Palmer Quarterly, 36,* 217–238.

Butler, P. (1981). *Self assertion for women.* San Francisco: Harper & Row.

Bybee, J., Glick, M., & Zigler, E. (1990). Differences across gender, grade level, and academic track in the content of the ideal self-image. *Sex Roles, 22,* 349–360.

Charney, R. (1978). *The development of personal pronouns.* Unpublished doctoral dissertation. University of Chicago.

Clemes, H., & Bean, R. (1981). *Self-esteem.* New York: G. P. Putnam and Sons.

Cooley, C. H. (1909). *Social Organization.* New York: Schocken Books.

Coopersmith, S. (1967). *The antecedents of self-esteem.* San Francisco: Freeman.

Coopersmith, S., & Gilberts, R. (1982). *Behavior academic self-esteem.* Palo Alto, CA: Consulting Psychologists Press.

Damon, W. (1983). *Social and personality development.* New York: Norton.

Damon, W., & Hart, D. (1982). The development of self-understanding from infancy through adolescence. *Child Development, 53,* 841–854.

Davidson, H., & Lange, G. (1970). Children's perceptions of their teacher's feelings toward them related to self-perception, school achievement, and behavior. *Journal of Experimental Education, 29,* 107–118.

Diener, E., & Srull, T. K. (1979). Self-awareness, psychological perspective and self-reinforcement in relation to personal and social standards. *Journal of Personality and Social Psychology, 24,* 413–423.

Dobbins, J. E. (1978). Effects of parental power on the developing self-esteem of pre-school age children 12–36 months of age. *Dissertation Abstracts International,* 1950–1951.

Dolan, L. (1981). The development of self-concept in the elementary school. In M. Lynch, A. Norem-Hebeisen, J. K. Gergen (Eds.), *Self-concept: Advances in theory and research.* Cambridge, MA: Ballinger.

Drummond, R., & Gilkison, B. (1989). Predictors of academic self-concept of older adults. *Psychological Reports, 65,* 771–774.

Dusek, J. B., & Flaherty, J. F. (1981). The development of self-concept during the adolescent years. *Monographs of the Society for Research in Child Development, 46,* 1–67.

Eato, L. E., & Lerner, R. M. (1981). Relations of physical and social environment perceptions to adolescent self-esteem. *The Journal of Genetic Psychology, 39,* 143–150.

Eder, R. A. (1989). The emergent personologist: The structure and content of 3½-, 5½-, and 7½-year-olds' concepts of themselves and other persons. *Child Development, 60,* 1218–1228.

Eder, R. A. (1990). Uncovering young children's psychological selves: Individual and developmental differences. *Child Development, 61,* 849–863.

Eder, R. A., Gerlack, S. G., & Perlmutter, M. (1987). In search of children's selves: Development of the specific and general components of the self-concept. *Child Development, 58,* 1044–1050.

Elrod, M. M., & Chase, S. J. (1980). Sex differences in self-esteem and parental behavior. *Psychological Reports, 46,* 719–727.

Enright, K., & Ruzicka, M. (1989). Relationships between perceived parental behavior and the self-esteem of gifted children. *Psychological Reports, 65,* 931–937.

Epstein, S. (1973). The self-concept revisited. *American Psychologist, 28,* 404–416.

Epstein, S. (1981). The unity principle versus the reality and pleasure principles. In M. Lynch, A. Norem-Hebeisen, and J. K. Gergen (Eds.), *Self-concept: Advances in theory and research.* Cambridge, MA: Ballinger.

Erikson, E. (1968). *Identity: Youth and crisis.* New York: W. W. Norton.

Fahey, M., & Phillips, S. (1981). The self-concept in middle childhood: Some baseline data. *Child Study Journal, 11,* 155–165.

Felson, R. (1981). Ambiguity and bias in the self-concept. *Social Psychology Quarterly, 44,* 64–69.

Fenson, L., & Ramsay, D. (1980). Decentration and integration of the child's play in the second year. *Child Development, 51,* 171–178.

Fillmore, L. W., & Britsch, S. (1988, June). *Early education for children from linguistic and cultural minority families.* Unpublished paper prepared for the Early Education Task Force of the National Association of State Boards of Education, University of California at Berkeley.

Fischer, K. W., & Lazerson, A. (1983). *Developmental psychology.* New York: Worth.

Gallup, G. C. (1977). Self-recognition in primates. *American Psychologist, 167,* 329–338.

Gallup, G. C. (1979). Self-recognition in chimpanzees and man. In M. Lewis and L. Rosenblum (Eds.), *The child and its family.* New York: Plenum.

Gecas, V. (1982). The self-concept. *Annual Review of Sociology, 8,* 1–33.

Geppert, U., & Kuster, U. (1983). The emergence of "wanting to do it oneself": A precursor of achievement motivation. *International Journal of Behavioral Development, 6,* 355–369.

Gergen, K. (1981). Theoretical issues in self-concept. In M. Lynch, A. Norem-Hebeisen, and J. K. Gergen (Eds.), *Self-concept advances in theory and research.* Cambridge, MA: Ballinger.

Grotevant, H. D., & Cooper, C. R. (1985). Patterns of interaction in family relationships and the development of identity exploration in adolescence. *Child Development, 56,* 415–428.

Gutmann, D. (1965). Women and the conception of ego strength. *Merrill-Palmer Quarterly, 11,* 229–240.

Hales, S. (1990, Winter). Valuing the self: Understanding the nature of self-esteem. *Saybrook Perspective,* 3–17.

Hamachek, D. E. (1978). *Encounters with the self.* New York: Holt, Rinehart and Winston.

Harper, L., & Huie, K. (1985). The effects of prior group experience, age, and familiarity on the quality and organization of preschoolers' social relationships. *Child Development, 56,* 704–717.

Harter, S. (1982). A cognitive-developmental approach to children's use of affect and trait labels. In F. Serafica (Ed.), *Social cognition and social relations in context.* New York: Guilford Press.

Harter, S. (1983). Developmental perspectives on the self system. In P. H. Mussen (Ed.), *Handbook of child psychology* (4th ed.) (Vol. 4) (pp. 275–385). New York: Wiley.

Harter, S. (1985). Competence as a dimension of self-evaluation: Toward a comprehensive model of self-worth. In R. Leahy (Ed.), *The development of the self* (pp. 55–121). San Diego, CA: Academic Press.

Harter, S., & Connell, J. P. (1982). A comparison of alternative models of the relationships between academic achievement and children's perceptions of competence, control and motivation orientation. In J. Nicholl (Ed.), *The development of achievement-related cognitions and behaviors.* Greenwich, CT: J.A.I. Press.

Hartup, W. W. (1989). Behavioral manifestations of children's friendships. In T. J. Berndt and G. W. Ladd (Eds.), *Peer relations in child development* (pp. 46–70). New York: Wiley.

Hartup, W. W. (1983). Peer relations. In P. H. Mussen (Ed.), *Handbook of child psychology* (4th ed.) (Vol. 4) (pp. 103–196). New York: Wiley.

Hauser, S. T., Powers, S. I., Noam, G., Jacobson, A. M., Weiss, B., & Follansbee, D. J. (1984). Familial contexts of adolescent ego development. *Child Development, 55,* 195–213.

Hay, D. F. (1979). Cooperative interactions and sharing among very young children and their parents. *Developmental Psychology, 15,* 647–653.

Heckhausen, J. (1988). Becoming aware of one's competence in the second year: Developmental progression within the mother-child dyad. *International Journal of Behavioral Development, 11*, 305–326.

Hetherington, E. M. (1979). Play and social interaction in children following divorce. *Journal of Social Issues, 35*, 26–49.

Howes, C., Unger, O., & Seidner, L. B. (1989). Social pretend play in toddlers: Parallels with social play and with solitary pretend. *Child Development, 60*, 77–84.

James, W. (1950). *The principles of psychology.* New York: Dover. (Original work published 1890)

Jones, G. P., & Dembo, M. H. (1989). Age and sex role differences in intimate friendships during childhood and adolescence. *Merrill-Palmer Quarterly, 35*, 445–457.

Jordan, J. V. (1986). The meaning of mutuality. *Work in Progress* (No. 23). Wellesley, MA: Stone Center for Developmental Services and Studies.

Kagan, J. (1981). *The second year.* Cambridge, MA: Harvard University Press.

Kagan, J., & Moss, H. (1983). *Birth to maturity: A study in psychological development.* New York: Wiley.

Kegan, R. (1982). *The evolving self.* Cambridge, MA: Harvard University Press.

Keller, A., Ford, L. H., & Meacham, J. A. (1978). Dimensions of self-concept in preschool children. *Developmental Psychology, 14*, 483–489.

Kihlstrom, J. F., Cantor, N., Albright, J. S., Chew, B. R., Klein, S. B., & Niedenthal, P. M. (1988). Information processing and the study of the self. In L. Berkowitz (Ed.), *Advances in experimental social psychology* (Vol. 21) (pp. 145–188). Orlando, FL: Academic Press.

Kizziar, J., & Hagedorn, J. (1979). *Search for acceptance: The adolescent and self-esteem.* Chicago: Nelson-Hall.

Koff, E., Rierdan, J., & Stubbs, M. L. (1990). Gender, body image, and self-concept in early adolescence. *Journal of Early Adolescence, 10*, 56–67.

Lackovic-Grgin, K., & Dekovic, M. (1990). The contribution of significant others to adolescents' self-esteem. *Adolescence, XXV*, 840–846.

Lecky, P. (1945). *Self-consistency: A theory of personality.* Hamden, CT: The Shoe String Press.

Levine, L. E. (1983). Mine: Self-definition in 2-year-old boys. *Developmental Psychology, 19*, 544–549.

Lewis, M. (1979). The self as a developmental concept. *Human Development, 22*, 416–419.

Lewis, M., & Brooks-Gunn, J. (Eds.). (1981). *Social cognition and the acquisition of self.* New York: Plenum.

Lewis, M., & Spanier, G. B. (1980). *Adolescent development: A life-span perspective.* New York: McGraw-Hill.

Lewis, M., Sullivan, M. W., Stanger, C., & Weiss, M. (1989). Self-development and self-conscious emotions. *Child Development, 60*, 146–156.

Livesley, W., & Bromley, D. B. (1973). *Person perception in childhood and adolescence.* New York: Wiley.

Loeb, R. C., Horst, L., & Horton, P. J. (1980). Family interaction patterns associated with self-esteem in preadolescent girls and boys. *Merrill-Palmer Quarterly, 26*, 203–217.

Lynch, M., Norem-Hebeisen, A., & Gergen, J. K. (Eds.). (1981). *Self-concept: Advances in theory and research.* Cambridge, MA: Ballinger.

Maccoby, E. E. (1980). *Social Development.* New York: Harcourt Brace Jovanovich.

Mahler, M., Pine, F., & Bergman, A. (1975). *The psychological birth of the human infant.* New York: Basic Books.

Mans, L. D., Cicchetti, D., & Sroufe, L. A. (1978). Mirror reaction of Down's syndrome infants and toddlers. *Child Development, 49*, 1247–1250.

Marcia, J. E. (1980). Identity in adolescence. In J. Adelson (Ed.), *Handbook of adolescent psychology* (pp. 159–187). New York: Wiley.

Marcia, J. E. (1988). *Identity diffusions differentiated.* Paper presented at the XXIV Meeting of the International Congress of Psychology. Sydney, Australia.

Markus, H. (1977). Self-schemata and processing information about the self. *Journal of Personality and Social Psychology, 35*, 63–78.

Markus, H. (1982). Self-schemata and processing information about the self. In M. Rosenberg and H. Kaplan (Eds.), *Social psychology of the self-concept.* Arlington Heights, IL: Harlan Davidson.

Markus, H., & Sentis, K. (1980). The self in social information processing. In J. Suls (Ed.), *Social psychological perspectives on the self.* Hillsdale, NJ: Erlbaum.

Marsh, H. W. (1989). Age and sex effects in multiple dimensions of self-concept: Preadolescence to early adulthood. *Journal of Educational Psychology, 81*, 417–430.

Marsh, H. W., Byrne, B. M., & Shavelson, R. J. (1988). A multifaceted academic self-concept: Its hierarchical structures and its relation to academic achievement. *Journal of Educational Psychology, 80*, 366–380.

Marsh, H. W., Smith, I. D., Marsh, M. R., & Owens, L. (1988). The transition from single-sex to coeducational high schools: Effect on multiple-dimensions of self-concept and on academic achievement. *American Educational Research Journal, 25*, 237–269.

McCall, R. B. (1974). Exploratory manipulation and play in the human infant. *Monographs of the Society for Research in Child Development, 39,* 185–197.

McDonald, K. A. (1980). Enhancing a child's positive self-concept. In T. Yawkey (Ed.), *The self-concept of the young child.* Provo, UT: Brigham Young University.

McGuire, W., & McGuire, C. V. (1980). Significant others in self-space: Sex differences and developmental trends in social self. In J. Suls (Ed.), *Social psychological perspectives on the self.* Hillsdale, NJ: Erlbaum.

McGuire, W., & Padawer-Swinger, A. (1976). Trait salience in the spontaneous self-concept. *Journal of Personality and Social Psychology, 33,* 743–754.

Miller, P. H., & Aloise, P. A. (1989). Young children's understanding of the psychological causes of behavior: A review. *Child Development, 60,* 257–285.

Miyamoto, S. F., & Dornbusch, S. (1956). A test of the symbolic interactionist hypothesis of self-conception. *American Journal of Sociology, 61,* 399–403.

Montemayor, R., & Eisen, M. (1977). The development of self-conceptions from childhood to adolescence. *Developmental Psychology, 13,* 314–319.

Morrison, T. L., & Lorence, J. L. (1978). Self-concept stability and change from late adolescence to early childhood. *Psychological Reports, 43,* 503–507.

Mortimer, J. T., & Lorence, J. (1981). Self-concept stability and change from late adolescence to early childhood. *Research in Community and Mental Health, 15,* 5–42.

Mueller, E. C., & Vandell, D. L. (1979). Infant-infant interaction. In J. Osofsky (Ed.), *Handbook of infant development.* New York: Wiley.

Mullener, N., & Laird, J. D. (1971). Some developmental changes in the organization of self-evaluations. *Developmental Psychology, 7,* 233–236.

Muuss, R. E. (1975). *Adolescent behavior and society.* New York: Random House.

Neisser, U. (1988). Five kinds of self-knowledge. *Philosophical Psychology, 1,* 35–59.

Offer, D., & Offer, J. B. (1975). *From teenage to young manhood.* New York: Basic Books.

Olver, R. R., Aries, E., & Batgos, J. (1990). Self–other differentiation and the mother-child relationship: The effects of sex and birth order. *Journal of Genetic Psychology, 150,* 311–321.

Pennebaker, J. W. (1980). Self-perception of emotion and internal sensation. In D. M. Wegner and R. Vallacher (Eds.), *The self in social psychology.* New York: Oxford University Press.

Piaget, J. (1962). *Play, dreams, and imitation in childhood.* New York: Norton.

Piaget, J. (1965). *The child's conception of the world.* Paterson, NJ: Littlefield, Adams.

Prawat, R. S., Grissom, S., & Parish, T. (1979). Affective development in children, grades 3 through 12. *Journal of Genetic Psychology, 135,* 37–49.

Purkey, W. W. (1978). *Inviting school success: A self-concept approach to teaching and learning.* Belmont, CA: Wadsworth.

Rogers, C. (1961). *On becoming a person.* Boston: Houghton-Mifflin.

Rosen, C. E. (1974). The effects of socio-dramatic play on problem-solving behavior among culturally disadvantaged preschool children. *Child Development, 45,* 920–927.

Rosenberg, M. (1979). *Conceiving the self.* New York: Basic Books.

Rosenberg, M. (1985). Self-concept and psychological well-being in adolescence. In R. Leahy (Ed.), *The development of the self* (pp. 205–246). New York: Academic Press.

Rosenberg, M. (1986). *Conceiving the self.* New York: Basic Books.

Rosenberg, M., & Rosenberg, F. (1981). The occupational self: A developmental study. In M. Lynch, A. Norem-Hebeisen, and K. J. Gergen (Eds.), *Self-concept: Advances in theory and research.* Cambridge, MA: Ballinger.

Rosenberg, M., & Rosenberg, F. (1982). Psychological selectivity in self-esteem formation. In M. Rosenberg and H. Kaplan (Eds.), *Social psychology of the self-concept.* Arlington Heights, IL: Harlan Davidson.

Rotenberg, K. J. (1982). Development of character constancy of self and other. *Child Development, 53,* 505–515.

Ruble, D. N. (1983). The development of social-comparison processes and their role in achievement-related self-socialization. In E. T. Higgins, D. Ruble, and W. W. Hartup (Eds.), *Social cognition and social development* (pp. 134–157). New York: Cambridge University Press.

Schlenker, B. R. (1980). *Impressive management.* Monterey, CA: Brooks/Cole.

Selman, R. (1980). *The growth of interpersonal understanding.* New York: Academic Press.

Shantz, C. U. (1983). Social cognition. In J. H. Flavell and E. M. Markman (Eds.), P. H. Mussen (Gen. Ed.). *Handbook of child psychology* (pp. 495–555). New York: Wiley.

Shavelson, R. J., & Bolus, R. (1982). Self-concept: The interplay of theory and methods. *Journal of Educational Psychology, 74,* 3–17.

Shavelson, R. J., Hubner, J. J., & Stanton, J. C. (1976). Self-concept: Validation of construct interpretations. *Review of Educational Research, 46,* 407–441.

Simmons, R. G., Blyth, D. A., Van Cleave, E. F., & Bush, D. M. (1979). Entry into early adolescence: The impact of school structure, puberty, and early dating on self-esteem. *American Sociology Review, 44,* 948–967.

Skinner, E. A. (1990). Age differences in the dimensions of perceived control during middle childhood: Implications for developmental conceptualizations and research. *Child Development, 61,* 1882–1890.

Smith, P., & Vollstedt, R. (1985). On defining play: An empirical study of the relationship between play and various play criteria. *Child Development, 56,* 1042–1050.

Spencer, M. B., Markstrom-Adams, C. (1990). Identity processes among racial and ethnic minority children in America. *Child Development, 61,* 290–300.

Sponseller, D. B., & Jaworski, A. P. (1979, April). *Social and cognitive complexity in young children's play.* Paper presented at the meeting of the American Educational Research Association, San Francisco.

Sprigle, H. A. (1980). The self-others concept. In T. Yawkey (Ed.), *The self-concept of the young child.* Provo, UT: Brigham Young University.

Squyres, E. M. (1979). Self-observation in one's own reflected image: A report. *Psychological Reports, 44,* 760–762.

Stipek, D. J., & Daniels, D. H. (1988). Declining perceptions of competence: A consequence of changes in the child or in the educational environment? *Journal of Educational Psychology, 80,* 352–356.

Stipek, D. B., Gralenski, H., & Kopp, C. (1990). Self-concept development in toddler years. *Developmental psychology, 26,* 972–977.

Streitmatter, J. L. (1988). Ethnicity as a mediating variable of early adolescent identity development. *Journal of Adolescence, 11,* 335–346.

Sullivan, H. S. (1953). *The interpersonal theory of psychiatry.* New York: W. W. Norton.

Suls, J., & Mullen, B. (1982). From the cradle to the grave: Comparison and self-evaluation across the life span. In J. Suls (Ed.), *Psychological perspectives on the self.* Hillsdale, NJ: Erlbaum.

Tesser, A., & Campbell, J. (1980). Self-definition. *Social Psychological Quarterly, 43,* 341–347.

van der Meulen, M. (1987). *Self-references in young children: Content, metadimensions, and puzzlement.* Groningen, Netherlands: Stichting Kinderstudies.

Wegner, D., & Vallacher, R. R. *The self in social psychology* New York: Oxford University Press, 1980.

Wylie, R. (1979). *The self-concept.* Vol. 2, *Theory and research on selected topics.* Lincoln: University of Nebraska Press.

Yamamoto, K. (1972). *The child and his self-image.* Boston: Houghton-Mifflin.

Yawkey, T. D. (1980). *The self-concept of the young child.* Provo, UT: Brigham Young University.

Young, T. R. (1972). *New sources of self.* New York: Pergaman Press.

Chapter 11

Adams, G. R., & Crane, P. (1980). An assessment of parents' and teachers' expectations of preschool children's social preference for attractive or unattractive children and adults. *Child Development, 51,* 224–231.

Ainsworth, M. (1973). The development of infant-mother attachment. In B. M. Caldwell and H. N. Ricciuti (Eds.), *Review of child development research* (vol. 3) (pp. 1–94). Chicago: University of Chicago Press.

Ainsworth, M. (1982). Attachment: Retrospect and prospect. In C. M. Parkes and J. Stevenson-Hinde (Eds.), *The place of attachment in human behavior* (pp. 3–30). New York: Basic.

Ainsworth, M., & Bell, S. M. (1970). Attachment, exploration, and separation: Illustrated by the behavior of one-year-olds in a strange situation. *Child Development, 41,* 49–67.

Ainsworth, M., Bell, S. M., & Slayton, D. J. (1974). Infant-mother attachment and social development: "Socialization" as a product of reciprocal responsiveness to signals. In M. P. Richards (Ed.), *The integration of a child into a social world* (pp. 17–57). London: Academic Press.

Ainsworth, M., Blehar, M., Waters, E., & Wall, S. (1978). *Patterns of attachment.* Hillsdale, NJ: Erlbaum.

Arend, R., Gove, F. L., & Sroufe, L. A. (1979). Continuity of individual adaptation from infancy to kindergarten: A predictive study of ego-resiliency and curiosity in preschoolers. *Child Development, 50,* 950–959.

Asher, S. R. (1978). Children's peer relations. In M. E. Lamb (Ed.), *Social and personality development.* New York: Holt, Rinehart and Winston.

Asher, S. R., & Coie, J. D. (Eds.) (1990). *Peer rejection in childhood.* New York: Cambridge University Press.

Asher, S. R., & Gottman, J. M. (Eds.). (1981). *The development of children's friendships.* New York: Cambridge University Press.

Asher, S. R., & Hymel, S. (1981). Children's social competence in peer relations: Sociometric and behavioral assessment. In J. D. Wine and M. D. Smye (Eds.), *Social Competence* (pp. 125–157). New York: Guilford.

Asher, S. R., Oden, S. L., & Gottman, J. M. (1977). Children's friendships in school settings. In L. G. Katz (Ed.), *Current topics in early childhood education* Vol. 1. Norwood, NJ: Ablex.

Asher, S. R., Parkhurst, J. T., Hymel, S., & Williams, G. A. (1990). Peer rejection and loneliness in childhood. In S. R. Asher and J. D. Coie (Eds.), *Peer rejection in childhood*. New York: Cambridge University Press.

Asher, S. R., & Renshaw, P. D. (1981). Children without friends: Social knowledge and social-skill training. In S. Asher and J. Gottman (Eds.), *The development of children's friendships* (pp. 273–296). New York: Cambridge University Press.

Asher, S. R., & Wheeler, V. A. (1985). Children's loneliness: A comparison of rejected and neglected peer states. *Journal of Consulting and Clinical Psychology, 53,* 500–505.

Ashlock, P., & Stephen, A. (1966). *Educational therapy in the elementary school.* Springfield, IL: Charles C Thomas.

Bates, J. E. (1980). The concept of difficult temperament. *Merrill-Palmer Quarterly, 26,* 299–319.

Bates, J. E., Maslin, C. A., & Frankel, K. A. (1985). Attachment security, mother-child interaction, and temperament as predictors of behavior-problem ratings at age three years. In I. Bretherton and E. Waters (Eds.), Growing points of attachment, theory and research. *Monographs of the Society for Research in Child Development, 50,* (2, Serial No. 209).

Baum, D. J. (1980). *Teenage pregnancy.* New York: Beaufort Books.

Baumrind, D. (1971). Current patterns of parental authority. *Developmental Psychological Monographs, 4* (1, Pt. 2).

Baumrind, D. (1980). New directions in socialization research. *American Psychologist, 35,* 639–652.

Baumrind, D. (1989). Rearing competent children. In W. Damon (Ed.), *Child development: Today and tomorrow* (pp. 349–375). San Francisco: Jossey-Bass.

Bell, R. Q. (1979). Parent-child and reciprocal influences. *American Psychologist, 34,* 821–826.

Bell, R. Q., & Harper, L. V. (1977). *Child effects on adults.* Hillsdale, NJ: Erlbaum.

Belsky, J. (1988). The "effects" of infant day care reconsidered. *Early Childhood Research Quarterly, 3,* 234–272.

Belsky, J., Lerner, R., & Spanier, G. (1984). *The child in the family.* Reading, MA: Addison-Wesley.

Belsky, J., Rovine, M., & Taylor, D. (1984). The Pennsylvania infant and family development project: III. The origins of individual differences in infant-mother attachment. Maternal and infant contributions. *Child Development, 55,* 718–728.

Berndt, T. J. (1982). The features and effects of friendship in early adolescence. *Child Development, 51,* 1447–1460.

Bernstein, R. (1981). The relationship between dimensions of delinquency and the development of self and peer perceptions. *Adolescence, XVI,* 543–556.

Binghma, C. R., Miller, B. C., & Adams, G. R. (1990). Correlates of age at first sexual intercourse in a national sample of women. *Journal of Adolescent Research, 5,* 18–33.

Black, B., & Hazen, N. L. (1990). Social status and patterns of communicaton in acquainted and unacquainted preschool children. *Developmental Psychology, 26,* 379–387.

Boskoff, A. (1982). Social failure in modern society: A reformulation and a tentative theoretical framework. *Sociological Inquiry, 52,* 88–95.

Bouvin, M., & Begin, G. (1989). Peer status and self-perception among early elementary school children: The case of rejected children. *Child Development, 60,* 591–596.

Bowlby, J. (1980). *Attachment.* New York: Basic Books.

Brazelton, T. B. (1979). Behavioral competence of the newborn infant. *Seminars in Perinatology, 27,* 532–545.

Brazelton, T. B., Koslowski, B., & Main, M. (1974). The origins of reciprocity: The early mother-infant interaction. In M. Lewis and L. A. Rosenblum (Eds.), *The effect of the infant on its caregiver.* New York: Wiley.

Brody, S., & Axelrod, S. (1978). *Mothers, fathers, and children.* New York: International Universities Press.

Bronson, G. W., & Pankey, W. B. (1977). On the distinction between fear and wariness. *Child Development, 48,* 1167–1183.

Brown, J., & Bakeman, R. (1980). Relationships of human mothers with their infants during the first year of life: Effects of prematurity. In R. W. Bell and W. P. Smotherman (Eds.), *Maternal influences and early behavior* (pp. 353–373). Holliswood, NY: Spectrum.

Cairns, R. B. (1990). Multiple metaphors for a singular idea. *Developmental Psychology, 27,* 23–26.

Caldwell, B. M. (1963). Mother-infant interaction in monomatric and polymatric families. *American Journal of Orthopsychiatry, 33,* 653–664.

Caruso, D. A. (1989). Attachment and exploration in infancy: Research and applied issues. *Early Childhood Research Quarterly, 4,* 117–132.

Carey, W. B., McCane-Sanford, T., & Davidson, E. C. (1981). Adolescent age and obstetric risk. *Seminars in Perinatology, 5,* 9–17.

Caspi, A., Elder, G. H., Jr., & Bem, D. J. (1987). Moving against the world: Life-course patterns of explosive children. *Developmental Psychology, 23,* 308–313.

Cassidy, J. (1988). Child-mother attachment and the self in six-year-olds. *Child Development, 59,* 121–135.

Centers for Disease Control. (1989, May 7). *AIDS weekly surveillance report.* Atlanta: Author.

Chapman, M. (1979). Listening to reason: Children's attentiveness and parental discipline. *Merrill-Palmer Quarterly, 25,* 251–263.

Chilman, C. S. (1983). Some psychosocial aspects of adolescent sexual and contraceptive behaviors in a changing American society. In J. B. Lancaster and B. A. Hamburg (Eds.), *School-age pregnancy and parenthood: Biosocial dimensions* (pp. 191–217). New York: Aldine DeGruyter.

Cohen, M. (1979). Statement of teenage pregnancy. *Pediatrics, 63,* 795–797.

Cohn, D. A. (1990). Child-mother attachment of six-year-olds and social competence at school. *Child Development, 61,* 152–162.

Coie, J. D. (1990). Toward a theory of peer rejection. In S. R. Asher and J. D. Coie (Eds.), *Peer rejection in childhood* (pp. 365–401). New York: Cambridge University Press.

Coie, J. D., & Dodge, K. A. (1983). Continuities and changes in children's social status: A five-year longitudinal study. *Merrill-Palmer Quarterly, 29,* 261–282.

Coie, J. D., & Dodge, K. A. (1988). Multiple sources of data on social behavior and social status in school: A cross-age comparison. *Child Development, 59,* 815–829.

Coie, J. D., Dodge, K. A., & Coppotelli, H. (1982). Dimensions and types of social status: A cross-age perspective. *Developmental Psychology, 18,* 557–570.

Coie, J. D., Dodge, K. A., Terry, R., & Wright, V. (1991). The role of aggression in peer relations: An analysis of aggressive episodes in boys' play groups. *Child Development, 62,* 812–826.

Coie, J. D., & Kupersmidt, J. B. (1983). A behavioral analysis of emerging social status in boys' groups. *Child Development, 54,* 1400–1416.

Cosaro, W. A. (1981). Friendship in the nursery school: Social organization in a peer environment. In S. R. Asher and J. M. Gottman, (Eds.), *The development of children's friendships.* New York: Cambridge University Press.

Cowen, E., Pederson, A., Babijian, H., Izzo, V., & Trost, M. (1973). Long-term follow-up of early detected vulnerable children. *Journal of Consulting and Clinical Psychology, 41,* 438–446.

Crick, N. R., & Ladd, G. W. (1990). Children's perceptions of the outcomes of social strategies: Do the ends justify being mean? *Developmental Psychology, 26,* 612–620.

Crockenberg, S., & Litman, C. (1990). Autonomy as competence in 2-year-olds: Maternal correlates of child defiance, compliance, and self-assertion. *Developmental Psychology, 26,* 961–971.

Csikszentmihalyi, M., Larson, R., & Prescott, S. (1977). The ecology of adolescent activity and experience. *The Journal of Youth and Adolescence, 6,* 281–294.

Custrini, R. J., & Feldman, R. (1989). Children's social competence and nonverbal encoding and decoding of emotions. *Journal of Clinical Child Psychology, 18,* 336–342.

Cvetkovich, G., & Grote, B. (1980). Psychological development and the social problem of teenage illegitimacy. In C. Chilman (Ed.), *Adolescent pregnancy and childbearing: Findings from research* (pp. 15–41). Washington, DC: U.S. Department of Health and Human Services.

Denham, S. A., McKinley, M., Couchoud, E. A., & Holt, R. W. (1990). Emotional and behavioral predictors of preschool peer ratings. *Child Development, 61,* 1145–1152.

Denham, S. A., Renwick, S. M., & Holt, R. W. (1991). Working and playing together: Prediction of preschool social-emotional competence from mother-child interaction. *Child Development, 62,* 242–249.

Dickstein, S., & Parke, R. D. (1988). Social referencing in infancy: A glance at fathers and marriage. *Child Development, 59,* 506–511.

DiClemente, R. J. (1990). The emergence of adolescents as a risk group for human immunodeficiency virus infection. *Journal of Adolescent Research, 5,* 7–17.

DiClemente, R. J., Forest, K., & Mickler, S. (1989, June). *College students' knowledge and attitudes about AIDS and changes in AIDS-preventative behaviors.* Presented at the Fifth International Conference on Acquired Immunodeficiency Syndrome. Montreal, Canada.

DiClemente, R. J., Zorn, J., & Temoshok, L. (1986). Adolescence and AIDS: A survey of knowledge, attitudes, beliefs about AIDS in San Francisco. *American Journal of Public Health, 76,* 1443–1445.

Dion, K. K. (1972). Physical attractiveness and evaluation of children's transgressions. *Journal of Personality and Social Psychology, 24,* 207–213.

Dion, K. K. (1973). Young children's stereotyping of facial attractiveness. *Developmental Psychology, 9,* 183–198.

Dishion, T. J., Patterson, G. R., Stoolmiller, M., & Skinner, M. L. (1991). Family, school, and behavioral antecedents to early adolescent involvement with antisocial peers. *Developmental Psychology, 27,* 172–180.

Dix, T., Ruble, D., & Zambarano, R. (1989). Mothers' implicit theories of discipline: Parent effects, and the attribution process. *Child Development, 60,* 1373–1391.

Dodge, K. A. (1983). Behavioral antecedents of peer social status. *Child Development, 54,* 1386–1399.

Dodge, K. A., Coie, J. D., & Brakke, N. P. (1982). Behavior patterns of socially rejected and neglected preadolescents: The roles of social approach and aggression. *Journal of Abnormal Child Psychology, 10,* 3, 389–410.

Dodge, K. A., & Frame, C. L. (1982). Social cognitive biases and deficits in aggressive boys. *Child Development, 53,* 620–635.

Dodge, K. A., Murphy, R. R., & Buchsbaum, K. (1984). The assessment of intention-cue detection skills in children: Implications for developmental psychology. *Child Development, 55,* 163–173.

Donovan, W. L., & Leavitt, L. A. (1985). Simulating conditions of learned helplessness: The effects of interventions and attributions. *Child Development, 56,* 594–603.

Dunphy, D. C. (1963). The social structure of urban adolescent peer groups. *Sociometry, 26,* 230–246.

Earn, B. M., & Sobol, M. P. (1990). A categorical analysis of children's attributions for social success and failure. *The Psychological Report, 40,* 173–185.

East, P. L., & Rook, K. S. (1992). Compensatory patterns of support among children's peer relationships: A test using school friends, nonschool friends, and siblings. *Developmental Psychology, 28,* 163–172.

Easterbrooks, M. A. (1989). Quality of attachment to mother and to father: Effects of perinatal risks status. *Child Development, 60,* 825–830.

Edelman, M. S., & Omark, D. R. (1973). Dominance hierarchies in young children. *Social Science Information, 43,* 237–250.

Edwards, R., Manstead, A. S. R., & McDonald, C. J. (1984). The relationship between children's sociometric status and ability to recognize facial expression of emotion. *European Journal of Social Psychology, 14,* 235–238.

Egeland, B., & Sroufe, L. A. (1981). Attachment and early maltreatment. *Child Development, 52,* 44–52.

Ehrenhaft, P. M., Wagner, J. L., & Herdman, R. C. (1989). Changing prognosis for very low birth weight infants. *Obstetrics and Gynecology, 74,* 528–535.

Eisen, M., Zellman, G. L., Leibowitz, A., Chow, W. K., & Evans, J. R. (1983). Factors discriminating pregnancy resolution decisions of unmarried adolescents. *Genetic Psychology Monographs, 108,* 69–95.

Emde, R. M., Gaensbauer, T., & Harmon, R. (1976). Emotional expression in infancy: A biobehavioral study. *Psychological Issues, 10* (Whole No. 1).

Emde, R. M., & Robinson, J. (1979). The first two months: Recent research in developmental psychobiology and the changing view of the newborn. In J. Noshpitz and J. Call (Eds.), *Basic handbook of child psychiatry.* New York: Basic Books.

Erickson, M., Egeland, B., & Sroufe, L. A. (1985). The relationship between quality of attachment and behavior problems in preschool in a high risk sample. In I. Bretherton and E. Waters (Eds.), *Growing points in attachment theory and research. Monographs of the Society for Research in Child Development, 50,* (1–2, Series No. 209), 147–186.

Erikson, E. (1950). *Childhood and society.* New York: W. W. Norton.

Field, T. M. (1977). Effects of early separation, interactive deficits and experimental manipulations of infant-mother face-to-face interaction. *Child Development, 48,* 763–771.

Field, T. M. (1982). Affective displays of high-risk infants during early interactions. In T. Field and A. Fogel (Eds.), *Emotion and early interaction* (pp. 101–125). Hillsdale, NJ: Erlbaum.

Forehand, R. (1977). Child noncompliance to parental requests: Behavioral analysis and treatment. In M. Hersen, R. M. Eisler, and P. M. Miller (Eds.), *Progress in behavior modification* (Vol. 5). New York: Academic Press.

Fraiberg, S. (1974). Blind infants and their mothers: An examination of the sign system. In M. Lewis and L. A. Rosenblum (Eds.), *The effect of the infant on its caregiver.* New York: Wiley.

French, D. (1988). Heterogeneity of peer-rejected boys: Aggressive and nonaggressive subtypes. *Child Development, 59,* 976–985.

French, D. (1990). Heterogeneity of peer-rejected girls. *Child Development, 61,* 2028–2031.

French, D., & Waas, G. A. (1985). Behavior problems of peer-neglected and peer-rejected elementary-age children: Parent and teacher perspectives. *Child Development, 56,* 246–252.

Freud, S. (1938). *An outline of psychoanalysis.* London: Hogarth.

Frodi, A. M., Bridges, L., & Grolnick, W. (1985). Correlates of master-related behavior: A short-term longitudinal study of infants in their second year. *Child Development, 56,* 1291–1298.

Frodi, A. M., & Lamb, M. (1978). Sex differences in responsiveness to infants: A developmental study of psychophysiological and behavioral responses. *Child Development, 49,* 1182–1188.

Frodi, A. M., Rahe, D. F., & Hartup, W. W. (1979). Rehabilitation of socially withdrawn preschool children through mixed-age and same-age socialization. *Child Development, 50,* 915–922.

Frodi, A. M., Thompson, R. (1985). Infants' affective responses in the strange situation: Effects of prematurity and of quality of attachment. *Child Development, 56,* 1280–1290.

Goldberg, S. (1977). Social competence in infancy: A model of parent-infant interaction. *Merrill-Palmer Quarterly, 23,* 163–177.

Goldberg, S. (1983). Parent-infant bonding: Another look. *Child Development, 54,* 1355–1382.

Goossens, F. A., & van Ijzendoorn, M. H. (1990). Quality of infants' attachments to professional caregivers: Relation to infant-parent attachment and day-care characteristics. *Child Development, 61,* 832–837.

Gottman, J. M., Gonso, J., & Rasmussen, B. (1975). Social interaction, social competence and friendship in children. *Child Development, 46,* 709–718.

Gottman, J. M., Gonso, J., & Schuler, P. (1976). Teaching social skills to isolated children. *Journal of Abnormal Child Psychology, 74,* 179–197.

Greenberg, M., & Morris, N. (1974). Engrossment: The newborn's impact upon the father. *American Journal of Orthopsychiatry, 44,* 520–531.

Greenberger, E., & Steinberg, L. (1986). *When teenagers work: The psychological and social costs of adolescent employment.* New York: Basic Books.

Grossman, F. K., Eichler, L. S., Winickoff, S. A., Anzalone, M. K., Gorseyeff, M., & Sargent, S. P. (1980). *Pregnancy, birth, and parenthood.* San Francisco: Jossey-Bass.

Guralnick, M. J., & Groom, J. M. (1990). The relationship between parent-rated behavior problems and peer relations in preschool children. *Early Education and Development, 1,* 266–278.

Gurucharri, C., Phelps, E., & Selman, R. (1984). Development of interpersonal understanding: A longitudinal and comparative study of normal and disturbed youths. *Journal of Consulting and Clinical Psychology, 52,* 26–36.

Harris, L. (1986). *American teens speak: Sex, myths, television, and birth control. The planned parenthood pull.* New York: Planned Parenthood Federation of America.

Hartup, W. W. (1989). Behavioral manifestations of children's friendships. In T. J. Berndt and G. W. Ladd (Eds.), *Peer relationships in child development* (pp. 46–70). New York: Wiley.

Hayes, C. D. (Ed.). (1987). *Risking the future: Adolescent sexuality, pregnancy and childbearing* (Vol. 1). Washington, DC: National Academy Press.

Hazen, N. L., & Black, B. (1989). Preschool peer communication skills: The role of social status and interaction context. *Child Development, 60,* 867–876.

Hechtman, L. (1989). Teenage mothers and their children: Risks and problems: A review. *Canadian Journal of Psychiatry, 34,* 569–581.

Hein, K. (1987). AIDS in adolescents: A rationale for concern. *New York State Journal of Medicine, 88,* 290–295.

Hein, K. (1988). *AIDS in adolescence: Exploring the challenge.* Paper presented at the National Invitation Conference on Adolescent AIDS, New York.

Hofferth, S. L., & Hayes, C. D. (Eds.). (1987). *Risking the future: Adolescent sexuality, pregnancy, and childbearing: Vol. 2. Working papers and statistical reports.* Washington, DC: National Academy Press.

Hogan, D. P., Hao, L., & Parish, W. L. (1990). Race, kin networks, and assistance to mother-headed families. *Social Forces, 68,* 797–812.

Howes, C. (1988). Peer interaction of young children. *Monographs of the Society for Research in Child Development, 53* (1, Serial No. 217).

Hymel, S. (1986). Interpretations of peer behavior: Affective bias in childhood and adolescence. *Child Development, 57,* 431–445.

Hymel, S., Rubin, K. H., Rowden, L., & LeMare, L. (1990). Children's peer relationships: Longitudinal prediction of internalizing and externalizing problems from middle to late childhood. *Child Development, 61,* 2004–2021.

Isabella, R. A., & Belsky, J. (1991). Interactional synchrony and the origins of infant-mother attachment: A replication study. *Child Development, 62,* 373–384.

Jacobson, S. W., & Frye, K. F. (1991). Effect of maternal social support on attachment: Experimental evidence. *Child Development, 62,* 572–582.

Jaslow, C. K. (1982). *Teenage pregnancy.* Ann Arbor, MI: ERIC/CAPS.

Johnson, D. W. (1981). *Reaching out.* Englewood Cliffs, NJ: Prentice-Hall.

Keane, S. P., Brown, K. P., & Crenshaw, T. M. (1990). Children's intention-cue detection as a function of maternal social behavior: Pathways to social rejection. *Developmental Psychology, 26,* 1004–1009.

Kegeles, S. M., Adler, N. E., & Irwin, C. E. (1988). Sexually active adolescents and condoms: Changes over one year in knowledge, attitudes, and use. *American Journal of Public Health, 78,* 460–465.

Kennell, J. H., Voos, D. K., & Klaus, M. H. (1979). Parent-infant bonding. In J. D. Osofsky (Ed.), *Handbook on infant development.* New York: Wiley.

Klaus, M., & Kennell, J. (1982). *Parent-infant bonding.* St. Louis: C. V. Mosby.

Kochanska, G., Kuczynski, L., Radke-Yarrow, M., & Darby-Welsch, J. (1987). Resolutions of control episodes between well and affectively ill mothers and their young children. *Journal of Abnormal Child Psychology, 15,* 441–456.

Kotelchuck, M. (1972). *The nature of the child's tie to his father.* Unpublished Ph.D. dissertation, Harvard University, Cambridge, MA.

Kotelchuck, M. (1981). The infant's relationship to the father: Experimental evidence. In M. E. Lamb (Ed.), *The role of the father in child development.* New York: Wiley.

Kuczynski, L., & Kochanska, G. (1990). Development of children's noncompliance strategies from toddlerhood to age 5. *Developmental Psychology, 26,* 398–408.

Kunst-Wilson, W., & Cronenwett, L. (1981). Nursing care for the emerging family: Promoting paternal behavior. *Research in Nursing and Health, 1,* 361–365.

Kupersmidt, J. B., & Coie, J. D. (1990). Preadolescent peer status, aggression, and school adjustment as predictors of externalizing problems in adolescence. *Child Development, 61,* 1350–1362.

Kupersmidt, J. B., Coie, J. D., & Dodge, K. A. (1990). Predicting disorder from peer social problems. In S. R. Asher and J. D. Coie (Eds.), *Peer rejection in childhood* (pp. 274–305). New York: Cambridge University Press.

Ladd, G. W. (1981). Effectiveness of social learning method for enhancing children's social interaction and peer acceptance. *Child Development, 52,* 171–178.

Ladd, G. W. (1983). Social networks of popular, average, and rejected children in school settings. *Merrill-Palmer Quarterly, 29,* 282–307.

Ladd, G. W., & Oden, S. L. (1979). The relationship between peer acceptance and children's ideas about helpfulness. *Child Development, 50,* 402–408.

Ladd, G. W., & Price, J. M. (1986). Promoting children's cognitive and social competence: The relation between parents' perceptions of task difficulty and children's perceived and actual competence. *Child Development, 57,* 446–460.

Ladd, G. W., & Price, J. M. (1987). Predicting children's social and school adjustment following the transition from preschool to kindergarten. *Child Development, 58,* 1168–1189.

Lamb, M. E. (1977). Father-infant and mother-infant interaction in the first year of life. *Child Development, 48,* 167–181.

Lamb, M. E., & Easterbrooks, M. A. (1981). Individual differences in parental sensitivity: Origins, components, and consequences. In M. E. Lamb and L. R. Sherrod (Eds.), *Infant social cognition: Empirical and theoretical considerations.* Hillsdale, NJ: Erlbaum.

Lamb, M. E., Elster, A. B., Peters, L. T., Kahn, J. S., & Tavare, J. (1986). *Characteristics of married and unmarried adolescent mothers and their parents.* Unpublished manuscript, University of Utah, Salt Lake City.

Lamb, M. E., Frodi, A. M., Hwang, C. P., & Frodi, M. (1983). Effects of paternal involvement on infant preferences for mothers and fathers. *Child Development, 54,* 450–458.

Lamb, M. E., & Sherrod, L. R. (Eds.). (1981). *Infant social cognition: Empirical and theoretical considerations.* Hillsdale, NJ: Erlbaum.

Langlois, J. H., & Downs, A. C. (1979). Peer relations as a function of physical attractiveness: The eye of the beholder or behavioral reality? *Child Development, 50,* 409–418.

Langlois, J. H., & Sawin, D. B. (1981). *Infant physical attractiveness as an elicitor of differential parent behaviors.* Paper presented at the meeting of Society for Research in Child Development, Boston.

Lanier, M., & McCarthy, B. (1989). AIDS awareness and the impact of AIDS education in juvenile corrections. *Criminal Justice and Behavior, 16,* 395–411.

Leavitt, L. A., & Donovan, W. (1979). Perceived infant temperament, locus of control, and maternal physiological response to infant gaze. *Journal of Research in Personality, 13,* 267–278.

Lerner, R. M., & Lerner, J. V. (1977). Effects of age, sex, and physical attractiveness on child-peer relations, academic performance, and elementary school adjustment. *Developmental Psychology, 13,* 585–590.

Lester, B. M., Hoffman, J., & Brazelton, T. B. (1985). The rhythmic structure of mother-infant interaction in term and preterm infants. *Child Development, 56,* 15–27.

Lewis, M., & Feiring, C. (1989). Infant, mother, and mother-infant interaction behavior and subsequent attachment. *Child Development, 60,* 831–837.

Leyser, Y., & Gottlieb, J. (1981). Improving the social status of rejected pupils. *Exceptional Children, 46,* 459–461.

Lieberman, A. F. (1977). Preschoolers' competence with a peer: Relations with attachment and peer experience. *Child Development, 48,* 1277–1287.

Lind, J., Vuorenkoski, V., & Wasz-Hockert, O. (1973). In N. Morris (Ed.), *Psychosomatic medicine in obstetrics and gynecology.* Basle, Switzerland: S. Karger.

Lozoff, M. M. (1974). Fathers and autonomy in women. In R. B. Kundsin (Ed.), *Women and success.* New York: Morrow.

Lutkenhaus, P., Grossmann, K. E., & Grossmann, K. (1985). Infant-mother attachment at twelve months and style of interaction with a stranger at the age of three. *Child Development, 56,* 1538–1542.

Lyons-Ruth, K., Connell, D. B., Grunebaum, H. U., & Botein, S. (1990). Infants at social risk: Maternal depression and family support services as mediators of infant development and security of attachment. *Child Development, 61,* 85–98.

Lytton, H. (1980). *Parent-child interaction: The socialization process observed in twin and singleton families.* New York: Plenum.

Maccoby, E. E., & Jacklin, C. M. (1974). The psychology of sex differences. Palo Alto, CA: Stanford University Press.

Maccoby, E. E., & Martin, J. A. (1983). Socialization in the context of the family: Parent-child interaction. In E. M. Hetherington (Ed.), *Handbook of child psychology* (pp. 1–102). New York: Wiley.

Main, M., Kaplan, N., & Cassidy, J. (1985). Security in infancy, childhood and adulthood: A move to the level of representation. In I. Bretherton and E. Waters (Eds.), *Growing points in attachment theory and research. Monographs of the Society for Research in Child Development, 50,* (Whole No. 209), 66–104.

Main, M., & Solomon, J. (1990). Procedures for identifying infants as disorganized/disoriented during the Ainsworth Strange Situation. In M. Greenberg, D. Cicchetti, and E. M. Cummings (Eds.), *Attachment during the preschool years.* Chicago: University of Chicago Press.

Main, M., & Weston, D. R. (1978). The quality of toddler's relationship to mother and to father. *Child Development, 49,* 1247–1250.

Malatesta, C. Z., Culver, C., Tesman, J. R., Shepard, B. (1989). The development of emotion expression during the first two years of life. *Monographs of the Society for Research in Child Development, 54,* Serial No. 219.

Mangelsdorf, S., Gunnar, M., Kestenbaum, R., Lang, S., & Andreas, D. (1990). Infant proneness-to-distress temperament, maternal personality and mother-infant attachment: Associations and goodness of fit. *Child Development, 61,* 820–831.

Martin, J. A. (1981). A longitudinal study of the consequences of early mother-infant interaction: A microanalytic approach. *Monographs of the Society for Research in Child Development, 46* (3, Serial No. 190).

Masters, J. C., & Furman, W. (1981). Popularity, individual friendship selection, and specific peer interaction among children. *Developmental Psychology, 17,* 344–350.

Matas, L., Arend, R., & Sroufe, L. A. (1978). Continuity of adaptation in the second year: The relationship between quality of attachment and later competence. *Child Development, 49,* 547–556.

McDavid, J. W., & Harari, H. (1966). Stereotyping of names and popularity in grade-school children. *Child Development, 37,* 453–459.

McDonald, M. A. (1978). Paternal behavior at first contact with the newborn in a birth environment without intrusions. *Birth Family Journal, 5,* 123–132.

Miller, K. (1990). Adolescents' same-sex and opposite-sex peer relations: Sex differences in popularity, perceived social competence, and social cognitive skills. *Journal of Adolescent Research, 5,* 222–241.

Miller, P. Y., & Simon, W. (1980). The development of sexuality in adolescence. In J. Adelson (Ed.), *Handbook of adolescent psychology.* New York: Wiley.

Mize, J., & Ladd, G. W. (1990). Toward the development of successful social skill training for preschool children. In S. R. Asher and J. D. Coie (Eds.), *Peer rejection in childhood.* New York: Cambridge University Press.

Mott, F. L., & Marsiglio, W. (1985). Early childbearing and completion of high school. *Family Planning Perspectives, 17,* 234–237.

Mueller, E., & Vandell, D. (1979). Infant-infant interaction. In J. Osofsky (Ed.), *Handbook of infant development.* New York: Wiley.

Mullis, R. L., & Mullis, A. K. (1989). Parents' reports of nine-year-old children: Reports of attitudes and behaviors. *Child Study Journal, 19,* 145–156.

Murray, A. D. (1979). Infant crying as an elicitor of parental behavior: An examination of two models. *Psychological Bulletin, 86,* 191–215.

National Research Council. (1987). *Risking the future: Adolescent sexuality, pregnancy, and childbearing.* Washington, DC: National Academy Press.

Newson, J., & Newson, E. (1968). *Four years old in an urban community*. London: Allen and Unwin.

Nicholson, J., Gist, J. F., Klein, R. D., & Standley, K. (1983). Outcomes of father involvement in pregnancy and birth. *Birth, 10*, 5–9.

Oden, S. L., & Asher, S. R. (1977). *Coaching children in social skills for friendship making*. Paper presented at the Biennial Meeting of the Society for Research in Child Development, Denver.

Ogbu, J. (1988). Black education: A cultural-ecological perspective. In H. P. McAdoo (Ed.), *Black families* (pp. 169–186). Beverly Hills: Sage.

Olweus, D. (1980). Familial and temperamental determinants of aggression behavior in adolescents: A causal analysis. *Developmental Psychology, 16*, 644–660.

Ooms, T. (Ed.). (1981). *Teenage pregnancy in a family context: Implications for policy*. Philadelphia: Temple University Press.

Overton, W. F. (1983). *The relationships between social and cognitive development*. NJ: Erlbaum.

Palkovitz, R. (1985). Lay-attitudes concerning fathers and "bonding." Cited in R. Palkovitz, Fathers' birth attendance, early contact and extended contact with their newborns: A critical review. *Child Development, 56*, 392–406.

Pannabecker, M. J., Emde, R. M., & Austin, B. C. (1982). The effect of early extended contact on father-newborn interaction. *Journal of Genetic Psychology, 141*, 7–17.

Parke, R. D. (1979). Perspectives of father-infant interaction. In J. D. Osofsky (Ed.), *Handbook of infant development*. New York: Wiley.

Parke, R. D. (1981). *Fathers*. Cambridge, MA: Harvard University Press.

Parke, R. D., MacDonald, K. B., Beitel, A., & Bhavnagri, N. (1988). The role of the family in the development of peer relationships. In R. D. Peters and R. J. McMahon (Eds.), *Marriage and families: Behavioral treatments and processes* (pp. 17–44). New York: Brunner-Mazel.

Parke, R. D., & Tinsley, B. J. (1987). Family interactions in infancy. In J. Osofsky (Ed.), *Handbook of infant development* (2nd ed.) (pp. 579–641). New York: Wiley.

Parker, J. G., & Asher, S. R. (1987). Peer relations and later personal adjustment: Are low-accepted children "at-risk"? *Psychological Bulletin, 102*, 357–389.

Parker, J. G., & Asher, S. R. (1988). *Peer group acceptance and the quality of children's best friendships*. Paper presented at the NATO Advanced Study Institute, "So-cial Competence in Developmental Perspective," Savoy, France.

Patterson, C. J., Cohn, D. A., & Kao, B. T. (1989). Maternal warmth as a protective factor against risks associated with peer rejection among children. *Development and Psychopathology, 1*, 21–38.

Patterson, C. J., Kupersmidt, J. B., & Griesler, P. C. (1990). Children's perceptions of self and of relationships with others as a function of sociometric status. *Child Development, 61*, 1335–1349.

Patterson, G. R. (1975). *Families: Applications of social learning to family life*. Champaign, IL: Research Press.

Patterson, G. R. (1982). *Coercive family process*. Eugene, OR: Castilia.

Patterson, G. R. (1986). Performance models for antisocial boys. *American Psychologist, 41*, 432–444.

Patterson, G. R., & Bank, L. (1989). Some amplifier and dampening mechanisms for pathologic processes in families. In M. Gunnar and E. Thelen (Eds.), *Systems and development: The Minnesota symposia on child psychology* (Vol. 22). Hillsdale, NJ: Erlbaum.

Patterson, G. R., DeBaryshe, B. D., & Ramsey, E. (1989). A developmental perspective on antisocial behavior. *American Psychologist, 44*, 329–335.

Pedersen, F. A. (1975). *Mother, father, and infant as an interactive system*. Paper presented at the Meeting of the American Psychological Association, Chicago.

Pedersen, F. A. (1982). Mother, father, and infant as an interactive system. In J. Belsky (Ed.), *In the beginning* (pp. 216–226). New York: Columbia University Press.

Pedersen F. A., & Robson, K. (1969). Father participation in infancy. *American Journal of Orthopsychiatry, 39*, 466–472.

Pederson, D. R., Moran, G., Sitko, C., Campbell, K., Ghesquire, K., & Acton, H. (1990). Maternal sensitivity and the security of infant-mother attachment: A Q-sort study. *Child Development, 61*, 1974–1983.

Peterson, G. H., Mehl, L. E., & Leiderman, P. (1979). The role of some birth-related variables in father attachment. *American Journal of Orthopsychiatry, 49*, 330–338.

Pettit, G. S., Bakski, A., Dodge, K. A., & Coie, J. D. (1990). The emergence of social dominance in young boys' play groups: Developmental differences and behavioral correlates. *Developmental Psychology, 26*, 1017–1025.

Pianta, R. C., Sroufe, L. A., & Egeland, B. (1989). Continuity and discontinuity in maternal sensitivity at 6, 24, and 42 months in a high-risk sample. *Child Development, 60*, 481–487.

Power, T. G., & Shanks, J. A. (1989). Parents as socializers: Maternal and paternal views. *Journal of Youth and Adolescence, 18,* 203–208.

Putallaz, M., & Gottman, J. M. (1981). An interactional model of children's entry into peer groups. *Child Development, 52,* 986–994.

Putallaz, M., & Sheppard, B. H. (1990). Social status and children's orientations to limited resources. *Child Development, 61,* 2022–2027.

Putallaz, M., & Wasserman, A. (1989). Children's naturalistic entry behavior and sociometric status: A developmental perspective. *Developmental Psychology, 25,* 297–305.

Radke-Yarrow, M., Cummings, E. M., Kuczynski, L., & Chapman, M. (1985). Patterns of attachment in two- and three-year-olds in normal families and families with parental depression. *Child Development, 56,* 884–893.

Ramey, D. C., & Farran, C. T. (1979). A compensatory education for disadvantaged children. *School Review, 87,* 171–189.

Ramey, C. T., & Ramey, S. L. (1990). Intensive educational intervention for children of poverty. *Intelligence, 14,* 1–9.

Reubens, B., Harrison, J., & Rupp, K. (1981). *The youth labor force, 1945–1995: A cross-national analysis.* Totowa, NJ: Allaheld, Osmun.

Roberts, J., & Baird, J. L., Jr. (1971). Parent ratings of behavioral patterns of children. *Vital and Health Statistics. Data from the National Health Survey* (Ser. 11, No. 108). Washington, DC: U.S. Government Printing Office.

Rode, S. S., Chang, P. N., Fisch, R. O., & Sroufe, L. A. (1981). Attachment patterns of infants separated at birth. *Developmental Psychology, 17,* 188–191.

Rodholm, M., & Larsson, K. (1979). Father-infant interaction at the first contact after delivery. *Early Human Development, 3,* 1–27.

Roff, M. (1966). *Some childhood and adolescent characteristics of adult homosexuals.* U.S. Army Medical Research and Developmental Command, Report No. 66–5.

Roff, M., Sells, S. B., & Golden, M. (1972). *Social adjustment and personality development in children.* Minneapolis: University of Minnesota Press.

Roscoe, B., & Kruger, T. (1990). AIDS: Late adolescents' knowledge and its influence on sexual behavior. *Adolescence, XXV,* 38–46.

Rubin, K. H., LeMare, L., & Lollis, S. (1990). Social withdrawal in childhood: Developmental pathways to peer rejection. In S. R. Asher and J. D. Coie (Eds.), *Peer rejection in childhood.* New York: Cambridge University Press.

Russell, A., & Finnie, V. (1990). Preschool children's social status and maternal instructions to assist group entry. *Developmental Psychology, 26,* 603–611.

Schaffer, H. R., & Emerson, P. E. (1964). The development of social attachments in infancy. *Monographs of the Society for Research in Child Development, 29,* (No. 94).

Segall, M. (1972). Cardiac responsibility to auditory stimulation in premature infants. *Nursing Research, 21,* 15–19.

Seitz, V., Rosenbaum, L. K., & Apfel, N. H. (1985). Effects of family support intervention: A ten-year follow-up. *Child Development, 56,* 376–391.

Shereshefsky, P. M., & Yarrow, L. J. (1973). *Psychological aspects of a first pregnancy and early post-natal adaptation.* New York: Raven Press.

Siegel, E., Bauman, K. E., Schaefer, E. S., Sanders, M. M., & Ingram, D. D. (1980). Hospital and home support during infancy: Impact on maternal attachment, child abuse and neglect and health care utilization. *Pediatrics, 66,* 183–190.

Simon, W., Berger, A. S., & Gagnon, J. S. (1972). Beyond anxiety and fantasy: The coital experiences of college youth. *Journal of Youth and Adolescence, 1,* 203–222.

Smetana, J. G. (1989). Adolescents' and parents' reasoning about actual family conflict. *Child Development, 60,* 1052–1067.

Smilgis, M. (1987, February 16). The big chill: Fear of AIDS. *Time,* 50–53.

Spitz, R. (1945). Hospitalism: An inquiry into the genesis of psychiatric conditions in early childhood. *Psychoanalytic Study of the Child, 1,* 53–74.

Sroufe, L. A. (1979). The coherence of individual development. *American Psychologist, 34,* 834–841.

Sroufe, L. A. (1983). Attachment classification from the perspective of infant-caregiver relationships and infant temperament. In M. Perlmutter (Ed.), *Minnesota Symposia in Child Psychology* (Vol. 16). Hillsdale, NJ: Erlbaum.

Sroufe, L. A. (1985). Attachment classification from the perspective of infant-caregiver relationships and infant temperament. *Child Development, 56,* 1–14.

Sroufe, L. A., & Fleeson, J. (1986). Attachment and the construction of relationships. In W. W. Hartup and Z. Rubin (Eds.), *Relationships and development* (pp. 51–72). Hillsdale, NJ: Erlbaum.

Sroufe, L. A., Schork, E., Motti, F., Lawroski, N., & La Frenier, P. (1984). The role of affect in social competence. In C. Izard, J. Kagan, & R. Zajonc (Eds.), *Emotions, cognition, and behavior*. Oxford: Oxford University Press.

Steinberg, L. (1988). *Noninstructional influences on high school student achievement: The contributions of parents, peers, extracurricular activities, and part-time work*. Madison, WI: National Center on Effective Secondary Schools.

Steinberg, L., & Dornbusch, S. M. (1990). Negative correlates of part-time employment during adolescence: Replication and elaboration. National Center on Effective Secondary Schools, Madison, WI.

Steinberg, L., Elmen, J., Mounts, N. (1989). Authoritative parenting, psychosocial maturity, and academic success among adolescents. *Child Development, 60,* 1424–1436.

Steinberg, L., Greenberger, E., Garduque, L., Ruggiero, M., & Vaux, A. (1982). Effects of working on adolescent development. *Developmental Psychology, 18,* 385–395.

Stern, D. N. (1974). Mother and infant at play: The dyadic interpretation involving facial, vocal, and gaze behaviors. In M. Lewis and L. Rosenblum (Eds.), *The effect of the infant on its caregiver*. New York: Wiley.

Strauss, C. E., Forehand, R., Frame, C. L., & Smith, K. (1984). Characteristics of children with extreme scores on the children's depression inventory. *Journal of Clinical Child Psychology, 13,* 227–231.

Strunin, L., & Hingson, R. (1987). Acquired immunodeficiency syndrome and adolescents: Knowledge, beliefs, attitudes, and behaviors. *Pediatrics, 79,* 825–828.

Styczynski, L. E., & Langlois, J. H. (1980). The effects of familiarity on behavioral stereotypes associated with physical attractiveness in young children. *Child Development, 48,* 1137–1141.

Suomi, S. J., & Harlow, H. (1975). The role and reason of peer relationships in Rhesus monkeys. In M. Lewis and L. A. Rosenblum (Eds.), *Friendships and peer relationships*. New York: Wiley.

Svejda, M., Campos, J. J., & Emde, R. (1980). Mother-infant "bonding": Failure to generalize. *Child Development, 51,* 775–779.

Tedesco, L. A., & Gaier, E. L. (1988). Friendship bonds in adolescence. *Adolescence, XXIII,* 126–139.

Teti, D. M., & Ablard, K. E. (1989). Security of attachment and infant-sibling relationships: A laboratory study. *Child Development, 60,* 1519–1528.

Thompson, L. A., Fagan, J. F., & Fulker, D. W. (1991). Longitudinal prediction of specific cognitive abilities from infant novelty preference. *Child Development, 62,* 530–538.

Thompson, R. A., Lamb, M., & Estes, D. (1982). Stability of infant-mother attachment and its relationship to changing life circumstances in an unselected middle-class sample. *Child Development, 53,* 144–148.

Thurman, Q., & Franklin, K. (1990). AIDS and college health: Knowledge, threats, prevention at a northeastern university. *Journal of American College Health, 38,* 179–184.

Tizard, B., Philips, J., & Plewis, I. (1976). Play in preschool centers. *Journal of Child Psychology and Psychiatry, 17,* 265–274.

Ulvedal, S. K., & Feeg, V. D. (1983). Pregnant teens who choose childbirth. *JOSH, 53,* 229–232.

Vaughn, B. E., & Waters, E. (1990). Attachment behavior at home and in the laboratory: Q-sort observations and strange situation classifications of one-year-olds. *Child Development, 61,* 1965–1973.

Walden, T. A., & Field, T. M. (1990). Preschool children's social competence and production and discrimination of affective expressions. *British Journal of Developmental Psychology, 8,* 65–76.

Washington, A. C. (1982). A cultural and historical perspective on pregnancy-related activity among U. S. teenagers. *Journal of Black Psychology, 9,* 1–28.

Waters, E., Kondo-Ikemura, K., Posada, G., & Richters, J. (1990). Learning to love: Mechanisms and milestones. In M. Gunnar (Ed.), *Minnesota symposia on child psychology* (pp. 217–255). Hillsdale, NJ: Erlbaum.

Yogman, M. W. (1982). Development of the father-infant relationship. In H. Fitzgerald (Ed.), *Theory and research in behavioral pediatrics* Vol. 1. New York: Plenum.

Zahavi, S., & Asher, S. R. (1978). The effects of verbal instructions on preschool children's aggressive behavior. *Journal of School Psychology, 16,* 146–153.

Zeskind, R. S. (1983). Production and spectral analysis of neonatal crying and its relations to other biobehavioral systems in the infant at risk. In T. Field and A. Sostek (Eds.), *Infants born at risk: Physiological, perceptual and cognitive processes*. New York: Grune and Stratton.

Chapter 12

American Bar Association (ABA). (1988). Commission on women in the professions. *Report to the House of Delegates*. Chicago: Author.

Ando, F. H. (1990). Women in Business. In S. E. Rix (Ed.), *The American Woman: 1990–1991* (pp. 222–230). New York: W. W. Norton.

Anthrop, J., & Allison, M. T. (1983). Role conflict and the high school female athlete. *Research Quarterly, 54,* 104–111.

Bandura, A. (1977). *Social learning theory.* Englewood Cliffs, NJ: Prentice-Hall.

Barnett, R. (1981). Parental sex-role attitudes and child-rearing values. *Sex Roles, 7,* 837–847.

Basnow, S. A. (1980). *Sex-role stereotypes: Traditions and alternatives.* Monterey, CA: Brooks/Cole.

Baumrind, D. (1980). New directions in socialization research. *American Psychologist, 35,* 639–652.

Bem, S. L. (1972). Self-perception theory. In L. Berkowitz (Ed.), *Advances in experimental social psychology* Vol. 6. New York: Academic Press.

Bem, S. L. (1975). Sex-role adaptability. *Journal of Personality and Social Psychology, 33,* 634–643.

Bem, S. L. (1979). Socialization influences on personality development in males and females. In M. M. Parks (Ed.), *APA master lecture series on issues of sex and gender in psychology.* Washington, DC: American Psychological Association.

Bem, S. L. (1983). Traditional sex roles are too restrictive. In B. Leone and M. T. O'Neill (Eds.), *Male/female roles.* St. Paul, MN: Greenhaven Press.

Bem, S. L. (1985). Androgyny and gender schema theory: A conceptual and empirical integration. *Nebraska Symposium on Motivation, 32,* 179–226.

Bem, S. L. (1989). Genital knowledge and gender constancy in preschool children. *Child Development, 60,* 649–662.

Bem, S. L., Martyna, W., & Watson, C. (1976). Sex typing and androgyny: Further explorations of the expressive domain. *Journal of Personality and Social Psychology, 34,* 1016–1023.

Bem, S. L., Von der Lippe, A., & Block, J. H. (1973). Sex role and socialization patterns: Some personality concomitants and environmental antecedents. *Journal of Consulting and Clinical Psychology, 41,* 321–24.

Beuf, F. A. (1979). Doctor, lawyer, household drudge. *Journal of Communication, 24,* 110–118.

Bigler, R. S., & Liben, L. S. (1990). The role of attitudes and interventions in gender-schematic processing. *Child Development, 61,* 1440–1452.

Block, J. H. (1979). *Personality development in males and females: The influence of differential socialization.* Paper presented as part of the Master Lecture Series at the Meeting of the American Psychological Association, New York.

Bornstein, M. H. (1989). Cross-cultural developmental comparisons: The case of Japanese-American infant and mother activities and interactions. What we know, what we need to know, and why we need to know it. *Developmental Review, 9,* 171–204.

Bowlby, J. (1980). *Attachment.* New York: Basic Books.

Brooks-Gunn, J., & Fisch, M. (1979). Early social development. In H. McGurk (Ed.), *Childhood social development.* London: Methren.

Broverman, I., & Broverman, D. M. (1972). Sex-role stereotypes: A current appraisal. *Journal of Social Issues, 28,* 59–78.

Brown, D. G. (1962). Sex-role preference. *Psychological Reports, 11,* 477–487.

Burge, P. L. (1982). The relationships between sex-role identity and self-concept of preschool children. *Child Study Journal, 12,* 249–257.

Burns, A. L., Mitchell, G., & Obradovich, S. (1989). Of sex roles and strollers: Female and male attention to toddlers at the zoo. *Sex Roles, 20,* 308–317.

Cairns, R. B. (1979). *Social development: The origins and plasticity of interchanges.* San Francisco: W. H. Freeman.

Caldera, Y. M., Huston, A. C., & O'Brien, M. (1989). Social interactions and play patterns of parents and toddlers with feminine, masculine, and neutral toys. *Child Development, 60,* 70–76.

Camp, S. L. (1988). (Ed.). *Country rankings of the status of women: Poor, powerless, and pregnant.* Washington, DC: Population Crisis Committee.

Cherry, L. (1975). The preschool child-teacher dyad: Sex differences in verbal interaction. *Child Development, 46,* 532–535.

Clarke-Stewart, K. A. (1978). And daddy makes three: The impact on mother and young child. *Child Development, 49,* 466–478.

Clarke-Stewart, K. A. (1980). The contribution to children's cognitive development in early childhood. In F. A. Pedersen (Ed.), *The father-infant relationship.* New York: Praeger.

Cohn, L. D. (1991). Sex differences in the course of personality development: A meta-analysis. *Psychological Bulletin, 109,* 252–266.

Condry, J., & Ross, D. F. (1985). Sex and aggression: The influence of gender label on the perception of aggression in children. *Child Development, 56,* 225–233.

Condry, S. M., Condry, J. C., & Pogatshnik, L. W. (1983). Sex differences: A study of the eye of the beholder. *Sex Roles, 9,* 697–704.

Constantinople, A. (1973). Masculinity-femininity: An exception to a famous dictum? *Psychological Bulletin, 80,* 389–407.

Coverman, S. (1985). Explaining husband's participation in domestic labor. *Sociological Quarterly, 26,* 81–97.

Crouch, J. G., & Neilson, P. B. (1989). Perceived child-rearing dimensions and assertiveness. *Adolescence, XXIV,* 133–145.

Damon, W. (1977). *The social world of the child.* San Francisco: Jossey-Bass.

Desertrain, G. S., & Weiss, M. R. (1988). Being female and athletic: A cause for conflict? *Sex Roles, 18,* 566–573.

Doescher, S. M., & Sugawara, A. I. (1990). Sex role flexibility and prosocial behavior among preschool children. *Sex Roles, 22,* 111–118.

Duncan, G. (1984). *Years of poverty, years of plenty.* Ann Arbor: University of Michigan, Survey Research Center, Institute for Social Research.

Eagly, A. H. (1987). *Sex differences in social behavior: A social role interpretation.* Hillsdale, NJ: Erlbaum.

Eagly, A. H., & Wood, W. (1982). Of gender stereotypes about social influence. *Journal of Personality and Social Psychology, 43,* 550–559.

Ehrhardt, A., & Meyer-Bahlburg, H. F. L. (1981). Effects of prenatal sex hormones on general-related behavior. *Science, 211,* 1312–1317.

Eisenberg, N., Murray E., & Hite, T. (1982). Children's reasoning regarding sex-type toy choices. *Child Development, 53,* 81–86.

Eisenberg, W., Wolchik, S., Hernandez, R., & Pasternack, J. (1985). Parental socialization of young children's play: A short-term longitudinal study. *Child Development, 56,* 1506–1513.

Entwisle, D. R., & Alexander, K. L. (1990). Beginning school math competence: Minority and majority comparisons. *Child Development, 61,* 454–471.

Entwisle, D. R., & Baker, D. P. (1983). Gender and young children's expectations for performance in arithmetic. *Developmental Psychology, 19,* 200–209.

Etaugh, C., & Harlow, H. (1975). Behaviors of male and female teachers as related to behaviors and attitudes of elementary school children. *The Journal of Genetic Psychology, 127,* 163–170.

Fagot, B. I. (1982). Adults as socializing agents. In T. Field (Ed.), *Review of human development.* New York: Wiley.

Fagot, B. I., & Hagan, R. (1985). Aggression in toddlers: Responses to the assertive acts of boys and girls. *Sex Roles, 12,* 341–351.

Fagot, B. I., & Hagan, R. (1991). Observations of parent's reactions to sex-stereotyped behaviors: Age and sex effects. *Child Development, 62,* 617–628.

Fagot, B. I., Hagan, R., Leinbach, M., & Kronsberg, S. (1985). Differential reactions to assertive and communicative acts of toddler boys and girls. *Child Development, 56,* 1499–1505.

Fagot, B. I., & Leinbach, M. (1989). The young child's gender schema: Environmental input, internal organization. *Child Development, 60,* 663–672.

Fields, S. (1983). *Like father, like daughter.* Boston: Little, Brown.

Fingerman, K. L. (1989). Sex and the working mother: Adolescent sexuality, sex role typing, and family background. *Adolescence, XXIV,* 1–18.

Fischer, J. L., & Narus, L. R., Jr. (1981). Sex-role development in late adolescence and adulthood. *Sex Roles, 7,* 97–105.

Freud, S. (1940). *An outline of psychoanalysis.* New York: W. W. Norton.

Freud, S. (1961). Female sexuality. In J. Strachey (Trans.), *The standard edition of the complete psychological works of Sigmund Freud.* London: Hogarth Press. (Original work published in 1931).

Freuh, R., & McGhee, P. H. (1975). Traditional sex-role development and amount of time spent watching television. *Developmental Psychology, 109,* 66–78.

Galambos, N. L., Almeida, D. M., & Petersen, A. C. (1990). Masculinity, femininity, and sex role attitudes in early adolescence: Exploring gender intensification. *Child Development, 61,* 1905–1914.

Geschwind, N., & Behan, P. O. (1984). Laterality, hormones and immunity. In N. Geschwind and A. M. Galaburda (Eds.), *Cerebral dominance: The biological foundations.* Cambridge, MA: Harvard University Press.

Goldberg, H. (1983). Men need liberating from masculine myths. In B. Leone and M. T. O'Neill (Eds.), *Male/female roles.* St. Paul, MN: Greenhaven Press.

Good, T. L., Sikes, J. N., & Brophy, T. (1973). Effects of teacher sex and student sex on classroom interaction. *Journal of Educational Psychology, 65,* 74–87.

Green, R. (1982). Sexual identity: Research strategies. *Archives of Sexual Behavior, 4,* 337–352.

Gross, L., & Jeffries-Fox, S. (1978). What do you want when you grow up little girl? In G. Tuchman (Ed.), *Hearth and home: Images of women in the mass media.* New York: Oxford University Press.

Hall, J. A., Braunwald, K. G., & Mroz, B. J. (1982). Gender, affect, and influences in a teaching situation. *Journal of Personality and Social Psychology, 34,* 281–292.

Hamburg, D. A., & Lunde, T. D. (1966). Sex hormones in the development of sex differences in human behavior. In E. E. Maccoby (Ed.), *The development of sex differences* (pp. 1–24). Palo Alto, CA: Stanford University Press.

Hammer, S. (1975). *Mothers and daughters.* New York: New York Times Book Co.

Hansen, G. L. (1982). Androgyny, sex-role orientation, and homosexism. *Journal of Psychology, 113,* 39–45.

Hartup, W. W. (1989). Behavioral manifestations of children's friendships. In T. J. Berndt and G. W. Ladd (Eds.), *Peer relationships in child development* (pp. 46–70). New York: Wiley.

Havighurst, R. J. (1983). Sex-role development. *Journal of Research and Development in Education, 16,* 60–65.

Hefner, R., Rebecca, M., Oleshansky, B. (1975). Development of sex role transcendence. *Human Development, 18,* 143–158.

Hetherington, E. M. (1966). Effects of paternal absence on sex-type behaviors in negro and white preadolescent males. *Journal of Personality and Social Psychology, 4,* 87–91.

Hetherington, E. M. (1972). Effects of father absence on personality development in adolescent daughters. *Developmental Psychology, 7,* 313–326.

Hetherington, E. M. (1979). Play and social interaction in children following divorce. *Journal of Social Issues, 35,* 26–49.

Hill, J. P., & Lynch, M. (1983). The intensification of gender-related roles expectations during early adolescence. In J. Brooks-Gunn & A. Petersen (Eds.), *Family puberty.* New York: Plenum Press.

Hock, E., McBride, S., & Ginezda, T. (1989). Maternal separation anxiety: Mother-infant separation from the maternal perspective. *Child Development, 60,* 793–802.

Hock, E., & Schirtzinger, M. B. (1992). Maternal separation anxiety: Its developmental course and relation to maternal mental health. *Child Development, 63,* 93–102.

Hoffman, L. (1979). Changes in family roles, socialization, and sex differences. *American Psychologist, 32,* 8, 644–657.

Hoffman, L. (1984). Maternal employment and the young child. In M. Perlmutter (Ed.), *Minnesota symposium in child psychology.* Hillsdale, NJ: Erlbaum.

Hoffman, L., & Saltzstein, H. D. (1967). Parent disposition and the child's moral development. *Journal of Personality and Social Psychology, 19,* 45–57.

Honig, A. (1991). Compliance, control, and discipline. In N. Lauter-Klatell (Ed.), *Readings in child development* (pp. 56–61). Mountain View, CA: Mayfield.

Horn, J. M., Plomin, R., & Rosenman, R. (1976). Heritability of personality traits in adult male twins. *Behavior Genetics, 6,* 17–30.

Huston, A. C. (1983). Sex-typing. In E. M. Hetherington (Ed.), *Handbook of child psychology.* New York: Wiley.

Hyde, J. S. (1984). How large are cognitive gender differences in aggression? A developmental meta-analysis. *Developmental Psychology, 20,* 722–736.

Hyde, J. S., & Linn, M. C. (1988). Are there sex differences in verbal abilities?: A meta-analysis. *Psychological Bulletin, 104,* 53–69.

Jacklin, C. N. (1989). Female and male: Issues of gender. *American Psychologist, 44,* 127–133.

Janman, K. (1989). One step behind: Current stereotypes of women, achievement, and work. *Sex Roles, 21,* 209–216.

Johnson, M. M. (1982). Fathers and femininity in daughters: A review of the research. *Sociology and Social Science Research, 67,* 1, 15–27.

Katz, P. A. (1986). Modification of children's gender-stereotyped behavior: General issues and research considerations. *Sex Roles, 14,* 591–602.

Katz, P. A., & Walsh, P. V. (1991). Modification of children's gender-stereotyped behavior. *Child Development, 62,* 338–351.

Kessler, S., & McKenna, W. (1978). *Gender: An ethnomethodological approach.* New York: Wiley.

Kimball, M. M. (1989). A new perspective on women's math achievement. *Psychological Bulletin, 105,* 198–214.

Kinoshita, J. (1991). Master of sex. *Discovery, 20,* 47–48.

Kohlberg, L. A. (1966). A cognitive-developmental analysis of children's sex-role concepts and attitudes. In E. E. Maccoby (Ed.), *The development of sex differences.* Palo Alto, CA: Stanford University Press.

Kohlberg, L. A., & Ullian, D. Z. (1974). Stages in the development of psychosexual concepts and attitudes. In R. C. Friedman, R. M. Richart, and R. L. Vande Wiele (Eds.), *Sex differences in behavior* (pp. 209–222). New York: Wiley.

Kotelchuck, M. (1981). The infant's relationship to the father: Experimental evidence. In M. E. Lamb (Ed.), *The role of the father in child development.* New York: Wiley.

Kuhn, D., Nash, S. C., & Brucken, L. (1978). Sex role concepts of two- and three-year-old children. *Child Development, 49,* 445–451.

Lamb, M. E. (1981). *The role of the father in child development.* New York: Wiley.

Lamb, M. E., Easterbrooks, M. A., & Holden, G. W. (1980). Reinforcement and punishment among preschoolers: Characteristics, effects, correlates. *Child Development, 51,* 1230–1236.

Lamke, L. K. (1982). Adjustment and sex-role orientation in adolescence. *Journal of Youth and Adolescence, 11,* 247–259.

Langlois, J. H., & Downs, A. C. (1980). Mothers, fathers, and peers as socialization agents of sex-typed behaviors in young children. *Child Development, 51,* 1237–47.

Lau, S. (1989). Sex role orientation and domains of self-esteem. *Sex Roles, 21,* 415–422.

Levine, S. (1967). Sex differences in the brain. In *Scientific American Readings, Psychobiology: The biological bases of behavior* (pp. 76–81). San Francisco: W. H. Freeman.

Levine, S. (1968). The effects of hormones in infants on CNS organization. In D. P. Kimble (Ed.), *Experience and capacity* Vol. 4. Washington, DC: Academy of Science.

Levinson, R. (1982). Teaching sex-roles. *Teaching Sociology, 10,* 78–80.

Levy-Shiff, R. (1982). The effects of father absence on young children in mother-headed families. *Child Development, 53,* 81–86.

Lewis, M., & Ban, P. (1977). Variance and invariance in the mother-infant interaction. In P. H. Leiderman, S. R. Tulkin, and A. Rosenfeld (Eds.), *Culture and infancy.* New York: Academic Press.

Lewis, M., & Weinraub, M. (1979). Origins of early sex-role development. *Sex Roles, 5,* 135–153.

Linn, M. C., & Petersen, A. C. (1985). Emergence and characteristics of sex differences in spatial ability: A meta-analysis. *Child Development, 56,* 1479–1498.

Linn, M. C., & Petersen, A. C. (1986). Meta-analyses of gender differences in spatial ability. In J. Hyde and M. Linn (Eds.), *The psychology of gender: Advances through meta-analysis* (pp. 67–101). Baltimore: Johns Hopkins University Press.

Linn, M. C., & Pulos, S. (1983). Male-female differences in predicting displaced volume strategy usage, aptitude relationships, and experience influences. *Journal of Research in Mathematics Education, 75,* 86–96.

Loehlin, J. C. (1985). Fitting heredity-environment models jointly to twin and adoption data from the California Psychological Inventory. *Behavior Genetics, 15,* 199–221.

Loehlin, J. C., & Nichols, B. C. (1976). *Heredity, environment, and personality.* Austin: University of Texas Press.

Loehlin, J. C., Willerman, L., & Horn, J. M. (1982). Personality resemblances between unwed mothers and their adopted-away offspring. *Journal of Personality and Social Psychology, 42,* 1089–1099.

Lott, B. (1989). Sexist discrimination as distancing behavior. *Psychology of Women Quarterly, 13,* 341–355.

Lott, B., & Lott, A. J. (1985). Learning theory in contemporary social psychology. In G. Lindzey and E. Aronson (Eds.), *The handbook of social psychology* (pp. 109–135). New York: Random House.

Lummis, M., & Stevenson, H. W. (1990). Gender differences in beliefs and achievement: A cross-cultural study. *Developmental Psychology, 26,* 354–363.

Lytton, H., & Romney, D. M. (1992). Parents' differential socialization of boys and girls: A meta-analysis. *Psychological Bulletin, 109,* 267–296.

Maccoby, E. E. (1980). *Social development.* New York: Harcourt Brace Jovanovich.

Maccoby, E. E., & Jacklin, C. N. (1974). *The psychology of sex differences.* Palo Alto, CA: Stanford University Press.

Markstrom-Adams, C. (1989). Androgyny and its relation to adolescent psychosocial well-being: A review of the literature. *Sex Roles, 21,* 325–340.

Marsh, H. W., & Jackson, S. A. (1986). Multidimensional self-concepts, masculinity, and femininity as a function of women's involvement in athletics. *Sex Roles, 15,* 391–415.

Martin, C. (1989). Children's use of gender-related information in making social judgments. *Developmental Psychology, 25,* 80–88.

Martin, C. L., & Halverson, C. (1981). A schematic processing model of sex typing and stereotyping in children. *Child Development, 52,* 1119–1134.

Martin, C. L., & Halverson, C. (1987). The roles of cognition in sex roles acquisition. In D. B. Carter (Ed.), *Current conceptions of sex roles and sex typing: Theory and research* (pp. 123–137). New York: Praeger.

Martin, C. L., & Little, J. K. (1990). The relation of gender understanding to children's sex-typed preferences and gender stereotypes. *Child Development, 61,* 1427–1439.

Martin, C. L., Wood, C. H., & Little, J. K. (1990). The development of gender stereotype components. *Child Development, 61,* 1891–1904.

Masica, D. N. (1982). Fetal feminization induced by androgen insensitivity in testicular feminizing syndrome. *Johns Hopkins Medical Journal, 124,* 105–114.

Massad, C. M. (1981). Sex roles identity and adjustment during adolescence. *Child Development, 52,* 1290–1298.

Matthews, W. (1981). Sex-role perception: Portrayal and perception in the fantasy play of young children. *Sex Roles, 7,* 979–987.

Mauldin, T., & Meeks, C. B. (1990). Sex differences in children's time use. *Sex Roles, 22,* 537–554.

McGuire, J. (1988). Gender stereotypes of parents with two-year-olds and beliefs about gender differences in behavior. *Sex Roles, 19,* 232–241.

McHale, S. M., Bartko, W. T., Crouter, A. C., & Perry-Jenkins, M. (1990). Children's housework and psychosocial functioning: The mediating effects of parents' sex-role behaviors and attitudes. *Child Development, 61,* 1413–1426.

McHale, S. M. & Huston, T. (1984). Men and women as parents: Sex role orientations, employment, and parental roles with infants. *Child Development, 55,* 1349–1361.

Mead, G. H. (1934). *Mind, self, and society.* Chicago: University of Chicago Press.

Meyer, B. (1980). The development of girls' sex-role attitudes. *Child Development, 51,* 508–514.

Mischel, W. (1966). A social learning view of sex differences in behavior. In E. E. Maccoby (Ed.), *The development of sex differences* (pp. 56–81). Palo Alto, CA: Stanford University Press.

Mitchell, J. E., Baker, L. A., & Jacklin, C. N. (1989). Masculinity and femininity in twin children: Genetic and environmental factors. *Child Development, 60,* 1475–1485.

Money, J., & Ehrhardt, A. A. (1972). *Man and woman: Boy and girl.* Baltimore: Johns Hopkins University Press.

Morrison, A. M., & Von Glinow, M. A. (1990). Women and minorities in management. *American Psychologist, 45,* 200–208.

National Committee on Pay Equity. (1989). *Briefing on the wage gap.* Washington, DC: Author.

Nelson, C. S., & Keith, J. G. (1990). Comparisons of female and male early adolescent sex role attitude and behavior development. *Adolescence, XXV,* 223–242.

O'Brien, M., & Huston, A. C. (1985). Development of sex-typed play behavior in toddlers. *Developmental Psychology, 21,* 855–871.

Olds, L. (1981). *Fully human.* Englewood Cliffs, NJ: Prentice-Hall.

Ollison, L. (1977). Socialization: Women, worth, and work. In C. Travis and C. Offir (Eds.), *The longest war.* New York: Harcourt Brace Jovanovich.

Orlofsky, J. D. (1982). Psychological androgyny, sex-typing, and sex-role ideology as predictors of male-female impersonal attraction. *Sex Roles, 8,* 1057–1073.

Orlofsky, J. D. (1983). Psychological and developmental perspectives in expectant and new parenthood. In

R. D. Parke (Ed.), *Review of child development research.* Chicago: University of Chicago Press.

Papageorgiou, A. B. (1983). My daddy might have loved me. *Educational Resources in Education.* Unpublished manuscript.

Parke, R. D. (1981). *Fathers.* Cambridge, MA: Harvard University Press.

Parke, R. D., & Asher, S. R. (1983). Social and personality development. *Annual Review of Psychology, 34,* 465–509.

Parke, R. D., & Sawin, D. B. (1980). The family in early infancy: Social interaction and attitudinal analysis. In F. Pedersen (Ed.), *The father-infant relationship: Observational studies in a family context.* New York: Praeger.

Parsons, J. E. (1982). Socialization of achievement attitudes and beliefs: Classroom influences. *Child Development, 53,* 322–339.

Parsons, T. (1955). Family structure and the socialization of the child. In T. Parsons and R. F. Bales (Eds.), *Family socialization and the interaction process* (pp. 35–131). Glencoe, IL: Free Press.

Paulsen, K., & Johnson, M. (1983). Sex-role attitudes and mathematical ability in 4th-, 8th-, and 11th-grade students from a high socioeconomic area. *Developmental Psychology, 19,* 210–214.

Pedersen, F. A. (1980). *The father-infant relationship: Observation studies in the family setting.* New York: Praeger.

Perloff, R. M. (1982). Mass media and sex-typing. *International Journal of Women's Studies, 5,* 265–273.

Pleck, J. H. (1975). Masculinity-femininity: Current and alternative paradigms. *Sex Roles, 5,* 161–77.

Pleck, J. H. (1979). The male sex role: Definitions, problems, and sources of change. In J. H. Williams (Ed.), *Psychology of women: Selected readings.* New York: W. W. Norton.

Pomerleau, A., Bolduc, D., Malcuit, G., & Cossette, L. (1990). Pink or blue: Environmental gender stereotypes in the first two years of life. *Sex Roles, 22,* 359–365.

Power, T. G., & Parke, R. D. (1983). Play as a context for early learning. In I. E. Sigel and L. M. Laosa (Eds.), *The family as a learning environment.* New York: Plenum.

Power, T. G., & Parke, R. D. (1985). Mother- and father-infant play: A developmental analysis. *Child Development, 56,* 1514–1524.

Radin, N. (1981). Child-rearing fathers in intact families. *Merrill-Palmer Quarterly, 27,* 489–514.

Radin, N., & Harold-Goldsmith, R. (1989). The involvement of selected unemployed and employed men with their children. *Child Development, 60,* 454–459.

Reis, H. T., & Wright, S. (1982). Knowledge of sex-role stereotypes in children aged three to five. *Sex Roles, 8,* 1049–1055.

Reuter, M. W., & Biller, H. B. (1973). Perceived paternal nurturance ability and personality adjustment among college males. *Journal of Consulting and Clinical Psychology, 40,* 339–342.

Rhode, D. L. (1989). *Justice and gender.* Cambridge, MA: Harvard University Press.

Rhode, D. L. (1990). Gender equality and employment policy. In S. E. Rix (Ed.), *The American woman: 1990–1991* (pp. 132–169). New York: W. W. Norton.

Richards, M. P. M., Dunn, J. F., & Antonis, B. (1977). Caretaking in the first year of life. *Child Care, Health and Development, 3,* 23–26.

Robinson, B. E., & Green, M. G. (1981). Beyond androgyny: The emergence of sex-role transcendence as a theoretical construct. *Developmental Review, 1,* 247–265.

Rose, R. M., Holeday, J. W., & Bernstein, I. S. (1978). Plasma testosterone, dominance rank, and aggressive behavior in Rhesus monkeys. *Nature, 231,* 366–368.

Rothschild, N. (1979). *Group as a mediator in the culturation process among young children.* Unpublished master's thesis. Annenberg School of Communications, University of Pennsylvania, Philadelphia.

Rubin, J. Z., Provenzano, F. J., & Luria, Z. (1974). The eye of the beholder: Parents' views on sex of newborns. *American Journal of Orthopsychiatry, 44,* 512–519.

Ruble, D., Balaban, T., & Cooper, J. (1981). Gender constancy and the effects of sex-typed televised toy commercials. *Child Development, 52,* 667–673.

Russell, G. (1978). The father role and its relation to masculinity, femininity, and androgyny. *Child Development, 49,* 1174–1181.

Sage, G. H., & Loudermilk, S. (1979). The female athlete and role conflict. *Research Quarterly, 50,* 88–96.

Schaffer, K. F. (1980). *Sex role issues in mental health.* Reading, MA: Addison-Wesley.

Schneider, A. M., & Tarshis, B. (1975). *Physiological psychology.* New York: Random House.

Serbin, L., & O'Leary, K. D. (1975). A comparison of teacher response to preacademic and problem behavior of boys and girls. *Child Development, 44,* 796–804.

Sidorowicz, L. S., & Lunney, G. S. (1980). Baby X revisited. *Sex Roles, 6,* 67–73.

Siegel, A. U. (1987). Are sons and daughters treated more differently by fathers than by mothers? *Developmental Review, 7,* 183–209.

Signorielli, N. (1989). Television and conceptions about sex roles: Maintaining conventionality and the status quo. *Sex Roles, 21,* 341–346.

Slaby, R. G., & Frey, K. S. (1975). Development of gender constancy and selective attention to same-sex models. *Child Development, 46,* 849–856.

Smith, C., & Lloyd, B. (1978). Maternal behavior and perceived sex of infant: Revisited. *Child Development, 49,* 1263–1266.

Snow, M. E., Jacklin, C. N., & Maccoby, E. E. (1983). Sex of child differences in father-child interaction at one year of age. *Child Development, 54,* 227–232.

Spence, J., & Helmreich, R. (1978). *Masculinity and femininity.* Austin: University of Texas Press.

Sprafkin, C., Serbin, L. A., & Elman, M. (1982). Sex-typing of play and psychological adjustment in young children: An empirical investigation. *Journal of Abnormal Child Psychology, 10,* 559–568.

Stattin, H., & Klackenberg-Larsson, I. (1990). The short- and long-term implications for parent-child relations of parents' prenatal preferences for their child's gender. *Developmental Psychology, 27,* 141–147.

Steenland, S. (1990). Behind the scenes: Women in television. In S. E. Rix (Ed.), *The American woman: 1990–1991* (pp. 231–237). New York: W. W. Norton.

Stein, A. H., & Friedrich, L. K. (1972). Television content and young children's behavior. In J. P. Murray (Ed.), *Television and social behavior: II. Television and social learning.* Washington, DC: U.S. Government Printing Office.

Steinberg, R. J., & Haignere, L. (1987). Equitable compensation: Methodological criteria for comparable worth. In C. Bose and G. Spitze (Eds.), *Ingredients for women's employment policy.* Albany: State University of New York Press.

Stevenson, H. W., & Lee, S. (1990). Contexts of achievement. *Monographs of the Society for Research in Child Development, 55,* Serial No. 221.

Stoddart, T., & Turiel, E. (1985). Children's concepts of cross-gender activities. *Child Development, 56,* 1241–1252.

Taylor, M., & Hall, J. A. (1982). Psychological androgyny: Theories, methods, conclusions. *Psychological Bulletin, 92,* 347–366.

Tortora, G. J., & Anagnostakos, N. P. (1984). *Principles of anatomy and physiology* (4th ed.). New York: Harper & Row.

Townsend, R. C. (1977). The competitive male as a loser. In A. Sargent (Ed.), *Beyond sex roles* (pp. 228–242). St. Paul: West.

Travis, G., & Offir, C. (Eds.). (1977). *The longest war.* New York: Harcourt Brace Jovanovich.

U.S. Bureau of the Census. (1983). *Childcare arrangements of working mothers: June 1982.* (Current Population Reports, Series T-23, No. 129). Washington, DC: U.S. Government Printing Office.

U.S. Bureau of Labor Statistics. (1984, January). *Employment and earnings.* Washington, DC: U.S. Government Printing Office.

U.S. Bureau of Labor Statistics. (1988, January). *Employment and earnings.* Washington, DC: U.S. Government Printing Office.

U.S. Bureau of Labor Statistics. (1989, January). *Employment and earnings.* Washington, DC: U.S. Government Printing Office.

U.S. Congress. House Committee on Small Business. 100th Congress, 2d session. (1988). *New economic realities: The rise of the woman entrepreneur.* Washington, DC: U.S. Government Printing Office.

Weinraub, M. (1980, August). *The changing role of the father.* Paper presented at the meeting of the American Psychological Association, Montreal.

Weitzman, N., Birns, B., & Friend, R. (1985). Traditional and nontraditional mothers' communication with their daughters and sons. *Child Development, 56,* 894–898.

Welch, R. L. (1979). Subtle sex-role cues in children's commercials. *Journal of Communication, 29,* 202–209.

Wells, K. (1980). Gender-role identity and psychological adjustment in adolescence. *Journal of Youth and Adolescence, 9,* 59–73.

Williams, F., La Rose, R., & Frost, F. (1981). *Children, television, and sex-role stereotyping.* New York: Praeger.

Zucker, K. J., & Torkos, H. (1989). Assessment of androgyny in children. *Annals of Sex Research, 2,* 187–203.

Zuckerman, D., & Sayre, D. H. (1982). Cultural sex-role expectations and children's sex-role concepts. *Sex Roles, 8,* 853–861.

Chapter 13

Abramovitch, R., Corter, C., & Lando, B. (1979). Sibling interaction in the home. *Child Development, 50,* 997–1003.

Abramovitch, R., Corter, C., & Pepler, P. (1981). Observations of mixed-sex sibling dyads. *Child Development, 51,* 1268–1271.

Adelson, J. (Ed.) (1980). *Handbook of adolescent psychology.* New York: Wiley.

Altshuler, J. L., & Ruble, D. N. (1989). Developmental changes in children's awareness of strategies for coping with uncontrollable stress. *Child Development, 60,* 1337–1349.

Armacost, R. L. (1989). Perceptions of stressors by high school students. *Journal of Adolescent Research, 4,* 443–461.

Ax, A. F. (1953). The physiological differentiation of fear and anger in humans. *Psychosomatic Medicine, 15,* 433–442.

Bamber, J. H. (1979). *The fears of adolescents.* New York: Academic.

Barrera, M. E., & Maurer, D. (1979). The perception of facial expression by the three-month-old child. *Child Development, 52,* 203–206.

Barrios, B. A., Hartmann, D. P., Shigetomi, C. (1981). Fears and anxieties in children. In E. J. Mash and L. G. Terdal (Eds.), *Behavioral assessment of childhood disorders.* New York: Guilford Press.

Bates, J. E. (1980). The concept of difficult temperament. *Merrill-Palmer Quarterly, 26,* 4, 299–319.

Bauer, D. H. (1976). An exploratory study of developmental changes in children's fears. *Journal of Child Psychology and Psychiatry, 17,* 69–74.

Baum, A., Singer, J. E., & Baum, C. (1981). Stress and the environment. *Journal of Social Issues, 37,* 4–10.

Blos, P. (1967). The second individuation process of adolescence. In R. S. Eissler et al. (Eds.), *Psychoanalytic study of the child* (Vol. 15). New York: International Universities Press.

Bowlby, J. (1973). *Separation: Anxiety and anger.* London: Hogarth.

Bowlby, J. (1980). *Attachment and loss: Vol. 3. Loss, sadness and depression.* New York: Basic Books.

Braungart, J. M., Plomin, R., DeFries, J. C., & Fulker, D. W. (1992). Genetic influence on tester-rated infant temperament as assessed by Bayley's Infant Behavior Record: Nonadoptive and adoptive siblings and twins. *Developmental Psychology, 28,* 40–47.

Bretherton, I., Fritz, J., Zahn-Waxler, C., & Ridgeway, D. (1986). Learning to talk about emotions: A functionalist perspective. *Child Development, 57,* 529–548.

Bridges, K. (1932). Emotional development in early infancy. *Child Development, 3,* 324–341.

Broberg, A., Lamb, M. E., & Hwang, P. (1990). Inhibition: Its stability and correlates in sixteen- to forty-month-old children. *Child Development, 61,* 1153–1163.

Buhrmester, D., & Furman, W. (1990). Perceptions of sibling relationships during middle childhood and adolescence. *Child Development, 61,* 1387–1398.

Buss, A. H., & Plomin, R. (1975). *A temperament theory of personality development.* New York: Wiley.

Buss, A. H., & Plomin, R. (1984). *Temperament: Early developing personality traits.* Hillsdale, NJ: Erlbaum.

Campos, J. J., Barrett, K. C., Lamb, M. E., Goldsmith, H. H., & Stenberg, C. (1983). Social emotional development. In P. H. Mussen (Ed.), *Handbook of child psychology,* 4th ed. (pp. 783–915). New York: Wiley.

Campos, J. J., Bertenthal, B. I., & Caplovitz, K. (1982). The interrelationship of affect and cognition in the visual cliff situations. In C. Izard, J. Kagan, and R. Zajonc (Eds.), *Emotion and Cognition.* New York: Plenum Press.

Charlesworth, W. R. (1969). The role of surprise in cognitive development. In D. Elkind and J. H. Flavell (Eds.), *Studies in cognitive development: Essays in honor of Jean Piaget* (pp. 257–314). London: Oxford University Press.

Chisholm, J. S. (1983). *Navajo infancy.* New York: Aldine.

Cohen, S. (1980). Afteraffects of stress on human performance and social behavior: A review of theory and research. *Psychological Bulletin, 87,* 578–604.

Cohn, J. F., & Tronick, E. Z. (1987). Mother-infant face-to-face interaction: The sequence of dyadic states at 3, 6, and 9 months. *Developmental Psychology, 23,* 68–77.

Cohn, J. F., & Tronick, E. Z. (1989). Specificity of infants' response to mothers' affective behavior. *Journal of the American Academy of Child and Adolescent Psychiatry, 28,* 242–248.

Compas, B., Howell, D. C., Phares, V., Williams, R. A., & Ledoux, N. (1989). Parent and child stress and symptoms: An integrative analysis. *Developmental Psychologist, 25,* 550–559.

Crumley, F. E. (1979). Adolescent suicide attempts. *Journal of the American Medical Association, 241,* 2404.

Cummings, E. M., Vogel, D., Cummings, J. S., & El-Sheikh, M. (1989). Children's responses to different forms of expression of anger between adults. *Child Development, 60,* 1392–1401.

Daniels, D., & Plomin, R. (1985). Origins of individual differences in infant shyness. *Developmental Psychology, 21,* 118–121.

deCatanzaro, D. (1981). *Suicide and self-damaging behavior.* New York: Academic Press.

DeLongis, A., Folkman, S., & Lazarus, R. S. (1988). The impact of daily stress on health and mood: Psychological and social resources as mediators. *Journal of Personality and Social Psychology, 54,* 486–495.

Denham, S. A., & Couchoud, E. A. (1990). Young preschoolers' understanding of emotions. *Child Study Journal, 20,* 171–192.

Dickstein, S., & Parke, R. D. (1988). Social referencing in infancy: A glance at fathers and marriage. *Child Development, 59,* 506–511.

Diener, E., Sandvick, E., & Larson, R. (1985). Age and sex effects for emotional intensity. *Developmental Psychology, 21,* 542–546.

Douvan, E., & Adelson, J. (1966). *The adolescent experience.* New York: Wiley.

Dubow, E. R., Tisak, J., Causey, D., Hryshko, A., & Reid, G. (1991). A two-year longitudinal study of stressful life events, social support, and social problem-solving skills: Contributions to children's behavioral and academic adjustment. *Child Development, 62,* 583–599.

Dunn, J., & Kendrick, C. (1980). The arrival of a sibling: Changes in patterns of interaction between mother and first-born child. *Journal of Child Psychology and Psychiatry, 21,* 119–132.

Dunn, J., & Munn, P. (1985). Becoming a family member: Family conflict and the development of social understanding in the second year. *Child Development, 56,* 480–492.

Fabes, R. A., & Eisenberg, N. (1992). Young children's coping with interpersonal anger. *Child Development, 63,* 116–128.

Fischer, J. L. (1981). Transitions in relationship style from adolescence to young adulthood. *Journal of Youth and Adolescence, 10,* 11–24.

Forman, B. D., Eidson, K., & Hagan, B. (1983). Measuring perceived stress in adolescents. *Adolescence, XXV,* 573–576.

Fox, V. (1977). Is adolescence a phenomenon of modern times? *Journal of Psychohistory, I,* 271–290.

Fraiberg, S. (1981). Blind infants and their mothers: An examination of the sign system. In S. R. Asher and J. M. Gottman (Eds.), *The development of children's friendships.* New York: Cambridge University Press.

Freedman, D. G. (1969). Ethnic differences in babies. *Human Nature, 2,* 36–43.

Freedman, D. G. (1974). *Human infancy: An evolutionary perspective.* Hillsdale, NJ: Erlbaum.

Freedman, D. G. (1979). *Human sociobiology: A holistic approach.* New York: Free Press.

Freud, A. (1958). *Psychoanalytic study of the child.* New York: International Universities Press.

Friedman, H. S., & Booth-Kewley, S. (1988). Validity of the Type A construct: A reprise. *Psychological Bulletin, 104,* 381–384.

Fromm, E. (1989). *The art of loving.* New York: Harper Collins.

Gaensbauer, T., Harmon, R., Cytryn, L., & McKnew, D. (1984). Social and affective development in infants with manic-depressive parents. *American Journal of Psychiatry, 141,* 223–229.

Gandour, M. J. (1989). Activity level as a dimension of temperament in toddlers: Its relevance for the organismic specificity hypothesis. *Child Development, 60,* 1092–1098.

Garcia-Coll, C. (1981). *Psychophysiological correlates of a tendency toward inhibition in infants.* Unpublished doctoral dissertation, Harvard University, Cambridge, MA.

Garcia-Coll, C., Kagan, J., & Reznick, J. S. (1984). Behavioral inhibition in young children. *Child Development, 55,* 1005–1019.

Garmezy, N., & Rutter, M. (Eds.). (1983). *Stress, coping, and development in children.* New York: McGraw-Hill.

Garmezy, N., & Tellegen, A. (1984). Studies of stress resistant children. In F. Morrison, D. Keating, and C. Ford (Eds.), *Applied developmental psychology* (pp. 231–287). New York: Academic Press.

Gherman, E. M. (1981). *Stress and the bottom line.* New York: AMACOM.

Goldsmith, H. H., & Campos, J. J. (1986). Fundamental issues in the study of early temperament: The Denver twin temperament study. In M. E. Lamb, A. L. Brown, and B. Rogoff (Eds.), *Advances in developmental psychology* (pp. 231–283). Hillsdale, NJ: Erlbaum.

Goldsmith, H. H., & Campos, J. J. (1990). The structure of temperamental fear and pleasure in infants: A psychometric perspective. *Child Development, 61,* 1944–1964.

Goldsmith, H. H., & Gottesman, I. I. (1981). Origins of variation in behavioral style: A longitudinal study of temperament in young twins. *Child Development, 52,* 91–103.

Greene, A. L. (1988). Early adolescents' perceptions of stress. *Journal of Early Adolescence, 8,* 391–403.

Grotevant, H. D., & Cooper, C. R. (1986). Individuation in family relationships: A perspective on individual differences in the development of identity and role-taking skill in adolescence. *Human Development, 29,* 82–100.

Hall, G. S. (1904). *Adolescence.* New York: Appleton.

Hamilton, P. (1989). *The interaction of depressed mothers and their three-month-old infants.* Unpublished doctoral dissertation. Boston University, Boston.

Haviland, J. M., & Lelwica, M. (1987). The induced affect response: 10-week-old infants' responses to three emotion expressions. *Developmental Psychology, 23,* 17–104.

Hendrin, H. (1982). *Suicide in America.* New York: W. W. Norton.

Hill, J. P., & Holmbeck, G. N. (1986). Attachment and autonomy during adolescence. In G. J. Whitehurst (Ed.), *Annals of child development* (Vol. 3) (pp. 145–189). Greenwich, CT: JAI.

Hill, J. P., & Palmquist, W. (1978). Social cognition and social relations in early adolescence. *International Journal of Behavioral Development, 1,* 1–36.

Hirshberg, L. M. (1990). When infants look to their parents: Twelve-month-olds' response to conflicting parental emotional signals. *Child Development, 61,* 1187–1191.

Hirshberg, L. M., & Svejda, M. (1990). Infants' social referencing of mothers compared to fathers. *Child Development, 61,* 1175–1191.

Hoffner, C., & Badzinski, D. M. (1989). Children's integration of facial and situational cues to emotion. *Child Development, 60,* 411–422.

Holahan, C. K., Holahan, C. J., & Belk, S. S. (1984). Adjustment in aging: The role of life stress, hassles, and self-efficacy. *Health Psychology, 3,* 315–328.

Holmes, T. H., & Rahe, R. H. (1967). The social readjustment rating scale. *Journal of Psychosomatic Research, 11,* 213–218.

Hubert, N., Wachs, T. (1985). Parental perceptions of the behavioral components of infant easiness/difficultness. *Child Development, 56,* 1525–1537.

Hubert, N., Wachs, T., Peters-Martin, P., & Gandour, M. J. (1982). The study of early temperament: Measurement and conceptual issues. *Child Development, 53,* 571–600.

Hunter, F., & Youniss, J. (1982). Changes in functions of three relations during adolescence. *Developmental Psychology, 18,* 806–811.

Izard, C. E. (1971). *The face of emotion.* New York: Appleton.

Izard, C. E. (1978). On the ontogenesis of emotions and emotion: Cognition relationships in infancy. In M. Lewis and L. A. Rosenblum (Eds.), *The development of affect* (pp. 163–199). New York: Plenum.

Izard, C. E. (1979). *The maximally discriminative facial movement scoring system.* Unpublished manuscript, University of Delaware, Newark. Cited in M. Harth and J. Campos (Eds.), *Handbook of child psychology* (1983). New York: Wiley.

Izard, C. E. (1982). *Human Emotions.* New York: Plenum, 1982.

Izard, C. E. (1983). *The maximally discriminative facial movement scoring system.* Unpublished manuscript,

University of Delaware, 1979. Cited in P. H. Mussen (Ed.), *Handbook of child psychology.* New York: Wiley.

Izard, C. E. (1990). Facial expressions and the regulation of emotions. *Journal of Personality and Social Psychology, 58,* 487–498.

Jerome, J. (1979, January 19). Catching them before suicide. *New York Times Magazine,* 30–32.

Jersild, A. (1968). *Child psychology* (6th ed.). Englewood Cliffs, NJ: Prentice-Hall.

Johnson, W., Emde, R. N., Pannabecker, B., Stenberg, C., & Davis, M. (1982). Maternal perception of infant emotion from birth to 18 months. *Infant Behavior and Development, 5,* 313–322.

Kagan, J., (1984). The idea of emotion in human development. In C. E. Izard, J. Kagan, and R. Zajonc (Eds.), *Emotion, cognition, and behavior* (pp. 38–72). New York: Cambridge University Press.

Kagan, J., & Moss, H. (1962). *Birth to maturity.* New York: Wiley.

Kagan, J., Reznick, J. S., & Snidman, N. (1987). The physiology and psychology of behavioral inhibition in children. *Child Development, 58,* 1459–1473.

Kagan, J., Reznick, J. S., Snidman, N., Gibbons, J., & Johnson, M. O. (1988). Childhood derivatives of inhibition and lack of inhibition to the unfamiliar. *Child Development, 59,* 1580–1589.

Kahn, J. H., Nursten, J. P., & Carrol, C. M. (1981). *Unwilling to school.* New York: Pergamon Press.

Kanner, A. D., Coyne, J. C., Schaefer, C., & Lazarus, R. S. (1981). Comparisons of two models of stress measurement: Daily hassles and uplifts versus major life events. *Journal of Behavioral Medicine, 4,* 1–39.

Kellerman, J. (1981). *Helping the fearful child.* New York: W. W. Norton.

Klein, P. S. (1989). Young children's understanding of love. *International Journal of Early Childhood, 21,* 29–34.

Klinnert, M. (1984). The regulation of infant behavior by maternal facial expression. *Infant Behavior and Development, 7,* 447–465.

Klos, D. S., & Loomis, D. F. (1978). A rating scale of intimate disclosure between late adolescents and their friends. *Psychological Reports, 42,* 815–820.

Knopf, I. J. (1979). *Childhood psychopathology.* Englewood Cliffs, NJ: Prentice-Hall.

Konopka, G. (1983). Adolescent suicide. *Exceptional Children, 49,* 5, 390–394.

Kopp, C. B. (1989). Regulation of distress and negative emotions: A developmental view. *Developmental Psychology, 25,* 343–354.

Korn, S. J. (1978, September). *Temperament, vulnerability, and behavior.* Paper presented at the Louisville Temperament Conference, Louisville, KY.

Korner, A., Zeanah, C. H., Linden, J., Berkowitz, R., Kraemer, H., & Agras, W., 1985). The relationship between neonatal and later activity and temperament. *Child Development, 56,* 38–42.

Kosky, R. (1983). Childhood suicidal behavior. *Journal of Child Psychology and Psychiatry, 24,* 3, 457–468.

Larson, R., Csikszentmihalyi, M., & Graef, R. (1980). Mood variability and the psychosocial adjustment of adolescents. *Journal of Youth and Adolescence, 9,* 469–490.

Larson, R., & Lampman–Petraitis, C. (1989). Daily emotional states as reported by children and adolescents. *Child Development, 60,* 1250–1260.

Lazarus, R. S. (1966). *Psychological stress and the coping process.* New York: McGraw-Hill.

Lazarus, R. S., & Launier, R. (1978). Stress-related transactions between person and environment. In L. A. Pervin and M. Lewis (Eds.), *Perspectives in interaction psychology.* New York: Plenum Press.

Lee, C., & Bates, J. (1985). Mother-child interaction at age two years and perceived difficult temperament. *Child Development, 56,* 1314–1325.

Levine, S. (1983). A psychobiological approach to the ontogeny of coping. In N. Garmezy and M. Rutter (Eds.), *Stress and coping in early childhood.* New York: McGraw-Hill.

Lewis, M. (1991). Emotional development in the young child. In N. Lauter-Klatell (Ed.), *Readings in child development* (pp. 51–55). Mountain View, CA: Mayfield.

Lewis, M., & Brooks, J. (1978). Self-knowledge and emotional development. In M. Lewis and L. A. Rosenblum (Eds.), *The development of affect* (pp. 205–226). New York: Plenum Press.

Lewis, M., & Michaelson, L. (1983). *Children's emotions and moods: Developmental theory and measurement.* New York: Plenum Press.

Lewis, M., & Rosenblum, L. A. (1978). *The development of affect.* New York: Plenum Press.

Lewis, M., Sullivan, M. W., Stanger, C., & Weiss, M. (1989). Self-development and self-conscious emotions. *Child Development, 60,* 146–156.

Ludemann, P. M. (1991). Generalized discrimination of positive facial expressions by seven- and ten-month-old infants. *Child Development, 62,* 55–67.

Luthar, S. S. (1991). Vulnerability and resilience: A study of high-risk adolescents. *Child Development, 62,* 600–616.

Main, M., Kaplan, N., & Cassidy, J. (1985). Security in infancy, childhood, and adulthood: A move to the level of respresentation. In I. Bretherton and E. Waters (Eds.), *Growing points of attachment theory and research* (pp. 66–104). *Monographs of the Society for Research in Child Development, 50* (Serial No. 209).

Malatesta, C. Z., Culver, C., Tesman, J. R., & Shepard, B. (1989). The development of emotion expression during the first two years of life. *Monographs of the Society for Research in Child Development, 54* (Serial No. 219).

Malatesta, C. Z., & Izard, C. E. (1984). The ontogenesis of human social signals: From biological imperative to symbol utilization. In N. A. Fox and R. J. Davidson (Eds.), *The psychobiology of affective development* (pp. 161–206). Hillsdale, NJ: Erlbaum.

Malatesta, C. Z., & Wilson, A. (1988). Emotion/cognition interaction in personality development: A discrete emotions, functionalist analysis. *British Journal of Social Psychology, 27*, 91–112.

Mann, J. J. (1987). *The suicidal patient: Biology and pharmacology.* Paper present at the annual meetings of the American Psychiatric Association, Chicago.

Matheny, A. P., Wilson, R. S., Dolan, A., & Krantz, J. (1981). Behavioral contrasts in twinships: Stability and patterns of differences in childhood. *Child Development, 52*, 579–588.

Matthews, K. A. (1979). Efforts to control by children and adults with the Type A coronary-prone behavior pattern. *Child Development, 50*, 842–847.

Matthews, K. A. (1988). CHD and Type A behaviors: Update on an alternative to Booth-Kewley and Friedman quantitative review. *Psychological Bulletin, 104*, 373–380.

Matthews, K. A., & Volkin, J. (1981). Efforts to excel and the Type A behavior pattern in children. *Child Development, 52*, 1283–1289.

McCall, R. B. (1979). Qualitative transitions in behavioral development in the first two years of life. In M. Bornstein and W. Kessen (Eds.), *Psychological development from infancy: Image to intention.* Hillsdale, NJ: Erlbaum.

McDevitt, S. C., & Carey, W. B. (1978). The measurement of temperament in 3 – 7 year old children. *Journal of Child Psychology and Psychiatry, 19*, 245–253.

Mechanic, D. (1978). *Students under stress: A study in the social psychology of adaptation.* Madison: University of Wisconsin Press.

Medeiros, D. C., Porter, B. J., & Welch, L. D. (1983). *Children under stress.* Englewood Cliffs, NJ: Prentice-Hall.

Meng, A., C. Henderson, C., Campos, J. J., & Emde, R. N. (1983). *The effects of background emotional elicitation on subsequent problem-solving in the toddler.* Unpublished manuscript, University of Denver, Denver.

Miller, M. S. (1982). *Child-stress.* New York: Doubleday.

Morris, R., & Kratochwill, T. R. (1983). *Treating children's fears and phobias.* New York: Pergamon Press.

Murphy, L. B. (1983). Issues in the development of emotion in infancy. In R. Plutchik and H. Kellerman (Eds.), *Emotion: Theory, research, and experimentation.* New York: Academic Press.

Nannis, E. D. (1988). Cognitive-developmental differences in emotional understanding. In E. D. Nannis and P. A. Cowan (Eds.), *New directions for child development: Developmental psychopathology and its treatment.* San Francisco: Jossey-Bass.

Nietzel, M. T., & Bernstein, D. A. (1981). Assessment of anxiety and fear. In M. Hersen and A. S. Bellack (Eds.), *Behavioral assessment: A practical handbook.* New York: Pergamon Press.

Offer, D., Ostrov, E., & Howard, K. I. (1981). *The adolescent.* New York: Basic Books.

Petersen, A. C. (1988). Adolescent development. *Annual Review of Psychology, 39*, 583–607.

Pfeffer, C., Plutchik. R., Mizruchi, M. (1983). Suicidal and assaultive behavior in children: Classification, measurement, and interrelations. *American Journal of Psychiatry, 140, 2*, 154–157.

Plomin, R. (1986). *Development, genetics, and psychology.* Hillsdale, NJ: Erlbaum.

Plutchik, R., & Kellerman, H. (Eds.). (1983). *Emotion: Theory, research, and experimentation.* New York: Academic Press.

Ratner, C. (1989). A social constructionist critique of the naturalistic theory of emotion. *The Journal of Mind and Behavior, 10*, 211–230.

Ray, L., & Johnson, N. (1983). Adolescent suicide. *The Personnel and Guidance Journal, 61*, 131–136.

Reichenbach, L., & Masters, J. C. (1983). Children's use of expressive and conceptual cues in judgments of emotions. *Child Development, 54*, 993–1004.

Ridgeway, D., Waters, E., & Kuczaj, S. A. (1985). The acquisition of emotion descriptive language: Receptive and productive vocabulary norms for ages 18 months to 6 years. *Developmental Psychology, 21*, 901–908.

Riese, M. L. (1990). Neonatal temperament in monozygotic and dizygotic pairs. *Child Development, 61*, 1230–1237.

Ritter, D. R., (1990). Adolescent suicide: Social competence and problem behavior of youth at high risk and low risk for suicide. *School Psychology Review, 19,* 83–95.

Rorty, A. (1980). *Explaining emotions.* Los Angeles: University of California Press.

Rosenblatt, J. (1981). Youth suicide. *Editorial Research Reports, 1,* 431–448.

Rothbart, M. K. (1981, April). *Infant temperament and early social interaction.* Paper presented at the meeting of the Society for Research in Child Development, Boston.

Rowlison, R. T., & Felner, R. D. (1988). Major life events, hassles, and adaptation in adolescence: Confounding in the conceptualization and measurement of life stress and adjustment revisited. *Journal of Personality and Social Psychology, 55,* 432–444.

Russell, J. A. (1990). The preschoolers' understanding of the causes and consequences of emotion. *Child Development, 61,* 1872–1881.

Russell, J. A., & Bullock, M. (1986). On the dimensions preschoolers use to interpret facial expressions of emotions. *Developmental Psychology, 22,* 97–102.

Rutter, M. (1983). Stress, coping, and development: Some issues and questions. In N. Garmezy and M. Rutter (Eds.), *Stress, coping and development in children.* New York: McGraw-Hill.

Rutter, M., Graham, P., Chadwick, F., & Yule, W. (1976). Adolescent turmoil: Fact or fiction? *Journal of Child Psychology and Psychiatry, 17,* 35–56.

Ryan, R. M., & Lynch, J. H. (1989). Emotional autonomy versus detachment: Revisiting the vicissitudes of adolescence and young adulthood. *Child Development, 60,* 340–356.

Sahler, O. J. Z., & McAnamey, E. R., (1981). *The child from 3 to 18.* St. Louis: Mosby.

Scarr, S., & Salapatek, P. (1970). Patterns of fear development during infancy. *Merrill-Palmer Quarterly, 16,* 53–87.

Selye, H. (1976) *The stress of life.* New York: McGraw-Hill. (Original work published in 1956.)

Selye, H. (1980). The stress concept today. In I. Kutash (Ed.), *Handbook on stress and anxiety.* San Francisco: Jossey-Bass.

Sheviakov, G. (1969). *Anger in children: Causes, characteristics, and considerations.* Washington, DC: Department of Elementary/Kindergarten/Nursery Education.

Smollar, J., & Youniss, J. (1985). *Transformation in adolescents' perceptions of parents.* Paper presented at the biennial meeting of the Society for Research in Child Development, Baltimore.

Snoek, D., & Rothblum, E. (1979). Self-disclosure among adolescents in relation to parental affection and control patterns. *Adolescence, 14,* 333–340.

Sprunger, L., Boyce, W. T., & Gaines, J. A. (1985). Family-infant congruence: Routines and rhythmicity in family adaptations to a young infant. *Child Development, 56,* 564–572.

Sroufe, L. A. (1979). Socioemotional development. In J. D. Osofsky (Ed.), *Handbook on infant development* (pp. 462–516). New York: Wiley.

Stapley, J. C., & Haviland, J. M. (1989). Beyond depression: Gender differences in normal adolescents' emotional experiences. *Sex Roles, 20,* 295–301.

Steinberg, L. (1981). Transformations in family relations at puberty. *Developmental Psychology, 17,* 833–840.

Steinberg, L. (1985a). *Adolescence.* New York: Knopf.

Steinberg, L. (1985b). Early temperamental antecedents of adult Type A behaviors. *Developmental Psychology, 21,* 1171–1180.

Steinberg, L. & Silverberg, S. (1986). The vicissitudes of autonomy in early adolescence. *Child Development, 57,* 841–851.

Stenberg, C., Campos, J. J., & Emde, R. (1983). The facial expression of anger in seven-month-old infants. *Child Development, 54,* 178–184.

Stifter, C. A. & Fox, N. (1986). Preschool children's ability to identify and label emotions. *Journal of Nonverbal Behavior, 10,* 255–266.

Stocker, C., Dunn, J., Plomin, R. (1989). Sibling relationships: Links with child temperament, maternal behavior, and family structure. *Child Development, 60,* 715–727.

Sullivan, M. W., & Lewis, M. (1989). Emotion and cognition in infancy: Facial expressions during contingency learning. *International Journal of Behavioral Development, 12,* 221–237.

Tavris, C. (1982). *Anger: The misunderstood emotion.* New York: Simon and Schuster.

Taylor, R. D., & Spiess, G. A. (1989). Effect of age on congruence between adults' and youths' ratings of life event stressors. *Psychological Reports, 65,* 1017–1018.

Thomas, A., & Chess, S. (1977). *Temperament and development.* New York: Brunner/Mazel.

Thomas, A., & Chess, S. (1980). *The dynamics of psychological development.* New York: Brunner/Mazel.

Thomas, A., Chess, S., & Birch, H. (1968). *Temperament and behavior disorders in children.* New York: New York University Press.

Thompson, R. A., & Lamb, M. E. (1984). Assessing qualitative dimensions of emotional responsiveness in infants: Separation reactions in the strange situation. *Infant Behavior and Development, 7*, 423–445.

Tishler, C. L., McKenry, P. C., & Morgan, K. C. (1981). Adolescent suicide attempts: Some significant factors. *Suicide Life Threatening Behavior, 11*, 31.

Trabasso, T., Stein, N. L., & Johnson, L. R. (1981). Children's knowledge of events: A causal analysis of story structure. In G. H. Bower (Ed.), *The psychology of learning and motivation* (pp. 237–282). New York: Academic Press.

Tronick. E. Z. (1989). Emotions and emotional communication in infants. *American Psychologist, 44*, 112–119.

Tronick, E. Z., & Cohn, J. F. (1989). Infant-mother face-to-face interaction: Age and gender differences in co-ordination and the occurrence of miscoordination. *Child Development, 60*, 85–92.

Vandell, D. L., Minnett, A. M., & Santrock, J. W. (1987). Age differences in sibling relationships during middle childhood. *Journal of Applied Developmental Psychology, 8*, 247–257.

Walden, T. A., & Field, T. M. (1982). Discrimination of facial expressions by preschool children. *Child Development, 53*, 1312–1319.

Walden, T. A., & Field, T. M. (1990). Preschool children's social competence and production and discrimination of affective expressions. *British Journal of Developmental Psychology, 8*, 65–76.

Walker-Andrews, A. S. (1988). Infants' perception of the affordances of expressive behaviors. In C. Rovee-Collier and L. Lipsitt (Eds.), *Advances in infancy research* (pp. 173–221). Norwood, NJ: Ablex.

Weinberg, K. (1989). *The relation between facial expressions of emotion and behavior in 6 month old infants.* Unpublished master's thesis, University of Massachusetts, Amherst.

Weinraub, M., & Lewis, M. (1977). The determinants of children's responses to separation. *Monographs of the Society for Research in Child Development, 42* (Serial No. 172).

Wenar, C. (1982). On negativism. *Human Development, 25*, 1–23.

Williams, J. W., & Stith, M. (1980). *Middle childhood behaviors and development.* New York: Macmillan.

Wilson, R. S., & Matheny, A. P. (1983). Assessment of temperament in infant twins. *Developmental Psychology, 19*, 2, 172–183.

Wilson, R. S., & Matheny, A. P. (1986). Behavior-genetics research in infant temperament: The Louisville twin study. In R. Plomin and J. Dunn (Eds.), *The study of temperament: Changes, continuities, and challenges* (pp. 81–97). Hillsdale, NJ: Erlbaum.

Work, W. C., Parker, G. R., & Cowen, E. L. (1990). The impact of life stressors on childhood adjustment: Multiple perspectives. *Journal of Community Psychology, 18*, 73–78.

Chapter 14

Achenbach, T. M., & Edelbrock, C. S. (1984). Psychopathology in childhood. *Annual Review of Psychology, 35*, 227–256.

Adams, D. (1977). Building moral dilemma activities. *Learning, 5*, 44–46.

Adelson, J. (Ed.). (1980). *Handbook of adolescent psychology.* New York: Wiley.

Arend, R., Gove, F. L., & Sroufe, L. A. (1979). Continuity of individual adaptation from infancy to kindergarten: A predictive study of ego-resiliency and curiosity in preschoolers. *Child Development, 50*, 950–959.

Bachman, J. G., Johnston, L. D., & O'Malley, P. M. (1987). *Monitoring the future: Questionnaire responses from the nation's high school seniors: 1986.* Ann Arbor: Institute for Social Research, University of Michigan.

Baran, S. J., Lawrence, J. C., & Courtright, J. A. (1979). Television drama as a facilitator of prosocial behavior: The Waltons. *Journal of Broadcasting, 23*, 277–283.

Baumrind, D. (1975). Early socialization and adolescent competence. In S. Dragastin and G. H. Elder (Eds.), *Adolescence in the life cycle.* New York: Wiley.

Bear, G., & Richards, H. C. (1981). Moral reasoning and conduct problems in the classroom. *Journal of Educational Psychology, 73*, 644–670.

Berling, K. (1981). *Moral development: The validity of Kohlberg's theory.* Stockholm, Sweden: Almquist and Wiksell International.

Berndt, T. (1979). Developmental changes in conformity to peers and parents. *Developmental Psychology, 15*, 608–616.

Berndt, T. J., & Berndt, E. G. (1975). Children's use of motives and intentionality in person perception and moral judgement. *Child Development, 46*, 904–912.

Blatt, M. M., & Kohlberg, L. (1975). The effects of classroom moral discussion upon children's level of moral judgement. *Journal of Moral Education, 2*, 129–161.

Bronfenbrenner, U. (1970). *Two worlds of childhood: U.S. and U.S.S.R.* New York: Russell Sage.

Bronfenbrenner, U. (1986). Ecology of the family as a context for human development: Research perspectives. *Developmental Psychology, 22*, 723–742.

Bussey, K. (1992). Lying and truthfulness: Children's definitions, standards, and evaluative reactions. *Child Development, 63*, 129–137.

Calabrese, R. L. (1987). Adolescence: A growth period conducive to alienation. *Adolescence, XXII,* 929–932.

Calabrese, R. L., & Adams, J. (1990). Alienation: A cause of juvenile delinquency. *Adolescence, XXV,* 334–342.

Caplan, M. Z., & Hay, D. F., (1989). Preschoolers' responses to peers' distress and beliefs about bystander intervention. *Journal of Child Psychology and Psychiatry, 30,* 231–242.

Colby, A. K., Kohlberg, L., Gibbs, J., & Lieberman, M. (1983). A longitudinal study of moral judgment. *Monographs of the Society for Research in Child Development, 48* (Serial No. 200).

Collins, W. A., & Getz, S. K. (1976). Children's social responses following modeled reactions to provocations: Prosocial effects of a television drama. *Journal of Personality, 44,* 488–500.

Columbia Broadcasting System. (1979). *Communicating with children through television: Studies of messages and other impressions conveyed by five children's programs.* New York: Author.

Damon, W. (1977). *The social world of the child.* San Francisco: Jossey-Bass.

Darley, J. M., & Shultz, T. R. (1990). Moral rules: Their content and acquisition. *Annual Review of Psychology, 41,* 525–556.

David, L. (1981). Feelings of guilt. DHHS Publication No. (ADM) 81–580. Washington, DC: U.S. Government Printing Office.

Devereux, E. C. (1970). The role of peer-group experience in moral development. *Child Psychology* (pp. 94–140). Minneapolis: University of Minnesota Press.

Dishion, T. J. (1990). The family ecology of boys' peer relations in middle childhood. *Child Development, 61,* 874–892.

Dishion, T. J., Patterson, G. R., Stoolmiller, M., & Skinner, M. L. (1991). Family, school, and behavioral antecedents to early adolescent involvement with antisocial peers. *Developmental Psychology, 27,* 172–180.

Dishion, T. J., Reid, J. B., & Patterson, G. R. (1988). Empirical guidelines for a family intervention for adolescent drug use. *Journal of Chemical Dependency Treatment, 2,* 181–216.

Dodge, K. A., Cole, J. D., & Brakke, N. P. (1982). Behavior patterns of socially rejected and neglected preadolescents: The roles of social approach and aggression. *Journal of Abnormal Child Psychology, 10,* 389–410.

Dworetzky, J. P. (1984). *Introduction to child development* (2nd ed.). St. Paul, MI: West.

Edwards, C. P. (1980). The comparative study of the development of moral judgment and reasoning. In R. L. Munroe, R. Munroe, and B. B. Whiting (Eds.), *Handbook of cross-cultural human development.* New York: Garland.

Eisenberg, J. (1986). *Altruistic emotion, cognition, and behavior.* Hillsdale, NJ: Erlbaum.

Eisenberg, N. (1989). Empathy and sympathy. In W. Damon (Ed.), *Child development today and tomorrow* (pp. 137–153). San Francisco: Jossey-Bass.

Eisenberg, N., & Strayer, J. (1987). Critical issues in the study of empathy. In N. Eisenberg and J. Strayer (Eds.), *Empathy and its development.* New York: Cambridge University Press.

Eisenberg-Berg, N., & Neal, C. (1979). Children's moral reasoning about their own spontaneous prosocial behavior. *Developmental Psychology, 15,* 228–229.

Ensminger, M. E. (1990). Sexual activity and problem behavior among black, urban adolescents. *Child Development, 61,* 2032–2046.

Erikson, E. (1980). *Identity and the life cycle.* New York: W. W. Norton.

Farrington, D. P. (1987). Early precursors of frequent offending. In J. Q. Wilson and G. C. Loury (Eds.), *From children to citizens: Vol. III. Families, schools, and delinquency prevention* (pp. 27–51). New York: Springer-Verlag.

Federal Bureau of Investigation. (1987). *Crime in the United States: Uniform crime reports, 1986.* Washington, DC: U.S. Government Printing Office.

Ferguson, T. J., Stegge, J., & Damhuis, I. (1991). Children's understanding of guilt and shame. *Child Development, 62,* 827–839.

Ferguson, T. J., & Rule, B. G. (1983). An attributional perspective on anger and aggression. In R. G. Green and E. I. Donnerstein (Eds.), *Aggression: Theoretical and empirical reviews* (pp. 41–74). New York: Academic Press.

Freedman, J. L., Wallington, S. A., & Bless, E. (1967). Compliance without pressure: The effect of guilt. *Journal of Personality and Social Psychology, 7,* 117–124.

Freud, S. (1964). An outline of psychoanalysis. In J. Strachey (Ed.), *The standard edition of the complete works of Sigmund Freud* (Vol. 23). London: Hogarth. (Original work published in 1940.)

Friedrich, L., & Stein, A. (1975). Prosocial television and young children: The effects of verbal labeling and role playing on learning and behavior. *Child Development, 46,* 27–38.

Froming, W., Allen, L., & Jensen, R. E. (1985). Altruism, role-taking, and self-awareness: The acquisition of norms governing altruistic behavior. *Child Development, 56,* 1223–1228.

Gabennesch, H. (1990). The perception of social conventionality by children and adults. *Child Development, 61,* 2047–2059.

Geiger, K. M., & Turiel, E. (1983). Disruptive school behavior and concepts of social convention in early adolescence. *Journal of Educational Psychology, 75,* 659–671.

Gilligan, C. (1982). *In a different voice.* Cambridge, MA: Harvard University Press.

Glueck, S., & Glueck, E. (1950). *Unraveling juvenile delinquency.* Cambridge, MA: Harvard University Press.

Grusec, J. E. (1981). Socialization processes and the development of altruism. In J. P. Rushton and R. M. Sorrentino (Eds.), *Altruism and helping behavior.* Hillsdale, NJ: Erlbaum.

Grusec, J. E., Saas-Kortsaak, P., & Simutis, Z. (1978). The role of example and moral exhortation in the training of altruism. *Child Development, 49,* 920–923.

Guerra, N. G. (1989). Consequential thinking and self-reported delinquency in high school students. *Criminal Justice and Behavior, 16,* 440–454.

Harris, S., Mussen, P. H., & Rutherford, E. (1976). Some cognitive, behavioral and personality correlates of maturity of moral judgment. *Journal of Genetic Psychology, 128,* 123–135.

Hartshorne, H., & May, M. A. (1928–1930). *Studies in the nature of character.* Vol. I.: *Studies in deceit.* New York: Macmillan.

Hartup W. W., & Coates, B. (1967). Imitation of a peer as a function of reinforcement from the peer group and rewardingness of the model. *Child Development, 38,* 1003–1016.

Hay, D. F., Murray, P., Cecire, S., & Nash, A. (1985). Social learning of social behavior in early life. *Child Development, 56,* 43–57.

Helwig, C. C., Tisak, M. S., & Turiel, E. (1990). Children's social reasoning in context: Reply to Gabennesch. *Child Development, 61,* 2068–2078.

Hoffman, M. L. (1971). Father-absence and conscience development. *Developmental Psychology, 4,* 400–406.

Hoffman, M. L. (1977). Moral internalization: Current theory and research. In. L. Berkowitz (Ed.), *Advances in experimental social psychology* (Vol. 10). New York: Academic Press.

Hoffman, M. L. (1980). Moral development in adolescence. In J. Adelson (Ed.), *Handbook of adolescent psychology.* New York: Wiley.

Hoffman, M. L. (1982). Affective and cognitive processes in moral internalization. In E. T. Higgins, D. M. Ruble, and W. W. Hartup (Eds.), *Social cognition and social behavior: Developmental perspectives.* Cambridge, England: Cambridge University Press.

Hoffman, M. L. (1983). Empathy, guilt and social cognition. In W. F. Overton (Ed.), *The relationship between social and cognitive development.* Hillsdale, NJ: Erlbaum.

Hoffman, M. L. (1984). Interaction of affect and cognition on empathy. In C. E. Izard, J. Kagan, and R. B. Zajonc (Eds.), *Emotions, cognition, and behavior.* Cambridge, England: Cambridge University Press.

Hoffman, M. L. (1987). The contribution of empathy to justice and moral judgment. In N. Eisenberg & J. Strayer (Eds.), *Empathy and its development.* New York: Cambridge University Press.

Hoffner, C., & Badzinski, D. (1989). Children's integration of facial situational cues to emotion. *Child Development, 60,* 411–422.

Holstein, C. (1968). *Parental concensus and interaction in relation to child's moral judgment.* Ph.D. dissertation, University of California, Berkeley.

Hughes, R., Tingle, B., & Sawin, C. (1981). Development of empathic understanding. *Child Development, 52,* 122–128.

Ianotti, R. J. (1978). Effect of role-taking experiences of role-taking, empathy, altruism, and aggression. *Developmental Psychology, 14,* 119–124.

Jensen, R. E., & Moore, S. G. (1977). The effect of attribute statements on cooperativeness and competitiveness in school-age boys. *Child Development, 48,* 305–307.

Knight, G. P., Kagan, J., & Raymond, B. (1982). Perceived parental practices and prosocial development. *The Journal of Genetic Psychology, 141,* 57–65.

Kohlberg, L. (1963). The development of children's orientations toward a moral order: I. Sequence in the development of moral thought. *Vita Humana, 6,* 11–33. New York: Karger.

Kohlberg, L. (1969). Stage and sequence: The cognitive-developmental approach to socialization. In D. Goslin (Ed.), *Handbook of socialization theory and research.* Chicago: Rand McNally.

Kohlberg, L. (1976). Moral stages and moralization: The cognitive-developmental approach. In T. Lickona (Ed.), *Moral development and behavior* (pp. 31–53). New York: Holt, Rinehart and Winston.

Kohlberg, L. (1978). *The meaning and measurement of moral development.* Invited address at the meetings of the American Psychological Association, Toronto.

Kohlberg, L. (1981). *The philosophy of moral development.* San Francisco: Harper & Row.

Kohlberg, L. (1984). *Essays on moral development:* Vol. 2. *The psychology of moral development.* San Francisco: Harper & Row.

Kohlberg, L., & Gilligan, C. (1972). The adolescent as a philosopher: The discovery of the self in a postconventional world. In J. Kagan and R. Coles (Ed.), *12 to 16: Early adolescence.* New York: W. W. Norton.

Kohlberg, L., & Kramer, R. (1969). Continuities and discontinuities in childhood moral development. *Human Development, 12,* 93–120.

Kwok, L., & Sing, L. (1989). Effects of self-concept and perceived disapproval of delinquent behavior in school children. *Journal of Youth and Adolescence, 18,* 345–359.

Leming, J. S. (1974). Moral reasoning, sense of control, and social political activism among adolsecents. *Adolescence, IX,* 507–528.

Lickona, T. (Ed.). (1976). *Moral development and moral behavior.* New York: Holt, Rinehart and Winston.

Loeber, R., & Dishion, T. J. (1983). Early predictors of male delinquency: A review. *Psychological Bulletin, 94,* 68–99.

Magnusson, D., Stottin, H., & Duner, A. (1982). Aggression and criminality in a longitudinal perspective. In S. A. Mednick (Ed.), *Antecedents of aggression and antisocial behavior.* Hingham, MA: Kluwer Boston.

McFalls, J. A., Jones, B. J., Gallager, B., & Rivera, J. (1985). Political orientation and occupational values of college youth, 1969 and 1981: A shift toward uniformity. *Adolescence, 20,* 696–713.

Mitchell, S., & Rosa, F. (1981). Boyhood behavior problems as precursors of criminality: A fifteen-year follow-up study. *Journal of Child Psychology and Psychiatry, 22,* 19–33.

Munsey, B. (1980). *Moral development, moral education, and Kohlberg.* Birmingham, AL: Religious Education Press.

Mussen, P. H., Rutherford, E., Harris, S., & Keasey, C. B. (1970). Honesty and altruism among preadolescents. *Developmental Psychology, 3,* 169–194.

Muuss, R. E. (1988). *Moral development, moral education, and Kohlberg.* Birmingham, AL: Religious Education Press.

Nelson, J. R., Smith, D. J., & Dodd, J. (1990). The moral reasoning of juvenile delinquents: A meta-analysis. *Journal of Abnormal Child Psychology, 18,* 231–239.

Nettler, G. (1982). *Lying, cheating, stealing.* Cincinnati: Anderson Publishing.

Osborne, S. G., & West D. J. (1978). The effectiveness of various predictors of criminal careers. *Journal of Adolescence, 1,* 101–117.

Paniagua, F. A. (1989). Lying by children: Why children say one thing, do another? *Psychological Reports, 64,* 971–984.

Patterson, G. R. (1982). *Coercive family processes.* Eugene, OR: Castilia Press.

Patterson, G. R., DeBaryshe, B. D., & Ramsey, E. (1989). A developmental perspective on antisocial behavior. *American Psychologist, 44,* 329–335.

Pearl, R. (1985). Children's understanding of others' need for help: Effects of problem explicitness and type. *Child Development, 56,* 735–745.

Peterson, C. C., Peterson, J. L., & Seeto, D. (1983). Developmental changes in ideas about lying. *Child Development, 54,* 1529–1535.

Piaget, J. (1932). *The moral judgment of the child.* London: Kegan Paul.

Piaget, J. (1963). *The child's conception of the world.* Patterson, NJ: Littlefield, Adams.

Piaget, J. (1965). *The moral judgment of the child.* (M. Gabain, Trans.). New York: Free Press.

Piaget, J. (1983). Piaget's theory. In W. Kessen (Ed.), P. H. Mussen (Series Ed.), *Handbook of child psychology:* Vol. 1. *History, theory, and methods* (pp. 103–128). New York: Wiley.

Piaget, J., & Inhelder, B. (1969). *The psychology of the child.* New York: Basic Books.

Poole, E. D., & Regoli R. M. (1979). Parental support, delinquent friends, and delinquency: A test of interaction effects. *Journal of Criminal Law and Criminology, 70,* 188–193.

Power, F. C., Higgins, A., & Kohlberg, L. (1989). *Lawrence Kohlberg's approach to moral education.* New York: Columbia University Press.

Pulkkinin, L. (1982). Search for alternatives to aggression in Finland. In A. F. Goldstein, and M. Segall (Eds.), *Aggression in global perspective.* New York: Pergamon Press.

Radke-Yarrow, M., & Zahn-Waxler, C. (1984). Roots, motives, and patterns in children's prosocial behavior. In E. Staub, D. Bartal, J. Karylowski, and J. Reykowski (Eds.), *Development and maintenance of prosocial behavior: International perspectives on positive behavior.* New York: Plenum Press.

Radke-Yarrow, M., Zahn-Waxler, C., & Chapman, M. (1983). Children's prosocial dispositions and behavior. In P. H. Mussen (Ed.), *Handbook of child psychology.* New York: Wiley.

Rest, J. R. (1979). *Development in judging moral issues.* Minneapolis: University of Minnesota Press.

Rest, J. R. (1983). Morality. In P. H. Mussen (Ed.), *Handbook of child psychology.* New York: Wiley.

Rheingold, H., Hay, D. F., & West, M. (1976). Sharing in the second year of life. *Child Development, 47,* 1148–58.

Roff, J. D., & Wirt, R. D. (1984). Childhood aggression and social adjustment as antecedents of delinquency. *Journal of Abnormal Child Psychology, 12,* 111–116.

Rosenkoetter, L. I., Huston, A. C., Wright, J. C. (1990). Television and the moral judgment of the young child. *Journal of Applied Developmental Psychology, 11,* 123–137.

Sawin, D. B. (1980). *A field study of children's reactions to distress in their peers.* Unpublished manuscript. University of Texas, Austin.

Sebald, H. (1989). Adolescents' peer orientation: Changes in the support system during the past three decades. *Adolescence, 24,* 937–946.

Shultz, T. R., & Schleifer, M. (1983). Towards a refinement of attribution concepts. In J. Jaspars, F. D. Fincham, and M. Hewstone (Eds), *Attribution theory and research: Conceptual, developmental and social dimensions* (pp. 37–62). London: Academic Press.

Simmons, C. V., & Wade, W. B. (1985). A comparative study of young people's ideals in five counties. *Adolescence, 20,* 889–898.

Simpson E. L. (1974). Moral development research: A case of scientific cultural bias. *Human Development, 17,* 81–106.

Smetana, J. G., Killen, M., & Turiel, E. (1991). Children's reasoning about interpersonal and moral conflicts. *Child Development, 62,* 629–644.

Snyder, J. J., & Patterson, G. R. (1986). The effects of consequences on patterns of social interaction: A quasi-experimental approach to reinforcement in natural interaction. *Child Development, 57,* 1257–1268.

Staub, E. (1979). Understanding and predicting social behavior with special emphasis on prosocial behavior. In J. H. Stevens and M. Mathews (Eds.), *Mother/child, father/child relationships.* Englewood Cliffs, NJ: Prentice-Hall.

Stouthamer-Loeber, M. (1986). Lying as a problem behavior in children: A review. *Clinical Psychology Review, 6,* 267–289.

Strichartz, A. F., & Burton, R. V. (1990). Lie and truth: A study of the development of the concept. *Child Development, 61,* 211–220.

Surber, C. F. (1977). Developmental processes in social inference: A verging of intentions and consequences in moral judgment. *Developmental Psychology, 13,* 654–665.

Thibault, J. P., & McKee, J. S., (1982). Practical parenting with Piaget. *Young Children, 38,* 18–20.

Thompson, R. A. (1987). Empathy and emotional understanding: The early development of empathy. In N. Eisenberg and J. Strayer (Eds.), *Empathy and its development.* Cambridge, England: Cambridge University Press.

Tompkins, S. S. (1963). *Affect, imagery, consciousness.* Vol. 2. *The negative affects.* New York: Springer Publishing.

Turiel, E. (1966). An experimental test of the sequentiality of developmental stages in the child's moral judgments. *Journal of Personality and Social Psychology, 3,* 611–618.

Turiel, E. (1972). Stage transition in moral development. In R. M. Travers (Ed.), *Second handbook of research on teaching.* Chicago: Rand McNally.

Turiel, E. (1990). Moral judgment, action, and development. *New directions for child development.* San Francisco: Jossey-Bass.

Walker, L. J. (1982). The sequentiality of Kohlberg's stages of moral development. *Child Development, 53,* 1330–1336.

Walker, L. J. (1984). Sex differences in the development of moral reasoning: A critical review. *Child Development, 55,* 677–691.

Walker, L. J. (1989). A longitudinal study of moral reasoning. *Child Development, 60,* 157–186.

Walker, L. J., & Taylor, J. H. (1991). Family interactions and the development of moral reasoning. *Child Development, 62,* 264–283.

White, C., Bushnell, N., & Regnemer, J. (1978). Moral development in Bahamian school children: A three-year examination of Kohlberg's stages of moral development. *Developmental Psychology, 14,* 58–65.

Whiting, J., & Whiting, B. (1975). *Children of six cultures.* Cambridge, MA: Harvard University Press.

Williams, J. W., & Stith, M. (1980). *Middle childhood behavior and development.* New York: Macmillan.

Youniss, J. (1980). *Parents and peers in social development.* Chicago: University of Chicago Press.

Zahn-Waxler, C. (1979). Child-rearing and children's prosocial initiations toward victims of distress. *Child Development, 50,* 319–330.

Zahn-Waxler, C., & Radke-Yarrow, M. (1979). *A developmental analysis of children's responses to emotions in others.* Paper presented at the biannual meeting of the Society for Research in Child Development, San Francisco.

Zahn-Waxler, C., Radke-Yarrow, M., Wagner, E., & Chapman, M. (1992). Development of concern for others. *Developmental Psychology, 28,* 126–136.

Zahn-Waxler, C., Robinson, J., & Emde, R. (1991, April). *The development and heritability of empathy.* Paper presented at the meeting of the Society for Research in Child Development, Seattle.

Zanna, M. P. (1988). *The development of judgments of responsibility of foreseeable and unforeseeable accidents and intentional harms.* Presented at the meeting of University of Waterloo Conference on Child Development, Ontario.

Zarbatany, L., Hartmann, D. P., & Gelfand, D. M. (1985). Why does children's generosity increase with age: Susceptibility to experimenter influence or altruism? *Child Development, 56,* 746–756.

Chapter 15

Aber, J. L., & Chicchetti, D. (1984). The socio-emotional development of maltreated children: An empirical and theoretical analysis. In H. Fitzgerald, B. Lester, and M. Yogman (Eds.), *Theory and research in behavioral pediatrics* (Vol. 2)(pp. 147–199). New York: Plenum.

Achenbach, R. M. (1982). *Developmental psychopathology.* New York: Wiley.

Adams-Tucker, C. (1982). Proximate effects of sexual abuse in childhood: A report of 28 children. *American Journal of Psychiatry, 139,* 1252–1256.

Adelson, J. (Ed.). (1980). *Handbook of Adolescent Psychiatry.* New York: Wiley.

Alcohol and health: New knowledge. (1974, June). Second special report to the United States Congress, National Institute on Alcohol Abuse and Alcoholism. U.S. Department of Health, Education and Welfare. Washington, DC: U.S. Government Printing Office, No. 1724–00399.

Algozzine, B. (1979). Social-emotional problems. In C. D. Mercer (Ed.), *Children and adolescents with learning disabilities.* Columbus, OH: Merrill.

American Medical Association. (1985). AMA diagnostic and treatment guidelines concerning child abuse and neglect. *Journal of the American Medical Association, 254,* 796–800.

American Psychiatric Association. (1987). *Diagnostic and Statistical Manual of Mental Disorders - Revised.* Washington, DC: American Psychiatric Association.

Amsterdam, B., Brill, M., Weisberg Bell, N., & Edwards, D. (1979). Coping with abuse: Adolescents' views. *Victimology, 4,* 278–284.

Ando, H., & Yoshimure, I. (1979). Effects of age on communication skill levels and prevalence of maladaptive behaviors and mentally retarded children. *Journal of Autism and Developmental Disorders, 9,* 83–94.

Asher, S., & Renshaw, P. (1981). Children with friends: Social knowledge and social skill training. In S. Asher and J. Gottman (Eds.), *The development of children's friendships.* New York: Cambridge University Press.

Bailey, G. W. (1989). Current perspectives on substance abuse in youth. *Journal of the American Academy of Adolescent Psychiatry, 28,* 151–162.

Bandura, A. (1977). *Social learning theory.* Englewood Cliffs, NJ: Prentice-Hall.

Bandura, A., & Walters, R. H. (1959). *Adolescent aggression.* New York: Ronald.

Bettelheim, B. (1977). *The empty fortress: Infantile autism and the birth of self.* Riverside, NJ: Free Press.

Bettes, B. A., Dusenbury, L., Kerner, J., James-Ortiz, S., & Botvin, G. J. (1990). Ethnicity and psychosocial factors in alcohol and tobacco use in adolescence. *Child Development, 61,* 557–565.

Block, J. A., Block, J., & Morrison, A. (1981). Parent agreement-disagreement on child rearing orientations and gender-related personality correlates in children. *Child Development, 52,* 965–974.

Boldizar, J. P., Perry, D. G., & Perry, L. C. (1989). Outcome values and aggression. *Child Development, 60,* 571–579.

Bolger, N., Downey, G., Walker, E., & Steininger, P. (1989). The onset of suicidal ideation in childhood and adolescence. *Journal of Youth and Adolescence, 18,* 175–188.

Botvin, G. J. (1987). Update on substance use prevention research. In National Institute on Drug Abuse, *Second triennial report on drug abuse to Congress.* Washington, DC: U.S. Government Printing Office.

Bousha, D. M. & Twentyman, C. T. (1984). Mother-child interactional study in abuse, neglect, and control groups: Naturalistic observations in the home. *Journal of Abnormal Psychology, 93,* 105–114.

Brent, D. A., Perper, J. A., Goldstein, C. E., Kolko, D. J., Allen, M. J., Allman, C. J., & Zelenak, J. P. (1989). Risk factors for adolescent suicide: Comparison of adolescent suicide victims with suicidal in-patients. *Archives of General Psychiatry, 45,* 581–588.

Bronfenbrenner, U. (1977). *Who needs parent education?* Paper prepared for Working Conference on Parent Education sponsored by Charles Stewart Mott Foundation, Flint, MI.

Brooke, J., & Whiteman, M. (1983). Stages of drug use in adolescence: Personality, peer, and family correlates. *Developmental Psychology, 19,* 269–277.

Brown, L. (1983). Status of child protective services in the U.S.: An analysis of issues and practice. In J. E. Leavitt (Ed.), *Child abuse and neglect: Research and innovation.* Boston: Martinus Nijhoff.

Brown, P., & Elliot, R. (1965). Control of aggression in a nursery school class. *Journal of Experimental Child Psychology, 2,* 103–107.

Bry, B. H. (1983). Predicting drug abuse: Review and reformulation. *The International Journal of the Addictions, 18,* 223–233.

Bry, B. H., McKeon, P., & Pandian, R. (1982). Extent of drug use as a function of number of risk factors. *Journal of Abnormal Psychology, 91,* 273–279.

Bryson, S. E., Smith, I. M., & Eastwood, D. (1988). Obstetrical suboptimality in autistic children. *Journal of the American Academy of Child Adolescent Psychiatry, 4,* 418–422.

Bukowski, W. M. (1990). Age differences in children's memory of information about aggressive, socially withdrawn, and prosocial boys and girls. *Child Development, 61,* 1326–1334.

Burgess, R. L., & Conger, R. D. (1978). Family interaction in abusive, neglectful, and normal families. *Child Development, 49,* 1163–1173.

Burgess, R. L., & Youngblade, L. M. (1988). Social incompetence and the intergenerational transmission of abusive parental practices. In G. T. Hotaling, D. Finkelhor, J. T. Kirkpatrick, and M. A. Straus (Eds.), *Family abuse and its consequences: New directions in research* (pp. 38–60). Newbury Park, CA: Sage.

Caffaro-Rouget, A., Long, R., & Van Santen, V. (1989). The impact of child sexual abuse on victims' adjustment. *Annals of Sex Research, 2,* 29–47.

Camras, L. A., Ribordy, S., Hill, J., Martino, S., Sachs, V., Spaccarelli, S., & Stefani, R. (1990). Maternal facial behavior and the recognition and production of emotional expression by maltreated and nonmaltreated children. *Developmental Psychology, 30,* 2, 304–312.

Carlson, G. A., & Rapport, M. D., (1989). Diagnosis classification issues in attention-deficit hyperactivity disorder. *Psychiatric Annals, 19,* 576–582.

Carman, R., Fitzgerald, B. J., & Holmgren, C. (1983). Drinking motivations and alcohol consumption among adolescent females. *The Journal of Psychology, 114,* 79–82.

Caspi, A., Elder, G. H., & Bem, D. J. (1988). Moving away from the world: Life-course patterns of shy children. *Developmental Psychology, 24,* 824–831.

Coleman, E. (1987). Child physical and sexual abuse among chemically dependent individuals. *Journal of Chemical Dependency, 1,* 27–38.

Coleman, H., & Collins, D. (1990). Treatment trilogy of father-daughter incest. *Child and Adolescent Social Work Journal, 7,* 339–355.

Conger, J. J., & Petersen, A. C. (1984). *Adolescent and youth: Psychological development in a changing world* (4th ed.). New York: Harper & Row.

Crittenden, P. (1985). Social networks, quality of child rearing and child development. *Child Development, 56,* 1299–1313.

Crumley, F. E. (1979). Adolescent suicide attempts. *JAMA, 241,* 2404.

Curran, D. K. (1987). *Adolescent suicidal behavior.* Washington, DC: Hemisphere Publishing.

Daly, M., & Wilson, M. (1985). Child abuse and other risks of not living with both parents. *Ethology and Sociobiology, 6,* 197–210.

de Cantanzaro, D. (1981). *Suicide and Self-Damaging Behavior.* New York: Academic Press.

De Casper, A. J., & Spence, M. J. (1986). Prenatal maternal speech influences on newborns' perception of speech sounds. *Infant Behavior and Development, 9,* 133–150.

D'Evelyn, K. (1970). *Meeting children's emotional needs: A guide for teachers.* Englewood Cliffs, NJ: Prentice-Hall.

De Frain, J., Taylor, J., & Ernst, L. (1982). *Coping with sudden infant death.* Lexington, MA: Lexington Books.

Dickstra, R. F. W. (1989). Suicide and the attempted suicide: An international perspective. *Acta Psychiatrica Scandanavia, 80,* 1–24.

Dodge, K. A. (1986). A social information-processing model of social competence in children. In M. Perlmutter (Ed.), *Minnesota Symposium on Child Psychology* (Vol. 18)(pp. 77–125). Hillsdale, NJ: Erlbaum.

Dodge, K. A., Coie, J. D., Pettit, G. S., & Price, J. M. (1990). Peer status and aggression in boys' groups: Developmental and contextual analyses. *Child Development, 61,* 1289–1309.

Duncan, P., Ritter, P., Dornbusch, S., Gross, R., & Carlsmith, J. (1983). The effects of pubertal timing on body image, school behavior and deviance. *Journal of Youth and Adolescence, 14,* 227–236.

Egeland, B., Breitenbucher, M., & Rosenberg, D. (1980). Prospective study of the significance of life stress in the etiology of child abuse. *Journal of Consulting and Clinical Psychology, 48,* 195–205.

Egeland, B., Jacobivitz, D., & Papatola, K. (1987). Intergenerational continuity of abuse. In R. J. Gelles and J. B. Lancaster (Eds.), *Child abuse and neglect: Biosocial dimensions* (pp. 255–276). New York: Aldine de Gruyter.

Epstein, L. H., & Chess, P. A. (1986). Behavior genetics of childhood obesity. *Behavior Therapy, 12,* 324–334.

Fay, W. H. (1979). Personal pronouns and the autistic child. *Journal of Autism and Developmental Disorders, 9,* 247–260.

Femina, D. D., Yeager, C. A., & Lewis, D. O. (1990). Child abuse: Adolescent records vs. adult recall. *Child Abuse and Neglect, 14,* 227–231.

Fernell, E., Gillberg, C., & von Wendt, I. (1990). Autistic symptoms in children with infantile hydrocephalus. *Acta Paediatrica Scandinavia, 43,* 227–335.

Ferrari, M., & Matthews, W. S. (1983). Self-recognition deficits in autism: Syndrome-specific or general developmental delay? *Journal of Autism and Developmental Disorders, 13,* 317–325.

Field, T. M., Dempsey, J. R., & Schuman, H. H. (1979). Developmental assessments of infants surviving the respiratory distress syndrome. In T. M. Field (Ed.), *Infants born at risk: Behavior and development.* Jamaica, NY: Spectrum.

Fishburne, P. M., & Cisin, I. (1980). *National survey on drug abuse: Main findings:* 1974, National Institute on Drug Abuse, DHHS Publication No. (ADM) 80-976. Washington, DC: U.S. Government Printing Office.

Friedman, R. M., Sandler, J., Hernandez, M., & Wolfe, D. A. (1981). Child abuse, In E. J. Mash and L. G. Terdal (Eds.), *Behavioral assessment of childhood disorders.* New York: Guilford Press.

Frodi, A. M. (1981). Contribution of infant characteristics to child abuse. *American Journal of Mental Deficiency, 85,* 341–349.

Garbarino, J., & Gillian, G. (1980). *Understanding abusive families.* Lexington, MA: Lexington Books.

Garber, H. J., Ritvo, E. R., Chiu, L. C., Griswold, V. J., Kashanian, A., Freeman, B. J., & Oldendorf, W. H. (1989). A magnetic resonance imaging study of autism: Normal fourth ventricle size and absence of pathology. *American Journal of Psychiatry, 146,* 532–534.

Garcia-Coll, C., Kagan, J., & Reznick, J. S. (1984). Behavioral inhibition in young children. *Child Development, 55,* 1005–1019.

Gelfand, D. M., Hartman, D. P., Lamb, A. K., Smith, C., Mahan, M. A., & Paul, S. C. (1974). The effects of adult models and described alternatives on children's choice of behavior management techniques. *Child Development, 45,* 585–593.

George, C., & Main, M. (1979). Social interactions of young abused children: Approach, avoidance, aggression. *Child Development, 50,* 306–318.

Gil, D. (1975). *Violence against children: Physical child abuse in the United States.* Cambridge, MA: Harvard University Press.

Gillberg, C. (1986). Onset at age 14 of a typical autistic syndrome. A case report of a girl with herpes encephalitis. *Journal of Autism and Developmental Disorders, 16,* 569–575.

Gillberg, C. (1989). Asperger syndrome in 23 Swedish children: A clinical study. *Developmental Medicine and Child Neurology, 31,* 520–531.

Gillberg, C. (1990). Autism and pervasive developmental disorders. *Journal of Psychology and Psychiatry, 31,* 99–119.

Gillberg, C., & Svendsen, P. (1987). Childhood psychosis and computed tomographic brain scan findings. *Journal of Autism and Developmental Disorders, 13,* 19–32.

Gittelman, R., Abikoff, H., Pollack, E., Klein, D., Katz S., & Mattes, J. (1980). A controlled trial of behavior modification and Methylphenidate in hyperactive children. In C. K. Whalen and B. Henker (Eds.), *Hyperactive children.* New York: Academic Press.

Grether, J. K., & Schulman, J. (1989). Sudden infant death syndrome and birth weight. *Journal of Pediatrics, 114,* 561–567.

Guerra, N. G., (1989). Consequential thinking and self-reported delinquency in high school youth. *Criminal Justice and Behavior, 16,* 440–454.

Guerra, N. G., & Slaby, R. G. (1989). Evaluative factors in social problem solving by aggressive boys. *Journal of Abnormal Child Psychology, 17,* 277–287.

Guerra, N. G., & Slaby, R. G. (1990). Cognitive mediators of aggression in adolescent offenders: 2. Intervention. *Developmental Psychology, 26,* 269–277.

Hagerman, R. (1990). Genes, chromosomes, and autism. In C. Gillberg (Ed.), *Autism, diagnosis and treatment.* New York: Plenum Press.

Hall, W. M. (1973). *Observational and interactive determinants of aggressive behavior in boys.* Ph.D. dissertation, Indiana University, Indianapolis.

Hartsough, C. S., & Lambert, N. (1982). Some environmental and familial correlates and antecedents of hyperactivity. *American Journal of Orthopsychiatry, 52,* 272–276.

Hechtman, L., & Weiss, G. (1983). Long-term outcome of hyperactive children. *American Journal of Orthopsychiatry, 53,* 522–541.

Hendrin, H. (1982). *Suicide in America.* New York: W. W. Norton.

Henker, B., & Whalen, C. K. (1989). Hyperactivity and attention deficits. *American Psychologist, 44,* 216–223.

Herold, S., Frackowiak, R. S. J., Le Couteur, A., Rutter, M., & Howlin, P. (1988). Cerebral blood flow and metabolism of oxygen and glucose in young autistic adults. *Psychological Medicine, 18,* 823–831.

Hersch, S. (1977). Epilogue. Future consideration and directions. In J. Schulterbrandt and A. Raskin (Eds.), *Depression in childhood: Diagnosis, treatment, and conceptual models* (pp. 147–152). New York: Raven.

Hertzig, M. E., Snow, M. E., New, E., & Shapiro, T. (1990). DSM-III and DSM-III-R diagnosis of autism and pervasive developmental disorder in nursery school children. *Journal of American Academy of Child Adolescent Psychiatry, 29,* 123–126.

Herzberger, S. D., & Tennen, H. (1983). Coping with abuse: Children's perspectives on their abusive treatment. In D. Finkelhor (Ed.), *The dark side of families.* Beverly Hills: Sage.

Hoberman, H. M., & Garfinkel, B. D. (1988). Suicide in children and adolescents. *Journal of the American Academy of Child Adolescence and Psychiatry, 27,* 689–695.

Hobson, R. P. (1988). Beyond cognition: A theory of autism. In G. Dawson (Ed.), *Autism: New perspectives on diagnosis, nature, and treatment.* New York: Guilford.

Hollister, L. E. (1983). Drug abuse in the United States: The past decade. *Drug and Alcohol Dependence, 11,* 49–53.

Holinger, P. A., & Luke, K. L. (1984). The epidemiology patterns of self-destructiveness in childhood, adolescence, and young adulthood. In H. S. Sudak, A. D. Ford, and N. B. Rushforth (Eds.), *Suicide in the young.* Boston: John Wright.

Honig, A. S. (1987). The shy child. *Young Children, 17,* 34–64.

Hotaling, G. T., Finkelhor, D., Kirkpatrick, J. T., & Straus, M. A. (Eds.). (1988). *Family abuse and its consequences: New directions in research.* Newbury Park, CA: Sage.

Howlin, P., & Rutter, M. (1987). *Treatment of autistic children.* New York: Wiley.

Jacobs, J. (1981). *Adolescent suicide.* New York: Wiley.

Janus, M. D., McCormick, A., Burgess, A. W., & Hartman, C. (1984). Adolescent runaways: Causes and consequences. Lexington, MA: Lexington Books.

Jerome, J. (1979, January 19). Catching them before suicide. *New York Times Magazine,* 30–32.

Jessor, R., & Jessor, S. L. (1978). Theory testing in longitudinal research on marijuana use. In D. B. Kandel (Ed.), *Longitudinal research on drug use: Empirical findings and methodological issues.* Washington, DC: Hemisphere.

Johnston, L. D., O'Malley, P. M., & Bachman, J. G. (1987). *National trends in drug use and related factors among American high school students and young adults. 1975–1986.* Rockville, MD: National Institute on Drug Abuse.

Junewicz, W. J. (1983). A protective posture toward emotional neglect and abuse. *Child Welfare, 62,* 240–252.

Kagan, J. (1989). Temperamental contributions to social behavior. *American Psychologist, 44,* 668–674.

Kagan, J., Reznick, J. S., & Snidman, N. (1988). Biological bases of childhood shyness. *Science, 240,* 167–171.

Kanner, L. (1943). Autistic disturbances of affective contact. *Nervous Child, 2,* 217–250.

Kanner, L. (1972). *Child psychiatry* (4th ed.). Springfield, IL: C. C. Thomas.

Kazdin, A. E., Moser, J., Colbus, D., & Bell, R. (1985). Depressive symptoms among physically abused and psychiatrically disturbed children. *Journal of Abnormal Psychology, 94,* 298–307.

Kellam, S. G. (1982). Social adaptation to first grade and teenage drug, alcohol, and cigarette use. *Journal of School, 52,* 301–306.

Kempe, C. H., Silverman, F. N., Steel, B. F., Droegemueller, W. & Silver, H. K. (1962). The battered child syndrome. *Journal of the American Medical Association, 181,* 17–24.

Kinard, E. M. (1980). Emotional development in physically abused children. *American Journal of Orthopsychiatry, 50,* 686–696.

Kizziar, J., & Hagedorn, J. (1979). *Search for acceptance: The adolescent and self-esteem.* Chicago: Nelson-Hall.

Klimes-Dougan, B., & Kistner, J. (1990). Physically abused preschoolers' responses to peers' distress. *Developmental Psychology, 26,* 599–602.

Koegel, R., Rincover, A., & Egel, A. (1982). *Educating and understanding autistic children.* San Diego: College-Hill.

Koegel, R., Schreibman, L., O'Neal, R., & Burke, J. (1983). The personality and family interaction characteristics of parents of autistic children. *Journal of Consulting and Clinical Psychology, 21,* 683–692.

Konopka, G. (1983). Adolescent suicide. *Exceptional Children, 49,* 5, 390–394.

Konstantareas, M. M., Zajdeman, H., Homatidis, S., McCabe, A. (1988). Maternal speech to verbal and higher functioning versus nonverbal and lower functioning autistic children. *Journal of Autism and Developmental Disorders, 18,* 647–656.

Kosky, R. (1983). Childhood suicidal behavior. *Journal of Child Psychology and Psychiatry, 24,* 3, 457–468.

Kovacs, M. (1990). Affective disorders in children and adolescents. *American Psychologist, 44,* 209–215.

Kovacs, M., & Gatsonis, C. (1989). Stability and change in childhood-onset depressive disorders: Longitudinal course as a diagnostic validator in L. N. Robins, J. L. Fleiss, and J. E. Barrett (Eds.), *The validity of psychiatric diagnosis* (pp. 57–75). New York: Raven.

Kreuz, I. E., & Rose, R. M. (1972). Assessment of aggressive behavior and plasma testosterone in a young criminal population. *Psychosomatic Medicine, 34,* 321–332.

Kufeldt, K., & Nimmo, M. (1987). Youth on the street: Abuse and neglect in the eighties. *Child Abuse and Neglect, 11,* 531–543.

Ladd, G. W., & Keeney, B. (1983). Intervention strategies and research with socially isolated children. *Small group behavior, 14,* 175–186.

Ladd, G. W., & Mize, J. (1983). A cognitive-social learning model of social skill training. *Psychological Review, 90,* 127–152.

Lambert, N., Sandoval, J., & Sassone, D. (1979). Prevalence of treatment regimens for children considered to be hyperactive. *American Journal of Orthopsychiatry, 49,* 482–490.

Larson, R., & Lampman-Petraitis, C. (1989). Daily emotional states as reported by children and adolescents. *Child Development, 60,* 1250–1260.

Levy, F., & Hobbes, G. (1982). A 30-month follow-up of hyperactive children. *Journal of the American Academy of Child Psychiatry, 21,* 243–246.

Lewis, R. A., Piercy, F. P., Sprenkle, D. H., & Trepper, T. S. (1990). Family-based interventions for helping drug-abusing adolescents. *Journal of Adolescent Research, 5,* 82–95.

Lipsitt, L. P. (1982). Perinatal indicators and psychophysiological precursors of crib death. In J. Belsky (Ed.), *In the beginning.* New York: Columbia University Press.

Lipsitt, L. P. (1990). Learning and memory in infants. *Merrill-Palmer Quarterly, 36,* 53–66.

Lipsitt, L. P., Sturner, W. Q., & Burke, P. M. (1979). Perinatal indicators and crib death. *Infant Behavior and Development, 2,* 325–329.

Lloyd, J. (1980). Life events and depressive disorder review: Events as predisposing factors. *Archives of General Psychiatry, 37,* 529–535.

Lotter, V. (1978). Follow-up studies, In M. Rutter & E. Schopler (Eds.), *Autism: A reappraisal of concepts and treatment.* New York: Plenum Press.

Lovaas, O. I. (1987). Behavioral treatment and normal educational and intellectual functioning in young autistic children. *Journal of Consulting and Clinical Psychology, 55,* 3–9.

Macfarland, J. W. (1964). Perspectives on personality consistency and change from the guidance study. *Vita Humana, 7,* 115–126.

Magnusson, D., Stottin, H., & Duner, A. (1982). Aggression and criminality in a longitudinal perspective. In S. A. Mednick (Ed.), *Antecedents of aggression and antisocial behavior.* Hingham, MA: Kluwer Boston.

Mann, J. J. (1987). *The suicidal patient: Biology and pharmacology.* Paper presented at the annual meeting of the American Psychiatric Association, Chicago.

Martin, B. (1975). Parent-child relations. In F. D. Horowitz (Ed.), *Review of child development research* (Vol. 4). Chicago: University of Chicago Press.

McAdoo, W. G., & DeMyer, W. K., (1978). Personality characteristics of parents. In M. Rutter and E. Schopler (Eds.), *Autism: A reappraisal of concepts and treatment.* New York: Plenum Press.

Milner, J. S., Robertson, K. R. & Rogers, D. L. (1990). Childhood history of abuse and adult child abuse potential. *Journal of Family Violence, 5,* 15–34.

Mitnick, M. F. (1983). Family sexual abuse and custody evaluation. *Conciliation Courts Review, 21,* 89–94.

Morse, C., Sahler, O., & Friedman, S. (1970). A three year follow-up of abused and neglected children. *American Journal of Disturbed Children, 120,* 439–446.

Murray, M., Swan, A. V., Johnson, M. R. D., & Bewley, B. R. (1983). Some factors associated with increased risk of smoking by children. *Journal of Child Psychology and Psychiatry, 24,* 223–232.

National Institute on Drug Abuse. (1977). *National survey on drug abuse: Main findings.* Washington, DC: U.S. Government Printing Office.

National Institute on Drug Abuse. (1987). *National household survey on drug abuse: Population estimates 1985.* Rockville, MD: Author.

Newcomb, M. D., & Bentler, P. M. (1989). Substance use and abuse among children and teenagers. *American Psychologist, 15,* 242–248.

Noll, R. B., Zucker, R. A., & Greenberg, G. S. (1990). Identification of alcohol by smell among preschoolers: Evidence for early socialization about drugs occurring in the home. *Child Development, 61,* 1520–1527.

O'Brien, S. (1980). *Child abuse: A crying shame.* Provo, UT: Brigham Young University Press.

Offer, D., Ostrov, E., & Howard, K. I. (1981). The adolescent. New York: Basic Books.

O'Leary, K. D., Pelham, W. E., Rosenbaum, A., & Price, G. (1976). Behavioral treatment of hyperkinetic children. *Clinical Pediatrics, 15,* 510–515.

Olweus, D. (1979). Stability and aggressive reaction patterns in males: A review. *Psychological Bulletin, 86,* 852–875.

Olweus, D. (1980). Familial and temperamental determinants of aggression behavior in adolescents—A causal analysis. *Developmental Psychology, 16,* 644–680.

Ottenbacher, K. J., & Cooper, H. M. (1983). Drug treatment of hyperactivity in children. *Developmental Medicine, 18,* 358–363.

Ounsted, C., Oppenheimer, R., & Lindsay, J. (1974). Aspects of bonding failure: The psychopathology and psychotherapeutic treatment of families of battered children. *Developmental Medicine and Child Neurology, 16,* 447–456.

Ozonoff, S., Pennington, B. F., & Rogers, S. J. (1990). Are there emotion perception deficits in young autistic children? *Journal of Child Psychology and Psychiatry, 31,* 343–361.

Parke, R. D., & Slaby, R. G. (1983). The development of aggression. In E. M. Hetherington (Ed.), P. H. Mussen (Series Ed.), *Handbook of child psychology: Vol. 4. Socialization, personality, and social development* (pp. 547–641). New York: Wiley.

Patterson, G. R. (1982). *Coercive family process.* Eugene, OR: Castalia.

Patterson, G. R., DeBaryshe, B. D., & Ramsey, F. (1989). A developmental perspective on antisocial behavior. *American Psychologist, 44,* 329–335.

Patterson, G. R., Littman, R. A., & Bricker, W. (1967). Assertive behavior in children: A step toward a theory of aggression. *Monographs of the Society for Research in Child Development, 35* (5, Serial No. 113).

Paul, B. (1987). Communication. In D. Cohen, A. M. Donnellan, & R. Paul (Eds.), *Handbook of autism and pervasive developmental disorders* (pp. 61–64). New York: Wiley.

Peck, D. (1981). Adolescent self-esteem, emotional learning disabilities, and significant others. *Adolescence, 62,* 443–449.

Peck, D. (1984). Official documentation of the black suicide experience. *Omega, 14,* 21–31.

Perry, D. G., Kusel, S. J., & Perry, L. C. (1988). Victims of peer aggression. *Developmental Psychology, 24,* 807–814.

Perry, D. G., Williard, J. C., & Perry, L. C. (1990). Peers' perceptions of the consequences that victimized children provide aggressors. *Child Development, 61,* 1310–1325.

Pfeffer, C., Plutchik, R., & Mizruchi, M. (1983). Suicidal and assaultive behavior in children: Classification, Measurement, and Interrelations. *American Journal of Psychiatry, 140,* 2, 154–157.

Plomin, R. (1986). *Development, genetics, and psychology.* Hillsdale, NJ: Erlbaum.

Plomin, R. (1990). *An introduction to human behavioral genetics.* Pacific Grove, CA: Brooks/Cole.

Plomin, R., & Daniels, D. (1987). Why are children in the same family so different from one another? *Behavioral and Brain Sciences, 10,* 1–16.

Plotkin, R. D., & Twentyman, C. T. (1982). *Cognitive mediation of child abuse.* Unpublished manuscript, University of Rochester, NY.

Polansky, N., Chalmers, M., Buttenweiser, C., & Williams, D. (1979). The isolation of the neglectful family. *American Journal of Orthopsychiatry, 49,* 149–152.

Powers, J. L., Eckenrode, J., & Jaklitsch, B. (1990). Maltreatment among runaway and homeless youth. *Child Abuse and Neglect, 14,* 87–98.

Pulkkinin, L. (1982). Search for alternatives to aggression in Finland. In A. F. Goldstein and M. Segall (Eds.), *Aggression in global perspective.* New York: Pergamon Press.

Rahdert, E. R., & Grabowski, J. (Eds.). (1988). *Adolescent drug abuse: Analysis of treatment research.* Washington, DC: U.S. Department of Health and Human Services, Public Health Service, Alcohol, Drug Abuse, and Mental Health Administration, National Institute on Drug Abuse.

Rapport, M. D., Quinn, S. O., DuPaul, G. J., Quinn, E. P., & Kelly, K. L. (1989). Attention deficit disorder with hyperactivity and methylphenidate: The effects of dose and mastery level on children's learning performance. *Journal of Abnormal Child Psychology, 17,* 669–689.

Ray, L., & Johnson, N. (1983). *Adolescent Suicide, Personnel and Guidance Journal, 61,* 131–136.

Reid, J. B., Taplin, P. S., & Lorber, R. A. (1981). A social interactional approach to the treatment of abusive families. In R. B. Stuart (Ed.), *Violent behavior: Social learning approaches to prediction, management, and treatment.* New York: Brunner/Mazel.

Rich, L. L. (1982). *Disturbed students*. Baltimore: University Park Press.

Risley, R. R., & Baer, D. M. (1973). Operant behavior modification: The deliberate development of behavior. In B. M. Caldwell & H. M. Ricciuti (Eds.), *Review of child development research*. Chicago: University of Chicago Press.

Ritter, D. R. (1990). Adolescent suicide: Social competence and problem behavior of youth at high risk and low risk for suicide. *School Psychology Review, 19,* 83–95.

Rogers, S. J., & Lewis, H. (1989). An effective day treatment model for young children with pervasive developmental disorders. *Journal of the American Academy of Child Adolescent Psychiatry, 28,* 207–214.

Rosenberg, M., & Reppucci, N. D. (1983). Abusive mothers: Perceptions of their own and their children's behavior. *Journal of Counseling and Clinical Psychology, 51,* 674–682.

Rosenblatt, J. (1981). Youth suicide. *Editorial Research Reports, 1,* 431–438.

Ross, D. M., & Ross, S. A. (1979). *Hyperactivity research theory: Theory and action.* New York: Wiley.

Ross, D. M., & Ross, S. A. (1982). *Hyperactivity: Current issues, research, and theory.* New York: Wiley.

Rutter, M. (1978). Diagnosis and definition of childhood autism. *Journal of Autism and Childhood Schizophrenia, 8,* 139–161.

Rutter, M. (1983). Cognitive deficits in the pathogenesis of autism. *Journal of Child Psychology and Psychiatry, 24,* 513–531.

Rutter, M. (1988). DSM-III-R: A postscript. M. Rutter, A. H. Tuma, and I. L. Lann (Eds.), *Assessment and diagnosis of child psychopathology* (pp. 453–464). New York: Guilford.

Saltman, J. (1977, February). The new alcoholics: Teenagers. Public Affairs Pamphlet No. 499.

Schecter, M. D., & Roberge, L. (1976). Sexual exploitation. In R. E. Helfer and C. F. Kempe (Eds.), *Child abuse and neglect.* Cambridge, MA: Ballinger.

Schopler, E., & Mesibov, G. B. (Eds.). (1984). *The effects of autism on the family.* New York: Plenum Press.

Schopler, E., & Mesibov, G. B. (Eds.). (1988). Introduction to diagnosis and assessment of autism. In *Diagnosis and assessment in autism* (pp. 3–14). New York: Plenum Press.

Schotte, D. E., & Clum, G. A. (1982). Suicide ideation in a college population: A test of a model. *Journal of Consulting and Clinical Psychology, 50,* 690–696.

Sears, R. R., Maccoby, E. E., & Levin, H. (1957). *Patterns of child rearing.* Evanston, IL: Harper & Row.

Segal, B., Huba, G. J., & Singer, J. L. (1980). Prediction of college drug use from personality and inner experience. *International Journal of the Addictions, 15,* 849–867.

Seidel, W. T., & Joschko, M. (1990). Evidence of difficulties in sustained attention in children with ADDH. *Journal of Abnormal Child Psychology, 18,* 217–229.

Sergeant, J. A., & Scholten, C. A. (1983). A stages information approach to hyperactivity. *Journal of Child Psychology and Psychiatry, 24,* 49–54.

Shneidman, E., Farberow, J., & Litman, R. (1976). *The psychology of suicide* (2nd ed.). New York: Jason Aronson.

Silber, J. J. (1986). Approaching the adolescent patient: Pitfalls and solutions. *Journal of Adolescent Health Care, 7,* 31–40.

Simon, N. G. (1983). New strategies for aggressive research. In E. C. Summell, M. Hahn, and J. Walters (Eds.), *Aggressive behavior: Genetic and neural approaches.* Hillsdale, NJ: Erlbaum.

Simons, R. L., Whitbeck, L. B., Conger, R. D., & Chyi-In, W. (1991). Intergenerational transmission of harsh parenting. *Developmental Psychology, 27,* 159–171.

Smith, G. M., & Fogg, G. P. (1978). Psychological predictors of early use, late use and nonuse of marijuana among teenage students. In D. B. Kandel (Ed.), *Longitudinal research on drug use: Empirical findings and methodological issues.* Washington, DC: Hemisphere.

Sroufe, L. A., & Rutter, M. (1984). The domain of developmental psychopathology. *Child Development, 55,* 17–29.

Stanton, M. D., Todd, T. C., Hard, D. B., Kirschner, S., Kleiman, J. I., Mowatt, D. T., Riley, P., Scott, S. M., & Van Deusen, M. M. (1978). Heroin addiction as a family phenomenon: A new conceptual model. *American Journal of Drug Abuse, 5,* 125–150.

Stark, A., Mandell, F., & Taeusch, H. (1978). Close encounters with SIDS. *Pediatrics, 61,* 664–665.

Steeles, C. M., & Josephs, R. A. (1990). Alcohol myopia: Its prized and dangerous effects. *American Psychologist, 45,* 921–933.

Steffenburg, S., & Gillberg, C. (1990). The etiology of autism. In C. Gillberg (Ed.), *Autism: Diagnosis and treatment.* New York: Plenum Press.

Sternac, L., & Segal, A. (1990). Adult sexual contact with children: An examination of cognitive factors. *Behavior Therapy, 20,* 573–584.

Swidler, H. J., & Walson, P. D. (1979). Hyperactivity: A current assessment. *Journal of Family Practice, 9,* 601–608.

Szatmari, P., Bartolucci, G., & Bremner, R. (1989). Asperger's syndrome and autism: Comparison of early history and outcome. *Developmental Medicine and Child Neurology, 31,* 709–720.

Tennes, K., Downey, K., & Vernadakis, A. (1977). Urinary control excretion rates and anxiety in normal one-year-old infants. *Psychosomatic Medicine and Child Neurology, 39,* 178–187.

Thompson, E. H., & Gongla, P. (1983). Single-parent families. In E. Macklin and R. Rubin (Eds.), *Contemporary families and alternate lifestyles.* Beverly Hills, CA: Sage.

Tieger, T. (1980). On the biological basis of sex differences in aggression. *Child Development, 51,* 943–963.

Tishler, C. L., McKenry, P. C., & Morgan, K. C. (1981). Adolescent suicide attempts: Some significant factors. *Suicide Life Threatening Behavior, 11,* 31.

Traub, G. S. (1983). Correlations of shyness with depression, anxiety, and academic performance. *Psychological Reports, 52,* 849–850.

Trickett, P. K., Aber, J. L., Carlson, V., & Cicchetti, D. (1991). Relationship of socioeconomic status to the etiology and developmental sequelae of physical child abuse. *Developmental Psychology, 27,* 148–158.

Trickett, P. K., & Susman, E. J. (1988). Parental perceptions of childrearing practices in physically abusive and nonabusive parents. *Developmental Psychology, 24,* 270–276.

Trites, R. L., & Laprade, K. (1983). Evidence for an independent syndrome of hyperactivity. *Journal of Child Psychology and Psychiatry, 24,* 573–586.

U.S. Department of Health and Human Services. (1988). *Study findings: Study of the national incidence & prevalence of child abuse and neglect.* Washington, DC: Author.

Van Dalen, A. (1989). The emotional consequences of physical child abuse. *Clinical Social Work Journal, 17,* 383–394.

Van Roosmalen, E., & McDaniel, S. (1989). Peer group influence as a factor in smoking behavior in adolescence. *Adolescence, 24,* 801–816.

Volkmar, F. R., & Nelson, D. S. (1990). Seizure disorders in autism. *Journal of the American Academy of Child Adolescent Psychiatry, 29,* 127–129.

Weidman, A. (1983). The compulsive adolescent substance abuser: Psychological differentiation and family process. *Journal of Drug Education, 13,* 161–172.

Weiss, G., & Hechtman, L. T. (1986). *Hyperactive children grown up.* New York: Guilford.

Windle, M. (1989). Substance use and abuse among adolescent runaways: A four-year follow-up study. *Journal of Youth and Adolescence, 18,* 331–344.

Windle, M., Miller-Tutzauer, C., Barnes, G. M., & Welte, J. (1991). Adolescent perceptions of help-seeking resources for substance abuse. *Child Development, 62,* 179–189.

Wing, L. (1990). Diagnosis of autism. In C. Gillberg (Ed.), *Autism: Diagnosis and treatment.* New York: Plenum Press.

Wing, L., & Attwood, A. (1987). Syndromes of autism and atypical development. In D. J. Cohen, A. M. Donnellan, and R. Paul (Eds.), *Handbook of autism and pervasive developmental disorders* (pp. 3–19). New York: Wiley.

Zametkin, A. J. (1989). The neurobiology of attention-deficit hyperactivity disorder. *Psychiatric Annals, 19,* 584–586.

Zenmore, R., & Rinholm, J. (1989). Vulnerability to depression as a function of parental rejection and control. *Canadian Journal of Behavioral Science, 21,* 364–376.

Zimbardo, P. G. (1978). *Shyness: What it is and what to do about it.* Reading, MA: Addison-Wesley.

Chapter 16

Bean, R., & Clemes, H. (1990). *How to discipline children without feeling guilty.* Los Angeles: Price Stern.

Bronfenbrenner, U., & Crouter, A. C. (1983). The evolution of environmental models in developmental research. In W. Kessen (Ed.), P. H. Mussen (Series Ed.), *Handbook of child psychology:* Vol. 1. *History, theory and methods* (4th ed.) (pp. 357–414). New York: Wiley.

Cairns, R. B., Cairns, B. D., & Neckerman, H. J. (1989). Early school dropout: Configurations and determinants, *Child Development, 60,* 1437–1452.

Dreikurs, R., & Soltz, V. (1964), *Children the challenge.* New York: Hawthorn Books.

Elliott, D., Voss, H., & Wendling, A. (1966). Capable dropouts and the social milieu of high school. *Journal of Educational Research, 60,* 180–186.

Erikson, E. (1968). *Identity: Youth and Crises.* New York: W. W. Norton.

Fine, M., & Rosenberg, P. (1983). Dropping out of high school: The ideology of school and work. *Journal of Education, 165,* 257–272.

Frankenberg, W. K., & Dodds, J. B. (1967). The Denver developmental screening test. *Journal of Pediatrics, 71,* 181–191.

Gesell, A. (1972). *The embryology of behavior: The beginnings of the human mind.* Westport, CT: Greenwood.

Gibson, E. J., & Walk, R. D. (1960). The visual cliff. *Scientific American, 202,* 64–71.

Gordon, T. (1991). *Discipline that works: Promoting self-discipline in children at home and at school.* New York: Dutton.

Marcia, J. E. (1980). Identity in adolescence. In J. Adelson (Ed.), *Handbook of adolescent psychology.* New York: Wiley.

U.S. Bureau of the Census. (1987). *Current Population Reports,* Ser. P-20. No. 413, *School enrollment-social and economic characteristics of students:* October 1983. Washington, DC: U. S. Government Printing Office.

U.S. Department of Health, Education and Welfare. (1979, September). *The urban high school reform initiative.* Washington, DC: Government Printing Office.

Wilson, W. J. (1987). *The truly disadvantaged.* Chicago: Chicago University Press.

Young, A. (1982, September). Labor force patterns of students, graduates, and dropouts. *Monthly Labor Review, 105,* 39–42.

Subject Index

ISBN 0-675-21336-3

9 780675 213363

90000>